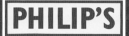

CW00428908

STREET
South
Hampshire

www.philips-maps.co.uk

First published in 1994 by

Philip's, a division of
Octopus Publishing Group Ltd
www.octopusbooks.co.uk
2-4 Heron Quays, London E14 4JP
An Hachette Livre UK Company
www.hachettelivre.co.uk

Third colour edition 2006
Second impression with revisions 2008
SHACC

ISBN 978-0-540-09488-2 (pocket)

© Philip's 2008

 **Ordnance Survey®**

This product includes mapping data licensed from
Ordnance Survey® with the permission of the
Controller of Her Majesty's Stationery Office.

© Crown copyright 2008. All rights reserved.
Licence number 100011710.

Ordnance Survey and the OS Symbol are
registered trademarks of Ordnance Survey, the
national mapping agency of Great Britain.

Printed and bound in China by Toppan

Contents

III **Key to map symbols**

IV **Key to map pages**

VI **Route planning**

VIII **Administrative and Postcode boundaries**

1 **Street maps** at 2⅔ inches to 1 mile

216 **Street map of Portsmouth city centre**
at 5⅓ inches to 1 mile

217 **Index** of towns and villages

220 **Index** of streets, hospitals, industrial estates, railway
stations, schools, shopping centres, universities
and places of interest

Digital Data

The exceptionally high-quality mapping found in this atlas is available as digital data in
TIFF format, which is easily convertible to other bitmapped (raster) image formats.

The index is also available in digital form as a standard database table. It contains all the
details found in the printed index together with the National Grid reference for the map
square in which each entry is named.

For further information and to discuss your requirements, please contact
victoria.dawbarn@philips-maps.co.uk

Symbol	Description		Symbol	Description
	Motorway with junction number		◆	**Ambulance station**
	Primary route – dual/single carriageway		◆	**Coastguard station**
	A road – dual/single carriageway		◆	**Fire station**
	B road – dual/single carriageway		◆	**Police station**
	Minor road – dual/single carriageway		✚	**Accident and Emergency entrance to hospital**
	Other minor road – dual/single carriageway		H	**Hospital**
	Road under construction		✜	**Place of worship**
	Tunnel, covered road		🄸	**Information Centre** (open all year)
	Rural track, private road or narrow road in urban area		🛒	**Shopping Centre**
	Gate or obstruction to traffic (restrictions may not apply at all times or to all vehicles)		P P&R	**Parking, Park and Ride**
	Path, bridleway, byway open to all traffic, road used as a public path		PO	**Post Office**
			⋏ 🚐	**Camping site, caravan site**
	Pedestrianised area		⏵ ⊠	**Golf course, picnic site**
DY7	**Postcode boundaries**		Prim Sch	**Important buildings, schools, colleges, universities and hospitals**
	County and unitary authority boundaries			**Built up area**
	Railway, tunnel, railway under construction			**Woods**
	Tramway, tramway under construction		River Medway	**Water name**
	Miniature railway			**River, weir, stream**
Walsall	**Railway station**			**Canal, lock, tunnel**
🚇	**Private railway station**			**Water**
South Shields	**Metro station**			**Tidal water**
🚊 🚊	**Tram stop, tram stop under construction**		Church	**Non-Roman antiquity**
◀●	**Bus, coach station**		ROMAN FORT	**Roman antiquity**

Acad	**Academy**	Inst	**Institute**	Recn Gd	**Recreation Ground**	
Allot Gdns	**Allotments**	Ct	**Law Court**			
Cemy	**Cemetery**	L Ctr	**Leisure Centre**	Resr	**Reservoir**	
C Ctr	**Civic Centre**	LC	**Level Crossing**	Ret Pk	**Retail Park**	
CH	**Club House**	Liby	**Library**	Sch	**School**	
Coll	**College**	Mkt	**Market**	Sh Ctr	**Shopping Centre**	
Crem	**Crematorium**	Meml	**Memorial**	TH	**Town Hall/House**	
Ent	**Enterprise**	Mon	**Monument**	Trad Est	**Trading Estate**	
Ex H	**Exhibition Hall**	Mus	**Museum**	Univ	**University**	
Ind Est	**Industrial Estate**	Obsy	**Observatory**	W Twr	**Water Tower**	
IRB Sta	**Inshore Rescue**	Pal	**Royal Palace**	Wks	**Works**	
	Boat Station	PH	**Public House**	YH	**Youth Hostel**	

87	**Adjoining page indicators and overlap bands**
237	The colour of the arrow and the band indicates the scale of the adjoining or overlapping page (see scales below)

	Railway or bus station building
	Place of interest
	Parkland

■ The small numbers around the edges of the maps identify the 1 kilometre National Grid lines
■ The dark grey border on the inside edge of some pages indicates that the mapping does not continue onto the adjacent page

The scale of the maps on the pages numbered in blue is 4.2 cm to 1 km • 2⅔ inches to 1 mile • 1: 23810

```
0        ¼           ½           ¾          1 mile
0    250m    500m    750m    1 kilometre
```

The scale of the maps on the pages numbered in red is 8.4 cm to 1 km • 5⅓ inches to 1 mile • 1: 11900

```
0        220 yards        440 yards        660 yards        ½ mile
0    125m    250m    375m    ½ kilometre
```

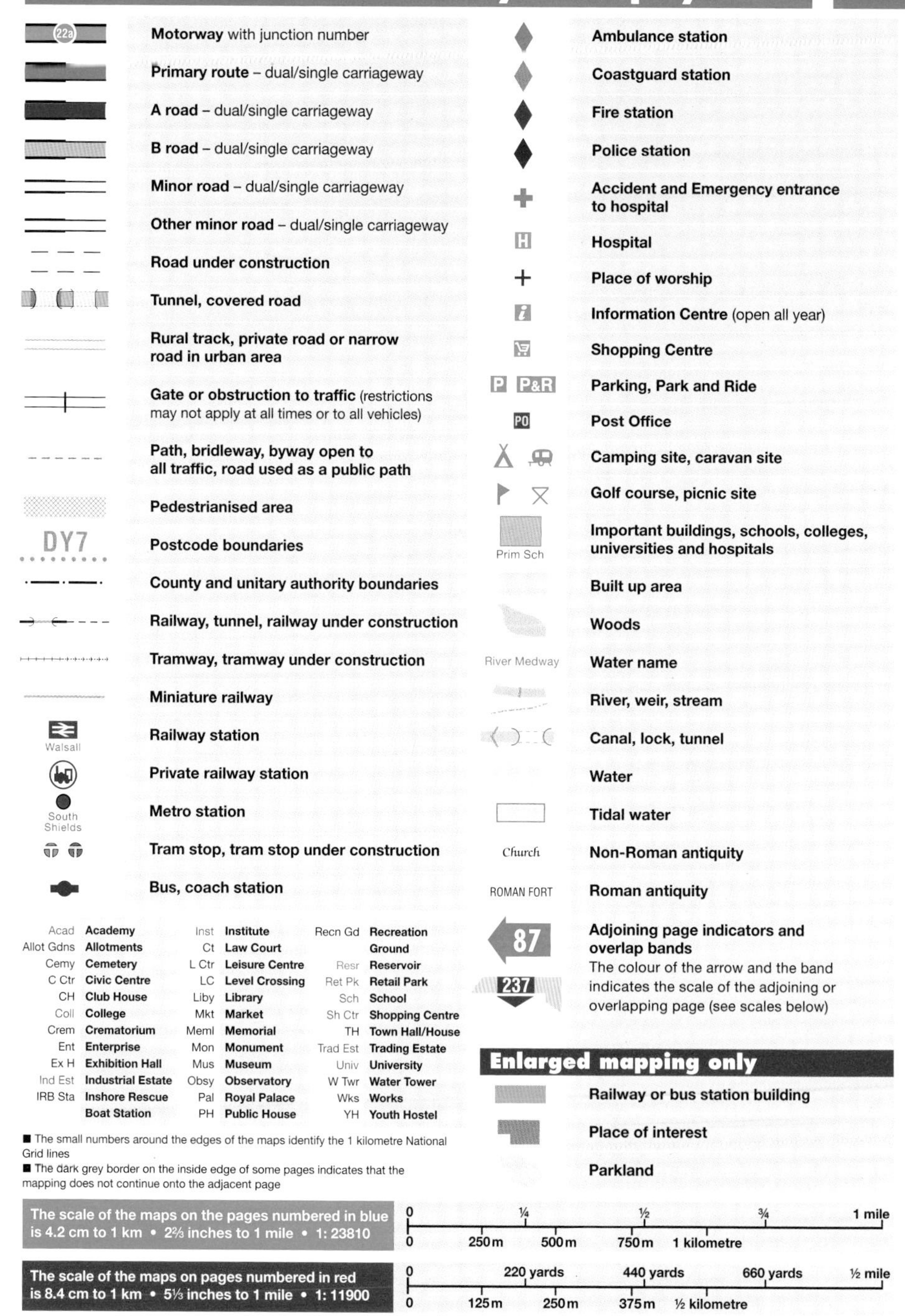

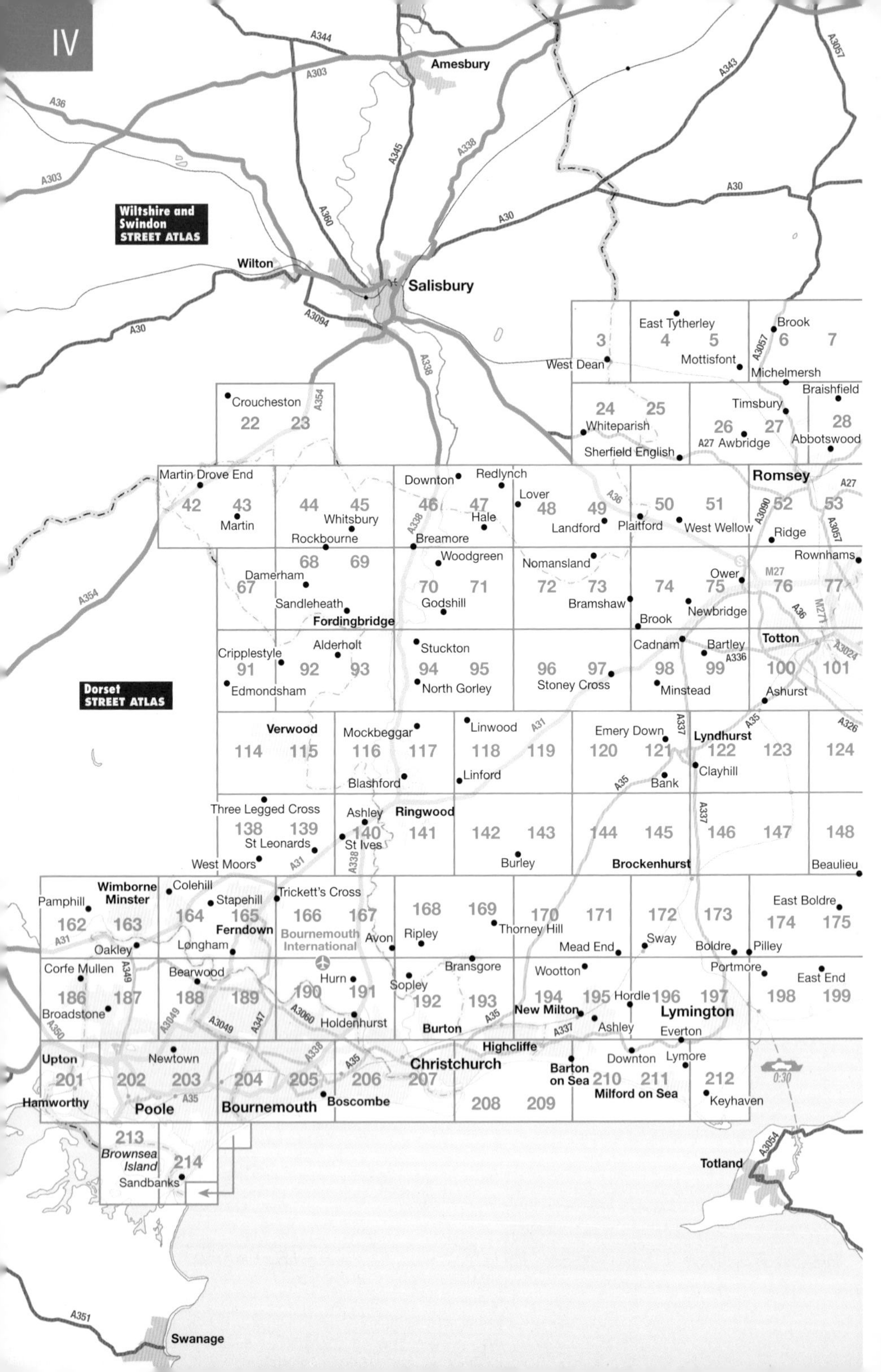
A344
A3057
Amesbury
A303
A343
A36
A345
A338
A303
A30
Wiltshire and Swindon STREET ATLAS
A360
A30
Wilton
Salisbury
A3094
A30
A338
East Tytherley
3
4
5
Brook
6
7
A3057
West Dean
Mottisfont
Michelmersh
Braishfield
A354
Croucheston
22
23
24
25
Whiteparish
Timsbury
26
27
28
Sherfield English
A27 Awbridge
Abbotswood
Martin Drove End
42
43
Martin
44
45
Whitsbury
Rockbourne
Downton
Redlynch
46
47
Hale
A338
Breamore
Lover
48
49
Landford
A36
50
51
Plaitford
West Wellow
Romsey
A27
A3090
52
53
Ridge
A3057
A354
68
69
Damerham
67
Sandleheath
Fordingbridge
Woodgreen
70
71
Godshill
Nomansland
72
73
Bramshaw
74
75
Ower
Brook
Newbridge
Rownhams
M27
76
77
A36
M271
Cripplestyle
Alderholt
91
92
93
Edmondsham
Stuckton
94
95
North Gorley
96
97
Stoney Cross
Cadnam
Bartley
98
99
A336
Minstead
Totton
100
101
A3024
Ashurst
Dorset STREET ATLAS
Verwood
114
115
Mockbeggar
116
117
Blashford
Linwood
118
119
A31
Linford
Emery Down
120
121
A337
Bank
A35
Lyndhurst
122
123
Clayhill
A35
A326
124
Three Legged Cross
138
139
St Leonards
West Moors
A31
Ashley
140
St Ives
A338
Ringwood
141
142
143
Burley
144
145
Brockenhurst
A337
146
147
148
Beaulieu
Pamphill
Wimborne Minster
162
163
A31
Oakley
Colehill
Stapehill
164
165
Ferndown
Longham
Trickett's Cross
166
167
Bournemouth International
Avon
168
169
Ripley
170
171
Thorney Hill
Mead End
172
173
Sway
Boldre
Pilley
East Boldre
174
175
Corfe Mullen
A349
186
187
Broadstone
A350
Bearwood
188
189
A3049
A3049
A347
Hurn
190
191
A3060
Holdenhurst
Sopley
192
193
Bransgore
Burton
A35
Wootton
194
195
New Milton
A337
Hordle
196
197
Ashley
Lymington
Everton
Portmore
198
199
East End
Upton
201
Hamworthy
Newtown
202
203
A35
Poole
204
Bournemouth
A338
205
A35
206
Boscombe
207
Christchurch
Highcliffe
208
209
Barton on Sea
Downton
210
211
Milford on Sea
Lymore
212
Keyhaven
0:30
213
Brownsea Island
214
Sandbanks
A3054
Totland
A351
Swanage

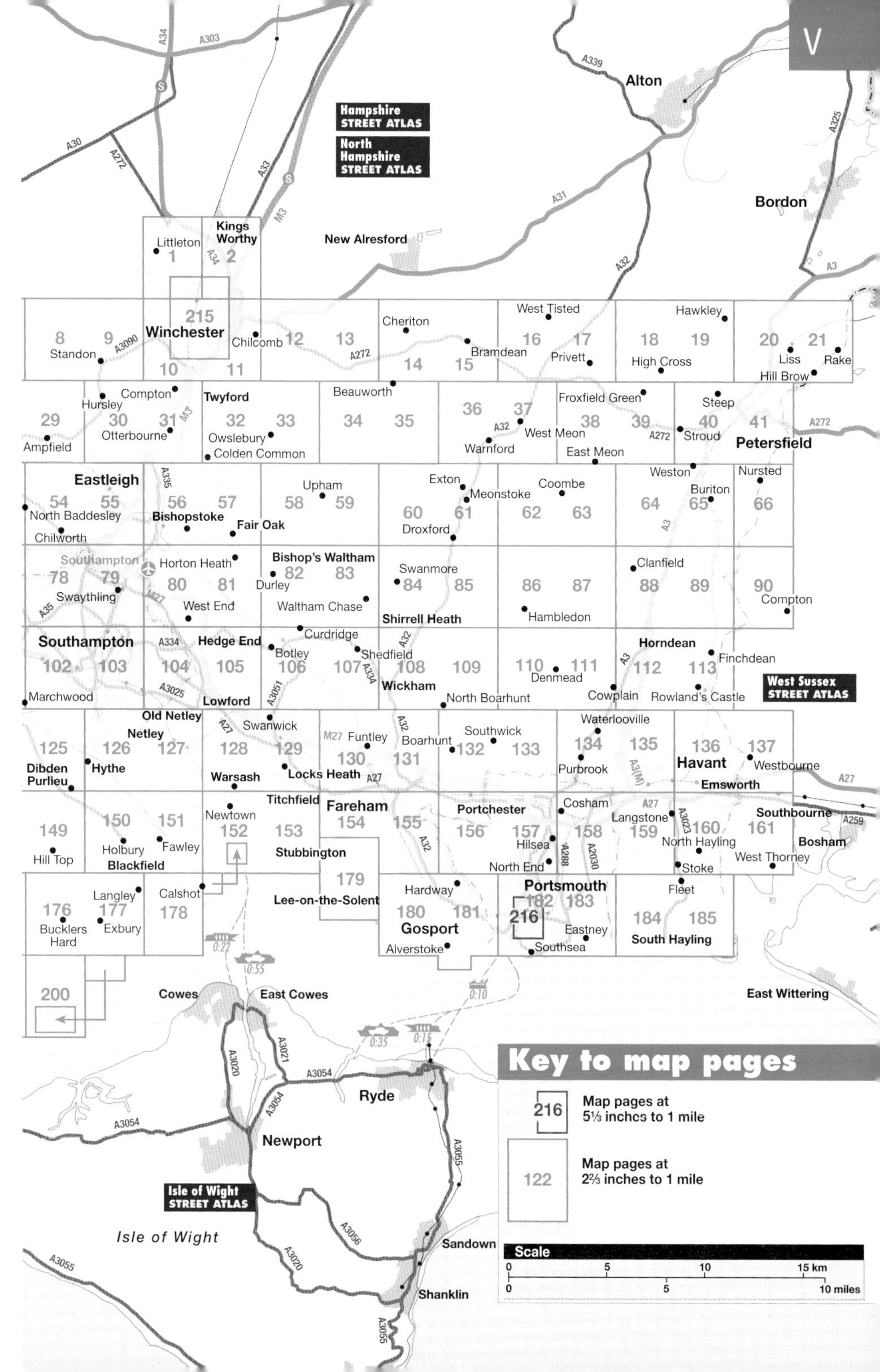
Key to map pages
216
Map pages at 5⅓ inches to 1 mile
122
Map pages at 2⅔ inches to 1 mile
Scale
0
5
10
15 km
0
5
10 miles
Hampshire STREET ATLAS
North Hampshire STREET ATLAS
West Sussex STREET ATLAS
Isle of Wight STREET ATLAS
Alton
Bordon
New Alresford
Littleton
Kings Worthy
Winchester
Chilcomb
Standon
Cheriton
Bramdean
West Tisted
Privett
Hawkley
High Cross
Liss
Rake
Hill Brow
Hursley
Compton
Twyford
Beauworth
Froxfield Green
Steep
Ampfield
Otterbourne
Owslebury
Colden Common
Warnford
West Meon
East Meon
Stroud
Petersfield
Eastleigh
North Baddesley
Chilworth
Bishopstoke
Fair Oak
Upham
Exton
Meonstoke
Droxford
Coombe
Weston
Buriton
Nursted
Southampton
Horton Heath
Bishop's Waltham
Durley
Swanmore
Clanfield
Compton
Swaythling
West End
Waltham Chase
Shirrell Heath
Hambledon
Curdridge
Hedge End
Botley
Shedfield
Wickham
Denmead
Horndean
Finchdean
Marchwood
Lowford
North Boarhunt
Cowplain
Rowland's Castle
Old Netley
Netley
Swanwick
Funtley
Boarhunt
Southwick
Waterlooville
Purbrook
Havant
Westbourne
Emsworth
Dibden Purlieu
Hythe
Warsash
Locks Heath
Titchfield
Fareham
Portchester
Cosham
Langstone
Southbourne
Bosham
Newtown
Hill Top
Holbury
Fawley
Blackfield
Stubbington
Hilsea
North End
North Hayling
Stoke
West Thorney
Langley
Calshot
Lee-on-the-Solent
Hardway
Portsmouth
Fleet
Bucklers Hard
Exbury
Gosport
Alverstoke
Eastney
Southsea
South Hayling
Cowes
East Cowes
East Wittering
Ryde
Newport
Isle of Wight
Sandown
Shanklin
0:22
0:55
0:10
0:35
0:15
A34
A303
A339
A30
A272
A33
M3
A31
A3
A32
A3090
A325
A335
A35
M27
A27
A334
A3025
A3051
A3(M)
A3023
A2030
A288
A259
A3054
A3020
A3021
A3055
A3056
1
2
215
8
9
10
11
12
13
14
15
16
17
18
19
20
21
29
30
31
32
33
34
35
36
37
38
39
40
41
54
55
56
57
58
59
60
61
62
63
64
65
66
78
79
80
81
82
83
84
85
86
87
88
89
90
102
103
104
105
106
107
108
109
110
111
112
113
125
126
127
128
129
130
131
132
133
134
135
136
137
149
150
151
152
153
154
155
156
157
158
159
160
161
176
177
178
179
180
181
182
183
184
185
216
200

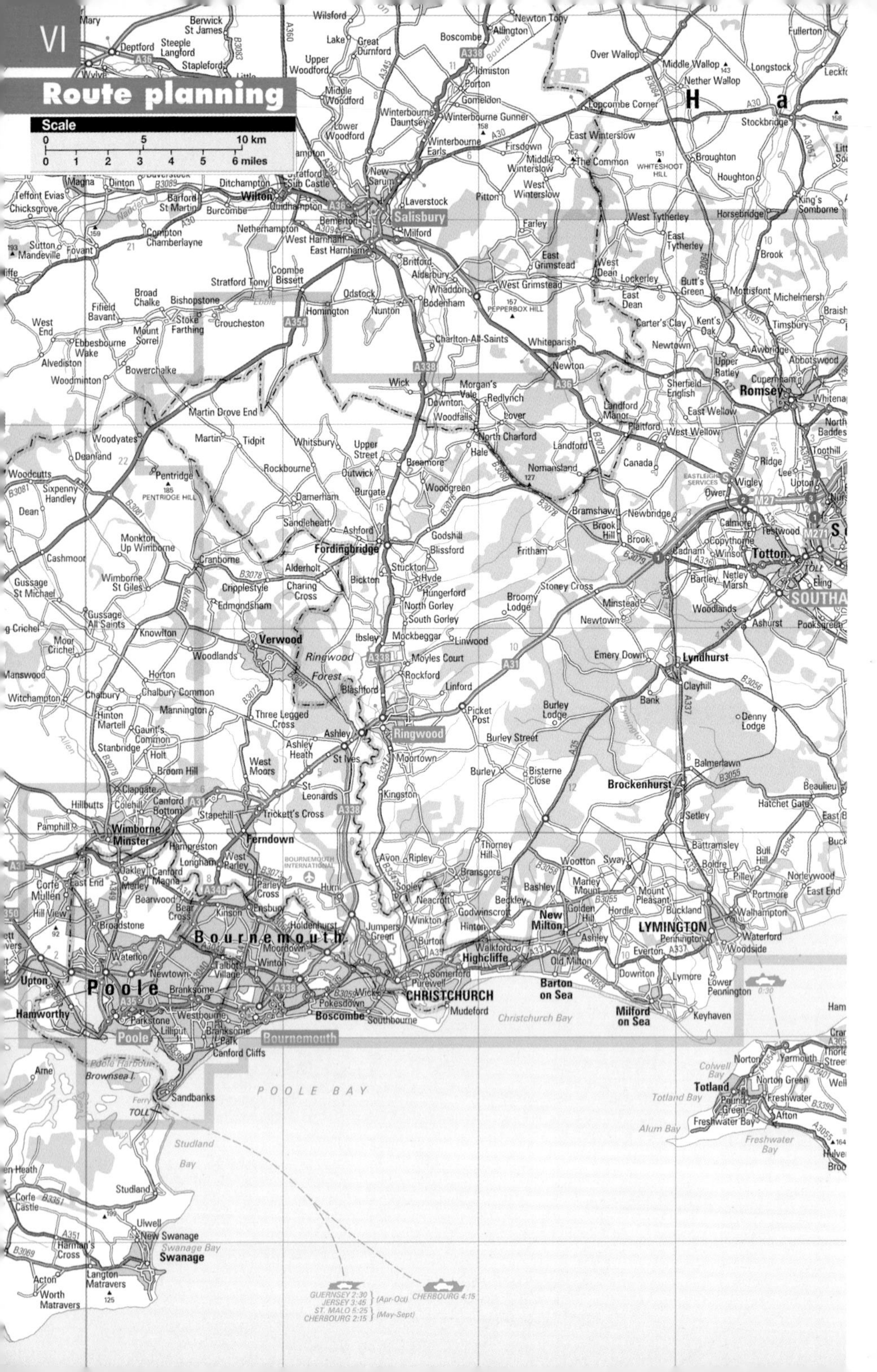

Route planning

Scale

Scale
0   5   10 km
0 1 2 3 4 5 6 miles

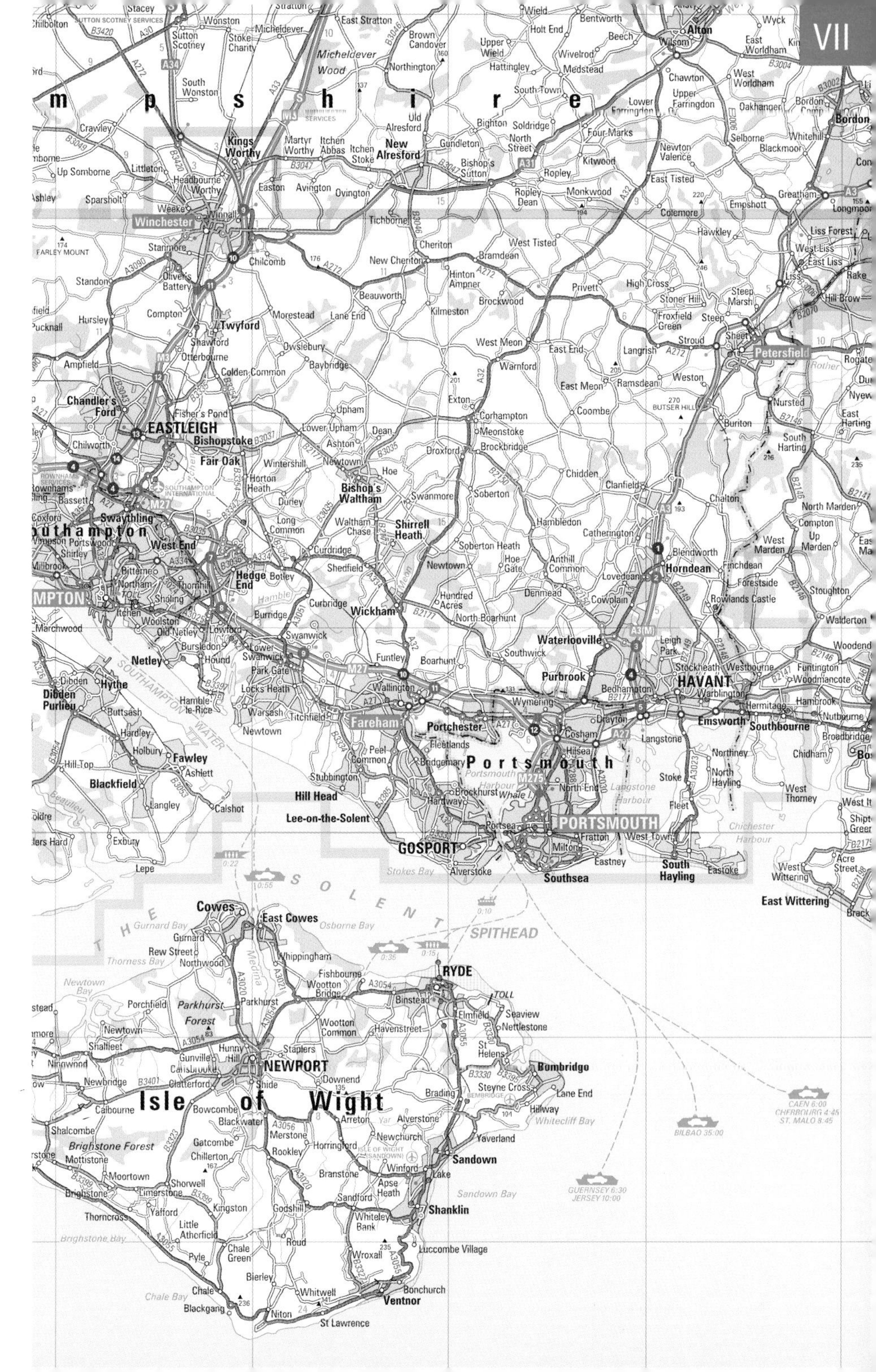
Hampshire
Isle of Wight
THE SOLENT
SPITHEAD
Winchester
EASTLEIGH
Southampton
Portsmouth
PORTSMOUTH
Petersfield
Fareham
GOSPORT
HAVANT
NEWPORT
RYDE
Cowes
East Cowes
Alton
Bordon
Kings Worthy
New Alresford
Chandler's Ford
Bishopstoke
Fair Oak
Twyford
West End
Hedge End
Botley
Bishop's Waltham
Shirrell Heath
Wickham
Waterlooville
Purbrook
Horndean
Emsworth
Southbourne
Portchester
Cosham
Hilsea
Southsea
South Hayling
Hill Head
Lee-on-the-Solent
Netley
Hythe
Dibden Purlieu
Fawley
Blackfield
Calshot
Burridge
Swanwick
Sandown
Shanklin
Ventnor
Bembridge
Brading
Seaview
St Helens
Yarmouth
Michelدever Wood
Micheldever Wood
Parkhurst Forest
Brighstone Forest
Southampton Water
Portsmouth Harbour
Langstone Harbour
Chichester Harbour
Osborne Bay
Gurnard Bay
Thorness Bay
Newtown Bay
Whitecliff Bay
Sandown Bay
Brighstone Bay
Chale Bay
Stokes Bay
East Wittering
West Wittering
Rowlands Castle
Clanfield
Catherington
Denmead
Soberton
Droxford
Meonstoke
Corhampton
Exton
West Meon
East Meon
Cheriton
Hinton Ampner
Bramdean
Ropley
Four Marks
Medstead
Chawton
Selborne
Liss
Steep
Sheet
Buriton
Chalton
Blendworth
Lovedean
Cowplain
Leigh Park
Bedhampton
Warblington
Westbourne
Hermitage
Stubbington
Titchfield
Warsash
Locks Heath
Park Gate
Sarisbury
Bursledon
Hamble-le-Rice
Woolston
Sholing
Bitterne
Swaythling
Shirley
Millbrook
Rownhams
Chilworth
Bassett
Ampfield
Hursley
Otterbourne
Shawford
Compton
Colden Common
Owslebury
Upham
Durley
Curdridge
Shedfield
Wootton Bridge
Binstead
Fishbourne
Whippingham
Northwood
Gurnard
Carisbrooke
Shorwell
Brighstone
Godshill
Wroxall
Niton
Whitwell
Chale
Blackgang
St Lawrence
Bonchurch
Luccombe Village
Lake
Arreton
Alverstone
Yaverland
Nettlestone
Elmfield
Havenstreet
CAEN 6:00
CHERBOURG 4:45
ST. MALO 8:45
BILBAO 35:00
GUERNSEY 6:30
JERSEY 10:00

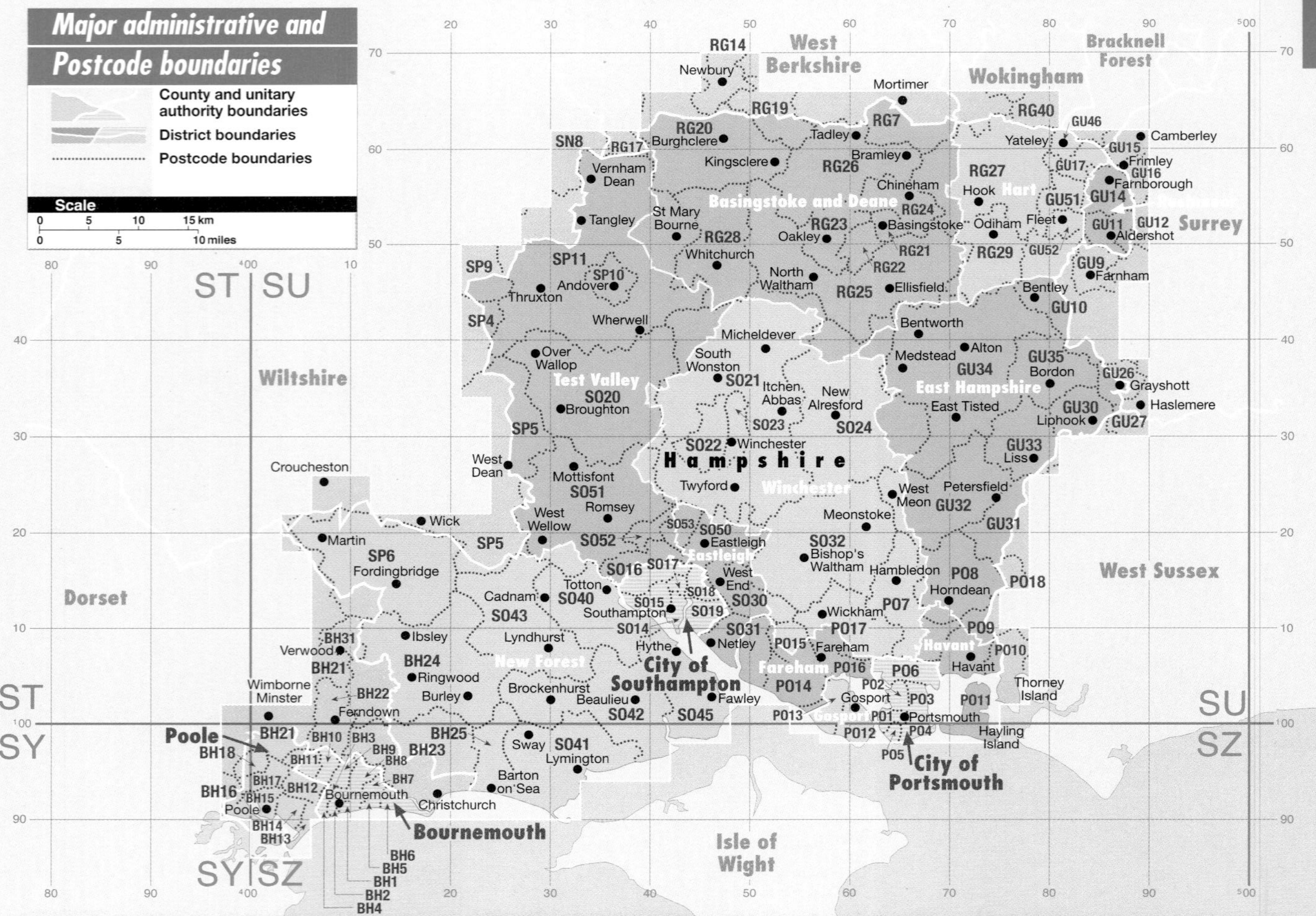

Major administrative and Postcode boundaries

County and unitary authority boundaries
District boundaries
Postcode boundaries

Scale

0   5   10   15 km
0   5   10 miles

2

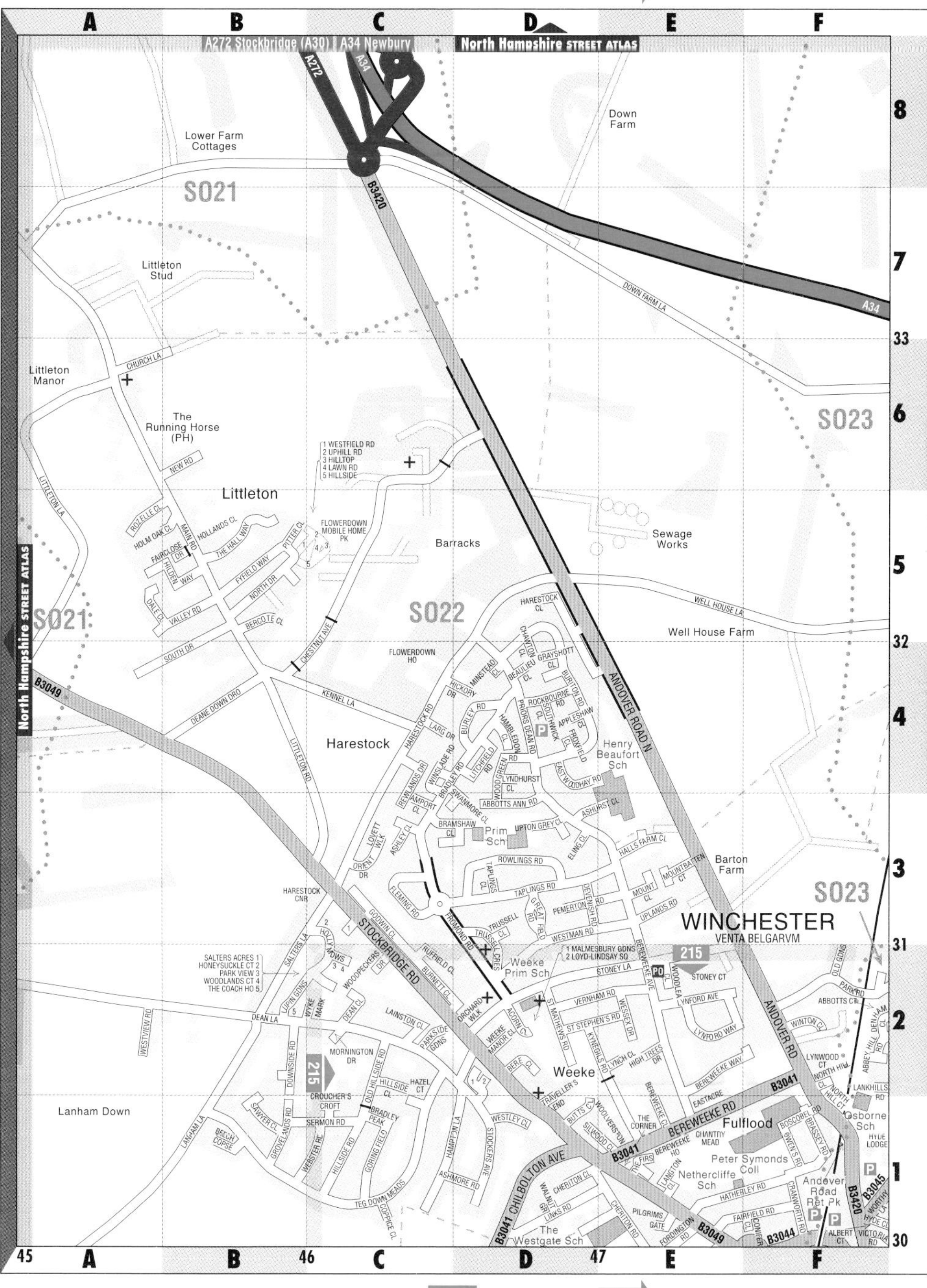
A
B
C
D
E
F
A272 Stockbridge (A30)
A34 Newbury
North Hampshire STREET ATLAS
A272
A34
8
7
6
5
4
3
2
1
33
32
31
30
45
46
47
Down Farm
Lower Farm Cottages
SO21
B3420
Littleton Stud
DOWN FARM LA
Littleton Manor
CHURCH LA
The Running Horse (PH)
SO23
1 WESTFIELD RD
2 UPHILL RD
3 HILLTOP
4 LAWN RD
5 HILLSIDE
NEW RD
Littleton
LITTLETON LA
ROZELLE CL
HOLM OAK CL
MAIN RD
HOLLANDS CL
THE HALL WAY
PITTER CL
FLOWERDOWN MOBILE HOME PK
Barracks
Sewage Works
FAIRCLOSE DR
HILDEN WAY
FYFIELD WAY
NORTH DR
DALE CL
VALLEY RD
BERCOTE CL
SO22
HARESTOCK CL
WELL HOUSE LA
Well House Farm
SOUTH DR
CHESTNUT AVE
FLOWERDOWN HO
CHAWTON CL
GRAYSHOTT CL
BEAULIEU CL
MINSTEAD CL
BURITON RD
B3049
DEANE DOWN DRO
KENNEL LA
HICKORY DR
ANDOVER ROAD N
ROCKBOURNE RD
SOUTHWICK CL
PRIORS DEAN RD
APPLESHAW CL
HARESTOCK RD
LARG DR
BURLEY RD
HAMBLEDON CL
FROXFIELD CL
Harestock
LITTLETON RD
WINSLADE RD
LITCHFIELD RD
Henry Beaufort Sch
BEWLANDS DR
BRADLEY RD
WOODGREEN RD
LYNDHURST CL
EAST WOODHAY RD
AMPORT CL
SWANMORE CL
ABBOTTS ANN RD
ASHURST CL
BRAMSHAW CL
Prim Sch
UPTON GREY CL
LOVETT WLK
ASHLEY CL
ELING CL
HALLS FARM CL
Barton Farm
ROWLINGS RD
ORIENT DR
TAPLINGS CL
MOUNTBATTEN CT
TAPLINGS RD
HARESTOCK CNR
FLEMING RD
GREAT FLD
PEMERTON RD
DEVENISH RD
MOUNT CL
UPLANDS RD
WINCHESTER
VENTA BELGARVM
GODWIN CL
TRUSSELL CL
WESTMAN RD
FROMOND RD
TRUSSELL CRES
STOCKBRIDGE RD
1 MALMESBURY GDNS
2 LOYD-LINDSAY SQ
215
SALTERS ACRES 1
HONEYSUCKLE CT 2
PARK VIEW 3
WOODLANDS CT 4
THE COACH HO 5
SALTERS LA
HOLLY MWS
RUFFIELD CL
Weeke Prim Sch
STONEY LA
BEREWEEKE AVE
PO
STONEY CT
OLD GDNS
PARK RD
WOODPECKERS DR
BURNETT CL
WOODLEA CL
LYNFORD AVE
ABBOTTS CT
LUPIN GDNS
WYKE MARK
ORCHARD WLK
ACORN CL
ST MATHEWS RD
VERNHAM RD
WESSEX DR
WINTON CL
DENHAM
WESTVIEW RD
DEAN LA
DEAN CL
LAINSTON CL
ST STEPHEN'S RD
LYNFORD WAY
PARKSIDE GDNS
WEEKE MANOR CL
KYNEGILS RD
ABBEY HILL
DOWNSIDE RD
MORNINGTON DR
BERE CL
LYNCH CL
HIGH TREES DR
LYNWOOD CT
NORTH HILL
HAZEL CT
OLD HILLSIDE RD
HILLSIDE CL
Weeke
BEREWEEKE WAY
NORTH HILL CT
LANKHILLS RD
CROUCHER'S CROFT
TRAVELLER'S END
B3041
Lanham Down
SAWYER CL
GROVELANDS RD
BRADLEY PEAK
WESTLEY CL
BUTTS CL
WOOLVERSTON
EASTACRE
BEREWEEKE RD
Fulflood
BOSCOBEL RD
BRASSEY RD
Osborne Sch
LANHAM LA
BEECH COPSE
SERMON RD
HAMPTON LA
STOCKERS AVE
SILWOOD CL
THE CORNER
BEREWEEKE CL
CHANTRY MEAD
OWEN'S RD
HYDE LODGE
WEBSTER RD
HILLSIDE RD
GORING FIELD
ASHMORE RD
CHILBOLTON AVE
THE FIRS
BEREWEEKE HO
Peter Symonds Coll
LANGTON CL
Nethercliffe Sch
Andover Road Ret Pk
B3045
TEG DOWN MEADS
COPPICE CL
WALNUT GR
CHERITON CL
LINKS RD
HATHERLEY RD
CRANWORTH RD
ANDOVER RD
B3420
P
The Westgate Sch
CHERITON RD
PILGRIMS GATE
FORDINGTON RD
B3049
FAIRFIELD RD
CONIFER CL
B3044
ALBERT CT
VICTORIA RD
HYDE CL
WORTHY LA

10
2

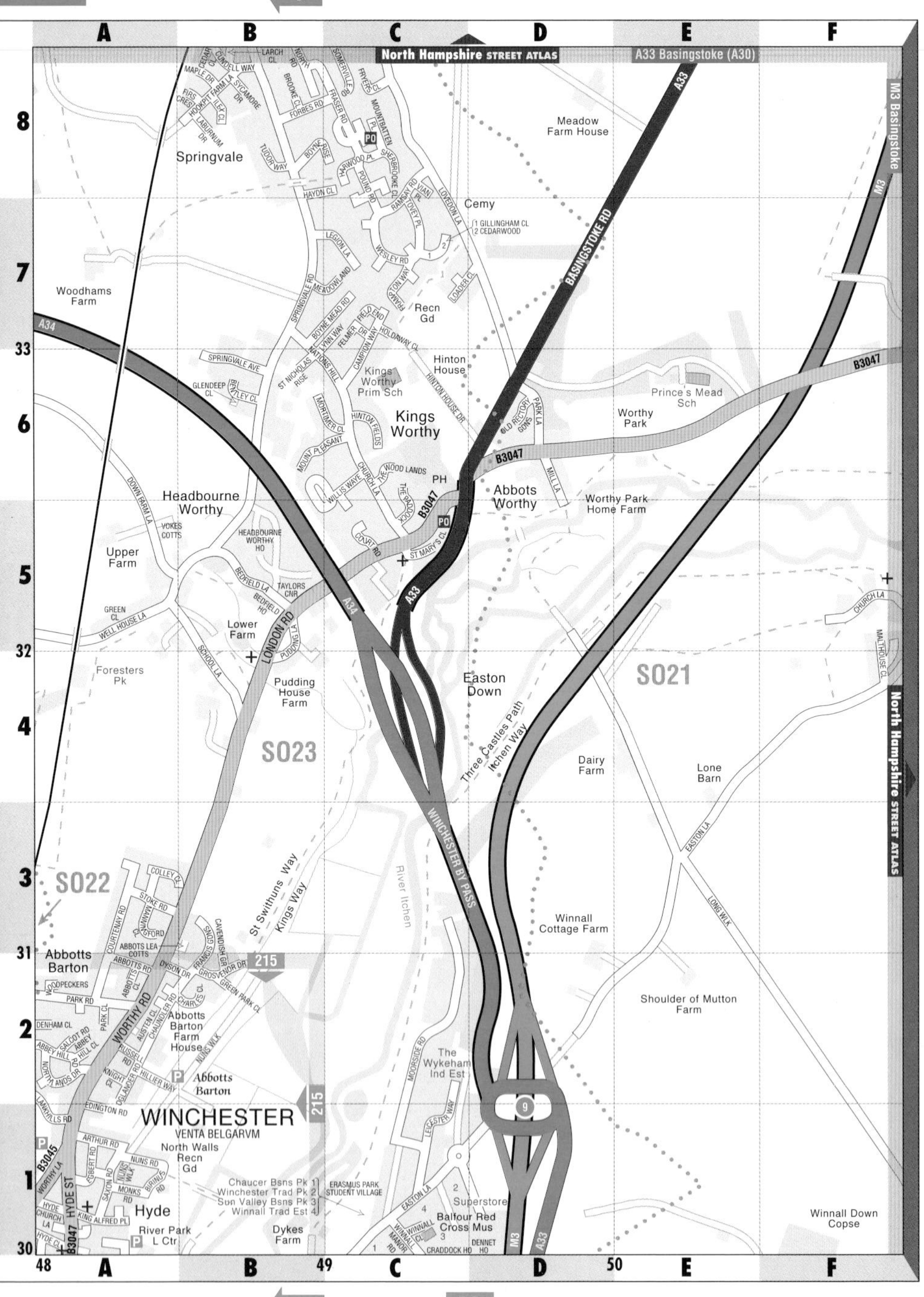
North Hampshire STREET ATLAS
A33 Basingstoke (A30)
M3 Basingstoke
Meadow Farm House
Springvale
Cemy
Woodhams Farm
Recn Gd
Hinton House
Kings Worthy Prim Sch
Kings Worthy
Prince's Mead Sch
Worthy Park
Headbourne Worthy
Abbots Worthy
Worthy Park Home Farm
Upper Farm
Lower Farm
Foresters Pk
Pudding House Farm
Easton Down
SO21
SO23
Three Castles Path
Itchen Way
Dairy Farm
Lone Barn
SO22
St Swithuns Way
Kings Way
River Itchen
WINCHESTER BY PASS
Winnall Cottage Farm
Abbotts Barton
Abbotts Barton Farm House
Shoulder of Mutton Farm
The Wykeham Ind Est
WINCHESTER
VENTA BELGARVM
North Walls Recn Gd
Chaucer Bsns Pk 1
Winchester Trad Pk 2
Sun Valley Bsns Pk 3
Winnall Trad Est 4
ERASMUS PARK STUDENT VILLAGE
Superstore
Balfour Red Cross Mus
Hyde
River Park L Ctr
Dykes Farm
Winnall Down Copse
BASINGSTOKE RD
LONDON RD
WORTHY RD
HYDE ST
A34
A33
B3047
M3
215
1
11

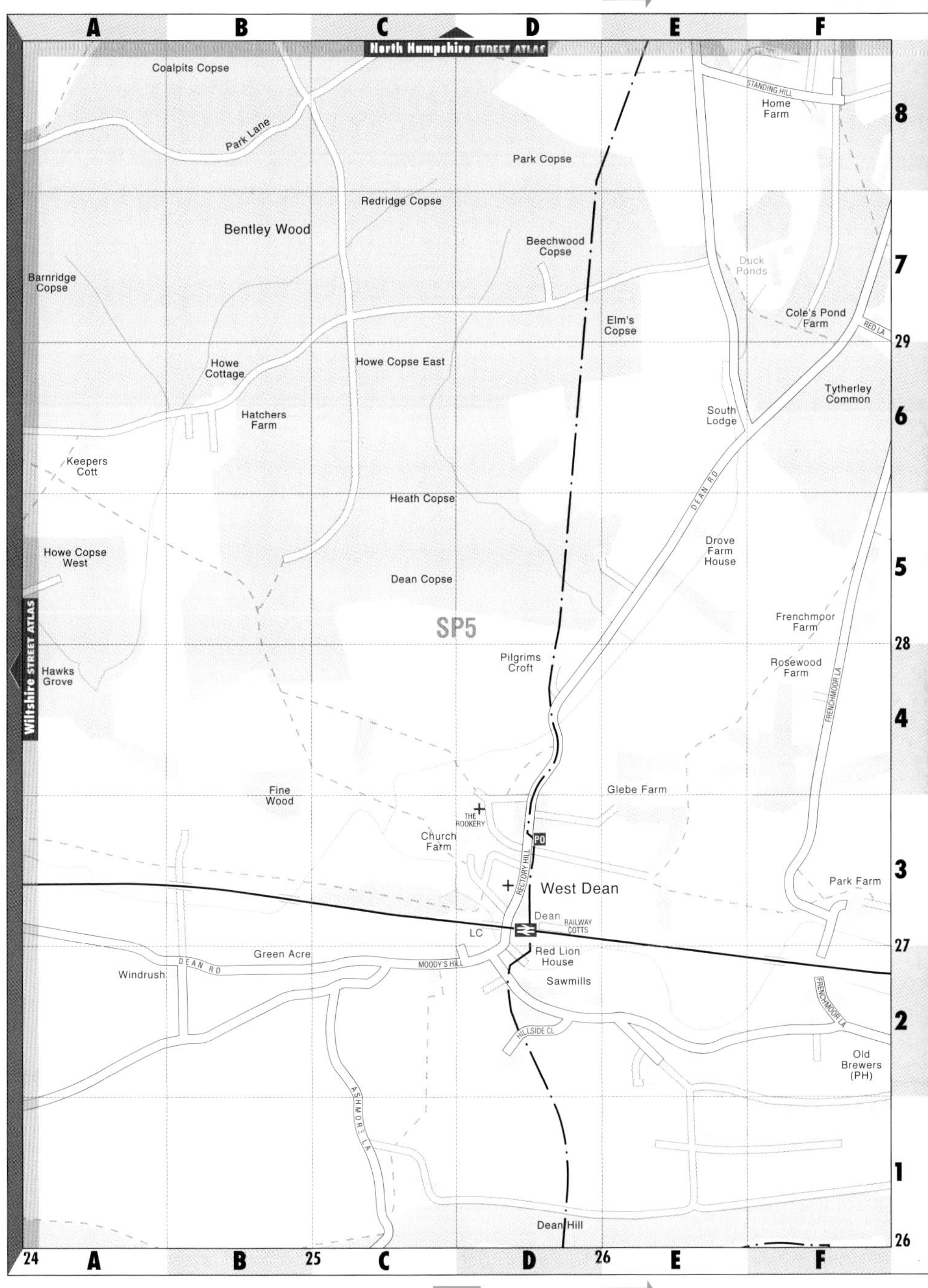

SP5

West Dean

Coalpits Copse

Park Lane

Park Copse

Redridge Copse

Bentley Wood

Beechwood Copse

Barnridge Copse

Elm's Copse

Home Farm

STANDING HILL

Duck Ponds

Cole's Pond Farm

RED LA

Howe Cottage

Howe Copse East

South Lodge

Tytherley Common

Hatchers Farm

Keepers Cott

Heath Copse

Drove Farm House

Howe Copse West

Dean Copse

Frenchmoor Farm

Hawks Grove

Pilgrims Croft

Rosewood Farm

FRENCHMOOR LA

DEAN RD

Fine Wood

Glebe Farm

Park Farm

THE ROOKERY

PO

Church Farm

Dean RAILWAY COTTS

LC

Red Lion House

Sawmills

Green Acre

MOODY'S HILL

Windrush

DEAN RD

HILLSIDE CL

Old Brewers (PH)

FRENCHMOOR LA

ASHMORE LA

Dean Hill

BESSLEY HILL

3

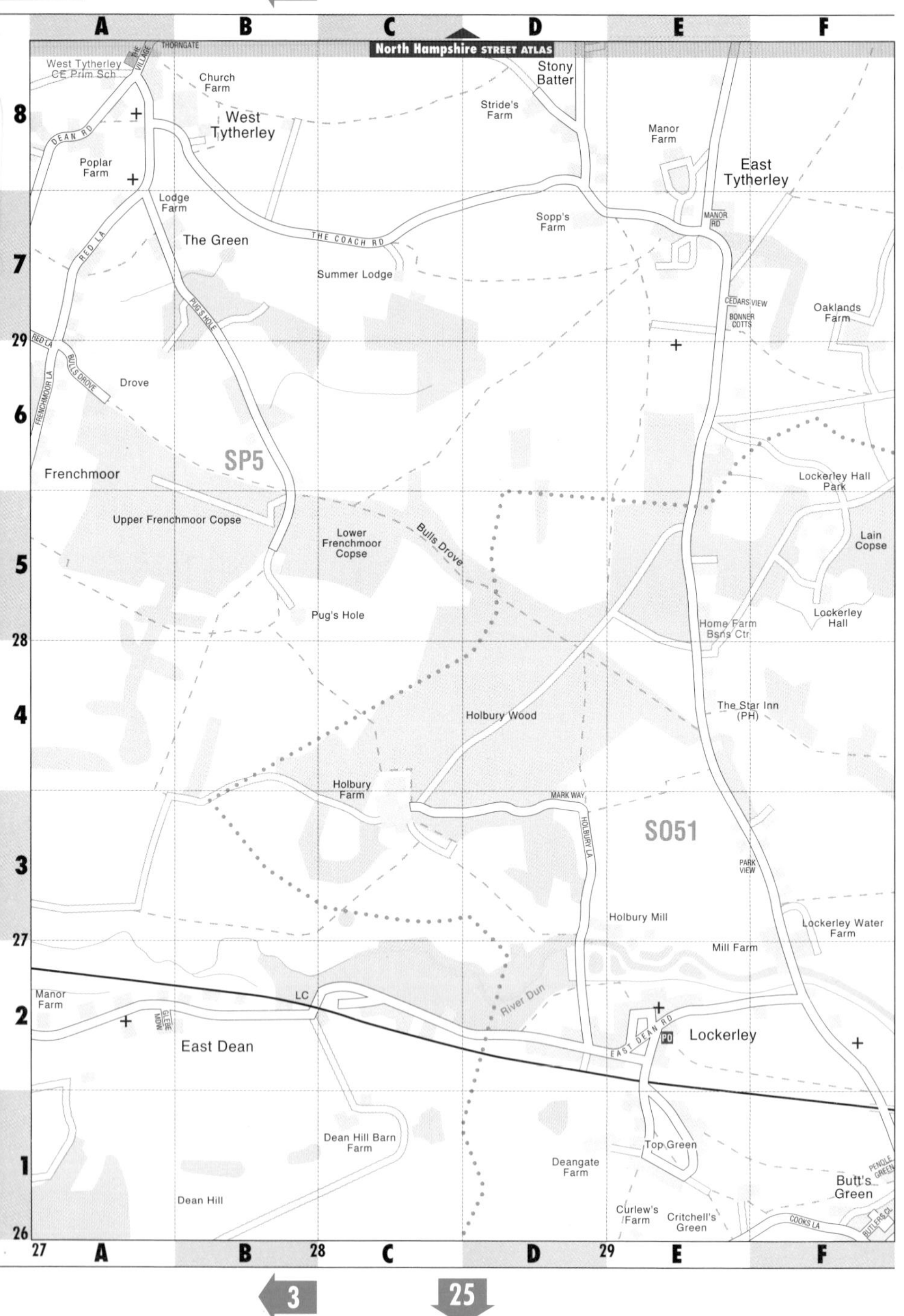
North Hampshire STREET ATLAS
A
B
C
D
E
F
8
7
29
6
5
28
4
3
27
2
1
26
27
28
29
THORNGATE
THE VILLAGE
West Tytherley
CE Prim Sch
Church
Farm
West
Tytherley
Stony
Batter
Stride's
Farm
Manor
Farm
East
Tytherley
DEAN RD
Poplar
Farm
Lodge
Farm
The Green
THE COACH RD
Sopp's
Farm
MANOR
RD
RED LA
Summer Lodge
PUG'S HOLE
CEDARS VIEW
BONNER
COTTS
Oaklands
Farm
RED LA
BULLS DROVE
FRENCHMOOR LA
Drove
SP5
Frenchmoor
Lockerley Hall
Park
Upper Frenchmoor Copse
Lower
Frenchmoor
Copse
Bulls Drove
Lain
Copse
Pug's Hole
Lockerley
Hall
Home Farm
Bsns Ctr
The Star Inn
(PH)
Holbury Wood
Holbury
Farm
MARK WAY
HOLBURY LA
SO51
PARK
VIEW
Holbury Mill
Lockerley Water
Farm
Mill Farm
Manor
Farm
LC
River Dun
GLEBE
MDW
East Dean
EAST DEAN RD
PO
Lockerley
Dean Hill Barn
Farm
Top Green
Deangate
Farm
PENDLE
GREEN
Butt's
Green
Dean Hill
Curlew's
Farm
Critchell's
Green
COOKS LA
BUTLERS CL

3

25

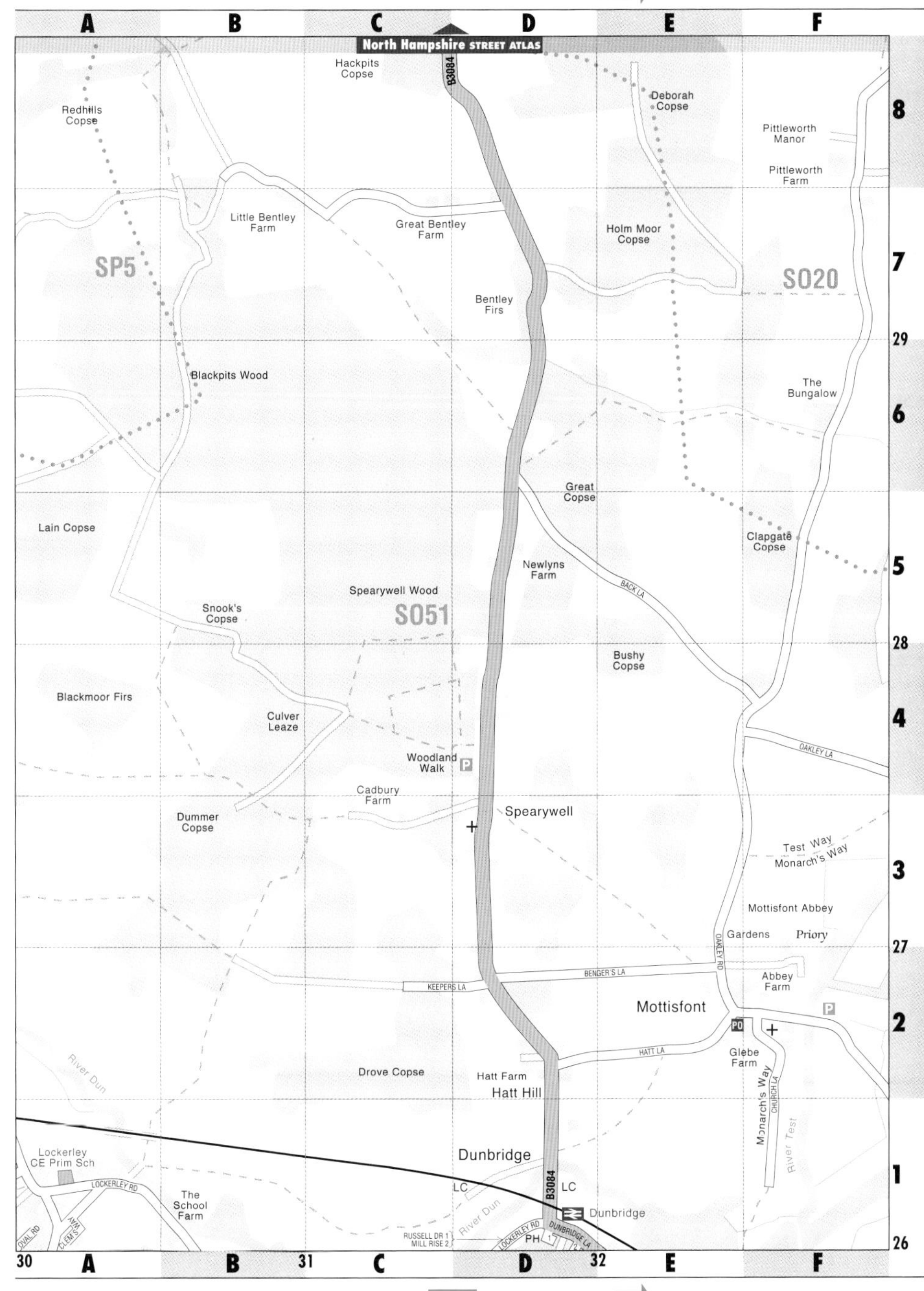

6

A **B** **C** **D** **E** **F**

8

Redhills
Copse

Hackpits
Copse

Deborah
Copse

Pittleworth
Manor

Pittleworth
Farm

Little Bentley
Farm

Great Bentley
Farm

Holm Moor
Copse

SP5

SO20

7

Bentley
Firs

29

Blackpits Wood

The
Bungalow

6

Great
Copse

Lain Copse

Newlyns
Farm

BACK LA

Clapgate
Copse

5

Snook's
Copse

Spearywell Wood

SO51

Bushy
Copse

28

Blackmoor Firs

Culver
Leaze

OAKLEY LA

4

Woodland
Walk P

Cadbury
Farm

Spearywell

Test Way
Monarch's Way

3

Dummer
Copse

Mottisfont Abbey

Gardens   Priory

OAKLEY RD

27

Abbey
Farm

KEEPERS LA

BENGER'S LA

Mottisfont

P

2

River Dun

Drove Copse

Hatt Farm

Hatt Hill

HATT LA

PO

Glebe
Farm

Monarch's Way

CHURCH LA

River Test

Lockerley
CE Prim Sch

LOCKERLEY RD

The
School
Farm

Dunbridge

LC

B3084

LC

1

COAL RD

JAMES
CL

RUSSELL DR 1
MILL RISE 2

LOCKERLEY RD

DUNBRIDGE LA

River Dun

PH

Dunbridge

26

30   **A**   **B**   31   **C**   **D**   32   **E**   **F**

6

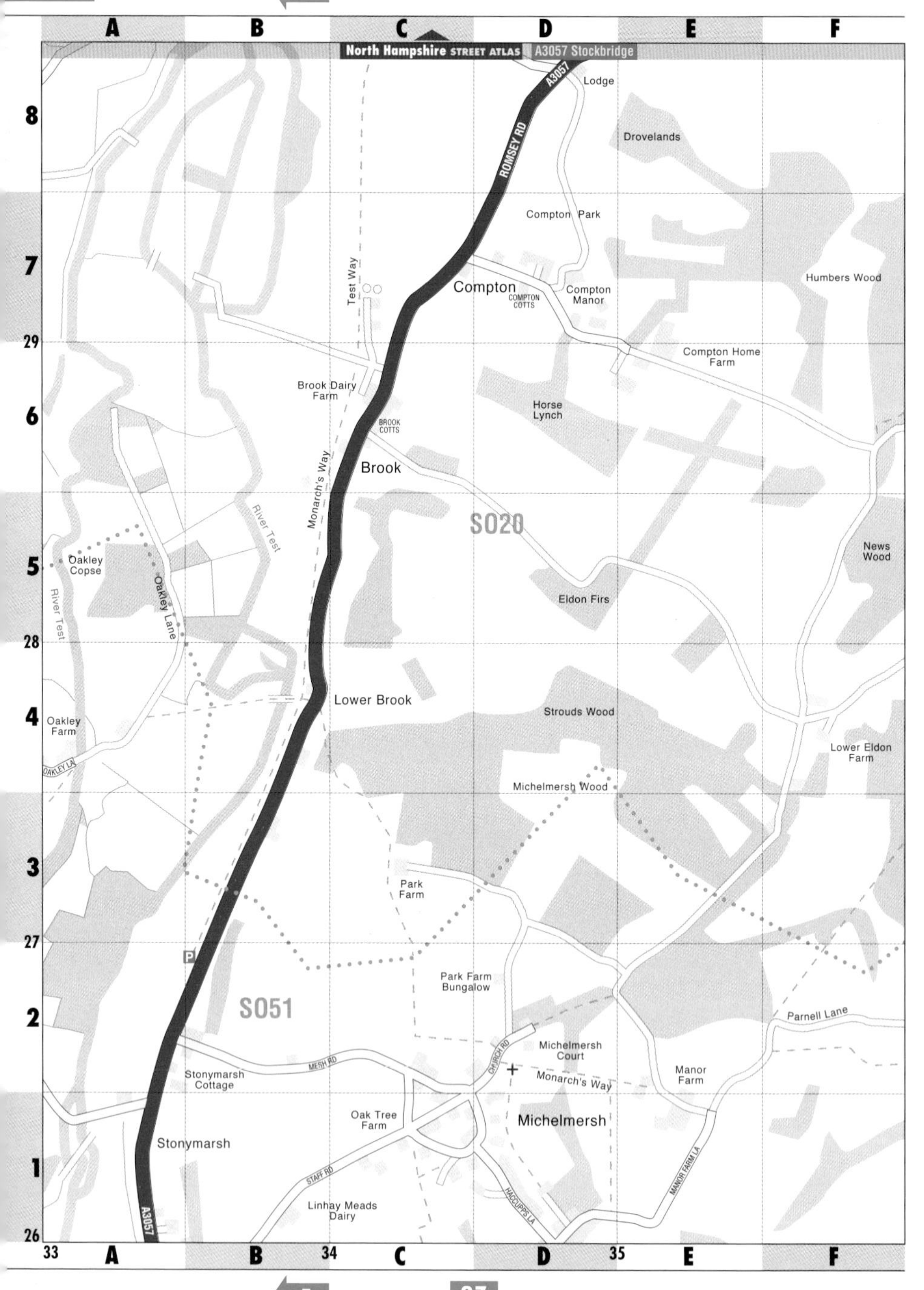

North Hampshire STREET ATLAS A3057 Stockbridge

A3057 Stockbridge

Lodge

Drovelands

Compton Park

Humbers Wood

Test Way

Compton

COMPTON COTTS

Compton Manor

Compton Home Farm

Brook Dairy Farm

BROOK COTTS

Horse Lynch

Monarch's Way

River Test

Brook

SO20

Oakley Copse

Oakley Lane

River Test

News Wood

Eldon Firs

28

Lower Brook

Strouds Wood

Oakley Farm

Lower Eldon Farm

OAKLEY LA

Michelmersh Wood

Park Farm

SO51

Park Farm Bungalow

Parnell Lane

Stonymarsh Cottage

MESH RD

Michelmersh Court

Monarch's Way

Manor Farm

Oak Tree Farm

Michelmersh

Stonymarsh

STAFF RD

Linhay Meads Dairy

HASDUPS LA

MANOR FARM LA

A3057

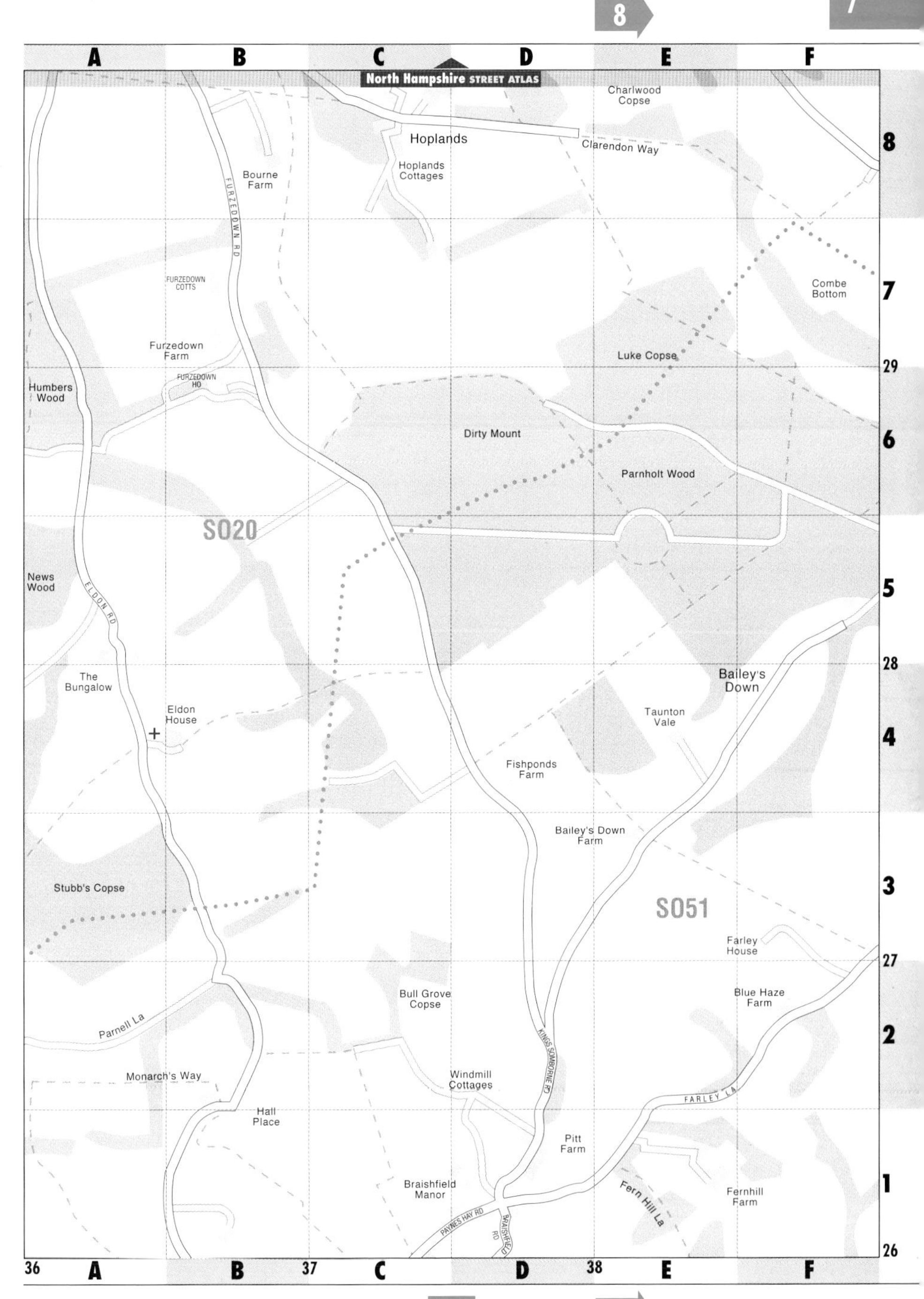

North Hampshire STREET ATLAS

A B C D E F

8

Charlwood
Copse
Hoplands
Clarendon Way
Hoplands
Cottages

Bourne
Farm

FURZEDOWN RD

7

FURZEDOWN
COTTS

Combe
Bottom

Luke Copse

29

Furzedown
Farm

FURZEDOWN
HO

Humbers
Wood

Dirty Mount

6

Parnholt Wood

SO20

News
Wood

ELDON RD

5

28

The
Bungalow

Eldon
House

Bailey's
Down

Taunton
Vale

4

Fishponds
Farm

Bailey's Down
Farm

SO51

Stubb's Copse

3

27

Farley
House

Parnell La

Bull Grove
Copse

Blue Haze
Farm

2

Monarch's Way

KINGS SOMBORNE RD

Windmill
Cottages

FARLEY LA

Hall
Place

Pitt
Farm

Braishfield
Manor

Fern Hill La

Fernhill
Farm

1

PAINES HAY RD

STOMP RD

26

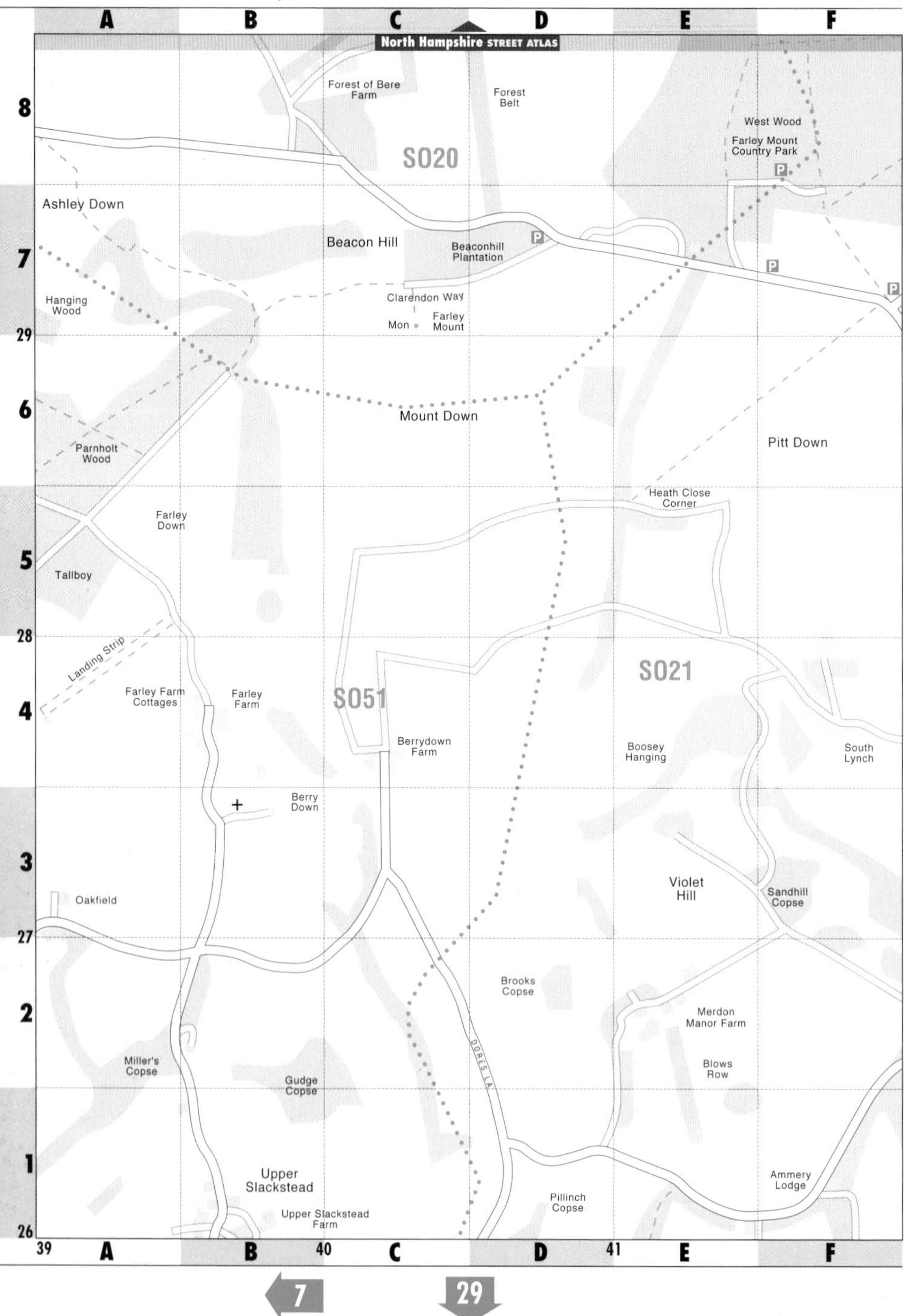
8

Forest of Bere
Farm

Forest
Belt

West Wood

Farley Mount
Country Park

P

SO20

Ashley Down

7

Beacon Hill

Beaconhill
Plantation

P

P

P

Hanging
Wood

Clarendon Way

29

Mon •

Farley
Mount

6

Mount Down

Pitt Down

Parnholt
Wood

Heath Close
Corner

Farley
Down

5

Tallboy

28

Landing Strip

SO021

4

Farley Farm
Cottages

Farley
Farm

SO51

Berrydown
Farm

Boosey
Hanging

South
Lynch

Berry
Down

+

3

Violet
Hill

Sandhill
Copse

Oakfield

27

Brooks
Copse

Merdon
Manor Farm

2

Miller's
Copse

Gudge
Copse

DORES LA

Blows
Row

1

Upper
Slackstead

Ammery
Lodge

26

Upper Slackstead
Farm

Pillinch
Copse

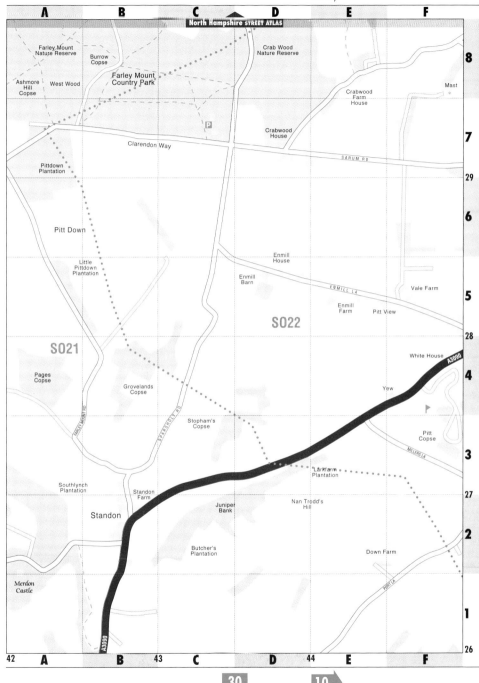

Farley Mount
Nature Reserve

Crab Wood
Nature Reserve

Burrow
Copse

Ashmore
Hill
Copse

West Wood

Farley Mount
Country Park

Crabwood
Farm
House

Mast

Crabwood
House

Clarendon Way

SARUM RD

Pittdown
Plantation

29

Pitt Down

Enmill
House

6

Little
Pittdown
Plantation

Enmill
Barn

Enmill
Farm

ENMILL LA

Vale Farm

5

SO22

Enmill
Farm

Pitt View

SO21

28

Pages
Copse

Grovelands
Copse

White House

A3090

Yew

4

FARLEY MOUNT RD

SPERSHOLT RD

Stopham's
Copse

Pitt
Copse

MILLERS LA

3

Southlynch
Plantation

Larkfarm
Plantation

27

Standon
Farm

Juniper
Bank

Nan Trodd's
Hill

Standon

Down Farm

2

Merdon
Castle

Butcher's
Plantation

PORT LA

1

A3090

26

9 1

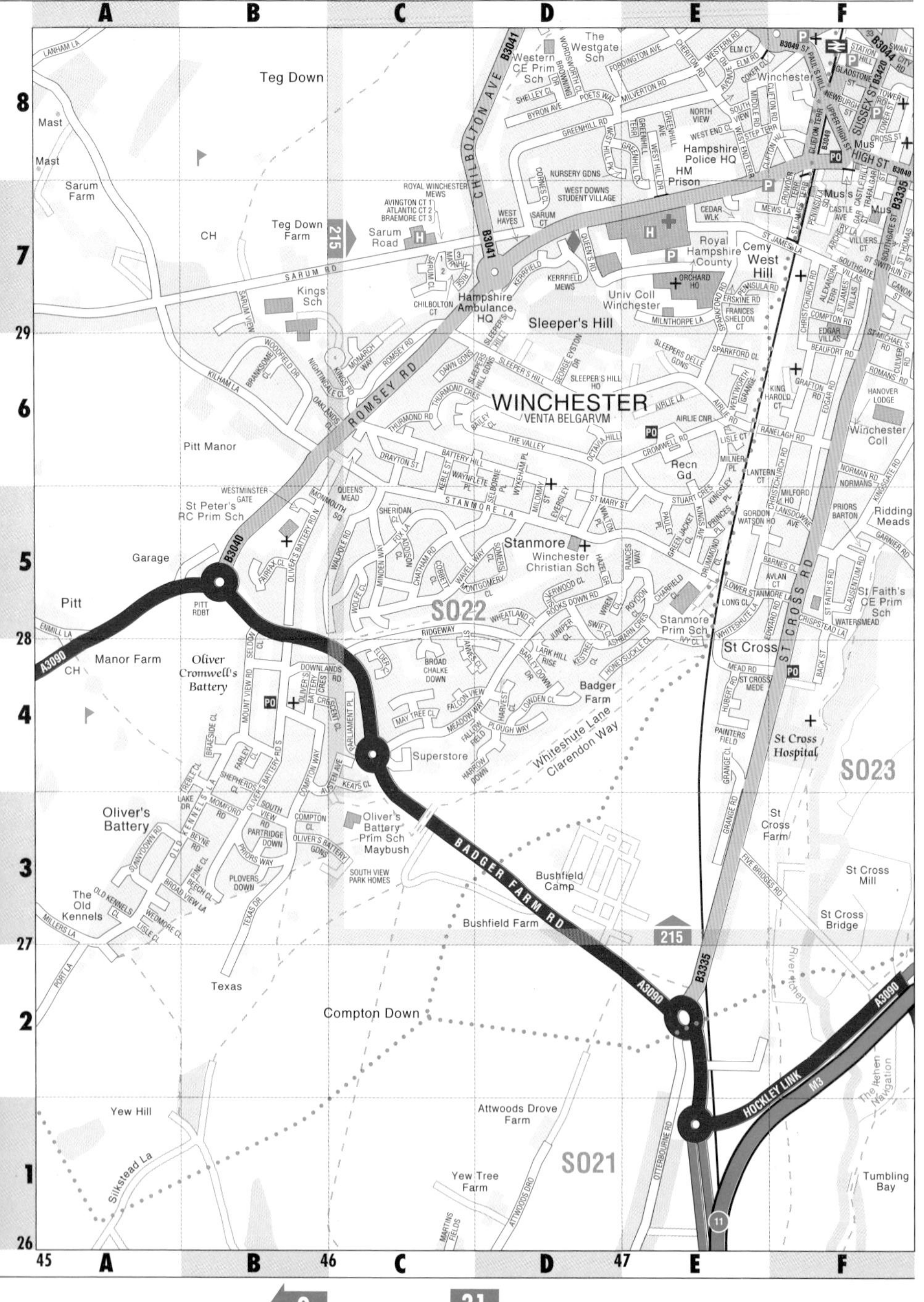

A B C D E F
8 7 29 6 5 28 4 3 27 2 1 26
45 46 47
Teg Down
Mast
Mast
Sarum Farm
CH
Teg Down Farm
215
Sarum Road
SARUM RD
Kings' Sch
Western CE Prim Sch
The Westgate Sch
Winchester
Hampshire Police HQ
HM Prison
Mus
HIGH ST
SUSSEX ST
B3041
B3040
B3044
B3335
CHILBOLTON AVE
WEST DOWNS STUDENT VILLAGE
ROYAL WINCHESTER MEWS
Royal Hampshire County
Cemy
West Hill
Univ Coll Winchester
Hampshire Ambulance HQ
Sleeper's Hill
ROMSEY RD
WINCHESTER
VENTA BELGARVM
Pitt Manor
St Peter's RC Prim Sch
Garage
Pitt
PITT RDBT
Manor Farm
CH
A3090
Oliver Cromwell's Battery
Stanmore
Winchester Christian Sch
Recn Gd
SO22
Stanmore Prim Sch
St Cross
ST CROSS RD
Badger Farm
Whiteshute Lane
Clarendon Way
Superstore
Winchester Coll
Ridding Meads
St Faith's CE Prim Sch
St Cross Hospital
SO23
Oliver's Battery
Oliver's Battery Prim Sch
Maybush
BADGER FARM RD
Bushfield Camp
Bushfield Farm
The Old Kennels
St Cross Farm
St Cross Mill
St Cross Bridge
Texas
Compton Down
River Itchen
HOCKLEY LINK
M3
Yew Hill
Silkstead La
Attwoods Drove Farm
SO21
Yew Tree Farm
Tumbling Bay
11

9 31

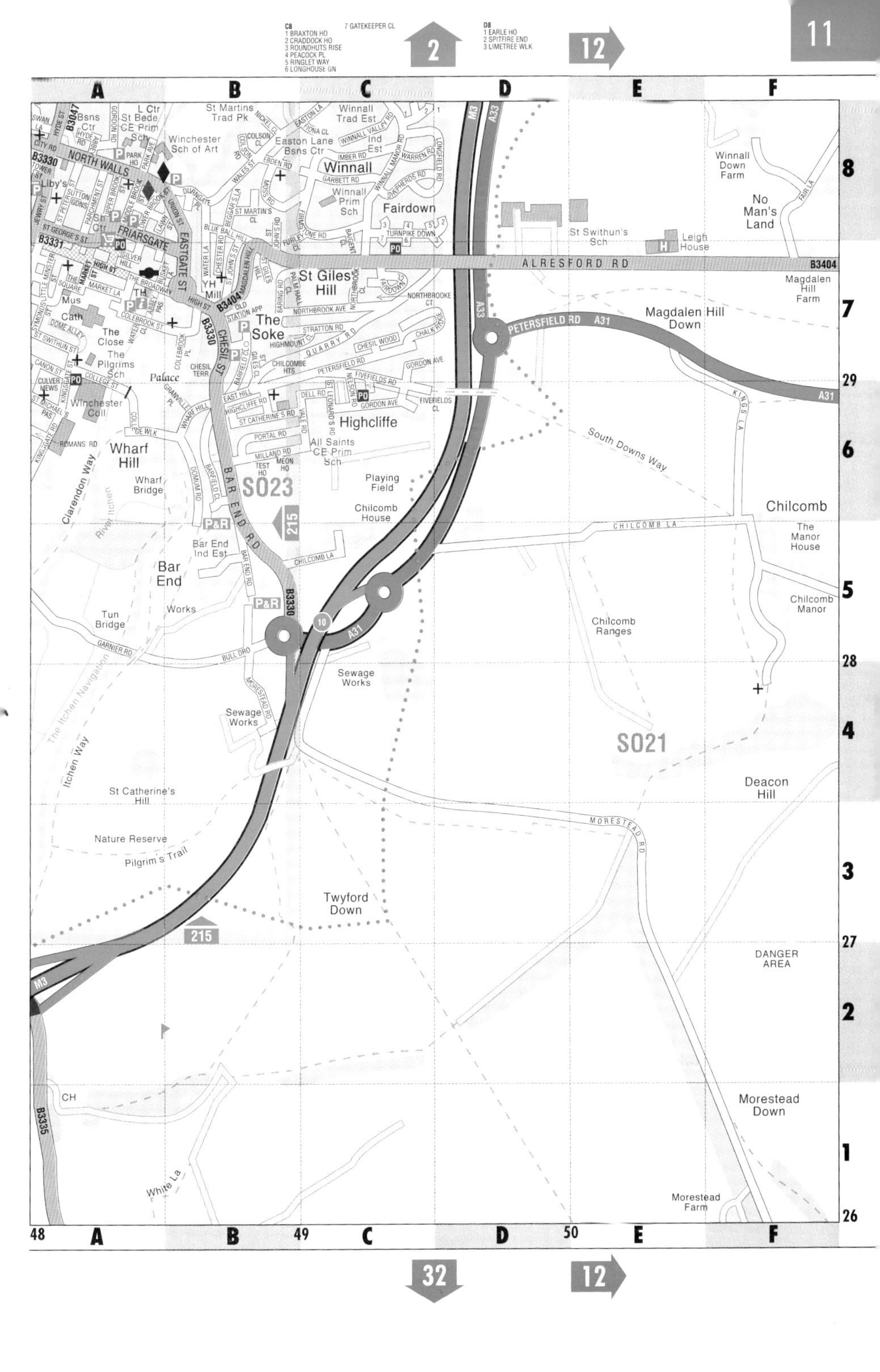
11
C8
1 BRAXTON HO
2 CRADDOCK HO
3 ROUNDHUTS RISE
4 PEACOCK PL
5 RINGLET WAY
6 LONGHOUSE GN
7 GATEKEEPER CL
2
D8
1 EARLE HO
2 SPITFIRE END
3 LIMETREE WLK
12
A
B
C
D
E
F
St Martins Trad Pk
Winnall Trad Est
L Ctr
Bsns Ctr
St Bede CE Prim Sch
Winchester Sch of Art
Easton Lane Bsns Ctr
Winnall Valley Rd Ind Est
Winnall
Winnall Prim Sch
Fairdown
Winnall Down Farm
No Man's Land
NORTH WALLS
FRIARSGATE
EASTGATE ST
Liby's
Ch Ctr
St Swithun's Sch
Leigh House
ALRESFORD RD
B3404
B3330
B3331
B3047
M3
A33
St Giles Hill
TURNPIKE DOWN
NORTHBROOK AVE
HIGH ST
THE BROADWAY
TH
YH Mill
Mus
Cath
The Close
The Pilgrims Sch
Palace
Winchester Coll
The Soke
CHESIL ST
PETERSFIELD RD
A31
Magdalen Hill Down
Magdalen Hill Farm
QUARRY RD
Highcliffe
All Saints CE Prim Sch
South Downs Way
Wharf Hill
Wharf Bridge
SO23
BAR END RD
215
Playing Field
Chilcomb House
Chilcomb
The Manor House
CHILCOMB LA
Clarendon Way
River Itchen
Bar End Ind Est
Bar End
Works
Tun Bridge
GARNIER RD
BULL DRO
Chilcomb Manor
Chilcomb Ranges
Sewage Works
Sewage Works
The Itchen Navigation
Itchen Way
SO21
St Catherine's Hill
Nature Reserve
Pilgrim's Trail
Deacon Hill
MORESTEAD RD
Twyford Down
DANGER AREA
CH
B3335
White La
Morestead Down
Morestead Farm
8
7
29
6
5
28
4
3
27
2
1
26
48
49
50
32
12

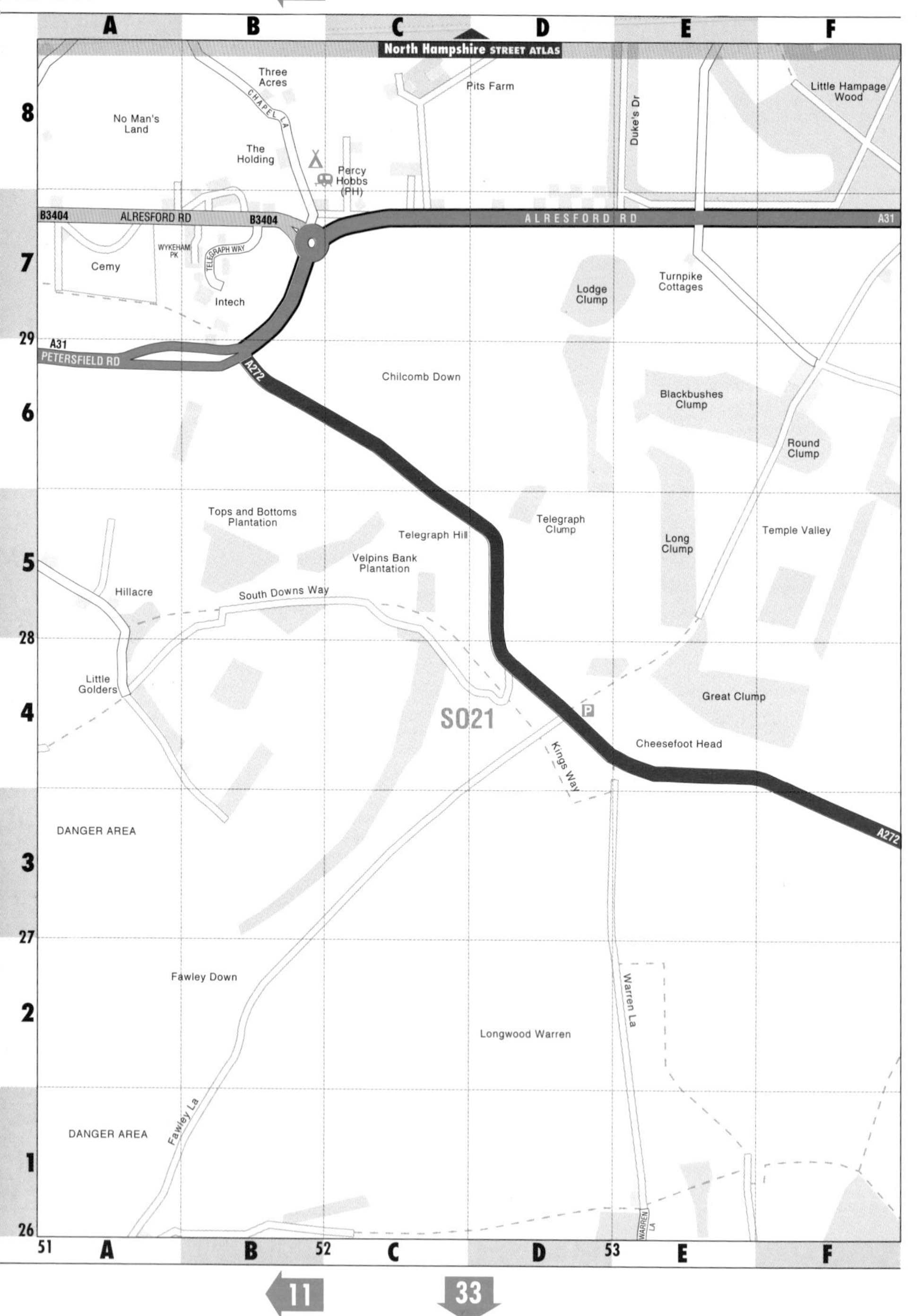

North Hampshire STREET ATLAS

8 · A · B · C · D · E · F

Three Acres

No Man's Land

Pits Farm

Little Hampage Wood

CHAPEL LA

The Holding

Percy Hobbs (PH)

B3404 ALRESFORD RD B3404

ALRESFORD RD A31

7 Cemy

WYKEHAM PK

TELEGRAPH WAY

Intech

Lodge Clump

Turnpike Cottages

29 A31 PETERSFIELD RD

A272

Chilcomb Down

Blackbushes Clump

6

Round Clump

Tops and Bottoms Plantation

Telegraph Hill

Telegraph Clump

Long Clump

Temple Valley

5 Velpins Bank Plantation

Hillacre

South Downs Way

28

Little Golders

Great Clump

4 SO21

Kings Way

Cheesefoot Head

DANGER AREA

3

27

Fawley Down

Warren La

2 Longwood Warren

A272

Fawley La

1 DANGER AREA

Warren La

26

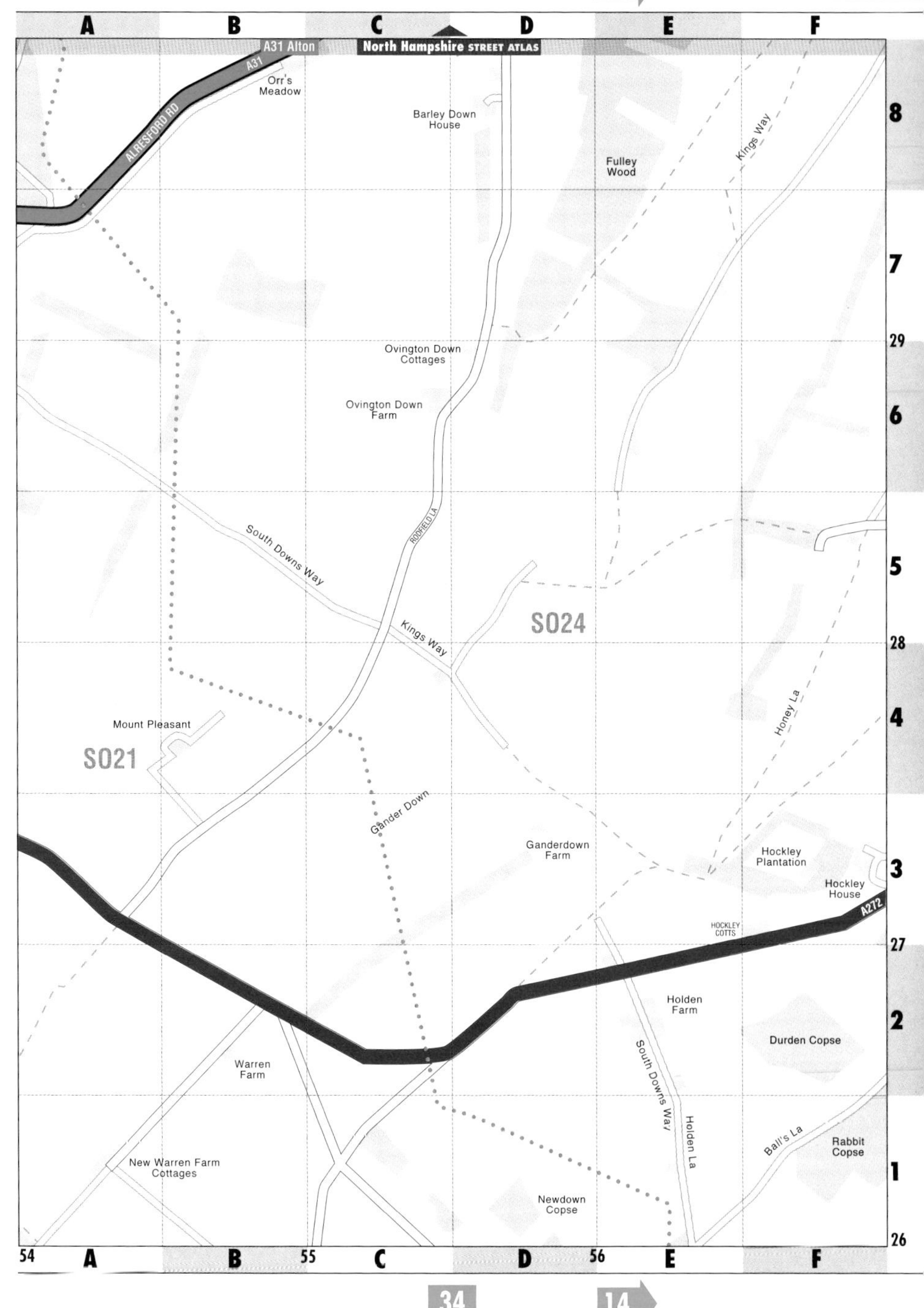

North Hampshire STREET ATLAS

A31 Alton

A31

ALRESFORD RD

Orr's Meadow

Barley Down House

Fulley Wood

Kings Way

8

7

Ovington Down Cottages

29

Ovington Down Farm

6

ROPPELD LA

South Downs Way

5

Kings Way

SO24

28

Honey La

Mount Pleasant

4

SO21

Gander Down

Ganderdown Farm

Hockley Plantation

Hockley House

3

A272

HOCKLEY COTTS

27

Holden Farm

Durden Copse

2

Warren Farm

South Downs Way

Holden La

Ball's La

Rabbit Copse

New Warren Farm Cottages

1

Newdown Copse

26

54   A   B   55   C   D   56   E   F

34

14

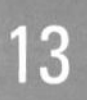

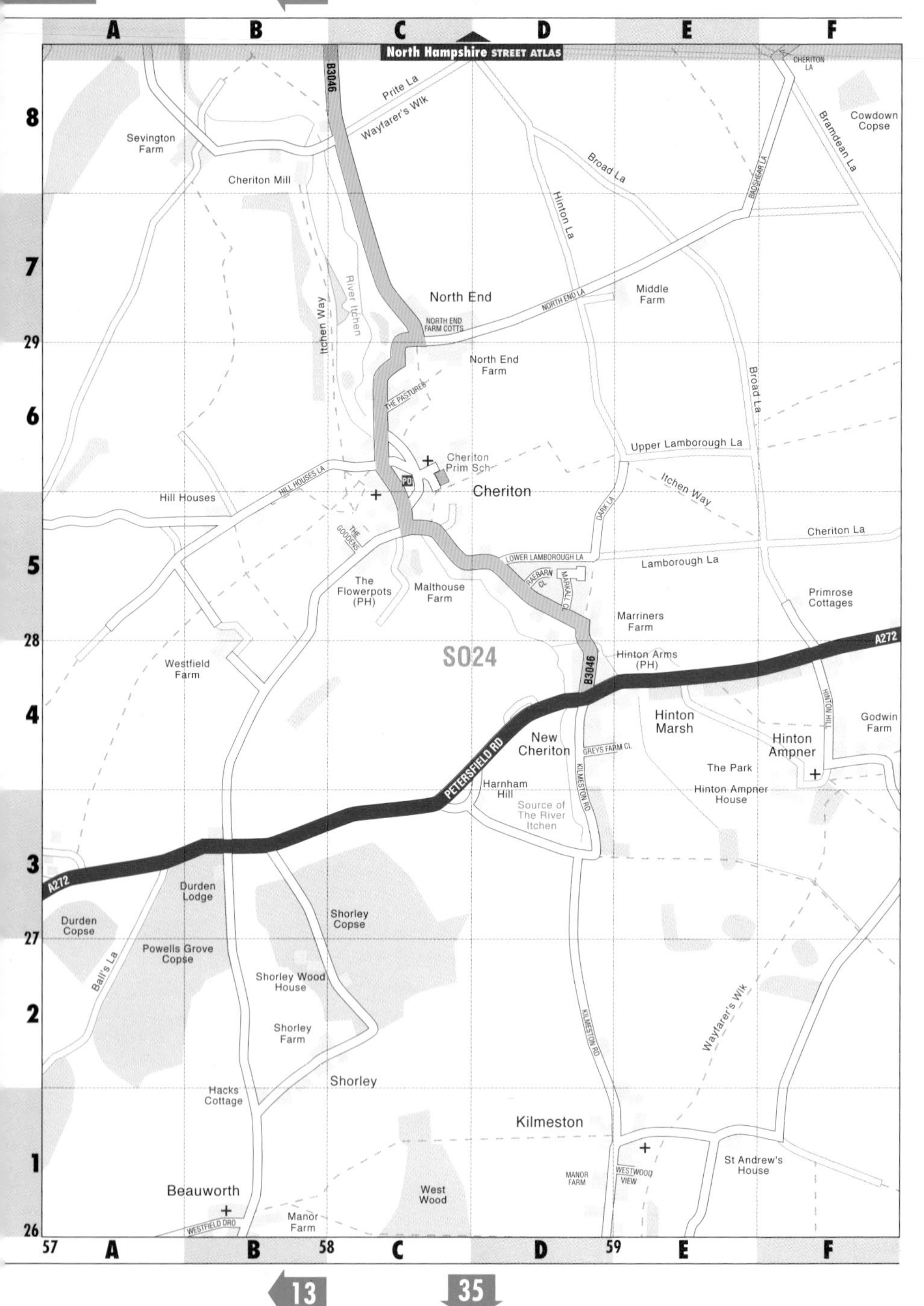

A B C D E F

8

7

29

6

5

28

4

3

27

2

1

26

Cheriton
La

Cowdown
Copse

Sevington
Farm

Cheriton Mill

Prite La

Wayfarer's Wlk

B3046

Broad La

Hinton La

Bramdean La

Broad La

River Itchen

Itchen Way

North End

NORTH END LA

Middle
Farm

NORTH END
FARM COTTS

North End
Farm

THE PASTURES

Upper Lamborough La

Itchen Way

Cheriton
Prim Sch

HILL HOUSES LA

Hill Houses

THE
GARDENS

Cheriton

Cheriton La

The
Flowerpots
(PH)

Malthouse
Farm

LOWER LAMBOROUGH LA

DARK LA

Lamborough La

Primrose
Cottages

OLD BARN
CL

MARSH LA

Marriners
Farm

Westfield
Farm

SO24

B3046

Hinton Arms
(PH)

A272

PETERSFIELD RD

New
Cheriton

GREYS FARM CL

Hinton
Marsh

Hinton
Ampner

Godwin
Farm

A272

Harnham
Hill

Source of
The River
Itchen

KILMESTON RD

The Park

HINTON HILL

Hinton Ampner
House

Durden
Copse

Durden
Lodge

Shorley
Copse

Ball's La

Powells Grove
Copse

Shorley Wood
House

Wayfarer's Wlk

Shorley
Farm

Hacks
Cottage

Shorley

Kilmeston

Beauworth

WESTFIELD DRO

Manor
Farm

West
Wood

MANOR
FARM

WESTWOOD
VIEW

St Andrew's
House

16

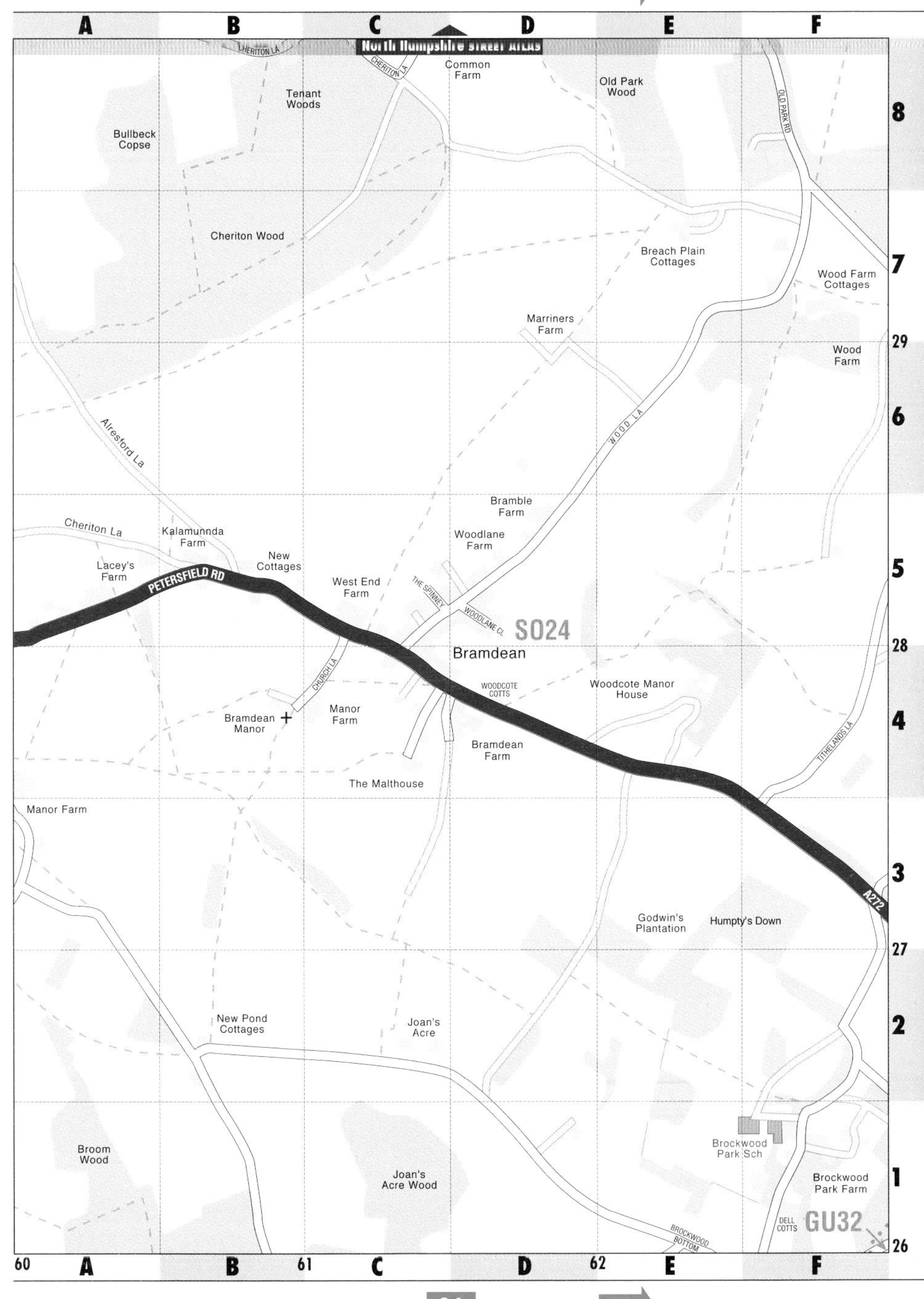

North Hampshire STREET ATLAS
A
B
C
D
E
F
CHERITON LA
Common Farm
Old Park Wood
OLD PARK RD
Tenant Woods
Bullbeck Copse
Cheriton Wood
Breach Plain Cottages
Wood Farm Cottages
Marriners Farm
Wood Farm
WOOD LA
Alresford La
Bramble Farm
Cheriton La
Kalamunnda Farm
Woodlane Farm
New Cottages
Lacey's Farm
PETERSFIELD RD
West End Farm
THE SPINNEY
WOODLANE CL
SO24
Bramdean
CHURCH LA
WOODCOTE COTTS
Woodcote Manor House
Bramdean Manor
Manor Farm
Bramdean Farm
TITHELANDS LA
The Malthouse
Manor Farm
A272
Godwin's Plantation
Humpty's Down
New Pond Cottages
Joan's Acre
Brockwood Park Sch
Broom Wood
Joan's Acre Wood
Brockwood Park Farm
DELL COTTS
GU32
BROCKWOOD BOTTOM
8
7
29
6
5
28
4
3
27
2
1
26
60
61
62

36
16

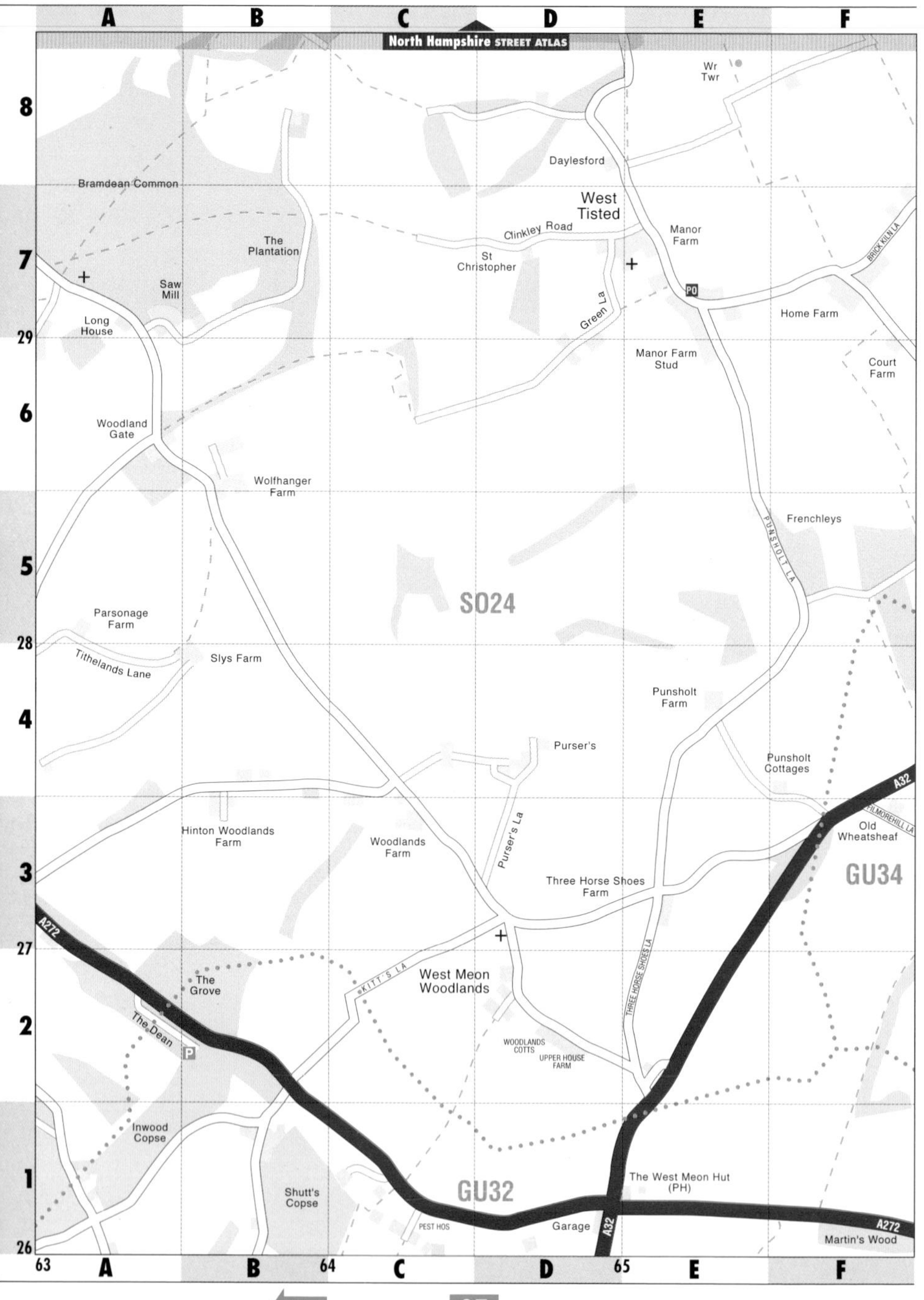

North Hampshire STREET ATLAS

A **B** **C** **D** **E** **F**

Wr
Twr

8

Daylesford

Bramdean Common

West
Tisted

7

The
Plantation

Clinkley Road

Manor
Farm

Saw
Mill

St
Christopher

PO

Long
House

29

Green La

Home Farm

Manor Farm
Stud

6

Court
Farm

Woodland
Gate

Wolfhanger
Farm

Frenchleys

5

SO24

Parsonage
Farm

28

Punsholt
Farm

Tithelands Lane

Slys Farm

4

Punsholt
Cottages

Purser's

A32

Hinton Woodlands
Farm

Woodlands
Farm

Old
Wheatsheaf

3

Purser's La

Three Horse Shoes
Farm

GU34

27

West Meon
Woodlands

The
Grove

Skitt's La

2

The Dean

WOODLANDS
COTTS

UPPER HOUSE
FARM

Three Horse Shoes La

Inwood
Copse

1

Shutt's
Copse

GU32

The West Meon Hut
(PH)

A272

26

PEST HOS

Garage

A32

Martin's Wood

63 **A** 64 **C** **D** 65 **E** **F**

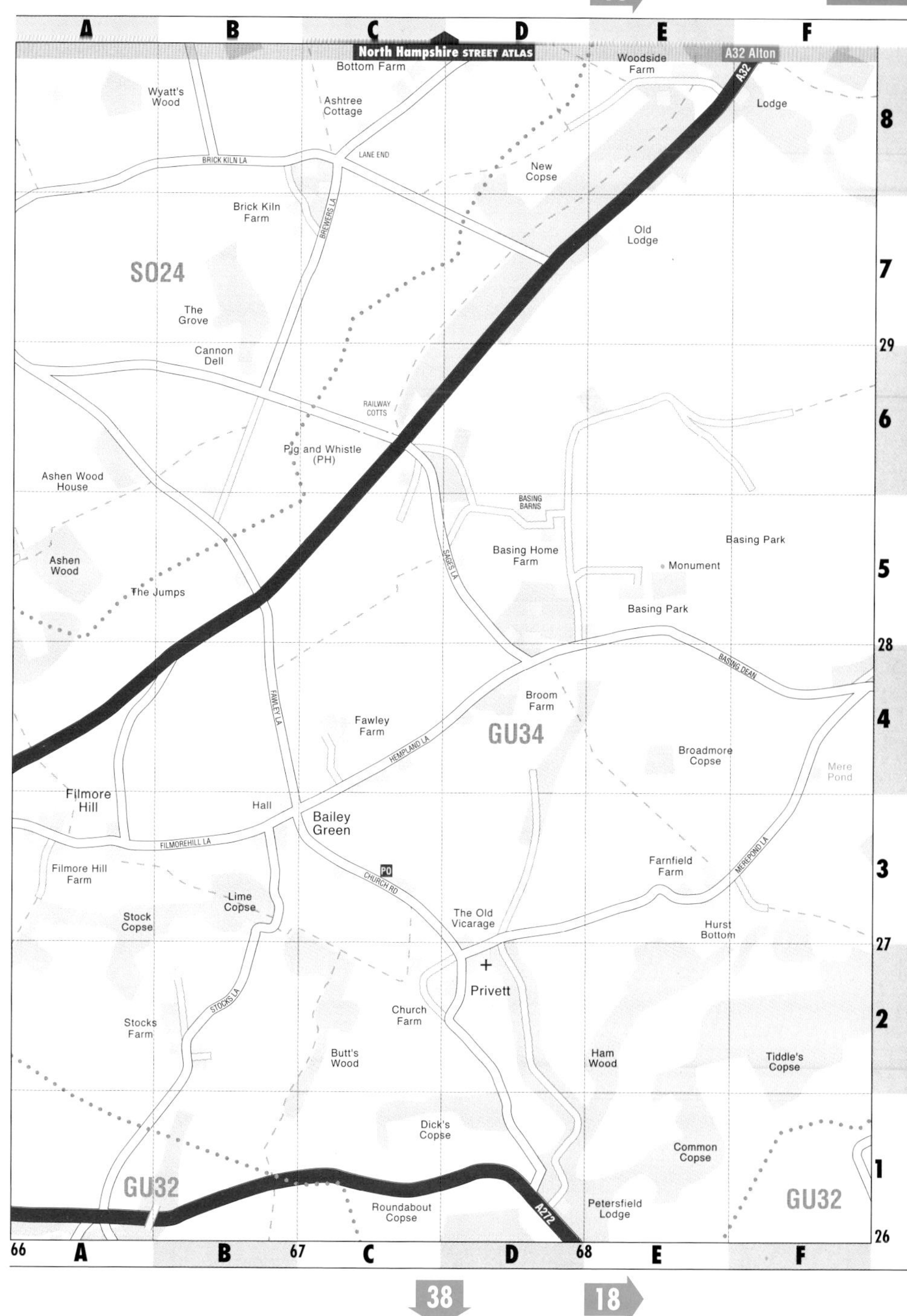

North Hampshire STREET ATLAS

Wyatt's Wood

Bottom Farm

Ashtree Cottage

Woodside Farm

A32 Alton

Lodge

BRICK KILN LA

LANE END

New Copse

8

Brick Kiln Farm

BICKINS LA

Old Lodge

SO24

7

The Grove

29

Cannon Dell

RAILWAY COTTS

6

Pig and Whistle (PH)

Ashen Wood House

BASING BARNS

Basing Home Farm

Basing Park

Ashen Wood

SORET LA

Monument

Basing Park

5

The Jumps

Basing Park

BASING DEAN

28

Broom Farm

4

Fawley Farm

HEMPLAND LA

GU34

Broadmore Copse

Mere Pond

FARLEY LA

Filmore Hill

Hall

Bailey Green

Farnfield Farm

MEREPOND LA

3

FILMOREHILL LA

CHURCH RD

PO

Filmore Hill Farm

Lime Copse

The Old Vicarage

Hurst Bottom

27

Stock Copse

+
Privett

Stocks Farm

STOCKS LA

Church Farm

2

Butt's Wood

Ham Wood

Tiddle's Copse

Dick's Copse

Common Copse

1

GU32

A272

Roundabout Copse

Petersfield Lodge

GU32

26

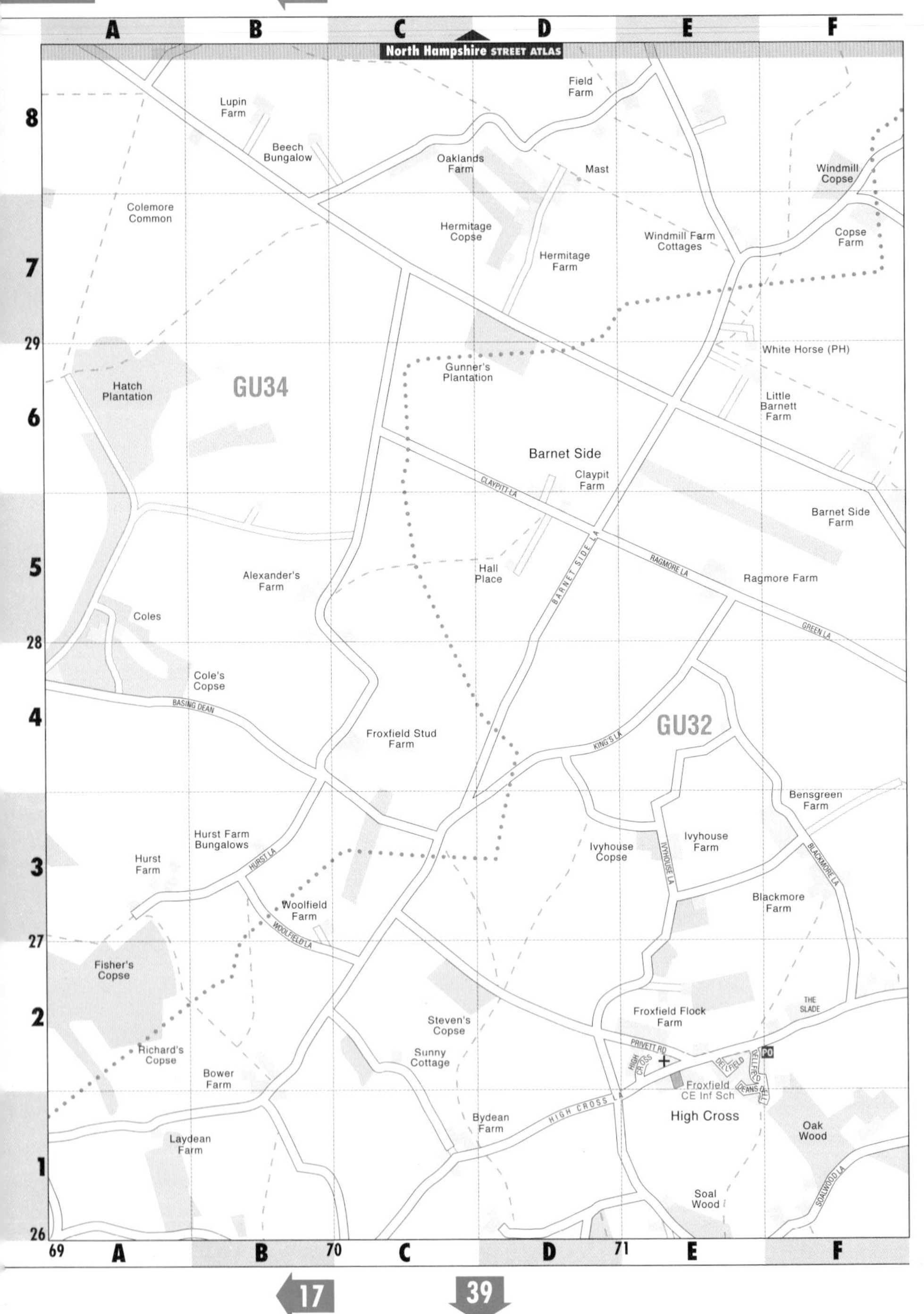

North Hampshire STREET ATLAS

A   B   C   D   E   F

8

Lupin Farm

Beech Bungalow

Field Farm

Oaklands Farm

Mast

Windmill Copse

Colemore Common

Hermitage Copse

Windmill Farm Cottages

Copse Farm

7

Hermitage Farm

29

GU34

Gunner's Plantation

White Horse (PH)

Hatch Plantation

Little Barnett Farm

6

Barnet Side

Claypit Farm

CLAYPIT LA

Barnet Side Farm

5

Alexander's Farm

Hall Place

BARNET SIDE

RAGMORE LA

Ragmore Farm

Coles

GREEN LA

28

Cole's Copse

BASING DEAN

4

Froxfield Stud Farm

KING'S LA

GU32

Bensgreen Farm

Hurst Farm Bungalows

HURST LA

Ivyhouse Copse

IVYHOUSE LA

Ivyhouse Farm

BLACKMORE LA

3

Hurst Farm

Woolfield Farm

WOOLFIELD LA

Blackmore Farm

27

Fisher's Copse

THE SLADE

2

Richard's Copse

Steven's Copse

Sunny Cottage

Froxfield Flock Farm

PRIVETT RD

PO

Bower Farm

Froxfield CE Inf Sch

Oak Wood

Bydean Farm

HIGH CROSS

High Cross

1

Laydean Farm

Soal Wood

SCHOOL LA

26

69 A   B 70 C   D 71 E   F

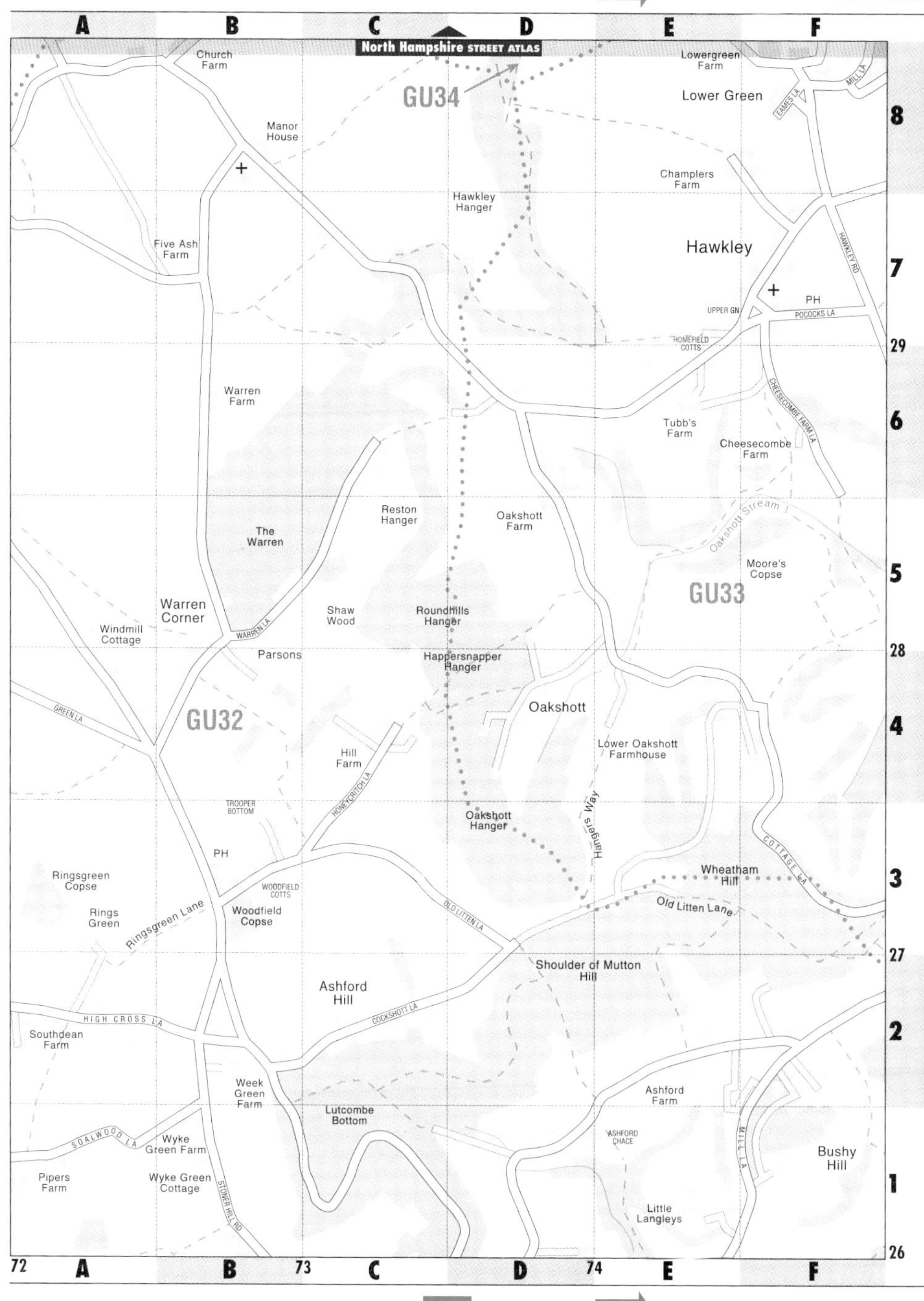

North Hampshire STREET ATLAS

GU34

Church Farm
Manor House
Five Ash Farm
Warren Farm
The Warren
Warren Corner
Windmill Cottage
Parsons
GU32
Shaw Wood
Hill Farm
TROOPER BOTTOM
PH
Ringsgreen Copse
Rings Green
Woodfield Copse
WOODFIELD COTTS
Ringsgreen Lane
Ashford Hill
Southdean Farm
HIGH CROSS LA
Week Green Farm
Lutcombe Bottom
SOALWOOD LA
Wyke Green Farm
Pipers Farm
Wyke Green Cottage

Hawkley Hanger
Reston Hanger
Oakshott Farm
Roundhills Hanger
Happersnapper Hanger
WARREN LA
Oakshott
Oakshott Hanger
Lower Oakshott Farmhouse
Hangers Way
OLD LITTEN LA
COCKSHOTT LA
Shoulder of Mutton Hill
Ashford Farm
ASHFORD CHACE
Little Langleys

Lowergreen Farm
Lower Green
Champlers Farm
Hawkley
PH
UPPER GN
POCOCKS LA
HOMEFIELD COTTS
Tubb's Farm
Cheesecombe Farm
Oakhout Stream
Moore's Copse
GU33
Wheatham Hill
Old Litten Lane
COTTAGE RD
Bushy Hill

MILL LA
FARRS LA
HAWKLEY RD
CHEESECOMBE FARM LA
MILL LA

GREEN LA
HORN CRITCH LA
STEINER'S HILL

72 A 73 B C 74 D E F

8
7
29
6
5
28
4
3
27
2
1
26

19

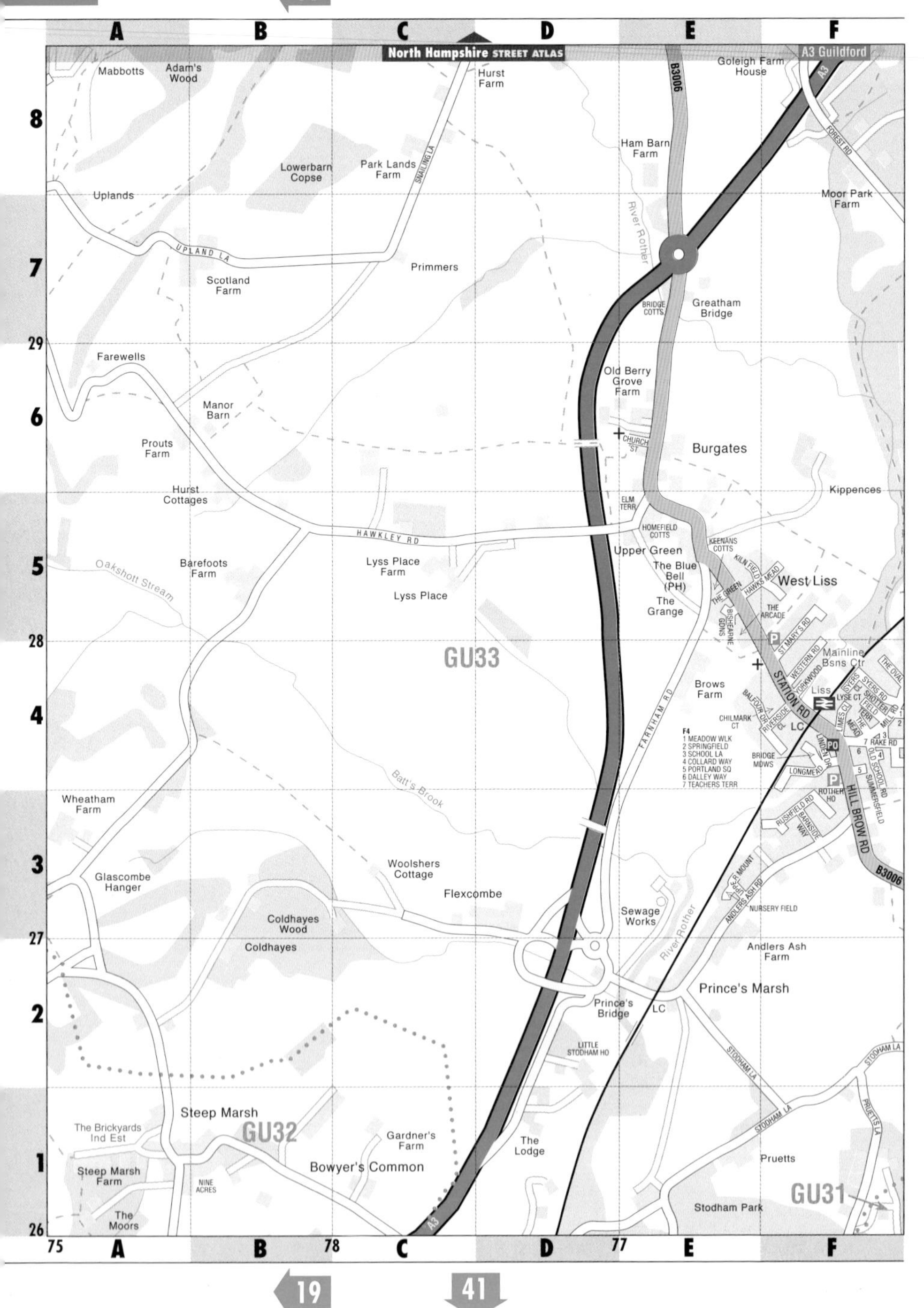

North Hampshire STREET ATLAS
A3 Guildford
A
B
C
D
E
F
8
7
29
6
5
28
4
3
27
2
1
26
75
78
77
Mabbotts
Adam's Wood
Hurst Farm
B3006
Goleigh Farm House
A3
FOREST RD
Ham Barn Farm
Lowerbarn Copse
Park Lands Farm
SNAILING LA
Uplands
Moor Park Farm
River Rother
UPLAND LA
Primmers
Scotland Farm
BRIDGE COTTS
Greatham Bridge
Farewells
Old Berry Grove Farm
Manor Barn
Prouts Farm
CHURCH ST
Burgates
Hurst Cottages
Kippences
ELM TERR
HOMEFIELD COTTS
HAWKLEY RD
KEENANS COTTS
Upper Green
Oakshott Stream
Barefoots Farm
Lyss Place Farm
The Blue Bell (PH)
West Liss
Lyss Place
The Grange
THE GREEN
HAWKS MEAD
THE ARCADE
ST MARY'S RD
BISHEARNE GDNS
P
GU33
Mainline Bsns Ctr
STATION RD
WESTERN RD
YORKWOOD
Brows Farm
Liss
LYSE CT
SYERS RD
THE OVAL
FARNHAM RD
CHILMARK CT
BALFOUR DR
RIVERSIDE CL
LC
F4
1 MEADOW WLK
2 SPRINGFIELD
3 SCHOOL LA
4 COLLARD WAY
5 PORTLAND SQ
6 DALLEY WAY
7 TEACHERS TERR
BRIDGE MDWS
LINDEN DR
PO
RAKE RD
LONGMEAD
OLD SCHOOL RD
ROTHER HO
SUMMERSFIELD
Batt's Brook
Wheatham Farm
RUSHFIELD RD
BARNSIDE WAY
HILL BROW RD
UPPER MOUNT
ANDLERS ASH RD
B3006
Glascombe Hanger
Woolshers Cottage
Flexcombe
Sewage Works
NURSERY FIELD
Coldhayes Wood
Coldhayes
River Rother
Andlers Ash Farm
Prince's Marsh
Prince's Bridge
LC
LITTLE STODHAM HO
STODHAM LA
Steep Marsh
The Brickyards Ind Est
GU32
Gardner's Farm
The Lodge
STODHAM LA
PRUETTS LA
Steep Marsh Farm
Bowyer's Common
Pruetts
NINE ACRES
GU31
The Moors
Stodham Park
A3

19

41

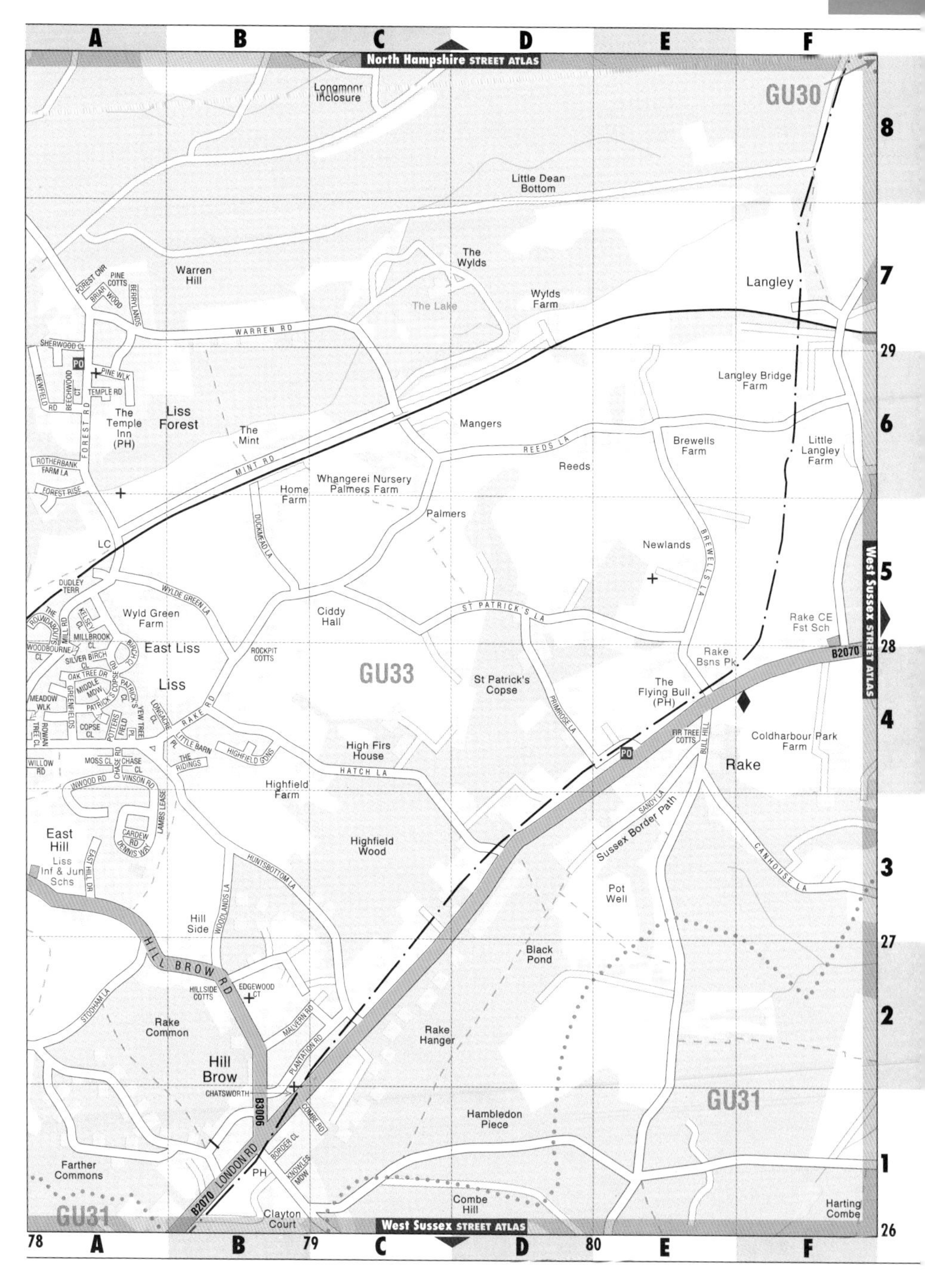

GU30

Longmoor Inclosure

Little Dean Bottom

The Wylds

Langley

Warren Hill

The Lake

Wylds Farm

WARREN RD

29

ROBERT CMN
PINE COTTS
BRUNEL WOOD
BERYL LANG

SHERWOOD CL
PO
PINE WLK
TEMPLE RD
BEECHWOOD
NEWFIELD RD

Liss Forest

The Temple Inn (PH)

The Mint

MINT RD

Langley Bridge Farm

6

ROTHERBANK FARM LA

FOREST RISE

Mangers

REEDS LA

Brewells Farm

Little Langley Farm

Home Farm

Whangerei Nursery
Palmers Farm

Reeds

LC

DUDLEY TERR

WYLDE GREEN LA

Palmers

Newlands

5

DUCKMEAD LA

Ciddy Hall

ST PATRICK'S LA

Wyld Green Farm

East Liss

Liss

ROCKPIT COTTS

GU33

St Patrick's Copse

Rake CE Fst Sch

Rake Bsns Pk

28

B2070

The Flying Bull (PH)

4

MEADOW WLK
ROWAN TREE CL
COPSE CL

LITTLE BARN
HIGHFIELD GDNS

High Firs House

PRIMROSE LA

FIR TREE COTTS

Coldharbour Park Farm

MOSS CL
CHASE CL
VINSON RD

HATCH LA

PO

Rake

Highfield Farm

BULL LA

East Hill

Liss Inf & Jun Schs

LAMBS LEASE

CARDEN RD
DENNIS WAY

HUNTSBOTTOM LA

Highfield Wood

SANDY LA

3

Pot Well

27

WOODLANDS LA

Hill Side

HILL BROW RD

Black Pond

CANHOUSE LA

HILL SIDE COTTS
EDGEWOOD RD

2

Rake Common

MALVERN RD

Rake Hanger

GU31

Hill Brow

CHATSWORTH

PLANTATION RD

Farther Commons

B3006

COMBE RD

Hambledon Piece

1

GU31

B2070 LONDON RD

PH

BORDER CL

Clayton Court

Combe Hill

Harting Combe

26

78   A   B   79   C   D   80   E   F

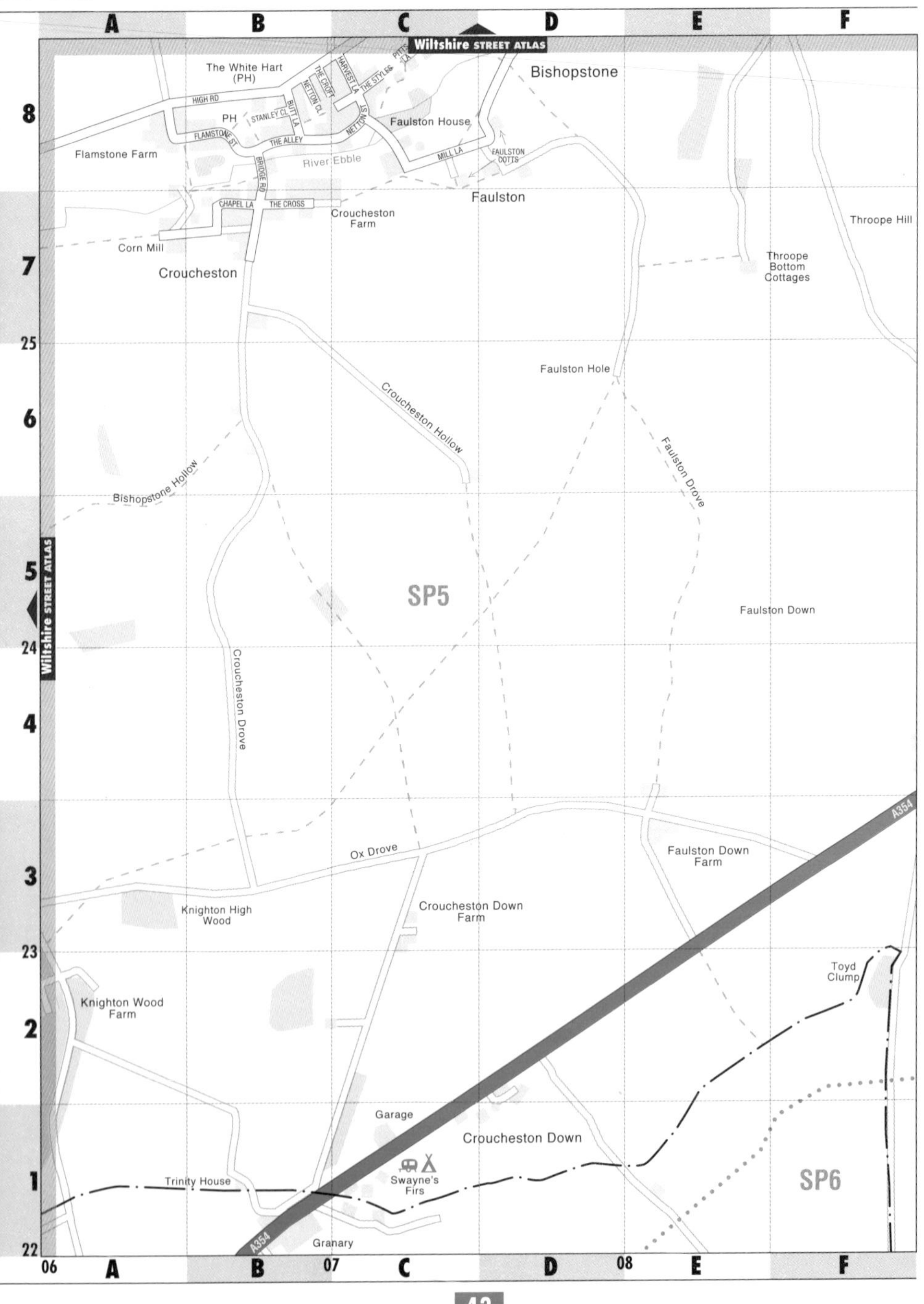

A   B   C   D   E   F

8

Bishopstone

The White Hart
(PH)

HIGH RD

PH

STANLEY CL

BUTT LA

THE CROFT

HARVEST LA

THE STYLES

PIT LA

METHER CL

Faulston House

FLAMSTO

THE ALLEY

MILL LA

FAULSTON
DOTTS

Flamstone Farm

BRIDGE RD

River Ebble

Faulston

CHAPEL LA   THE CROSS

Croucheston
Farm

Throope Hill

7

Corn Mill

Croucheston

Throope
Bottom
Cottages

25

Faulston Hole

6

Croucheston Hollow

Faulston Drove

Bishopstone Hollow

5

SP5

Faulston Down

24

Croucheston Drove

4

A354

3

Ox Drove

Faulston Down
Farm

Knighton High
Wood

Croucheston Down
Farm

23

Toyd
Clump

Knighton Wood
Farm

2

Garage

Croucheston Down

SP6

1

Trinity House

Swayne's
Firs

Granary

22

06   A   B   07   C   D   08   E   F

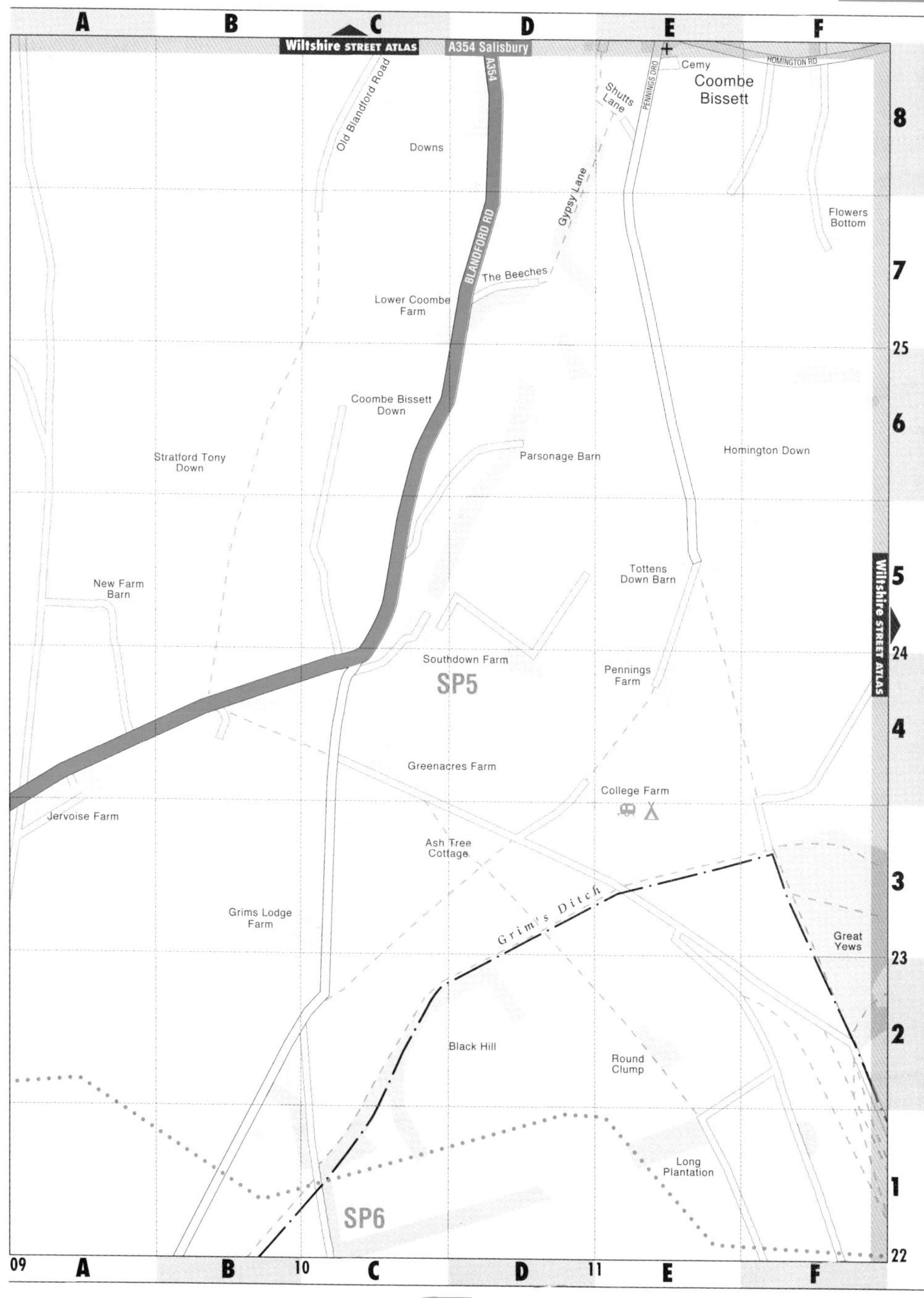

A354 Salisbury

Old Blandford Road

Downs

A354

Cemy

Shutts
Lane

HOMINGTON RD

Coombe
Bissett

PENNINGS DRO

Gypsy Lane

Flowers
Bottom

8

BLANDFORD RD

The Beeches

7

Lower Coombe
Farm

25

Coombe Bissett
Down

6

Stratford Tony
Down

Parsonage Barn

Homington Down

New Farm
Barn

Tottens
Down Barn

5

Wiltshire STREET ATLAS

24

Southdown Farm

SP5

Pennings
Farm

4

Greenacres Farm

College Farm

Jervoise Farm

Ash Tree
Cottage

3

Grims Lodge
Farm

Grim's Ditch

Great
Yews

23

Black Hill

Round
Clump

2

Long
Plantation

1

SP6

22

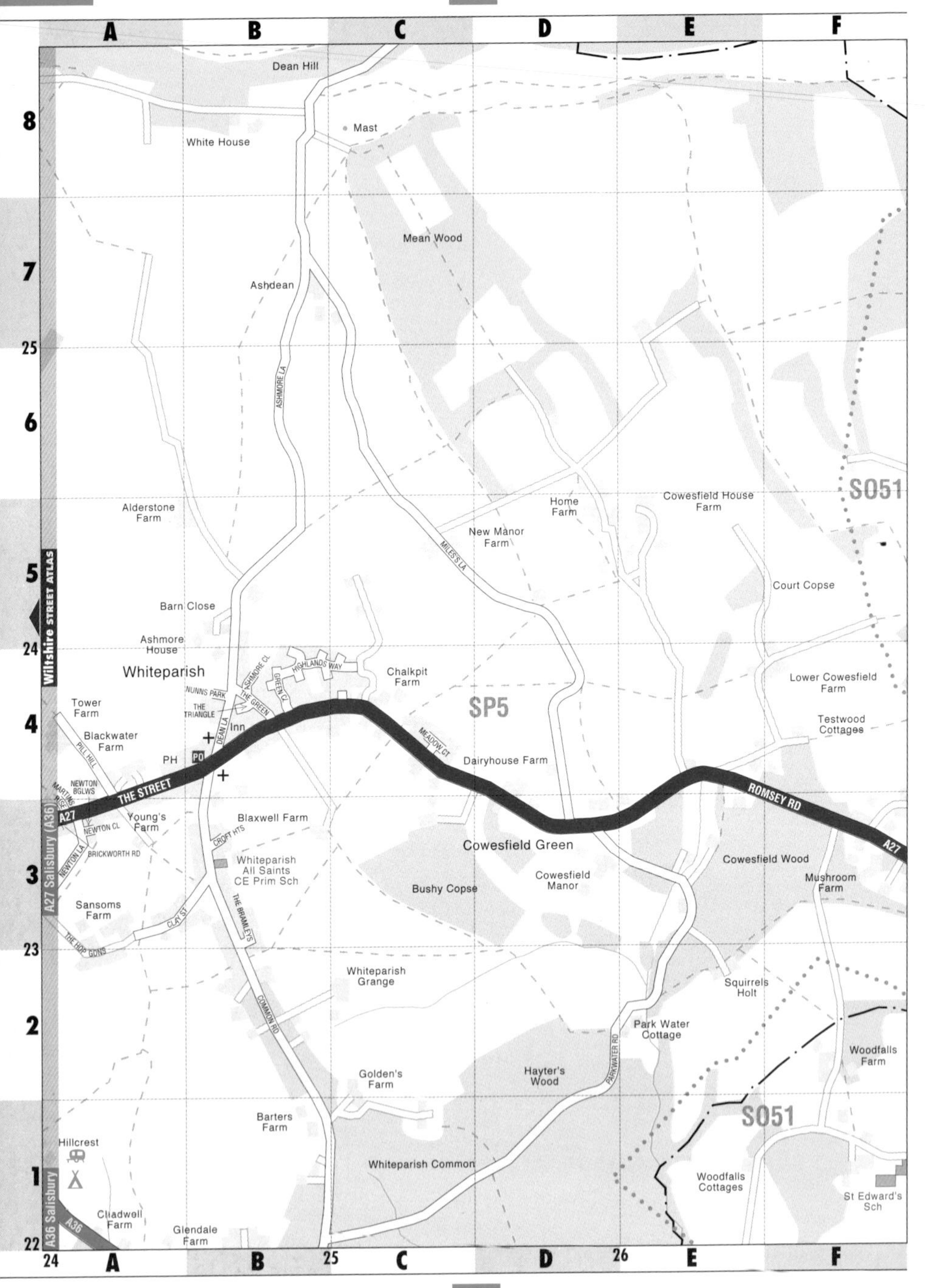

A   B   C   D   E   F

Dean Hill

8

White House

Mast

Mean Wood

7

Ashdean

25

ASHMORE LA

6

SO51

Alderstone
Farm

Home
Farm

Cowesfield House
Farm

5

New Manor
Farm

MEES LA

Court Copse

Barn Close

24

Ashmore
House

Lower Cowesfield
Farm

Whiteparish

HIGHLANDS WAY

Chalkpit
Farm

SP5

Testwood
Cottages

Tower
Farm

NUNNS PARK

ASHMORE CL

DREES CL

THE TRIANGLE

4

Blackwater
Farm

GRANT AV

PH

PO

MEADOW CT

Dairyhouse Farm

ROMSEY RD

A27

THE STREET

NEWTON LA

Young's
Farm

Blaxwell Farm

NEWTON CL

CROFT HTS

Cowesfield Green

Cowesfield Wood

Mushroom
Farm

BRICKWORTH RD

3

Whiteparish
All Saints
CE Prim Sch

Bushy Copse

Cowesfield
Manor

Sansoms
Farm

EUCLS ST

THE BRAMLETS

Squirrels
Holt

THE TOP DOWNS

23

Whiteparish
Grange

COMMON RD

Park Water
Cottage

Woodfalls
Farm

2

Golden's
Farm

Hayter's
Wood

SO51

Barters
Farm

1

Hillcrest

Whiteparish Common

Woodfalls
Cottages

St Edward's
Sch

A36 Salisbury

Cladwell
Farm

Glendale
Farm

22

A   B   **25**   C   D   **26**   E   F

A27 Salisbury (A36)

Wiltshire STREET ATLAS

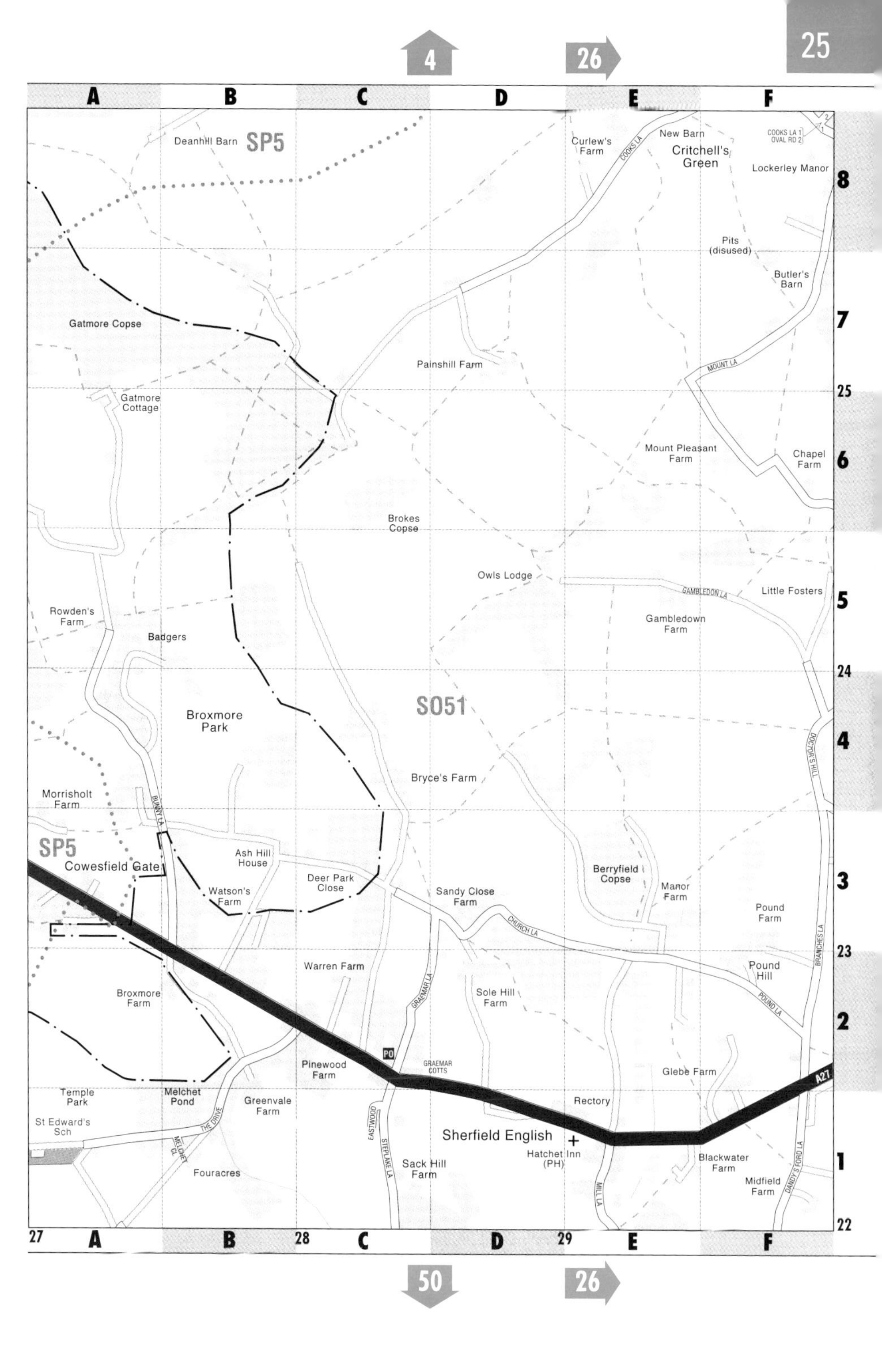

A B C D E F

SP5

Deanhill Barn

Curlew's Farm

New Barn
Critchell's Green

COOKS LA 1
OVAL RD 2

Lockerley Manor 8

Gatmore Copse

Pits
(disused)

Butler's Barn 7

Gatmore Cottage

Painshill Farm

MOUNT LA

25

Mount Pleasant Farm

Chapel Farm 6

Brokes Copse

Owls Lodge

GAMBLEDON LA

Little Fosters 5

Rowden's Farm

Gambledown Farm

24

Badgers

SO51

Broxmore Park

4

Morrisholt Farm

Bryce's Farm

BUNNY LA

Ash Hill House

Berryfield Copse

Manor Farm

Pound Farm 3

SP5

Cowesfield Gate

Watson's Farm

Deer Park Close

Sandy Close Farm

CHURCH LA

POUND LA

BRANCHES LA

Pound Hill 23

Warren Farm

GRAEMAR LA

Sole Hill Farm

Pound Hill 2

Broxmore Farm

Pinewood Farm

PO

GRAEMAR COTTS

Glebe Farm

A27

Temple Park

Melchet Pond

Greenvale Farm

THE DRIVE

Rectory

Sherfield English

Blackwater Farm 1

St Edward's Sch

Fouracres

EAST DOWN LA

STEPLAKE LA

Sack Hill Farm

Hatchet Inn (PH)

MILL LA

Midfield Farm

DAMYS FORD LA

22

27 A 28 B C 28 D 29 E F

25
5

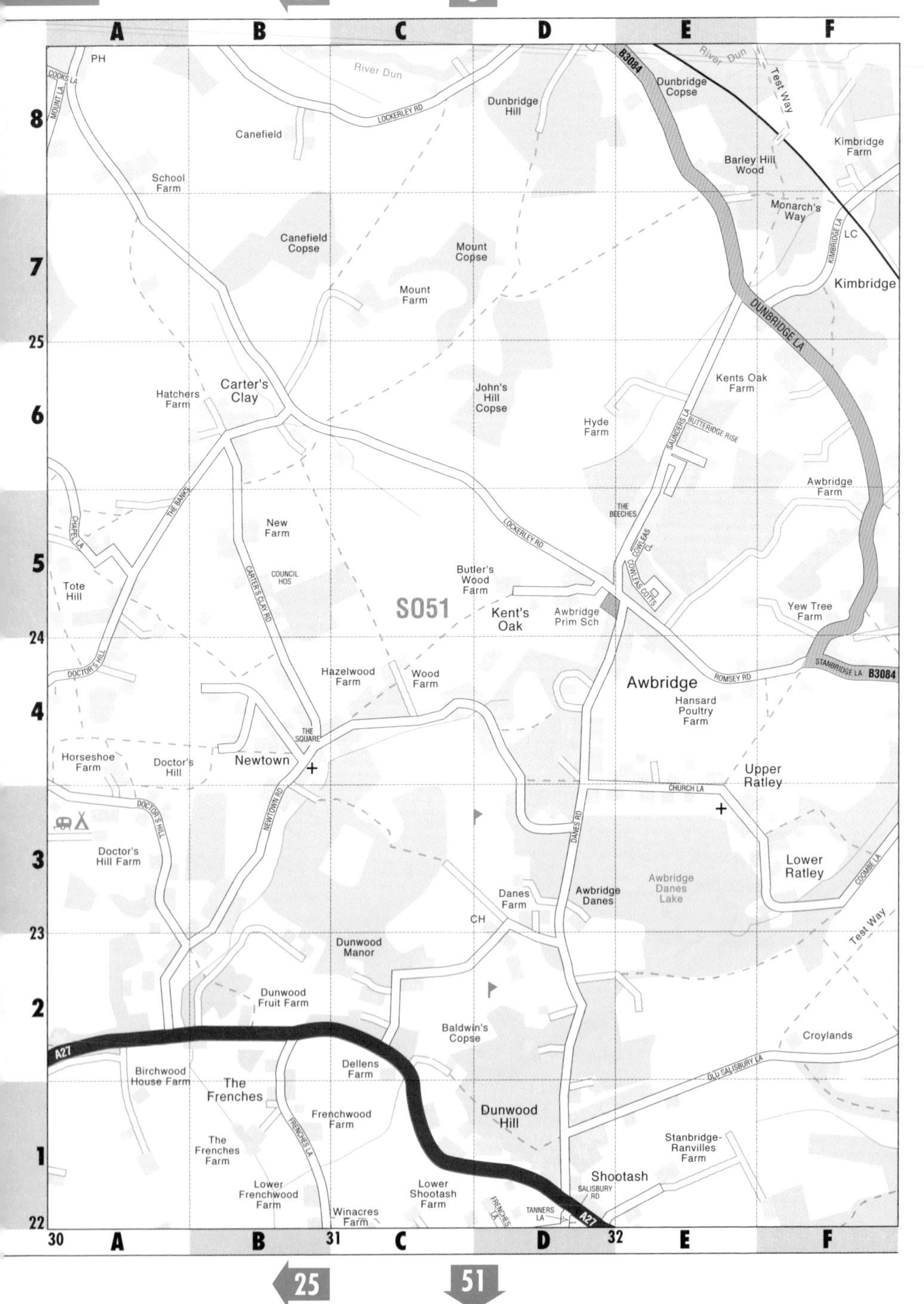

A
B
C
D
E
F
PH
COOKS LA
MOUNT LA
River Dun
LOCKERLEY RD
Dunbridge Hill
B3084
Dunbridge Copse
Test Way
Canefield
Kimbridge Farm
Barley Hill Wood
School Farm
Monarch's Way
KIMBRIDGE LA
LC
Canefield Copse
Mount Copse
Kimbridge
Mount Farm
DUNBRIDGE LA
Kents Oak Farm
Hatchers Farm
Carter's Clay
John's Hill Copse
Hyde Farm
SAUNDERS LA
BUTTERIDGE RISE
Awbridge Farm
THE BANKS
New Farm
THE BEECHES
CHAPEL LA
CARTER'S CLAY RD
COUNCIL HOS
LOCKERLEY RD
COWLEAS CL
COWLEAS COTTS
Butler's Wood Farm
Tote Hill
S051
Kent's Oak
Awbridge Prim Sch
Yew Tree Farm
DOCTOR'S HILL
Hazelwood Farm
Wood Farm
Awbridge
ROMSEY RD
STANBRIDGE LA
B3084
Hansard Poultry Farm
THE SQUARE
Horseshoe Farm
Doctor's Hill
Newtown
Upper Ratley
CHURCH LA
DOCTOR'S HILL
NEWTOWN RD
DANES RD
Doctor's Hill Farm
Lower Ratley
COOMBE LA
Awbridge Danes Lake
Danes Farm
Awbridge Danes
CH
Test Way
Dunwood Manor
Dunwood Fruit Farm
Baldwin's Copse
Croylands
A27
Dellens Farm
Birchwood House Farm
The Frenches
OLD SALISBURY LA
Frenchwood Farm
Dunwood Hill
FRENCHES LA
The Frenches Farm
Stanbridge-Ranvilles Farm
Shootash
Lower Frenchwood Farm
Lower Shootash Farm
SALISBURY RD
Winacres Farm
FRENCHES LA
TANNERS LA
A27
8
7
25
6
5
24
4
3
23
2
1
22
30
31
32

25
51

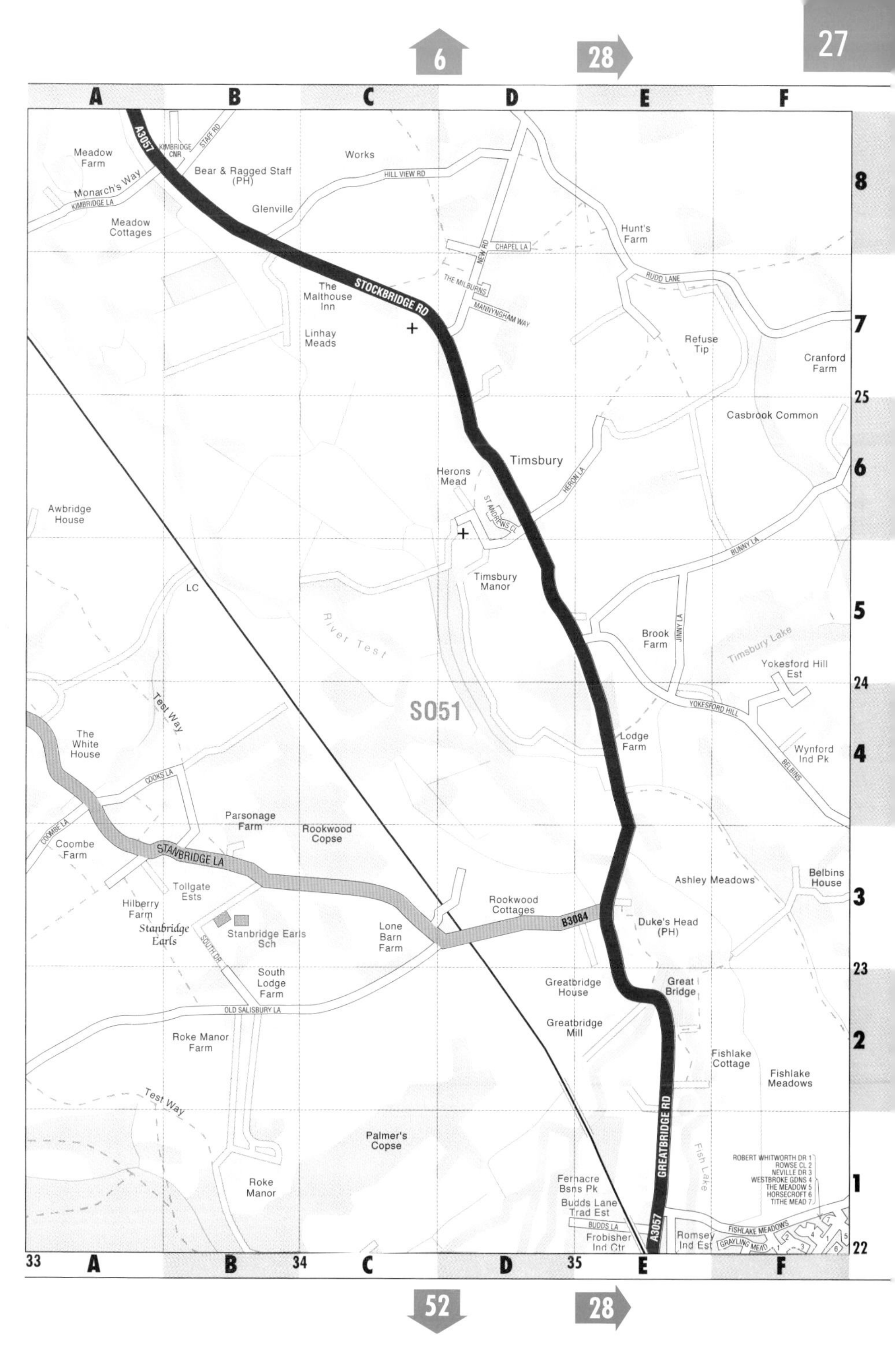
6
28
A
B
C
D
E
F
8
7
6
5
4
3
2
1
25
24
23
22
33
34
35
A3057
KIMBRIDGE CNR
STAFF RD
Meadow Farm
Monarch's Way
KIMBRIDGE LA
Bear & Ragged Staff (PH)
Works
HILL VIEW RD
Glenville
Meadow Cottages
Hunt's Farm
CHAPEL LA
NEW RD
THE MILBURNS
MANNYNGHAM WAY
RUDD LANE
The Malthouse Inn
STOCKBRIDGE RD
Linhay Meads
Refuse Tip
Cranford Farm
Casbrook Common
Timsbury
Herons Mead
HERON LA
ST ANDREWS CL
Awbridge House
BUNNY LA
Timsbury Manor
LC
River Test
Brook Farm
JINNY LA
Timsbury Lake
Yokesford Hill Est
YOKESFORD HILL
SO51
Test Way
The White House
Lodge Farm
Wynford Ind Pk
BELBINS
COOKS LA
COOMBE LA
Coombe Farm
Parsonage Farm
Rookwood Copse
STANBRIDGE LA
Ashley Meadows
Belbins House
Tollgate Ests
Hilberry Farm
Stanbridge Earls
Stanbridge Earls Sch
SOUTH DR
Lone Barn Farm
Rookwood Cottages
B3084
Duke's Head (PH)
South Lodge Farm
Greatbridge House
Great Bridge
OLD SALISBURY LA
Greatbridge Mill
Roke Manor Farm
Fishlake Cottage
Fishlake Meadows
Test Way
Palmer's Copse
GREATBRIDGE RD
Fish Lake
ROBERT WHITWORTH DR 1
ROWSE CL 2
NEVILLE DR 3
WESTBROKE GDNS 4
THE MEADOW 5
HORSECROFT 6
TITHE MEAD 7
Roke Manor
Fernacre Bsns Pk
Budds Lane Trad Est
BUDDS LA
Frobisher Ind Ctr
A3057
Romsey Ind Est
FISHLAKE MEADOWS
GRAYLING MEAD

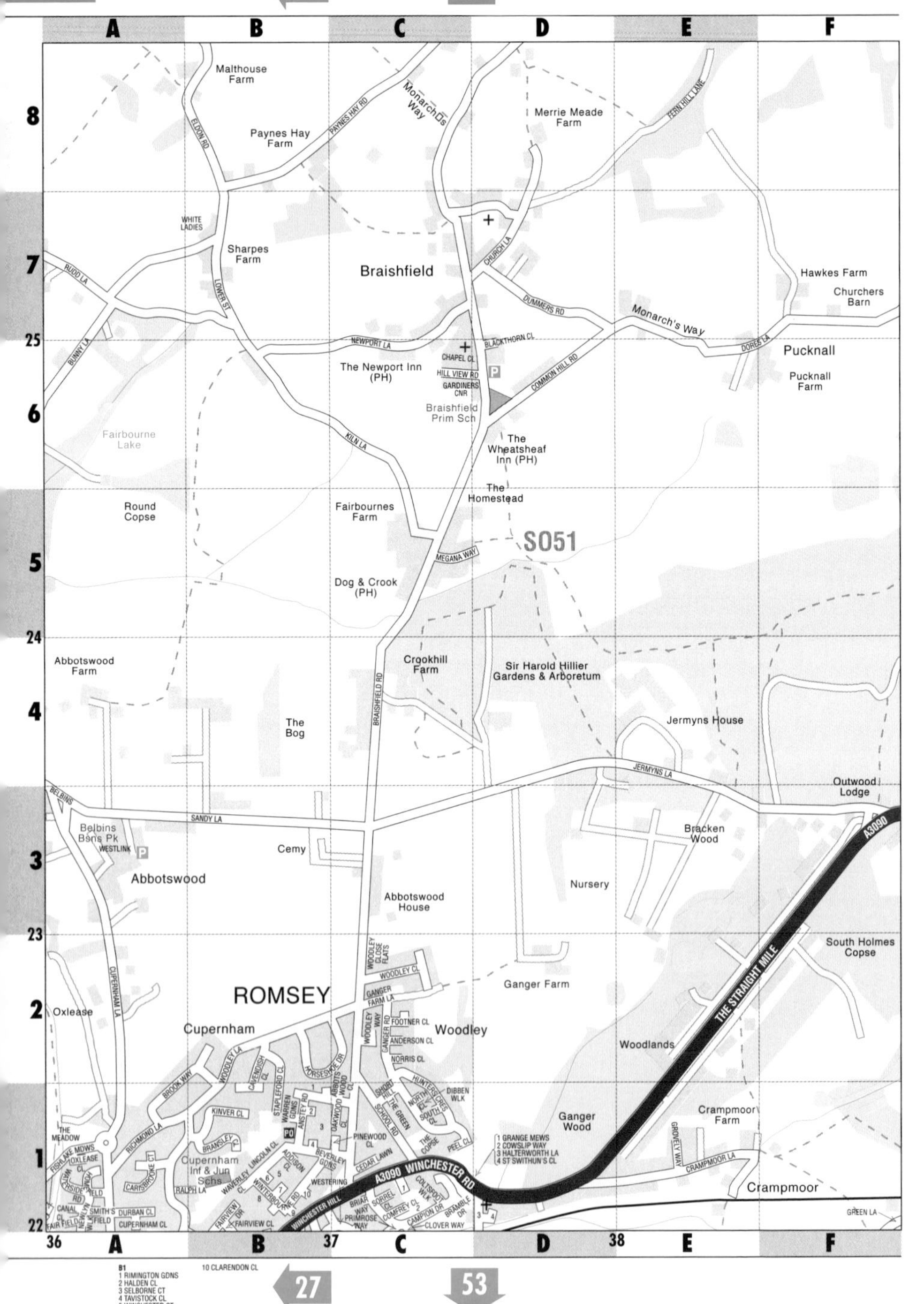

27

7

A **B** **C** **D** **E** **F**

8

Malthouse
Farm

Monarch's Way

Merrie Meade
Farm

FERN HILL LANE

ELSON RD

PAYNES HAY RD

Paynes Hay
Farm

WHITE
LADIES

7

Sharpes
Farm

Braishfield

Hawkes Farm

Churchers
Barn

RUDD LA

LOWER ST

CHURCH LA

DUMMERS RD

Monarch's Way

DOREY LA

25

BUNNY LA

NEWPORT LA

CHAPEL CL

BLACKTHORN CL

Pucknall

The Newport Inn
(PH)

HILL VIEW RD

GARDINERS
CNR

COMMON HILL RD

Pucknall
Farm

6

Fairbourne
Lake

KILN LA

Braishfield
Prim Sch

The
Wheatsheaf
Inn (PH)

The
Homestead

Round
Copse

Fairbournes
Farm

SO51

5

Dog & Crook
(PH)

MEGANA WAY

24

Abbotswood
Farm

BRAISHFIELD RD

Crookhill
Farm

Sir Harold Hillier
Gardens & Arboretum

4

The
Bog

Jermyns House

JERMYNS LA

Outwood
Lodge

A3090

3

BELBINS

SANDY LA

Belbins
Boris Pk

WESTLINN

Cemy

Bracken
Wood

Abbotswood

Nursery

THE STRAIGHT MILE

South Holmes
Copse

23

Abbotswood
House

CUPERNHAM LA

WOODLEY
CLOSE
FLATS

WOODLEY CL

South Holmes
Copse

2

Oxlease

ROMSEY

GANGER
FARM LA

WOODLEY WAY

Ganger Farm

Woodley

Woodlands

Crampmoor
Farm

Cupernham

FOOTNER CL

ANDERSON CL

NORRIS CL

Ganger
Wood

GRINDEY WAY

CRAMPMOOR LA

BROOK WAY

KINVER CL

DIBBEN
WLK

HUNTS CL

THE BRIDES

PEEL CL

1 GRANGE MEWS
2 COWSLIP WAY
3 HALTERWORTH LA
4 ST SWITHUN S CL

Crampmoor

1

THE
MEADOW

Cupernham
Inf & Jun
Schs

PO

PINEWOOD
CL

CADET LAWN

A3090 WINCHESTER RD

GREEN LA

22

CANAL

SMITH'S
FIELD

DURBAN CL

Cupernham CL

RALPH LA

WINCHESTER HILL

FAIRVIEW CL

BRIAR
WAY

PRIMROSE
WAY

SORREL
CL

COURTNEY CL

CAMPION DR

CLOVER WAY

CANDOVER
DR

36

A **B** **C** **D** **E** **F**

27

37

53

38

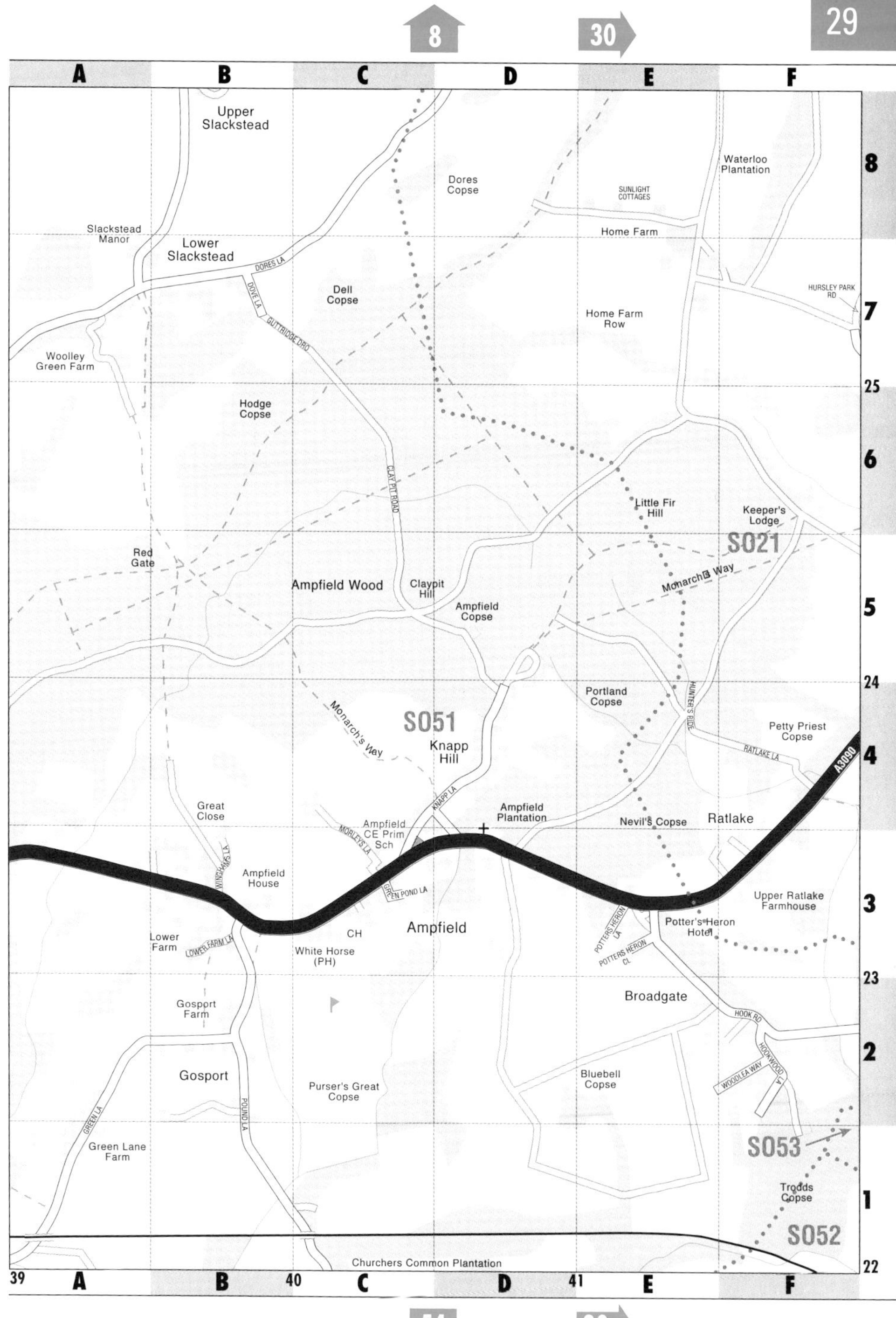

A   B   C   D   E   F

Upper
Slackstead

Dores
Copse

SUNLIGHT
COTTAGES

Waterloo
Plantation

8

Slackstead
Manor

Lower
Slackstead

Home Farm

HURSLEY PARK
RD

DORES LA

Dell
Copse

Home Farm
Row

7

Woolley
Green Farm

GUTTRIDGE DRO

DOLE LA

25

Hodge
Copse

6

CLAYPIT ROAD

Little Fir
Hill

Keeper's
Lodge

SO21

Red
Gate

Ampfield Wood

Claypit
Hill

Ampfield
Copse

Monarch's Way

5

24

Portland
Copse

HUNTER'S RIDGE

Petty Priest
Copse

RATLAKE LA

Monarch's Way

SO51

Knapp
Hill

4

A3090

Great
Close

KNAPP LA

Ampfield
Plantation

Nevil's Copse

Ratlake

WINDMILL LA

Ampfield CE Prim
Sch

MORLEYS LA

Ampfield
House

GREEN POND LA

Upper Ratlake
Farmhouse

3

Lower
Farm

LOWER FARM LA

CH

White Horse
(PH)

Ampfield

POTTERS HERON LA

POTTERS HERON
CL

Potter's Heron
Hotel

23

Gosport
Farm

Broadgate

HOOK RD

2

Gosport

POUND LA

Purser's Great
Copse

Bluebell
Copse

WOOD LA WAY

Green Lane
Farm

GREEN LA

SO53

SO52

Trodds
Copse

1

Churchers Common Plantation

22

39   A   B   40   C   D   41   E   F

A B C D E F

8

PORT LA

KEBLE CL

King's Head Inn

CATWAYS
HEATHCOTE PL

COLLINS LA

Shawlands Farm

7

Cemy

PO

Hursley Park

Hursley

PELICAN CT

MERCURY CL
SOUTH RD

HURSLEY PARK RD

Parsonage Farm

BUNSTEAD LA

Monarch's Way

25

HURSLEY PARK RD

6

John Keble CE Prim Sch

BUNSTEAD

POLES LA

Upper Silkstead Farm

Silkstead

B3043

Brooks Copse

Brooks Way

SO21

Weedacre Copse

P

Lower Silkstead Farmhouse

5

Hursley Forest

Windmill Copse

24

A3090

Ladwell

Red House

Strowdens Copse

Wells Row

Freemanties Copse

4

Kent's Copse

Field House

Cranbury Park

Hawstead Farm

Home Farm

Cranbury House

Great Pond

3

Hocombe Plantation

SO53

Hocombe

Hocombe Bridge

23

ROTHVILLE PL

Hocombe Upper Plantation

HOOK RD

HURSLEY RD

HOCOMBE RD

Castle Copse

Upper Pond

The Castle

SO051

HOOK WATER CL
HOOK WATER RD

HOCOMBE PARK GL

CHARNWOOD GL

HOCOMBE WOOD RD

ASHDOWN

RANZAL RD

Lower Pond

2

SO052

BEECH

BEECHWOOD CRES

TITHEWOOD CL

CHARNWOOD CL

CHARNWOOD CL

ELM

HAZEL CL

WALNUT

WOODLANDS CL

COULTAE RD

SHERWOOD RD

WESTERN RD

GROSVENOR RD

1

WHEELHOUSE CVN PK
ST JAMES CVN PK

THE KING EDWARD CVN PK

PO

STEWART HO

QUEEN'S RD

GORDON RD

Hiltingbury

HILTINGBURY CL

HAKWOOD RD

MALCOLM RD

HEATHERDENE RD

Recn Gd

PINE RD

Cemy

Cuckoo Bushes

Hiltingbury Jun Sch

Hiltingbury Inf Sch

OAKWOOD

HILTINGBURY RD

FRESHWATER RD

MALTBES RD

WINCHESTER RD

22

THE WOODLANDS

THE TANYARDS

B3043

42 A B 43 C D 44 E F

B1
1 AMPFIELD CT
2 HURSLEY CT
3 ASHTON PL
4 HILTINGBURY CT
5 CHILLINGTON GDNS
6 VANBURGH WAY
7 LAURISTON DR
8 CRANBORNE GDNS
9 STRATFIELD DR
10 ALBURY PL
11 APSLEY PL
12 ORMESBY DR
13 SIMPKINS CT
14 OAKLANDS

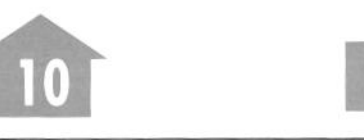

10
32

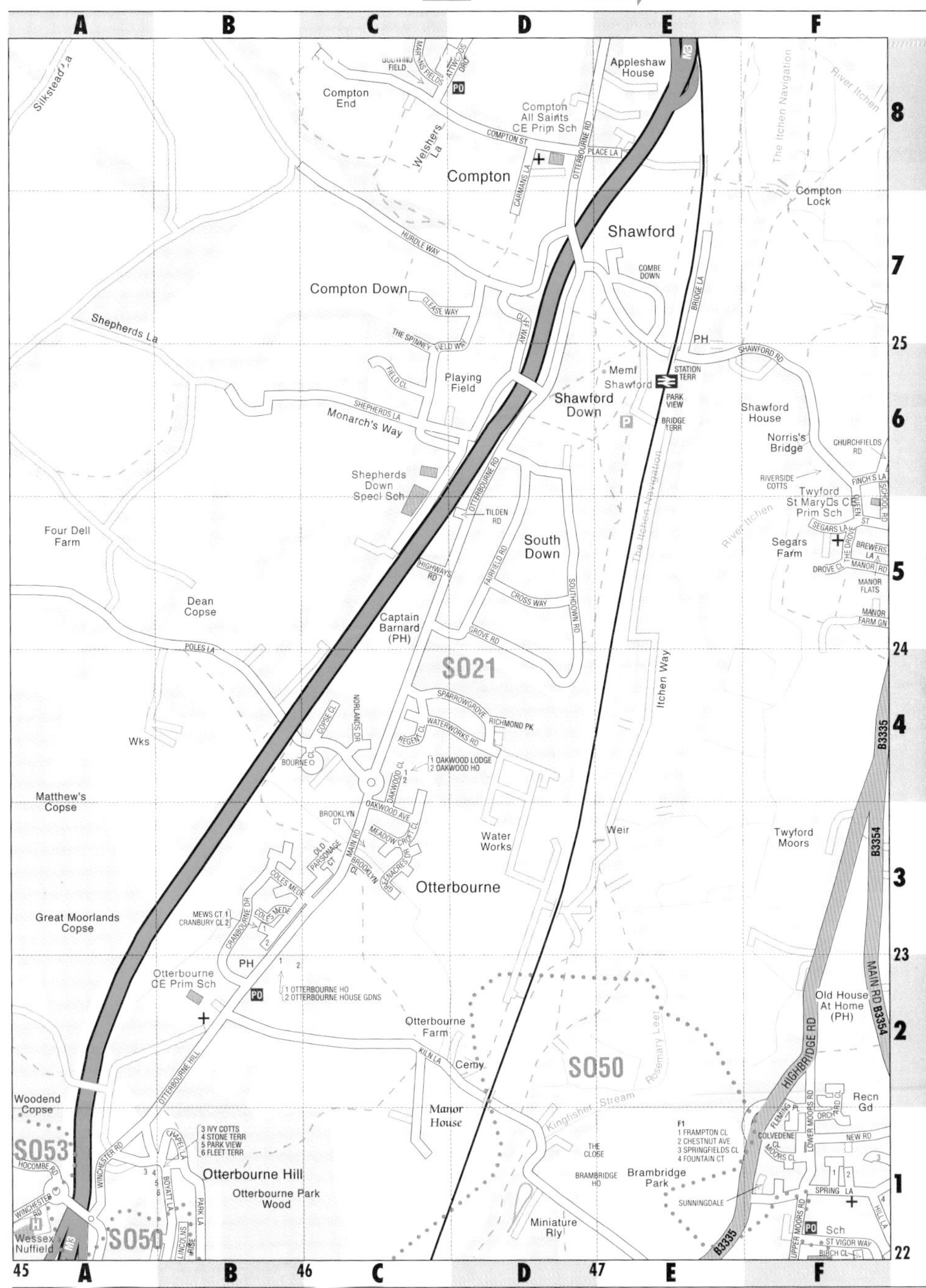

A
B
C
D
E
F
Silkstead La
Compton End
Appleshaw House
Compton All Saints CE Prim Sch
COMPTON ST
PLACE LA
OTTERBOURNE RD
Welshers La
Compton
CARMANS LA
Compton Lock
The Itchen Navigation
River Itchen
Shawford
HURDLE WAY
COMBE DOWN
Compton Down
CLEASE WAY
THE SPINNEY
FIELD WY
CLIFF WAY
BRIDGE LA
Shepherds La
PH
SHAWFORD RD
Playing Field
FIELD CL
Meml
Shawford
STATION TERR
PARK VIEW
BRIDGE TERR
Shawford Down
SHEPHERDS LA
Monarch's Way
Shawford House
Norris's Bridge
CHURCHFIELDS RD
RIVERSIDE COTTS
FINCH'S LA
Twyford St Mary's CE Prim Sch
SCHOOL RD
Shepherds Down Specl Sch
OTTERBOURNE RD
TILDEN RD
Four Dell Farm
South Down
SEGARS LA
THE DROVE
Segars Farm
BREWERS LA
DROVE CL
MANOR RD
MANOR FLATS
MANOR FARM GN
HIGHWAYS RD
FAIRFIELD RD
CROSS WAY
SOUTHDOWN RD
Dean Copse
Captain Barnard (PH)
GROVE RD
POLES LA
SO21
Itchen Way
SPARROWGROVE
RICHMOND PK
WATERWORKS RD
REGENT CL
COPSE CL
NORLANDS DR
Wks
BOURNE CL
1 OAKWOOD LODGE
2 OAKWOOD HO
OAKWOOD CL
Matthew's Copse
OAKWOOD AVE
BROOKLYN CT
MEADOW CROFT CL
Water Works
Weir
Twyford Moors
B3335
B3354
OLD PARSONAGE CT
MAIN RD
BROOKLYN CL
GREENACRES DR
COLES MEDE
Otterbourne
MEWS CT
CRANBURY CL
CRANBOURNE DR
Great Moorlands Copse
PH
1 OTTERBOURNE HO
2 OTTERBOURNE HOUSE GDNS
Otterbourne CE Prim Sch
Otterbourne Farm
Old House At Home (PH)
MAIN RD B3354
HIGHBRIDGE RD
Rosemary Leet
KILN LA
Cemy
SO50
OTTERBOURNE HILL
Woodend Copse
Manor House
Kingfisher Stream
Recn Gd
FLEMING PL
ORCHARD CL
LOWER MOORS RD
NEW RD
COLVEDENE CL
MOORS CL
F1
1 FRAMPTON CL
2 CHESTNUT AVE
3 SPRINGFIELDS CL
4 FOUNTAIN CT
SO53
HOCOMBE RD
WINCHESTER RD
3 IVY COTTS
4 STONE TERR
5 PARK VIEW
6 FLEET TERR
CHAPEL LA
THE CLOSE
Otterbourne Hill
BOYATT LA
Otterbourne Park Wood
PARK LA
BRAMBRIDGE HO
Brambridge Park
SUNNINGDALE
SPRING LA
HILL LA
WINCHESTER RD
Wessex Nuffield
M3
SO50
LINCOLNS RISE
Miniature Rly
UPPER MOORS RD
Sch
ST VIGOR WAY
BIRCH CL
8
7
25
6
5
24
4
3
23
2
1
22
45
46
47
56
32

31
11

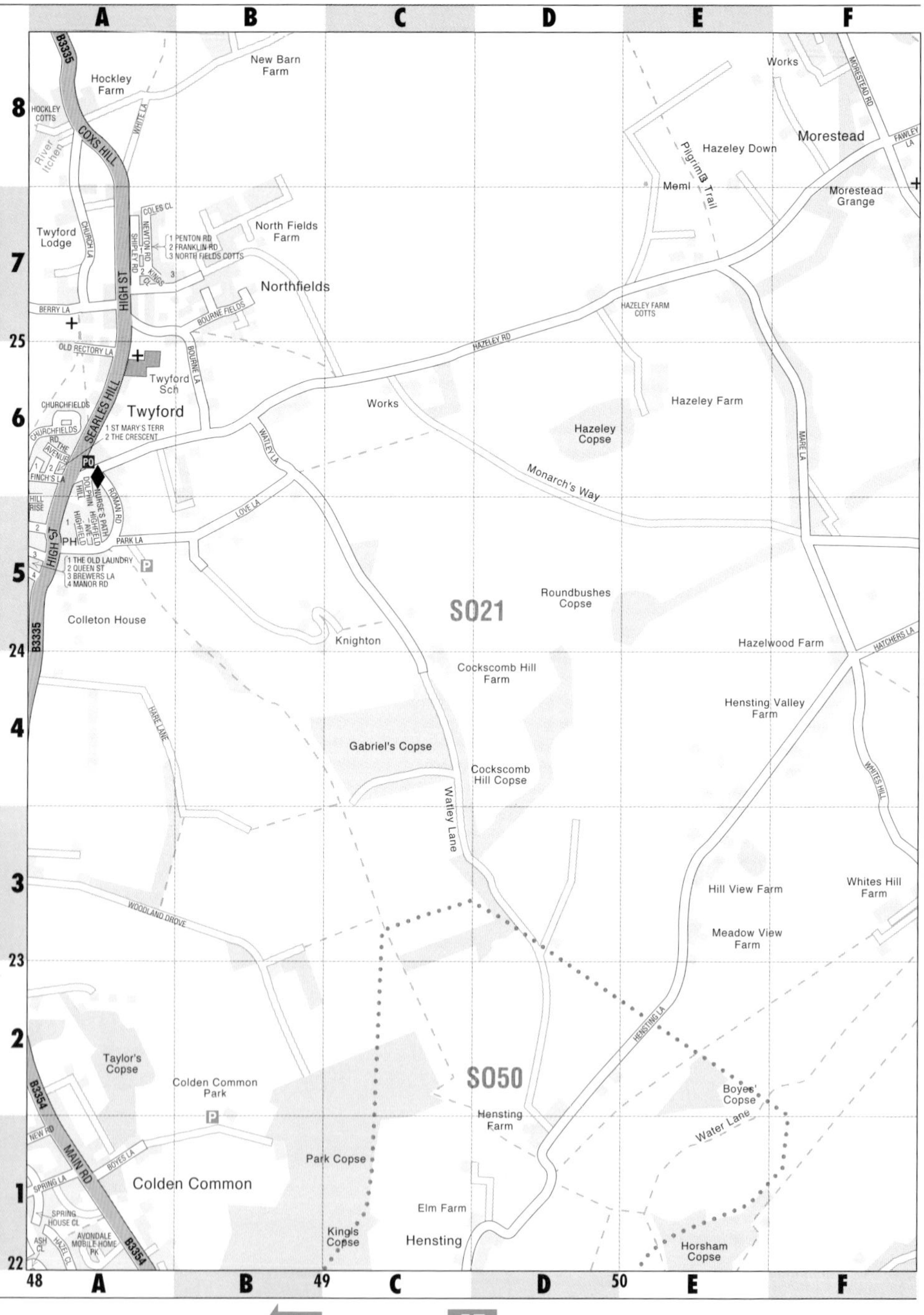
A
B
C
D
E
F
Hockley Farm
New Barn Farm
Works
Morestead
Hazeley Down
Pilgrims' Trail
Meml
Morestead Grange
Twyford Lodge
North Fields Farm
Northfields
1 PENTON RD
2 FRANKLIN RD
3 NORTH FIELDS COTTS
BERRY LA
OLD RECTORY LA
HIGH ST
COXS HILL
SEARLES HILL
BOURNE FIELDS
BOURNE LA
HAZELEY RD
HAZELEY FARM COTTS
Twyford Sch
Twyford
Works
Hazeley Farm
Hazeley Copse
Monarch's Way
1 ST MARY'S TERR
2 THE CRESCENT
WATLEY LA
LOVE LA
PARK LA
1 THE OLD LAUNDRY
2 QUEEN ST
3 BREWERS LA
4 MANOR RD
Colleton House
SO21
Roundbushes Copse
Knighton
Hazelwood Farm
HATCHERS LA
Cockscomb Hill Farm
Hensting Valley Farm
MARE LA
Gabriel's Copse
Cockscomb Hill Copse
HARE LANE
Watley Lane
WHITES HILL
Hill View Farm
Whites Hill Farm
WOODLAND DROVE
Meadow View Farm
HENSTING LA
Taylor's Copse
Colden Common Park
SO50
Boyes' Copse
Hensting Farm
Water Lane
B3335
B3354
MAIN RD
NEW RD
BOYES LA
SPRING LA
Colden Common
Park Copse
Elm Farm
King's Copse
Hensting
Horsham Copse
AVONDALE MOBILE HOME PK
48
49
50
22
23
24
25

31
57

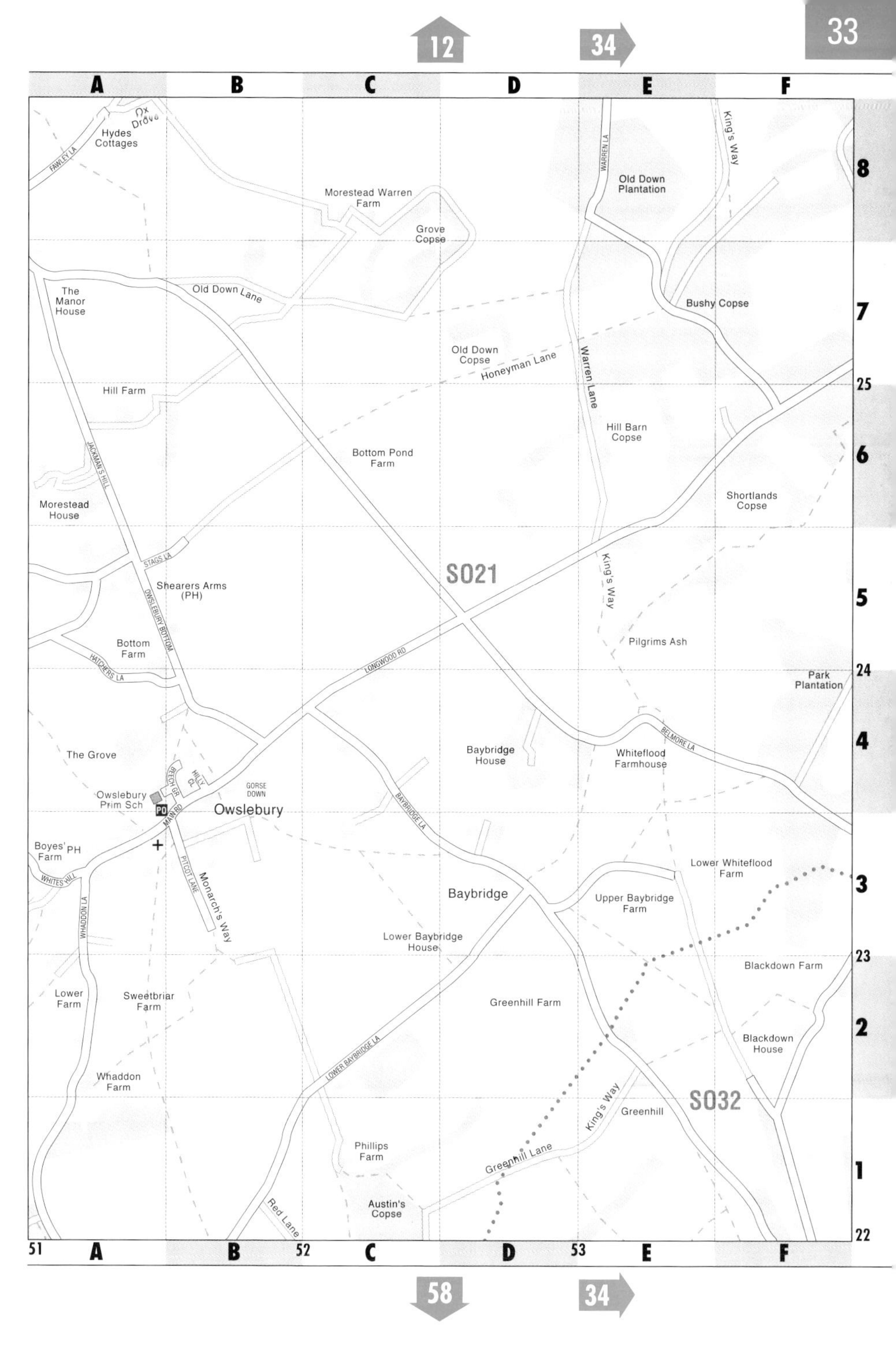
12
34
A
B
C
D
E
F
Ox Drove
Hydes Cottages
FAWLEY LA
Morestead Warren Farm
Grove Copse
WARREN LA
Old Down Plantation
King's Way
8
The Manor House
Old Down Lane
Bushy Copse
7
Old Down Copse
Honeyman Lane
Warren Lane
Hill Farm
25
Hill Barn Copse
JACKMAN'S HILL
Bottom Pond Farm
6
Morestead House
Shortlands Copse
STAGS LA
SO21
King's Way
Shearers Arms (PH)
OWSLEBURY BOTTOM
5
Bottom Farm
Pilgrims Ash
HATCHERS LA
LONGWOOD RD
24
Park Plantation
Baybridge House
Whiteflood Farmhouse
BELMORE LA
4
The Grove
BEECH GR
HILLY CL
GORSE DOWN
Owslebury Prim Sch
PO
MAIN RD
Owslebury
BAYBRIDGE LA
Boyes' Farm
PH
WHITES HILL
PITCOT LANE
Monarch's Way
Lower Whiteflood Farm
3
WHADDON LA
Baybridge
Upper Baybridge Farm
Lower Baybridge House
23
Blackdown Farm
Lower Farm
Sweetbriar Farm
Greenhill Farm
2
Blackdown House
LOWER BAYBRIDGE LA
Whaddon Farm
SO32
King's Way
Greenhill
Phillips Farm
Greenhill Lane
1
Austin's Copse
Red Lane
22
51
52
53
58
34

33
13

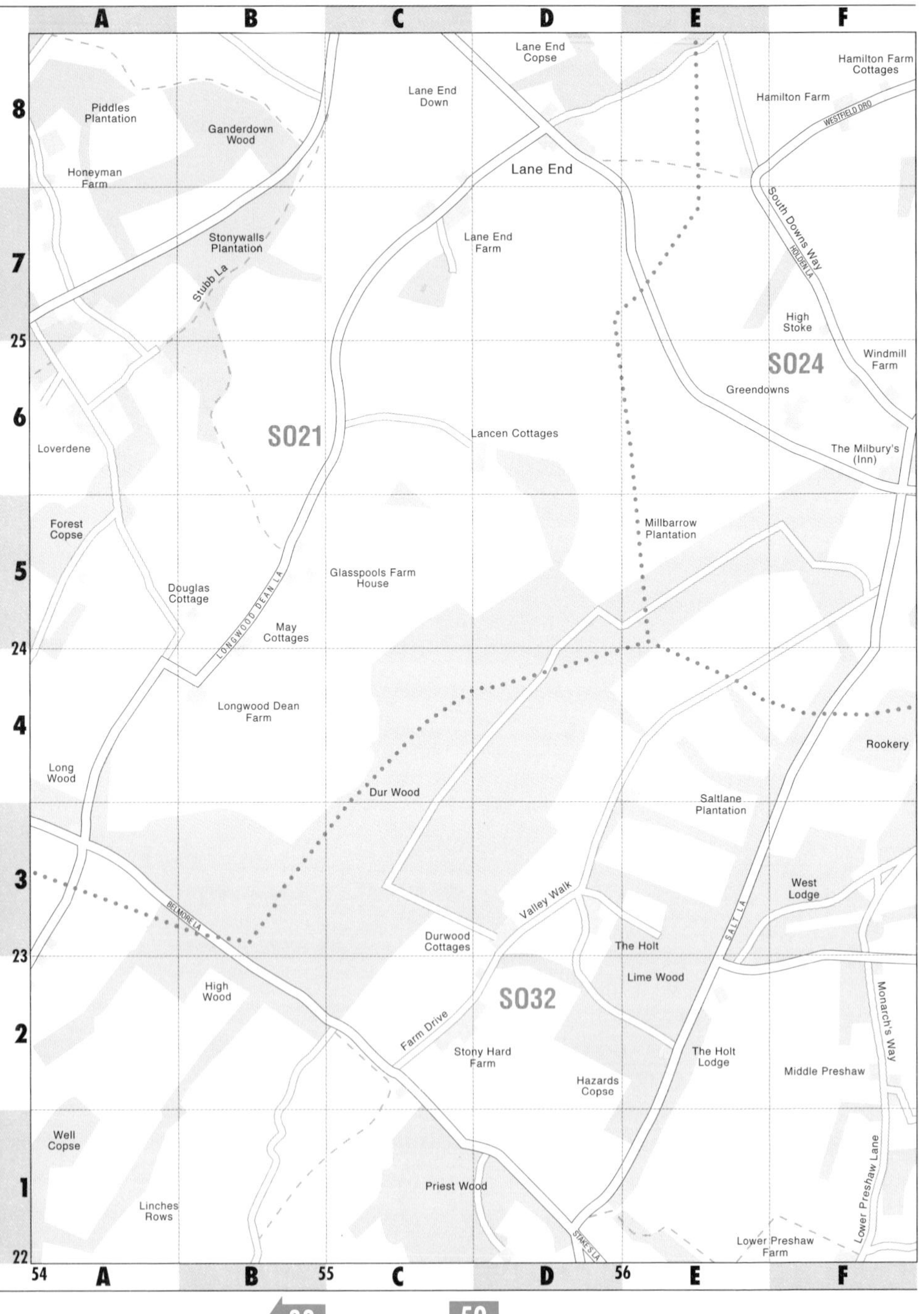
A
B
C
D
E
F
8
7
25
6
5
24
4
3
23
2
1
22
54
55
56
Lane End Copse
Hamilton Farm Cottages
Hamilton Farm
Lane End Down
Piddles Plantation
Ganderdown Wood
Honeyman Farm
WESTFIELD DRO
Lane End
South Downs Way
HOLDEN LA
Lane End Farm
Stonywalls Plantation
Stubb La
High Stoke
Windmill Farm
SO24
Greendowns
Loverdene
SO21
Lancen Cottages
The Milbury's (Inn)
Forest Copse
Millbarrow Plantation
Glasspools Farm House
Douglas Cottage
LONGWOOD DEAN LA
May Cottages
Longwood Dean Farm
Rookery
Long Wood
Dur Wood
Saltlane Plantation
West Lodge
BELMORE LA
Valley Walk
SALT LA
Durwood Cottages
The Holt
Lime Wood
High Wood
SO32
Monarch's Way
Farm Drive
Stony Hard Farm
The Holt Lodge
Middle Preshaw
Hazards Copse
Well Copse
Priest Wood
Lower Preshaw Lane
Linches Rows
STAKES LA
Lower Preshaw Farm

33
59

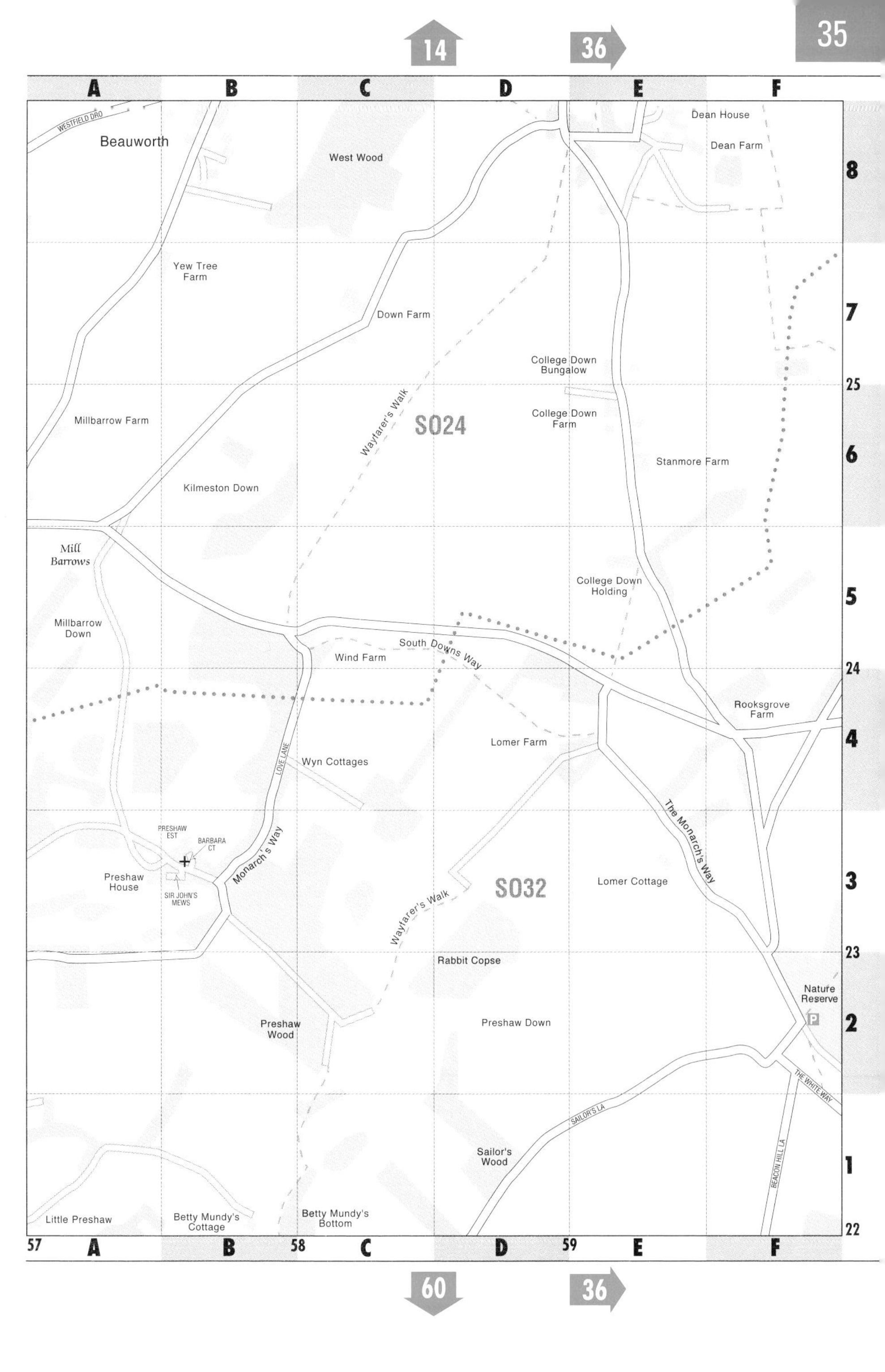

A   B   C   D   E   F

8

WESTFIELD DRO

Beauworth

West Wood

Dean House

Dean Farm

7

Yew Tree
Farm

Down Farm

25

Waylarer's Walk

SO24

Millbarrow Farm

College Down
Bungalow

College Down
Farm

6

Kilmeston Down

Stanmore Farm

Mill
Barrows

5

Millbarrow
Down

College Down
Holding

South Downs Way

Wind Farm

24

Rooksgrove
Farm

LOVE LANE

Wyn Cottages

Lomer Farm

4

Monarch's Way

PRESHAW
EST

BARBARA
CT

Preshaw
House

SIR JOHN'S
MEWS

Waylarer's Walk

SO32

Lomer Cottage

The Monarch's Way

3

23

Rabbit Copse

Nature
Reserve

Preshaw Down

Preshaw
Wood

2

THE WHITE WAY

SAILOR'S LA

Sailor's
Wood

1

BEACON HILL LA

Little Preshaw

Betty Mundy's
Cottage

Betty Mundy's
Bottom

22

35
15

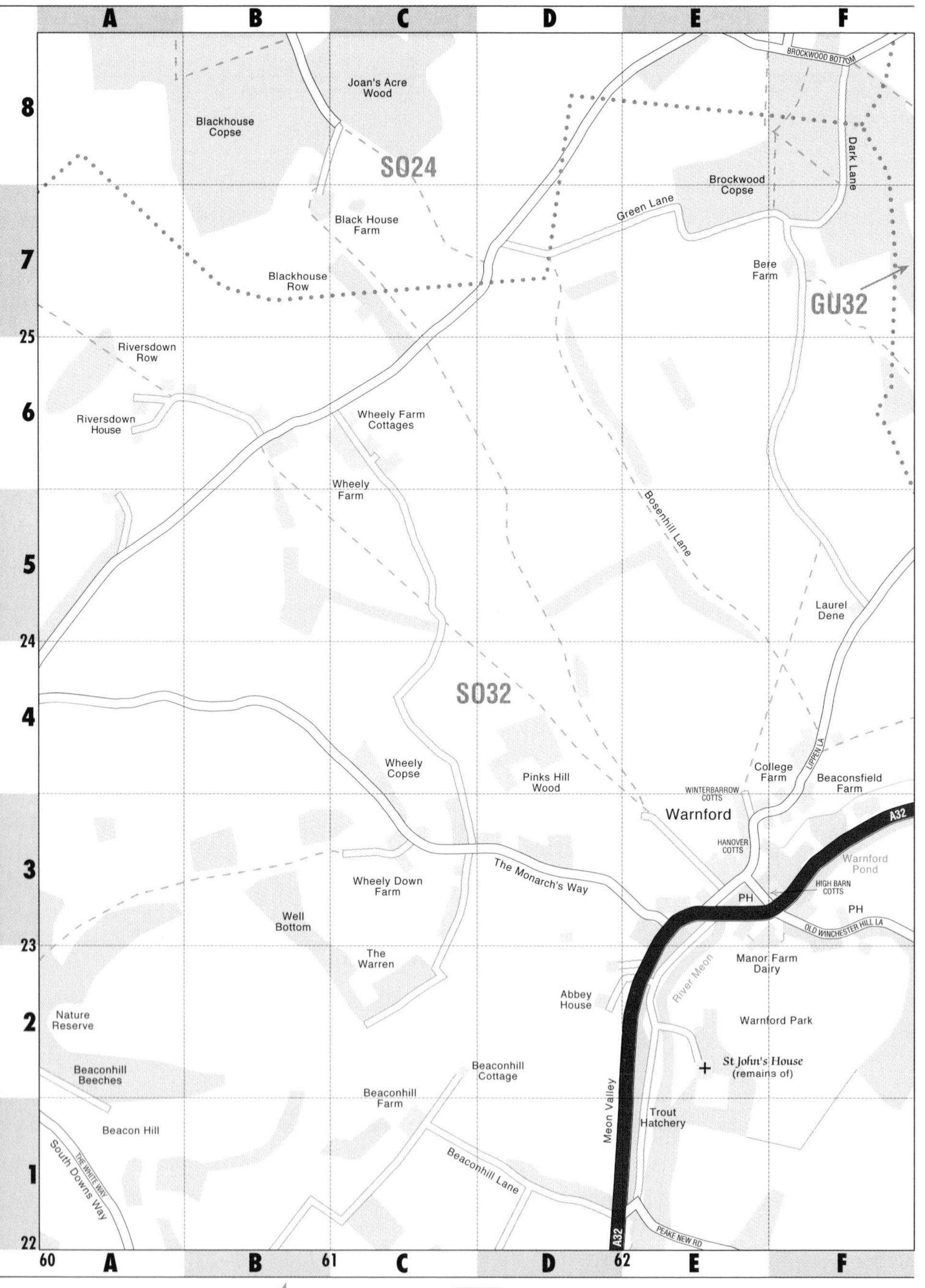
A
B
C
D
E
F
8
7
25
6
5
24
4
3
23
2
1
22
60
61
62
Joan's Acre Wood
Blackhouse Copse
SO24
BROCKWOOD BOTTOM
Dark Lane
Brockwood Copse
Green Lane
Black House Farm
Blackhouse Row
Bere Farm
GU32
Riversdown Row
Riversdown House
Wheely Farm Cottages
Wheely Farm
Bosenhill Lane
Laurel Dene
SO32
LIPPEN LA
Wheely Copse
Pinks Hill Wood
College Farm
Beaconsfield Farm
WINTERBARROW COTTS
Warnford
A32
HANOVER COTTS
Warnford Pond
The Monarch's Way
HIGH BARN COTTS
PH
PH
OLD WINCHESTER HILL LA
Wheely Down Farm
Well Bottom
The Warren
Manor Farm Dairy
River Meon
Abbey House
Nature Reserve
Warnford Park
Beaconhill Beeches
Beaconhill Cottage
St John's House (remains of)
Beaconhill Farm
Meon Valley
Trout Hatchery
Beacon Hill
THE WHITE WAY
South Downs Way
Beaconhill Lane
PEAKE NEW RD
A32

35
61

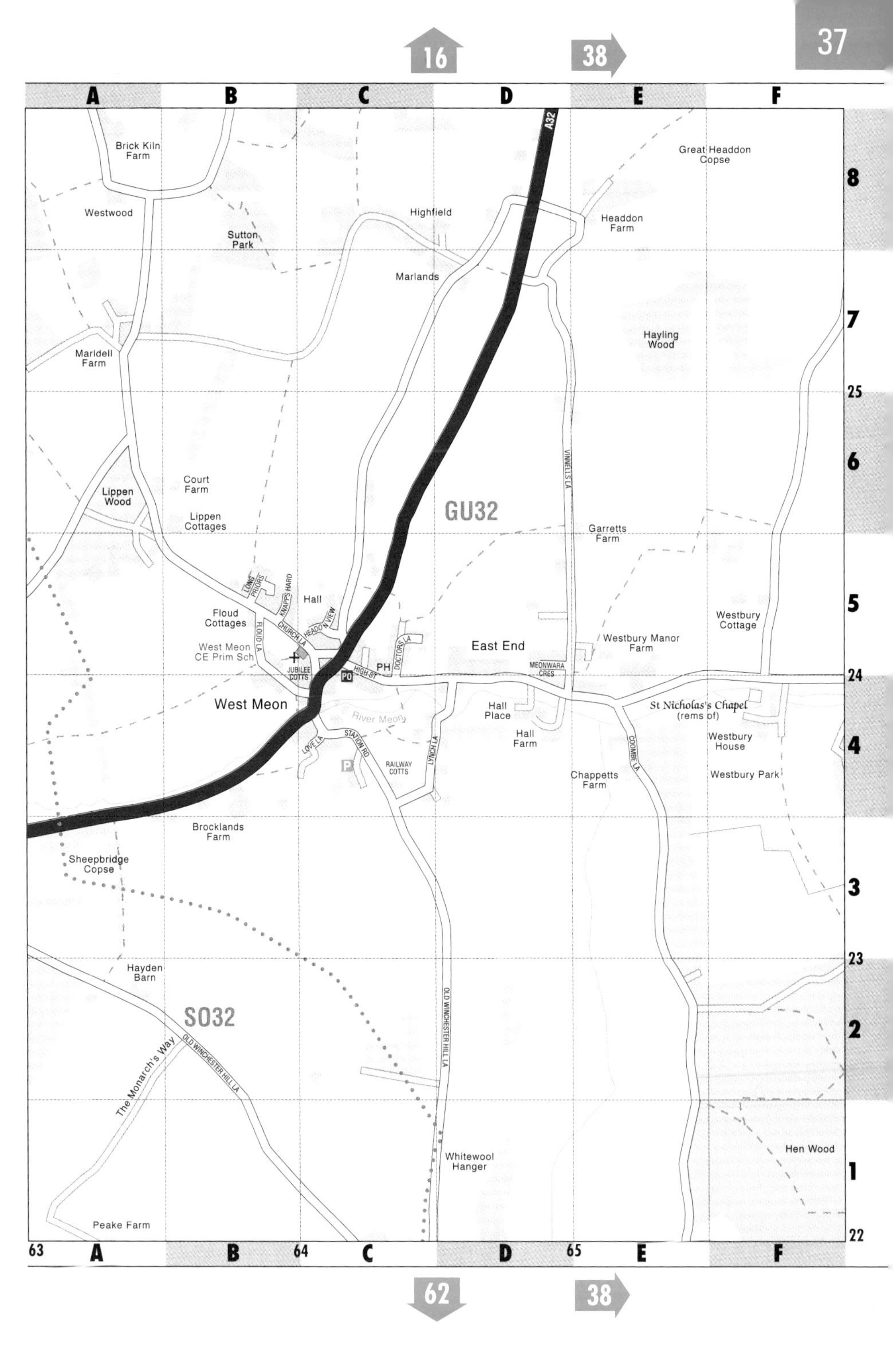
16
38
A
B
C
D
E
F
A32
Brick Kiln Farm
Great Headdon Copse
Westwood
Sutton Park
Highfield
Headdon Farm
Marlands
Marldell Farm
Hayling Wood
Lippen Wood
Court Farm
Lippen Cottages
GU32
VINNELLS LA
Garretts Farm
LONG PRIORS
KNAPPS HARD
Hall
Floud Cottages
HEADON VIEW
CHURCH LA
FLOUD LA
Westbury Cottage
West Meon CE Prim Sch
DOCTORS LA
East End
Westbury Manor Farm
JUBILEE COTTS
PO
HIGH ST
PH
MEONWARA CRES
West Meon
River Meon
Hall Place
St Nicholas's Chapel (rems of)
LOVE LA
STATION RD
LYNCH LA
Hall Farm
COOMBE LA
Westbury House
P
RAILWAY COTTS
Chappetts Farm
Westbury Park
Brocklands Farm
Sheepbridge Copse
Hayden Barn
SO32
The Monarch's Way
OLD WINCHESTER HILL LA
Whitewool Hanger
Hen Wood
Peake Farm
8
7
25
6
5
24
4
3
23
2
1
22
63
64
65
62
38

GU34

GU32

Arbor Trees Farm
Redwood Cottage
Red Wood
Peak Farm
Kingsland Copse
Great Copyhold Copse
Old Down
Old Down Farm
War Hill
Warhill Cottage
Park House
Upper Bordean House
Upper Bordean Farm
Bordean Barn
Tigwell Copse
Mare Pond
Trenleygrove Plantation
Trenley Grove
Burrow Plantation
Tigwell Cottages
Tigwell Farm
East Lodge
Bereleigh Cottage
Orchard Plantation
Riplington
Park Cottages
River Meon
Drayton House
Bereleigh House
Park Farm
Riplington Hanger
Drayton Farm
Park Cottages
Drayton Cottages
Drayton
Horsedown Farm
Drayton Mill
Mascoombe Bottom
Emmet's Down
Drayton Down
Chalk Dell Cottages
Park Hill
Hen Wood
Hatmaker Lane
Middle Down
Sewage Works
Vineyard Hole
Frogmore
Gravel Lane
1 FORBES ALMSHOUSES
2 TEMPLE LA
3 WESTBROOKE COTTS
Court House
EAME'S COTTS
Yew Down
PARK VISTA
THE CROSS
THE GREEN
CHIDDEN
HIGH VIEW
CHAPEL ST
HIGH ST
CHURCH ST
WASHHOUSE LA
GLENTHORNE MEADOW
PH
PO
GREENWAY
East Meon
East Meon CE Prim Sch

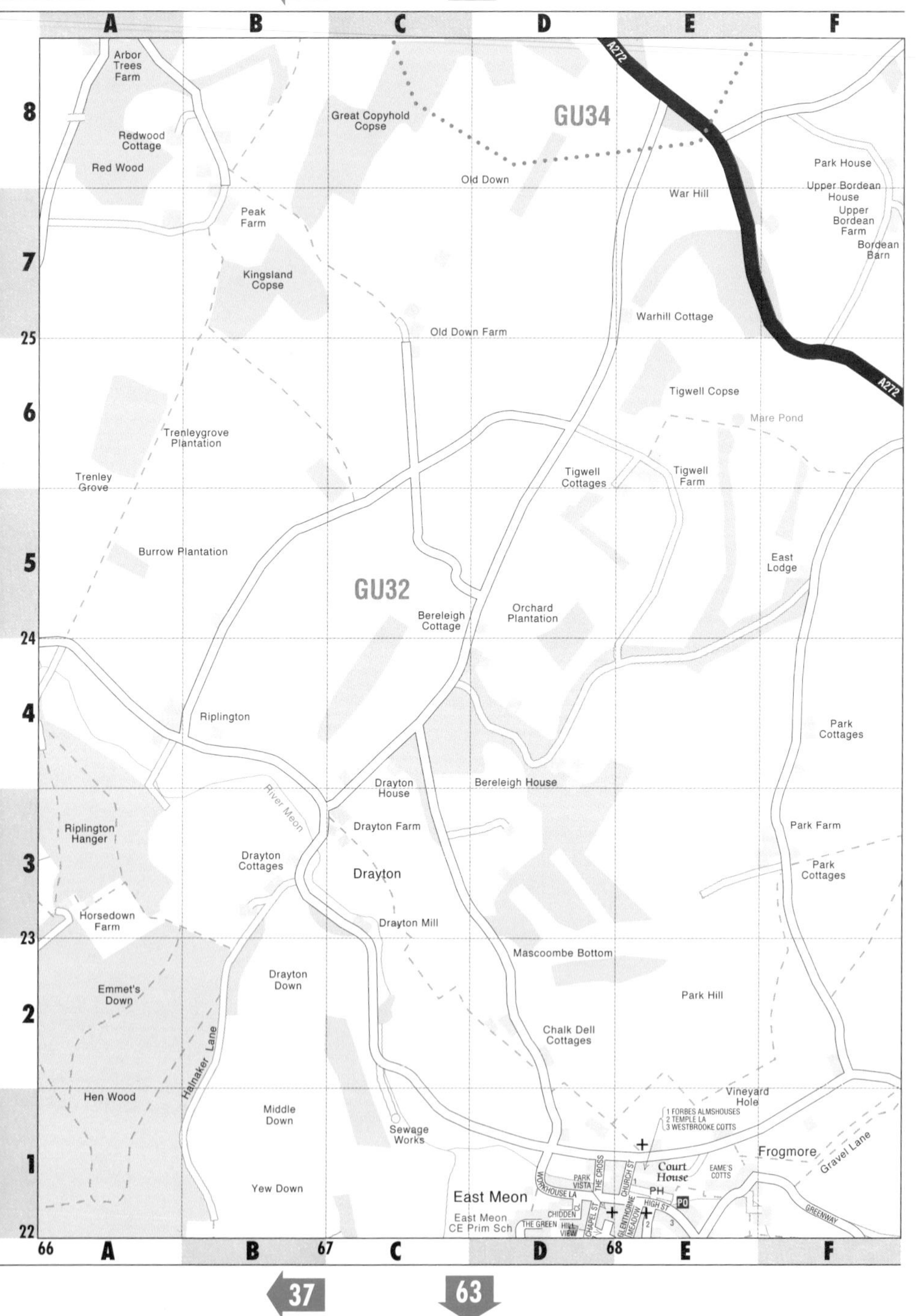

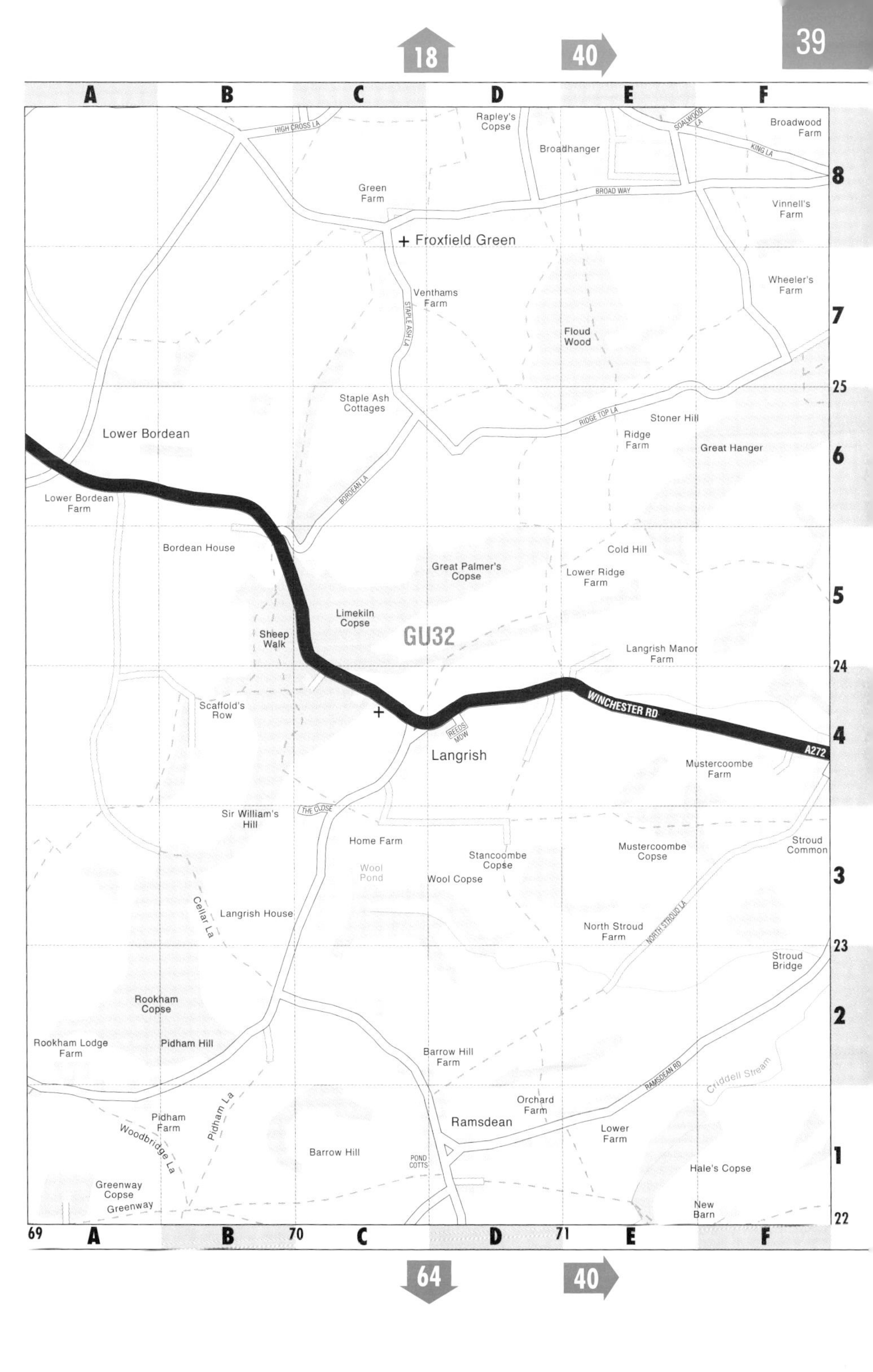

A   B   C   D   E   F

HIGH CROSS LA

Rapley's Copse

Broadhanger

SCALWOOD LA

KING LA

Broadwood Farm

Green Farm

BROAD WAY

Vinnell's Farm

8

+ Froxfield Green

Wheeler's Farm

Venthams Farm

Floud Wood

7

STAPLE ASH LA

Staple Ash Cottages

RIDGE TOP LA

Stoner Hill

25

Lower Bordean

Ridge Farm

Great Hanger

6

Lower Bordean Farm

BORDEAN LA

Bordean House

Great Palmer's Copse

Cold Hill

Lower Ridge Farm

5

Limekiln Copse

GU32

Sheep Walk

Langrish Manor Farm

24

Scaffold's Row

+

WINCHESTER RD

4

A272

BEECH MDW

Langrish

Mustercoombe Farm

Sir William's Hill

THE CLOSE

Home Farm

Stancoombe Copse

Mustercoombe Copse

Stroud Common

3

Cellar La

Wool Pond

Wool Copse

North Stroud Farm

NORTH STROUD LA

23

Langrish House

Rookham Copse

Stroud Bridge

2

Rookham Lodge Farm

Pidham Hill

Pidham La

Barrow Hill Farm

Orchard Farm

RAMSDEAN RD

Criddell Stream

Pidham Farm

Woodbridge La

Ramsdean

Lower Farm

Hale's Copse

1

Barrow Hill

POND COTTS

Greenway Copse

Greenway

New Barn

22

39 19

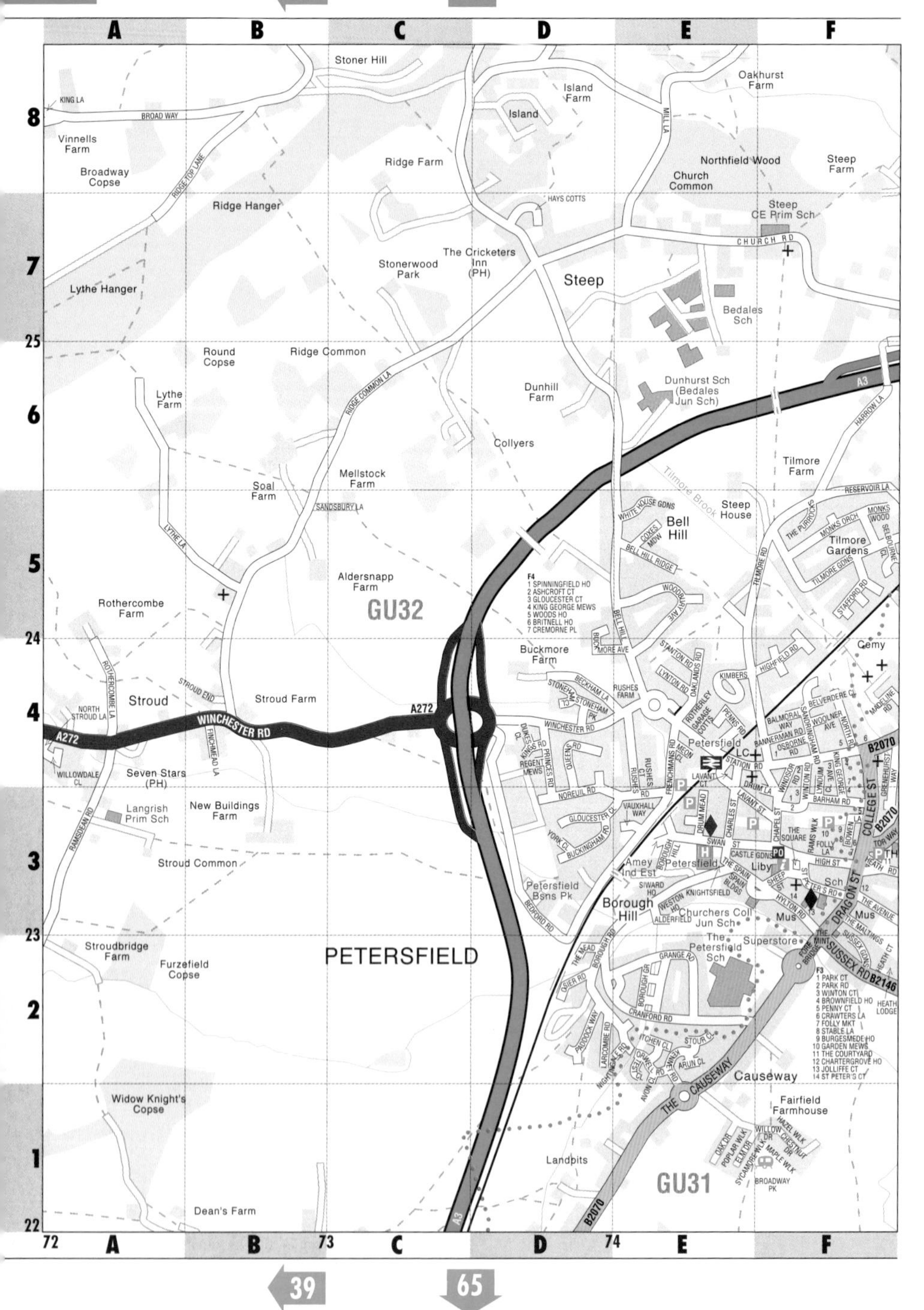

A B C D E F
8 7 6 5 4 3 2 1
25 24 23 22
72 73 74
KING LA
BROAD WAY
Vinnells Farm
Broadway Copse
RIDGE-TOP LANE
Ridge Hanger
Stoner Hill
Island Farm
Island
MILL LA
Oakhurst Farm
Ridge Farm
Northfield Wood
Church Common
Steep Farm
HAYS COTTS
Steep CE Prim Sch
CHURCH RD
Lythe Hanger
Stonerwood Park
The Cricketers Inn (PH)
Steep
Bedales Sch
Round Copse
Ridge Common
Lythe Farm
RIDGE COMMON LA
Dunhill Farm
Dunhurst Sch (Bedales Jun Sch)
A3
HARROW LA
Collyers
Tilmore Farm
Soal Farm
Mellstock Farm
SANDSBURY LA
Tilmore Brook
WHITE HOUSE GDNS
Bell Hill
Steep House
RESERVOIR LA
LYTHE LA
COXES MDW
BELL HILL RIDGE
THE PURROCKS
MONKS ORCH
MONKS WOOD
Tilmore Gardens
TILMORE GDNS
SELBOURNE
TILMORE RD
STAFFORD RD
Aldersnapp Farm
WOODBURY AVE
Rothercombe Farm
GU32
F4
1 SPINNINGFIELD HO
2 ASHCROFT CT
3 GLOUCESTER CT
4 KING GEORGE MEWS
5 WOODS HO
6 BRITNELL HO
7 CREMORNE PL
BELL HILL
BUCKMORE AVE
STANTON RD
LYNTON RD
OAKLANDS RD
KIMBERS
HIGHFIELD RD
Cemy
Buckmore Farm
ROTHERCOMBE LA
STROUD END
Stroud
Stroud Farm
STONEHAM CL
BECKHAM LA
STONEHAM PK
RUSHES FARM
ROTHERLEY
GARAGE COTTS
PENNS RD
BELVEDERE CL
MADELINE RD
NORTH STROUD LA
A272
WINCHESTER RD
FINCHMEAD LA
WINCHESTER RD
DUKES CL
KINGS RD
PRINCES RD
QUEENS RD
REGENT MEWS
RUSHES CT
RUSHES RD
FRENCHMANS RD
MEON CL
Petersfield
LC
STATION RD
LAVANT CT
BALMORAL WAY
SANDRINGHAM RD
WOOLNER AVE
NORTH RD
BANNERMAN RD
OSBORNE RD
B2070
GRENEHURST WAY
WILLOWDALE CL
Seven Stars (PH)
NOREUIL RD
DRUM MEAD
DRUM LA
WINDSOR RD
WINTON RD
LYNDUM
KING GEORGE AVE
BARHAM RD
Langrish Prim Sch
New Buildings Farm
GLOUCESTER CL
VAUXHALL WAY
CHARLES ST
LAVANT ST
CHAPEL ST
RAMS WLK
THE SQUARE
FOLLY LA
BOWEN LA
COLLEGE ST
RAMSDEAN RD
YORK CL
BUCKINGHAM RD
BOROUGH HILL
SWAN ST
CASTLE GDNS
HIGH ST
Stroud Common
Amey Ind Est
Petersfield
THE SPAIN
SPAIN BLDGS
Liby
SHEEP ST
ST PETER'S RD
Sch
Mus
Petersfield Bsns Pk
SIWARD HO
KNIGHTSFIELD
WESTON RD
Borough Hill
HYLTON RD
DRAGON ST
THE AVENUE
THE MALTINGS
BEDFORD RD
ALDERFIELD
Churchers Coll Jun Sch
Mus
Stroudbridge Farm
PETERSFIELD
The Petersfield Sch
Superstore
THE MINT
SUSSEX GDNS
HEATH CT
THE MEAD
BOROUGH RD
GRANGE RD
FORE BRIDGE
SUSSEX RD
B2146
Furzefield Copse
OSIER RD
BOROUGH GR
F3
1 PARK CT
2 PARK RD
3 WINTON CT
4 BROWNFIELD HO
5 PENNY CT
6 CRAWTERS LA
7 FOLLY MKT
8 STABLE LA
9 BURGESMEDE HO
10 GARDEN MEWS
11 THE COURTYARD
12 CHARTERGROVE HO
13 JOLLIFFE CT
14 ST PETER'S CT
HEATH LODGE
CRANFORD RD
PADDOCK WAY
LARCOMBE RD
ITCHEN CL
STOUR CL
ARUN CL
NIGHTINGALE RD
TEST CL
ORWELL RD
KENNET RD
AVON
THE CAUSEWAY
Causeway
Widow Knight's Copse
Fairfield Farmhouse
WILLOW DR
HAZEL WLK
CHESTNUT DR
MAPLE WLK
OAK DR
POPLAR WLK
ELM DR
SYCAMORE WLK
BROADWAY PK
Landpits
GU31
Dean's Farm
B2070

39 65

20

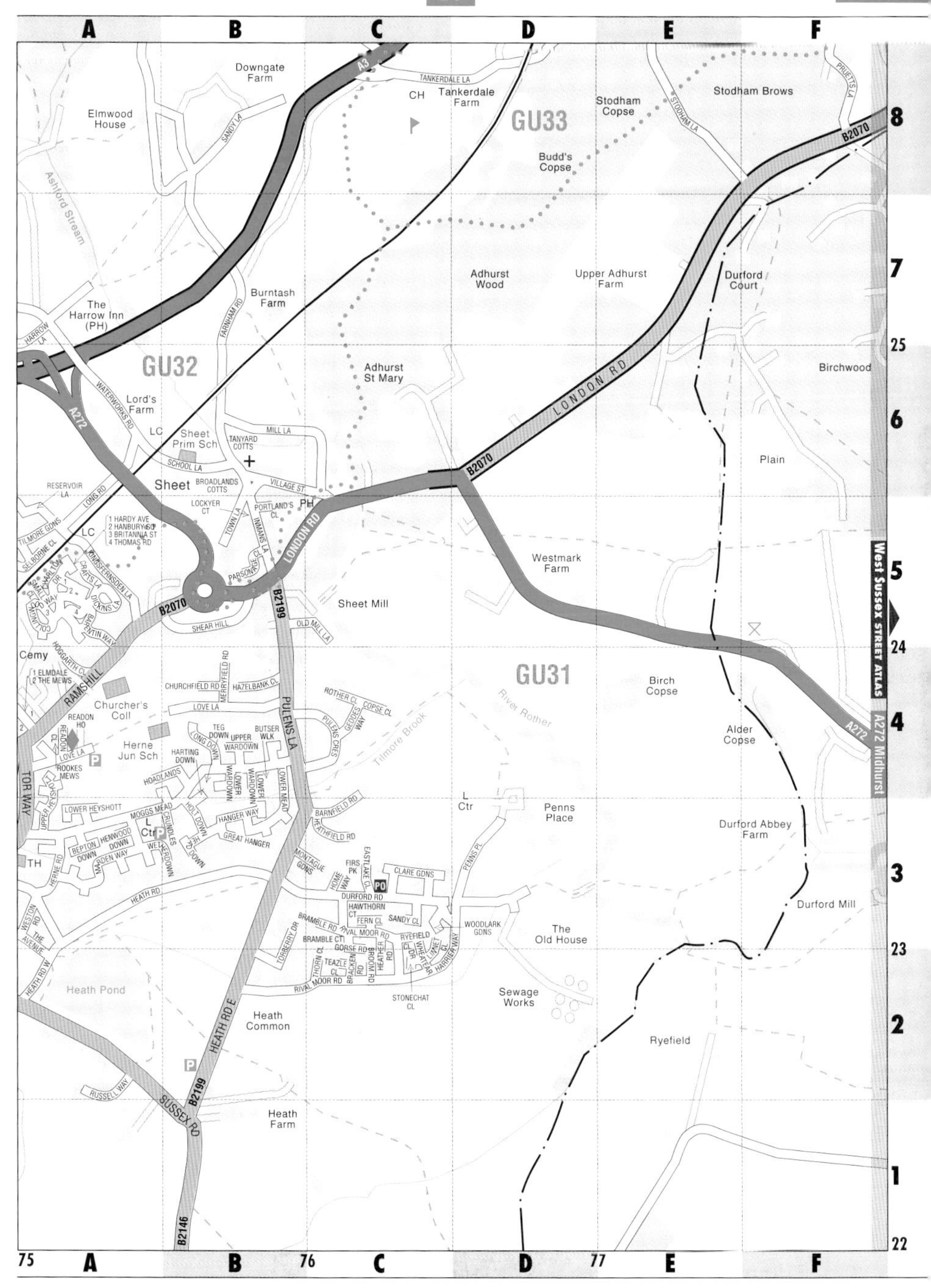

Downgate Farm
Elmwood House
Tankerdale Farm
TANKERDALE LA
GU33
Stodham Copse
Stodham Brows
Budd's Copse
Ashford Stream
Adhurst Wood
Upper Adhurst Farm
Durford Court
Burntash Farm
The Harrow Inn (PH)
GU32
Adhurst St Mary
LONDON RD
B2070
Birchwood
Lord's Farm
Sheet Prim Sch
Sheet
Plain
Westmark Farm
Sheet Mill
West Sussex STREET ATLAS
Cemy
GU31
Birch Copse
River Rother
Tilmore Brook
Churcher's Coll
Herne Jun Sch
Alder Copse
A272 Midhurst
Penns Place
Durford Abbey Farm
Durford Mill
The Old House
Sewage Works
Heath Pond
Heath Common
Ryefield
Heath Farm
PULENS LA
HEATH RD E
SUSSEX RD
RAMSHILL
TOR WAY
HEATH RD
B2199
B2146
A3
A272

66

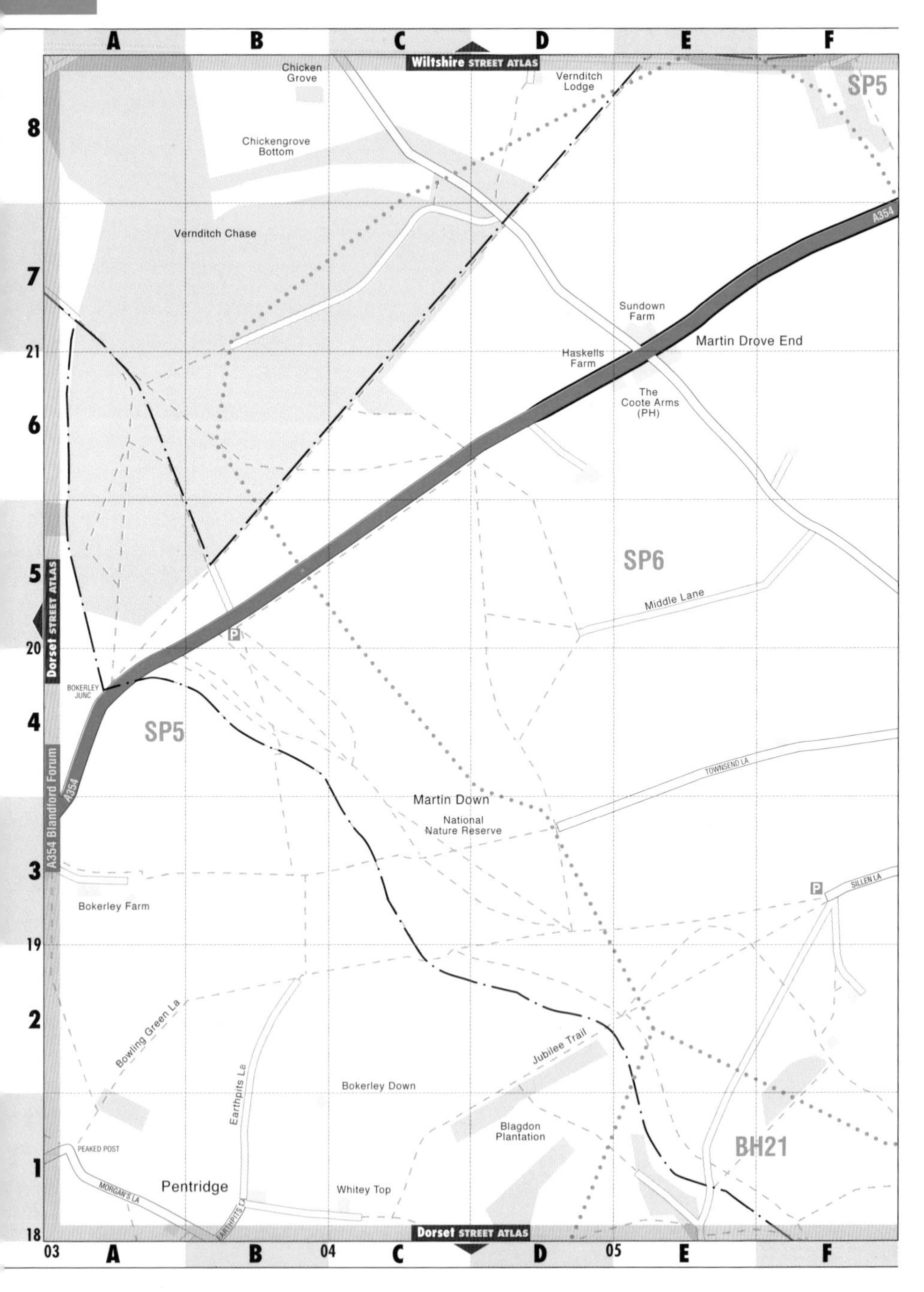

SP5

A354

21

Chicken Grove

Chickengrove Bottom

Vernditch Chase

Vernditch Lodge

Sundown Farm

Haskells Farm

Martin Drove End

The Coote Arms (PH)

SP6

Middle Lane

BOKERLEY JUNC

SP5

A354

TOWNSEND LA

Martin Down

National Nature Reserve

SILLEN LA

Bokerley Farm

Bowling Green La

Earthpits La

Bokerley Down

Jubilee Trail

BH21

PEAKED POST

Blagdon Plantation

MORGAN'S LA

Pentridge

EARTHPITS LA

Whitey Top

03   A   B   04   C   D   05   E   F

18

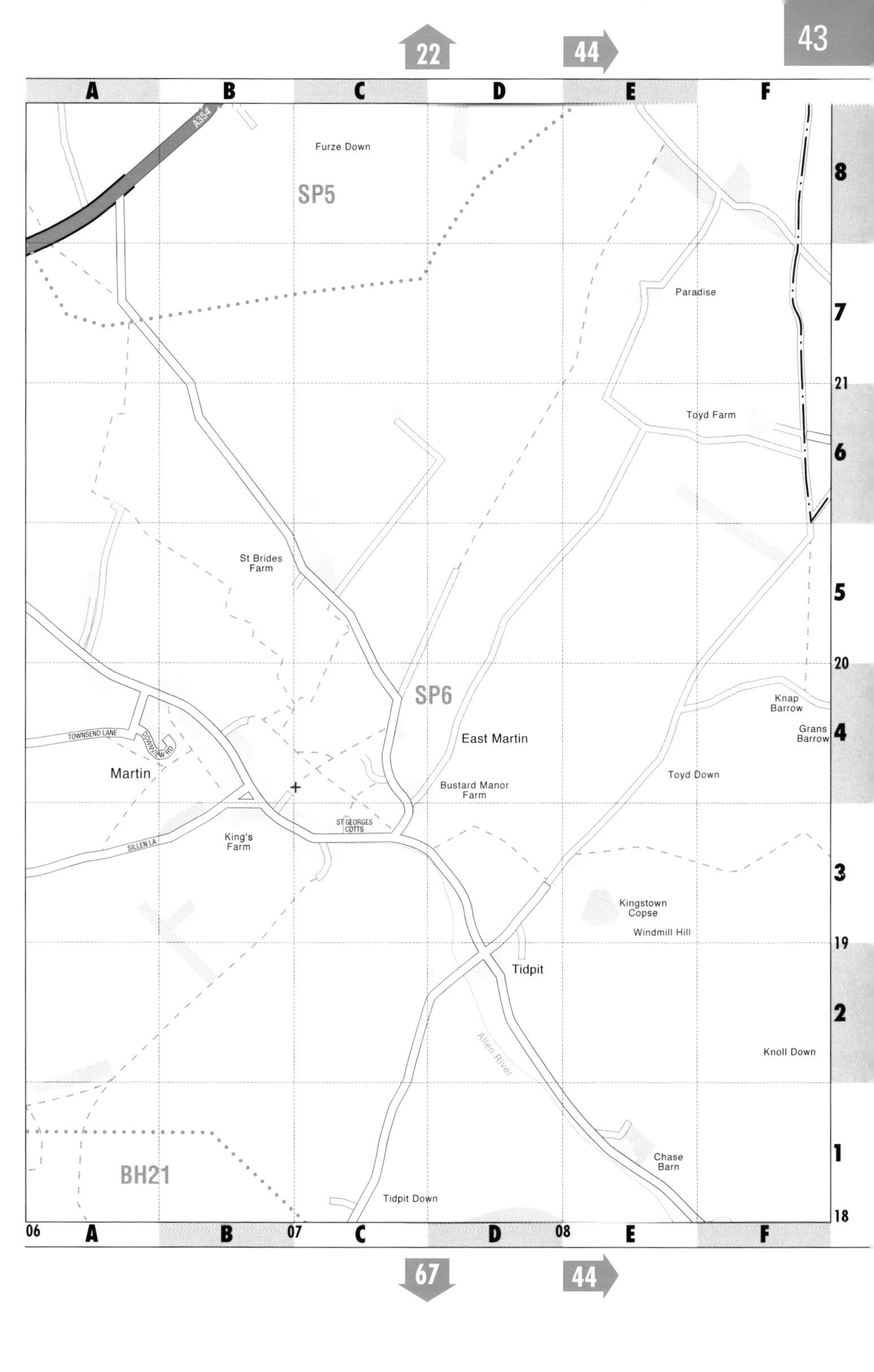
22
44
A
B
C
D
E
F
8
7
21
6
5
20
4
3
19
2
1
18
A354
Furze Down
SP5
Paradise
Toyd Farm
St Brides
Farm
SP6
Knap
Barrow
Grans
Barrow
East Martin
TOWNSEND LANE
DOWNVIEW RD
Martin
Bustard Manor
Farm
Toyd Down
ST GEORGES
COTTS
King's
Farm
SILLEN LA
Kingstown
Copse
Windmill Hill
Tidpit
Allen River
Knoll Down
Chase
Barn
BH21
Tidpit Down
06
07
08
67
44

43
23

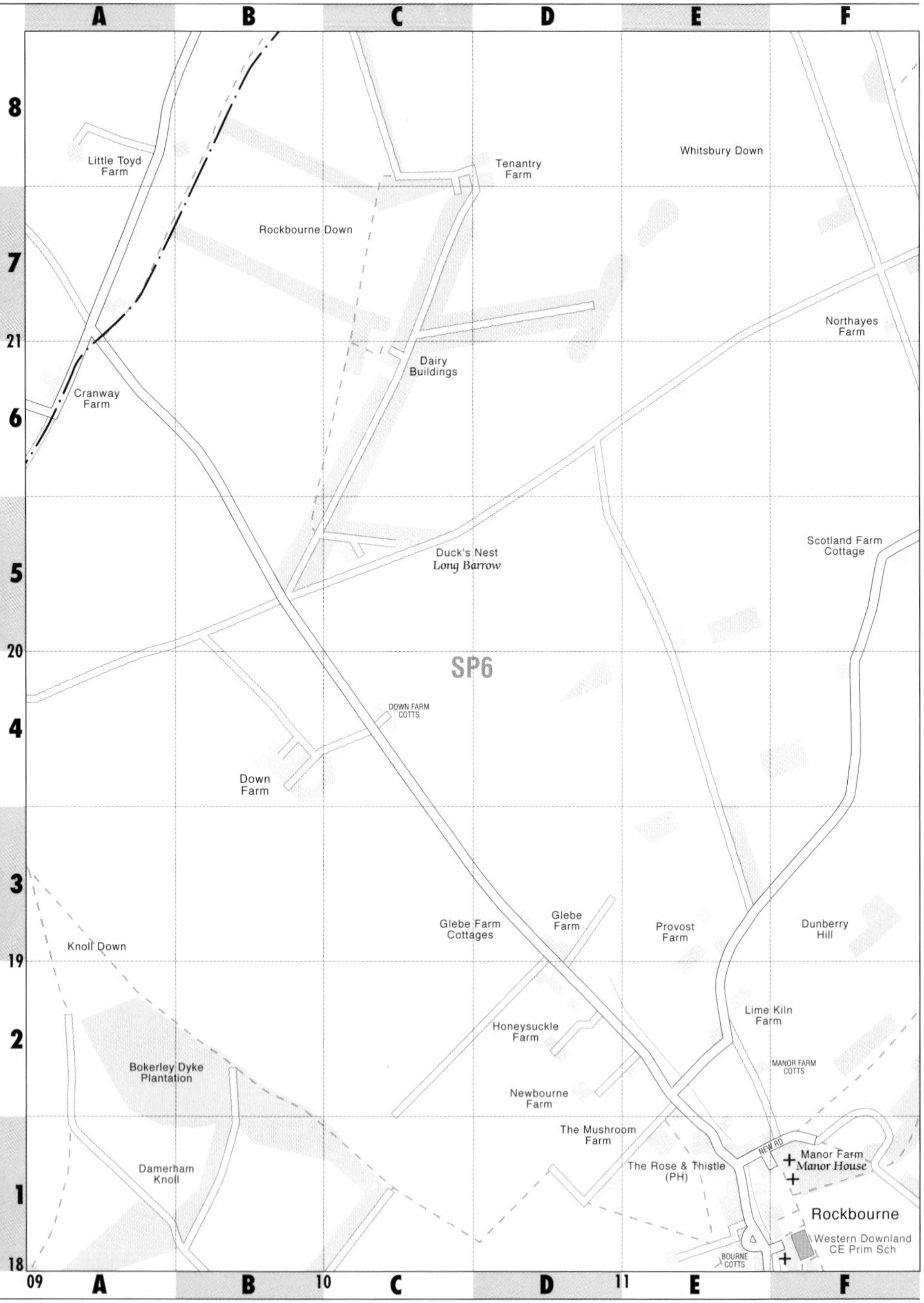

	A	B	C	D	E	F

8

Little Toyd Farm

Tenantry Farm

Whitsbury Down

Rockbourne Down

7

Northayes Farm

21

Dairy Buildings

Cranway Farm

6

Duck's Nest *Long Barrow*

Scotland Farm Cottage

5

20

SP6

DOWN FARM COTTS

4

Down Farm

3

Glebe Farm Cottages

Glebe Farm

Provost Farm

Dunberry Hill

Knoll Down

19

Lime Kiln Farm

2

Honeysuckle Farm

MANOR FARM COTTS

Bokerley Dyke Plantation

Newbourne Farm

The Mushroom Farm

NEW RD

Manor Farm
Manor House

1

Damerham Knoll

The Rose & Thistle (PH)

Rockbourne

Western Downland CE Prim Sch

18

BOURNE COTTS

09	A	B	10	C	D	11	E	F

43
68

46

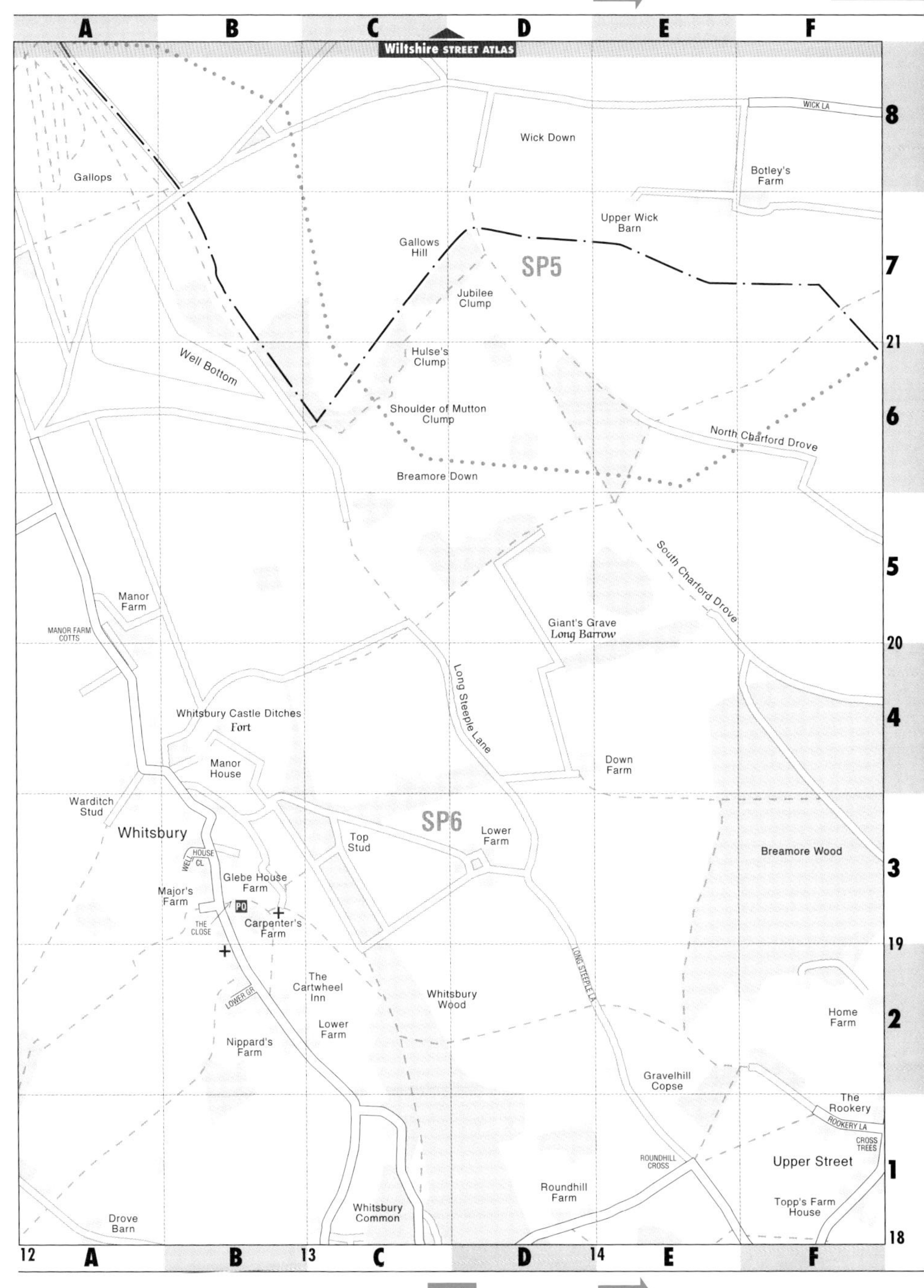

WICK LA

Wick Down

Botley's
Farm

Gallops
Farm

Upper Wick
Barn

Gallows
Hill

SP5

Jubilee
Clump

Hulse's
Clump

Well Bottom

North Charford Drove

Shoulder of Mutton
Clump

Breamore Down

South Charford Drove

Manor
Farm

Giant's Grave
Long Barrow

MANOR FARM
COTTS

Long Steeple Lane

Whitsbury Castle Ditches
Fort

Down
Farm

Manor
House

Warditch
Stud

Whitsbury

SP6

Breamore Wood

HOUSE
CL

Top
Stud

Lower
Farm

Glebe House
Farm

Major's
Farm

PO

THE
CLOSE

Carpenter's
Farm

The
Cartwheel
Inn

Whitsbury
Wood

LONG STEEPLE LA

Nippard's
Farm

Lower
Farm

Home
Farm

Gravelhill
Copse

The
Rookery

ROOKERY LA

CROSS
TREES

Drove
Barn

Whitsbury
Common

Roundhill
Farm

ROUNDHILL
CROSS

Upper Street

Topp's Farm
House

45

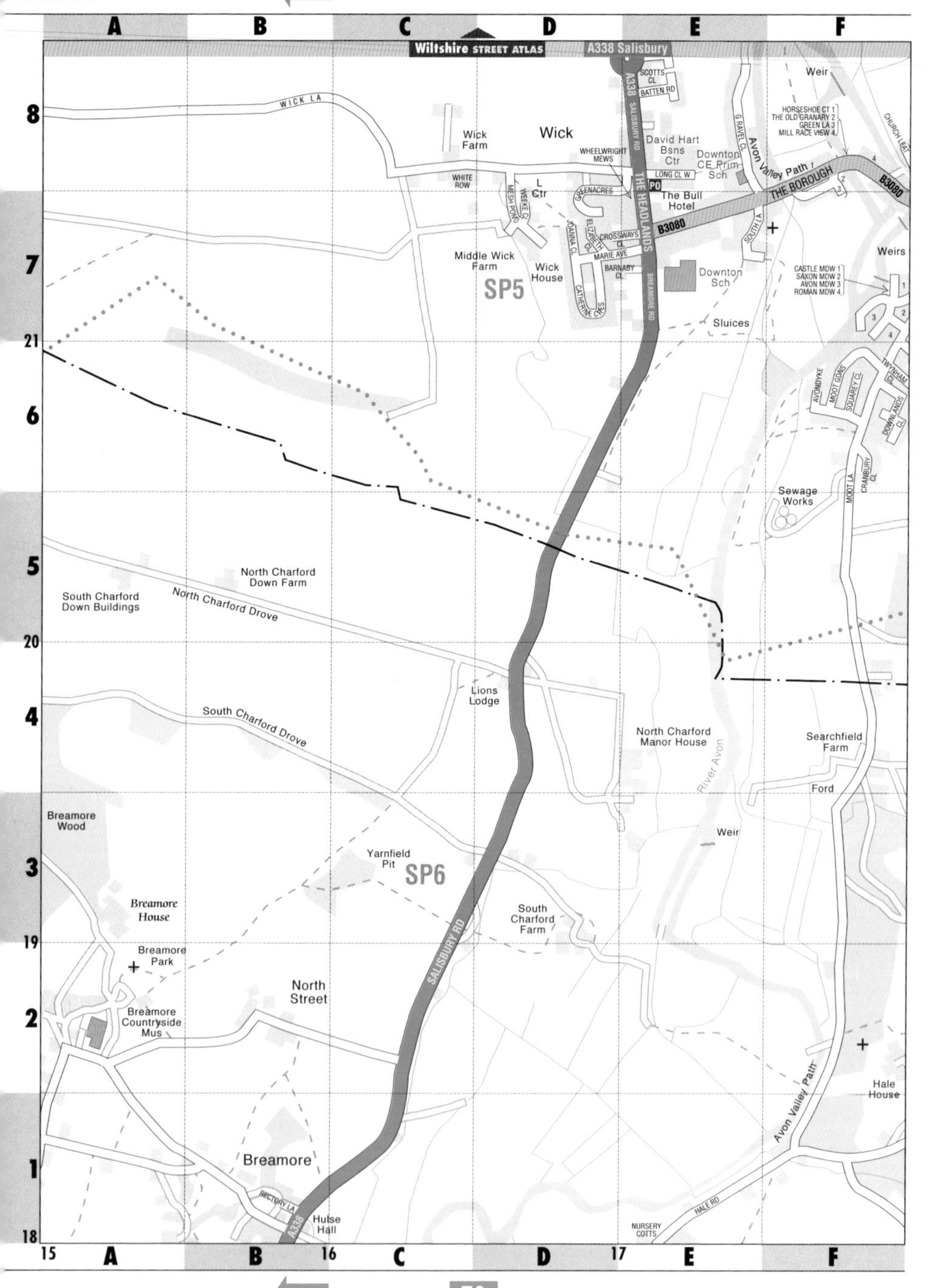
Wiltshire STREET ATLAS
A338 Salisbury
WICK LA
Wick Farm
Wick
SCOTTS CL
BATTEN RD
SALISBURY RD
A338
THE HEADLANDS
WHEELWRIGHT MEWS
David Hart Bsns Ctr
Downton CE Prim Sch
LONG CL W
PO
The Bull Hotel
WHITE ROW
L Ctr
MESH POND
WEEKE CL
GREENACRES
JOANNA CL
ELIZABETH CL
CROSSWAYS CL
MARIE AVE
BARNABY CL
CATHERINE CRES
B3080
THE BOROUGH
Avon Valley Path
SOUTH LA
G RAVEL CL
Weir
HORSESHOE CT 1
THE OLD GRANARY 2
GREEN LA 3
MILL RACE VIEW 4
CHURCH LEAT
Weirs
CASTLE MDW 1
SAXON MDW 2
AVON MDW 3
ROMAN MDW 4
Middle Wick Farm
Wick House
SP5
Downton Sch
Sluices
BREAMORE RD
AVONDYKE
MOOT GDNS
SQUAREY CL
TWYNHAM CL
DOWNLANDS CL
Sewage Works
MOOT LA
CRANBURY CL
North Charford Down Farm
South Charford Down Buildings
North Charford Drove
Lions Lodge
South Charford Drove
North Charford Manor House
River Avon
Searchfield Farm
Ford
Breamore Wood
Weir
Yarnfield Pit
SP6
Breamore House
South Charford Farm
SALISBURY RD
Breamore Park
North Street
Breamore Countryside Mus
Avon Valley Path
Hale House
Breamore
RECTORY LA
A338
Hulse Hall
NURSERY COTTS
HALE RD
A B C D E F
8 7 21 6 5 20 4 3 19 2 1 18
15 16 17

45
70

48

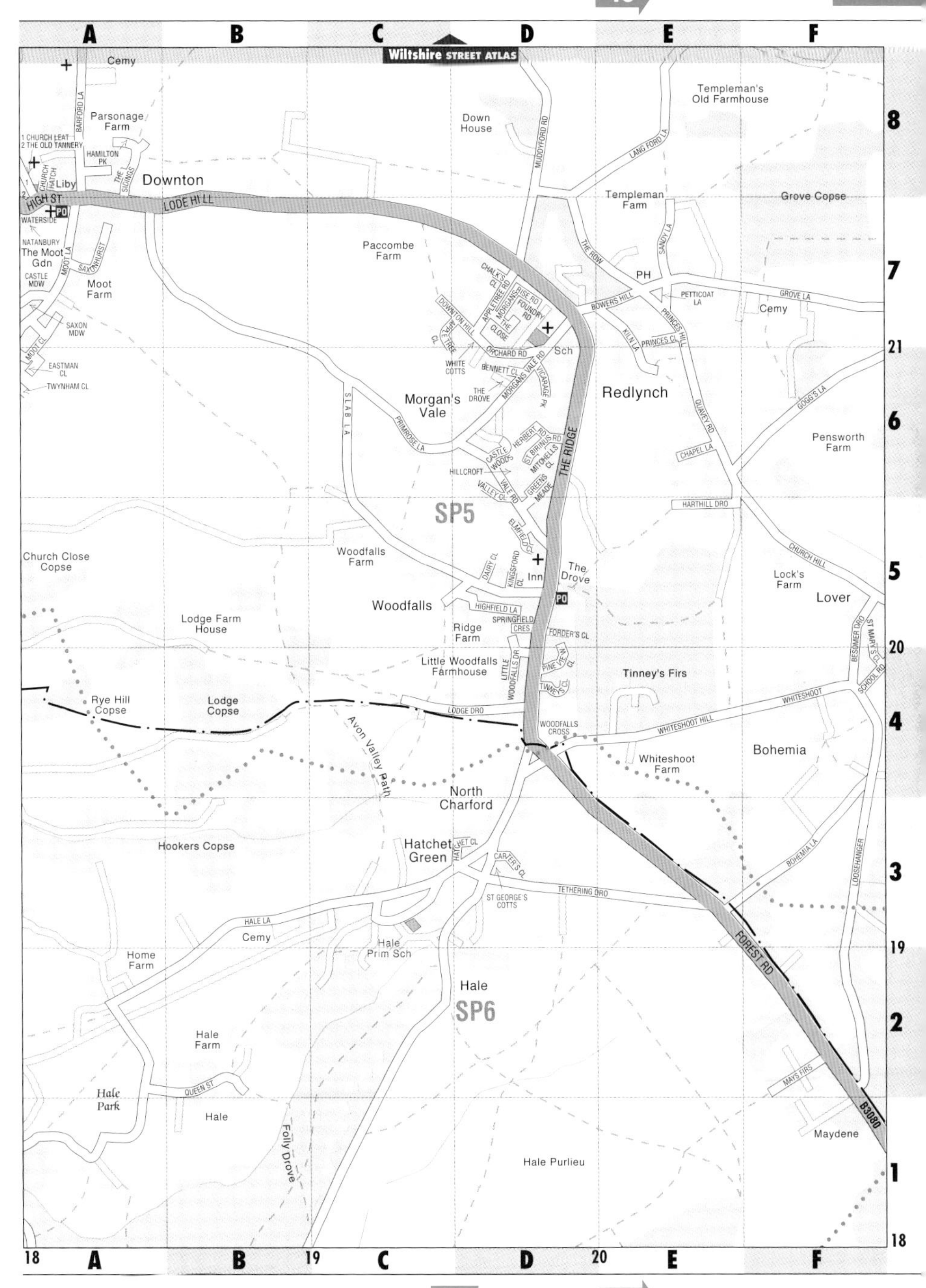
A
B
C
D
E
F
Wiltshire STREET ATLAS
Cemy
Parsonage Farm
BARFORD LA
1 CHURCH LEAT
2 THE OLD TANNERY
HAMILTON PK
THE SIDINGS
CHURCH HATCH
Liby
Downton
HIGH ST
PO
LODE HILL
WATERSIDE
NATANBURY
The Moot Gdn
MOOT LA
SAXONHURST
CASTLE MDW
Moot Farm
SAXON MDW
MOOT CL
EASTMAN CL
TWYNHAM CL
Down House
MUDDYFORD RD
Templeman's Old Farmhouse
LANG FORD LA
Templeman Farm
Grove Copse
SANDY LA
THE ROW
Paccombe Farm
PH
CHALK'S CL
APPLETREE RD
MORGANS RISE RD
FOUNDRY RD
THE CLOSE
DOWNTON HILL
APPLE TREE CL
ORCHARD RD
BOWERS HILL
PETTICOAT LA
GROVE LA
Cemy
PRINCES HILL
KILN LA
PRINCES CL
Sch
WHITE COTTS
BENNETT CL
MORGANS VALE RD
VICARAGE PK
THE DROVE
Morgan's Vale
Redlynch
SLAB LA
PRIMROSE LA
GOGG'S LA
QUAVEY RD
Pensworth Farm
CASTLE WOODS
HERBERT RD
ST BIRINUS RD
MITCHELLS CL
THE RIDGE
CHAPEL LA
HILLCROFT
VALLEY CL
VALE RD
GREENS MEADE
HARTHILL DRO
SP5
ELMFIELD CL
Church Close Copse
Woodfalls Farm
DAIRY CL
KINGSFORD CL
Inn
The Drove
CHURCH HILL
Lock's Farm
Lover
Woodfalls
PO
HIGHFIELD LA
SPRINGFIELD CRES
Lodge Farm House
Ridge Farm
FORDER'S CL
BESOMER DRO
ST MARY'S CL
SCHOOL RD
Little Woodfalls Farmhouse
LITTLE WOODFALLS DR
PINE VIEW CL
TINNEYS CL
Tinney's Firs
WHITESHOOT
Rye Hill Copse
Lodge Copse
LODGE DRO
WHITESHOOT HILL
Avon Valley Path
WOODFALLS CROSS
Whiteshoot Farm
Bohemia
North Charford
Hookers Copse
Hatchet Green
HATCHET CL
CARTER'S CL
BOHEMIA LA
LOOSEHANGER
ST GEORGE'S COTTS
TETHERING DRO
HALE LA
Cemy
Hale Prim Sch
FOREST RD
Home Farm
Hale
SP6
Hale Farm
MAYS FIRS
Hale Park
QUEEN ST
Hale
B3080
Maydene
Folly Drove
Hale Purlieu
8
7
21
6
5
20
4
3
19
2
1
18
18
19
20

71
48

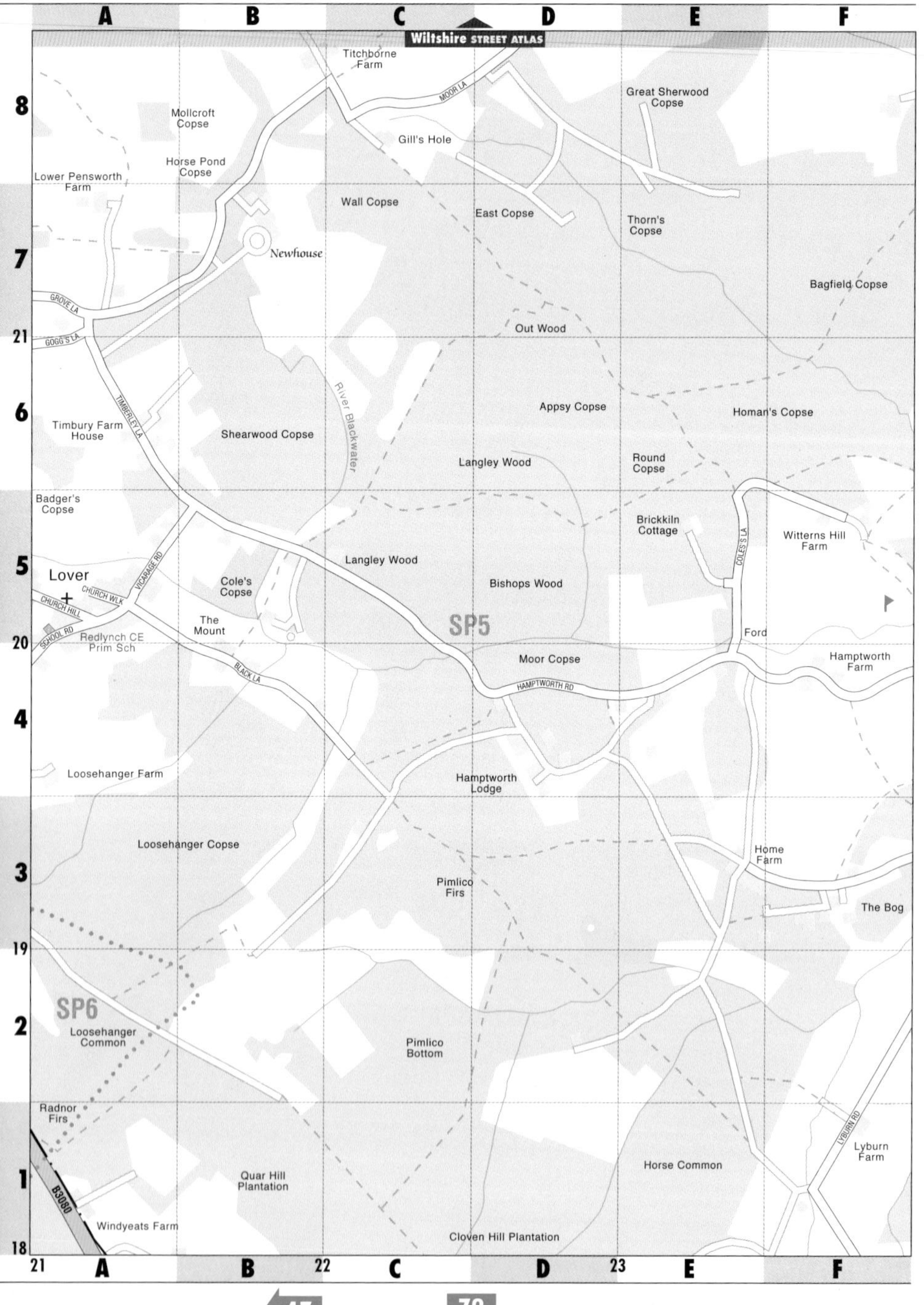

Wiltshire STREET ATLAS

A **B** **C** **D** **E** **F**

8

Titchborne
Farm

MOOR LA

Great Sherwood
Copse

Mollcroft
Copse

Horse Pond
Copse

Gill's Hole

Lower Pensworth
Farm

Wall Copse

East Copse

Thorn's
Copse

7

Newhouse

GROVE LA

Bagfield Copse

21

GOGG'S LA

Out Wood

6

TIMBURY LA

Timbury Farm
House

Shearwood Copse

River Blackwater

Appsy Copse

Homan's Copse

Langley Wood

Round
Copse

Badger's
Copse

Langley Wood

Brickkiln
Cottage

Witterns Hill
Farm

LA STYLES

5

Lover

CHURCH WLK

MORGANS RD

Cole's
Copse

Bishops Wood

SP5

CHURCH HILL

The
Mount

Ford

Hamptworth
Farm

SCHOOL RD

20

Redlynch CE
Prim Sch

BLACK LA

Moor Copse

HAMPTWORTH RD

4

Loosehanger Farm

Hamptworth
Lodge

3

Loosehanger Copse

Pimlico
Firs

Home
Farm

The Bog

19

SP6

2

Loosehanger
Common

Pimlico
Bottom

Radnor
Firs

LYBURN RD

Lyburn
Farm

B3080

1

Quar Hill
Plantation

Horse Common

Windyeats Farm

Cloven Hill Plantation

18

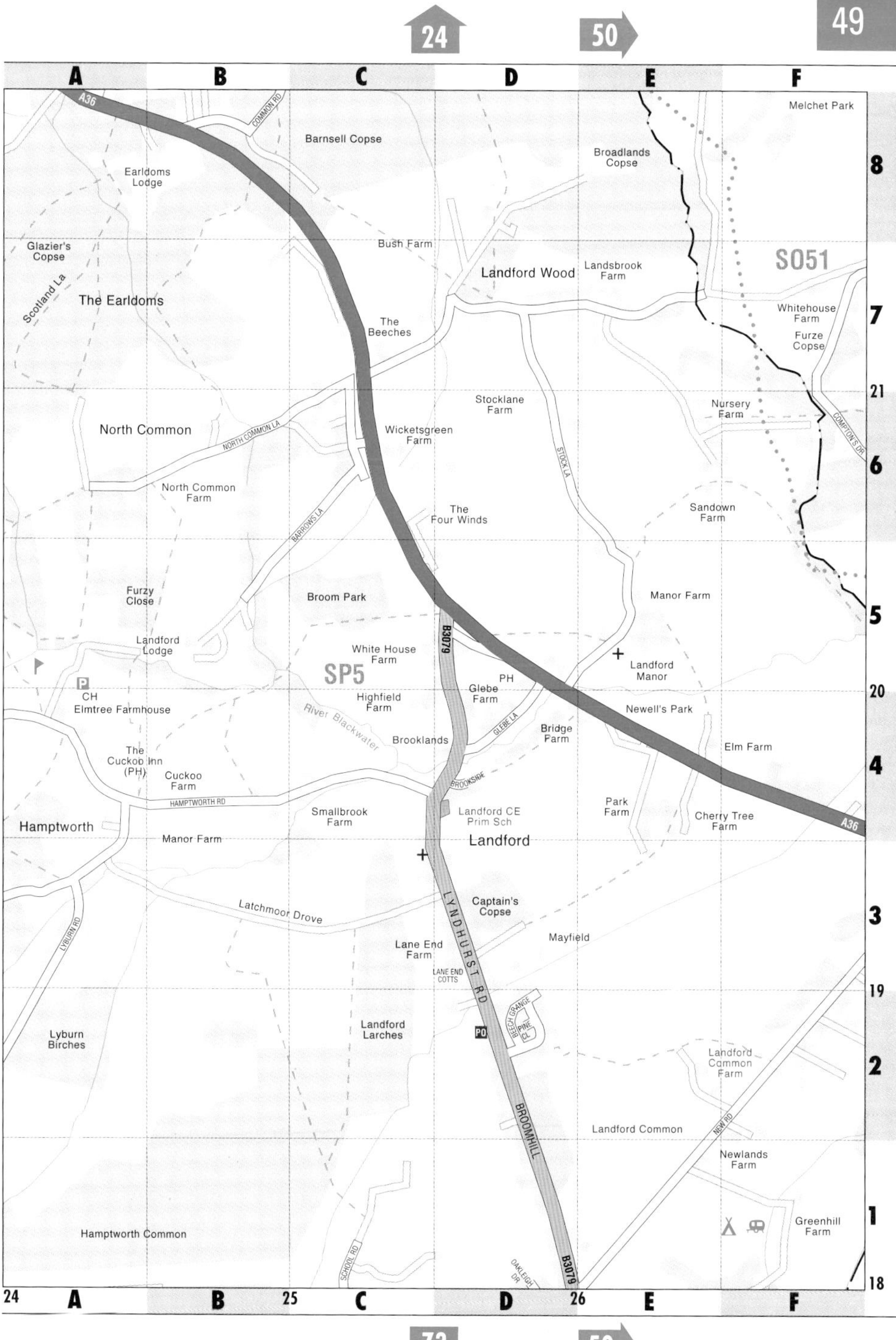

A B C D E F

8

Melchet Park

Broadlands
Copse

Barnsell Copse

Earldoms
Lodge

A36

Bush Farm

Landford Wood

Landsbrook
Farm

SO51

Glazier's
Copse

Whitehouse
Farm

7

The Earldoms

Scotland La

Furze
Copse

The
Beeches

21

Stocklane
Farm

North Common

NORTH COMMON LA

Wicketsgreen
Farm

Nursery
Farm

6

North Common
Farm

STOCKA

BARROWS LA

COMPTONS DR

The
Four Winds

Sandown
Farm

Furzy
Close

Broom Park

Manor Farm

5

Landford
Lodge

White House
Farm

SP5

Landford
Manor

20

CH

P

Elmtree Farmhouse

Highfield
Farm

B3079

Glebe
Farm

PH

Newell's Park

Elm Farm

River Blackwater

GLEBE LA

Bridge
Farm

4

The
Cuckoo Inn
(PH)

Brooklands

BROOKSIDE

Cuckoo
Farm

HAMPTWORTH RD

Smallbrook
Farm

Landford CE
Prim Sch

Park
Farm

Cherry Tree
Farm

A36

Hamptworth

Manor Farm

Landford

Latchmoor Drove

LYNDHURST RD

Captain's
Copse

3

Lane End
Farm

Mayfield

LANE END
COTTS

19

LYBURN RD

Lyburn
Birches

Landford
Larches

PO

GRANGE

PINE VW

HELEN'S CL

Landford
Common
Farm

NEW RD

2

BROOKHILL

Landford Common

Newlands
Farm

1

Hamptworth Common

SCHOOL RD

OAK END DR

B3079

Greenhill
Farm

18

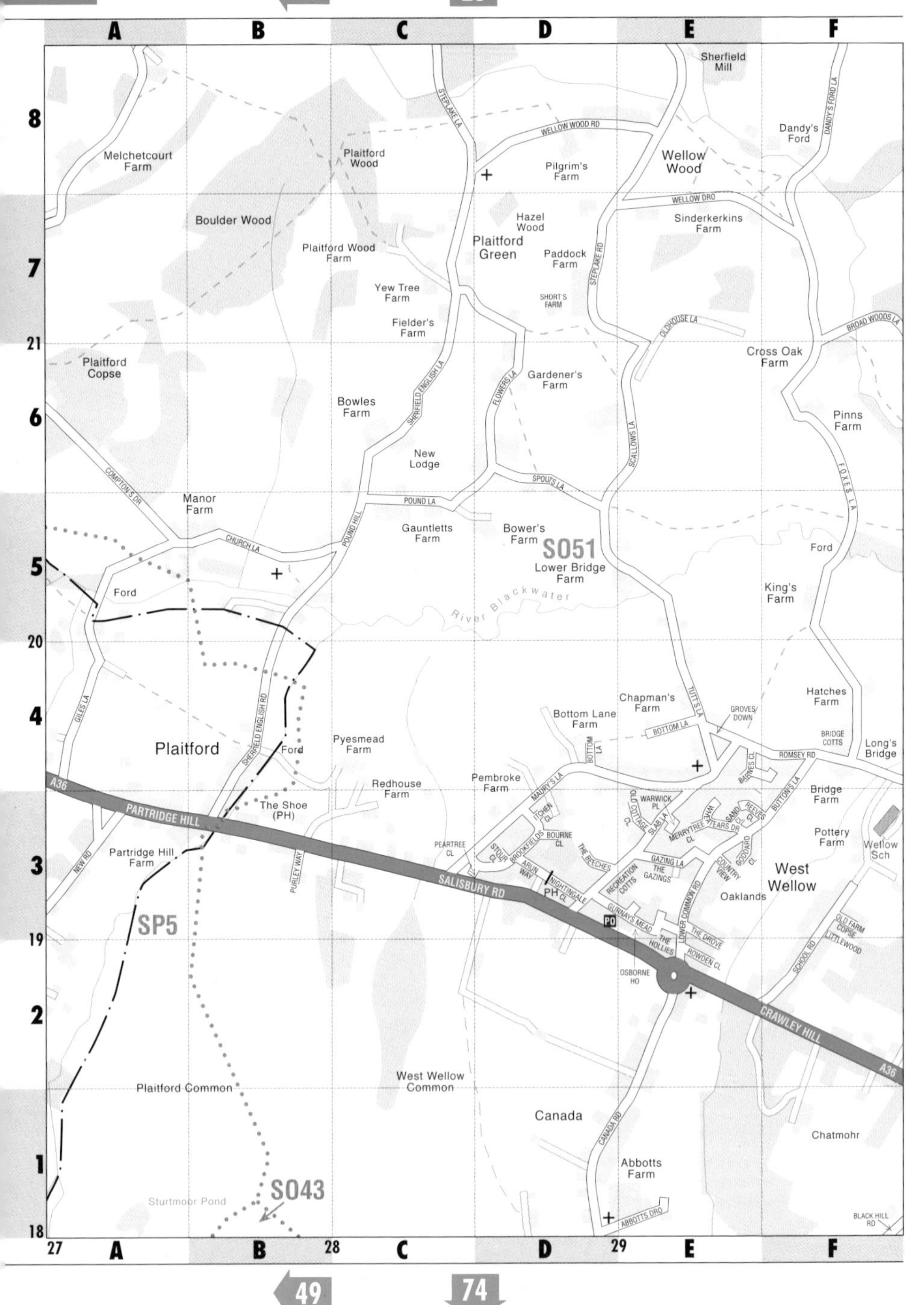
49
25
Sherfield Mill
Melchetcourt Farm
Plaitford Wood
Pilgrim's Farm
Wellow Wood
Dandy's Ford
Boulder Wood
Hazel Wood
Sinderkerkins Farm
Plaitford Wood Farm
Plaitford Green
Paddock Farm
Yew Tree Farm
Fielder's Farm
Plaitford Copse
Cross Oak Farm
Gardener's Farm
Bowles Farm
Pinns Farm
New Lodge
Manor Farm
Gauntletts Farm
Bower's Farm
SO51
Lower Bridge Farm
Ford
King's Farm
River Blackwater
Chapman's Farm
Hatches Farm
Bottom Lane Farm
Plaitford
Pyesmead Farm
Long's Bridge
Redhouse Farm
Pembroke Farm
Bridge Farm
The Shoe (PH)
Pottery Farm
Wellow Sch
Partridge Hill Farm
West Wellow
Oaklands
SP5
West Wellow Common
Plaitford Common
Canada
Chatmohr
Abbotts Farm
Sturtmoor Pond
SO43
A36
PARTRIDGE HILL
SALISBURY RD
CRAWLEY HILL
74

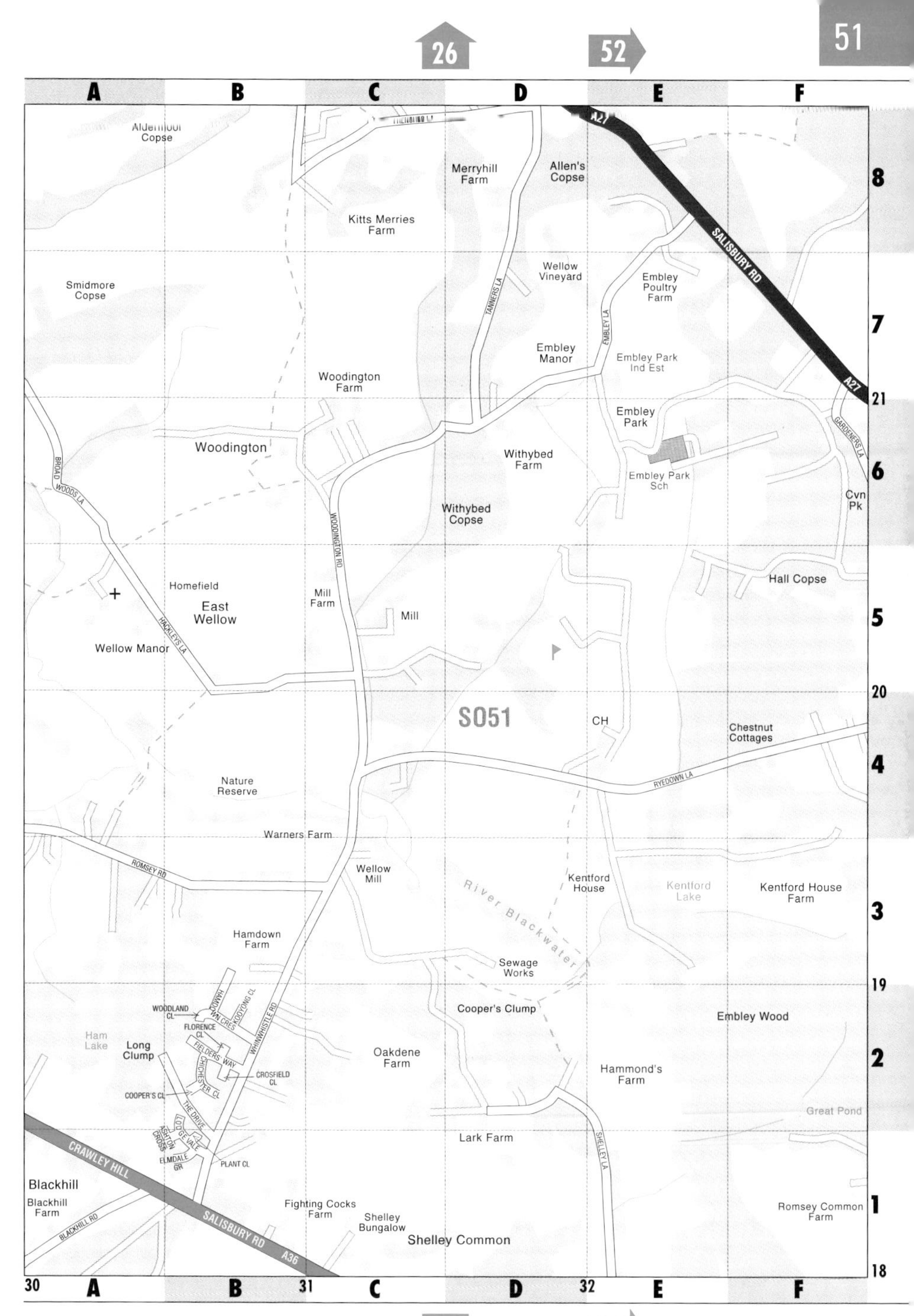

A B C D E F

8

7

21

6

Cvn
Pk

5

20

4

3

19

2

1

18

Aldermoor
Copse

Merryhill
Farm

Allen's
Copse

Kitts Merries
Farm

A27

SALISBURY RD

Smidmore
Copse

Wellow
Vineyard

Embley
Poultry
Farm

TANNERS LA

OMBLEY LA

Embley Park
Ind Est

A27

GARDENER LA

Woodington
Farm

Embley
Manor

Woodington

Embley
Park

Embley Park
Sch

Withybed
Farm

WOODINGTON RD

Withybed
Copse

Hall Copse

Homefield

HACKLEYS LA

East
Wellow

Mill
Farm

Mill

+

Wellow Manor

SO51

CH

Chestnut
Cottages

Nature
Reserve

RYEDOWN LA

Warners Farm

ROMSEY RD

Wellow
Mill

River Blackwater

Kentford
House

Kentford
Lake

Kentford House
Farm

Hamdown
Farm

Ham
Lake

Long
Clump

WOODLAND
CL

FLORENCE

SELBORNE WAY

GROSFIELD
CL

COOPER'S CL

THE GREEN

NIGHTINGALE CL

OATING CL

WHITENDALE CL

ELMDALE
GR

PLANT CL

Sewage
Works

Cooper's Clump

Embley Wood

Oakdene
Farm

Hammond's
Farm

Great Pond

SHELLEY LA

Lark Farm

Blackhill

CRAWLEY HILL

Blackhill
Farm

BLACKHILL RD

SALISBURY RD

A36

Fighting Cocks
Farm

Shelley
Bungalow

Shelley Common

Romsey Common
Farm

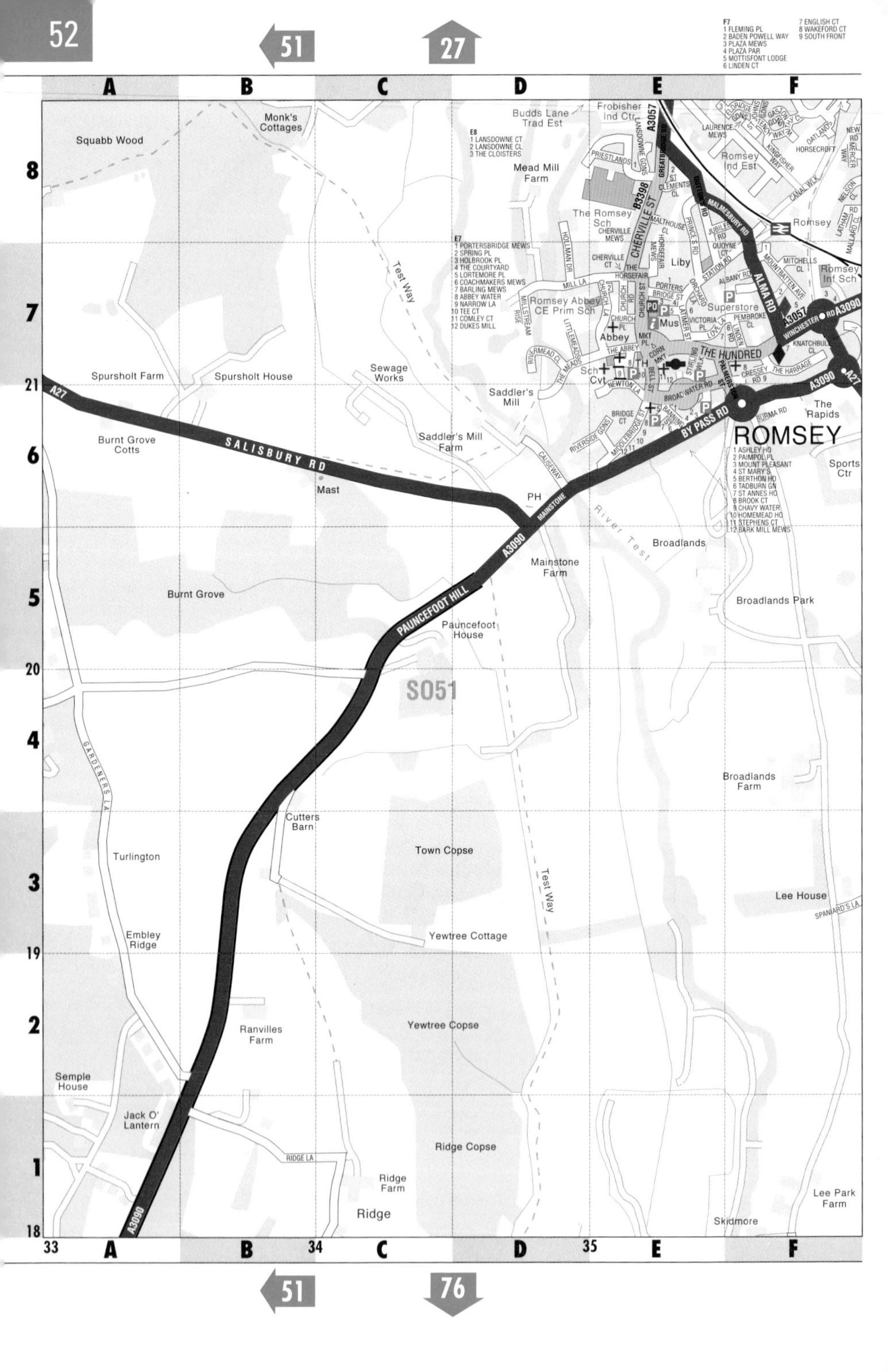
51
27
F7
1 FLEMING PL
2 BADEN POWELL WAY
3 PLAZA MEWS
4 PLAZA PAR
5 MOTTISFONT LODGE
6 LINDEN CT
7 ENGLISH CT
8 WAKEFORD CT
9 SOUTH FRONT
E8
1 LANSDOWNE CT
2 LANSDOWNE CL
3 THE CLOISTERS
E7
1 PORTERSBRIDGE MEWS
2 SPRING PL
3 HOLBROOK PL
4 THE COURTYARD
5 LORTEMORE PL
6 COACHMAKERS MEWS
7 BARLING MEWS
8 ABBEY WATER
9 NARROW LA
10 TEE CT
11 COMLEY CT
12 DUKES MILL
F6
1 ASHLEY HO
2 PAIMPOL PL
3 MOUNT PLEASANT
4 ST MARY'S
5 BERTHON HO
6 TADBURN GN
7 ST ANNES HO
8 BROOK CT
9 CHAVY WATER
10 HOMEMEAD HO
11 STEPHENS CT
12 BARK MILL MEWS
Squabb Wood
Monk's Cottages
Budds Lane Trad Est
Frobisher Ind Ctr
Mead Mill Farm
Romsey Ind Est
Romsey
The Romsey Sch
Liby
Romsey Abbey CE Prim Sch
Superstore
Mus
Abbey
Romsey Inf Sch
Spursholt Farm
Spursholt House
Sewage Works
Saddler's Mill
Sch
Cvt
TH
The Rapids
ROMSEY
Burnt Grove Cotts
SALISBURY RD
Saddler's Mill Farm
Mast
PH
Sports Ctr
Broadlands
Mainstone Farm
Burnt Grove
Broadlands Park
PAUNCEFOOT HILL
Pauncefoot House
SO51
Broadlands Farm
Cutters Barn
Turlington
Town Copse
Test Way
Lee House
Embley Ridge
Yewtree Cottage
Ranvilles Farm
Yewtree Copse
Semple House
Jack O' Lantern
Ridge Copse
RIDGE LA
Ridge Farm
Ridge
Lee Park Farm
Skidmore
River Test
GARDENERS LA
A27
A3090
A3057
B3398
CHERVILLE ST
THE HUNDRED
BY PASS RD
ALMA RD
MAINSTONE
CAUSEWAY
BROADWATER RD
51
76

28
54

A
B
C
D
E
F
8
7
21
6
5
20
4
3
19
2
1
18
36
37
38
Harefield
Romsey Jun Sch
Romsey
WINCHESTER HILL
A3090
WINCHESTER RD
LC
Stroud Sch
GREEN LA
Willow Farm
Halterworth
HALTERWORTH LA
1 FABER MEWS
2 BRICKWOODS CL
3 STRONGS CL
KENNETT CL
Halterworth Com Prim Sch
Warren Farm
4 MINDEN HO
5 BLENHEIM HO
6 NORMANDY HO
7 SALERNO HO
Cemy
1 GROSVENOR CT
2 MONTFORT COLLEGE
PO
MAPLE CL
ELMTREE GDNS
ALDER CL
BOTLEY RD
PH
HIGHWOOD LA
Whitenap Farm
Whitenap
The Mountbatten Sch & Language Coll
The Quadrangle
Brooklyn
North Baddesley
HEATHERVIEW CL 1
LINDEN WLK 2
A27
S051
LUZBOROUGH LA
The Premier Ctr
Park Ct
The Triton Ctr
Abbey Ent Ctr
Scrag Hill
Beggarspath Wood
Luzborough Plantation
SOUTHAMPTON RD
Parker's Moor
S052
A3057
Lower Ashfield Farm
Ashfield
Hoe Farm
HOE LA
Upper Ashfield Farm
SPANIARD'S LA
LEE LA
Telegraph Wood
Lower Toothill
Toot Hill
Packridge Farm
Upper Toothill
TOOTHILL RD
PACKRIDGE LA
LEE DRO
Middle Farm
UPPER TOOTHILL RD
ROWNHAMS LA
Mast
Lee Manor Farm Cottage
Nightingale Wood
S016

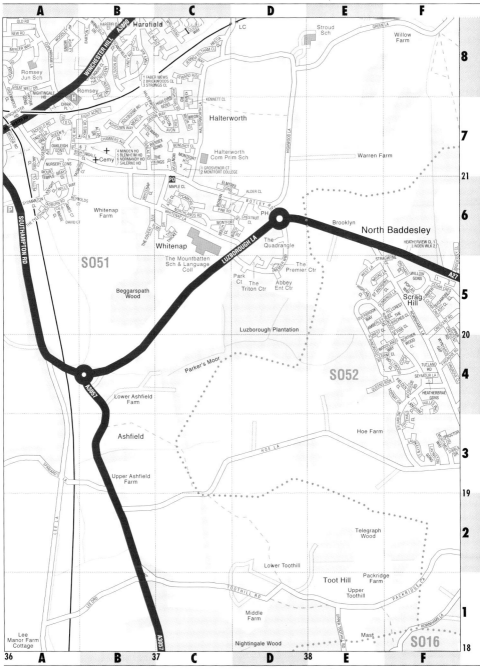

53
29

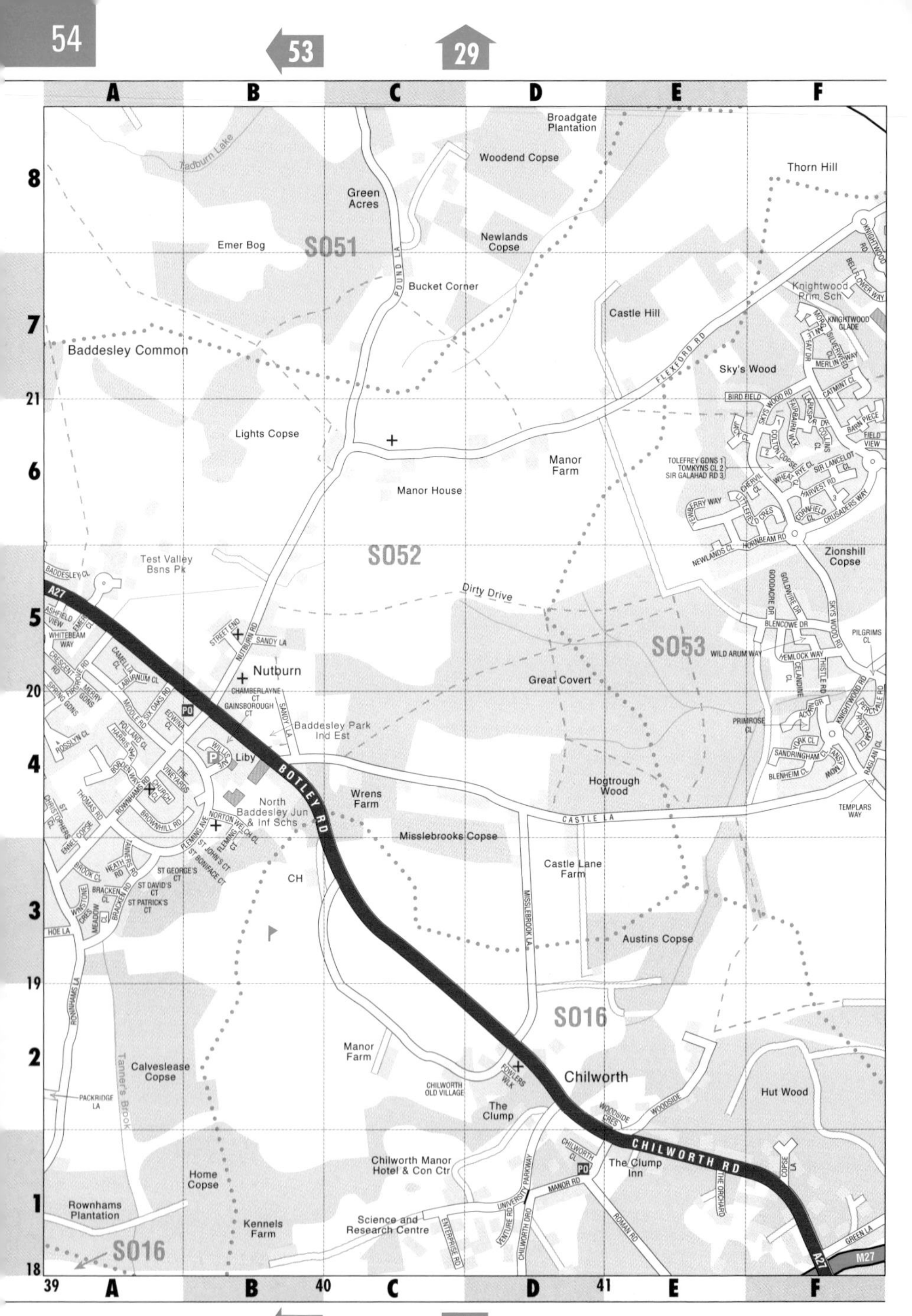
A
B
C
D
E
F
8
7
21
6
5
20
4
3
19
2
1
18
39
40
41
Broadgate Plantation
Woodend Copse
Tadburn Lake
Thorn Hill
Green Acres
Emer Bog
SO51
Newlands Copse
POUND LA
Bucket Corner
Knightwood Prim Sch
Castle Hill
Baddesley Common
FLEXFORD RD
Sky's Wood
Lights Copse
Manor Farm
Manor House
TOLEFREY GDNS 1
TOMKYNS CL 2
SIR GALAHAD RD 3
Test Valley Bsns Pk
SO52
Zionshill Copse
BADDESLEY CL
A27
Dirty Drive
NEWLANDS CL
HORNBEAM RD
SKYS WOOD RD
BLENCOWE DR
SO53
WILD ARUM WAY
HEMLOCK WAY
PILGRIMS CL
STREET END
SANDY LA
NUTBURN RD
Nutburn
Great Covert
CHAMBERLAYNE CT
GAINSBOROUGH CT
Baddesley Park Ind Est
PRIMROSE CL
Liby
BOTTLEY RD
Hogtrough Wood
Wrens Farm
North Baddesley Jun & Inf Schs
CASTLE LA
TEMPLARS WAY
Misslebrooks Copse
Castle Lane Farm
CH
MISSLEBROOK LA
Austins Copse
HOE LA
SO16
ROWNHAMS LA
Manor Farm
Tanner's Brook
Calveslease Copse
Chilworth
Hut Wood
PACKRIDGE LA
CHILWORTH OLD VILLAGE
The Clump
WOODSIDE
CHILWORTH RD
Chilworth Manor Hotel & Con Ctr
The Clump Inn
Home Copse
Rownhams Plantation
Science and Research Centre
Kennels Farm
UNIVERSITY PARKWAY
MANOR RD
ROMAN RD
THE ORCHARD
GREEN LA
M27
SO16

53
78

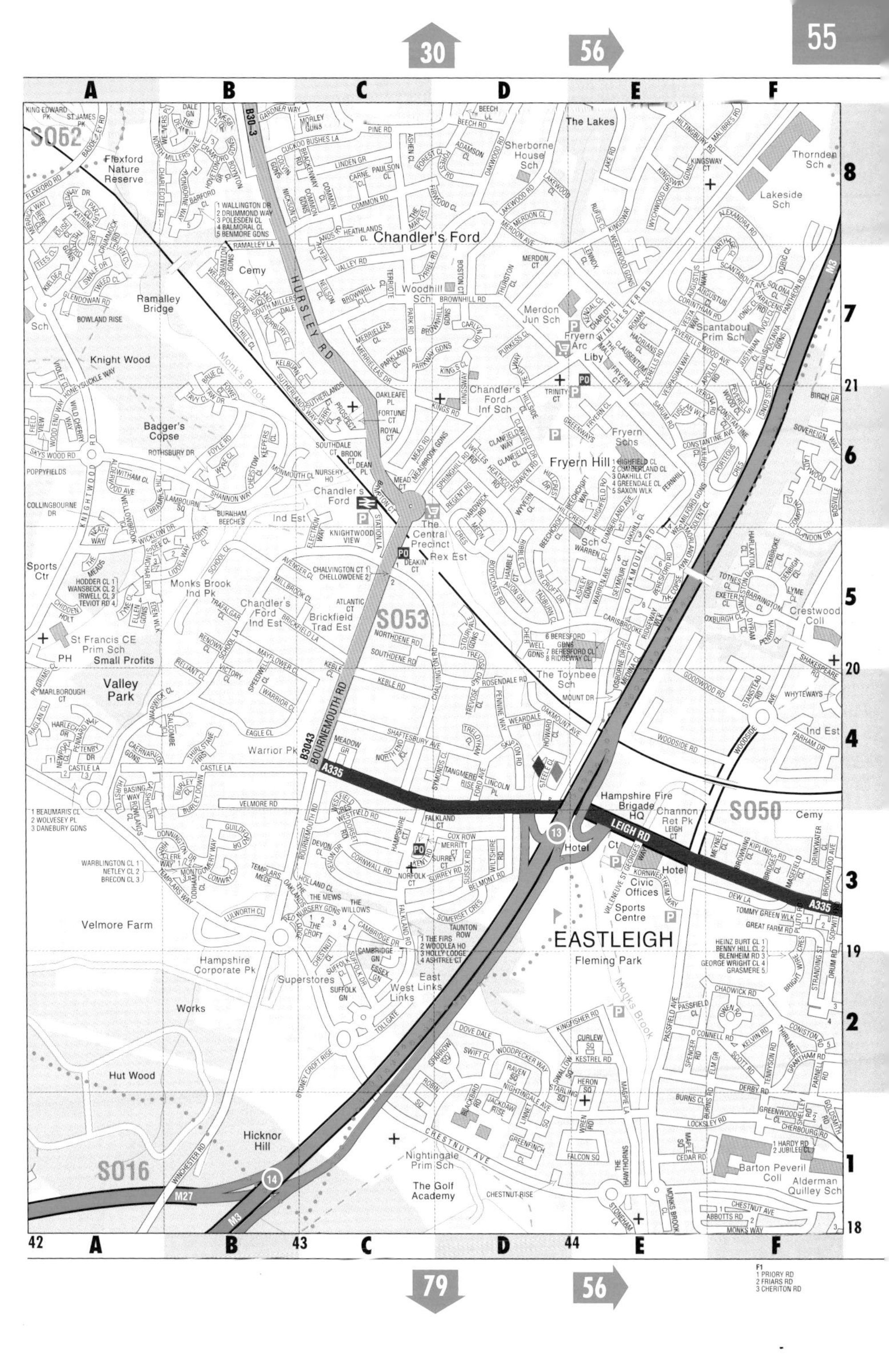
30
56
A
B
C
D
E
F
8
7
21
6
5
20
4
3
19
2
1
18
42
43
44
SO52
SO53
SO50
SO16
Flexford Nature Reserve
Ramalley Bridge
Knight Wood
Badger's Copse
Cemy
Chandler's Ford
HURSLEY RD
The Lakes
Sherborne House Sch
Thornden Sch
Lakeside Sch
Merdon Jun Sch
Fryern Arc
Liby
Woodhill Sch
Scantabout Prim Sch
Chandler's Ford Inf Sch
Fryern Schs
Fryern Hill
The Central Precinct
Rex Est
Ind Est
Monks Brook Ind Pk
Chandler's Ford Ind Est
Brickfield Trad Est
Sports Ctr
St Francis CE Prim Sch
Small Profits
PH
Valley Park
Warrior Pk
Crestwood Coll
The Toynbee Sch
BOURNEMOUTH RD
B3043
A335
LEIGH RD
M3
M27
Hampshire Fire Brigade HQ
Channon Ret Pk
Hotel
Civic Offices
Sports Centre
EASTLEIGH
Fleming Park
Monks Brook
Velmore Farm
Hampshire Corporate Pk
Superstores
West Links
East Links
Works
Hut Wood
Hicknor Hill
Nightingale Prim Sch
The Golf Academy
Barton Peveril Coll
Alderman Quilley Sch
Ind Est
Cemy
1 WALLINGTON DR
2 DRUMMOND WAY
3 POLESDEN CL
4 BALMORAL CL
5 BENMORE GDNS
1 HIGHFIELD CL
2 CUMBERLAND CL
3 OAKHILL CL
4 GREENDALE CL
5 SAXON WLK
6 BERESFORD GDNS
7 BERESFORD CL
8 RIDGEWAY CL
1 BEAUMARIS CL
2 WOLVESEY PL
3 DANEBURY GDNS
WARBLINGTON CL 1
NETLEY CL 2
BRECON CL 3
HODDER CL 1
WANSBECK CL 2
IRWELL CL 3
TEVIOT RD 4
1 THE FIRS
2 WOODLEA HO
3 HOLLY LODGE
4 ASHTREE CT
HEINZ BURT CL 1
BENNY HILL CL 2
BLENHEIM RD 3
GEORGE WRIGHT CL 4
GRASMERE 5
1 HARDY RD
2 JUBILEE CL
79
56
F1
1 PRIORY RD
2 FRIARS RD
3 CHERITON RD

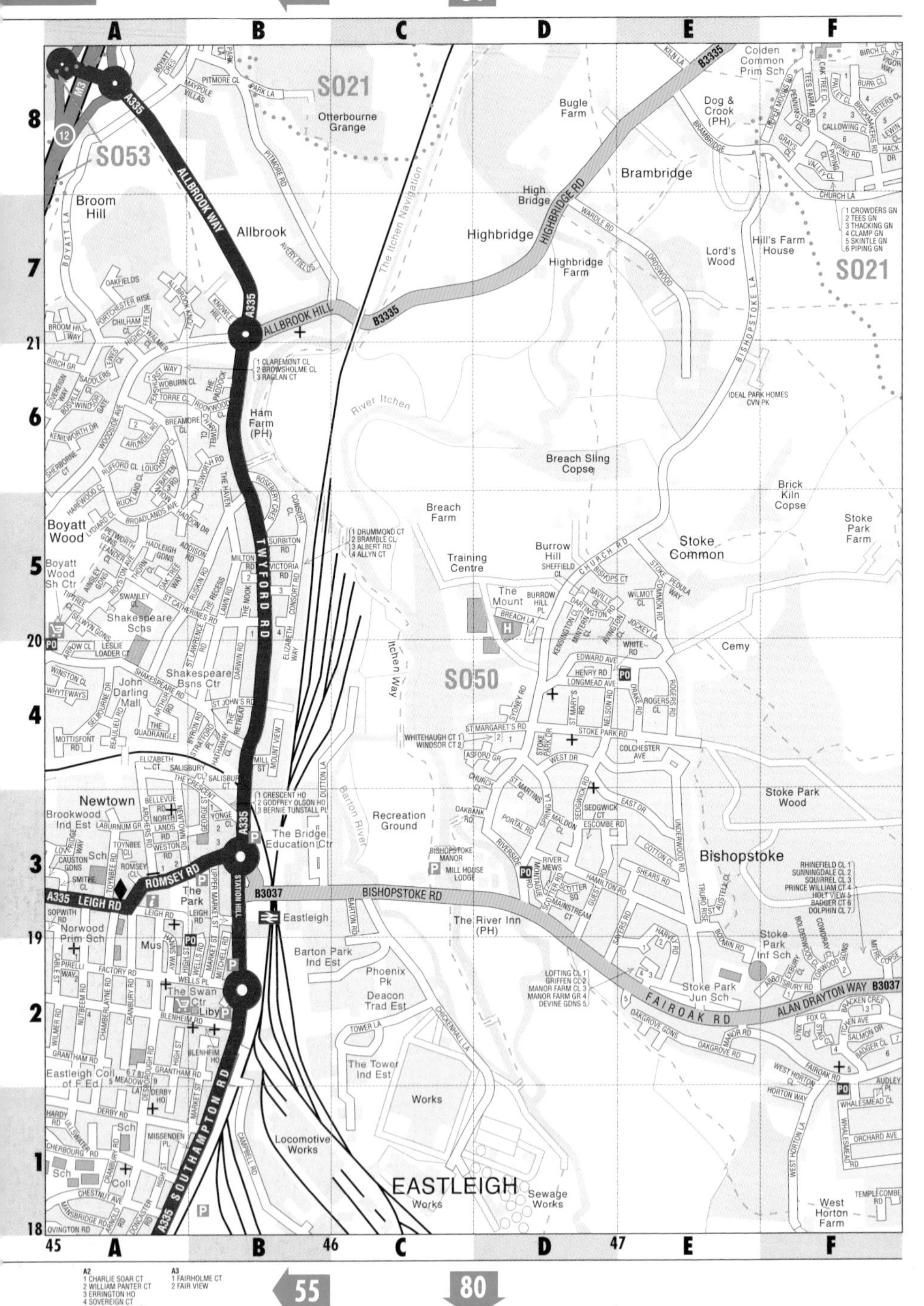

A2
1 CHARLIE SOAR CT
2 WILLIAM PANTER CT
3 ERRINGTON HO
4 SOVEREIGN CT
5 MAPLELEAF GDNS
6 THE PASTURES
7 THE CROFT
8 THE SPINNEY
9 GRANTHAM CT

A3
1 FAIRHOLME CT
2 FAIR VIEW

32
58

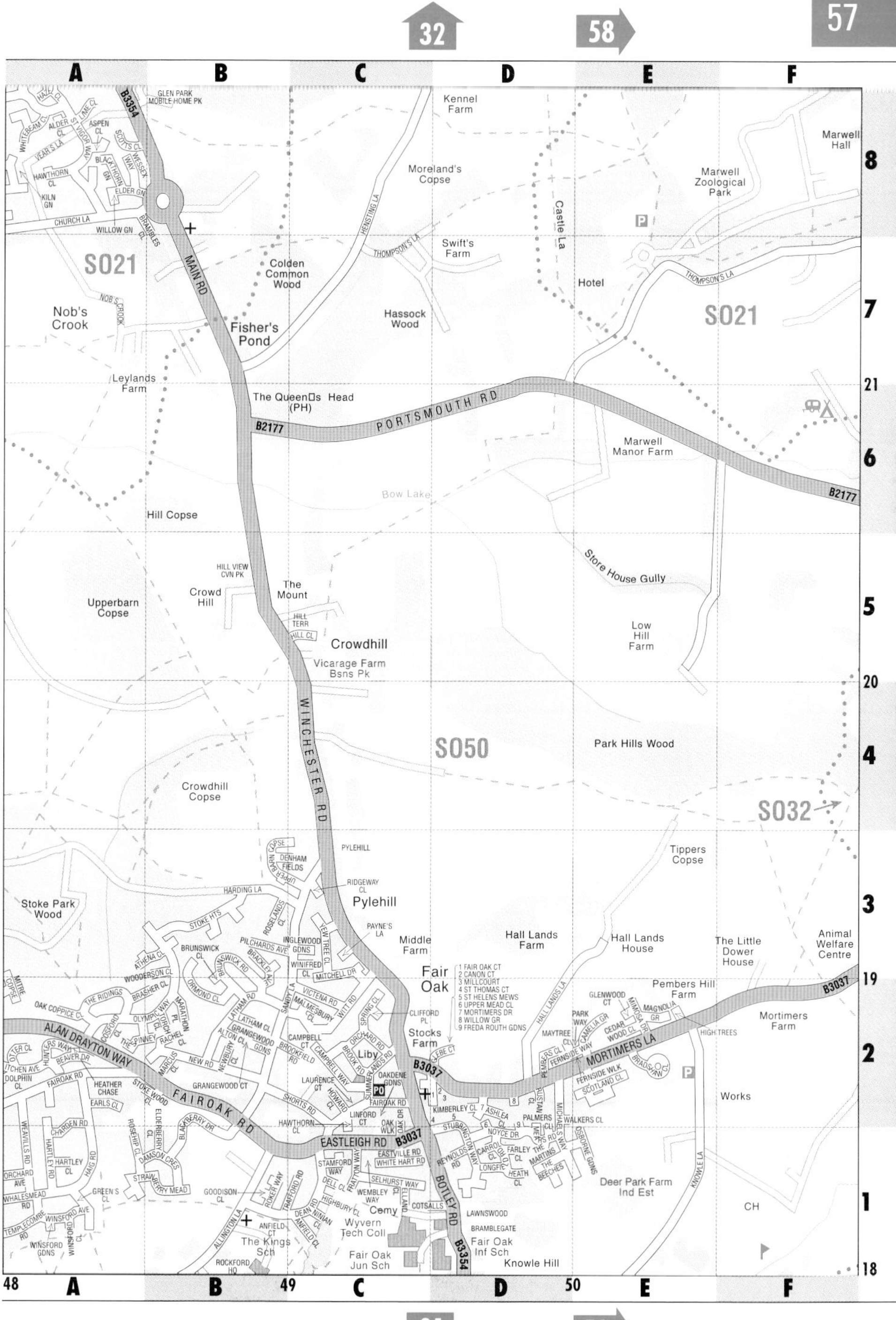
A
B
C
D
E
F
8
7
21
6
5
20
4
3
19
2
1
18
48
49
50
B3354
GLEN PARK MOBILE HOME PK
HAZEL CL
WHITEBEAM CL
ALDER CL
ST VIGOR WAY
LIME CL
ASPEN CL
SCOTTS CL
WESSEX WAY
YEW'S LA
BLACKTHORN GN
HAWTHORN CL
KILN GN
ELDER GN
CHURCH LA
WILLOW GN
BRAMBLES CL
Kennel Farm
Moreland's Copse
Marwell Hall
Marwell Zoological Park
HENSTING LA
Castle La
THOMPSON'S LA
Swift's Farm
SO21
Colden Common Wood
MAIN RD
Hotel
NOB'S CROOK
Nob's Crook
Fisher's Pond
Hassock Wood
SO21
Leylands Farm
The Queen's Head (PH)
B2177
PORTSMOUTH RD
Marwell Manor Farm
B2177
Bow Lake
Hill Copse
Store House Gully
HILL VIEW CVN PK
Crowd Hill
The Mount
Upperbarn Copse
HILL TERR
HILL CL
Crowdhill
Low Hill Farm
Vicarage Farm Bsns Pk
WINCHESTER RD
SO50
Park Hills Wood
Crowdhill Copse
SO32
PYLEHILL
Tippers Copse
UPPER BARN COPSE
DENHAM FIELDS
RIDGEWAY CL
HARDING LA
Stoke Park Wood
Pylehill
STOKE HTS
ROSELANDS CL
YEW TREE CL
PAYNE'S LA
Middle Farm
Hall Lands Farm
Hall Lands House
The Little Dower House
Animal Welfare Centre
BRUNSWICK CL
PILCHARDS AVE
INGLEWOOD GDNS
ATHENA CL
BRUNSWICK RD
BRACKLEY AVE
WINIFRED CL
MITCHELL DR
Fair Oak
1 FAIR OAK CT
2 CANON CT
3 MILLCOURT
4 ST THOMAS CT
5 ST HELENS MEWS
6 UPPER MEAD CL
7 MORTIMERS DR
8 WILLOW GR
9 FREDA ROUTH GDNS
WOODERSON CL
MITRE COPSE
BRASHER CL
ORMOND CL
VICTENA RD
THE RIDINGS
SANDY LA
WITT RD
OAK COPPICE CL
MALMESBURY CL
SPRING CL
CLIFFORD PL
HALL LANDS LA
GLENWOOD CT
MIMOSA DR
MAGNOLIA GR
Pembers Hill Farm
B3037
Mortimers Farm
HIGH TREES
ALAN DRAYTON WAY
OLYMPIC WAY
TORCH CL
MARATHON PL
RACHEL CL
LATHAM RD
LATHAM CL
GRANGEWOOD GDNS
ALTON CL
THE PINNEY
CAMPBELL CT
ORCHARD RD
Stocks Farm
GLEBE CT
PARK WAY
CAMELIA GR
CEDAR WOOD CL
MAYTREE CL
FERNSIDE WAY
MORTIMERS LA
BRADSHAW CL
OTTER CL
HUNTERS WAY
BEAVER DR
MARCUS CL
NEW RD
NEWBURY CL
BROOKFIELD RD
CAMPBELL WAY
BROOK RD
SUMMERLANDS RD
Liby
B3037
PEMBERS CL
FERNSIDE WLK
SCOTLAND CL
KITCHEN AVE
DOLPHIN CL
FAIROAK RD
HEATHER CHASE
STOKE WOOD CL
GRANGEWOOD CT
LAURENCE CT
HOWARD CL
OAKDENE GDNS
PO
Works
EARLS CL
FAIROAK RD
SHORTS RD
FAIROAK RD
KIMBERLEY CL
ASHLEA CL
PALMERS CL
TRISTAN CL
MICHAELS WAY
WALKERS CL
WEAVILLS RD
CHARDEN RD
ELDERBERRY CL
BLACKBERRY DR
LINFORD CT
HAWTHORN CL
OAK WLK
OAK DR
STUBBINGTON WAY
NOYCE DR
FARLEY CL
MEADS RD
OSBORNE GDNS
HARTLEY RD
HARTLEY CL
HAIG RD
ROSEHIP CL
DAMSON CRES
EASTLEIGH RD
B3037
EASTVILLE RD
WHITE HART RD
REYNOLDS RD
CARROL CL
LONGFIELD
HEATH CL
MARTINS THE
THE BEECHES
ORCHARD AVE
STRAWBERRY MEAD
STAMFORD WAY
FRATTON WAY
DELL CL
SELHURST WAY
BOTLEY RD
Deer Park Farm Ind Est
KNOWLE LA
WHALESMEAD RD
GREEN'S CL
GOODISON CL
ROKER WAY
TRAFFORD RD
WEMBLEY WAY
HIGHBURY CL
ELLAND CL
COTSALLS
CH
TEMPLECOMBE RD
WINSFORD AVE
WINSFORD CL
DEAN RD
NINIAN CL
ANFIELD CL
Cemy
Wyvern Tech Coll
LAWNSWOOD
BRAMBLEGATE
WINSFORD GDNS
ALLINGTON LA
ANFIELD CT
The Kings Sch
Fair Oak Inf Sch
B3354
ROCKFORD HO
Fair Oak Jun Sch
Knowle Hill

81
58

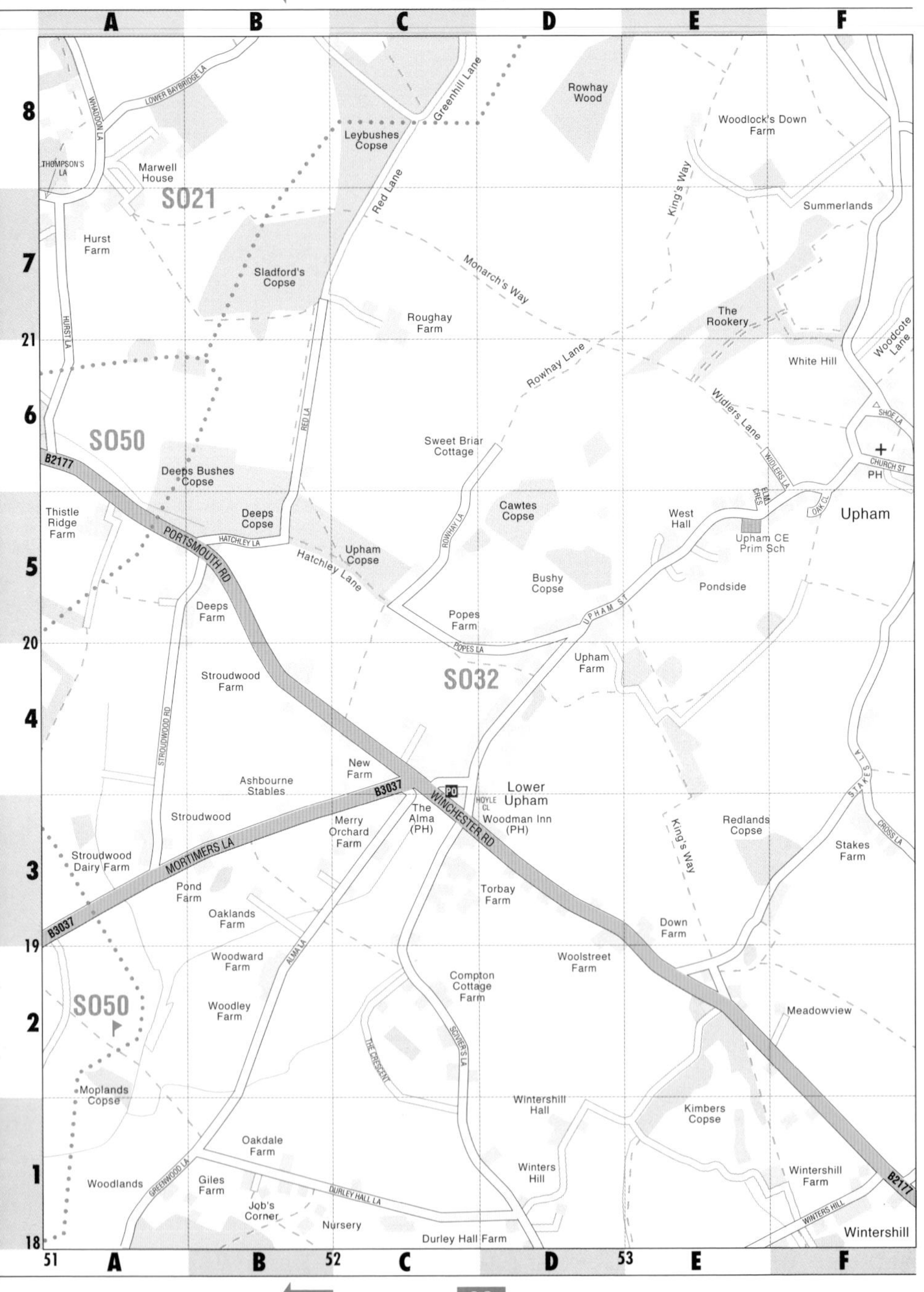

SO21

Marwell House

THOMPSON'S LA

Hurst Farm

Sladford's Copse

SO50

HURST LA

B2177

Thistle Ridge Farm

Deeps Bushes Copse

Deeps Copse

PORTSMOUTH RD

HATCHLEY LA

Hatchley Lane

Upham Copse

Deeps Farm

Stroudwood Farm

STROUDWOOD RD

Ashbourne Stables

New Farm

B3037

Stroudwood

Merry Orchard Farm

The Alma (PH)

MORTIMERS LA

Stroudwood Dairy Farm

B3037

Pond Farm

Oaklands Farm

Woodward Farm

ALMA LA

SO50

Moplands Copse

Woodley Farm

THE CRESCENT

Woodlands

Giles Farm

Oakdale Farm

GREENWOOD LA

Job's Corner

Nursery

DURLEY HALL LA

Durley Hall Farm

LOWER BAYBRIDGE LA

WHADDON LA

Leybushes Copse

Greenhill Lane

Red Lane

Red Lane

RED LA

Roughay Farm

Sweet Briar Cottage

Cawtes Copse

BOURNE LA

Popes Farm

POPES LA

SO32

WINCHESTER RD

PO

HOYLE CL

Lower Upham

Woodman Inn (PH)

Torbay Farm

SCURES LA

Compton Cottage Farm

Wintershill Hall

Winters Hill

Rowhay Wood

Monarch's Way

Rowhay Lane

Bushy Copse

Upham Farm

UPHAM ST

Upham Farm

King's Way

Woolstreet Farm

Woodlock's Down Farm

King's Way

The Rookery

White Hill

Widlers Lane

WIDLERS LA

West Hall

Upham CE Prim Sch

Pondside

Redlands Copse

Down Farm

Meadowview

Kimbers Copse

Summerlands

Woodcote Lane

SHOE LA

CHURCH ST

PH

OAK CL

PUMP LANE

Upham

FT STA LA

ORMS LA

Stakes Farm

Wintershill Farm

WINTERS HILL LA

B2177

Wintershill

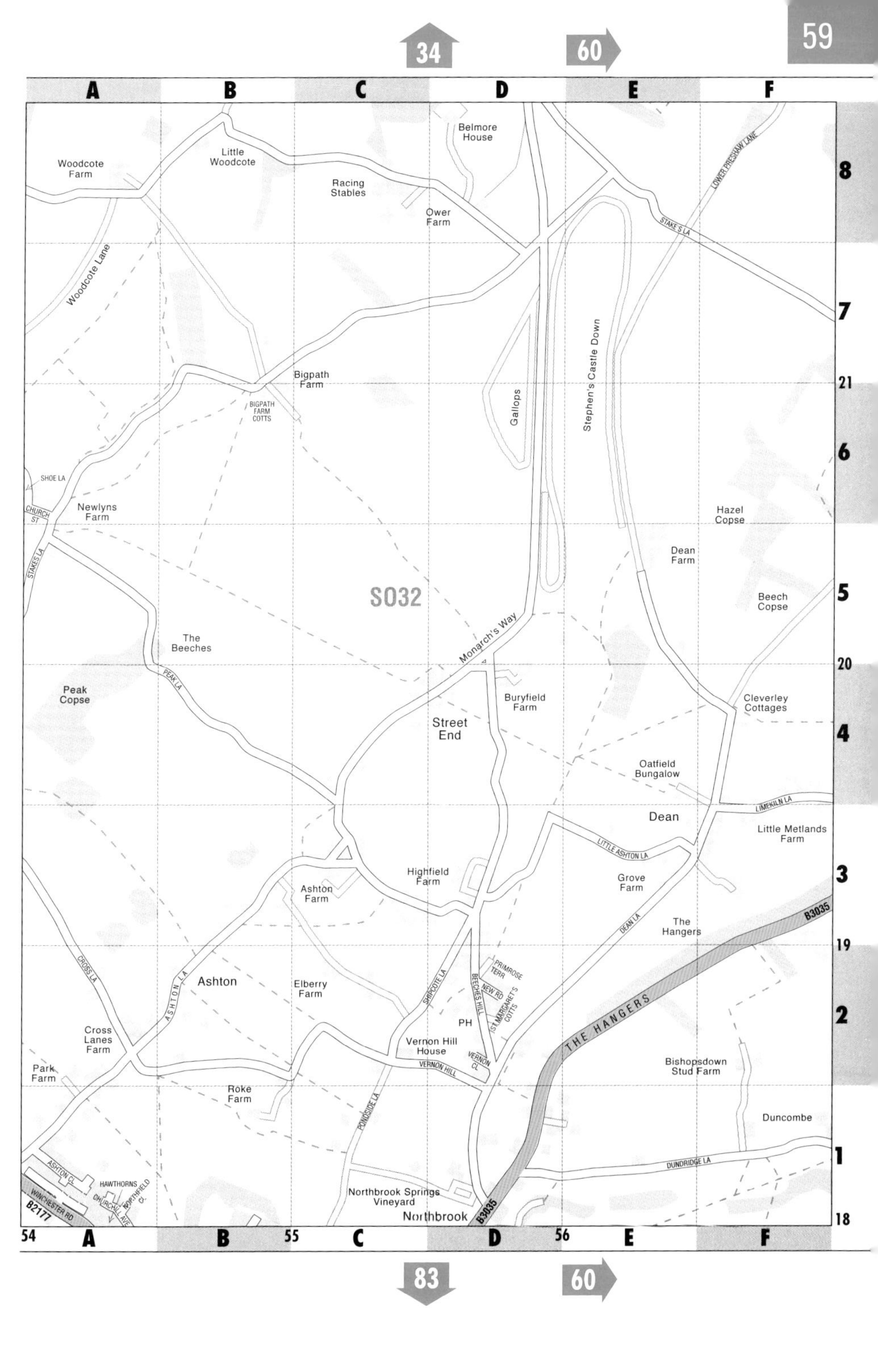
59
34
60
A
B
C
D
E
F
Belmore House
Woodcote Farm
Little Woodcote
Racing Stables
Ower Farm
LOWER PRESHAW LANE
STAKE'S LA
8
Woodcote Lane
7
Stephen's Castle Down
Bigpath Farm
BIGPATH FARM COTTS
Gallops
21
6
SHOE LA
CHURCH ST
Newlyns Farm
Hazel Copse
STAKES LA
Dean Farm
SO32
5
Beech Copse
Monarch's Way
The Beeches
Peak Copse
PEAK LA
20
Buryfield Farm
Cleverley Cottages
Street End
4
Oatfield Bungalow
LIMEKILN LA
Dean
Little Metlands Farm
LITTLE ASHTON LA
Highfield Farm
Ashton Farm
Grove Farm
3
B3035
The Hangers
DEAN LA
19
CROSS LA
PRIMROSE TERR
NEW RD
BEECHES HILL
ST MARGARET'S COTTS
Ashton
Elberry Farm
SHIPCOTE LA
ASHTON LA
2
PH
Cross Lanes Farm
Vernon Hill House
THE HANGERS
VERNON CL
Bishopsdown Stud Farm
Park Farm
VERNON HILL
Roke Farm
PONDSIDE LA
Duncombe
1
DUNDRIDGE LA
ASHTON CL
HAWTHORNS
NORTHFIELD CL
CHURCHILL AVE
WINCHESTER RD
B2177
Northbrook Springs Vineyard
Northbrook
B3035
18
54
55
56
83
60

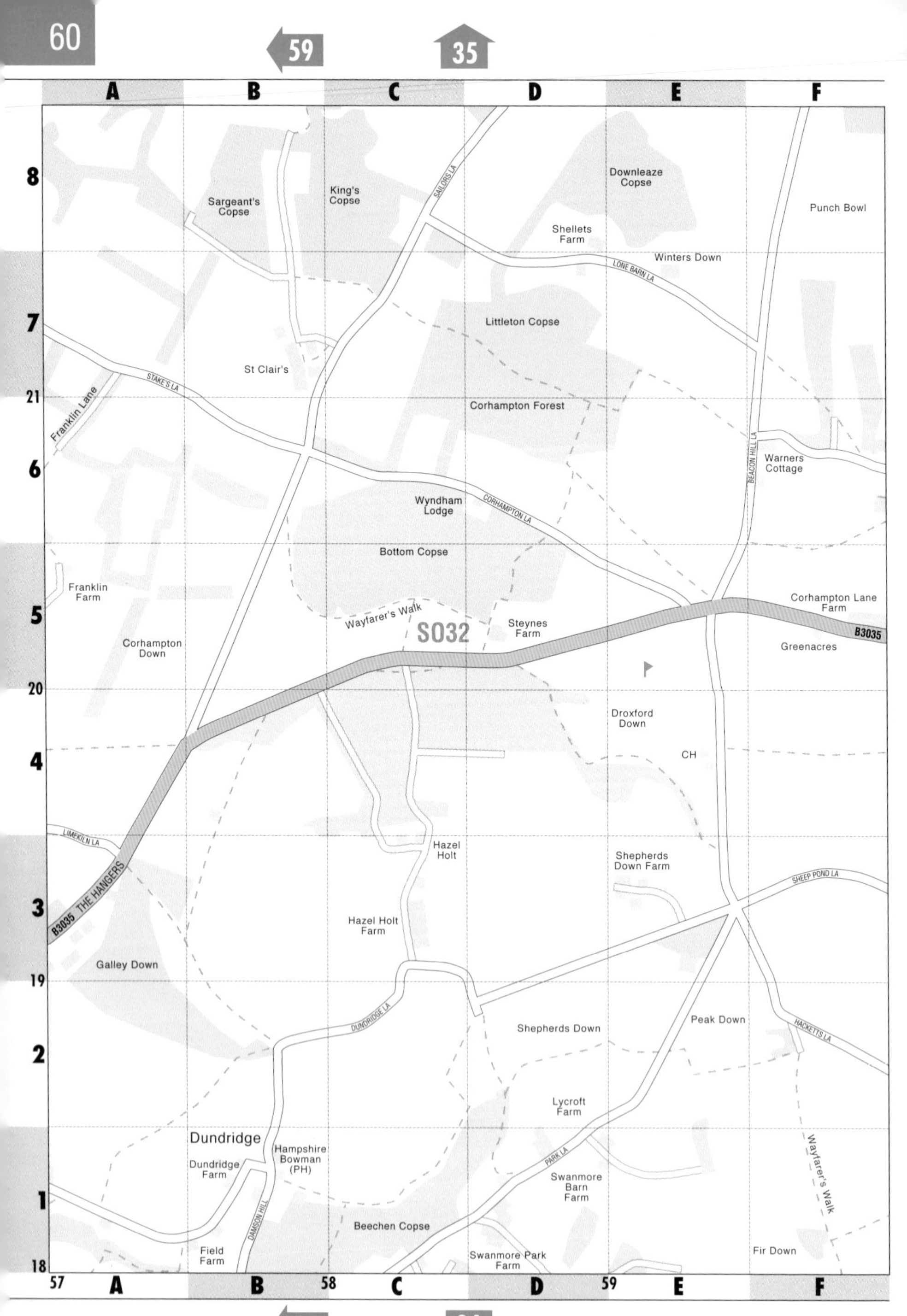

A **B** **C** **D** **E** **F**

8

Sargeant's Copse

King's Copse

Downleaze Copse

Punch Bowl

Shellets Farm

Winters Down

7

Littleton Copse

St Clair's

LONE BARN LA

21

Franklin Lane

STAKE'S LA

Corhampton Forest

BEACON HILL LA

Warners Cottage

6

Wyndham Lodge

CORHAMPTON LA

Franklin Farm

Bottom Copse

5

Wayfarer's Walk

SO32

Steynes Farm

Corhampton Lane Farm

B3035

Corhampton Down

Greenacres

20

Droxford Down

4

CH

LIMEKILN LA

THE HANGERS

Hazel Holt

Shepherds Down Farm

SHEEP POND LA

3

B3035

Hazel Holt Farm

Galley Down

19

DUNDRIDGE LA

Shepherds Down

Peak Down

HACKETTS LA

2

Lycroft Farm

Wayfarer's Walk

Dundridge

Hampshire Bowman (PH)

PARK LA

1

Dundridge Farm

Swanmore Barn Farm

DANSON HILL

Beechen Copse

Fir Down

18

Field Farm

Swanmore Park Farm

57 **A** **B** 58 **C** **D** 59 **E** **F**

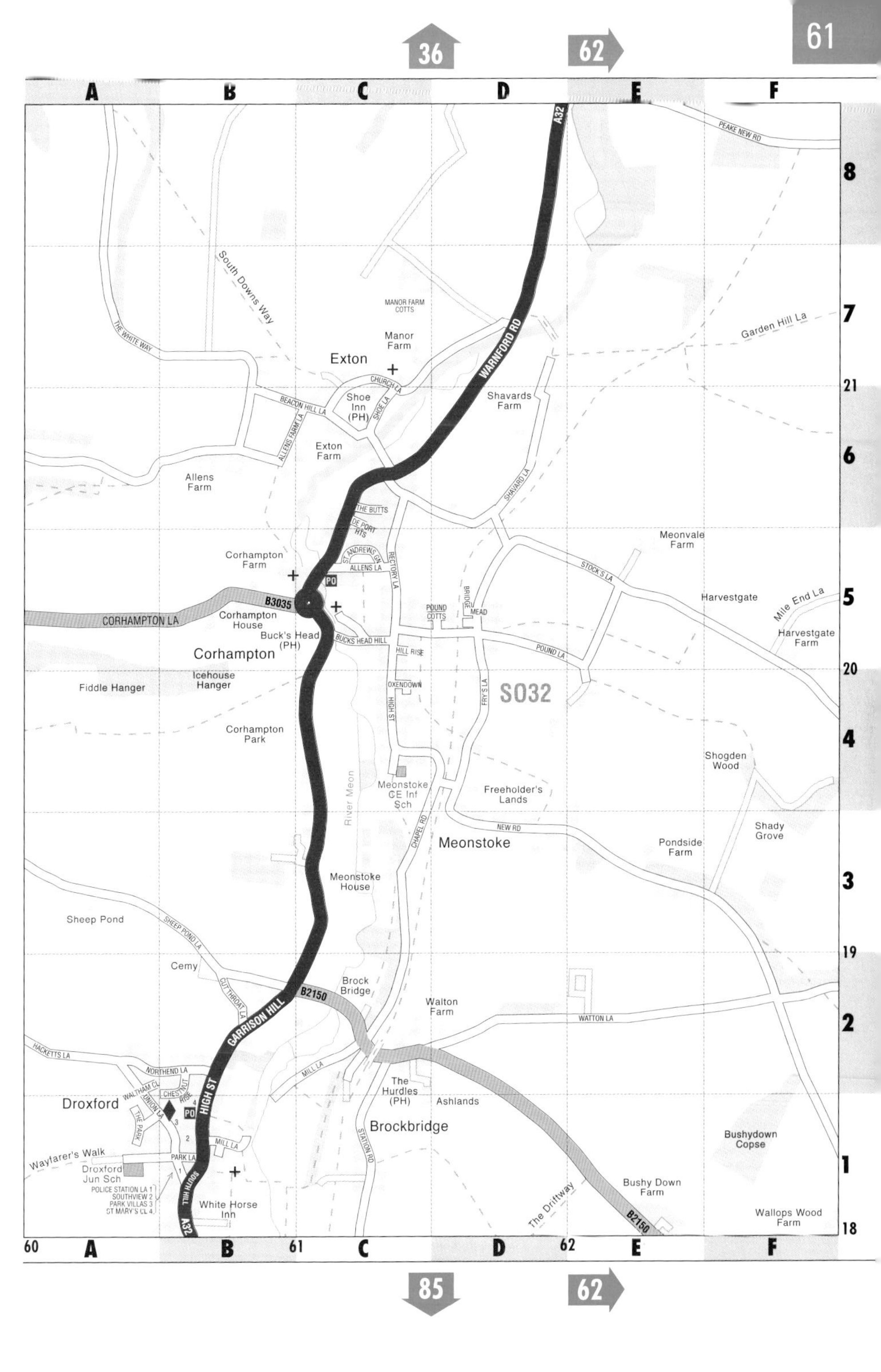
36
62
A
B
C
D
E
F
8
7
21
6
5
20
4
3
19
2
1
18
60
61
62
A32
PEAKE NEW RD
South Downs Way
THE WHITE WAY
MANOR FARM COTTS
Manor Farm
Exton
CHURCH LA
WARNFORD RD
Garden Hill La
Shavards Farm
BEACON HILL LA
Shoe Inn (PH)
SHOE LA
ALLENS FARM LA
Exton Farm
Allens Farm
SHAVARD LA
THE BUTTS
DE PORT HTS
Meonvale Farm
ST ANDREWS GN
ALLENS LA
RECTORY LA
Corhampton Farm
STOCK'S LA
PO
BRIDGE
MEAD
POUND COTTS
Harvestgate
Mile End La
B3035
CORHAMPTON LA
Corhampton House
Buck's Head (PH)
BUCKS HEAD HILL
Harvestgate Farm
HILL RISE
POUND LA
Corhampton
Icehouse Hanger
Fiddle Hanger
OXENDOWN
HIGH ST
FRY'S LA
SO32
Corhampton Park
Shogden Wood
River Meon
Meonstoke CE Inf Sch
Freeholder's Lands
NEW RD
CHAPEL RD
Meonstoke
Pondside Farm
Shady Grove
Meonstoke House
Sheep Pond
SHEEP POND LA
Cemy
CUT THROAT LA
GARRISON HILL
B2150
Brock Bridge
Walton Farm
WATTON LA
HACKETTS LA
NORTHEND LA
MILL LA
WALTHAM CL
CHESTNUT RISE
UNION LA
The Hurdles (PH)
Ashlands
Droxford
THE PARK
HIGH ST
Brockbridge
STATION RD
MILL LA
Bushydown Copse
Wayfarer's Walk
PARK LA
Droxford Jun Sch
POLICE STATION LA 1
SOUTHVIEW 2
PARK VILLAS 3
ST MARY'S CL 4
SOUTH HILL
White Horse Inn
Bushy Down Farm
The Driftway
Wallops Wood Farm
85
62

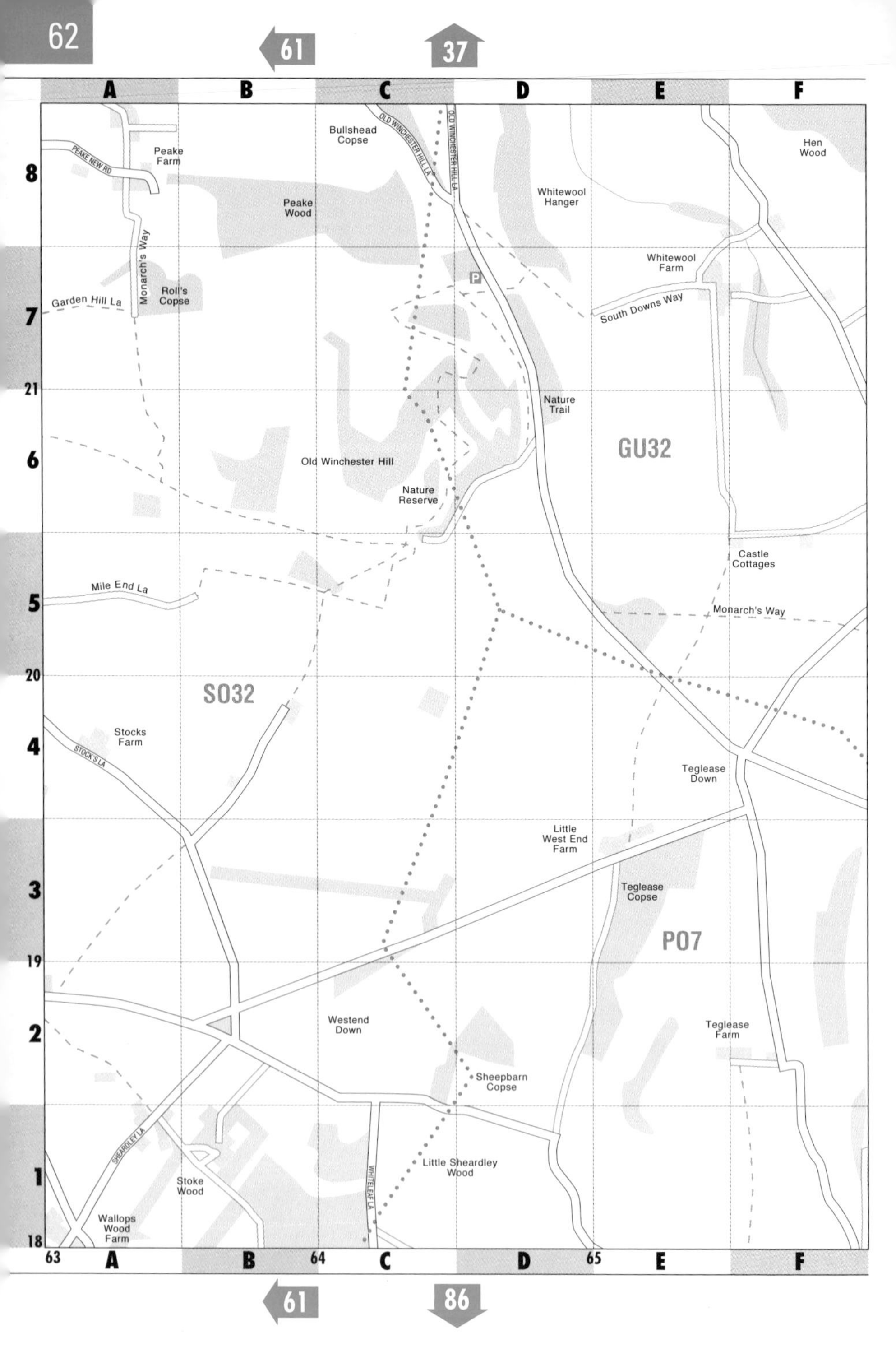
61
37
A
B
C
D
E
F
8
7
21
6
5
20
4
3
19
2
1
18
63
64
65
Peake Farm
PEAKE NEW RD
Bullshead Copse
OLD WINCHESTER HILL LA
Hen Wood
Whitewool Hanger
Peake Wood
Monarch's Way
Whitewool Farm
Garden Hill La
Roll's Copse
South Downs Way
Nature Trail
GU32
Old Winchester Hill
Nature Reserve
Castle Cottages
Mile End La
Monarch's Way
SO32
Stocks Farm
STOCK'S LA
Teglease Down
Little West End Farm
Teglease Copse
PO7
Westend Down
Teglease Farm
Sheepbarn Copse
SHEARDLEY LA
Little Sheardley Wood
WHITELEAF LA
Stoke Wood
Wallops Wood Farm
61
86

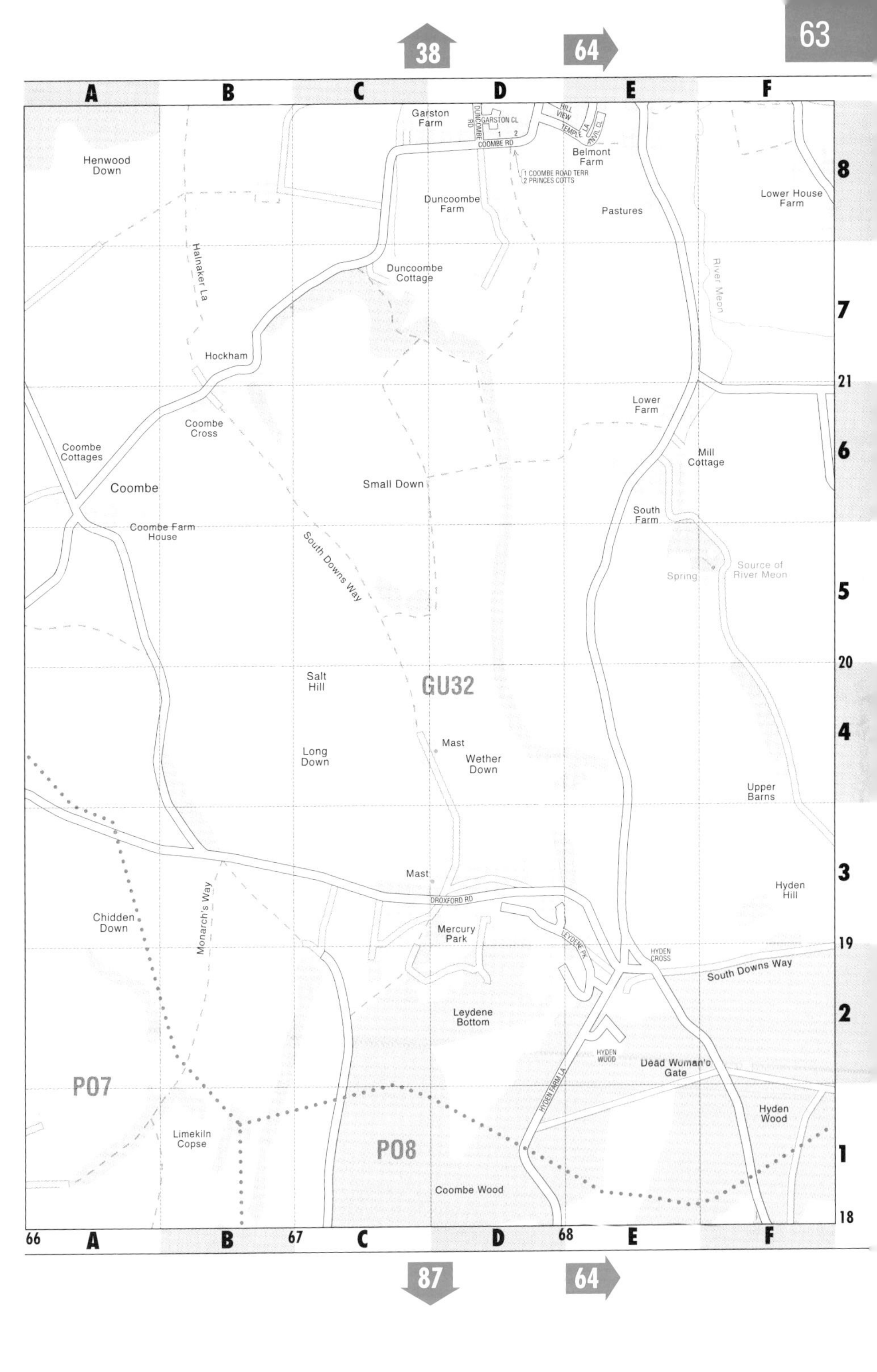

A B C D E F

8
7
21
6
5
20
4
3
19
2
1
18

Henwood
Down

Garston
Farm

Belmont
Farm

HILL
VIEW

TEMPLE

GARSTON CL.

DUNCOMBE RD

COOMBE RD

1 2

1 COOMBE ROAD TERR
2 PRINCES COTTS

Lower House
Farm

Duncoombe
Farm

Pastures

Halnaker La

River Meon

Duncoombe
Cottage

Hockham

Lower
Farm

Coombe
Cross

Coombe
Cottages

Mill
Cottage

Coombe

Small Down

South
Farm

Coombe Farm
House

South Downs Way

Source of
River Meon

Spring

Salt
Hill

GU32

Long
Down

Mast

Wether
Down

Upper
Barns

Mast

DROXFORD RD

Chidden
Down

Monarch's Way

Mercury Park

LEYDENE LA

Hyden
Hill

HYDEN
CROSS

South Downs Way

19

Leydene
Bottom

P07

HYDEN
WOOD

Dead Woman's
Gate

HYDEN FARM LA

Limekiln
Copse

P08

Hyden
Wood

Coombe Wood

66 A B 67 C D 68 E F

63
39

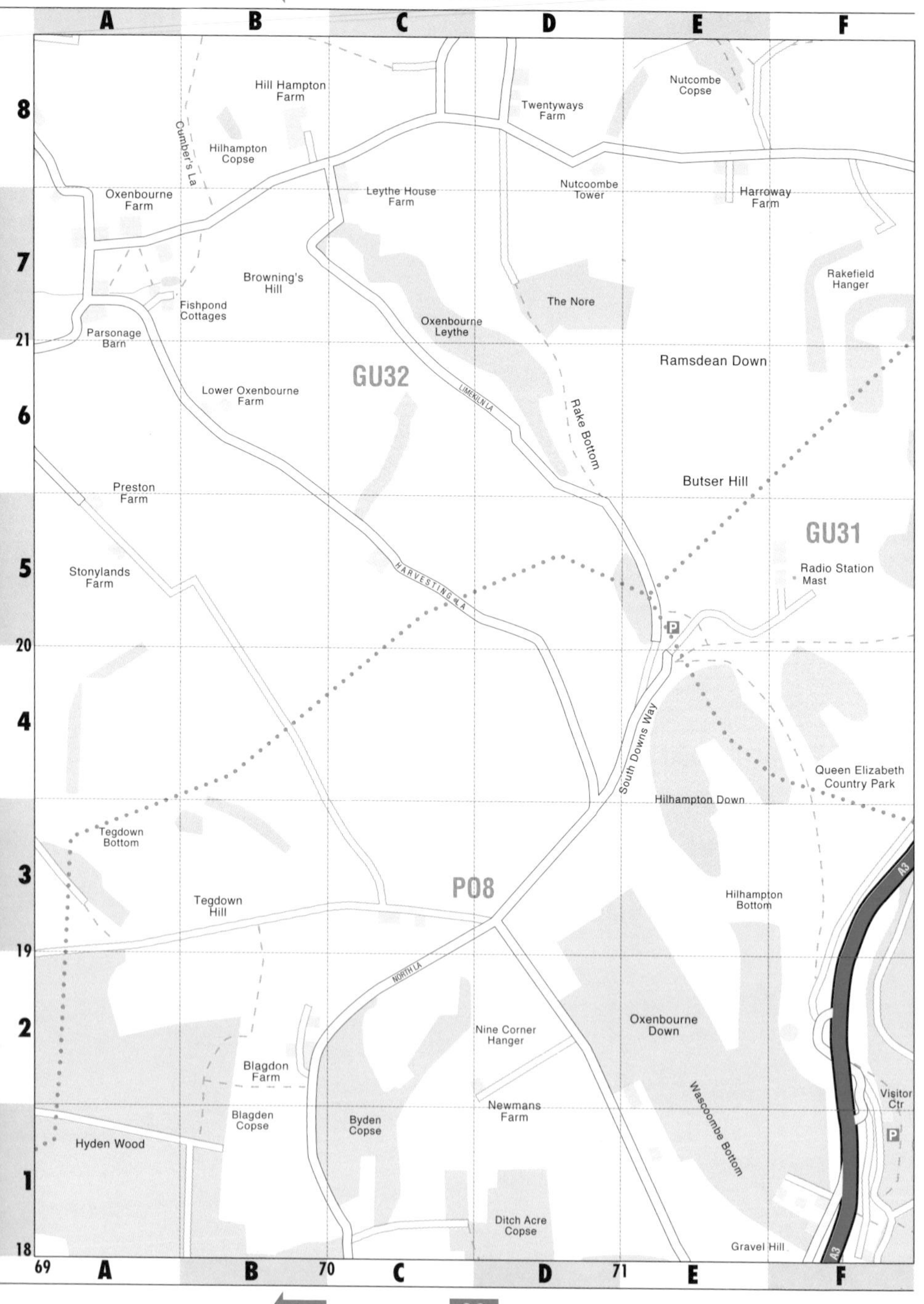
A
B
C
D
E
F
8
7
21
6
5
20
4
3
19
2
1
18
69
70
71
Hill Hampton Farm
Twentyways Farm
Nutcombe Copse
Cumber's La
Hilhampton Copse
Oxenbourne Farm
Leythe House Farm
Nutcoombe Tower
Harroway Farm
Browning's Hill
Fishpond Cottages
The Nore
Rakefield Hanger
Parsonage Barn
Oxenbourne Leythe
Ramsdean Down
GU32
Lower Oxenbourne Farm
LIMEKILN LA
Rake Bottom
Preston Farm
Butser Hill
GU31
Stonylands Farm
HARVESTING LA
Radio Station Mast
South Downs Way
Queen Elizabeth Country Park
Hilhampton Down
Tegdown Bottom
Tegdown Hill
PO8
Hilhampton Bottom
A3
NORTH LA
Nine Corner Hanger
Oxenbourne Down
Blagdon Farm
Visitor Ctr
Blagden Copse
Byden Copse
Newmans Farm
Wascoombe Bottom
Hyden Wood
Ditch Acre Copse
Gravel Hill

63
88

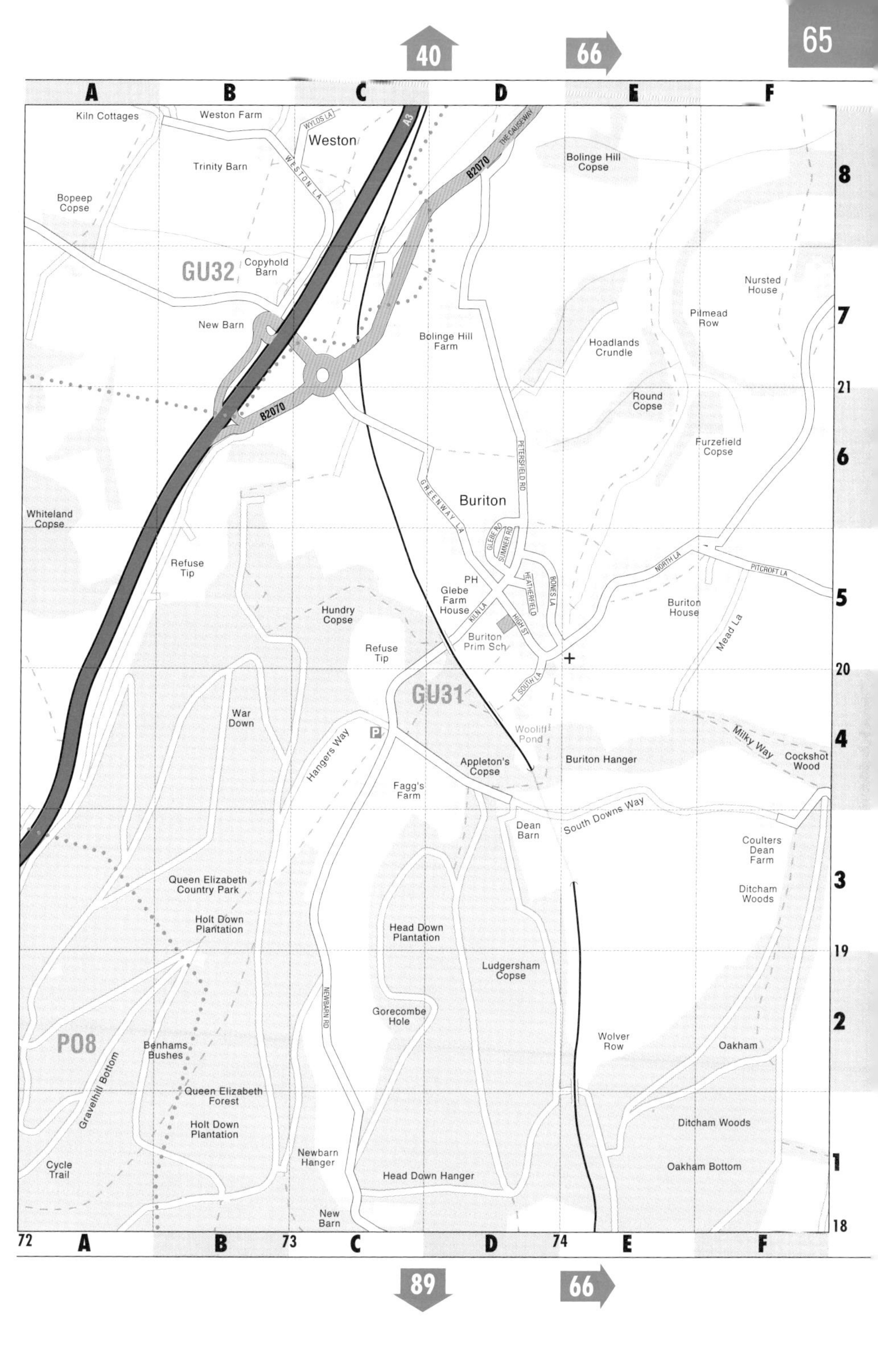
40
66
A
B
C
D
E
F
Kiln Cottages
Weston Farm
WYLDS LA
Weston
A3
THE CAUSEWAY
WESTON LA
B2070
Trinity Barn
Bolinge Hill
Copse
Bopeep
Copse
8
GU32
Copyhold
Barn
Nursted
House
Pilmead
Row
7
New Barn
Bolinge Hill
Farm
Hoadlands
Crundle
21
B2070
Round
Copse
Furzefield
Copse
PETERSFIELD RD
6
GREENWAY LA
Buriton
Whiteland
Copse
GLEBE RD
SUMNER RD
Refuse
Tip
NORTH LA
PITCROFT LA
HEATHERFIELD
BONES LA
PH
Glebe
Farm
House
5
Hundry
Copse
Buriton
House
KILN LA
HIGH ST
Mead La
Buriton
Prim Sch
Refuse
Tip
20
SOUTH LA
GU31
War
Down
Wooliff
Pond
4
Milky Way
Hangers Way
Appleton's
Copse
Buriton Hanger
Cockshot
Wood
Fagg's
Farm
South Downs Way
Dean
Barn
Coulters
Dean
Farm
3
Queen Elizabeth
Country Park
Ditcham
Woods
Holt Down
Plantation
Head Down
Plantation
19
Ludgersham
Copse
NEWBARN RD
Gorecombe
Hole
2
PO8
Benhams
Bushes
Wolver
Row
Oakham
Gravelhill Bottom
Queen Elizabeth
Forest
Holt Down
Plantation
Ditcham Woods
1
Newbarn
Hanger
Cycle
Trail
Oakham Bottom
Head Down Hanger
New
Barn
18
72
A
B
73
C
D
74
E
F
89
66

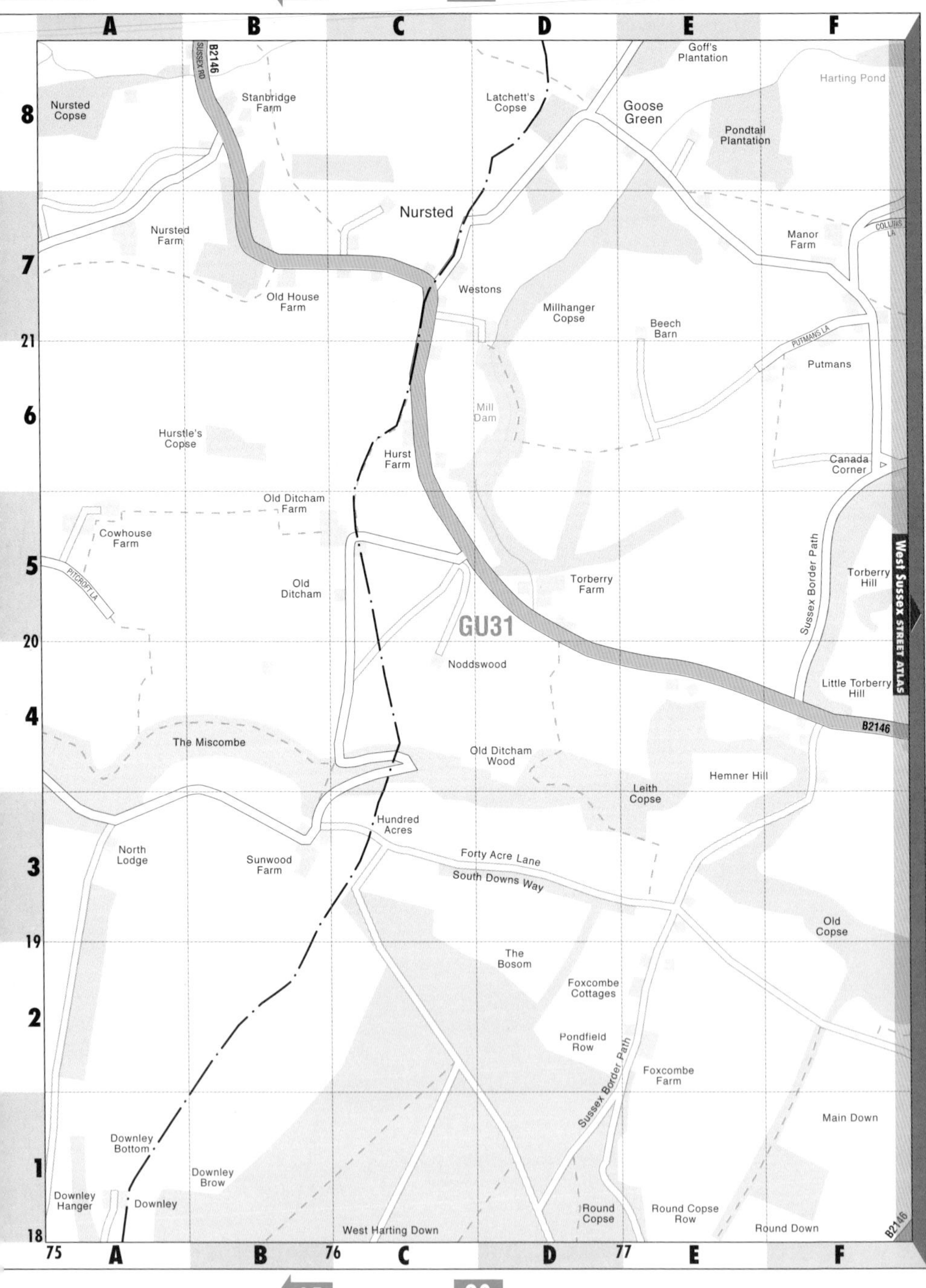

West Sussex Street Atlas

B2146

Nursted Copse

Stanbridge Farm

Latchett's Copse

Goff's Plantation

Goose Green

Harting Pond

Pondtail Plantation

Nursted Farm

Nursted

Manor Farm

COLUMS LA

Old House Farm

Westons

Millhanger Copse

Beech Barn

PUTMANS LA

Putmans

Hurstle's Copse

Hurst Farm

Mill Dam

Canada Corner

Old Ditcham Farm

Cowhouse Farm

Old Ditcham

Torberry Farm

Sussex Border Path

Torberry Hill

PITCROFT LA

GU31

Little Torberry Hill

Noddswood

B2146

The Miscombe

Old Ditcham Wood

Hemner Hill

North Lodge

Hundred Acres

Leith Copse

Sunwood Farm

Forty Acre Lane

South Downs Way

Old Copse

The Bosom

Foxcombe Cottages

Pondfield Row

Sussex Border Path

Foxcombe Farm

Main Down

Downley Bottom

Downley Brow

Downley Hanger

Downley

West Harting Down

Round Copse

Round Copse Row

Round Down

B2146

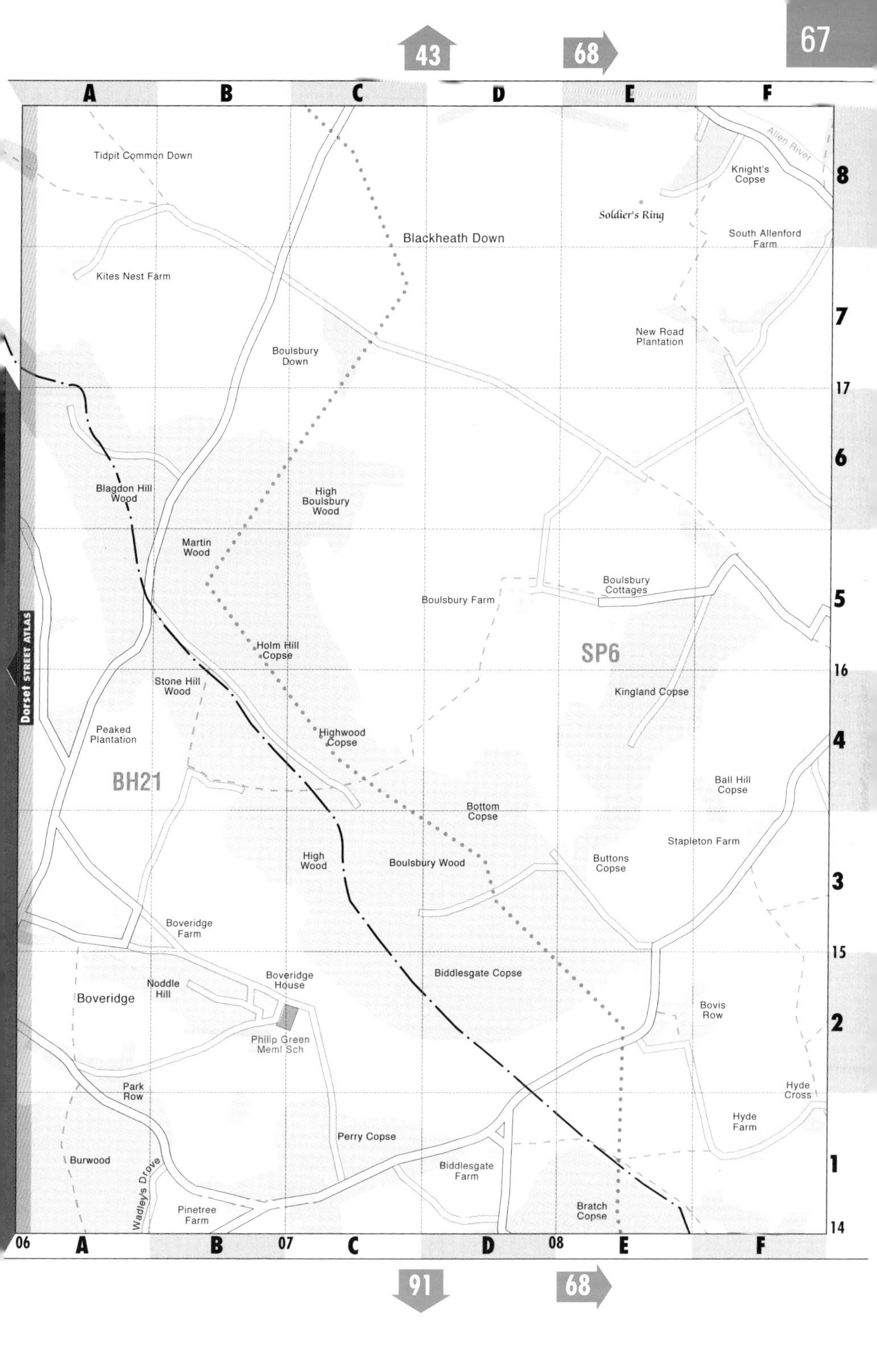

A **B** **C** **D** **E** **F**

Tidpit Common Down

Knight's Copse

8

Allen River

Soldier's Ring

South Allenford Farm

Blackheath Down

Kites Nest Farm

7

New Road Plantation

Boulsbury Down

17

6

Blagdon Hill Wood

High Boulsbury Wood

Martin Wood

Boulsbury Cottages

5

Boulsbury Farm

Holm Hill Copse

SP6

Stone Hill Wood

16

Kingland Copse

Peaked Plantation

Highwood Copse

4

Ball Hill Copse

BH21

Bottom Copse

Stapleton Farm

High Wood

Boulsbury Wood

Buttons Copse

3

Boveridge Farm

15

Biddlesgate Copse

Noddle Hill

Boveridge House

Bovis Row

2

Boveridge

Philip Green Meml Sch

Park Row

Hyde Cross

Hyde Farm

Burwood

Perry Copse

1

Biddlesgate Farm

Pinetree Farm

Bratch Copse

14

Wadleys Drove

A **B** **C** **D** **E** **F**
06   07   08

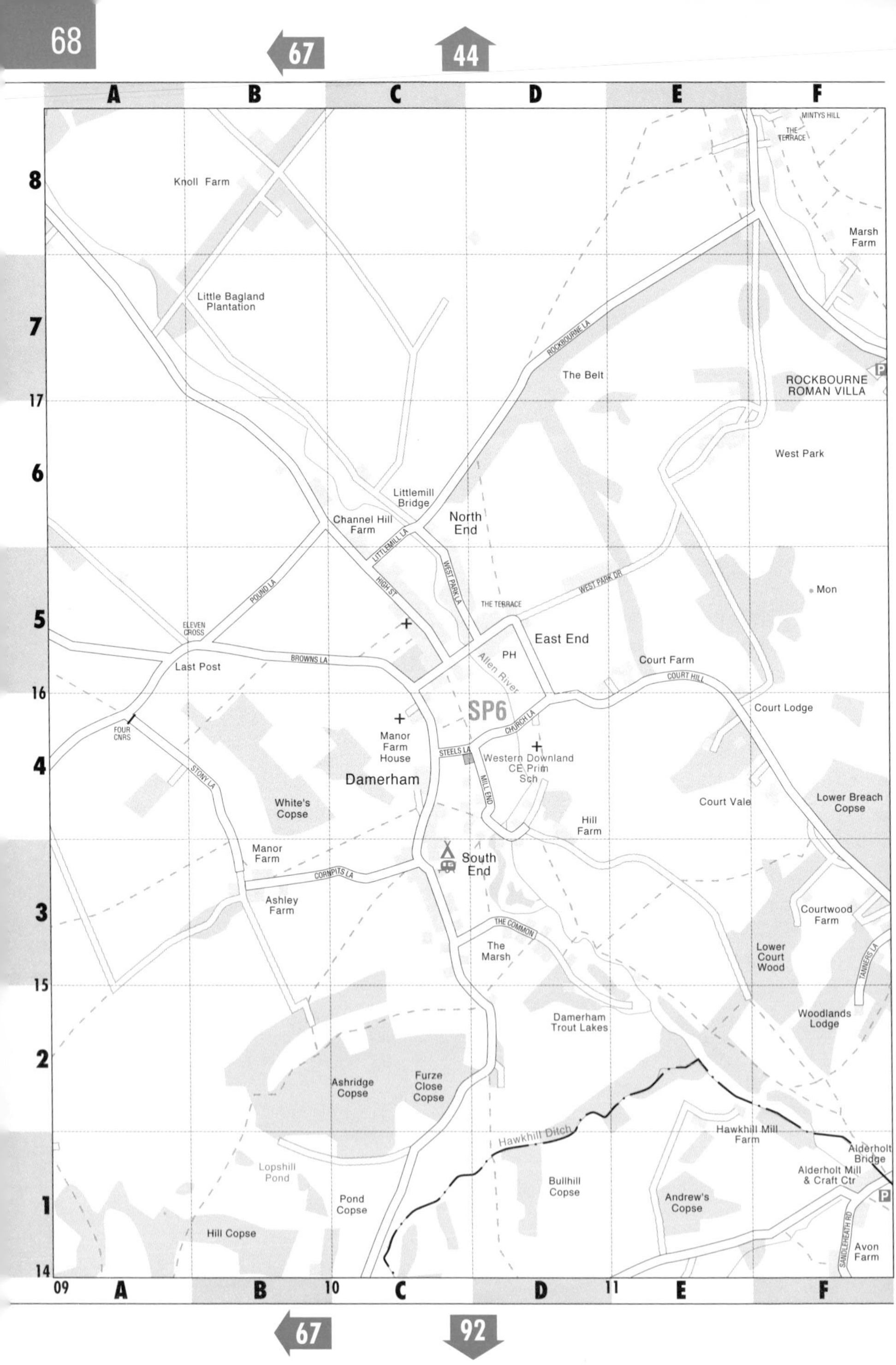

A B C D E F

8

Knoll Farm

MINTYS HILL
THE TERRACE

Marsh Farm

Little Bagland Plantation

7

ROCKBOURNE LA

The Belt

ROCKBOURNE ROMAN VILLA

17

West Park

6

Littlemill Bridge

Channel Hill Farm

North End

LITTLEMILL LA

WEST PARK LA

HIGH ST

POUND LA

WEST PARK DR

Mon

THE TERRACE

5

ELEVEN CROSS

BROWNS LA

Alton River

PH

East End

Court Farm

COURT HILL

Court Lodge

Last Post

16

SP6

FOUR CNRS

Manor Farm House

CHURCH LA

Western Downland CE Prim Sch

STEELS LA

Court Vale

Lower Breach Copse

4

ESTON LA

Damerham

MILL END

White's Copse

Hill Farm

Manor Farm

CORBINS LA

South End

Court wood Farm

3

Ashley Farm

THE COMMON

The Marsh

Lower Court Wood

TANNERS LA

Woodlands Lodge

15

Damerham Trout Lakes

2

Ashridge Copse

Furze Close Copse

Hawkhill Ditch

Hawkhill Mill Farm

Alderholt Bridge

Lopshill Pond

Pond Copse

Bullhill Copse

Andrew's Copse

Alderholt Mill & Craft Ctr

1

Hill Copse

BARNETHEATH RD

Avon Farm

14

09 A B 10 C D 11 E F

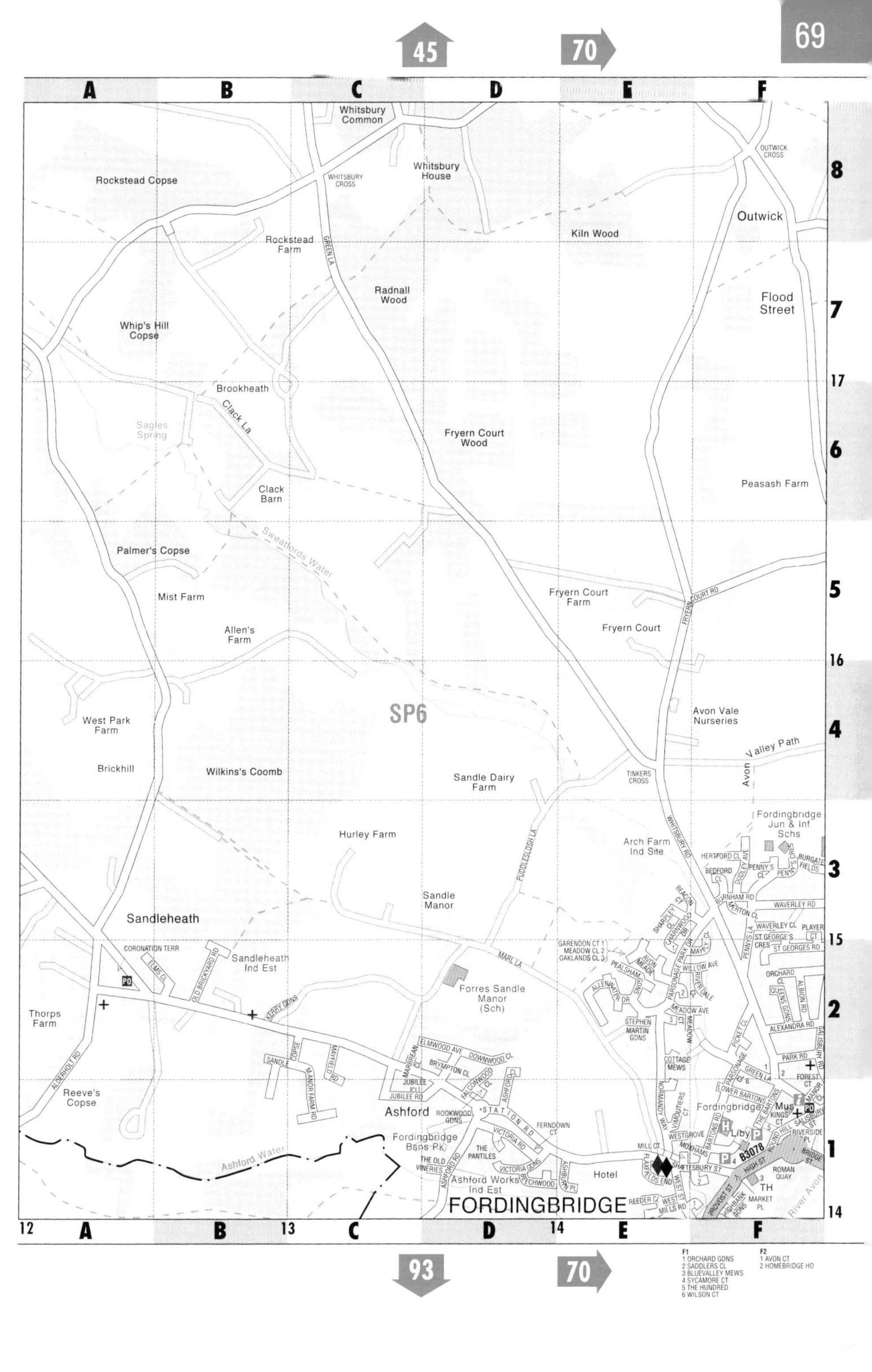

45

A　B　C　D　E　F

8

Whitsbury
Common

Rockstead Copse

WHITSBURY
CROSS

Whitsbury
House

Kiln Wood

Outwick

OUTWICK
CROSS

Rockstead
Farm

Radnall
Wood

Flood
Street

7

17

Whip's Hill
Copse

GREEN LA

Brookheath

Clack La

Fryern Court
Wood

Peasash Farm

6

Sagles
Spring

Clack
Barn

Sweatfords Water

Palmer's Copse

Fryern Court
Farm

FRYERN COURT RD

5

Mist Farm

Fryern Court

16

Allen's
Farm

SP6

Avon Vale
Nurseries

Avon Valley Path

4

West Park
Farm

TINKERS
CROSS

Avon

Brickhill

Wilkins's Coomb

Sandle Dairy
Farm

WHITSBURY RD

Arch Farm
Ind Site

Fordingbridge
Jun & Inf
Schs

3

Hurley Farm

HERTFORD CL

BURGATE
FIELDS

PENNY'S
CL

BEDFORD

PENS

Sandle
Manor

PUDDLESLOSH LA

RANHAM RD

WAVERLEY RD

WAVERLEY CL

PLAYER

Sandleheath

SMART

ST GEORGE'S
CRES

ST GEORGES RD

CORONATION TERR

ELMS CL

Sandleheath
Ind Est

MARL LA

GARENDON CT 1
MEADOW CL 2
OAKLANDS CL 3

PEALSHAM

MAY'S

ORCHARD

GLEBE GDNS

ALBION RD

15

Thorps
Farm

PO

DERRICK GDNS

KERRY GDNS

Forres Sandle
Manor
(Sch)

GLENAY DR

MEADOW AVE

WILLOW AVE

COTTAGE
MEWS

STEPHEN
MARTIN
GDNS

PARK RD

ALEXANDRA RD

FOREST
CT

SALISBURY RD

2

Reeve's
Copse

ASHDENHOLT RD

Ashford
Water

SANDLE

MAYFIELD RD

SANDLE FARM RD

MARIAN

ELMWOOD AVE

DOWNWOOD CL

BRYMPTON CL

JUBILEE
CLO

GREEN LA

LOWER BARTONS

Fordingbridge

Mus

PO

FOREST
ST

KINGS

RIVERSIDE

Reeve's
Copse

JUBILEE RD

Ashford

ROOKWOOD
GDNS

STATION RD

FERNDOWN
CT

VICTORIA RD

WESTGROVE

MORANT

Lby

WEST ST

ROMAN
QUAY

B3078

BRIDGE
ST

1

Fordingbridge Bsns Pk

THE
PANTILES

VICTORIA GDNS

RICHWOOD

Hotel

WEST END

HIGH ST

WHITSBURY ST

TH

ROMAN
QUAY

MARKET
PL

Ashford Works
Ind Est

REEDER CL

MILLS RD

WEST ST

PROSPECT PL

FORDINGBRIDGE

River Avon

14

12　A　B　13　C　D　14　E　F

F1
1 ORCHARD GDNS
2 SADDLERS CL
3 BLUEVALLEY MEWS
4 SYCAMORE CT
5 THE HUNDRED
6 WILSON CT

F2
1 AVON CT
2 HOMEBRIDGE HO

69
46

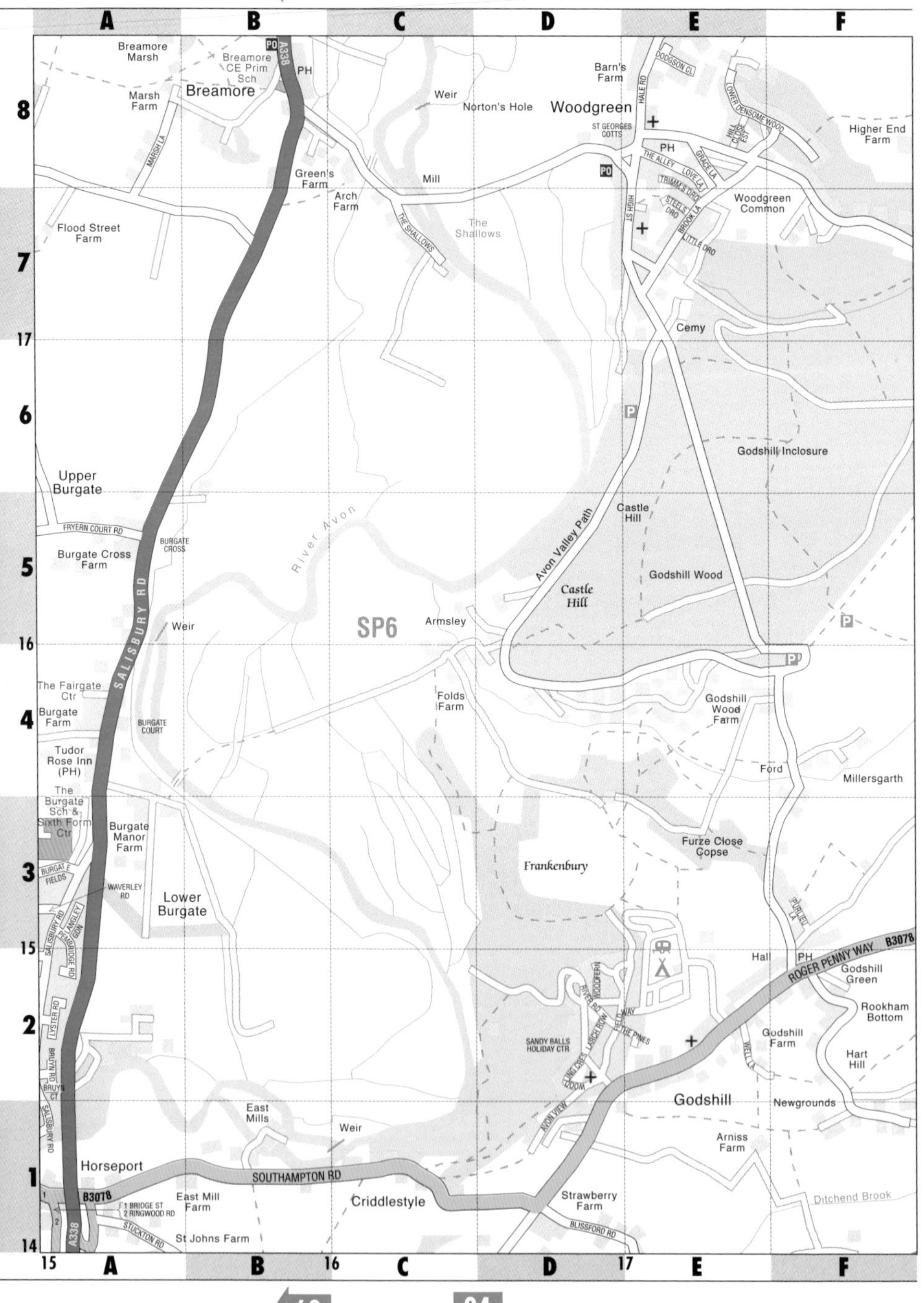
Breamore Marsh
Breamore CE Prim Sch
Breamore
Marsh Farm
Green's Farm
Arch Farm
Flood Street Farm
Weir
Norton's Hole
Mill
The Shallows
Woodgreen
Barn's Farm
Woodgreen Common
Higher End Farm
Cemy
Godshill Inclosure
Upper Burgate
FRYERN COURT RD
Burgate Cross Farm
BURGATE CROSS
River Avon
Avon Valley Path
Castle Hill
Godshill Wood
SP6
Armsley
SALISBURY RD
The Fairgate Ctr
Burgate Farm
Tudor Rose Inn (PH)
The Burgate Sch & Sixth Form Ctr
Burgate Manor Farm
Lower Burgate
Folds Farm
Godshill Wood Farm
Ford
Millersgarth
Furze Close Copse
Frankenbury
SANDY BALLS HOLIDAY CTR
ROGER PENNY WAY
B3078
Godshill Green
Rookham Bottom
Godshill Farm
Hart Hill
Godshill
Newgrounds
Arniss Farm
East Mills
Horseport
SOUTHAMPTON RD
East Mill Farm
Criddlestyle
Strawberry Farm
St Johns Farm
Ditchend Brook
BLISSFORD RD
STUCKTON RD
A338

69
94

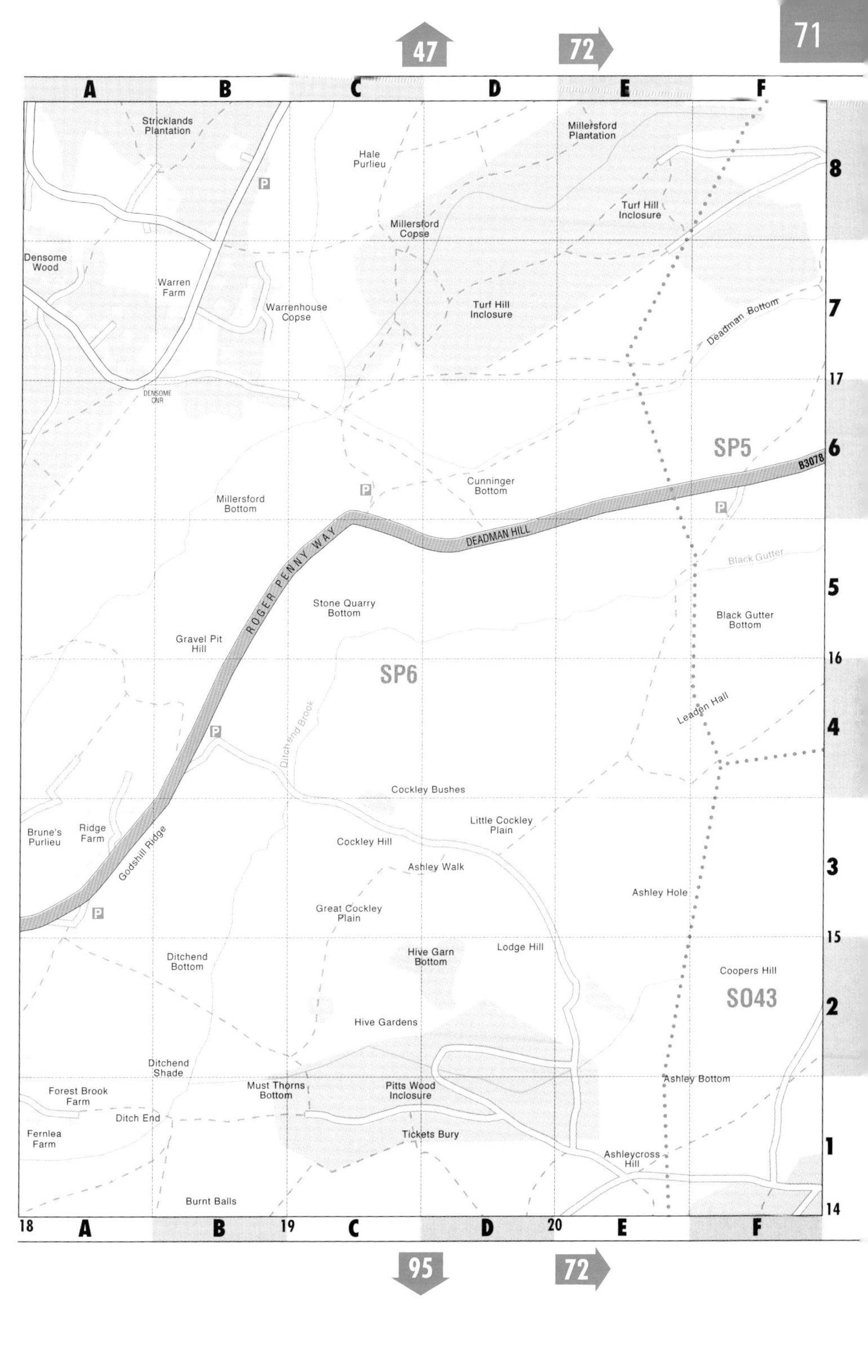
47
72
95
72
A
B
C
D
E
F
8
7
17
6
5
16
4
3
15
2
1
14
18
19
20
Stricklands Plantation
Hale Purlieu
Millersford Plantation
Turf Hill Inclosure
Millersford Copse
Densome Wood
Warren Farm
Warrenhouse Copse
Turf Hill Inclosure
Deadman Bottom
DENSOME CNR
SP5
B3078
Cunninger Bottom
Millersford Bottom
DEADMAN HILL
ROGER PENNY WAY
Black Gutter
Stone Quarry Bottom
Black Gutter Bottom
Gravel Pit Hill
SP6
Ditchend Brook
Leaden Hall
Cockley Bushes
Little Cockley Plain
Brune's Purlieu
Ridge Farm
Godshill Ridge
Cockley Hill
Ashley Walk
Ashley Hole
Great Cockley Plain
Hive Garn Bottom
Lodge Hill
Ditchend Bottom
Coopers Hill
SO43
Hive Gardens
Ditchend Shade
Ashley Bottom
Forest Brook Farm
Must Thorns Bottom
Pitts Wood Inclosure
Ditch End
Fernlea Farm
Tickets Bury
Ashleycross Hill
Burnt Balls

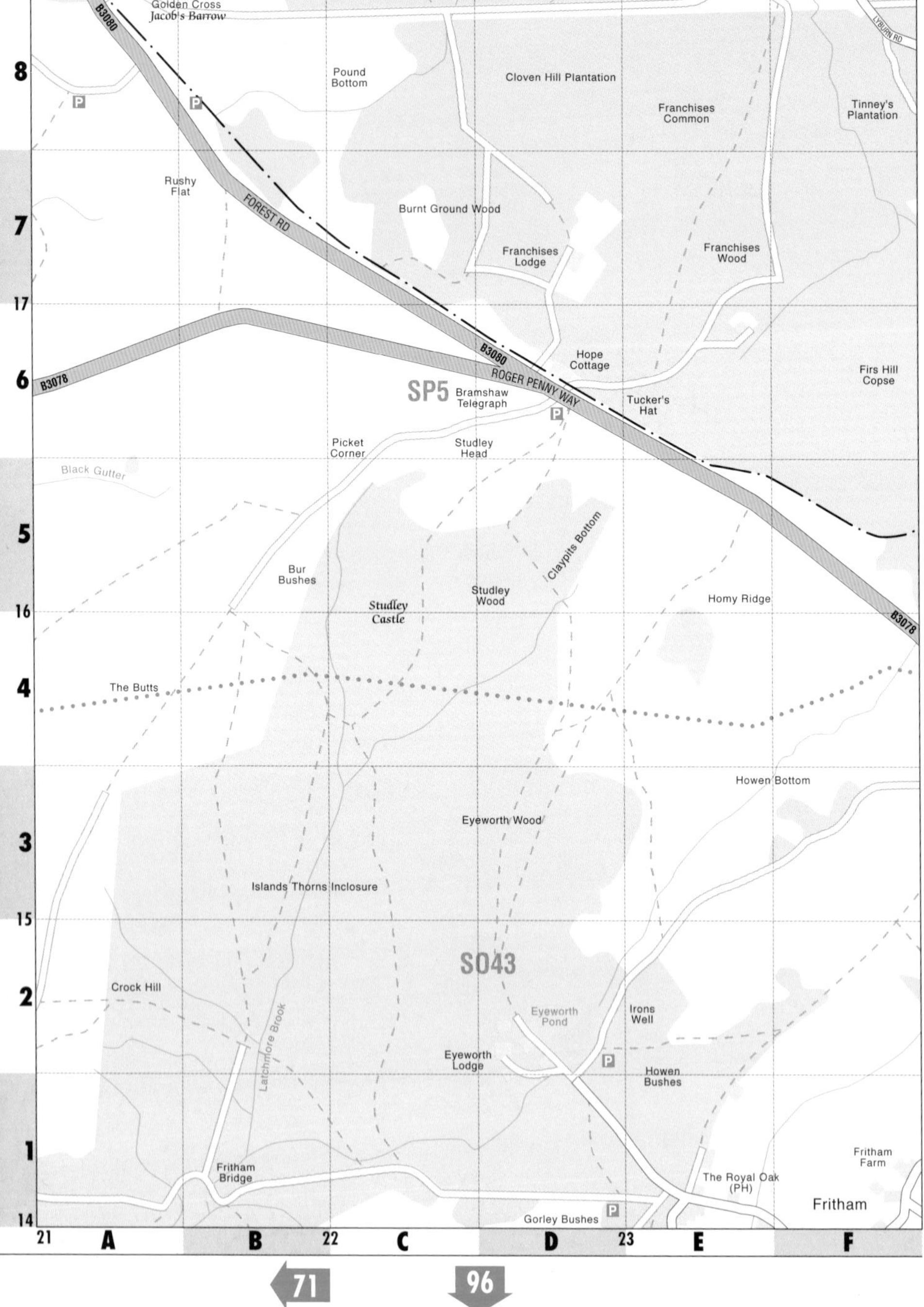

A B C D E F

8

Golden Cross
Jacob's Barrow

P P

Pound
Bottom

Cloven Hill Plantation

Franchises
Common

Tinney's
Plantation

B3080

Rushy
Flat

FOREST RD

7

Burnt Ground Wood

Franchises
Lodge

Franchises
Wood

17

B3080

ROGER PENNY WAY

Hope
Cottage

Firs Hill
Copse

6

B3078

SP5

Bramshaw
Telegraph

Tucker's
Hat

Picket
Corner

Studley
Head

Black Gutter

5

Bur
Bushes

Studley
Castle

Studley
Wood

Claypits Bottom

Homy Ridge

16

B3078

4

The Butts

Howen Bottom

3

Eyeworth Wood

Islands Thorns Inclosure

15

SO43

2

Crock Hill

Latchmore Brook

Eyeworth
Pond

Irons
Well

Eyeworth
Lodge

P

Howen
Bushes

1

Fritham
Bridge

The Royal Oak
(PH)

Fritham
Farm

P

Fritham

14

Gorley Bushes

21 A B 22 C D 23 E F

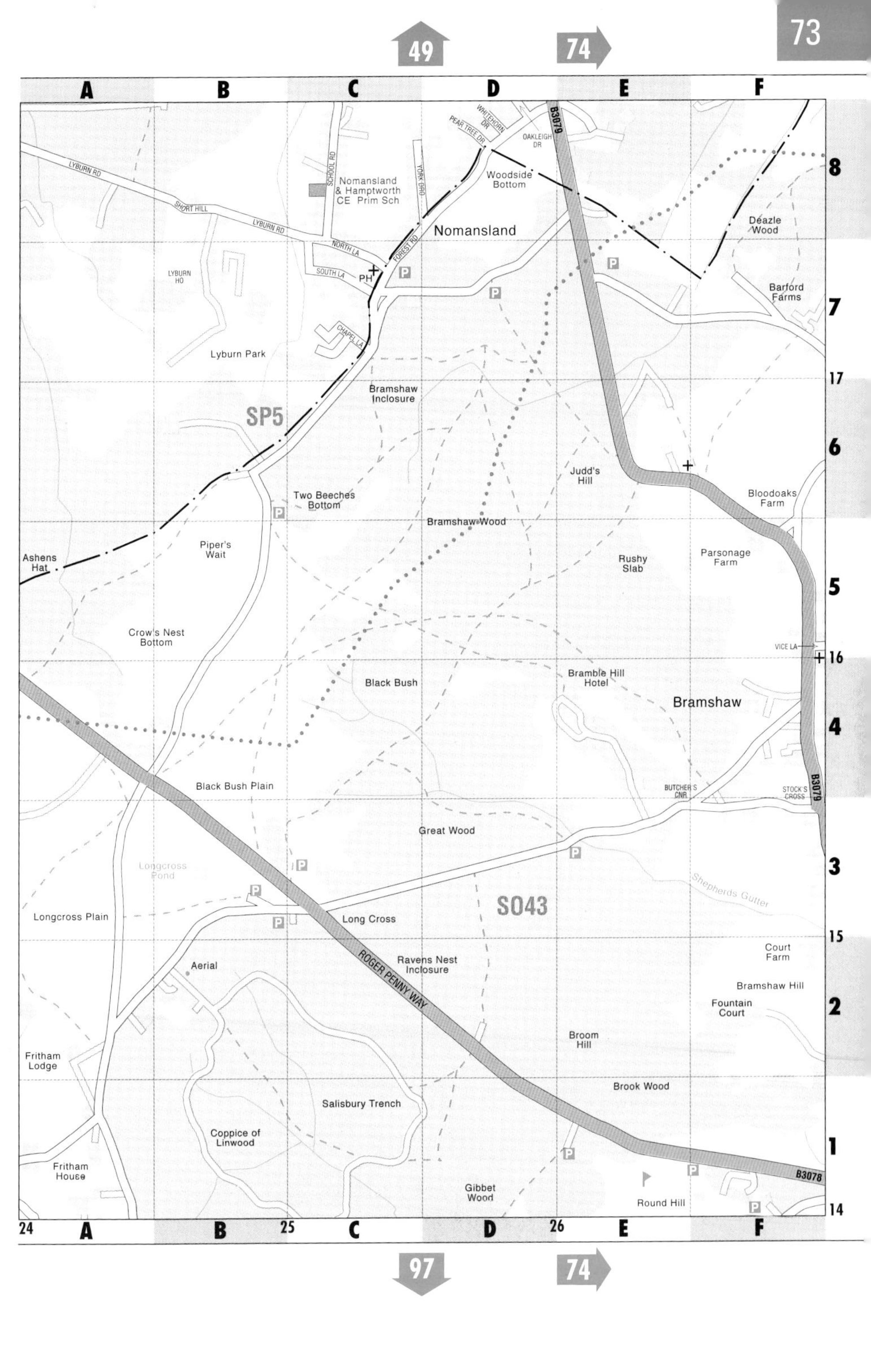
49
74
A
B
C
D
E
F
LYBURN RD
SHORT HILL
SCHOOL RD
YORK GRO
WHITEHORN DR
PEAR TREE DR
OAKLEIGH DR
B3079
Nomansland & Hamptworth CE Prim Sch
Woodside Bottom
Nomansland
NORTH LA
FOREST RD
SOUTH LA
PH
LYBURN HO
CHAPEL LA
Lyburn Park
Deazle Wood
Barford Farms
Bramshaw Inclosure
SP5
Judd's Hill
Two Beeches Bottom
Bramshaw Wood
Bloodoaks Farm
Piper's Wait
Ashens Hat
Rushy Slab
Parsonage Farm
Crow's Nest Bottom
VICE LA
Black Bush
Bramble Hill Hotel
Bramshaw
Black Bush Plain
BUTCHER'S CNR
STOCK'S CROSS
Great Wood
Longcross Pond
Shepherds Gutter
S043
Longcross Plain
Long Cross
Court Farm
Aerial
Ravens Nest Inclosure
ROGER PENNY WAY
Bramshaw Hill
Fountain Court
Broom Hill
Fritham Lodge
Brook Wood
Salisbury Trench
Coppice of Linwood
Fritham House
Gibbet Wood
Round Hill
B3078
8
7
17
6
5
16
4
3
15
2
1
14
24
25
26
97
74

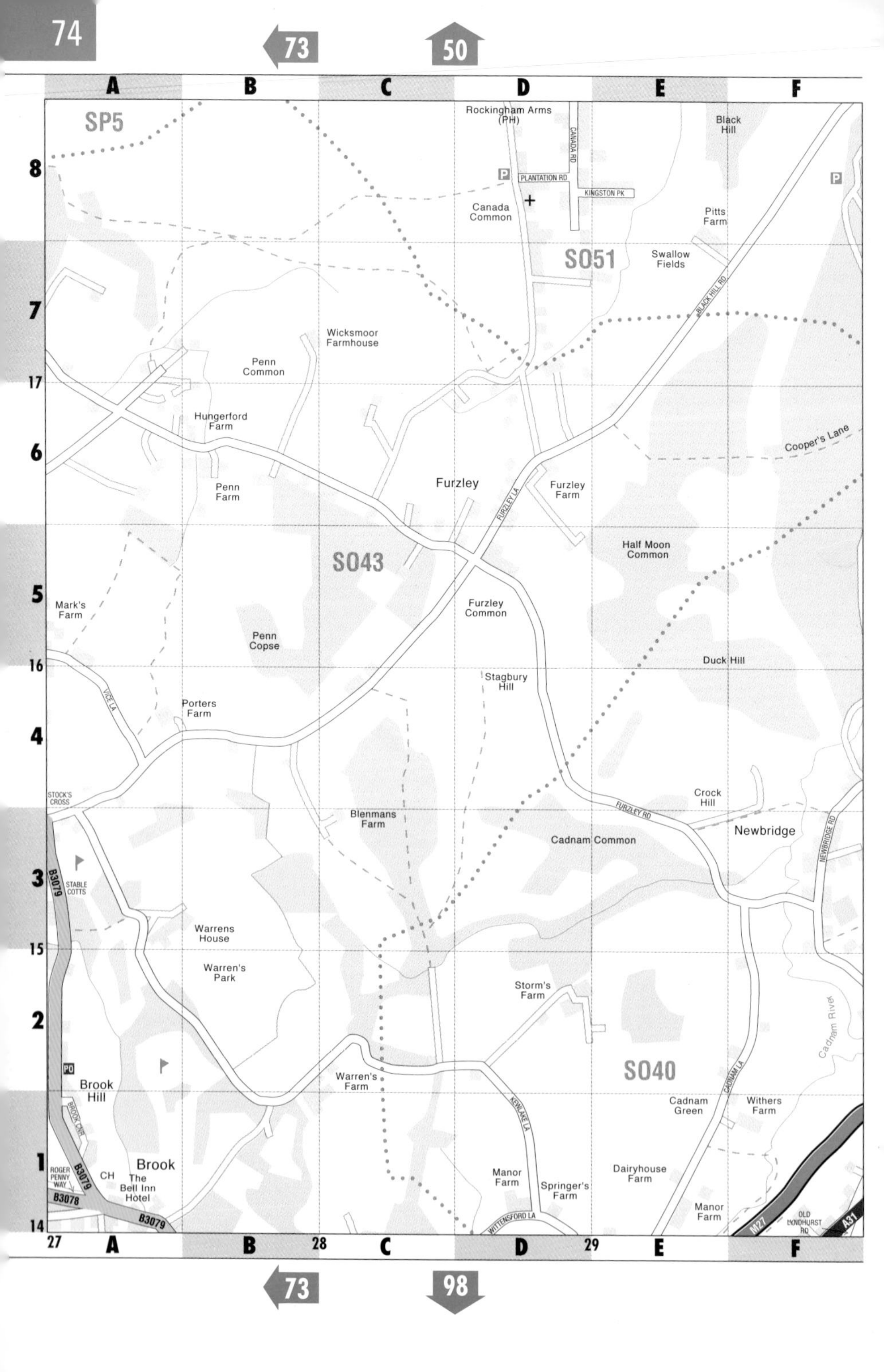
74
73
50
A
B
C
D
E
F
SP5
Rockingham Arms
(PH)
CANADA RD
PLANTATION RD
KINGSTON PK
Canada
Common
Black
Hill
Pitts
Farm
SO51
Swallow
Fields
BLACK HILL RD
8
7
17
6
5
16
4
3
15
2
1
14
Wicksmoor
Farmhouse
Penn
Common
Hungerford
Farm
Cooper's Lane
Penn
Farm
Furzley
FURZLEY LA
Furzley
Farm
Half Moon
Common
SO43
Mark's
Farm
Penn
Copse
Furzley
Common
Duck Hill
Stagbury
Hill
VICE LA
Porters
Farm
STOCK'S
CROSS
Crock
Hill
FURZLEY RD
Blenmans
Farm
Newbridge
Cadnam Common
NEWBRIDGE RD
B3079
STABLE
COTTS
Warrens
House
Warren's
Park
Storm's
Farm
Cadnam River
PO
SO40
Brook
Hill
Warren's
Farm
KEWLAKE LA
CADNAM LA
Cadnam
Green
Withers
Farm
BROOK CNR
Brook
CH
ROGER
PENNY
WAY
The
Bell Inn
Hotel
B3078
Manor
Farm
Springer's
Farm
Dairyhouse
Farm
Manor
Farm
WITTENSFORD LA
M27
OLD
LYNDHURST
RD
A31
27
28
29
98

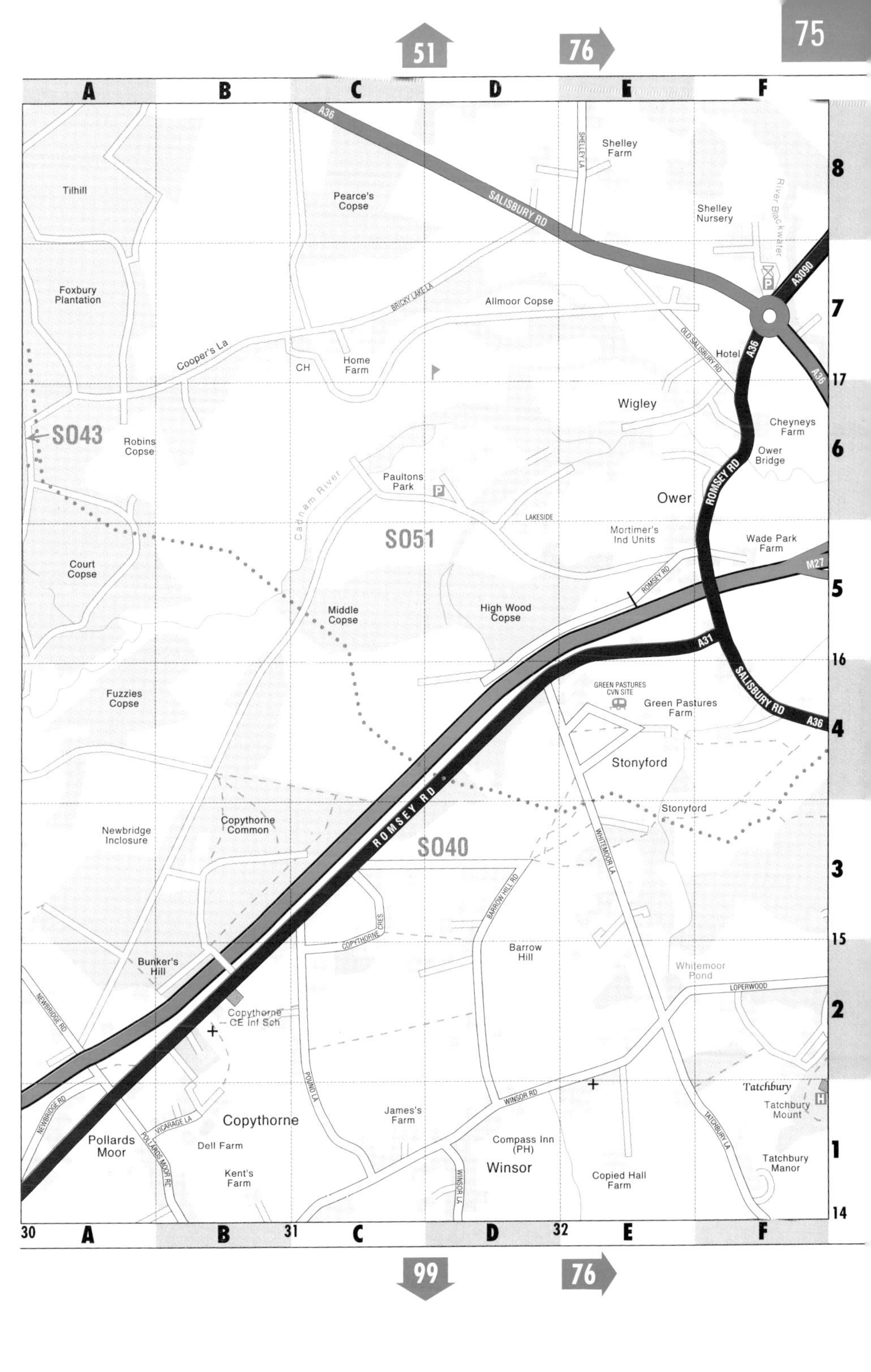
51
76
A
B
C
D
E
F
8
7
17
6
5
16
4
3
15
2
1
14
30
31
32
99
A36
SALISBURY RD
SHELLEY LA
Shelley Farm
Shelley Nursery
River Blackwater
A3090
Tilhill
Pearce's Copse
Foxbury Plantation
BRICKY LAKE LA
Allmoor Copse
Cooper's La
CH
Home Farm
OLD SALISBURY RD
Hotel
Wigley
Cheyneys Farm
Ower Bridge
SO43
Robins Copse
Paultons Park
Cadnam River
ROMSEY RD
Ower
LAKESIDE
SO51
Mortimer's Ind Units
Wade Park Farm
Court Copse
M27
Middle Copse
High Wood Copse
A31
Fuzzies Copse
GREEN PASTURES CVN SITE
Green Pastures Farm
Stonyford
Newbridge Inclosure
Copythorne Common
SO40
WHITEMOOR LA
BARROW HILL RD
COPYTHORNE CRES
Barrow Hill
Bunker's Hill
Whitemoor Pond
LOPERWOOD
NEWBRIDGE RD
Copythorne CE Inf Sch
Tatchbury
Tatchbury Mount
POUND LA
WINSOR RD
VICARAGE LA
Copythorne
James's Farm
TATCHBURY LA
Pollards Moor
POLLARDS MOOR RD
Dell Farm
Compass Inn (PH)
Winsor
WINSOR LA
Copied Hall Farm
Tatchbury Manor
Kent's Farm

75
52

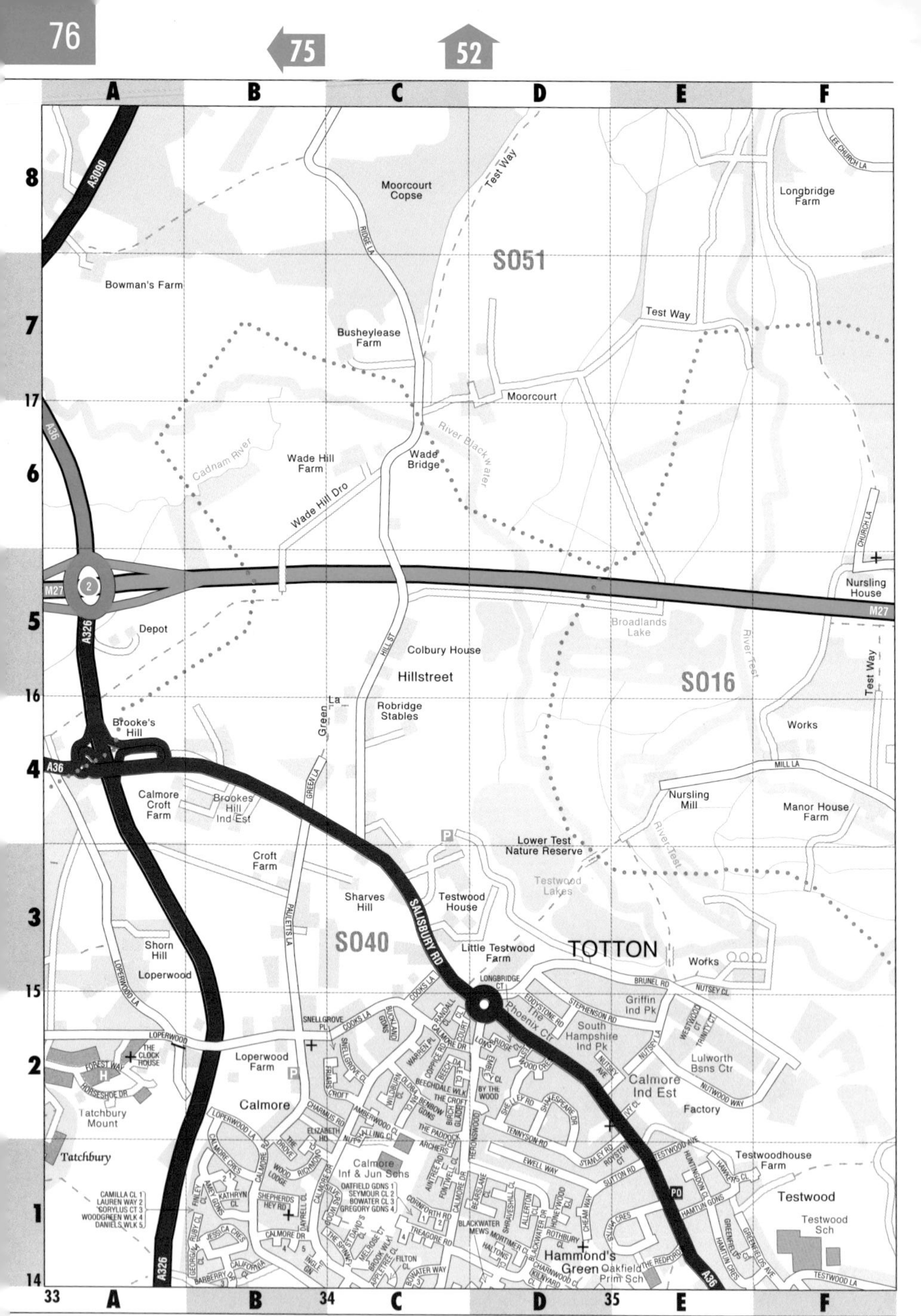
A
B
C
D
E
F
8
7
6
5
4
3
2
1
17
16
15
14
33
34
35
A3090
A36
M27
A326
SALISBURY RD
Moorcourt Copse
Test Way
Longbridge Farm
SO51
Bowman's Farm
Busheylease Farm
Moorcourt
Wade Hill Farm
Wade Bridge
Wade Hill Dro
Cadnam River
River Blackwater
Nursling House
Depot
Broadlands Lake
Colbury House
Hillstreet
SO16
Robridge Stables
Brooke's Hill
Works
Nursling Mill
Manor House Farm
Calmore Croft Farm
Brookes Hill Ind Est
Croft Farm
Lower Test Nature Reserve
Testwood Lakes
Sharves Hill
Testwood House
SO40
Shorn Hill
Loperwood
Little Testwood Farm
TOTTON
Griffin Ind Pk
South Hampshire Ind Pk
Loperwood Farm
Calmore
Calmore Ind Est
Lulworth Bsns Ctr
Factory
Tatchbury Mount
Tatchbury
Calmore Inf & Jun Schs
Testwoodhouse Farm
Testwood
Testwood Sch
Hammond's Green
Oakfield Prim Sch
CAMILLA CL 1
LAUREN WAY 2
CORYLUS CT 3
WOODGREEN WLK 4
DANIELS WLK 5
OATFIELD GDNS 1
SEYMOUR CL 2
BOWATER CL 3
GREGORY GDNS 4

75
100

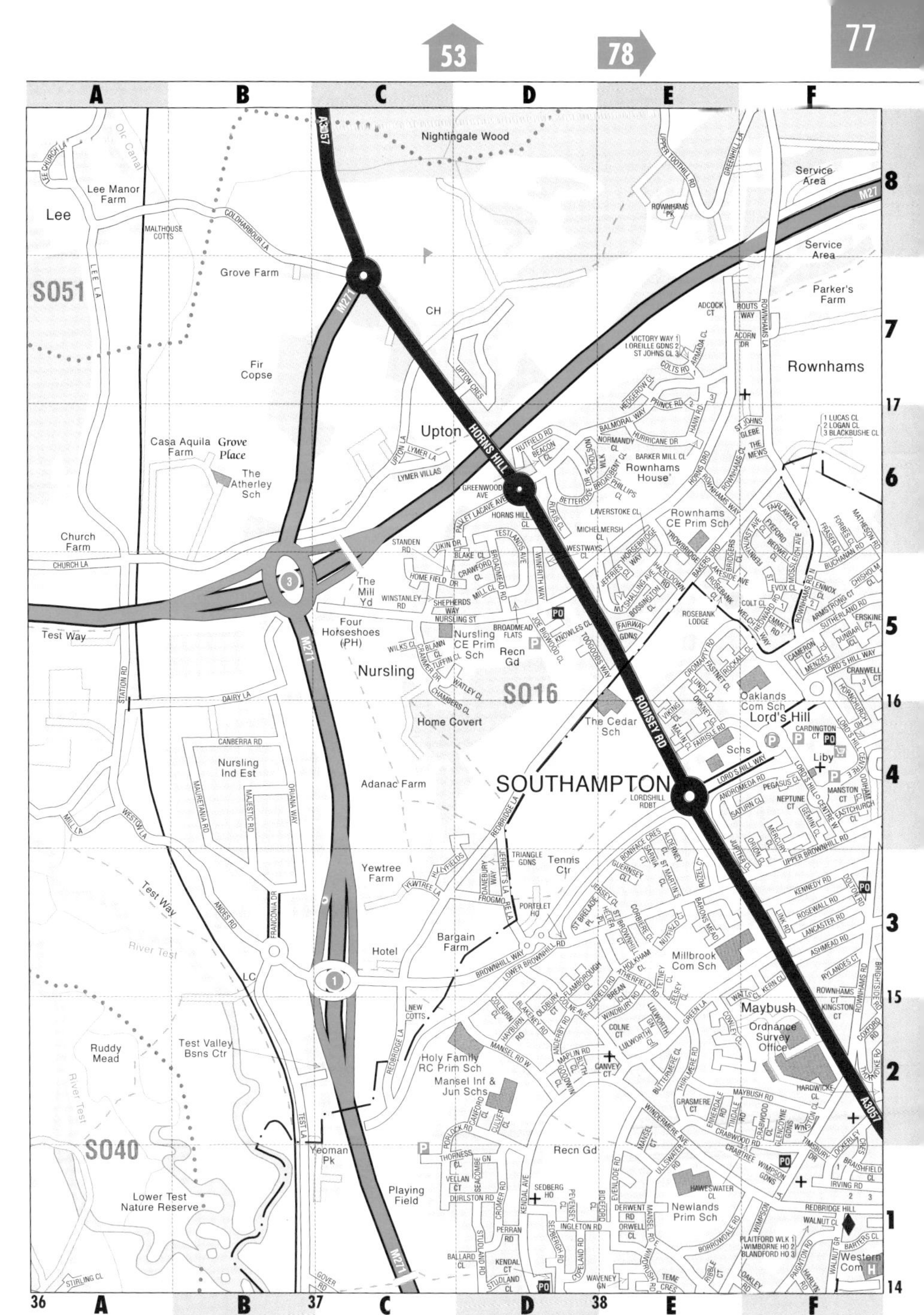
53
78
Nightingale Wood
Lee Manor Farm
Lee
Grove Farm
SO51
Service Area
Parker's Farm
Rownhams
Fir Copse
Upton
Casa Aquila Farm
Grove Place
The Atherley Sch
Rownhams House
Rownhams CE Prim Sch
Church Farm
The Mill Yd
Test Way
Four Horseshoes (PH)
Nursling CE Prim Sch
Recn Gd
Nursling
SO16
Home Covert
Oaklands Com Sch
Lord's Hill
The Cedar Sch
Nursling Ind Est
Schs
Adanac Farm
SOUTHAMPTON
Yewtree Farm
Tennis Ctr
Bargain Farm
Hotel
Millbrook Com Sch
Maybush
Ordnance Survey Office
Ruddy Mead
Test Valley Bsns Ctr
Holy Family RC Prim Sch
Mansel Inf & Jun Schs
SO40
Yeoman Pk
Recn Gd
Playing Field
Lower Test Nature Reserve
Newlands Prim Sch
Western Com
M27
M271
A3057
HORNS HILL
ROMSEY RD
River Test
101
78

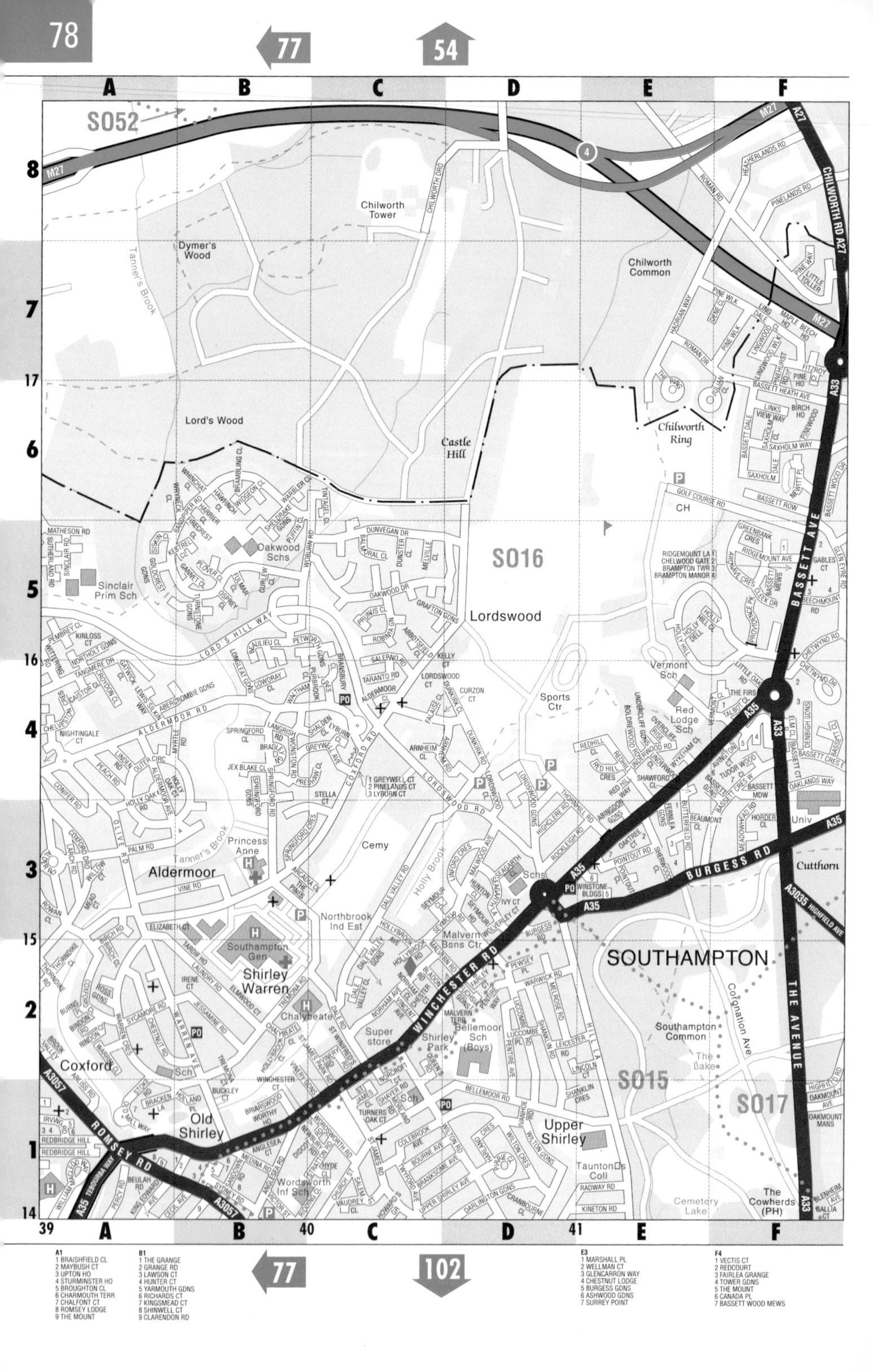
78
77
54
SO52
M27
A27
CHILWORTH RD A27
Chilworth Tower
Dymer's Wood
Tanner's Brook
Chilworth Common
Lord's Wood
Castle Hill
Chilworth Ring
SO16
Oakwood Schs
Sinclair Prim Sch
Lordswood
Vermont Sch
Sports Ctr
Red Lodge Sch
BASSETT AVE
A33
A35
BURGESS RD
Cutthorn
Univ
Princess Anne
Aldermoor
Cemy
Northbrook Ind Est
Southampton Gen
Shirley Warren
Chalybeate
Super store
Malvern Bsns Ctr
WINCHESTER RD
SOUTHAMPTON
Southampton Common
Coronation Ave
The Lake
THE AVENUE
SO15
SO17
Coxford
Old Shirley
Shirley Park
Bellemoor Sch (Boys)
Upper Shirley
Taunton's Coll
Wordsworth Inf Sch
ROMSEY RD
A3057
Cemetery Lake
The Cowherds (PH)
A3035
39
40
41
77
102
A1
1 BRAISHFIELD CL
2 MAYBUSH CT
3 UPTON HO
4 STURMINSTER HO
5 BROUGHTON CL
6 CHARMOUTH TERR
7 CHALFONT CT
8 ROMSEY LODGE
9 THE MOUNT
B1
1 THE GRANGE
2 GRANGE RD
3 LAWSON CT
4 HUNTER CT
5 YARMOUTH GDNS
6 RICHARDS CT
7 KINGSMEAD CT
8 SHINWELL CT
9 CLARENDON RD
E3
1 MARSHALL PL
2 WELLMAN CT
3 GLENCARRON WAY
4 CHESTNUT LODGE
5 BURGESS GDNS
6 ASHWOOD GDNS
7 SURREY POINT
F4
1 VECTIS CT
2 REDCOURT
3 FAIRLEA GRANGE
4 TOWER GDNS
5 THE MOUNT
6 CANADA PL
7 BASSETT WOOD MEWS

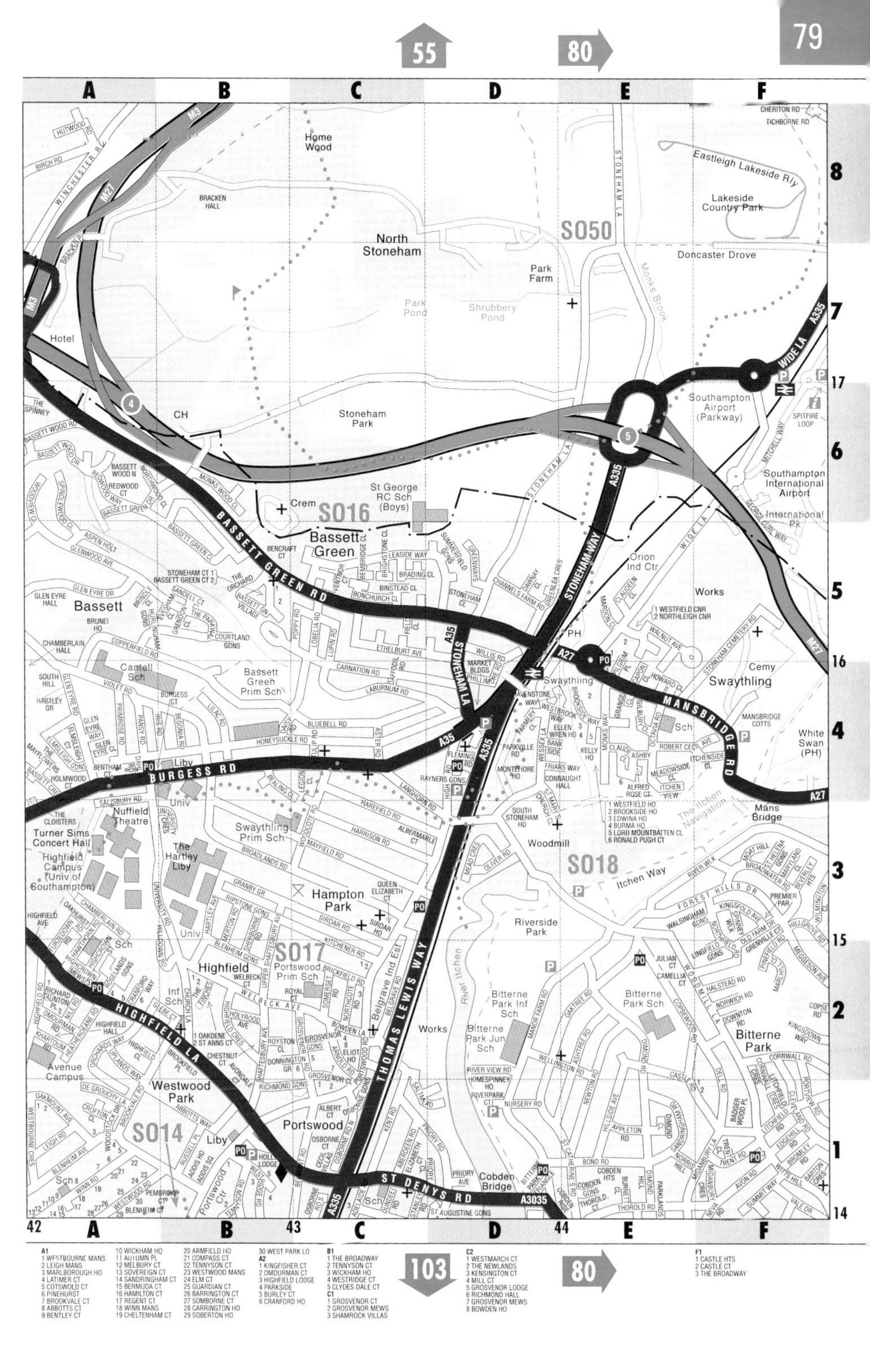

A1
1 WESTBOURNE MANS
2 LEIGH MANS
3 MARLBOROUGH HO
4 LATIMER CT
5 COTSWOLD CT
6 PINEHURST
7 BROOKVALE CT
8 ABBOTTS CT
9 BENTLEY CT

10 WICKHAM HO
11 AUTUMN PL
12 MELBURY CT
13 SOVEREIGN CT
14 SANDRINGHAM CT
15 BERMUDA CT
16 HAMILTON CT
17 REGENT CT
18 WINN MANS
19 CHELTENHAM HO

20 ARMFIELD HO
21 COMPASS CT
22 TENNYSON CT
23 WESTWOOD MANS
24 ELM CT
25 GUARDIAN CT
26 BARRINGTON CT
27 SOMBORNE CT
28 CARRINGTON HO
29 SOBERTON HO

30 WEST PARK LO

B1
1 THE BROADWAY
2 TENNYSON CT
3 WICKHAM HO
4 WESTRIDGE CT
5 CLYDES DALE CT
C1
1 GROSVENOR CT
2 GROSVENOR MEWS
3 SHAMROCK VILLAS

A2
1 KINGFISHER CT
2 OMDURMAN CT
3 HIGHFIELD LODGE
4 PARKSIDE
5 BURLEY CT
6 CRANFORD HO

C2
1 WESTMARCH CT
2 THE NEWLANDS
3 KENSINGTON CT
4 MILL CT
5 GROSVENOR LODGE
6 RICHMOND HALL
7 GROSVENOR MEWS
8 BOWDEN HO

F1
1 CASTLE HTS
2 CASTLE CT
3 THE BROADWAY

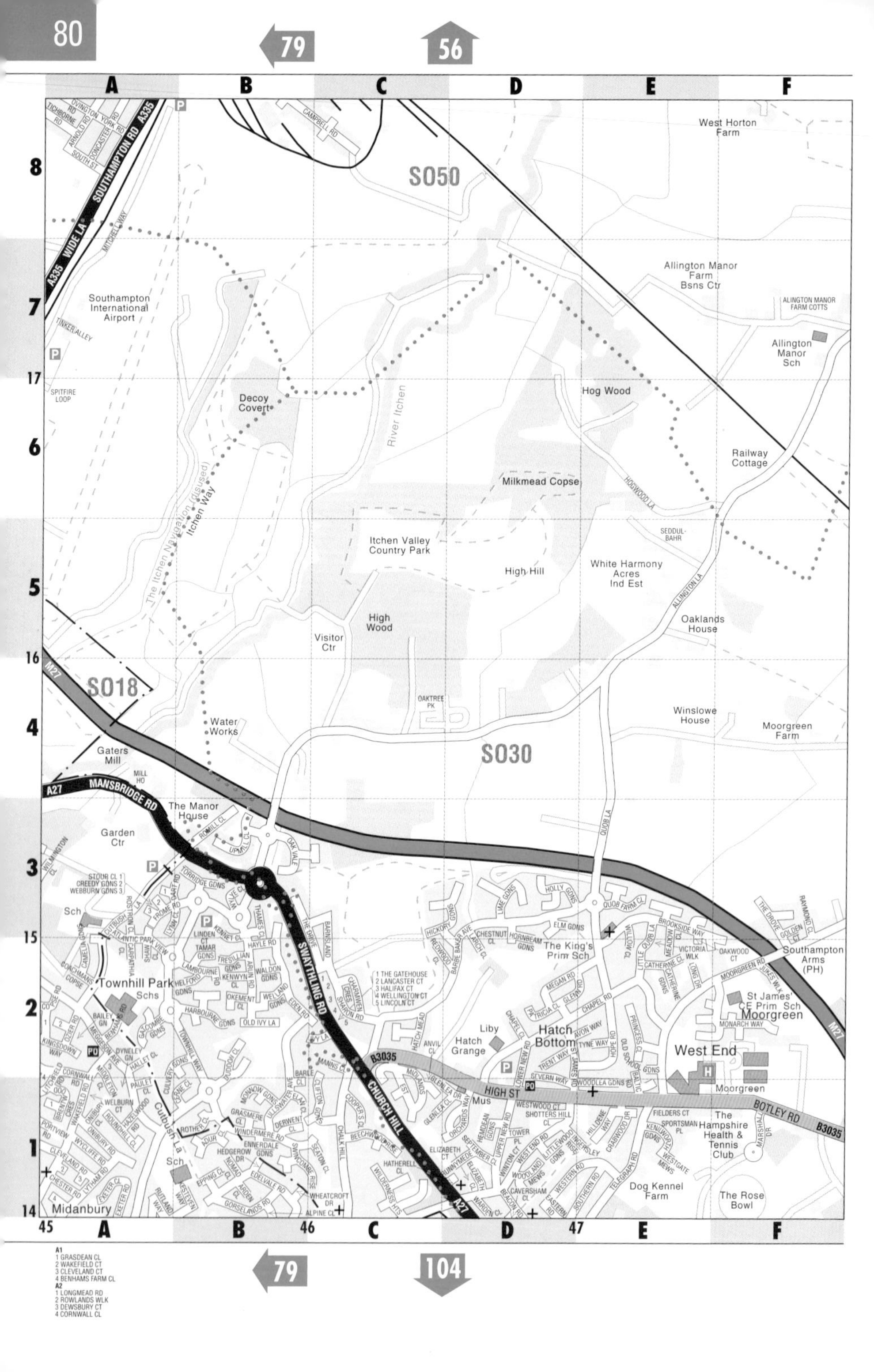

57

82

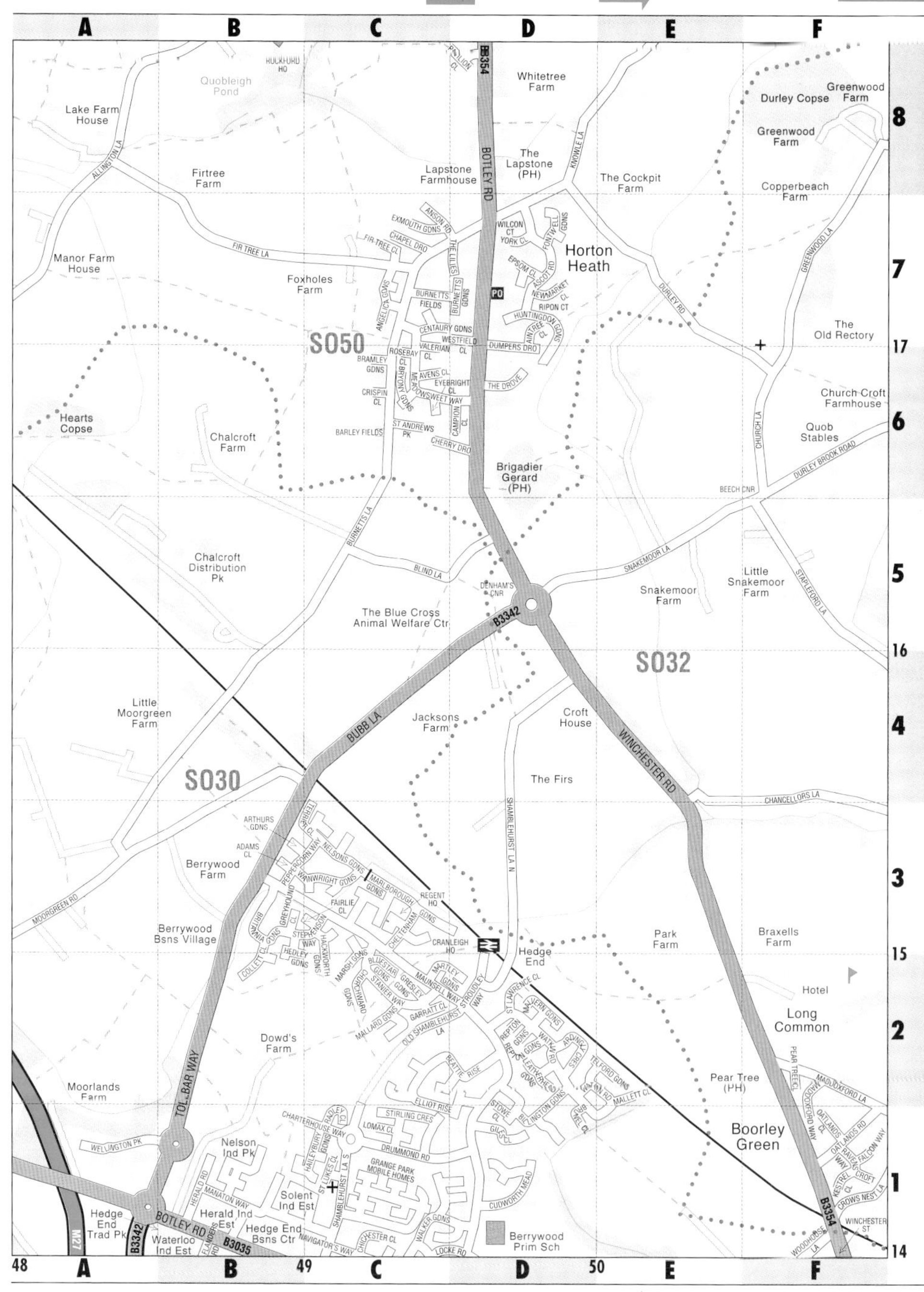

A
B
C
D
E
F
8
7
17
6
5
16
4
3
15
2
1
14
48
49
50
Lake Farm House
Quobleigh Pond
Whitetree Farm
Durley Copse
Greenwood Farm
Greenwood Farm
B3354
BOTLEY RD
ALLINGTON LA
Firtree Farm
Lapstone Farmhouse
The Lapstone (PH)
KNOWLE LA
The Cockpit Farm
Copperbeach Farm
FIR TREE LA
EXMOUTH GDNS
ANSON RD
CHAPEL DRO
FIR TREE CL
THE LILIES
WILCON CT
YORK CL
FONTWELL GDNS
EPSOM CL
ASCOT RD
Horton Heath
Manor Farm House
Foxholes Farm
ANGELICA GDNS
BURNETTS FIELDS
BURNETTS GDNS
PO
NEWMARKET CL
RIPON CT
HUNTINGDON GDNS
AINTREE CL
DURLEY RD
GREENWOOD LA
The Old Rectory
SO50
CENTAURY GDNS
WESTFIELD
VALERIAN CL
DUMPERS DRO
ROSEBAY CL
BRAMLEY GDNS
BRYONY GDNS
AVENS CL
EYEBRIGHT CL
MEADOWSWEET WAY
THE DROVE
CRISPIN CL
CAMPION CL
Hearts Copse
Chalcroft Farm
BARLEY FIELDS
ST ANDREWS PK
CHERRY DRO
Church Croft Farmhouse
Quob Stables
CHURCH LA
DURLEY BROOK ROAD
Brigadier Gerard (PH)
BEECH CNR
BURNETTS LA
Chalcroft Distribution Pk
BLIND LA
SNAKEMOOR LA
Little Snakemoor Farm
Snakemoor Farm
STAPLEFORD LA
DENHAM'S CNR
The Blue Cross Animal Welfare Ctr
B3342
SO32
Little Moorgreen Farm
BUBB LA
Jacksons Farm
Croft House
WINCHESTER RD
SO30
The Firs
SHAMBLEHURST LA N
CHANCELLORS LA
ARTHURS GDNS
ADAMS CL
TERRIER CL
NELSONS GDNS
PEPPERCORN WAY
Berrywood Farm
WAINWRIGHT GDNS
MARLBOROUGH GDNS
REGENT HO
MOORGREEN RD
FAIRLIE CL
GREYHOUND CL
CHELTENHAM GDNS
Berrywood Bsns Village
STEPHENSON WAY
CRANLEIGH HO
Park Farm
Braxells Farm
HEDLEY GDNS
HACKWORTH GDNS
Hedge End
COLLETT CL
MARSH GDNS
BLUESTAR GDNS
GRESLEY GDNS
MARTLEY GDNS
STROUDLEY WAY
ST LAWRENCE CL
CHURCHWARD GDNS
STANIER WAY
MALLARD GDNS
MAUNSELL WAY
GARRATT CL
OLD SHAMBLEHURST LA
MALVERN GDNS
Hotel
Long Common
TOLL BAR WAY
Dowd's Farm
REPTON GDNS
REPTON CL
WATKIN RD
ARDINGLY CRES
BEATTIE RISE
LEATHERHEAD GDNS
TELFORD GDNS
Pear Tree (PH)
PEAR TREE CL
MAUNSELL WAY
WALTON RD
MALLETT CL
Moorlands Farm
ELLIOT RISE
STOWE CL
BILLINGTON GDNS
OXFORD WAY
OXFORD LA
CHARTERHOUSE WAY
RADLEY CL
STIRLING CRES
GILES CL
BIRWELL CL
OATLANDS RD
LOMAX CL
HAILEYBURY GDNS
DRUMMOND RD
Boorley Green
RAVENS WAY
FALDON WAY
CROFT
WELLINGTON PK
Nelson Ind Pk
GRANGE PARK MOBILE HOMES
HERALD RD
ST LUKES CL
SHAMBLEHURST LA S
Solent Ind Est
CUDWORTH MEAD
KESTREL CL
CROWS NEST LA
MANATON WAY
Herald Ind Est
B3354
WINCHESTER ST
Hedge End Trad Pk
M27
B3342
BOTLEY RD
B3035
Waterloo Ind Est
FLANDERS RD
Hedge End Bsns Ctr
NAVIGATOR'S WAY
CHICHESTER CL
WALKER GDNS
LOCKE RD
Berrywood Prim Sch
WOODHOUSE LA

105

82

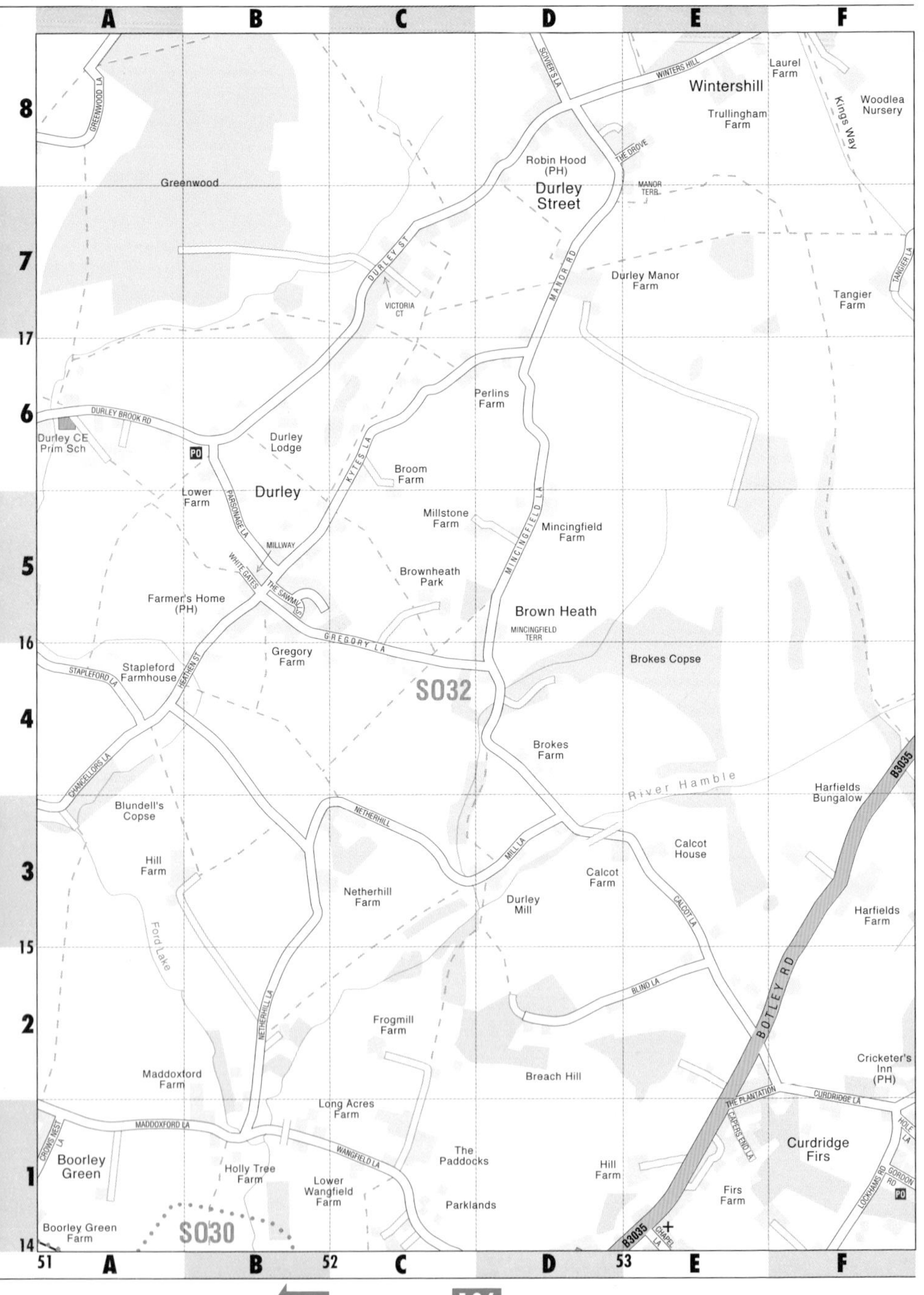

Wintershill

Laurel Farm

Woodlea Nursery

Winters Hill

Schools La

The Grove

Durley St

Manor Rd

Kings Way

Tangier La

Greenwood La

Robin Hood (PH)

Durley Street

Trullingham Farm

Manor Terr.

Durley Manor Farm

Tangier Farm

Greenwood

Victoria Ct

Durley Brook Rd

Durley CE Prim Sch

PO

Durley Lodge

Perlins Farm

Kyles La

Broom Farm

Mincingfield La

Durley

Lower Farm

Passingbrs La

Millstone Farm

Mincingfield Farm

Millway

Brownheath Park

White Gates

The Sawmill

Farmer's Home (PH)

Brown Heath

Mincingfield Terr.

Brokes Copse

Stapleford La

Stapleford Farmhouse

Gregory La

Gregory Farm

Somerset

SO32

Brokes Farm

River Hamble

Harfields Bungalow

B3035

Chapel End La

Blundell's Copse

Netherhill

Mill La

Calcot House

Calcot La

Harfields Farm

Hill Farm

Netherhill Farm

Durley Mill

Calcot Farm

Botley Rd

Ford Lake

Netherhill La

Frogmill Farm

Blind La

Cricketer's Inn (PH)

Maddoxford Farm

Long Acres Farm

Breach Hill

The Plantation

Chapel End La

Curdridge La

Curdridge Firs

Cross Rd

Maddoxford La

Wangfield La

The Paddocks

Hill Farm

Firs Farm

Lockhams Rd

Gordon Rd

PO

Boorley Green

Holly Tree Farm

Lower Wangfield Farm

Parklands

Chapel La

B3035

Boorley Green Farm

SO30

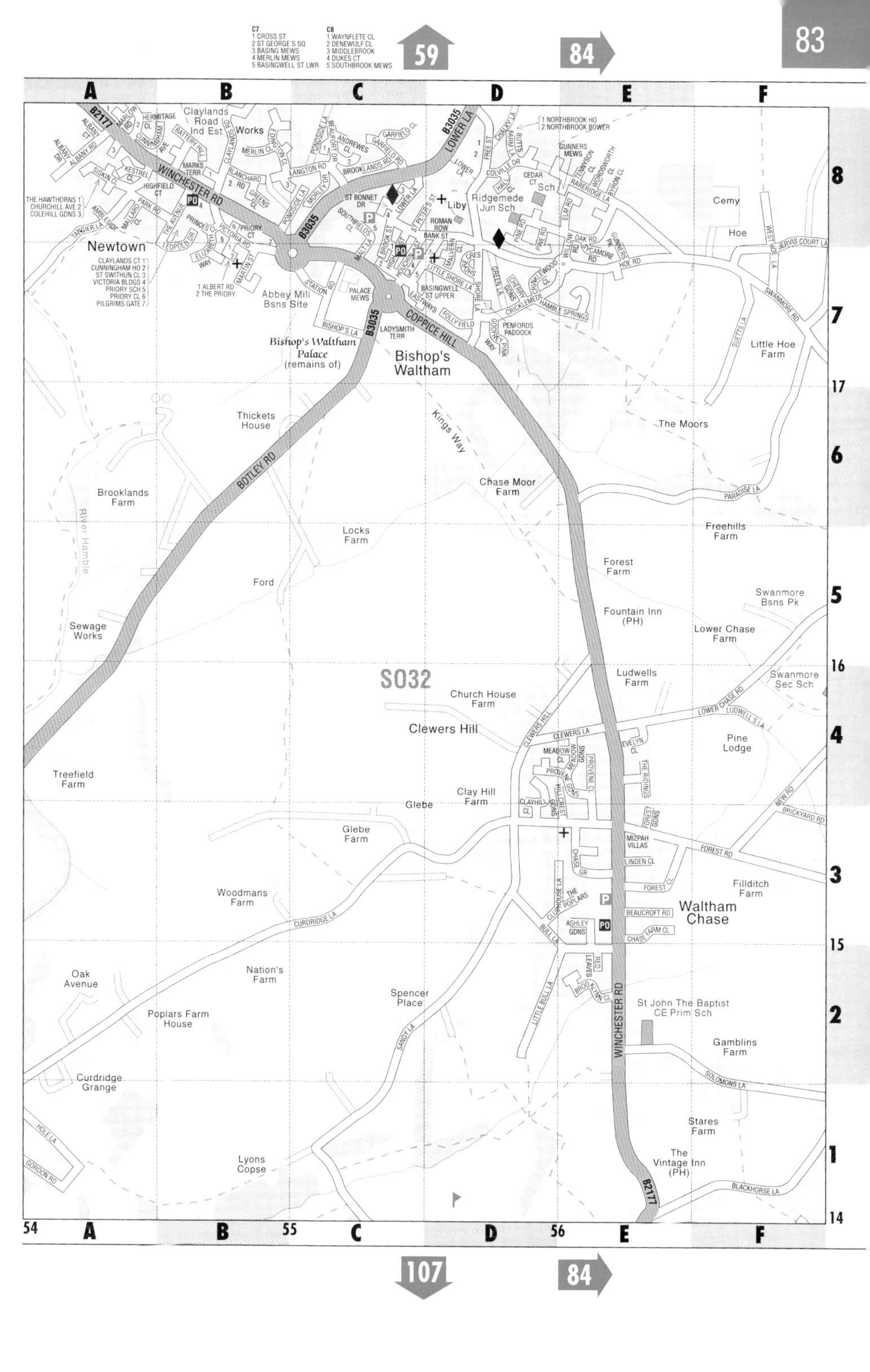
C7
1 CROSS ST
2 ST GEORGE'S SQ
3 BASING MEWS
4 MERLIN MEWS
5 BASINGWELL ST LWR
C8
1 WAYNFLETE CL
2 DENEWULF CL
3 MIDDLEBROOK
4 DUKES CT
5 SOUTHBROOK MEWS
59
84
1 NORTHBROOK HO
2 NORTHBROOK BOWER
THE HAWTHORNS 1
CHURCHILL AVE 2
COLEHILL GDNS 3
CLAYLANDS CT 1
CUNNINGHAM HO 2
ST SWITHUN CL 3
VICTORIA BLDGS 4
PRIORY SCH 5
PRIORY CL 6
PILGRIMS GATE 7
1 ALBERT RD
2 THE PRIORY
Newtown
Claylands Road Ind Est
Works
WINCHESTER RD
B2177
B3035
LOWER LA
COPPICE HILL
Abbey Mill Bsns Site
Bishop's Waltham Palace (remains of)
Bishop's Waltham
Ridgemede Jun Sch
Liby
Sch
Cemy
Hoe
HOE RD
JERVIS COURT LA
SWANMORE RD
Little Hoe Farm
Thickets House
Kings Way
The Moors
BOTLEY RD
Chase Moor Farm
PARADISE LA
Brooklands Farm
River Hamble
Locks Farm
Freehills Farm
Forest Farm
Ford
Swanmore Bsns Pk
Fountain Inn (PH)
Sewage Works
Lower Chase Farm
SO32
Ludwells Farm
Swanmore Sec Sch
Church House Farm
LOWER CHASE RD
Clewers Hill
CLEWERS LA
Pine Lodge
Treefield Farm
Clay Hill Farm
Glebe
Glebe Farm
NEW RD
BRICKYARD RD
FOREST RD
Woodmans Farm
Fillditch Farm
Waltham Chase
CURDRIDGE LA
Oak Avenue
Nation's Farm
Spencer Place
Poplars Farm House
St John The Baptist CE Prim Sch
WINCHESTER RD
Gamblins Farm
Curdridge Grange
SOLOMONS LA
Stares Farm
HOLE LA
GORDON RD
Lyons Copse
The Vintage Inn (PH)
BLACKHORSE LA
A
B
C
D
E
F
54
55
56
14
15
16
17
1
2
3
4
5
6
7
8
107
84

83
60

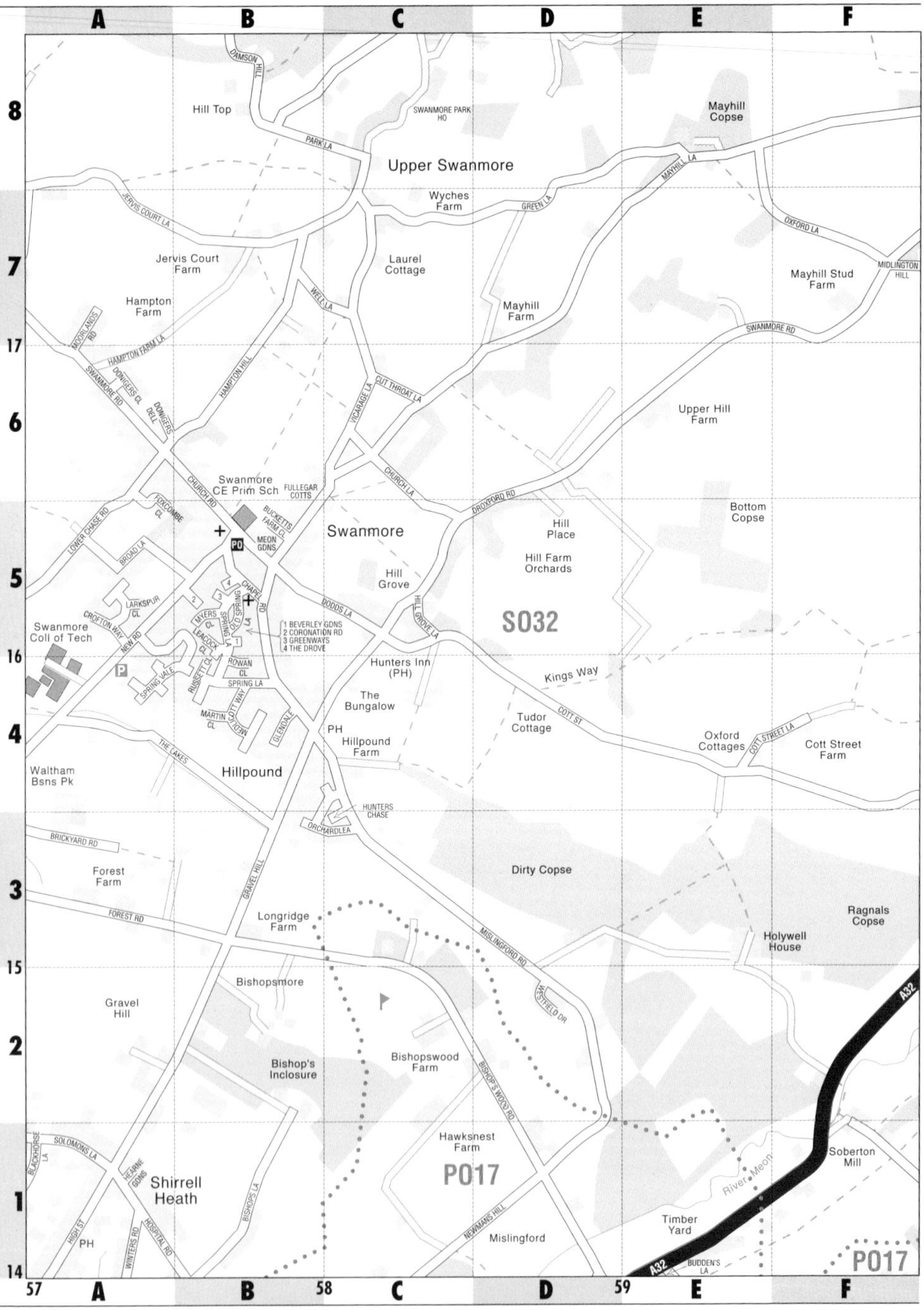

A   **B**   **C**   **D**   **E**   **F**

DAMSON HILL

Hill Top

SWANMORE PARK HO

Mayhill Copse

PARK LA

Upper Swanmore

Wyches Farm

MAYHILL LA

GREEN LA

OXFORD LA

JERVIS COURT LA

Jervis Court Farm

Laurel Cottage

MILL LA

Mayhill Stud Farm

MIDLINGTON HILL

Hampton Farm

HAMPTON FARM LA

Mayhill Farm

SWANMORE RD

WOODS MOSS

SPARROWS LEE

SWANMORE RD

DONKEYS HILL LANE

HAMPTON HILL

CUT THROAT LA

VICARAGE LA

Upper Hill Farm

FORSCOMBE CL

CHURCH RD

Swanmore CE Prim Sch

FULLEGAR COTTS

BUCKETTS FARM

CHURCH LA

DROXFORD RD

Hill Place

Bottom Copse

LOWER CHASE RD

BROAD LA

Swanmore

MEON GDNS

PO

Hill Grove

BODDEA LA

Hill Farm Orchards

SO32

Swanmore Coll of Tech

LARKSPUR CL

CROFTON AVE

NEW RD

1 BEVERLEY GDNS
2 CORONATION RD
3 GREENWAYS
4 THE DROVE

HILL GROVE LA

Kings Way

COTT ST

Oxford Cottages

COTT STREET LA

Cott Street Farm

P

SPRING VALE

ROMAN CL

SPRING LA

Hunters Inn (PH)

The Bungalow

PH

Hillpound Farm

Tudor Cottage

Waltham Bsns Pk

MARTIN CL

CEMETERY LA

GLEN CL

THE LAKES

Hillpound

HUNTERS CHASE

FINCHARDLEA

BRICKYARD RD

GRAVEL HILL

Forest Farm

Dirty Copse

Ragnals Copse

FOREST RD

Longridge Farm

MISLINGFORD RD

Holywell House

Bishopsmore

WHITELEY DR

A32

Gravel Hill

Bishop's Inclosure

Bishopswood Farm

BISHOP'S PASS RD

SOLOMONS LA

BLACKHOUSE LA

LOWER CHASE RD

BISHOPS LA

Hawksnest Farm

PO17

River Meon

Soberton Mill

HIGH ST

WINTERS RD

HOSPITAL RD

Shirrell Heath

NEWMANS HILL

Mislingford

Timber Yard

A32

BUDDEN'S LA

PO17

PH

57   **A**   **B**   **58**   **C**   **D**   **59**   **E**   **F**

83
108

61
86

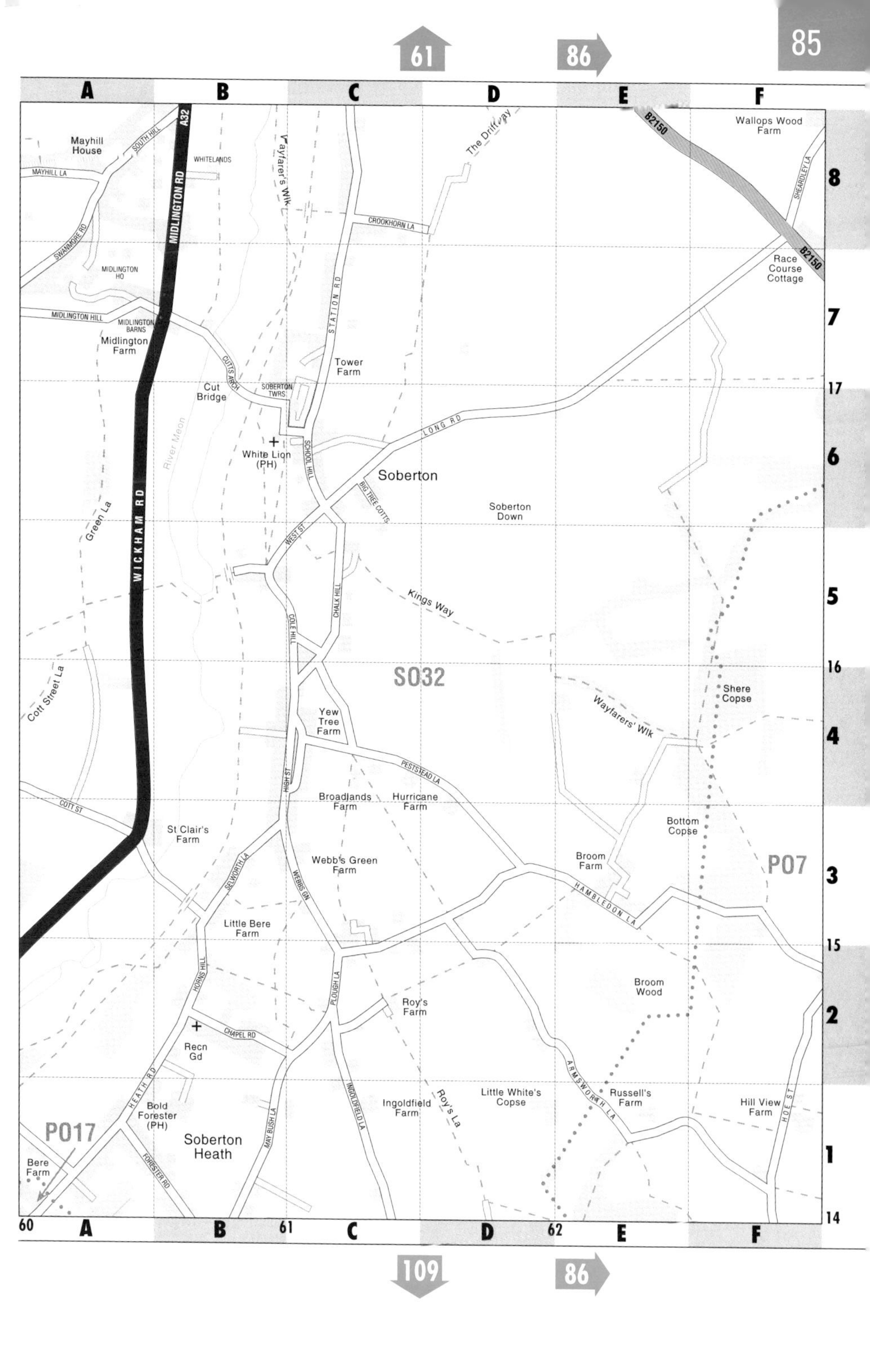
A
B
C
D
E
F
8
7
17
6
5
16
4
3
15
2
1
14
60
61
62
Mayhill House
MAYHILL LA
SOUTH HILL
A32
MIDLINGTON RD
WHITELANDS
Wayfarer's Wlk
The Driftway
B2150
Wallops Wood Farm
SHEARDLEY LA
CROOKHORN LA
SWANMORE RD
MIDLINGTON HO
STATION RD
Race Course Cottage
MIDLINGTON HILL
MIDLINGTON BARNS
Midlington Farm
CUTTS ARCH
Tower Farm
Cut Bridge
SOBERTON TWRS
River Meon
LONG RD
White Lion (PH)
SCHOOL HILL
Soberton
BIG TREE COTTS
Soberton Down
Green La
WICKHAM RD
WEST ST
Kings Way
CHALK HILL
COLE HILL
SO32
Cott Street La
Shere Copse
Wayfarers' Wlk
Yew Tree Farm
HIGH ST
PESTSTEAD LA
COTT ST
Broadlands Farm
Hurricane Farm
St Clair's Farm
Bottom Copse
Broom Farm
Webb's Green Farm
PO7
SELWORTH LA
WEBBS GN
HAMBLEDON LA
Little Bere Farm
HORNS HILL
Broom Wood
PLOUGH LA
Roy's Farm
CHAPEL RD
Recn Gd
ARMSWORTH LA
HEATH RD
INGOLDFIELD LA
Roy's La
Little White's Copse
Russell's Farm
Ingoldfield Farm
Hill View Farm
HOE ST
Bold Forester (PH)
PO17
Soberton Heath
MAY BUSH LA
Bere Farm
FORESTER RD

109
86

85
62

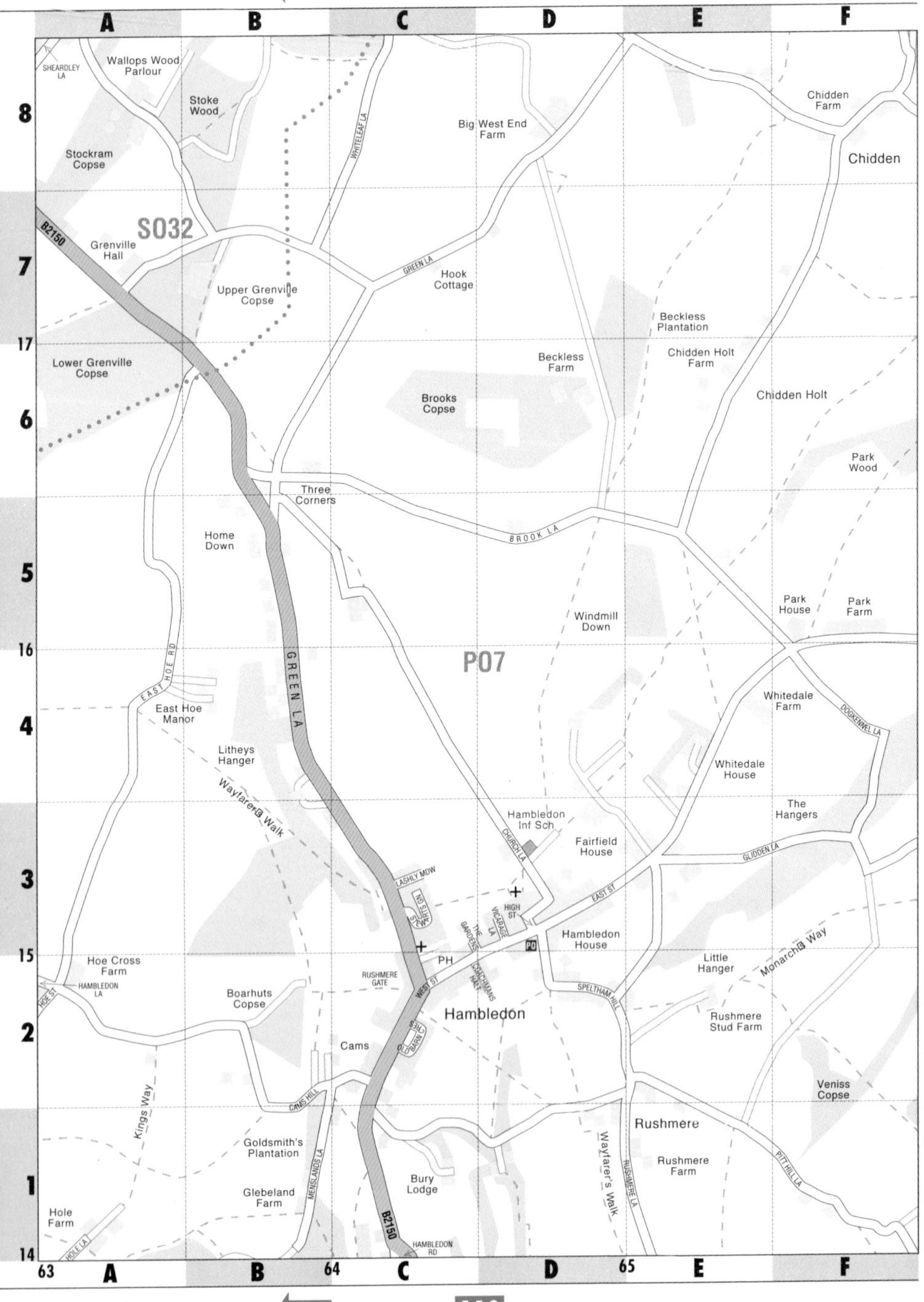
A
B
C
D
E
F
8
7
17
6
5
16
4
3
15
2
1
14
63
64
65
SHEARDLEY LA
Wallops Wood Parlour
Stoke Wood
Stockram Copse
WHITELEAF LA
Big West End Farm
Chidden Farm
Chidden
B2150
SO32
Grenville Hall
GREEN LA
Hook Cottage
Upper Grenville Copse
Beckless Plantation
Chidden Holt Farm
Beckless Farm
Lower Grenville Copse
Brooks Copse
Chidden Holt
Park Wood
Three Corners
Home Down
BROOK LA
Park House
Park Farm
Windmill Down
PO7
EAST HOE RD
East Hoe Manor
Whitedale Farm
DOGKENNEL LA
Litheys Hanger
Whitedale House
Wayfarer's Walk
The Hangers
Hambledon Inf Sch
CHURCH LA
Fairfield House
LASHLY MDW
GLIDDEN LA
EAST ST
HIGH ST
VICARAGE LA
THE GARDENS
Hambledon House
Monarch's Way
PH
Hoe Cross Farm
HAMBLEDON LA
HOE ST
RUSHMERE GATE
WEST ST
COLDHARBOUR HILL
SPELTHAM HILL
Little Hanger
Boarhuts Copse
Hambledon
Rushmere Stud Farm
Cams
OLD BARN
Kings Way
CAMS HILL
Veniss Copse
Rushmere
Goldsmith's Plantation
MENSLANDS LA
Wayfarer's Walk
RUSHMERE LA
Rushmere Farm
PITT HILL LA
Bury Lodge
Glebeland Farm
Hole Farm
HOLE LA
HAMBLEDON RD

85
110

63
88

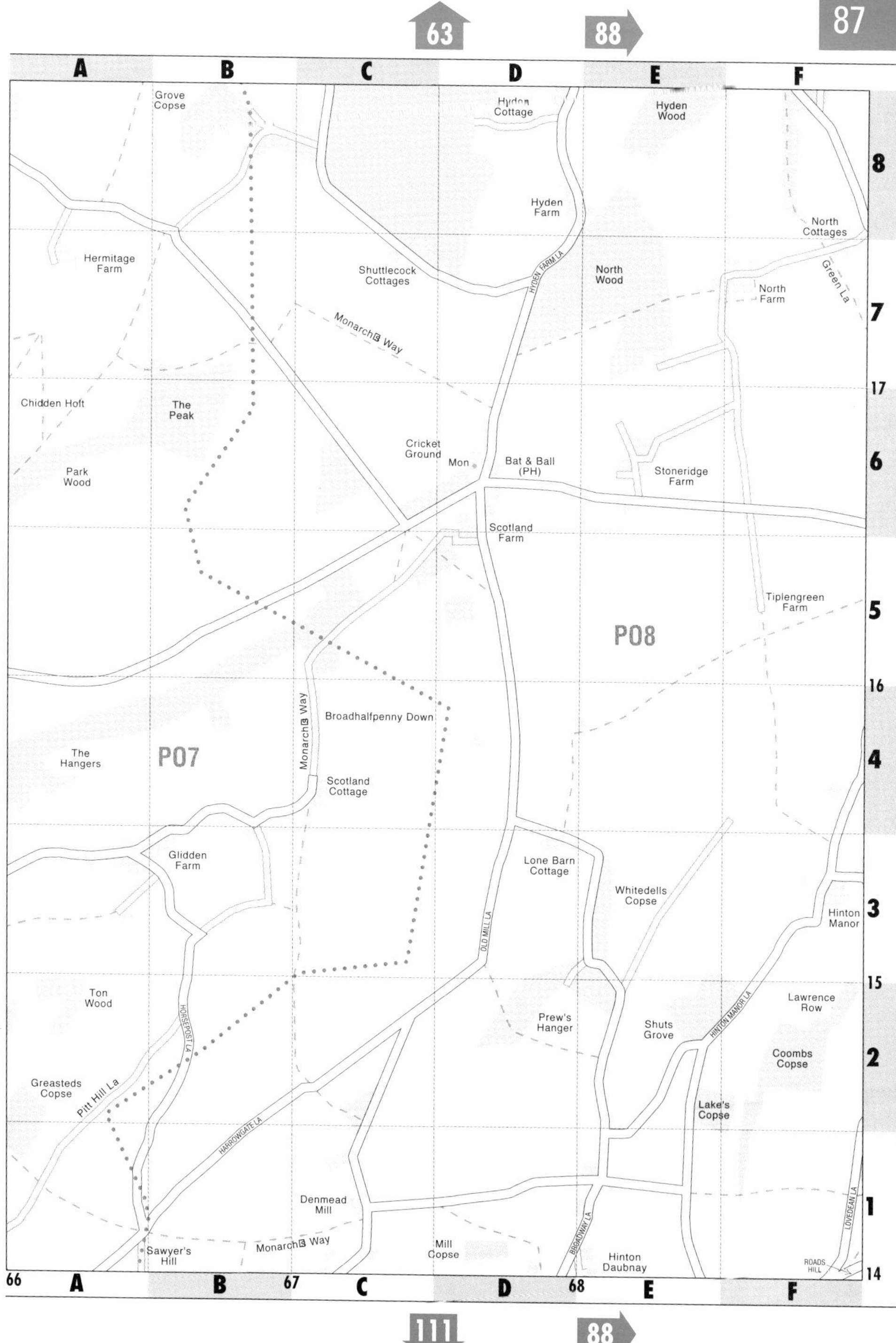
A
B
C
D
E
F
Grove Copse
Hydon Cottage
Hyden Wood
8
Hyden Farm
North Cottages
Hermitage Farm
Shuttlecock Cottages
HYDEN FARM LA
North Wood
North Farm
Green La
7
Monarch's Way
17
Chidden Hoft
The Peak
Cricket Ground
Mon
Bat & Ball (PH)
Park Wood
Stoneridge Farm
6
Scotland Farm
Tiplengreen Farm
5
PO8
16
Monarch's Way
Broadhalfpenny Down
The Hangers
PO7
Scotland Cottage
4
Glidden Farm
Lone Barn Cottage
Whitedells Copse
OLD MILL LA
3
Hinton Manor
15
Ton Wood
Lawrence Row
HORSEPOST LA
Prew's Hanger
Shuts Grove
HINTON MANOR LA
2
Coombs Copse
Greasteds Copse
Pitt Hill La
Lake's Copse
HARROWGATE LA
Denmead Mill
1
LOVEDEAN LA
Monarch's Way
Mill Copse
BROADWAY LA
Sawyer's Hill
Hinton Daubnay
ROADS HILL
14
66
67
68

111
88

87
64

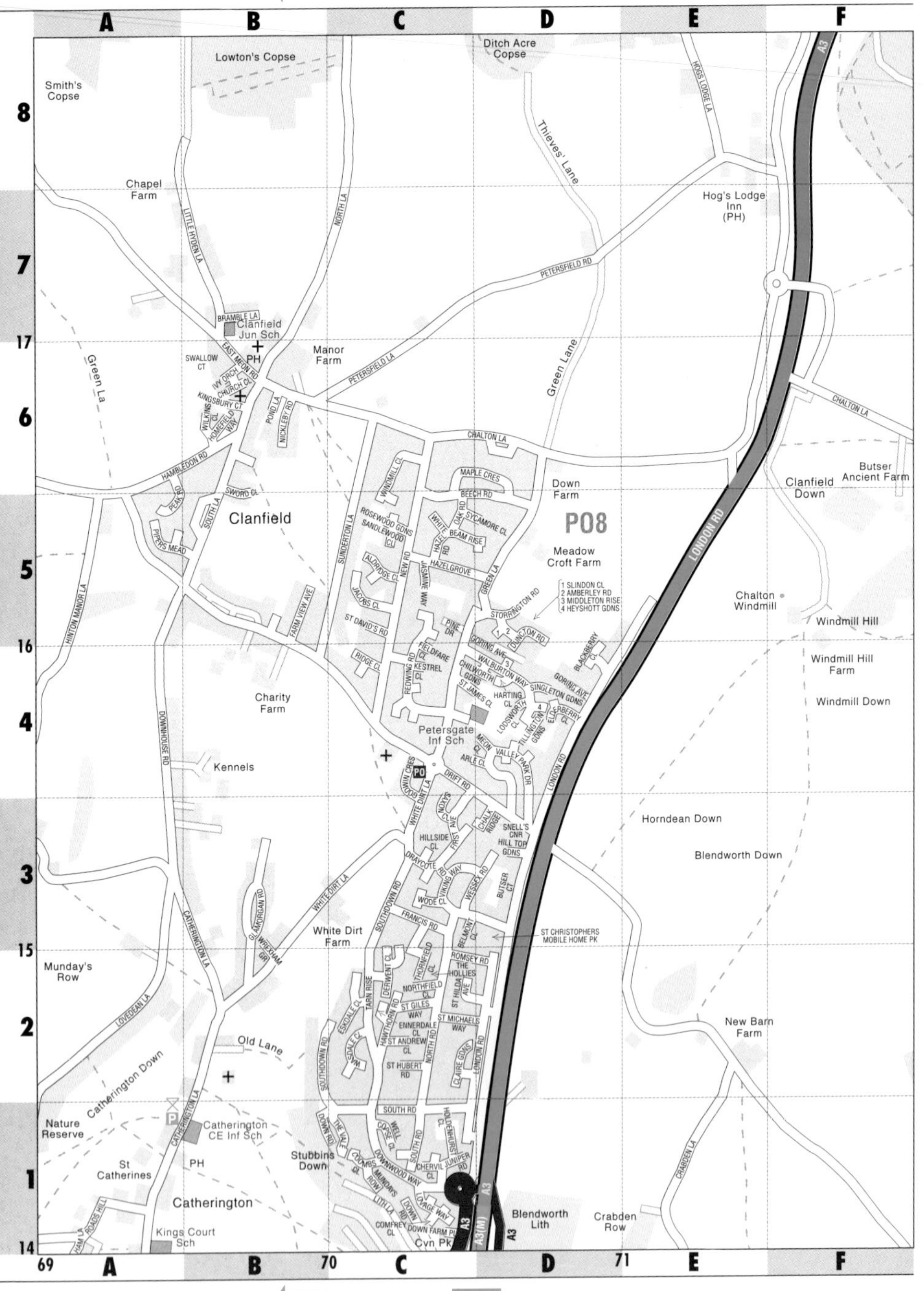
Lowton's Copse
Ditch Acre Copse
Smith's Copse
Thieves' Lane
HOGS LODGE LA
Chapel Farm
Hog's Lodge Inn (PH)
LITTLE HYDEN LA
NORTH LA
PETERSFIELD RD
BRAMBLE LA
Clanfield Jun Sch
Manor Farm
Green Lane
Green La
CHALTON LA
HAMBLEDON RD
Down Farm
Clanfield Down
Butser Ancient Farm
Clanfield
PO8
LONDON RD
Meadow Croft Farm
Chalton Windmill
Windmill Hill
Windmill Hill Farm
Windmill Down
HINTON MANOR LA
Charity Farm
Petersgate Inf Sch
Kennels
DOWNHOUSE RD
Horndean Down
Blendworth Down
White Dirt Farm
WHITE DIRT LA
ST CHRISTOPHERS MOBILE HOME PK
Munday's Row
Old Lane
New Barn Farm
Catherington Down
Nature Reserve
Catherington CE Inf Sch
Stubbins Down
St Catherines
Catherington
Kings Court Sch
Blendworth Lith
Crabden Row
CRABDEN LA
1 SLINDON CL
2 AMBERLEY RD
3 MIDDLETON RISE
4 HEYSHOTT GDNS
A3
A3(M)

87
112

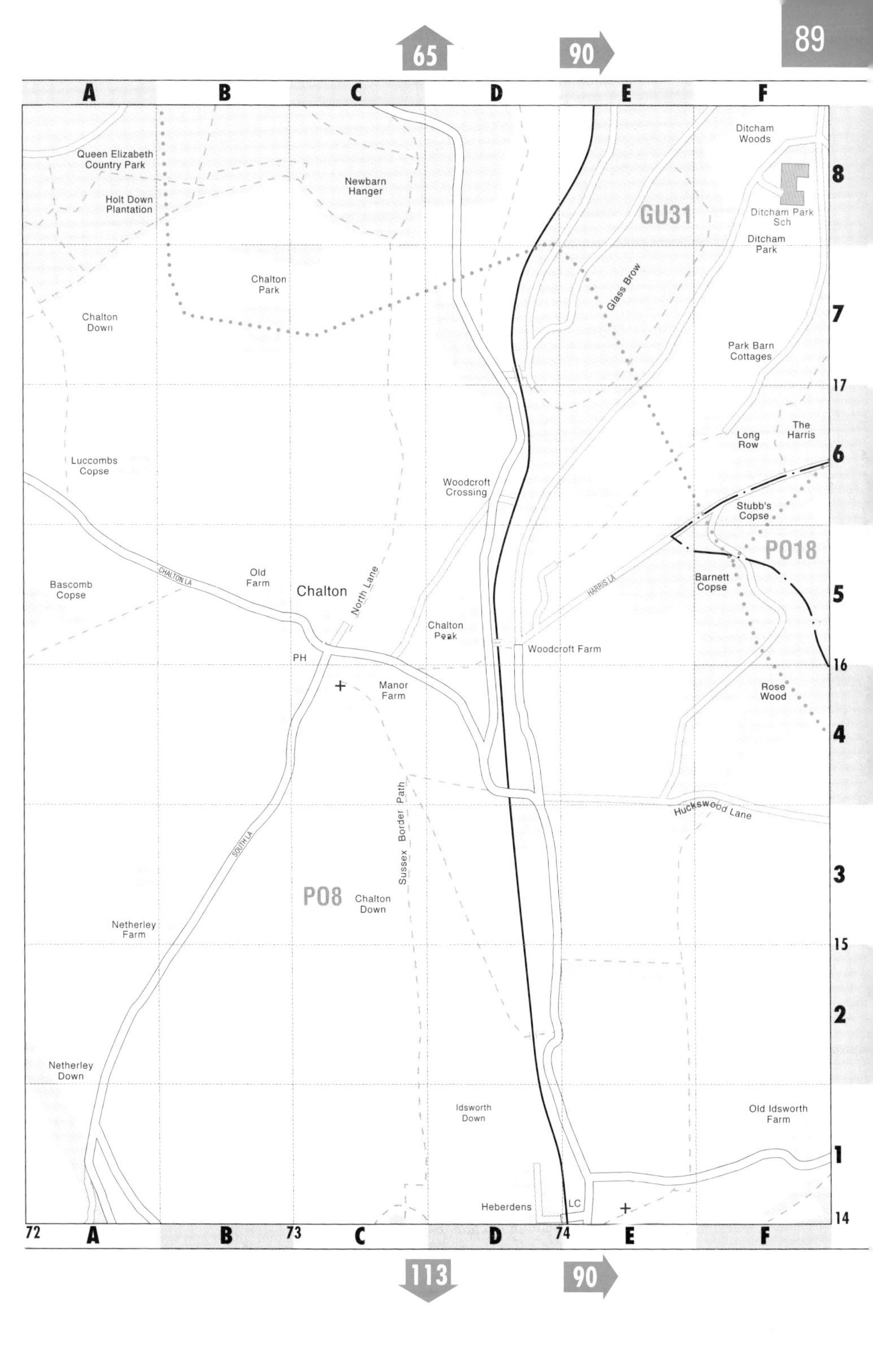

65
90
A
B
C
D
E
F
Ditcham Woods
8
Queen Elizabeth Country Park
Newbarn Hanger
Holt Down Plantation
GU31
Ditcham Park Sch
Ditcham Park
Chalton Park
Glass Brow
Chalton Down
7
Park Barn Cottages
17
Long Row
The Harris
Luccombs Copse
6
Woodcroft Crossing
Stubb's Copse
PO18
Old Farm
Bascomb Copse
CHALTON LA
Chalton
North Lane
HARRIS LA
Barnett Copse
5
Chalton Peak
Woodcroft Farm
PH
16
Manor Farm
Rose Wood
4
Hucksswood Lane
Sussex Border Path
SOUTH LA
3
PO8
Chalton Down
Netherley Farm
15
2
Netherley Down
Idsworth Down
Old Idsworth Farm
1
Heberdens
LC
14
72
73
74
113
90

89
66

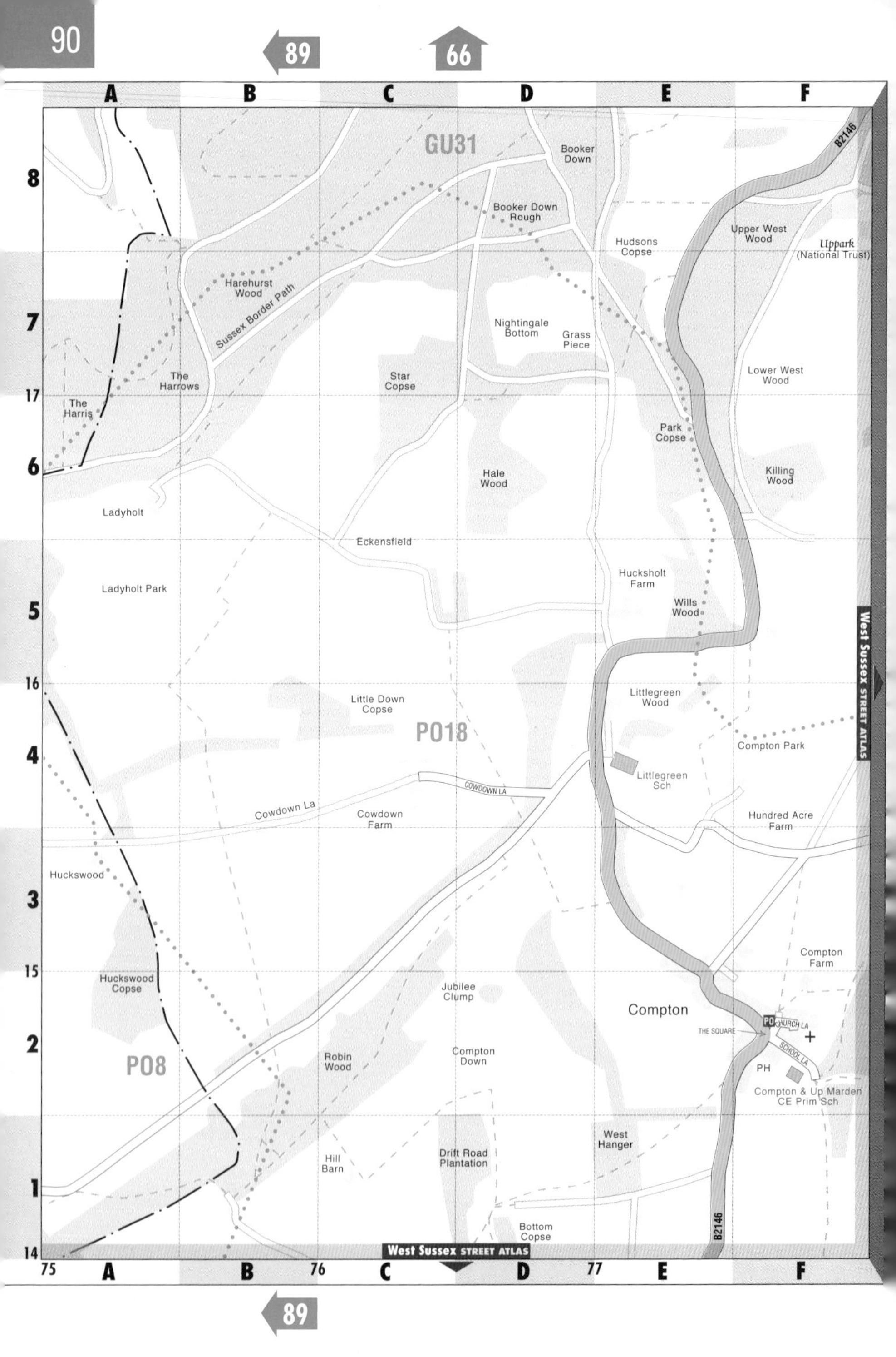
A
B
C
D
E
F
GU31
Booker Down
Booker Down Rough
B2146
Upper West Wood
Uppark (National Trust)
Hudsons Copse
Harehurst Wood
Sussex Border Path
Nightingale Bottom
Grass Piece
Lower West Wood
The Harrows
Star Copse
The Harris
Park Copse
Hale Wood
Killing Wood
Ladyholt
Eckensfield
Huckholt Farm
Ladyholt Park
Wills Wood
Littlegreen Wood
Little Down Copse
PO18
Compton Park
Littlegreen Sch
COWDOWN LA
Cowdown La
Cowdown Farm
Hundred Acre Farm
Huckswood
Compton Farm
Huckswood Copse
Jubilee Clump
Compton
PO
CHURCH LA
THE SQUARE
SCHOOL LA
Robin Wood
Compton Down
PH
PO8
Compton & Up Marden CE Prim Sch
West Hanger
Hill Barn
Drift Road Plantation
Bottom Copse
B2146
8
7
17
6
5
16
4
3
15
2
1
14
75
76
77
West Sussex STREET ATLAS

89

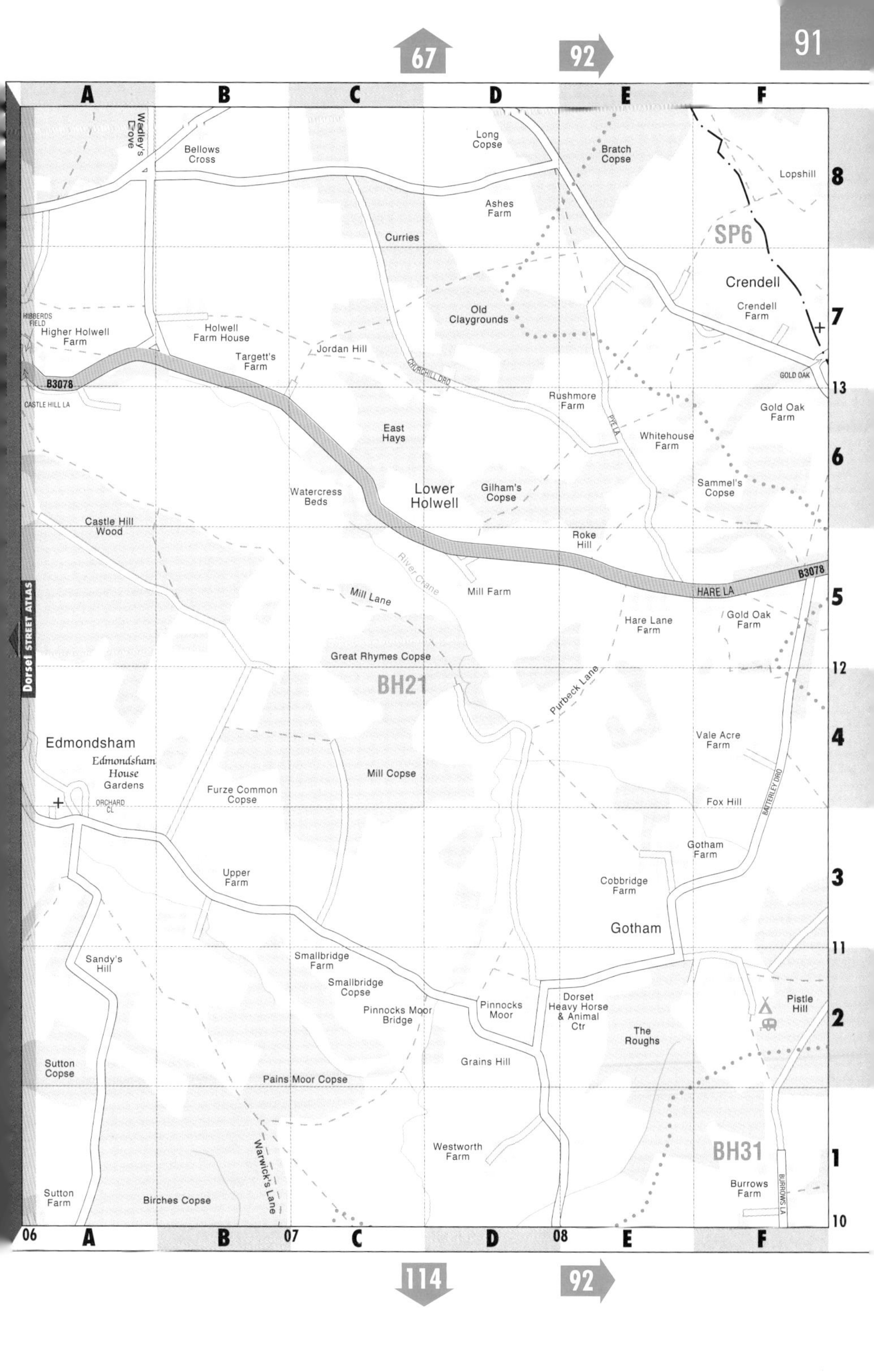
67
92
A
B
C
D
E
F
Wadley's Drove
Bellows Cross
Long Copse
Bratch Copse
Lopshill
8
Ashes Farm
Curries
SP6
Crendell
Crendell Farm
7
HIBBERDS FIELD
Higher Holwell Farm
Holwell Farm House
Old Claygrounds
Targett's Farm
Jordan Hill
CHURCHILL DRO
GOLD OAK
13
B3078
CASTLE HILL LA
Rushmore Farm
Gold Oak Farm
East Hays
PYE LA
Whitehouse Farm
6
Watercress Beds
Lower Holwell
Gilham's Copse
Sammel's Copse
Castle Hill Wood
Roke Hill
River Crane
B3078
HARE LA
Mill Farm
Mill Lane
5
Hare Lane Farm
Gold Oak Farm
Great Rhymes Copse
BH21
12
Purbeck Lane
Vale Acre Farm
4
Edmondsham
Edmondsham House Gardens
Mill Copse
Furze Common Copse
ORCHARD CL
Fox Hill
BATTERLEY DRO
Gotham Farm
Upper Farm
Cobbridge Farm
3
Gotham
11
Sandy's Hill
Smallbridge Farm
Smallbridge Copse
Pinnocks Moor Bridge
Pinnocks Moor
Dorset Heavy Horse & Animal Ctr
Pistle Hill
2
The Roughs
Sutton Copse
Grains Hill
Pains Moor Copse
Westworth Farm
BH31
1
Warwick's Lane
Burrows Farm
BURROWS LA
Sutton Farm
Birches Copse
10
06
07
08
Dorset STREET ATLAS
114
92

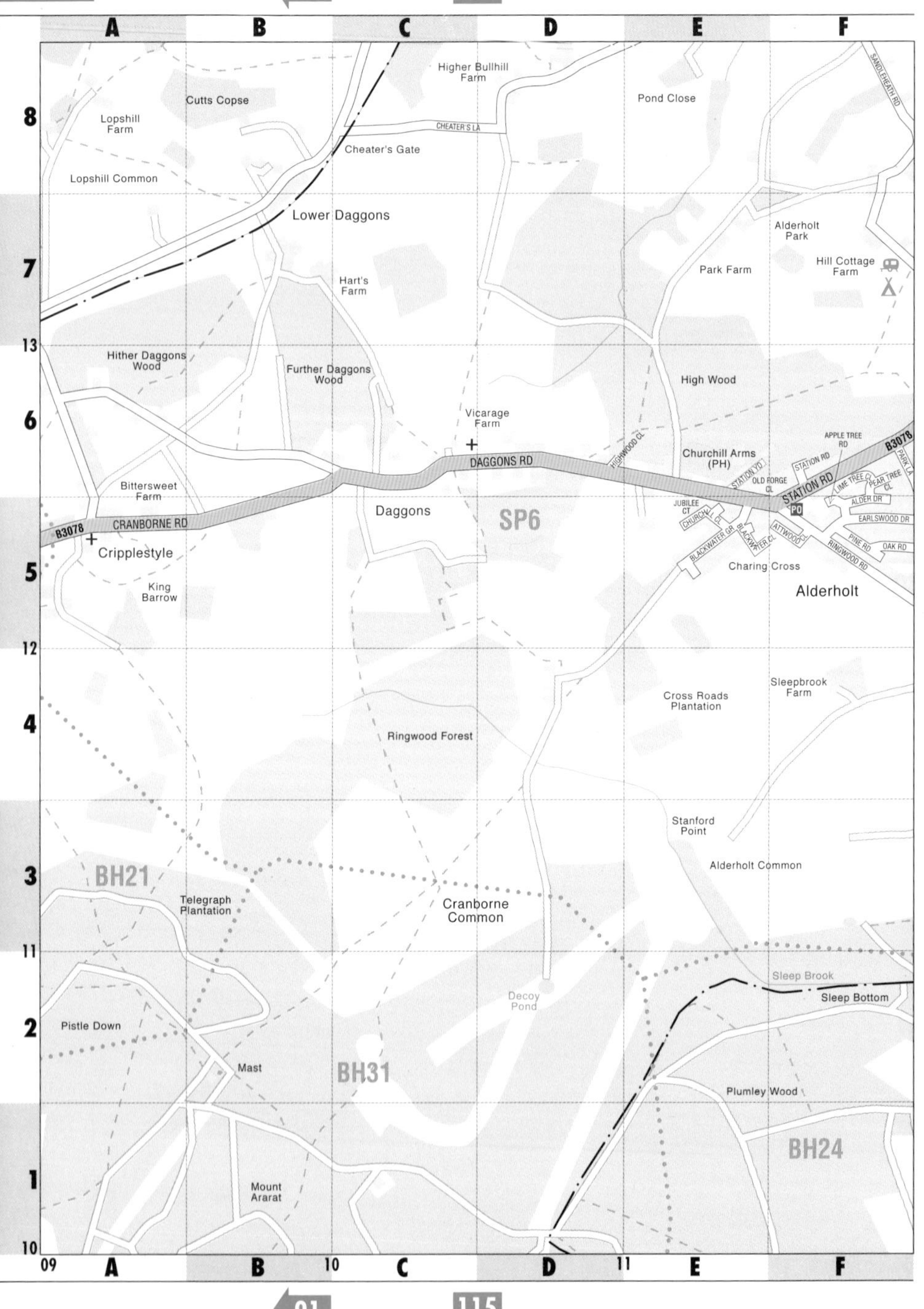

A | B | C | D | E | F

8
Lopshill Farm
Cutts Copse
Higher Bullhill Farm
Pond Close
CHEATER'S LA
Cheater's Gate
Lopshill Common
Lower Daggons
Alderholt Park
Hill Cottage Farm

7
Hart's Farm
Park Farm

13
Hither Daggons Wood
Further Daggons Wood
High Wood

6
Vicarage Farm
DAGGONS RD
PUGMOOR CL
Churchill Arms (PH)
APPLE TREE RD
STATION RD
B3078
STATION YD
STATION RD
OLD FORGE CL
Bittersweet Farm
Daggons
SP6
STATION RD
PO
LIME TREE CL
PEAR TREE CL
ALDER DR
B3078
CRANBORNE RD
JUBILEE CT
CHURCH
BLACKWATER DR
BLACK TREE CL
ATTWOOD
EARLSWOOD DR
Cripplestyle
PINE RD
OAK RD
RINGWOOD RD

5
King Barrow
Charing Cross
Alderholt

12
Cross Roads Plantation
Sleepbrook Farm

4
Ringwood Forest
Stanford Point
Alderholt Common

3
BH21
Telegraph Plantation
Cranborne Common

11
Decoy Pond
Sleep Brook
Sleep Bottom

2
Pistle Down
Mast
BH31
Plumley Wood

1
Mount Ararat
BH24

10
09
A | B | C | D | E | F
10
11

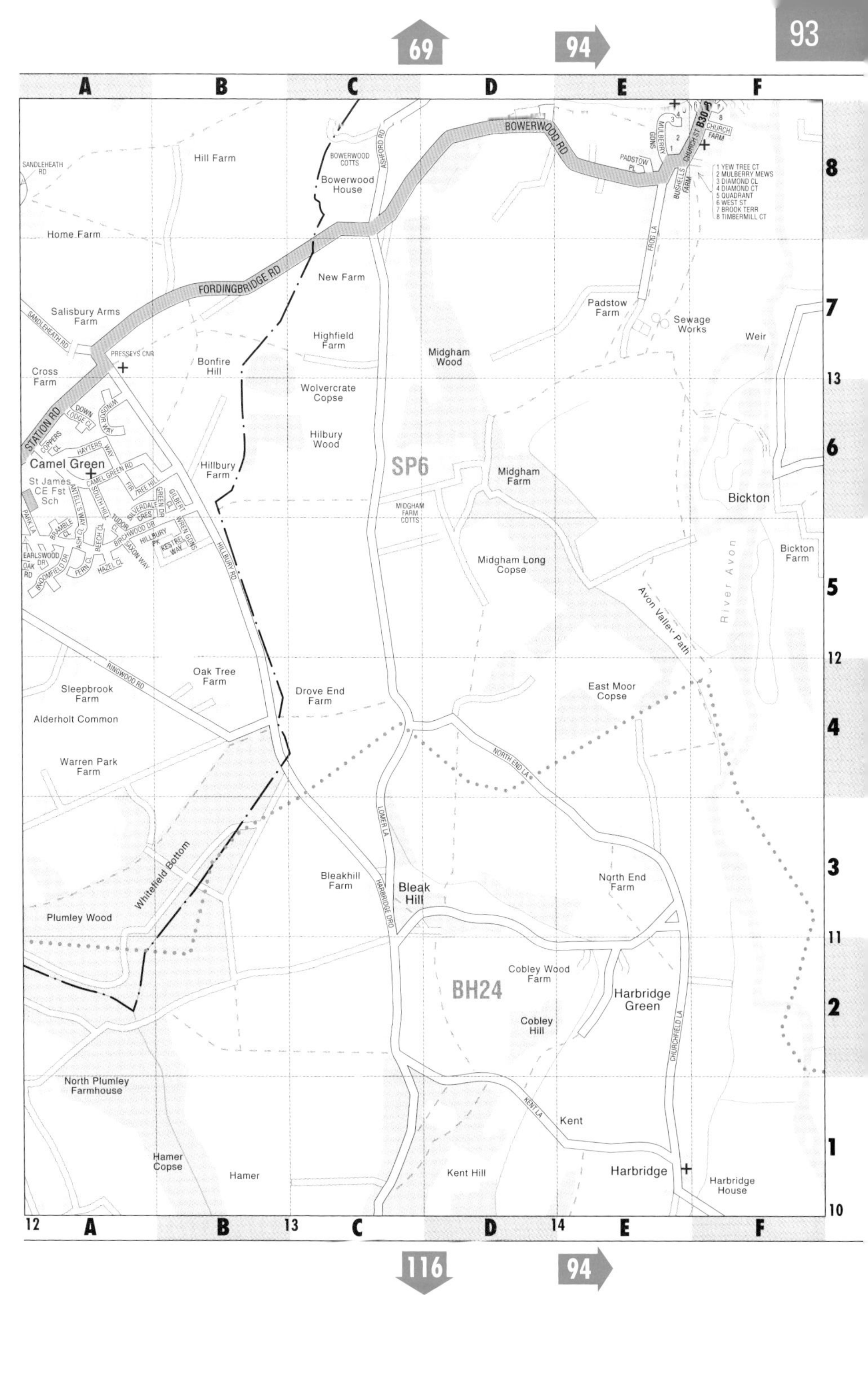
69
94
A
B
C
D
E
F
8
7
6
5
4
3
2
1
13
12
11
10
14
Hill Farm
Bowerwood House
BOWERWOOD COTTS
ASHFORD RD
BOWERWOOD RD
MULBERRY GDNS
CHURCH ST
B3078
CHURCH FARM
PADSTOW PL
BUSHELLS FARM
1 YEW TREE CT
2 MULBERRY MEWS
3 DIAMOND CL
4 DIAMOND CT
5 QUADRANT
6 WEST ST
7 BROOK TERR
8 TIMBERMILL CT
SANDLEHEATH RD
Home Farm
FORDINGBRIDGE RD
New Farm
FROG LA
Salisbury Arms Farm
Highfield Farm
Padstow Farm
Sewage Works
Weir
PRESSEYS CNR
Bonfire Hill
Midgham Wood
Cross Farm
Wolvercrate Copse
STATION RD
Hilbury Wood
Camel Green
St James CE Fst Sch
Hillbury Farm
SP6
Midgham Farm
Bickton
MIDGHAM FARM COTTS
HILLBURY RD
Midgham Long Copse
Bickton Farm
River Avon
Avon Valley Path
RINGWOOD RD
Oak Tree Farm
Sleepbrook Farm
Drove End Farm
East Moor Copse
Alderholt Common
NORTH END LA
Warren Park Farm
LOMER LA
Whitefield Bottom
Bleakhill Farm
HARBRIDGE DRO
Bleak Hill
North End Farm
Plumley Wood
Cobley Wood Farm
BH24
Harbridge Green
Cobley Hill
CHURCHFIELD LA
North Plumley Farmhouse
KENT LA
Kent
Hamer Copse
Hamer
Kent Hill
Harbridge
Harbridge House
116
94

93
70

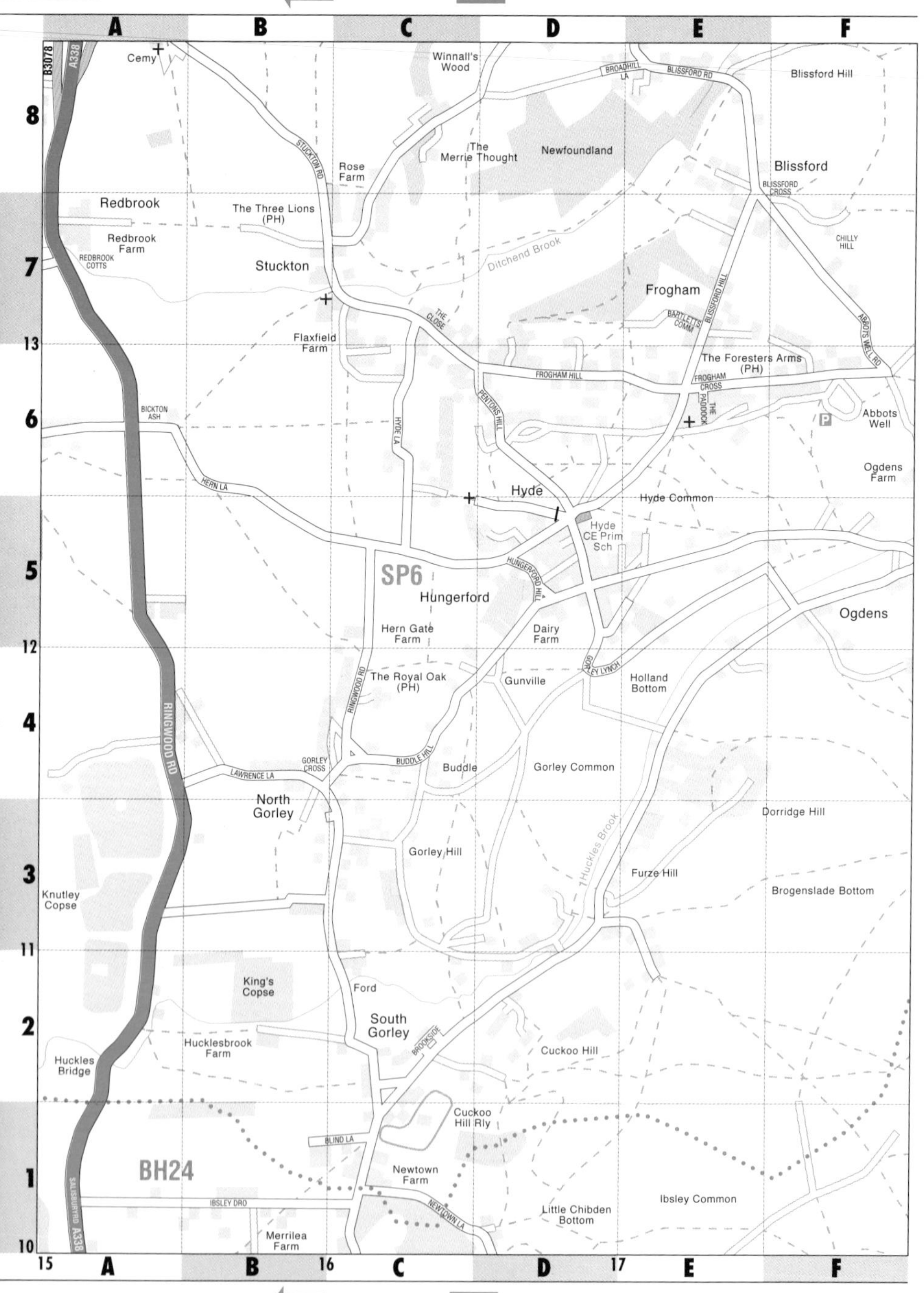
A
B
C
D
E
F
8
7
13
6
5
12
4
3
11
2
1
10
15
16
17
B3078
A338
Cemy
Winnall's Wood
BROADHILL LA
BLISSFORD RD
Blissford Hill
STUCKTON RD
Rose Farm
The Merrie Thought
Newfoundland
Blissford
BLISSFORD CROSS
Redbrook
The Three Lions (PH)
Redbrook Farm
REDBROOK COTTS
Stuckton
Ditchend Brook
CHILLY HILL
Frogham
BLISSFORD HILL
BARTLETTS COMM
THE CLOSE
Flaxfield Farm
ABBOTS WELL RD
The Foresters Arms (PH)
FROGHAM HILL
FROGHAM CROSS
THE PADDOCK
BICKTON ASH
HYDE LA
PENTONS HILL
Abbots Well
Ogdens Farm
HERN LA
Hyde
Hyde Common
Hyde CE Prim Sch
SP6
HUNGERFORD HILL
Hungerford
Ogdens
Hern Gate Farm
Dairy Farm
GORLEY LYNCH
RINGWOOD RD
The Royal Oak (PH)
Gunville
Holland Bottom
RINGWOOD RD
BUDDLE HILL
GORLEY CROSS
LAWRENCE LA
Buddle
Gorley Common
North Gorley
Dorridge Hill
Huckles Brook
Gorley Hill
Furze Hill
Knutley Copse
Brogenslade Bottom
King's Copse
Ford
South Gorley
BROOKSIDE
Hucklesbrook Farm
Cuckoo Hill
Huckles Bridge
Cuckoo Hill Rly
BLIND LA
BH24
Newtown Farm
SALISBURY RD
NEWTOWN LA
IBSLEY DRO
Ibsley Common
Little Chibden Bottom
Merrilea Farm

93
117

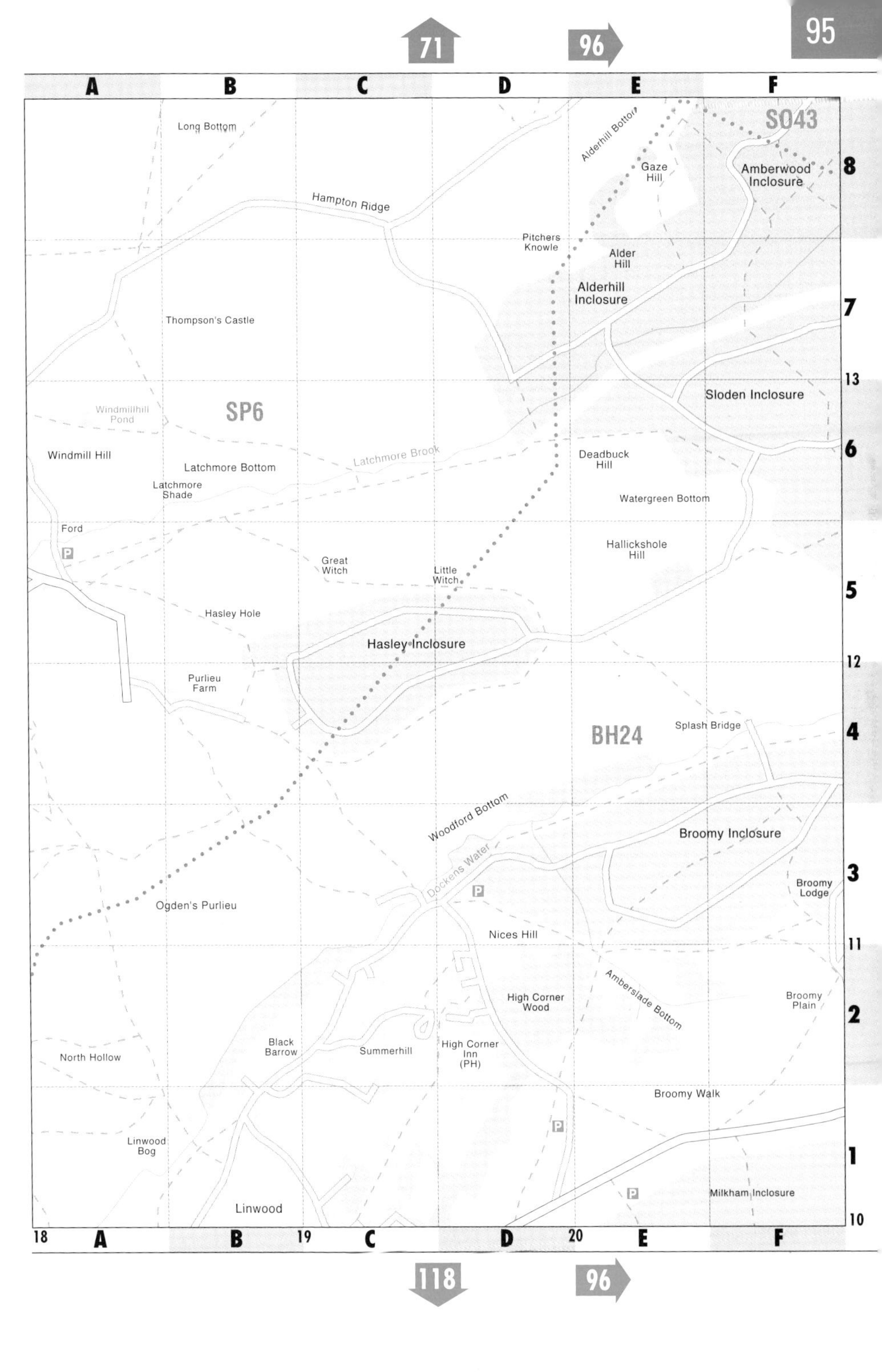
71
96
A
B
C
D
E
F
Long Bottom
Alderhill Bottom
SO43
Gaze Hill
Amberwood Inclosure
8
Hampton Ridge
Pitchers Knowle
Alder Hill
Alderhill Inclosure
7
Thompson's Castle
13
Sloden Inclosure
Windmillhill Pond
SP6
Windmill Hill
Latchmore Brook
Deadbuck Hill
6
Latchmore Bottom
Latchmore Shade
Watergreen Bottom
Ford
Hallickshole Hill
Great Witch
Little Witch
5
Hasley Hole
Hasley Inclosure
12
Purlieu Farm
BH24
Splash Bridge
4
Woodford Bottom
Broomy Inclosure
Dockens Water
3
Broomy Lodge
Ogden's Purlieu
Nices Hill
11
Amberslade Bottom
High Corner Wood
Broomy Plain
2
Black Barrow
Summerhill
High Corner Inn (PH)
North Hollow
Broomy Walk
Linwood Bog
1
Milkham Inclosure
Linwood
10
18
19
20
118
96

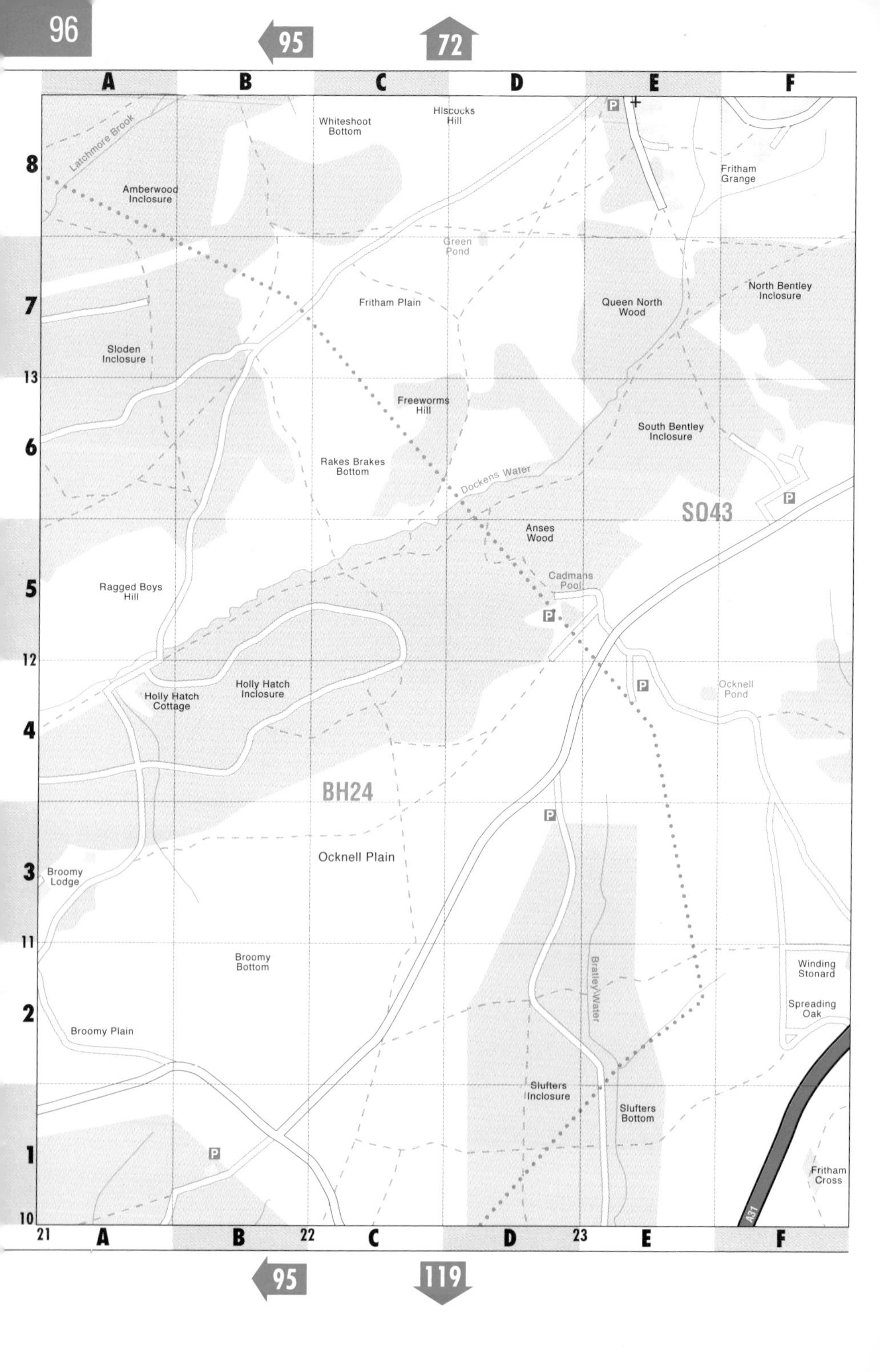
95
72
A
B
C
D
E
F
Latchmore Brook
Whiteshoot
Bottom
Hiscocks
Hill
Fritham
Grange
8
Amberwood
Inclosure
Green
Pond
7
Fritham Plain
Queen North
Wood
North Bentley
Inclosure
Sloden
Inclosure
13
Freeworms
Hill
6
South Bentley
Inclosure
Rakes Brakes
Bottom
Dockens Water
SO43
Anses
Wood
5
Ragged Boys
Hill
Cadmans
Pool
12
Holly Hatch
Inclosure
Holly Hatch
Cottage
Ocknell
Pond
4
BH24
Ocknell Plain
3
Broomy
Lodge
11
Broomy
Bottom
Bratley Water
Winding
Stonard
2
Spreading
Oak
Broomy Plain
Slufters
Inclosure
Slufters
Bottom
1
Fritham
Cross
A31
10
21
A
B
22
C
D
23
E
F
95
119

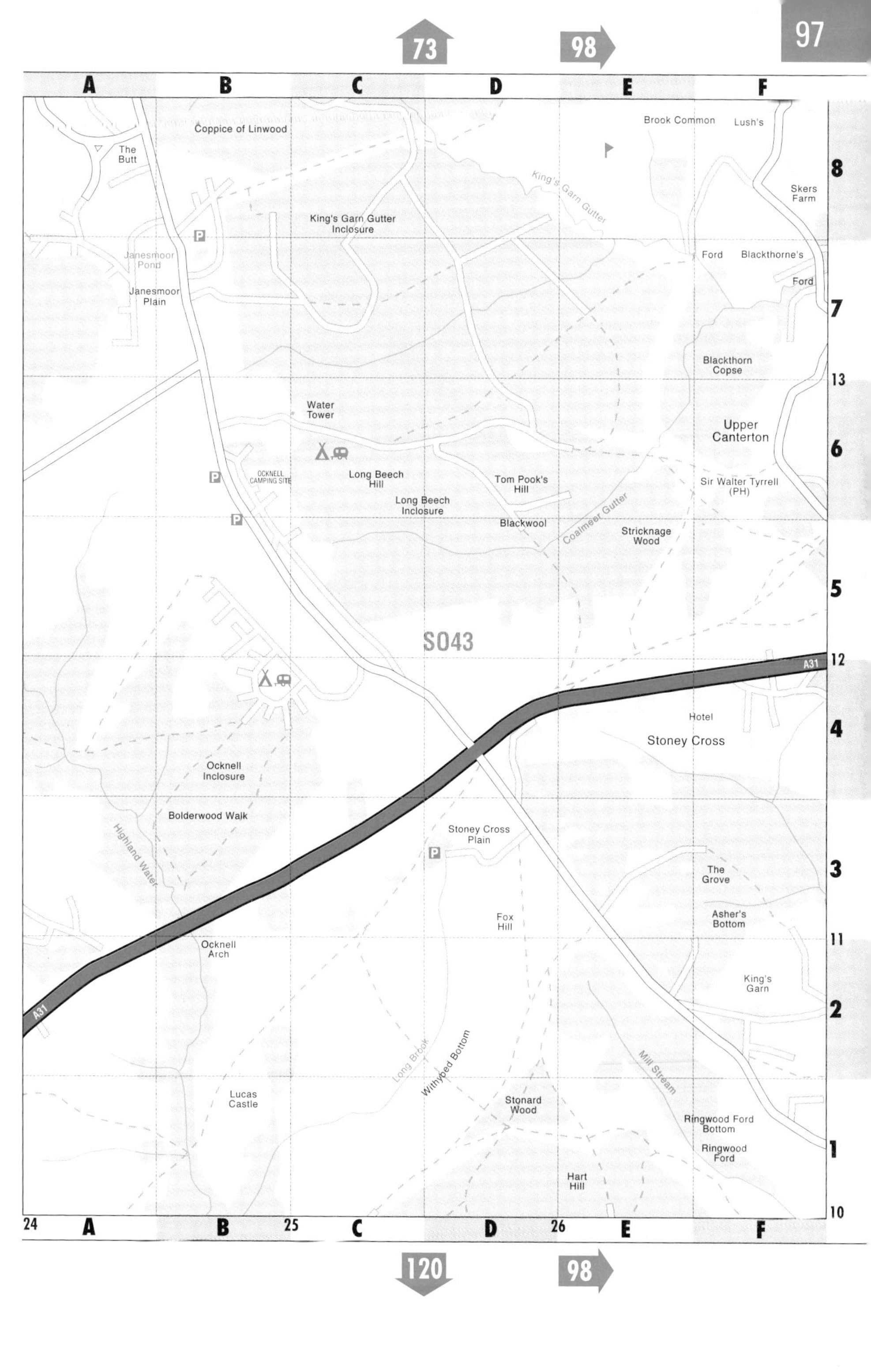

A   B   C   D   E   F

8

Coppice of Linwood

Brook Common   Lush's

The
Butt

Skers
Farm

King's Garn Gutter

King's Garn Gutter
Inclosure

Ford   Blackthorne's

Janesmoor
Pond

Ford

7

Janesmoor
Plain

13

Water
Tower

Blackthorn
Copse

Upper
Canterton

6

OCKNELL
CAMPING SITE

Long Beech
Hill

Tom Pook's
Hill

Sir Walter Tyrrell
(PH)

Long Beech
Inclosure

Blackwool

Coalmeer Gutter

Stricknage
Wood

5

SO43

12

A31

Hotel

4

Stoney Cross

Ocknell
Inclosure

Bolderwood Walk

Stoney Cross
Plain

The
Grove

3

Highland Water

Asher's
Bottom

11

Ocknell
Arch

Fox
Hill

King's
Garn

2

Long Brook

Withybed Bottom

Mill Stream

Lucas
Castle

Stonard
Wood

Ringwood Ford
Bottom

Ringwood
Ford

1

A31

Hart
Hill

10

97
74

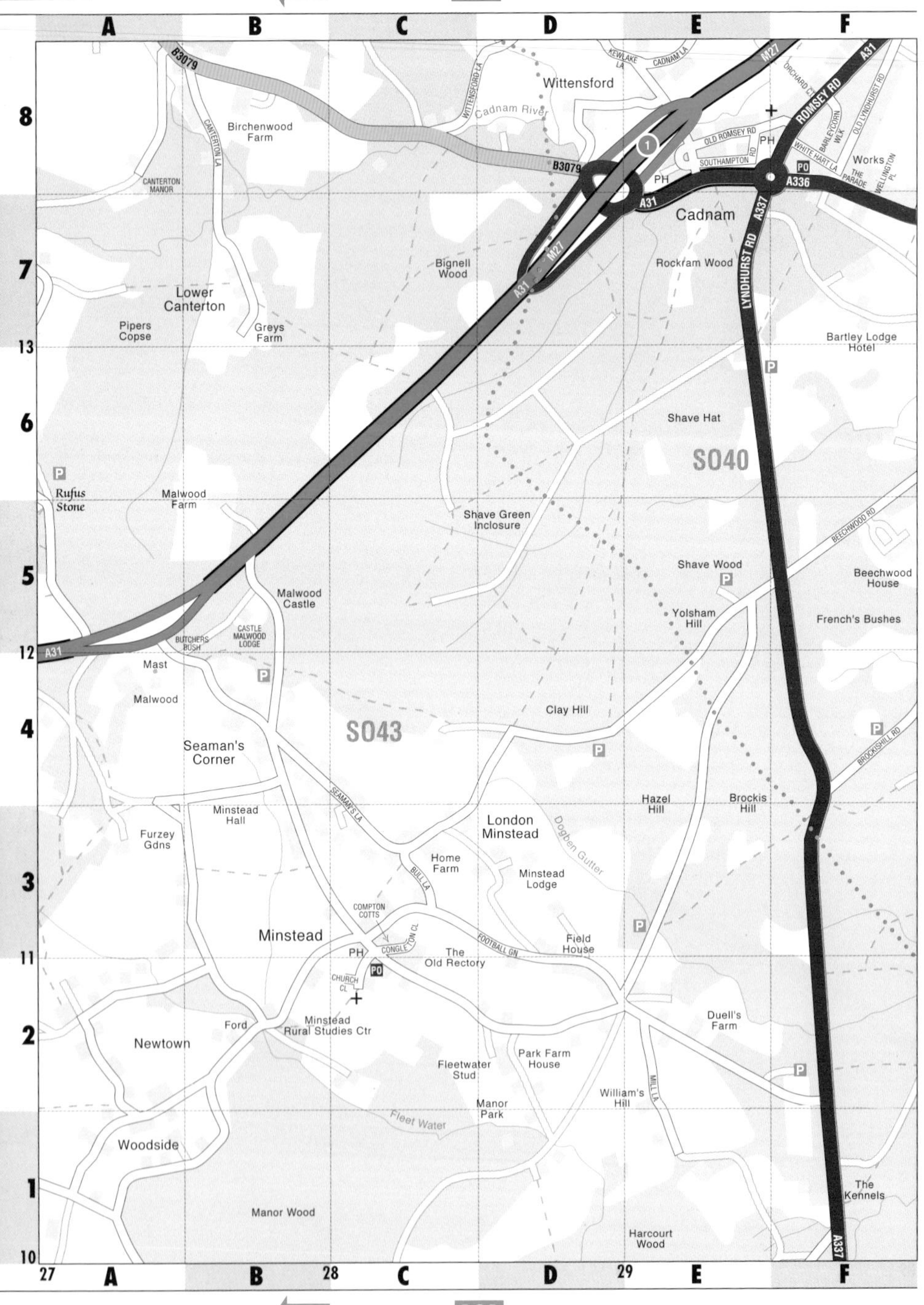
A
B
C
D
E
F
8
7
13
6
5
12
4
3
11
2
1
10
27
28
29
B3079
M27
A31
A336
A337
ROMSEY RD
LYNDHURST RD
Wittensford
Cadnam River
Birchenwood Farm
CANTERTON LA
CANTERTON MANOR
WITTENSFORD LA
KEWLAKE LA
CADNAM LA
ORCHARD CL
OLD LYNDHURST RD
BARLEYCORN WLK
WHITE HART LA
OLD ROMSEY RD
SOUTHAMPTON RD
PH
PO
Works
THE PARADE
WELLINGTON PL
Cadnam
Rockram Wood
Bignell Wood
Lower Canterton
Pipers Copse
Greys Farm
Bartley Lodge Hotel
Shave Hat
SO40
Rufus Stone
Malwood Farm
Shave Green Inclosure
BEECHWOOD RD
Shave Wood
Beechwood House
Malwood Castle
Yolsham Hill
French's Bushes
BUTCHERS BUSH
CASTLE MALWOOD LODGE
Mast
Malwood
Clay Hill
SO43
Seaman's Corner
BROCKISHILL RD
SEAMAN'S LA
Minstead Hall
Hazel Hill
Brockis Hill
Furzey Gdns
London Minstead
Dogben Gutter
Home Farm
BULL LA
Minstead Lodge
COMPTON COTTS
Minstead
CONGLETON CL
FOOTBALL GN
Field House
The Old Rectory
CHURCH CL
Duell's Farm
Ford
Newtown
Minstead Rural Studies Ctr
Park Farm House
Fleetwater Stud
William's Hill
MILL LA
Manor Park
Fleet Water
Woodside
The Kennels
Manor Wood
Harcourt Wood

97
121

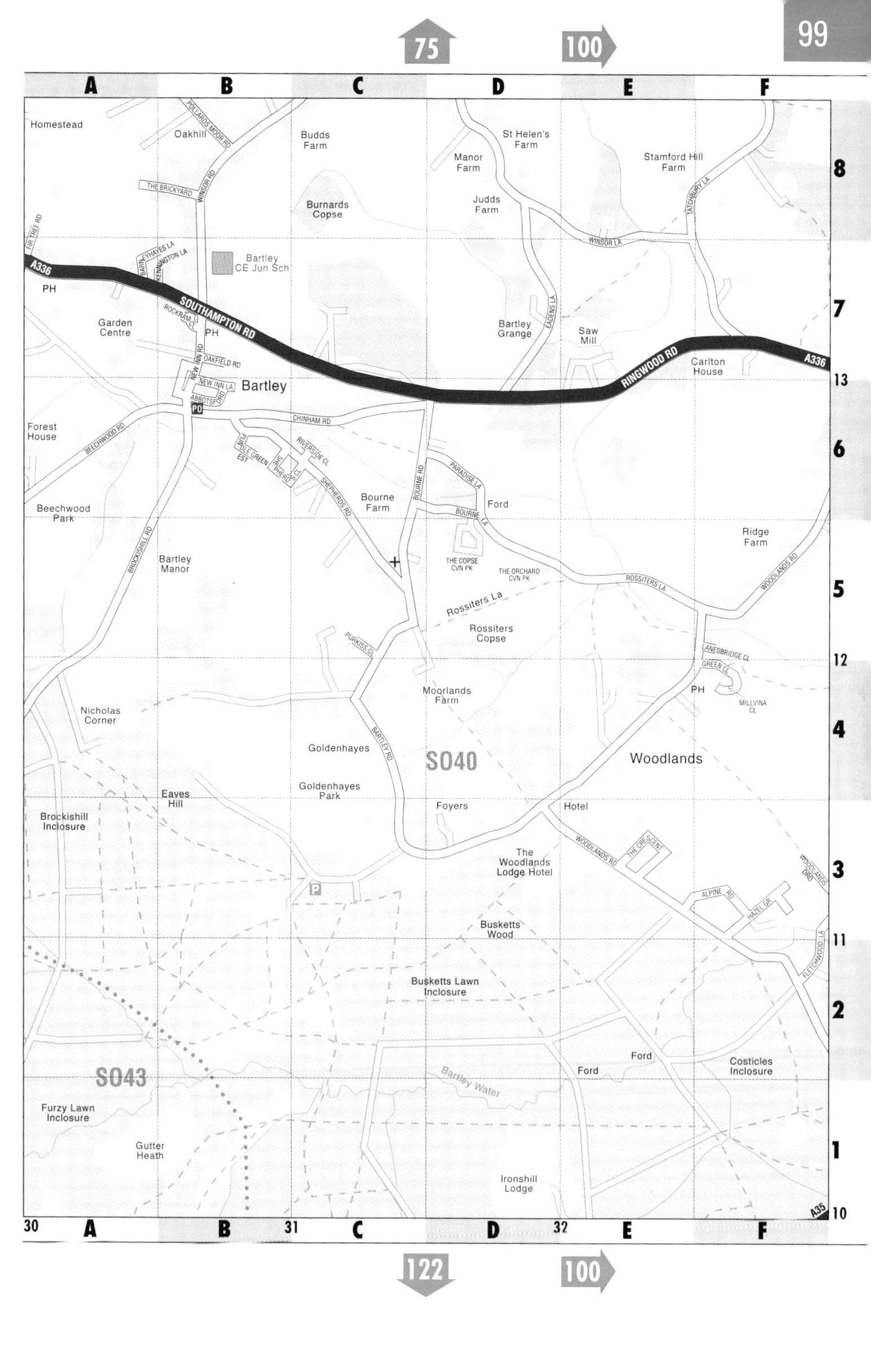
75
100
A
B
C
D
E
F
Homestead
Oakhill
POLLARDS MOOR RD
Budds Farm
Manor Farm
St Helen's Farm
Stamford Hill Farm
THE BRICKYARD
WINSOR RD
Burnards Copse
Judds Farm
TATCHBURY LA
FIR TREE RD
Bartley CE Jun Sch
WINSOR LA
A336
PH
SOUTHAMPTON RD
ROCKRAM CL
Garden Centre
PH
EADENS LA
Bartley Grange
Saw Mill
NEW INN RD
OAKFIELD RD
RINGWOOD RD
Carlton House
A336
NEW INN LA
Bartley
ABBOTSFORD
PO
CHINHAM RD
Forest House
BEECHWOOD RD
RIVERSIDE CL
PINDLE GREEN EST
PARADISE LA
BOURNE RD
SHEPHERDS RD
Bourne Farm
Ford
Beechwood Park
BOURNE LA
Ridge Farm
BROCKISHILL RD
Bartley Manor
THE COPSE CVN PK
THE ORCHARD CVN PK
ROSSITERS LA
WOODLANDS RD
Rossiters La
Rossiters Copse
PURKISS CL
LANESBRIDGE CL
GREEN CL
PH
Moorlands Farm
MILLVINA CL
Nicholas Corner
BARTLEY RD
Goldenhayes
SO40
Woodlands
Eaves Hill
Goldenhayes Park
Brockishill Inclosure
Foyers
Hotel
The Woodlands Lodge Hotel
WOODLANDS RD
THE CRESCENT
WOODLANDS DRO
P
ALPINE RD
HAZEL GR
Busketts Wood
FLETCHWOOD LA
Busketts Lawn Inclosure
Ford
Costicles Inclosure
Ford
SO43
Bartley Water
Furzy Lawn Inclosure
Gutter Heath
Ironshill Lodge
A35
8
7
13
6
5
12
4
3
11
2
1
10
30
31
32
122
100

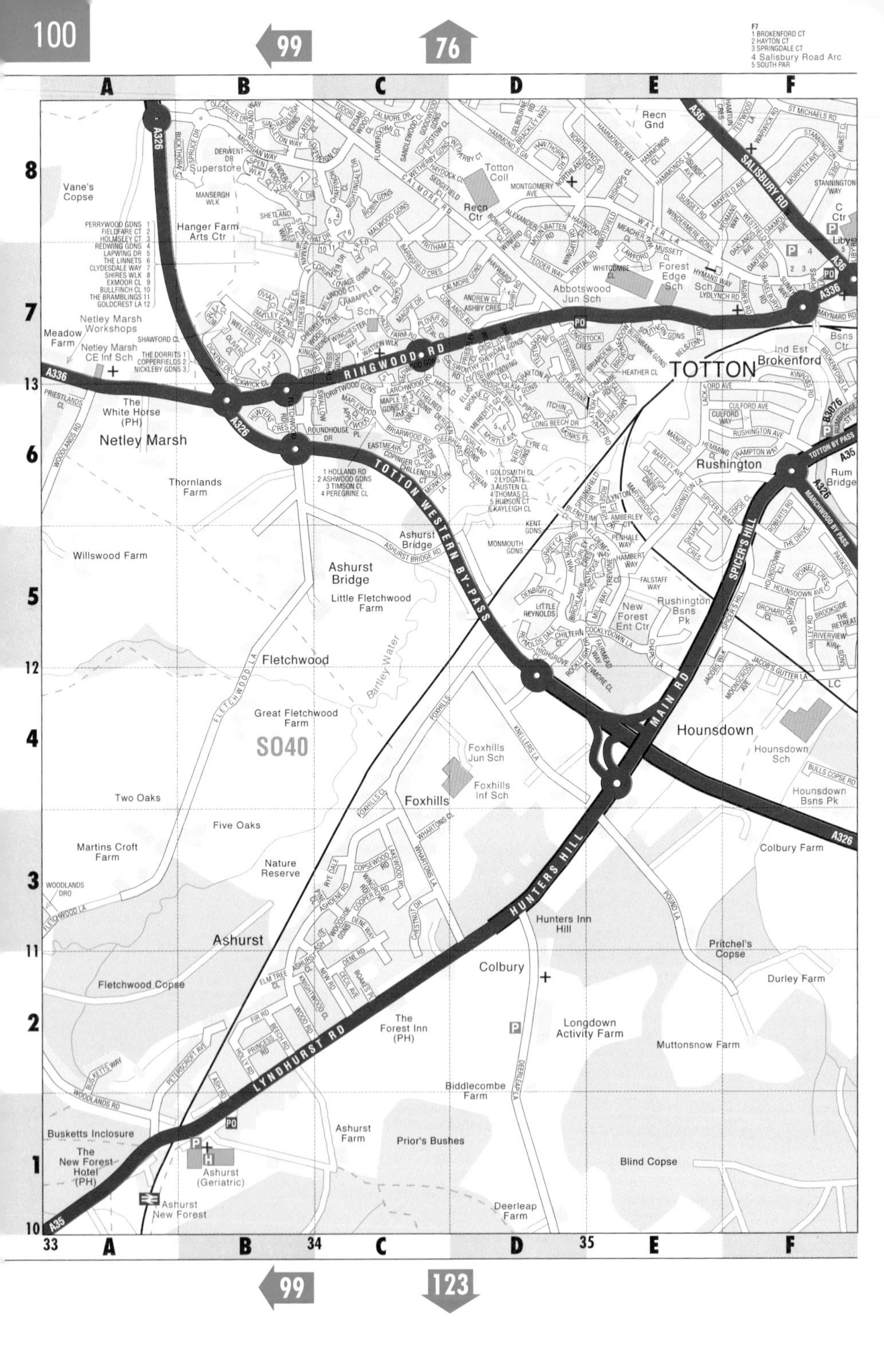

99
76
F7
1 BROKENFORD CT
2 HAYTON CT
3 SPRINGDALE CT
4 Salisbury Road Arc
5 SOUTH PAR
TOTTON
Netley Marsh
Rushington
Hounsdown
Fletchwood
Ashurst
Colbury
Foxhills
S040
Ashurst Bridge
Vane's Copse
Hanger Farm Arts Ctr
Superstore
Totton Coll
Recn Ctr
Recn Gnd
Abbotswood Jun Sch
Forest Edge Sch
Netley Marsh Workshops
Meadow Farm
Netley Marsh CE Inf Sch
The White Horse (PH)
Thornlands Farm
Willswood Farm
Little Fletchwood Farm
Great Fletchwood Farm
Two Oaks
Five Oaks
Martins Croft Farm
Nature Reserve
Fletchwood Copse
Foxhills Jun Sch
Foxhills Inf Sch
New Forest Ent Ctr
Rushington Bsns Pk
Hounsdown Sch
Hounsdown Bsns Pk
Colbury Farm
Hunters Inn Hill
Pritchel's Copse
Durley Farm
The Forest Inn (PH)
Longdown Activity Farm
Muttonsnow Farm
Biddlecombe Farm
Ashurst Farm
Prior's Bushes
Blind Copse
Deerleap Farm
Busketts Inclosure
The New Forest Hotel (PH)
Ashurst (Geriatric)
Ashurst New Forest
Brokenford
Ind Est
Bsns Ctr
Rum Bridge
RINGWOOD RD
TOTTON WESTERN BY-PASS
LYNDHURST RD
HUNTERS HILL
MAIN RD
SPICER'S HILL
SALISBURY RD
A326
A336
A36
A35
B3076
1 HOLLAND RD
2 ASHWOOD GDNS
3 TIMSON CL
4 PEREGRINE CL
1 GOLDSMITH CL
2 LYDGATE
3 AUSTEN CL
4 THOMAS CL
5 HUDSON CT
6 KAYLEIGH CL
1 PERRYWOOD GDNS
2 FIELDFARE CT
3 HOLMSLEY CT
4 REDWING GDNS
5 LAPWING DR
6 THE LINNETS
7 CLYDESDALE WAY
8 SHIRES WLK
9 EXMOOR CL
10 BULLFINCH CL
11 THE BRAMBLINGS
12 GOLDCREST LA
1 THE DORRITS
2 COPPERFIELDS
3 NICKLEBY GDNS
A B C D E F
8 7 6 5 4 3 2 1
13 12 11 10
33 34 35
99
123

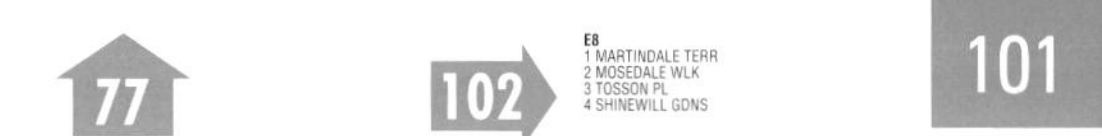

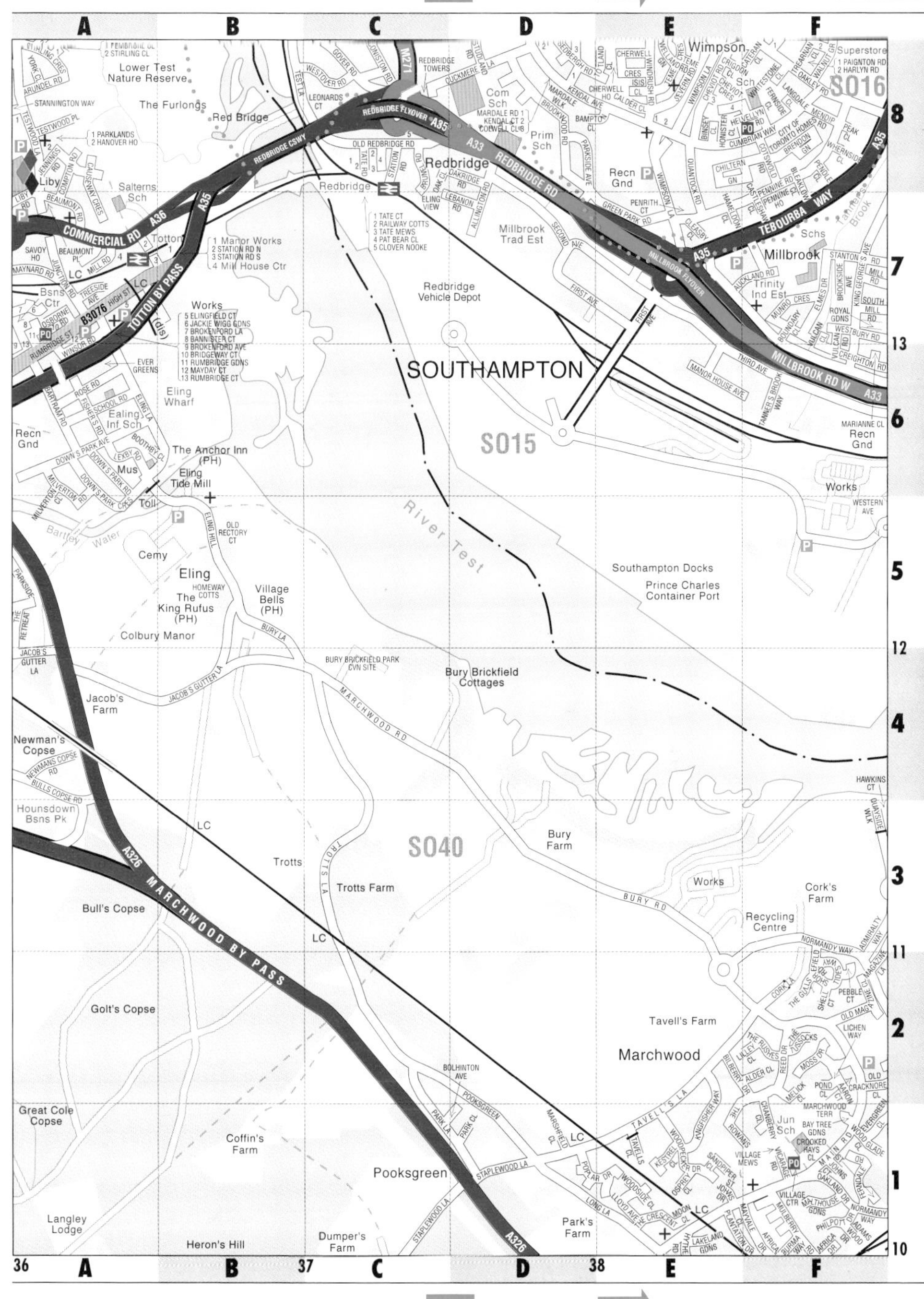

SOUTHAMPTON

SO15

SO16

SO40

Wimpson

Redbridge

Millbrook

Marchwood

Eling

Pooksgreen

River Test

Southampton Docks
Prince Charles
Container Port

77
102
124
102

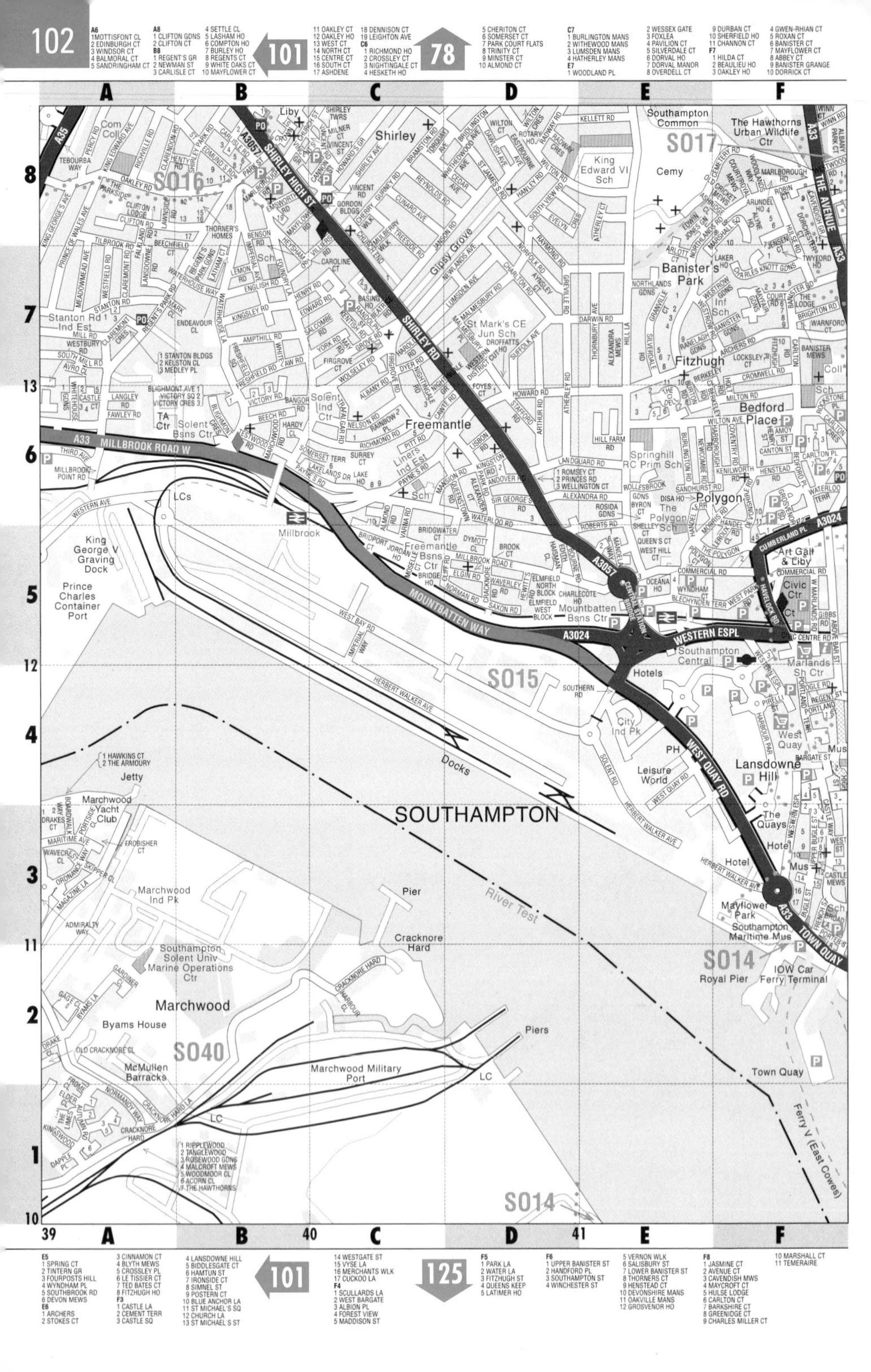

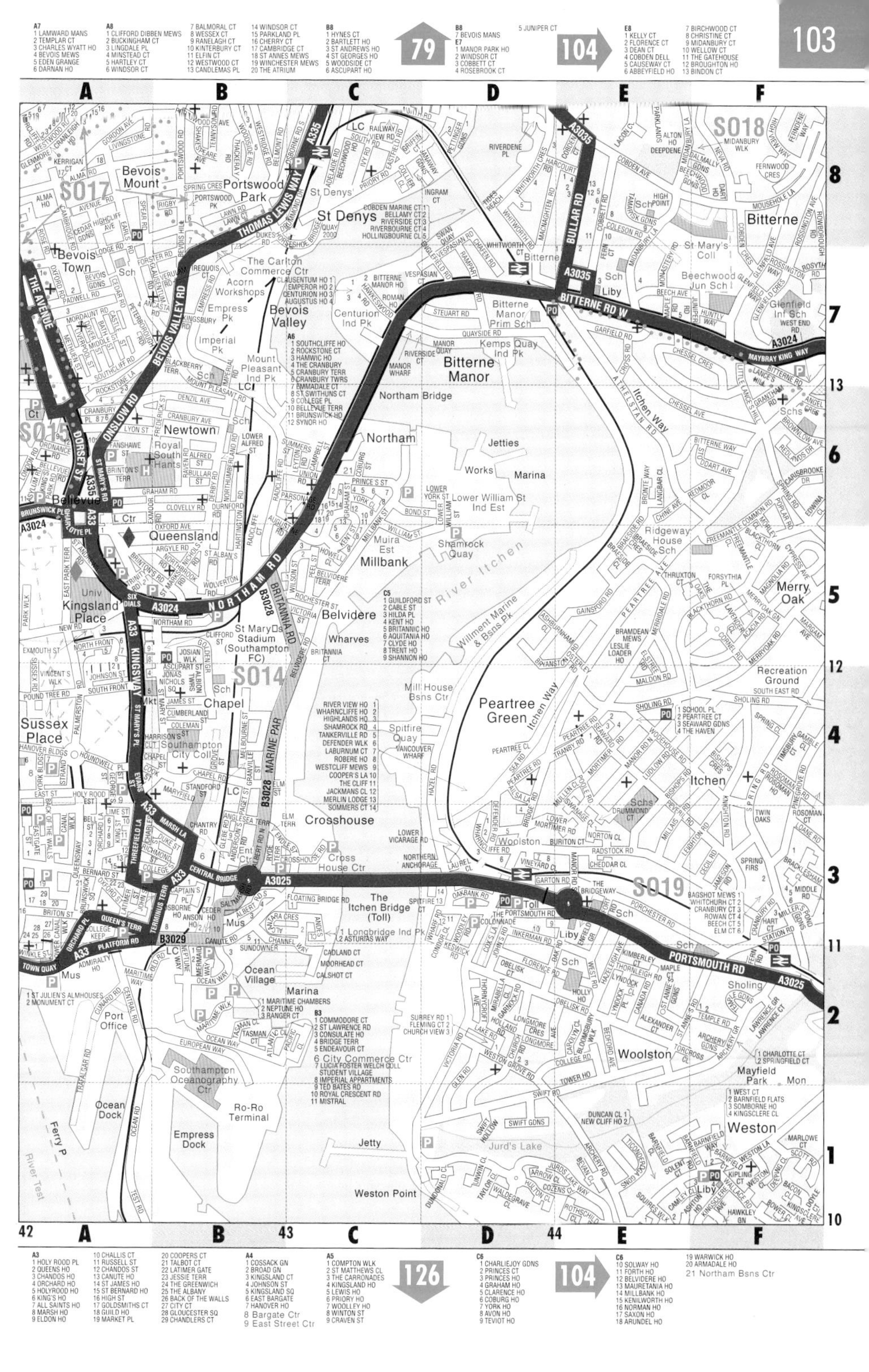
A7
1 LAMWARD MANS
2 TEMPLAR CT
3 CHARLES WYATT HO
4 BEVOIS MEWS
5 EDEN GRANGE
6 DARNAN HO
A8
1 CLIFFORD DIBBEN MEWS
2 BUCKINGHAM CT
3 LINGDALE PL
4 MINSTEAD CT
5 HARTLEY CT
6 WINDSOR CT
7 BALMORAL CT
8 WESSEX CT
9 RANELAGH CT
10 KINTERBURY CT
11 ELFIN CT
12 WESTWOOD CT
13 CANDLEMAS PL
14 WINDSOR CT
15 PARKLAND PL
16 CHERRY CT
17 CAMBRIDGE CT
18 ST ANNES MEWS
19 WINCHESTER MEWS
20 THE ATRIUM
B8
1 HYNES CT
2 BARTLETT HO
3 ST ANDREWS HO
4 ST GEORGES HO
5 WOODSIDE CT
6 ASCUPART HO
79
B8
7 BEVOIS MANS
E7
1 MANOR PARK HO
2 WINDSOR CT
3 COBBETT CT
4 ROSEBROOK CT
5 JUNIPER CT
104
E8
1 KELLY CT
2 FLORENCE CT
3 DEAN CT
4 COBDEN DELL
5 CAUSEWAY CT
6 ABBEYFIELD HO
7 BIRCHWOOD CT
8 CHRISTINE CT
9 MIDANBURY CT
10 WELLOW CT
11 THE GATEHOUSE
12 BROUGHTON HO
13 BINDON CT
A B C D E F
8 7 13 6 5 12 4 3 11 2 1 10
42 43 44
Bevois Mount
SO17
Portswood Park
St Denys
Bevois Town
The Carlton Commerce Ctr
Acorn Workshops
Empress Pk
Imperial Pk
Bevois Valley
Centurion Ind Pk
Mount Pleasant Ind Pk
Bitterne Manor
Kemps Quay Ind Pk
Bitterne Manor Prim Sch
Bitterne
SO18
St Mary's Coll
Beechwood Jun Sch
Glenfield Inf Sch
Northam Bridge
Northam
Jetties
Works
Marina
Lower William St Ind Est
Newtown
Royal South Hants
Bellevue
Queensland
SO15
Muira Est
Millbank
Shamrock Quay
River Itchen
Itchen Way
Ridgeway House Sch
Merry Oak
Kingsland Place
Univ
St Mary's Stadium (Southampton FC)
Belvidere
Wharves
Willment Marine & Bsns Pk
SO14
Chapel
Mill House Bsns Ctr
Recreation Ground
Sussex Place
Southampton City Coll
Spitfire Quay
Vancouver Wharf
Peartree Green
Itchen
Crosshouse
Cross House Ctr
Woolston
SO19
The Itchen Bridge (Toll)
Ocean Village
Marina
Port Office
Sholing
Southampton Oceanography Ctr
Woolston
Mayfield Park
Ocean Dock
Ro-Ro Terminal
Empress Dock
Jetty
Jurd's Lake
Weston
Weston Point
River Test
THOMAS LEWIS WAY
BEVOIS VALLEY RD
BITTERNE RD W
BULLAR RD
NORTHAM RD
BRITANNIA RD
MARINE PAR
KINGSWAY
DORSET ST
THE AVENUE
ONSLOW RD
CENTRAL BRIDGE
PORTSMOUTH RD
MAYBRAY KING WAY
PLATFORM RD
TOWN QUAY
A3
1 HOLY ROOD PL
2 QUEENS HO
3 CHANDOS HO
4 ORCHARD HO
5 HOLYROOD HO
6 KING'S HO
7 ALL SAINTS HO
8 MARSH HO
9 ELDON HO
10 CHALLIS CT
11 RUSSELL ST
12 CHANDOS ST
13 CANUTE HO
14 ST JAMES HO
15 ST BERNARD HO
16 HIGH ST
17 GOLDSMITHS CT
18 GUILD HO
19 MARKET PL
20 COOPERS CT
21 TALBOT CT
22 LATIMER GATE
23 JESSIE TERR
24 THE GREENWICH
25 THE ALBANY
26 BACK OF THE WALLS
27 CITY CT
28 GLOUCESTER SQ
29 CHANDLERS CT
A4
1 COSSACK GN
2 BROAD GN
3 KINGSLAND CT
4 JOHNSON ST
5 KINGSLAND SQ
6 EAST BARGATE
7 HANOVER BLDGS
8 Bargate Ctr
9 East Street Ctr
A5
1 COMPTON WLK
2 ST MATTHEWS CL
3 THE CARRONADES
4 KINGSLAND HO
5 LEWIS HO
6 PRIORY HO
7 WOOLLEY HO
8 WINTON ST
9 CRAVEN ST
126
C6
1 CHARLIEJOY GDNS
2 PRINCES CT
3 PRINCES HO
4 GRAHAM HO
5 CLARENCE HO
6 COBURG HO
7 YORK HO
8 AVON HO
9 TEVIOT HO
104
C6
10 SOLWAY HO
11 FORTH HO
12 BELVIDERE HO
13 MAURETANIA HO
14 MILLBANK HO
15 KENILWORTH HO
16 NORMAN HO
17 SAXON HO
18 ARUNDEL HO
19 WARWICK HO
20 ARMADALE HO
21 Northam Bsns Ctr

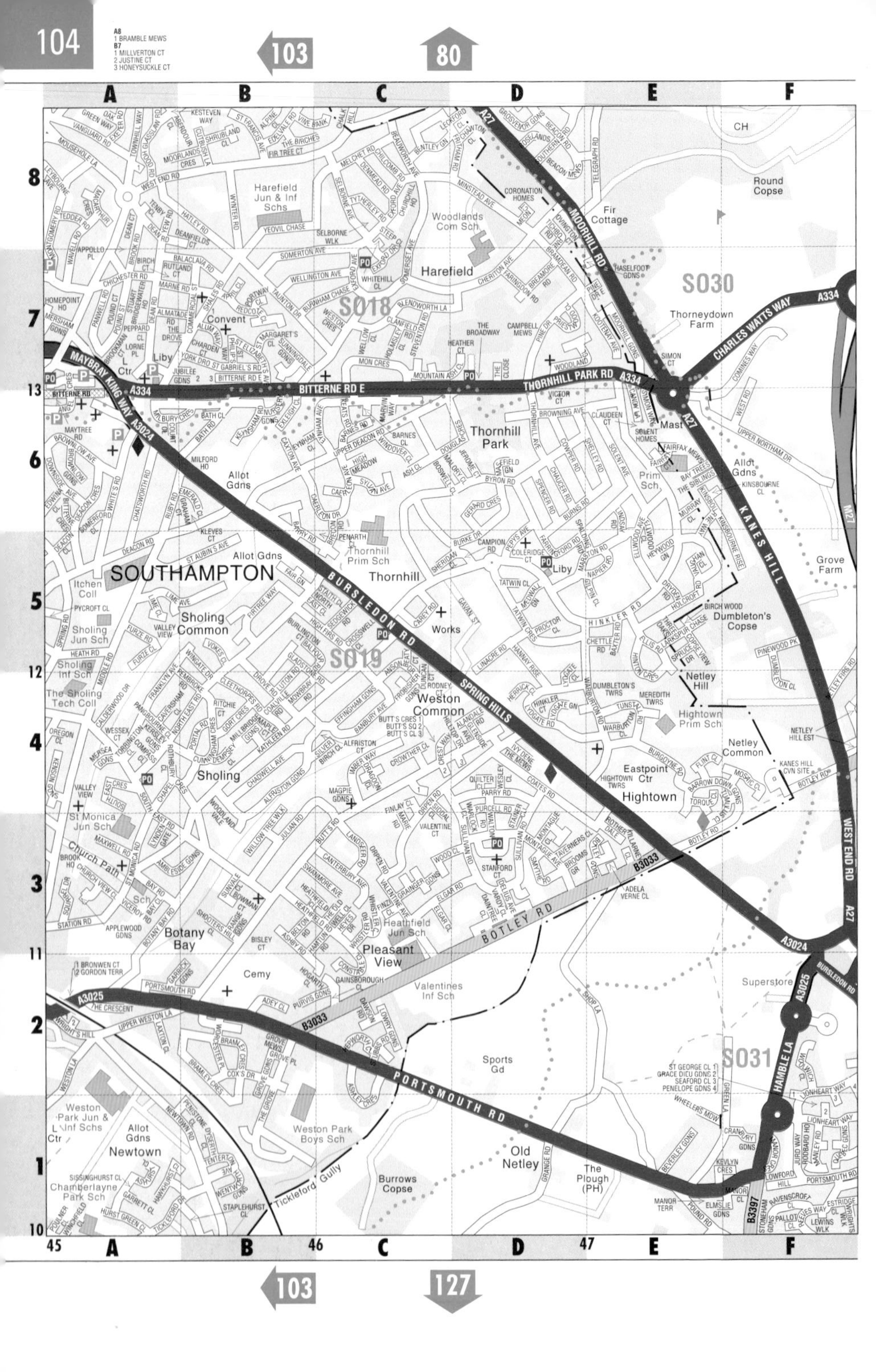

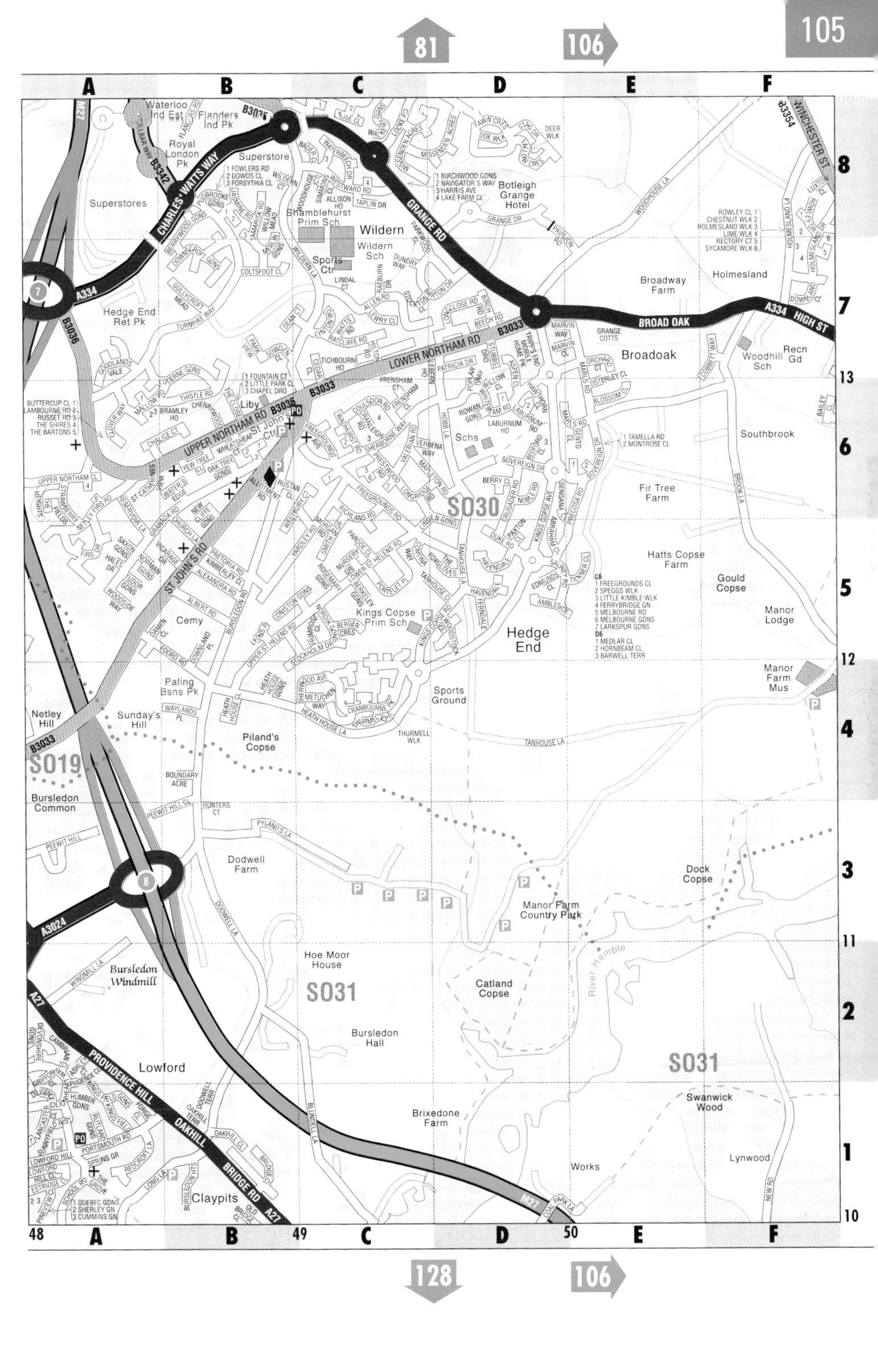
81
106
A
B
C
D
E
F
8
7
13
6
5
12
4
3
11
2
1
10
48
49
50
128
106
Waterloo Ind Est
Flanders Ind Pk
Royal London Pk
Superstore
Superstores
CHARLES' WATTS WAY
B3035
B3342
M27
A334
B3036
Hedge End Ret Pk
Shamblehurst Prim Sch
Wildern
Wildern Sch
Sports Ctr
GRANGE RD
Botleigh Grange Hotel
1 BIRCHWOOD GDNS
2 NAVIGATOR'S WAY
3 HARRIS AVE
4 LAKE FARM CL
1 FOWLERS RD
2 DOWDS CL
3 FORSYTHIA CL
WOODHOUSE LA
B3354
WINCHESTER ST
ROWLEY CL 1
CHESTNUT WLK 2
HOLMESLAND WLK 3
LIME WLK 4
RECTORY CT 5
SYCAMORE WLK 6
Broadway Farm
Holmesland
BROAD OAK
A334 HIGH ST
Broadoak
Woodhill Sch
Recn Gd
B3033
LOWER NORTHAM RD
UPPER NORTHAM RD
1 FOUNTAIN CT
2 LITTLE PARK CL
3 CHAPEL DRO
Liby
St John's Ctr
PO
BUTTERCUP CL 1
LAMBOURNE HO 2
RUSSET HO 3
THE SHIRES 4
THE BARTONS 5
Schs
Southbrook
1 TAMELLA RD
2 MONTROSE CL
Fir Tree Farm
SO30
ST JOHN'S RD
Hatts Copse Farm
Gould Copse
Manor Lodge
C6
1 FREEGROUNDS CL
2 SPEGGS WLK
3 LITTLE KIMBLE WLK
4 FERRYBRIDGE GN
5 MELBOURNE RD
6 MELBOURNE GDNS
7 LARKSPUR GDNS
D6
1 MEDLAR CL
2 HORNBEAM CL
3 BARWELL TERR
Kings Copse Prim Sch
Hedge End
Cemy
Paling Bsns Pk
Manor Farm Mus
Sports Ground
Netley Hill
Sunday's Hill
Piland's Copse
TANHOUSE LA
SO19
Bursledon Common
Dodwell Farm
Manor Farm Country Park
Dock Copse
A3024
Hoe Moor House
SO31
Catland Copse
River Hamble
Bursledon Windmill
A27
Bursledon Hall
PROVIDENCE HILL
Lowford
OAKHILL
Brixedone Farm
Swanwick Wood
BRIDGE RD
Claypits
Works
Lynwood
COAL PARK LA
1 QUEBEC GDNS
2 SHERLEY GN
3 CUMMINS GN

105
82

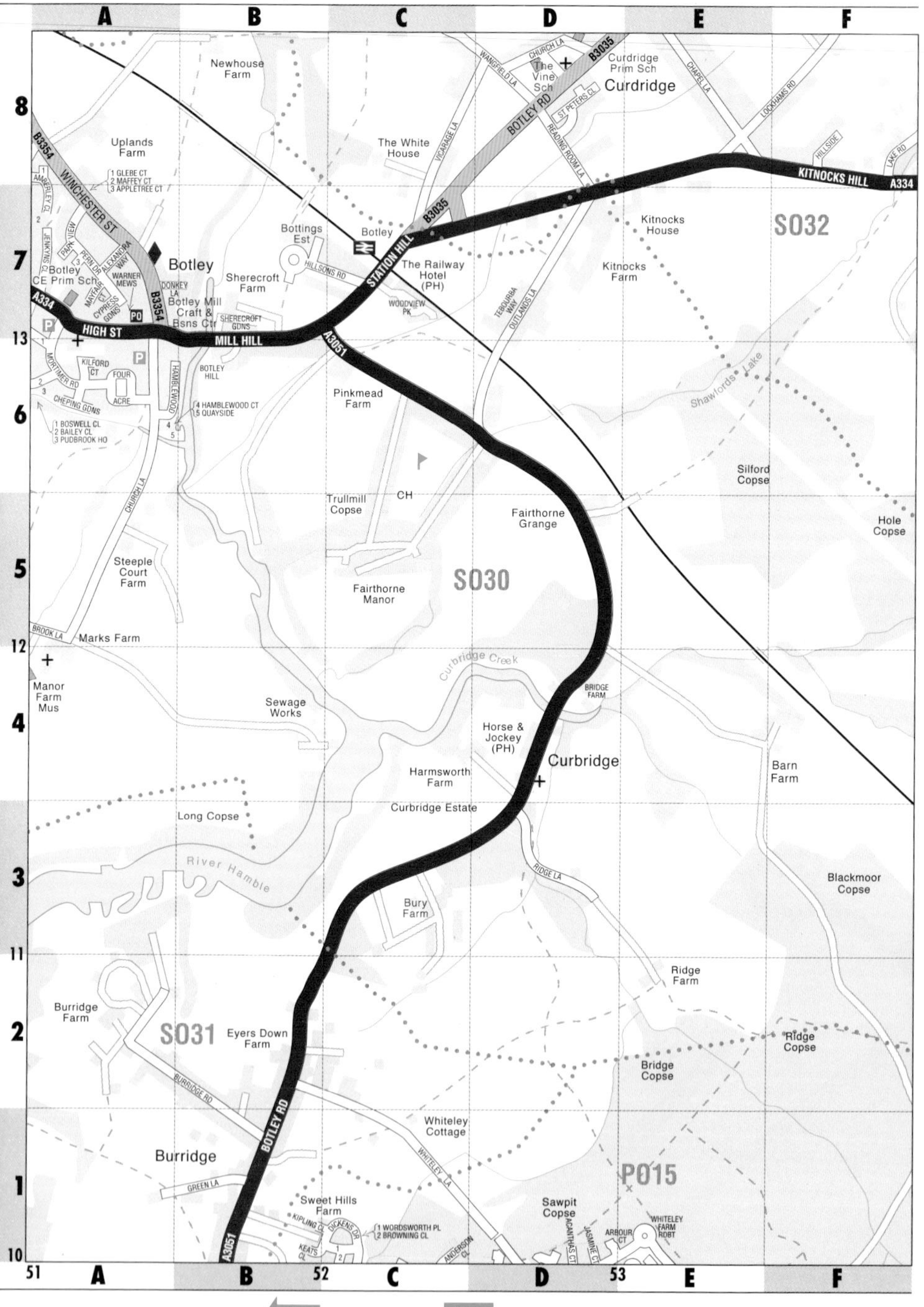
A
B
C
D
E
F
Newhouse Farm
Uplands Farm
The White House
Curdridge Prim Sch
Curdridge
The Vine Sch
CHURCH LA
WANGFIELD LA
B3035
BOTLEY RD
ST PETERS CL
VICARAGE LA
READING ROOM LA
CHAPEL LA
LOCKHAMS RD
HILLSIDE
LAKE RD
KITNOCKS HILL
A334
B3354
WINCHESTER ST
1 GLEBE CT
2 MAFFEY CT
3 APPLETREE CT
Bottings Est
Botley
STATION HILL
The Railway Hotel (PH)
Kitnocks House
Kitnocks Farm
SO32
Botley
Botley CE Prim Sch
Shercroft Farm
HILLSONS RD
WARNER MEWS
DONKEY LA
Botley Mill Craft & Bsns Ctr
SHERECROFT GDNS
WOODVIEW PK
TEBOURBA WAY
OUTLANDS LA
HIGH ST
MILL HILL
A3051
KILFORD CT
FOUR ACRE
BOTLEY HILL
HAMBLEWOOD
4 HAMBLEWOOD CT
5 QUAYSIDE
MORTIMER RD
CHEPING GDNS
1 BOSWELL CL
2 BAILEY CL
3 PUDBROOK HO
Pinkmead Farm
Shawfords Lake
Silford Copse
CHURCH LA
Trullmill Copse
CH
Fairthorne Grange
Hole Copse
Steeple Court Farm
SO30
Fairthorne Manor
BROOK LA
Marks Farm
Manor Farm Mus
Curbridge Creek
BRIDGE FARM
Sewage Works
Horse & Jockey (PH)
Curbridge
Barn Farm
Harmsworth Farm
Curbridge Estate
Long Copse
River Hamble
RIDGE LA
Blackmoor Copse
Bury Farm
Ridge Farm
Burridge Farm
SO31
Eyers Down Farm
Ridge Copse
Bridge Copse
BURRIDGE RD
BOTLEY RD
Whiteley Cottage
Burridge
WHITELEY LA
PO15
GREEN LA
Sweet Hills Farm
Sawpit Copse
KIPLING CL
DICKENS DR
1 WORDSWORTH PL
2 BROWNING CL
KEATS CL
ANDERSON CL
ACANTHAS CT
JASMINE CT
ARBOUR CT
WHITELEY FARM RDBT
A3051
8
7
13
6
5
12
4
3
11
2
1
10
51
52
53

105
129

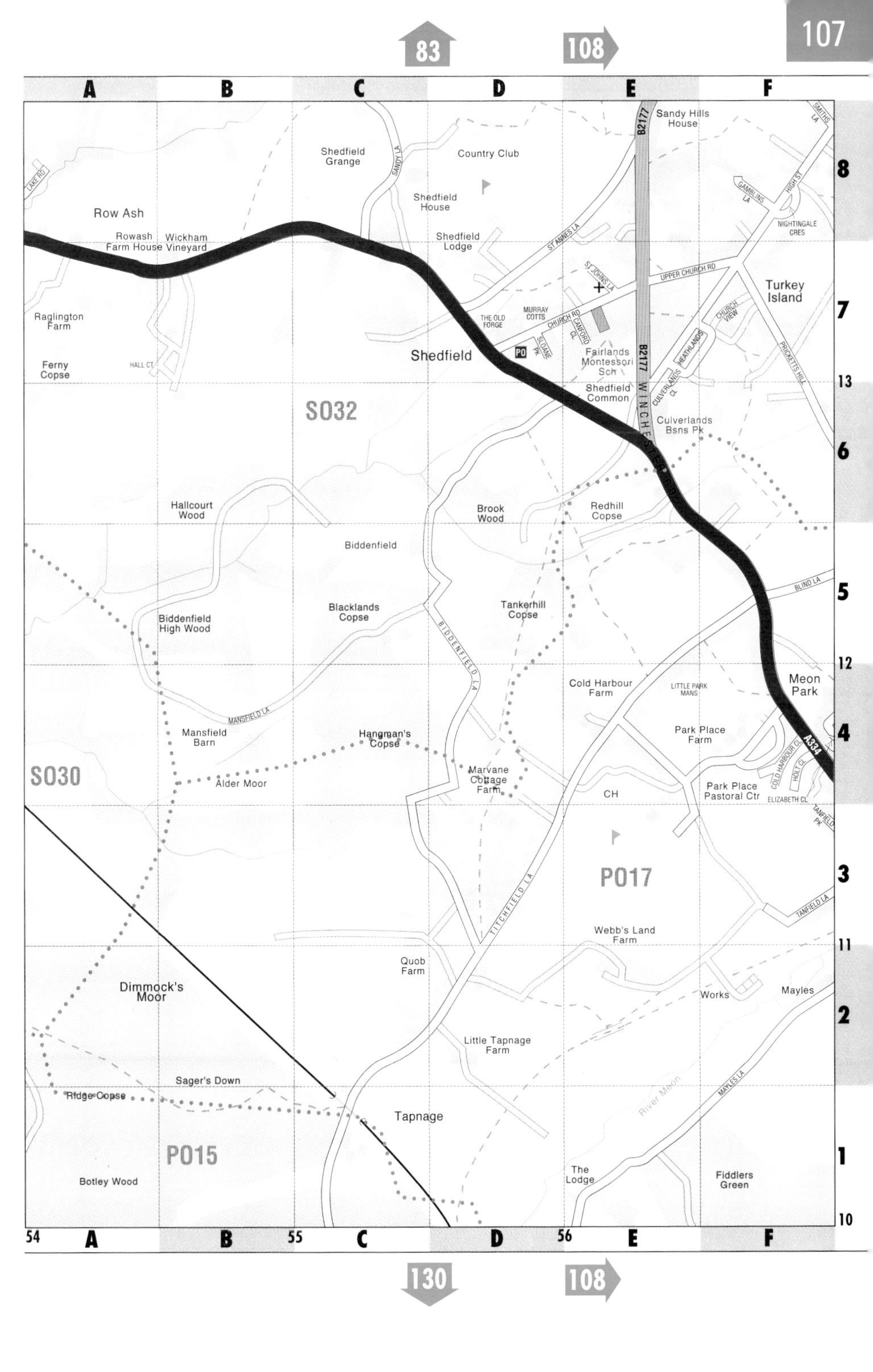
83
108
A
B
C
D
E
F
8
7
13
6
5
12
4
3
11
2
1
10
LAKE RD
Row Ash
Rowash Farm House
Wickham Vineyard
Raglington Farm
Ferny Copse
HALL CT
Shedfield Grange
SANDY LA
Country Club
Shedfield House
Shedfield Lodge
ST ANNES LA
ST JOHNS LA
B2177
Sandy Hills House
SMITHS LA
GAMBLINS LA
HIGH ST
NIGHTINGALE CRES
UPPER CHURCH RD
Turkey Island
CHURCH VIEW
THE OLD FORGE
MURRAY COTTS
CHURCH RD
CANFORD CL
SLOANE PK
Shedfield
Fairlands Montessori Sch
HEATHLANDS
CULVERLANDS CL
PRICKETT'S HILL
Shedfield Common
WINCHESTER RD
Culverlands Bsns Pk
SO32
Hallcourt Wood
Brook Wood
Redhill Copse
Biddenfield
BLIND LA
Biddenfield High Wood
Blacklands Copse
Tankerhill Copse
BIDDENFIELD LA
Cold Harbour Farm
LITTLE PARK MANS
Meon Park
MANSFIELD LA
Mansfield Barn
Hangman's Copse
Park Place Farm
A334
SO30
Alder Moor
Marvane Cottage Farm
CH
Park Place Pastoral Ctr
COLD HARBOUR CL
HOLT CL
ELIZABETH CL
TANFIELD PK
TITCHFIELD LA
PO17
TANFIELD LA
Webb's Land Farm
Quob Farm
Dimmock's Moor
Works
Mayles
Little Tapnage Farm
Sager's Down
Ridge Copse
River Meon
MAYLES LA
Tapnage
PO15
The Lodge
Fiddlers Green
Botley Wood
54
55
56
130
108

107
84

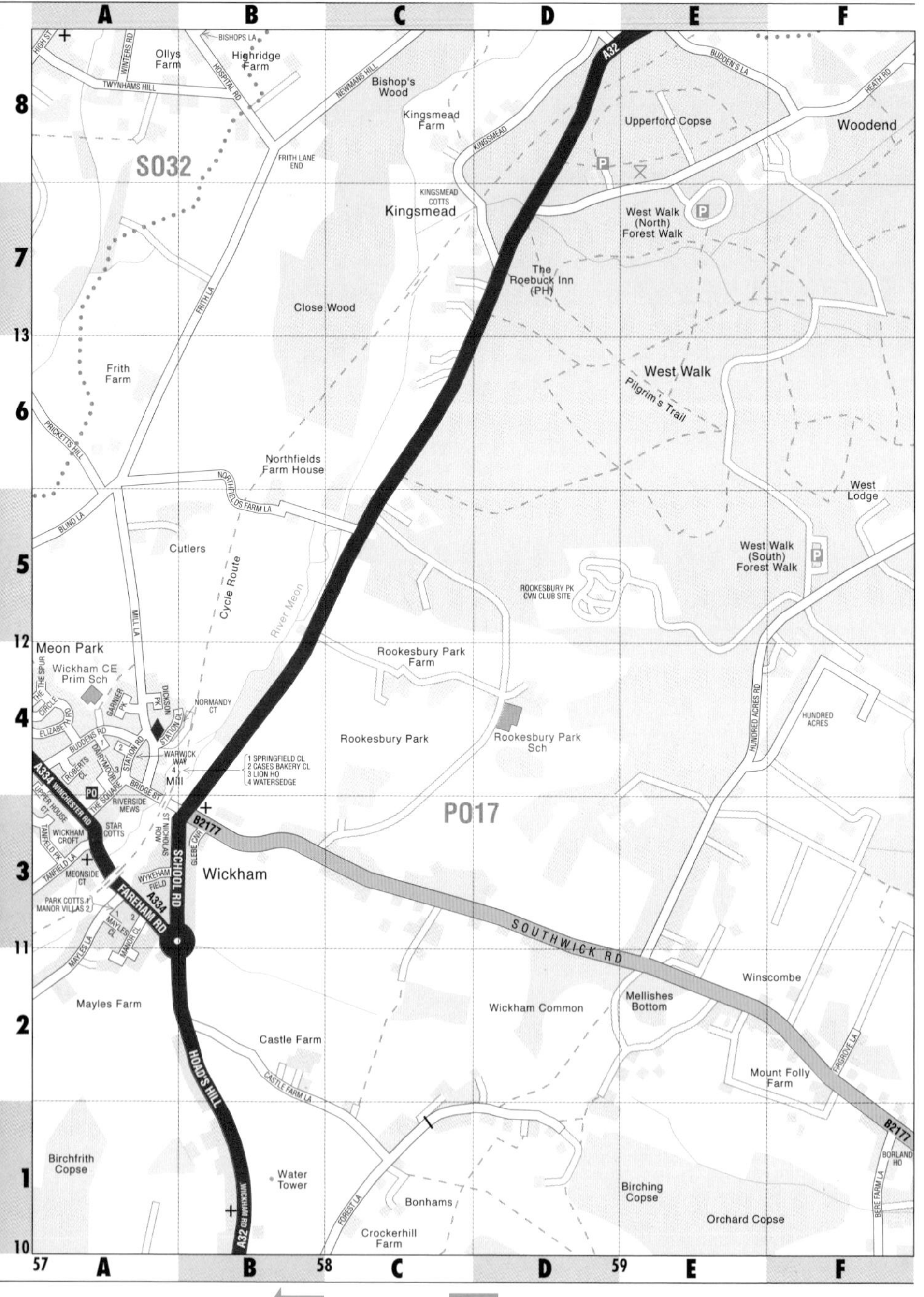
A
B
C
D
E
F
8
7
13
6
5
12
4
3
11
2
1
10
57
58
59
Ollys Farm
Highridge Farm
TWYNHAMS HILL
WINTERS RD
HOSPITAL RD
BISHOPS LA
HIGH ST
Bishop's Wood
NEWMANS HILL
Kingsmead Farm
KINGSMEAD
A32
BUDDEN'S LA
HEATH RD
Upperford Copse
Woodend
SO32
FRITH LANE END
KINGSMEAD COTTS
Kingsmead
West Walk (North) Forest Walk
The Roebuck Inn (PH)
Close Wood
FRITH LA
Frith Farm
West Walk
Pilgrim's Trail
PRICKETTS HILL
Northfields Farm House
NORTHFIELDS FARM LA
West Lodge
BLIND LA
Cutlers
Cycle Route
West Walk (South) Forest Walk
ROOKESBURY PK CVN CLUB SITE
MILL LA
River Meon
Meon Park
Wickham CE Prim Sch
Rookesbury Park Farm
THE SPUR
CIRCLE
ELIZABETH RD
GARNIER PK
DICKSON PK
NORMANDY CT
STATION CT
HUNDRED ACRES RD
HUNDRED ACRES
BUDDENS RD
Rookesbury Park
Rookesbury Park Sch
ROBERTS CL
DAIRYMOOR
STATION RD
WARWICK WAY
1 SPRINGFIELD CL
2 CASES BAKERY CL
3 LION HO
4 WATERSEDGE
Mill
A334 WINCHESTER RD
UPPER HOUSE CT
PO
THE SQUARE
BRIDGE ST
RIVERSIDE MEWS
PO17
B2177
STAR COTTS
ST NICHOLAS ROW
WICKHAM CROFT
TANFIELD PK
TANFIELD LA
MEONSIDE CT
SCHOOL RD
GLEBE CNR
Wickham
WYKEHAM FIELD
PARK COTTS 1
MANOR VILLAS 2
FAREHAM RD
A334
MAYLES CL
MANOR CL
MAYLES LA
SOUTHWICK RD
Winscombe
Mayles Farm
Mellishes Bottom
Wickham Common
Castle Farm
HOAD'S HILL
CASTLE FARM LA
Mount Folly Farm
HAGROVE LA
B2177
BORLAND HO
Birchfrith Copse
Water Tower
Birching Copse
BERE FARM LA
Bonhams
FOREST LA
Orchard Copse
WICKHAM RD
A32
Crockerhill Farm

107
131

85
110

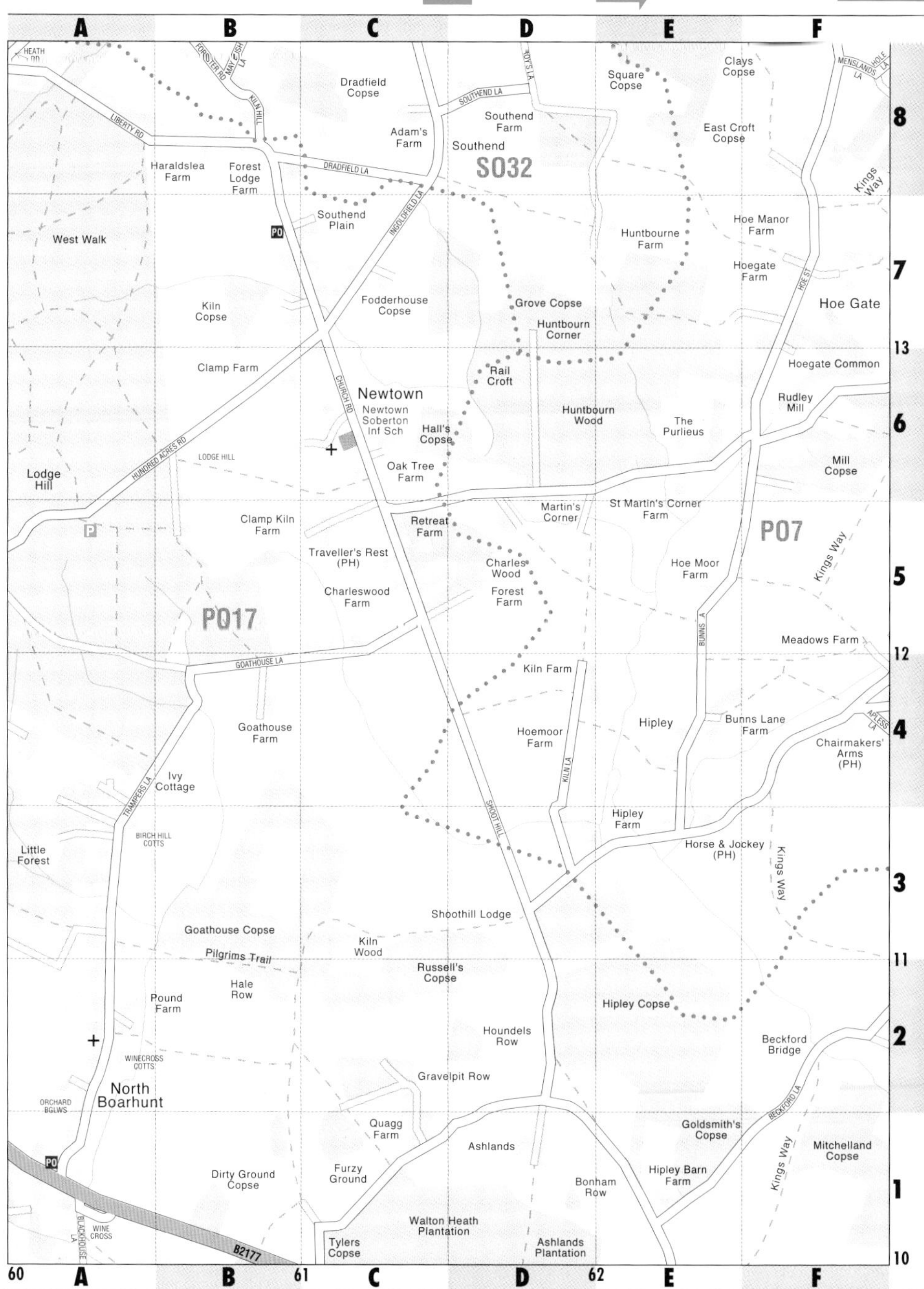

Dradfield Copse
Adam's Farm
Southend Farm
Southend
SO32
Square Copse
Clays Copse
East Croft Copse
Haraldslea Farm
Forest Lodge Farm
DRADFIELD LA
LIBERTY RD
KILN HILL
SOUTHEND LA
INGOLDFIELD LA
West Walk
Southend Plain
Huntbourne Farm
Hoe Manor Farm
Hoegate Farm
Hoe Gate
HOE ST
Kiln Copse
Fodderhouse Copse
Grove Copse
Huntbourn Corner
Hoegate Common
Clamp Farm
Rail Croft
Newtown
Newtown Soberton Inf Sch
CHURCH RD
Hall's Copse
Huntbourn Wood
The Purlieus
Rudley Mill
Mill Copse
HUNDRED ACRES RD
LODGE HILL
Lodge Hill
Oak Tree Farm
Martin's Corner
St Martin's Corner Farm
Clamp Kiln Farm
Retreat Farm
PO7
Kings Way
Traveller's Rest (PH)
Charles Wood
Hoe Moor Farm
Charleswood Farm
Forest Farm
PO17
Meadows Farm
BUNNS LA
GOATHOUSE LA
Kiln Farm
Goathouse Farm
Hoemoor Farm
Hipley
Bunns Lane Farm
Chairmakers' Arms (PH)
Ivy Cottage
TRAMPERS LA
KILN LA
BIRCH HILL COTTS
SHOOT HILL
Hipley Farm
Horse & Jockey (PH)
Little Forest
Shoothill Lodge
Goathouse Copse
Kiln Wood
Pilgrims Trail
Russell's Copse
Pound Farm
Hale Row
Hipley Copse
Houndels Row
Beckford Bridge
WINECROSS COTTS
Gravelpit Row
North Boarhunt
ORCHARD BGLWS
Quagg Farm
Ashlands
Goldsmith's Copse
BECKFORD LA
Mitchelland Copse
Furzy Ground
Dirty Ground Copse
Bonham Row
Hipley Barn Farm
Walton Heath Plantation
Tylers Copse
Ashlands Plantation
BLACKHOUSE LA
WINE CROSS
B2177
A B C D E F
8 7 6 5 4 3 2 1
13 12 11 10
60 61 62

109
86

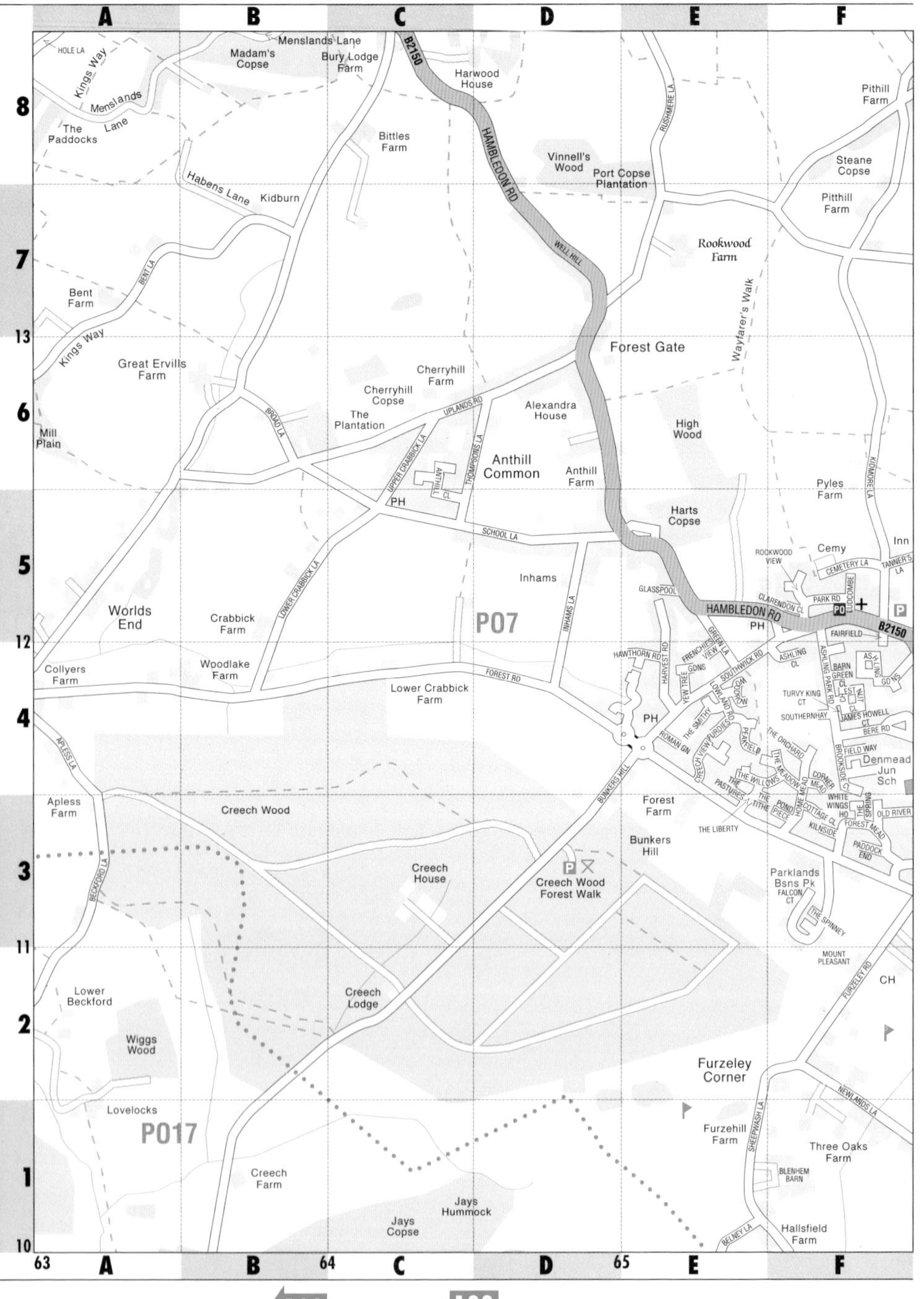
A
B
C
D
E
F
8
7
13
6
5
12
4
3
11
2
1
10
63
64
65
HOLE LA
Kings Way
Menslands Lane
Madam's Copse
Bury Lodge Farm
B2150
Harwood House
Menslands Lane
The Paddocks
Bittles Farm
HAMBLEDON RD
RUSHMERE LA
Pithill Farm
Vinnell's Wood
Port Copse Plantation
Steane Copse
Habens Lane
Kidburn
Pitthill Farm
WELL HILL
Rookwood Farm
BENT LA
Bent Farm
Wayfarer's Walk
Kings Way
Great Ervills Farm
Forest Gate
Cherryhill Farm
Cherryhill Copse
Alexandra House
Mill Plain
BROAD LA
The Plantation
UPLANDS RD
High Wood
Anthill Common
Anthill Farm
UPPER CRABBICK LA
ANTHILL CL
THOMPSONS LA
PH
KIDMORE LA
Pyles Farm
Harts Copse
SCHOOL LA
Cemy
Inn
ROOKWOOD VIEW
CEMETERY LA
TANNER'S LA
Inhams
LOWER CRABBICK LA
GLASSPOOL
PARK RD
LUDCOMBE
PO
P
Worlds End
Crabbick Farm
PO7
INHAMS LA
CLARENDON CL
HAMBLEDON RD
PH
FAIRFIELD
B2150
Collyers Farm
Woodlake Farm
HAWTHORN RD
HARVEST RD
FRENCHIES VIEW
GREEN LA
SOUTHWICK RD
ASHLING CL
ASHLING PARK RD
BARN GREEN CL
ASHLING GDNS
YEW TREE GDNS
FOREST RD
Lower Crabbick Farm
LOWLAND RD
WOODROW
TURVY KING CT
CHESTNUT CL
THE SMITHY
PH
SOUTHERNHAY
JAMES HOWELL CT
BERE RD
APLESS LA
ROMAN GN
PURDIES
PEAKFIELD
THE ORCHARD
FIELD WAY
CREECH VIEW
BROOKSIDE CL
Denmead Jun Sch
THE MEADOW
CORNER MEAD
THE WILLOWS
THE PASTURES
BUNKERS HILL
Apless Farm
Creech Wood
Forest Farm
THE TITHE
POND PIECE
HOME MEAD
COTTAGE CL
WHITE WINGS HO
THE SPRING
OLD RIVER
FOREST MEAD
THE LIBERTY
KILNSIDE
Bunkers Hill
PADDOCK END
BECKFORD LA
Creech House
P
Creech Wood Forest Walk
Parklands Bsns Pk
FALCON CT
THE SPINNEY
MOUNT PLEASANT
FURZELEY RD
CH
Lower Beckford
Creech Lodge
Wiggs Wood
Furzeley Corner
NEWLANDS LA
Lovelocks
PO17
Furzehill Farm
SHEEPWASH LA
Three Oaks Farm
Creech Farm
BLENHEM BARN
Jays Hummock
Jays Copse
BELNEY LA
Hallsfield Farm

109
133

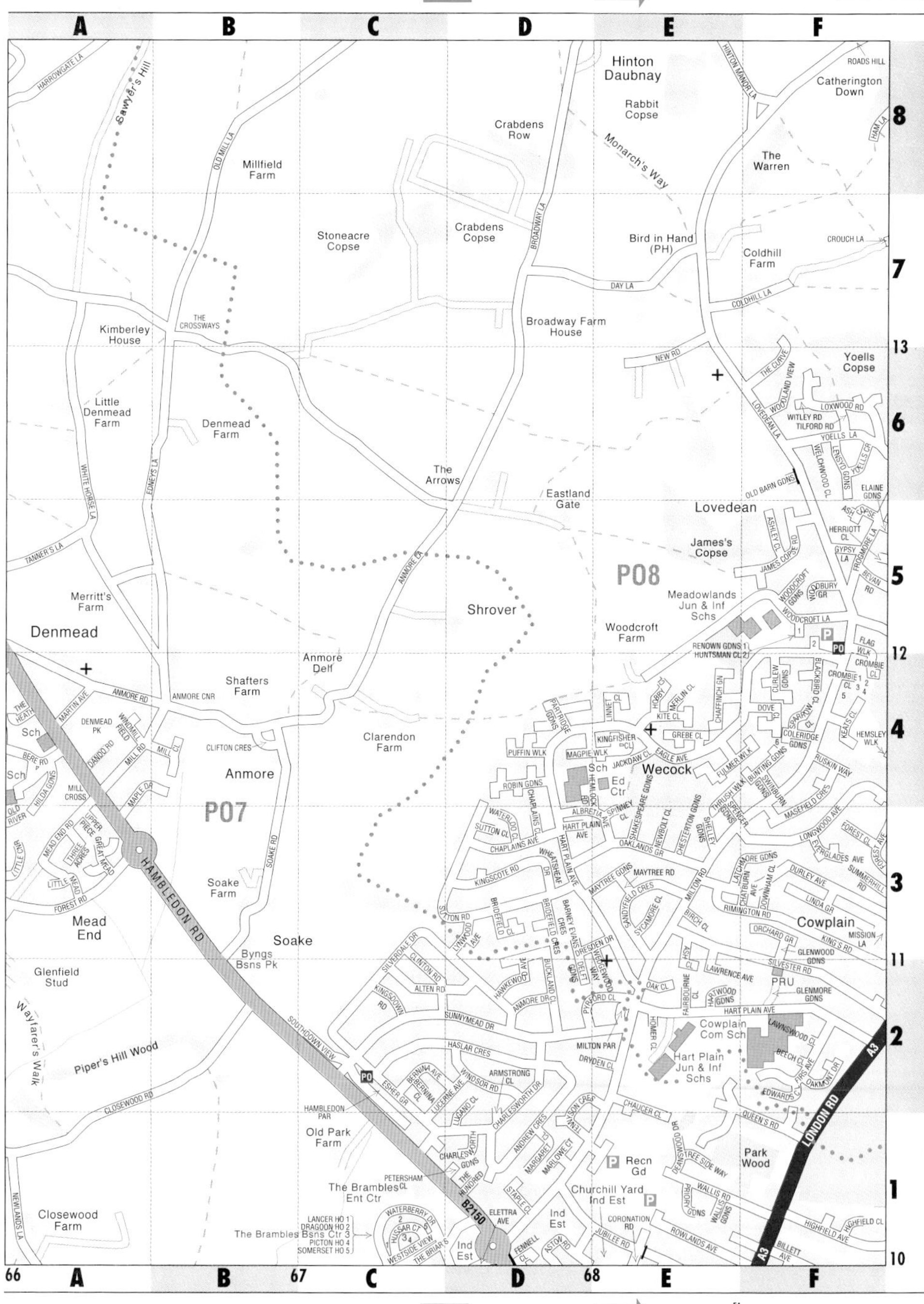

F4
1 THAMES CT
2 AVON CT
3 HAMBLE CT
4 ITCHEN CT
5 BEAULIEU CT
6 PATRICK HOWARD-DOBSON CT

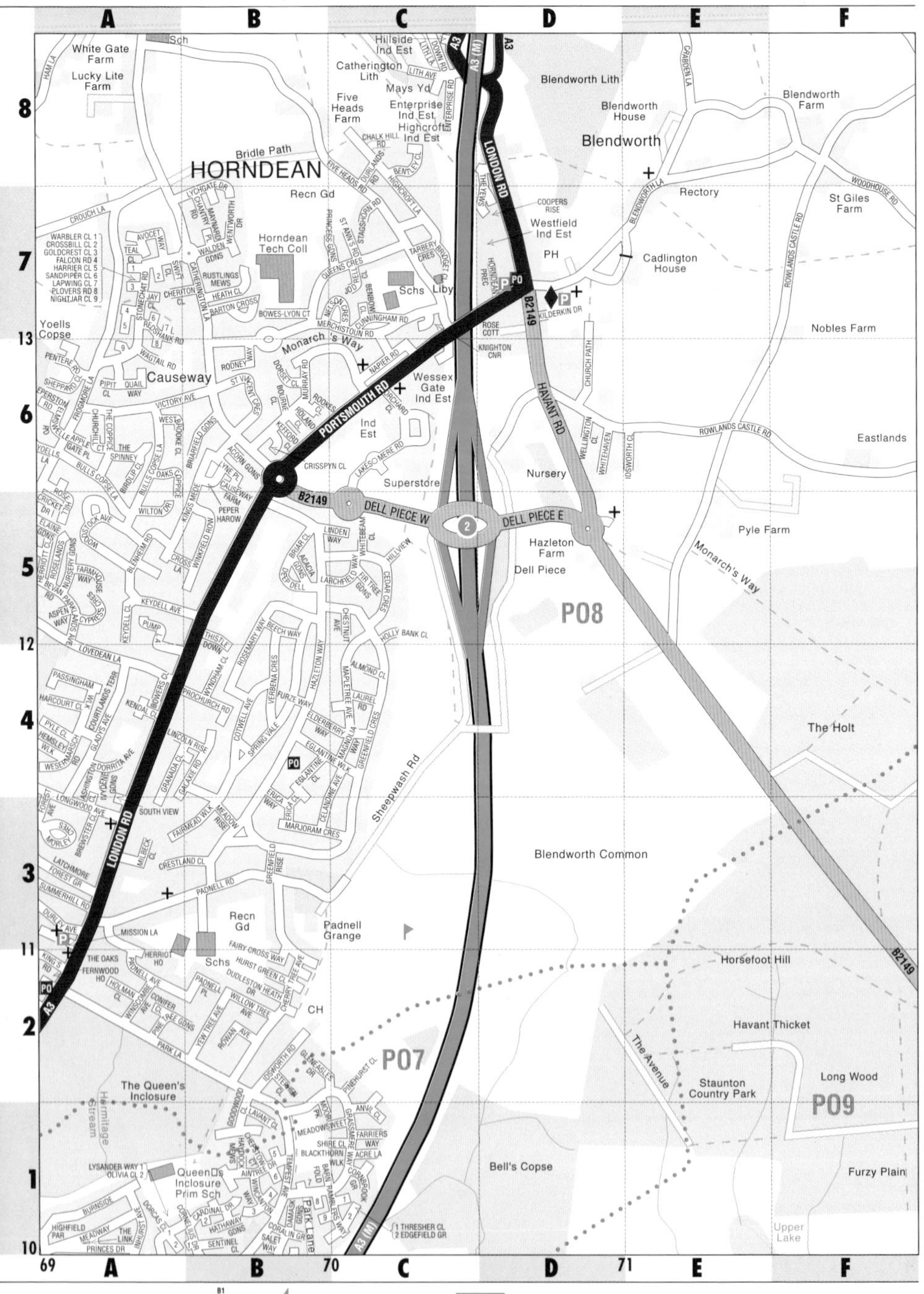

89

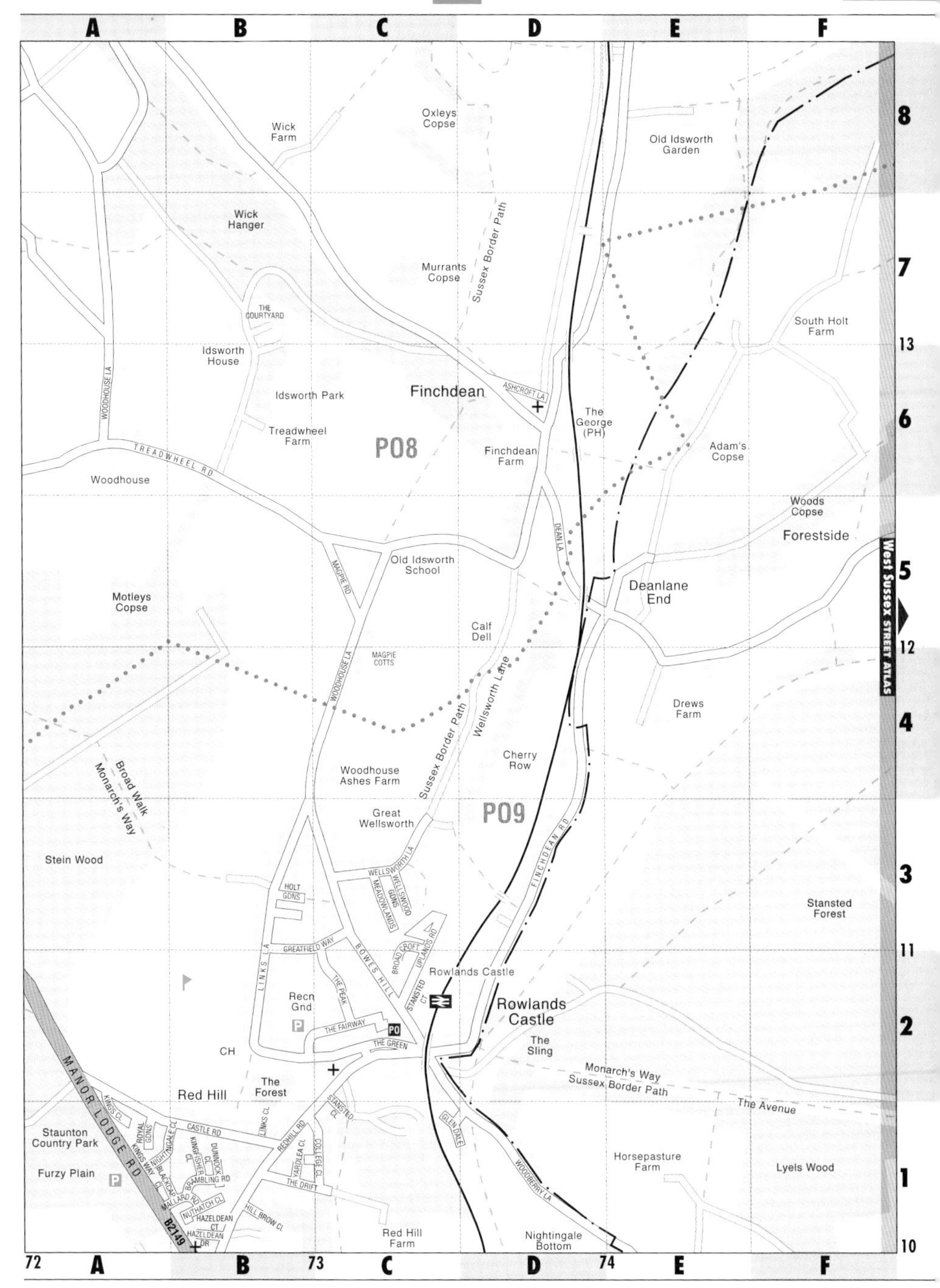
A
B
C
D
E
F
Wick Farm
Oxleys Copse
Old Idsworth Garden
8
Wick Hanger
Sussex Border Path
Murrants Copse
7
South Holt Farm
THE COURTYARD
Idsworth House
13
Idsworth Park
Finchdean
ASHCROFT LA
The George (PH)
WOODHOUSE LA
Treadwheel Farm
PO8
Finchdean Farm
Adam's Copse
6
TREADWHEEL RD
Woodhouse
Woods Copse
DEAN LA
Forestside
MAGPIE RD
Old Idsworth School
West Sussex STREET ATLAS
5
Motleys Copse
Deanlane End
Calf Dell
12
MAGPIE COTTS
WOODHOUSE LA
Wellsworth Lane
Drews Farm
Sussex Border Path
4
Cherry Row
Broad Walk
Monarch's Way
Woodhouse Ashes Farm
Great Wellsworth
PO9
FINCHDEAN RD
Stein Wood
WELLSWORTH LA
WELLSWOOD GDNS
MEADOWLANDS
HOLT GDNS
3
Stansted Forest
GREATFIELD WAY
BROADCROFT
UPLANDS RD
LINKS LA
BOWES HILL
11
Rowlands Castle
THE PEAK
Recn Gnd
STANSTED CT
Rowlands Castle
2
THE FAIRWAY
PO
The Sling
THE GREEN
CH
Monarch's Way
Sussex Border Path
MANOR LODGE RD
The Forest
Red Hill
The Avenue
KINGS CL
STANSTED CL
Staunton Country Park
ROYAL GDNS
CASTLE RD
LINKS CL
GLEN DALE
KINGS WAY
NIGHTINGALE CL
KINGFISHER CL
DUNNOCK CL
REDHILL RD
YARDLEA CL
COLLEGE CL
Horsepasture Farm
Furzy Plain
BLACKCAP CL
BRAMBLING RD
Lyels Wood
1
THE DRIFT
WOODBERRY LA
MALLARD RD
NUTHATCH CL
HILL BROW CL
HAZELDEAN CT
HAZELDEAN DR
B2149
Red Hill Farm
Nightingale Bottom
10
72
73
74

136

91

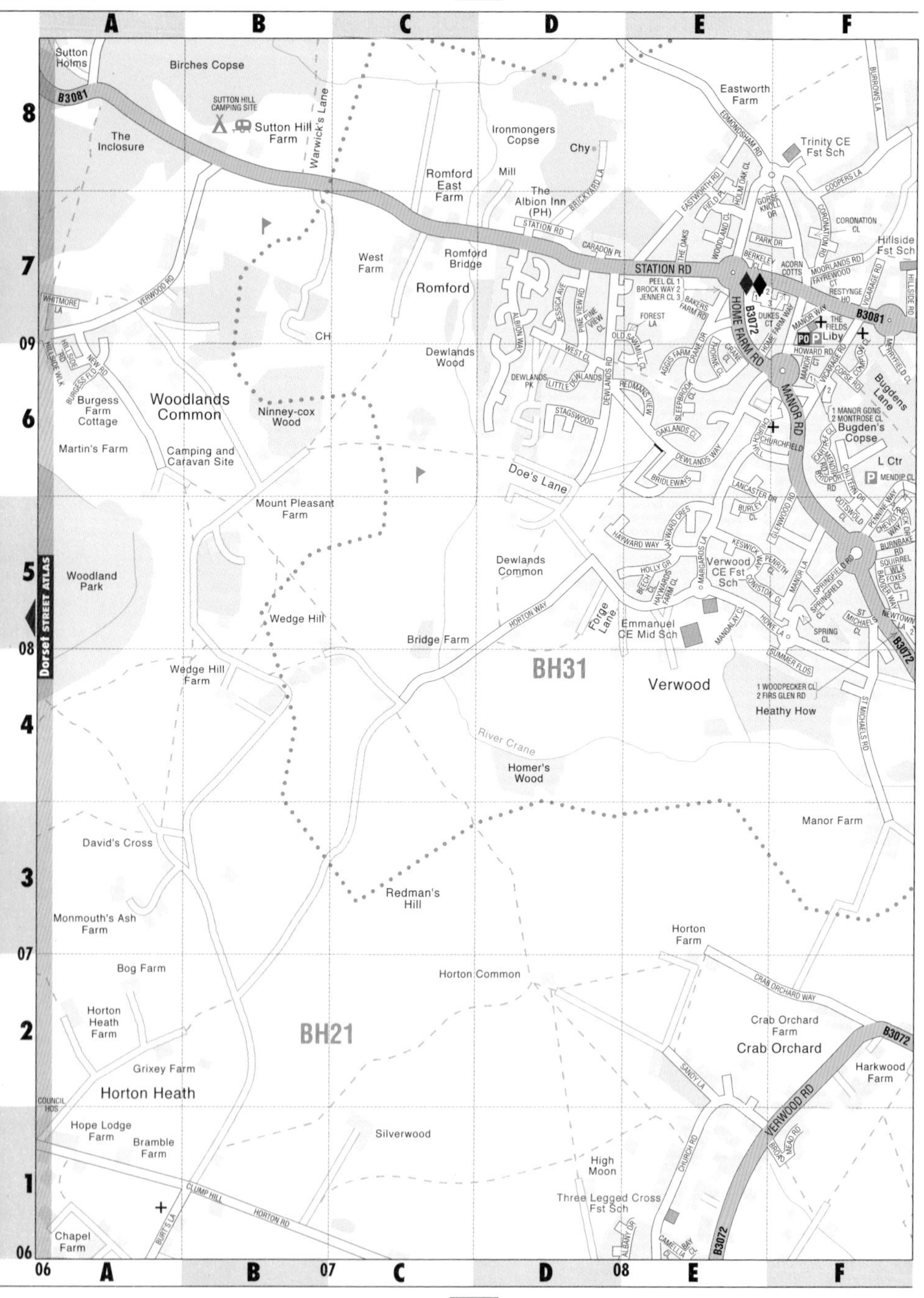
Sutton Holms
Birches Copse
B3081
SUTTON HILL CAMPING SITE
Sutton Hill Farm
The Inclosure
Warwick's Lane
Ironmongers Copse
Chy
Eastworth Farm
Trinity CE Fst Sch
Romford East Farm
Mill
The Albion Inn (PH)
STATION RD
West Farm
Romford Bridge
Romford
STATION RD
Hillside Fst Sch
CH
Dewlands Wood
Woodlands Common
Ninney-cox Wood
Burgess Farm Cottage
Martin's Farm
Camping and Caravan Site
Doe's Lane
Mount Pleasant Farm
Dewlands Common
Woodland Park
Wedge Hill
Bridge Farm
Forge Lane
Emmanuel CE Mid Sch
Verwood CE Fst Sch
BH31
Verwood
Wedge Hill Farm
Heathy How
River Crane
Homer's Wood
Manor Farm
David's Cross
Redman's Hill
Monmouth's Ash Farm
Horton Farm
Horton Common
Bog Farm
Horton Heath Farm
BH21
Crab Orchard Farm
Crab Orchard
Grixey Farm
Horton Heath
Harkwood Farm
Hope Lodge Farm
Bramble Farm
Silverwood
High Moon
Three Legged Cross Fst Sch
Chapel Farm
CLUMP HILL
HORTON RD
VERWOOD RD
B3072
MANOR RD
HOME FARM RD
Bugden's Copse
Bugdens Lane
L Ctr
Liby
Dorset STREET ATLAS

92
116

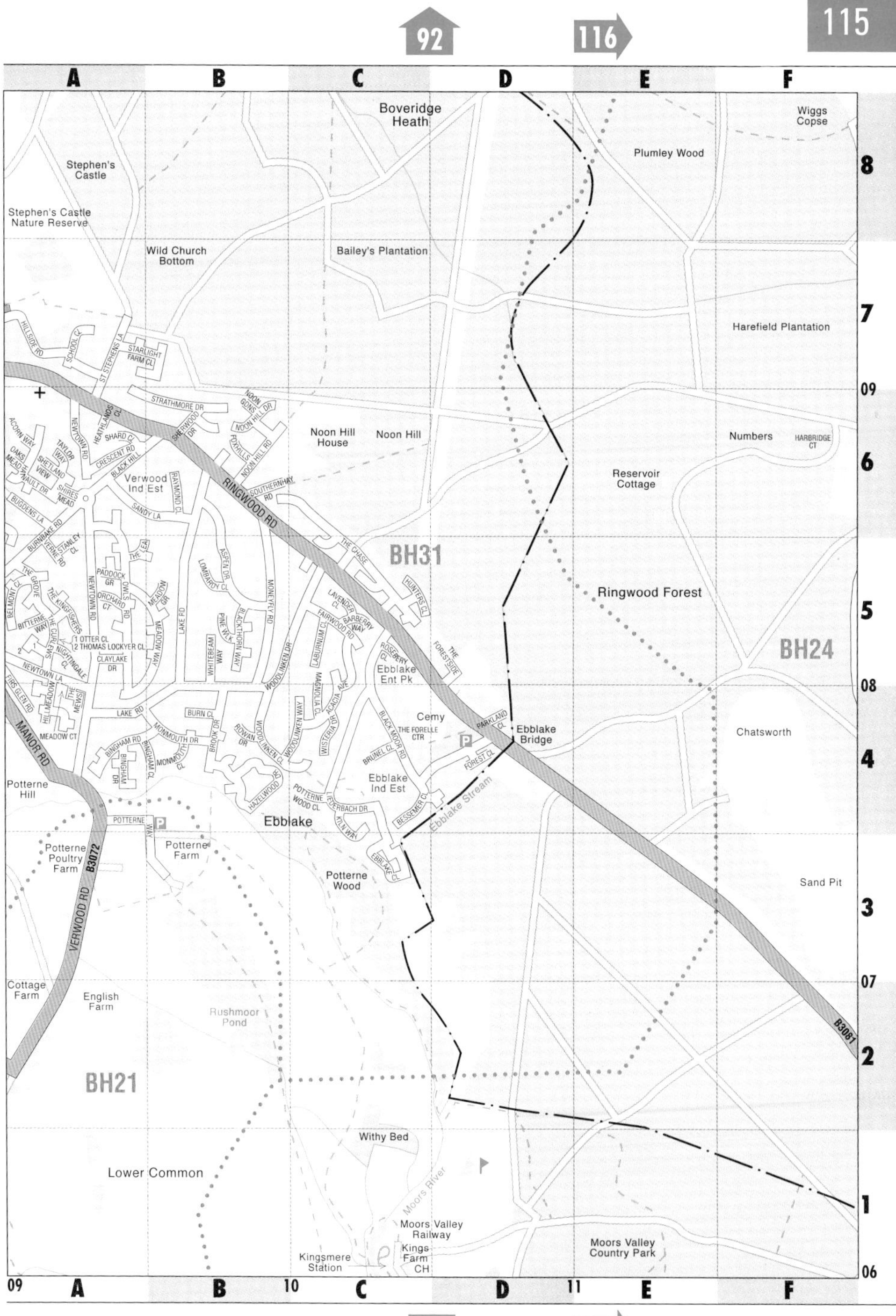
Boveridge Heath
Stephen's Castle
Stephen's Castle Nature Reserve
Wild Church Bottom
Bailey's Plantation
Plumley Wood
Wiggs Copse
Harefield Plantation
Noon Hill House
Noon Hill
Numbers
Reservoir Cottage
Verwood Ind Est
RINGWOOD RD
BH31
Ringwood Forest
BH24
Ebblake Ent Pk
Cemy
Ebblake Bridge
Chatsworth
Ebblake Ind Est
Ebblake Stream
Ebblake
Potterne Hill
Potterne Poultry Farm
Potterne Farm
Potterne Wood
Sand Pit
VERWOOD RD
B3072
MANOR RD
B3081
Cottage Farm
English Farm
Rushmoor Pond
BH21
Withy Bed
Lower Common
Moors River
Moors Valley Railway
Kings Farm CH
Kingsmere Station
Moors Valley Country Park

139
116

A B C D E F

8

Gravel Pit

Turmer
Hill

Harbridge
Farm

Ibsley
Bridge

Avon Valley Path

Weir

Turmer

Harbridge
Lodge

PH

Plumley
Farm

7

Lower
Turmer

Mill Stream

09

Turmer Brook

6

SHEPHERDS LA

Shepherds
Cottage

SHEPHERDS HILL

Home
Wood

Dog Kennel
Wood

Gravel
Pit

Ibsley
Water

CHESTNUT AVE

Riverbank
Covert

Whitehoe
Cottages

New Barn
Cottages

Old
Somerley

Ellingham

5

Ellingham
Farm

+

Somerley
Park

The
Bothy

ELLINGHAM DR

New
Bridge

ELLINGHAM
CROSS

ELLINGHAM DRO

Nursery
Cottages

ICA DR

BH24

SALISBURY RD

08

Broad Close
Covert

4

Somerley

Old Laundry
Cottage

Gravel
Works

Park
Cottage

The Belt

3

Ringwood
Forest

River Avon

Meadow
Lake

Blashford
Farm

A338

DUNCOMBE DR

Sand
Pit

07

Dockens Water

SALISBURY RD

2

B3081

ASHLEY DR

Sunderton
Wood

Weir

Lifeland
Copse

Upper Hurst
Farm

VERWOOD RD.

Duncombe
Lodge

Ashley
Farm

King Stream

Gouldings
Farm

1

B3081

Baker's
Hanging

Up
Mead

Hurst Old
Farm

Lin Brook

06

12 A B 13 C D 14 E F

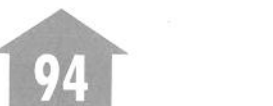

94
118
141
118

A   **B**   **C**   **D**   **E**   **F**

SALISBURY RD A338

Ibsley Manor Farm

Cottage Plantation

Great Bottom

8

NEW RD

PO

CUFNELLS CL

Summerlug Hill

Whitefield Plantation

Linwood Bog

Ibsley

Hearns Plantation

Cross Lanes Farm

Mockbeggar Farm

Digden Bottom

MOCKBEGGAR LA

Mockbeggar

CROSS LANES

7

Ibsley House

09

Avon Valley Path

Newlands Plantation

Dockens Water

Rodens Bottom

6

Fir Walk

Moyles Court Sch
Ford

Big Whitemoor Bottom

ELLINGHAM DRO

Rockford Common

Wood Sorrel

Little Whitemoor Bottom

5

08

Alice Lisle Inn (PH)

P

Rockford

Rockford Green

BH24

Waterslade Farm

4

Blashford Lakes Study Ctr

IVY LA

Ivy Lake

Bigsburn Hill

Water Slade Bottom

A338

Sailing Club

Rockford Farm

Highwood

3

SNAILS LA

Bracken Hill

Forest Edge Farm

Highwood Copse

HIGHWOOD RD

LINFORD HO

Blashford

Linbrook Almshouses

07

Highwood Farm

Linbrook View

Linford

WOOLMER LA

SYCAMORE CT 1
OLD FARM CL 2

Lin Brook

Linbank Farm

2

Headlands Bsns Pk

Northfield Lake

P

STILLWATER PK

North Poulner

Hangersley

ST AUBYNS LA

NORTH POULNER RD

SHAW RD

LAWRENCE RD

Burcomb

Headlands Adventure Ctr

Kingfisher Lake

Poulner Inf & Jun Schs

ROSS RD

BURCOMBE LA

Hangersley Hill

1

A338

SALISBURY

HURST RD

NORTHFIELD RD

SEYMOUR GDNS

PO

BUTLERS LA

LINFORD RD

Forest Corner Farm

06

LINBROOK CT

MEADOW CL

HAMPTON DR

HAWKINS CL

1 GRENVILLE CL
2 DRAKE CL
3 FROBISHER CL
4 CHICHESTER RD
5 POULNER PK

15   **A**   16   **B**   **C**   17   **D**   **E**   **F**

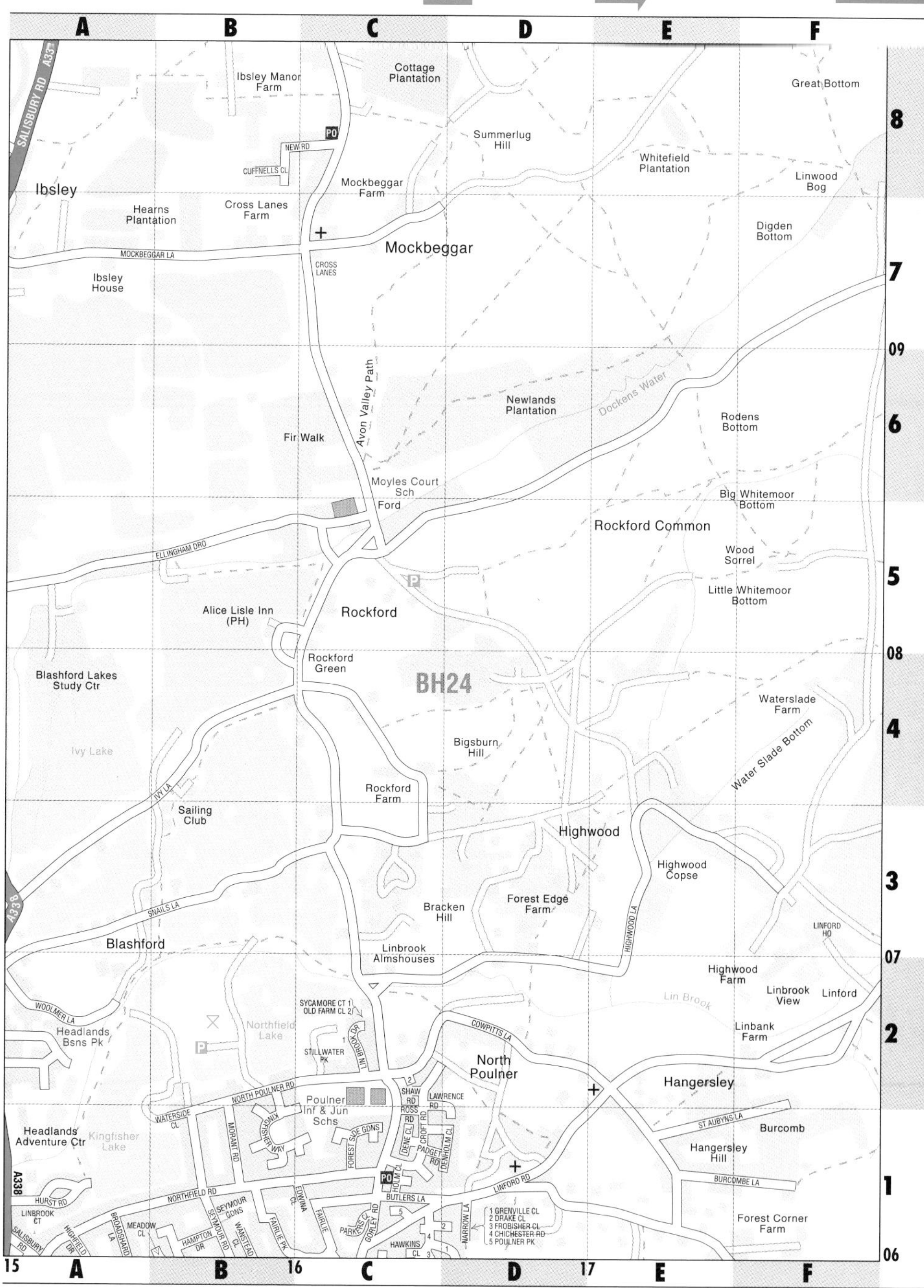

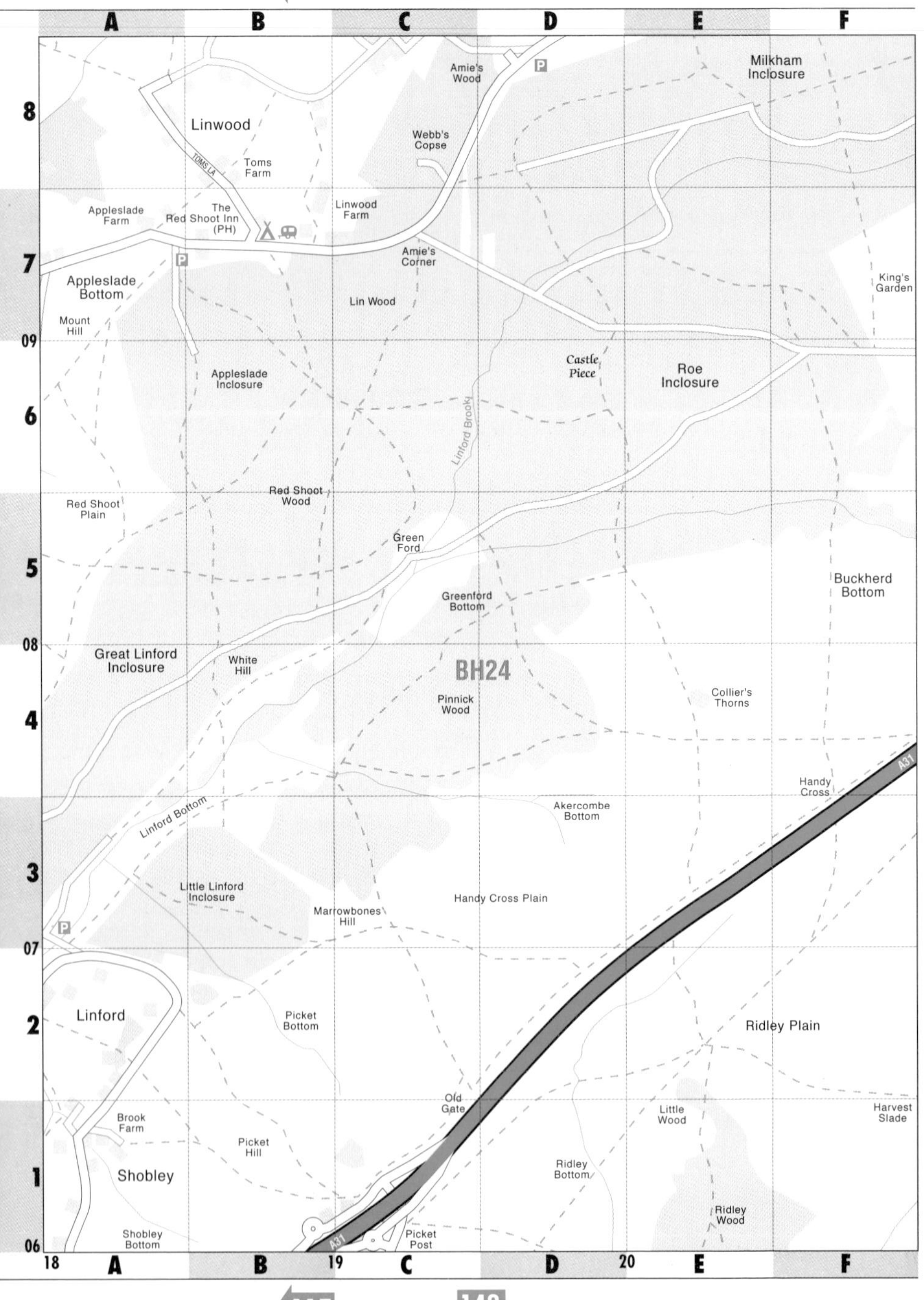

117
95

| A | B | C | D | E | F |

8

Linwood

Amie's
Wood

P

Milkham
Inclosure

Webb's
Copse

Toms
Farm

Appleslade
Farm

TOMS LA

The
Red Shoot Inn
(PH)

Linwood
Farm

King's
Garden

7

P

Amie's
Corner

Appleslade
Bottom

Lin Wood

09

Mount
Hill

Appleslade
Inclosure

Castle
Piece

Roe
Inclosure

6

Linford Brook

Red Shoot
Plain

Red Shoot
Wood

5

Green
Ford

Buckherd
Bottom

Greenford
Bottom

08

Great Linford
Inclosure

White
Hill

BH24

Collier's
Thorns

4

Pinnick
Wood

Handy
Cross

A31

Akercombe
Bottom

3

Linford Bottom

Little Linford
Inclosure

Handy Cross Plain

Marrowbones
Hill

07

P

Ridley Plain

2

Linford

Picket
Bottom

Old
Gate

Little
Wood

Harvest
Slade

Brook
Farm

Picket
Hill

Ridley
Bottom

1

Shobley

Picket
Hill

Ridley
Wood

06

Shobley
Bottom

A31

Picket
Post

| 18 | A | B | 19 | C | D | 20 | E | F |

117
142

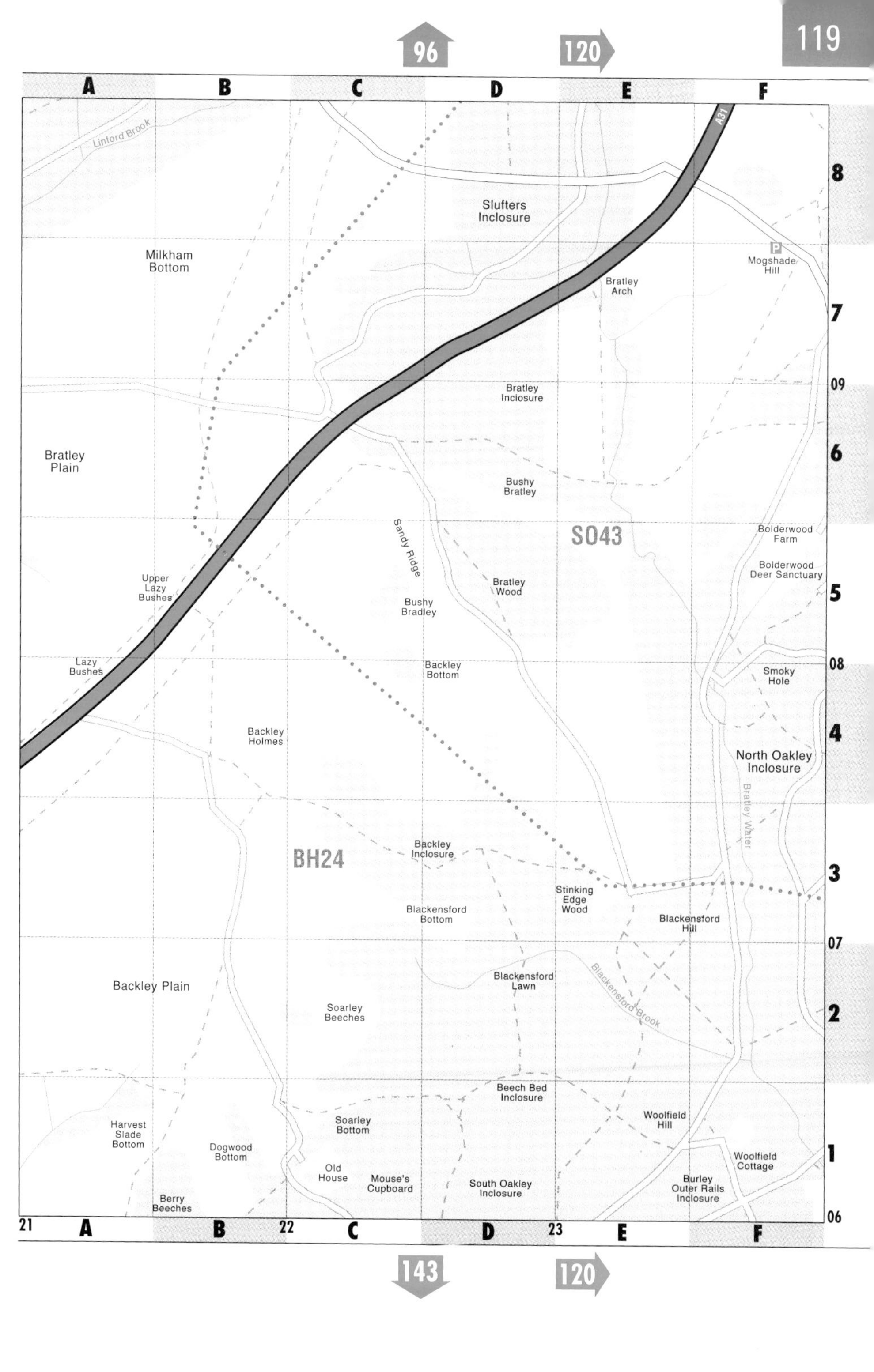
96
120
A
B
C
D
E
F
Linford Brook
A31
8
Slufters Inclosure
Milkham Bottom
Mogshade Hill
Bratley Arch
7
09
Bratley Inclosure
Bratley Plain
6
Bushy Bratley
Sandy Ridge
SO43
Bolderwood Farm
Upper Lazy Bushes
Bratley Wood
Bolderwood Deer Sanctuary
5
Bushy Bradley
Lazy Bushes
Backley Bottom
08
Smoky Hole
Backley Holmes
4
North Oakley Inclosure
Bratley Water
Backley Inclosure
BH24
3
Stinking Edge Wood
Blackensford Bottom
Blackensford Hill
07
Blackensford Lawn
Backley Plain
Blackensford Brook
Soarley Beeches
2
Beech Bed Inclosure
Harvest Slade Bottom
Soarley Bottom
Woolfield Hill
Dogwood Bottom
1
Woolfield Cottage
Old House
Mouse's Cupboard
South Oakley Inclosure
Burley Outer Rails Inclosure
Berry Beeches
06
21
22
23
143
120

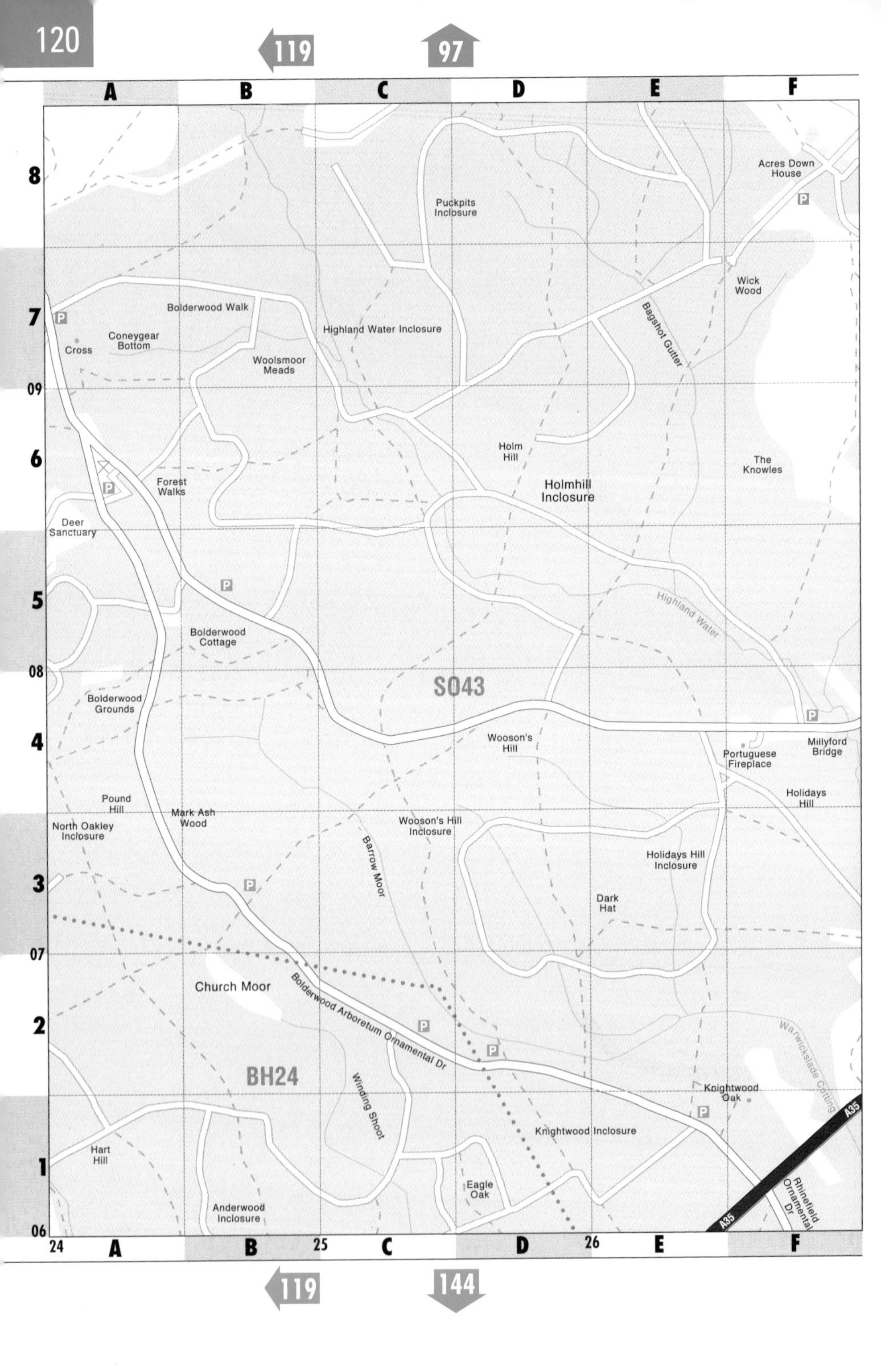

119
97

A **B** **C** **D** **E** **F**

8

Acres Down
House

Puckpits
Inclosure

7
Bolderwood Walk

Wick
Wood

Cross
Coneygear
Bottom

Highland Water Inclosure

Bagshot Gutter

Woolsmoor
Meads

09

6

Holm
Hill

The
Knowles

Holmhill
Inclosure

Forest
Walks

Deer
Sanctuary

5

Highland Water

Bolderwood
Cottage

08

SO43

Bolderwood
Grounds

4

Wooson's
Hill

Millyford
Bridge

Portuguese
Fireplace

Pound
Hill

Mark Ash
Wood

Wooson's Hill
Inclosure

Holidays
Hill

North Oakley
Inclosure

Barrow Moor

Holidays Hill
Inclosure

3

Dark
Hat

07

Church Moor

Bolderwood Arboretum Ornamental Dr

2

BH24

Winding Shoot

Knightwood
Oak

Knightwood Inclosure

Warwickslade Cutting

A35

1

Hart
Hill

Eagle
Oak

Rhinefield
Ornamental Dr

A35

Anderwood
Inclosure

06

24   **A**   **B**   25   **C**   **D**   26   **E**   **F**

119
144

98
122

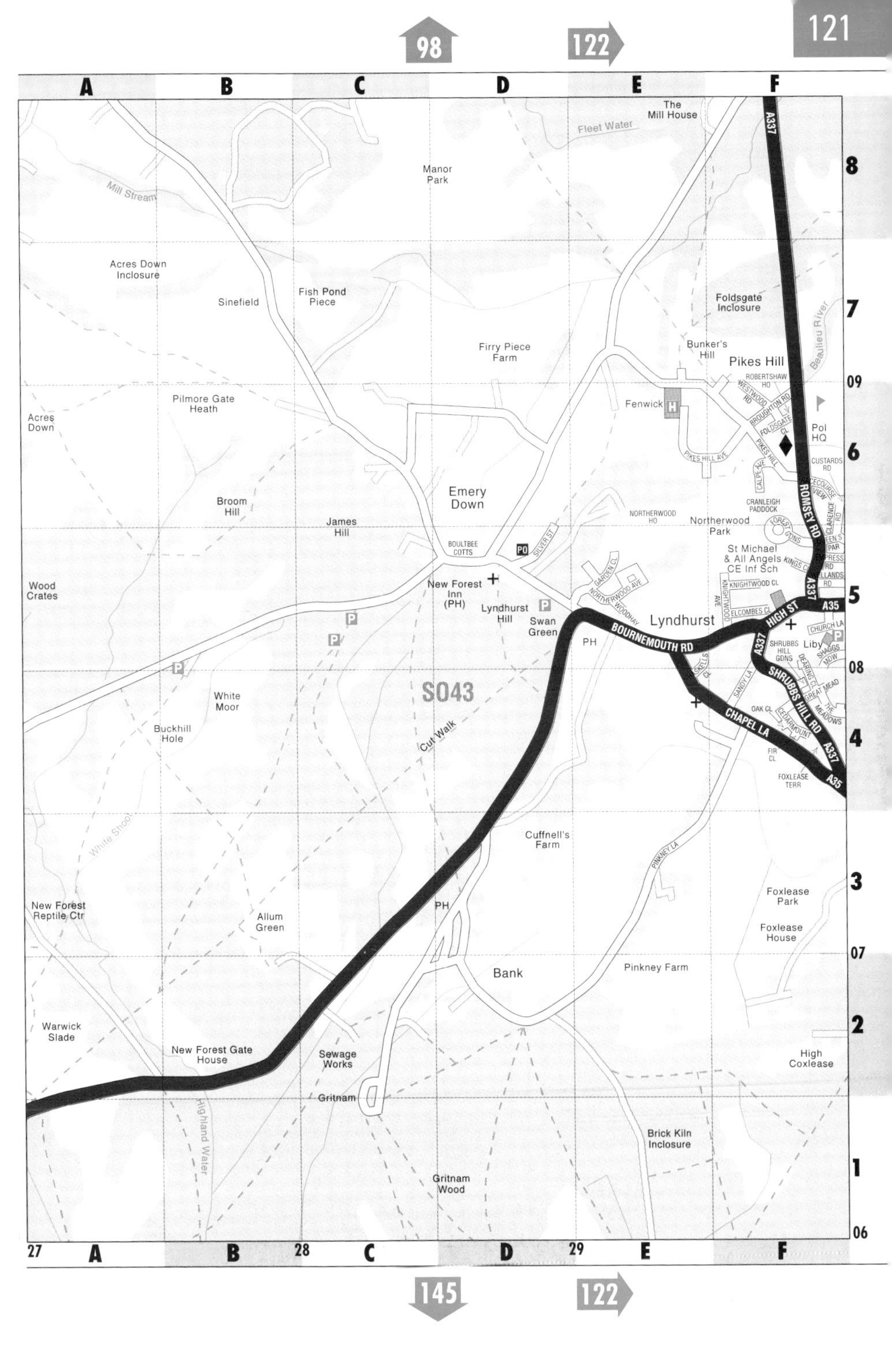
A
B
C
D
E
F
The Mill House
Fleet Water
A337
8
Manor Park
Mill Stream
Acres Down Inclosure
Sinefield
Fish Pond Piece
Foldsgate Inclosure
7
Beaulieu River
Firry Piece Farm
Bunker's Hill
Pikes Hill
ROBERTSHAW HO
09
WESTWOOD RD
BROUGHTON RD
Pilmore Gate Heath
Fenwick
Acres Down
FOLDSGATE CL
Pol HQ
PIKES HILL
6
PIKES HILL AVE
CALPE AVE
CUSTARDS RD
RACECOURSE VIEW
Emery Down
ROMSEY RD
CRANLEIGH PADDOCK
Broom Hill
NORTHERWOOD HO
Northerwood Park
CLARENCE RD
James Hill
FOREST GDNS
BOULTBEE COTTS
PO
SILVER ST
St Michael & All Angels CE Inf Sch
KINGS CL
EMPRESS RD
WELLANDS RD
New Forest Inn (PH)
GARDEN CL
NORTHERWOOD AVE
KNIGHTWOOD CL
Wood Crates
KNIGHTWOOD AVE
5
A35
Lyndhurst Hill
Swan Green
NORTHERWOOD
WOODHAY
ELCOMBES CL
HIGH ST
Lyndhurst
CHURCH LA
BOURNEMOUTH RD
PH
SHRUBBS HILL GDNS
Liby
SHAGGS MDW
08
DEARING CL
SHRUBBS HILL RD
SANDY LA
GREAT MEAD
S043
White Moor
THE MEADOWS
OAK CL
CEDARMOUNT
CHAPEL LA
Buckhill Hole
Cut Walk
4
FIR CL
FOXLEASE TERR
White Shoot
Cuffnell's Farm
PINKNEY LA
3
Foxlease Park
New Forest Reptile Ctr
PH
Allum Green
Foxlease House
07
Bank
Pinkney Farm
Warwick Slade
2
High Coxlease
New Forest Gate House
Sewage Works
Gritnam
Highland Water
Brick Kiln Inclosure
1
Gritnam Wood
06
27
28
29

145
122

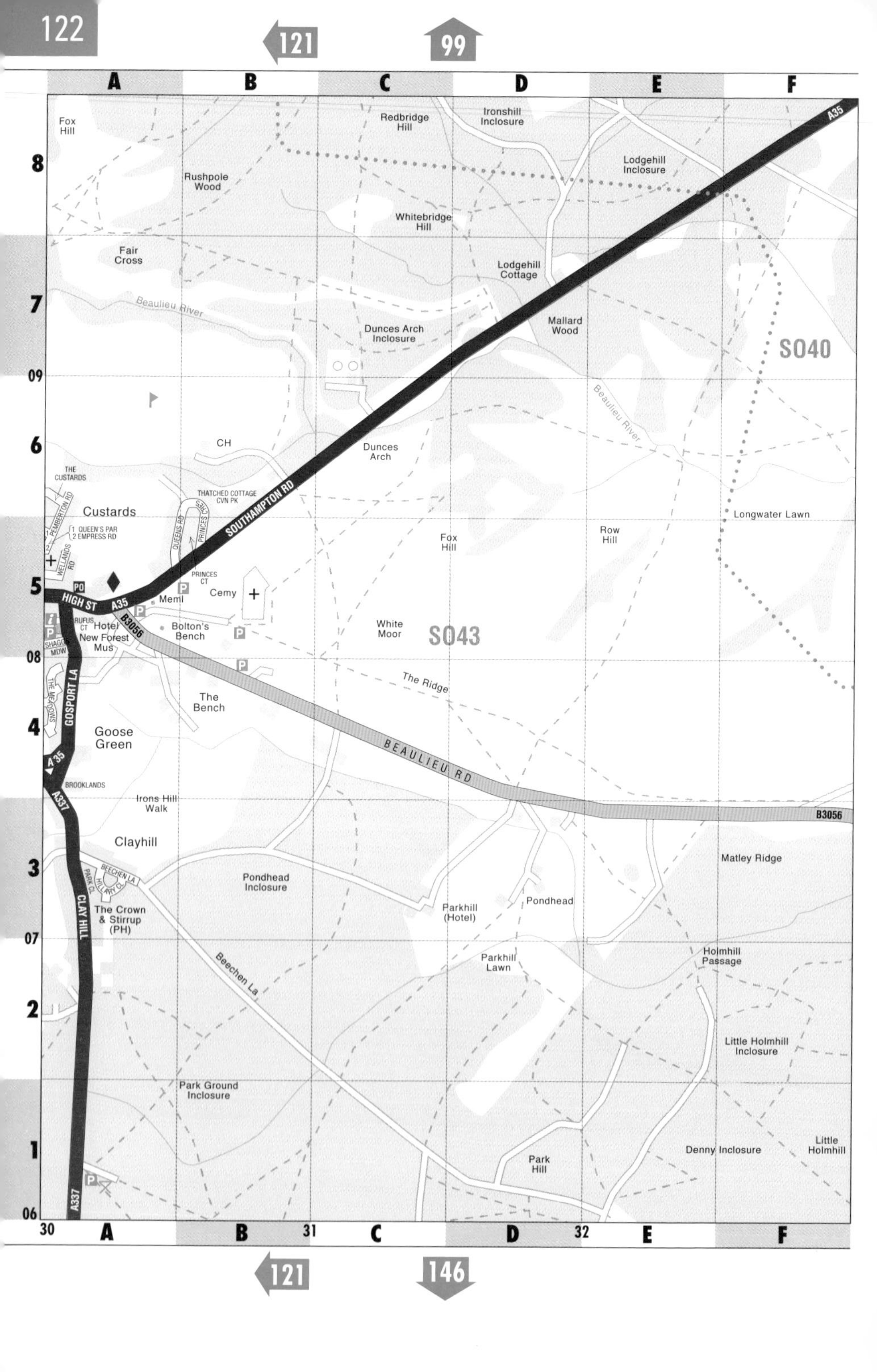

A B C D E F

8

Fox
Hill

Redbridge
Hill

Ironshill
Inclosure

Rushpole
Wood

Lodgehill
Inclosure

Whitebridge
Hill

7

Fair
Cross

Beaulieu River

Lodgehill
Cottage

SO40

Dunces Arch
Inclosure

Mallard
Wood

Beaulieu River

09

6

CH

Dunces
Arch

Longwater Lawn

THE
CUSTARDS

SOUTHAMPTON RD

THATCHED COTTAGE
CVN PK

Custards

QUEENS RD

Fox
Hill

Row
Hill

1 QUEEN'S PAR
2 EMPRESS RD

PEMBERTON RD

PRINCES RD

5

PO

A35

PRINCES
CT

Meml

Cemy

White
Moor

SO43

HIGH ST

B3056

Boltons
Bench

RUFUS
CT Hotel
New Forest
Mus

08

SHAGGS
MDW

P

The
Bench

The Ridge

4

GOSPORT LA

Goose
Green

BEAULIEU RD

A35

BROOKLANDS

Irons Hill
Walk

B3056

Clayhill

Matley Ridge

3

BEECHEN LA

Pondhead
Inclosure

Parkhill
(Hotel)

Pondhead

Holmhill
Passage

CLAY HILL

The Crown
& Stirrup
(PH)

Beechen La

Parkhill
Lawn

07

Little Holmhill
Inclosure

2

Park Ground
Inclosure

Park
Hill

Denny Inclosure

Little
Holmhill

1

A337

06

30 A 31 B C 32 D E F

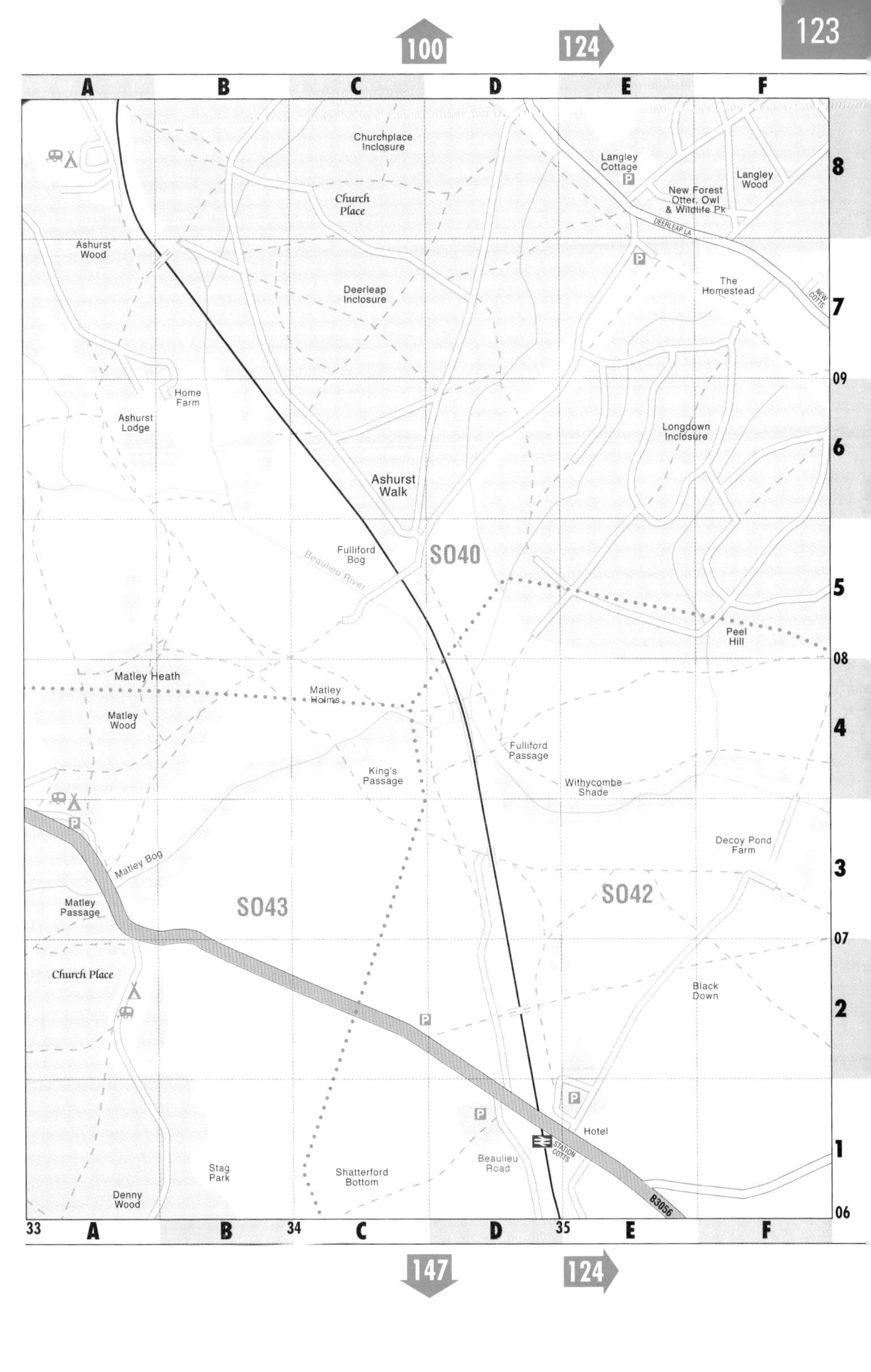
100
124
A
B
C
D
E
F
8
7
09
6
5
08
4
3
07
2
1
06
33
34
35
Churchplace Inclosure
Church Place
Langley Cottage
Langley Wood
New Forest Otter, Owl & Wildlife Pk
DEERLEAP LA
Ashurst Wood
Deerleap Inclosure
The Homestead
NEW COTTS
Home Farm
Ashurst Lodge
Longdown Inclosure
Ashurst Walk
Fulliford Bog
SO40
Beaulieu River
Peel Hill
Matley Heath
Matley Holms
Matley Wood
Fulliford Passage
King's Passage
Withycombe Shade
Decoy Pond Farm
Matley Bog
Matley Passage
SO43
SO42
Church Place
Black Down
Hotel
STATION COTTS
Stag Park
Shatterford Bottom
Beaulieu Road
Denny Wood
B3056
147
124

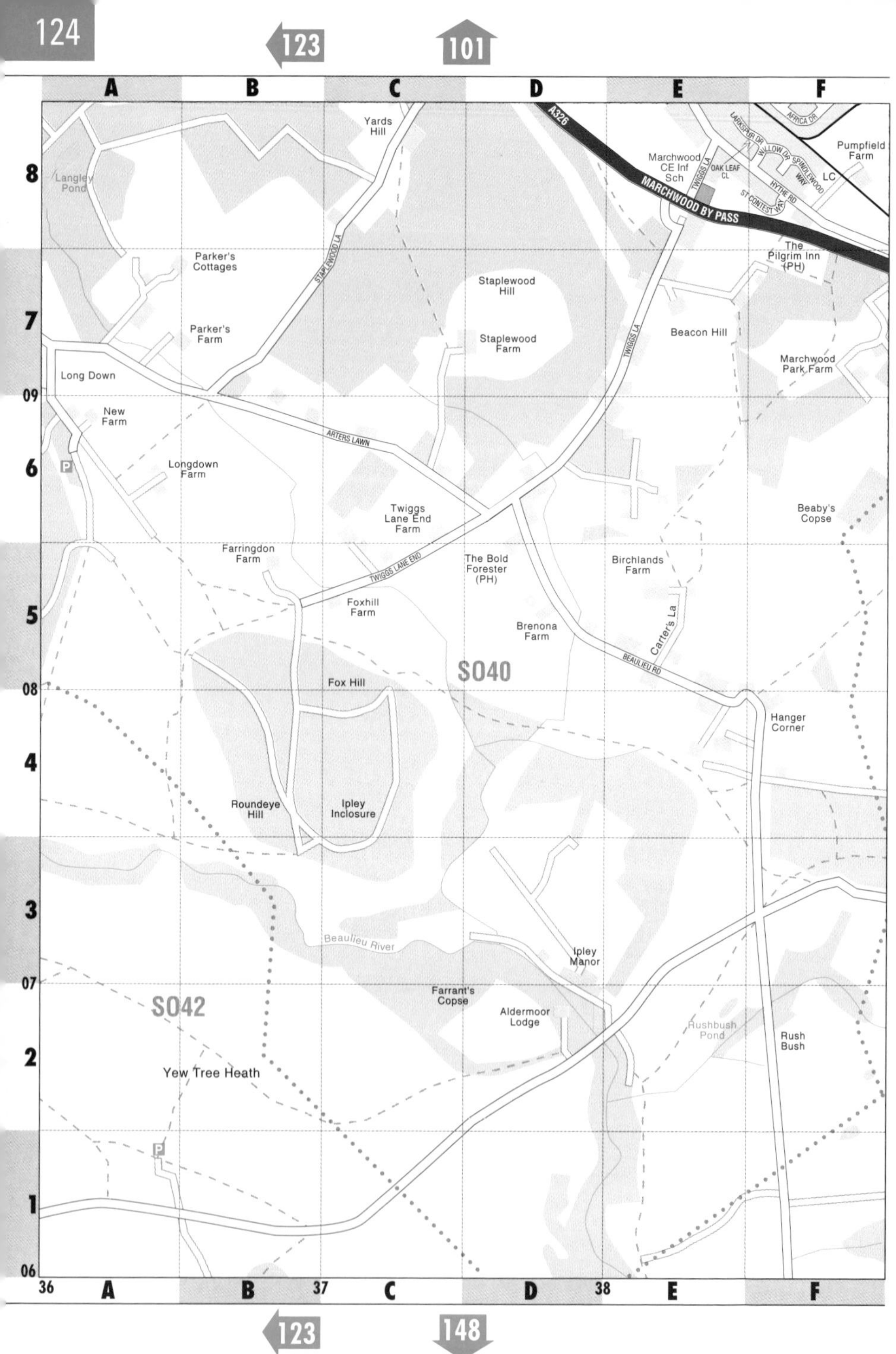

8

7

09

6

5

08

4

3

07

2

1

06

A B C D E F

Langley
Pond

Parker's
Cottages

Parker's
Farm

Long Down

New
Farm

Longdown
Farm

Farringdon
Farm

Fox Hill

Roundeye
Hill

Ipley
Inclosure

Foxhill
Farm

Twiggs
Lane End
Farm

The Bold
Forester
(PH)

Brenona
Farm

Birchlands
Farm

SO40

Yards
Hill

Staplewood
Hill

Staplewood
Farm

Staplewood
Hill

Beacon Hill

A326

MARCHWOOD BY PASS

Marchwood
CE Inf
Sch

OAK LEAF
CL

LC

Pumpfield
Farm

The
Pilgrim Inn
(PH)

Marchwood
Park Farm

Beaby's
Copse

Carter's La

BEAULIEU RD

Hanger
Corner

STEM WOOD LA

ARTERS LAWN

TWIGGS LANE END

TWIGGS LA

Beaulieu River

SO42

Yew Tree Heath

Farrant's
Copse

Aldermoor
Lodge

Ipley
Manor

Rushbush
Pond

Rush
Bush

36 A B 37 C D 38 E F

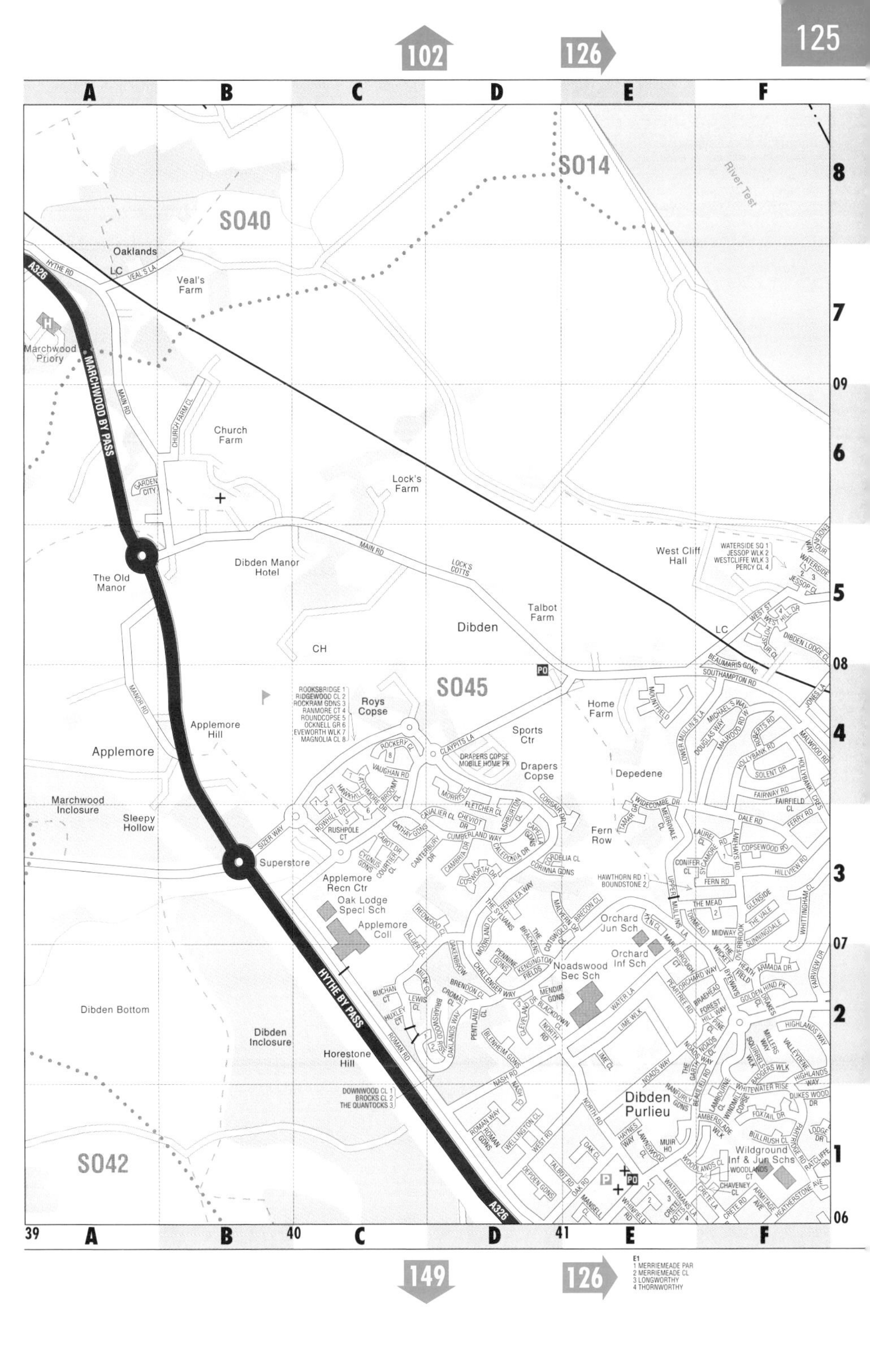

102
126
A
B
C
D
E
F
8
7
09
6
5
08
4
3
07
2
1
06
39
40
41
SO40
SO14
SO45
SO42
River Test
Oaklands
HYTHE RD
LC
VEAL'S LA
Veal's Farm
A326
Marchwood Priory
MARCHWOOD BY PASS
MAIN RD
CHURCH FARM CL
Church Farm
GARDEN CITY
Lock's Farm
MAIN RD
LOCK'S COTTS
The Old Manor
Dibden Manor Hotel
Talbot Farm
Dibden
CH
PO
West Cliff Hall
WATERSIDE SQ 1
JESSOP WLK 2
WESTCLIFFE WLK 3
PERCY CL 4
WATERSIDE
JESSOP CL
WEST ST
LC
DIBDEN LODGE CL
BEAUMARIS GDNS
SOUTHAMPTON RD
MANOR RD
ROOKSBRIDGE 1
RIDGEWOOD CL 2
ROCKRAM GDNS 3
RANMORE CT 4
ROUNDCOPSE 5
OCKNELL GR 6
EVEWORTH WLK 7
MAGNOLIA CL 8
Roys Copse
Applemore Hill
Applemore
Home Farm
Sports Ctr
MOUNTFIELD
LOWER MULLINS LA
DOUGLAS WAY
MICHAEL'S WAY
MALWOOD RD W
ROBERTS RD
MALWOOD RD
HOLLYBANK RD
HOLLYBANK CRES
CLAYPITS LA
ROCKERY CL
VAUGHAN RD
DRAPERS COPSE MOBILE HOME PK
Drapers Copse
Depedene
SOLENT DR
FAIRWAY RD
FAIRFIELD CL
Marchwood Inclosure
Sleepy Hollow
HAWKHILL
LATCHMORE DR
BROOMY CL
MORRIS CL
FLETCHER CL
ASHBURTON CL
CORSAIR DR
WIDECOMBE DR
TAMAR GR
MERRIVALE CL
DALE RD
FERRY RD
ROWHILL DR
RUSHPOLE CT
CAVALIER CL
CHEVIOT DR
CATHAY GDNS
CUMBERLAND WAY
CAPELLA GDNS
CALEDONIA DR
Fern Row
LAUREL CL
SYCAMORE RD
LANEHAYS RD
COPSEWOOD RD
SIZER WAY
CABOT DR
CYGNUS GDNS
COURTIER CL
CANTERBURY DR
CAMBRIA DR
CORDELIA CL
CORINNA GDNS
CONIFER CL
HILLVIEW RD
Superstore
COSWORTH DR
HAWTHORN RD 1
BOUNDSTONE 2
FERN RD
UPPER MULLINS LA
Applemore Recn Ctr
Oak Lodge Specl Sch
FERNLEA WAY
THE SYLVANS
MALVERN DR
BRECON CL
THE MEAD
TORMEAD
GLENSIDE
THE VALE
WHITTINGHAM CL
Applemore Coll
REDWOOD CL
ALDER CL
MOORLAND CL
THE BRACKENS
THE COTSWOLD CL
Orchard Jun Sch
LYN CL
MARLBOROUGH CT
MIDWAY
OVERBROOK
SUNNINGDALE
THE WICKET
OAKENBROW
PENNINE GDNS
KENSINGTON FIELDS
Orchard Inf Sch
FAIRVIEW DR
HEATH FIELD
ARMADA DR
HYTHE BY PASS
MILNE CL
CHALLENGER WAY
Noadswood Sec Sch
ORCHARD WAY
BYEWAYS
GOLDEN HIND PK
BUCHAN CT
LEWIS CL
BRENDON CL
MENDIP GDNS
PEARTREE RD
BRAEHEAD
HUXLEY CT
CROMALT CL
BRIARSWOOD RISE
PENTLAND CL
CLEVELAND DR
BLACKDOWN CL
WATER LA
FOREST HILL WAY
PINE CL
DRAKES CL
Dibden Bottom
ROMAN RD
OAKLANDS WAY
NORTH RD
LIME WLK
HIGHLANDS WAY
Dibden Inclosure
Horestone Hill
BLENHEIM GDNS
LIME CL
NOADS WAY
THE GARTH
NOADS CL
MILLERS WAY
SQUIRRELS WLK
VALLEYDENE
BADGERS WLK
NASH RD
NASH CL
HIGHLANDS WAY
WHITEWATER RISE
DOWNWOOD CL 1
BROCKS CL 2
THE QUANTOCKS 3
Dibden Purlieu
RANFURLY GDNS
BEAULIEU RD
LAMBOURNE CL
WINDMILL COPSE
DUKES WOOD DR
FOXTAIL DR
ROMAN WAY
ROMAN GDNS
WELLINGTON CL
WEST RD
HAYNES WAY
LAWNSWOOD CL
AMBERSLADE WLK
BULLRUSH CL
PARTRIDGE RD
LODGE DR
Muir Ho
OAK CL
Wildground Inf & Jun Schs
RATCLIFFE RD
WOODLANDS CL
WOODLANDS CT
DEPEDEN GDNS
TALBOT RD
OAK RD
P
PO
CHAVENEY CL
ARMITAGE AVE
HEATHERSTONE AVE
MANSELL CL
WHINFIELD
WATERMANS LA
CRETE COTTS
CRETE LA
CRETE RD
A326
149
126
E1
1 MERRIEMEADE PAR
2 MERRIEMEADE CL
3 LONGWORTHY
4 THORNWORTHY

SO14

Docks
QE2
Passenger
Terminal
Mast

Ferry

Weston Shelf

Weston
Hard

SO19

ROTHSCHILD
CL

WESTON LA

SEAFIELD RD

INTERNATIONAL WAY

HARTLEY GN

CLIFF RD

SPRINGFIELD RD

SPASHOTT RD

HURSTBOURNE
PL

CANBERRA
TWRS

HARCLESE AVE

Weston
Shore
Inf Sch

Weston
Park

RIVERSDALE CL	1
SQUIRES WLK	2
HAMPTON TWRS	3
HAVRE TWRS	4
OSLO TWRS	5
COPENHAGEN TWRS	6
ROTTERDAM TWRS	7
WESTON CT	8
GRATELEY CL	9
DRAYTON CL	10

Solent Way

SO31

MARINA
VIEW

ABBEY HILL

Hythe
Marina

WHITE
HEATHER
CT

ENDEAVOUR WAY

VELSHEDA
CT

ASTRA
CT

SHAMROCK WAY

ENDEAVOUR WAY

WEST ST

Hythe Pier Rly

Hythe Pier

Hythe
Hard

Hythe

Southampton Water

1 WATERSIDE	10 COURT HOUSE CL
2 MOUNT HOUSE CL	11 LAWRENCE HO
3 HAZELDALE VILLAS	12 MARINER MEWS
4 HOMEBOROUGH HO	13 HANOVER CT
5 DRUMMOND CT	14 THE SYCAMORES
6 ADMIRALS WAY	15 FAIRFIELD CL
7 MARSH PAR	16 GREEN CL
8 NEW MARSH HO	17 HOLLYBANK CL
9 DRUMMOND RD	18 TRAFALGAR HO

DIBDEN
LODGE CL

Hythe
Prim Sch

PO

LC

Liby

Pier

Waterside
Heritage
Ctr

SO45

HOWARD
OLIVER

HOLLYBANK CRES

KELVIN

LANGDOWN

ABBEY RD

ASHFORD CRES

LANGDOWN RD

GRAYS

HARTLEY
GDNS

Solent Way

FAIRVIEW CL

Langdown
Firs

LANGDOWN
FIRS

WINDRUSH WAY

GREEN LEAF

Langdown

LC

BEAULIEU RD

PO

CURLEW
WLK

CURLEW
CL

Hythe

H

HIGHLANDS CL

SILVERDALE CL

D'MONT

Waterside
Prim Sch

Furzey
Piece

SPINNEY
DALE

FROST LA

HART HILL

FROG'S
HALL

LODGE CL

ELIZABETH
GDNS

BUTTERCUP
WAY

HEATHERTON
GDNS

WILDGROUND LA

WEST RD

EAST RD

Furzedown
Farm

Hotel

Frostlane

Kitcher's
Copse

Forest Lodge

Crampool Copse

Works

A1		A2		B1
1 HARTLEY WLK		1 FAIRVIEW PAR		1 NELSON CT
2 SILVERS END		2 KNIGHTSTONE GRANGE		2 FURZEDOWN MEWS
3 ANDREW CL		3 HIGHLANDS WAY		3 TRAFALGAR WAY
4 WILDGROUND LA		4 FRAYSLEA		4 HAMILTON MEWS
5 NORTHBOURNE CL				
6 SHOBLANDS WAY				
7 SANDILANDS WAY				

104
128
A
B
C
D
E
F
SO19
SO31
Chamberlayne Park Sch
West Wood
Abbey Fruit Park Ind Est
The Roll Call (PH)
Ridge Farm
Kestrel Farm
Priors Heath Copse
Butlocks Heath
The Grange (PH)
Schs
Netley Abbey
Netley Castle (Conv Home)
Abbey Hall
Netley
Hound Farm
Hound Corner Fruit Farm
Hound Corner Ecology Park
Hound
Netley Court Sch
Liby
Hamble Com Sports Coll
Hamble
Police Training Ctr
Min Rly
Royal Victoria Country Park
The Park Heritage Ctr
West Wood
Cemy
Hamble Prim Sch
Recn Gd
Airfield (disused)
Hamble Court Bsns Pk
Works
Hamble Cliff
Southampton Water
Solent Way
Ensign Pk
Mitchell Point
Works
Depot
Hamble Common
HAMBLE LA
B3397
1 DRAYTON CL
2 LONGSTOCK CL
3 LAMBERHURST CL
THE KESTRELS 1
RATHDORA MEWS 2
CHAMBERLAYNE RD 3
ASH CL 4
MAPLE CL 5
NIGHTINGALE CL 6
BATCHELOR GN 7
WOODLAND VIEW 8
THE OAKS 9
FOUNDRY CRES 10
SHORWELL 1
NETTLESTONE 2
MANCHESTER RD 1
ROSS MEWS 2
VICTORIA CT 3
ENGLEFIELD CT 4
GARFIELD RD 5
WYKEHAM CL 6
WINCHESTER CL 7
HOLMES CL 8
MORTIMER CL 9
CHAMBERLAYNE HO 10
CRICHTON HO 11
ASHBURTON HO 12
CHANDLERS PL 13
SPINNAKER CT 14
THE MARINERS 15
8
7
09
6
5
08
4
3
07
2
1
06
45
46
47
151
128

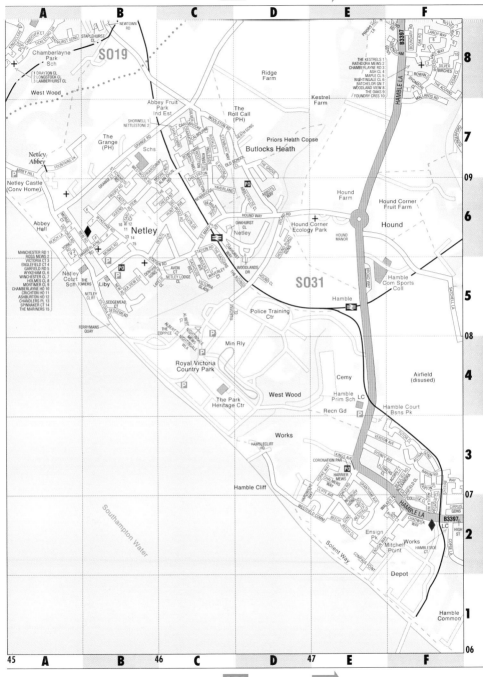

Map

A B C D E F

8

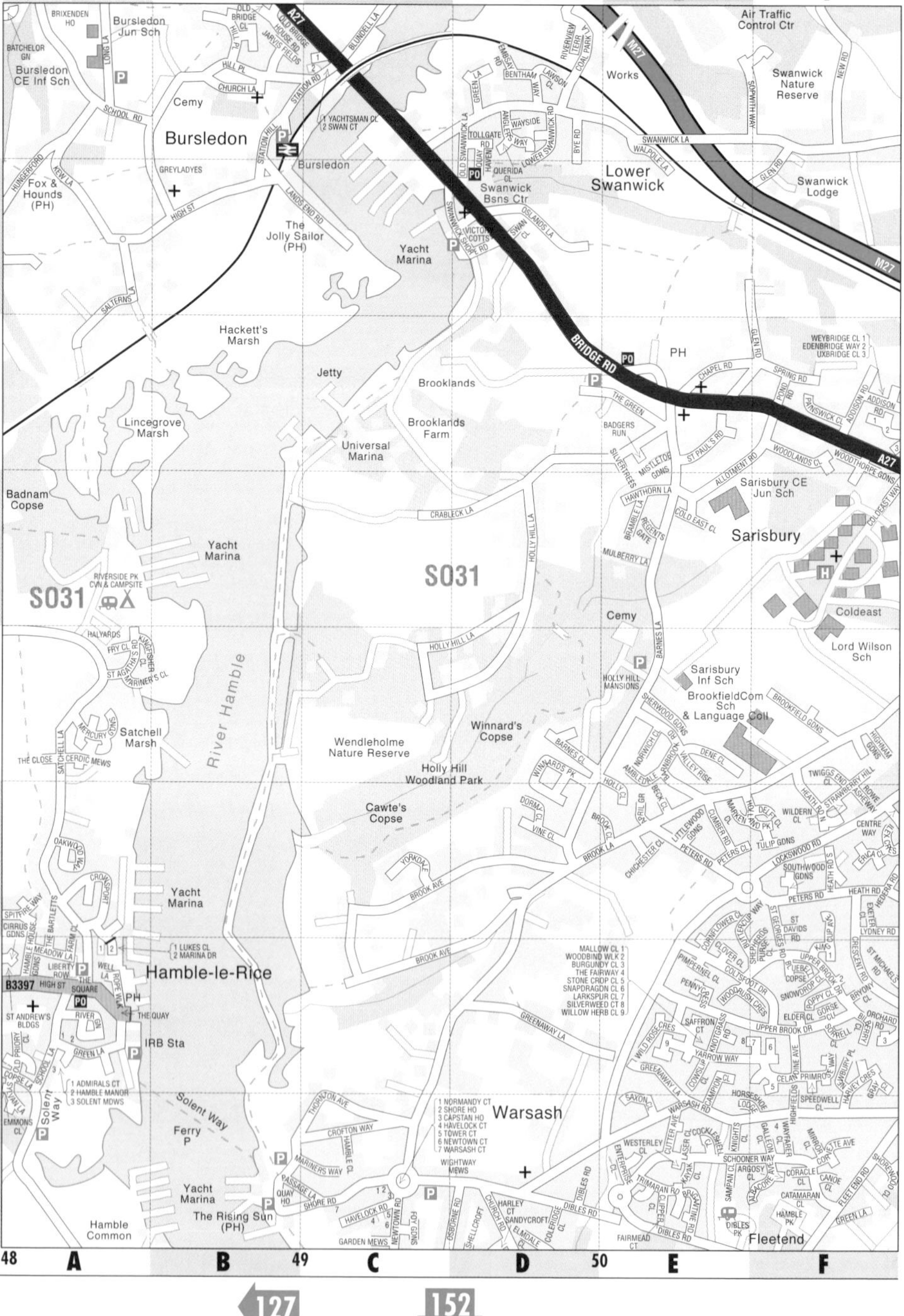

Brixenden Ho
Bursledon Jun Sch
OLD BRIDGE
M27
BLINDHE LA
Air Traffic Control Ctr
Swanwick Nature Reserve
BATCHELOR GN
Bursledon CE Inf Sch
Cemy
SCHOOL RD
HILL PL
CHURCH LA
Bursledon
Bentham
Works
Lower Swanwick
Swanwick Lodge
SWANWICK LA

7

Fox & Hounds (PH)
GREYLADYES
HIGH ST
The Jolly Sailor (PH)
1 YACHTSMAN CT
2 SWAN CT
Bursledon
TOLLGATE RD
QUERIDA CL
Swanwick Bsns Ctr
WAYSIDE
SWAN CL
Yacht Marina
1 VICTORY CL
2 COTTS
PO
CHAPEL RD
SPRING RD
PH
GLEN RD
M27
A27

09

SALTERNS
Hackett's Marsh
Jetty
Brooklands
PH
THE GREEN
BADGERS RUN
WEYBRIDGE CL 1
EDENBRIDGE WAY 2
UXBRIDGE CL 3
WOODHAVEN GDNS

6

Lincegrove Marsh
Universal Marina
Brooklands Farm
ST PAUL'S LA
MISTLETOE GDNS
HAWTHORN LA
Sarisbury CE Jun Sch
Sarisbury
EAST COAST RD

5

Badnam Copse
Yacht Marina
RIVERSIDE PK CVN & CAMPSITE
CRABLECK LA
SO31
MULBERRY LA
Coldeast
Lord Wilson Sch

08

SO31
HALYARDS
FRY CL
ST MARINER'S CL
HOLLY HILL LA
Cemy
BARNES LA
Sarisbury Inf Sch
Sarisbury Infant
BrookfieldCom Sch & Language Coll
BROOKFIELD GDNS

4

THE CLOSE
CERDIC MEWS
Satchell Marsh
River Hamble
Winnard's Copse
HOLLY HILL MANSIONS
SHERWOOD GDNS
DENE CL
TWIGGS END
WILDERN LA
CENTRE WAY

3

OAKWOOD
CROFT RD
Wendleholme Nature Reserve
Holly Hill Woodland Park
Cawte's Copse
YORK LA
BROOK AVE
BROOK LA
PETERS RD
CHICHESTER CL
LITTLEWOOD GDNS
TULIP GDNS
LOCKSHEATH RD
SOUTHWOOD GDNS
HEATH RD

07

CIRRUS GDNS
MEADOW LA
1 LUKES CL
2 MARINA DR
Yacht Marina
WELL LA
HIGH ST
Hamble-le-Rice
BROOK AVE
MALLOW CL 1
WOODBIND WLK 2
BURGUNDY CL 3
THE FAIRWAY 4
STONE CROP CL 5
SNAPDRAGON CL 6
LARKSPUR CL 7
SILVERWEED CL 8
WILLOW HERB CL 9
PEARTREE
COLTSFOOT CL
PIMPERNEL CL
ELDER CL CORSE
ORCHARD
UPPER BROOK DR

2

B3397
ST ANDREW'S BLDGS
SQUARE
PO
RIVER
PH
THE QUAY
IRB Sta
GREENAWAY LA
SAXON
YARROW WAY
SPEEDWELL CL
HORSE
ST MICHAELS

1

EMMONS CL
Solent Way
1 ADMIRALS CT
2 HAMBLE MANOR
3 SOLENT MDWS
Ferry P
CROFTON WAY
HAMBLE LA
PASSAGE LA
QUAY HO
SHORE RD
1 NORMANDY CT
2 SHORE HO
3 CAPSTAN HO
4 HAVELOCK CT
5 TOWER CT
6 NEWTOWN CT
7 WARSASH CT
WIGHTWAY MEWS
Warsash
HARLEY CT
SANDYCROFT
WESTERLEY CT
SCHOONER WAY
ARGOSY CL
CORACLE CL
CANOE CL
CATAMARAN CL
HAMBLE PK

06

Hamble Common
Yacht Marina
The Rising Sun (PH)
GARDEN MEWS
DIBLES RD
FAIRMEAD CT
GREEN LA
DIBLES
Fleetend

48 A B 49 C D 50 E F

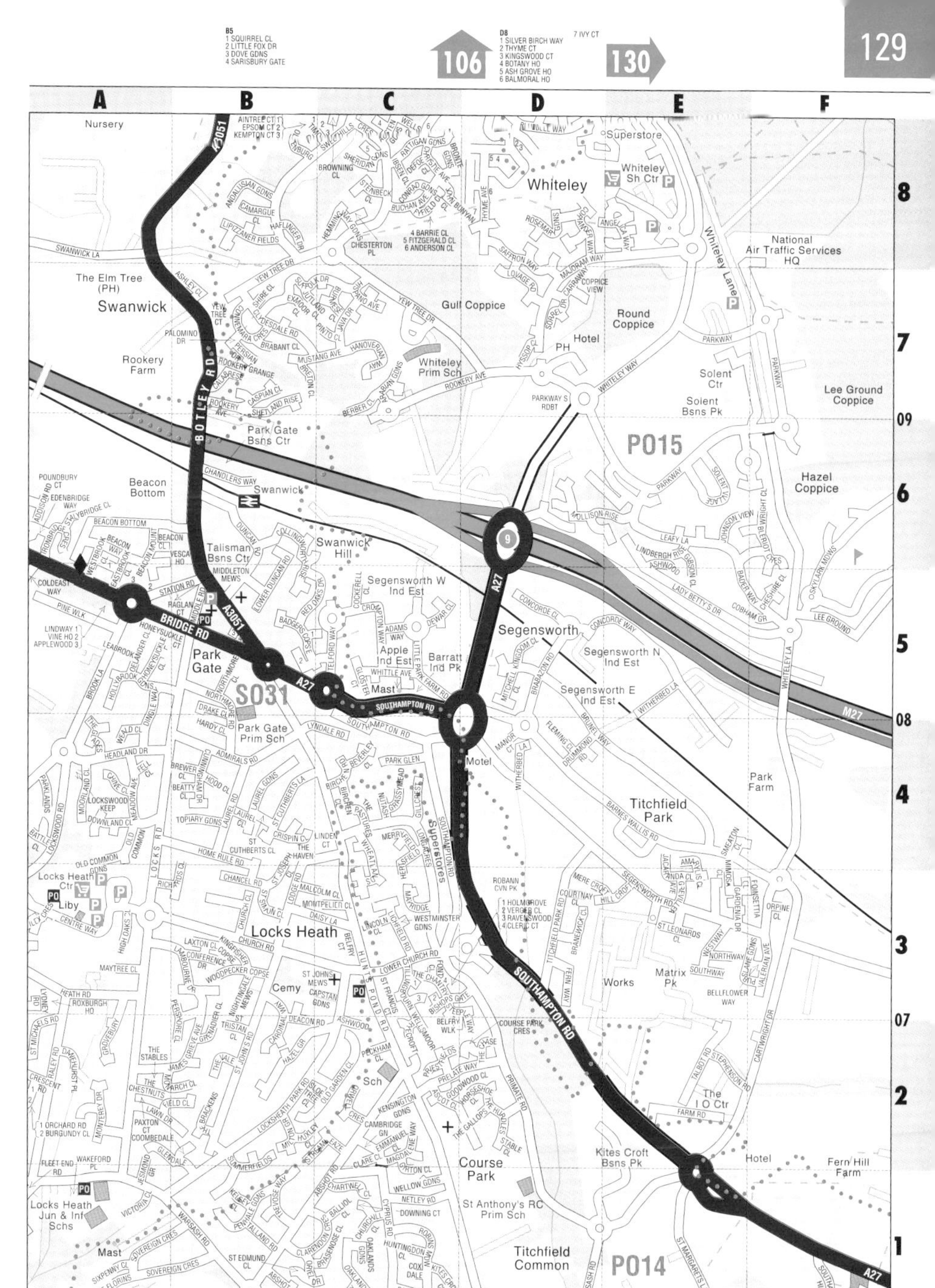

B5
1 SQUIRREL CL
2 LITTLE FOX DR
3 DOVE GDNS
4 SARISBURY GATE

106

7 IVY CT

D8
1 SILVER BIRCH WAY
2 THYME CT
3 KINGSWOOD CT
4 BOTANY HO
5 ASH GROVE HO
6 BALMORAL HO

130

129

107

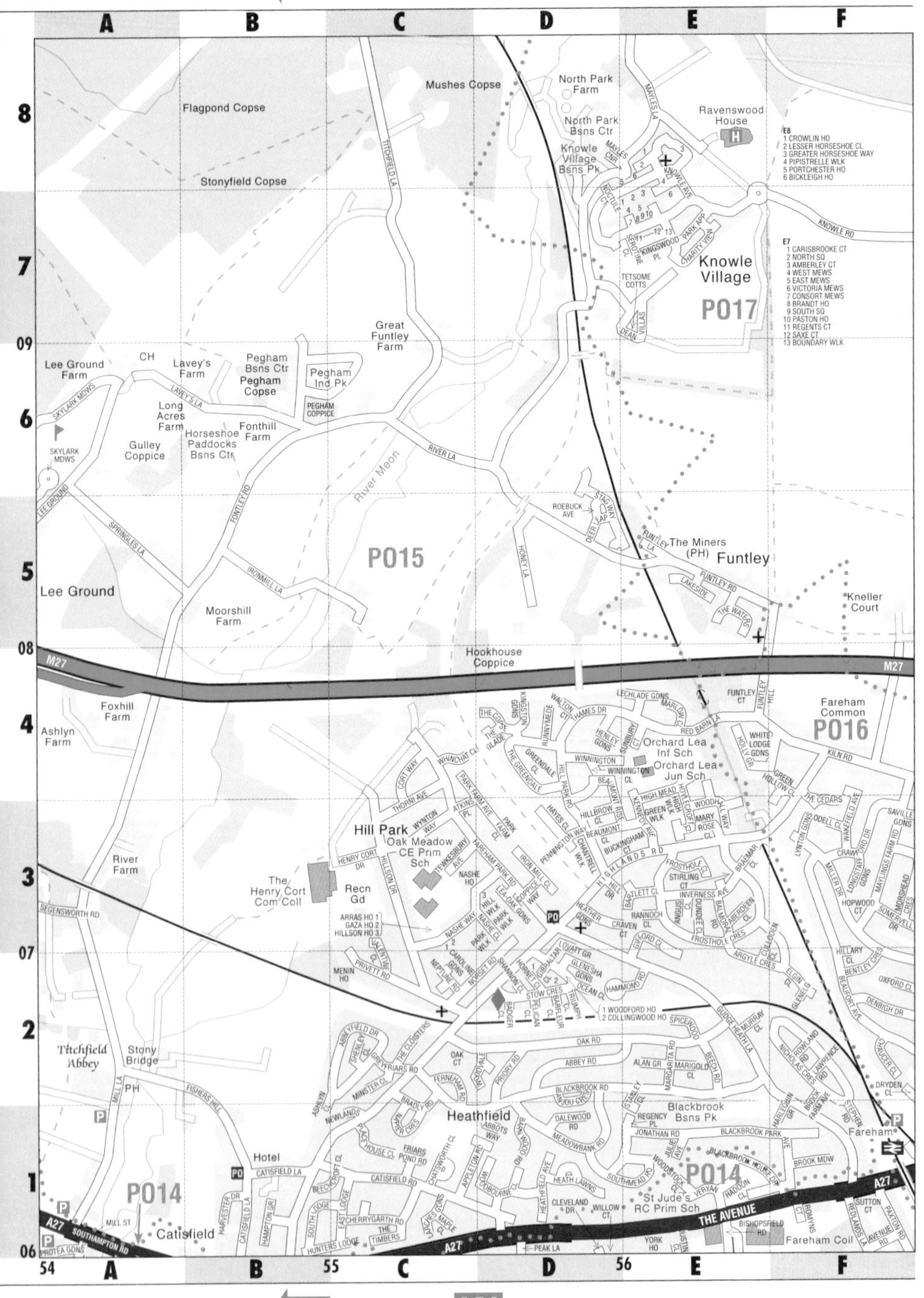

A
B
C
D
E
F
8
7
09
6
5
08
4
3
07
2
1
06
54
55
56
Flagpond Copse
Mushes Copse
North Park Farm
North Park Bsns Ctr
Knowle Village Bsns Pk
Ravenswood House
E8
1 CROWLIN HO
2 LESSER HORSESHOE CL
3 GREATER HORSESHOE WAY
4 PIPISTRELLE WLK
5 PORTCHESTER HO
6 BICKLEIGH HO
Stonyfield Copse
TITCHFIELD LA
MAYLES LA
MAYLES CNR
NOCTULE CT
KNOWLE AVE
KNOWLE RD
SEROTINE CL
KINGSWOOD PL
PARK APP
CHARITY VW
Knowle Village
TETSOME COTTS
PO17
DEAN VILLAS
E7
1 CARISBROOKE CT
2 NORTH SQ
3 AMBERLEY CT
4 WEST MEWS
5 EAST MEWS
6 VICTORIA MEWS
7 CONSORT MEWS
8 BRANDT HO
9 SOUTH SQ
10 PASTON HO
11 REGENTS CT
12 SAXE CT
13 BOUNDARY WLK
Great Funtley Farm
Lee Ground Farm
CH
Lavey's Farm
Pegham Bsns Ctr
Pegham Copse
Pegham Ind Pk
PEGHAM COPPICE
SKYLARK MDWS
LAVEY'S LA
Long Acres Farm
Horseshoe Paddocks Bsns Ctr
Fonthill Farm
Gulley Coppice
River Meon
RIVER LA
LEE GROUND
SPRINGLES LA
FONTLEY RD
ROEBUCK AVE
STAG WAY
DEER LEAP
HONEY LA
FUNTLEY LA
The Miners (PH)
Funtley
FUNTLEY RD
LAKESIDE
THE WATERS
PO15
Kneller Court
Lee Ground
IRONMILL LA
Moorshill Farm
Hookhouse Coppice
M27
Foxhill Farm
Ashlyn Farm
LECHLADE GDNS
MARLOW CT
FUNTLEY CT
FUNTLEY HILL
Fareham Common
PO16
KINGSTON GDNS
WALTON CT
THAMES DR
RED BARN LA
THE COPSE
THE GLADE
RUNNYMEDE
HENLEY GDNS
SUNBURY CT
Orchard Lea Inf Sch
Orchard Lea Jun Sch
WHITE LODGE GDNS
HOLLY GR
KILN RD
WHINCHAT CL
GREENDALE CL
THE GREENDALE
WINNINGTON
WINNINGTON CL
GREEN HOLLOW CL
THE CEDARS
CORT WAY
THORNI AVE
PARK FARM AVE
HILL PARK RD
HIGH MEAD
HOYLECROFT CL
WOODHALL WAY
WYNTON WAY
ATKINS PL
PARK FARM CL
HAYES CL
HILLBROW CL
MARY ROSE CL
LYNTON GDNS
ODELL CL
WAKEFIELD AVE
SAVILLE GDNS
Hill Park
Oak Meadow CE Prim Sch
PENNINGTON WAY
BEAUMONT CL
BUCKINGHAM CT
HIGHLANDS RD
CRAWFORD DR
MAYLINGS FARM RD
HENRY CORT DR
TEWKESBURY AVE
FAREHAM PARK RD
IRON MILL CL
CHANTRELL WLK
FROSTHOLE CL
BRAEMAR CL
MILLER DR
LONGSTAFF GDNS
The Henry Cort Com Coll
Recn Gd
HILLSON DR
NASHE HO
COPPICE WAY
LEA-OAK GDNS
STIRLING CT
INVERNESS AVE
DUNDEE CL
BALMORAL RD
ABERDEEN CL
HOPWOOD CT
SOMERVELL DR
MORSHEAD CRES
River Farm
SEGENSWORTH RD
ARRAS HO 1
GAZA HO 2
HILLSON HO 3
NASHE WAY
HILL WLK
PARK WLK
PO
HEATHER GDNS
RANNOCH CL
CRAVEN CT
FROSTHOLE CRES
ANGUS CL
CULLODEN CL
ARGYLE CRES
VALENTINE CL
CAROLINE GDNS
NORSET RD
SHANNON CL
HORNET CL
GIBRALTAR CL
LOVATT GR
GLENESHA GDNS
GIFFORD CL
HAMMOND RD
ELGIN CL
GLENELG
HILLARY CL
BENTLEY CRES
OXFORD CL
MENIN HO
PRIVETT RD
NEPTUNE RD
STOW CRES
OCEAN CL
BEAUFORT AVE
DENBIGH DR
BADGER CL
PELICAN CL
BARFLEUR CL
TRIUMPH CL
1 WOODFORD HO
2 COLLINGWOOD HO
SPICEWOOD
GUDGE HEATH LA
MURRAY CL
ROWLAND RD
LAWRENCE RD
NICHOLAS CRES
CHAUCER CL
Titchfield Abbey
Stony Bridge
ABBEYFIELD DR
SHENLEY CL
THE CLOISTERS
OAK RD
GREYFRIARS RD
OAK CT
ABBEY RD
PRIORY RD
ALAN GR
MARIGOLD CL
MARGARITA RD
BEECH RD
DRYDEN CL
MILL LA
PH
FISHERS HILL
MINSTER CL
FERNEHAM RD
BLACKBROOK RD
STANLEY CL
Blackbrook Bsns Pk
HARLEQUIN GR
BROOK FARM AVE
STEPHEN RD
ASHLYN CL
NEWLANDS
BRADLY RD
Heathfield
DALEWOOD RD
REGENCY PL
JONATHAN RD
BLACKBROOK PARK AVE
Fareham
P
NAPIER CRES
PLACE HOUSE CL
ABBOTS WAY
BARNWOOD RD
MEADOWBANK RD
JULIE AVE
BLACKBROOK HOUSE DR
BROOK MDW
Hotel
FRIARS POND RD
CHATSWORTH CL
APPLETON RD
HEATHFIELD AVE
SOUTHMEAD RD
WOODSTOCK
PO14
PO
CATISFIELD LA
BEECHCROFT CL
CATISFIELD RD
WOODBOURNE CL
HEATH LAWNS
VERYAN
HADDON CL
A27
PO14
HARVESTER DR
HAMPTON GR
CLEVELAND DR
WILLOW CT
St Jude's RC Prim Sch
THE AVENUE
SUTTON CT
PAXTON RD
MILL ST
A27 SOUTHAMPTON RD
Catisfield
SOUTH LODGE
EAST LODGE
CHERRYGARTH RD
THE TIMBERS
LARCHES GDNS
MAPLE CL
BISHOPSFIELD RD
ROMYNS CT
REDLANDS LA
AVENUE RD
PROTEA GDNS
HUNTERS LODGE
A27
PEAK LA
YORK HO
AUSTIN CT
Fareham Coll

129

154

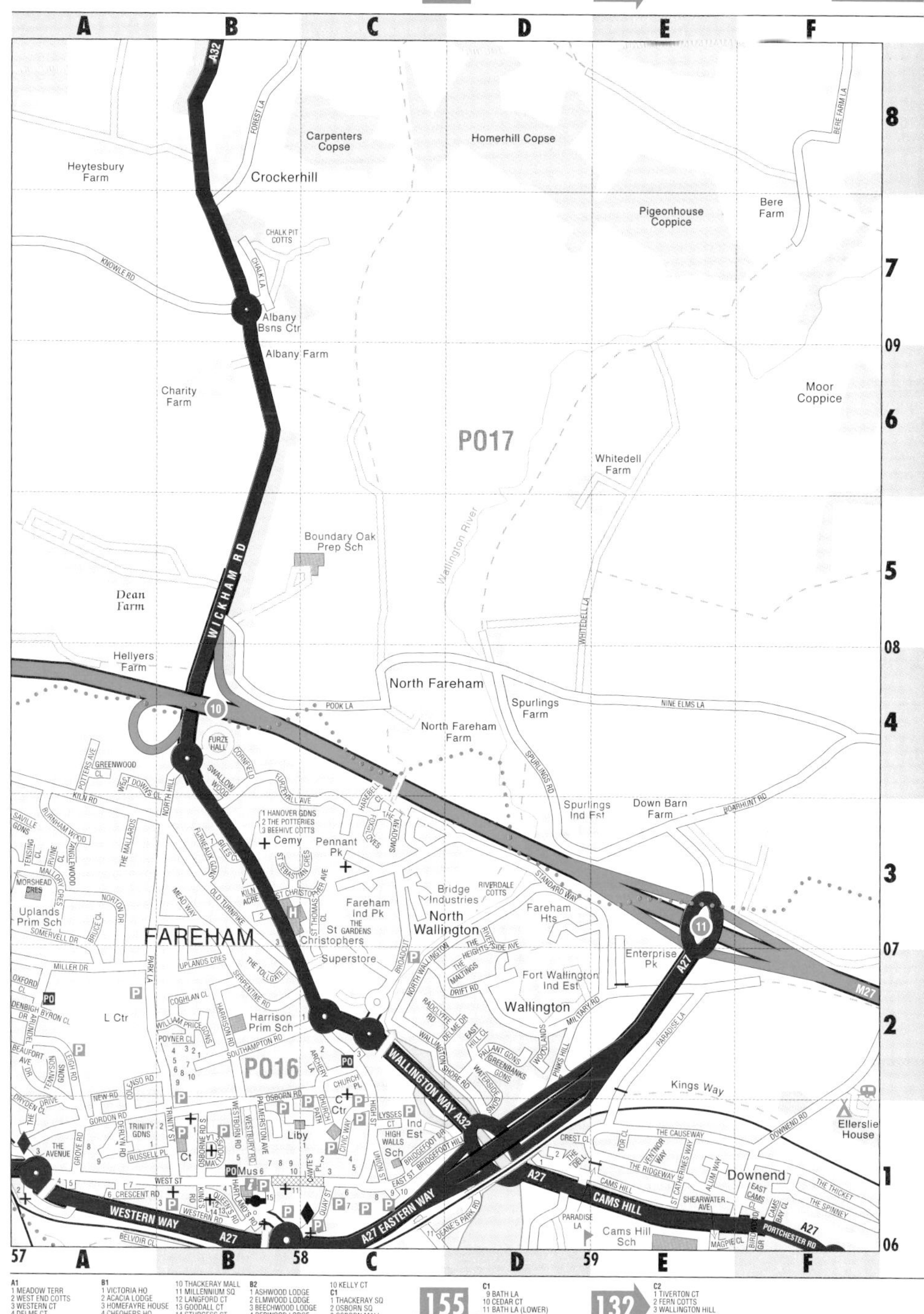

A B C D E F

8
7
09
6
08
4
5
08
4
3
07
2
07
1
06

Heytesbury Farm

Carpenters Copse

Homerhill Copse

Crockerhill

Pigeonhouse Coppice

Bere Farm

Moor Coppice

CHALK PIT COTTS

A32

Albany Bsns Ctr

Albany Farm

Charity Farm

P017

Whitedell Farm

Dean Farm

WICKHAM RD

Boundary Oak Prep Sch

Wallington River

Hellyers Farm

North Fareham

Spurlings Farm

NINE ELMS LA

POOK LA

North Fareham Farm

Spurlings Ind Est

Down Barn Farm

FURZE HALL

SWALLOW WD

10

GREENWOOD

KILN RD

Cemy

1 HANOVER GDNS
2 THE POTTERIES
3 BEEHIVE COTTS

Pennant Pk

Bridge Industries

RIVERDALE COTTS

Fareham Hts

Fort Wallington Ind Est

Enterprise Pk

11

Fareham Ind Pk

FAREHAM

Uplands Prim Sch

MORSHEAD CRES

THE St Christophers GARDENS

North Wallington

STANDARD WAY

M27

A27

Superstore

Wallington

Harrison Prim Sch

P016

Liby

Kings Way

Ellerslie House

WALLINGTON WAY A32

THE CAUSEWAY

Ct Ctr.

Ind High Est WALLS Sch

Downend

EAST CAMS

WESTERN WAY

A27

A27 EASTERN WAY

CAMS HILL

Cams Hill Sch

A27

PORTCHESTER RD

57   A   58   C   D   59   E   F

A1
1 MEADOW TERR
2 WEST END COTTS
3 WESTERN CT
4 DELME CT
5 MAYTREE RD
6 THE GILLIES
7 BURY RD
8 FAREGROVE CT
9 RICHES MEWS

B1
1 VICTORIA HO
2 ACACIA LODGE
3 HOMEFAYRE HOUSE
4 CHEQHERS HO
5 MORESBY CT
6 SAVDY BLDGS
7 DELME SQ
8 WESTBURY MALL
9 WESTBURY SQ
10 THACKERAY MALL
11 MILLENNIUM SQ
12 LANGFORD CT
13 GOODALL CT
14 STURGESS CT
15 HARPER WAY

B2
1 ASHWOOD LODGE
2 ELMWOOD LODGE
3 BEECHWOOD LODGE
4 REDWOOD LODGE
5 PINEWOOD LODGE
6 CEDARWOOD LODGE
7 BIRCHWOOD LODGE
8 NORTHWOOD SQ
9 DARREN CT
10 KELLY CT

C1
1 THACKERAY SQ
2 OSBORN SQ
3 OSBORN MALL
4 CROAD CT
5 CONSORT CT
6 WESTQUAY HO
7 ADELAIDE PL
8 MADISON CT

C1
9 BATH LA
10 CEDAR CT
11 BATH LA (LOWER)

C2
1 TIVERTON CT
2 FERN COTTS
3 WALLINGTON HILL

D1
1 WALLINGTON SHORE RD
2 CHARLEMONT DR

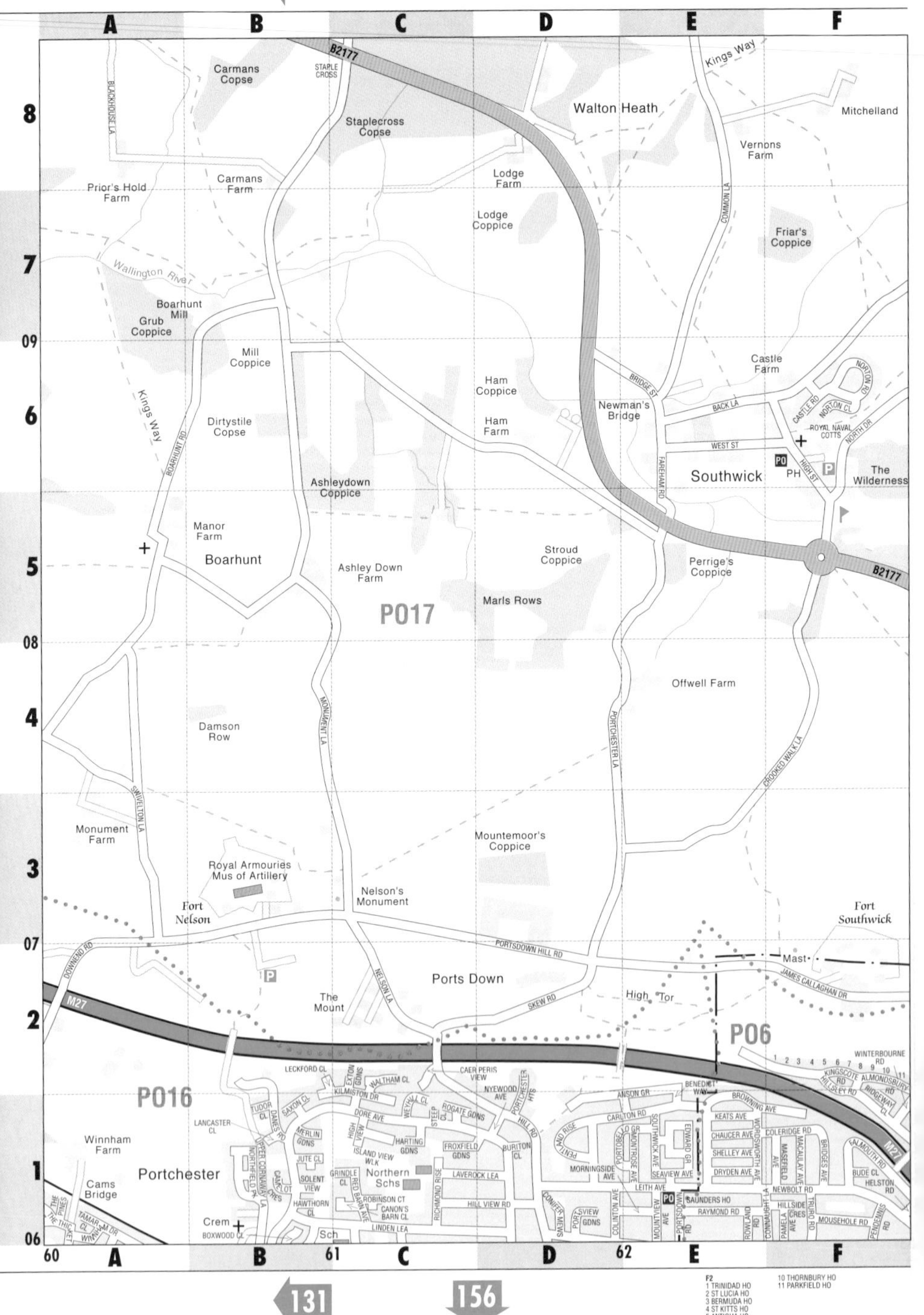

A   **B**   **C**   **D**   **E**   **F**

B2177

Carmans Copse

Staplecross Copse

STAPLE CROSS

Walton Heath

Kings Way

Mitchelland

8

BLACKHOUSE LA

Vernons Farm

Prior's Hold Farm

Carmans Farm

Lodge Farm

Lodge Coppice

Friar's Coppice

7

Wallington River

COMMON LA

Boarhunt Mill

Grub Coppice

Mill Coppice

Ham Coppice

Castle Farm

09

Kings Way

BOARHUNT RD

Dirtystile Copse

Ham Farm

Newman's Bridge

BRIDGE ST

BACK LA

MORSON RD

NORTH RD

MARION RD

ROYAL NAVAL COTTS

WEST ST

6

Ashleydown Coppice

Manor Farm

Boarhunt

Ashley Down Farm

Southwick

PO

PH

P

The Wilderness

FAREHAM RD

5

PO17

Stroud Coppice

Perrige's Coppice

B2177

Marls Rows

Damson Row

Offwell Farm

PORTCHESTER LA

4

SKELTON LA

MONUMENT LA

Monument Farm

CROOKHORN LA

Mountemoor's Coppice

3

Royal Armouries Mus of Artillery

Nelson's Monument

Fort Southwick

Fort Nelson

P

PORTSDOWN HILL RD

Mast

JAMES CALLAGHAN DR

07

DORKING RD

Ports Down

The Mount

NELSON LA

SKEW RD

High Tor

PO6

2

M27

PO16

WINTERBOURNE RD

KINGS RD

ALMONDSBURY RD

1 2 3 4 5 6 7 8 9

LECKFORD CL

CAER PERIS VIEW

NYEWOOD AVE

ANSON GR

CARLTON RD

BROWNING AVE

COLERIDGE RD

MASEFIELD AVE

KINGSLEY RD

M27

Winnham Farm

Cams Bridge

Portchester

WALTHAM CL

KILMISTON DR

DUNE AVE

ROGATE GDNS

FROXFIELD GDNS

BURITON CL

HILL RD

KEATS AVE

CHAUCER AVE

SHELLEY AVE

DRYDEN AVE

MACAULAY RD

BRIDGES AVE

BUDE CL

HELSTON RD

1

LANCASTER CL

ISLAND VIEW WLK

HARTING GDNS

LAVEROCK LEA

Northern Schs

SEAVIEW AVE

LEITH AVE

MORNINGSIDE

NEWBOLT RD

HILLSIDE CRES

MOUSEHOLE RD

JUTE CL

SOLENT VIEW

GRINDLE CL

Crem

HAWTHORN CL

ROBINSON CT

CANON'S BARN CL

LINDEN LEA

HILL VIEW RD

SAUNDERS HO

RAYMOND HO

SVIEW GDNS

BOXWOOD CL

Sch

06

60   **A**   **B**   **61**   **C**   **D**   **62**   **E**   **F**

F2
1 TRINIDAD HO
2 ST LUCIA HO
3 BERMUDA HO
4 ST KITTS HO
5 ANTIGUA HO
6 FOXCOTE HO
7 KINGSODTE HO
8 ALMONDSBURY HO
9 OAKLANDS HO
10 THORNBURY HO
11 PARKFIELD HO

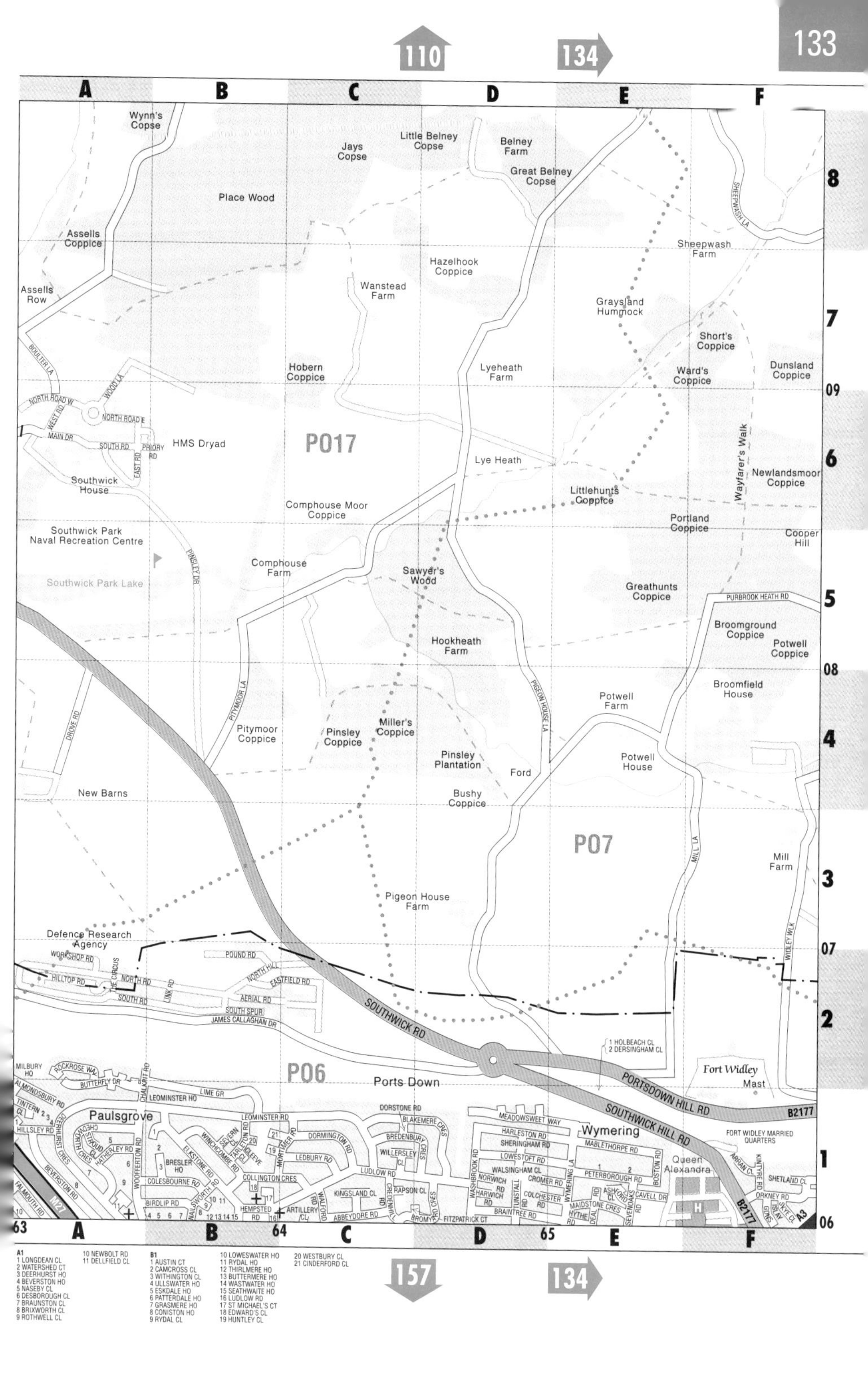

Wynn's Copse

Place Wood

Jays Copse

Little Belney Copse

Belney Farm

Great Belney Copse

Assells Coppice

Assells Row

Hazelhook Coppice

Wanstead Farm

Sheepwash Farm

Grays/land Hummock

Short's Coppice

Dunsland Coppice

Hobern Coppice

Lyeheath Farm

Ward's Coppice

Newlandsmoor Coppice

HMS Dryad

P017

Lye Heath

Littlehunts Coppice

Wayfarer's Walk

Cooper Hill

Southwick House

Comphouse Moor Coppice

Portland Coppice

Southwick Park Naval Recreation Centre

Comphouse Farm

Sawyer's Wood

Greathunts Coppice

Purbrook Heath Rd

Southwick Park Lake

Hookheath Farm

Broomground Coppice

Potwell Coppice

Broomfield House

Pitymoor Coppice

Pinsley Coppice

Miller's Coppice

Pinsley Plantation

Ford

Potwell Farm

Potwell House

New Barns

Bushy Coppice

P07

Mill Farm

Pigeon House Farm

Defence Research Agency

Workshop Rd

Hilltop Rd

North Rd

South Rd

Pound Rd

North Hill

Eastfield Rd

Aerial Rd

South Spur

James Callaghan Dr

Southwick Rd

1 Holbeach Cl
2 Dersingham Cl

Fort Widley Mast

Milbury Ho

Rockrose Way

Butterfly Dr

Leominster Ho

Lime Gr

P06

Ports Down

Portsdown Hill Rd

Southwick Hill Rd

Fort Widley Married Quarters

B2177

Paulsgrove

Dorstone Rd

Blakemere Dr

Meadowsweet Way

Harleston Rd

Sheringham Rd

Lowestoft Rd

Mablethorpe Rd

Wymering

Queen Alexandra

Leominster Rd

Dormington Rd

Bredenbury

Willersley Rd

Ledbury Rd

Ludlow Rd

Walsingham Cl

Norwich

Peterborough Rd

Ashton

Colchester

Harwich

Cromer Rd

Tunstall

Cavell Rd

Shetland Cl

Orkney Rd

Bresler Ho

Colesbourne Rd

Collington Cres

Kingsland Cl

Rapson Cl

Braintree Rd

Maidstone Cres

Hythe

Birdlip Rd

Hempsted

Artillery Cl

Abbeydore Rd

Brom

Fitzpatrick Ct

A3

B2177

63   64   65

A   B   C   D   E   F

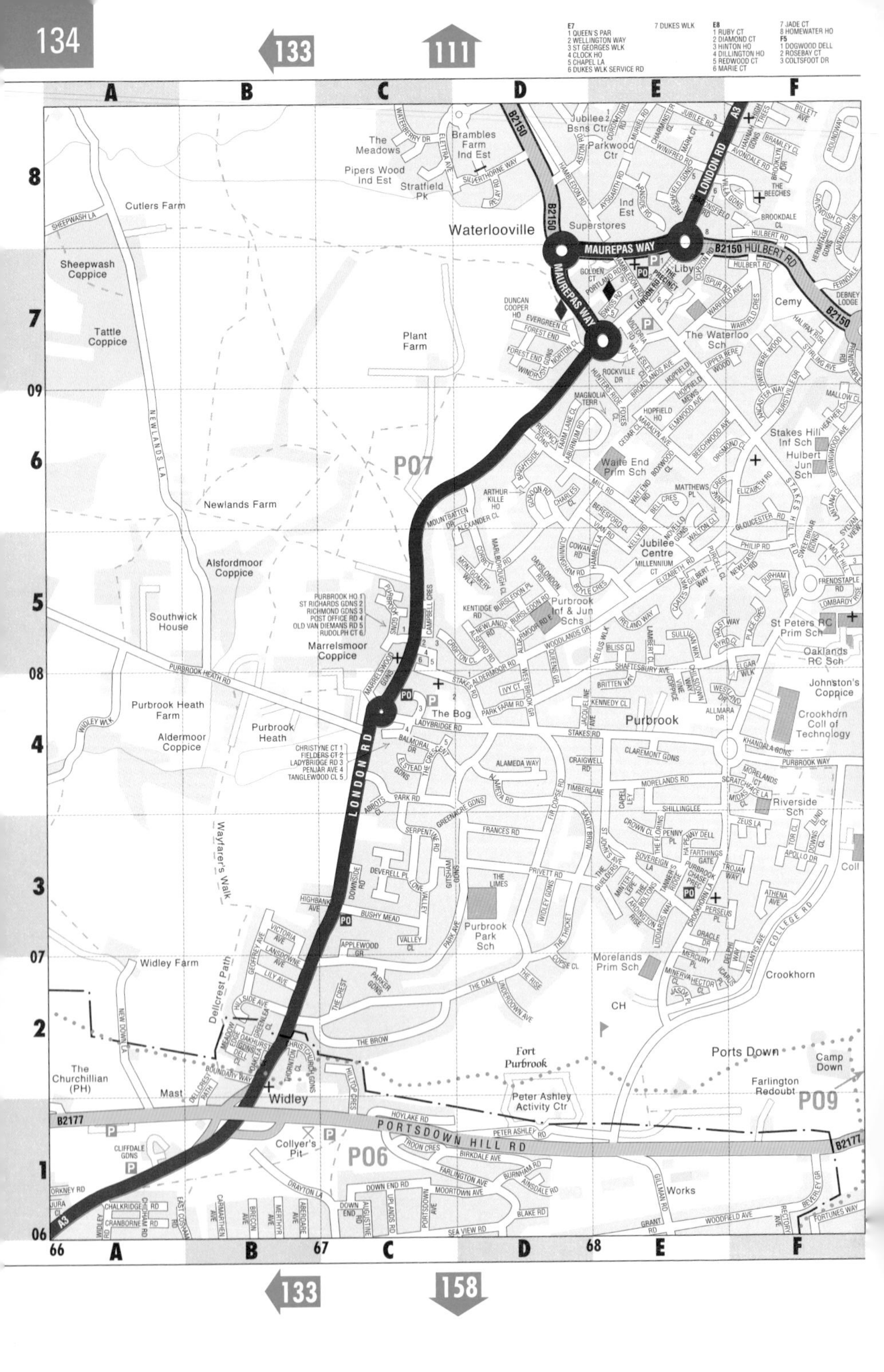
134
133
111
E7
1 QUEEN'S PAR
2 WELLINGTON WAY
3 ST GEORGES WLK
4 CLOCK HO
5 CHAPEL LA
6 DUKES WLK SERVICE RD
7 DUKES WLK
E8
1 RUBY CT
2 DIAMOND CT
3 HINTON HO
4 DILLINGTON HO
5 REDWOOD CT
6 MARIE CT
7 JADE CT
8 HOMEWATER HO
F5
1 DOGWOOD DELL
2 ROSEBAY CT
3 COLTSFOOT DR
A
B
C
D
E
F
8
7
09
6
5
08
4
3
07
2
1
06
66
67
68
The Meadows
Brambles Farm Ind Est
Pipers Wood Ind Est
Stratfield Pk
Jubilee Bsns Ctr
Parkwood Ctr
Ind Est
Superstores
Waterlooville
Cutlers Farm
SHEEPWASH LA
Sheepwash Coppice
Tattle Coppice
MAUREPAS WAY
B2150
HULBERT RD
LONDON RD
A3
Liby
Cemy
DUNCAN COOPER HO
Plant Farm
The Waterloo Sch
NEWLANDS LA
PO7
Waite End Prim Sch
Stakes Hill Inf Sch
Hulbert Jun Sch
Newlands Farm
Alsfordmoor Coppice
Jubilee Centre
Southwick House
Purbrook Inf & Jun Schs
Marrelsmoor Coppice
PURBROOK HO 1
ST RICHARDS GDNS 2
RICHMOND GDNS 3
POST OFFICE RD 4
OLD VAN DIEMANS RD 5
RUDOLPH CT 6
St Peters RC Prim Sch
Oaklands RC Sch
Johnston's Coppice
PURBROOK HEATH RD
Purbrook Heath Farm
Aldermoor Coppice
Purbrook Heath
The Bog
Purbrook
Crookhorn Coll of Technology
CHRISTYNE CT 1
FIELDERS CT 2
LADYBRIDGE RD 3
PENJAR AVE 4
TANGLEWOOD CL 5
STAKES RD
PURBROOK WAY
Riverside Sch
Wayfarer's Walk
The Limes
Purbrook Park Sch
Morelands Prim Sch
Coll
Crookhorn
Widley Farm
Dellcrest Path
CH
Fort Purbrook
Ports Down
Camp Down
The Churchillian (PH)
Mast
Widley
Peter Ashley Activity Ctr
Farlington Redoubt
PO9
B2177
PORTSDOWN HILL RD
Collyer's Pit
PO6
Works
CLIFFDALE GDNS
158

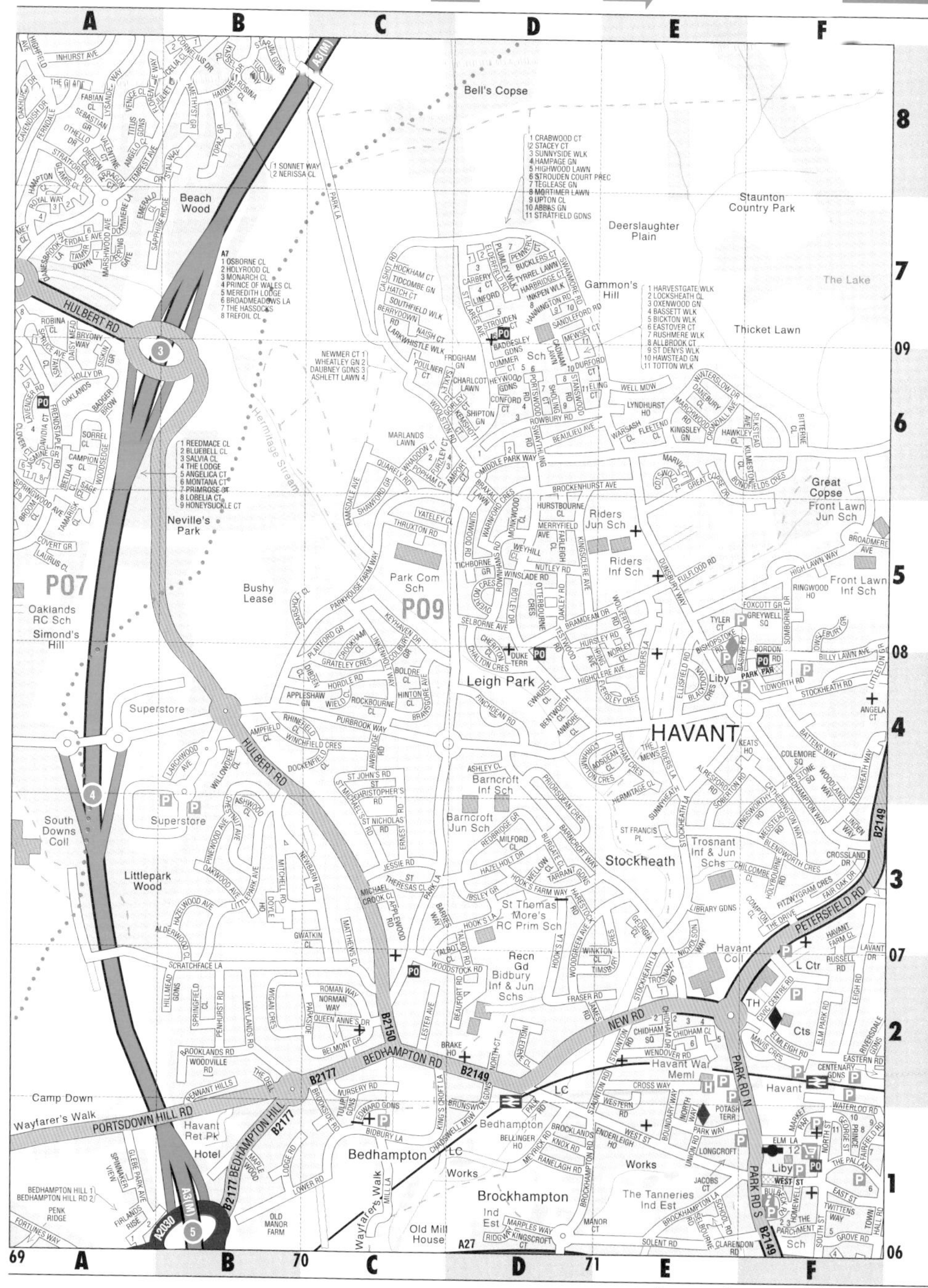

E2
1 BROOKFIELD CL
2 CHIDHAM WLK
3 WHYKE CT
4 COMPTON CT
5 WESTBOURNE CT
6 THE FORUM

F1
1 MILESTONE POINT
2 WATERMILL CT
3 SPRINGWELL
4 SLINDON GDNS
5 GROVE CT
6 EMPIRE CT
7 FAIRFIELD TERR
8 MANOR CL
9 EAST VIEW TERR

10 WELLINGTON CT
11 NORTH STREET ARC
12 Meridian Ctr

135 113

Durrants

Rowlands Castle
St JohnΩs CE
Prim Sch
Durrants
PRU

MANOR LODGE RD

Gipsies
Plain

PARK VIEW 1
CHESTNUT CT 2
WHICHERS GATE RD 3

Staunton
Country Park

Hammond's Lands
Coppice

Mays Coppice
Farm

Sandpit
Roundell

STUBBERMERE

Staunton Park
Com Sch

Sewage
Works

Shuffles
Plantation

Blackbush
Copse

Sussex Border Path

BROXHEAD RD 1
WOODDINGTON CL 2

MIDDLE PARK WAY

Vistors
Ctr

Leigh Park
Gardens

KEN
BERRY
CT

Southleigh Forest

Barton's
Copse

PO9

ANDOVER HO
EXBURY CT

Portsmouth
(Bupa)

Hollybank
House

Football
Gd

West
Leigh

HAVANT

Nest
Bsns Pk

Ind Est

Hemsley
House

East Leigh
House

Southleigh
Park

LONG COPSE CT 1
BIRCH TREE CL 2
CHURCHILL DRS
WALLROCK WLK 4
THE GREENWAY 5
WOODROFFE WLK 6
LAURENCE GN 7

FARRINGDON RD

REDLYNCH

Forsythia

Azalea cl

Fuschia cl

Downley
Point

The
Oakwood
Ctr

St AlbanΩs
CE Prim Sch

Locks
Farm

Home
Farm
Barn

WOODFIELD CL

CROSSLAND DR

Hayward
Bsns Ctr

1 SOLENT HO
2 LANGSTONE HO
3 CHICHESTER HO
4 FLEXFORD GDNS
5 GAULTER CL
6 HODGES CL

Rowan rd

Bramble cl

Camelia cl

1 WEAVERS GN
2 SPINDLE WARREN
3 BLADON CL
4 MARLBOROUGH PK

BARWELL GR 8
PANTON CL 9
GODWIN CL 10
ALLENDALE AVE 11
HEDGEROW GDNS 12

Ind Est

Kenwood
Bsns Pk

Swallow

Kingfisher
ct

Southleigh
Farm

Nursery

PO10

St James
CE Prim Sch

HEATHERTON MEWS 1
SILVERTREES 2
AVALON CT 3
WESTBOURNE AVE 4

Denvilles

Manor
Farm

Motel

EMSWORTH

Warblington
Sch

Warblington

Warblington

Emsworth
Prim Sch

Glenwood
Sch

Emsworth
(MALVERN MEWS)

SULTAN

Mus

ROMAN
WAY

HAVANT RD

A259

A27

135 160

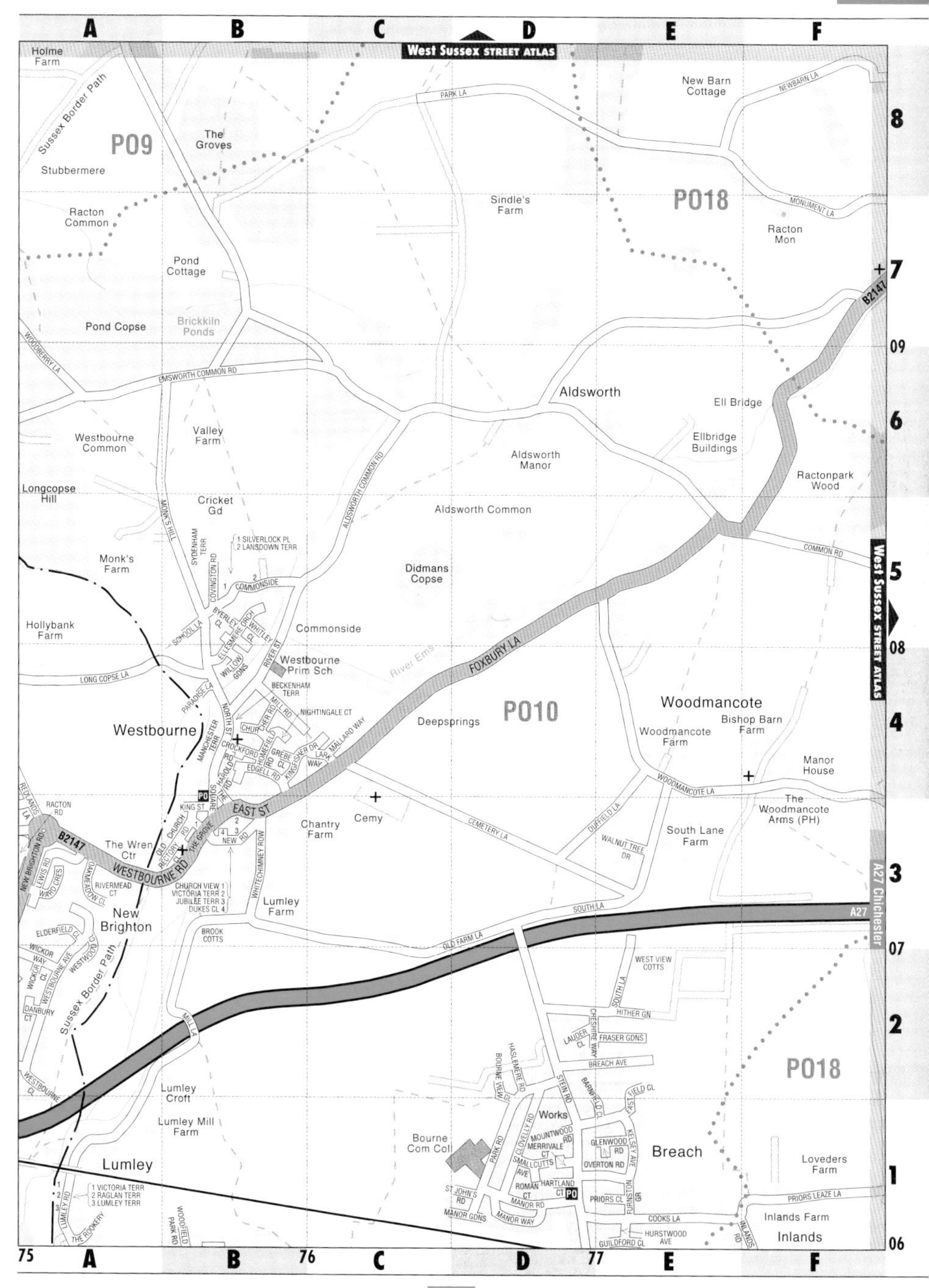
West Sussex STREET ATLAS
Holme Farm
Sussex Border Path
PO9
The Groves
Stubbermere
Racton Common
Pond Cottage
Pond Copse
Brickkiln Ponds
PARK LA
New Barn Cottage
NEWBARN LA
Sindle's Farm
PO18
MONUMENT LA
Racton Mon
B2147
EMSWORTH COMMON RD
WOODBERRY LA
Aldsworth
Ell Bridge
Ellbridge Buildings
Westbourne Common
Valley Farm
Aldsworth Manor
Ractonpark Wood
Longcopse Hill
Cricket Gd
MONK'S HILL
ALDSWORTH COMMON RD
Aldsworth Common
COMMON RD
Monk's Farm
1 SILVERLOCK PL
2 LANSDOWN TERR
SYDENHAM TERR
COVINGTON RD
COMMONSIDE
Didmans Copse
Hollybank Farm
Commonside
SCHOOL LA
Westbourne Prim Sch
RIVER ST
River Ems
FOXBURY LA
LONG COPSE LA
BECKENHAM TERR
NIGHTINGALE CT
PARADISE LA
MILL RD
MALLARD WAY
Westbourne
NORTH ST
MANCHESTER TERR
Deepsprings
PO10
Woodmancote
Bishop Barn Farm
Woodmancote Farm
Manor House
CROCKFORD RD
EDGELL RD
KINGFISHER DR
LARK WAY
WOODMANCOTE LA
REDLANDS LA
RACTON RD
KING ST
EAST ST
Cemy
The Woodmancote Arms (PH)
Chantry Farm
CEMETERY LA
DUFFIELD LA
South Lane Farm
WALNUT TREE DR
The Wren Ctr
NEW RD
WESTBOURNE RD
WHITECHIMNEY ROW
NEW BRIGHTON RD
RIVERMEAD CT
CHURCH VIEW 1
VICTORIA TERR 2
JUBILEE TERR 3
DUKES CL 4
Lumley Farm
A27 Chichester
A27
SOUTH LA
New Brighton
ELDERFIELD CL
BROOK COTTS
OLD FARM LA
WEST VIEW COTTS
SOUTH LA
HITHER GN
LAUDER CL
FRASER GDNS
CHESHIRE WAY
BREACH AVE
HASLEMERE RD
BOURNE VIEW
MILL LA
WESTBOURNE CL
Lumley Croft
Lumley Mill Farm
Works
EAST FIELD CL
PO18
Bourne Com Coll
PARK RD
CLOVELLY RD
MOUNTWOOD RD
MERRIVALE CT
SMALLCUTTS AVE
GLENWOOD RD
OVERTON RD
KELSEY AVE
Breach
Loveders Farm
Lumley
1 VICTORIA TERR
2 RAGLAN TERR
3 LUMLEY TERR
LUMLEY RD
THE ROOKERY
WOODFIELD PARK RD
ST JOHN'S RD
ROMAN CT
HARTLAND CT
MANOR RD
MANOR GDNS
MANOR WAY
PRIORS CL
FURNSTON GR
PRIORS LEAZE LA
Inlands Farm
Inlands
COOKS LA
HURSTWOOD AVE
GUILDFORD CL
INLANDS RD
A B C D E F
8 7 09 6 5 08 4 3 07 2 1 06
75 76 77

114

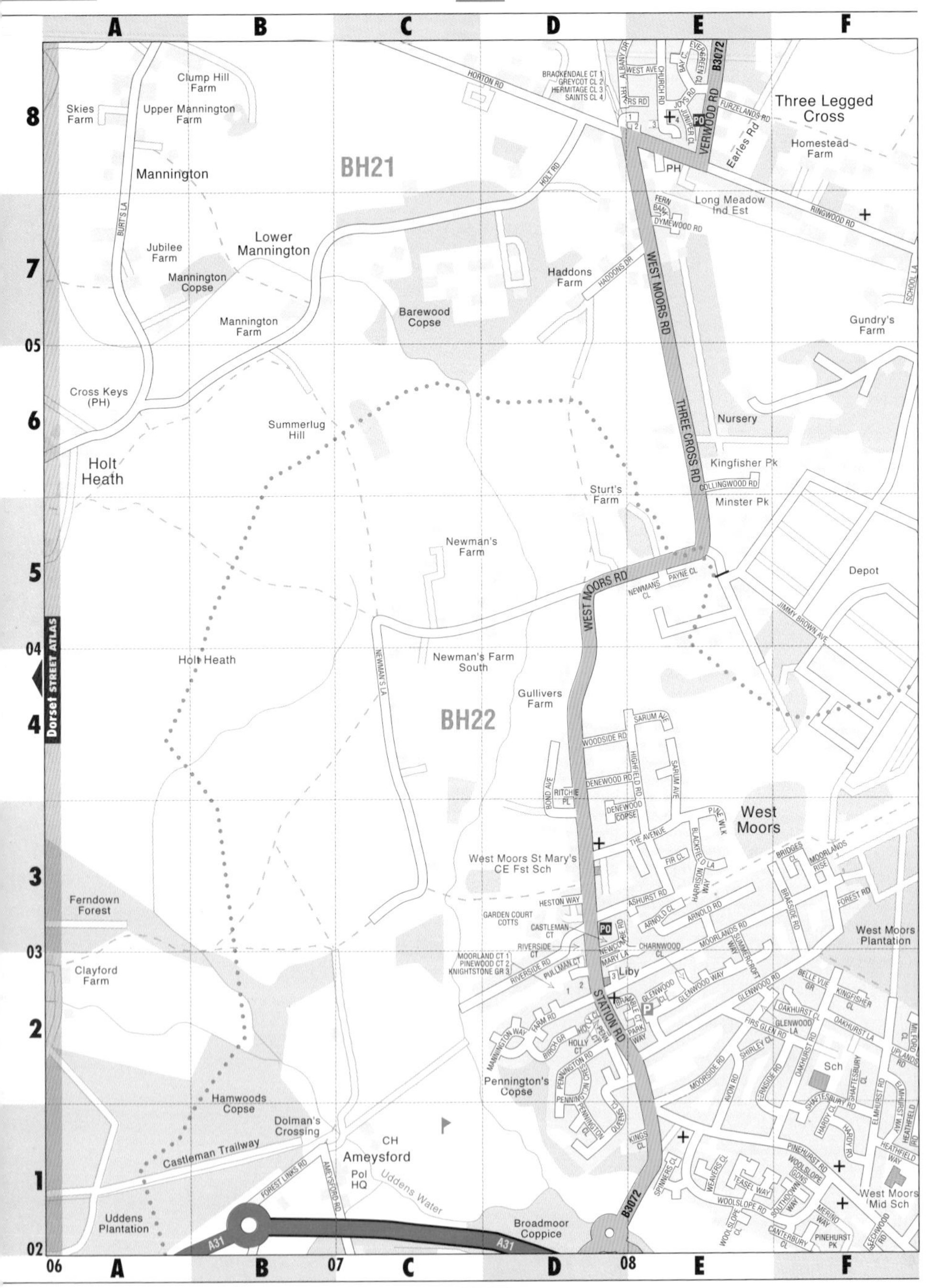
A
B
C
D
E
F
8
7
05
6
5
04
4
3
03
2
1
02
06
07
08
Clump Hill Farm
Skies Farm
Upper Mannington Farm
Mannington
BH21
HORTON RD
BRACKENDALE CT 1
GREYCOT CL 2
HERMITAGE CL 3
SAINTS CL 4
ALBANY DR
WEST AVE
CHURCH RD
EVERGREEN CL
B3072
VERWOOD RD
FURZELANDS RD
Three Legged Cross
Earles Rd
Homestead Farm
PO
PH
HOLT RD
FERN BANK
DYMEWOOD RD
Long Meadow Ind Est
RINGWOOD RD
BURT'S LA
Jubilee Farm
Lower Mannington
Mannington Copse
Mannington Farm
Barewood Copse
Haddons Farm
HADDONS DR
WEST MOORS RD
SCHOOL LA
Gundry's Farm
Cross Keys (PH)
THREE CROSS RD
Nursery
Summerlug Hill
Holt Heath
Kingfisher Pk
COLLINGWOOD RD
Minster Pk
Sturt's Farm
Newman's Farm
NEWMANS CL
PAYNE CL
Depot
JIMMY BROWN AVE
NEWMAN'S LA
Newman's Farm South
Gullivers Farm
BH22
SARUM AVE
WOODSIDE RD
HIGHFIELD RD
DENEWOOD RD
BOND AVE
RITCHIE PL
DENEWOOD COPSE
PINE WLK
West Moors
THE AVENUE
BLACKFIELD LA
FIR CL
HARRISON WAY
BRIDGES CL
MOORLANDS RISE
West Moors St Mary's CE Fst Sch
Ferndown Forest
HESTON WAY
ASHURST RD
BRAESIDE RD
FOREST RD
GARDEN COURT COTTS
CASTLEMAN CT
ARNOLD CL
ARNOLD RD
West Moors Plantation
RIVERSIDE CT
NEWCOMBE RD
CHARNWOOD CL
MOORLANDS RD
SUMMERCROFT WAY
MOORLAND CT 1
PINEWOOD CT 2
KNIGHTSTONE GR 3
RIVERSIDE RD
PULLMAN CT
MARY LA
Clayford Farm
Liby
GLENWOOD WAY
GLENWOOD RD
BELLE VUE GR
KINGFISHER CL
STATION RD
GLENWOOD CL
OAKHURST CL
OAKHURST LA
MANNINGTON WAY
FARM RD
BIRCH GR
HOLLY CT
FIRS GLEN RD
GLENWOOD LA
MILFORD CL
UPLANDS RD
PARK WAY
SHIRLEY CL
OAKHURST RD
PENNINGTON RD
PENNINGTON CRES
Pennington's Copse
MOORSIDE RD
AVON RD
FERNSIDE RD
Sch
SHAFTESBURY CL
ELMHURST RD
HEATHFIELD WAY
Hamwoods Copse
SHAFTESBURY RD
HARDY CL
HARDY RD
HEATHFIELD RD
Dolman's Crossing
QUEENS CL
CH
KINGS CL
Castleman Trailway
Ameysford
PINEHURST RD
FOREST LINKS RD
AMEYSFORD RD
Pol HQ
SPINNERS CL
WEAVERS CL
TEASEL WAY
WOOLSLOPE GDNS
West Moors Mid Sch
Uddens Water
SOUTHDOWN WAY
WOOLSLOPE RD
MERINO WAY
Uddens Plantation
Broadmoor Coppice
WOOLSLOPE CL
CANTERBURY CL
PINEHURST PK
BEECHWOOD RD
A31
P

165

115 140

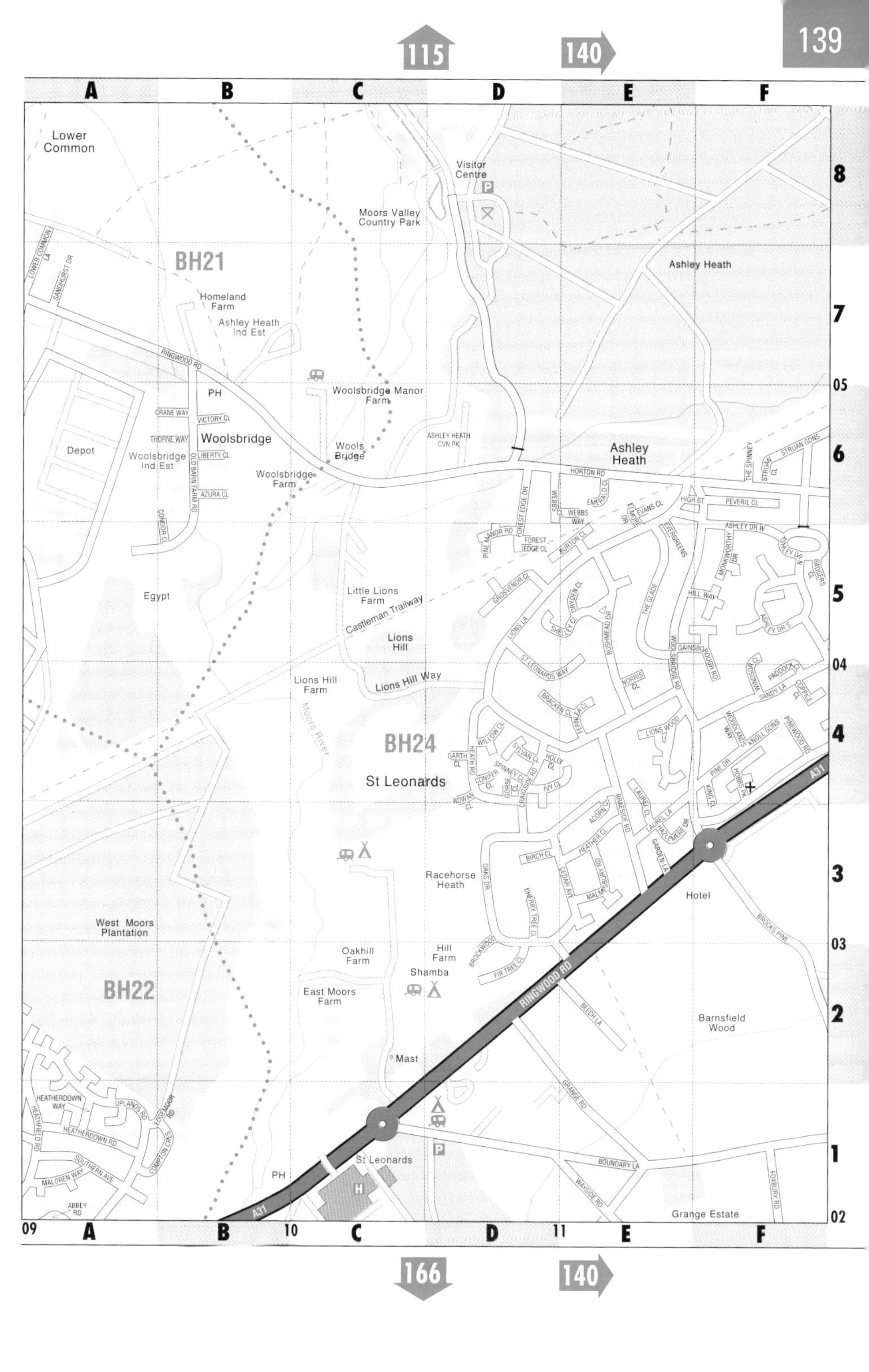
A B C D E F
8 7 6 5 4 3 2 1
05 04 03 02
09 10 11
Lower Common
Visitor Centre
Moors Valley Country Park
BH21
Ashley Heath
Homeland Farm
Ashley Heath Ind Est
LOWER COMMON LA
SANDHURST DR
RINGWOOD RD
PH
CRANE WAY
VICTORY CL
THORNE WAY
Woolsbridge
LIBERTY CL
Depot
Woolsbridge Ind Est
OLD BARN FARM RD
AZURA CL
CONDOR CL
Woolsbridge Manor Farm
Wools Bridge
Woolsbridge Farm
ASHLEY HEATH CVN PK
Ashley Heath
HORTON RD
THE SPINNEY
STRUAN CL
STRUAN GDNS
FOREST EDGE DR
WEBBS CL
WEBBS WAY
EMERALD CL
ELMORE DR
EVANS CL
HIGH ST
PEVERIL CL
PINE MANOR RD
FOREST EDGE CL
BURTON CL
EVERGREENS
ASHLEY DR W
MONKWORTHY DR
ASHLEY DR N
BADGERS CL
Egypt
Little Lions Farm
Castleman Trailway
GROSVENOR CL
DRYDEN CL
BUSHMEAD DR
THE GLADE
HILL WAY
LIONS LA
SHELLEY CL
ASHLEY DR S
Lions Hill
Lions Hill Farm
Lions Hill Way
ST LEONARDS WAY
NORRIS CL
WOOLSBRIDGE RD
GAINSBOROUGH RD
WINDSOR CL
PADDOCK CL
SANDY LA
COPPICE CL
BRACKEN CL
FERNLEA CL
Moors River
BH24
WILLOW CL
LIONS WOOD
WOODLANDS WAY
KNOLL GDNS
PINEWOOD RD
GARTH CL
HEATH RD
SYLVAN CL
HOLLY CL
St Leonards
CONIFER CL
SPINNEY CL
GORSE CL
CRAIGSIDE RD
IVY CL
PINE DR
HOBBS PK
KING CL
ROWAN CL
BRAESIDE RD
LAUREL CL
LAUREL LA
HAZEL
MERE DR
ACORN CL
A31
HEATHER CL
GARDEN LA
BIRCH CL
Racehorse Heath
OAKS DR
CEDAR AVE
MALMESBURY RD
Hotel
BROCKS PINE
CHERRY TREE CL
West Moors Plantation
Oakhill Farm
Hill Farm
BROCKWOOD
FIR TREE CL
Shamba
BH22
East Moors Farm
RINGWOOD RD
BEECH LA
Barnsfield Wood
Mast
HEATHERDOWN WAY
UPLANDS RD
EDGEMOOR RD
GRANGE RD
HEATHFIELD RD
HEATHERDOWN RD
COMPTON CRES
SOUTHERN AVE
P
St Leonards
BOUNDARY LA
MALOREN WAY
PH
H
WAYSIDE RD
FOXBURY RD
ABBEY RD
A31
Grange Estate

166 140

139
116

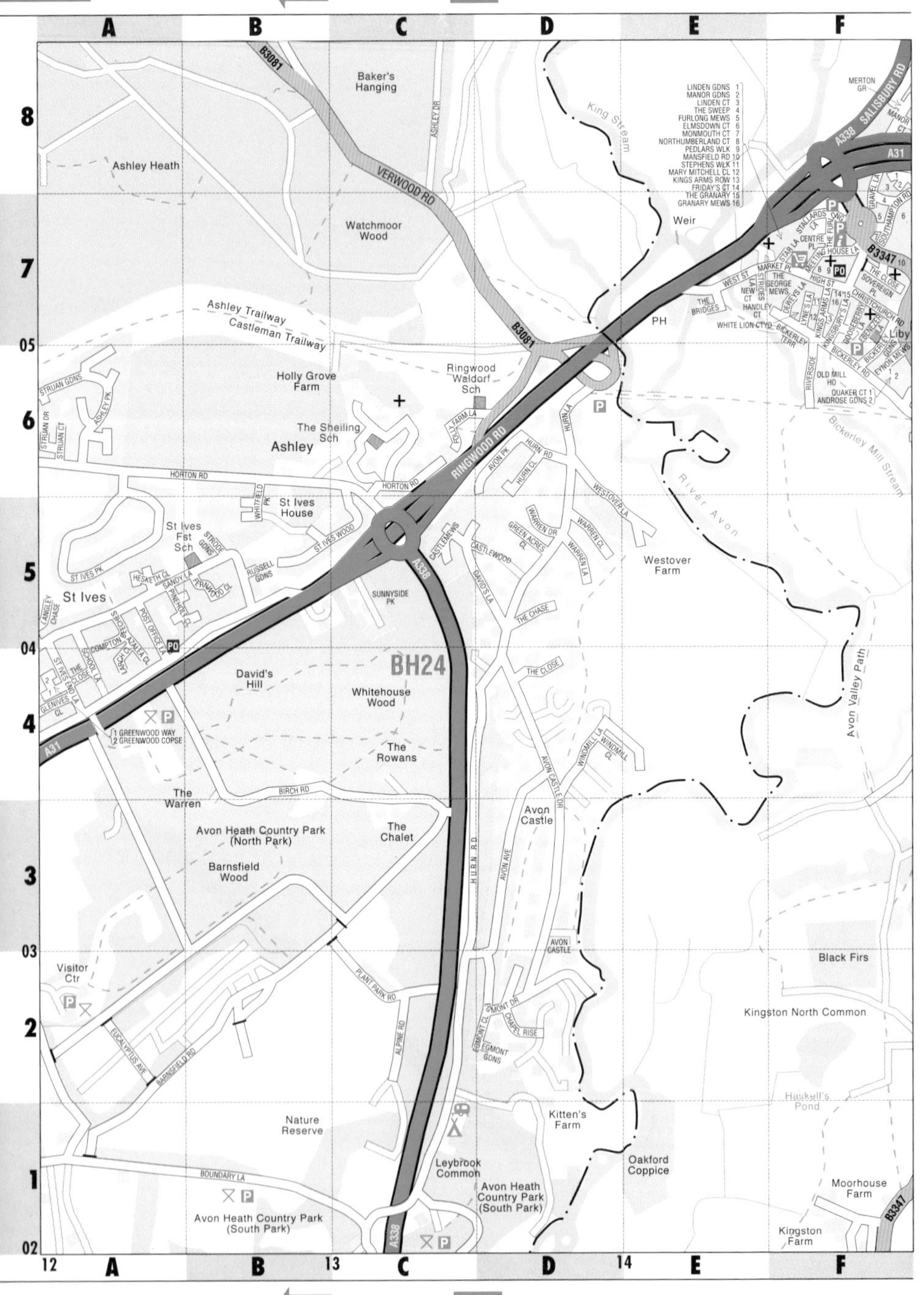
Baker's Hanging
Ashley Heath
Watchmoor Wood
VERWOOD RD
B3081
ASHLEY DR
King Stream
Weir
PH
Ashley Trailway
Castleman Trailway
Holly Grove Farm
Ringwood Waldorf Sch
The Sheiling Sch
Ashley
HORTON RD
RINGWOOD RD
St Ives House
St Ives Fst Sch
St Ives
SUNNYSIDE PK
BH24
David's Hill
Whitehouse Wood
The Rowans
The Warren
BIRCH RD
Avon Heath Country Park (North Park)
Barnsfield Wood
The Chalet
Avon Castle
Westover Farm
River Avon
Bickerley Mill Stream
Avon Valley Path
Visitor Ctr
PLANT PARK RD
ALPINE RD
EUCALYPTUS AVE
BARNSFIELD RD
Nature Reserve
BOUNDARY LA
Avon Heath Country Park (South Park)
Leybrook Common
Avon Heath Country Park (South Park)
Kitten's Farm
Oakford Coppice
Black Firs
Kingston North Common
Haskell's Pond
Moorhouse Farm
Kingston Farm
A31
A338
B3347
SALISBURY RD
LINDEN GDNS 1
MANOR GDNS 2
LINDEN CT 3
THE SWEEP 4
FURLONG MEWS 5
ELMSDOWN CT 6
MONMOUTH CT 7
NORTHUMBERLAND CT 8
MANSFIELD RD 10
PEDLARS WLK 9
STEPHENS WLK 11
MARY MITCHELL CL 12
KINGS ARMS ROW 13
FRIDAY'S CT 14
THE GRANARY 15
GRANARY MEWS 16
1 GREENWOOD WAY
2 GREENWOOD COPSE
A B C D E F
8 7 05 6 5 04 4 3 03 2 1 02
12 13 14

139
167

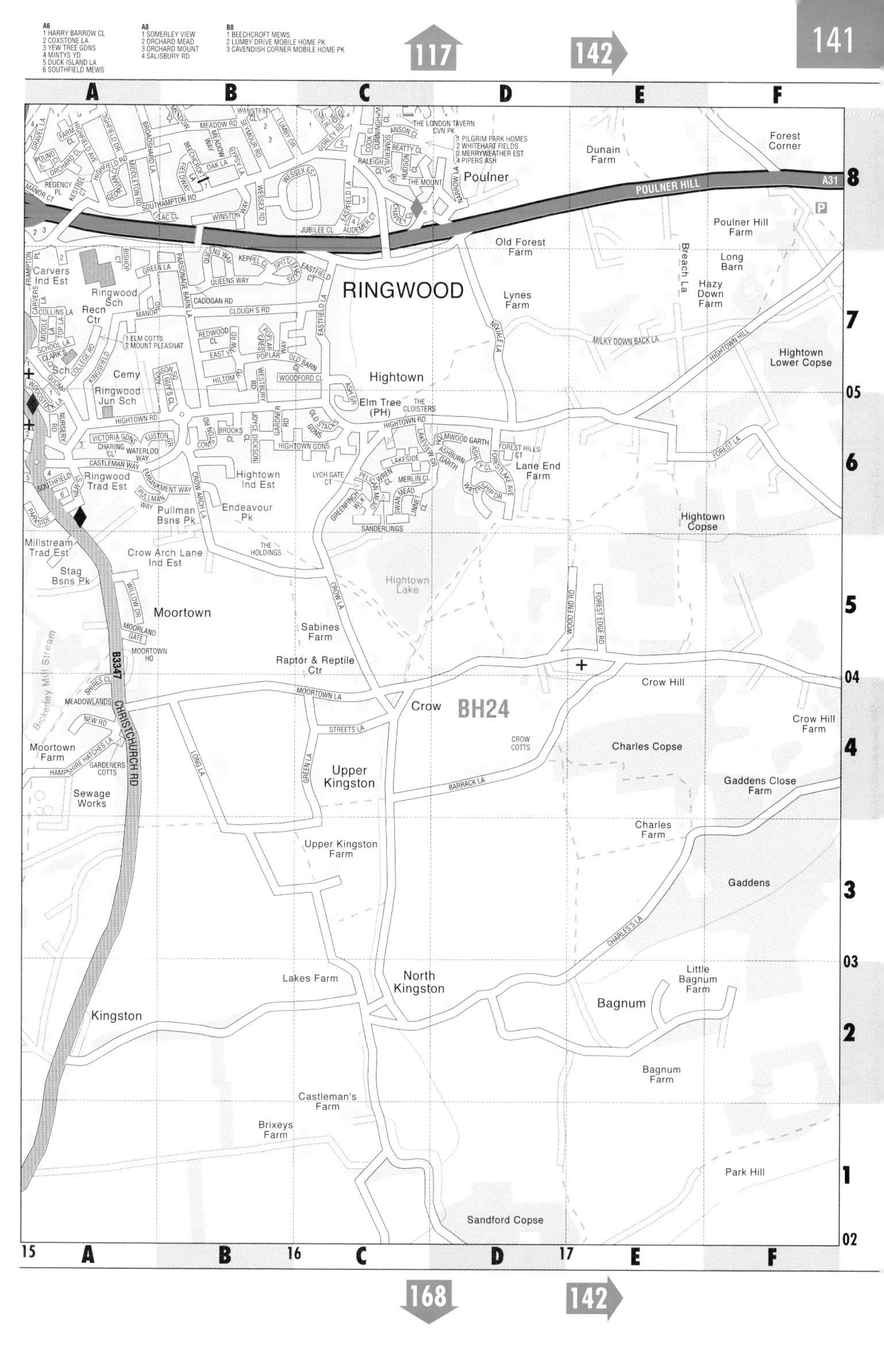

117 142

A6
1 HARRY BARROW CL
2 COXSTONE LA
3 YEW TREE GDNS
4 MINTYS YD
5 DUCK ISLAND LA
6 SOUTHFIELD MEWS

A8
1 SOMERLEY VIEW
2 ORCHARD MEAD
3 ORCHARD MOUNT
4 SALISBURY RD

B8
1 BEECHCROFT MEWS
2 LUMBY DRIVE MOBILE HOME PK
3 CAVENDISH CORNER MOBILE HOME PK

RINGWOOD

Poulner

POULNER HILL

A31

BH24

1 PILGRIM PARK HOMES
2 WHITEHART FIELDS
8 MERRYWEATHER EST
4 PIPERS ASH

THE LONDON TAVERN
CVN PK

Dunain
Farm

Forest
Corner

Poulner Hill
Farm

Long
Barn

Hazy
Down
Farm

Hightown
Lower Copse

Old Forest
Farm

Lynes
Farm

Hightown

Elm Tree
(PH)

THE
CLOISTERS

Lane End
Farm

Hightown
Copse

Hightown
Ind Est

Hightown
Lake

Pullman
Bsns Pk

Endeavour
Pk

Crow Arch Lane
Ind Est

THE
HOLDINGS

Millstream
Trad Est

Stag
Bsns Pk

Ringwood
Trad Est

Moortown

Sabines
Farm

Raptor & Reptile
Ctr

Moortown
Ho

Crow

Crow Hill

Crow Hill
Farm

Moortown
Farm

Sewage
Works

GARDENERS
COTTS

Upper
Kingston

CROW
COTTS

Charles Copse

Gaddens Close
Farm

Upper Kingston
Farm

Charles
Farm

Gaddens

Lakes Farm

North
Kingston

Little
Bagnum
Farm

Kingston

Bagnum

Castleman's
Farm

Bagnum
Farm

Brixeys
Farm

Park Hill

Sandford Copse

Carvers
Ind Est

Ringwood
Sch

Ringwood
Recn
Ctr

Cemy

Ringwood
Jun Sch

Victoria Gdns

Charing
Cross

Waterloo
Way

Castleman Way

Hightown
Ind Est

Hightown
Gdns

Hightown Rd

15 16 17

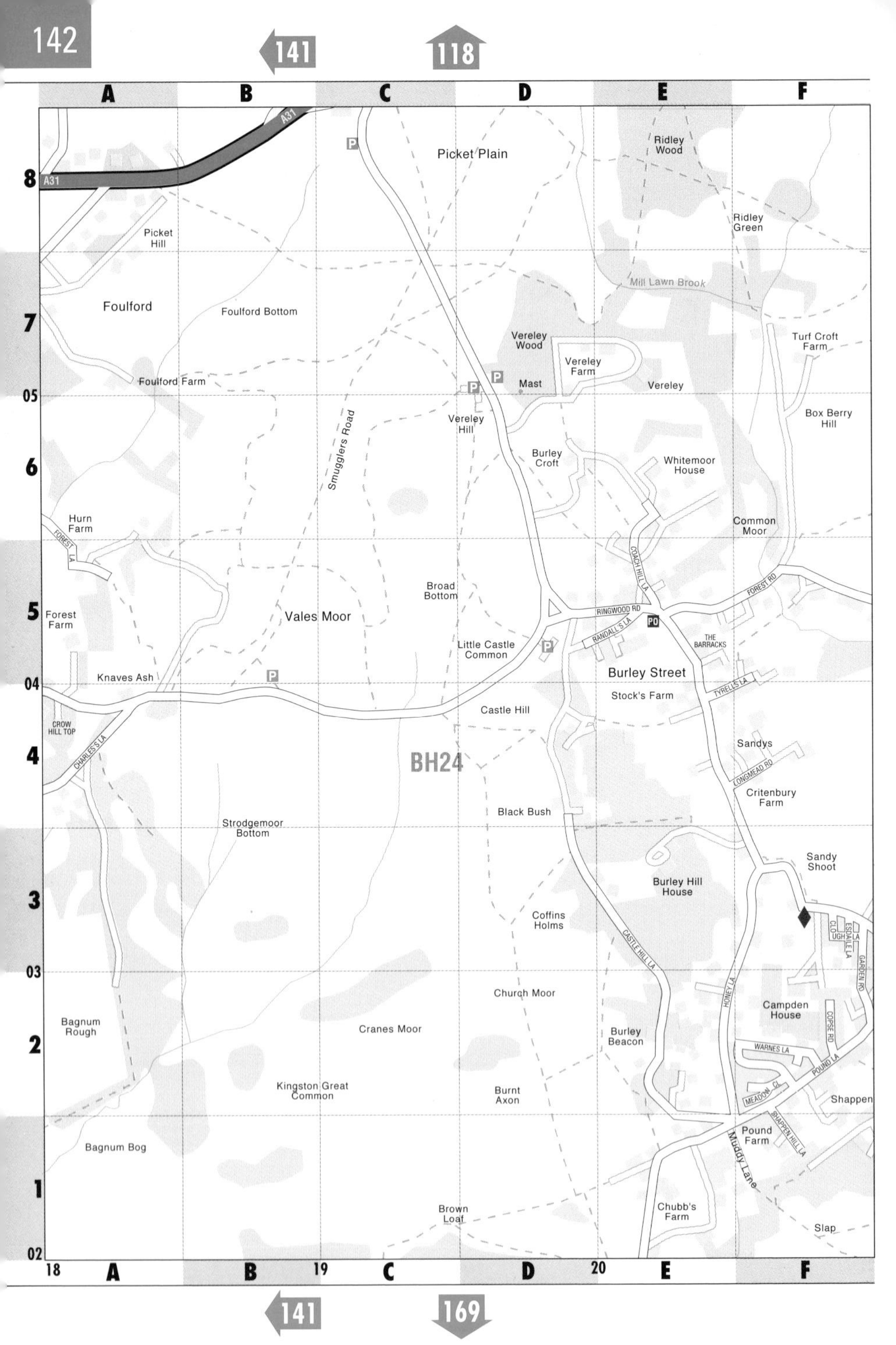

A   **B**   **C**   **D**   **E**   **F**

A31

8

A31

Picket Plain

Ridley Wood

Ridley Green

Picket Hill

Foulford

Foulford Bottom

7

Mill Lawn Brook

Turf Croft Farm

Foulford Farm

05

Vereley Wood

Vereley Farm

Mast

Vereley

Box Berry Hill

Vereley Hill

Smugglers Road

Burley Croft

Whitemoor House

6

Hurn Farm

FOREST LA

Common Moor

Broad Bottom

Vales Moor

5

Forest Farm

Little Castle Common

RINGWOOD RD

RANDALL'S LA

CHURCH HILL LA

PO

THE BARRACKS

FOREST RD

04

Knaves Ash

P

Burley Street

Stock's Farm

TYRELLS LA

CROW HILL TOP

Castle Hill

Sandys

CHARLES LA

4

BH24

LONGMEAD RD

Critenbury Farm

Strodgemoor Bottom

Black Bush

Sandy Shoot

Burley Hill House

3

Coffins Holms

CASTLE HILL LA

◆

ESH LA
OLD

ESH LA

GARDEN RD

03

Bagnum Rough

Church Moor

Campden House

HOBB LA

COPSE RD

2

Cranes Moor

Burley Beacon

WARNES LA

POUND LA

Kingston Great Common

Burnt Axon

MEADOW CL

Shappen

Pound Farm

SHAPPEN HILL LA

MUDDY LANE

1

Bagnum Bog

Brown Loaf

Chubb's Farm

Slap

02

18   **A**   **B**   **19**   **C**   **D**   **20**   **E**   **F**

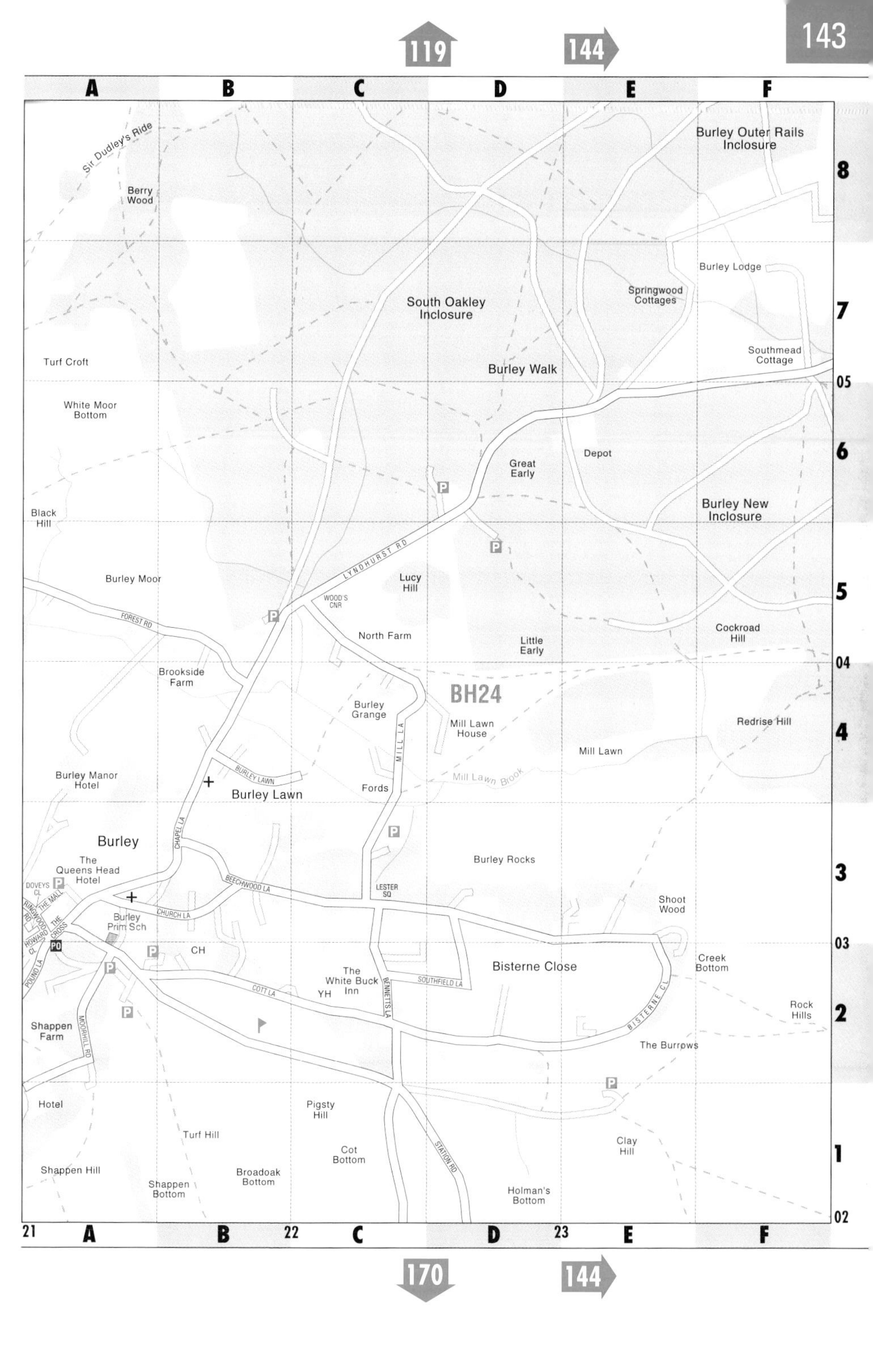
119
144
A
B
C
D
E
F
Sir Dudley's Ride
Berry Wood
Burley Outer Rails Inclosure
8
Burley Lodge
Springwood Cottages
South Oakley Inclosure
7
Turf Croft
Southmead Cottage
Burley Walk
05
White Moor Bottom
Depot
6
Great Early
Burley New Inclosure
Black Hill
LYNDHURST RD
Lucy Hill
Burley Moor
5
WOOD'S CNR
FOREST RD
North Farm
Little Early
Cockroad Hill
04
Brookside Farm
BH24
Burley Grange
Redrise Hill
Mill Lawn House
4
MILL LA
Mill Lawn
BURLEY LAWN
Burley Manor Hotel
Burley Lawn
Fords
Mill Lawn Brook
Burley
Burley Rocks
The Queens Head Hotel
CHAPEL LA
3
DOVEYS CL
THE MALL
BEECHWOOD LA
LESTER SQ
Shoot Wood
RINGWOOD RD
THE CROSS
CHURCH LA
Burley Prim Sch
HOWARD CL
PO
CH
03
Creek Bottom
Bisterne Close
POUND LA
The White Buck Inn
SOUTHFIELD LA
COTT LA
YH
BENNETTS LA
BISTERNE CL
Rock Hills
2
Shappen Farm
MOORHILL RD
The Burrows
Hotel
Pigsty Hill
Turf Hill
Clay Hill
Cot Bottom
STATION RD
1
Shappen Hill
Broadoak Bottom
Shappen Bottom
Holman's Bottom
02
21
22
23
170
144

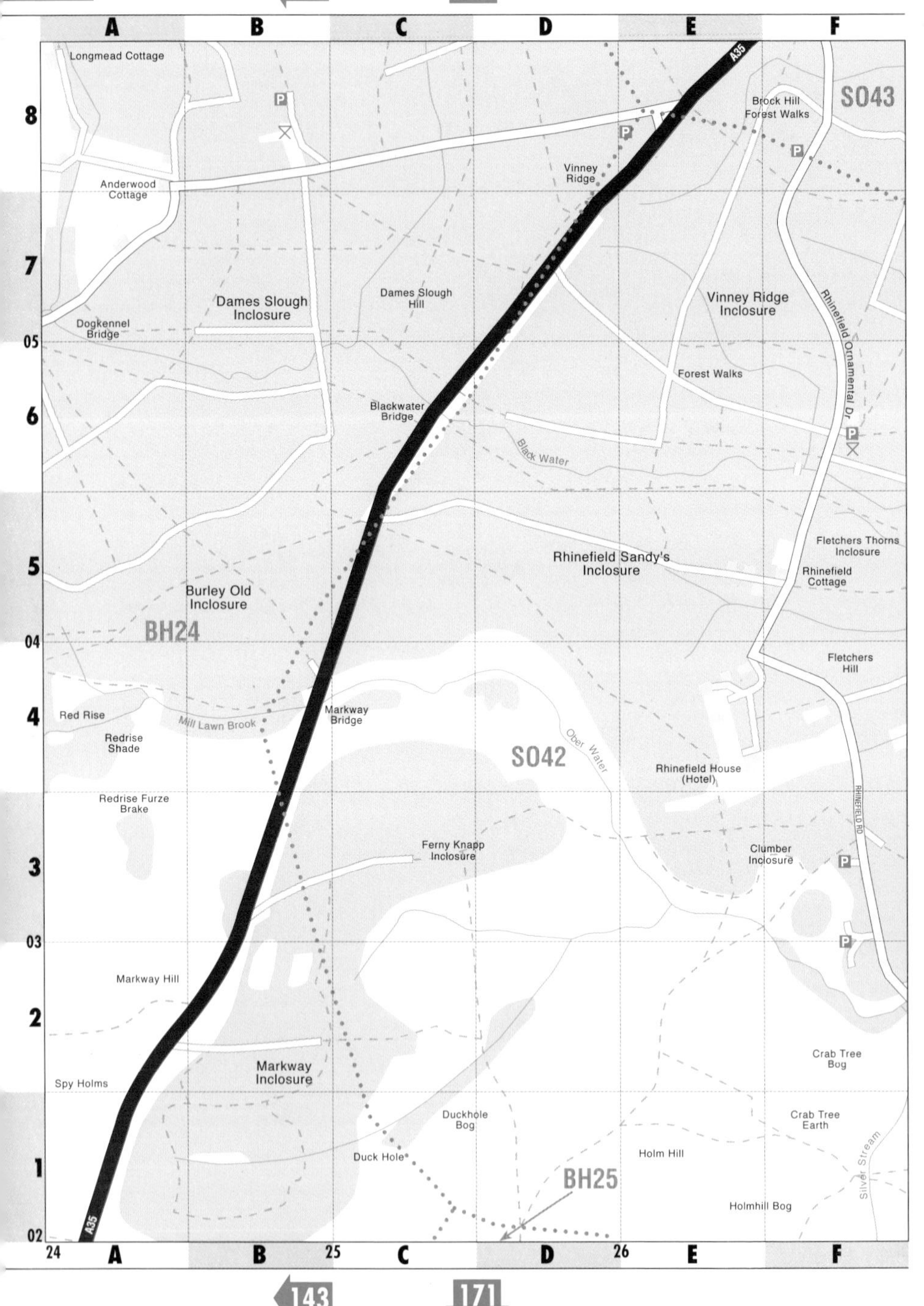

A   B   C   D   E   F

Longmead Cottage

8

Anderwood
Cottage

7

Dames Slough
Inclosure

Dogkennel
Bridge

05

6

Blackwater
Bridge

Black Water

5

Burley Old
Inclosure

BH24

04

4

Red Rise

Redrise
Shade

Mill Lawn Brook

Redrise Furze
Brake

Markway Hill

2

Spy Holms

Markway
Inclosure

Dames Slough
Hill

Markway
Bridge

Ferny Knapp
Inclosure

Duckhole
Bog

Duck Hole

1

Vinney
Ridge

Brock Hill
Forest Walks

A35

Vinney Ridge
Inclosure

Forest Walks

Rhinefield Sandy's
Inclosure

SO42

Ober Water

Rhinefield House
(Hotel)

Clumber
Inclosure

Holm Hill

BH25

Holmhill Bog

Rhinefield Ornamental Dr.

Fletchers Thorns
Inclosure

Rhinefield
Cottage

Fletchers
Hill

RHINEFIELD RD

Crab Tree
Bog

Crab Tree
Earth

Silver Stream

A35

24   A   B   25   C   D   26   E   F

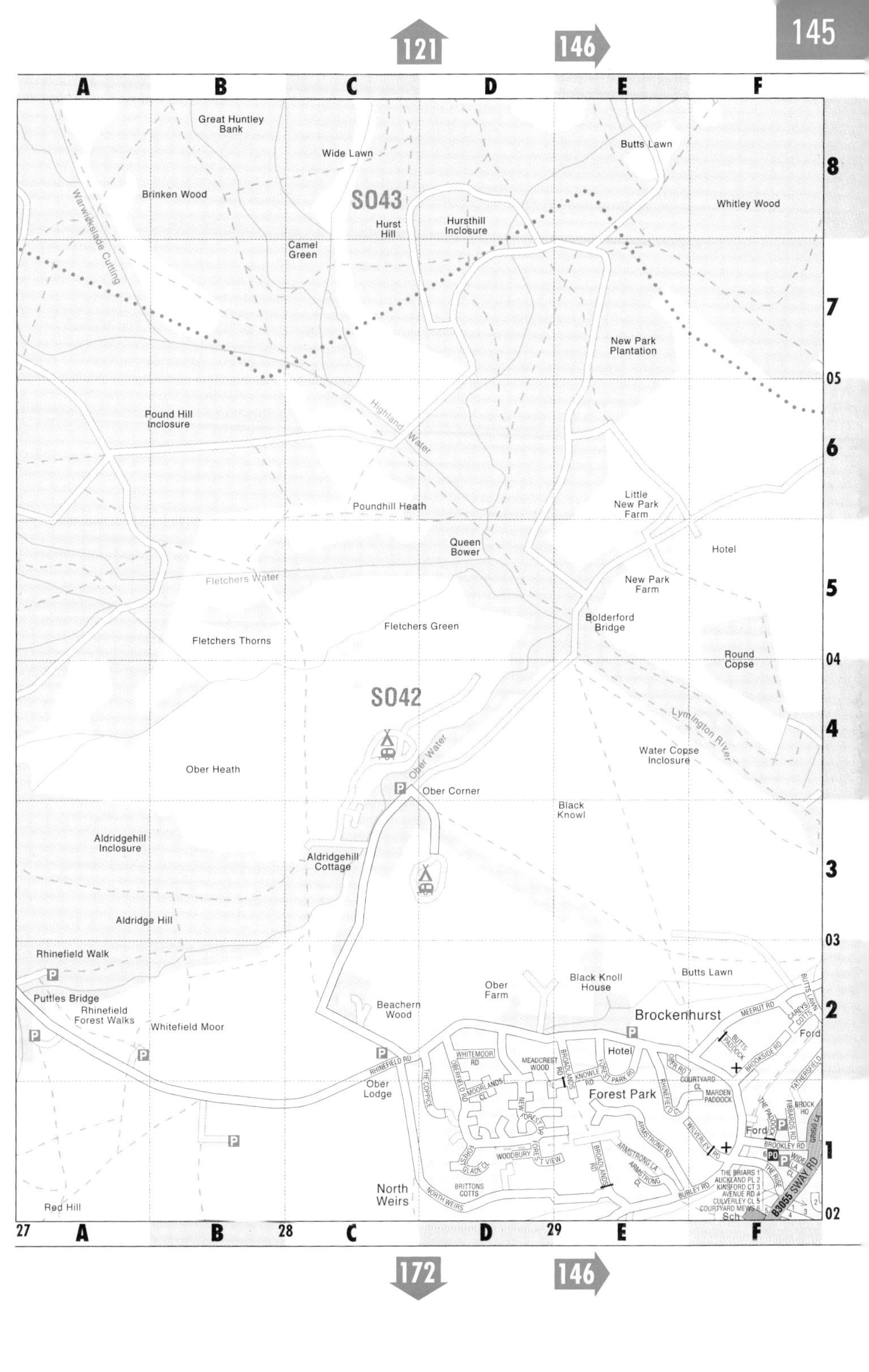
121
146
A
B
C
D
E
F
Great Huntley Bank
Wide Lawn
Butts Lawn
Brinken Wood
SO43
Hurst Hill
Hursthill Inclosure
Whitley Wood
Warwickslade Cutting
Camel Green
New Park Plantation
Pound Hill Inclosure
Highland Water
Poundhill Heath
Little New Park Farm
Queen Bower
Hotel
Fletchers Water
New Park Farm
Bolderford Bridge
Fletchers Thorns
Fletchers Green
Round Copse
SO42
Lymington River
Ober Water
Water Copse Inclosure
Ober Heath
Ober Corner
Black Knowl
Aldridgehill Inclosure
Aldridgehill Cottage
Aldridge Hill
Rhinefield Walk
Black Knoll House
Butts Lawn
Ober Farm
Puttles Bridge
Beachern Wood
Brockenhurst
Rhinefield Forest Walks
Whitefield Moor
Hotel
Ford
Ober Lodge
Forest Park
North Weirs
Red Hill
Sch
B3055 SWAY RD
RHINEFIELD RD
WHITEMOOR RD
MEADCREST WOOD
BROADLANDS RD
KNOWLE RD
FOREST PARK RD
MEERUT RD
BUTTS PADDOCK
BROOKSIDE RD
CAREYS COTTS
FATHERSFIELD
OBER RD
COURTYARD CL
MARDEN PADDOCK
RHINEFIELD CL
THE PADDOCK
FIBBARDS RD
BROCK HO
GRIGG LA
MOORLANDS CL
OBERFIELD RD
THE COPPICE
NEW FOREST DR
ARMSTRONG RD
WILVERLEY RD
BROOKLEY RD
WIDE LA CL
ARMSTRONG LA
ARMSTRONG CL
BROADLANDS RD
FOREST GLADE CL
WOODBURY
FOREST VIEW
BRITTONS COTTS
NORTH WEIRS
BURLEY RD
THE RISE
THE BRIARS 1
AUCKLAND PL 2
KINSFORD CT 3
AVENUE RD 4
CULVERLEY CL 5
COURTYARD MEWS 6
PO
8
7
05
6
5
04
4
3
03
2
1
02
27
28
29
172
146

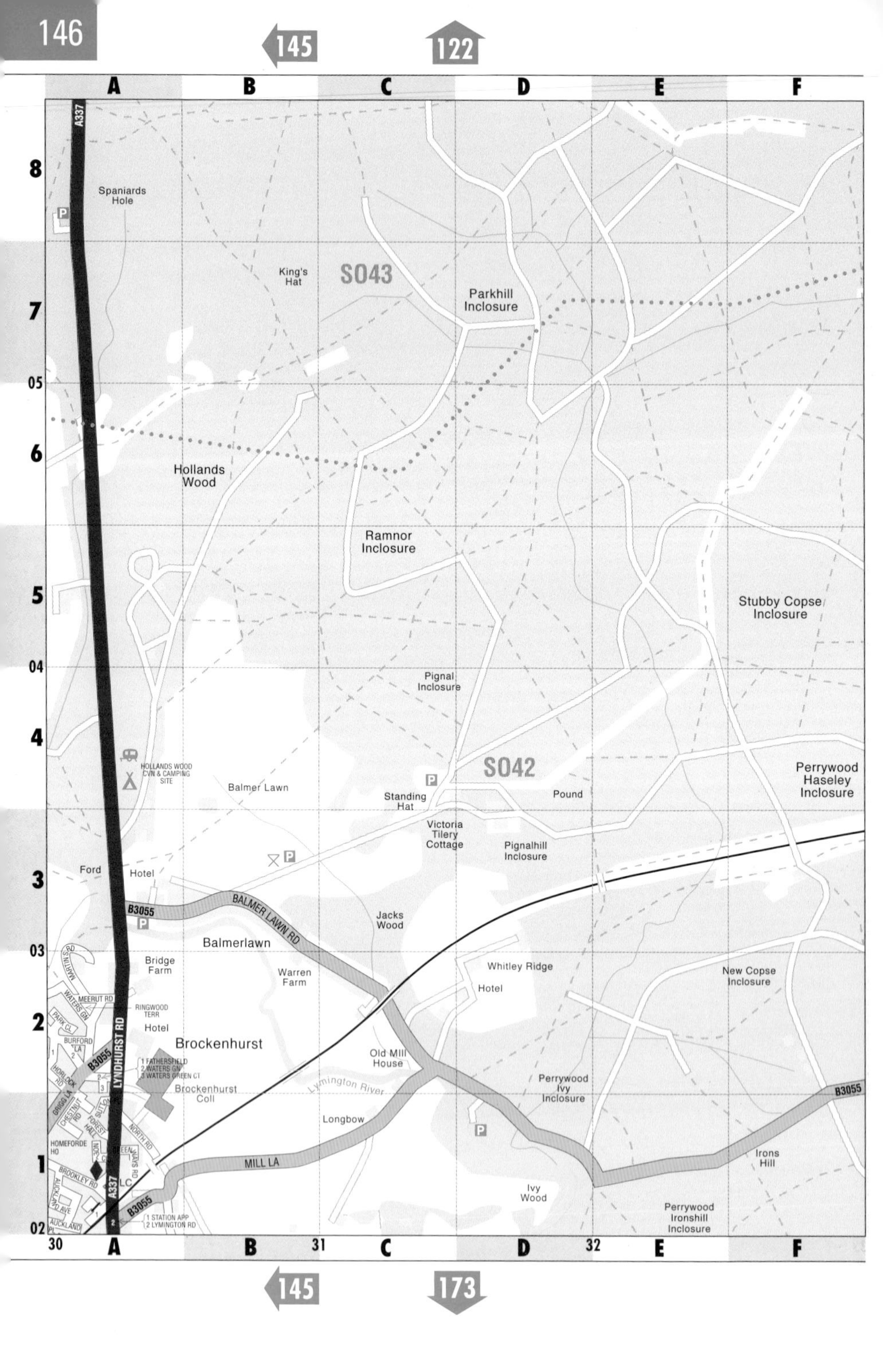

145
122
A
B
C
D
E
F
8
7
05
6
5
04
4
3
03
2
1
02
30
31
32
A337
Spaniards Hole
King's Hat
SO43
Parkhill Inclosure
Hollands Wood
Ramnor Inclosure
Stubby Copse Inclosure
Pignal Inclosure
HOLLANDS WOOD CVN & CAMPING SITE
SO42
Balmer Lawn
Standing Hat
Pound
Perrywood Haseley Inclosure
Victoria Tilery Cottage
Pignalhill Inclosure
Ford
Hotel
B3055
BALMER LAWN RD
Jacks Wood
Balmerlawn
Bridge Farm
Warren Farm
Whitley Ridge
New Copse Inclosure
Hotel
RINGWOOD TERR
Hotel
Brockenhurst
LYNDHURST RD
1 FATHERSFIELD
2 WATERS GN
3 WATERS GREEN CT
Brockenhurst Coll
Old Mill House
Lymington River
Perrywood Ivy Inclosure
B3055
Longbow
Irons Hill
MILL LA
Ivy Wood
Perrywood Ironshill Inclosure
1 STATION APP
2 LYMINGTON RD
145
173

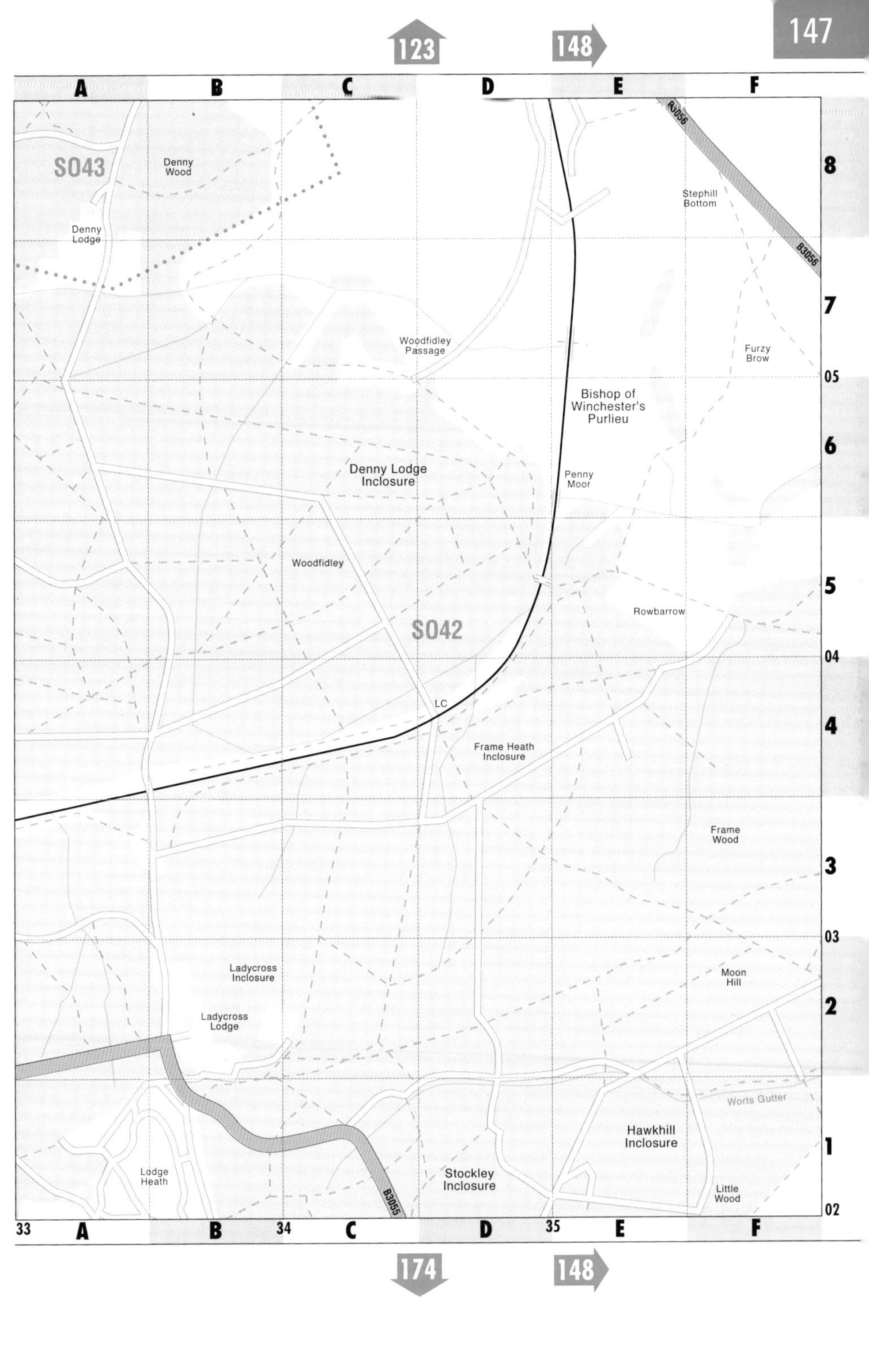

123
148
A
B
C
D
E
F
8
7
05
6
5
04
4
3
03
2
1
02
33
34
35
174
SO43
Denny Wood
Denny Lodge
B3056
Stephill Bottom
Furzy Brow
Woodfidley Passage
Bishop of Winchester's Purlieu
Denny Lodge Inclosure
Penny Moor
Woodfidley
SO42
Rowbarrow
LC
Frame Heath Inclosure
Frame Wood
Ladycross Inclosure
Moon Hill
Ladycross Lodge
Worts Gutter
Hawkhill Inclosure
Lodge Heath
Stockley Inclosure
Little Wood
B3055

147
124

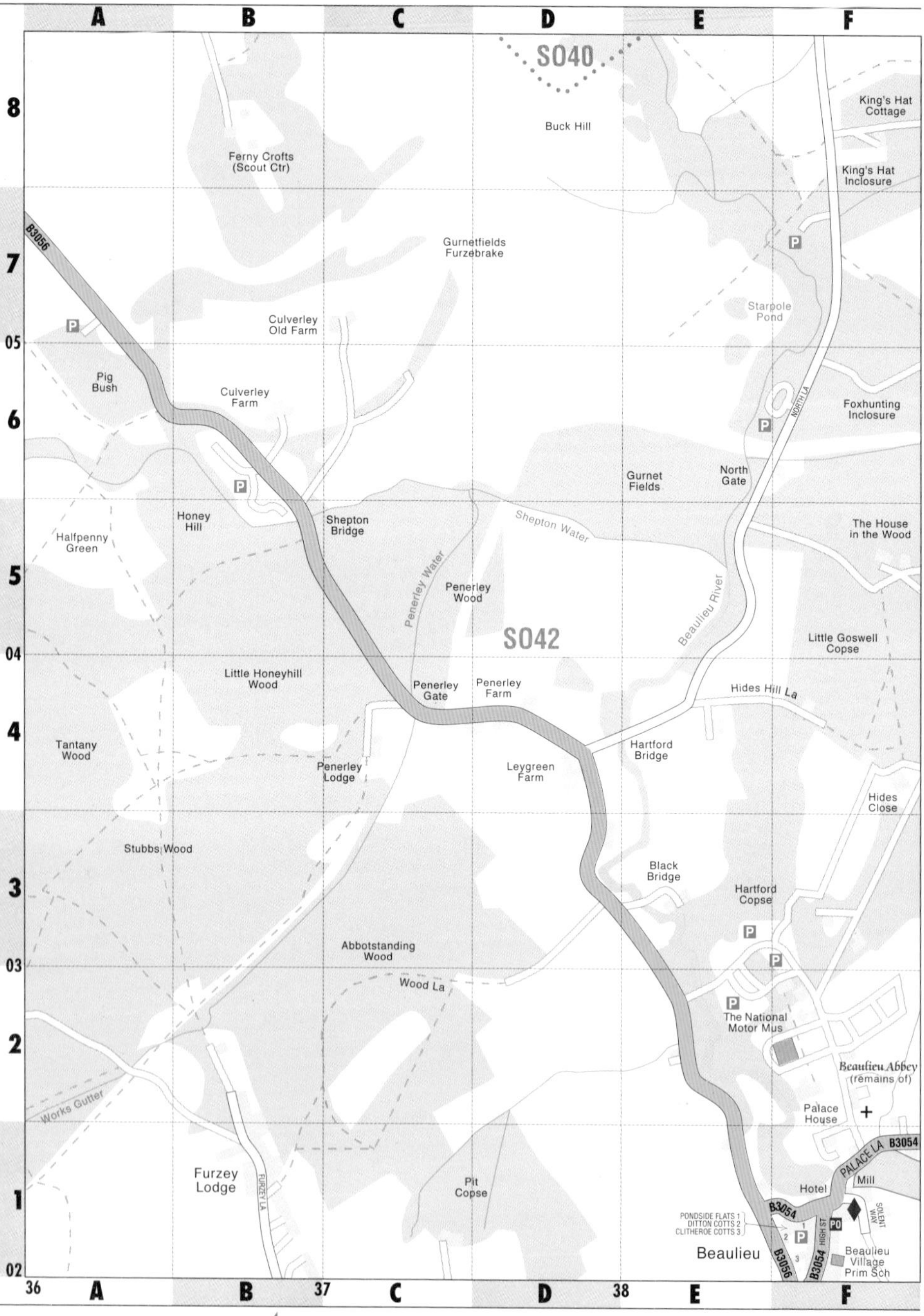

| | A | B | C | D | E | F |

SO40

King's Hat Cottage

8

Buck Hill

Ferny Crofts (Scout Ctr)

King's Hat Inclosure

Gurnetfields Furzebrake

7

P

B3056

Starpole Pond

05

P

Culverley Old Farm

Pig Bush

Culverley Farm

Foxhunting Inclosure

6

P

NORTH LA

Honey Hill

Shepton Bridge

Shepton Water

Gurnet Fields

North Gate

The House in the Wood

Halfpenny Green

Penerley Water

Penerley Wood

Beaulieu River

5

Little Goswell Copse

04

Little Honeyhill Wood

SO42

Penerley Gate

Penerley Farm

Hides Hill La

4

Tantany Wood

Penerley Lodge

Leygreen Farm

Hartford Bridge

Hides Close

Stubbs Wood

Black Bridge

3

Hartford Copse

03

Abbotstanding Wood

Wood La

P

P

2

P

The National Motor Mus

Beaulieu Abbey (remains of)

Works Gutter

Palace House

FURZEY LA

Furzey Lodge

Pit Copse

PALACE LA

B3054

Mill

1

Hotel

B3054

SOLENT WAY

02

Beaulieu

PONDSIDE FLATS 1
DITTON COTTS 2
CLITHEROE COTTS 3

HIGH ST

B3056

B3054

PO

Beaulieu Village Prim Sch

| 36 | A | | B | 37 | C | | D | 38 | E | | F |

147
175

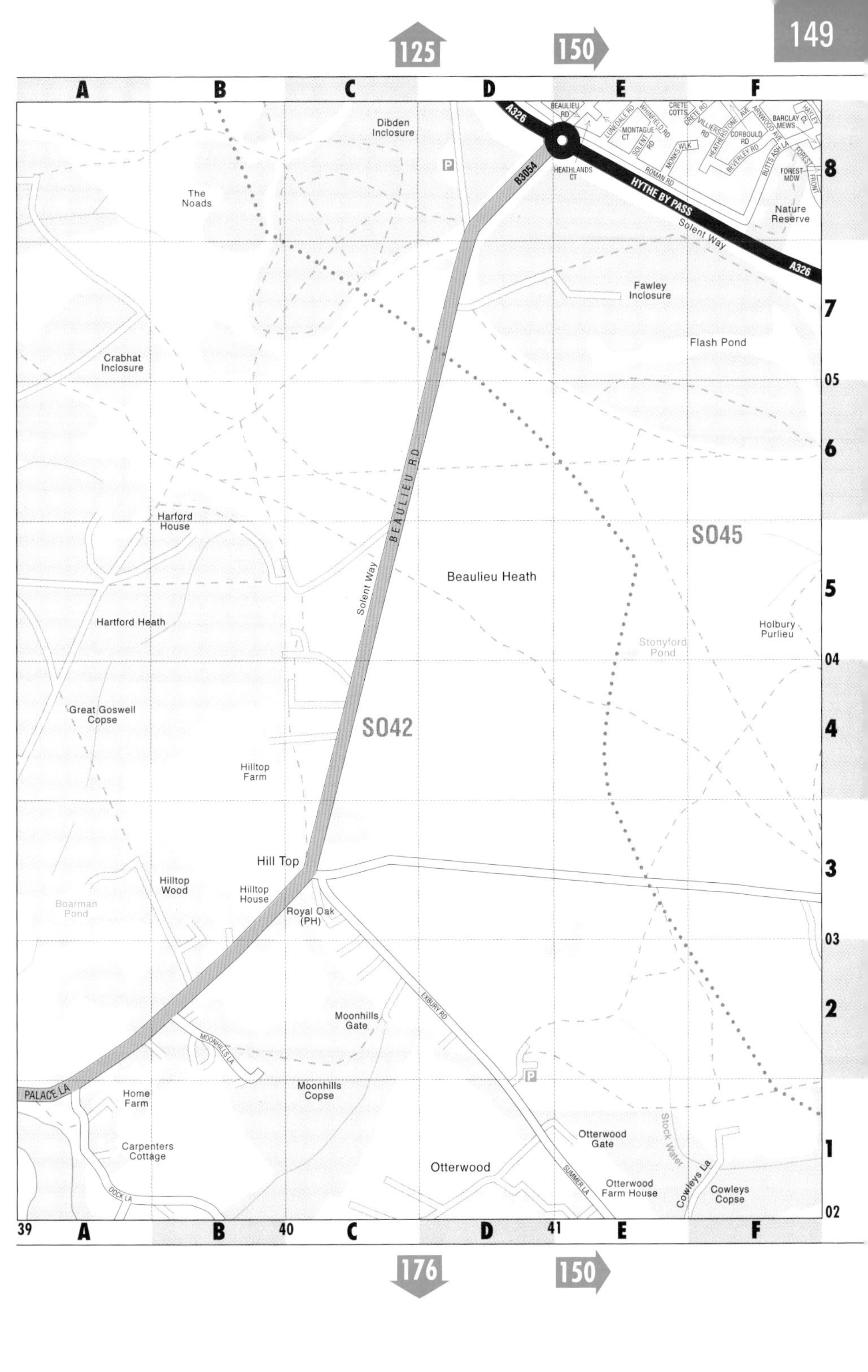
125
150
A
B
C
D
E
F
8
7
05
6
5
04
4
3
03
2
1
02
39
40
41
A326
BEAULIEU RD
LUNEDALE RD
WHINFIELD RD
MONTAGUE CT
SOLENT RD
CRETE COTTS
CRETE RD
VILLIERS RD
HEATHERSTONE AVE
CORBOULD RD
ARNWOOD AVE
BARCLAY MEWS
HAYLEY CL
BEVERLEY RD
BUTTS ASH LA
FOREST FRONT
FOREST MDW
MONKS WLK
ROMAN RD
HEATHLANDS CT
HYTHE BY PASS
B3054
Dibden Inclosure
The Noads
Nature Reserve
Solent Way
Fawley Inclosure
Flash Pond
Crabhat Inclosure
S045
Harford House
Beaulieu Heath
BEAULIEU RD
Solent Way
Hartford Heath
Stonyford Pond
Holbury Purlieu
Great Goswell Copse
S042
Hilltop Farm
Hill Top
Hilltop Wood
Hilltop House
Boarman Pond
Royal Oak (PH)
EXBURY RD
Moonhills Gate
MOONHILLS LA
PALACE LA
Home Farm
Moonhills Copse
Carpenters Cottage
DOCK LA
Otterwood
Otterwood Gate
SUMMER LA
Otterwood Farm House
Stock Water
Cowleys La
Cowleys Copse
176
150

149 126

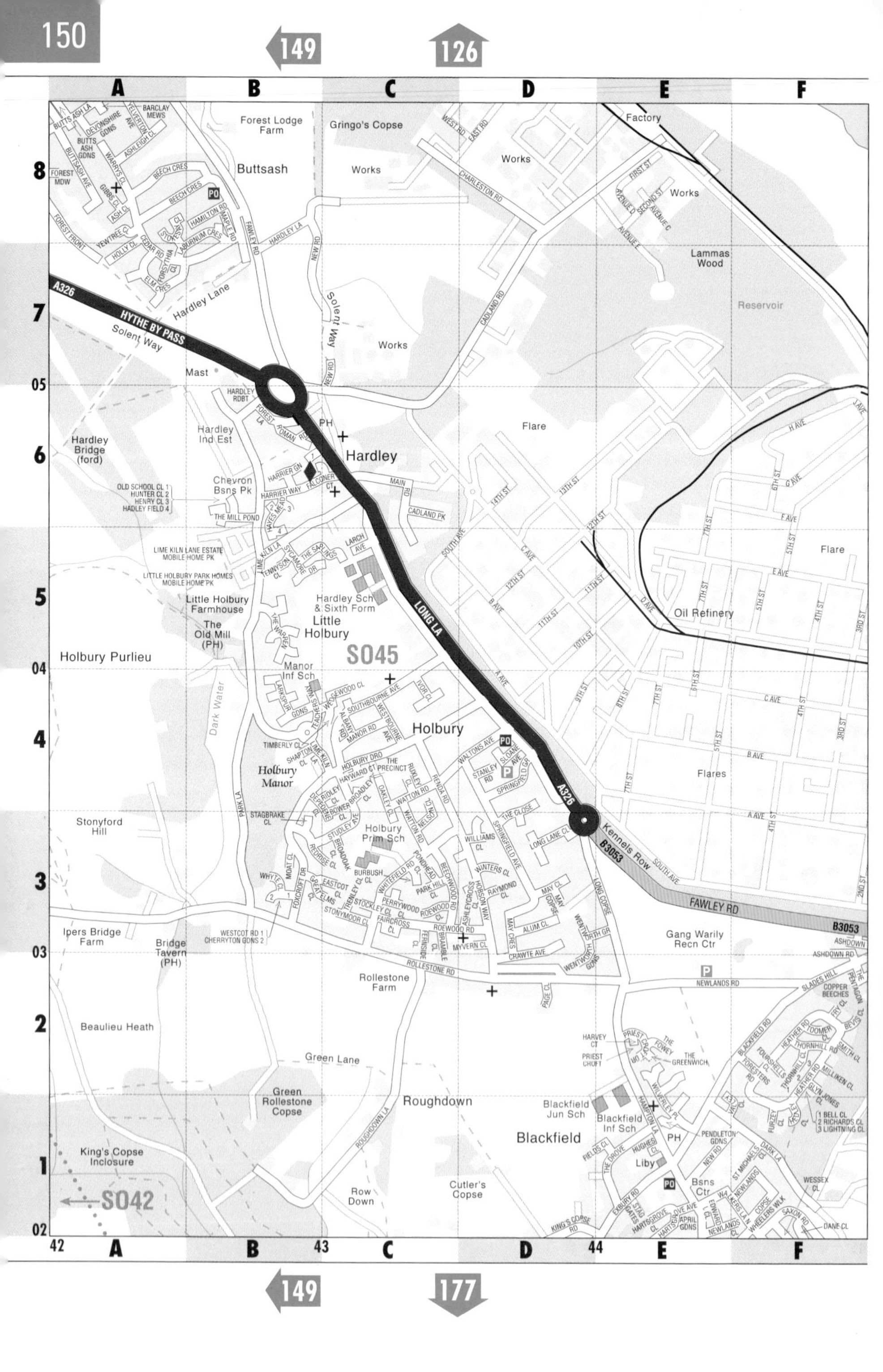
Forest Lodge Farm
Gringo's Copse
Buttsash
Works
Factory
Lammas Wood
Reservoir
HYTHE BY PASS
A326
Hardley Lane
Solent Way
Mast
HARDLEY RDBT
Hardley Ind Est
Hardley Bridge (ford)
Hardley
Chevron Bsns Pk
Flare
Oil Refinery
LONG LA
Hardley Sch & Sixth Form
Little Holbury
Little Holbury Farmhouse
The Old Mill (PH)
Holbury Purlieu
SO45
Manor Inf Sch
Holbury
Holbury Manor
Dark Water
Stonyford Hill
Holbury Prim Sch
Flares
Kennels Row
B3053
FAWLEY RD
Gang Warily Recn Ctr
Ipers Bridge Farm
Bridge Tavern (PH)
ROLLESTONE RD
Rollestone Farm
NEWLANDS RD
Beaulieu Heath
Green Lane
Green Rollestone Copse
Roughdown
Blackfield Jun Sch
Blackfield Inf Sch
Blackfield
King's Copse Inclosure
SO42
Row Down
Cutler's Copse
Liby
Bsns Ctr

149 177

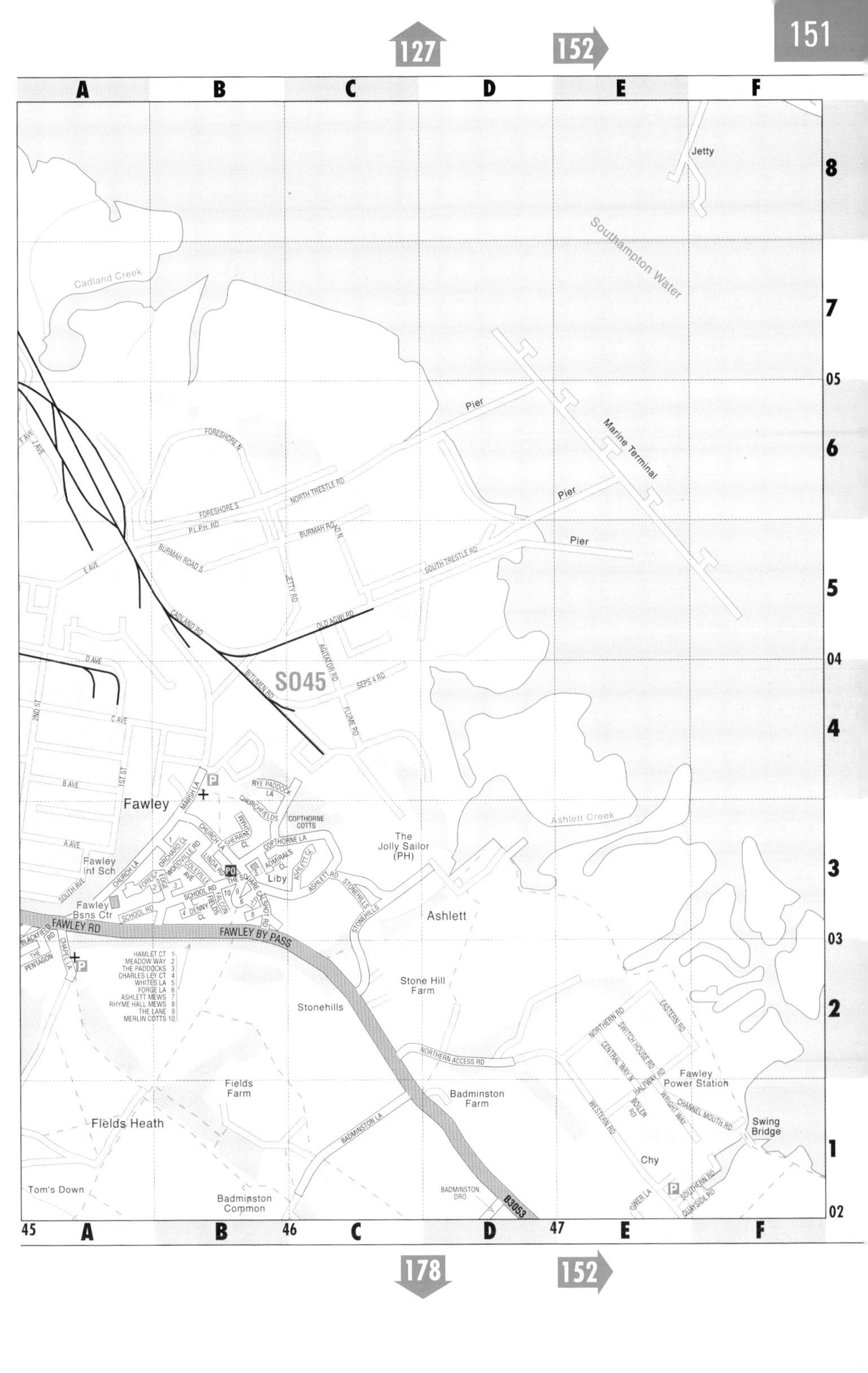
127
152
Jetty
Southampton Water
Cadland Creek
Pier
Marine Terminal
Pier
Pier
FORESHORE N
NORTH TRESTLE RD
FORESHORE S
PL P.H. RD
BURMAH RD
BURMAH ROAD S
SOUTH TRESTLE RD
E AVE
JETTY RD
CADLAND RD
OLD AGWI RD
D AVE
BITUMEN RD
AGITATOR RD
SEPS 4 RD
SO45
FLUME RD
2ND ST
C AVE
1ST ST
B AVE
RYE PADDOCK LA
MARSH LA
Fawley
CHURCHFIELDS
COPTHORNE COTTS
A AVE
CHURCH LA
COPTHORNE LA
The Jolly Sailor (PH)
Ashlett Creek
Fawley Inf Sch
ORCHARD CL
WOODVILLE RD
ADMIRALS CL
ASHLETT CL
Liby
ASHLETT RD
STONEHILLS
COLEVILLE AVE
SCHOOL RD
CALSHOT RD
THE SQUARE
SOUTH AVE
Fawley Bsns Ctr
SCHOOL RD
DENNY CL
FIELDS
FALCON
Ashlett
FAWLEY RD
FAWLEY BY PASS
BLACKFIELD RD
THE PENTAGON
CHAPEL LA
HAMLET CT 1
MEADOW WAY 2
THE PADDOCKS 3
CHARLES LEY CT 4
WHITES LA 5
FORGE LA 6
ASHLETT MEWS 7
RHYME HALL MEWS 8
THE LANE 9
MERLIN COTTS 10
Stone Hill Farm
Stonehills
NORTHERN RD
EASTERN RD
SWITCH HOUSE RD
CENTRAL WAY N
NORTHERN ACCESS RD
Fields Farm
Badminston Farm
HALFWAY RD
Fawley Power Station
WESTERN RD
BOILER RD
WRIGHT WAY
CHANNEL MOUTH RD
Fields Heath
BADMINSTON LA
Swing Bridge
Chy
Tom's Down
Badminston Common
BADMINSTON DRO
B3053
SOUTHERN RD
QUAYSIDE RD
A B C D E F
8 7 05 6 5 04 4 3 03 2 1 02
45 46 47
178
152

151
128

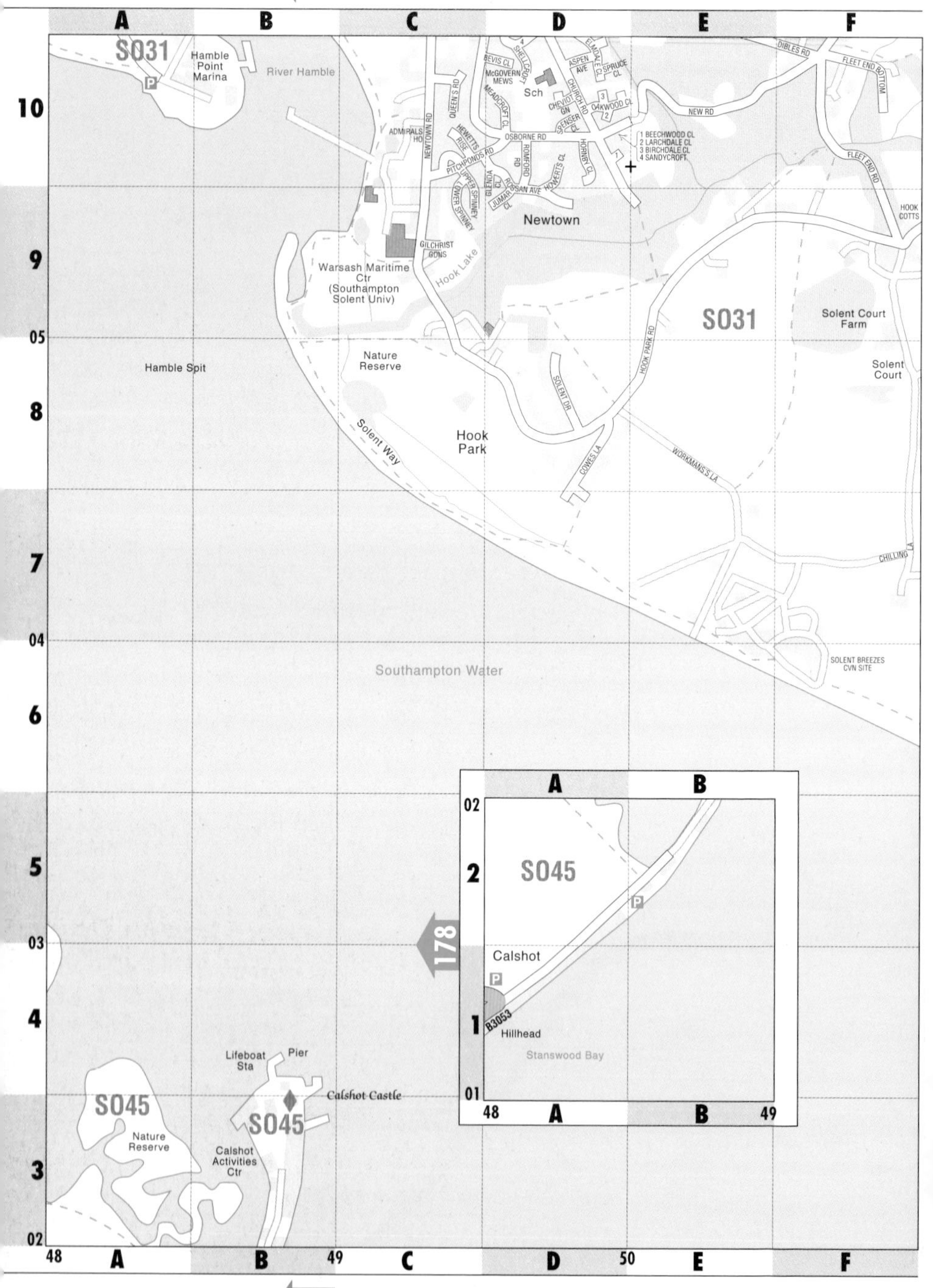
SO31
Hamble Point Marina
River Hamble
Admirals Ho
Newtown Rd
Queen's Rd
Hewetts Rise
Pitchponds Rd
Upper Spinney
Lower Spinney
Glenda Cl
Jumar Cl
Russan Ave
Howerts Cl
Romford Rd
Osborne Rd
Meadcroft Cl
Bevis Cl
McGovern Mews
Shellcroft
Sch
Aspen Ave
Elmdale Cl
Spruce Cl
Cheviot Gn
Church Rd
Spenser Cl
Oakwood Cl
Hornby Cl
New Rd
Dibles Rd
Fleet End Bottom
Fleet End Rd
1 Beechwood Cl
2 Larchdale Cl
3 Birchdale Cl
4 Sandycroft
Newtown
Gilchrist Gdns
Warsash Maritime Ctr (Southampton Solent Univ)
Hook Lake
Hook Cotts
SO31
Solent Court Farm
Solent Court
Hamble Spit
Nature Reserve
Hook Park Rd
Solent Dr
Solent Way
Hook Park
Cowes La
Workmans's La
Chilling La
Southampton Water
Solent Breezes Cvn Site
SO45
Calshot
B3053
Hillhead
Stanswood Bay
Lifeboat Sta
Pier
Calshot Castle
SO45
Nature Reserve
Calshot Activities Ctr
SO45
A
B
C
D
E
F
10
9
05
8
7
04
6
5
03
4
3
02
48
49
50
1
2
01

178
151

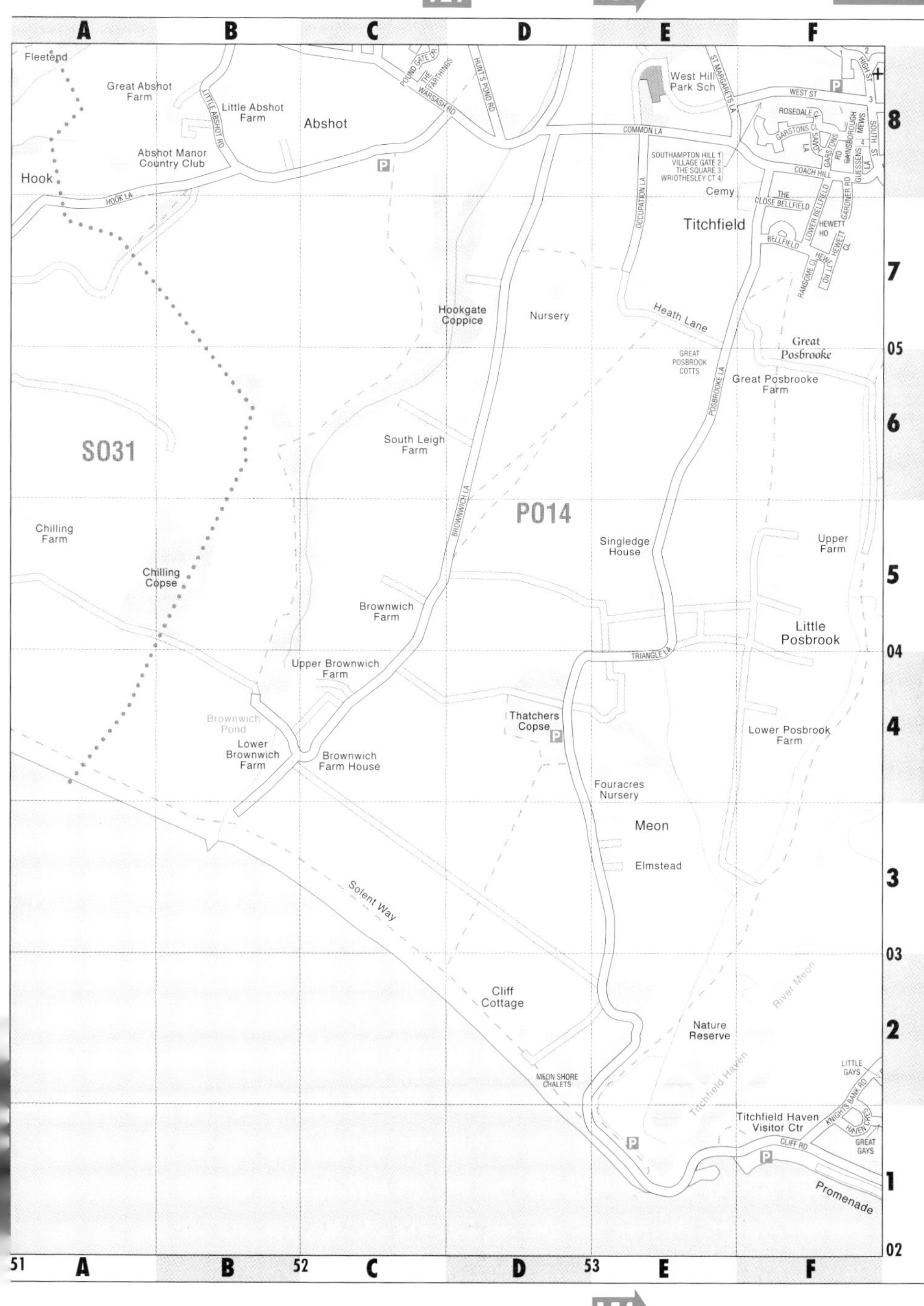

Fleetend

Great Abshot
Farm

Little Abshot
Farm

Abshot

Abshot Manor
Country Club

Hook

HOOK LA

LITTLE ABSHOT RD

POND GATE RD
THE TITHINGS
THE MARGASONS RD
HUNTS POND RD

COMMON LA

OCCUPATION LA

West Hill
Park Sch

WEST ST

ST MARGARETS LA

ROSEDALE CL
GLADSTONES CL
GASCOIGNE LA
PASSION CL
ST MARKS LA
GRANGE MEWS

COACH HILL

SOUTHAMPTON HILL 1
VILLAGE GATE 2
THE SQUARE 3
WRIOTHESLEY CT 4

Cemy

Titchfield

THE
CLOSE BELLFIELD

BELLFIELD

LOWER BELLFIELD
LOWER BELLFIELD
HEWETT
HD
HEWETT
PARSONAGE CL
GARDNER LA

Hookgate
Coppice

Nursery

Heath Lane

Great
Posbrooke

GREAT
POSBROOK
COTTS

Great Posbrooke
Farm

POSBROOK LA

SO31

South Leigh
Farm

PO14

Chilling
Farm

Chilling
Copse

BROWNWICH LA

Brownwich
Farm

Upper Brownwich
Farm

Brownwich
Pond

Lower
Brownwich
Farm

Brownwich
Farm House

Solent Way

Singledge
House

Upper
Farm

Little
Posbrook

TRIANGLE LA

Thatchers
Copse

Lower Posbrook
Farm

Fouracres
Nursery

Meon

Elmstead

Cliff
Cottage

MEON SHORE
CHALETS

River Meon

Nature
Reserve

Titchfield Haven

Titchfield Haven
Visitor Ctr

HAVEN BANK CL
TRACEY DR

CLIFF RD

LITTLE
GAYS

GREAT
GAYS

Promenade

05

7

05

6

5

04

4

3

03

2

1

02

51   52   53
A   B   C   D   E   F

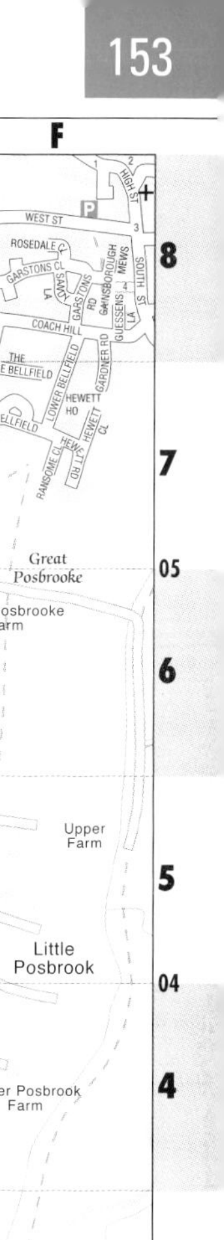

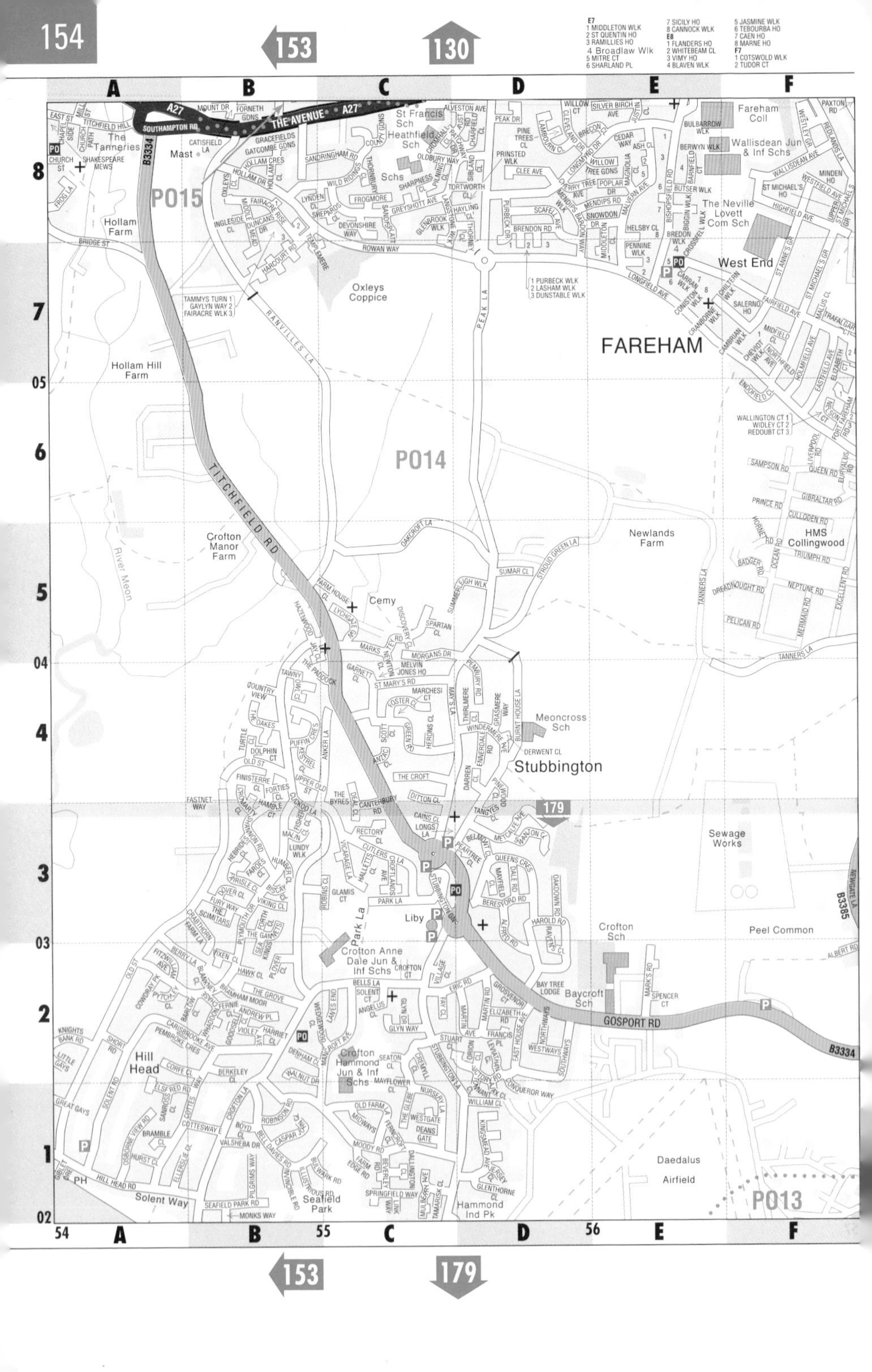

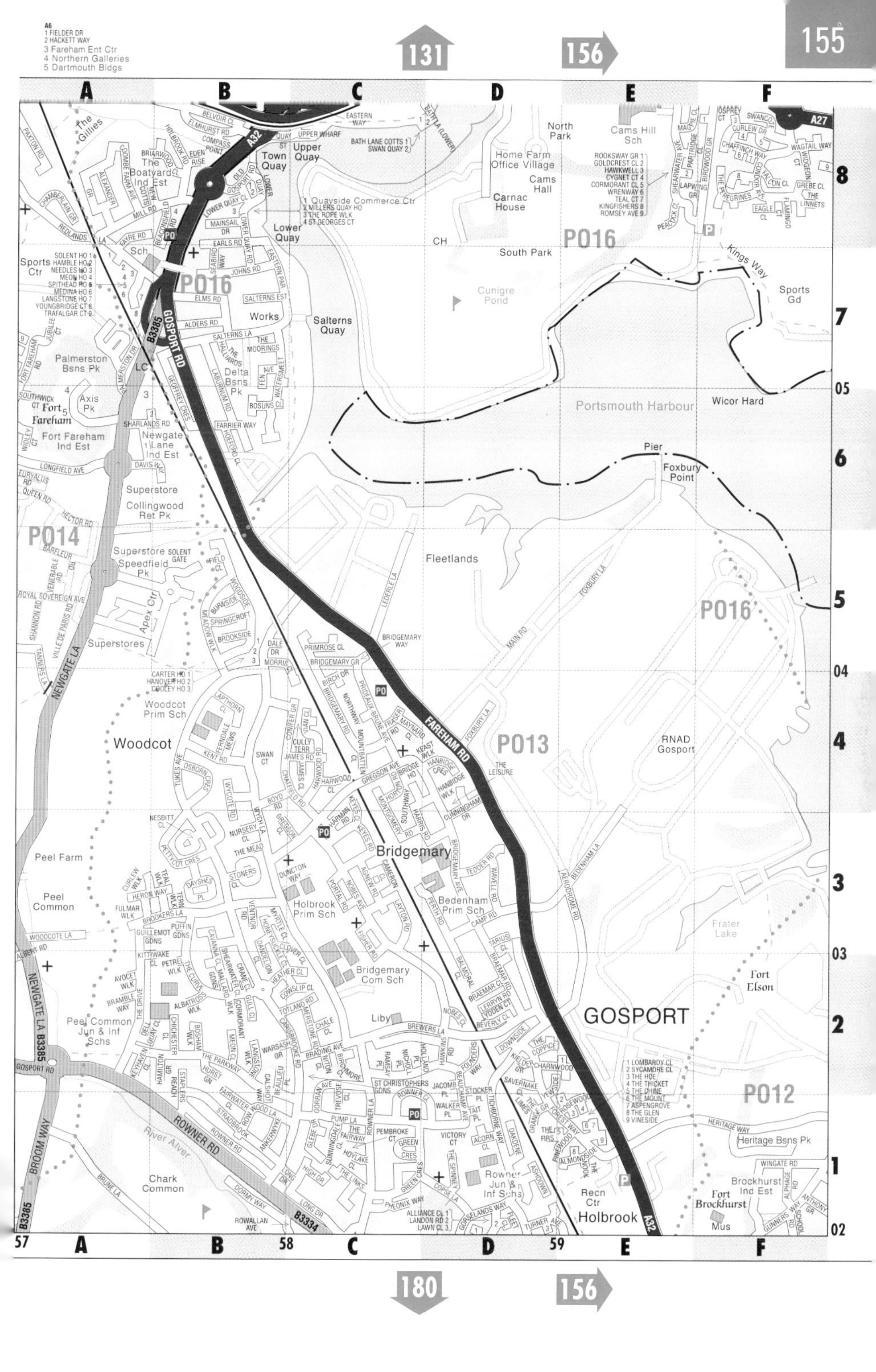
155
131
156
180
156
A6
1 FIELDER DR
2 HACKETT WAY
3 Fareham Ent Ctr
4 Northern Galleries
5 Dartmouth Bldgs
A
B
C
D
E
F
57
58
59
02
03
04
05
1
2
3
4
5
6
7
8
A32
A27
B3385
B3334
PO16
PO14
PO13
PO12
GOSPORT
Portsmouth Harbour
The Gillies
The Boatyard Ind Est
Town Quay
Upper Quay
Lower Quay
Salterns Quay
North Park
Home Farm Office Village
Cams Hill Sch
Cams Hall
Carnac House
South Park
Cunigre Pond
Kings Way
Sports Gd
Wicor Hard
Pier
Foxbury Point
Sports Ctr
Palmerston Bsns Pk
Axis Pk
Fort Fareham
Fort Fareham Ind Est
Newgate Lane Ind Est
Delta Bsns Pk
Works
Superstore
Collingwood Ret Pk
Superstore
Speedfield Pk
Apex Ctr
Superstores
Fleetlands
RNAD Gosport
Woodcot
Woodcot Prim Sch
Bridgemary
Holbrook Prim Sch
Bedenham Prim Sch
Bridgemary Com Sch
Liby
Peel Farm
Peel Common
Peel Common Jun & Inf Schs
Frater Lake
Fort Elson
Chark Common
River Alver
Rowner Jun & Inf Schs
Recn Ctr
Holbrook
Heritage Bsns Pk
Brockhurst Ind Est
Fort Brockhurst
Mus
GOSPORT RD
FAREHAM RD
NEWGATE LA
ROWNER RD
BROOM WAY
1 Quayside Commerce Ctr
2 MILLERS QUAY HO
3 THE ROPE WLK
4 ST GEORGES CT
ROOKSWAY GR 1
GOLDCREST CL 2
HAWKWELL 3
CYGNET CT 4
CORMORANT CL 5
WRENWAY 6
TEAL CT 7
KINGFISHERS 8
ROMSEY AVE 9
SOLENT HO 1
HAMBLE HO 2
NEEDLES HO 3
MEON HO 4
SPITHEAD HO 5
MEDINA HO 6
LANGSTONE HO 7
YOUNGBRIDGE CT 8
TRAFALGAR CT 9
CARTER HO 1
HANOVER HO 2
COOLEY HO 3
1 LOMBARDY CL
2 SYCAMORE CL
3 THE HOE
4 THE THICKET
5 THE CHINE
6 THE MOUNT
7 ASPENGROVE
8 THE GLEN
9 VINESIDE
ALLIANCE CL 1
LANDON RD 2
LAWN CL 3

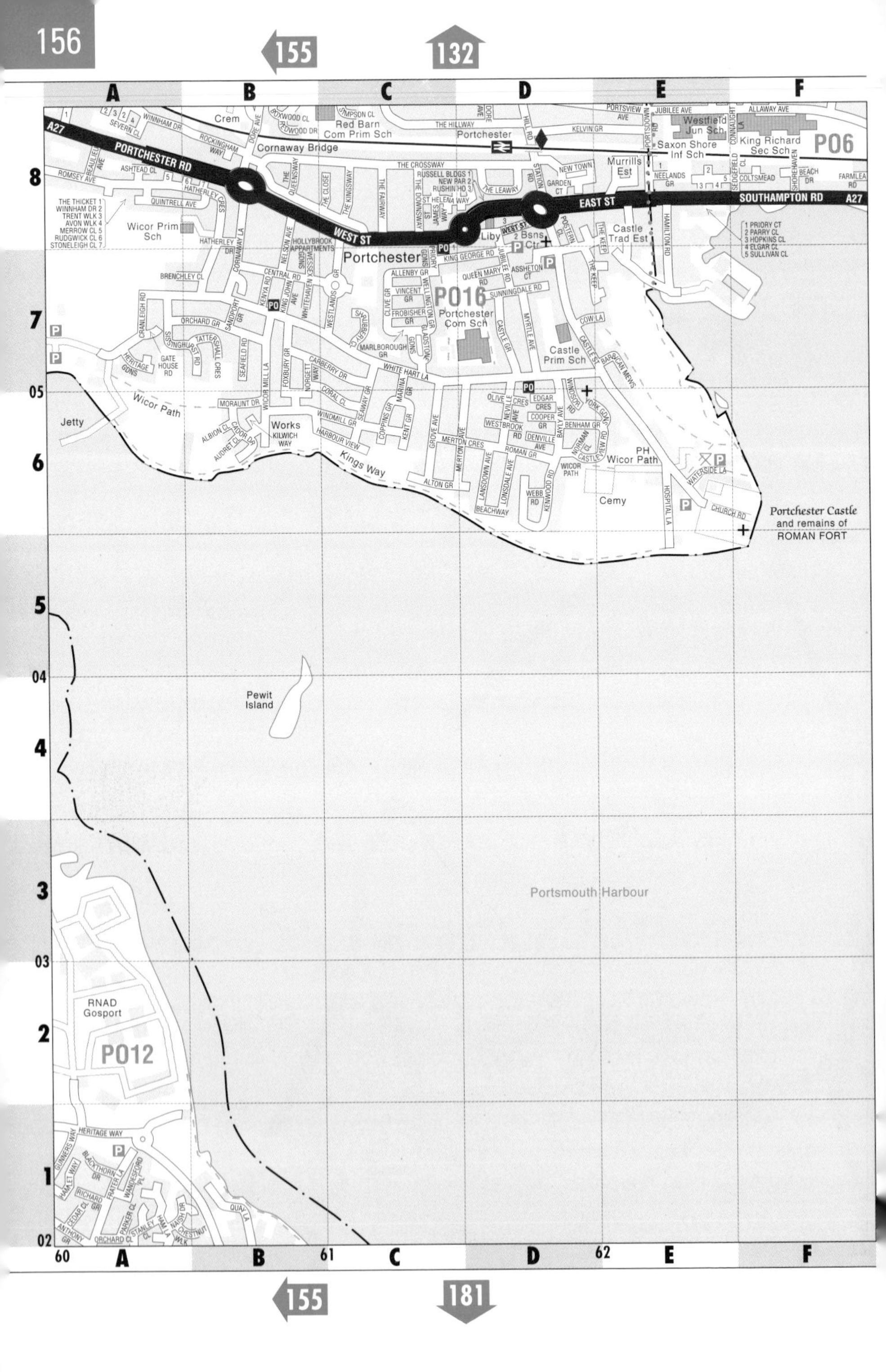
155
132
A
B
C
D
E
F
A27
PORTCHESTER RD
Crem
Cornaway Bridge
Red Barn
Com Prim Sch
Portchester
Westfield
Jun Sch
Saxon Shore
Inf Sch
King Richard
Sec Sch
PO6
Murrills
Est
WEST ST
EAST ST
SOUTHAMPTON RD
Wicor Prim
Sch
Liby
Bsns
Ctr
Castle
Trad Est
Portchester
PO16
Portchester
Com Sch
Castle
Prim Sch
THE THICKET 1
WINNHAM DR 2
TRENT WLK 3
AVON WLK 4
MERROW CL 5
RUDGWICK CL 6
STONELEIGH CL 7
1 PRIORY CT
2 PARRY CL
3 HOPKINS CL
4 ELGAR CL
5 SULLIVAN CL
Wicor Path
Jetty
Works
Kings Way
PH
Wicor Path
Cemy
Portchester Castle
and remains of
ROMAN FORT
Pewit
Island
Portsmouth Harbour
RNAD
Gosport
PO12
HERITAGE WAY
QUAY LA
8
7
05
6
5
04
4
3
03
2
1
02
60
61
62
155
181

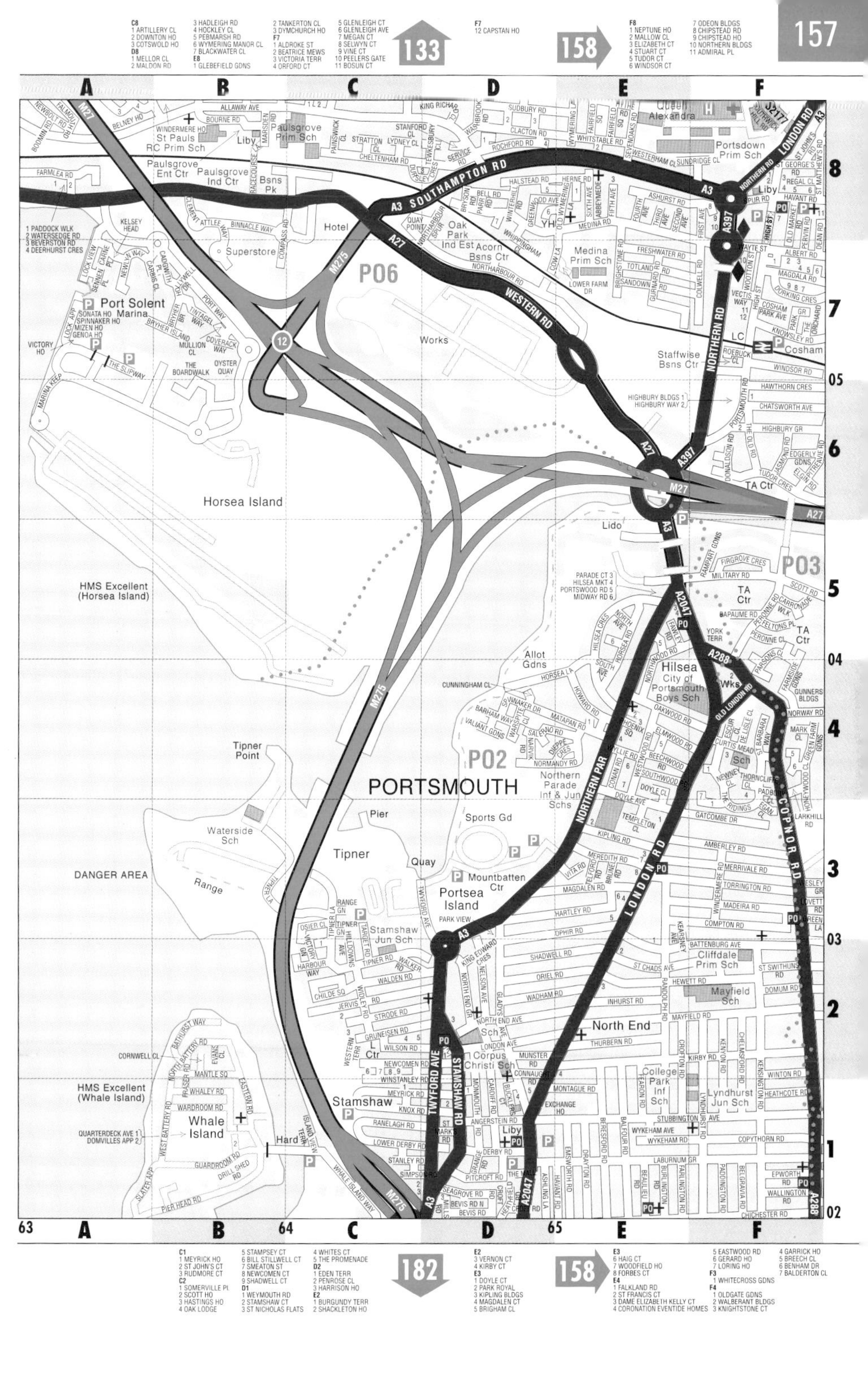

157
C8
1 ARTILLERY CL
2 DOWNTON HO
3 COTSWOLD HO
D8
1 MELLOR CL
2 MALDON RD
3 HADLEIGH RD
4 HOCKLEY CL
5 PEBMARSH RD
6 WYMERING MANOR CL
7 BLACKWATER CL
E8
1 GLEBEFIELD GDNS
2 TANKERTON CL
3 DYMCHURCH HO
F7
1 ALDROKE ST
2 BEATRICE MEWS
3 VICTORIA TERR
4 ORFORD CT
5 GLENLEIGH CT
6 GLENLEIGH AVE
7 MEGAN CT
8 SELWYN CT
9 VINE CT
10 PEELERS GATE
11 BOSUN CT
133
F7
12 CAPSTAN HO
158
F8
1 NEPTUNE HO
2 MALLOW CL
3 ELIZABETH CT
4 STUART CT
5 TUDOR CT
6 WINDSOR CT
7 ODEON BLDGS
8 CHIPSTEAD RD
9 CHIPSTEAD HO
10 NORTHERN BLDGS
11 ADMIRAL PL
A B C D E F
8 7 05 6 5 04 4 3 03 2 1 02
63 64 65
PORTSMOUTH
PO6
PO2
PO3
Port Solent Marina
Horsea Island
HMS Excellent (Horsea Island)
HMS Excellent (Whale Island)
Whale Island
Tipner Point
Tipner
Waterside Sch
DANGER AREA
Range
Paulsgrove Ent Ctr
Paulsgrove Ind Ctr
Paulsgrove Prim Sch
St Pauls RC Prim Sch
Superstore
Hotel
Oak Park Ind Est
Acorn Bsns Ctr
Medina Prim Sch
Queen Alexandra
Portsdown Prim Sch
Works
Staffwise Bsns Ctr
Cosham
Lido
Hilsea
City of Portsmouth Boys Sch
Allot Gdns
Northern Parade Inf & Jun Schs
Sports Gd
Pier
Quay
Mountbatten Ctr
Portsea Island
Stamshaw Jun Sch
Stamshaw
Corpus Christi Sch
North End
Cliffdale Prim Sch
Mayfield Sch
College Park Inf Sch
Lyndhurst Jun Sch
SOUTHAMPTON RD
WESTERN RD
NORTHERN RD
LONDON RD
NORTHERN PAR
COPNOR RD
TWYFORD AVE
STAMSHAW RD
M27
M275
A27
A3
A397
A2047
A288
C1
1 MEYRICK HO
2 ST JOHN'S CT
3 RUDMORE CT
C2
1 SOMERVILLE PL
2 SCOTT HO
3 HASTINGS HO
4 OAK LODGE
5 STAMPSEY CT
6 BILL STILLWELL CT
7 SMEATON ST
8 NEWCOMEN CT
9 SHADWELL CT
D1
1 WEYMOUTH RD
2 STAMSHAW CT
3 ST NICHOLAS FLATS
4 WHITES CT
5 THE PROMENADE
D2
1 EDEN TERR
2 PENROSE CL
3 HARRISON HO
E2
1 BURGUNDY TERR
2 SHACKLETON HO
182
E2
3 VERNON CT
4 KIRBY CT
E3
1 DOYLE CT
2 PARK ROYAL
3 KIPLING BLDGS
4 MAGDALEN CT
5 BRIGHAM CL
158
E3
6 HAIG CT
7 WOODFIELD HO
8 FORBES CT
E4
1 FALKLAND RD
2 ST FRANCIS CT
3 DAME ELIZABETH KELLY CT
4 CORONATION EVENTIDE HOMES
5 EASTWOOD RD
6 GERARD HO
7 LORING HO
F3
1 WHITECROSS GDNS
F4
1 OLDGATE GDNS
2 WALBERANT BLDGS
3 KNIGHTSTONE CT
4 GARRICK HO
5 BREECH CL
6 BENHAM DR
7 BALDERTON CL

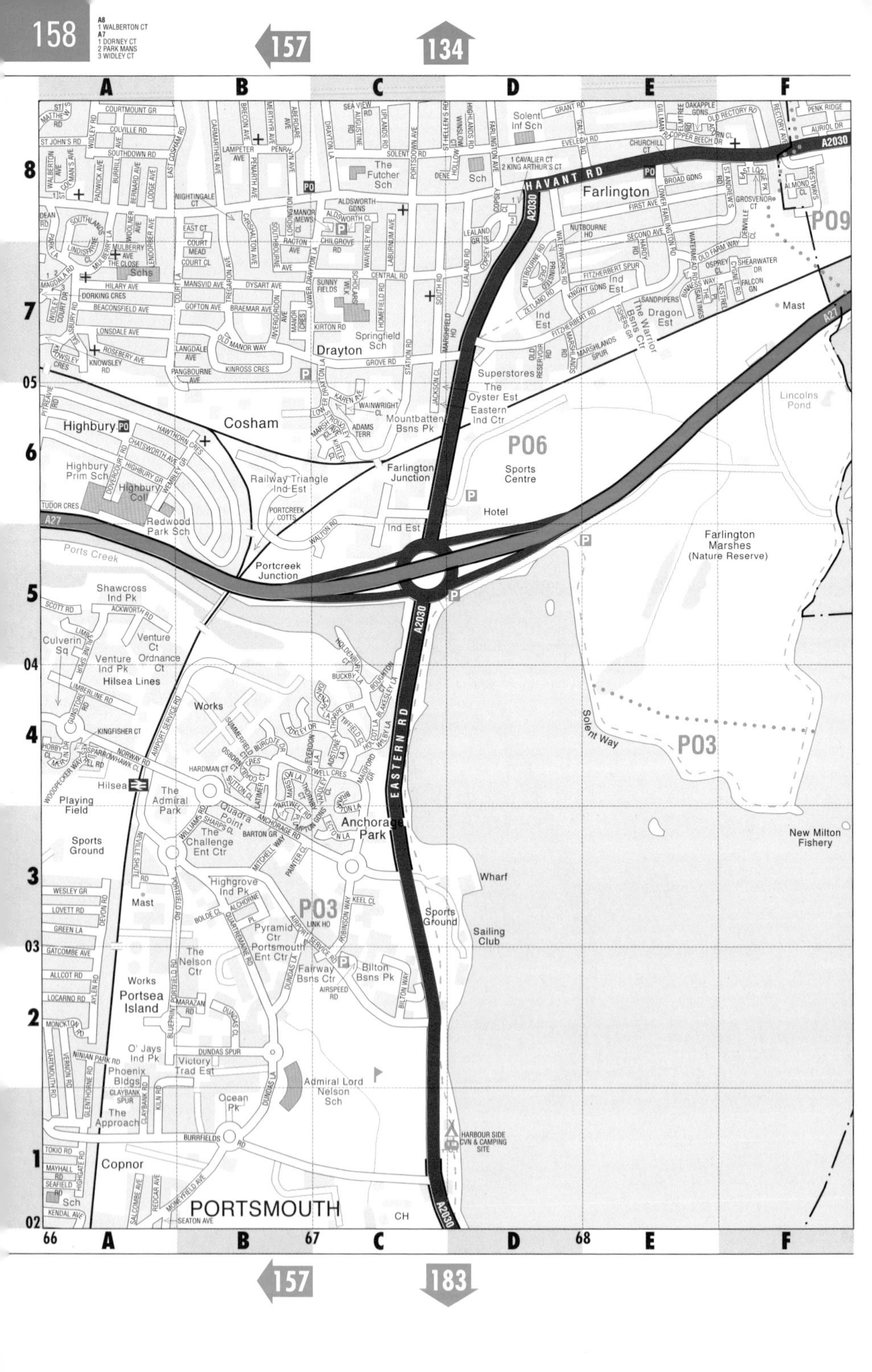
158
A8
1 WALBERTON CT
A7
1 DORNEY CT
2 PARK MANS
3 WIDLEY CT
157
134
A
B
C
D
E
F
8
7
05
6
5
04
4
3
03
2
1
02
66
67
68
183
COURTMOUNT GR
COLVILLE RD
ST JOHN'S RD
SOUTHDOWN RD
PADWICK AVE
BURRILL AVE
BERNARD AVE
LODGE AVE
EAST COSHAM RD
CARMARTHEN AVE
BRECON AVE
LAMPETER AVE
PENARTH AVE
MERTHYR AVE
ABERDARE AVE
DRAYTON LA
SEA VIEW RD
AUGUSTINE RD
UPLANDS RD
PORTSDOWN AVE
SOLENT RD
ST HELEN'S RD
HIGHLANDS RD
FARLINGTON AVE
Solent Inf Sch
GRANT RD
GATT RD
EVELEGH RD
CHURCHILL CT
OAKAPPLE GDNS
OLD RECTORY RD
RECTORY AVE
PENK RIDGE
AURIOL DR
A2030
The Futcher Sch
Sch
1 CAVALIER CT
2 KING ARTHUR'S CT
HAVANT RD
Farlington
BROAD GDNS
FIRST AVE
LOWER FARLINGTON RD
ST ANDREW'S RD
GROSVENOR CT
ALMOND CL
PO9
NIGHTINGALE CT
ALDSWORTH GDNS
MANOR MEWS
CHILGROVE RD
SOUTHBOURNE AVE
RACTON AVE
WAVERLEY RD
LABURNUM AVE
LEALAND GR
COPSEY CL
NUTBOURNE HO
SECOND AVE
OLD FARM WAY
SHEARWATER DR
SOUTHLANDS
LINDISFARNE CL
MULBERRY AVE
THE CLOSE
Schs
EAST CT
COURT MEAD
COURT CL
CARSHALTON AVE
HILARY AVE
DORKING CRES
BEACONSFIELD AVE
MANSVID AVE
DYSART AVE
GOFTON AVE
BRAEMAR AVE
SUNNY FIELDS
CENTRAL RD
HOMEFIELD RD
SOUTH RD
LEALAND RD
FITZHERBERT SPUR
KNIGHT GDNS
Ind Est
SANDPIPERS
The Warrior Bsns Ctr
Dragon Est
Mast
A27
LONSDALE AVE
OLD MANOR WAY
KIRTON RD
Springfield Sch
Drayton
ROSEBERY AVE
KNOWSLEY RD
LANGDALE AVE
KINROSS CRES
GROVE RD
PANGBOURNE AVE
MARSHFIELD HO
FITZHERBERT RD
MARSHLANDS SPUR
Superstores
The Oyster Est
Eastern Ind Ctr
Lincolns Pond
KAREN AVE
WAINWRIGHT CL
Mountbatten Bsns Pk
ADAMS TERR
JACKSON CL
Highbury
Cosham
HAWTHORN CRES
CHATSWORTH AVE
Highbury Prim Sch
Highbury Coll
PO6
Sports Centre
Railway Triangle Ind Est
Farlington Junction
Hotel
TUDOR CRES
Redwood Park Sch
PORTCREEK COTTS
WALTON RD
Ind Est
Ports Creek
Farlington Marshes
(Nature Reserve)
Portcreek Junction
Shawcross Ind Pk
SCOTT RD
ACKWORTH RD
Culverin Sq
Venture Ct
Ordnance Ct
Venture Ind Pk
Hilsea Lines
LIMBERLINE RD
HOLDENBURY CT
BUCKBY LA
BOUGHTON CT
Works
EASTERN RD
KINGFISHER CT
NORWAY RD
AIRPORT SERVICE RD
Solent Way
PO3
HARDMAN CT
Hilsea
The Admiral Park
Playing Field
Quadra Point
ANCHORAGE RD
Anchorage Park
The Challenge Ent Ctr
BARTON GR
MITCHELL WAY
Sports Ground
New Milton Fishery
Wharf
WESLEY GR
LOVETT RD
GREEN LA
DEVON RD
Mast
Highgrove Ind Pk
KEEL CL
Sports Ground
Sailing Club
GATCOMBE AVE
ALLCOT RD
Pyramid Ctr
Portsmouth Ent Ctr
The Nelson Ctr
Fairway Bsns Ctr
Bilton Bsns Pk
Works
Portsea Island
AIRSPEED RD
BILTON WAY
LOCARNO RD
AYLEN RD
MONCKTON RD
MARAZAN RD
DUNDAS CL
O' Jays Ind Pk
DUNDAS SPUR
Victory Trad Est
NINIAN PARK RD
Phoenix Bldgs
CLAYBANK SPUR
Admiral Lord Nelson Sch
The Approach
Ocean Pk
DUNDAS LA
HARBOUR SIDE CVN & CAMPING SITE
BURRFIELDS RD
TOKIO RD
MAYHALL RD
SEAFIELD RD
Copnor
Sch
KENDAL AVE
PORTSMOUTH
SEATON AVE
CH

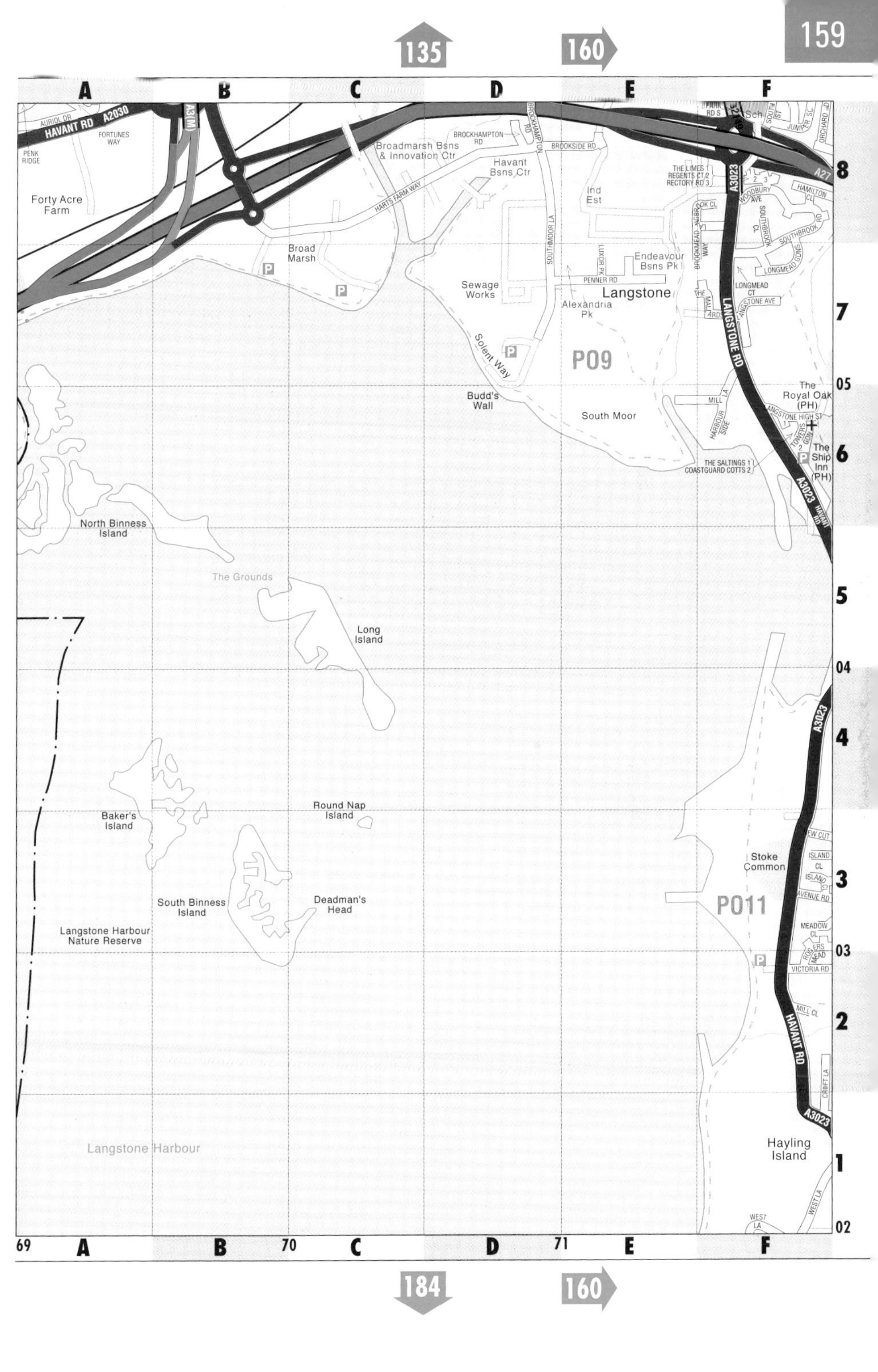

A   B   C   D   E   F

HAVANT RD A2030

AUDIT DR

PENK RIDGE

FORTUNES WAY

8

Forty Acre Farm

Broad Marsh

Broadmarsh Bsns & Innovation Ctr

BROCKHAMPTON RD

HART'S FARM WAY

Havant Bsns Ctr

BROOKSIDE RD

SOUTHBROOK LA

Ind Est

The Limes 1
Regents Ct 2
Rectory Rd 3

School

A3023

A27

COOK CL

SOUTHBROOK

LANGMEAD

AVEBURY

HAMILTON

7

Sewage Works

LUMLEY RD

PENNER RD

Langstone

Alexandria Pk

Endeavour Bsns Pk 1

PO9

LANGSTONE RD

LONGMEAD CT

LANGSTONE AVE

05

Solent Way

Budd's Wall

South Moor

The Royal Oak (PH)

MILL

LANGSTONE HIGH ST

6

North Binness Island

The Grounds

P

The Saltings 1
Coastguard Cotts 2

The Ship Inn (PH)

A3023

5

04

Long Island

A3023

4

Baker's Island

Round Nap Island

NEW CUT

ISLAND CL

ISLAND

AVENUE RD

Stoke Common

PO11

3

03

South Binness Island

Deadman's Head

MEADOW CL

VICTORIA RD

P

Langstone Harbour Nature Reserve

MILL CL

HAVANT RD

2

Langstone Harbour

A3023

Hayling Island

1

WEST LA

ORBIT LA

02

69   A   B   70   C   D   71   E   F

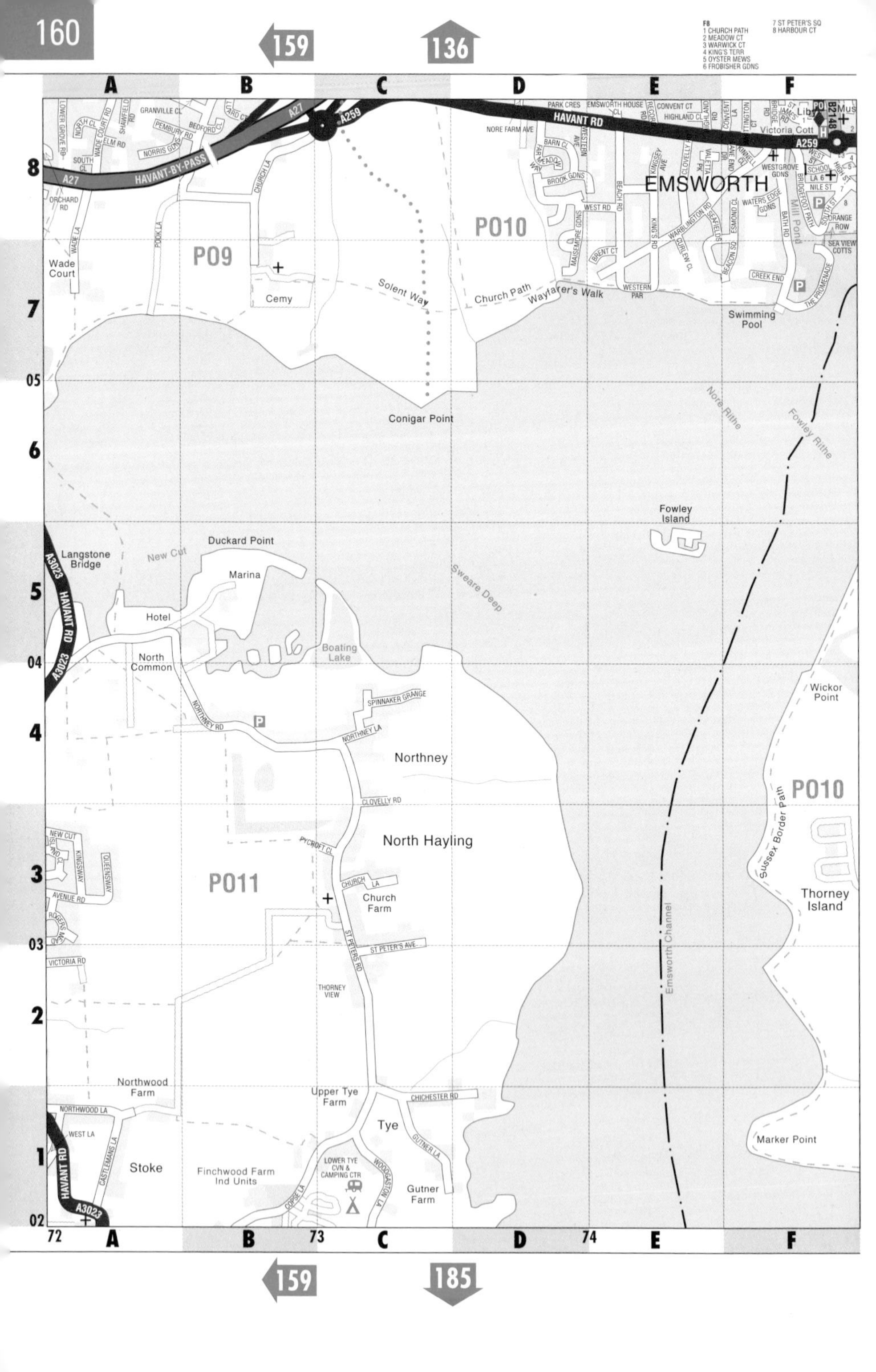
159
136
F8
1 CHURCH PATH
2 MEADOW CT
3 WARWICK CT
4 KING'S TERR
5 OYSTER MEWS
6 FROBISHER GDNS
7 ST PETER'S SQ
8 HARBOUR CT
A
B
C
D
E
F
8
7
05
6
5
04
4
3
03
2
1
02
72
73
74
A27
HAVANT-BY-PASS
A259
HAVANT RD
B2148
EMSWORTH
PO9
PO10
PO11
Wade Court
Cemy
Solent Way
Church Path
Wayfarer's Walk
Swimming Pool
Conigar Point
Nore Rithe
Fowley Rithe
Fowley Island
Langstone Bridge
New Cut
Duckard Point
Marina
Sweare Deep
Hotel
North Common
Boating Lake
A3023
Wickor Point
NORTHNEY RD
SPINNAKER GRANGE
NORTHNEY LA
Northney
CLOVELLY RD
North Hayling
PYCROFT CL
CHURCH LA
Church Farm
ST PETER'S AVE
ST PETERS RD
THORNEY VIEW
Emsworth Channel
Sussex Border Path
Thorney Island
Northwood Farm
Upper Tye Farm
CHICHESTER RD
Tye
GUTNER LA
NORTHWOOD LA
WEST LA
CASTLEMANS LA
Stoke
Finchwood Farm Ind Units
LOWER TYE CVN & CAMPING CTR
WOODGASTON LA
COPSE LA
Gutner Farm
Marker Point
Mill Pond
185

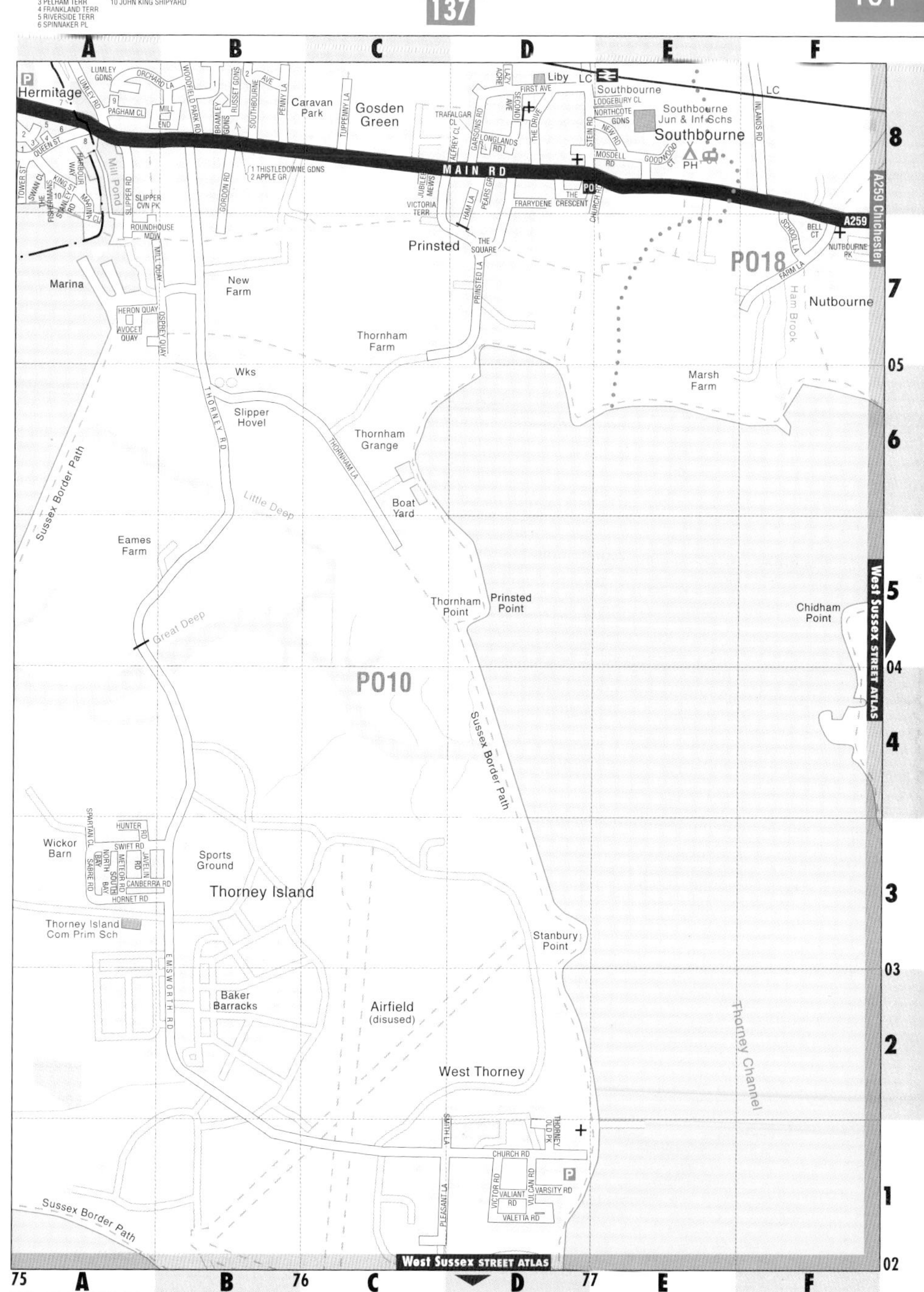
Hermitage
Caravan Park
Gosden Green
Liby
Southbourne
Southbourne Jun & Inf Schs
MAIN RD
A259
A259 Chichester
Prinsted
PO18
Nutbourne
Marina
New Farm
Thornham Farm
Wks
Slipper Hovel
Thornham Grange
Marsh Farm
Boat Yard
Little Deep
Eames Farm
Sussex Border Path
Great Deep
Thornham Point
Printed Point
Chidham Point
PO10
West Sussex STREET ATLAS
Wickor Barn
Sports Ground
Thorney Island
Thorney Island Com Prim Sch
Stanbury Point
Baker Barracks
Airfield (disused)
West Thorney
Thorney Channel
CHURCH RD
Sussex Border Path

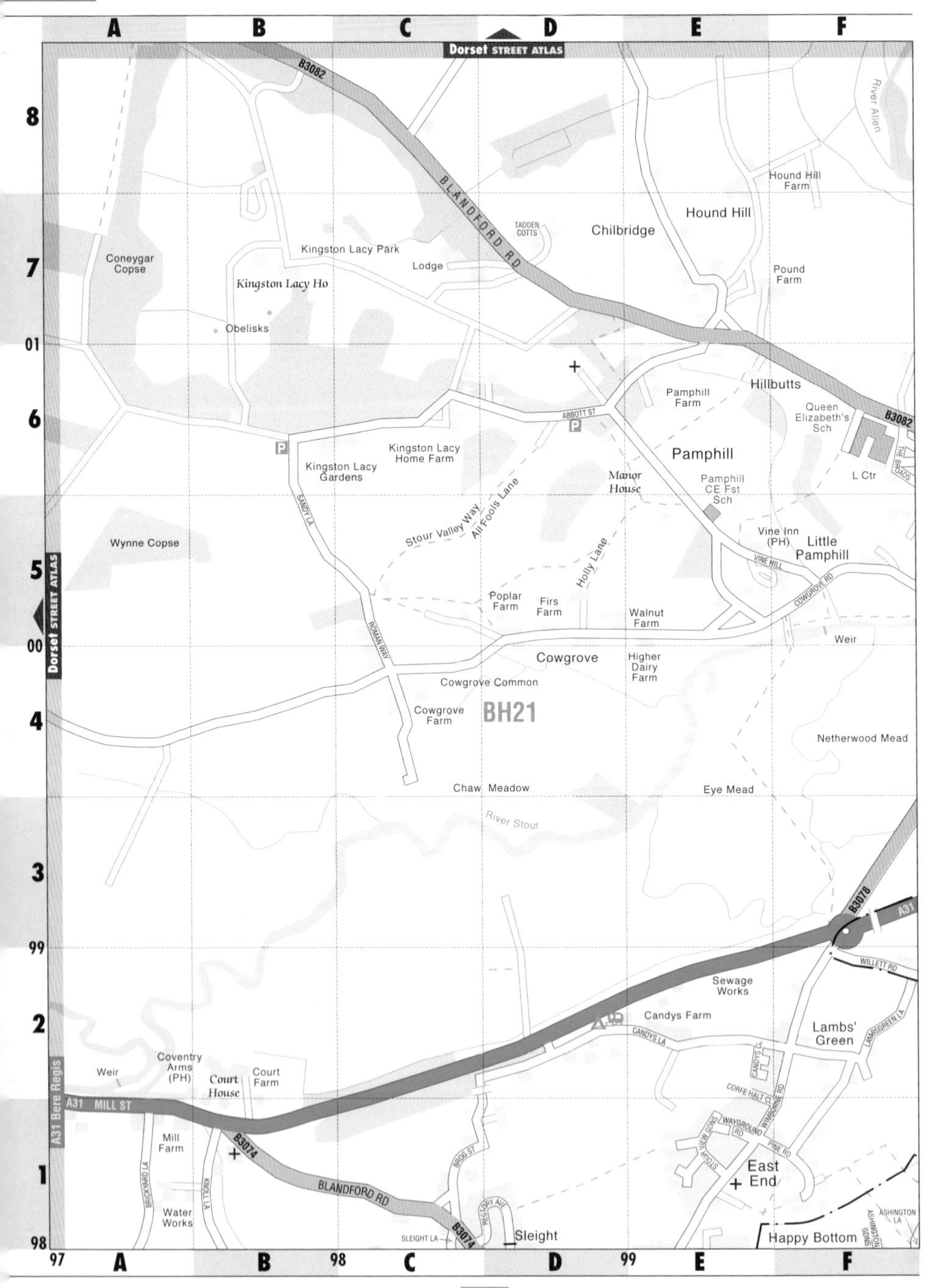

A B C D E F

8

7

01

6

5

00

4

3

99

2

1

98

97 A B 98 C D 99 E F

Dorset STREET ATLAS

B3082

BLANDFORD RD

River Allen

Hound Hill Farm

Hound Hill

Chilbridge

TADDEN COTTS

Coneygar Copse

Kingston Lacy Park

Lodge

Pound Farm

Kingston Lacy Ho

Obelisks

Hillbutts

Pamphill Farm

Queen Elizabeth's Sch

B3082

Kingston Lacy Home Farm

Kingston Lacy Gardens

ABBOTT ST

Pamphill

L Ctr

Manor House

Pamphill CE Fst Sch

Stour Valley Way

All Fools Lane

Vine Inn (PH)

Little Pamphill

VINE HILL

Wynne Copse

Holly Lane

COWGROVE RD

Poplar Farm

Firs Farm

Walnut Farm

Weir

Cowgrove

Higher Dairy Farm

Cowgrove Common

BH21

Netherwood Mead

Cowgrove Farm

Chaw Meadow

Eye Mead

River Stout

B3078

A31

WILLETT RD

Sewage Works

Candys Farm

CANDYS LA

Lambs' Green

MARSHGREEN LA

A31

Coventry Arms (PH)

Weir

Court House

Court Farm

CANDYS LA

A31 Bere Regis

MILL ST

Mill Farm

B3074

BLANDFORD RD

BLANDFORD RD

BRIG ST

CORFE HALT CLOSE RD

WAYGROUND

PINE RD

East End

Water Works

KNOLL LA

B3074

SLEIGHT LA

Sleight

Happy Bottom

ASHINGTON LA

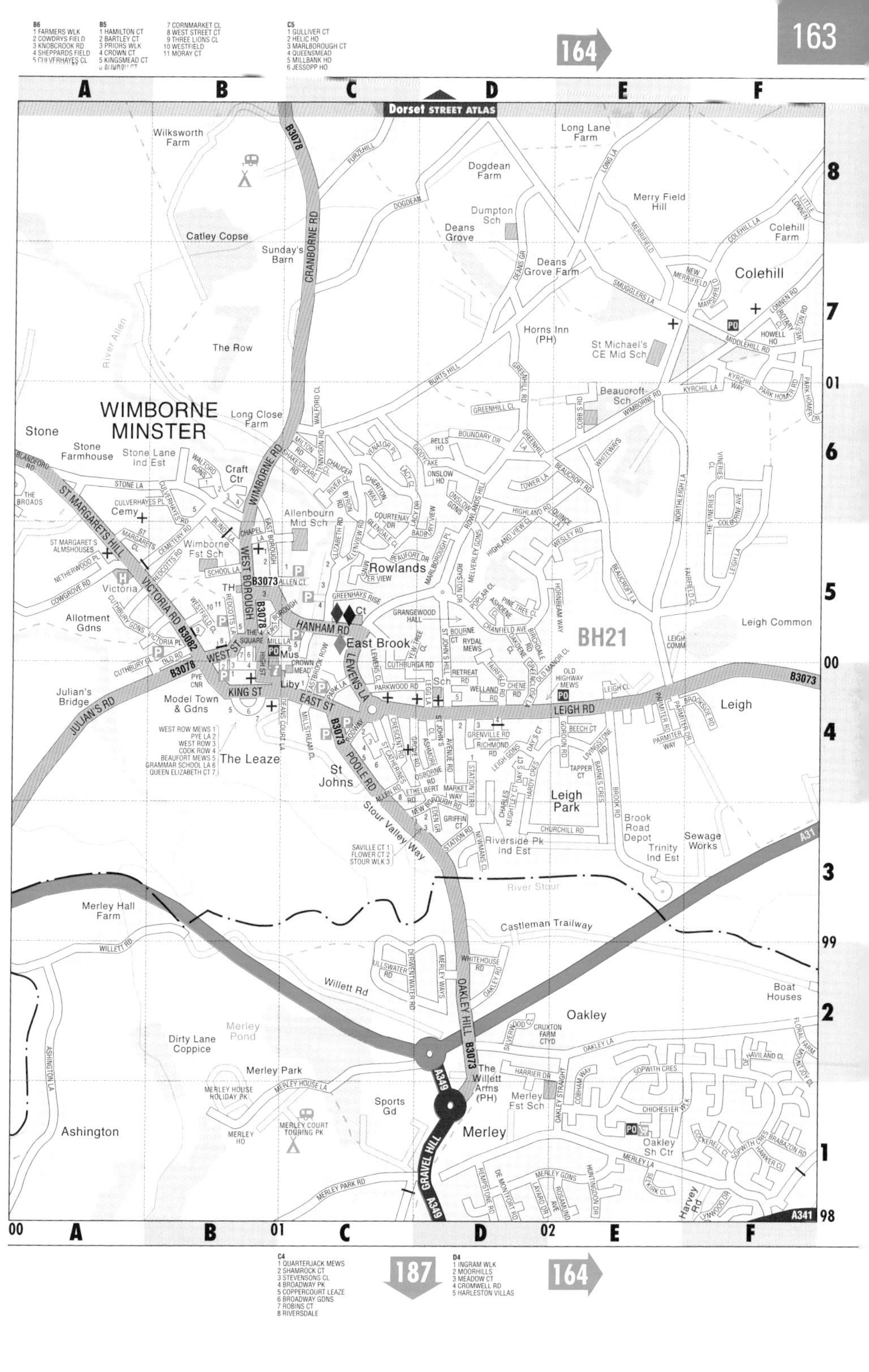
163
164
Dorset STREET ATLAS
B6
1 FARMERS WLK
2 COWDRYS FIELD
3 KNOBCROOK RD
4 SHEPPARDS FIELD
5 CULVERHAYES CL
B5
1 HAMILTON CT
2 BARTLEY CT
3 PRIORS WLK
4 CROWN CT
5 KINGSMEAD CT
7 CORNMARKET CL
8 WEST STREET CT
9 THREE LIONS CL
10 WESTFIELD
11 MORAY CT
C5
1 GULLIVER CT
2 HELIC HO
3 MARLBOROUGH CT
4 QUEENSMEAD
5 MILLBANK HO
6 JESSOPP HO
WIMBORNE MINSTER
Wilksworth Farm
Catley Copse
Sunday's Barn
The Row
River Allen
Long Close Farm
Stone
Stone Farmhouse
Stone Lane Ind Est
Craft Ctr
Cemy
Wimborne Fst Sch
Allenbourn Mid Sch
Victoria
Allotment Gdns
Julian's Bridge
Model Town & Gdns
The Leaze
St Johns
East Brook
Rowlands
Long Lane Farm
Dogdean Farm
Dumpton Sch
Deans Grove
Deans Grove Farm
Horns Inn (PH)
St Michael's CE Mid Sch
Merry Field Hill
Colehill Farm
Colehill
Beaucroft Sch
BH21
Leigh Common
Leigh
Leigh Park
Brook Road Depot
Trinity Ind Est
Sewage Works
Riverside Pk Ind Est
Stour Valley Way
River Stour
Castleman Trailway
Merley Hall Farm
Willett Rd
Merley Pond
Dirty Lane Coppice
Merley Park
MERLEY HOUSE HOLIDAY PK
MERLEY COURT TOURING PK
MERLEY HO
Ashington
Sports Gd
Merley
The Willett Arms (PH)
Merley Fst Sch
Oakley
Oakley Sh Ctr
Boat Houses
Harvey Rd
CRANBORNE RD
WIMBORNE RD
WEST BOROUGH
HANHAM RD
KING ST
EAST ST
POOLE RD
LEIGH RD
VICTORIA RD
ST MARGARETS HILL
JULIAN'S RD
OAKLEY HILL
GRAVEL HILL
WEST ROW MEWS 1
PYE LA 2
WEST ROW 3
COOK ROW 4
BEAUFORT MEWS 5
GRAMMAR SCHOOL LA 6
QUEEN ELIZABETH CT 7
SAVILLE CT 1
FLOWER CT 2
STOUR WLK 3
B3078
B3073
B3082
A349
A31
A341
00
01
02
98
99
2
3
4
5
6
7
8
A
B
C
D
E
F
C4
1 QUARTERJACK MEWS
2 SHAMROCK CT
3 STEVENSONS CL
4 BROADWAY PK
5 COPPERCOURT LEAZE
6 BROADWAY GDNS
7 ROBINS CT
8 RIVERSDALE
187
164
D4
1 INGRAM WLK
2 MOORHILLS
3 MEADOW CT
4 CROMWELL RD
5 HARLESTON VILLAS

163

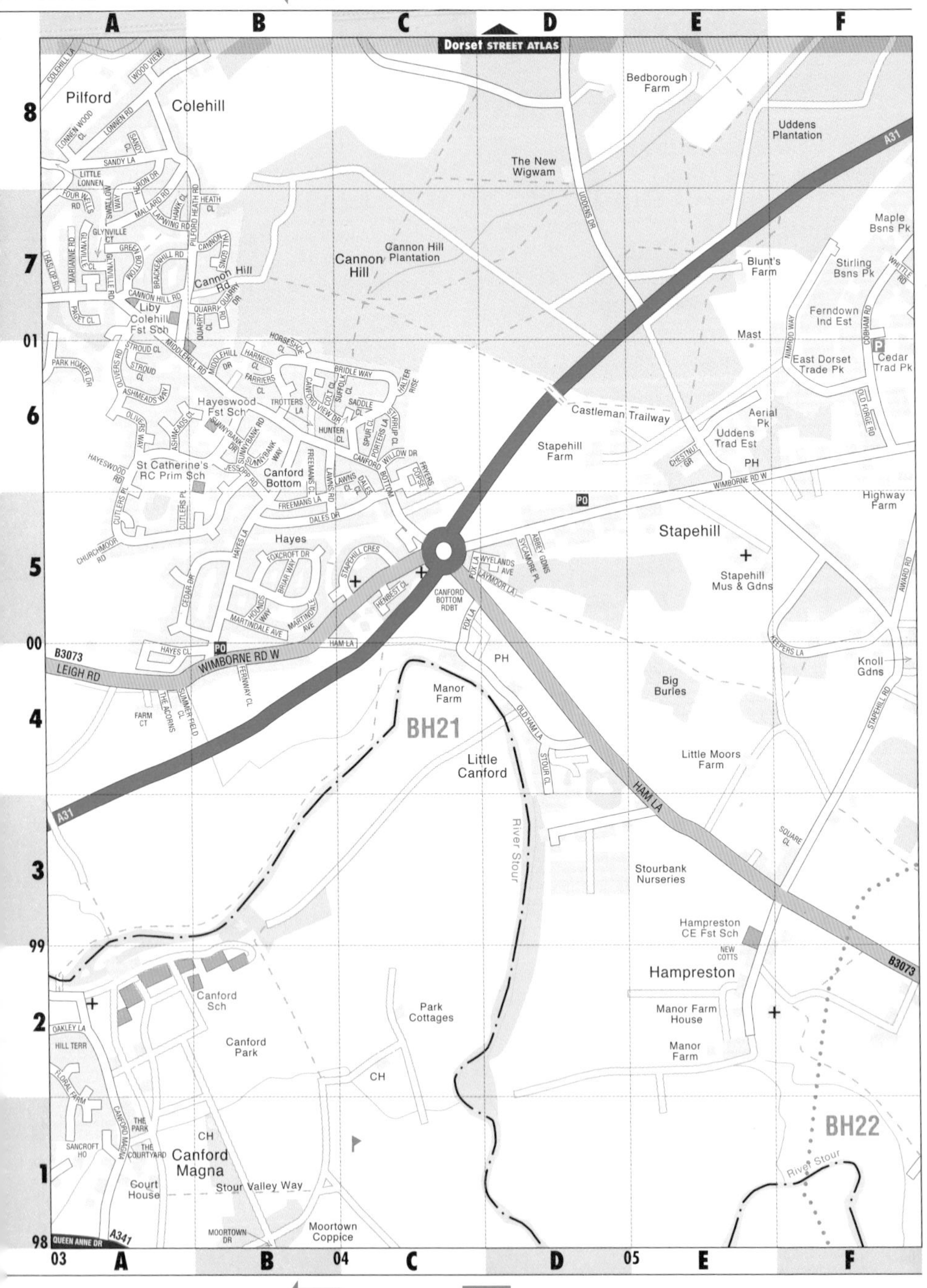
Dorset STREET ATLAS
Pilford
Colehill
Bedborough Farm
Uddens Plantation
The New Wigwam
A31
Cannon Hill
Cannon Hill Plantation
Cannon Hill Rd
Liby
Colehill Fst Sch
Blunt's Farm
Maple Bsns Pk
Stirling Bsns Pk
Ferndown Ind Est
Mast
East Dorset Trade Pk
Cedar Trad Pk
Hayeswood Fst Sch
Castleman Trailway
Aerial Pk
Uddens Trad Est
Stapehill Farm
PH
St Catherine's RC Prim Sch
Canford Bottom
WIMBORNE RD W
Highway Farm
Hayes
Stapehill
Stapehill Mus & Gdns
CANFORD BOTTOM RDBT
B3073
LEIGH RD
PH
Knoll Gdns
Manor Farm
Big Burles
BH21
Little Canford
Little Moors Farm
HAM LA
River Stour
Stourbank Nurseries
Hampreston CE Fst Sch
B3073
Hampreston
Canford Sch
Park Cottages
Manor Farm House
Canford Park
Manor Farm
CH
BH22
CH
Canford Magna
River Stour
Court House
Stour Valley Way
A341
Moortown Coppice
QUEEN ANNE DR

163

188

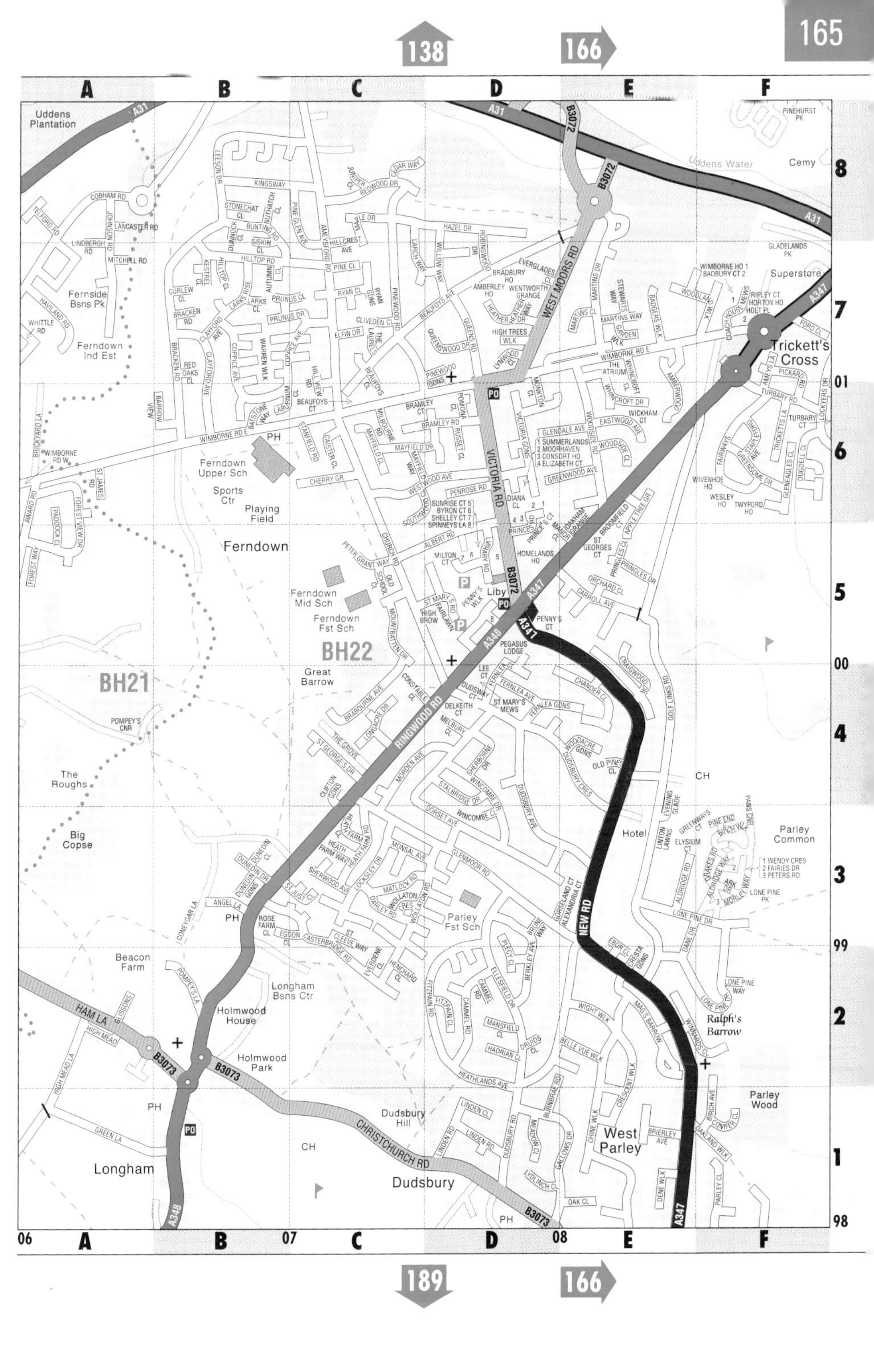
138
166
A
B
C
D
E
F
Uddens Plantation
A31
B3072
Uddens Water
Cemy
PINEHURST PK
8
COBHAM RD
TELFORD RD
JOHNSON RD
LANCASTER RD
LINDBERGH RD
MITCHELL RD
Fernside Bsns Pk
HAVILAND RD
WHITTLE RD
Ferndown Ind Est
LEESON DR
KINGSWAY
STONECHAT CL
NUTHATCH CL
DUNNOCK CL
BUNTING RD
SISKIN CL
HILLTOP RD
KESTREL CL
HILLTOP CL
AUTUMN RD
CURLEW CL
BRACKEN RD
LARKS RISE
LARKS CL
PRUNUS CL
PRUNUS DR
CLAYFORD AVE
COPPICE AVE
WARREN WLK
RED OAKS CL
BRACKEN RD
BARROW VIEW
BATSTONE WAY
PINE GLEN AVE
AMEYSFORD RD
HILLCREST AVE
PINE CL
RYAN CL
RYAN GDNS
JUNIPER CL
CEDAR WAY
REDWOOD DR
LE DR
HAZEL DR
LARCH WAY
WILLOW WAY
ROBINSWOOD DR
PINEWOOD RD
CLIVEDEN CL
ELFIN DR
THE LAURELS
BEAUFOYS AVE
BEAUFOYS CL
BEAUFOYS CT
HILLVIEW RD
QUEENSWOOD DR
QUEENS RD
PINEWOOD GDNS
BRADBURY HO
AMBERLEY HO
WENTWORTH GRANGE
EVERGLADES CL
HEATHER DR
HEATHER WAY
HIGH TREES WLK
LYNWOOD CL
WEST MOORS RD
MARTINS DR
MARTINS CL
STEWARTS WAY
MARTINS WAY
GARDEN WLK
BADGERS WLK
WIMBORNE RD E
THE ATRIUM
WHINCROFT CL
WHINCROFT DR
AMBERWOOD
WOODLAND WLK
WIMBORNE HO 1
BADBURY CT 2
COACH HOUSE MEWS
RIPLEY CT
HORTON HO
HOLT PL
GLADELANDS PK
Superstore
A347
7
FORD CL
Trickett's Cross
AMEYS LA
PICKARD RD
TURBARY RD
LOCKYERS DR
TURBARY CT
01
TRICKETTS LA
FAIRWAYS
STAPLE CL
GREENSOME DR
GLENEAGLES CL
DUGDELL CL
WIVENHOE HO
WESLEY HO
TWYFORD HO
6
BRICKYARD LA
WIMBORNE RD W
ST JAMES RD
AWARD RD
FOREST VIEW DR
PADDOCK CL
FOREST WAY
PH
Ferndown Upper Sch
Sports Ctr
Playing Field
Ferndown
STAMFIELD RD
CAISTER CL
MILBOURNE RD
MAYFIELD RD
MAYFIELD CL
MAYFIELD DR
MAYFIELD WAY
BRAMLEY CT
BRAMLEY RD
POMONA CL
RUSSET CL
PO
VICTORIA RD
MONKTON CL
VICTORIA GDNS
GLENDALE AVE
1 SUMMERLANDS
2 MOORHAVEN
3 CONSORT HO
4 ELIZABETH CT
WOODSIDE RD
EASTWOOD AVE
WICKHAM CT
WOODSIDE CL
GREENWOOD AVE
CHERRY GR
WESTWOOD AVE
PENROSE RD
SOUTHWOOD
SUNRISE CT 5
BYRON CT 6
SHELLEY CT 7
SPINNEYS LA 8
DIANA CL
PRINCES CT
OAKHAM GRANGE
BROOMFIELD CT
APPLE TREE GR
ST GEORGES CT
PRINGLES CL
PRINGLES DR
ALBERT RD
PETER GRANT WAY
CHURCH RD
OLD SCHOOL CL
MILTON CT
LIBRARY RD
HOMELANDS HO
B3072
ORCHARD CL
CARROLL AVE
Ferndown Mid Sch
Ferndown Fst Sch
P
PENNY'S WLK
Liby
ST MARY'S RD
FAIRLAWN
HIGH BROW
PENNY'S CT
5
BH22
MOUNTBATTEN DR
A348
PEGASUS LODGE
CRAIGWOOD DR
GOLF LINKS RD
00
BH21
Great Barrow
CONSTABLE CL
LEE CT
FERNLEA CL
FERNLEA AVE
CHANDER CL
DUDSWAY CT
DELKEITH CT
ST MARY'S MEWS
FERNLEA GDNS
BRABOURNE AVE
LONGACRE DR
RINGWOOD RD
MELBURY CL
POMPEY'S CNR
4
THE GROVE
ST GEORGE'S DR
MORDEN AVE
SHERBORNE DR
WOODACRE GDNS
OLD PINES CL
DUDSBURY CRES
CH
The Roughs
CLIFTON GDNS
WINCOMBE DR
STALBRIDGE DR
DUDSBURY AVE
DORSET AVE
WINCOMBE CL
EVENING GLADE
LINTON LAWNS
Hotel
GREENWAYS CT
PINE END
BIRCH WY
PARIS CNR
ELYSIUM CT
Parley Common
Big Copse
HEATH FARM CL
HEATH FARM RD
HEATH FARM WAY
MONSAL AVE
GLENMOOR RD
DUNEDIN CL
DUNEDIN DR
DUNEDIN GDNS
SHERWOOD AVE
LOCKSLEY DR
MATLOCK RD
WOLLATON CRES
WOLLATON RD
DARLEY RD
ST JUST CL
GORSELAND CT
ALEXANDRIA CT
NEW RD
ALDRIDGE RD
CRAKES RD
ALDRIDGE WAY
ARK DR
MORLEY WAY
1 WENDY CRES
2 FAIRIES DR
3 PETERS RD
LONE PINE PK
3
CONEYGAR LA
ANGEL LA
PH
ROSE FARM CL
EGDON CL
CASTERBRIDGE RD
ST CLEEVE WAY
EVERDENE CL
HENCHARD CL
Parley Fst Sch
PLECY CL
BERKLEY AVE
BRUNE WAY
EBOR CL
CRESTA GDNS
LONE PINE DR
DANE DR
99
Beacon Farm
POMPEY'S LA
Longham Bsns Ctr
Holmwood House
FITZPAIN RD
FITZPAIN CL
CAMMEL RD
ELLESFIELD DR
LONE PINE WAY
2
HAM LA
GLISSONS
HIGH MEAD
B3073
MANSFIELD CL
DRUIDS CL
HADRIAN CL
WIGHT WLK
MAG'S BARROW
WINIFREDS CL
Ralph's Barrow
BELLE VUE WLK
Holmwood Park
HEATHLANDS AVE
BURNBRAE RD
CRESCENT WLK
HIGH MEAD LA
PH
Dudsbury Hill
LINDEN CL
LINDEN RD
DUDSBURY RD
MEADOW CL
GALLOWS DR
CHINE WLK
BIRCH AVE
CONIFER CL
Parley Wood
GREEN LA
PO
CHRISTCHURCH RD
West Parley
BRIERLEY AVE
OAKLAND WLK
CH
Longham
Dudsbury
LYDLINCH CL
DENE WLK
PARLEY CL
1
A348
OAK CL
PH
98
06
07
08
189
166

165
139

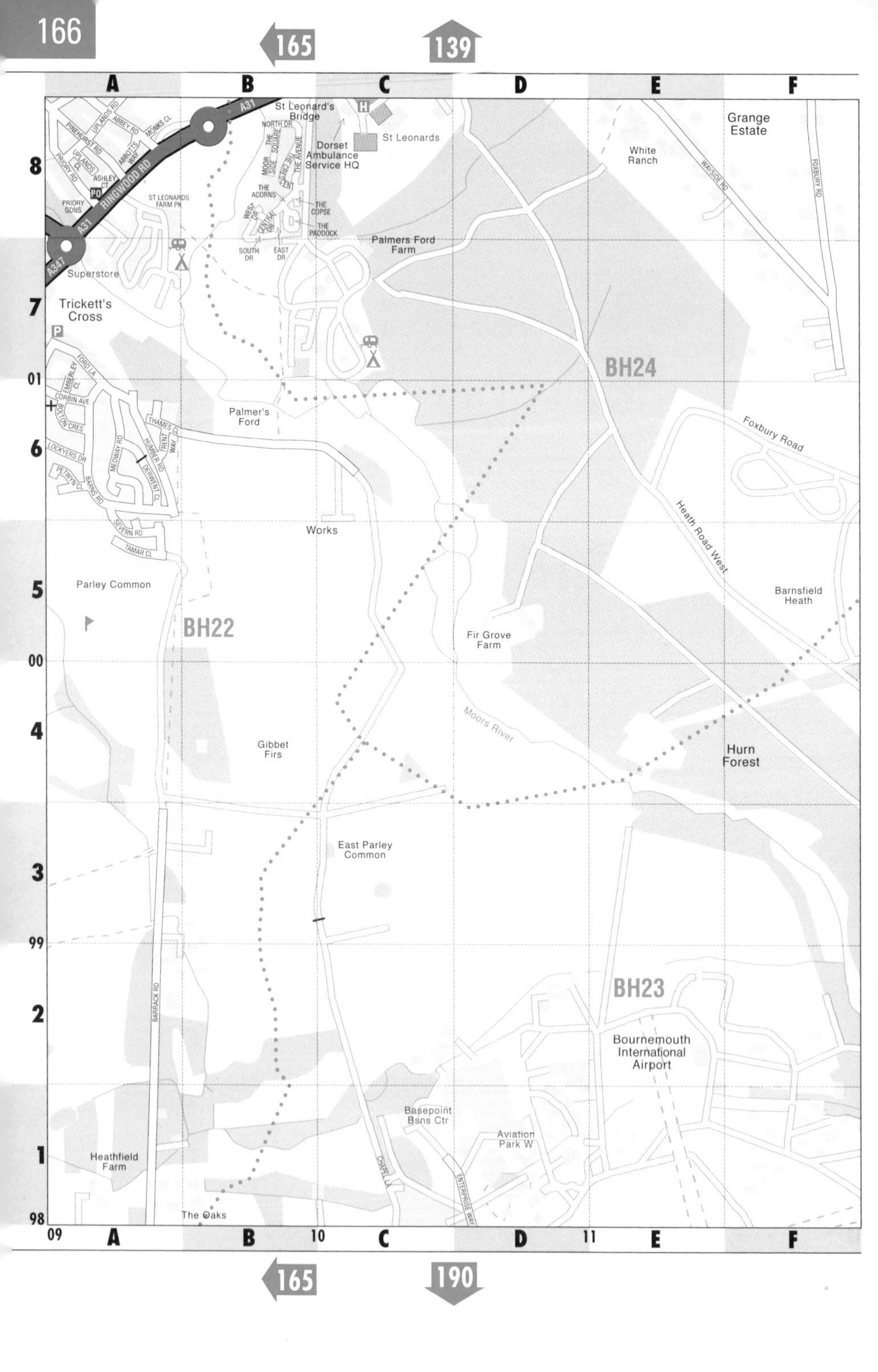
A
B
C
D
E
F
St Leonard's Bridge
St Leonards
Dorset Ambulance Service HQ
Grange Estate
White Ranch
Palmers Ford Farm
Superstore
Trickett's Cross
BH24
Palmer's Ford
Foxbury Road
Works
Heath Road West
Parley Common
Barnsfield Heath
BH22
Fir Grove Farm
Moors River
Gibbet Firs
Hurn Forest
East Parley Common
BH23
Bournemouth International Airport
Basepoint Bsns Ctr
Aviation Park W
Heathfield Farm
The Oaks
RINGWOOD RD
A31
A347
BARRACK RD
CHAPEL LA
ENTERPRISE WAY
WAYSIDE RD
FOXBURY RD
8
7
01
6
5
00
4
3
99
2
1
98
09
10
11

165
190

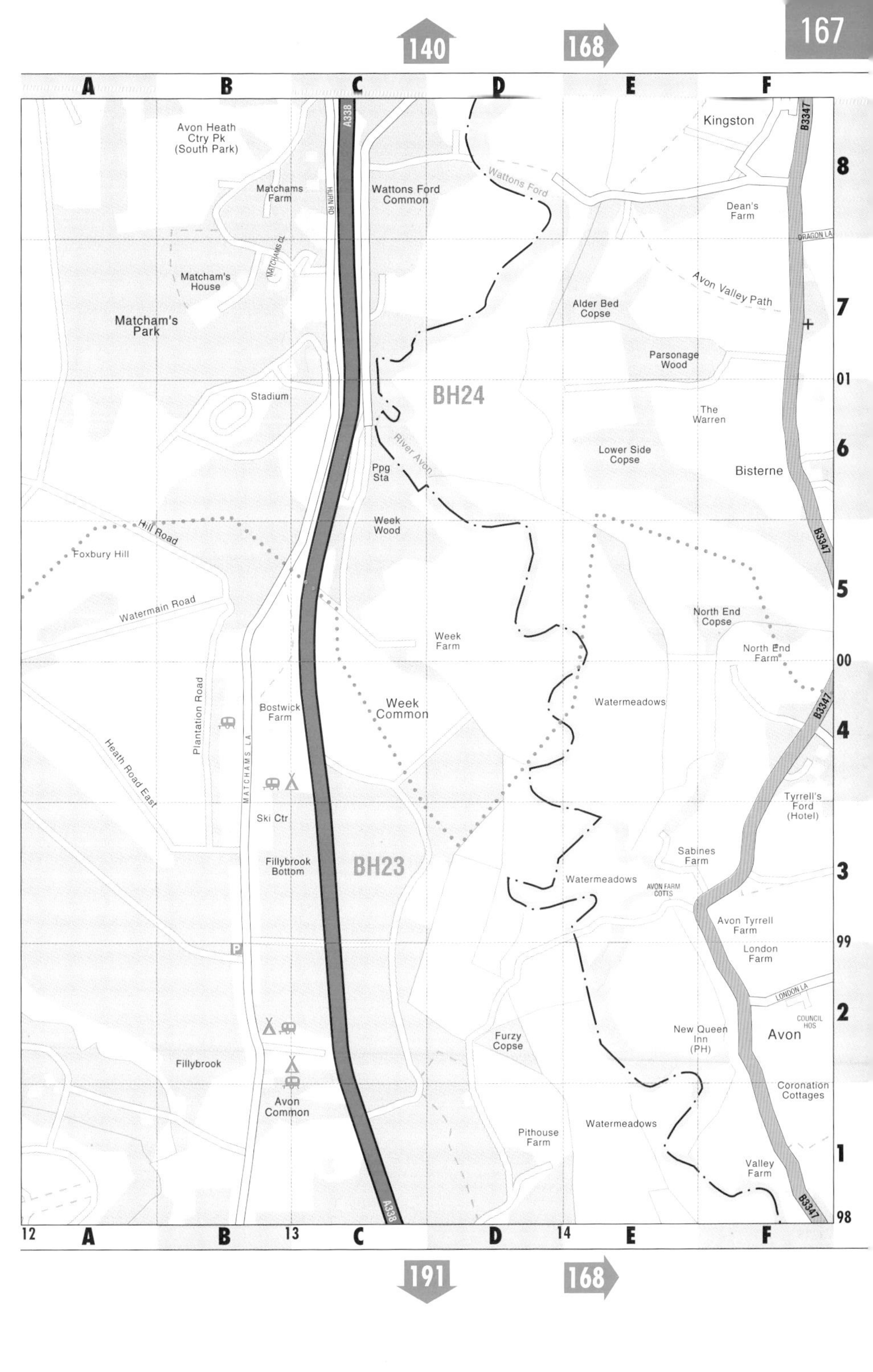
140
168
A
B
C
D
E
F
Avon Heath
Ctry Pk
(South Park)
Kingston
B3347
A338
8
Wattons Ford
Matchams
Farm
HURN RD
Wattons Ford
Common
Dean's
Farm
DRAGON LA
MATCHAMS CL
Matcham's
House
Avon Valley Path
7
Alder Bed
Copse
Matcham's
Park
Parsonage
Wood
01
Stadium
BH24
The
Warren
River Avon
Lower Side
Copse
6
Ppg
Sta
Bisterne
Week
Wood
Hill Road
Foxbury Hill
B3347
5
Watermain Road
North End
Copse
Week
Farm
North End
Farm
00
Plantation Road
Bostwick
Farm
Week
Common
Watermeadows
B3347
4
Heath Road East
MATCHAMS LA
Tyrrell's
Ford
(Hotel)
Ski Ctr
Sabines
Farm
Fillybrook
Bottom
BH23
3
Watermeadows
AVON FARM
COTTS
Avon Tyrrell
Farm
99
P
London
Farm
LONDON LA
2
COUNCIL
HOS
New Queen
Inn
(PH)
Avon
Furzy
Copse
Fillybrook
Coronation
Cottages
Avon
Common
Watermeadows
Pithouse
Farm
1
Valley
Farm
A338
B3347
98
12
13
14
191
168

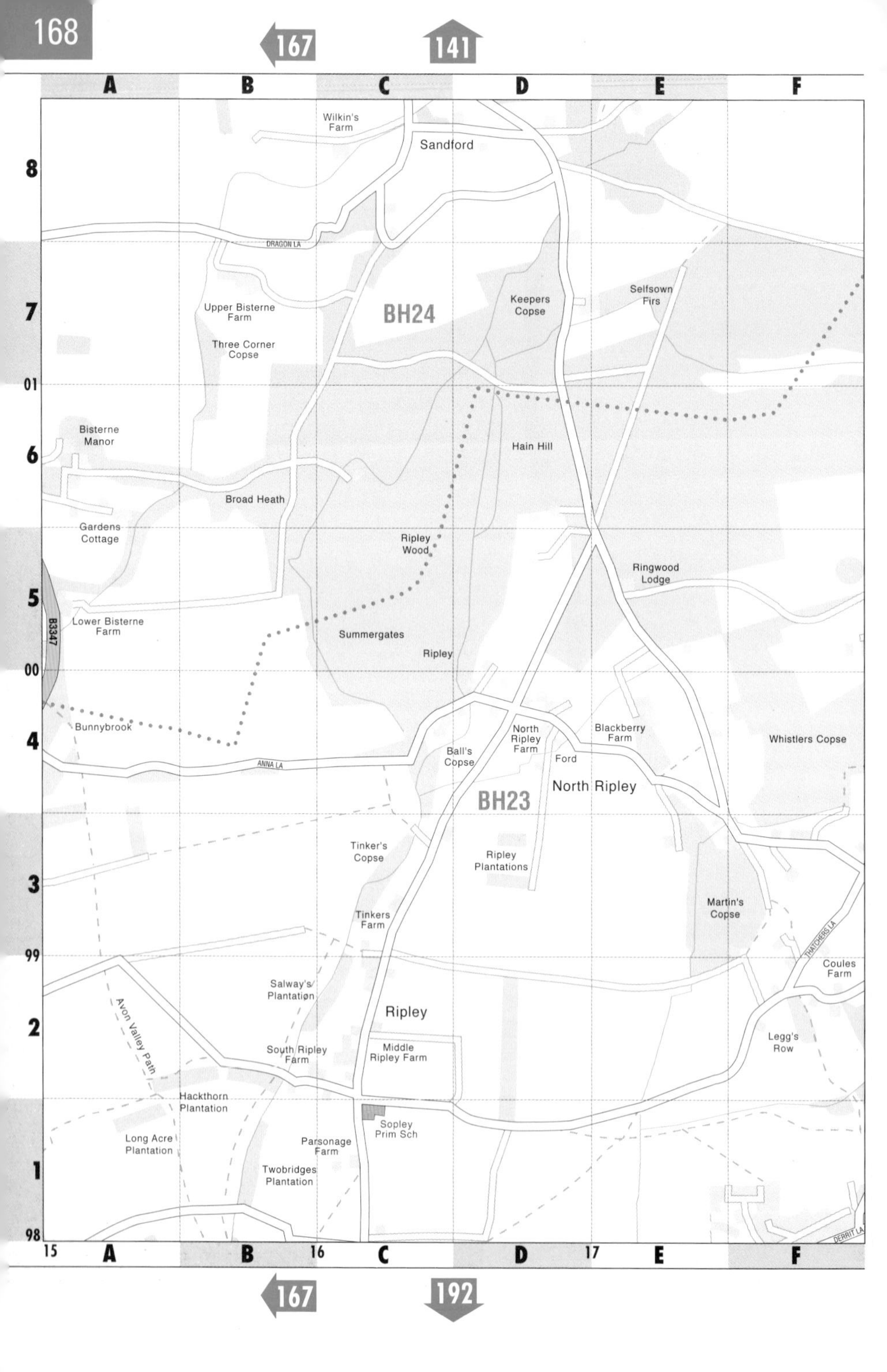

167
141

| | A | B | C | D | E | F |

8

Wilkin's Farm

Sandford

DRAGON LA

7

Upper Bisterne Farm

BH24

Keepers Copse

Selfsown Firs

Three Corner Copse

01

Bisterne Manor

Hain Hill

6

Broad Heath

Gardens Cottage

Ripley Wood

Ringwood Lodge

5

B3347

Lower Bisterne Farm

Summergates

Ripley

00

Bunnybrook

4

ANNA LA

Ball's Copse

North Ripley Farm

Blackberry Farm

Whistlers Copse

Ford

North Ripley

BH23

Tinker's Copse

Ripley Plantations

Martin's Copse

3

Tinkers Farm

Coules Farm

99

Salway's Plantation

Avon Valley Path

Ripley

2

South Ripley Farm

Middle Ripley Farm

Legg's Row

Hackthorn Plantation

Long Acre Plantation

Parsonage Farm

Sopley Prim Sch

1

Twobridges Plantation

DEBRITT LA

98

| 15 | A | B | 16 | C | D | 17 | E | F |

167
192

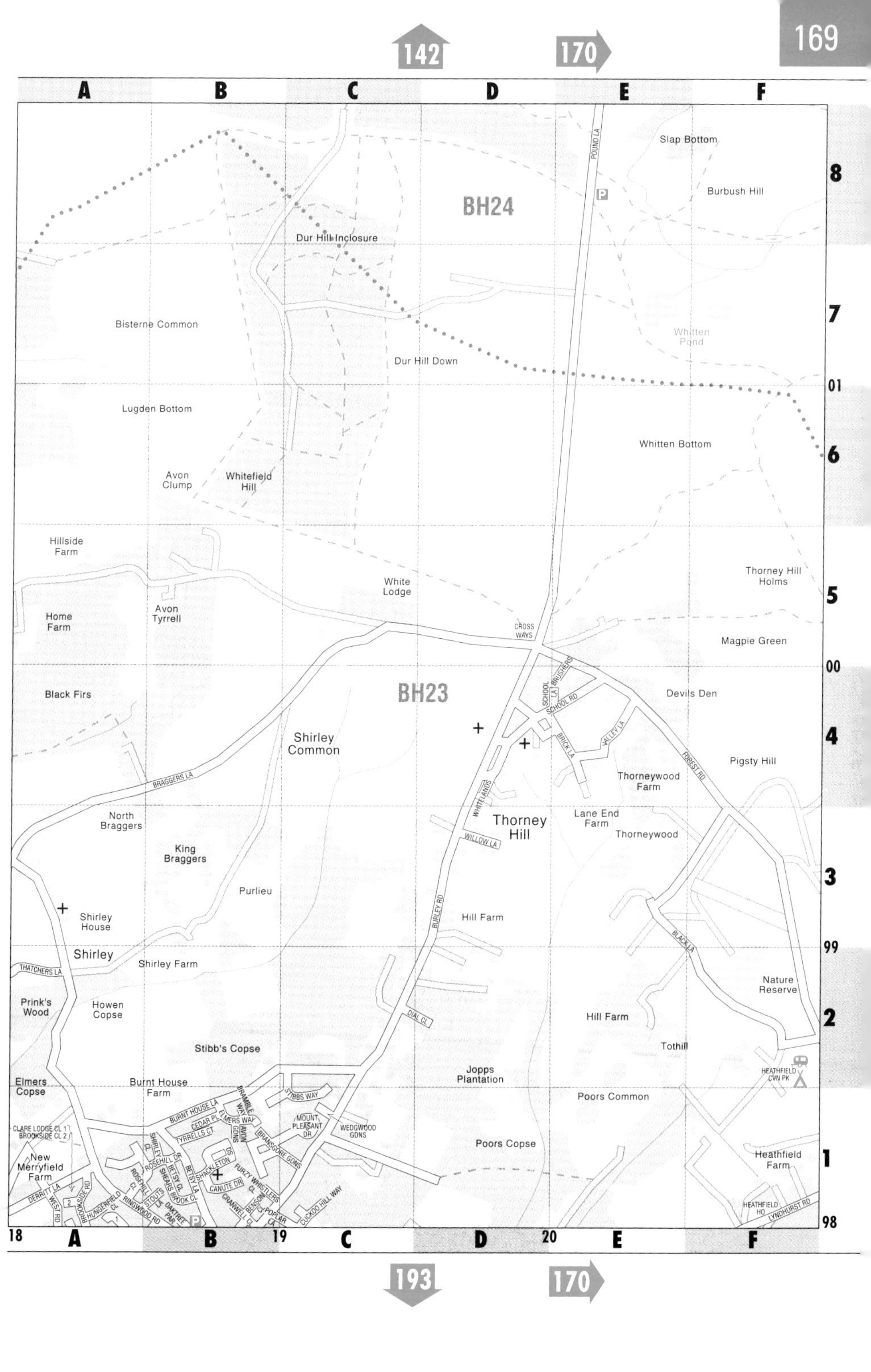
142
170
A
B
C
D
E
F
8
7
01
6
5
00
4
3
99
2
1
98
BH24
BH23
Slap Bottom
Burbush Hill
POUND LA
Dur Hill Inclosure
Bisterne Common
Whitten Pond
Dur Hill Down
Lugden Bottom
Whitten Bottom
Avon Clump
Whitefield Hill
Hillside Farm
Thorney Hill Holms
White Lodge
Home Farm
Avon Tyrrell
CROSS WAYS
Magpie Green
Black Firs
Devils Den
SCHOOL LA
BRUSHERS
SCHOOL RD
Shirley Common
BRICK LA
VALLEY LA
Pigsty Hill
FOREST RD
BRAGGERS LA
Thorneywood Farm
WHITELANDS
North Braggers
Thorney Hill
Lane End Farm
Thorneywood
WILLOW LA
King Braggers
Purlieu
Shirley House
BURLEY RD
Hill Farm
BLACK LA
Shirley
Shirley Farm
THATCHERS LA
Nature Reserve
Prink's Wood
Howen Copse
DIAL CL
Hill Farm
Stibb's Copse
Tothill
Jopps Plantation
HEATHFIELD CVN PK
Elmers Copse
Burnt House Farm
Poors Common
STIBBS WAY
BURNT HOUSE LA
BRAMBLE WAY
CEDAR PL
ELMERS WAY
MOUNT PLEASANT DR
WEDGWOOD GDNS
CLARE LODGE CL 1
BROOKSIDE CL 2
TYRRELLS CT
AVON GDNS
BRANSGORE GDNS
Poors Copse
New Merryfield Farm
ROSEHILL DR
SHACKLETON SQ
FURZY WHISTLERS CL
Heathfield Farm
CANUTE DR
DERRITT LA
WEST RD
BROOKSIDE RD
HUNGERFORD CL
RINGWOOD RD
STOUTS LA
OAKTREE PDE
BENSON CL
POPLAR LA
CUCKOO HILL WAY
HEATHFIELD HQ
LYNDHURST RD
18
19
20
193
170

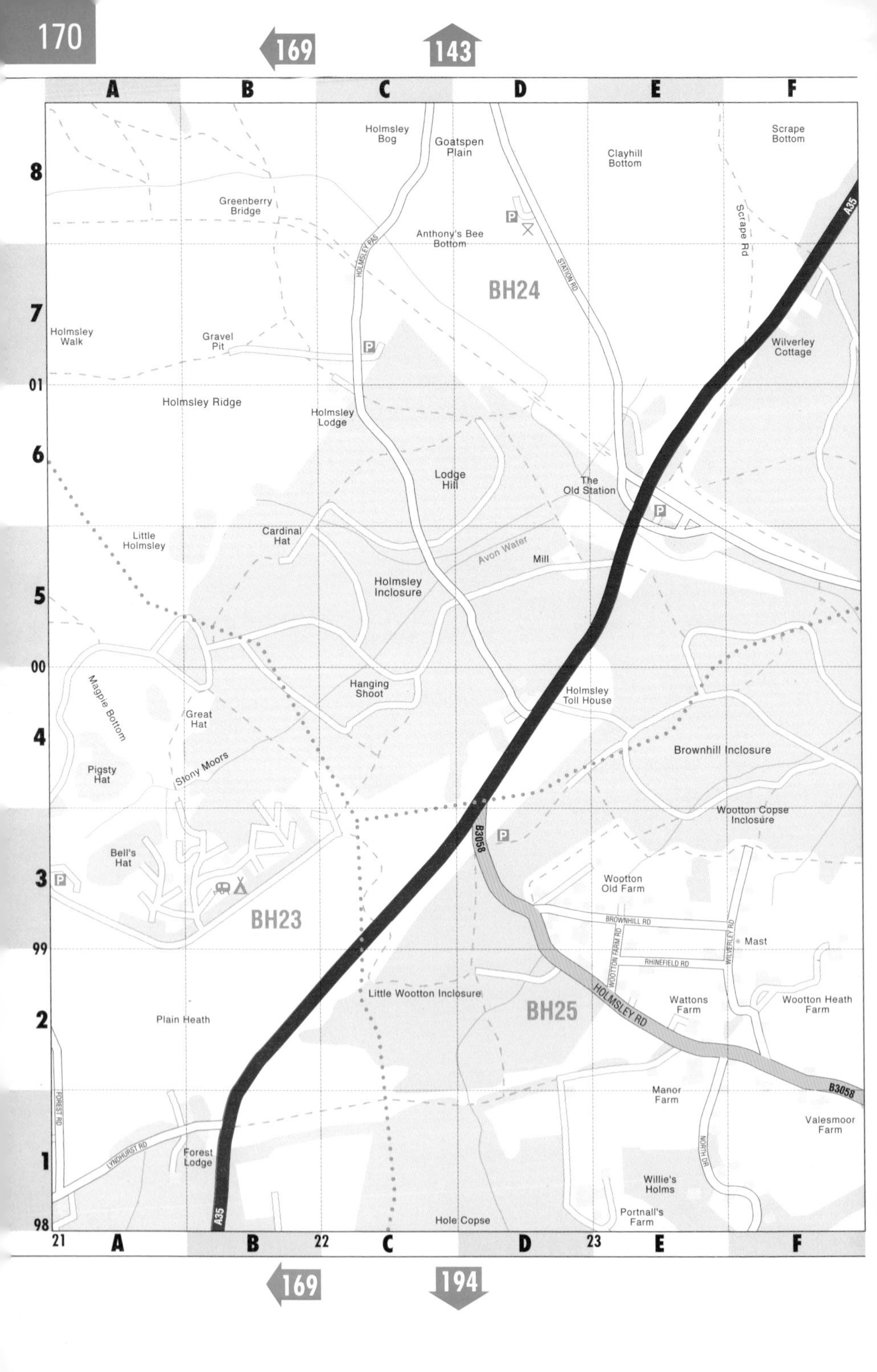
Holmsley Bog
Goatspen Plain
Clayhill Bottom
Scrape Bottom
Greenberry Bridge
Anthony's Bee Bottom
HOLMSLEY PAS
STATION RD
Scrape Rd
A35
BH24
Holmsley Walk
Gravel Pit
Wilverley Cottage
Holmsley Ridge
Holmsley Lodge
Lodge Hill
The Old Station
Little Holmsley
Cardinal Hat
Avon Water
Mill
Holmsley Inclosure
Magpie Bottom
Hanging Shoot
Holmsley Toll House
Great Hat
Stony Moors
Brownhill Inclosure
Pigsty Hat
Wootton Copse Inclosure
B3058
Bell's Hat
Wootton Old Farm
BH23
BROWNHILL RD
WOOTTON FARM RD
WILVERLEY RD
Mast
RHINEFIELD RD
Little Wootton Inclosure
BH25
HOLMSLEY RD
Wattons Farm
Wootton Heath Farm
Plain Heath
Manor Farm
FOREST RD
Valesmoor Farm
LYNDHURST RD
Forest Lodge
NORTH DR
Willie's Holms
Portnall's Farm
Hole Copse

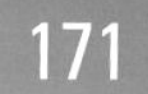

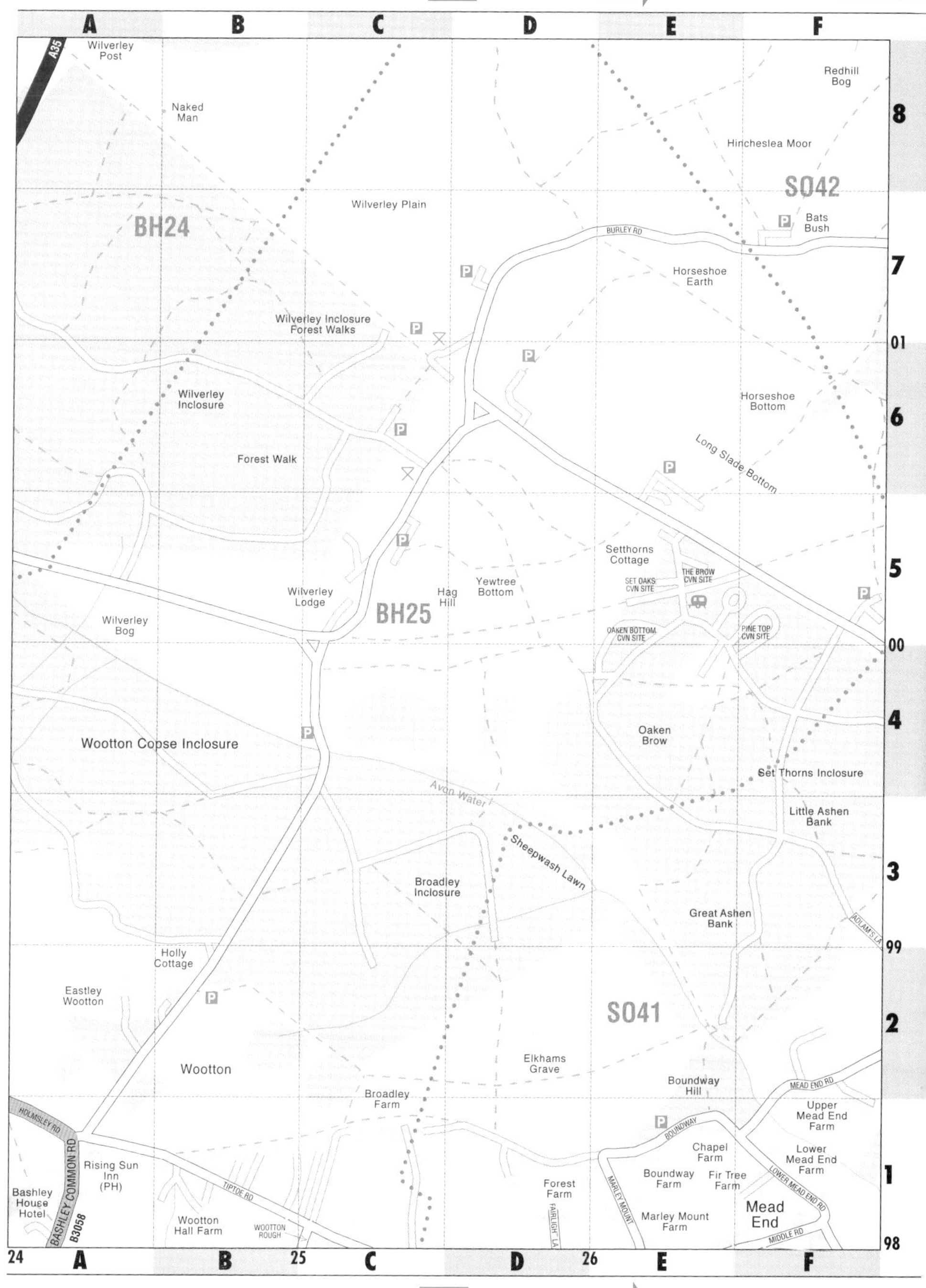

144
172
A
B
C
D
E
F
A35
Wilverley Post
Naked Man
Redhill Bog
Hincheslea Moor
SO42
8
Wilverley Plain
BH24
Bats Bush
BURLEY RD
Horseshoe Earth
7
Wilverley Inclosure Forest Walks
01
Wilverley Inclosure
Horseshoe Bottom
6
Forest Walk
Long Slade Bottom
Setthorns Cottage
5
SET OAKS CVN SITE
THE BROW CVN SITE
Wilverley Lodge
Hag Hill
Yewtree Bottom
BH25
Wilverley Bog
OAKEN BOTTOM CVN SITE
PINE TOP CVN SITE
00
4
Oaken Brow
Wootton Copse Inclosure
Set Thorns Inclosure
Avon Water
Little Ashen Bank
Sheepwash Lawn
3
Broadley Inclosure
Great Ashen Bank
ADLAM'S LA
99
Holly Cottage
Eastley Wootton
SO41
2
Elkhams Grave
Wootton
Boundway Hill
MEAD END RD
Broadley Farm
Upper Mead End Farm
HOLMSLEY RD
BOUNDWAY
Chapel Farm
Lower Mead End Farm
Rising Sun Inn (PH)
1
Boundway Farm
Fir Tree Farm
LOWER MEAD END RD
TIPTOE RD
Forest Farm
MARLEY MOUNT
Bashley House Hotel
BASHLEY COMMON RD
Mead End
Marley Mount Farm
Wootton Hall Farm
B3058
FAIRLIGHT LA
WOOTTON ROUGH
MIDDLE RD
98
24
25
26
195
172

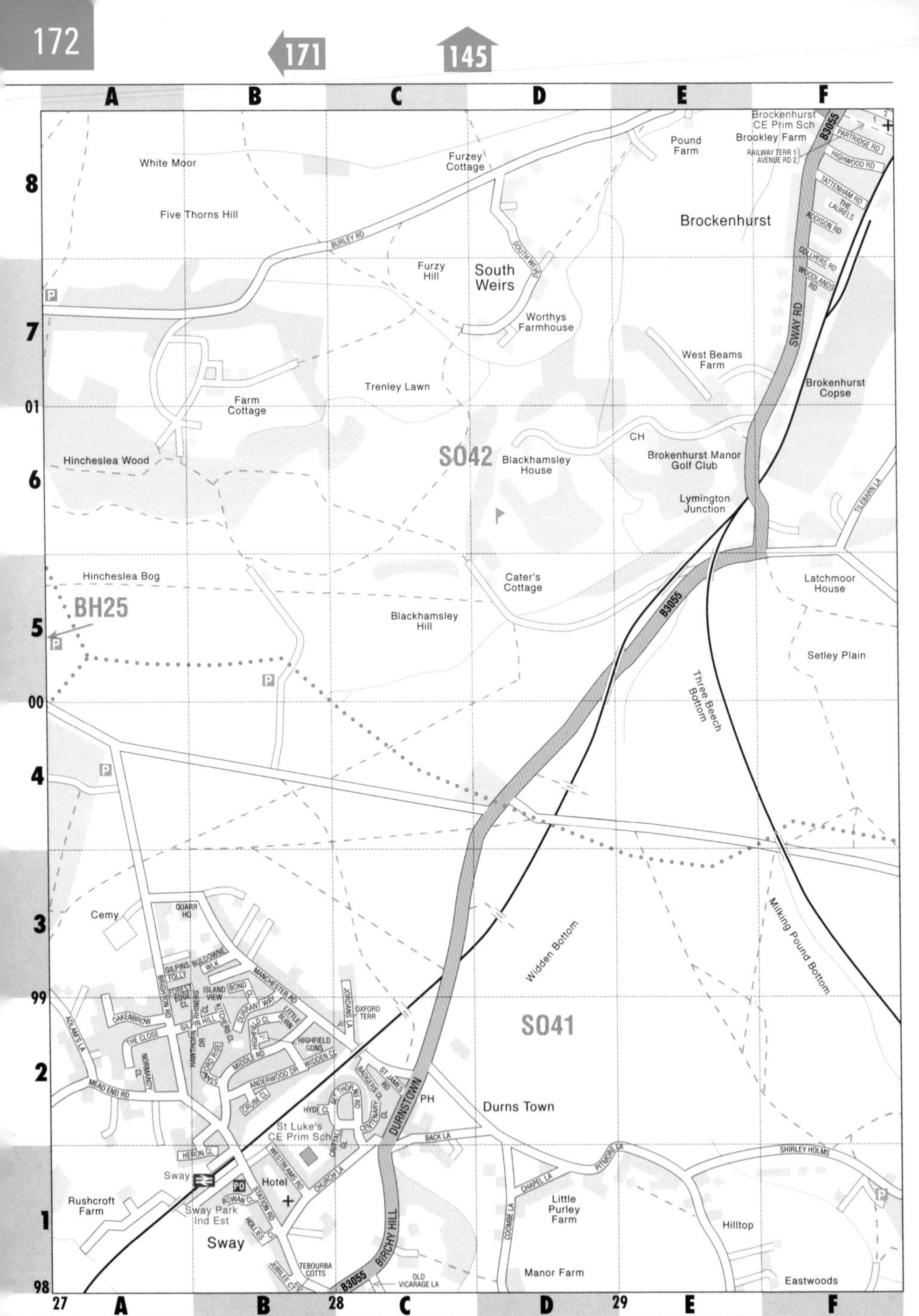
A
B
C
D
E
F
8
7
01
6
5
00
4
3
99
2
1
98
27
28
29
White Moor
Five Thorns Hill
BURLEY RD
Furzey Cottage
Pound Farm
Brockenhurst CE Prim Sch
Brookley Farm
B3055
PARTRIDGE RD
RAILWAY TERR 1
AVENUE RD 2
HIGHWOOD RD
TATTENHAM RD
THE LAURELS
ADDISON RD
Brockenhurst
COLLYERS RD
WOODLANDS RD
SOUTH WEIRS
Furzy Hill
South Weirs
Worthys Farmhouse
SWAY RD
West Beams Farm
Trenley Lawn
Farm Cottage
Brokenhurst Copse
CH
Brokenhurst Manor Golf Club
Hinchesleа Wood
SO42
Blackhamsley House
Lymington Junction
TILEBARN LA
Hinchesleа Bog
Cater's Cottage
Latchmoor House
BH25
Blackhamsley Hill
Setley Plain
Three Beech Bottom
Cemy
QUARR HO
Milking Pound Bottom
Widden Bottom
GILPINS FOLLY
BULDOWNE WLK
MANCHESTER RD
BRIGHTON RD
FOREST EDGE CL
ISLAND VIEW
BOND CL
JORDANS LA
OXFORD TERR
RHINERS CL
DURRANT WAY
LITTLE BURN
ADLAMS LA
OAKENBROW
GILPIN HILL
KITCHERS CL
SO41
THE CLOSE
HAWTHORN DR
HIGHFIELD GDNS
NORMANDY CL
STANFORD RISE
MIDDLE RD
WIDDEN CL
ST JAMES RD
ANDERWOOD DR
BADGERS CL
DURNSTOWN
MEAD END RD
CRUSE CL
SETTHORNS RD
PH
HYDE CL
CENTENARY CL
Durns Town
St Luke's CE Prim Sch
CRITTALL CL
BACK LA
HERON CL
WESTREAMS RD
PITMORE LA
SHIRLEY HOLMS
Sway
PO
Hotel
CHURCH LA
CHAPEL LA
Rushcroft Farm
ROWAN CL
STATION RD
Little Purley Farm
Sway Park Ind Est
BIRCHY HILL
Hilltop
COOMBE LA
Sway
HOLLIES CL
TEBOURBA COTTS
JUBILEE CT
B3055
OLD VICARAGE LA
Manor Farm
Eastwoods

146
174

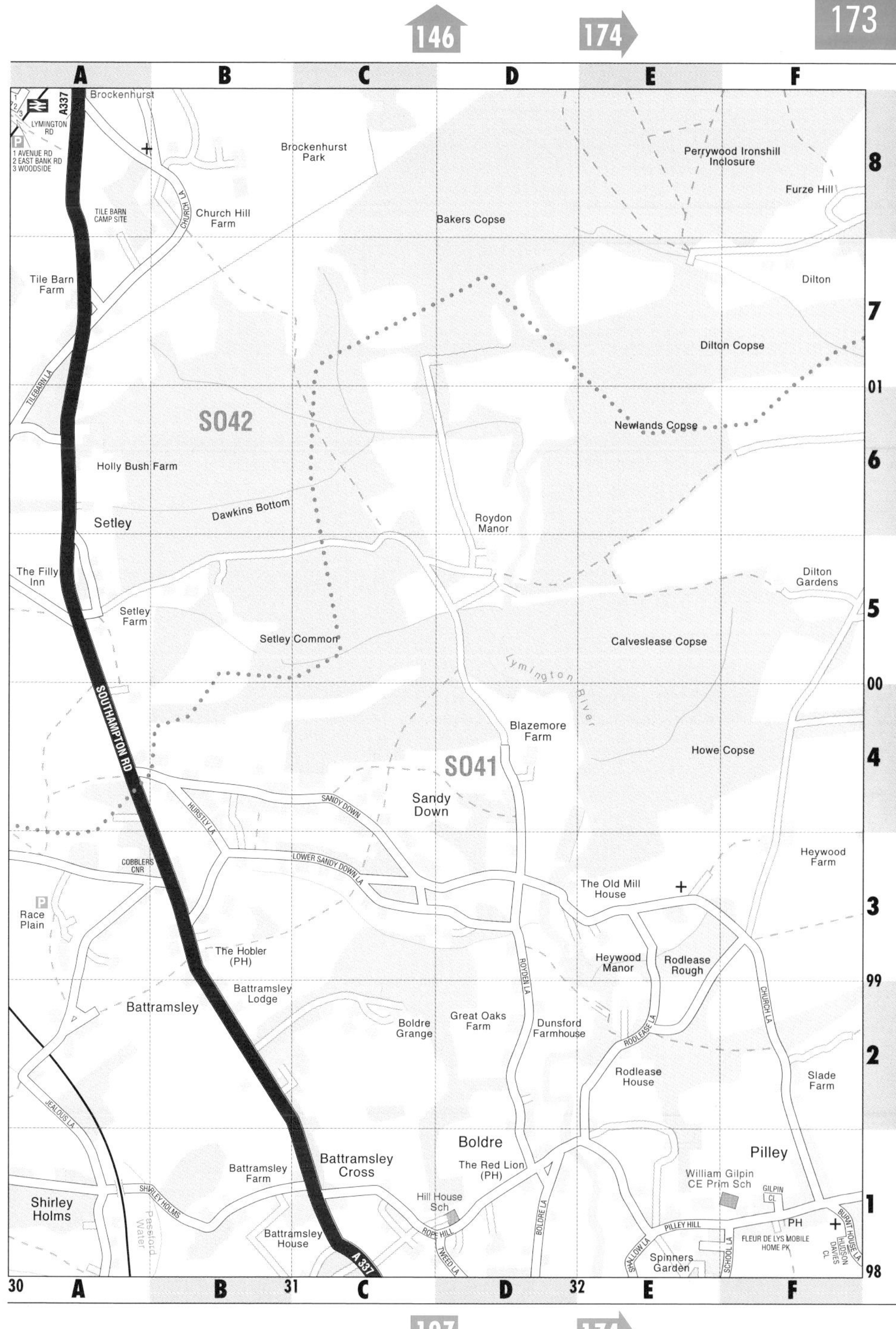
A
B
C
D
E
F
Brockenhurst
A337
LYMINGTON RD
1 AVENUE RD
2 EAST BANK RD
3 WOODSIDE
Brockenhurst Park
Perrywood Ironshill Inclosure
Furze Hill
TILE BARN CAMP SITE
CHURCH LA
Church Hill Farm
Bakers Copse
Tile Barn Farm
Dilton
Dilton Copse
TILEBARN LA
SO42
Newlands Copse
Holly Bush Farm
Dawkins Bottom
Setley
Roydon Manor
The Filly Inn
Dilton Gardens
Setley Farm
Setley Common
Calveslease Copse
Lymington River
SOUTHAMPTON RD
Blazemore Farm
Howe Copse
SO41
Sandy Down
SANDY DOWN
HURSTLY LA
COBBLERS CNR
LOWER SANDY DOWN LA
Heywood Farm
The Old Mill House
Race Plain
The Hobler (PH)
ROYDEN LA
Heywood Manor
Rodlease Rough
Battramsley Lodge
Battramsley
Boldre Grange
Great Oaks Farm
Dunsford Farmhouse
RODLEASE LA
CHURCH LA
Rodlease House
Slade Farm
JEALOUS LA
Boldre
Battramsley Cross
Battramsley Farm
The Red Lion (PH)
Pilley
William Gilpin CE Prim Sch
Shirley Holms
SHIRLEY HOLMS
Passford Water
Hill House Sch
GILPIN CL
ROPE HILL
BOLDRE LA
PILLEY HILL
PH
Battramsley House
TWEED LA
A 337
SHALLOW LA
Spinners Garden
SCHOOL LA
FLEUR DE LYS MOBILE HOME PK
HUDSON DAVIES CL
BURNT HOUSE LA
8
7
01
6
5
00
4
3
99
2
1
98
30
31
32

197
174

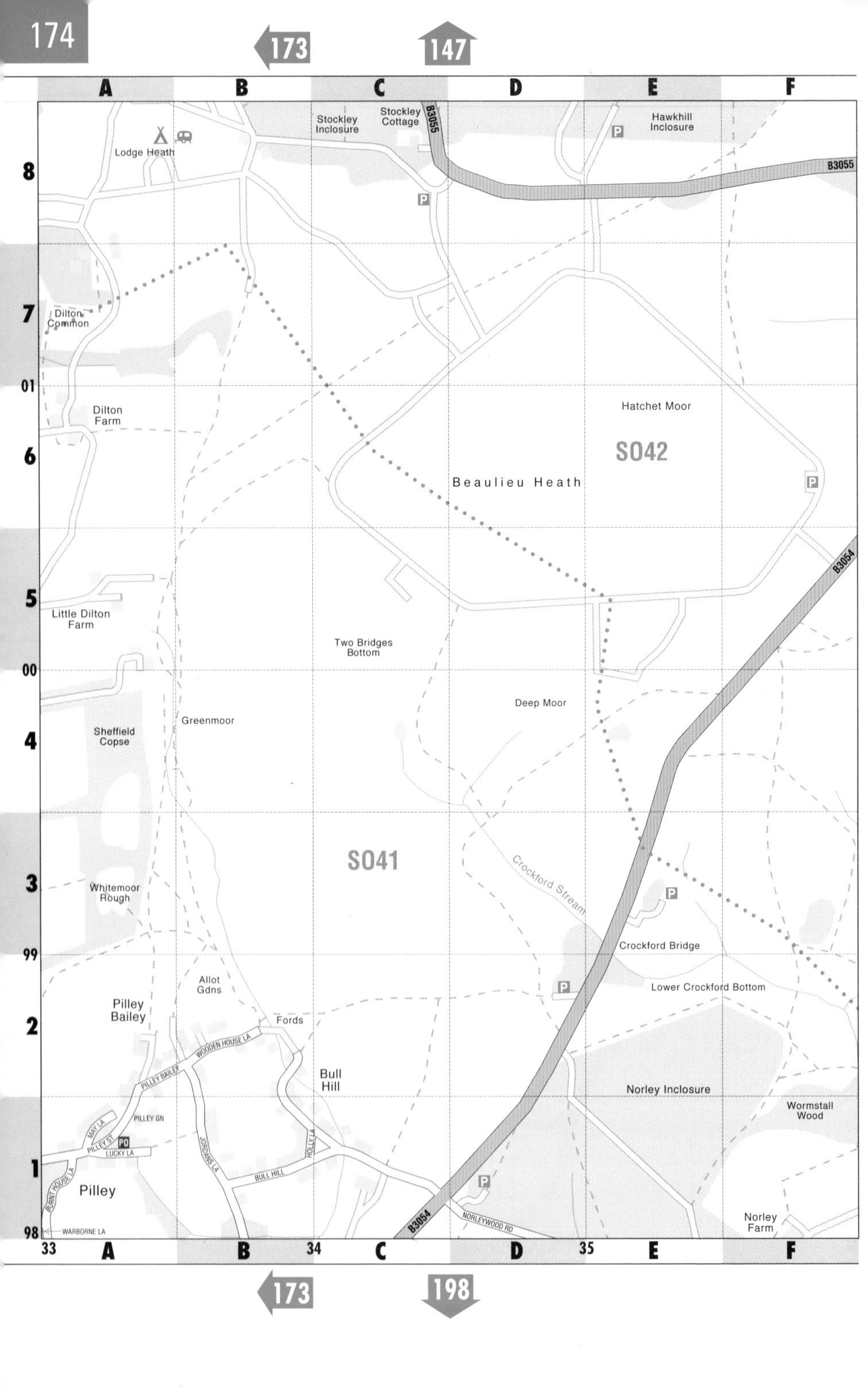
173
147
A
B
C
D
E
F
8
7
01
6
5
00
4
3
99
2
1
98
33
34
35
Lodge Heath
Stockley Inclosure
Stockley Cottage
B3055
Hawkhill Inclosure
P
Dilton Common
Dilton Farm
Hatchet Moor
SO42
Beaulieu Heath
B3054
Little Dilton Farm
Two Bridges Bottom
Deep Moor
Sheffield Copse
Greenmoor
SO41
Whitemoor Rough
Crockford Stream
Crockford Bridge
Lower Crockford Bottom
Allot Gdns
Pilley Bailey
Fords
WOODEN HOUSE LA
PILLEY BAILEY
Bull Hill
Norley Inclosure
Wormstall Wood
MAY LA
PILLEY GN
PILLEY ST
PO
LUCKY LA
JORDANS LA
HOLLY LA
BULL HILL
BURNT HOUSE LA
Pilley
WARBORNE LA
NORLEYWOOD RD
Norley Farm
173
198

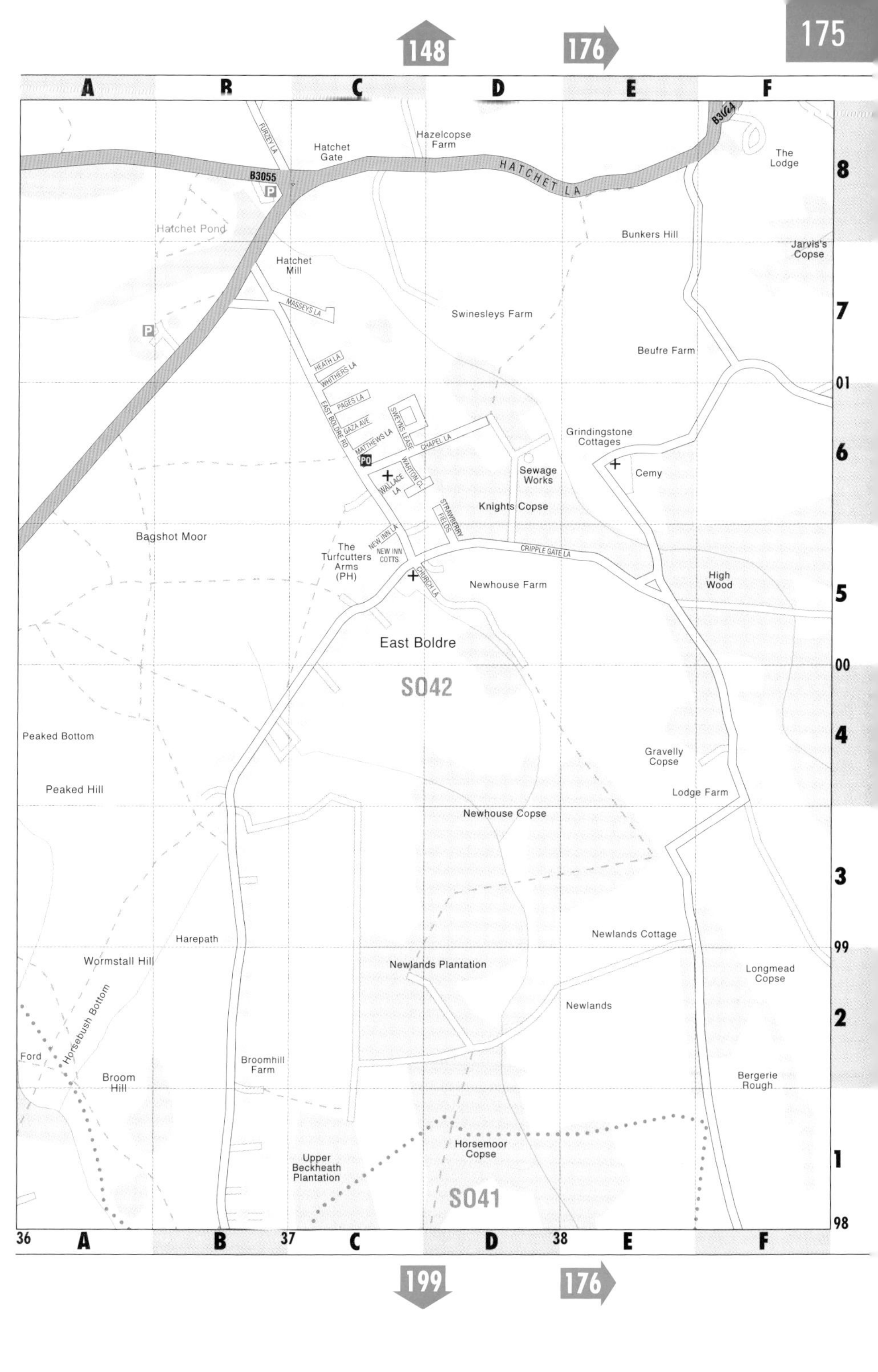

B3054

The Lodge

HATCHET LA

8

Hatchet Gate

Hazelcopse Farm

B3055

P

Hatchet Pond

Bunkers Hill

Jarvis's Copse

Hatchet Mill

MASSEYS LA

Swinesleys Farm

7

P

Beufre Farm

01

HEATH LA

SMITHERS LA

PAGES LA

EAST BOLDRE RD

GAZA AVE

MATTHEWS LA

CHAPEL LA

SCHOOL LA

Grindingstone Cottages

6

PO

WALLACE LA

WATERS LA

Cemy

Sewage Works

Knights Copse

STRAWBERRY FIELDS

Bagshot Moor

The Turfcutters Arms (PH)

NEW INN LA

NEW INN COTTS

CHURCH LA

CRIPPLE GATE LA

High Wood

5

Newhouse Farm

East Boldre

SO42

00

Peaked Bottom

Gravelly Copse

4

Peaked Hill

Lodge Farm

Newhouse Copse

3

Newlands Cottage

99

Harepath

Wormstall Hill

Horsebush Bottom

Newlands Plantation

Newlands

Longmead Copse

2

Ford

Broom Hill

Broomhill Farm

Bergerie Rough

Upper Beckheath Plantation

Horsemoor Copse

1

SO41

98

175
149

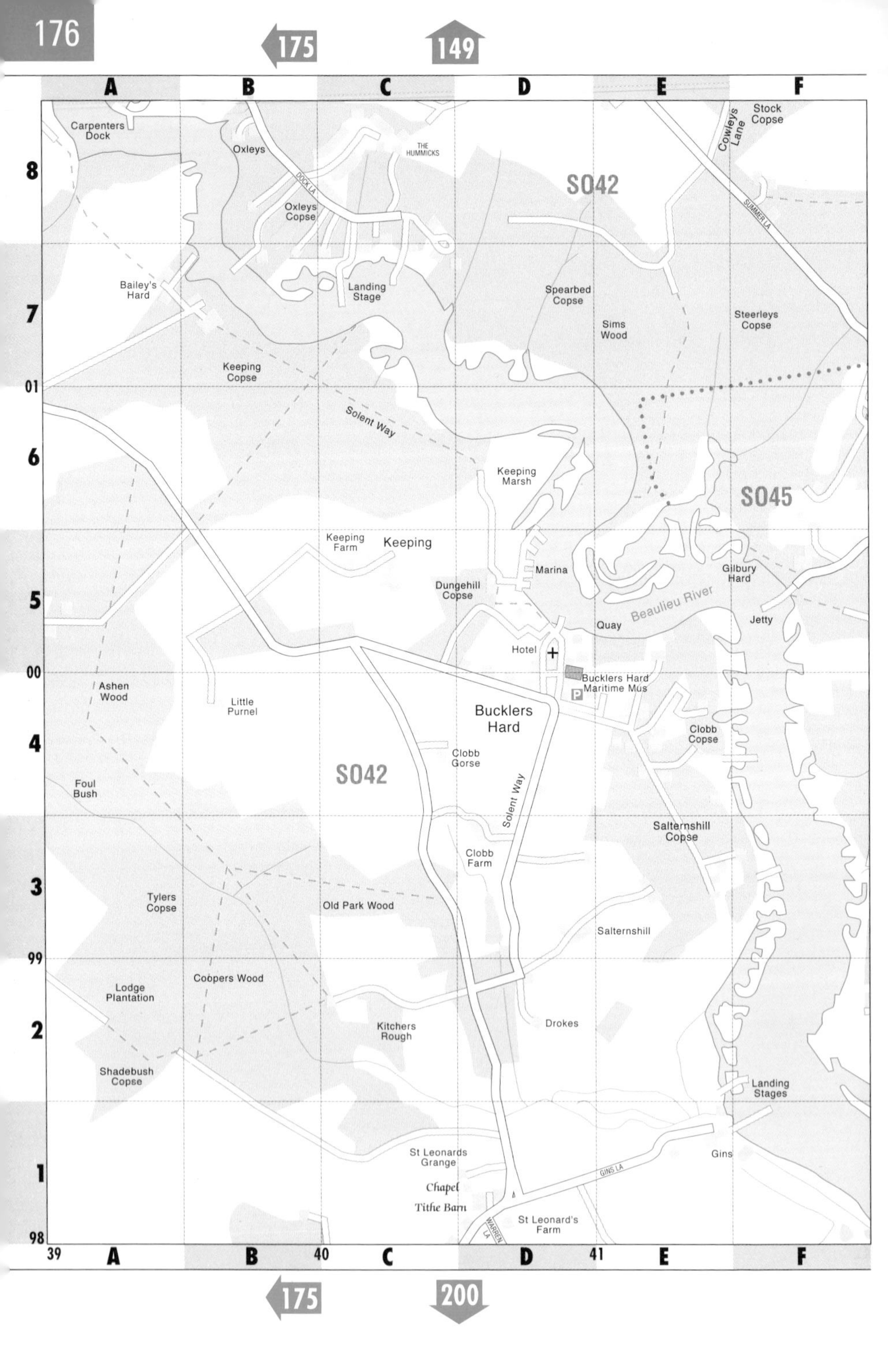
A
B
C
D
E
F
8
7
01
6
5
00
4
3
99
2
1
98
39
40
41
Carpenters Dock
Oxleys
THE HUMMICKS
DOCK LA
Oxleys Copse
S042
Cowleys Lane
Stock Copse
SUMMER LA
Bailey's Hard
Landing Stage
Spearbed Copse
Sims Wood
Steerleys Copse
Keeping Copse
Solent Way
Keeping Marsh
S045
Keeping Farm
Keeping
Marina
Gilbury Hard
Dungehill Copse
Beaulieu River
Quay
Jetty
Hotel
Bucklers Hard Maritime Mus
Ashen Wood
Little Purnel
Bucklers Hard
Clobb Copse
Clobb Gorse
S042
Foul Bush
Solent Way
Saltemshill Copse
Clobb Farm
Tylers Copse
Old Park Wood
Salternshill
Coopers Wood
Lodge Plantation
Drokes
Kitchers Rough
Shadebush Copse
Landing Stages
St Leonards Grange
GINS LA
Gins
Chapel
Tithe Barn
WARREN LA
St Leonard's Farm

175
200

150
178

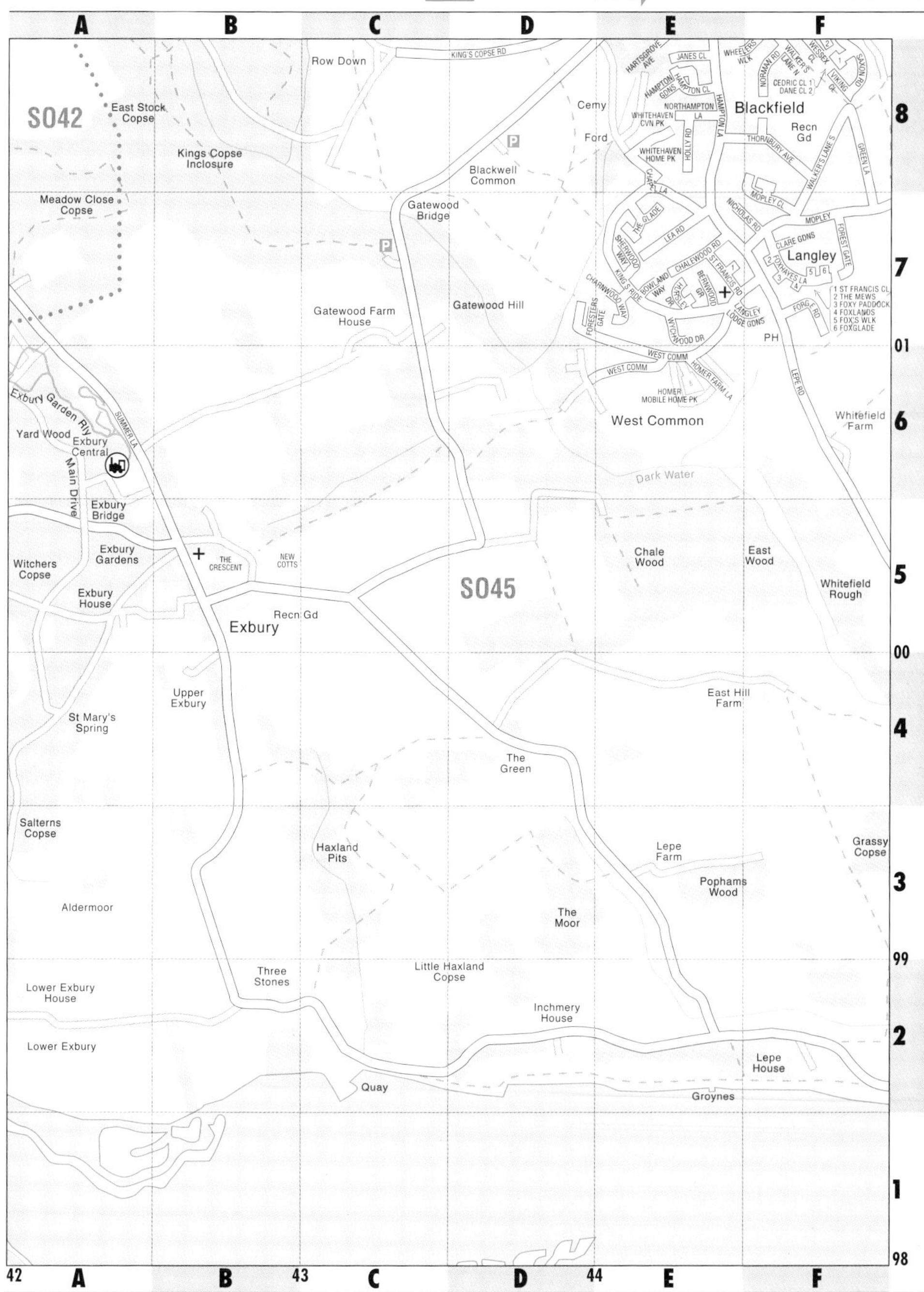

A
B
C
D
E
F
8
7
01
6
5
00
4
3
99
2
1
98
42
43
44
SO42
SO45
East Stock Copse
Kings Copse Inclosure
Meadow Close Copse
Row Down
KING'S COPSE RD
Cemy
Ford
Blackwell Common
Gatewood Bridge
Gatewood Farm House
Gatewood Hill
HARTSGROVE AVE
JANES CL
HAMPTON GDNS
HAMPTON CL
NORTHAMPTON LA
HAMPTON LA
WHITEHAVEN CVN PK
WHITEHAVEN HOME PK
HOLLY RD
WHEELERS WLK
NORMAN RD
WALKER'S LANE N
WESSEX CL
SAXON RD
VIKING CL
CEDRIC CL
DANE CL
Blackfield
Recn Gd
THORNBURY AVE
WALKER'S LANE S
GREEN LA
CHAPEL LA
THE GLADE
LEA RD
NICHOLAS RD
MOPLEY CL
MOPLEY
CLARE GDNS
FOREST GATE
Langley
FOXHAYES LA
SHERWOOD WAY
KINGS RIDE
CHARNWOOD WAY
FORESTERS GATE
ROWLAND WAY
CHALEWOOD RD
ST FRANCIS RD
BERNWOOD GR
WYCHWOOD DR
LANGLEY LODGE GDNS
FORGE RD
1 ST FRANCIS CL
2 THE MEWS
3 FOXY PADDOCK
4 FOXLANDS
5 FOX'S WLK
6 FOXGLADE
PH
WEST COMM
HOMER FARM LA
HOMER MOBILE HOME PK
West Common
LEPE RD
Whitefield Farm
Exbury Garden Rly
SUMMER LA
Yard Wood
Exbury Central
Main Drive
Exbury Bridge
Dark Water
Exbury Gardens
Witchers Copse
THE CRESCENT
NEW COTTS
Chale Wood
East Wood
Whitefield Rough
Exbury House
Recn Gd
Exbury
Upper Exbury
St Mary's Spring
East Hill Farm
The Green
Salterns Copse
Haxland Pits
Lepe Farm
Grassy Copse
Pophams Wood
Aldermoor
The Moor
Three Stones
Little Haxland Copse
Lower Exbury House
Inchmery House
Lower Exbury
Lepe House
Quay
Groynes

178

177
151

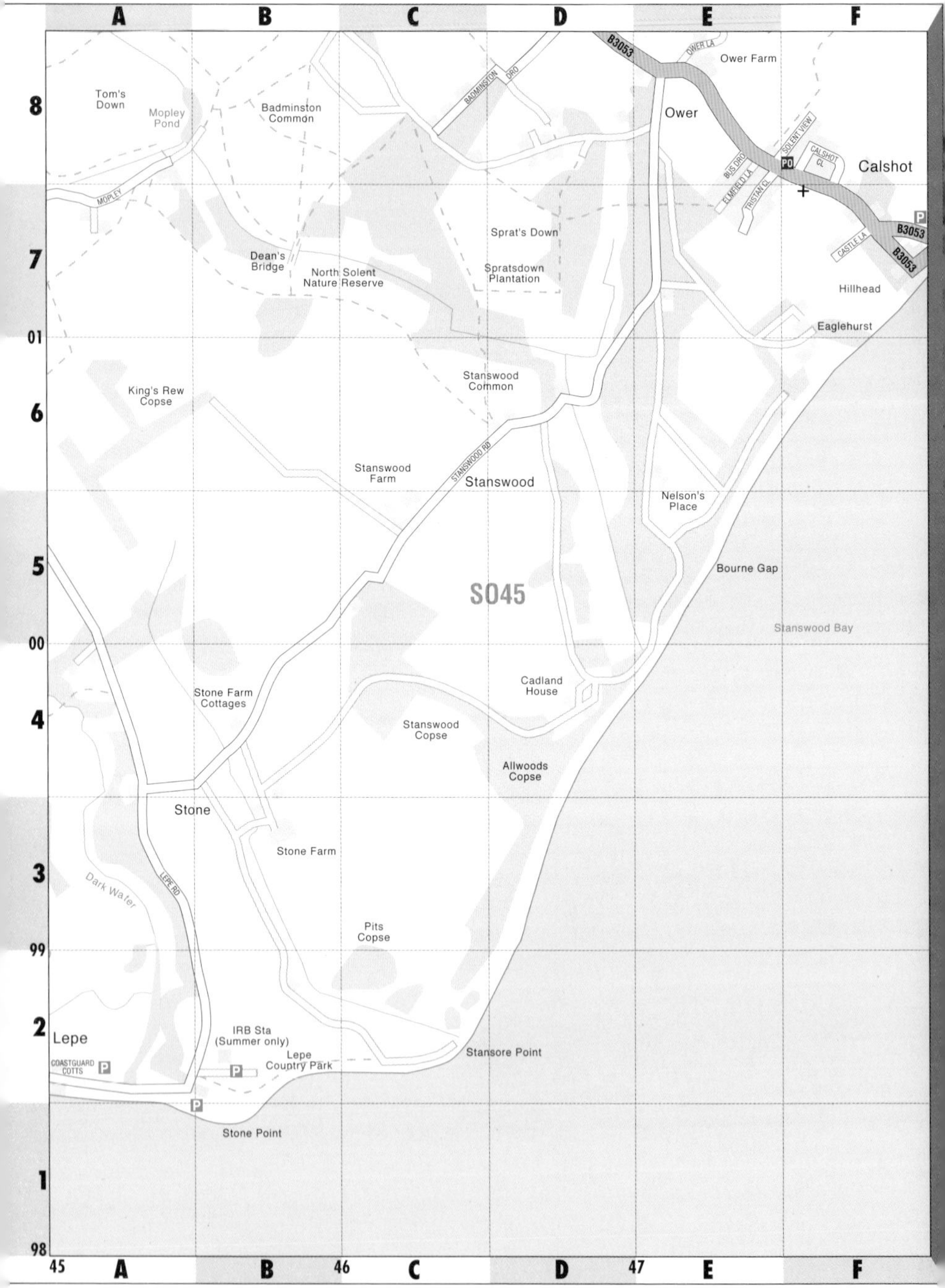

A **B** **C** **D** **E** **F**

8

B3053

OWER LA

Ower Farm

Tom's Down

Mopley Pond

Badminston Common

Ower

SOLENT VIEW

CALSHOT CL

Calshot

BARN CRES

ELMFIELD LA

THE MALL

PO

7

MOPLEY

Dean's Bridge

North Solent Nature Reserve

Sprat's Down

Spratsdown Plantation

CASTLE LA

B3053

B3053

Hillhead

Eaglehurst

01

King's Rew Copse

Stanswood Common

6

Stanswood Farm

STANSWOOD RD

Stanswood

Nelson's Place

5

SO45

Bourne Gap

Stanswood Bay

00

Stone Farm Cottages

Cadland House

4

Stanswood Copse

Allwoods Copse

Stone

3

Dark Water

LEPE RD

Stone Farm

99

Pits Copse

2

Lepe

IRB Sta (Summer only)

COASTGUARD COTTS

P

P

Lepe Country Park

Stansore Point

P

Stone Point

1

98

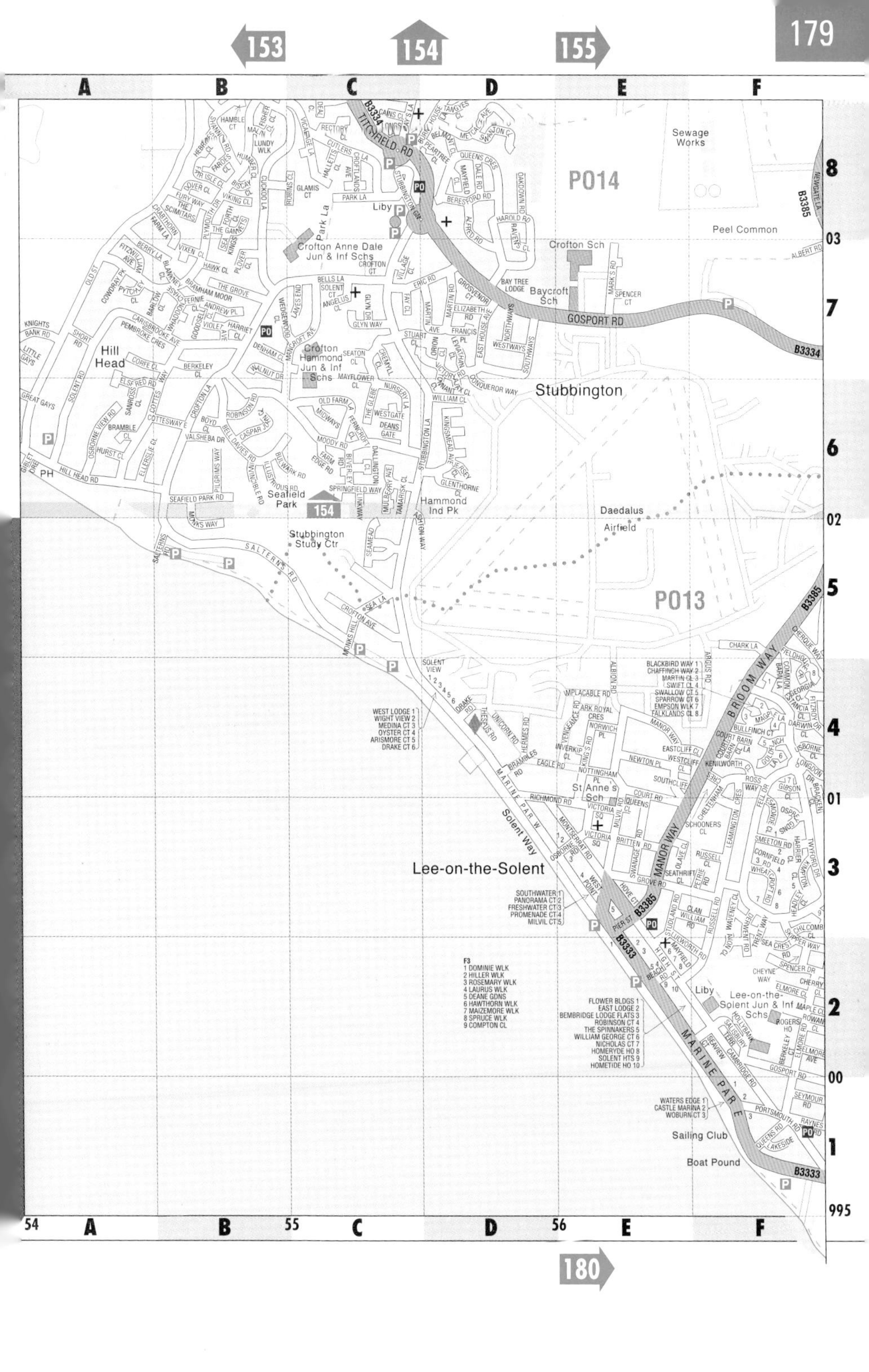
153
154
155
A
B
C
D
E
F
8
03
7
6
02
5
4
01
3
2
00
1
995
54
55
56
180
Sewage Works
PO14
Peel Common
B3385
B3334
TITCHFIELD RD
GOSPORT RD
Crofton Sch
Baycroft Sch
Crofton Anne Dale Jun & Inf Schs
Liby
Park La
Hill Head
Crofton Hammond Jun & Inf Schs
Stubbington
Seafield Park
Hammond Ind Pk
Daedalus Airfield
Stubbington Study Ctr
PO13
SALTERNS RD
CROFTON AVE
SEA LA
HILL HEAD RD
STUBBINGTON LA
ASHTON WAY
BROOM WAY
MANOR WAY
St Anne's Sch
Solent Way
MARINE PARADE W
Lee-on-the-Solent
B3333
Lee-on-the-Solent Jun & Inf Schs
MARINE PARADE
Sailing Club
Boat Pound
WEST LODGE 1
WIGHT VIEW 2
MEDINA CT 3
OYSTER CT 4
ARISMORE CT 5
DRAKE CT 6
SOUTHWATER 1
PANORAMA CT 2
FRESHWATER CT 3
PROMENADE CT 4
MILVIL CT 5
F3
1 DOMINIE WLK
2 HILLER WLK
3 ROSEMARY WLK
4 LAURUS WLK
5 DEANE GDNS
6 HAWTHORN WLK
7 MAIZEMORE WLK
8 SPRUCE WLK
9 COMPTON CL
FLOWER BLDGS 1
EAST LODGE 2
BEMBRIDGE LODGE FLATS 3
ROBINSON CT 4
THE SPINNAKERS 5
WILLIAM GEORGE CT 6
NICHOLAS CT 7
HOMERYDE HO 8
SOLENT HTS 9
HOMETIDE HO 10
BLACKBIRD WAY 1
CHAFFINCH WAY 2
MARTIN CL 3
SWIFT CL 4
SWALLOW CT 5
SPARROW CT 6
EMPSON WLK 7
FALKLANDS CL 8
WATERS EDGE 1
CASTLE MARINA 2
WOBURN CT 3

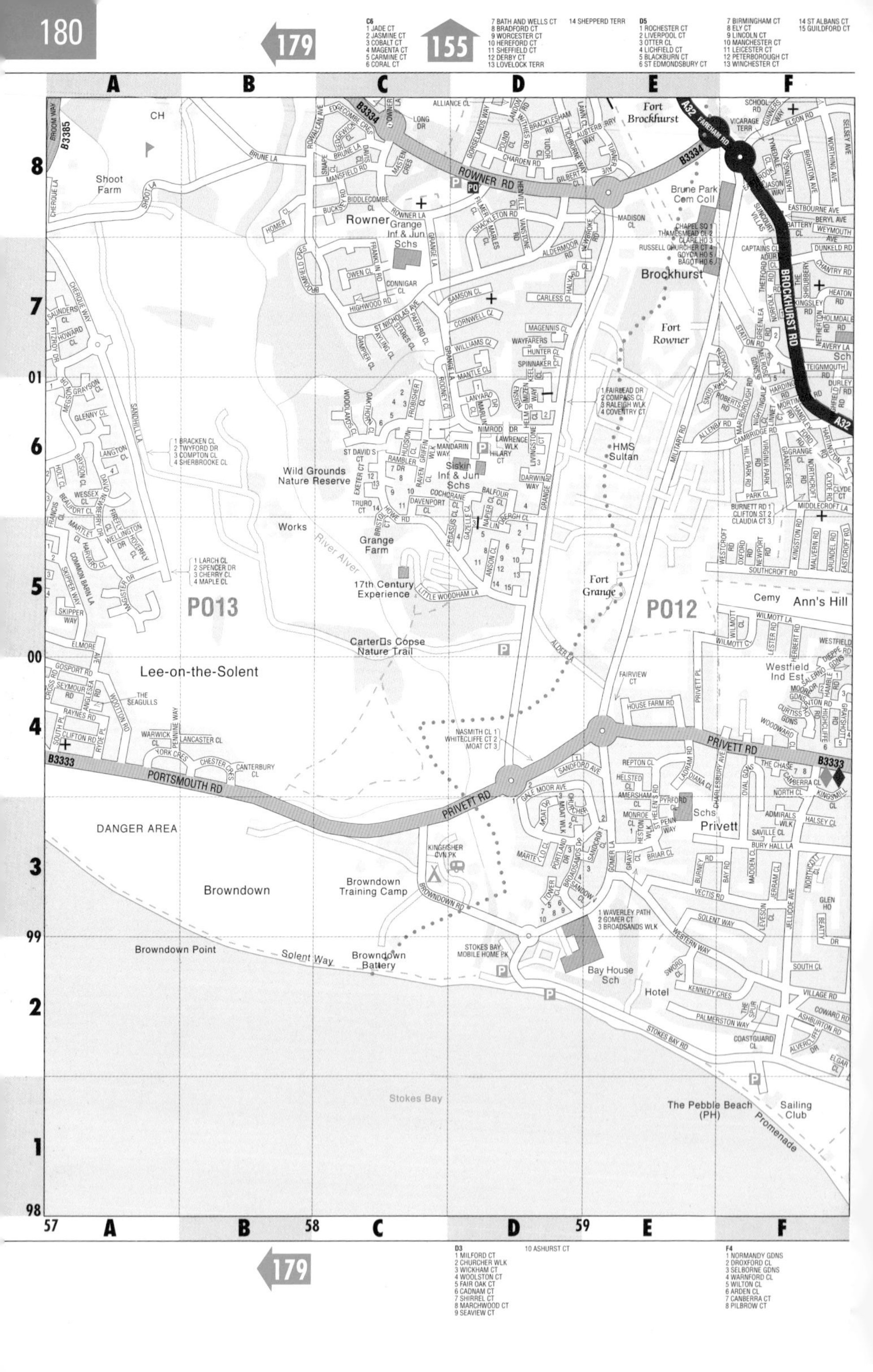
179
155
C6
1 JADE CT
2 JASMINE CT
3 COBALT CT
4 MAGENTA CT
5 CARMINE CT
6 CORAL CT
7 BATH AND WELLS CT
8 BRADFORD CT
9 WORCESTER CT
10 HEREFORD CT
11 SHEFFIELD CT
12 DERBY CT
13 LOVELOCK TERR
14 SHEPPERD TERR
D5
1 ROCHESTER CT
2 LIVERPOOL CT
3 OTTER CL
4 LICHFIELD CT
5 BLACKBURN CT
6 ST EDMONDSBURY CT
7 BIRMINGHAM CT
8 ELY CT
9 LINCOLN CT
10 MANCHESTER CT
11 LEICESTER CT
12 PETERBOROUGH CT
13 WINCHESTER CT
14 ST ALBANS CT
15 GUILDFORD CT
A B C D E F
Shoot Farm
Rowner
Grange Inf & Jun Schs
Fort Brockhurst
Brune Park Cem Coll
Brockhurst
Fort Rowner
ROWNER RD
BROCKHURST RD
A32
B3334
B3385
B3333
HMS Sultan
Wild Grounds Nature Reserve
Siskin Inf & Jun Schs
Works
Grange Farm
River Alver
17th Century Experience
Fort Grange
PO13
PO12
Cemy
Ann's Hill
Carter's Copse Nature Trail
Lee-on-the-Solent
Westfield Ind Est
PORTSMOUTH RD
PRIVETT RD
Privett
DANGER AREA
Browndown
Browndown Training Camp
Browndown Point
Solent Way
Browndown Battery
Bay House Sch
Hotel
Stokes Bay
The Pebble Beach (PH)
Sailing Club
Promenade
57 58 59
98 99 00 01
1 2 3 4 5 6 7 8
179
D3
1 MILFORD CT
2 CHURCHER WLK
3 WICKHAM CT
4 WOOLSTON CT
5 FAIR OAK CT
6 CADNAM CT
7 SHIRREL CT
8 MARCHWOOD CT
9 SEAVIEW CT
10 ASHURST CT
F4
1 NORMANDY GDNS
2 DROXFORD CL
3 SELBORNE GDNS
4 WARNFORD CL
5 WILTON CL
6 ARDEN CL
7 CANBERRA CL
8 PILBROW CT

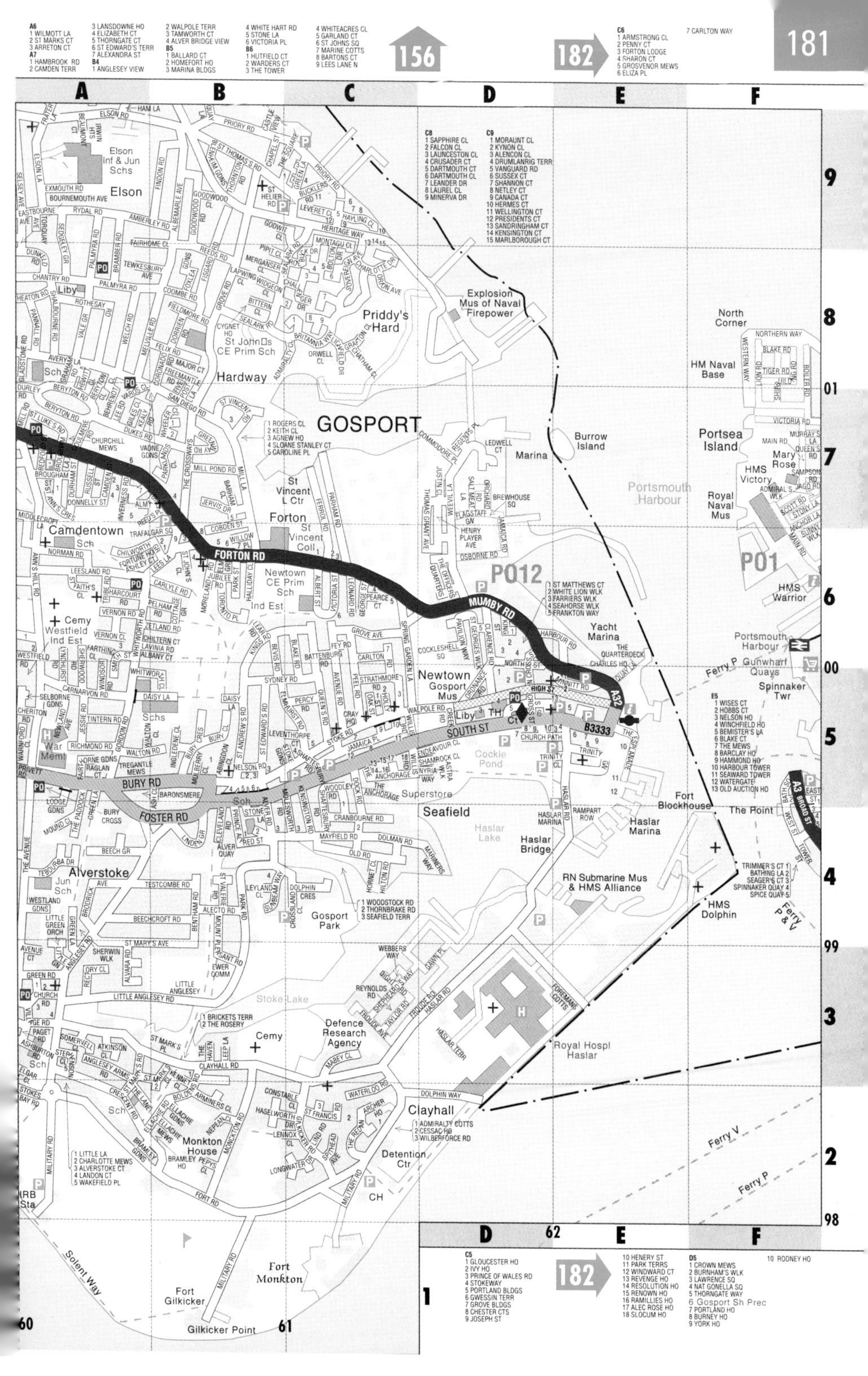

A6
1 WILMOTT LA
2 ST MARKS CT
3 ARRETON CT
A7
1 HAMBROOK RD
2 CAMDEN TERR
3 LANSDOWNE HO
4 ELIZABETH CT
5 THORNGATE CT
6 ST EDWARD'S TERR
7 ALEXANDRA ST
B4
1 ANGLESEY VIEW
2 WALPOLE TERR
3 TAMWORTH CT
4 ALVER BRIDGE VIEW
B5
1 BALLARD CT
2 HOMEFORT HO
3 MARINA BLDGS
4 WHITE HART RD
5 STONE LA
6 VICTORIA PL
B6
1 HUTFIELD CT
2 WARDERS CT
3 THE TOWER
4 WHITEACRES CL
5 GARLAND CT
6 ST JOHNS SQ
7 MARINE COTTS
8 BARTONS CT
9 LEES LANE N
156
182
C6
1 ARMSTRONG CL
2 PENNY CT
3 FORTON LODGE
4 SHARON CT
5 GROSVENOR MEWS
6 ELIZA PL
7 CARLTON WAY
A
B
C
D
E
F
C8
1 SAPPHIRE CL
2 FALCON CL
3 LAUNCESTON CL
4 CRUSADER CT
5 DARTMOUTH CT
6 DARTMOUTH CL
7 LEANDER DR
8 LAUREL CL
9 MINERVA DR
C9
1 MORAUNT CL
2 KYNON CL
3 ALENCON CL
4 DRUMLANRIG TERR
5 VANGUARD RD
6 SUSSEX CT
7 SHANNON CT
8 NETLEY CT
9 CANADA CT
10 HERMES CT
11 WELLINGTON CT
12 PRESIDENTS CT
13 SANDRINGHAM CT
14 KENSINGTON CT
15 MARLBOROUGH CT
Elson
Elson Inf & Jun Schs
Priddy's Hard
Explosion Mus of Naval Firepower
North Corner
HM Naval Base
Hardway
GOSPORT
1 ROGERS CL
2 KEITH CL
3 AGNEW HO
4 SLOANE STANLEY CT
5 CAROLINE PL
Burrow Island
Marina
Portsea Island
HMS Victory
Mary Rose
Royal Naval Mus
Portsmouth Harbour
St Vincent L Ctr
Forton
St Vincent Coll
Camdentown
FORTON RD
Newtown CE Prim Sch
PO12
PO1
HMS Warrior
MUMBY RD
1 ST MATTHEWS CT
2 WHITE LION WLK
3 FARRIERS WLK
4 SEAHORSE WLK
5 FRANKTON WAY
Cemy
Westfield Ind Est
Yacht Marina
Portsmouth Harbour
Gunwharf Quays
Spinnaker Twr
Newtown
Gosport Mus
E5
1 WISES CT
2 HOBBS CT
3 NELSON HO
4 WINCHFIELD HO
5 BEMISTER'S LA
6 BLAKE CT
7 THE MEWS
8 BARCLAY HO
9 HAMMOND HO
10 HARBOUR TOWER
11 SEAWARD TOWER
12 WATERGATE
13 OLD AUCTION HO
SOUTH ST
B3333
A32
BURY RD
FOSTER RD
Cockle Pond
Superstore
Seafield
Haslar Lake
Haslar Bridge
Haslar Marina
Fort Blockhouse
The Point
Alverstoke
RN Submarine Mus & HMS Alliance
HMS Dolphin
TRIMMER'S CT 1
BATHING LA 2
SEAGER'S CT 3
SPINNAKER QUAY 4
SPICE QUAY 5
1 WOODSTOCK RD
2 THORNBRAKE RD
3 SEAFIELD TERR
Gosport Park
Stoke Lake
Defence Research Agency
Royal Hospl Haslar
1 BRICKETS TERR
2 THE ROSERY
Cemy
Clayhall
1 ADMIRALTY COTTS
2 CESSAC HO
3 WILBERFORCE RD
Monkton House
1 LITTLE LA
2 CHARLOTTE MEWS
3 ALVERSTOKE CT
4 LANDON CT
5 WAKEFIELD PL
Detention Ctr
CH
Ferry V
Ferry P
Fort Monkton
Fort Gilkicker
Gilkicker Point
Solent Way
60
61
62
9
8
01
7
6
00
5
4
99
3
2
98
1
C5
1 GLOUCESTER HO
2 IVY HO
3 PRINCE OF WALES RD
4 STOKEWAY
5 PORTLAND BLDGS
6 GWESSIN TERR
7 GROVE BLDGS
8 CHESTER CTS
9 JOSEPH ST
182
10 HENERY ST
11 PARK TERRS
12 WINDWARD CT
13 REVENGE HO
14 RESOLUTION HO
15 RENOWN HO
16 RAMILLIES HO
17 ALEC ROSE HO
18 SLOCUM HO
D5
1 CROWN MEWS
2 BURNHAM'S WLK
3 LAWRENCE SQ
4 NAT GONELLA SQ
5 THORNGATE WAY
6 Gosport Sh Prec
7 PORTLAND HO
8 BURNEY HO
9 YORK HO
10 RODNEY HO

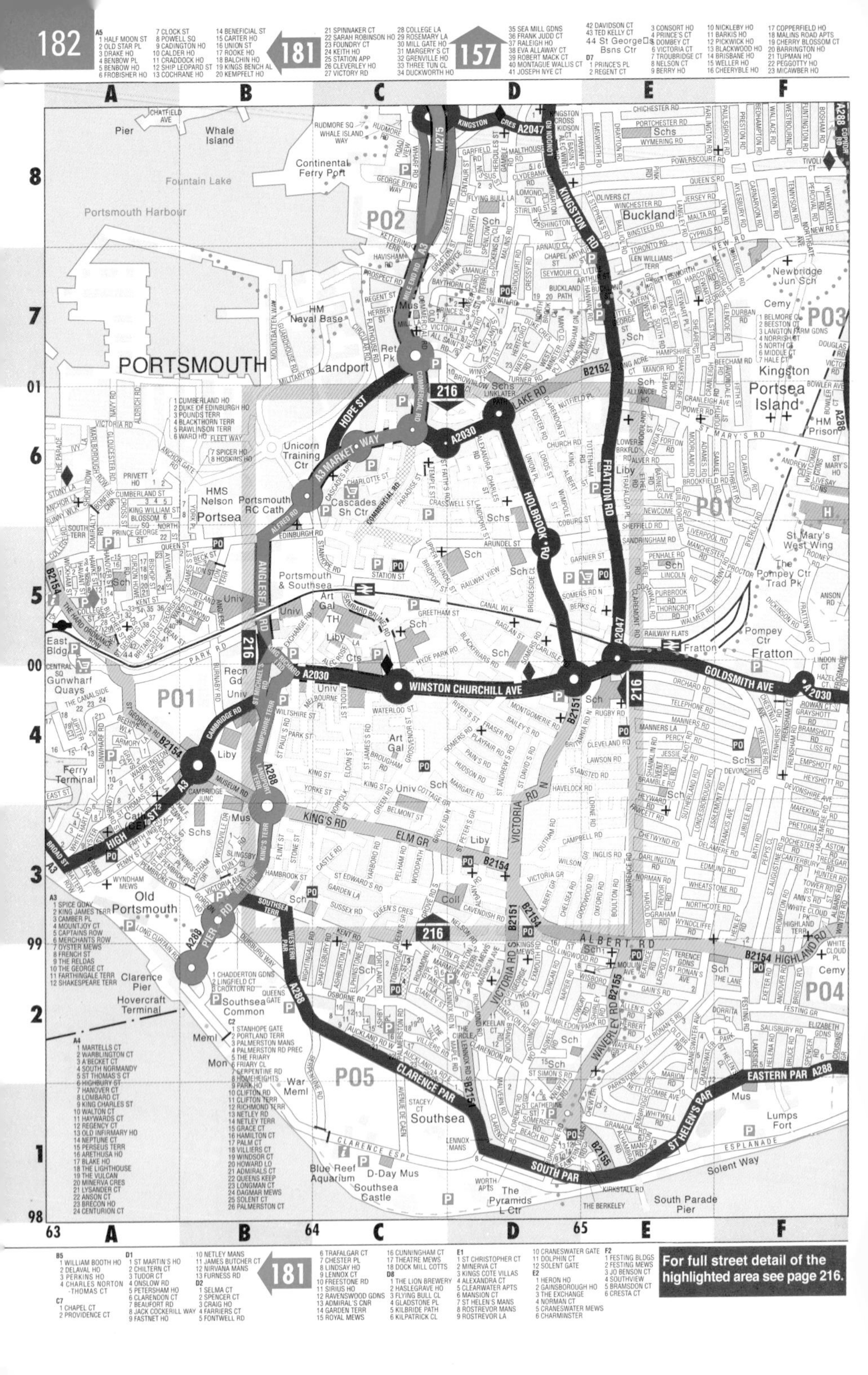

182
A5
1 HALF MOON ST
2 OLD STAR PL
3 DRAKE HO
4 BENBOW PL
5 BENBOW HO
6 FROBISHER HO
7 CLOCK ST
8 POWELL SQ
9 CADINGTON HO
10 CALDER HO
11 CRADDOCK HO
12 SHIP LEOPARD ST
13 COCHRANE HO
14 BENEFICIAL ST
15 CARTER HO
16 UNION ST
17 ROOKE HO
18 BALCHIN HO
19 KINGS BENCH AL
20 KEMPFELT HO
181
21 SPINNAKER CT
22 SARAH ROBINSON HO
23 FOUNDRY CT
24 KEITH HO
25 STATION APP
26 CLEVERLEY HO
27 VICTORY RD
28 COLLEGE LA
29 ROSEMARY LA
30 MILL GATE HO
31 MARGERY'S CT
32 GRENVILLE HO
33 THREE TUN CL
34 DUCKWORTH HO
157
35 SEA MILL GDNS
36 FRANK JUDD CT
37 RALEIGH HO
38 EVA ALLAWAY CT
39 ROBERT MACK CT
40 MONTAGUE WALLIS CT
41 JOSEPH NYE CT
42 DAVIDSON CT
43 TED KELLY CT
44 St George□s Bsns Ctr
D7
1 PRINCE'S PL
2 REGENT CT
3 CONSORT HO
4 PRINCE'S CT
5 DOMBEY CT
6 VICTORIA CT
7 TROUBRIDGE CT
8 NELSON CT
9 BERRY HO
10 NICKLEBY HO
11 BARKIS HO
12 PICKWICK HO
13 BLACKWOOD HO
14 BRISBANE HO
15 WELLER HO
16 CHEERYBLE HO
17 COPPERFIELD HO
18 MALINS ROAD APTS
19 CHERRY BLOSSOM CT
20 BARRINGTON HO
21 TUPMAN HO
22 PEGGOTTY HO
23 MICAWBER HO
A B C D E F
8 7 01 6 5 00 4 3 99 2 1 98
Pier
Whale Island
Continental Ferry Port
Fountain Lake
Portsmouth Harbour
P02
HM Naval Base
PORTSMOUTH
Landport
Buckland
Kingston
Portsea Island
HM Prison
Newbridge Jun Sch
P03
Unicorn Training Ctr
HMS Nelson
Portsea
Portsmouth RC Cath
Cascades Sh Ctr
Portsmouth & Southsea
P01
St Mary's West Wing
The Pompey Ctr Trad Pk
Pompey Ctr
Fratton
East Bldg
Gunwharf Quays
Ferry Terminal
WINSTON CHURCHILL AVE
GOLDSMITH AVE
KING'S RD
ELM GR
ALBERT RD
HIGHLAND RD
VICTORIA RD N
FRATTON RD
KINGSTON RD
HOLBROOK RD
HOPE ST
MARKET WAY
ANGLESEA RD
HAMPSHIRE TERR
HIGH ST
PIER RD
CLARENCE PAR
SOUTH PAR
EASTERN PAR
ST HELEN'S PAR
Old Portsmouth
216
A3
1 SPICE QUAY
2 KING JAMES TERR
3 CAMBER PL
4 MOUNTJOY CT
5 CAPTAINS ROW
6 MERCHANTS ROW
7 OYSTER MEWS
8 FRENCH ST
9 THE RELDAS
10 THE GEORGE CT
11 FARTHINGALE TERR
12 SHAKESPEARE TERR
Clarence Pier
Hovercraft Terminal
Southsea Common
1 CHADDERTON GDNS
2 LINGFIELD CT
3 CROXTON RD
A4
1 MARTELLS CT
2 WARBLINGTON CT
3 A'BECKET CT
4 SOUTH NORMANDY
5 ST THOMAS'S CT
6 HIGHBURY ST
7 HANOVER CT
8 LOMBARD CT
9 KING CHARLES ST
10 WALTON CT
11 HAYWARDS CT
12 REGENCY CT
13 OLD INFIRMARY HO
14 NEPTUNE CT
15 PERSEUS TERR
16 ARETHUSA HO
17 BLAKE HO
18 THE LIGHTHOUSE
19 THE VULCAN
20 MINERVA CRES
21 LYSANDER CT
22 ANSON CT
23 BRECON HO
24 CENTURION CT
C2
1 STANHOPE GATE
2 PORTLAND TERR
3 PALMERSTON MANS
4 PALMERSTON RD PREC
5 THE FRIARY
6 FRIARY CL
7 SERPENTINE RD
8 HOMEHEIGHTS
9 PARK HO
10 CLIFTON RD
11 CLIFTON TERR
12 RICHMOND TERR
13 NETLEY RD
14 NETLEY TERR
15 GRACE CT
16 HAMILTON CT
17 PALM CT
18 VILLIERS CT
19 WINDSOR CT
20 HOWARD LO
21 ADMIRALS CT
22 QUEENS KEEP
23 LONGMAN CT
24 DAGMAR MEWS
25 SOLENT CT
26 PALMERSTON CT
P05
Southsea
P04
Lumps Fort
Blue Reef Aquarium
D-Day Mus
Southsea Castle
The Pyramids L Ctr
South Parade Pier
Solent Way
63 A B 64 C D 65 E F
B5
1 WILLIAM BOOTH HO
2 DELAVAL HO
3 PERKINS HO
4 CHARLES NORTON -THOMAS CT
C7
1 CHAPEL CT
2 PROVIDENCE CT
D1
1 ST MARTIN'S HO
2 CHILTERN CT
3 TUDOR CT
4 ONSLOW RD
5 PETERSHAM HO
6 CLARENDON CT
7 BEAUFORT RD
8 JACK COCKERILL WAY
9 FASTNET HO
10 NETLEY MANS
11 JAMES BUTCHER CT
12 NIRVANA MANS
13 FURNESS RD
D2
1 SELMA CT
2 SPENCER CT
3 CRAIG HO
4 FARRIERS CT
5 FONTWELL RD
181
6 TRAFALGAR CT
7 CHESTER PL
8 LINDSAY HO
9 LENNOX CT
10 FREESTONE RD
11 SIRIUS HO
12 RAVENSWOOD GDNS
13 ADMIRAL'S CNR
14 GARDEN TERR
15 ROYAL MEWS
16 CUNNINGHAM CT
17 THEATRE MEWS
18 DOCK MILL COTTS
D8
1 THE LION BREWERY
2 HASLEGRAVE HO
3 FLYING BULL CL
4 GLADSTONE PL
5 KILBRIDE PATH
6 KILPATRICK CL
E1
1 ST CHRISTOPHER CT
2 MINERVA CT
3 KINGS COTE VILLAS
4 ALEXANDRA CT
5 CLEARWATER APTS
6 MANSION CT
7 ST HELEN'S MANS
8 ROSTREVOR MANS
9 ROSTREVOR LA
10 CRANESWATER GATE
11 DOLPHIN CT
12 SOLENT GATE
E2
1 HERON HO
2 GAINSBOROUGH HO
3 THE EXCHANGE
4 NORMAN CT
5 CRANESWATER MEWS
6 CHARMINSTER
F2
1 FESTING BLDGS
2 FESTING MEWS
3 JO BENSON CT
4 SOUTHVIEW
5 BRAMSDON CT
6 CRESTA CT
For full street detail of the highlighted area see page 216.

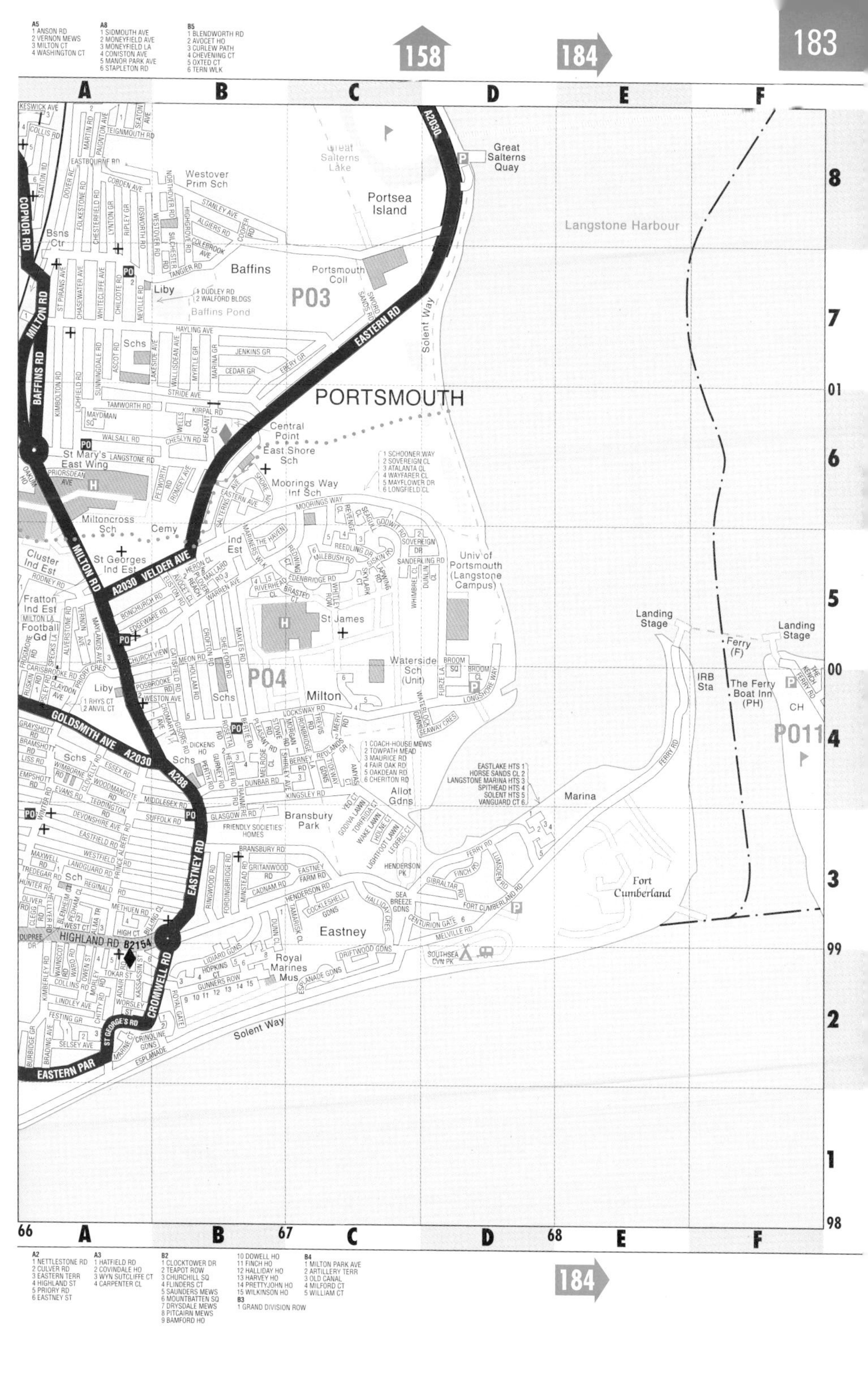

158
184

PORTSMOUTH

Langstone Harbour

Great Salterns Lake

Portsea Island

Great Salterns Quay

PO3

PO4

PO11

Baffins

Milton

Eastney

Fort Cumberland

Marina

Langstone Harbour

184

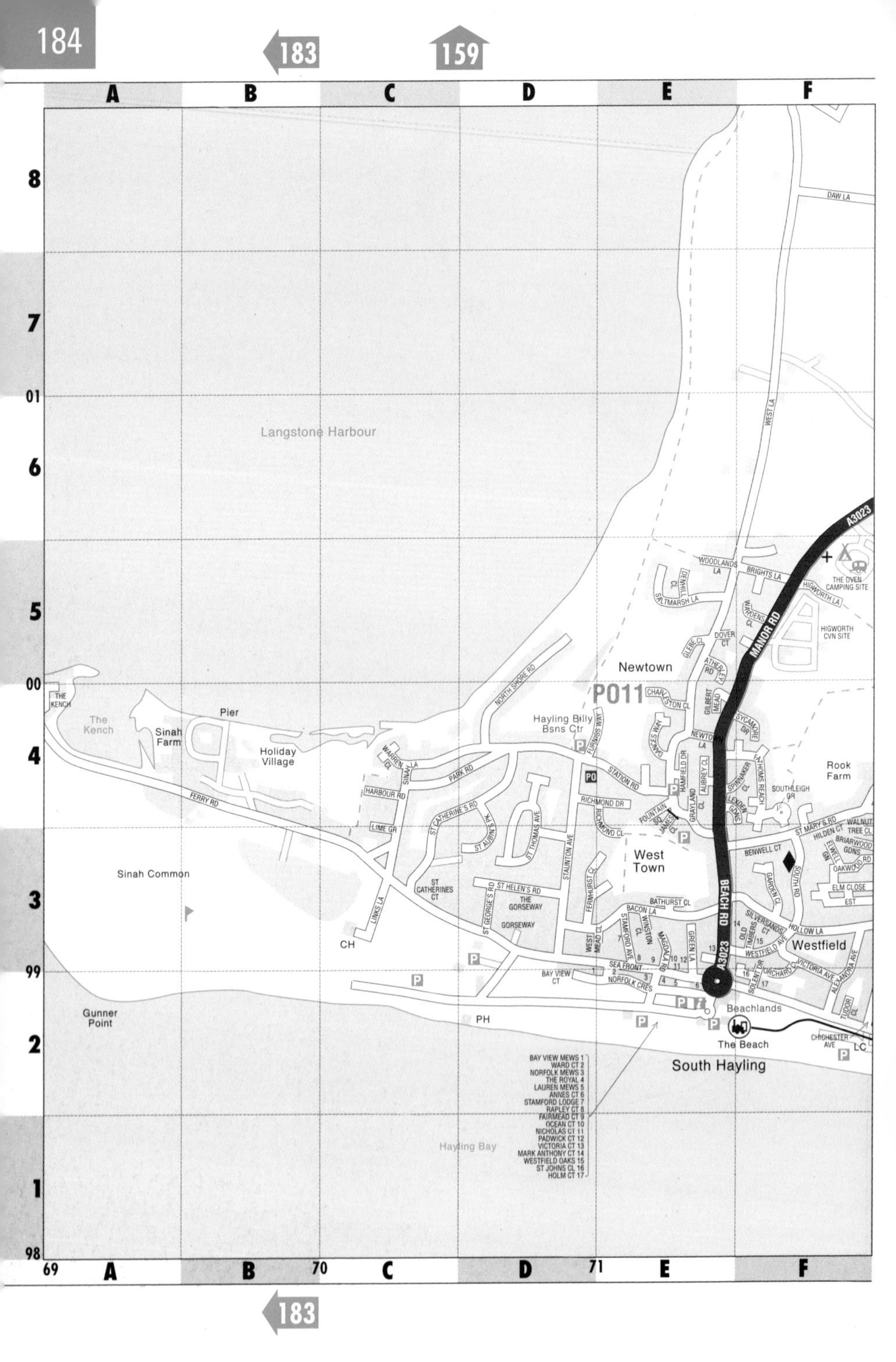

8
7
01
6
5
00
4
3
99
2
1
98

A　　B　　C　　D　　E　　F

Langstone Harbour

DAW LA

A3023

WOODLANDS LA
BRIGHTS LA
THE OVEN CAMPING SITE
HIGWORTH LA
HIGWORTH CVN SITE

ST MARSH LA
WEST LA
MANOR RD

DOVER CT

Newtown

P011

Hayling Billy
Bsns Ctr

Rook
Farm

NORTH SHORE RD

PO

STATION RD

RICHMOND DR

WARREN LA

HARBOUR RD

PARK RD

The Kench

The
Kench

Sinah
Farm

Pier

Holiday
Village

FERRY RD

LIME GR

ST CATHERINE'S RD

ST THOMAS AVE

STAUNTON AVE

RICHMOND CL

POINTOUT

GRAYLAND

ST MARY'S RD
HILDEN CT
WALNUT TREE CL
BRIARWOOD GDNS
OAKWOOD RD
ELM CLOSE EST
SOUTHLEIGH GR

BENWELL CT

West
Town

Sinah Common

LINKS LA

CH

ST CATHERINES CT

ST GEORGE'S RD

ST HELEN'S RD
THE GORSEWAY
GORSEWAY

ST AUBIN'S

FERNWAYS CL

BACON LA

BATHURST CL

BEACH RD

A3023

GARDEN LA

ON HILL'S

HOLLOW LA
OLD

Westfield

VICTORIA AVE

CHICHESTER AVE
LC

Gunner
Point

P

P

BAY VIEW
CT

PH

WEST MEAD

SEA FRONT

NORFOLK CRES

P

P

P

Beachlands

The Beach

South Hayling

BAY VIEW MEWS 1
WARD CT 2
NORFOLK MEWS 3
THE ROYAL 4
LAUREN MEWS 5
ANNES CT 6
STAMFORD LODGE 7
RAPLEY CT 8
FAIRMEAD CT 9
OCEAN CT 10
NICHOLAS CT 11
PADWICK CT 12
VICTORIA CT 13
MARK ANTHONY CT 14
WESTFIELD OAKS 15
ST JOHNS CT 16
HOLM CT 17

Hayling Bay

160

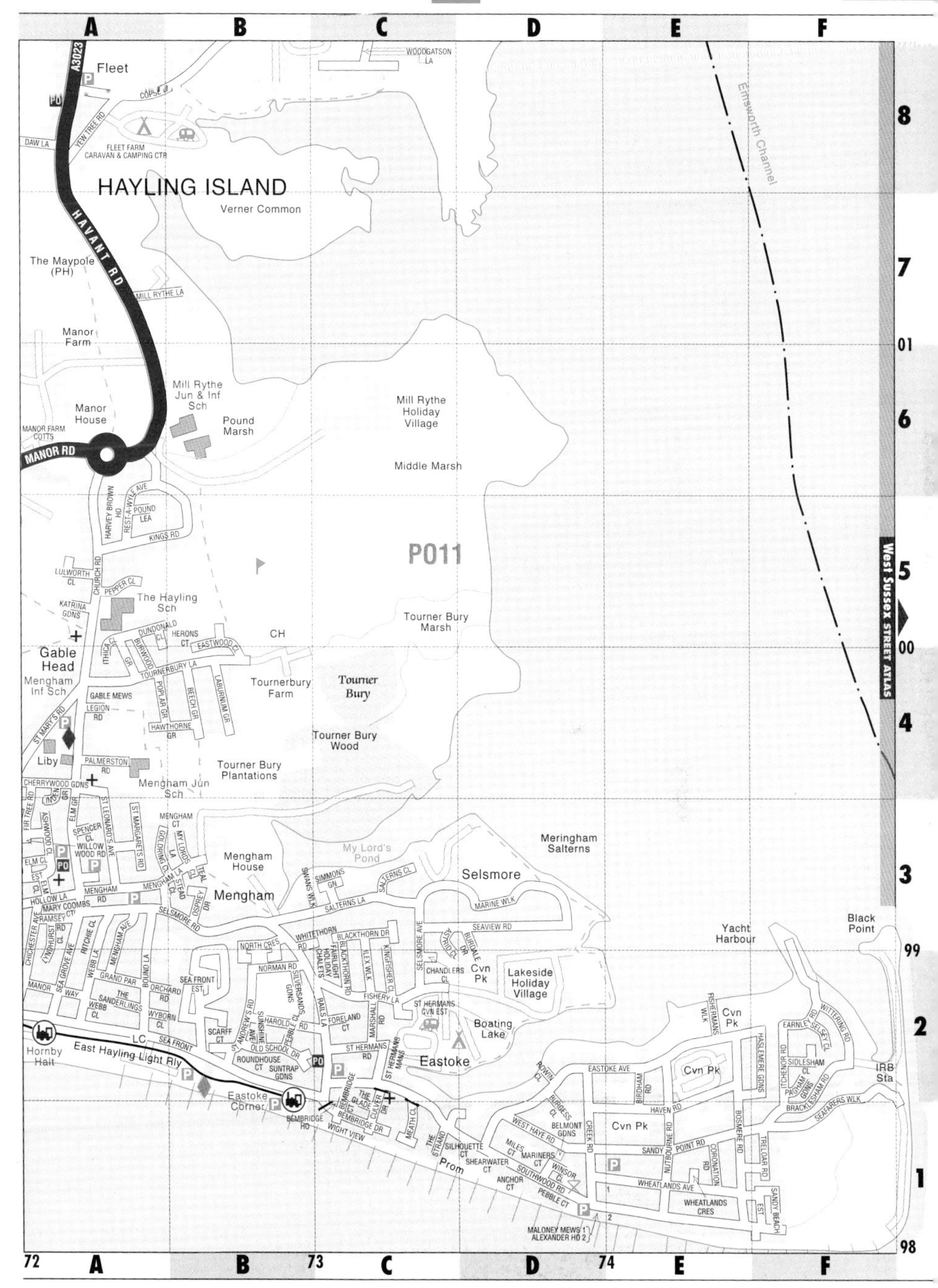
A
B
C
D
E
F
Fleet
A3023
WOODGATSON LA
COPSE LA
YEW TREE RD
DAW LA
FLEET FARM CARAVAN & CAMPING CTR
HAYLING ISLAND
Verner Common
Emsworth Channel
HAVANT RD
The Maypole (PH)
MILL RYTHE LA
Manor Farm
Mill Rythe Jun & Inf Sch
Manor House
Pound Marsh
Mill Rythe Holiday Village
MANOR FARM COTTS
MANOR RD
Middle Marsh
HARVEY BROWN RD
REST-A-WYLE AVE
POUND LEA
KINGS RD
PO11
LULWORTH CL
CHURCH RD
PEPPER CL
The Hayling Sch
KATRINA GDNS
Tourner Bury Marsh
DUNDONALD CL
HERONS CT
EASTWOOD CL
CH
Gable Head
ITHICA CL
BURWOOD GR
TOURNERBURY LA
Mengham Inf Sch
Tournerbury Farm
Tourner Bury
GABLE MEWS
POPLAR GR
BEECH GR
LABURNUM GR
LEGION RD
HAWTHORNE GR
ST MARY'S RD
Tourner Bury Wood
Liby
PALMERSTON RD
Tourner Bury Plantations
Mengham Jun Sch
CHERRYWOOD GDNS
FIR TREE RD
LINDEN GR
ELM GR
ST LEONARD'S AVE
ST MARGARETS RD
MENGHAM CT
ASHWOOD CL
SPENCER CL
WILLOW WOOD RD
GOLDRING CL
MY LORDS LA
Meringham Salterns
My Lord's Pond
Mengham House
ELM CL
Selsmore
EST
MENGHAM RD
MENGHAM LA
STEAD CL
TEAL CL
SIMMONS GN
SALTERNS CL
SWANS WLK
Mengham
HOLLOW LA
MARY COOMBS CT
RAMSEY CT
OSPREY DR
SALTERNS LA
MARINE WLK
SELSMORE RD
SEAVIEW RD
CHICHESTER AVE
LYNDHURST RD
RITCHIE CL
MENGHAM AVE
WHITETHORN RD
BLACKTHORN DR
Yacht Harbour
Black Point
NORTH CRES
FAIRLIGHT CHALETS
BLACKTHORN RD
SELSMORE AVE
ASTROS CL
BURDALE DR
99
SEA GROVE AVE
WEBB LA
BOUND LA
NORMAN RD
ILEX WLK
KINGFISHER CL
CHANDLERS CL
Cvn Pk
Lakeside Holiday Village
SEA FRONT EST
GRAND PAR
ORCHARD RD
SILVERSANDS GDNS
MANOR WAY
THE SANDERLINGS
FISHERY LA
WEBB CL
ST ANDREW'S RD
SUNSHINE AVE
RAILS LA
FORELAND CT
MARSHALL RD
ST HERMANS CVN EST
FISHERMANS WLK
WYBORN CL
HAROLD RD
PEBBLE CL
Boating Lake
EARNLEY RD
WITTERING RD
SELSEY CL
LC
SEA FRONT
SCARFF CT
Hornby Halt
East Hayling Light Rly
OLD SCHOOL DR
ST HERMANS RD
ST HERMANS MANS
HASLEMERE GDNS
ITCHENOR RD
SIDLESHAM CL
IRB Sta
ROUNDHOUSE CT
SUNTRAP GDNS
Eastoke
ROWIN CL
EASTOKE AVE
BIRDHAM RD
PAGHAM GDNS
BRACKLESHAM RD
Eastoke Corner
BEMBRIDGE CT
THE GLADE
CULVER DR
SEAFARERS WLK
BEMBRIDGE HO
BEMBRIDGE DR
MEATH CL
BURGESS CL
HAVEN RD
BOSMERE RD
WIGHT VIEW
THE STRAND
SILHOUETTE CT
WEST HAYE RD
BELMONT GDNS
CREEK RD
Cvn Pk
NUTBOURNE RD
SANDY POINT RD
CORONATION RD
TRELOAR RD
SHEARWATER CT
MILES CT
MARINERS CT
Prom
WINSOR CL
SOUTHWOOD RD
WHEATLANDS AVE
ANCHOR CT
PEBBLE CT
WHEATLANDS CRES
SANDY BEACH EST
MALONEY MEWS 1
ALEXANDER HO 2
8
7
01
6
5
00
4
3
2
1
98
72
73
74
West Sussex STREET ATLAS

162

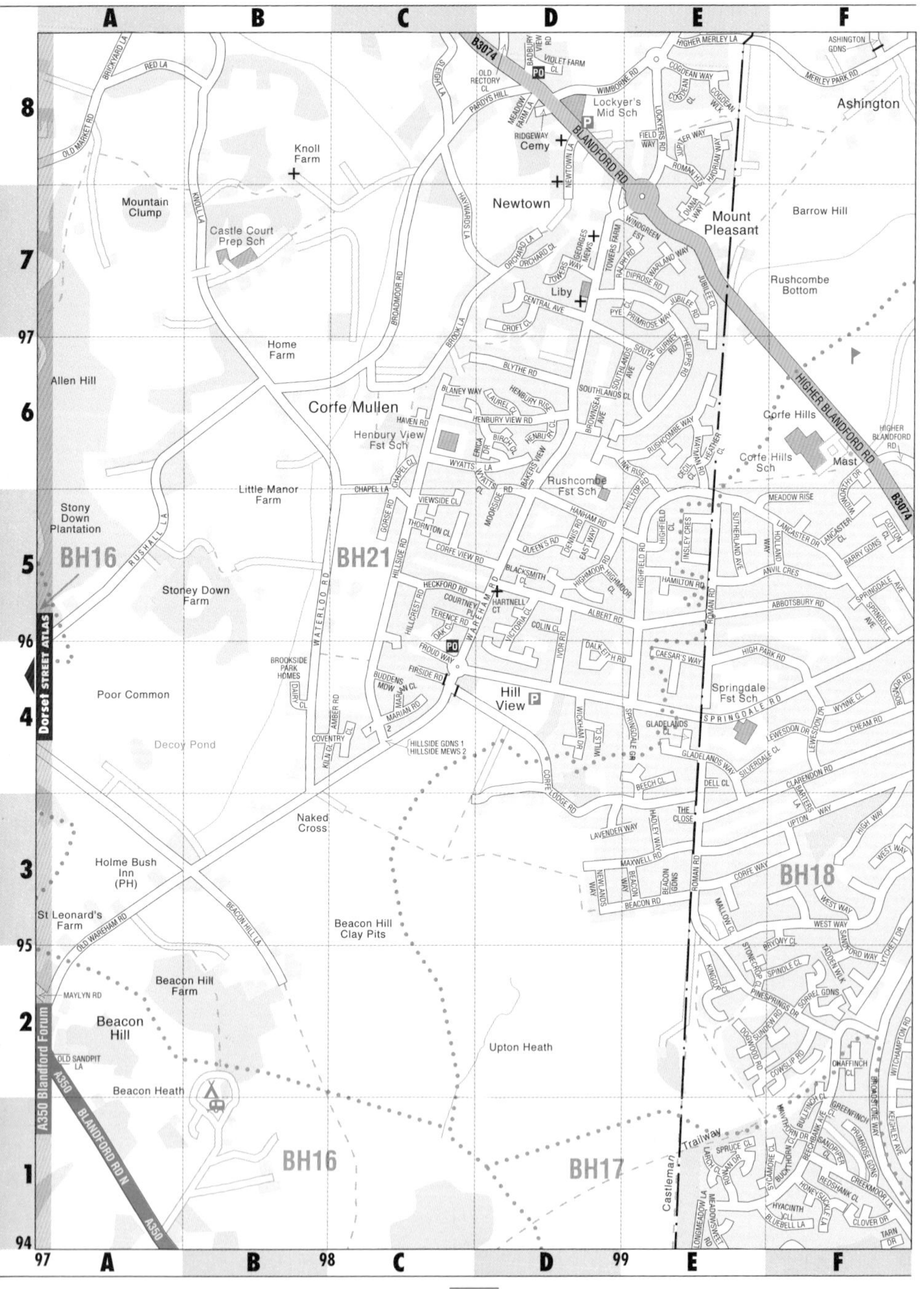
A
B
C
D
E
F
8
7
97
6
5
96
4
3
95
2
1
94
98
99
Ashington
Barrow Hill
Mount Pleasant
Rushcombe Bottom
Lockyer's Mid Sch
Ridgeway Cemy
Newtown
Knoll Farm
Mountain Clump
Castle Court Prep Sch
Liby
Home Farm
Allen Hill
Corfe Mullen
Henbury View Fst Sch
Corfe Hills
Corfe Hills Sch
Mast
Rushcombe Fst Sch
Little Manor Farm
Stony Down Plantation
BH16
BH21
Stoney Down Farm
Poor Common
Decoy Pond
Hill View
Springdale Fst Sch
Naked Cross
Holme Bush Inn (PH)
St Leonard's Farm
Beacon Hill Clay Pits
BH18
Beacon Hill Farm
Beacon Hill
Upton Heath
Beacon Heath
BH16
BH17
Castleman Trailway
B3074
BLANDFORD RD
HIGHER BLANDFORD RD
A350 BLANDFORD RD N
A350 Blandford Forum
Dorset STREET ATLAS
HIGHER MERLEY LA
MERLEY PARK RD
ASHINGTON GDNS
WIMBORNE RD
COGDEAN WAY
VIOLET FARM CL
BADBURY VIEW RD
OLD RECTORY CL
PARDYS HILL
SLEIGHT LA
RED LA
BRICKYARD LA
OLD MARKET RD
KNOLL LA
HAYWARDS LA
BROADMOOR RD
BROOK LA
ORCHARD LA
ORCHARD CL
CENTRAL AVE
CROFT CL
BLYTHE RD
BLANEY WAY
HENBURY RISE
HENBURY VIEW RD
HAVEN RD
WYATTS LA
CHAPEL LA
CHAPEL CL
VIEWSIDE CL
THORNTON CL
GORSE RD
HILLSIDE RD
CORFE VIEW RD
QUEEN'S RD
HANHAM RD
MOORSIDE RD
HECKFORD RD
COURTNEY PL
TERENCE RD
HILLCREST RD
BLACKSMITH CL
HARTNELL CT
WAREHAM RD
VICTORIA CL
COLIN CL
IVOR RD
ALBERT RD
DALKEITH RD
CAESAR'S WAY
FROUD WAY
FIRSIDE RD
BUDDENS MDW
MARIAN RD
BROOKSIDE PARK HOMES
DAIRY CL
AMBER RD
COVENTRY CL
KILN CL
WATERLOO RD
HILLSIDE GDNS 1
HILLSIDE MEWS 2
WICKHAM DR
WILLIS CL
SPRINGDALE GR
GLADELANDS CL
GLADELANDS WAY
SPRINGDALE RD
CORFE LODGE RD
BEECH CL
DELL CL
THE CLOSE
LAVENDER WAY
HADLEY WAY
MAXWELL RD
NEWLANDS WAY
BEACON WAY
BEACON GDNS
BEACON RD
ROMAN RD
CORFE WAY
UPTON WAY
HIGH WAY
WEST WAY
MALLOW CL
BRYONY CL
STONECROP CL
SPINDLE CL
SANDFORD WAY
TADDEN WLK
LYTCHETT DR
KINGCUP CL
PINESPRINGS DR
SORREL GDNS
DOGWOOD RD
SUNDEW RD
COWSLIP RD
CHAFFINCH CL
WITCHAMPTON RD
BROADSTONE WAY
KEIGHLEY AVE
GREENFINCH
BULLFINCH CL
HAWTHORN DR
BEECHBANK AVE
SANDPIPER CL
PRIMROSE GDNS
CREEKMOOR LA
REDSHANK CL
HONEYSUCKLE LA
HYACINTH CL
BLUEBELL LA
CLOVER DR
TARN DR
SPRUCE CL
LARCH CL
ROWAN DR
SYCAMORE CL
BUCKTHORN CL
LONGMEADOW LA
MEADOWSWEET RD
CLARENDON RD
BARTERS LA
SILVERDALE CL
LEWESDON DR
WYNNE CL
CHEAM RD
HIGH PARK RD
ABBOTSBURY RD
SPRINGDALE AVE
ANVIL CRES
HAMILTON RD
HIGHFIELD RD
HIGHFIELD CL
INSLEY CRES
SUTHERLAND AVE
HOLLAND WAY
LANCASTER DR
LANCASTER CL
BARRY GDNS
COTTON CL
MEADOW RISE
WIDWORTHY DR
HIGHER BLANDFORD RD
HIGHMOOR RD
HIGHMOOR CL
EAST WAY
DENNIS RD
HILLTOP RD
LINK RISE
CECIL CL
HEATHER CL
WAYMAN RD
RUSHCOMBE WAY
SOUTHLANDS CL
SOUTHLANDS AVE
BROWNSEA AVE
SOUTH RD
GURNEY RD
PHELIPS RD
PRIMROSE WAY
PYE CL
JUBILEE RD
JUBILEE CL
DIPROSE RD
WARLAND WAY
RALPH RD
TOWERS FARM
WINDGREEN EST
TOWERS WAY
GEORGES MEWS
NEWTOWN LA
MEADOW FARM LA
FIELD WAY
LOCKYERS RD
JUPITER WAY
ROMAN HTS
HADRIAN WAY
DIANA WAY
COGDEAN CL
COGDEAN WLK
RUSHALL LA
BEACON HILL LA
OLD WAREHAM RD
MAYLYN RD
OLD SANDPIT LA
PO
P

201

163
188

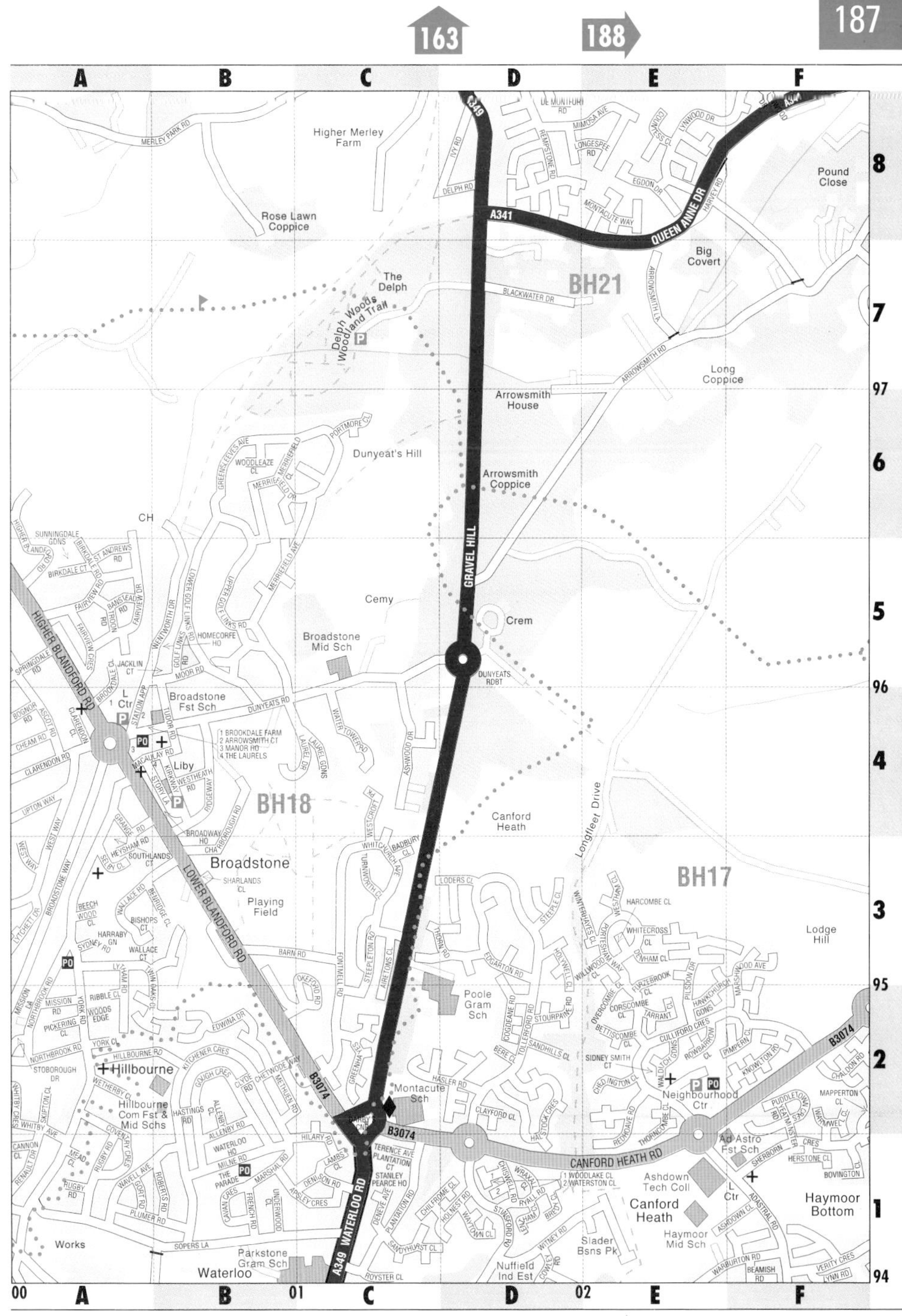
A
B
C
D
E
F
8
7
97
6
5
96
4
3
95
2
1
94
00
01
02
Higher Merley Farm
MERLEY PARK RD
Rose Lawn Coppice
The Delph
Delph Woods Woodland Trail
BH21
BLACKWATER DR
A349
A341
QUEEN ANNE DR
DELPH RD
IVY RD
MIMOSA AVE
LONGESPEE RD
REMPSTONE RD
EGDON DR
MONTACUTE WAY
LYNWOOD DR
HARVEY RD
Pound Close
Big Covert
ARROWSMITH LA
ARROWSMITH RD
Long Coppice
Arrowsmith House
Dunyeat's Hill
Arrowsmith Coppice
GRAVEL HILL
Cemy
Crem
DUNYEATS RDBT
Broadstone Mid Sch
Broadstone Fst Sch
DUNYEATS RD
PORTMORE CL
WOODLEAZE CL
MERRIEFIELD CL
MERRIEFIELD DR
MERRIEFIELD AVE
GREENSLEEVES AVE
LOWER GOLF LINKS RD
UPPER GOLF LINKS RD
HOMECORFE HO
MOOR RD
GOLF LINKS RD
WENTWORTH DR
CH
SUNNINGDALE GDNS
ST ANDREWS RD
BIRKDALE CT
BIRKDALE RD
FAIRVIEW RD
FAIRVIEW DR
FAIRVIEW CRES
BANSTEAD RD
TROON RD
BROOKDALE CL
JACKLIN CT
SPRINGDALE RD
HIGHER BLANDFORD RD
L Ctr
Liby
1 BROOKDALE FARM
2 ARROWSMITH CT
3 MANOR RD
4 THE LAURELS
BOGNOR RD
ASCOT RD
CHEAM RD
CLARENDON RD
CLARENDON CL
STATION APP
TUDOR RD
MACAULAY RD
KIRKWAY
STORY LA
WESTHEATH RD
RIDGEWAY
UPTON WAY
WEST WAY
BROADSTONE WAY
BH18
WATERTOWER RD
LAUREL DR
LAUREL GDNS
ASHWOOD DR
Canford Heath
Longfleet Drive
BROADWAY HO
SCARBOROUGH RD
GRANGE RD
HEYSHAM RD
SOUTHLANDS CT
Broadstone
SHARLANDS CL
LOWER BLANDFORD RD
Playing Field
BEECH WOOD CL
WALLACE RD
BEHRIDGE CL
BISHOPS CT
HARRABY GN
SYDNEY RD
WALLACE CT
WESTCROFT PK
WHITCHURCH AVE
BADBURY CL
TURNWORTH CL
LODERS CL
STEEPLE CL
BH17
HARCOMBE CL
WHITECROSS CL
DENHAM CL
WINTERHAYES CL
Lodge Hill
BARN RD
STEEPLETON RD
AIRETONS CL
FONTMELL RD
OKEFORD RD
THORN RD
EDGARTON RD
HOLTWELL CL
WILLWOOD CL
FURZEBROOK CL
PILSDON DR
MARSHWOOD AVE
Poole Gram Sch
CORSCOMBE CL
TARRANT CL
HAWKCHURCH GDNS
BETTISCOMBE CL
CULLIFORD CRES
ROWBARROW CL
PIMPERN CL
KNOWLTON RD
COGDEANE RD
TOLLERFORD RD
STOURPAINE RD
SANDHILLS CL
BERE CL
OVERCOMBE CL
SIDNEY SMITH CT
CHEDINGTON CL
MISSION RD
NORTHBROOK RD
YORK RD
RIBBLE CL
WOODS EDGE
PICKERING CL
YORK CL
HILLBOURNE RD
NORTHBROOK RD
STOBOROUGH DR
Hillbourne
KITCHENER CRES
EDWINA DR
CHETWODE WAY
B3074
GOUGH CRES
CLYDE RD
METHUEN RD
Hillbourne Com Fst & Mid Schs
WETHERBY CL
HASTINGS RD
ALLENBY CL
ALLENBY RD
WATERLOO HO
MILNE RD
THE PARADE
MARSHAL RD
WHITBY AVE
SKIPTON CL
COVENTRY CRES
RUGBY RD
MEAD CL
CANNON CL
RENAULT DR
WAVELL AVE
GORT RD
ROBERTS RD
PLUMER RD
CAVAN CRES
FRENCH RD
UNDERWOOD CL
APSLEY CRES
DENISON RD
HILARY RD
LAMBS CL
Montacute Sch
HASLER RD
CLAYFORD CL
HALSTOCK CRES
REDHOAVE RD
THORNCOMBE CL
Neighbourhood Ctr
MAPPERTON CL
PUDDLETOWN CRES
YEATMINSTER RD
WARMWELL CL
CHALDON RD
CANFORD HEATH RD
TERENCE AVE
PLANTATION CT
STANLEY PEARCE HO
DENEVE AVE
PLANTATION RD
CHILFROME CL
HOLNEST RD
WAYTOWN CL
CHISWELL RD
WRAXALL CL
RYALL RD
STINSFORD RD
LENTHAM CL
BRIDE CL
1 WOODLAKE CL
2 WATERSTON CL
Ad Astro Fst Sch
SHERBORN CRES
HERSTONE CL
BOVINGTON CL
Ashdown Tech Coll
Canford Heath
L Ctr
ASHDOWN CL
ADASTRAL RD
Haymoor Bottom
Haymoor Mid Sch
WITNEY RD
COWLEY RD
Slader Bsns Pk
Nuffield Ind Est
Works
SOPERS LA
Parkstone Gram Sch
Waterloo
A349 WATERLOO RD
SANDYHURST CL
ROYSTER CL
WARBURTON RD
BEAMISH RD
VERITY CRES
LYNN RD

202
188

187 164

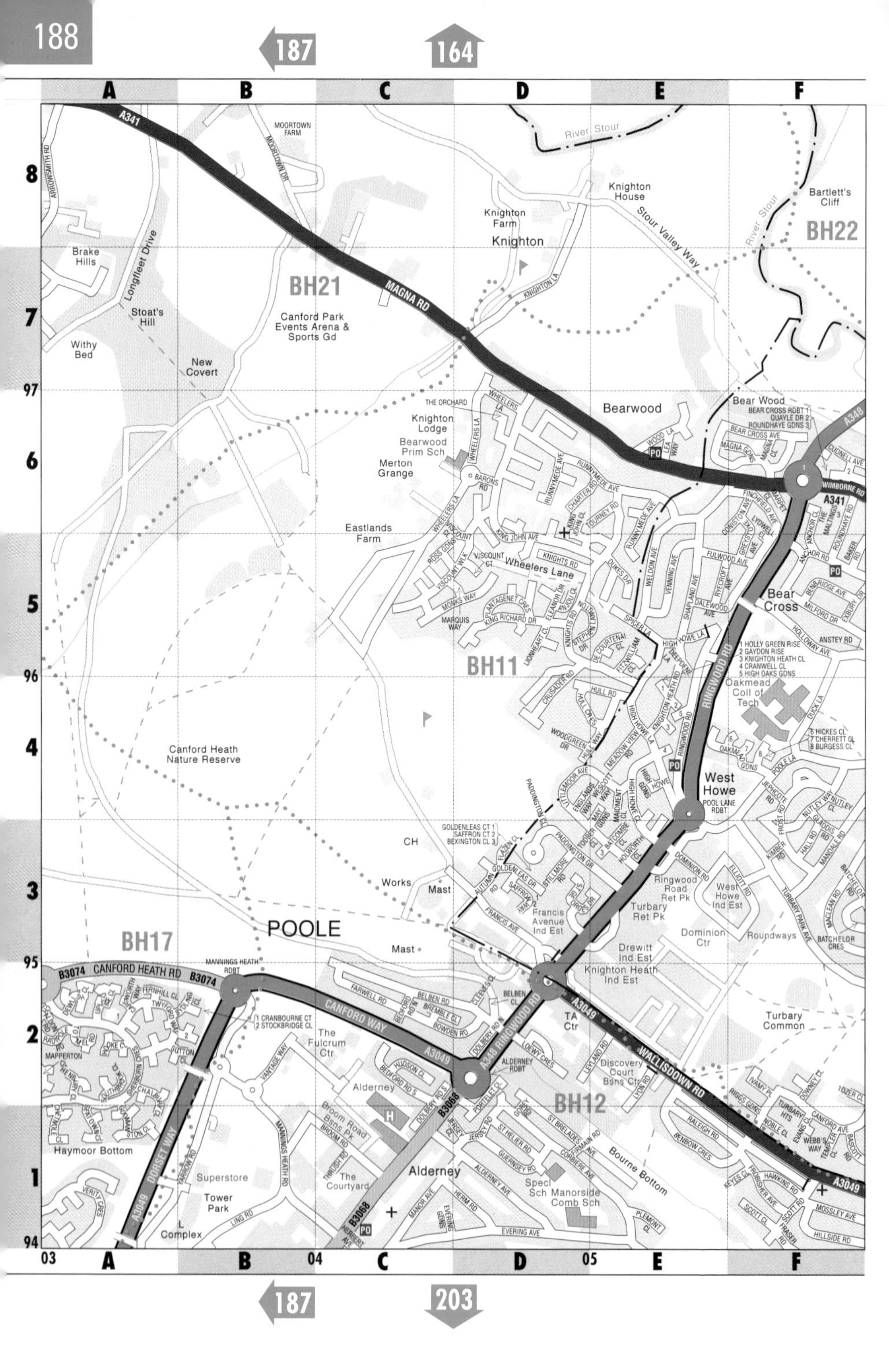
A341
MAGNA RD
BH21
BH22
BH11
BH17
BH12
POOLE
Knighton
Knighton House
Knighton Farm
Stour Valley Way
River Stour
Bartlett's Cliff
Brake Hills
Longfleet Drive
Stoat's Hill
Withy Bed
New Covert
Canford Park Events Arena & Sports Gd
Bearwood
Bear Wood
Knighton Lodge
Bearwood Prim Sch
Merton Grange
Eastlands Farm
Wheelers Lane
Bear Cross
Oakmead Coll of Tech
West Howe
Canford Heath Nature Reserve
CH
Works
Mast
Francis Avenue Ind Est
Ringwood Road Ret Pk
Turbary Ret Pk
West Howe Ind Est
Dominion Ctr
Roundways
Drewitt Ind Est
Knighton Heath Ind Est
Turbary Common
TA Ctr
Discovery Court Bsns Ctr
The Fulcrum Ctr
Alderney
Broom Road Bsns Pk
The Courtyard
Superstore
Tower Park
L Complex
Haymoor Bottom
Specl Sch
Manorside Comb Sch
Bourne Bottom
B3074 CANFORD HEATH RD
CANFORD WAY
A3049
WALLISDOWN RD
RINGWOOD RD
DORSET WAY
B3068
A348
WIMBORNE RD
POOL LANE RDBT
MANNINGS HEATH RDBT
ALDERNEY RDBT
BEAR CROSS RDBT

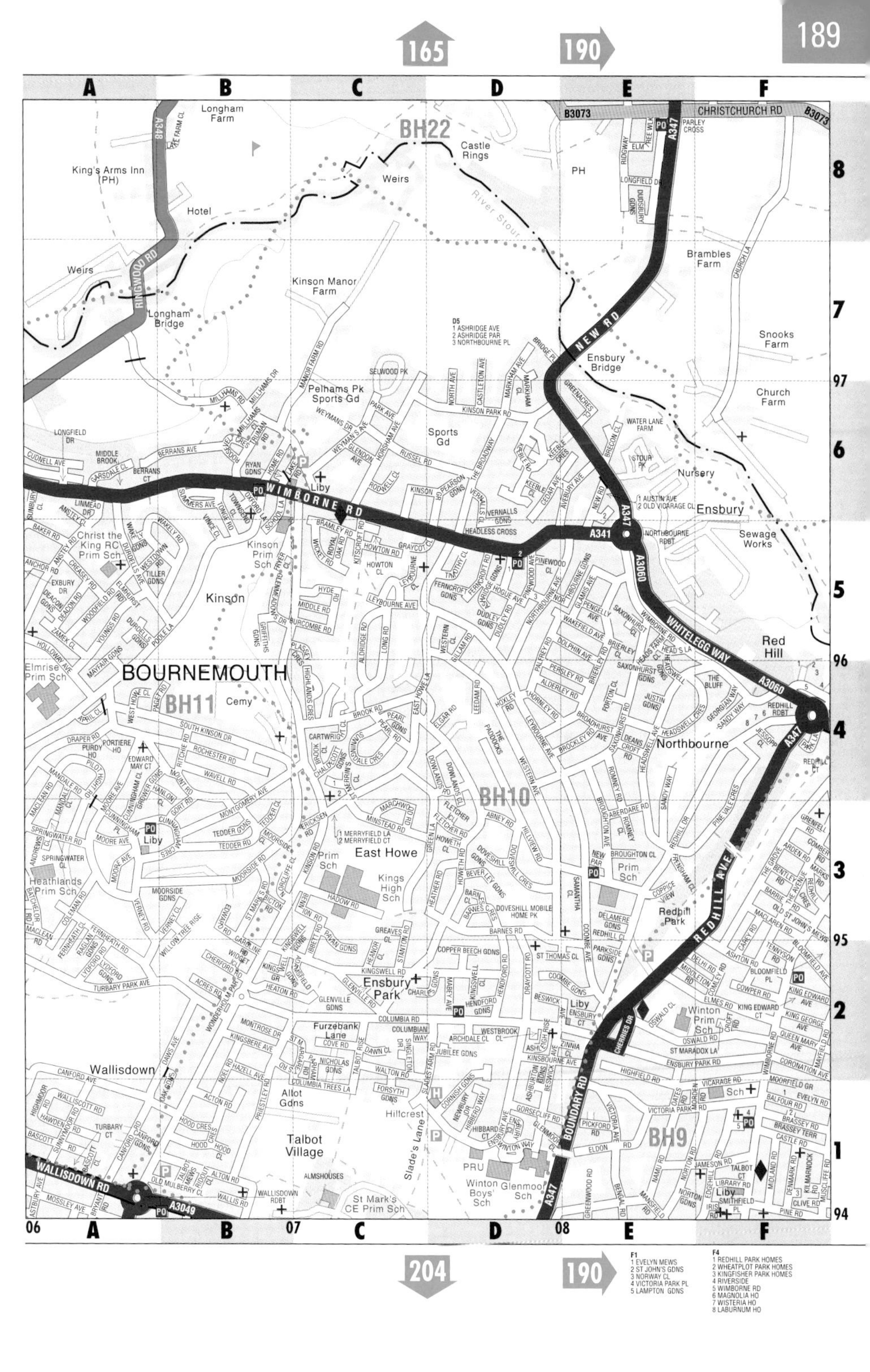

F1
1 EVELYN MEWS
2 ST JOHN'S GDNS
3 NORWAY CL
4 VICTORIA PARK PL
5 LAMPTON GDNS

F4
1 REDHILL PARK HOMES
2 WHEATPLOT PARK HOMES
3 KINGFISHER PARK HOMES
4 RIVERSIDE
5 WIMBORNE RD
6 MAGNOLIA HO
7 WISTERIA HO
8 LABURNUM HO

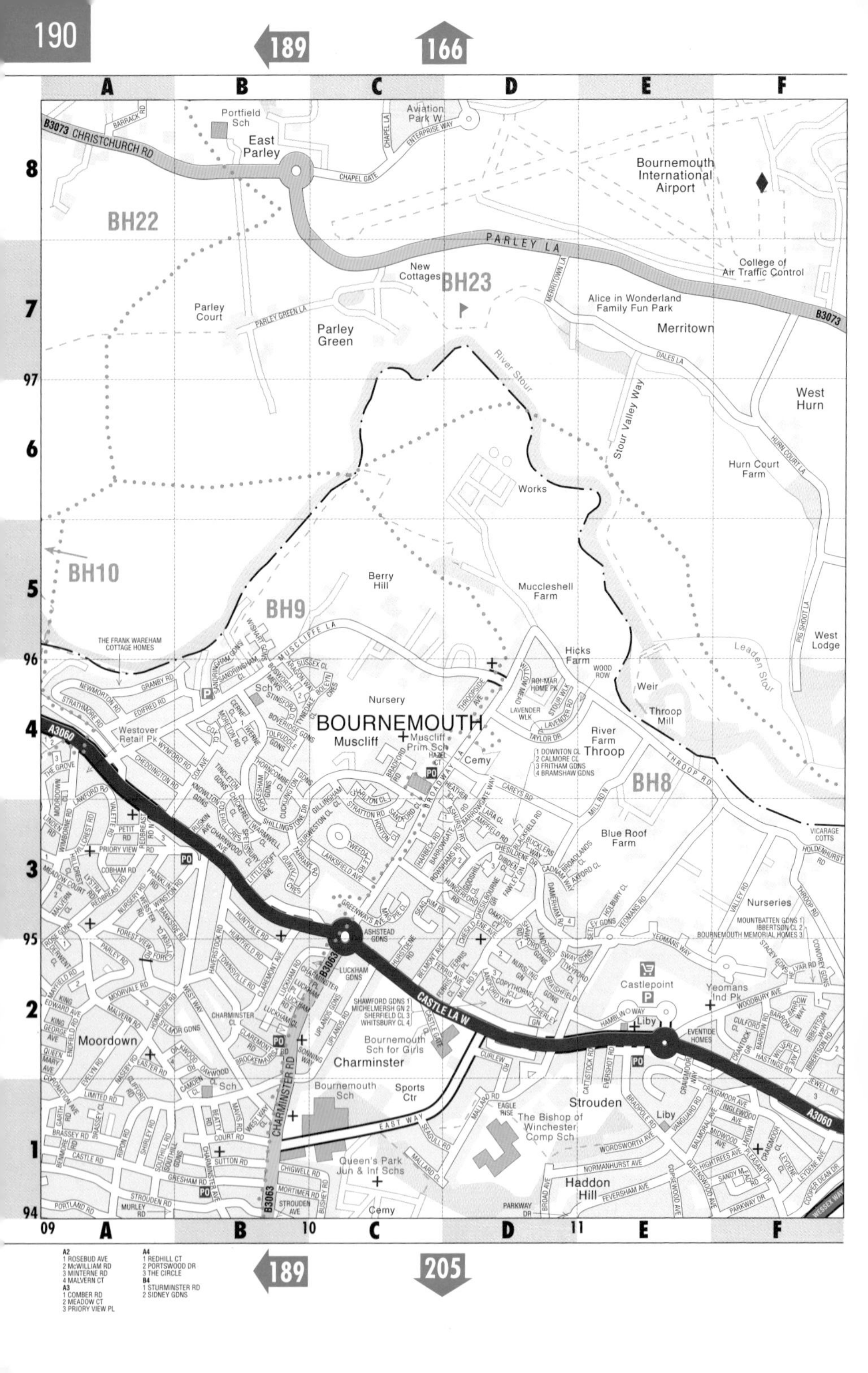
190
189
166
A
B
C
D
E
F
8
7
97
6
5
96
4
3
95
2
1
94
09
10
11
B3073 CHRISTCHURCH RD
BARRACK RD
Portfield Sch
East Parley
Aviation Park W
CHAPEL LA
ENTERPRISE WAY
CHAPEL GATE
Bournemouth International Airport
BH22
PARLEY LA
New Cottages
BH23
College of Air Traffic Control
MERRITOWN LA
Alice in Wonderland Family Fun Park
B3073
Parley Court
PARLEY GREEN LA
Parley Green
Merritown
DALES LA
River Stour
Stour Valley Way
West Hurn
HURN COURT LA
Hurn Court Farm
Works
BH10
Berry Hill
Muccleshell Farm
BH9
PIG SHOOT LA
West Lodge
THE FRANK WAREHAM COTTAGE HOMES
MUSCLIFFE LA
Hicks Farm
WOOD ROW
Leaden Stour
Weir
Throop Mill
Nursery
BOURNEMOUTH
Muscliff
Muscliff Prim Sch
Westover Retail Pk
A3060
Cemy
River Farm
Throop
THROOP RD
BH8
1 DOWNTON CL
2 CALMORE CL
3 FRITHAM GDNS
4 BRAMSHAW GDNS
BROADWAY LA
CAREYS RD
MILL RD N
Blue Roof Farm
VICARAGE COTTS
HOLDENHURST RD
Nurseries
MOUNTBATTEN GDNS 1
IBBERTSON CL 2
BOURNEMOUTH MEMORIAL HOMES 3
YEOMANS RD
YEOMANS WAY
Castlepoint
Yeomans Ind Pk
WOODBURY AVE
B3063
CASTLE LA W
SHAWFORD GDNS 1
MICHELMERSH GN 2
SHERFIELD CL 3
WHITSBURY CL 4
Bournemouth Sch for Girls
Charminster
Moordown
Liby
EVENTIDE HOMES
Bournemouth Sch
Sports Ctr
CHARMINSTER RD
EAST WAY
EAGLE RISE
The Bishop of Winchester Comp Sch
Strouden
Liby
A3060
Queen's Park Jun & Inf Schs
WORDSWORTH AVE
NORMANHURST AVE
Haddon Hill
FEVERSHAM AVE
Cemy
PARKWAY DR
WESSEX WAY
A
B
C
D
E
F
A2
1 ROSEBUD AVE
2 McWILLIAM RD
3 MINTERNE RD
4 MALVERN CT
A3
1 COMBER RD
2 MEADOW CT
3 PRIORY VIEW PL
A4
1 REDHILL CT
2 PORTSWOOD DR
3 THE CIRCLE
B4
1 STURMINSTER RD
2 SIDNEY GDNS
189
205

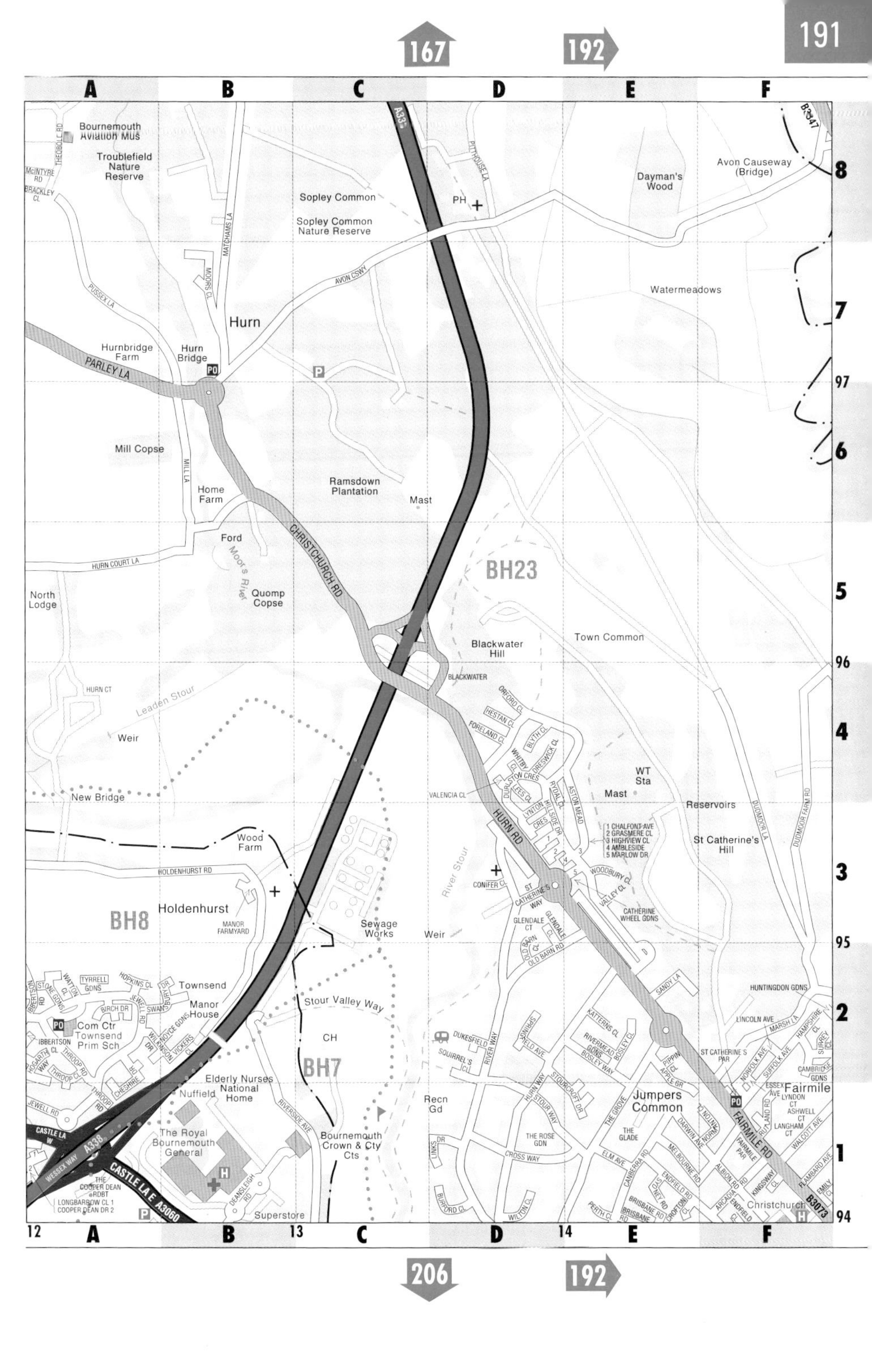
167
192
A
B
C
D
E
F
Bournemouth Aviation Mus
Troublefield Nature Reserve
Sopley Common
Sopley Common Nature Reserve
PH
Dayman's Wood
Avon Causeway (Bridge)
Watermeadows
Hurn
Hurnbridge Farm
Hurn Bridge
PARLEY LA
AVON CSWY
MATCHAMS LA
MOORS CL
PUSSEX LA
PITHOUSE LA
A338
B3347
Mill Copse
MILL LA
Home Farm
Ramsdown Plantation
Mast
Ford
Moors River
HURN COURT LA
CHRISTCHURCH RD
Quomp Copse
North Lodge
BH23
Blackwater Hill
Town Common
BLACKWATER
HURN CT
Leaden Stour
Weir
New Bridge
WT Sta
Mast
Reservoirs
St Catherine's Hill
HURN RD
VALENCIA CL
1 CHALFONT AVE
2 GRASMERE CL
3 HIGHVIEW CL
4 AMBLESIDE
5 MARLOW DR
Wood Farm
HOLDENHURST RD
Holdenhurst
BH8
MANOR FARMYARD
Sewage Works
Weir
River Stour
CONIFER CL
ST CATHERINE'S WAY
WOODBURY CL
VALLEY CL
CATHERINE WHEEL GDNS
GLENDALE CT
OLD BARN RD
SANDY LA
DUDMOOR LA
DUDMOOR FARM RD
HUNTINGDON GDNS
Townsend
Manor House
Stour Valley Way
Com Ctr
Townsend Prim Sch
CH
BH7
DUKESFIELD
SQUIRREL'S CL
RIVER WAY
LINCOLN AVE
ST CATHERINE'S PAR
Elderly Nurses National Home
Nuffield
Recn Gd
Jumpers Common
Fairmile
The Royal Bournemouth General
Bournemouth Crown & Cty Cts
THE ROSE GDN
CROSS WAY
THE GLADE
FAIRMILE RD
B3073
CASTLE LA W
WESSEX WAY
CASTLE LA E A3060
THE COOPER DEAN RDBT
LONGBARROW CL 1
COOPER DEAN DR 2
Superstore
Christchurch
8
7
97
6
5
96
4
3
95
2
1
94
12
13
14
206
192

191
168

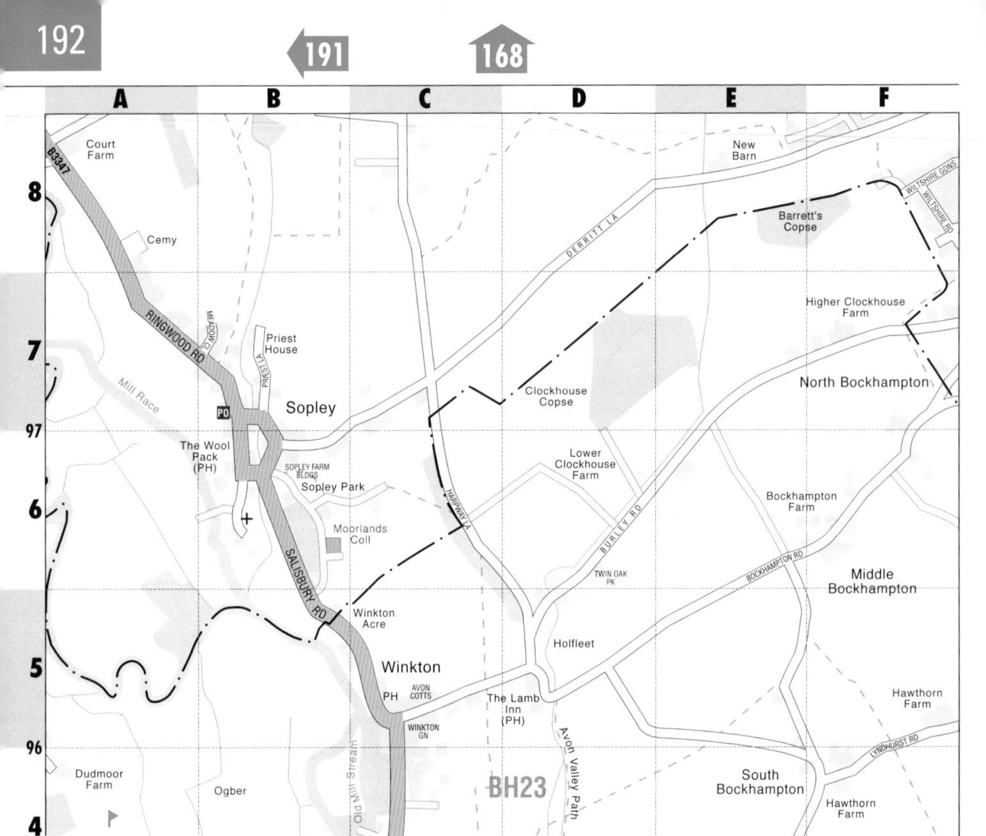
A
B
C
D
E
F
8
7
97
6
5
96
4
3
95
2
1
94
15
16
17
Court Farm
B3347
Cemy
RINGWOOD RD
MEADOW CL
Priest House
PRIEST LA
Mill Race
PO
Sopley
The Wool Pack (PH)
SOPLEY FARM BLDGS
Sopley Park
Moorlands Coll
SALISBURY RD
Winkton Acre
Winkton
PH
AVON COTTS
WINKTON GN
Old Mill Stream
Dudmoor Farm
Ogber
WINKTON HO
JOPPS CNR
New Barn
Barrett's Copse
WILTSHIRE GDNS
WILTSHIRE RD
DERRITT LA
Higher Clockhouse Farm
North Bockhampton
Clockhouse Copse
Lower Clockhouse Farm
HARPWAY LA
BURLEY RD
Bockhampton Farm
BOCKHAMPTON RD
TWIN OAK PK
Middle Bockhampton
Holfleet
The Lamb Inn (PH)
Avon Valley Path
BH23
Hawthorn Farm
LYNDHURST RD
South Bockhampton
Hawthorn Farm
HAWTHORN RD
Waterditch Farm
WATERDITCH RD
BURTONCROFT
MORLEY CL
Burton CE Prim Sch
River Avon
CHESTNUT WAY
KIRKHAM AVE
HARRISON CL
CAMPBELL RD
PARK CL
FARWELL CL
KATHERINE CHANCE CL
BURTON HALL
Coward's Marsh
Winkton Common
BIRCH AVE
AVON VIEW RD
AVON VIEW PAR
WINKTON CL
HEATHLANDS CL
BURTON HALL PL
THE LINDENS
PRESTON LA
REDCLIFFE CL
COWLEYS RD
PRIORY VIEW RD
MOORCROFT AVE
SALISBURY RD
VICARAGE WAY
SUMMERFIELD CL 1
BARLANDS CL 2
BURNHAM RD
PITTMORE RD
WOODSTOCK RD
VINNEYS CL
Burton Green Farm
HILL LA
MEADOW LA
FERN CL
CRABTREE CL
FOOTNERS LA
WHITEHAYES RD
THE GREEN
Burton
HUNTINGDON GDNS
SUFFOLK AVE
MARSH LA
STONY LA
WHITEHAYES CL
BODOWEN CL
BODOWEN RD
TREEBYS CL
HOLLY GDNS
SUMMERS LA
WALCOTT AVE
Works
FLAMBARD AVE
HAWORTH CL
WILDFELL CL
VILLETTE CL
BRONTE AVE
BRANWELL CL
EMILY CL
ANNE CL
CALKIN CL
QUEENSMEAD
RIMBURY WAY
MARTINS HILL CL
SHORTS CL
MARTINS HILL LA
ALDER CL
MEDLAR CL
GORDON WAY
BURTON HO
BURTON CL
Burton Farm
SANDY PLOT
B3347
PH
AMBURY LA

191
207

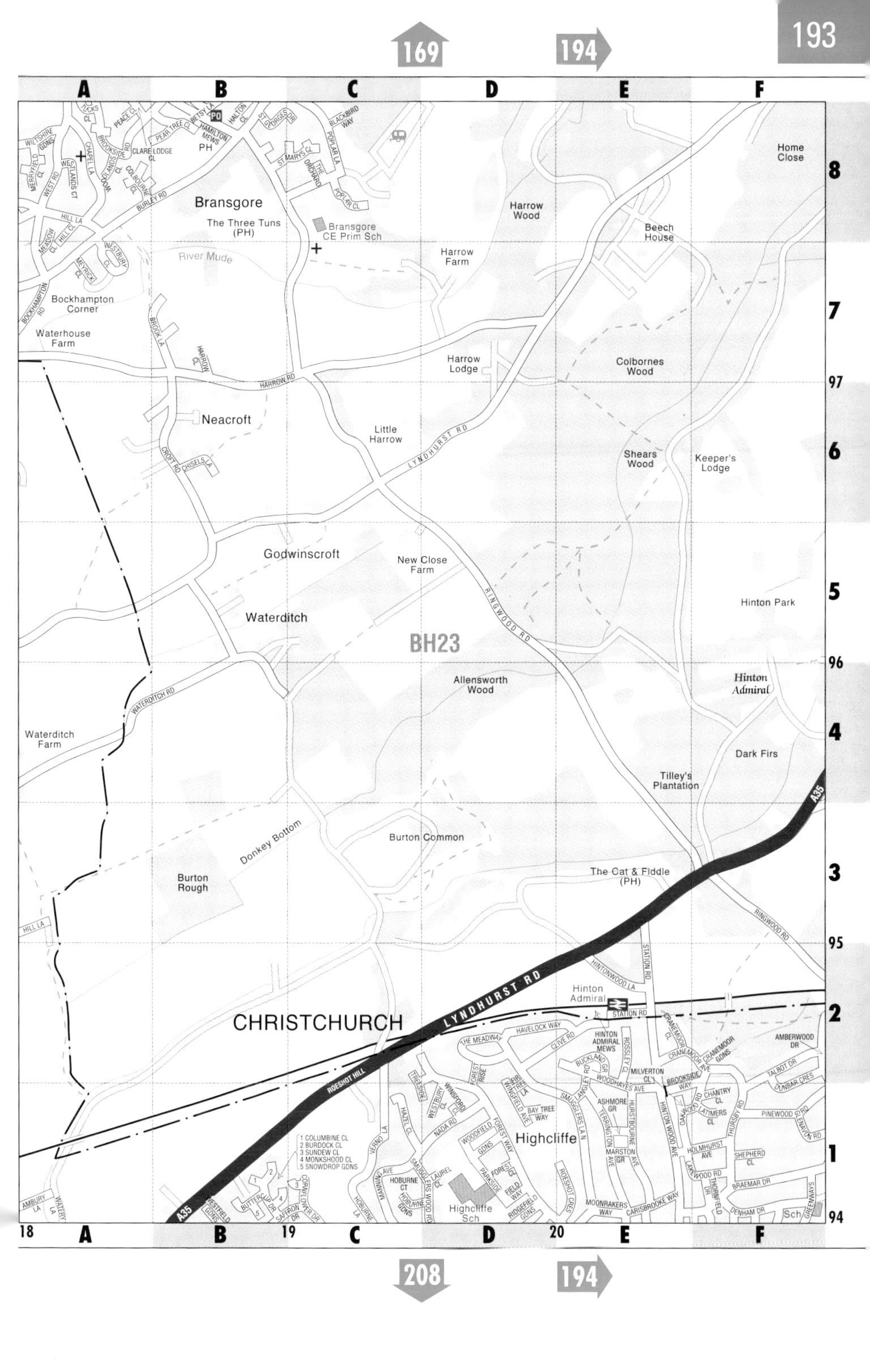
169
194
A
B
C
D
E
F
Bransgore
The Three Tuns (PH)
Bransgore CE Prim Sch
River Mude
Harrow Wood
Harrow Farm
Beech House
Home Close
Bockhampton Corner
Waterhouse Farm
Harrow Lodge
Colbornes Wood
HARROW RD
Neacroft
Little Harrow
LYNDHURST RD
Shears Wood
Keeper's Lodge
Godwinscroft
New Close Farm
Waterditch
BH23
RINGWOOD RD
Hinton Park
Allensworth Wood
Hinton Admiral
WATERDITCH RD
Waterditch Farm
Dark Firs
Tilley's Plantation
Burton Common
Donkey Bottom
Burton Rough
The Cat & Fiddle (PH)
A35
HILL LA
STATION RD
HINTONWOOD LA
Hinton Admiral
CHRISTCHURCH
LYNDHURST RD
ROESHOT HILL
Highcliffe
Highcliffe Sch
1 COLUMBINE CL
2 BURDOCK CL
3 SUNDEW CL
4 MONKSHOOD CL
5 SNOWDROP GDNS
8
7
97
6
5
96
4
3
95
2
1
94
18
19
20
208
194

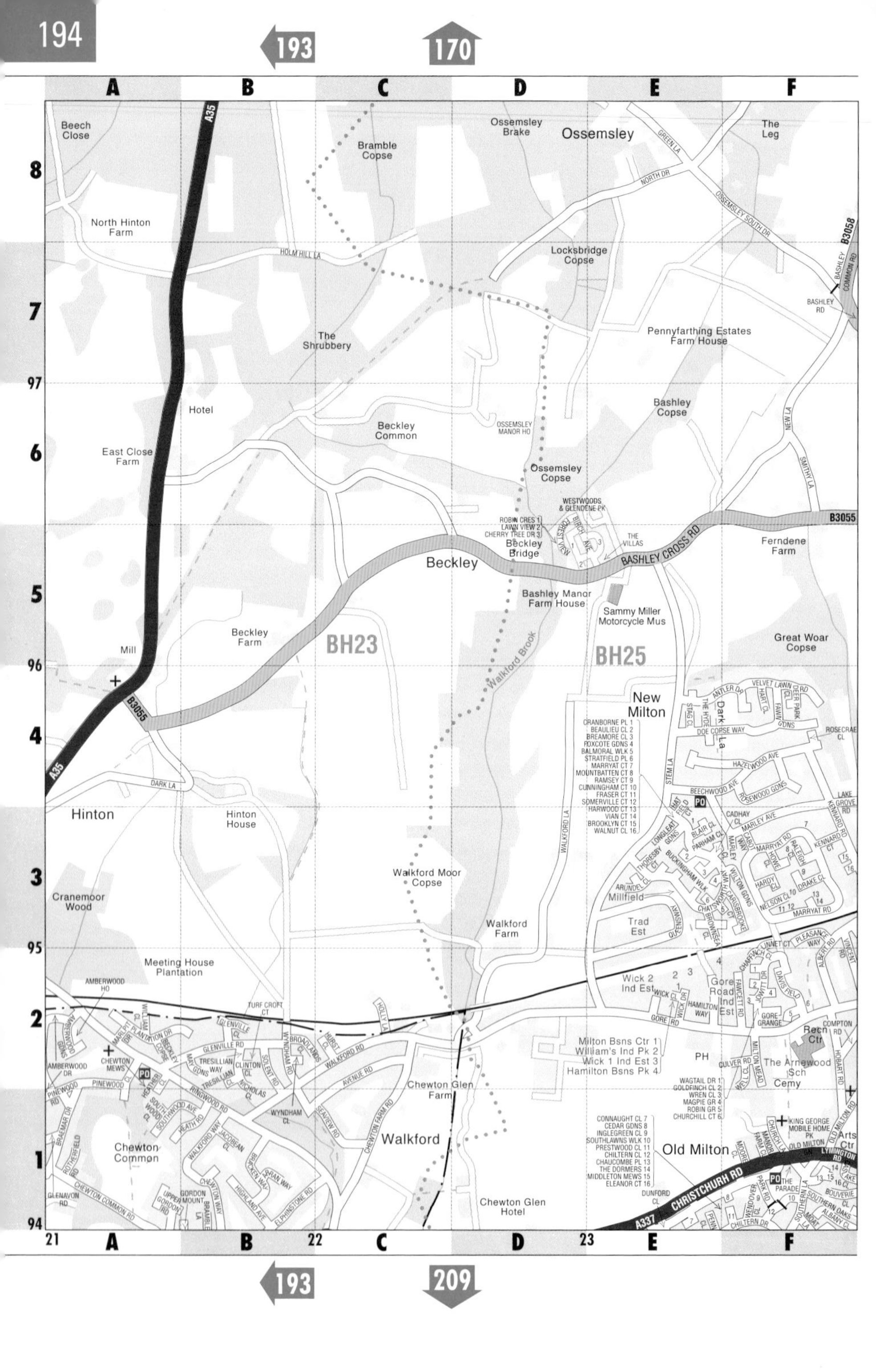
Beech Close
Bramble Copse
Ossemsley Brake
Ossemsley
The Leg
North Hinton Farm
HOLM HILL LA
Locksbridge Copse
NORTH DR
OSSEMSLEY SOUTH DR
GREEN LA
B3058
BASHLEY COMMON RD
BASHLEY RD
The Shrubbery
Pennyfarthing Estates Farm House
Hotel
Beckley Common
OSSEMSLEY MANOR HO
Bashley Copse
NEW LA
SMITHY LA
East Close Farm
Ossemsley Copse
WESTWOODS & GLENDENE PK
B3055
Ferndene Farm
Beckley Bridge
Beckley
BASHLEY CROSS RD
THE VILLAS
Bashley Manor Farm House
Sammy Miller Motorcycle Mus
Beckley Farm
BH23
BH25
Great Woar Copse
Mill
Walkford Brook
New Milton
A35
Hinton
Hinton House
DARK LA
Walkford Moor Copse
Cranemoor Wood
Walkford Farm
Millfield
Trad Est
Meeting House Plantation
Wick 2 Ind Est
Gore Road Ind Est
AMBERWOOD HO
Rech Ctr
The Arnewood Sch
Cemy
Chewton Glen Farm
Walkford
Old Milton
Chewton Common
Chewton Glen Hotel
CHRISTCHURCH RD
A337
LYMINGTON RD
Milton Bsns Ctr 1
William's Ind Pk 2
Wick 1 Ind Est 3
Hamilton Bsns Pk 4
CRANBORNE PL 1
BEAULIEU CL 2
BREAMORE CL 3
FOXCOTE GDNS 4
BALMORAL WLK 5
STRATFIELD PL 6
MARRYAT CT 7
MOUNTBATTEN CT 8
RAMSEY CT 9
CUNNINGHAM CT 10
FRASER CT 11
SOMERVILLE CT 12
HARWOOD CT 13
VIAN CT 14
BROOKLYN CT 15
WALNUT CL 16
WAGTAIL DR 1
GOLDFINCH CL 2
WREN CL 3
MAGPIE GR 4
ROBIN GR 5
CHURCHILL CT 6
CONNAUGHT CL 7
CEDAR GDNS 8
INGLEGREEN CL 9
SOUTHLAWNS WLK 10
PRESTWOOD CL 11
CHILTERN CL 12
CHAUCOMBE PL 13
THE DORMERS 14
MIDDLETON MEWS 15
ELEANOR CT 16
ROBIN CRES 1
LAWN VIEW 2
CHERRY TREE DR 3
A B C D E F
8 7 6 5 4 3 2 1
97 96 95 94
21 22 23

A B C D E F

8
7
97
6
5
96
4
3
95
2
1
94

Bashley
B3058
Marlpit Farm
Marlpit La
Wootton
St John's Rd
Bashley Park
Fball Gd
PO
Danelea
Tiptoe Prim Sch
PO
Tiptoe
Marley Mount
Middle Rd
Broadley House
Arnewood Common
Deemster Farm
Crabbswood Farm
Crabbswood La
Vale View Pk
Brockhills Farm
Northover La
Oak Farm
The Plough (PH)
Arnewood Bridge Rd
B3055
Meadow Farm
Danestream Farm
Sway Rd
Danebury Farm
Tiptoe Farm
Fernhill Gate
Bashley Cross Rd
Kamptee Copse
Woodlands Way
Harris Badgers Copse
Stanley Pk (CVN & Chalet Site)
Stanley's Copse
Drkes Stream
Taggs La
Hordle Grange
BH25
Vaggs Farm
SO41
Ballard Coll
Ballard Sch
Duplock Ho 10
Pine Ho 11
Lake-View Manor Rd
Lake Grove Rd
PO
Meadow Rd
Pennywell Gdns
1 Summertrees Ct
2 Dinham Ct
3 Blackthorn Way
4 Coppice Cl
Golden Hill Farm
Wellingtonia Gdns
Penny's Cnr
Silver St
Three Bells (PH)
PO
Ashley La
Fernhill La
New Milton
Kelsall Gdns
Park View Mews
Park View Gate
Avenue Rd
Ashley Inf Sch
Lavender Farm
Westmoreland Ct
Hordle
Wisbech Way
Ashley Jun Sch
Ashley
Noah's Ark Farm
Golden Hill
Liby
Parkland
Stannington Ct
Superstore
New Milton Schs
A337
Cemy
Spring La
Autumn Copse
Glen Spr
Peter's Farm
White Croft
Breakhill Copse
Sand and Gravel Pit
Lymington Rd
Hooper's Hill
A337
Ashley Manor Farm
Angel La
B3058
24 A 25 B C 26 D E F

210 196

A1
1 KEATS HO
2 SHENSTONE CT
3 CLIFTON CT
4 WINSTON CT
5 SOLENT LO
6 WINSTON PAR
7 BOUVERIE CL
8 EDMUNDS CL
9 BARTON COURT AVE
10 SPINDLEWOOD CL

9 SHELLEY HO
10 BYRON HO
A7
1 VINCENT RD
2 CHARLOTTE CT
3 DANESTEAD HO
4 ELM CT
5 CASSELLES CT
6 HOMEFIELD HO
8 ELIOT HO

A3
1 HEATHER LO
2 RUSSELL CT
3 DANESTEAD HO
4 OSBOURNE HO
5 HOMEHILL HO
6 MALLARD BLDGS
7 RICHMOND CT

8 PEGASUS CT
9 BEAU CT
B1
1 HAZEL CT
2 ST DENYS
3 DUDLEY PL
4 CHERRY TREE CT
5 YEW TREE CT
6 GREENWOODS

R2
1 SPENCER CT
2 ORCHARD LEIGH
3 CORNERWAYS CT
4 JACMAR CT
5 ASHLEY ARNEWOOD CT
6 YEOMANS LODGE
7 WESTCROFT PAR
8 ELIZABETH CT
9 WAVERLEY HO

B3
1 TANGLEWOOD CT
2 ALVANDI GDNS
3 ASHTON CT
4 MORANT CT
5 TREVONE
6 FREMINGTON CT
7 YORK PL
8 FAIRCOURT
9 MERLEWOOD CT

B3
10 CONWAY CT
11 STIRLING CT

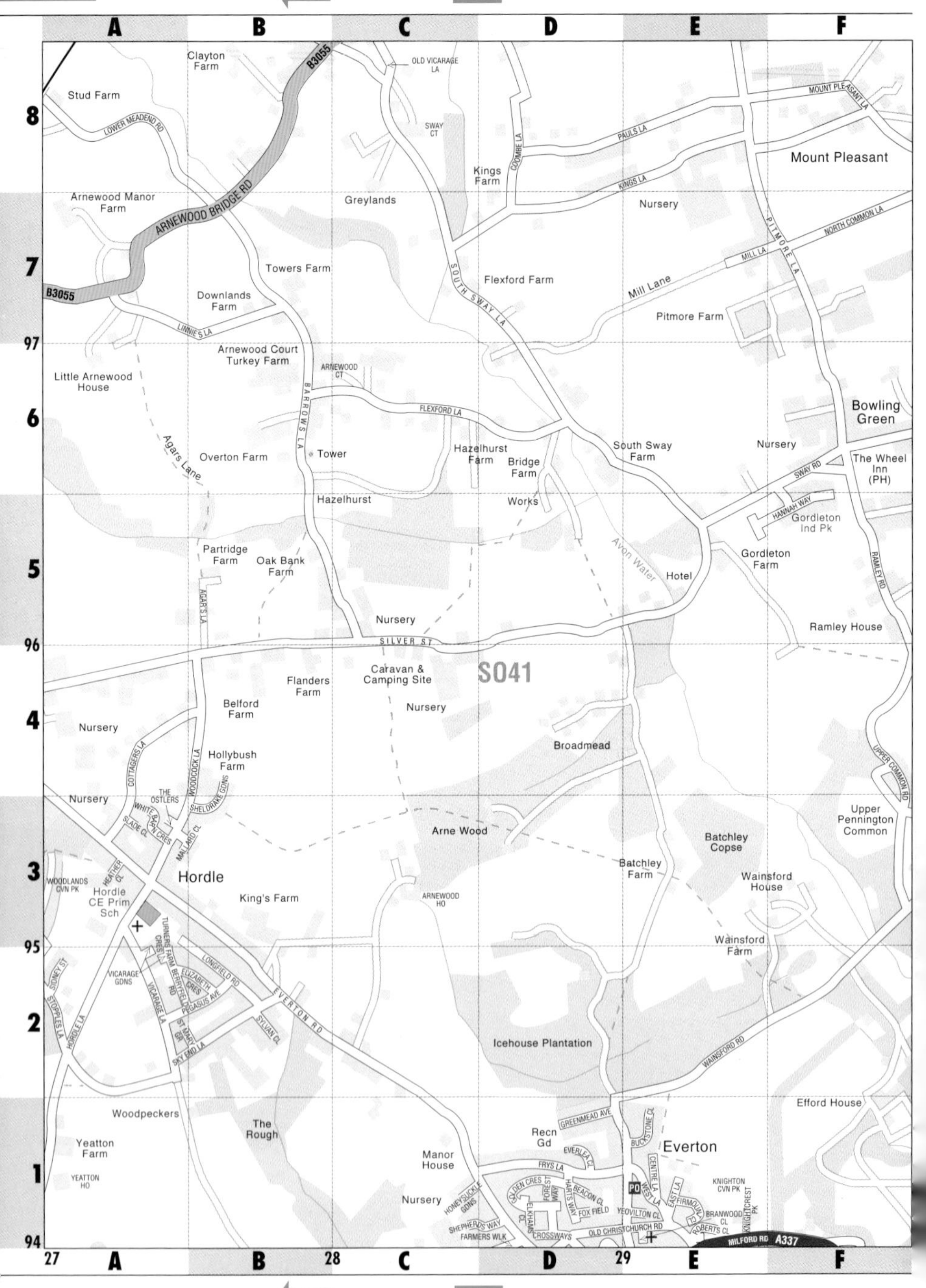
Clayton Farm
Stud Farm
B3055
LOWER MEADEND RD
OLD VICARAGE LA
SWAY CT
MOUNT PLEASANT LA
PAULS LA
Mount Pleasant
Kings Farm
COOMBE LA
KINGS LA
Arnewood Manor Farm
ARNEWOOD BRIDGE RD
Greylands
Nursery
PITMORE LA
NORTH COMMON LA
MILL LA
Towers Farm
SOUTH SWAY LA
Flexford Farm
Mill Lane
Downlands Farm
LINNIES LA
Pitmore Farm
Arnewood Court Turkey Farm
ARNEWOOD CT
Little Arnewood House
BARROWS LA
FLEXFORD LA
Bowling Green
Agars Lane
Overton Farm
Tower
Hazelhurst Farm
Bridge Farm
South Sway Farm
Nursery
The Wheel Inn (PH)
SWAY RD
Hazelhurst
Works
HANNAH WAY
Gordleton Ind Pk
Partridge Farm
Oak Bank Farm
Avon Water
Gordleton Farm
Hotel
RAMLEY RD
AGAR'S LA
Nursery
Ramley House
SILVER ST
Caravan & Camping Site
Flanders Farm
SO41
Belford Farm
Nursery
Nursery
Hollybush Farm
Broadmead
COTTAGERS LA
WOODCOCK LA
UPPER COMMON RD
Nursery
THE OSTLERS
SHELDRAKE GDNS
WHITE BARN CRES
SLADE CL
MALLARD CL
Arne Wood
Upper Pennington Common
Batchley Copse
WOODLANDS CVN PK
HEATHER CL
Hordle
Batchley Farm
Wainsford House
Hordle CE Prim Sch
King's Farm
ARNEWOOD HO
TURNERS FARM CRES
Wainsford Farm
SIDNEY ST
VICARAGE GDNS
BERRYFIELD RD
ELIZABETH CRES
LONGFIELD RD
PEGASUS AVE
EVERTON RD
STOPPLES LA
HORDLE LA
VICARAGE LA
ST MARYS GR
SYLVAN CL
SKY END LA
Icehouse Plantation
WAINSFORD RD
Woodpeckers
Efford House
GREENMEAD AVE
The Rough
Recn Gd
BUCKSTONE CL
Yeatton Farm
Manor House
EVERLEA CL
Everton
YEATTON HO
FRYS LA
CENTRE LA
KNIGHTON CVN PK
GOLDEN CRES
FOREST WAY
HARTS WAY
BEACON CL
PO
WEST LA
EAST LA
FIRMOUNT CL
KNIGHTCREST PK
Nursery
HONEYSUCKLE GDNS
ELKHAMS CL
FOX FIELD
YEOVILTON CL
BRANWOOD CL
SHEPHERDS WAY
CROSSWAYS
OLD CHRISTCHURCH RD
ROBERTS CL
FARMERS WLK
MILFORD RD
A337
A B C D E F
8 7 97 6 5 96 4 3 95 2 1 94
27 28 29

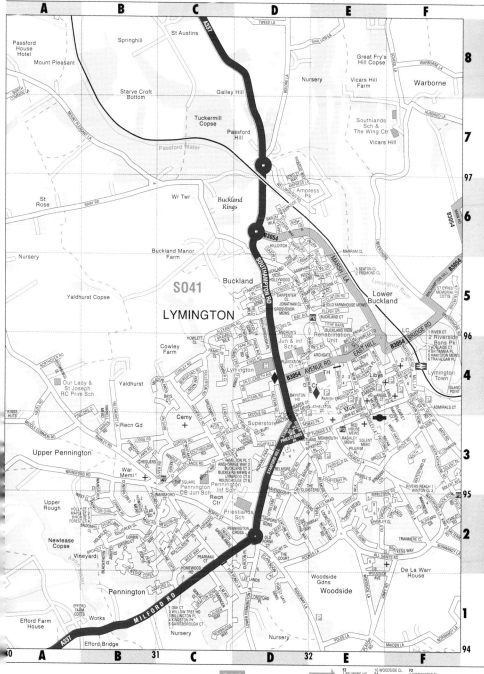

A B C D E F

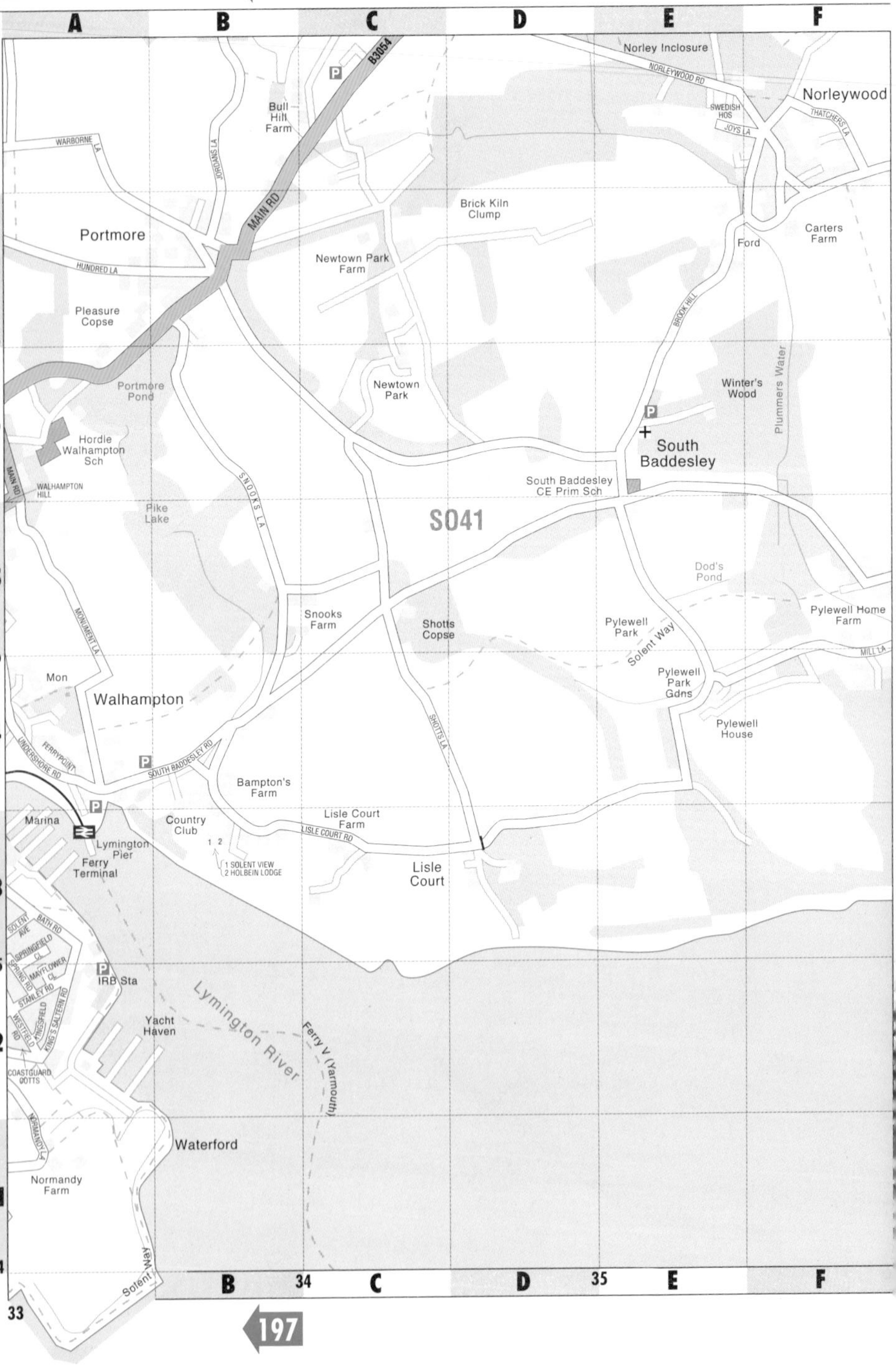

8
B3054
Norley Inclosure
NORLEYWOOD RD
Bull Hill Farm
SWEDISH HOS
JOYS LA
THATCHERS LA
Norleywood

Brick Kiln Clump

7
WARBORNE LA
Portmore
HUNDRED LA
MAIN RD
Newtown Park Farm
Ford
Carters Farm

97
Pleasure Copse

6
Portmore Pond
SNOOKS LA
Newtown Park
Winter's Wood
Plummers Water
P
+ South Baddesley
Hordle Walhampton Sch
WALHAMPTON HILL
MAIN RD
Pike Lake
South Baddesley CE Prim Sch

SO41

5
MONUMENT LA
Snooks Farm
Shotts Copse
Pylewell Park
Dod's Pond
Solent Way
Pylewell Home Farm
MILL LA

96
Mon
Walhampton
Pylewell Park Gdns
Pylewell House

4
FERRYPOINT
UNDERSHORE RD
P
SOUTH BADDESLEY RD
Bampton's Farm
SHOTTS LA
Lisle Court Farm
LISLE COURT RD

Marina
P
Lymington Pier
Ferry Terminal
Country Club
1 2
1 SOLENT VIEW
2 HOLBEIN LODGE
Lisle Court

3
COLLOT AVE
BATH RD
SPRINGFIELD
MAYFLOWER
STANLEY RD
ROSSFIELD
P IRB Sta

95
Yacht Haven

2
COASTGUARD COTTS
Lymington River
Ferry (Yarmouth)

1
Normandy Farm
Waterford

94
SOLENT WAY

33
B 34 C D 35 E F

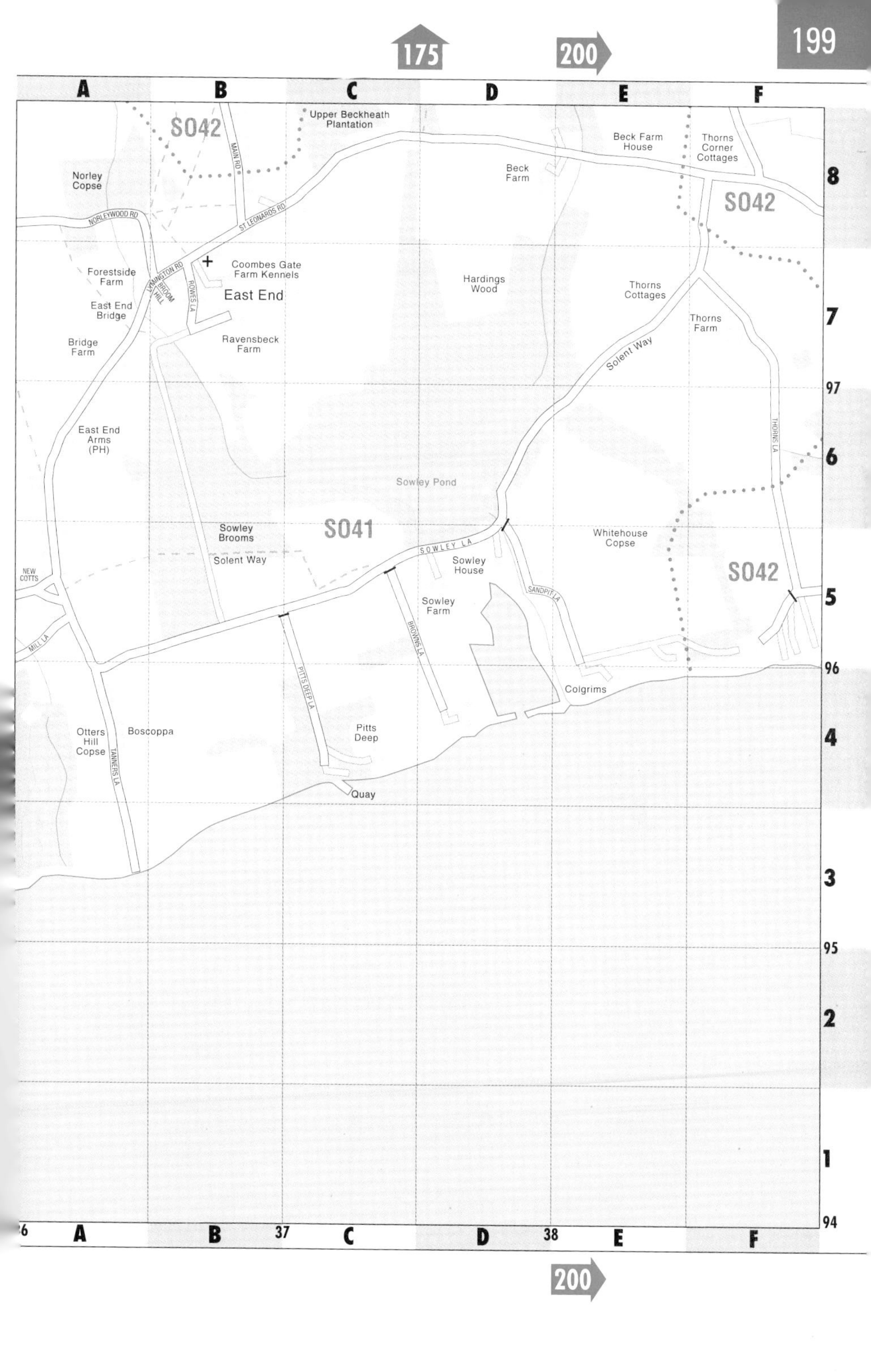
175
200
A
B
C
D
E
F
SO42
Upper Beckheath Plantation
MAIN RD
Norley Copse
NORLEYWOOD RD
ST LEONARDS RD
Beck Farm House
Thorns Corner Cottages
Beck Farm
8
SO42
Forestside Farm
LYMINGTON RD
BROOM HILL
ROWES LA
Coombes Gate Farm Kennels
East End
Hardings Wood
Thorns Cottages
East End Bridge
7
Thorns Farm
Bridge Farm
Ravensbeck Farm
Solent Way
97
East End Arms (PH)
THORNS LA
6
Sowley Pond
Sowley Brooms
SO41
Whitehouse Copse
SOWLEY LA
Sowley House
NEW COTTS
Solent Way
SO42
SANDPIT LA
Sowley Farm
5
MILL LA
BROWNS LA
PITTS DEEP LA
96
Colgrims
Otters Hill Copse
Boscoppa
Pitts Deep
4
TANNERS LA
Quay
3
95
2
1
94
36
37
38
200

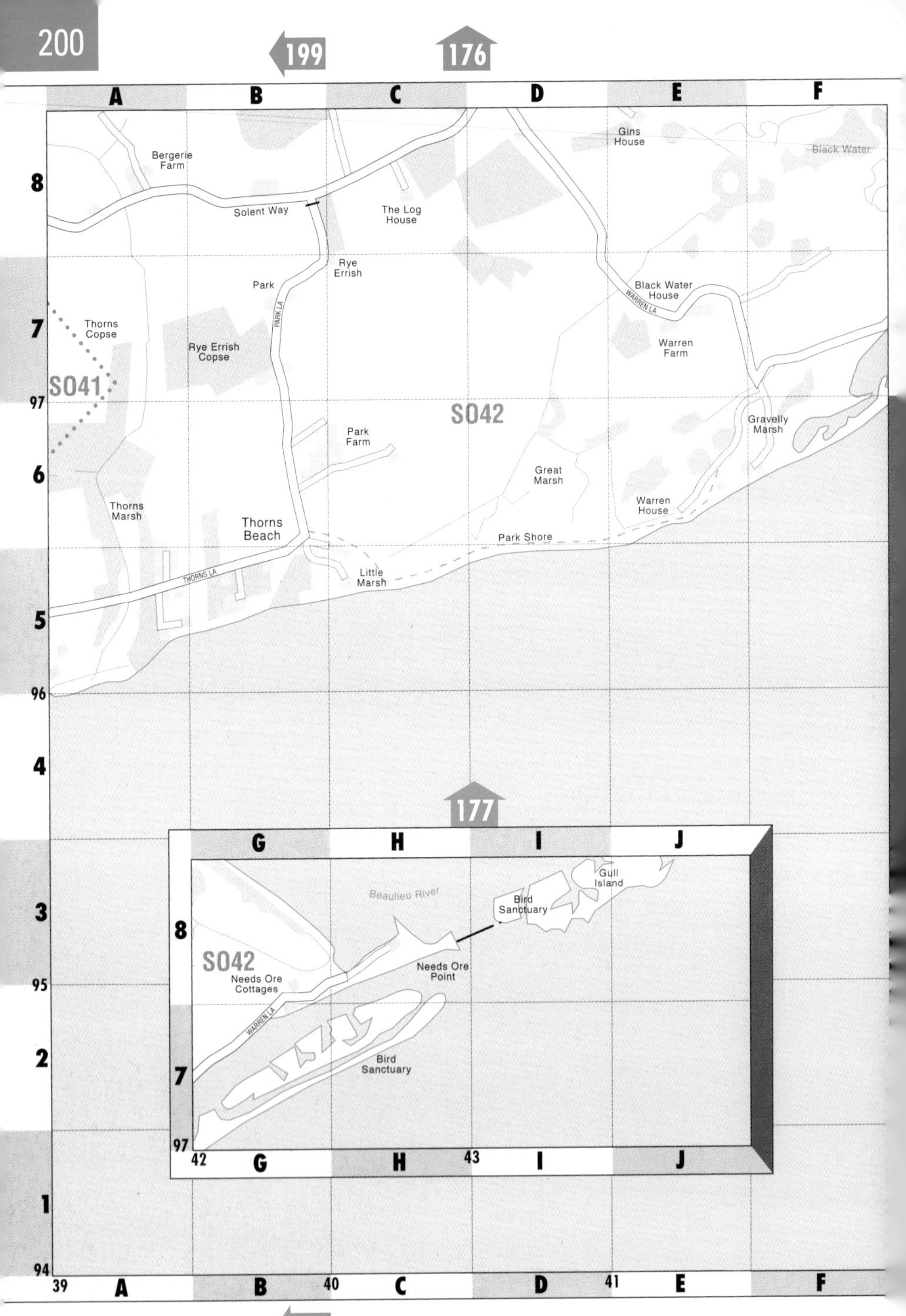

A   B   C   D   E   F

8

Bergerie
Farm

Gins
House

Black Water

Solent Way

The Log
House

Rye
Errish

Park

7

Thorns
Copse

Rye Errish
Copse

Black Water
House

WARREN LA

Warren
Farm

SO41

97

SO42

Gravelly
Marsh

6

Park
Farm

Great
Marsh

Warren
House

Thorns
Marsh

Thorns
Beach

Park Shore

Little
Marsh

THORNS LA

5

96

4

G   H   I   J

Gull
Island

Beaulieu River

Bird
Sanctuary

3

8

SO42

95

Needs Ore
Cottages

Needs Ore
Point

WARREN LA

2

7

Bird
Sanctuary

97

42   G   H   43   I   J

1

94

39   A   B   40   C   D   41   E   F

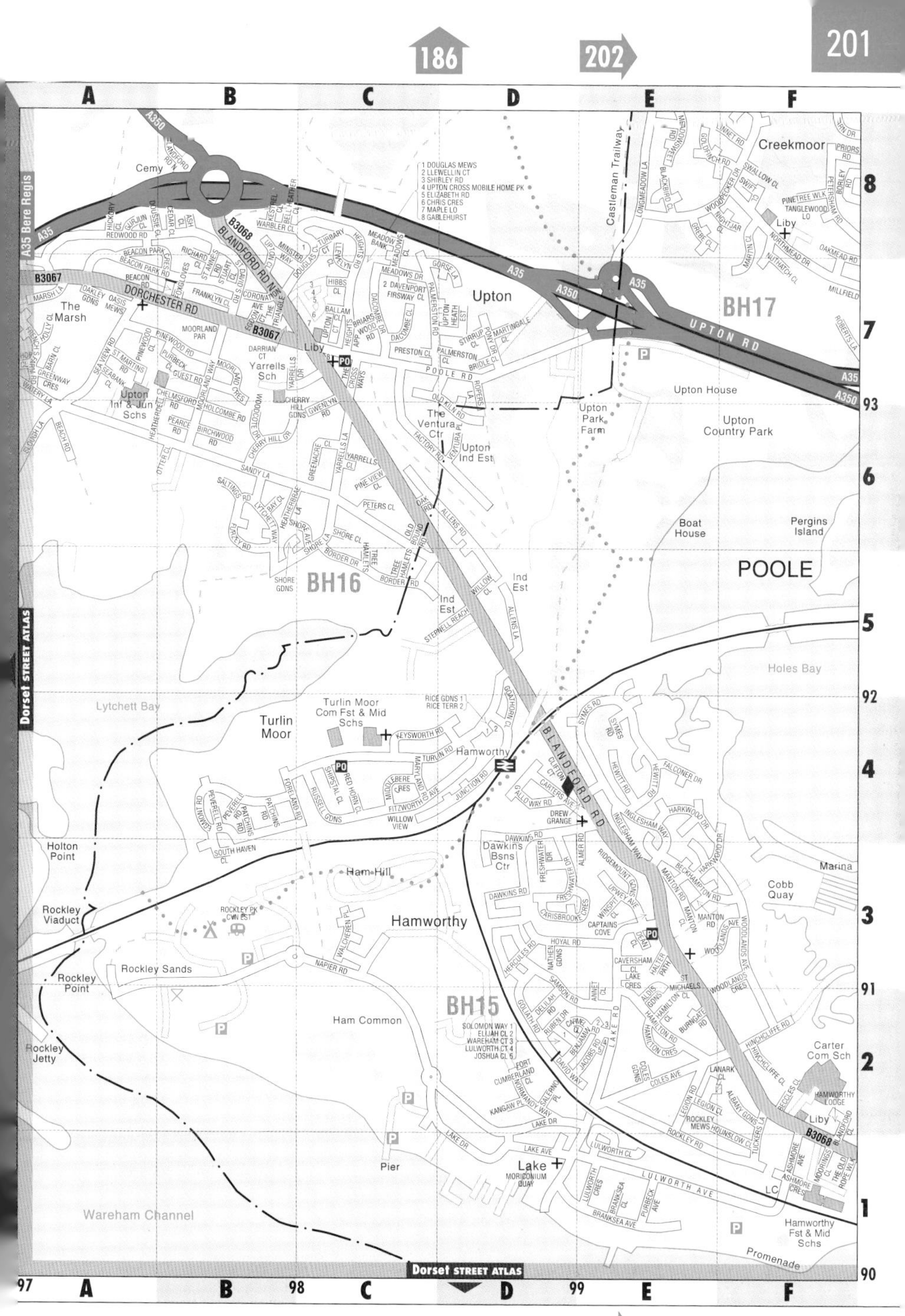

1 DOUGLAS MEWS
2 LLEWELLIN CT
3 SHIRLEY RD
4 UPTON CROSS MOBILE HOME PK
5 ELIZABETH RD
6 CHRIS CRES
7 MAPLE LO
8 GARLEHURST

Creekmoor

Upton

BH17

Upton House

Upton Park Farm

Upton Country Park

POOLE

Boat House

Pergins Island

Holes Bay

BH16

The Marsh

Upton Inf & Jun Schs

Yarrells Sch

The Ventura Ctr

Upton Ind Est

Lytchett Bay

Turlin Moor

Turlin Moor Com Fst & Mid Schs

RICE GDNS 1
RICE TERR 2

Ind Est

Ind Est

Hamworthy

BLANDFORD RD

Holton Point

Ham Hill

Dawkins Bsns Ctr

Marina

Cobb Quay

Rockley Viaduct

ROCKLEY PK C W FST

Hamworthy

DREW GRANGE

Captains Cove

Rockley Point

Rockley Sands

Napier Rd

Ham Common

BH15

SOLOMON WAY 1
ELIJAH CL 2
WAREHAM CT 3
LULWORTH CL 4
JOSHUA CL 5

Lanark

Carter Com Sch

Rockley Jetty

Pier

Lake

MORICONIUM DGW

Hamworthy Lodge

B3068

LC

Wareham Channel

Hamworthy Fst & Mid Schs

Promenade

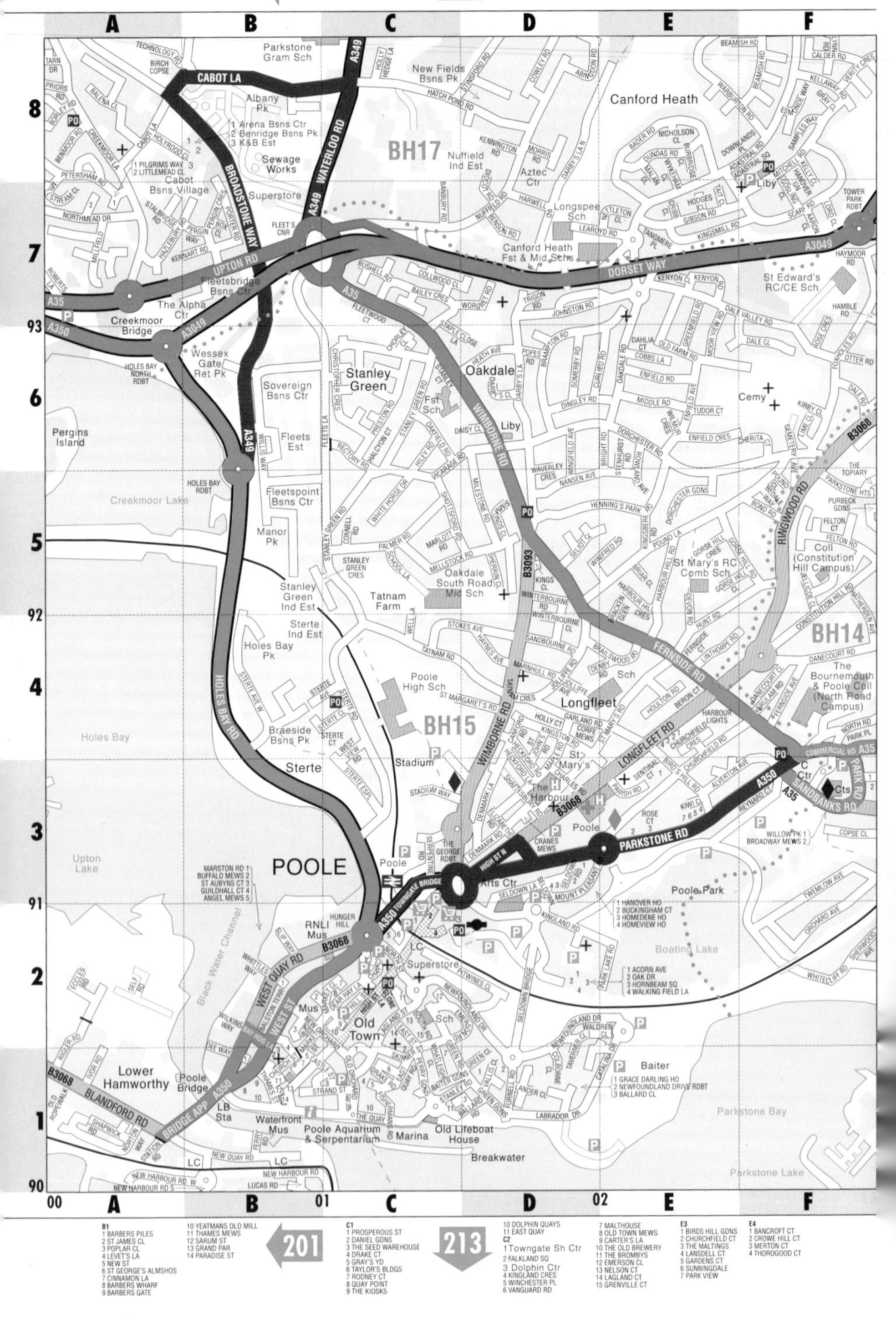

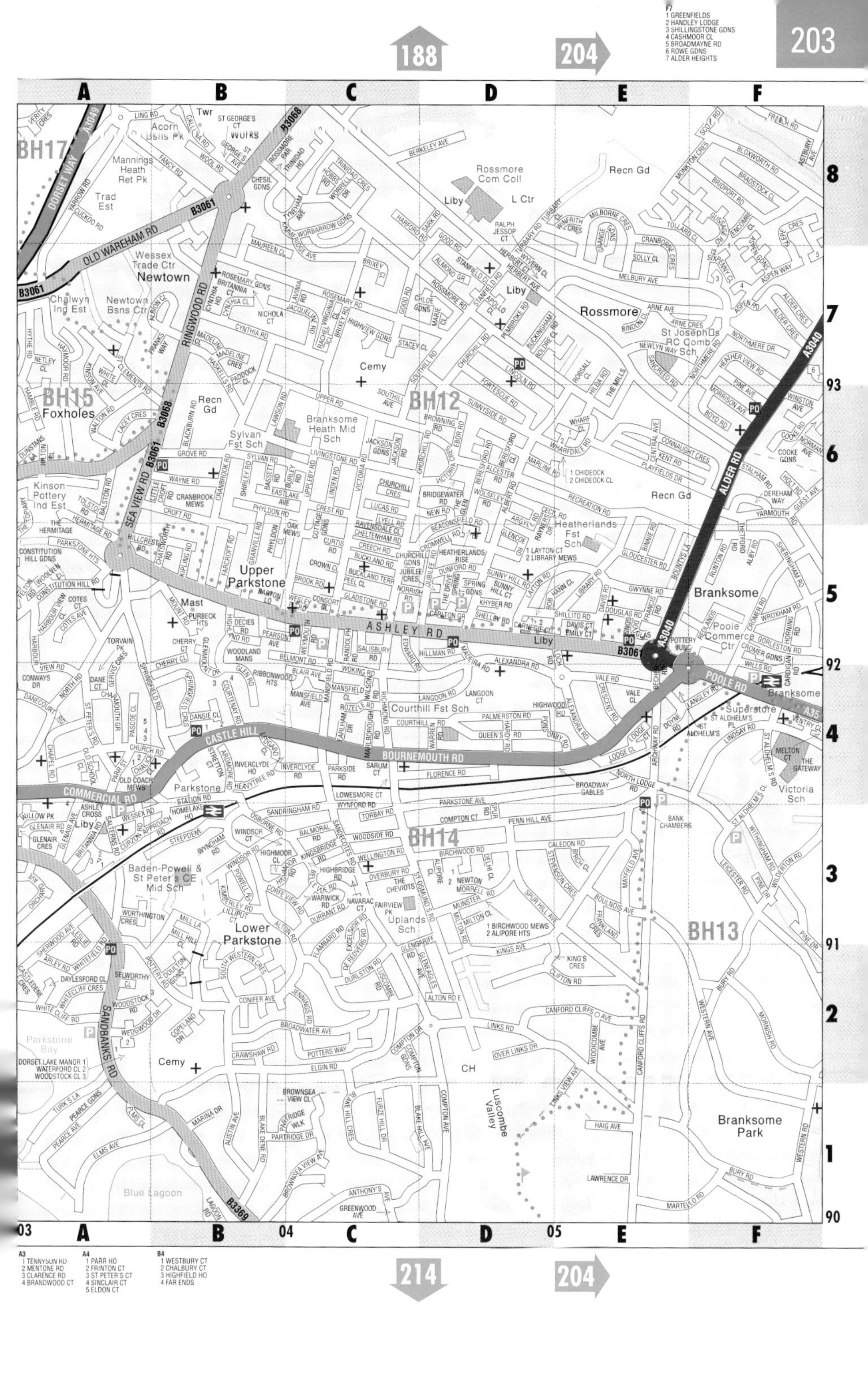
203
188
204
F7
1 GREENFIELDS
2 HANDLEY LODGE
3 SHILLINGSTONE GDNS
4 CASHMOOR CL
5 BROADMAYNE RD
6 ROWE GDNS
7 ALDER HEIGHTS
A
B
C
D
E
F
8
7
93
6
5
92
4
3
91
2
1
90
03
04
05
BH17
BH15
BH12
BH14
BH13
Acorn Bsns Pk
Manning's Heath Ret Pk
Trad Est
Wessex Trade Ctr
Newtown
Chalwyn Ind Est
Newtown Bsns Ctr
Foxholes
Kinson Pottery Ind Est
Rossmore Com Coll
Liby
L Ctr
Recn Gd
Rossmore
St Joseph's RC Comb Sch
Cemy
Branksome Heath Mid Sch
Sylvan Fst Sch
Upper Parkstone
Mast
Heatherlands Fst Sch
Branksome
Poole Commerce Ctr
Superstore
Victoria Sch
Courthill Fst Sch
Parkstone
Baden-Powell & St Peter's CE Mid Sch
Lower Parkstone
Uplands Sch
Parkstone Bay
Blue Lagoon
Luscombe Valley
Branksome Park
CH
DORSET WAY
A3049
B3061
B3068
OLD WAREHAM RD
RINGWOOD RD
SEA VIEW RD
ASHLEY RD
CASTLE HILL
BOURNEMOUTH RD
COMMERCIAL RD
SANDBANKS RD
B3369
ALDER RD
A3040
POOLE RD
A35
CANFORD CLIFFS RD
WESTERN AVE
PENN HILL AVE
ALEXANDRA RD
CONSTITUTION HILL RD
214
204
A3
1 TENNYSON RD
2 MENTONE RD
3 CLARENCE RD
4 BRANDWOOD CT
A4
1 PARR HO
2 FRINTON CT
3 ST PETER'S CT
4 SINCLAIR CT
5 ELDON CT
B4
1 WESTBURY CT
2 CHALBURY CT
3 HIGHFIELD HO
4 FAR ENDS

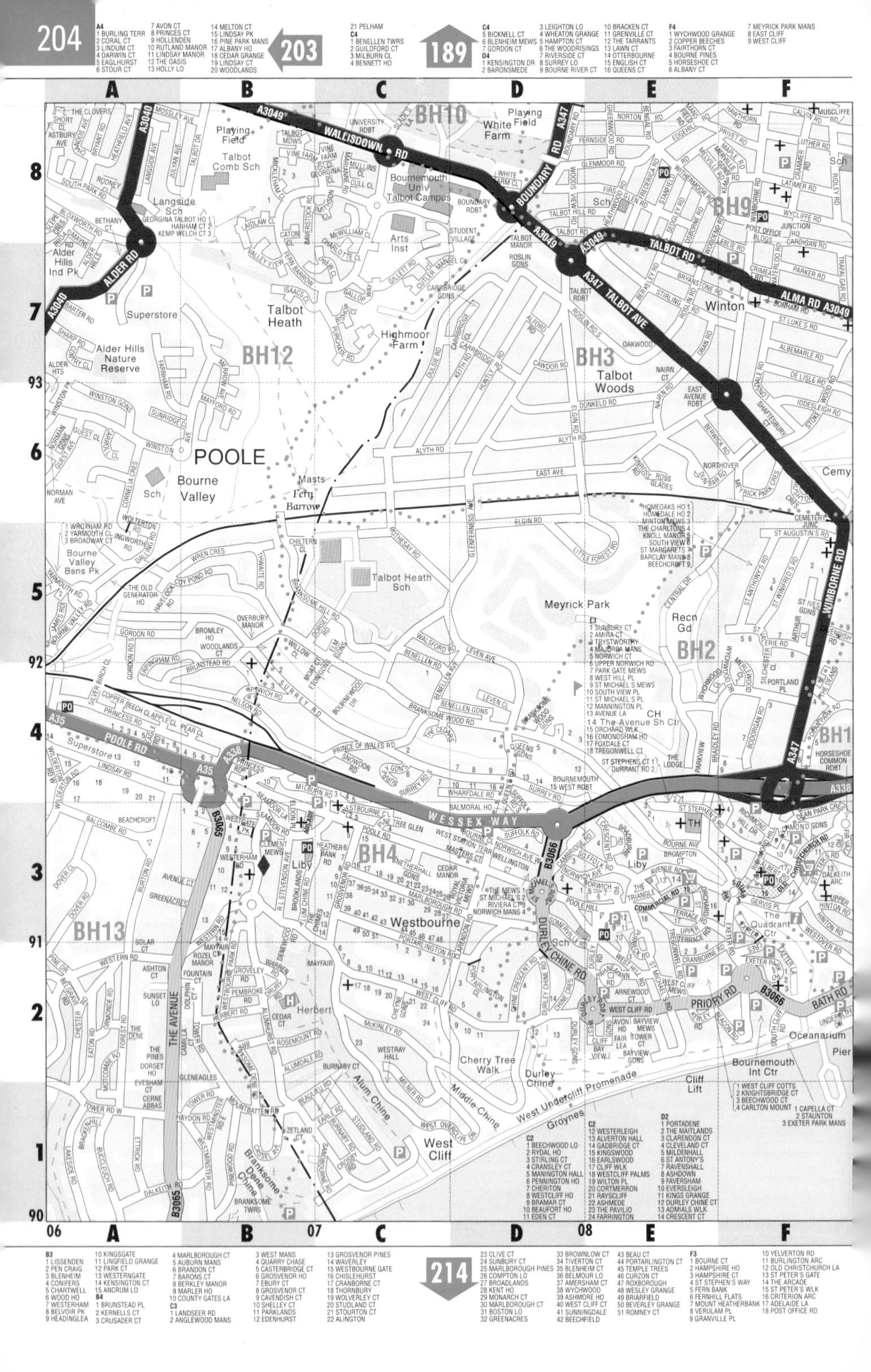

204
A4
1 BURLING TERR
2 CORAL CT
3 LINDUM CT
4 DARWIN CT
5 EAGLHURST
6 STOUR CT
7 AVON CT
8 PRINCES CT
9 HOLLENDEN
10 RUTLAND MANOR
11 LINDSAY MANOR
12 THE OASIS
13 HOLLY LO
14 MELTON CT
15 LINDSAY PK
16 PINE PARK MANS
17 ALBANY HO
18 CEDAR GRANGE
19 LINDSAY CT
20 WOODLANDS
203
21 PELHAM
C4
1 BENELLEN TWRS
2 GUILDFORD CT
3 MILBURN CL
4 BENNETT HO
189
C4
5 BICKNELL CT
6 BLENHEIM MEWS
7 GORDON CT
D4
1 KENSINGTON DR
2 BARONSMEDE
3 LEIGHTON LO
4 WHEATON GRANGE
5 HAMPTON CT
6 THE WOODRISINGS
7 RIVERSIDE CT
8 SURREY LO
9 BOURNE RIVER CT
10 BRACKEN CT
11 GRENVILLE CT
12 THE TARRANTS
13 LAWN CT
14 OTTERBOURNE
15 ENGLISH CT
16 QUEENS CT
F4
1 WYCHWOOD GRANGE
2 COPPER BEECHES
3 FAIRTHORN CT
4 BOURNE PINES
5 HORSESHOE CT
6 ALBANY CT
7 MEYRICK PARK MANS
8 EAST CLIFF
9 WEST CLIFF
A B C D E F
8
7
93
6
5
92
4
3
91
2
1
90
06 07 08
BH10
BH12
BH3
BH9
BH2
BH4
BH13
BH1
POOLE
Talbot Heath
Talbot Woods
Winton
Westbourne
Meyrick Park
Alder Hills Ind Pk
Alder Hills Nature Reserve
Bourne Valley
Bourne Valley Bsns Pk
Talbot Comb Sch
Bournemouth Univ Talbot Campus
Arts Inst
Talbot Heath Sch
White Farm
Highmoor Farm
Fern Barrow
Recn Gd
Cherry Tree Walk
Durley Chine
Alum Chine
Middle Chine
Branksome Dene Chine
West Cliff
West Undercliff Promenade
Groynes
Bournemouth Int Ctr
Oceanarium
Pier
Cliff Lift
The Quadrant Ctr
Herbert
Cemy
Superstore
WALLISDOWN RD
TALBOT RD
TALBOT AVE
ALMA RD
WIMBORNE RD
POOLE RD
WESSEX WAY
DURLEY CHINE RD
PRIORY RD
BATH RD
THE AVENUE
ALDER RD
BOUNDARY RD
A3049
A3040
A347
A35
A338
B3065
B3066
E3
1 SUNBURY CT
2 AMIRA CT
3 TRYSTWORTHY
4 MAJORCA MANS
5 NORWICH CT
6 UPPER NORWICH RD
7 PARK GATE MEWS
8 WEST HILL PL
9 ST MICHAEL'S MEWS
10 SOUTH VIEW PL
11 ST MICHAEL'S PL
12 MANNINGTON PL
13 AVENUE LA
14 The Avenue Sh Ctr
15 ORCHARD WLK
16 EDMONDSHAM HO
17 FOXDALE CT
18 TREGONWELL CT
C2
1 BEECHWOOD LO
2 RYDAL HO
3 STIRLING CT
4 CRANSLEY CT
5 MANINGTON HALL
6 PENNINGTON HO
7 CHERITON
8 WESTCLIFF HO
9 BRAMAR CT
10 BEAUFORT HO
11 EDEN CT
C2
12 WESTERLEIGH
13 ALVERTON HALL
14 GADBRIDGE CT
15 KINGSWOOD
16 EARLSWOOD
17 CLIFF WLK
18 WESTCLIFF PALMS
19 WILTON PL
20 CORTMERRON
21 RAYSCLIFF
22 ASHMEDE
23 THE PAVILIO
24 FARRINGTON
D2
1 PORTADENE
2 THE MAITLANDS
3 CLARENDON CT
4 CLEVELAND CT
5 MILDENHALL
6 ST ANTONY'S
7 RAVENSHALL
8 ASHDOWN
9 FAVERSHAM
10 EVERSLEIGH
11 KINGS GRANGE
12 DURLEY CHINE CT
13 ADMIALS WLK
14 CRESCENT CT
1 WEST CLIFF COTTS
2 KNIGHTSBRIDGE CT
3 BEECHWOOD CT
4 CARLTON MOUNT
1 CAPELLA CT
2 STAUNTON
3 EXETER PARK MANS
B3
1 LISSENDEN
2 PEN CRAIG
3 BLENHEIM
4 CONIFERS
5 CHARTWELL
6 WOOD HO
7 WESTERHAM
8 BELVOIR PK
9 HEADINGLEA
10 KINGSGATE
11 LINGFIELD GRANGE
12 PARK CT
13 WESTERNGATE
14 KENSINGTON CT
15 ANCRUM LO
B4
1 BRUNSTEAD PL
2 KERNELLS CT
3 CRUSADER CT
4 MARLBOROUGH CT
5 AUBURN MANS
6 BRANDON CT
7 BARONS CT
8 BERKLEY MANOR
9 MARLER HO
10 COUNTY GATES LA
C3
1 LANDSEER RD
2 ANGLEWOOD MANS
3 WEST MANS
4 QUARRY CHASE
5 CASTERBRIDGE CT
6 GROSVENOR HO
7 EBURY CT
8 GROSVENOR CT
9 CAVENDISH CT
10 SHELLEY CT
11 PARKLANDS
12 EDENHURST
13 GROSVENOR PINES
14 WAVERLEY
15 WESTBOURNE GATE
16 CHISLEHURST
17 CRANBORNE CT
18 THORNBURY
19 WOLVERLEY CT
20 STUDLAND CT
21 STOURTON CT
22 ALINGTON
214
23 CLIVE CT
24 SUNBURY CT
25 MARLBOROUGH PINES
26 COMPTON LO
27 BROADLANDS
28 KENT HO
29 MONARCH CT
30 MARLBOROUGH CT
31 BOSTON LO
32 GREENACRES
33 BROWNLOW CT
34 TIVERTON CT
35 BLENHEIM CT
36 BELMOUR LO
37 AMERSHAM CT
38 WYCHWOOD
39 ASHMORE HO
40 WEST CLIFF CT
41 SUNNINGDALE
42 BEECHFIELD
43 BEAU CT
44 PORTARLINGTON CT
45 TEMPLE TREES
46 CURZON CT
47 ROXBOROUGH
48 WESLEY GRANGE
49 BRIARFIELD
50 BEVERLEY GRANGE
51 ROMNEY CT
F3
1 BOURNE CT
2 HAMPSHIRE HO
3 HAMPSHIRE CT
4 ST STEPHEN'S WAY
5 FERN BANK
6 FERNHILL FLATS
7 MOUNT HEATHERBANK
8 VERULAM PL
9 GRANVILLE PL
10 YELVERTON RD
11 BURLINGTON ARC
12 OLD CHRISTCHURCH LA
13 ST PETER'S GATE
14 THE ARCADE
15 ST PETER'S WLK
16 CRITERION ARC
17 ADELAIDE LA
18 POST OFFICE RD

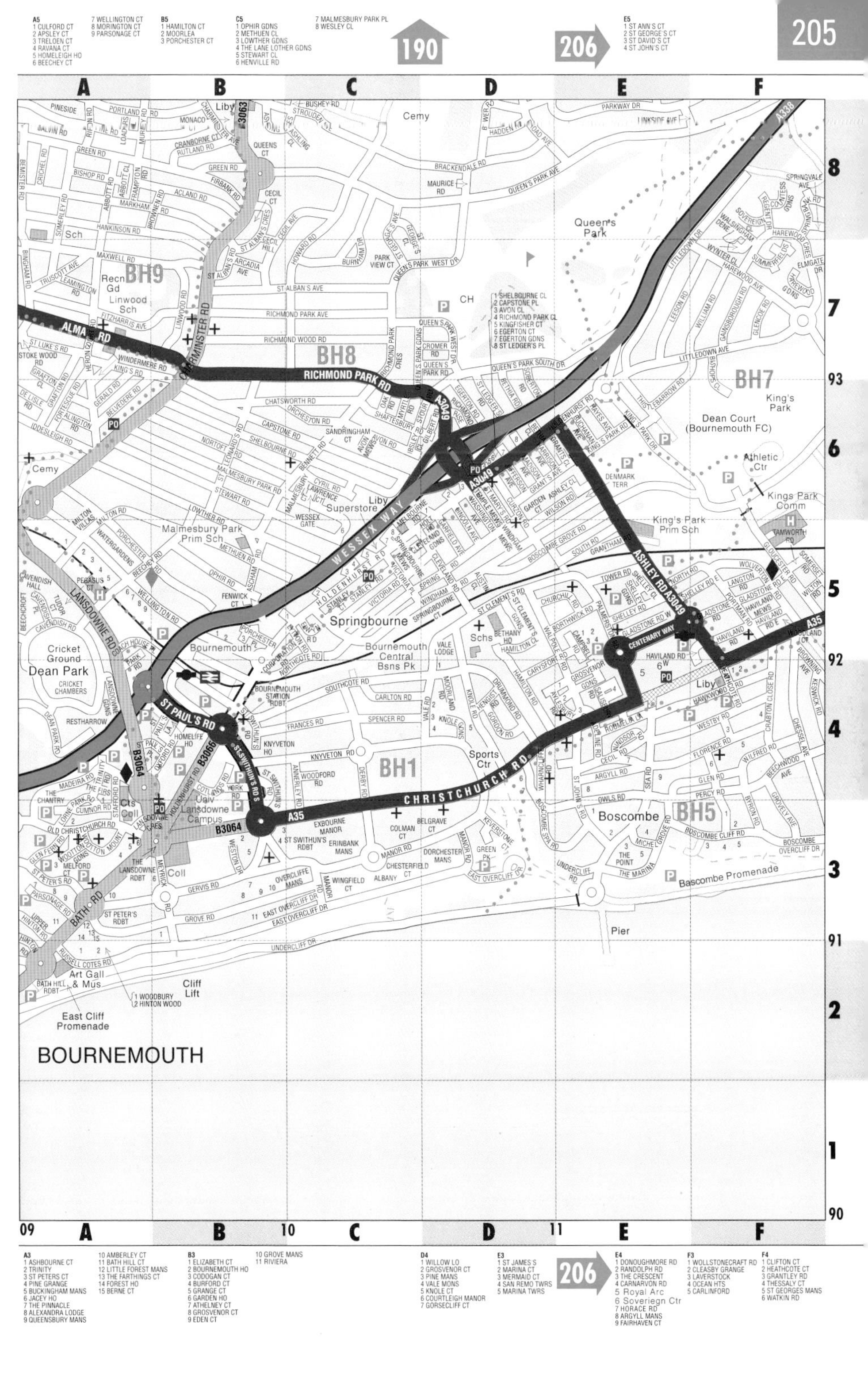
A5
1 CULFORD CT
2 APSLEY CT
3 TRELOEN CT
4 RAVANA CT
5 HOMELEIGH HO
6 BEECHEY CT
7 WELLINGTON CT
8 MORINGTON CT
9 PARSONAGE CT
B5
1 HAMILTON CT
2 MOORLEA
3 PORCHESTER CT
C5
1 OPHIR GDNS
2 METHUEN CL
3 LOWTHER GDNS
4 THE LANE LOTHER GDNS
5 STEWART CL
6 HENVILLE RD
7 MALMESBURY PARK PL
8 WESLEY CL
190
206
E5
1 ST ANN'S CT
2 ST GEORGE'S CT
3 ST DAVID'S CT
4 ST JOHN'S CT
A
B
C
D
E
F
8
7
93
6
5
92
4
3
91
2
1
90
09
10
11
BH9
BH8
BH7
BH1
BH5
Cemy
Queen's Park
Recn Gd
Linwood Sch
Sch
CH
Dean Court (Bournemouth FC)
King's Park
Athletic Ctr
Kings Park Comm
King's Park Prim Sch
Malmesbury Park Prim Sch
Liby
Superstore
Springbourne
Bournemouth
Bournemouth Central Bsns Pk
Cricket Ground
Dean Park
Schs
Sports Ctr
Univ Lansdowne Campus
Cts Coll
Coll
Boscombe
Pier
Bascombe Promenade
Art Gall & Mus
Cliff Lift
East Cliff Promenade
BOURNEMOUTH
ALMA RD
CHARMINSTER RD
RICHMOND PARK RD
WESSEX WAY
ASHLEY RD A3049
CHRISTCHURCH RD
ST PAUL'S RD
LANSDOWNE RD
BATH RD
HOLDENHURST RD
CENTENARY WAY
QUEEN'S PARK AVE
QUEEN'S PARK SOUTH DR
LITTLEDOWN AVE
ST ALBAN'S AVE
RICHMOND PARK AVE
RICHMOND WOOD RD
MALMESBURY PARK RD
GERVIS RD
GROVE RD
EAST OVERCLIFF DR
UNDERCLIFF DR
A338
A3049
A35
B3063
B3064
B3066
1 SHELBOURNE CL
2 CAPSTONE PL
3 AVON CL
4 RICHMOND PARK CL
5 KINGFISHER CT
6 EGERTON CT
7 EGERTON GDNS
8 ST LEDGER'S PL
1 WOODBURY
2 HINTON WOOD
A3
1 ASHBOURNE CT
2 TRINITY
3 ST PETERS CT
4 PINE GRANGE
5 BUCKINGHAM MANS
6 JACEY HO
7 THE PINNACLE
8 ALEXANDRA LODGE
9 QUEENSBURY MANS
10 AMBERLEY CT
11 BATH HILL CT
12 LITTLE FOREST MANS
13 THE FARTHINGS CT
14 FOREST HO
15 BERNE CT
B3
1 ELIZABETH CT
2 BOURNEMOUTH HO
3 CODOGAN CT
4 BURFORD CT
5 GRANGE CT
6 GARDEN HO
7 ATHELNEY CT
8 GROSVENOR CT
9 EDEN CT
10 GROVE MANS
11 RIVIERA
D4
1 WILLOW LO
2 GROSVENOR CT
3 PINE MANS
4 VALE MONS
5 KNOLE CT
6 COURTLEIGH MANOR
7 GORSECLIFF CT
E3
1 ST JAMES'S
2 MARINA CT
3 MERMAID CT
4 SAN REMO TWRS
5 MARINA TWRS
206
E4
1 DONOUGHMORE RD
2 RANDOLPH RD
3 THE CRESCENT
4 CARNARVON RD
5 Royal Arc
6 Soveriegn Ctr
7 HORACE RD
8 ARGYLL MANS
9 FAIRHAVEN CT
F3
1 WOLLSTONECRAFT RD
2 CLEASBY GRANGE
3 LAVERSTOCK
4 OCEAN HTS
5 CARLINFORD
F4
1 CLIFTON CT
2 HEATHCOTE CT
3 GRANTLEY RD
4 THESSALY CT
5 ST GEORGES MANS
6 WATKIN RD

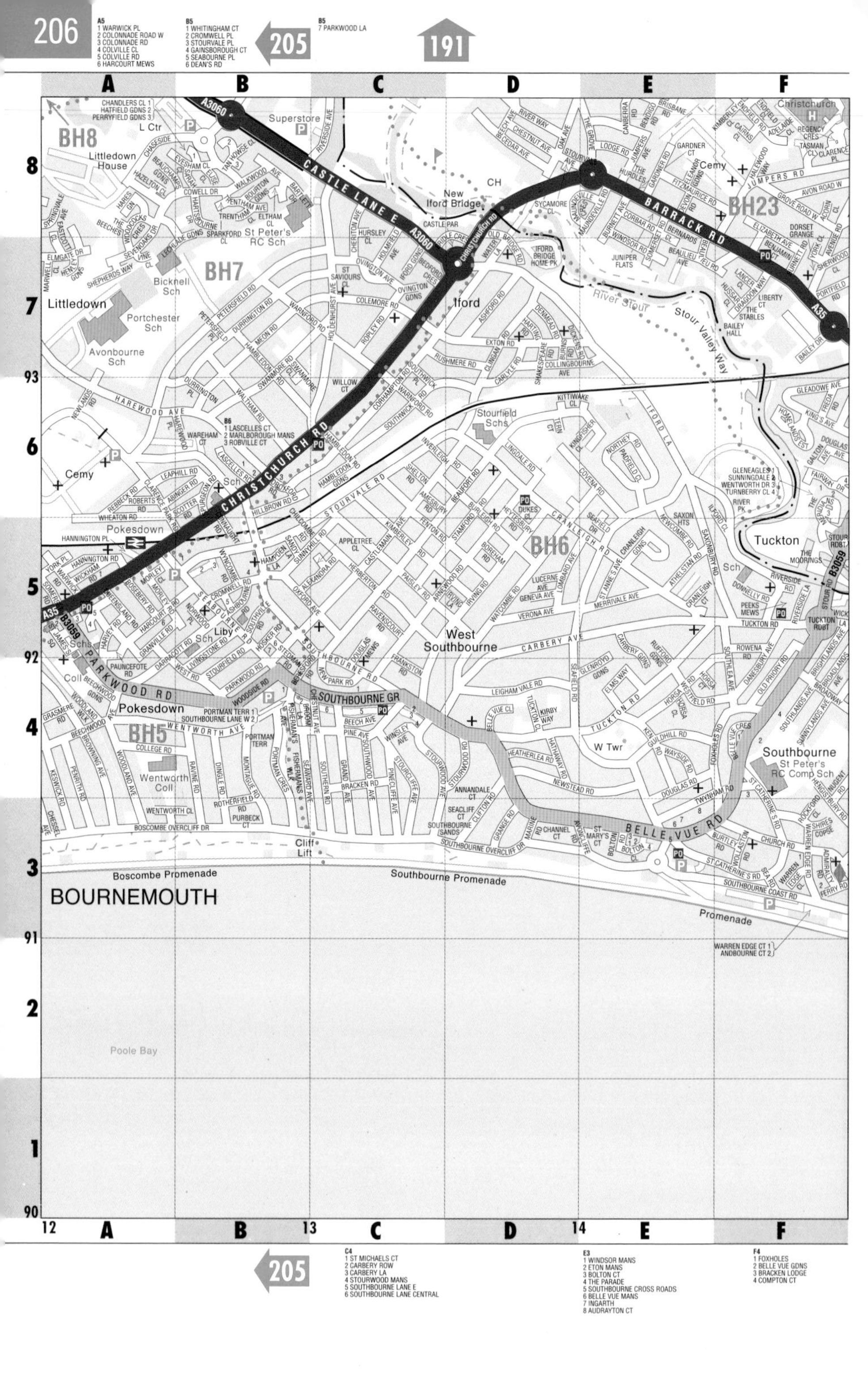

A5
1 WARWICK PL
2 COLONNADE ROAD W
3 COLONNADE RD
4 COLVILLE CL
5 COLVILLE RD
6 HARCOURT MEWS
B5
1 WHITINGHAM CT
2 CROMWELL PL
3 STOURVALE PL
4 GAINSBOROUGH CT
5 SEABOURNE PL
6 DEAN'S RD
205
B5
7 PARKWOOD LA
191
A
B
C
D
E
F
BH8
Littledown House
L Ctr
Superstore
CASTLE LANE E
A3060
New Iford Bridge
CH
Christchurch
Cemy
BARRACK RD
BH23
BH7
St Peter's RC Sch
Bicknell Sch
Littledown
Portchester Sch
Avonbourne Sch
Iford
River Stour
Stour Valley Way
CHRISTCHURCH RD
Stourfield Schs
Cemy
Pokesdown
BH6
Tuckton
A35
B3059
PARKWOOD RD
SOUTHBOURNE GR
West Southbourne
CARBERY AVE
Liby
Pokesdown
BH5
WENTWORTH AVE
Wentworth Coll
Southbourne
St Peter's RC Comp Sch
BELLE VUE RD
W Twr
Cliff Lift
Boscombe Promenade
Southbourne Promenade
Promenade
BOURNEMOUTH
Poole Bay
WARREN EDGE CT 1
ANDBOURNE CT 2
12
13
14
A
B
C
D
E
F
205
C4
1 ST MICHAELS CT
2 CARBERY ROW
3 CARBERY LA
4 STOURWOOD MANS
5 SOUTHBOURNE LANE E
6 SOUTHBOURNE LANE CENTRAL
E3
1 WINDSOR MANS
2 ETON MANS
3 BOLTON CT
4 THE PARADE
5 SOUTHBOURNE CROSS ROADS
6 BELLE VUE MANS
7 INGARTH
8 AUDRAYTON CT
F4
1 FOXHOLES
2 BELLE VUE GDNS
3 BRACKEN LODGE
4 COMPTON CT

A5	A6	A7	B6	E6	E7	F8	
1 MARINA VIEW 2 THE MOORINGS 3 SWAN GN 4 KINGFISHERS 5 WATERMEAD 6 MALMSBURY CL	1 HOMESTOUR HO 2 ORCHARD MEWS 3 ST ANDREWS 4 RIVERLAND CT	1 WINSTON CT 2 KENILWORTH CT 3 ARTHUR LA 4 MULBERRY CT 5 MITRE CT	1 POUND LA 2 MILLHAMS STREET N 3 THE CLOISTERS 4 PRIORY VIEW CT 5 SILVER ST	1 FRANCESCA LO 2 GILLION CT 3 ROSEDALE CL	1 STRETE MOUNT 2 PUREWELL CT 3 CURL CL 4 FRANCESCA GRANGE 5 FRANCESCA CT	1 SOUTHDOWN CT 2 MALVERN CT 3 PURBECK CT 4 MENDIP CT 5 CHILTERN CT 6 COTSWOLD CT	7 QUANTOCK CT 8 PENNINE CT 9 WENLOCK CT

192   **208**   **207**

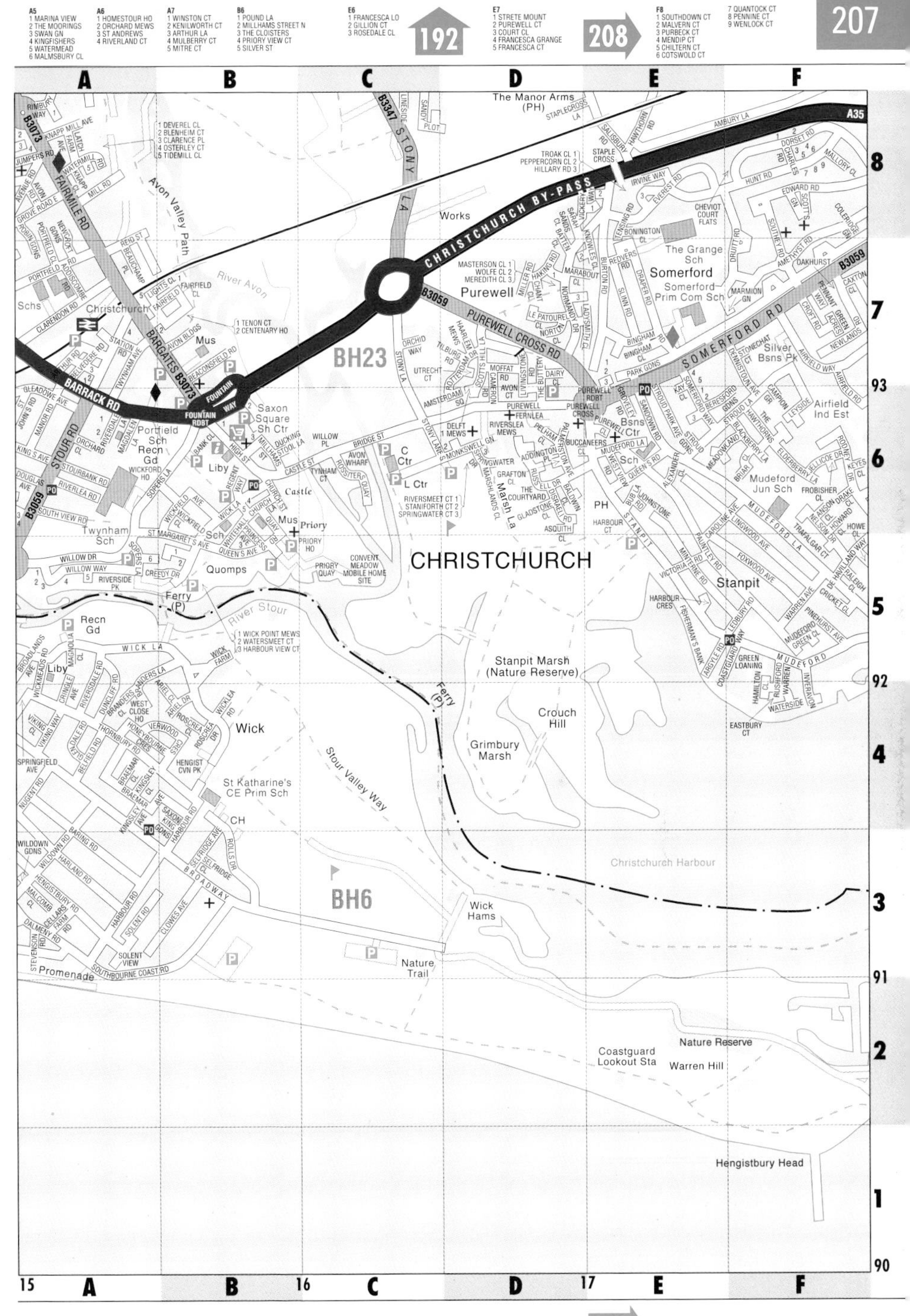

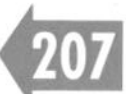

207
193

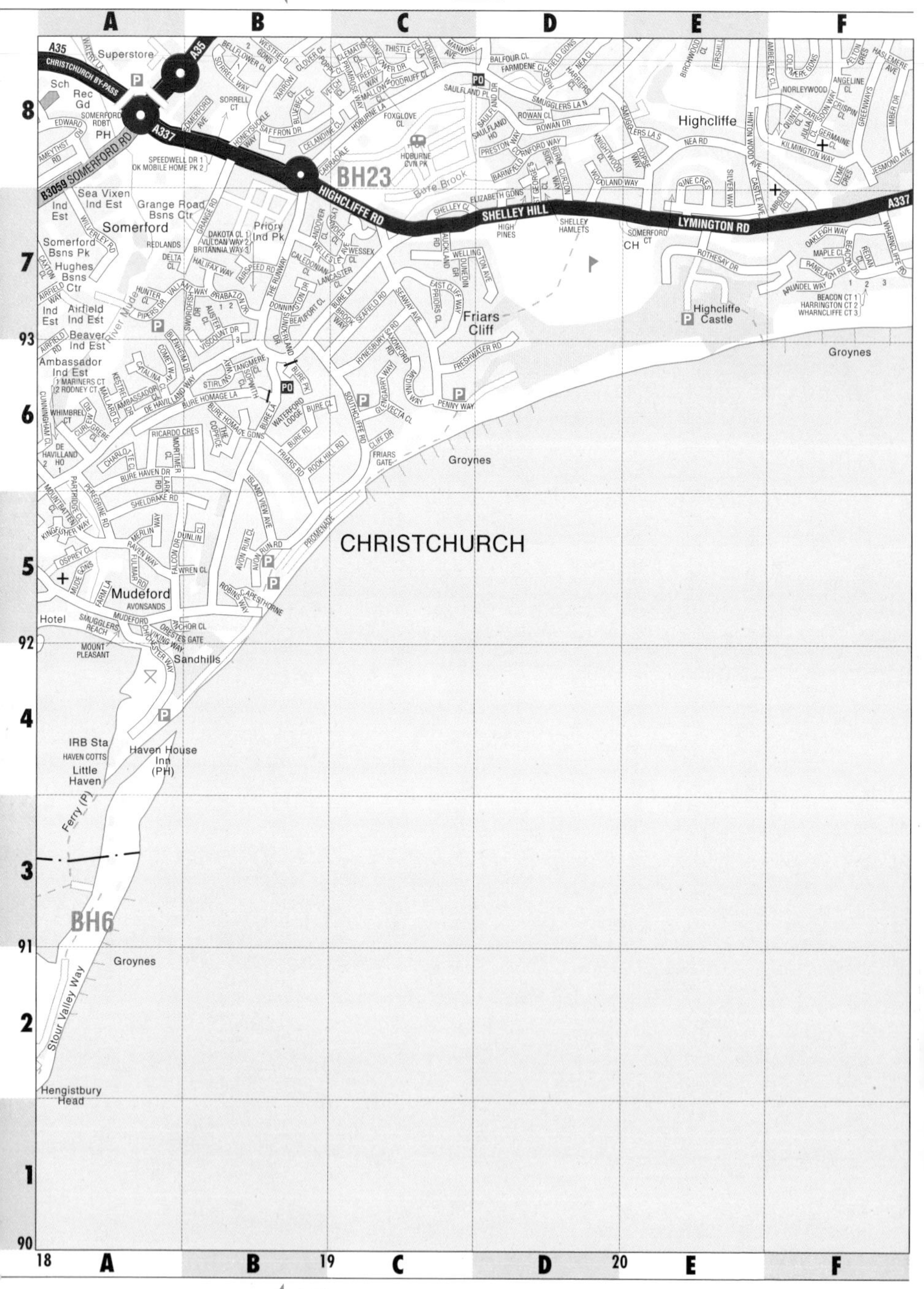

A
B
C
D
E
F
8
7
93
6
5
92
4
3
91
2
1
90
18
19
20
A35
Superstore
CHRISTCHURCH BY-PASS
Sch
Rec Gd
SOMERFORD RDBT
PH
A337
B3059 SOMERFORD RD
SPEEDWELL DR 1
OK MOBILE HOME PK 2
Sea Vixen Ind Est
Ind Est
Grange Road Bsns Ctr
Somerford
Somerford Bsns Pk
Hughes Bsns Ctr
Airfield Ind Est
Ind Est
Beaver Ind Est
Ambassador Ind Est
1 MARINERS CT
2 ROONEY CT
Priory Ind Pk
DAKOTA CL 1
VULCAN WAY 2
BRITANNIA WAY 3
REDLANDS
River Mude
BH23
HIGHCLIFFE RD
SHELLEY HILL
LYMINGTON RD
HIGH PINES
SHELLEY HAMLETS
SOMERFORD CT
CH
Highcliffe
Highcliffe Castle
HOBURNE CVN PK
Bure Brook
Friars Cliff
FRIARS GATE
Groynes
BEACON CT 1
HARRINGTON CT 2
WHARNCLIFFE CT 3
CHRISTCHURCH
PROMENADE
Mudeford
AVONSANDS
Hotel
MOUNT PLEASANT
Sandhills
IRB Sta
HAVEN COTTS
Little Haven
Haven House Inn (PH)
Ferry (P)
BH6
Groynes
Stour Valley Way
Hengistbury Head

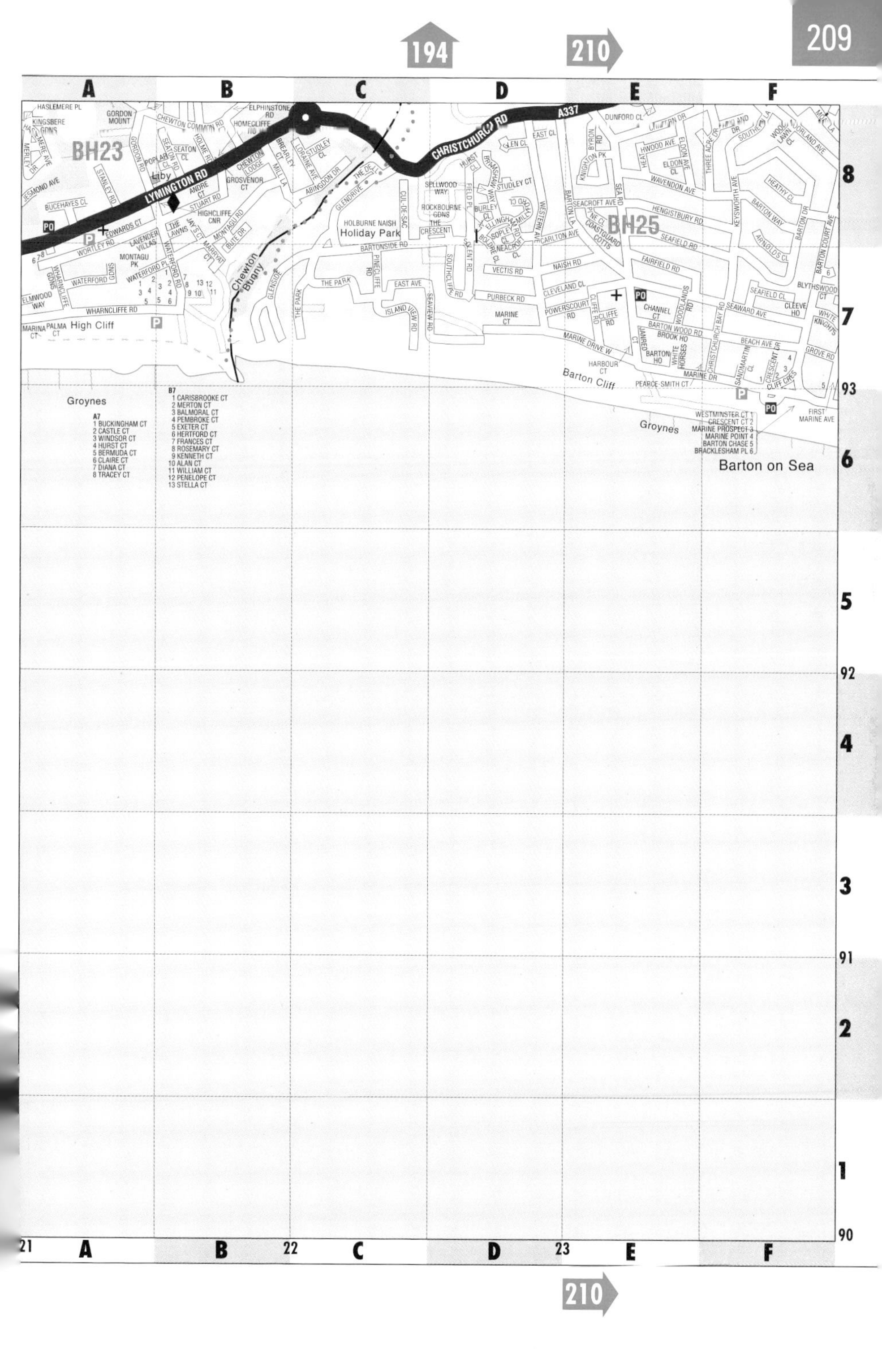

194

210

BH23

BH25

Groynes

A7
1 BUCKINGHAM CT
2 CASTLE CT
3 WINDSOR CT
4 HURST CT
5 BERMUDA CT
6 CLAIRE CT
7 DIANA CT
8 TRACEY CT

B7
1 CARISBROOKE CT
2 MERTON CT
3 BALMORAL CT
4 PEMBROKE CT
5 EXETER CT
6 HERTFORD CT
7 FRANCES CT
8 ROSEMARY CT
9 KENNETH CT
10 ALAN CT
11 WILLIAM CT
12 PENELOPE CT
13 STELLA CT

Groynes

WESTMINSTER CT 1
CRESCENT CT 2
MARINE PROSPECT 3
MARINE POINT 4
BARTON CHASE 5
BRACKLESHAM PL 6

FIRST
MARINE AVE

Barton on Sea

Holburne Naish
Holiday Park

Barton Cliff

209
195

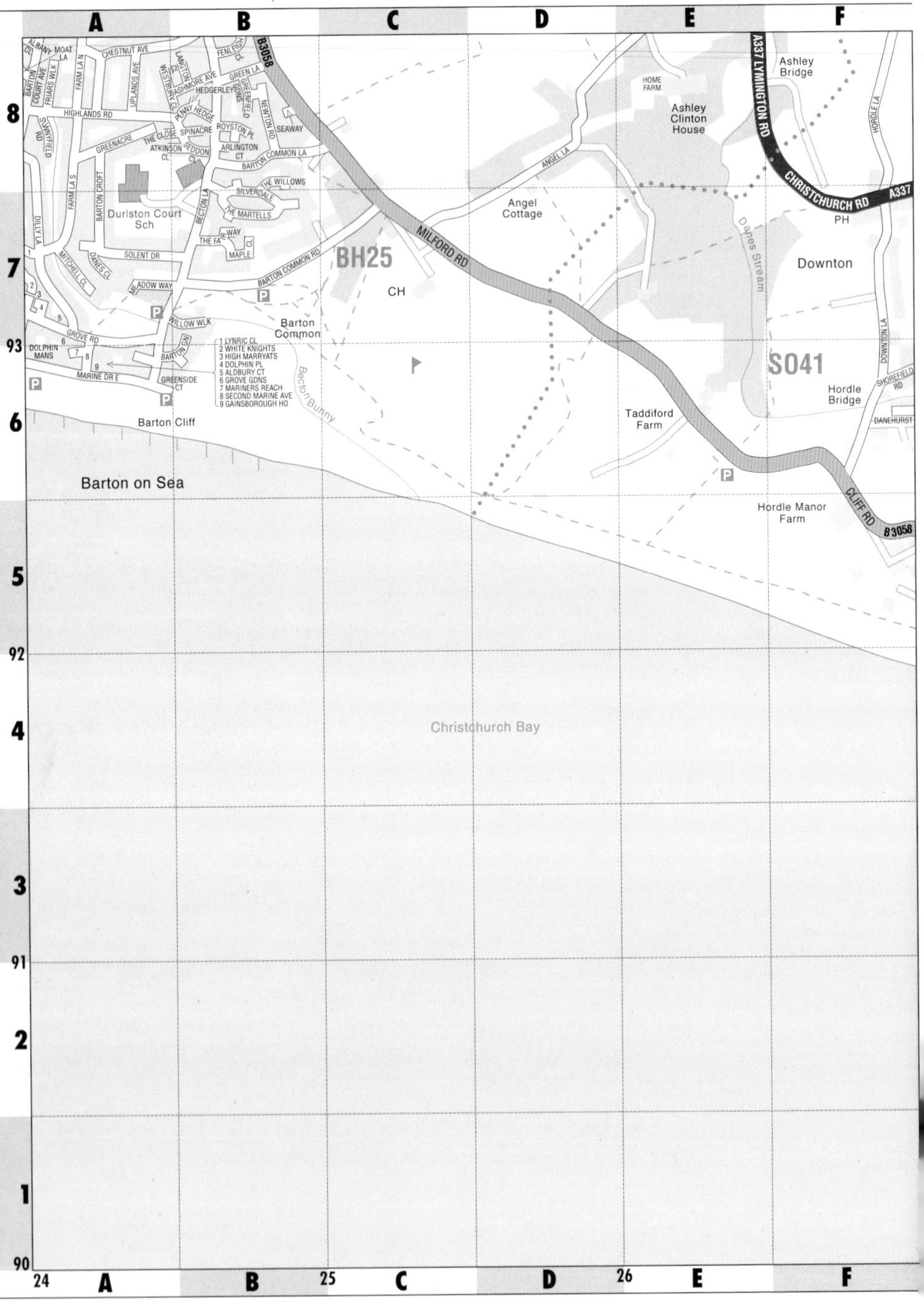

A B C D E F

8

B3058

ALBANY CL
MOAT LA
FRIARS WK
ASHLEY PK
CHESTNUT AVE
LANGSTONE AVE
WESTOVER RD
BASHMORE AVE
HEDGERLEY
GREEN LA
NEWTON RD
FENTON
SEAWAY
HIGHLANDS RD
GREENMEACRE
PONY HEDGE
ROYSTON PL
BARTON COMMON LA
THE CLOSE
SPINACRE
ARLINGTON CT
THE WILLOWS
ATKINSON CL
UPLANDS AVE

HOME FARM

Ashley Bridge

Ashley Clinton House

A337 LYMINGTON RD

CHRISTCHURCH RD   A337

PH

Duriston Court Sch

SILVERDALE
THE MARTELLS
BECTON LA
FIR WAY
THE FAIRWAY
MAPLE

Angel Cottage

ANGEL LA

Downton

SOLENT DR

MEADOW WAY

BARTON COMMON RD

MILFORD RD

7

BH25

CH

S041

Dares Stream

Hordle Bridge

SHOREFIELD RD

GROVE RD

WILLOW WLK

Barton Common

1 LYNRIC CL
2 WHITE KNIGHTS
3 HIGH MARRYATS
4 DOLPHIN PL
5 ALDBURY CT
6 GROVE GDNS
7 MARINERS REACH
8 SECOND MARINE AVE
9 GAINSBOROUGH HO

YEOVIL RD
DANEHURST

93

DOLPHIN MANS

Becton Bunny

Taddiford Farm

GREENSIDE CT
MARINE DR E

Barton Cliff

Hordle Manor Farm

6

CLIFF RD

B3058

Barton on Sea

5

92

4

Christchurch Bay

3

91

2

1

90

24   **A**   **B**   25   **C**   **D**   26   **E**   **F**

209

196
212

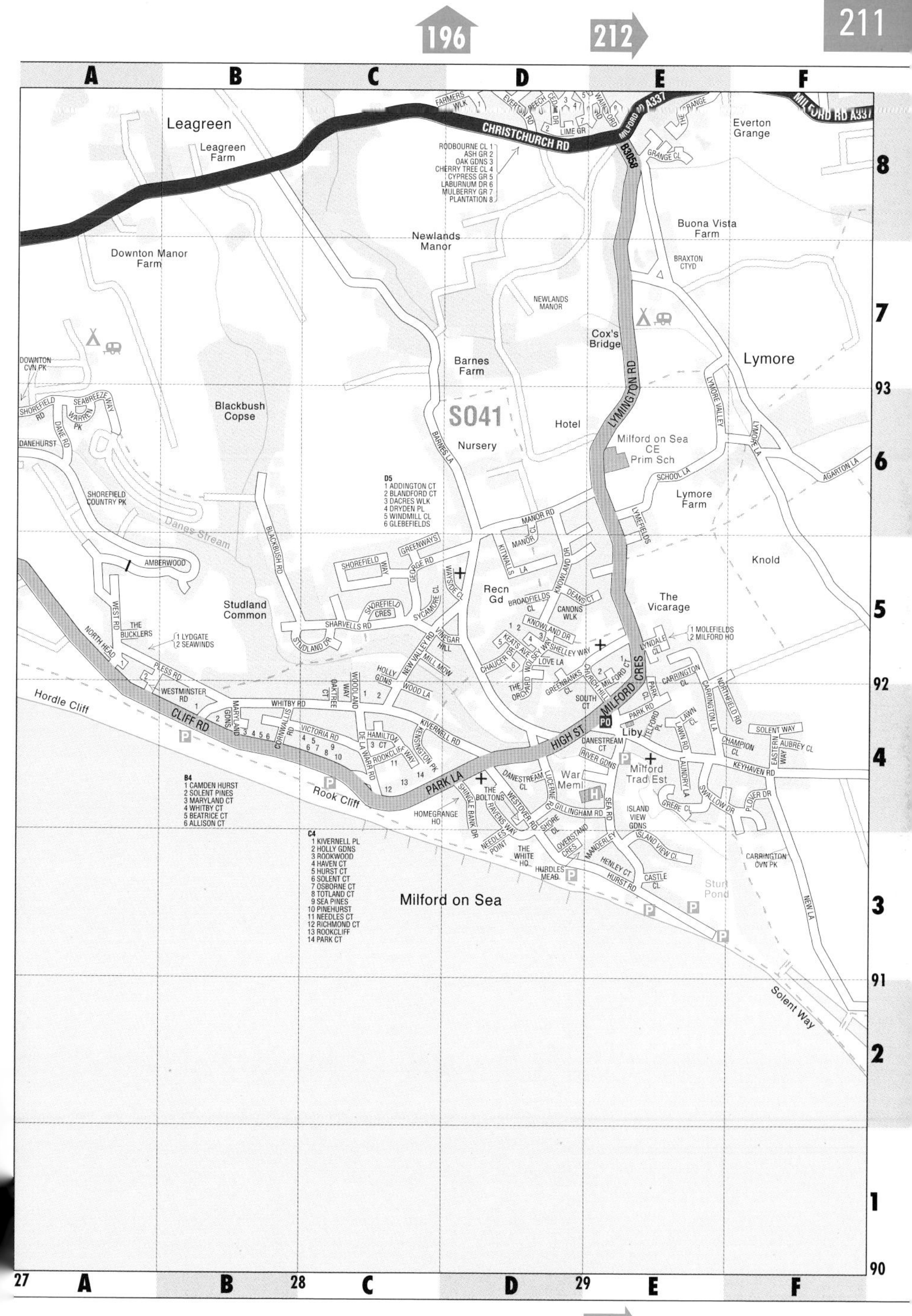
A
B
C
D
E
F
Leagreen
Leagreen Farm
CHRISTCHURCH RD
MILFORD RD A337
B3058
FARMERS WLK
EVERTON RD
BEECH
CEDAR DR
LIME GR
THE GRANGE
GRANGE CL
Everton Grange
RODBOURNE CL 1
ASH GR 2
OAK GDNS 3
CHERRY TREE CL 4
CYPRESS GR 5
LABURNUM DR 6
MULBERRY GR 7
PLANTATION 8
8
Downton Manor Farm
Newlands Manor
Buona Vista Farm
BRAXTON CTYD
NEWLANDS MANOR
7
Cox's Bridge
Lymore
DOWNTON CVN PK
Barnes Farm
93
SHOREFIELD RD
SEABREEZE WAY
WARREN PK
Blackbush Copse
SO41
Hotel
LYMINGTON RD
LYMORE VALLEY
LYMORE LA
DANE RD
DANEHURST
BARNES LA
Nursery
Milford on Sea CE Prim Sch
AGARTON LA
6
SCHOOL LA
D5
1 ADDINGTON CT
2 BLANDFORD CT
3 DACRES WLK
4 DRYDEN PL
5 WINDMILL CL
6 GLEBEFIELDS
Lymore Farm
SHOREFIELD COUNTRY PK
MANOR RD
Danes Stream
BLACKBUSH RD
GREENWAYS
MANOR CL
KITTIWALLS LA
LYMEFIELDS
AMBERWOOD
SHOREFIELD WAY
GEORGE RD
WAYSIDE CL
Recn Gd
KNOWLAND DR
Knold
Studland Common
SHOREFIELD CRES
SYCAMORE CL
BROADFIELDS CL
DEANS CT
CANONS WLK
The Vicarage
5
WEST RD
THE BUCKLERS
SHARVELLS RD
VINEGAR HILL
KNOWLAND DR
1 MOLEFIELDS
2 MILFORD HO
NORTH HEAD
1 LYDGATE
2 SEAWINDS
STUDLAND DR
NEW VALLEY RD
KEATS AVE
WOLSEY WAY
SHELLEY WAY
LYNDALE CL
MILL MDW
CHAUCER DR
LOVE LA
PLESS RD
HOLLY GDNS
OAKTREE CT
WOODLAND WAY
WOOD LA
THE ORCHARD
GREENBANKS CL
CHURCH HILL
MILFORD CT
MILFORD CRES
CARRINGTON CL
CARRINGTON LA
NORTHFIELD RD
92
WESTMINSTER RD
Hordle Cliff
WHITBY RD
SOUTH CT
PARK CL
PARK RD
TELFORD PL
LAWN CL
LAWN RD
CLIFF RD
MARYLAND GDNS
CORNWALLIS RD
VICTORIA RD
HAMILTON CT
KENSINGTON PK
KIVERNELL RD
HIGH ST
PO
Liby
SOLENT WAY
AUBREY CL
DANESTREAM CT
CHAMPION CL
EASTERN WAY
DE LA WARR RD
ROOKCLIFF WAY
RIVER GDNS
Milford Trad Est
KEYHAVEN RD
4
B4
1 CAMDEN HURST
2 SOLENT PINES
3 MARYLAND CT
4 WHITBY CT
5 BEATRICE CT
6 ALLISON CT
PARK LA
DANESTREAM CL
LUCERNE RD
War Meml
LAUNDRY LA
Rook Cliff
SHINGLE BANK DR
THE BOLTONS
WESTOVER RD
GILLINGHAM RD
SEA RD
GREBE CL
SWALLOW DR
PLOVER DR
HOMEGRANGE HO
RAVENS WAY
SHORE CL
ISLAND VIEW GDNS
C4
1 KIVERNELL PL
2 HOLLY GDNS
3 ROOKWOOD
4 HAVEN CT
5 HURST CT
6 SOLENT CT
7 OSBORNE CT
8 TOTLAND CT
9 SEA PINES
10 PINEHURST
11 NEEDLES CT
12 RICHMOND CT
13 ROOKCLIFF
14 PARK CT
NEEDLES POINT
THE WHITE HO
OVERSTRAND CRES
MANDERLEY
ISLAND VIEW CL
CARRINGTON CVN PK
HURDLES MEAD
HENLEY CT
HURST RD
CASTLE CL
Sturt Pond
NEW LA
Milford on Sea
3
91
Solent Way
2
1
90
27
28
29

212

211
197

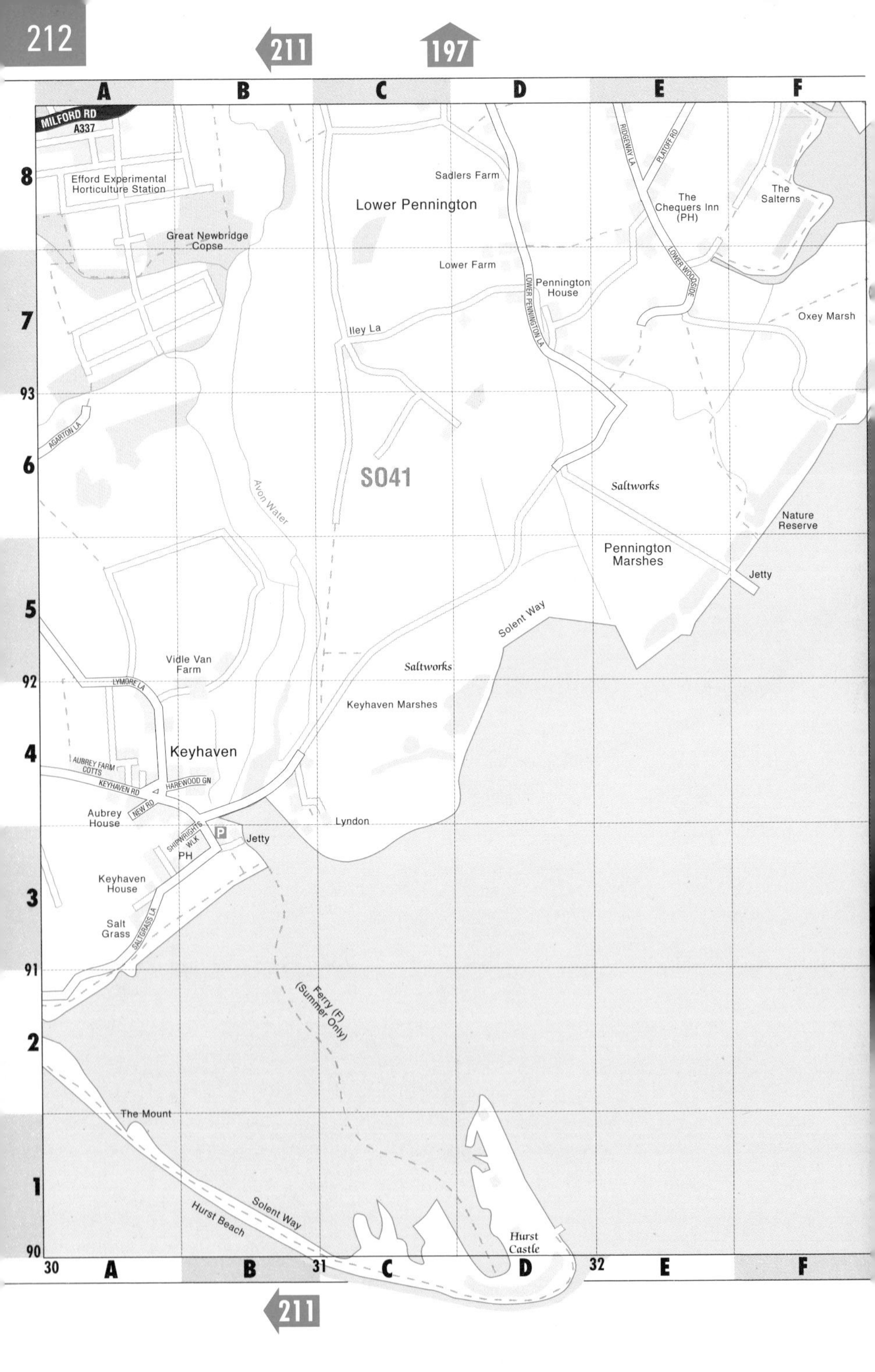
MILFORD RD
A337
Efford Experimental Horticulture Station
Great Newbridge Copse
Sadlers Farm
Lower Pennington
Lower Farm
Pennington House
LOWER PENNINGTON LA
RIDGEWAY LA
PLATOFF RD
The Chequers Inn (PH)
The Salterns
LOWER WOODSIDE
Oxey Marsh
Iley La
AGARTON LA
SO41
Avon Water
Saltworks
Nature Reserve
Pennington Marshes
Jetty
Solent Way
Vidle Van Farm
LYMORE LA
Saltworks
Keyhaven Marshes
Keyhaven
AUBREY FARM COTTS
KEYHAVEN RD
HAREWOOD GN
NEW RD
Aubrey House
SHIPWRIGHTS WLK
P
Jetty
PH
Lyndon
Keyhaven House
Salt Grass
SALTGRASS LA
Ferry (F) (Summer Only)
The Mount
Solent Way
Hurst Beach
Hurst Castle
A B C D E F
8 7 93 6 5 92 4 3 91 2 1 90
30 31 32

211

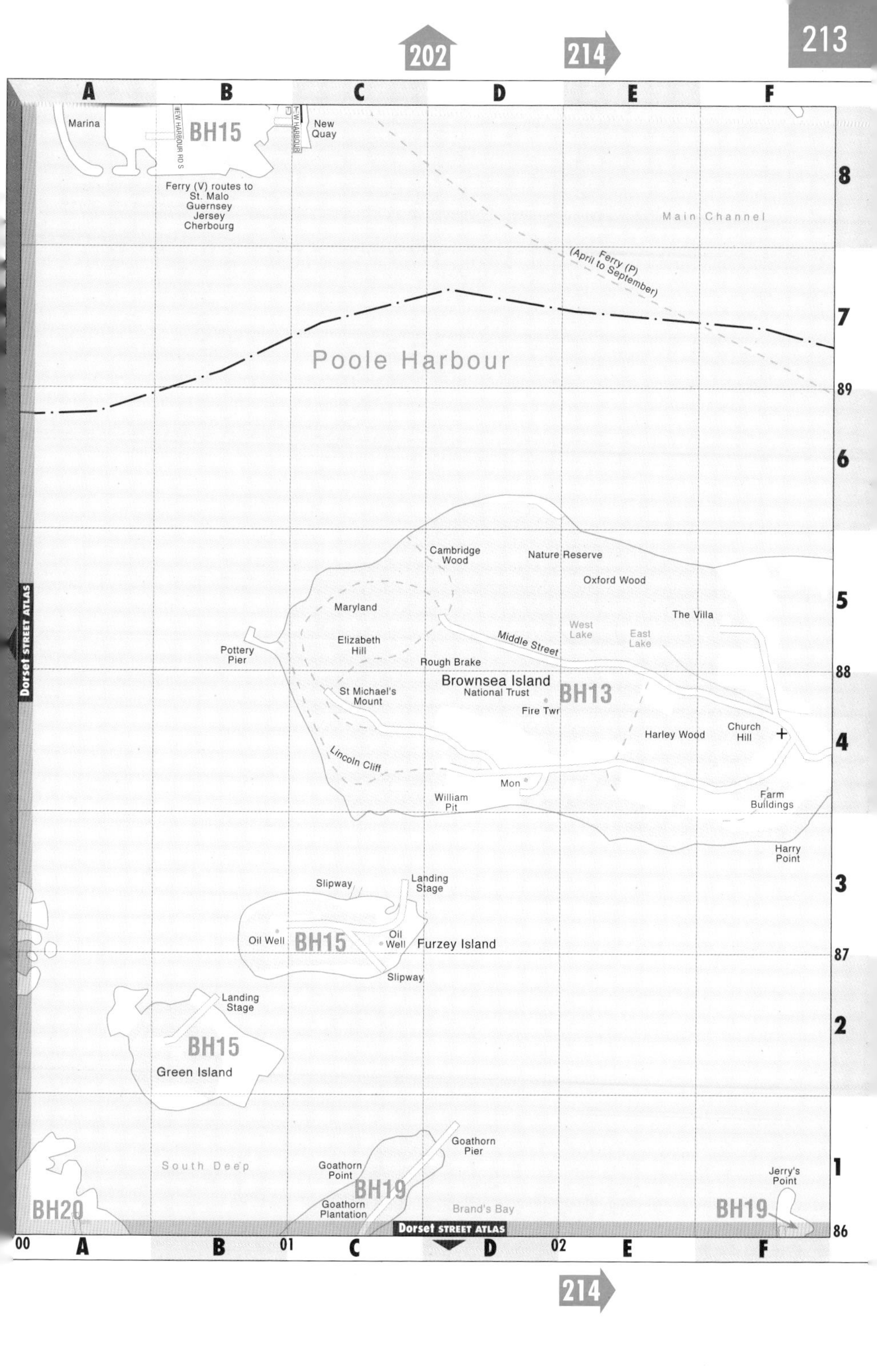

A   B   C   D   E   F

Marina

BH15

New
Quay

Ferry (V) routes to
St. Malo
Guernsey
Jersey
Cherbourg

8

Main Channel

Ferry (P)
(April to September)

7

Poole Harbour

89

6

Cambridge
Wood   Nature Reserve

Oxford Wood

5

Maryland   The Villa

West   East
Lake   Lake

Elizabeth   Middle Street
Hill   88

Pottery   Rough Brake
Pier
Brownsea Island
St Michael's   National Trust   **BH13**
Mount   Fire Twr

Harley Wood   Church
Hill   +   4

Lincoln Cliff

Mon
Farm
William   Buildings
Pit

Harry
Point

3

Slipway   Landing
Stage

Oil Well **BH15** Oil   Furzey Island
Well   87

Slipway

Landing
Stage
2

BH15

Green Island

1

Goathorn
Pier

South Deep   Goathorn
Point   **BH19**

BH20   Goathorn   Brand's Bay   Jerry's   **BH19**
Plantation   Point

86
A   B   C   D   E   F

Dorset STREET ATLAS

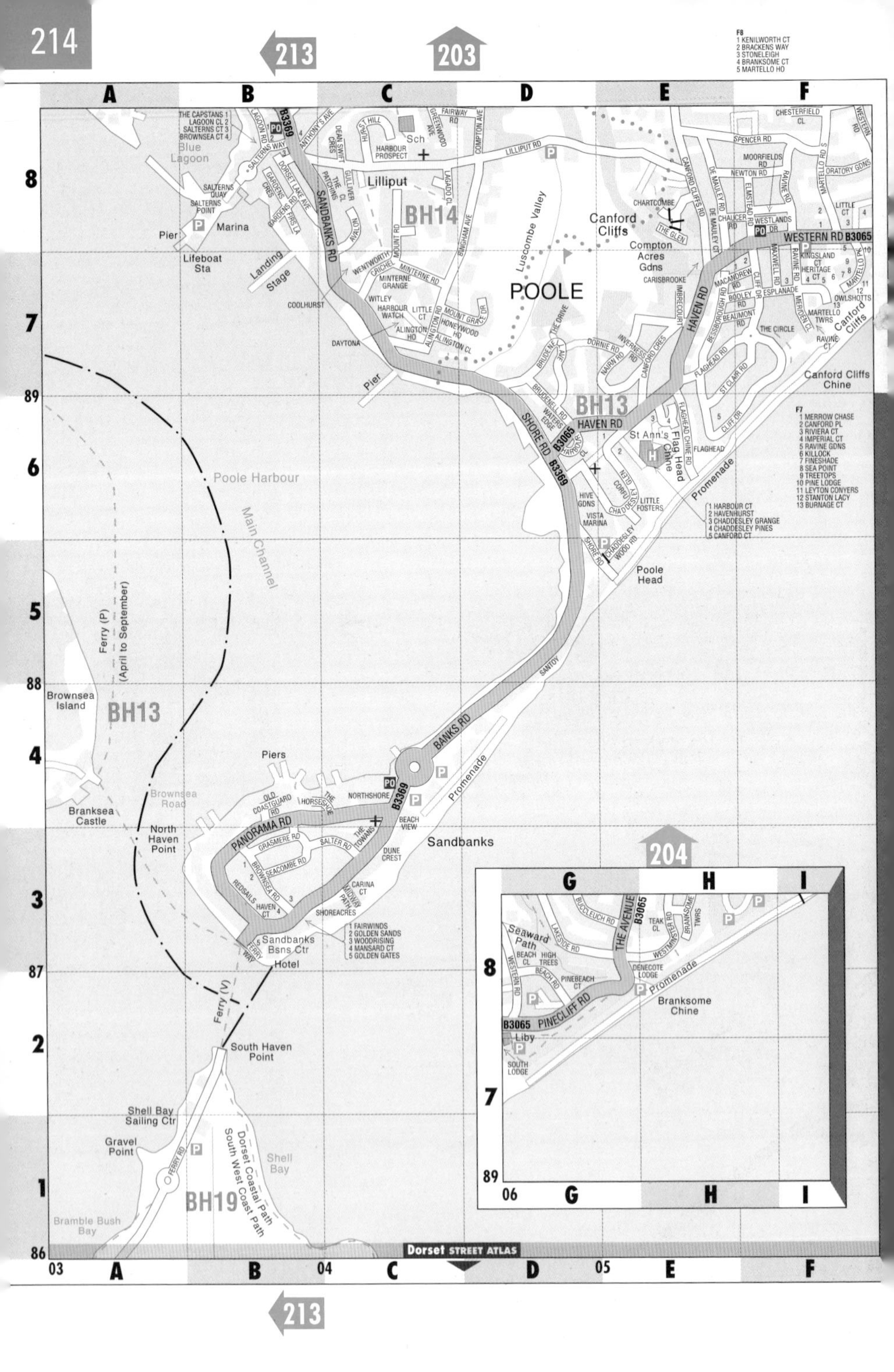
213
203
F8
1 KENILWORTH CT
2 BRACKENS WAY
3 STONELEIGH
4 BRANKSOME CT
5 MARTELLO HO
Lilliput
BH14
POOLE
Canford Cliffs
Compton Acres Gdns
Luscombe Valley
Poole Harbour
Main Channel
BH13
Brownsea Island
Branksea Castle
North Haven Point
Piers
Sandbanks
Sandbanks Bsns Ctr
Hotel
South Haven Point
Shell Bay Sailing Ctr
Gravel Point
Shell Bay
BH19
Bramble Bush Bay
Dorset Coastal Path
South West Coast Path
Ferry (P) (April to September)
Ferry (V)
Poole Head
Canford Cliffs Chine
St Ann's
Flag Head Chine
Promenade
SANDBANKS RD
SHORE RD
BANKS RD
HAVEN RD
WESTERN RD
PANORAMA RD
B3369
B3065
F7
1 MERROW CHASE
2 CANFORD PL
3 RIVIERA CT
4 IMPERIAL CT
5 RAVINE GDNS
6 KILLOCK
7 FINESHADE
8 SEA POINT
9 TREETOPS
10 PINE LODGE
11 LEYTON CONYERS
12 STANTON LACY
13 BURNAGE CT
1 HARBOUR CT
2 HAVENHURST
3 CHADDESLEY GRANGE
4 CHADDESLEY PINES
5 CANFORD CT
1 FAIRWINDS
2 GOLDEN SANDS
3 WOODRISING
4 MANSARD CT
5 GOLDEN GATES
204
Seaward Path
Branksome Chine
THE AVENUE
PINECLIFF RD
Liby
Dorset STREET ATLAS
213

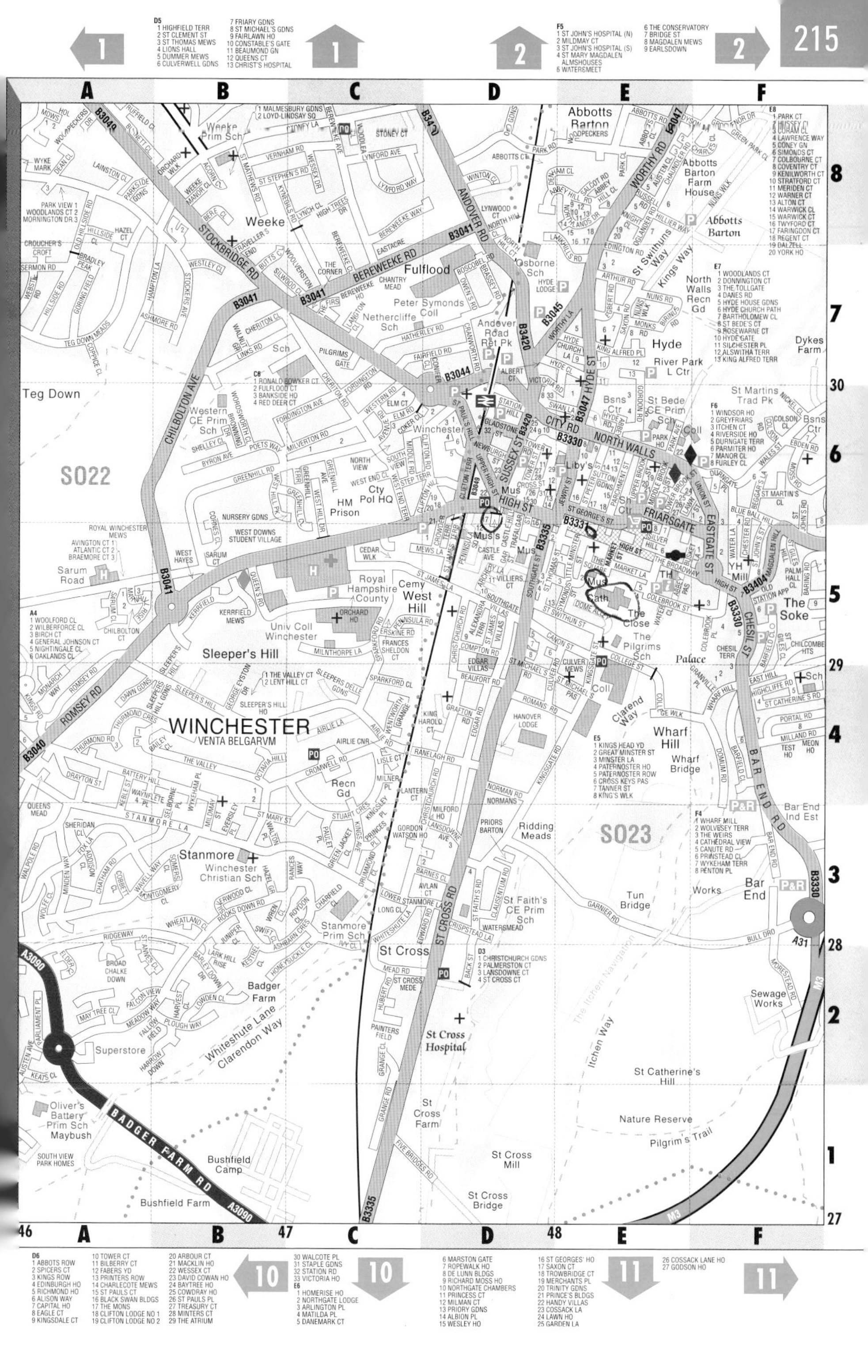
D5
1 HIGHFIELD TERR
2 ST CLEMENT ST
3 ST THOMAS MEWS
4 LIONS HALL
5 DUMMER MEWS
6 CULVERWELL GDNS
7 FRIARY GDNS
8 ST MICHAEL'S GDNS
9 FAIRLAWN HO
10 CONSTABLE'S GATE
11 BEAUMOND GN
12 QUEENS CT
13 CHRIST'S HOSPITAL
F5
1 ST JOHN'S HOSPITAL (N)
2 MILDMAY CT
3 ST JOHN'S HOSPITAL (S)
4 ST MARY MAGDALEN ALMSHOUSES
5 WATERSMEET
6 THE CONSERVATORY
7 BRIDGE ST
8 MAGDALEN MEWS
9 EARLSDOWN
E8
1 PARK CT
2 HUSSEY CL
3 CURAM CL
4 LAWRENCE WAY
5 CONEY GN
6 SIMONDS CT
7 COLBOURNE CT
8 COVENTRY CT
9 KENILWORTH CT
10 STRATFORD CT
11 MERIDEN CT
12 WARNER CT
13 ALTON CT
14 WARWICK CL
15 WARWICK CT
16 TWYFORD CT
17 FARINGDON CT
18 REGENT CT
19 DALZELL
20 YORK HO
E7
1 WOODLANDS CT
2 DONNINGTON CT
3 THE TOLLGATE
4 DANES RD
5 HYDE HOUSE GDNS
6 HYDE CHURCH PATH
7 BARTHOLOMEW CL
8 ST BEDE'S CT
9 ROSEWARNE CT
10 HYDE GATE
11 SILCHESTER PL
12 ALSWITHA TERR
13 KING ALFRED TERR
F6
1 WINDSOR HO
2 GREYFRIARS
3 ITCHEN CT
4 RIVERSIDE HO
5 DURNGATE TERR
6 PARMITER HO
7 MANOR CL
8 FURLEY CT
C8
1 RONALD BOWKER CT
2 FULFLOOD CT
3 BANKSIDE HO
4 RED DEER CT
A4
1 WOOLFORD CL
2 WILBERFORCE CL
3 BIRCH CT
4 GENERAL JOHNSON CT
5 NIGHTINGALE CL
6 OAKLANDS CL
E5
1 KINGS HEAD YD
2 GREAT MINSTER ST
3 MINSTER LA
4 PATERNOSTER HO
5 PATERNOSTER ROW
6 CROSS KEYS PAS
7 TANNER ST
8 KING'S WLK
F4
1 WHARF MILL
2 WOLVESEY TERR
3 THE WEIRS
4 CATHEDRAL VIEW
5 CANUTE RD
6 PRINSTEAD CL
7 WYKEHAM TERR
8 FENTON PL
D3
1 CHRISTCHURCH GDNS
2 PALMERSTON CT
3 LANSDOWNE CT
4 ST CROSS CT
WINCHESTER
VENTA BELGARVM
S022
S023
Weeke
Fulflood
Abbotts Barton
Teg Down
Sleeper's Hill
Stanmore
St Cross
Badger Farm
Hyde
The Soke
Bar End
Wharf Hill
St Catherine's Hill
Nature Reserve
Pilgrim's Trail
Itchen Way
The Itchen Navigation
Whiteshute Lane
Clarendon Way
St Cross Hospital
St Cross Farm
St Cross Mill
St Cross Bridge
Bushfield Camp
Bushfield Farm
Oliver's Battery Prim Sch
Maybush
Superstore
Sewage Works
Royal Hampshire County
HM Prison
Peter Symonds Coll
Nethercliffe Sch
Univ Coll Winchester
Winchester Christian Sch
Stanmore Prim Sch
St Faith's CE Prim Sch
Western CE Prim Sch
Andover Road Ret Pk
Cty Pol HQ
Cemy
West Hill
The Close
The Pilgrims Sch
Palace
Ridding Meads
Tun Bridge
Whart Bridge
Bar End Ind Est
Dykes Farm
St Martins Trad Pk
North Walls Recn Gd
River Park L Ctr
St Bede CE Prim Sch
Osborne Sch
Sarum Road
Recn Gd
STOCKBRIDGE RD
BEREWEEKE RD
ANDOVER RD
WORTHY RD
HYDE ST
CITY RD
NORTH WALLS
HIGH ST
FRIARSGATE
EASTGATE ST
CHESIL ST
BAR END RD
ST CROSS RD
ROMSEY RD
CHILBOLTON AVE
BADGER FARM RD
SOUTHGATE ST
SUSSEX ST
ST JAMES LA
B3040
B3041
B3049
B3044
B3045
B3047
B3420
B3330
B3331
B3335
B3404
A3090
M3
D6
1 ABBOTS ROW
2 SPICERS CT
3 KINGS ROW
4 EDINBURGH HO
5 RICHMOND HO
6 ALISON WAY
7 CAPITAL HO
8 EAGLE CT
9 KINGSDALE CT
10 TOWER CT
11 BILBERRY CT
12 FABERS YD
13 PRINTERS ROW
14 CHARLECOTE MEWS
15 ST PAULS CT
16 BLACK SWAN BLDGS
17 THE MONS
18 CLIFTON LODGE NO 1
19 CLIFTON LODGE NO 2
20 ARBOUR CT
21 MACKLIN HO
22 WESSEX CT
23 DAVID COWAN HO
24 BAYTREE HO
25 COWDRAY HO
26 ST PAULS PL
27 TREASURY CT
28 MINTERS CT
29 THE ATRIUM
30 WALCOTE PL
31 STAPLE GDNS
32 STATION RD
33 VICTORIA HO
E6
1 HOMERISE HO
2 NORTHGATE LODGE
3 ARLINGTON PL
4 MATILDA PL
5 DANEMARK CT
6 MARSTON GATE
7 ROPEWALK HO
8 DE LUNN BLDGS
9 RICHARD MOSS HO
10 NORTHGATE CHAMBERS
11 PRINCESS CT
12 MILMAN CT
13 PRIORY GDNS
14 ALBION PL
15 WESLEY HO
16 ST GEORGES' HO
17 SAXON CT
18 TROWBRIDGE CT
19 MERCHANTS PL
20 TRINITY GDNS
21 PRINCE'S BLDGS
22 HANDY VILLAS
23 COSSACK LA
24 LAWN HO
25 GARDEN LA
26 COSSACK LANE HO
27 GODSON HO

1 1 2 2 10 10 11 11

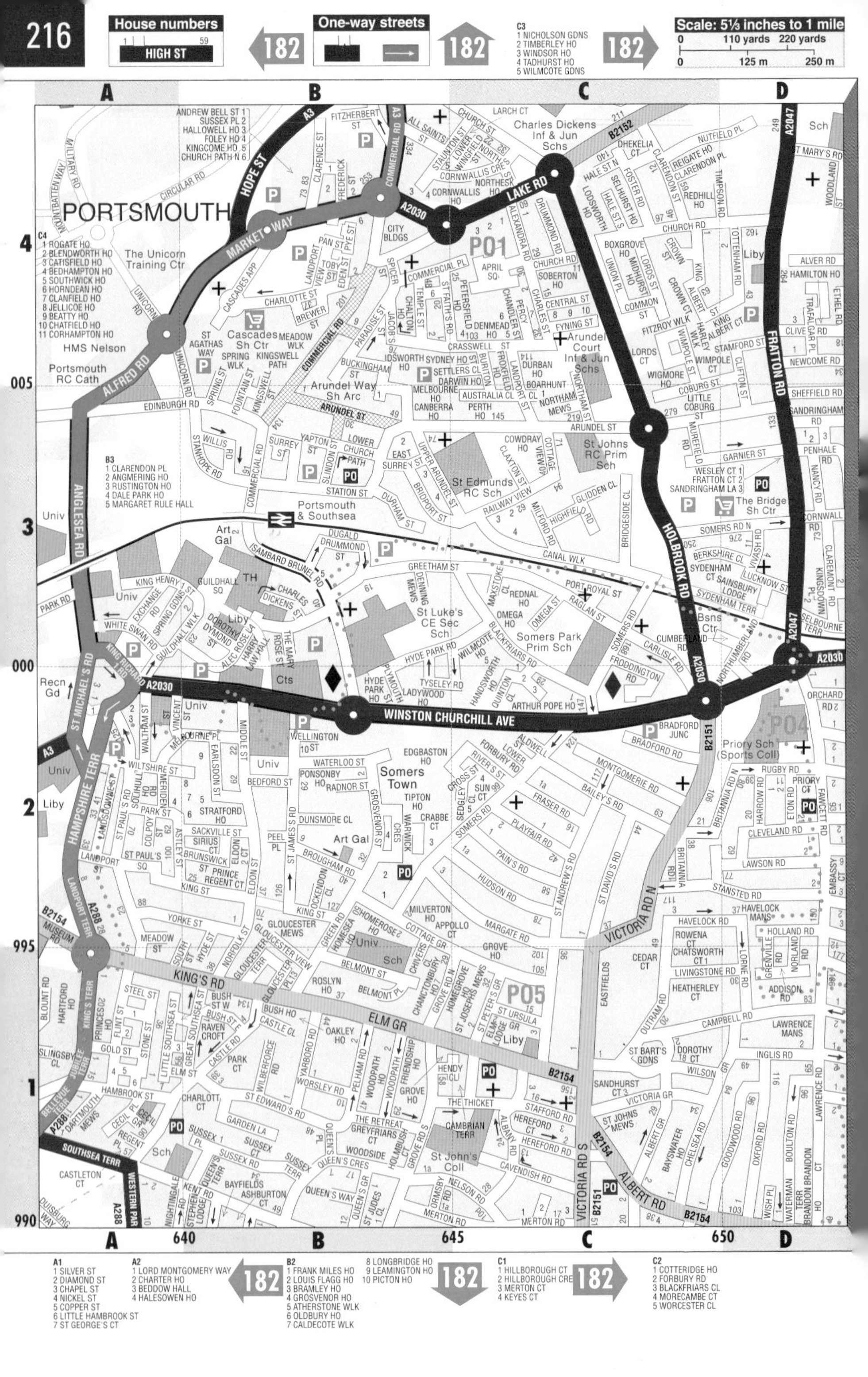
216
House numbers
HIGH ST
182
One-way streets
182
C3
1 NICHOLSON GDNS
2 TIMBERLEY HO
3 WINDSOR HO
4 TADHURST HO
5 WILMCOTE GDNS
182
Scale: 5⅓ inches to 1 mile
110 yards 220 yards
125 m 250 m
A
B
C
D
ANDREW BELL ST 1
SUSSEX PL 2
HALLOWELL HO 3
FOLEY HO 4
KINGCOME HO 5
CHURCH PATH N 6
PORTSMOUTH
C4
1 ROGATE HO
2 BLENDWORTH HO
3 CATISFIELD HO
4 BEDHAMPTON HO
5 SOUTHWICK HO
6 HORNDEAN HO
7 CLANFIELD HO
8 JELLICOE HO
9 BEATTY HO
10 CHATFIELD HO
11 CORHAMPTON HO
The Unicorn Training Ctr
HMS Nelson
Portsmouth RC Cath
Charles Dickens Inf & Jun Schs
Cascades Sh Ctr
Arundel Way Sh Arc
Arundel Court Inf & Jun Schs
St Johns RC Prim Sch
St Edmunds RC Sch
B3
1 CLARENDON PL
2 ANGMERING HO
3 RUSTINGTON HO
4 DALE PARK HO
5 MARGARET RULE HALL
Portsmouth & Southsea
WESLEY CT 1
FRATTON CT 2
SANDRINGHAM LA 3
The Bridge Sh Ctr
St Luke's CE Sec Sch
Somers Park Prim Sch
Priory Sch (Sports Coll)
Somers Town
St John's Coll
PO1
PO4
PO5
MARKET WAY
HOPE ST
COMMERCIAL RD
LAKE RD
HOLBROOK RD
FRATTON RD
ANGLESEA RD
ALFRED RD
WINSTON CHURCHILL AVE
HAMPSHIRE TERR
KING'S RD
ELM GR
VICTORIA RD N
VICTORIA RD S
ALBERT RD
SOUTHSEA TERR
ARUNDEL ST
CANAL WLK
A
640
B
645
C
650
D
A1
1 SILVER ST
2 DIAMOND ST
3 CHAPEL ST
4 NICKEL ST
5 COPPER ST
6 LITTLE HAMBROOK ST
7 ST GEORGE'S CT
A2
1 LORD MONTGOMERY WAY
2 CHARTER HO
3 BEDDOW HALL
4 HALESOWEN HO
182
B2
1 FRANK MILES HO
2 LOUIS FLAGG HO
3 BRAMLEY HO
4 GROSVENOR HO
5 ATHERSTONE WLK
6 OLDBURY HO
7 CALDECOTE WLK
8 LONGBRIDGE HO
9 LEAMINGTON HO
10 PICTON HO
182
C1
1 HILLBOROUGH CT
2 HILLBOROUGH CRES
3 MERTON CT
4 KEYES CT
182
C2
1 COTTERIDGE HO
2 FORBURY RD
3 BLACKFRIARS CL
4 MORECAMBE CT
5 WORCESTER CL

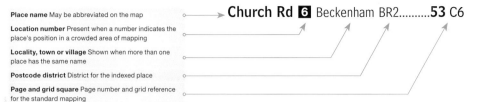

Place name May be abbreviated on the map

Location number Present when a number indicates the place's position in a crowded area of mapping

Locality, town or village Shown when more than one place has the same name

Postcode district District for the indexed place

Page and grid square Page number and grid reference for the standard mapping

Church Rd **6** Beckenham BR2.........**53** C6

Public and commercial buildings are highlighted in magenta. Places of interest are highlighted in blue with a star *

Abbreviations used in the index

Acad	**Academy**	Comm	**Common**	Gd	**Ground**	L	**Leisure**	Prom	**Promenade**
App	**Approach**	Cott	**Cottage**	Gdn	**Garden**	La	**Lane**	Rd	**Road**
Arc	**Arcade**	Cres	**Crescent**	Gn	**Green**	Liby	**Library**	Recn	**Recreation**
Ave	**Avenue**	Cswy	**Causeway**	Gr	**Grove**	Mdw	**Meadow**	Ret	**Retail**
Bglw	**Bungalow**	Ct	**Court**	H	**Hall**	Meml	**Memorial**	Sh	**Shopping**
Bldg	**Building**	Ctr	**Centre**	Ho	**House**	Mkt	**Market**	Sq	**Square**
Bsns, Bus	**Business**	Ctry	**Country**	Hospl	**Hospital**	Mus	**Museum**	St	**Street**
Bvd	**Boulevard**	Cty	**County**	HQ	**Headquarters**	Orch	**Orchard**	Sta	**Station**
Cath	**Cathedral**	Dr	**Drive**	Hts	**Heights**	Pal	**Palace**	Terr	**Terrace**
Cir	**Circus**	Dro	**Drove**	Ind	**Industrial**	Par	**Parade**	TH	**Town Hall**
Cl	**Close**	Ed	**Education**	Inst	**Institute**	Pas	**Passage**	Univ	**University**
Cnr	**Corner**	Emb	**Embankment**	Int	**International**	Pk	**Park**	Wk, Wlk	**Walk**
Coll	**College**	Est	**Estate**	Intc	**Interchange**	Pl	**Place**	Wr	**Water**
Com	**Community**	Ex	**Exhibition**	Junc	**Junction**	Prec	**Precinct**	Yd	**Yard**

Index of localities, towns and villages

A

Abbotswood 28 A3
Abbotts Barton 215 C8
Abshot 153 C8
Alderholt 92 F5
Aldermoor 78 A3
Alderney 188 C1
Aldsworth 137 D6
Allbrook 56 B7
Alverstoke 181 A4
Ameysford 138 C1
Ampfield 29 C3
Anchorage Park 158 C3
Anmore 111 B4
Ann's Hill 180 F5
Anthill Common 110 D6
Applemore 125 A4
Appleslade Bottom .. 118 A4
Ashfield 53 B3
Ashford 69 C1
Ashington 163 A1
Ashlett 151 D3
Ashley
  New Milton 195 D3
  St Leonards 140 B6
Ashley Heath 139 E6
Ashton 59 B2
Ashurst 100 B3
Ashurst Bridge 100 C5
Avon 167 F2
Avon Castle 140 D3
Awbridge 26 E4

B

Baffins 183 B7
Bagnum 141 E2
Balmerlawn 146 B3
Banister's Park 102 E7
Bank 121 D2
Bar End 215 F3
Bartley 99 B6
Barton on Sea 209 F6
Bashley 179 A5
Bassett 79 A5
Battramsley 173 B2
Battramsley Cross .. 173 C1
Baybridge 33 D3
Beacon Hill 186 A2

Bear Cross 188 F5
Bearwood 188 E6
Beaulieu 148 E1
Beauworth 34 A8
Beckley 194 C5
Bedford Place 102 F6
Bedhampton 135 C1
Bellevue 103 A6
Bell Hill 40 E5
Belvidere 103 C5
Bevois Mount 103 A8
Bevois Town 103 A7
Bevois Valley 103 B7
Bickton 93 F6
Bishopstoke 56 E3
Bishopstone 22 D8
Bishop's Waltham ... 83 C7
Bisterne 167 F6
Bisterne Close 143 D2
Bitterne 103 F8
Bitterne Manor 103 D7
Bitterne Pk 79 F2
Blackfield 150 D1
Blackwater 191 D4
Blashford 117 A3
Bleak Hill 93 C3
Blendworth 112 D8
Blissford 94 F8
Boarhunt 132 B5
Bohemia 47 F4
Boldre 173 D1
Boorley Green 81 F2
Borough Hill 40 E3
Boscombe 205 E3
Botany Bay 104 A3
Botley 106 B7
Bourne Valley 204 B6
Bournemouth 205 A2
Boveridge 67 A2
Bowling Green 196 F6
Boyatt Wood 56 A5
Braishfield 28 C7
Brambridge 56 E8
Bramdean 15 C4
Bramshaw 73 F4
Branksome 203 F5
Branksome Park ... 203 F1
Bransgore 193 A8
Breach 137 E1
Breamore 70 B8
Bridgemary 155 C3
Broadgate 29 E2

Broadoak 105 E7
Broadstone 187 B3
Brockbridge 61 C1
Brockenhurst 145 E2
Brockhampton 135 D1
Brockhurst 180 E7
Brokenford 100 F7
Brook 74 A1
Brook Hill 74 A2
Broom Hill 56 A7
Brown Heath 82 D5
Buckland
  Lymington 197 D5
  Portsmouth 182 E8
Bucklers Hard 200 D4
Bunstead 30 D6
Buriton 65 D6
Burley 143 A3
Burley Lawn 143 B4
Burley Street 142 E5
Burridge 106 B1
Bursledon 128 B8
Burton 192 D2
Butlocks Heath 127 D7
Buttsash 150 B8

C

Cadnam 98 E7
Calmore 76 B2
Calshot 178 F8
Camdentown 181 A6
Camel Green 93 A6
Canada 50 D1
Canford Cliffs 214 E8
Canford Heath 187 E1
Canford Magna 164 A1
Carter's Clay 26 B6
Catherington 88 B1
Catisfield 130 A1
Causeway
  Horndean 112 A6
  Petersfield 40 F7
Chalton 89 C5
Chandler's Ford 55 C8
Chapel 103 B4
Charminster 190 C2
Cheriton 14 D6
Chidden 86 F8
Chilbridge 162 E7
Chilcomb 11 F6

Chilworth 54 D2
Christchurch 207 D5
Clanfield 88 B5
Clayhall 181 D2
Clayhill 122 A3
Claypits 105 B1
Clewers Hill 83 D4
Colbury 100 D2
Colden Common 32 A1
Colehill 164 B8
Compton
  Brook 6 D7
  Horndean 90 E1
  Shawford 31 D8
Compton Down 31 C7
Coombe Bissett 23 E8
Copnor 158 A1
Copythorne 75 B1
Corfe Mullen 186 C6
Corhampton 61 B5
Cosham 158 B6
Course Park 129 D2
Coweslield Gate 25 D1
Cowgrove 162 D4
Cowplain 111 F3
Coxford 78 A2
Crab Orchard 114 F2
Crampmoor 28 F1
Creekmoor 201 F8
Crendell 91 F7
Criddlestyle 70 C1
Cripplestyle 92 A5
Critchell's Green 25 D1
Crockerhill 131 B8
Crosshouse 103 C3
Croucheston 22 B7
Crow 141 C4
Crowhill 57 C5
Crowsfield Green ... 24 D3
Cupernham 28 B2
Curbridge 106 D4
Curdridge 106 D8
Curdridge Firs 82 F1
Custards 122 A6

D

Daggons 92 C5
Damerham 68 C4
Dean 59 E3
Deanlane End 113 E5

Dean Park 205 A4
Denmead 111 A5
Denvilles 136 B2
Dibden 125 D5
Dibden Purlieu 125 E1
Downend 131 F1
Downton
  Milford on Sea 210 F7
  Redlynch 47 A8
Drayton
  Cosham 158 C7
  East Meon 38 C3
Droxford 61 A1
Dudsbury 165 C1
Dunbridge 5 D1
Dundridge 60 B1
Dunwood Hill 26 D1
Durley 82 B5
Durley Street 82 D7
Durns Town 172 D2
Durrants 136 B8

E

East Boldre 175 C5
East Brook 163 C5
East Dean 4 B2
East End
  Corfe Mullen 162 E1
  Damerham 68 D5
  East Boldre 199 B7
East Howe 189 C5
Eastleigh 56 C1
East Meon 38 D1
Eastney 183 C3
Eastoke 185 C2
Easton Down 2 D4
East Parley 190 B8
East Tytherley 4 E8
Ebblake 115 C3
Edmondsham 91 A4
Eling 101 B5
Ellingham 116 E5
Elson 181 A9
Emery Down 121 D6
Emsworth 136 E2
Ensbury 189 F6
Ensbury Park 189 C2
Everton 196 E1
Exbury 177 B5
Exton 61 C7

1

1st St SO45 . . . . .151 A4

2

2nd St SO45 . . . . .151 A4

3

3rd St SO45 . . . . .150 F4

4

4th St SO45 . . . . .150 F4

5

5th St Blackfield SO45 . . . .150 E4
Fawley SO45 . . . . .150 F5

6

6th St Fawley SO45 . . . . . . .150 E4
Fawley SO45 . . . . .150 F6

7

7th St Fawley SO45 . . . . . . .150 E4
Fawley SO45 . . . . .150 E5

8

8th St Fawley SO45 . . . . . . .150 E4

9

9th St SO45 . . . . .150 D4

1

10th St SO45 . . . . .150 D5
11th St SO45 . . . . .150 D5
12th St SO45 . . . . .150 D5
13th St SO45 . . . . .150 D6
14th St SO45 . . . . .150 D6
17th Century Experience*
PO13 . . . . .180 C5

A

A Ave SO45 . . . . .150 D4
A'Becket Ct **3** PO1 . . . .182 A4
Aaron Cl BH17 . . . . .202 F7
Aaron Ct SO40 . . . . .101 F2
Abbas Gn PO9 . . . . .135 D7
Abbey Cl SO45 . . . . .126 A3
Abbey Ct **3** SO15 . . . . . . .102 F7
Abbey Ent Ctr SO51 . . . . . . .53 D5
Abbey Fruit Park Ind Est
SO31 . . . . .127 C7
Abbey Gdns BH21 . . . . .164 D5
Abbey Hill SO31 . . . . .127 A7
Abbey Hill Cl SO23 . . . . . . .215 E8
Abbey Mill Bsns Site
SO32 . . . . .83 C7
Abbey Pas SO23 . . . . .215 E5
Abbey Rd Fareham PO15 . .130 D2
West Moors BH22 . . . . .166 A8
Abbey The SO51 . . . . .52 E7
Abbey Water **3** SO51 . . . . .52 E7
Abbeydore Rd PO6 . . . . . . .133 C1
Abbeyfield Dr PO15 . . . . . .130 C2
Abbeyfield Ho **3** SO18 . .103 E8
Abbeyfields Cl SO31 . . . . . .127 D6
Abbeymede PO6 . . . . .157 E8
Abbots Cl
Christchurch BH23 . . . . . . .208 F7
Waterlooville PO7 . . . . .134 C4
Abbots Lea Cotts SO23 . . . . .2 B3
Abbots Row **1** SO22 . . . .215 D6
Abbots Way
Fareham PO15 . . . . .130 D1
Netley SO31 . . . . .127 D6
Abbots Well Rd SP6 . . . . . . .94 F7
Abbotsbury Rd
Bishopstoke SO52 . . . . .56 F2
Corfe Mullen BH18 . . . . . . .186 F5
Abbotsfield SO40 . . . . .100 E8
Abbotsfield Cl SO16 . . . . . . .78 C5
Abbotsford SO40 . . . . .99 B6
Abbotstone Ave PO9 . . . . . .136 A4
Abbotswood Cl SO51 . . . . . .28 C1
Abbotswood Jun Sch
SO40 . . . . .100 E7
Abbott Cl BH9 . . . . .205 A8
Abbott Rd BH9 . . . . .205 A8
Abbott St BH21 . . . . .162 D6
Abbotts Ann Rd SO22 . . . . . .1 D3
Abbotts Cl SO23 . . . . .215 E8
Abbotts Ct
6 Southampton SO17 . . . . .79 A1

Abbotts Ct continued
Winchester SO22 . . . . .215 D8
Abbotts Dro SO51 . . . . .50 E1
Abbotts Rd Eastleigh SO50 .55 F1
Winchester SO23 . . . . .215 E8
Abbotts Way
Southampton SO17 . . . . .79 B1
West Moors BH22 . . . . .166 A8
Abercrombie Gdns SO16 . .78 A4
Aberdare Ave PO6 . . . . .158 B8
Aberdare Rd BH10 . . . . .189 E3
Aberdeen Cl PO15 . . . . .130 E3
Aberdeen Rd SO17 . . . . .79 C1
Aberdour Cl SO18 . . . . .104 B8
Abingdon Cl PO12 . . . . .181 B5
Abingdon Dr BH23 . . . . . . .209 C8
Abingdon Gdns SO16 . . . . . .78 E3
Abingdon Rd BH17 . . . . . . .202 D8
Abinger Rd BH7 . . . . .206 B6
Abney Rd BH10 . . . . .189 D3
Above Bar St SO14 . . . . . . .102 F5
Abraham Cl SO30 . . . . .105 D5
Abshot Cl PO14 . . . . .129 B1
Abshot Rd PO14 . . . . .129 B1
Acacia Ave BH31 . . . . .115 C4
Acacia Gdns PO8 . . . . .111 E8
Acacia Lodge **2** PO16 . .131 B1
Acacia Rd Hordle SO41 . . . .195 F3
Southampton SO19 . . . . . . .103 F5
Acanthas Ct PO15 . . . . .106 D1
Acer Way PO9 . . . . .136 B4
Ackworth Rd PO3 . . . . .158 A5
Acland Rd BH9 . . . . .205 B8
Acorn Ave BH15 . . . . .202 D2
Acorn Bsns Ctr PO6 . . . . . .157 D7
Acorn Bsns Pk BH12 . . . . .203 B8
Acorn Cl
Christchurch BH23 . . . . . . .206 F8
Farlington PO6 . . . . .158 E8
Gosport PO13 . . . . .155 D1
Marchwood SO40 . . . . .102 A1
New Milton BH25 . . . . .195 C4
St Leonards BH24 . . . . .139 E3
Winchester SO22 . . . . .215 B8
Acorn Cotts BH31 . . . . .114 F7
Acorn Ct SO31 . . . . .127 F3
Acorn Dr SO16 . . . . .77 F7
Acorn Gdns PO8 . . . . .112 B6
Acorn Gr SO53 . . . . .54 F4
Acorn Way BH31 . . . . .115 A6
Acorn Workshops SO14 . .103 B7
Acorns The
Bursledon SO31 . . . . .127 F8
West Moors BH24 . . . . .166 B8
Wimborne Minst BH21 . . . .164 A4
Acre La PO7 . . . . .112 C1
Acres Rd BH11 . . . . .189 B2
Acton Rd BH10 . . . . .189 B1
Ad Astro Fst Sch BH17 . . . .187 F1
Adair Rd PO4 . . . . .183 A2
Adames Rd PO1 . . . . .182 E6
Adams Cl SO30 . . . . .81 B3
Adams Rd SO45 . . . . .126 A2
Adams Terr PO6 . . . . .158 C6
Adams Way PO15 . . . . .204 B5
Adams Wood Dr SO40 . . . .101 F1
Adamsfield Gdns BH10 . . .189 C2
Adamson Cl SO53 . . . . .55 D8
Adastral Rd BH17 . . . . .202 F8
Adastral Sq BH17 . . . . .202 F8
Adcock Ct SO16 . . . . .77 E7
Adderbury Ave PO10 . . . . . .136 F3
Addington Cl SO41 . . . . .211 D5
Addington Pl BH23 . . . . . . .207 D6
Addis Ho SO17 . . . . .79 B1
Addis Sq SO17 . . . . .79 B1
Addiscombe Rd BH23 . . . . .207 A7
Addison Cl Romsey SO51 . . .28 B1
Winchester SO22 . . . . .215 A3
Addison Rd
Brockenhurst SO42 . . . . . . .172 E8
Eastleigh SO50 . . . . .56 B5
Locks Heath SO31 . . . . .129 A6
Portsmouth PO4 . . . . .216 D1
Sarisbury SO31 . . . . .128 F6
Addison Sq BH24 . . . . .141 B7
Adela Verne Cl SO19 . . . . . .104 E3
Adelaide Cl BH23 . . . . .206 F8
Adelaide Ct SO41 . . . . .197 F4
Adelaide La **17** BH1 . . . .204 F3
Adelaide Pl **7** PO16 . . . .131 C1
Adelaide Rd SO17 . . . . .103 C8
Adeline Rd BH1,BH5 . . . . . .205 E4
Adey Cl SO19 . . . . .104 B2
Adhurst Rd PO9 . . . . .136 A4
Adlam's La SO41 . . . . .222 F7
Admiral Lord Nelson Sch
PO3 . . . . .158 B1
Admiral Park The PO3 . . . .158 A4
Admiral Pl **11** PO6 . . . . .157 F8
Admiral's Cnr **13** PO5 . .182 D2
Admiral's Wlk PO1 . . . . .181 F7
Admirals Ct
Hamble-le-R SO31 . . . . .128 A2
Lymington SO41 . . . . .197 F4
2 Portsmouth PO5 . . . . .182 C2
Admirals Ho SO31 . . . . .152 C10
Admirals Rd SO31 . . . . .129 B4
Admirals Way SO45 . . . . . . .126 A5
Admirals Wlk
Bournemouth BH2 . . . . . . .204 D2
Gosport PO12 . . . . .180 F3
Admiralty Cl PO12 . . . . .181 C8
Admiralty Cotts PO12 . . . . .181 C2
Admiralty Ho SO14 . . . . . . .103 A2
Admiralty Rd
Bournemouth BH6 . . . . . . .206 F3

Admiralty Rd continued
Portsmouth PO1 . . . . .182 A5
Admiralty Way SO40 . . . . . .101 F3
Adsdean Cl PO6 . . . . .135 E4
Adstone La PO3 . . . . .158 C4
Adur Cl Gosport PO12 . . . . .180 F7
West End SO18 . . . . .80 B1
Aerial Pk BH21 . . . . .164 E6
Aerial Rd PO6 . . . . .133 B2
Aerodrome Rd PO13 . . . . . .155 E3
Africa Dr SO40 . . . . .124 F8
Agar's La SO41 . . . . .196 B5
Agarton La SO41 . . . . .211 F6
Aggis Farm BH21 . . . . .114 E6
Agincourt Rd PO2 . . . . .182 D7
Agitator Rd SO45 . . . . .151 C4
Agnew Ho PO12 . . . . .181 B7
Agnew Rd PO13 . . . . .155 C3
Aikman La SO40 . . . . .100 B7
Ailsa La SO19 . . . . .103 D4
Ainsdale Rd PO6 . . . . .134 D1
Ainsley Gdns SO50 . . . . .56 A5
Aintree Cl SO40 . . . . .81 D7
Aintree Ct SO31 . . . . .129 B8
Aintree Dr PO7 . . . . .112 B1
Aintree Rd SO40 . . . . .76 C1
Airetons Cl BH18 . . . . .187 C3
Airfield Ind Est
Christchurch BH23 . . . . . . .207 F6
Christchurch BH23 . . . . . . .208 A7
Airfield Rd BH23 . . . . .207 F6
Airfield Way BH23 . . . . .207 F7
Airlie Ct SO22 . . . . .215 C4
Airlie La SO22 . . . . .215 C4
Airlie Rd SO22 . . . . .215 C4
Airport Service Rd
Portsmouth PO3 . . . . .158 A4
Portsmouth PO3 . . . . .158 B3
Airspeed Rd
Christchurch BH23 . . . . . . .208 B7
Portsmouth PO3 . . . . .158 C2
Ajax Cl PO14 . . . . .179 D6
Akeshill Cl BH25 . . . . .195 B5
Alameda Rd PO7 . . . . .134 D4
Alameda Way PO7 . . . . .134 D4
Alan Chun Ho SO31 . . . . . . .127 C7
Alan Cl **10** BH23 . . . . . . .209 B7
Alan Drayton Way SO50 . .56 F7
Alan Gr PO15 . . . . .130 E2
Alandale Rd SO40 . . . . .104 D4
Albacore Ave SO31 . . . . . . .128 F1
Albany Bh1 . . . . .205 C3
Albany Bsns Ctr PO17 . . . .131 B7
Albany Cl BH25 . . . . .194 F1
Albany Ct
Bishop's Waltham SO32 . . . .83 A8
6 Bournemouth BH2 . . .204 F4
Gosport PO12 . . . . .181 B6
Albany Dr
Bishop's Waltham SO32 . . . .83 A8
Three Legged Cross BH21 . .114 E1
Albany Gdns BH15 . . . . .201 F2
Albany Ho **17** BH13 . . . .204 A4
Albany Park Ct SO17 . . . . . .102 F8
Albany Pk BH17 . . . . .202 B8
Albany Rd
Bishop's Waltham SO32 . . . .83 A8
Holbury SO45 . . . . .150 C4
Portsmouth PO5 . . . . .216 C1
Romsey SO51 . . . . .52 F7
Southampton SO15 . . . . . . .102 C6
Albany The **23** SO14 . . . .102 F3
Albatross Wlk PO13 . . . . . .155 B2
Albemarle Ave PO12 . . . . . .181 B9
Albemarle Rd BH3 . . . . .204 F7
Albermarle Ct SO17 . . . . . . .79 C3
Albert Cl SO31 . . . . .127 C5
Albert Ct
Southampton SO17 . . . . .79 C1
Albert Gr PO5 . . . . .216 C1
Albert Rd
Bishop's Waltham SO32 . . . .83 A7
Bournemouth BH1 . . . . . . .204 F3
Corfe Mullen BH21 . . . . . . .186 D5
Cosham PO6 . . . . .157 F7
Eastleigh SO50 . . . . .56 B5
Ferndown BH22 . . . . .161 F3
Hedge End SO30 . . . . .105 B5
New Milton BH25 . . . . .194 F2
Poole BH12 . . . . .203 D6
Portsmouth PO4,PO5 . . . . .182 E2
Stubbington PO14 . . . . .179 F7
Albert Rd N SO14 . . . . .103 B3
Albert Rd S SO14 . . . . .103 B3
Albert St PO12 . . . . .181 C6
Albion Cl Poole BH22 . . . . . .203 B7
Portchester PO16 . . . . .156 B6
Albion Pl
3 Southampton SO14 . .102 F4
14 Winchester SO23 . . .215 E6
Albion Rd
Christchurch BH23 . . . . . . .191 F1
Edgebridge SP6 . . . . .69 F2
Lee-on-t-S PO13 . . . . .179 E4
Albion Twrs SO14 . . . . .103 B4
Albion Way BH31 . . . . .114 D7
Albretia Ave PO8 . . . . .111 E3
Albury Pl **10** SO53 . . . . . . .30 B1
Alby Rd BH12 . . . . .203 F5
Alcantara Cres SO14 . . . . . .103 B3
Alcester Rd BH12 . . . . .203 D6
Alchorne Pl PO3 . . . . .158 B3
Aldbury Ct BH25 . . . . .210 A7
Alder Cl Burton BH23 . . . . .192 D1
Colden Common SO21 . . . . .57 A8
Hythe SO45 . . . . .125 C2
Marchwood SO40 . . . . .101 F2

Alder Cl continued
Romsey SO51 . . . . .53 D6
Alder Cres BH12 . . . . .203 F7
Alder Dr SP6 . . . . .92 F5
Alder Hill Dr SO40 . . . . .100 B8
Alder Hills BH12 . . . . .204 A8
Alder Hills Ind Pk BH12 . .204 A7
Alder Hills Nature Reserve*
BH12 . . . . .204 A7
Alder Mts BH12 . . . . .188 D1
Alder La PO12,PO13 . . . . . .180 D5
Alder Rd Poole BH12 . . . . . .203 F6
Southampton SO16 . . . . .78 A3
Alderfield GU32 . . . . .40 E3
Alderholt Mill & Craft Ctr*
SP6 .68 F1
Alderholt Rd SP6 . . . . .69 A2
Alderley Rd BH10 . . . . .189 D4
Alderman Quilley Sch
SO50 . . . . .55 F1
Alderman Quilley Sch The
SO50 . . . . .56 A1
Aldermoor Ave SO16 . . . . . .78 A4
Aldermoor Cl SO16 . . . . .78 C4
Aldermoor Rd
Gosport PO13 . . . . .180 D7
Southampton SO16 . . . . .78 B4
Waterlooville PO7 . . . . .134 D5
Aldermoor Rd E PO7 . . . . . .134 D5
Alderney Ave BH12 . . . . . . .188 D1
Alderney Cl SO16 . . . . .77 E4
Alderney Hospl BH12 . . . . .188 D2
Alderney Rdbt BH12 . . . . . .188 D2
Alders Rd PO16 . . . . .155 B7
Aldershot Ho **31** PO9 . . .136 B5
Alderwood Ave SO53 . . . . . .55 A6
Alderwood Cl PO9 . . . . .135 B3
Aldis Gdns BH15 . . . . .201 E2
Aldrich Rd PO1 . . . . .182 A6
Aldridge Cl PO8 . . . . .88 C5
Aldridge Rd
Bournemouth BH10 . . . . . .189 C5
Ferndown BH22 . . . . .165 E3
Aldridge Way BH22 . . . . . . .165 F3
Aldroke St **1** PO6 . . . . . . .157 F7
Aldsworth Cl PO6 . . . . .158 C8
Aldsworth Common Rd
PO10 . . . . .137 C6
Aldsworth Gdns PO6 . . . . . .158 C8
Aldwell St PO5 . . . . .216 C2
Alec Rose Ho **17** PO12 . .181 C5
Alec Rose La PO1 . . . . .216 B3
Alec Wintle Ho PO2 . . . . . . .182 D8
Alecto Rd PO12 . . . . .181 B4
Alencon Cl **3** PO12 . . . . .181 C9
Alexander Cl
Christchurch BH23 . . . . . . .207 E6
Totton SO40 . . . . .100 D8
Waterlooville PO7 . . . . .134 D6
Alexander Ct
Southampton SO15 . . . . . . .102 D6
Southampton,Woolston
SO19 . . . . .103 E2
Alexander Gr PO16 . . . . .155 A8
Alexander Ho PO11 . . . . . . .185 E1
Alexandra Ave PO11 . . . . . .184 F2
Alexandra Cl SO45 . . . . .126 A4
Alexandra Ct
Hamble-le-R SO31 . . . . .127 F3
4 Portsmouth PO4 . . . . .182 E1
Alexandra Lodge **8**
BH1 . . . . .205 A3
Alexandra Mews SO31 . . . .102 E7
Alexandra Rd
Bournemouth BH6 . . . . . . .206 C5
Chandler's Ford SO53 . . . . . .55 F8
Fordingbridge SP6 . . . . .69 F2
Hedge End SO30 . . . . .105 B5
Hythe SO45 . . . . .126 A4
Lymington SO41 . . . . .197 C5
Poole BH14 . . . . .203 D5
Portsmouth PO1 . . . . .216 C4
Southampton SO15 . . . . . . .102 E6
Alexandra St **7** PO12 . . . .181 A7
Alexandra Terr SO23 . . . . . .215 D5
Alexandra Way SO30 . . . . . .106 A7
Alexandria Cl BH21 . . . . . . .186 D5
Alexandria Pk PO9 . . . . .159 E7
Alford Rd BH3 . . . . .204 D7
Alfred Cl SO40 . . . . .100 C7
Alfred Rd
Portsmouth PO1 . . . . .216 A4
Stubbington PO14 . . . . .179 D8
Alfred Rose Ct SO18 . . . . . . .79 E4
Alfred St SO14 . . . . .103 B6
Alfrey Cl PO10 . . . . .136 F6
Alfriston Ct SO19 . . . . .104 C4
Alfriston Gdns SO19 . . . . . .104 B4
Algiers Rd PO3 . . . . .183 B8
Alhambra Rd PO4 . . . . .182 E1
Alice in Wonderland Family
Fun Pk* BH23 . . . . .190 E7
Alington **22** BH4 . . . . .203 E8
Alington Cl BH14 . . . . .214 C7
Alington Ho BH14 . . . . .214 C7
Alington Manor Farm Cotts
SO50 . . . . .80 F7
Alington Rd
Bournemouth BH3 . . . . . . .205 A6
Poole BH14 . . . . .214 C7
Alipore Cl BH14 . . . . .203 D3
Alipore Rd BH14 . . . . .203 D3
Alison Way **12** SO22 . . . .215 D6
All Saint's Rd PO1 . . . . .182 D7
All Saints CE Prim Sch
SO23 . . . . .215 E4
All Saints Ho **7** SO14 . . .103 A3
All Saints Rd SO41 . . . . .197 F2

All Saints' St PO1 . . . . . . .216 B4
Allan Gr SO51 . . . . .53 B7
Allaway Ave PO6 . . . . .157 B8
Allbrook Ct PO9 . . . . .135 D6
Allbrook Hill SO50 . . . . .56 B7
Allbrook Knoll SO50 . . . . . . .56 A7
Allbrook Way SO50 . . . . .56 B7
Allcot Rd PO3 . . . . .158 A2
Allen Ct BH21 . . . . .163 C5
Allen Rd Hedge End SO30 . .105 C7
Wimborne Minst BH21 . . . .163 C4
Allen's Rd PO4 . . . . .182 E2
Allenbourn Mid Sch
BH21 . . . . .163 C5
Allenby Cl BH17 . . . . .187 B2
Allenby Gr PO16 . . . . .156 C2
Allenby Rd Gosport PO12 . .180 E6
Poole BH17 . . . . .187 B2
Allendale Ave PO10 . . . . . . .136 E3
Allens Farm La SO32 . . . . . .61 B6
Allens La Meonstoke SO32 .61 C5
Upton BH16 . . . . .201 E5
Allens Rd BH16 . . . . .201 D6
Allenview Rd BH21 . . . . . . .163 C5
Allenwater Dr SP6 . . . . .69 E2
Allerton Cl SO40 . . . . .76 D1
Alley The Bishopstone SP5 . .22 B8
Woodgreen SP6 . . . . .70 E8
Alliance Cl PO13 . . . . .180 D8
Alliance Ho PO1 . . . . .182 E6
Allington La SO30 . . . . .80 E5
Allington Manor Farm Bsns
Ctr SO50 . . . . .80 E7
Allington Manor Sch
SO50 . . . . .80 F7
Allington Rd SO15 . . . . .101 C3
Allison Ct **6** SO41 . . . . . .211 B4
Allison Ho SO30 . . . . .105 C8
Allmara Dr PO7 . . . . .134 F4
Allotment Rd
Hedge End SO30 . . . . .105 B6
Sarisbury SO31 . . . . .128 E6
Allyn Ct SO50 . . . . .56 B5
Alma Ho SO14 . . . . .103 A8
Alma La SO32 . . . . .58 B2
Alma Rd
Bournemouth BH9 . . . . . . .205 A7
Romsey SO51 . . . . .52 D8
Southampton SO14 . . . . . . .103 A8
Alma St PO12 . . . . .181 B7
Alma Terr PO4 . . . . .183 A3
Almatade Rd SO18 . . . . .104 A7
Almer Rd BH15 . . . . .201 E3
Almond Cl Havant PO9 . . . .158 C7
Waterlooville PO8 . . . . .112 C4
Almond Ct **8** SO15 . . . . .102 C6
Almond Gr BH12 . . . . .203 D7
Almond Rd SO15 . . . . .102 C6
Almondsbury Ho **8**
PO6 . . . . .132 F2
Almondsbury Rd PO6 . . . . .132 F2
Almondside PO13 . . . . .155 E1
Almshouses BH10 . . . . .189 C1
Alpha Ctr The BH17 . . . . . .202 B7
Alphage Rd PO12 . . . . .155 F1
Alpine Cl SO18 . . . . .79 F2
Alpine Rd
St Leonards BH24 . . . . .140 C2
Woodlands SO40 . . . . .99 F3
Alresford Rd
Chilcomb SO21 . . . . .12 D7
Havant PO9 . . . . .135 E4
Winchester SO23 . . . . .11 D7
Alsford Rd PO7 . . . . .134 D5
Alswitha Terr **12** SO23 . .215 E2
Alten Rd PO7 . . . . .111 C2
Althorpe Dr PO3 . . . . .158 C4
Alton Cl SO50 . . . . .57 B2
Alton Ct **16** SO23 . . . . . . .215 E8
Alton Gr PO16 . . . . .156 C6
Alton Ho SO18 . . . . .103 E8
Alton Rd
Bournemouth BH10 . . . . . .189 B1
Poole BH14 . . . . .203 C3
Alton Rd E BH14 . . . . .203 D2
Alum Chine Rd BH4 . . . . . .204 B3
Alum Cl SO45 . . . . .150 D3
Alum Way
Porchester PO16 . . . . .131 E1
Southampton SO18 . . . . .80 A3
Alumdale Rd BH4 . . . . .204 B2
Alumhurst Rd BH4 . . . . .204 A2
Alvandi Gdns **2** BH25 . . .195 B3
Alvara Rd PO12 . . . . .181 A4
Alver Bridge View **4**
PO12 . . . . .181 B4
Alver Quay PO12 . . . . .181 B4
Alver Rd Gosport PO12 . . . .181 B4
Portsmouth PO1 . . . . .182 D7
Alvercliffe Dr PO12 . . . . . . .180 F2
Alverstoke CE Jun Sch
PO12 . . . . .181 A4
Alverstoke Com Inf Sch
PO12 . . . . .181 A3
Alverstoke Ct PO12 . . . . . . .181 A3
Alverstone Rd PO4 . . . . .183 A3
Alverton Ave PO14 . . . . .202 F3
Alverton Hall **18** BH4 . . .204 B3
Alveston Ave PO14 . . . . . . .154 D8
Alyne Ho SO15 . . . . .101 F6
Alyth Rd BH3 . . . . .204 D7
Amado Cl PO15 . . . . .129 E6
Ambassador Cl BH23 . . . . . .208 A6
Ambassador Ind Est
BH23 . . . . .208 A6
Amber Rd BH21 . . . . .186 C4
Amberley Cl Botley SO30 . .106 A8
Christchurch BH23 . . . . . . .208 F8

Amberley Cl *continued*
North Baddesley SO52 …53 E5
Amberley Ct
10 Bournemouth BH1 …205 A3
3 Knowle Village PO17 …130 E7
Totton SO40 …100 E6
Amberley Ho BH22 …165 D7
Amberley Rd
Clanfield PO8 …88 D5
Gosport PO12 …181 A9
Portsmouth PO2 …157 F3
Amberslade Wlk SO45 …125 F1
Amberwood
Ferndown BH22 …165 E7
Milford on S SO41 …211 B5
Amberwood Cl SO40 …76 C2
Amberwood Dr BH23 …193 F2
Amberwood Gdns BH23 …194 A2
Amberwood Ho BH23 …194 A2
Ambledale SO31 …128 E4
Ambleside
Bishop's Waltham SO32 …83 A8
Christchurch BH23 …191 E3
Hedge End SO30 …105 D5
Ambleside Gdns SO19 …104 A3
Ambleside Rd SO41 …197 F3
Ambury La BH23 …207 F8
Amersham Cl PO12 …180 E4
Amersham Ct 37 BH4 …204 C3
Amesbury Rd BH6 …206 C6
Amethyst Gr PO7 …135 B8
Amethyst Rd BH23 …207 F7
Amey Gdns SO40 …76 B1
Amey Ind Est GU32 …40 E3
Ameys La BH22 …165 F7
Ameysford Rd
Ameysford BH22 …138 B1
Ferndown BH22 …165 C7
Amira Ct 2 BH2 …204 E3
Amoy St SO15 …102 F6
Ampfield CE Prim Sch
SO51 …29 C3
Ampfield Cl PO9 …135 B4
Ampfield Ct 1 SO53 …30 B1
Ampfield Rd BH8 …190 D3
Amport Cl SO22 …1 C3
Amport Ct PO9 …135 D6
Ampress La SO41 …197 D6
Ampress Pk SO41 …197 D6
Ampthill Rd SO15 …102 B7
Amsterdam Sq BH23 …207 D6
Amyas Ct PO4 …183 C4
Ancasta Rd SO14 …103 B7
Anchor Cl
Bournemouth BH11 …188 F6
Christchurch BH23 …208 A5
Anchor Ct PO11 …185 D1
Anchor Gate Rd PO1 …182 A6
Anchor La PO1 …182 A6
Anchor Mews SO41 …197 E4
Anchor Rd BH11 …188 F5
Anchorage Rd PO3 …158 B3
Anchorage The PO12 …181 C5
Anchorage Way SO41 …197 D3
Ancrum Lo 15 BH4 …204 B3
Andalusian Gdns PO15 …129 B8
Andbourne Ct BH6 …206 F3
Anderby Rd SO16 …77 D2
Anderson Cl Havant PO9 …136 A3
Romsey SO51 …28 C2
Swanwick PO15 …129 C8
Anderson's Rd SO14 …103 B3
Anderwood Dr SO41 …172 B2
Andes Cl SO14 …103 C3
Andes Rd SO16 …77 B3
Andlers Ash Rd GU33 …20 E3
Andover Cl BH23 …208 B7
Andover Ho PO9 …136 A5
Andover Rd
Portsmouth PO4 …182 F2
Southampton SO15 …102 D6
Winchester SO23 …215 D8
Andover Road N SO22 …1 E4
Andover Road Ret Pk
SO23 …215 D7
Andre Ct BH23 …209 B8
Andrew Bell St PO1 …216 B4
Andrew Cl
3 Hythe SO45 …126 A1
Portsmouth PO1 …182 F6
Totton SO40 …100 D7
Andrew Cres PO7 …111 D1
Andrew La BH25 …195 D2
Andrew Pl PO14 …179 B7
Andrew's Lodge SO41 …197 D5
Andrewes Cl SO32 …83 C8
Andrews Cl BH11 …189 A3
Andromeda Rd SO16 …77 F4
Androse Gdns BH24 …140 F6
Anfield Cl SO50 …57 C1
Anfield Ct SO50 …57 B1
Angel Cres SO18 …104 A6
Angel Ct SO41 …197 E4
Angel La
Barton on S BH25 …210 D8
Ferndown BH22 …165 B3
Angel Mews BH15 …202 B2
Angela Ct PO9 …135 F4
Angelica Ct PO7 …135 A6
Angelica Gdns SO50 …81 C7
Angelica Way PO15 …129 E8
Angeline Cl BH23 …208 F8
Angelo Cl PO7 …135 A8
Angelus Cl PO14 …179 C7
Angerstein Rd PO2 …157 D1
Anglers Way SO31 …128 D8
Anglesea PO1 …182 B5
Anglesea Ct SO15 …78 B1
Anglesea Rd
Lee-on-t-S PO13 …180 A4
Portsmouth PO1 …216 A3
Southampton SO15 …78 B1
Anglesea Terr SO14 …103 B3
Anglesey Arms Rd
PO12 …181 A3
Anglesey Rd PO12 …181 A3
Anglesey View 1 PO12 …181 B4
Anglewood Mans 2
BH4 …204 C3
Anglo-European Coll of
Chiropractic BH5 …206 A4
Angmering Ho 2 PO1 …216 B3
Angus Cl PO15 …130 E3
Anjou Cl BH11 …188 D5
Anjou Cres PO15 …130 D2
Anker La PO14 …154 C4
Ankerwyke PO13 …155 B1
Anmore Cl PO9 …135 D4
Anmore Cnr PO7 …111 B4
Anmore Dr PO7 …111 D2
Anmore La PO7,PO8 …111 C5
Anmore Rd PO7 …111 A4
Ann's Hill Rd PO12 …181 A6
Anna La BH23 …168 B4
Annandale Ct BH6 …206 D4
Anne Cl BH23 …192 A1
Anne Cres PO7 …134 E6
Annerley Rd BH1 …205 C4
Annes Ct PO11 …184 E2
Annet Cl BH15 …201 E2
Anson Cl
Christchurch BH23 …207 F6
Gosport PO13 …180 D5
Ringwood BH24 …141 C8
Anson Ct 22 PO1 …182 A4
Anson Dr SO19 …104 C5
Anson Gr PO16 …132 E1
Anson Ho SO14 …103 B3
Anson Rd
Horton Heath SO50 …81 C7
1 Portsmouth PO4 …183 A5
Anstey Cl BH11 …189 A6
Anstey Rd
Bournemouth BH11 …189 A5
Romsey SO51 …28 B1
Antell's Way SP6 …93 A6
Anthill Cl PO7 …110 C6
Anthony Gr PO12 …156 A1
Anthony Way PO10 …136 F3
Anthony's Ave BH14 …203 C1
Antigua Ho 5 PO6 …132 F2
Antler Dr BH25 …194 E4
Anton Cl SO51 …53 C7
Anvil Cl East Meon GU32 …63 E8
Waterlooville PO7 …112 C1
West End SO30 …80 C2
Anvil Cres BH18 …186 F5
Anvil Ct PO4 …183 A4
Anzac Cl PO14 …154 C4
Apex Ctr PO14 …155 A5
Apless La PO7 …110 A4
Apollo Cl BH12 …203 D7
Apollo Dr PO7 …134 F3
Apollo Rd SO53 …55 F7
Apple Cl BH13 …204 A4
Apple Gr
Christchurch BH23 …191 E2
Emsworth PO10 …161 B8
Apple Ind Est PO15 …129 C5
Apple Tree Cl SP5 …47 D7
Apple Tree Gr BH22 …165 E6
Apple Tree Rd SP6 …92 F5
Applegate Pl PO8 …112 A6
Applemore Coll SO45 …125 C3
Appleshaw Cl SO22 …1 D4
Appleshaw Gn PO9 …135 C4
Appleslade Way BH25 …195 B5
Appleton Rd
Fareham PO15 …130 D1
Southampton SO18 …79 E1
Appletree Cl
Bournemouth BH6 …206 C5
New Milton BH25 …195 A1
Totton SO40 …76 C1
Appletree Ct SO30 …106 A7
Appletree Rd SP5 …47 D7
Applewood SO31 …129 A5
Applewood Gdns SO19 …104 A3
Applewood Gr PO7 …134 C3
Applewood Pl SO40 …100 C6
Applewood Rd PO9 …135 C3
Appollo Ct PO5 …216 B2
Appollo Pl SO18 …104 A7
Approach Rd BH14 …203 B3
Approach The PO3 …158 A1
April Cl
Bournemouth BH11 …189 A4
Southampton SO18 …104 B7
April Gdns SO45 …150 E1
April Gr SO31 …128 E3
April Sq PO1 …216 C4
Apsley Cres BH17 …187 C1
Apsley Ct 2 BH8 …205 A5
Apsley Pl 11 SO53 …30 B1
Apsley Rd PO4 …183 A4
Aquila Way SO31 …127 F2
Aquitania Ho 6 SO14 …103 C5
Arabian Gdns PO15 …129 C7
Aragon Way BH9 …190 B4
Arbour Ct Whiteley PO15 …106 E1
20 Winchester SO22 …215 D6
Arcade BH4 …204 B3
Arcade The
14 Bournemouth BH1 …204 F3
Liss GU33 …20 E5
Arcadia Ave BH8 …205 B7
Arcadia Cl SO16 …78 B3
Arcadia Rd BH23 …191 F1
Arch Farm Ind Site SP6 …69 E3
Archdale Cl BH10 …189 D2
Archer Ho PO12 …181 C2
Archers 1 SO15 …102 E6
Archers Cl SO40 …76 C1
Archers Rd Eastleigh SO50 …56 A3
Southampton SO15 …102 F7
Archery Gdns SO19 …103 F2
Archery Gr SO19 …103 F2
Archery La
Fareham PO16 …131 C2
Winchester SO23 …215 D5
Archery Rd SO19 …103 E1
Archgate SO41 …197 E4
Archway Rd BH14 …203 E4
Arden Cl
6 Gosport PO12 …180 F4
Southampton SO18 …80 B1
Arden Rd BH9 …189 F3
Arden Wlk BH25 …195 B2
Ardingly Cres SO30 …81 D2
Ardington Rise PO7 …134 E3
Ardmore Rd BH14 …203 B4
Ardnave Cres SO16 …78 F5
Arena Bsns Ctr BH17 …202 B8
Arethusa Ho 16 PO1 …182 A4
Argosy Cl SO31 …128 F1
Argus Rd PO13 …179 F4
Argyle Cres PO15 …130 F2
Argyle Rd
Christchurch BH23 …207 E5
Southampton SO14 …103 B5
Argyll Mans 8 BH5 …205 E4
Argyll Rd
Bournemouth BH5 …205 E4
Poole BH12 …203 D6
Ariel Cl BH6 …207 B4
Ariel Dr BH6 …207 B4
Ariel Rd PO1 …182 E5
Arismore Ct PO13 …179 D4
Ark Dr BH22 …165 F3
Ark Royal Cres PO13 …179 E4
Arle Cl PO8 …88 C4
Arley Rd BH14 …203 A2
Arlington Ct BH25 …210 B8
Arlington Pl 3 SO23 …215 E6
Arliss Rd SO16 …78 A1
Arlott Ct SO15 …102 E7
Armada Cl SO16 …77 E7
Armada Dr SO45 …125 F2
Armadale Ho 20 SO14 …103 C6
Armfield Ho 20 SO17 …79 A1
Arminers Cl PO12 …181 B2
Armitage Ave SO45 …125 F1
Armory La PO1 …182 A4
Armoury The SO40 …102 A3
Armstrong Cl
Brockenhurst SO42 …145 E1
1 Gosport PO12 …181 C6
Waterlooville PO7 …111 D1
Armstrong Ct SO16 …77 F5
Armstrong La SO42 …145 E1
Armstrong Rd SO42 …145 E1
Armsworth La PO7,SO32 …85 E1
Arnaud Cl PO2 …182 D7
Arne Ave BH12 …203 E7
Arne Cres BH12 …203 F7
Arnewood Bridge Rd
SO41 …196 B7
Arnewood Ct
Bournemouth BH2 …204 E2
Sway SO41 …196 C6
Arnewood Ho SO41 …196 C3
Arnewood Rd BH6 …206 D5
Arnewood Sch The
BH25 …194 F2
Arnheim Cl SO16 …78 C4
Arnheim Rd SO16 …78 D4
Arnold Cl BH22 …138 E3
Arnold Rd Eastleigh SO50 …80 A8
Southampton SO17 …79 C2
West Moors BH22 …138 E3
Arnolds Cl BH25 …209 F8
Arnside Rd PO7 …134 E8
Arnwood Ave SO45 …149 F8
Arragon Ct PO7 …135 A8
Arran Cl PO6 …133 F1
Arran Way BH23 …194 B1
Arras Ho PO15 …130 C3
Arreton SO31 …127 C6
Arreton Ct 3 PO12 …181 A6
Arrow Cl Eastleigh SO50 …56 A4
Southampton SO19 …103 D1
Arrowsmith Ct BH18 …187 A4
Arrowsmith La BH21 …187 E7
Arrowsmith Rd BH21 …187 E7
Arters Lawn SO40 …124 C6
Arthur Cl BH2 …204 F5
Arthur Kille Ho PO7 …134 D6
Arthur La 3 BH23 …207 A7
Arthur Pope Ho PO5 …216 C2
Arthur Rd
Christchurch BH23 …207 A7
Eastleigh SO50 …56 A4
Southampton SO15 …102 D6
Winchester SO23 …215 E7
Arthur St PO2 …182 E7
Arthurs Gdns SO30 …81 B3
Artillery Cl 1 PO6 …157 C8
Artillery Terr 2 PO4 …183 B4
Arts Inst of Bournemouth The
BH12 …204 C8
Arun Cl GU31 …40 E2
Arun Rd SO18 …80 B2
Arun Way SO51 …50 D3
Arundel Cl BH25 …194 E3
Arundel Ct Inf Sch PO1 …216 C4
Arundel Ct Jun Sch
PO1 …216 C4
Arundel Dr PO16 …131 A2
Arundel Ho
Southampton,Banister's Pk
SO15 …102 F8
18 Southampton,Northam
SO14 …103 C6
Arundel Rd Eastleigh SO50 …56 A6
Gosport PO12 …180 F5
Totton SO40 …101 A8
Arundel St PO1 …216 C3
Arundel Way BH23 …208 F7
Arundel Way Sh Arc
PO1 …216 B3
Ascham Rd BH8 …205 B5
Ascot Cl PO14 …129 C2
Ascot Rd
Broadstone BH18 …187 A4
Horton Heath SO50 …81 D7
Portsmouth PO3 …183 A7
Ascupart Ho 6 SO17 …103 B8
Ascupart St SO14 …103 B4
Asford Gr SO50 …56 D4
Ash Cl Alderholt SP6 …93 A5
Bursledon SO31 …127 F8
Colden Common SO21 …32 A1
Fareham PO14 …154 E8
Gosport PO12 …181 B5
Hythe SO45 …150 A8
North Baddesley SO52 …53 F5
Romsey SO51 …53 C6
Southampton SO19 …104 C6
Upton BH16 …201 B8
Waterlooville PO8 …111 E2
Ash Copse PO8 …111 F5
Ash Gr Ashurst SO40 …100 C3
Hordle SO41 …211 D8
Ringwood BH24 …141 C6
Ash Grove Ho 5 PO15 …129 D8
Ash Rd SO40 …100 B2
Ashbarn Cres SO22 …215 C3
Ashbourne Ct 1 BH1 …205 A3
Ashbourne Rd BH5 …206 B5
Ashbridge Rise SO53 …30 B1
Ashburn Garth BH24 …141 D6
Ashburn Pl SP6 …69 E1
Ashburnham Cl SO19 …103 D5
Ashburton Cl SO45 …125 D3
Ashburton Ct PO5 …216 B1
Ashburton Gdns BH10 …189 D1
Ashburton Ho SO31 …127 B6
Ashburton Rd
Gosport PO12 …180 F2
Portsmouth PO5 …182 C2
Ashby Cres SO40 …100 D7
Ashby Pl PO5 …182 C2
Ashby Rd
Southampton SO19 …104 B3
Totton SO40 …100 D7
Ashcroft Ct 2 GU32 …40 F4
Ashcroft La PO8 …113 D6
Ashdene 17 SO15 …102 B8
Ashdene Cl BH21 …163 D5
Ashdene Rd SO40 …100 C3
Ashdown
8 Bournemouth BH2 …204 D2
Fawley SO45 …150 F3
Gosport PO13 …155 D1
Ashdown Cl
Chandler's Ford SO53 …30 C2
Poole BH17 …187 F1
Ashdown Dr SO53 …30 C2
Ashdown Rd
Blackfield SO45 …150 F2
Chandler's Ford SO53 …30 C2
Ashdown Tech Coll
BH17 …187 E1
Ashdown Way SO51 …53 B7
Ashdown Wlk BH25 …195 C2
Ashe Rd PO9 …136 B5
Ashen Cl SO53 …55 C8
Ashfield View SO52 …54 A5
Ashford Chace GU32 …19 E1
Ashford Cl
Fordingbridge SP6 …69 D1
Portsmouth PO6 …133 E1
Ashford Cres SO45 …126 B3
Ashford Rd
Bournemouth BH6 …206 D7
Fordingbridge SP6 …93 C8
Ashford Works Ind Est
SP6 …69 D1
Ashington Cl PO8 …112 A3
Ashington Gdns BH21 …186 F8
Ashington La BH21 …163 A1
Ashington Pk BH25 …195 B1
Ashlea Cl SO50 …57 D2
Ashleigh Cl SO45 …150 A8
Ashleigh Rise BH10 …189 D2
Ashlet Gdns BH25 …195 D4
Ashlett Cl SO45 …151 C3
Ashlett Lawn PO9 …135 C6
Ashlett Mews SO45 …151 B3
Ashlett Rd SO45 …151 C3
Ashley Arnewood Ct 5
BH25 …195 B2
Ashley Cl
Bournemouth BH1 …205 E6
Havant PO9 …135 D4
Horndean PO8 …111 F5
Ringwood BH24 …141 D6
Swanwick SO31 …129 B7
Winchester SO22 …1 C3
Ashley Common Rd
BH25 …195 C4
Ashley Cres SO19 …104 C1
Ashley Cross BH14 …203 A4
Ashley Ct
Bursledon SO31 …105 A2
Gosport PO12 …181 A6
West Moors BH22 …166 A8
Ashley Dr BH24 …116 C3
Ashley Drive N BH24 …139 F5
Ashley Drive S BH24 …139 F5
Ashley Drive W BH24 …139 F5
Ashley Gdns
Chandler's Ford SO53 …55 E5
Waltham Chase SO32 …83 E3
Ashley Heath Cvn Pk
BH24 …139 D6
Ashley Heath Ind Est
BH21 …139 B7
Ashley Ho SO51 …52 E6
Ashley Inf Sch BH25 …195 D3
Ashley Jun Sch BH25 …195 C3
Ashley La
Hordle BH25,SO41 …195 E4
Lymington SO41 …197 E3
Ashley Mdws SO51 …53 A8
Ashley Meads BH25 …195 D4
Ashley Pk BH24 …140 A6
Ashley Rd
Bournemouth BH1 …205 E5
New Milton BH25 …195 C3
Poole BH14 …203 C5
Ashleycross Cl SO45 …150 D3
Ashling Cl
Bournemouth BH8 …205 C8
Denmead PO7 …110 F4
Ashling Cres BH8 …205 B8
Ashling Gdns PO7 …110 F4
Ashling La PO2 …157 D1
Ashling Park Rd PO7 …110 F4
Ashlyn Cl PO15 …130 C2
Ashmead 22 BH4 …204 C2
Ashmead Rd SO16 …77 F3
Ashmeads Cl BH21 …164 A6
Ashmeads Way BH21 …164 A6
Ashmore BH21 …163 D4
Ashmore Ave
Barton on S BH25 …210 B8
Hamworthy BH15 …201 F1
Ashmore Cl SP5 …24 B4
Ashmore Cres BH15 …201 F1
Ashmore Gr BH23 …193 E1
Ashmore Ho 39 BH4 …204 C3
Ashmore La SP5 …24 B6
Ashmore Rd SO22 …215 B7
Ashridge Ave 1 BH10 …189 D5
Ashridge Cl SO15 …102 F8
Ashridge Gdns BH10 …189 D5
Ashridge Par 2 BH10 …189 D5
Ashstead Gdns BH8 …190 C3
Ashtead Cl PO16 …156 A8
Ashton Cl SO32 …59 A1
Ashton Cross SO51 …51 B1
Ashton Ct
3 New Milton BH25 …195 B3
Poole BH13 …204 A2
Ashton Ho SO19 …103 F1
Ashton La SO32 …59 B2
Ashton Pl 3 SO53 …30 B1
Ashton Rd BH9 …189 F2
Ashton Way PO14 …179 C5
Ashtree Cl BH25 …195 D2
Ashtree Ct SO53 …55 C3
Ashtree Rd SO18 …79 E2
Ashurst Bridge Rd
SO40 …100 C5
Ashurst Cl Ashurst SO40 …100 B2
Southampton SO19 …104 A1
Winchester SO22 …1 D3
Ashurst Ct 10 PO12 …180 D3
Ashurst Hospl (Geriatric)
SO40 …100 B1
Ashurst New Forest Sta
SO40 …100 A1
Ashurst Rd
Bournemouth BH8 …190 D3
Cosham PO6 …157 E8
West Moors BH22 …138 E3
Ashwell Ct BH23 …191 F1
Ashwood Titchfield SO31 …129 C2
Whiteley PO15 …129 E5
Ashwood Cl Havant PO9 …135 B3
South Hayling PO11 …185 A3
Ashwood Dr BH18 …187 C4
Ashwood Gdns
6 Southampton SO16 …78 E3
Totton SO40 …100 C7
Ashwood Lodge 1
PO16 …131 B2
Aspen Ave SO31 …152 D10
Aspen Cl
Colden Common SO21 …57 A8
Hedge End SO30 …105 D7
Aspen Dr BH31 …115 B5
Aspen Gdns BH12 …203 F7
Aspen Holt SO16 …79 A5
Aspen Pl BH25 …195 B1
Aspen Rd BH12 …203 F7
Aspen Way Poole BH12 …203 F7
Waterlooville PO8 …112 A5
Aspen Wlk SO40 …100 B8
Aspengrove PO13 …155 E1
Asquith Cl BH23 …207 D6
Assheton Ct PO16 …156 D7
Astbury Ave BH12 …204 A8
Aster Rd SO16 …79 C4
Astley St PO5 …216 A2
Aston Mead BH23 …191 E4

Aston Rd Portsmouth PO4 .182 F3
Waterlooville PO7 .111 D1
Astra Ct SO45 .126 A5
Astra Wlk PO12 .181 D5
Astral Gdns SO31 .127 F3
Astrid Cl PO11 .185 C3
Asturias Way SO14 .103 C3
Asylum Rd SO15 .103 A6
Atalanta Cl PO4 .183 C5
Atheling Rd SO45 .126 A4
Athelney Ct 7 BH1 .205 B3
Athelstan Rd
Bournemouth BH6 .206 E5
Southampton SO19 .103 E6
Athelston Ct SO41 .197 D3
Athena Ave PO7 .134 F3
Athena Cl SO50 .57 B3
Atherfield Rd SO16 .77 E3
Atherley Ct SO15 .102 E8
Atherley Rd
South Hayling PO11 .184 E5
Southampton SO15 .102 D6
Atherley Sch The SO16 .77 B6
Atherstone Wlk 5 PO5 .216 B2
Atkins Pl PO15 .130 C3
Atkinson Cl
Barton on S BH25 .210 B8
Gosport PO12 .181 A3
Atlantic Cl SO14 .103 B2
Atlantic Ct
Chandler's Ford SO53 .55 C5
Winchester SO22 .215 A5
Atlantic Park View SO18 .80 A2
Atlantis Ave PO7 .134 F2
Atrium The
Ferndown BH22 .165 E7
20 Southampton SO17 .103 A8
29 Winchester SO23 .215 D6
Attwood Cl SP6 .92 F5
Attwoods Dro SO21 .10 D1
Aubrey Cl
Milford on S SO41 .211 F4
South Hayling PO11 .184 E4
Aubrey Farm Cotts
SO41 .212 A4
Auburn Mans 5 BH13 .204 B4
Auckland Ave SO42 .146 A1
Auckland Pl SO42 .146 A1
Auckland Rd
Christchurch BH23 .208 C7
Southampton SO15 .101 F7
Auckland Rd E PO5 .182 C2
Auckland Rd W PO5 .182 C2
Audemer Ct BH24 .141 C8
Audley Pl SO50 .56 F1
Audrayton Ct 8 BH6 .206 E3
Audret Cl PO16 .156 B6
Augustine Rd
Cosham PO6 .158 C8
Southampton SO14 .103 B6
Augustus Cl SO53 .55 E7
Augustus Ho SO18 .103 C7
Augustus Way SO53 .55 E7
Auriol Dr PO9 .159 A8
Aust Rd PO14 .154 D8
Austen Ave
Bournemouth BH10 .189 E6
Winchester SO22 .215 A2
Austen Cl Totton SO40 .100 D6
Winchester SO23 .215 E8
Austen Gdns PO15 .129 C8
Auster Cl BH23 .208 B7
Austerberry Way PO13 .180 E8
Austin Ave BH14 .203 B1
Austin Cl BH1 .205 D5
Austin Ct 1 PO6 .133 B1
Australia Cl PO1 .216 C3
Autumn Cl BH22 .165 B7
Autumn Copse BH25 .195 D2
Autumn Pl 11 SO17 .79 A1
Autumn Rd
Bournemouth BH11 .188 D3
Marchwood SO40 .102 A1
Avalon BH14 .214 C8
Avalon Ct PO10 .136 F2
Avebury Ave BH10 .189 E6
Avebury Gdns SO53 .30 A1
Avenger Cl SO53 .55 B5
Avens Cl SO50 .81 C6
Avenue C SO45 .150 E8
Avenue Campus (Univ of Southampton) SO17 .79 A2
Avenue Ct Gosport PO12 .181 A3
Poole BH13 .204 B3
2 Southampton SO17 .102 F8
Avenue D SO45 .150 E8
Avenue De Caen PO5 .182 C1
Avenue E SO45 .150 E8
Avenue La 18 BH2 .204 E3
Avenue Rd
Bournemouth BH2 .204 E3
Brockenhurst SO42 .172 F8
Christchurch BH23 .206 F7
Gosport PO12 .181 C5
Lymington SO41 .197 E4
New Milton BH25 .195 A3
North Hayling PO11 .160 A3
Southampton SO14 .103 A8
Walkford BH23 .194 C2
Wimborne Minst BH21 .163 D4
Winchester SO22 .215 C6
Avenue Sh Ctr The 14
BH2 .204 E3
Avenue The
Bishop's Waltham SO32 .83 B8
Avenue The *continued*
Bournemouth BH9 .189 F3
Fareham PO14 .130 E1
Gosport PO12 .181 A4
Petersfield GU31 .40 F3
Poole BH13 .204 A2
Southampton SO17 .78 F2
Twyford SO21 .32 A6
West Moors BH22 .138 E3
West Moors BH24 .166 B8
Avery Fields SO50 .56 B7
Avery La PO12 .181 A8
Aviation Park W
East Parley BH23 .190 C8
Hurn BH23 .166 D1
Avington Cl SO50 .56 D5
Avington Ct
Southampton SO16 .78 F4
Winchester SO22 .215 A5
Avington Gn PO9 .136 B6
Avlan Ct SO23 .215 D3
Avocet Cl PO4 .183 B5
Avocet Ho 2 PO4 .183 B5
Avocet Quay PO10 .161 A7
Avocet Way PO8 .112 A7
Avocet Wlk PO13 .155 A2
Avon Ave BH24 .140 D3
Avon Bldgs BH23 .207 B7
Avon Castle BH24 .140 D3
Avon Castle Dr BH24 .140 D3
Avon Cl
Bournemouth BH8 .205 D6
Lee-on-t-S PO13 .179 F2
Lymington SO41 .197 C3
Petersfield GU31 .40 E2
Avon Cotts BH23 .192 C5
Avon Cres SO51 .53 C7
Avon Cswy BH23 .191 C7
Avon Ct
Christchurch BH23 .207 C6
1 Fordingbridge SP6 .69 F2
Netley SO31 .127 C5
2 Waterlooville PO8 .111 F4
7 Poole BH13 .204 A4
Avon Farm Cotts BH23 .167 E3
Avon Gdns BH23 .169 B1
Avon Gn SO53 .55 D5
Avon Heath Ctry Park Visitor Ctr* BH24 .140 A2
Avon Heath Ctry Pk (North Pk)* BH24 .140 B3
Avon Heath Ctry Pk (South Pk)* BH24 .167 B8
Avon Ho
Bournemouth BH2 .204 E2
8 Southampton SO14 .103 C6
Avon Mdw SP5 .46 F7
Avon Meade SP6 .69 E2
Avon Mews BH8 .205 C6
Avon Pk BH24 .140 D6
Avon Rd
Bournemouth BH8 .205 C6
Southampton SO18 .79 F1
West Moors BH22 .138 E2
Avon Road E BH23 .207 A8
Avon Road W BH23 .206 F8
Avon Run Cl BH23 .208 B5
Avon Run Rd BH23 .208 B5
Avon View SP6 .70 D1
Avon View Par BH23 .192 C3
Avon View Rd BH23 .192 C3
Avon Way SO30 .80 E2
Avon Wharf BH23 .207 C5
Avon Wlk PO16 .156 A8
Avonborne Way SO53 .55 B8
Avonbourne Sch BH7 .206 A7
Avoncliffe Rd BH6 .206 E3
Avondale Ct SO17 .79 B2
Avondale Mobile Home Pk
SO21 .32 A1
Avondale Rd
Portsmouth PO1 .182 F7
Waterlooville PO7 .134 F8
Avondyke SP5 .46 F6
Avonsands BH23 .208 A5
Avro Cl SO15 .102 A7
Avro Ct SO31 .127 F2
Award Rd
Ferndown BH21 .164 F5
Wimborne Minst BH21 .165 A6
Awbridge Prim Sch
SO51 .26 D5
Awbridge Rd PO9 .135 C4
Axford Cl BH8 .190 D3
Axis Pk PO14 .155 A6
Aylen Rd PO3 .158 A2
Aylesbury Rd
Bournemouth BH1 .205 E4
Portsmouth PO2 .182 F8
Ayling Cl PO13 .180 C7
Aylward St PO1 .182 A5
Aynsley Ct SO15 .102 D7
Aysgarth Rd PO7 .134 E8
Aysha Cl BH25 .195 B1
Azalea Cl Havant PO9 .136 C4
St Leonards BH24 .140 A5
Aztec Ctr BH17 .202 D8
Azura Cl BH21 .139 B6

B

B Ave Fawley SO45 .150 F4
Holbury SO45 .150 D5
Back La Mottisfont SO51 .5 E5
Southwick PO17 .132 E6
Sway SO41 .172 C2
Back of the Walls 26
SO14 .103 A3
Back St SO23 .215 D2
Bacon Cl SO19 .103 F1
Bacon La PO11 .184 E3
Badbury Cl BH18 .187 C3
Badbury Ct BH22 .165 F7
Badbury View BH21 .163 D5
Badbury View Rd BH21 .186 D8
Baddesley Cl SO52 .53 F6
Baddesley Gdns PO9 .135 D6
Baddesley Park Ind Est
SO52 .54 B4
Baddesley Rd SO53 .30 A1
Baden Cl BH25 .195 B1
Baden Powell Way 2
SO51 .52 F7
Baden-Powell & St Peter's CE Mid Sch BH14 .203 B3
Bader Cl SO30 .105 C8
Bader Rd BH17 .202 E8
Bader Way PO15 .129 F5
Badger Brow PO7 .135 A6
Badger Cl
Bishopstoke SO50 .56 F2
Fareham PO15 .130 D2
Badger Ct SO50 .56 F2
Badger Farm Rd SO22 .215 B1
Badger Rd PO14 .154 F5
Badger Way BH31 .114 F5
Badger Wood Pl SO18 .79 F1
Badgers Cl
St Leonards BH24 .139 F5
Sway SO41 .172 C2
Badgers Copse
Locks Heath SO31 .129 B5
New Milton BH25 .195 C6
Badgers Run SO31 .128 E6
Badgers The SO31 .127 C6
Badgers Wlk
Ferndown BH22 .165 E7
Hythe SO45 .125 F2
Badminston Dro SO45 .178 C8
Badminston La SO45 .151 C1
Badshear La SO24 .14 F8
Baffins Rd PO3 .183 A6
Bagber Rd SO40 .100 F7
Bagot Ho PO12 .180 F6
Bagshot Mews SO19 .103 F3
Baigent Cl SO23 .11 C8
Bailey Cl Botley SO30 .106 A6
New Milton BH25 .195 D4
Winchester SO22 .215 B4
Bailey Cres BH15 .202 C7
Bailey Dr BH23 .206 F7
Bailey Gn SO18 .80 A2
Bailey Hall BH23 .206 F7
Bailey's Rd PO5 .216 C2
Baiter Gdns BH15 .202 C1
Baker Rd BH11 .189 A5
Baker St PO1 .182 D7
Bakers Dro SO16 .77 E5
Bakers Farm Rd BH31 .114 E7
Bakers View BH21 .186 D6
Balaclava Rd SO18 .104 B7
Balchin Ho 18 PO1 .182 A5
Balcombe Rd BH13 .204 A3
Balderton Cl 7 PO2 .157 F4
Baldwin Cl BH23 .207 D6
Balena Cl BH17 .202 A8
Balfour Cl
Christchurch BH23 .208 D8
Gosport PO13 .180 D6
Balfour Dr GU33 .20 F4
Balfour Rd
Bournemouth BH9 .189 F1
Portsmouth PO2 .157 E1
Southampton SO19 .104 C5
Balfour Red Cross Mus*
SO23 .2 C1
Ballam Cl BH16 .201 C7
Ballard Cl
New Milton BH25 .195 B4
Poole BH15 .202 D1
Southampton SO16 .77 D1
Ballard Coll BH25 .195 A4
Ballard Ct 1 PO12 .181 B5
Ballard Rd BH15 .202 D1
Ballard Sch BH25 .195 A4
Balliol Cl PO14 .129 C1
Balliol Rd PO2 .182 E8
Balmer Lawn Rd SO42 .146 B3
Balmoral Ave BH8 .190 E1
Balmoral Cl
Chandler's Ford SO53 .55 B8
Gosport PO13 .155 D2
Southampton SO16 .78 C5
Balmoral Ct
3 Christchurch BH23 .209 B7
7 Southampton SO17 .103 A8
4 Southampton,Millbrook
SO15 .102 A6
Balmoral Dr PO7 .134 C4
Balmoral Ho
Bournemouth BH2 .204 D3
6 Whiteley PO15 .129 D8
Balmoral Rd
Fareham PO15 .130 E3
Poole BH14 .203 C3
Balmoral Way
Petersfield GU32 .40 F4
Rownhams SO16 .77 E6
Balmoral Wlk BH25 .194 F3
Balston Rd BH14 .203 A6
Balston Terr BH15 .202 B2
Baltic Rd SO30 .80 E1
Bambridge Pk Gdn Ctr Miniature Rly* SO50 .31 D1
Bamford Ho 9 PO4 .183 B2
Bampton Cl SO16 .101 E8
Bampton Ct SO53 .55 C6
Banbury Ave SO19 .104 C4
Banbury Rd BH17 .202 C7
Bancroft Ct 1 BH15 .202 E4
Bangor Rd SO15 .102 B6
Banister Ct 6 SO15 .102 F7
Banister Gdns SO15 .102 F7
Banister Grange 9
SO15 .102 F7
Banister Inf Sch SO15 .102 F7
Banister Mews SO15 .102 F7
Banister Rd SO15 .102 F7
Bank Chambers BH14 .203 E3
Bank Cl BH23 .207 B6
Bank Side SO18 .79 D4
Bank St SO32 .83 D8
Bankhill Dr SO41 .197 D5
Banks Rd BH13 .214 C4
Banks The SO51 .26 A5
Bankside SO41 .197 D6
Bankside Ho 3 SO22 .215 C6
Bankside Rd BH9 .190 A3
Bankview SO41 .197 D6
Bannerman Rd GU32 .40 F4
Banning St SO51 .52 E6
Bannister Ct SO40 .101 A7
Banstead Rd BH18 .187 A5
Bapaume Rd PO3 .157 F5
Bar End Ind Est SO23 .215 F3
Bar End Rd SO23 .215 F4
Bar Gate Mus* SO14 .102 F4
Barbara Ct SO32 .35 B3
Barbe Baker Ave SO30 .80 D2
Barberry Dr SO40 .76 B1
Barberry Way BH31 .115 C5
Barbers Gate 9 BH15 .202 B1
Barbers Piles 1 BH15 .202 B1
Barbers Wharf 8 BH15 .202 B1
Barbican Mews PO16 .156 E7
Barclay Ho 8 PO12 .181 E5
Barclay Mans BH2 .204 F5
Barclay Mews
Hythe SO45 .149 F8
Hythe SO45 .150 A8
Bardon Way PO14 .154 D8
Barentin Way GU31 .41 A5
Barfield Cl SO23 .215 F4
Barfields SO41 .197 E4
Barfields Ct 2 SO41 .197 E4
Barfleur Cl PO15 .130 D2
Barfleur Rd PO14 .155 A5
Barford Cl SO53 .55 B8
Barford La SP5 .47 A8
Bargate Ctr 8 SO14 .103 A4
Bargate St SO14 .102 F4
Bargates BH23 .207 B7
Barham Cl PO12 .181 B7
Barham Rd GU32 .40 F3
Barham Way PO2 .157 D4
Baring Rd
Bournemouth BH6 .207 A3
Winchester SO23 .215 F5
Bark Mill Mews SO51 .52 E6
Barker Mill Cl SO16 .77 E6
Barkis Ho 11 PO1 .182 D7
Barkshire Ct 7 SO15 .102 F8
Barlands Cl BH23 .192 C2
Barle Cl SO18 .80 B1
Barley Down Dr SO22 .215 B2
Barley Fields SO50 .81 C6
Barleycorn Wlk SO40 .98 F8
Barling Mews 7 SO51 .52 E7
Barlow Cl PO14 .179 B7
Barn Cl Emsworth PO10 .160 D8
Upton BH16 .201 A7
Barn Fold PO7 .112 B1
Barn Green Cl PO7 .110 F4
Barn Piece SO53 .54 F6
Barn Rd BH18 .187 B3
Barn Wood Rd PO15 .130 D1
Barnaby Cl SP5 .46 D7
Barnbrook Rd SO31 .128 E4
Barncroft Inf Sch PO9 .135 D3
Barncroft Jun Sch PO9 .135 D3
Barncroft Way PO9 .135 D3
Barnes Cl
Bournemouth BH10 .189 D3
Sarisbury SO31 .128 D4
Southampton SO18 .104 C6
West Wellow SO51 .50 E4
Winchester SO23 .215 D3
Barnes Cres
Bournemouth BH10 .189 D3
Wimborne Minst BH21 .163 E4
Barnes La
Milford on S SO41 .211 C6
Sarisbury SO31 .128 E4
Barnes Rd
Bournemouth BH10 .189 D3
Portsmouth PO1 .182 E6
Southampton SO19 .104 C6
Barnes Wallis Rd PO15 .129 E4
Barnes Way PO9 .135 C3
Barnet Side La GU32,
GU34 .18 D5
Barney Evans Cres PO8 .111 D3
Barneyhayes La SO40 .99 A7
Barnfield BH23 .208 D8
Barnfield Cl
Breach PO10 .137 E1
Southampton SO19 .103 E1
Barnfield Ct
Fareham PO14 .154 E8
Southampton SO19 .103 F1
Barnfield Flats SO19 .103 F1
Barnfield Rd
Petersfield GU31 .41 C3
Southampton SO19 .103 F1
Barnfield Way SO19 .103 F1
Barns Rd BH22 .166 A6
Barnsfield Cres SO40 .100 C7
Barnsfield Rd BH24 .140 B2
Barnside Way GU33 .20 F3
Barnsland SO30 .80 C2
Baron Rd SO31 .127 F3
Barons Ct 7 BH12 .204 B4
Barons Mead SO16 .77 E3
Barons Rd BH11 .188 D6
Baronsmede 2 BH2 .204 D4
Baronsmere PO12 .181 A5
Barrack La BH24 .141 D4
Barrack Rd
Christchurch BH23 .206 E8
Ferndown BH22 .166 A2
Barracks The BH24 .142 E5
Barratt Ind Pk PO15 .129 C5
Barrie Cl PO15 .129 C8
Barrie Rd BH9 .189 F3
Barrington Cl SO50 .55 F5
Barrington Ct 26 SO17 .79 A1
Barrington Ho 20 PO1 .182 D7
Barrow Down Gdns
SO19 .104 E4
Barrow Dr BH8 .190 F2
Barrow Hill Rd SO40 .75 D3
Barrow Rd BH8 .190 F2
Barrow View BH22 .165 B6
Barrow Way BH8 .190 F2
Barrowgate Rd BH8 .190 D3
Barrowgate Way BH8 .190 D3
Barrows La Landford SP5 .49 C6
Sway SO41 .196 B6
Barrs Ave BH25 .195 B4
Barrs Wood Dr BH25 .195 B4
Barrs Wood Rd BH25 .195 B4
Barry Gdns BH18 .186 F5
Barry Rd SO19 .104 B5
Barter Rd BH12 .204 A7
Barters Cl SO16 .77 F1
Barters La BH18 .186 F3
Bartholomew Cl 7
SO23 .215 E7
Bartlett Cl PO15 .130 E3
Bartlett Dr BH7 .206 B8
Bartlett Ho 2 SO17 .103 B8
Bartletts Comm SP6 .94 E7
Bartletts The SO31 .128 A2
Bartley Ave SO40 .100 E6
Bartley CE Jun Sch SO40 .99 B7
Bartley Ct 2 BH21 .163 B5
Bartley Rd SO40 .99 C4
Barton Chase BH25 .209 F7
Barton Cl SO51 .53 B8
Barton Common La
BH25 .210 B8
Barton Common Rd
BH25 .210 B7
Barton Court Ave BH25 .210 A8
Barton Court Rd BH25 .195 A1
Barton Cres SO18 .79 F1
Barton Croft BH25 .210 A7
Barton Cross PO8 .112 B7
Barton Dr
Barton on S BH25 .209 F8
Hamble-le-R SO31 .127 F3
Hedge End SO30 .105 D7
Barton Gn BH25 .210 B6
Barton Gr PO3 .158 B3
Barton Ho BH25 .209 E7
Barton La BH25 .209 E8
Barton Lo BH12 .203 B5
Barton Park Ind Est SO50 .56 B2
Barton Peveril Coll SO50 .55 F1
Barton Rd SO50 .56 C3
Barton Way BH25 .209 F8
Barton Wood Rd BH25 .209 E7
Bartons Ct 8 PO12 .181 B6
Bartons Rd
Fordingbridge SP6 .69 F1
Havant PO9 .136 B4
Bartons The
Fordingbridge SP6 .69 F1
Hedge End SO30 .105 A6
Bartonside Rd BH25 .209 C7
Bartram Rd SO40 .101 A6
Barwell Gr PO10 .136 E3
Barwell Terr 3 SO30 .105 D6
Bascott Cl BH11 .189 A1
Bascott Rd BH11 .189 A1
Basepoint Bsns Ctr
BH23 .166 C1
Basepoint Ent Ctr SO14 .103 B3
Bashley Common Rd
BH25 .195 A8
Bashley Cross Rd BH25 .194 E5
Bashley Dr BH25 .195 B6
Bashley Rd BH25 .195 A6
Basin St PO2 .182 D8
Basing Barns GU34 .17 D5
Basing Dean GU34 .17 E4
Basing Ho SO15 .102 C7
Basing Mews 3 SO32 .83 C7
Basing Rd PO9 .135 E4
Basing Way SO53 .55 A4
Basingstoke Rd SO21,SO23 .2 D7
Basingwell St Lwr 5
SO32 .83 C7
Basingwell St Upper
SO32 .83 D7
Bassett Ave SO16 .78 F5
Bassett Cl SO16 .78 F4
Bassett Cres E SO16 .78 F4
Bassett Cres W SO16 .78 F3

Bassett Ct SO16 78 F4
Bassett Dale SO16 78 F6
Bassett Gdns SO16 78 F4
Bassett Gn Village SO16 79 B5
Bassett Green Cl SO16 79 B5
Bassett Green Ct SO16 79 B5
Bassett Green Dr SO16 79 A6
Bassett Green Prim Sch SO16 79 B4
Bassett Green Rd SO16 79 B5
Bassett Heath Ave SO16 78 F6
Bassett Mdw SO16 78 F4
Bassett Mews SO16 78 F5
Bassett Rd BH12 203 B6
Bassett Row SO16 78 F6
Bassett Wlk PO9 135 D6
Bassett Wood Dr SO16 79 A6
Bassett Wood Mews 7 SO16 78 F4
Bassett Wood N SO16 79 A6
Bassett Wood Rd SO16 79 A6
Batchelor Cres BH11 188 F3
Batchelor Gn SO31 127 F8
Batchelor Rd BH11 189 A3
Batcombe Cl BH11 188 E3
Bath & Wells Ct 7 PO13 180 C6
Bath Cl SO19 104 B6
Bath Hill Ct 11 BH1 205 A3
Bath Hill Rdbt BH1 205 A2
Bath La 9 PO16 131 C1
Bath La (lower) 11 PO16 131 C1
Bath Lane Cotts PO16 155 C8
Bath Rd
Bournemouth BH1 205 A3
Emsworth PO10 160 F8
Lymington SO41 198 A3
Portsmouth PO4 182 F3
Southampton SO19 104 B6
Bath Sq PO1 181 F5
Bath St SO14 103 A7
Bathing La PO1 181 F5
Bathurst Cl PO11 184 E3
Bathurst Way PO2 157 B2
Batstone Way BH22 165 B6
Batten Cl BH23 207 D7
Batten Rd SP5 46 E8
Battenburg Ave PO2 157 F2
Battenburg Rd PO12 181 C6
Battens Way PO9 135 F4
Batterley Dro BH21 91 F4
Battery Cl PO12 180 F8
Battery Hill
Bishop's Waltham SO32 83 B8
Winchester SO22 215 A4
Battery Row PO1 182 A3
Battle Cl SO31 129 A4
Battramsley Cross SO41 173 C1
Baverstock Rd BH12 204 B8
Baxter Rd SO19 104 E5
Bay Cl Southampton SO19 104 A3
Three Legged Cross BH21 138 E8
Upton BH16 201 B6
Bay Hog La BH15 202 B2
Bay House Sch PO12 180 E2
Bay Rd Gosport PO12 180 F3
Southampton SO19 104 A3
Bay Tree Gdns SO40 101 F1
Bay Tree Lodge PO14 179 D7
Bay Tree Way BH23 193 D1
Bay Trees SO19 104 E6
Bay View BH2 204 E2
Bay View Ct PO11 184 D2
Bay View Mews PO11 184 D2
Baybridge La SO21 33 C4
Baybridge Rd PO9 136 B5
Baycroft Sch PO14 179 E7
Bayfields PO5 216 B1
Bayly Ave PO16 156 D6
Baynton Ho SO41 197 D4
Bays Ct SO41 197 C4
Bays Rd SO41 197 C3
Bayswater Ho PO5 216 C1
Baythorn Cl PO2 182 D7
Baytree Ho 24 SO23 215 D6
Bayview Gdns BH2 204 E2
Bayview Mews BH2 204 E2
Beach Ave BH25 209 F7
Beach Cl BH13 214 G8
Beach Dr PO6 156 F8
Beach La SO31 127 A6
Beach Rd
Emsworth PO10 160 E8
Lee-on-t-S PO13 179 E2
Poole BH13 214 G8
Portsmouth PO5 182 D1
South Hayling PO11 184 E3
Upton BH16 201 A6
Beach View BH13 214 C4
Beachcroft BH13 204 A3
Beachlands Sta* PO11 184 F2
Beachway PO16 156 D6
Beacon Bottom SO31 129 A6
Beacon Cl Everton SO41 196 D1
Locks Heath SO31 129 A6
Rownhams SO16 77 D6
Beacon Ct
Christchurch BH23 208 F7
Fordingbridge SP6 69 E3
Beacon Dr BH23 208 F7
Beacon Gdns BH18 186 E3
Beacon Hill La
Corfe Mullen BH21 186 B3
Droxford SO32 60 F6
Meonstoke SO32 61 C6
Beacon Mews SO30 104 D8
Beacon Mount SO31 129 A6
Beacon Park Cres BH16 201 A8
Beacon Park Rd BH16 201 B7
Beacon Rd
Bournemouth BH2 204 F2
Broadstone BH18 186 E3
Upton BH16 201 B7
West End SO30 104 D8
Beacon Sq PO10 160 F7
Beacon Way
Broadstone BH18 186 E3
Locks Heath SO31 129 A6
Beaconsfield Ave PO6 158 A7
Beaconsfield Rd
Christchurch BH23 207 B7
Fareham PO16 155 B8
Poole BH12 203 D6
Waterlooville PO7 134 E8
Bealing Cl SO16 79 B4
Beamish Rd BH17 202 F8
Bear Cross Ave BH11 188 F6
Bear Cross Rdbt BH11 188 F6
Bear Mus The* GU31 40 F3
Bearslane Cl SO40 76 D1
Bearwood Prim Sch BH11 188 C6
Beasant Cl PO3 183 B6
Beatrice Ct 5 SO41 211 B4
Beatrice Mews 2 PO6 157 F7
Beatrice Rd
Portsmouth PO4 182 E2
Southampton SO15 102 C7
Beattie Rise SO30 81 D2
Beatty Cl
Locks Heath SO31 129 B4
Ringwood BH24 141 C8
Beatty Dr PO12 180 F2
Beatty Ho 9 PO1 216 C4
Beatty Rd BH9 190 B1
Beaty Ct SO19 104 C5
Beau Ct
43 Bournemouth BH4 204 C3
9 New Milton BH25 195 A3
Beauchamp Ave PO13 155 D1
Beauchamp Pl BH23 207 A7
Beauchamps Gdns BH7 206 A8
Beaucroft La BH21 163 E5
Beaucroft Rd
Waltham Chase SO32 83 E3
Wimborne Minst BH21 163 E6
Beaucroft Sch BH21 163 E6
Beaufort Ave PO16 130 F2
Beaufort Cl
Christchurch BH23 208 B7
Lee-on-t-S PO13 180 A6
Beaufort Dr
Bishop's Waltham SO32 83 C8
Wimborne Minst BH21 163 C5
Beaufort Ho 10 BH4 204 C2
Beaufort Mews BH21 163 B4
Beaufort Rd
Bournemouth BH6 206 D6
Havant PO9 135 D2
7 Portsmouth PO5 182 D1
Winchester SO23 215 D4
Beaufoys Ave BH22 165 D7
Beaufoys Cl BH22 165 C7
Beaufoys Ct BH22 165 C6
Beaulieu Abbey* SO42 148 F2
Beaulieu Ave
Christchurch BH23 206 E7
Havant PO9 135 D6
Portchester PO16 156 A8
Beaulieu Cl
New Milton BH25 194 E3
Southampton SO16 78 B5
Winchester SO22 1 D4
Beaulieu Ct 5 PO8 111 F4
Beaulieu Ho 2 SO15 102 F7
Beaulieu Pl PO13 155 B2
Beaulieu Rd
Beaulieu SO42,SO45 149 C6
Bournemouth BH4 204 B1
Christchurch BH23 206 E7
Dibden Purlieu SO45 125 F1
Eastleigh SO50 56 A4
Hamble-le-R SO31 127 F3
Hythe SO45 125 F1
Lyndhurst SO43 122 C4
Marchwood SO40 124 E5
Portsmouth PO2 157 E1
Beaulieu Road Sta SO42 123 D1
Beaulieu Village Prim Sch SO42 148 F1
Beaumaris Cl SO53 55 A4
Beaumaris Gdns SO45 125 F5
Beaumond Gn 11 SO23 215 D5
Beaumont Cl
Fareham PO15 130 D3
Southampton SO16 78 E3
Beaumont Ct PO12 181 A9
Beaumont Pl SO40 101 A7
Beaumont Rd
Poole BH13 214 F7
Totton SO40 101 A7
Beaumont Rise PO15 130 D4
Beauworth Ave SO18 104 C8
Beaver Dr SO50 57 A2
Beaver Ind Est BH23 208 A7
Beccles Cl BH15 201 F2
Becher Rd BH14 203 E4
Beck Cl SO31 128 E3
Beck St PO1 182 B5
Beckenham Terr PO10 137 B4
Beckford La PO17 109 F2
Beckham La GU32 40 D4
Beckhampton Rd BH15 201 E3
Beckley Copse BH23 194 A2
Becton La BH25 210 B7
Becton Mead BH25 195 B1
Bedale Way BH15 202 F5
Bedales Sch GU32 40 E7
Beddow Hall 3 PO5 216 A2
Bedenham La PO13 155 E3
Bedenham Prim Sch PO13 155 D3
Bedfield Ho SO23 2 B5
Bedfield La SO23 2 B5
Bedford Ave SO19 103 E2
Bedford Cl
Fordingbridge SP6 69 F3
Havant PO9 160 B8
Hedge End SO30 105 D6
Bedford Cres BH7 206 C7
Bedford Pl SO15 102 F6
Bedford Rd GU32 40 D3
Bedford Rd N BH12 188 C2
Bedford Rd S BH12 188 C2
Bedford St Gosport PO12 181 A7
Portsmouth PO5 216 B2
Bedhampton Hill PO9 135 B1
Bedhampton Hill Rd PO9 135 A1
Bedhampton Ho 4 PO1 216 C4
Bedhampton Rd
Havant PO9 135 C2
Portsmouth PO2 182 F8
Bedhampton Sta PO9 135 D1
Bedhampton Way PO9 135 F4
Bedwell Cl SO16 77 F6
Beech Ave
Bournemouth BH6 206 C4
Christchurch BH23 206 D8
Southampton SO18 103 E7
Beech Cl Alderholt SP6 93 A5
Broadstone BH18 186 E4
Chandler's Ford SO53 55 D8
Hamble-le-R SO31 127 E2
Hordle SO41 211 D8
Romsey SO51 53 C6
Verwood BH31 114 E5
Waterlooville PO8 111 F2
Winchester SO22 10 B3
Beech Cnr SO32 81 F6
Beech Copse SO22 1 B1
Beech Cres SO45 150 A8
Beech Ct
Southampton SO19 103 F3
Wimborne Minst BH21 163 E4
Beech Gdns SO31 127 E2
Beech Gr Gosport PO12 181 A4
Owslebury SO21 33 B4
South Hayling PO11 185 B4
Beech Grange SP5 49 D2
Beech Ho SO16 78 F7
Beech La BH24 139 E2
Beech Rd Ashurst SO40 100 B2
Chandler's Ford SO53 55 D8
Clanfield PO8 88 D5
Fareham PO15 130 E2
Hedge End SO30 105 D7
Southampton SO15 102 B6
Beech Way PO8 112 B5
Beech Wood Cl BH18 187 A3
Beecham Rd PO1 182 F7
Beechbank Ave BH17 186 F1
Beechcroft BH1 205 A5
Beechcroft Cl
Chandler's Ford SO53 55 D6
Fareham PO15 130 C1
Beechcroft La BH24 141 B8
Beechcroft Mews 1 BH24 141 B8
Beechcroft Rd PO12 181 B4
Beechcroft Way SO53 55 E6
Beechdale Cl SO40 76 D2
Beechdale Wlk SO40 76 C2
Beechen La SO43 122 A3
Beeches Hill SO32 59 D2
Beeches The
Awbridge SO51 26 E5
Bournemouth BH7 206 A8
Fair Oak SO50 57 D1
Waterlooville PO7 134 F8
West Wellow SO51 50 D3
Beechey Ct 6 BH8 205 A5
Beechey Rd BH8 205 A5
Beechfield 42 BH4 204 C3
Beechfield Ct SO15 102 B8
Beechmount Rd SO16 78 F5
Beechwood SP6 69 D1
Beechwood Ave
Bournemouth BH5 206 A4
New Milton BH25 194 F4
Waterlooville PO7 134 E6
Beechwood Cl
Chandler's Ford SO53 30 A1
Warsash SO31 152 D10
Beechwood Cres SO53 30 B2
Beechwood Ct
Bournemouth BH2 204 E2
Liss GU33 21 A6
Beechwood Gdns
Bournemouth BH5 206 A4
Southampton SO18 103 F8
Beechwood Ho SO17 103 C8
Beechwood Jun Sch SO18 103 F7
Beechwood La BH24 143 B3
Beechwood Lo 1 BH4 204 C2
Beechwood Lodge 3 PO16 131 B2
Beechwood Rd
Bartley SO40 99 A6
Holbury SO45 150 C3
Beechwood Rd *continued*
Portsmouth PO2 157 E4
West Moors BH22 138 F1
Beechwood Rise SO18 80 C1
Beechwood Way SO45 125 C2
Beechworth Rd 1 PO9 136 A1
Beehive Cotts PO16 131 B3
Beehive Wlk PO1 182 A4
Beeston Ct PO1 182 E7
Beggar's La SO23 215 F6
Begonia Rd SO16 79 B4
Behrendt Cl PO12 181 A7
Belben Cl BH12 188 D2
Belben Rd BH12 188 C2
Belbins SO51 27 F4
Belbins Bsns Pk SO51 28 A3
Belfield Rd BH6 207 A4
Belfry Ct SO31 129 C3
Belfry Wlk PO14 129 C2
Belgrave Ct BH1 205 D3
Belgrave Ind Est SO17 79 C2
Belgrave Rd Poole BH13 204 A2
Southampton SO17 79 C2
Belgravia Rd PO2 157 F1
Bell Cl SO45 150 F2
Bell Cres PO7 134 E6
Bell Ct PO18 161 F7
Bell Davies Rd PO14 179 B6
Bell Heather Cl BH16 201 B8
Bell Hill GU32 40 E5
Bell Hill Ridge GU32 40 E5
Bell Rd PO6 157 D8
Bell St Romsey SO51 52 E7
Southampton SO14 103 A3
Bellair Ho PO9 136 A1
Bellair Rd PO9 136 A1
Bellamy Ct SO17 103 D8
Belle Vue Cl BH6 206 D4
Belle Vue Cres BH6 206 F4
Belle Vue Gdns 2 BH6 206 F4
Belle Vue Gr BH22 138 F2
Belle Vue Mans 6 BH6 206 E3
Belle Vue Rd
Bournemouth BH6 206 E3
Poole BH14 203 C3
Belle Vue Wlk BH22 165 E2
Bellemoor Rd SO15 78 D1
Bellemoor Sch (Boys) SO15 78 D2
Bellevue La PO10 136 F2
Bellevue Rd
Eastleigh SO50 56 A3
Southampton SO15 103 A6
Bellevue Terr
Portsmouth PO5 216 A1
10 Southampton SO14 103 A6
Bellfield PO14 153 F7
Bellflower Cl BH23 208 B8
Bellflower Way
Chandler's Ford SO53 54 F7
Titchfield PO15 129 F3
Bellinger Ho PO9 135 D1
Bells Ho BH21 163 D6
Bells La PO14 179 C7
Belmont Ave BH8 190 C2
Belmont Cl Horndean PO8 88 C3
Hythe SO45 126 A2
Stubbington PO14 179 D8
Verwood BH31 115 A5
Belmont Gdns PO11 185 D1
Belmont Gr PO9 135 C2
Belmont Pl PO5 216 B1
Belmont Rd
Chandler's Ford SO53 55 D3
New Milton BH25 195 C4
Poole BH14 203 C5
Southampton SO17 79 C1
Belmont St PO5 216 B1
Belmore Cl PO1 182 E7
Belmore Ct SO41 197 D3
Belmore Ho 1 SO41 197 E2
Belmore La
Lymington SO41 197 E3
Owslebury SO21 33 E4
Upham SO21,SO32 34 B3
Belmore Rd SO41 197 D3
Belmour Lo 36 BH4 204 C3
Belney Ho PO6 157 A8
Belney La PO7 110 E1
Belstone Rd SO40 100 E7
Belton Rd SO19 104 B3
Belvedere Rd
Bournemouth BH3 205 A6
Christchurch BH23 207 A7
Hythe SO45 126 A2
Belverdere Cl GU32 40 F4
Belvidere Ho 12 SO14 103 C6
Belvidere Rd SO14 103 C5
Belvidere Terr SO14 103 C5
Belvoir Cl PO16 155 B8
Belvoir Pk 8 BH13 204 B3
Bembridge SO31 127 C6
Bembridge Cl SO16 79 C5
Bembridge Cres PO4 182 E1
Bembridge Ct PO11 185 C1
Bembridge Dr PO11 185 C1
Bembridge Ho PO11 185 C1
Bembridge Lodge Flats PO13 179 E2
Bemister Rd BH9 205 A8
Bemister's La 5 PO12 181 E5
Benbow Cl PO8 112 C7
Benbow Cres BH12 188 E1
Benbow Gdns SO40 76 C2
Benbow Ho 5 PO1 182 A5
Benbow Pl 4 PO1 182 A5
Benbridge Ave BH11 188 F5
Bencraft Ct SO16 79 B5
Bendigo Rd BH23 206 E8
Benedict Cl SO51 53 C7
Benedict Way PO16 132 E1
Beneficial St 14 PO1 182 A5
Benellen Ave BH4 204 C4
Benellen Gdns BH4 204 D4
Benellen Rd BH4 204 C5
Benellen Twrs 1 BH4 204 C4
Bengal Rd BH9 204 E8
Benger's La SO51 5 E2
Benham Dr 6 PO3 157 F4
Benham Gr PO16 156 D6
Benhams Farm Cl 4 SO18 80 A1
Benhams Rd SO18 80 A2
Benjamin Ct BH23 206 F7
Benjamin Rd BH15 201 D2
Benmoor Rd BH17 202 A8
Benmore Cl BH25 195 C2
Benmore Gdns SO53 55 B8
Benmore Rd BH9 190 A1
Bennett Cl SP5 47 D6
Bennett Ho 4 BH4 204 C4
Bennett Rd BH8 205 C6
Bennetts La BH24 143 C2
Bennion Rd BH10 189 C3
Benny Hill Cl SO50 55 F3
Benridge Bsns Pk BH17 202 B8
Benridge Cl BH18 187 A3
Benson Cl BH23 169 B1
Benson Rd Poole BH17 202 D7
Southampton SO15 102 B8
Bent La PO7 110 A7
Bentham Ct SO16 79 A4
Bentham Rd PO12 181 B4
Bentham Way SO31 128 D8
Bentley Cl Horndean PO8 112 C8
Kings Worthy SO23 2 B6
Bentley Cres PO16 130 F2
Bentley Ct Havant PO9 136 B5
9 Southampton SO17 79 A1
Bentley Gn SO18 104 C8
Bentley Rd BH9 189 F3
Bentley Way SO41 197 D6
Bentworth Cl PO9 135 D4
Benwell Ct PO11 184 F3
Bepton Down GU31 41 A3
Berber Cl PO15 129 C7
Bercote Cl SO22 1 B5
Bere Cl
Chandler's Ford SO53 55 A8
Poole BH17 187 D2
Winchester SO22 215 B8
Bere Farm La PO17 131 F8
Bere Rd PO7 110 F4
Beresford Cl
Chandler's Ford SO53 55 E5
Poole BH12 203 D6
Waterlooville PO7 134 E6
Beresford Gdns
Chandler's Ford SO53 55 E5
Christchurch BH23 207 E6
Beresford Rd
Bournemouth BH5 206 B4
Chandler's Ford SO53 55 E5
Lymington SO41 197 C4
Poole BH12 203 D6
Portsmouth PO2 157 E1
Stubbington PO14 179 D8
Bereweeke Ave SO22 215 C8
Bereweeke Cl SO22 215 C7
Bereweeke Ho SO22 215 C7
Bereweeke Rd SO22 215 C7
Bereweeke Way SO22 215 C8
Bergen Cres SO30 105 C5
Berkeley Ave BH12 203 D8
Berkeley Cl
Southampton SO15 102 F7
Stubbington PO14 179 B7
Verwood BH31 114 E7
Berkeley Ct PO13 179 F2
Berkeley Gdns SO30 105 C5
Berkeley Rd
Bournemouth BH3 204 E7
Southampton SO15 102 F6
Berkeley Sq PO9 136 B1
Berkeley The PO5 182 E1
Berkley Ave BH22 165 D2
Berkley Manor 8 BH13 204 B4
Berkshire Cl PO1 216 D3
Bermuda Ct
5 Christchurch BH23 209 A7
15 Southampton SO17 79 A1
Bermuda Ho 3 PO6 132 F2
Bernard Ave PO6 158 A8
Bernard Powell Ho PO9 136 A1
Bernard St SO14 103 A3
Bernards Cl BH23 206 E8
Berne Ct 15 BH1 205 A3
Berney Rd PO4 183 C4
Bernie Tunstall Pl SO50 56 B3
Bernina Ave PO7 111 C2
Bernina Cl PO7 111 C2
Bernwood Gr SO45 177 E7
Beron Ct BH15 202 E4
Berrans Ave BH11 189 B6
Berrans Ct BH11 189 A6
Berry Cl SO30 105 D6
Berry Ho 9 PO1 182 D7
Berry La
Stubbington PO14 179 A7
Twyford SO21 32 A7
Berrydown Rd PO9 135 C7
Berryfield Rd SO41 196 A2
Berrylands GU33 21 A7

Berrywood Bsns Village SO30 81 B3
Berrywood Gdns SO30 105 B8
Berrywood Prim Sch SO30 81 D1
Berthon Ho SO51 52 E6
Bertie Rd PO4 183 B4
Bertram Rd BH25 195 C4
Berwick Rd BH3 204 E6
Berwyn Wlk PO14 154 E8
Beryl Ave PO12 180 F8
Beryton Cl PO12 181 A7
Beryton Rd PO12 181 A7
Besomer Dro SP5 47 F5
Bessborough Rd BH13 214 E7
Bessemer Cl BH31 115 C4
Beswick Ave BH10 189 D2
Bethany Ct BH12 204 A7
Bethany Ho BH1 205 D5
Bethany Jun CE Sch BH1 205 D5
Bethia Cl BH8 205 D6
Bethia Rd BH8 205 D6
Betsy Cl BH23 169 B1
Betsy La BH23 169 B1
Betteridge Dr SO16 77 D6
Bettesworth Rd PO1 182 E7
Bettiscombe Cl BH17 187 E2
Betula Cl PO7 135 A6
Beulah Rd SO16 78 A1
Bevan Cl SO19 103 E1
Bevan Rd PO8 111 F5
Beverley Cl SO31 129 C4
Beverley Gdns
Bournemouth BH10 189 D3
Bursledon SO31 104 E1
Romsey SO51 28 B1
Swanmore SO32 84 B5
Beverley Gr PO6 134 F1
Beverley Grange 50 BH4 204 C3
Beverley Hts SO18 79 F3
Beverley Rd Hythe SO45 149 F8
Stubbington PO14 179 C6
Beverly Cl PO13 155 D2
Beverston Ho 4 PO6 133 A1
Beverston Rd PO6 133 A1
Bevis Cl Blackfield SO45 150 F2
Warsash SO31 152 D10
Bevis Rd Gosport PO12 181 B6
Portsmouth PO2 157 D1
Bevis Rd N PO2 157 D1
Bevois Gdns SO14 103 A7
Bevois Hill SO14 103 B8
Bevois Mans 7 SO14 103 B8
Bevois Mews 4 SO14 103 A7
Bevois Town Prim Sch SO14 103 A7
Bevois Valley Rd SO14 103 B7
Bexington Cl BH11 188 E3
Beyne Rd SO22 10 B3
Bickerley Gdns BH24 140 F6
Bickerley Rd BH24 140 F6
Bickerley Terr BH24 140 F7
Bickleigh Ho 6 PO17 130 E8
Bicknell Ct 5 BH4 204 C4
Bicknell Sch BH7 206 A7
Bickton Ash SP6 94 A6
Bickton Wlk PO9 135 D6
Bicton Rd BH11 189 B3
Bidbury Inf Sch PO9 135 D2
Bidbury Jun Sch PO9 135 D2
Bidbury La PO9 135 C1
Biddenfield La SO32, PO17 107 D5
Biddlecombe Cl PO13 180 C8
Biddlesgate Ct 5 SO14 102 F3
Bideford Cl SO16 77 E1
Big Tree Cotts SO32 85 C6
Biggin Wlk PO14 154 E8
Bigpath Farm Cotts SO32 59 B6
Bilberry Cl SO31 128 F2
Bilberry Ct 11 SO22 215 D6
Bilberry Dr SO40 101 E2
Bill Stillwell Ct 6 PO2 157 C2
Billett Ave PO7 111 F1
Billing Cl PO4 183 B3
Billington Gdns SO30 81 D1
Billington Pl SO41 197 D2
Billy Lawn Ave PO9 135 F4
Bilton Bsns Pk PO3 158 C2
Bilton Way PO3 158 C2
Bindon Cl Poole BH12 203 E7
Southampton SO16 78 A2
Bindon Ct 13 SO18 103 E8
Bindon Rd SO16 78 A2
Bingham Ave BH14 214 D8
Bingham Cl
Christchurch BH23 207 E7
Verwood BH31 115 B4
Bingham Dr
Lymington SO41 197 E3
Verwood BH31 115 A4
Bingham Rd
Bournemouth BH9 205 A7
Christchurch BH23 207 E7
Verwood BH31 115 A4
Binnacle Way PO6 157 B8
Binness Way PO6 158 E7
Binnie Rd BH12 203 E5
Binsey Cl SO16 101 E8
Binstead Cl SO16 79 C5
Binsteed Rd PO2 182 E8
Birch Ave Beckley BH25 194 D5
Burton BH23 192 C3
Birch Ave *continued*
Ferndown BH22 165 F1
Birch Cl
Colden Common SO21 56 F8
Corfe Mullen BH21 186 D6
Liss GU33 21 A4
Poole BH14 203 E3
Romsey SO51 53 D6
Southampton SO16 78 A2
St Leonards BH24 139 D3
Waterlooville PO8 111 E3
Birch Copse BH17 202 A8
Birch Ct Lymington SO41 197 B2
Southampton SO18 104 A7
3 Winchester SO22 215 A4
Birch Dale SO45 126 B2
Birch Dr
Bournemouth BH8 191 A2
Gosport PO13 155 C4
Birch Gr Eastleigh SO50 56 A6
Old Milton BH25 195 A1
West Moors BH22 138 D2
Birch Hill Cotts PO17 109 A3
Birch Ho SO16 78 F7
Birch Rd Chilworth SO16 79 A8
Hedge End SO30 105 D7
Southampton SO16 78 A3
St Leonards BH24 140 B4
Birch Tree Cl PO10 136 F4
Birch Tree Dr PO10 136 F4
Birch Wlk BH22 165 F3
Birch Wood SO19 104 E5
Birchdale Cl SO31 152 D10
Birchdale Rd BH21 163 D5
Birchen Cl SO31 129 C4
Birchen Rd SO31 129 C4
Birches Cl The SO52 53 F5
Birches The SO18 104 B8
Birchglade SO40 76 C2
Birchlands SO40 100 D5
Birchmore Cl PO13 155 C2
Birchwood Cl BH23 208 E8
Birchwood Ct 7 SO18 103 E8
Birchwood Dr SP6 93 A5
Birchwood Gdns SO30 105 C8
Birchwood Lodge 7 PO16 131 B2
Birchwood Mews BH14 203 D3
Birchwood Rd
Poole BH14 203 D3
Upton BH16 201 B6
Birchy Hill SO41 172 C1
Bird Field SO53 54 F7
Bird's Hill Rd BH15 202 E3
Birdham Rd PO11 185 E2
Birdlip Cl PO8 112 A6
Birdlip Rd PO6 133 B1
Birds Hill Gdns 1 BH15 202 E3
Birdwood Gr PO16 155 F8
Birinus Rd SO23 215 E7
Birkdale Ave PO6 134 D1
Birkdale Ct BH18 187 A5
Birkdale Rd BH18 187 A5
Birmingham Ct 7 PO13 180 D5
Biscay Cl PO14 179 B8
Bishearne Gdns GU33 20 E5
Bishop Cl BH12 204 C7
Bishop Ct BH24 141 A8
Bishop of Winchester Comp Sch The BH8 190 D1
Bishop Rd BH9 205 A8
Bishop St PO1 182 A5
Bishop's La SO32 83 C7
Bishop's Waltham Inf Sch SO32 83 D8
Bishop's Waltham Pal* SO32 83 C7
Bishop's Wood Rd PO17, SO32 84 D2
Bishops Cl
Bournemouth BH7 205 F7
Totton SO40 100 E8
Bishops Cres SO19 103 F4
Bishops Ct
Bishopstoke SO50 56 D5
Broadstone BH18 187 A3
Bishops Gate PO14 129 D3
Bishops La SO32 84 B1
Bishops Rd SO19 103 E4
Bishopsfield Rd PO14 154 E8
Bishopstoke La SO50 56 E7
Bishopstoke Manor SO50 56 C3
Bishopstoke Rd
Eastleigh SO50 56 C3
Havant PO9 135 E5
Bisley Ct SO19 104 B3
Bisterne Cl BH24 143 E2
Bittern Cl PO12 181 B8
Bitterne CE Inf Sch SO19 103 F6
Bitterne CE Jun Sch SO19 103 F6
Bitterne Cl PO9 135 F6
Bitterne Cres SO19 104 A6
Bitterne Manor Ho SO18 103 C7
Bitterne Manor Prim Sch SO18 103 D7
Bitterne Park Inf Sch SO17 79 D2
Bitterne Park Jun Sch SO17 79 D2
Bitterne Park Sch SO18 79 E2
Bitterne Park Triangle SO18 79 D1
Bitterne Rd SO18 104 A6
Bitterne Rd E SO18 104 C7
Bitterne Rd W SO18 103 E7
Bitterne Sta SO18 103 D7
Bitterne Way
Lymington SO41 197 D2
Southampton SO19 103 F6
Verwood BH31 115 A5
Bitumen Rd SO45 151 B4
Black Hill BH31 115 A6
Black Hill Rd SO43,SO51 74 E7
Black La Bransgore BH23 169 E3
Redlynch SP5 48 B4
Black Moor Rd BH31 115 C4
Black Swan Bldgs 16 SO22 215 D6
Blackberry Cl PO8 88 D4
Blackberry Dr SO50 57 B1
Blackberry La BH23 207 F6
Blackberry Terr SO14 103 B7
Blackbird Cl
Broadstone BH17 201 E8
Waterlooville PO8 111 F4
Blackbird Rd SO50 55 D2
Blackbird Way
Bransgore BH23 193 C8
Lee-on-t-S PO13 179 F4
Blackbrook Bsns Pk PO15 130 E1
Blackbrook House Dr PO14 130 E1
Blackbrook Park Ave PO15 130 E1
Blackbrook Rd PO15 130 D2
Blackburn Ct 5 PO13 180 D5
Blackburn Rd BH12 203 B6
Blackbush Rd SO41 211 B5
Blackbushe Cl SO16 77 F5
Blackcap Cl PO9 113 A1
Blackdown Cl SO45 125 D2
Blackdown Cres PO9 135 E4
Blackfield Inf Sch SO45 150 E1
Blackfield Jun Sch SO45 150 E1
Blackfield La BH22 138 E3
Blackfield Rd
Blackfield SO45 150 F2
Bournemouth BH8 190 D3
Blackfriars Cl 3 PO5 216 C2
Blackfriars Rd PO5 216 C3
Blackhorse La SO32 83 F1
Blackhouse La
North Boarhunt PO17 132 A8
Soberton PO17 109 A1
Blackmoor Wlk 2 PO9 136 B5
Blackmore La GU32 18 F3
Blacksmith Cl BH21 186 D5
Blackthorn Cl
Braishfield SO51 28 D6
Lymington SO41 197 B2
Southampton SO19 103 F5
Blackthorn Dr
Gosport PO12 156 A1
South Hayling PO11 185 C3
Blackthorn Gn SO21 57 A8
Blackthorn Rd
South Hayling PO11 185 C2
Southampton SO19 103 F5
Blackthorn Terr PO1 182 A6
Blackthorn Way
New Milton BH25 195 D4
Verwood BH31 115 B5
Blackthorn Wlk PO7 112 C1
Blackwater BH23 191 D4
Blackwater Cl
Alderholt SP6 92 E5
7 Cosham PO6 157 D8
Blackwater Dr
Oakley BH21 187 D7
Totton SO40 76 D1
Blackwater Gr SP6 92 E5
Blackwater Mews SO40 76 D1
Blackwood Ho 13 PO1 182 D7
Bladon Cl PO9 136 C3
Bladon Rd SO16 78 C2
Blair Ave BH14 203 C4
Blair Cl BH25 194 E3
Blake Cl SO16 77 D5
Blake Ct 6 PO12 181 E5
Blake Dene Rd BH14 203 B1
Blake Hill Ave BH14 203 D1
Blake Hill Cres BH14 203 C1
Blake Ho 17 PO1 182 A4
Blake Rd Cosham PO6 134 D1
Gosport PO12 181 C6
Portsmouth PO1 181 F8
Blakemere Cres PO6 133 D1
Blakeney Rd SO16 77 D2
Blakesley La PO3 158 C4
Blanchard Rd SO32 83 B8
Blandford Cl BH15 201 F2
Blandford Ct 2 SO41 211 D5
Blandford Ho SO16 77 F1
Blandford Rd
Coombe Bissett SP5 23 D7
Corfe Mullen BH21 186 D8
Hamworthy BH16 201 D4
Pamphill BH21 162 D7
Blandford Rd N
Upton BH16 201 B7
Upton BH16 201 B8
Blaney Way BH21 186 C6
Blankney Cl PO14 179 B7
Blann Cl SO16 77 C5
Blashford Lakes Study Ctr BH24 117 A4
Blaven Wlk 4 PO14 154 E8
Bleaklow Cl SO16 101 F8
Blechynden Terr SO15 102 E5
Blencowe Dr SO53 54 F5
Blendworth Cres PO9 135 F3
Blendworth Ho 2 PO1 216 C4
Blendworth La
Blendworth PO8 112 E7
Southampton SO18 104 C7
Blendworth Rd 1 PO4 183 B5
Blenheim 3 BH13 204 B3
Blenheim Ave SO17 79 A1
Blenheim Cl
Chandler's Ford SO53 54 F4
Totton SO40 100 E6
Blenheim Cres SO41 195 F4
Blenheim Ct
35 Bournemouth BH4 204 C3
Christchurch BH23 207 A8
Portsmouth PO4 183 A3
Southampton SO17 79 A1
Blenheim Dr BH23 208 B6
Blenheim Gdns
Gosport PO12 181 B9
Havant PO9 136 C2
Hythe SO45 125 D2
Southampton SO17 79 B2
Blenheim Ho
Eastleigh SO50 56 B2
Romsey SO51 53 B7
Blenheim Mews 6 BH4 204 C4
Blenheim Rd
Eastleigh SO50 56 A2
Waterlooville PO8 112 A5
Blenhem Barn PO7 110 F1
Bleriot Cres PO15 129 F6
Blighmont Ave SO15 102 B6
Blighmont Cres SO15 102 B6
Blind La Curdridge SO32 82 E2
Horton Heath SO30 81 C5
Ibsley SP6 94 C1
Wickham PO17 107 F5
Wimborne Minst BH21 163 B5
Bliss Cl PO7 134 E5
Blissford Cl PO9 136 B5
Blissford Cross SP6 94 E8
Blissford Hill SP6 94 E7
Blissford Rd SP6 94 E8
Bloomfield Ave BH9 189 F2
Bloomfield Pl BH9 189 F2
Bloomsbury Wlk SO19 103 E2
Blossom Cl SO30 105 E6
Blossom Sq PO1 182 A6
Blount Rd PO1 182 B3
Bloxworth Rd BH12 203 F8
Blue Anchor La 10 SO14 102 F3
Blue Ball Hill SO23 215 F6
Blue Reef Aquarium* PO5 182 C1
Bluebell Cl
Christchurch BH23 208 B8
Waterlooville PO7 135 A6
Bluebell Copse SO31 128 F2
Bluebell La BH17 186 F1
Bluebell Rd SO16 79 C4
Bluebell Way PO15 129 D8
Blueprint Portfield Rd PO3 158 A2
Bluestar Gdns SO30 81 C2
Bluevalley Mews 3 SP6 69 F1
Bluff The BH10 189 F4
Blundell La SO31 105 C1
Blyth Cl
Christchurch BH23 191 D4
Southampton SO16 77 D2
Blyth Mews 4 SO15 102 E6
Blythe Rd BH21 186 D6
Blythswood Ct BH25 209 F7
Boakes Pl SO40 100 C2
Boardwalk The PO6 157 B7
Boardwalk Way SO40 102 A3
Boarhunt Cl PO1 216 C3
Boarhunt Rd
Boarhunt PO17 132 A6
Fareham PO17 131 E3
Boatyard Ind Est The PO16 155 A8
Bob Hann Cl BH12 203 D5
Bockhampton Rd BH23 192 E6
Bodley Rd BH13 214 F7
Bodmin Rd
Bishopstoke SO50 56 E2
Portchester PO6 157 A8
Bodorgan Rd BH2 204 F4
Bodowen Cl BH23 192 D2
Bodowen Rd BH23 192 D1
Bodycoats Rd SO53 55 D5
Bognor Rd BH18 186 F4
Bohemia La SP5,SP6 47 F3
Boiler Rd Fawley SO45 151 E1
Portsmouth PO1 181 F8
Bokerley Junc SP5 42 A4
Bolde Cl PO3 158 B3
Boldens Rd PO12 181 B2
Bolderwood Arboretum Ornamental Dr* BH24, SO43 120 C2
Bolderwood Cl SO50 56 F2
Bolderwood Deer Sanctuary* SO43 120 A6
Boldre Cl
Barton on S BH25 209 D8
Havant PO9 135 C4
Poole BH12 203 D7
Boldre La SO41 197 D8
Boldrewood Rd SO16 78 E4
Boleyn Cres BH9 190 C4
Bolhinton Ave SO40 101 D1
Bolton Cl BH6 206 E3
Bolton Cres BH22 166 A6
Bolton Ct 3 BH6 206 E3
Bolton Dr PO12 181 C8
Bolton Rd BH6 206 E3
Boltons The
Milford on S SO41 211 D4
Waterlooville PO7 134 E3
Bonchurch Cl SO16 79 C5
Bonchurch Rd PO4 183 A5
Bond Ave BH22 138 D4
Bond Cl SO41 172 B3
Bond Rd Poole BH15 202 F5
Southampton SO18 79 E1
Bond St SO14 103 C6
Bondfields Cres PO9 135 F6
Bones La GU31 65 D5
Bonfire Cnr PO1 182 A6
Bonham Rd BH9 204 F7
Boniface Cl SO40 100 D8
Boniface Cres SO16 77 E4
Bonington Cl BH23 207 E8
Bonner Cotts SP5 4 E7
Boothby Cl SO40 101 A6
Bordean La GU32 39 C6
Borden Way SO52 54 A4
Border Cl GU33 21 B1
Border Dr BH16 201 C5
Border Rd BH16 201 C5
Bordon Rd PO9 135 F5
Boreham Rd BH6 206 D5
Borland Ho PO17 108 F1
Borough Gr GU32 40 E2
Borough Hill GU32 40 E3
Borough Rd GU32 40 D2
Borough The SP5 46 F8
Borrowdale Rd SO16 77 E1
Borthwick Rd BH1 205 E5
Boscobel Rd SO22 215 D7
Boscombe Cliff Rd BH5 205 F3
Boscombe Grove Rd BH1 205 D5
Boscombe Overcliff Dr BH5 206 A3
Boscombe Spa Rd BH5 205 D3
Bosham Rd PO2 182 F8
Bosham Wlk PO13 155 B2
Bosley Cl BH23 191 E2
Bosley Way BH23 191 E2
Bosmere Gdns PO10 136 E1
Bosmere Jun Sch PO9 159 F8
Bosmere Rd PO11 185 E1
Bossington Cl SO16 77 E5
Boston Ct SO53 55 D7
Boston Lo 31 BH4 204 C3
Boston Rd PO6 133 E1
Bosun Ct 11 PO6 157 F7
Bosuns Cl PO16 155 B6
Bosville SO50 56 A6
Boswell Cl Botley SO30 106 A6
Southampton SO19 104 C6
Bosworth Mews BH9 190 B4
Botany Bay Rd SO19 104 A3
Botany Ho 4 PO15 129 D8
Botley CE Prim Sch SO30 106 A7
Botley Dr PO9 135 D5
Botley Gdns SO19 104 E3
Botley Hill SO30 106 B6
Botley Mill Craft & Bsns Ctr SO30 106 B7
Botley Rd
Bishop's Waltham SO32 83 B6
Curdridge SO32 82 F2
Fair Oak SO50 57 D1
Hedge End SO30 81 B1
Horton Heath SO50 81 D7
North Baddesley SO52 54 B4
Romsey SO51,SO52 53 D6
Southampton SO19 104 D3
Swanwick SO31 129 B7
Botley Sta SO30 106 C7
Bottings Est SO30 106 B7
Bottom La
West Wellow SO51 50 D4
West Wellow SO51 50 E4
Boughton Ct PO3 158 C4
Boulnois Ave BH14 203 E3
Boultbee Cotts SO43 121 D5
Boulter La PO17 133 A7
Boulton Rd PO5 216 D1
Bound La PO11 185 A2
Boundary Acre SO31 105 B4
Boundary Cl SO15 101 F7
Boundary Dr BH21 163 D6
Boundary La BH24 139 E1
Boundary Oak Prep Sch PO17 131 C5
Boundary Rd
Bournemouth BH10 189 E1
Bursledon SO31 127 F8
Boundary Rdbt BH3, BH10 204 D8
Boundary Way
Cosham PO6 134 B2
Havant PO9 135 E1
Boundary Wlk 13 PO17 130 E7
Boundstone SO45 125 F3
Boundway SO41 171 E1
Bountys La BH12 203 E5
Bourne Ave
Bournemouth BH2 204 E3
Southampton SO15 78 C1
Bourne Cl
Bournemouth BH2 204 D3
Otterbourne SO21 31 C4
Waterlooville PO8 112 B6
West Wellow SO51 50 D3
Bourne Com Coll PO10 137 D1
Bourne Cotts SP6 44 E1
Bourne Ct
1 Bournemouth BH2 204 F3
Wimborne Minst BH21 163 D5

Bourne Fields SO21 32 B7
Bourne La Bartley SO40 99 D6
Twyford SO21 32 B6
Bourne Pines 4 BH2 204 F4
Bourne Rd Bartley SO40 99 C6
Cosham PO6 157 B8
Southampton SO15 102 D5
Bourne River Ct 9 BH4 204 D4
Bourne Valley Bsns Pk BH12 204 A5
Bourne Valley Rd BH12 204 A5
Bourne View Cl PO10 137 D2
Bournemouth & Poole Coll (Constitution Hill Campus) The BH14 202 F5
Bournemouth & Poole Coll (North Road Campus) The BH14 202 F4
Bournemouth & Poole Coll Annexe The BH1 205 A3
Bournemouth & Poole Coll The BH1 205 B3
Bournemouth Ave PO12 181 A9
Bournemouth Aviation Mus* BH23 191 A8
Bournemouth Central Bsns Pk BH1 205 C5
Bournemouth Ho
2 Bournemouth BH1 205 B3
7 Havant PO9 136 A5
Bournemouth Int Ctr* BH2 204 F2
Bournemouth International Airport BH23 190 E8
Bournemouth Learning Support Centre PRU BH10 189 D1
Bournemouth Meml Homes BH8 190 F1
Bournemouth Nuffield Derwent Suite BH7 191 B1
Bournemouth Nuffield Hospl The BH8 205 A5
Bournemouth Rd
Chandler's Ford SO53 55 C4
Lyndhurst SO43 121 E5
Poole BH14 203 D4
Bournemouth Sch BH8 190 C1
Bournemouth Sch for Girls BH8 190 C2
Bournemouth Sta BH8 205 B4
Bournemouth Station Rdbt BH8 205 B4
Bournemouth Univ (Lansdowne Campus) BH1 205 B3
Bournemouth Univ (Talbot Campus) BH12 204 C8
Bournemouth West Rdbt BH2 204 D3
Bournewood Dr BH4 204 C4
Bourton Gdns BH7 206 B8
Bouverie Cl 7 BH25 195 A1
Boveridge Gdns BH9 190 B4
Bovington Cl BH17 187 F1
Bowater Cl SO40 76 C1
Bowater Way SO40 76 C1
Bowcombe SO31 127 C7
Bowden Ho 8 SO17 79 C2
Bowden La SO17 79 C2
Bowden Rd BH12 188 C2
Bowen La GU31 40 F3
Bower Cl Holbury SO45 150 C3
Southampton SO19 103 F1
Bower Rd BH8 205 D8
Bowers Cl PO8 112 A4
Bowers Hill SP5 47 E7
Bowerwood Cotts SP6 93 C8
Bowerwood Rd SP6 93 D8
Bowes Hill PO9 113 C3
Bowes-Lyon Ct PO8 112 B7
Bowland Rise
Chandler's Ford SO53 55 A7
New Milton BH25 195 C2
Bowland Way SO45 177 E7
Bowler Ave PO1 182 F6
Bowler Ct PO1 182 F6
Bowman Ct SO19 104 B3
Box Cl BH17 202 B7
Boxgrove Ho PO1 216 C4
Boxwood Cl
Portchester PO16 132 B1
Waterlooville PO7 134 E6
Boyatt Cres SO50 56 A8
Boyatt La SO50 56 A7
Boyatt Wood Sh Ctr SO50 56 A5
Boyd Cl PO14 179 B6
Boyd Rd Gosport PO13 155 B4
Poole BH12 203 F6
Boyes La SO21 32 A1
Boyle Cres PO7 134 D5
Boyne Mead Rd SO23 2 C7
Boyne Rise SO23 2 B8
Boynton Cl SO53 55 B8
Brabant Cl PO15 129 B7
Brabazon Dr BH23 208 B7
Brabazon Rd
Locks Heath PO15 129 D5
Merley BH21 163 F1
Brabourne Ave BH22 165 C4
Bracken Cl
Lee-on-t-S PO13 180 A6
North Baddesley SO52 54 A3
St Leonards BH24 139 D4
Bracken Cres SO50 56 F2
Bracken Ct 10 BH4 204 D4
Bracken Glen BH15 202 E5
Bracken Hall SO16 79 B8
Bracken Heath 8 PO7 112 B1
Bracken La SO16 78 A1
Bracken Lodge 3 BH6 206 F4
Bracken Pl SO16 79 A7
Bracken Rd
Bournemouth BH6 206 C4
Ferndown BH22 165 B7
North Baddesley SO52 54 A3
Petersfield GU31 41 C2
Bracken Way BH23 194 B1
Brackendale Ct BH21 138 E8
Brackendale Rd BH8 205 D8
Brackenhill BH13 204 A1
Brackenhill Rd BH21 164 A7
Brackens The
Hythe SO45 125 D3
Locks Heath SO31 129 B2
Brackens Way
Lymington SO41 197 F2
2 Poole BH13 214 F8
Brackenway Rd SO53 55 C8
Bracklesham Cl SO19 103 F3
Bracklesham Pl BH25 209 F7
Bracklesham Rd
Gosport PO13 180 D8
South Hayling PO11 185 F2
Brackley Ave SO50 57 B3
Brackley Cl BH23 191 A8
Brackley Way SO40 100 D8
Bradburne Rd BH2 204 E3
Bradbury Ho BH22 165 D7
Bradford Ct 8 PO13 180 C6
Bradford Junc PO5 216 C2
Bradford Rd
Bournemouth BH9 190 C4
Portsmouth PO5 216 C2
Brading Ave
Gosport PO13 155 C2
Portsmouth PO4 183 A2
Brading Cl SO16 79 C5
Bradley Ct 10 PO9 136 B6
Bradley Gn SO16 78 B4
Bradley Peak SO22 215 A7
Bradley Rd SO22 1 C4
Bradly Rd PO15 130 C1
Bradpole Rd BH8 190 E1
Bradshaw Cl SO50 57 E2
Bradstock Cl BH12 203 F8
Braehead SO45 125 F2
Braemar Ave
Bournemouth BH6 207 A4
Cosham PO6 158 B7
Braemar Cl
Bournemouth BH6 207 A4
Fareham PO15 130 E3
Gosport PO13 155 D2
Braemar Dr BH23 193 F1
Braemar Rd PO13 155 D2
Braemore Ct SO22 215 A5
Braeside Bsns Pk BH15 202 B4
Braeside Cl
Southampton SO19 103 E5
Winchester SO22 10 B4
Braeside Cres SO19 103 E5
Braeside Rd
Southampton SO19 103 E5
St Leonards BH24 139 E3
West Moors BH22 138 F3
Braggers La BH23 169 B4
Braidley Rd BH2 204 E4
Brailswood Rd BH15 202 E4
Braintree Rd PO6 133 D1
Braishfield Cl SO16 77 F1
Braishfield Gdns BH8 190 D2
Braishfield Prim Sch SO51 28 D6
Braishfield Rd
Havant PO9 136 A4
Romsey SO51 28 C4
Brake Ho PO9 135 D2
Bramar Ct 9 BH4 204 C2
Bramber Rd PO12 181 A8
Bramble Cl Alderholt SP6 93 A5
Eastleigh SO50 56 B5
Havant PO9 136 C3
Holbury SO45 150 C3
Stubbington PO14 179 A6
Bramble Ct
Petersfield GU31 41 C3
West Moors BH22 138 E2
Bramble Dr SO51 28 C1
Bramble Hill SO53 55 A6
Bramble La Clanfield PO8 88 B7
Sarisbury SO31 128 E5
Walkford BH23 194 B1
Bramble Mews 1 SO18 104 A8
Bramble Rd
Petersfield GU31 41 C3
Portsmouth PO4 182 E4
Bramble Way
Bransgore BH23 169 B1
Gosport PO13 155 A2
Bramble Wlk SO41 197 C4
Bramblegate SO50 57 D1
Brambles Bsns Ctr The PO7 111 C1
Brambles Cl SO21 57 A8
Brambles Ent Ctr The PO7 111 C1
Brambles Farm Ind Est PO7 134 D8
Brambles Rd PO13 179 D4
Brambling Cl SO16 78 B6
Brambling Rd PO9 113 B1
Bramblings The SO40 100 C7
Brambridge SO50 56 E8
Brambridge Ho SO50 31 D1
Bramdean Dr PO9 135 D5
Bramdean Mews SO19 103 E5
Bramdean Rd SO18 104 D7
Bramham Moor PO14 179 B7
Bramley Cl
Lymington SO41 197 E2
Waterlooville PO7 134 F8
Bramley Cres SO19 104 B2
Bramley Ct BH22 165 C6
Bramley Gdns
Emsworth PO10 161 B8
Gosport PO12 181 B2
Horton Heath SO50 81 C6
Bramley Ho
Gosport PO12 181 B2
Hedge End SO30 105 B6
3 Portsmouth PO5 216 B2
Bramley Rd
Bournemouth BH10 189 C5
Ferndown BH22 165 D6
Bramleys The SP5 24 B3
Brampton La PO3 158 C4
Brampton Manor SO16 78 F5
Brampton Rd BH15 202 D6
Brampton Twr SO16 78 F5
Bramsdon Ct 5 PO4 182 F2
Bramshaw Cl SO22 1 C3
Bramshaw Ct 18 PO9 136 B5
Bramshaw Gdns BH8 190 D3
Bramshaw Way BH25 209 D8
Bramshott Rd
Portsmouth PO4 182 F4
Southampton SO19 126 F8
Bramston Rd SO15 102 C8
Branches La SO51 25 F3
Branders Cl BH6 207 A4
Branders La BH6 207 B5
Brandon Ct
6 Poole BH12 204 B4
Portsmouth PO5 216 D1
Brandon Ho PO5 216 D1
Brandon Rd PO5 182 D2
Brandt Ho 8 PO17 130 E7
Brandwood Ct 4 BH14 203 A3
Branewick Cl PO15 129 D3
Branksea Ave BH15 201 E1
Branksea Cl BH15 201 E1
Branksome Ave SO15 78 C1
Branksome Cl
New Milton BH25 195 B2
Winchester SO22 10 B6
Branksome Ct 4 BH13 214 F8
Branksome Dene Rd BH4 204 B2
Branksome Heath Mid Sch BH12 203 C6
Branksome Hill Rd BH4 204 B5
Branksome Sta BH12 203 F4
Branksome Twrs BH13 214 H8
Branksome Wood Gdns BH2 204 D4
Branksome Wood Rd BH2,BH4 204 C4
Bransbury Cl SO16 78 C4
Bransbury Rd PO4 183 B3
Bransgore Ave PO9 135 C4
Bransgore CE Prim Sch BH23 193 C8
Bransgore Gdns BH23 169 C1
Bransley Cl SO51 28 B1
Branwell Cl BH23 192 A1
Branwood Cl SO41 196 E1
Brasenose Cl PO14 129 C1
Brasher Cl SO50 57 A2
Brassey Cl BH9 190 A1
Brassey Rd
Bournemouth BH9 190 A1
Winchester SO22 215 D7
Brassey Terr BH9 189 F1
Brasted Ct PO4 183 C5
Braunston Cl 7 PO6 133 A1
Braxall Lawn PO9 135 D6
Braxton Ctyd SO41 211 E7
Braxton Ho 1 SO23 11 C8
Breach Ave PO10 137 E2
Breach La SO50 56 D5
Breamore CE Prim Sch SP6 70 B8
Breamore Cl
Eastleigh SO50 56 A6
New Milton BH25 194 E3
Breamore Countryside Mus* SP6 46 A2
Breamore Ho* SP6 46 A3
Breamore Rd
Downton SP5 46 E7
Southampton SO18 104 D7
Brean Cl SO16 77 E2
Brearley Ct BH23 209 B8
Brecon Ave PO6 158 B8
Brecon Cl
Bournemouth BH10 189 E6
Chandler's Ford SO53 55 B3
Fareham PO14 154 E8
Hythe SO45 125 E3
New Milton BH25 195 C2
Brecon Ho 23 PO1 182 A4
Brecon Rd SO19 104 C5
Bredenbury Cres PO6 133 C1
Bredon Wlk PO14 154 E8
Bredy Cl BH17 187 D1
Breech Cl 5 PO3 157 F4
Bremble Cl BH12 188 C2
Brenchley Cl PO16 156 B7
Brendon Cl SO45 125 D2
Brendon Gn SO16 101 F8
Brendon Rd PO14 154 D8
Brent Ct PO10 160 E7
Brentwood Cres SO18 80 A1
Breton Cl PO15 129 B7
Brewells La GU33 21 E5
Brewer Cl SO31 129 B4
Brewer St PO1 216 B4
Brewers La
Gosport PO13 155 D2
Twyford SO21 31 F5
West Tisted SO24 17 C7
Brewhouse Sq PO12 181 D7
Brewster Cl PO8 112 A3
Briar Cl
Christchurch BH23 207 F6
Gosport PO12 180 E3
Poole BH15 202 E5
Waterlooville PO8 112 B5
Briar Way Romsey SO51 28 C1
Wimborne Minst BH21 164 B5
Briar Wood GU33 21 A7
Briar's The PO7 111 C1
Briardene Ct SO40 100 E7
Briarfield 49 BH4 204 C3
Briarfield Gdns PO8 112 B6
Briars The SO42 145 F1
Briarswood SO16 78 B1
Briarswood Rd BH16 201 C7
Briarswood Rise SO45 125 D2
Briarwood Cl PO16 155 B8
Briarwood Gdns PO11 184 F3
Briarwood Rd SO40 100 C6
Brick Kiln La SO24 17 B8
Brick La BH23 169 E4
Brickets Terr PO12 181 B3
Brickfield La
Chandler's Ford SO53 55 C5
Lymington SO41 197 F5
Brickfield Rd SO17 79 C2
Brickfield Trad Est SO53 55 C5
Brickmakers Rd SO21 56 F8
Brickwoods Cl SO51 53 B8
Brickworth Rd SP5 24 A3
Bricky Lake La SO51 75 C7
Brickyard La
Corfe Mullen BH21 162 A1
Ferndown BH22 165 A6
Verwood BH31 114 D7
Brickyard Rd SO32 84 A3
Brickyard The SO40 99 B8
Brickyards Ind Est The GU32 20 A1
Bridefield Cl PO8 111 D3
Bridefield Cres PO8 111 D3
Bridge App BH15 202 B1
Bridge Cl SO31 105 B1
Bridge Cotts Liss GU33 20 E7
West Wellow SO51 50 F4
Bridge Ct SO51 52 E6
Bridge Education Ctr The SO50 56 B3
Bridge Farm SO30 106 D4
Bridge Ho Gosport PO13 155 C4
Southampton SO15 102 C5
Bridge Industries PO16 131 C3
Bridge La SO21 31 E7
Bridge Mdws GU33 20 F4
Bridge Mead SO32 61 D5
Bridge Pl BH10 189 D7
Bridge Rd Bishopstone SP5 22 B8
Bursledon SO31 105 B1
Emsworth PO10 136 F1
Locks Heath SO31 129 B5
Lymington SO41 197 F5
Romsey SO51 53 A7
Sarisbury SO31 128 D6
Southampton SO19 103 D3
Bridge Sh Ctr The PO1 216 D3
Bridge St
Christchurch BH23 207 C6
Fordingbridge SP6 69 F1
Southwick PO17 132 E6
Titchfield PO14 154 A7
Wickham PO17 108 A3
7 Winchester SO23 215 F5
Bridge Terr Compton SO21 31 E6
4 Southampton SO14 103 B3
Bridgefoot Dr PO16 131 C1
Bridgefoot Hill PO16 131 C1
Bridgefoot Path PO10 160 F8
Bridgemary Ave PO13 155 D3
Bridgemary Com Sch PO13 155 C2
Bridgemary Gr PO13 155 C5
Bridgemary Rd PO13 155 C4
Bridgemary Way PO13 155 C5
Bridgers Cl SO16 77 E5
Bridges Ave PO6 132 F1
Bridges Cl Eastleigh SO50 55 F3
West Moors BH22 138 F3
Bridges The BH24 140 E7
Bridgeside Cl PO1 216 C3
Bridget Cl PO8 112 C7
Bridgewater Rd BH12 203 D6
Bridgeway Ct SO40 101 A7
Bridgeway The SO19 103 E3
Bridgwater Ct SO15 102 D5
Bridle Cl BH16 201 D7
Bridle Cres BH7 206 D7
Bridle Way BH21 164 C6
Bridleways BH31 114 E6
Bridlington Ave SO15 102 D8
Bridport Ct SO15 102 C5
Bridport Rd Poole BH12 203 F8
Verwood BH31 114 F6
Bridport St PO1 216 B3
Brierley Ave BH22 165 E1
Brierley Cl BH10 189 E5
Brierley Rd BH10 189 E4
Brigantine Rd SO31 128 E1
Brigham Cl 5 PO2 157 E3
Brighstone Cl SO16 79 C5
Bright Rd BH15 202 E6
Bright Wire Cres SO50 55 F2
Brightlands Ave BH6 206 F5
Brighton Ave PO12 180 F8
Brighton Rd
Southampton SO15 102 F7
Sway SO41 172 A3
Brights La PO11 184 F5
Brightside PO7 134 D6
Brightside Rd SO16 77 F3
Brightstone Rd PO6 157 E7
Brindle Cl SO16 79 A5
Brinsons Cl BH23 192 C3
Brinton La SO45 126 A5
Brinton's Rd SO14 103 B5
Brinton's Terr SO14 103 A6
Brisbane Ho 14 PO1 182 D7
Brisbane Rd BH23 191 E1
Bristol Ct PO13 180 C6
Bristol Rd PO4 182 F2
Britain St PO1 182 A5
Britannia Ct Poole BH12 203 B7
Southampton,Bitterne Manor SO14 103 C5
Britannia Gdns SO30 81 B3
Britannia Pl SO41 197 F4
Britannia Rd Poole BH14 203 A3
Portsmouth PO5 216 C2
Southampton SO14 103 B5
Britannia Rd N PO5 216 D2
Britannia St GU31 41 A5
Britannia Way
Christchurch BH23 208 B7
Gosport PO12 181 C8
Britannic Ho 5 SO14 103 C5
Britnell Ho 6 GU31 40 F4
Briton St SO14 103 A3
Britten Rd PO13 179 E3
Britten Way PO7 134 E4
Brittons Cotts SO42 145 D1
Brixey Cl BH12 203 C7
Brixey Rd BH12 203 C7
Brixworth Cl 8 PO6 133 A1
Broad Ave BH8 205 D8
Broad Chalke Down SO22 215 A2
Broad Croft PO9 113 C3
Broad Gdns PO6 158 E8
Broad Gn 2 SO14 103 A4
Broad La Denmead PO7 110 B6
Lymington SO41 197 F2
North Baddesley SO52 53 E5
Southampton SO14 102 F3
Swanmore SO32 84 A5
Broad Mead Rd BH21 114 F1
Broad Oak SO30 105 E7
Broad St PO1 181 F4
Broad View La SO22 10 A3
Broad Way
Froxfield Green GU32 39 E8
Hamble-le-R SO31 127 E5
Broad Woods La SO51 51 A6
Broadbent Cl SO16 77 E6
Broadcut PO16 131 C2
Broadfields Cl SO41 211 D5
Broadhill La SP6 94 E8
Broadhurst Ave BH10 189 E4
Broadlands*
Romsey SO51 52 E5
27 Bournemouth BH4 204 C3
Broadlands Ave
Bournemouth BH6 206 F4
Eastleigh SO50 56 A5
Waterlooville PO7 134 E7
Broadlands Cl
Bournemouth BH8 190 D3
Walkford BH23 194 B2
Broadlands Cotts GU32 41 B6
Broadlands Rd
Brockenhurst SO42 145 E1
Brockenhurst SO42 145 E2
Southampton SO17 79 B3
Broadlaw Wlk 4 PO14 154 E7
Broadley Cl SO45 150 C4
Broadly Cl SO41 197 B2
Broadmarsh Bsns & Innovation Ctr PO9 159 C8
Broadmayne Rd BH12 204 A8
Broadmead Cl 2 SO41 197 F2
Broadmead Flats SO16 77 D5
Broadmead Rd SO16 77 D5
Broadmeadow Cl SO40 100 E7
Broadmeadows La 6 PO7 135 A7
Broadmere Ave PO9 135 F5
Broadmoor Rd BH21 186 C7
Broadoak Cl SO45 150 C3
Broads The BH21 162 F6
Broadsands Dr PO12 180 D3
Broadsands Wlk PO12 180 E3
Broadshard La BH24 141 A8
Broadstone Fst Sch BH18 187 B4
Broadstone Mid Sch BH18 187 C5
Broadstone Way
Broadstone BH17 186 F1
Poole BH17 202 B7
Broadwater Ave BH14 203 C2
Broadwater Rd
Romsey SO51 52 E6
Southampton SO18 79 F3
Broadway BH6 207 B3

Broadway Ct BH12 204 A5
Broadway Gables BH14 203 E4
Broadway Gdns 6 BH21 163 C4
Broadway Ho BH18 187 B4
Broadway La
Bournemouth BH8 190 C4
Horndean PO8 111 D7
Broadway Mews BH14 202 F3
Broadway Pk
Petersfield GU31 40 F1
4 Wimborne Minst BH21 163 C4
Broadway The
3 Bitterne Pk SO18 79 F1
Bournemouth BH10 189 D6
1 Portswood SO17 79 B1
Southampton,Thornhill Pk SO18 104 D7
Winchester SO23 215 E5
Brock Hill Forest Wlks* SO43 144 F8
Brock Ho SO42 145 F1
Brock Way BH31 114 E7
Brockenhurst Ave PO9 135 D6
Brockenhurst CE Prim Sch SO42 172 F8
Brockenhurst Coll SO42 146 A2
Brockenhurst Rd BH9 190 B2
Brockenhurst Sta SO42 173 A8
Brockhampton La PO9 135 E1
Brockhampton Rd
Havant PO9 135 D1
Langstone PO9 159 D8
Brockhills La BH25 195 C6
Brockhurst Ind Est PO12 155 F1
Brockhurst Inf Sch PO12 180 F7
Brockhurst Jun Sch PO12 181 A8
Brockhurst Rd PO12 180 F7
Brockishill Rd SO40 99 A5
Brocklands PO9 135 D1
Brockley Rd BH10 189 E4
Brocks Cl SO45 125 D2
Brocks Pine BH24 139 F3
Brockwood BH24 139 D2
Brockwood Bottom SO24 36 F8
Brockwood Park Sch SO24 15 F1
Brodrick Ave PO12 181 A4
Brog St BH21 162 C1
Brokenford Ave SO40 101 A7
Brokenford Bsns Ctr SO40 100 F7
Brokenford Ct 1 SO40 100 F7
Brokenford La SO40 100 F7
Brombys The 11 BH15 202 C2
Bromley Ho BH12 204 B5
Bromley Rd SO18 79 F1
Brompton Ct BH2 204 E3
Brompton Rd PO4 182 F3
Bromyard Cres PO6 133 D1
Bronte Ave BH23 192 A1
Bronte Cl SO40 100 D6
Bronte Gdns PO15 129 C8
Bronte Way SO19 103 E6
Bronwen Ct SO19 104 A2
Brook Ave
New Milton BH25 195 B4
Warsash SO31 128 C3
Brook Ave N BH25 195 B4
Brook Cl
Bournemouth BH10 189 C4
North Baddesley SO52 54 A3
Sarisbury SO31 128 E3
Brook Cnr SO43 74 A1
Brook Cotts Compton SO20 6 C6
Westbourne PO10 137 B3
Brook Ct
Chandler's Ford SO53 55 C6
Romsey SO51 52 E6
Southampton SO15 102 D5
Brook Dr BH31 115 B4
Brook Farm Ave PO15 130 F1
Brook Gdns PO10 160 D8
Brook Hill SO41 198 E7
Brook Ho
Barton on S BH25 209 E7
Southampton SO19 104 A3
Brook La Botley SO30 105 F6
Bransgore BH23 193 B7
Corfe Mullen BH21 186 C6
Hambledon PO7 86 D5
Locks Heath SO31 129 A5
Warsash SO31 128 D3
Woodgreen SP6 70 E7
Brook Mdw PO15 130 F1
Brook Rd
Bournemouth BH10 189 C4
Fair Oak SO50 57 C2
Lymington SO41 197 F2
Poole BH12 203 C5
Southampton SO18 104 A7
Wimborne Minst BH21 163 E4
Brook Road Depot BH21 163 E3
Brook St SO32 83 C8
Brook Terr SP6 93 F8
Brook Valley SO16 78 A2
Brook Way
Christchurch BH23 208 C7
Romsey SO51 28 A1
Brook Wlk SO40 76 C1
Brookdale Cl
Broadstone BH18 187 A4
Waterlooville PO7 134 F8
Brookdale Farm BH18 187 A4
Brooke Cl SO23 2 B8
Brookers La PO13 155 B3
Brookes Hill Ind Est SO40 76 B4
Brookfield Cl 1 PO9 135 E2
Brookfield Com Sch & Language Coll SO31 128 E4
Brookfield Gdns SO31 128 F4
Brookfield Pl SO17 79 B2
Brookfield Rd
Fair Oak SO50 57 B2
Portsmouth PO1 182 E6
Brookfields SO51 50 D3
Brookland Cl SO41 197 C3
Brooklands
Bournemouth BH4 204 B3
Lyndhurst SO43 122 A4
Brooklands Rd
Bishop's Waltham SO32 83 C8
Havant PO9 135 B2
Brooklyn Cl SO21 31 C3
Brooklyn Ct
New Milton BH25 194 F3
Otterbourne SO21 31 C3
Brooklyn Dr PO7 134 F8
Brooklynn Cl SO32 83 E2
Brookman Ct SO18 104 A7
Brookmead Way PO9 159 F8
Brooks Cl BH24 141 B6
Brooks Sh Ctr The SO23 215 E6
Brookside Gosport PO13 155 B5
Ibsley SP6 94 C2
Landford SP5 49 D4
Totton SO40 100 F5
Brookside Ave SO15 101 F7
Brookside Cl
Bransgore BH23 169 A1
Denmead PO7 110 F4
Brookside Ho SO18 79 E4
Brookside Park Homes BH21 186 B4
Brookside Rd
Bransgore BH23 193 A8
Brockenhurst SO42 145 F2
Havant,Bedhampton PO9 135 C1
Langstone PO9 159 E8
Wimborne Minst BH21 163 F4
Brookside Way
Christchurch BH23 193 E1
Southampton SO18 79 E4
West End SO30 80 E3
Brookvale Ct 7 SO17 79 A1
Brookvale Rd SO17 79 A1
Brookwood Ave SO50 55 F3
Brookwood Ind Est SO50 56 A3
Brookwood Rd SO16 101 D8
Broom Cl
Portsmouth PO4 183 D4
Waterlooville PO7 135 A5
Broom Hill SO41 199 B7
Broom Hill Way SO50 56 A7
Broom La BH6 206 B4
Broom Rd
Petersfield GU31 41 C2
Poole BH12 188 C1
Broom Road Bsns Pk BH12 188 C1
Broom Sq PO4 183 D5
Broom Way
Gosport PO13,PO14 155 A1
Lee-on-t-S PO13 179 F4
Broomfield Cres PO13 180 B7
Broomfield Ct BH22 165 E6
Broomfield Dr SP6 93 A5
Broomfield La SO41 197 E4
Broomhill SP5 49 D2
Broomhill Cl SO41 197 B2
Brooms Gr SO19 104 D3
Broomy Cl SO45 125 C4
Brougham La PO12 181 A7
Brougham Rd PO5 216 B2
Brougham St PO12 181 A7
Broughton Ave BH10 189 E3
Broughton Cl
Bournemouth BH10 189 E3
5 Southampton SO16 78 A1
Broughton Ho 12 SO18 103 E8
Broughton Rd SO43 121 F6
Brow Cvn Site The BH25 171 E5
Brow The PO7 134 C2
Browndown Rd PO13 180 C3
Brownen Rd BH9 205 B8
Brownfield Ho 4 GU31 40 F3
Brownhill Cl SO53 55 C7
Brownhill Ct SO16 77 E3
Brownhill Gdns SO53 55 D7
Brownhill Rd
Chandler's Ford SO53 55 D7
New Milton BH25 170 E3
North Baddesley SO52 54 A4
Brownhill Way SO16 77 D3
Browning Ave
Bournemouth BH5 206 A4
Portchester PO6 132 E1
Southampton SO19 104 D6
Browning Cl
Eastleigh SO50 55 F3
Swanwick PO15 129 C8
Totton SO40 100 D7
Browning Dr SO22 215 B6
Browning Rd BH12 203 D6
Brownings Cl SO41 197 A4
Brownlow Ave SO19 104 A6
Brownlow Cl PO1 182 D7
Brownlow Ct 33 BH4 204 C3
Brownlow Gdns SO19 104 A6
Browns La Damerham SP6 68 B5
East End SO41 199 C5
Brownsea Ave BH21 186 D6
Brownsea Cl BH25 194 E3
Brownsea Ct BH14 214 B8
Brownsea Island (NT)* BH15 213 D4
Brownsea Rd BH13 214 B3
Brownsea View Ave BH14 203 C1
Brownsea View Cl BH14 203 C1
Brownwich La PO14 153 D5
Browsholme Cl SO50 56 A6
Broxburn Cl SO53 30 E1
Broxhead Rd PO9 136 A6
Bruce Cl PO16 131 A3
Bruce Rd PO4 182 F2
Brudenell Ave BH13 214 D7
Brudenell Rd BH13 214 D6
Brue Cl SO53 55 B7
Brune La PO13 180 C8
Brune Park Com Coll PO12 180 E8
Brune Way BH22 165 D3
Brunei Ho SO16 79 A5
Brunel Cl Hedge End SO30 81 D1
Verwood BH31 115 C4
Brunel Rd
Portsmouth PO2 157 E3
Southampton SO15 101 C8
Totton SO40 76 E3
Brunel Way PO15 129 D4
Brunstead Pl 1 BH12 204 B4
Brunstead Rd BH12 204 B4
Brunswick Cl SO50 57 B3
Brunswick Gdns PO9 135 D2
Brunswick Ho 11 SO15 103 A6
Brunswick Pl
Lymington SO41 197 E4
Southampton SO15 103 A6
Brunswick Rd SO50 57 B3
Brunswick Sq SO14 103 A3
Brunswick St PO5 216 B2
Brushers BH23 169 E4
Bruyn Ct SP6 70 A2
Bruyn Rd SP6 70 A2
Bryanston Rd SO19 103 E5
Bryanstone Rd BH3 204 E7
Bryant Rd BH12 204 A8
Bryher Br PO6 157 B7
Bryher Island PO6 157 B7
Brympton Cl SP6 69 D2
Bryony Cl
Broadstone BH18 186 F3
Locks Heath SO31 128 F2
Bryony Gdns SO50 81 C6
Bryony Way PO7 135 A7
Bryson Cl PO13 180 A6
Bryson Rd PO6 157 D8
Bub La BH23 207 E6
Bubb La SO30 81 C4
Buccaneers Cl BH23 207 E6
Buccleuch Rd BH13 204 A1
Bucehayes Cl BH23 209 A8
Buchan Ave PO15 129 C8
Buchan Ct SO45 125 C2
Buchanan Ave BH7 205 E6
Buchanan Rd SO16 77 F5
Buckby La PO3 158 C4
Bucketts Farm Cl SO32 84 B5
Buckingham Ct
1 Christchurch BH23 209 A7
Fareham PO15 130 E3
Poole BH15 202 D3
2 Southampton SO17 103 A8
Buckingham Gn PO1 182 D7
Buckingham Mans 5 BH1 205 A3
Buckingham Rd
Petersfield GU32 40 D3
Poole BH12 203 D7
Buckingham St PO1 216 B4
Buckingham Wlk BH25 194 E3
Buckland Cl
Eastleigh SO50 56 A5
Waterlooville PO7 111 D2
Buckland Ct SO41 197 E5
Buckland Dene SO41 197 D5
Buckland Gdns SO40 76 C2
Buckland Gr BH23 193 E2
Buckland Path PO2 182 D7
Buckland Rd BH12 203 C5
Buckland St PO2 182 E7
Buckland Terr BH12 203 C5
Buckland View SO41 197 E5
Bucklers Ct Havant PO9 135 D7
Lymington SO41 197 D3
Portsmouth PO2 157 D1
Bucklers Hard Maritime Mus* SO42 176 D5
Bucklers Mews SO41 197 D3
Bucklers Rd PO12 181 C9
Bucklers The SO41 211 A5
Bucklers Way BH8 190 D3
Buckley Ct SO16 78 B1
Buckmore Ave GU32 40 D4
Bucks Head Hill SO32 61 C5
Bucksey Rd PO13 180 C8
Buckstone Cl SO41 196 E1
Buckthorn Cl
Broadstone BH17 186 F1
Totton SO40 100 B8
Budden's La PO17 108 E8
Buddens Mdw BH21 186 C4
Buddens Rd PO17 108 A4
Buddle Hill SP6 94 C4
Budds La SO51 27 E1
Budds Lane Trad Est SO51 27 E1
Bude Cl PO6 132 F1
Buffalo Mews BH15 202 B2
Bugdens La BH31 115 A6
Bugle St SO14 102 F3
Bulbarrow Wlk PO14 154 E8
Bulbeck Rd PO9 135 F1
Buldowne Wlk SO41 172 B3
Bull Dro SO23 215 F3
Bull Hill Boldre SO41 174 B1
Rake GU33 21 E4
Bull La Minstead SO43 98 C3
Waltham Chase SO32 83 D3
Bullar Rd SO18 103 E8
Bullar St SO14 103 B6
Bullfinch Cl
Broadstone BH17 186 F1
Totton SO40 100 C7
Bullfinch Ct PO13 179 F4
Bullrush Cl SO45 125 F1
Bulls Copse La PO8 112 A6
Bulls Copse Rd SO40 101 A4
Bulls Dro SP5 4 A6
Bulwark Rd PO14 179 B6
Bunkers Hill PO7 110 D4
Bunns La PO7 109 E5
Bunny La
Michelmersh SO51 27 F5
Sherfield English SO51 25 A4
Bunstead La SO21 30 D7
Bunting Gdns PO8 111 F4
Bunting Rd BH22 165 B8
Burbidge Gr PO4 183 A2
Burbridge Cl BH17 202 E8
Burbush Cl SO45 150 C3
Burcombe La BH24 117 F1
Burcombe Rd BH10 189 C5
Burcote Dr PO3 158 B4
Burdale Dr PO11 185 D3
Burdock Cl BH23 193 B1
Bure Cl BH23 208 B6
Bure Haven Dr BH23 208 A6
Bure Homage Gdns BH23 208 B6
Bure Homage La BH23 208 B6
Bure La BH23 208 B6
Bure Pk BH23 208 B6
Bure Rd BH23 208 B6
Burford Cl BH23 191 D1
Burford Ct 4 BH1 205 B3
Burford La SO42 146 A2
Burgate Cl PO9 135 D3
Burgate Cross SP6 70 A5
Burgate Ct SP6 70 A4
Burgate Fields SP6 70 A3
Burgate Sch & Sixth Form Ctr The SP6 70 A3
Burgesmede Ho 9 GU32 40 F3
Burgess Cl
Bournemouth BH11 188 F4
South Hayling PO11 185 D1
Burgess Ct SO16 79 B4
Burgess Fld BH21 114 A6
Burgess Gdns 5 SO16 78 E3
Burgess Rd
Southampton SO16 79 B4
Upper Shirley SO16 78 D3
Burghclere Rd
Havant PO9 136 B6
Southampton SO19 126 F8
Burgoyne Rd
Portsmouth PO5 182 D1
Southampton SO19 104 E4
Burgundy Cl SO31 128 F2
Burgundy Terr 1 PO2 157 E2
Buriton Cl PO16 132 D1
Buriton Ct SO19 103 E3
Buriton Prim Sch GU31 65 D5
Buriton Rd SO22 1 D4
Buriton St PO1 216 C4
Burke Dr SO19 104 D5
Burleigh Rd
Bournemouth BH6 206 D5
Portsmouth PO1 182 F7
Burley Cl
Barton on S BH25 209 D8
Chandler's Ford SO53 55 B4
14 Havant PO9 136 B6
Totton SO40 100 B7
Verwood BH31 114 E5
Burley Ct 5 SO17 79 A2
Burley Down SO53 55 B4
Burley Ho 7 SO16 102 B8
Burley Lawn BH24 143 B4
Burley Prim Sch BH24 143 A3
Burley Rd
Bransgore BH23 193 A8
Bransgore,Thorney Hill BH23 169 D3
Brockenhurst SO42 172 C8
Poole BH12 203 C6
Winchester SO22 1 D4
Winkton BH23 192 D6
Burling Terr 1 BH13 204 A4
Burlington Arc 11 BH1 204 F3
Burlington Ct SO19 104 B5
Burlington Mans 1 SO15 102 C7
Burlington Rd
Portsmouth PO2 157 E1
Southampton SO15 102 E6
Burma Ho SO18 79 E4
Burma Rd SO51 52 F6
Burma Way SO40 101 F1
Burmah Road N SO45 151 C5
Burmah Road S SO45 151 B5
Burmese Cl PO15 129 C7
Burn Cl BH31 115 B4
Burnaby Ct BH4 204 C1
Burnaby Rd
Bournemouth BH4 204 C1
Portsmouth PO1 182 B4
Burnage Ct 13 BH13 214 F7
Burnbake Rd BH31 115 A5
Burnbank Gdns SO40 100 E7
Burnbrae Rd BH22 165 D1
Burnett Ave BH23 206 E8
Burnett Cl Hythe SO45 126 B2
Southampton SO18 79 E1
Winchester SO22 215 A8
Burnett Rd
Christchurch BH23 206 F7
Gosport PO12 180 F6
Burnetts Fields SO50 81 C7
Burnetts Gdns SO50 81 D7
Burnetts La SO30 81 C5
Burney Ho 8 PO12 181 D5
Burney Rd PO12 180 E3
Burngate Rd BH15 201 E2
Burnham Beeches SO53 55 B6
Burnham Chase SO18 104 C7
Burnham Dr BH8 205 C7
Burnham Rd
Burton BH23 192 C2
Cosham PO6 134 D1
Fordingbridge SP6 69 F3
Burnham Wood PO16 131 A3
Burnham's Wlk 2 PO12 181 D5
Burnleigh Gdns BH25 195 C4
Burns Cl SO50 55 E1
Burns Pl SO16 78 A2
Burns Rd
Bournemouth BH6 206 D7
Eastleigh SO50 55 F1
Southampton SO19 104 D6
Burnside
Christchurch BH23 208 D8
Gosport PO13 155 B5
Waterlooville PO7 112 A1
Burnt House La
Boldre SO41 174 A1
Bransgore BH23 169 B1
Stubbington PO14 154 D4
Burr Cl SO21 56 F8
Burrard Gr SO41 197 F2
Burrfields Rd PO3 158 B1
Burridge Rd SO31 106 A2
Burrill Ave PO6 158 A8
Burrow Hill Pl SO50 56 D5
Burrows Cl PO9 136 A3
Burrows La BH31 114 F8
Bursledon CE Inf Sch SO31 128 A8
Bursledon Ho 4 BH25 195 A2
Bursledon Hts SO31 105 B1
Bursledon Jun Sch SO31 128 A8
Bursledon Pl PO7 134 D5
Bursledon Rd
Hedge End SO30 105 B5
Southampton SO19,SO31 104 C5
Waterlooville PO7 134 D5
Bursledon Sta SO31 128 B8
Bursledon Windmill* SO31 105 A2
Burt's Hill BH21 163 D7
Burt's La BH21 138 A7
Burtley Rd BH6 206 F3
Burton CE Prim Sch BH23 192 C3
Burton Cl Burton BH23 192 C1
St Leonards BH24 139 E5
Burton Hall BH23 192 C3
Burton Hall Pl BH23 192 D3
Burton Ho BH23 192 D1
Burton Rd
Christchurch BH23 207 E7
Poole BH13 204 A3
Southampton SO15 102 E6
Burtoncroft BH23 192 C3
Burwood Gr PO11 185 A4
Bury Brickfield Park Cvn Site SO40 101 C4
Bury Cl PO12 181 B5
Bury Cres PO12 181 B5
Bury Cross PO12 181 A5
Bury Farm SO30 106 C3
Bury Hall La PO12 180 F3
Bury Ho 7 PO16 131 A1
Bury La SO40 101 B5
Bury Rd Gosport PO12 181 A5
Marchwood SO40 101 E3
Poole BH13 203 F1
Poole BH13 203 F2
Bus Dro SO45 178 E8
Bush Ho PO5 216 B1
Bush St E PO5 216 B1
Bush St W PO5 216 B1
Bushell Rd BH15 202 C7
Bushells Farm SP6 93 E8
Bushey Rd BH8 190 C1
Bushmead Dr BH24 139 E5
Bushy Mead PO7 134 C3
Busket La SO23 215 E5
Busketts Way SO40 100 A2
Butcher St PO1 182 A5
Butcher's Cnr SO43 73 E4
Butchers Bush SO43 98 B5
Bute Dr BH23 209 B8
Butlers Cl SO51 4 F1
Butlers La BH24 117 C1
Butser Ancient Farm* PO8 88 F6

Butser Ct P08 . . . . .88 D3
Butser Wlk
 Fareham PO14 . . . . .154 E8
 Petersfield GU31 . . . . .41 B4
Butt La SP5 . . . . .22 B8
Butt's CI SO19 . . . . .104 C4
Butt's Cres SO19 . . . . . . .104 C4
Butt's Rd SO19 . . . . .104 C3
Butt's Sq SO19 . . . . .104 C4
Buttercup CI
 Hedge End SO30 . . . . . .105 A6
 Hythe SO45 . . . . .126 A1
Buttercup Dr BH23 . . . . . .193 B1
Buttercup Way SO31 . . . .128 E3
Butterfield Rd SO16 . . . . . .78 E3
Butterfly Dr PO6 . . . . .133 A1
Butteridge Rise SO51 . . . .26 E6
Buttermere Ho 1 PO6 . . .133 B1
Buttery The BH23 . . . . . .207 D7
Button's La SO51 . . . . .50 F3
Butts Ash Gdns SO45 . . . .126 A1
Butts Ash La SO45 . . . . . .150 A8
Butts Bridge Hill SO45 . . .126 A2
Butts CI SO22 . . . . .61 C6
Butts Farm La SO32 . . . . . .83 D8
Butts Lawn SO42 . . . . . . .145 F2
Butts Paddock SO42 . . . . .145 F2
Butts The SO32 . . . . .61 C6
Buttsash Ave SO45 . . . . . .150 A8
Buttsbridge Rd SO45 . . . .126 A1
By Pass Rd SO51 . . . . .52 E6
By The Wood SO40 . . . . . . .76 D2
Byams La SO40 . . . . .102 A2
Bye Rd SO31 . . . . .128 D8
Byerley CI PO10 . . . . .137 B5
Byerley Rd PO1 . . . . .182 F5
Byeways SO45 . . . . .125 F2
Byngs Byes Pk PO7 . . . . . .111 B2
Byrd CI PO7 . . . . .134 E5
Byres The PO14 . . . . .154 C4
Byron Ave SO22 . . . . .215 B6
Byron CI
 Bishop's Waltham SO32 . . .83 E8
 Fareham PO16 . . . . .131 A2
Byron Ct Ferndown BH22 .165 D5
 Southampton SO15 . . . . .102 E6
Byron Ho 10 BH25 . . . . . .195 A2
Byron Rd
 Barton on S BH25 . . . . . .209 E8
 Bournemouth BH5 . . . . . .205 F3
 Eastleigh SO50 . . . . .56 B4
 Portsmouth PO2 . . . . . . .182 F8
 Southampton SO19 . . . . .104 D6
 Wimborne Minst BH21 . . .163 C6

C

C Ave SO45 . . . . .150 D5
Cable St Eastleigh SO50 . . .56 A2
 Southampton SO14 . . . . .103 C5
Cabot Bsns Village
 BH17 . . . . .202 A7
Cabot Dr SO45 . . . . .125 C3
Cabot La BH17 . . . . .202 B8
Cabot Way PO15 . . . . . . .194 F3
Cadgwith PI PO6 . . . . . . .157 B7
Cadhay CI BH25 . . . . .194 F3
Cadington Ho 2 PO11 . . .182 A5
Cadland Ct SO14 . . . . . . .103 E2
Cadland Pk SO45 . . . . . . .126 A8
Cadland Rd Fawley SO45 .151 B5
 Fawley,Buttsash SO45 . . .150 D7
Cadnam Ct 6 PO12 . . . . .180 D3
Cadnam La SO40 . . . . .74 F2
Cadnam Lawn PO9 . . . . . .135 D6
Cadnam Rd SO45 . . . . . . .183 B3
Cadnam Way BH8 . . . . . . .190 D3
Cadogan Rd BH24 . . . . . .141 B7
Cador Dr PO16 . . . . .156 B6
Caen Ho 5 PO14 . . . . . . .154 E8
Caer Peris View PO16 . . . .132 C2
Caerleon Ave SO19 . . . . .104 C6
Caerleon Dr SO19 . . . . . .104 C6
Caernarvon Gdns SO53 . . .55 A4
Caesar's Way BH18 . . . . . .186 C4
Cains CI PO14 . . . . .179 C8
Caird Ave BH25 . . . . .195 C2
Cairns CI BH23 . . . . .206 F8
Cairo Terr PO2 . . . . .182 D7
Caister CI BH22 . . . . .165 C6
Caistor CI SO16 . . . . .78 A4
Calabrese SO31 . . . . .129 B7
Calbourne SO31 . . . . .127 C7
Calcot La SO32 . . . . .82 E3
Caldecote Wlk 7 PO5 . . .216 B2
Calder CI SO16 . . . . .101 E8
Calder Ho 10 PO1 . . . . . .182 A5
Calder Rd DI/17 . . . . .202 F8
Calderwood Dr SO19 . . . .104 A4
Caledon Rd BH14 . . . . . . .203 E3
Caledonia Dr SO45 . . . . . .125 D3
Caledonian CI BH23 . . . . .208 B7
California CI SO40 . . . . .76 B1
Calkin CI BH23 . . . . .192 A1
Callowing CI SO21 . . . . . . .58 F8
Calluna Rd BH12 . . . . . . .203 B8
Calmore CI BH8 . . . . .190 D3
Calmore Cres SO40 . . . . . .76 C2
Calmore Dr SO40 . . . . . . .100 C8
Calmore Gdns SO40 . . . . .100 D7
Calmore Ind Est SO40 . . . .76 E2
Calmore Inf Sch SO40 . . . .76 C1
Calmore Jun Sch SO40 . . .76 C1
Calmore Rd SO40 . . . . . . .100 C8
Calpe SO43 . . . . .121 F6

Calshot Activities Ctr
 SO45 . . . . .152 B3
Calshot Castle* SO45 . . .152 B2
Calshot CI SO45 . . . . .178 F8
Calshot Ct SO14 . . . . .103 C2
Calshot Dr SO53 . . . . .55 A4
Calshot Rd Fawley SO45 . .151 B3
 Havant PO9 . . . . .136 C7
Calshot Way PO13 . . . . . .155 B1
Calvin Rd BH9 . . . . .204 F8
Camargue CI PO15 . . . . . .129 B8
Camber PI 3 PO1 . . . . . . .182 A3
Cambria Dr SO45 . . . . . . .125 D3
Cambrian CI SO31 . . . . . .105 A2
Cambrian Terr PO5 . . . . . .216 C1
Cambrian Wlk PO14 . . . . .154 F7
Cambridge Ct 11 SO14 . . .103 A8
Cambridge Dr SO53 . . . . . .55 C3
Cambridge Gdns BH23 . . .191 F2
Cambridge Gn
 Chandler's Ford SO53 . . . .55 C2
 Titchfield PO14 . . . . .129 C2
Cambridge Junc PO1 . . . .182 B4
Cambridge Rd
 Bournemouth BH2 . . . . . .204 D3
 Gosport PO12 . . . . .180 F6
 Lee-on-t-S PO13 . . . . . . .179 F2
 Portsmouth PO1 . . . . . . .182 B4
 Southampton SO14 . . . . .103 A8
Camcross CI 2 PO6 . . . . .133 B1
Camden CI BH9 . . . . .190 B1
Camden Hurst 1 SO41 . . .211 B4
Camden St PO12 . . . . .181 A7
Camden Terr 2 PO12 . . . .181 A7
Camel Green Rd SP6 . . . . .93 A6
Camelia CI PO9 . . . . .136 C3
Camelia Gdns SO40 . . . . . .80 A2
Camelia Gr SO50 . . . . .57 E2
Camellia CI
 North Baddesley SO52 . . . .54 A5
 Three Legged Cross BH21 .114 E1
Camellia Ct SO18 . . . . .79 E2
Camellia Gdns BH25 . . . . .195 B2
Camelot Cres PO13 . . . . . .132 B1
Cameron Ct PO13 . . . . . . .155 C3
Cameron Ct SO16 . . . . .77 F5
Cameron Rd BH23 . . . . . .207 D7
Camilla Ct SO40 . . . . .76 B1
Camilla Ct BH13 . . . . .204 B2
Camley CI SO19 . . . . .103 E1
Cammel Rd BH22 . . . . . . .165 D2
Camp Rd PO13 . . . . .155 D3
Campbell Cres PO7 . . . . . .134 C5
Campbell Ct SO50 . . . . . . .57 C2
Campbell Mews SO18 . . . .104 D7
Campbell Rd
 Bournemouth BH1 . . . . . .205 E5
 Burton BH23 . . . . .192 C3
 Eastleigh SO50 . . . . .56 B1
 Portsmouth PO5 . . . . . . .216 D1
Campbell St SO14 . . . . . . .103 C6
Campbell Way SO50 . . . . . .57 C2
Campion CI
 Horton Heath SO50 . . . . . .81 D6
 Locks Heath SO31 . . . . . .128 E2
 Waterlooville PO7 . . . . . .135 A6
Campion Dr SO51 . . . . .28 C1
Campion Gr SO31 . . . . . . .207 F6
Campion Rd SO19 . . . . . . .104 C6
Campion Way
 Kings Worthy SO23 . . . . . . .2 C7
 Lymington SO41 . . . . . . .197 E5
Cams Bay CI PO16 . . . . . .131 F1
Cams Hill Hambledon PO7 . .86 B2
 Portchester PO16 . . . . . . .131 E1
Cams Hill Sch PO16 . . . . . .155 E8
Canada CI 9 PO12 . . . . . .181 C9
Canada PI 6 SO31 . . . . . .129 B7
Canada Rd
 Southampton SO19 . . . . .103 E2
 West Wellow SO51 . . . . . .50 D1
Canal CI SO51 . . . . .28 A1
Canal Wlk
 Portsmouth PO1 . . . . . . .216 C3
 Romsey SO51 . . . . .52 F8
 Southampton SO14 . . . . .103 A3
Canalside The PO1 . . . . . .182 A4
Canberra Cl PO12 . . . . . . .180 F4
Canberra Ct 7 PO12 . . . . .180 F4
Canberra Ho PO1 . . . . . . .216 B3
Canberra Rd
 Christchurch BH23 . . . . . .191 E1
 Nursling SO16 . . . . .77 B4
 Thorney Island PO10 . . . .161 A3
Canberra Twrs SO19 . . . . .103 A8
Candlemas PI 18 SO17 . . .103 A8
Candover Ct SO19 . . . . . . .127 A8
Candy La SO18 . . . . .104 E6
Candys CI BH21 . . . . .162 E2
Candys La BH21 . . . . .162 E2
Canford Ave PO14 . . . . . .154 F7
Canford Bottom BH21 . . . .164 C6
Canford Bottom Rdbt
 BH21 . . . . .164 C5
Canford CI
 Shedfield SO32 . . . . .107 E7
 Southampton SO16 . . . . . .77 D2
Canford Cliffs Ave BH14 . .203 E2
Canford Cliffs Rd BH13 . . .203 E2
Canford Cres BH13 . . . . . .214 E7
Canford Ct BH13 . . . . .214 E6
Canford Gdns BH11 . . . . .189 A1
Canford Heath Fst & Mid
 Schs BH17 . . . . .202 D7
Canford Heath Nature
 Reserve* BH11 . . . . . . .188 B4
Canford Heath Rd BH17 . .187 E1
Canford Magna BH21 . . . .164 A1

Canford Park Events Arena &
 Sports Gd* BH21 . . . . .188 B7
Canford PI 2 BH13 . . . . . .214 F7
Canford Rd
 Bournemouth BH11 . . . . .189 A1
 Poole BH15 . . . . .202 B8
Canford Sch BH21 . . . . . .164 B2
Canford View Dr BH21 . . .164 B6
Canford Way BH12 . . . . . .188 C2
Canhouse La GU31,GU33 . .21 F3
Cannock Wlk 8 PO14 . . . .154 E7
Cannon CI BH18 . . . . .187 A1
Cannon Hill Gdns BH21 . . .164 B7
Cannon Hill Rd BH21 . . . .164 A7
Cannon Ho SO41 . . . . . . .197 E4
Cannon St
 Lymington SO41 . . . . . . .197 E4
 Southampton SO15 . . . . .102 C8
Canoe CI SO31 . . . . .128 F1
Canon Ct SO50 . . . . .57 C2
Canon St SO23 . . . . .215 E5
Canon's Barn CI PO16 . . .132 C1
Canons Wlk SO41 . . . . . . .211 D5
Cantell Sch SO16 . . . . .79 A4
Canterbury Ave SO19 . . . .104 C3
Canterbury CI
 Lee-on-t-S PO13 . . . . . . .180 B4
 West Moors BH22 . . . . . .138 F1
Canterbury Dr SO45 . . . . .125 D3
Canterbury Rd
 Portsmouth PO4 . . . . . . .182 F3
 Stubbington PO14 . . . . . .154 C4
Canterton La SO43 . . . . . . .98 B8
Canterton Manor SO43 . . . .98 A8
Canton St SO15 . . . . .102 F6
Canute Dr BH23 . . . . .169 B1
Canute Ho 6 SO14 . . . . . .103 A3
Canute Rd
 Southampton SO14 . . . . .103 B3
 Winchester SO23 . . . . . . .215 F4
Canvey Ct SO16 . . . . .77 E2
Capel Ley PO7 . . . . .134 E4
Capella Ct BH21 . . . . .204 F2
Capella Gdns SO45 . . . . . .125 D3
Capers End La SO32 . . . . . .82 E1
Capesthorne BH23 . . . . . .206 E7
Capital Ho 7 SO22 . . . . . .215 D6
Capon CI SO18 . . . . .79 E4
Capstan Gdns SO31 . . . . .129 C3
Capstan Ho
 12 Cosham PO6 . . . . . . .157 F7
 Warsash SO31 . . . . .128 C1
Capstans The BH14 . . . . .214 B8
Capstone PI BH8 . . . . .205 B6
Capstone Rd BH8 . . . . . . .205 B6
Captain's Row SO41 . . . . .197 F4
Captains CI PO12 . . . . . . .180 F7
Captains Cove BH15 . . . . .201 E3
Captains PI SO14 . . . . . . .103 B3
Captains Row 5 PO1 . . . .182 A3
Caradon PI BH31 . . . . . . .114 D7
Carausius Way PO16 . . . . .156 C7
Carbery Ave BH6 . . . . . . .206 D5
Carbery Ct PO9 . . . . .135 D7
Carbery Gdns BH6 . . . . . .206 E5
Carbery La 3 BH6 . . . . . .206 E5
Carbery Row 2 BH6 . . . . .206 C4
Carbis CI PO6 . . . . .157 A7
Carbis Rd GU33 . . . . .21 A3
Cardigan Rd
 Bournemouth BH9 . . . . . .204 F8
 Poole BH12 . . . . .203 F4
Cardinal Dr PO7 . . . . .112 B1
Cardinal Way SO31 . . . . . .129 B2
Cardington Ct SO16 . . . . . .77 F4
Carey Rd
 Bournemouth BH9 . . . . . .189 F3
 Poole BH15 . . . . .202 C5
Careys Cotts SO42 . . . . . .145 F2
Careys Rd BH8 . . . . .190 D4
Carina Ct BH13 . . . . .214 C5
Carisbrooke Netley SO31 . .127 C7
 Poole BH15 . . . . .214 E7
Carisbrooke Ave PO14 . . .179 B7
Carisbrooke Cl BH9 . . . . . .190 C2
Carisbrooke Cres
 Chandler's Ford SO53 . . . .55 B6
 Hamworthy BH15 . . . . . .201 D3
Carisbrooke Ct
 1 Christchurch BH23 . . . .209 B7
 1 Knowle Village PO17 . . .130 E7
 New Milton BH25 . . . . . .194 F3
 Romsey SO51 . . . . .28 A1
Carisbrooke Dr SO19 . . . .103 F6
Carisbrooke Rd
 Gosport PO12 . . . . .155 C2
 Portsmouth PO4 . . . . . . .183 A4
Carisbrooke Way BH23 . . .193 E1
Carless CI PO13 . . . . .180 D7
Carlinford 5 BH5 . . . . . . .205 F3
Carlisle Ct 3 SO16 . . . . . .102 B8
Carlisle Rd
 Portsmouth PO5 . . . . . . .216 C3
 Southampton SO16 . . . . .102 B8
Carlton Ave BH25 . . . . . . .209 D8
Carlton Commerce Ctr The
 SO14 . . . . .103 B7
Carlton Cres SO15 . . . . . .102 F6
Carlton Ct 3 BH12 . . . . . .203 D5
Carlton Ho SO41 . . . . .197 E4
Carlton Mount BH2 . . . . . .204 E2
Carlton PI SO15 . . . . .102 F7
Carlton Rd
 Bournemouth BH1 . . . . . .205 C4
 Gosport PO12 . . . . .181 C6
 Portchester PO16 . . . . . . .132 E1
 Southampton SO15 . . . . .102 F7

Carlton Way 7 PO12 . . . .181 C6
Carlyle Rd
 Bournemouth BH6 . . . . . .206 D6
 Gosport PO12 . . . . .181 B6
Carlyn Dr SO53 . . . . .55 D7
Carmans La SO21 . . . . .31 D8
Carmarthen Ave PO6 . . . .158 B8
Carmel CI BH15 . . . . .201 D2
Carmiln Cl 1 PO12 . . . . . .180 C4
Carnarvon Rd
 4 Bournemouth BH1 . . . .205 E4
 Gosport PO12 . . . . .181 A5
 Portsmouth PO2 . . . . . . .182 F8
Carnation Rd SO16 . . . . . . .79 C4
Carne CI SO53 . . . . .55 C8
Carne PI PO6 . . . . .157 A7
Carnegie CI BH12 . . . . . . .203 D5
Caroline Ave BH23 . . . . . .207 F6
Caroline Ct SO15 . . . . . . .102 B7
Caroline Gdns PO15 . . . . .130 C2
Caroline PI PO12 . . . . . . .181 B7
Caroline Rd BH11 . . . . . . .189 B2
Carolyn CI SO19 . . . . .103 E2
Carpathia CI SO18 . . . . . . .80 A2
Carpenter CI Hythe SO45 .126 A4
 Lymington SO41 . . . . . . .197 D5
 4 Portsmouth PO4 . . . . .183 A3
Carradale BH23 . . . . .208 B8
Carran Wlk PO14 . . . . . . .154 E7
Carraway PO15 . . . . .129 D7
Carrbridge CI BH3 . . . . . .204 D7
Carrbridge Gdns BH3 . . . .204 D7
Carrbridge Rd BH3 . . . . . .204 D7
Carrick Way BH25 . . . . . . .195 C2
Carrington CI SO41 . . . . . .211 E5
Carrington Ho 22 SO17 . . .79 A1
Carrington La SO41 . . . . . .211 E5
Carroll CI SO50 . . . . .57 D1
Carroll Ave BH22 . . . . . . .165 E5
Carroll CI BH12 . . . . .204 A6
Carronade Wlk PO13 . . . .157 F5
Carronades The 3
 SO14 . . . . .103 A5
Carshalton Ave PO6 . . . . .158 B8
Carsworth Way BH17 . . . .188 A2
Carter Com Sch BH15 . . . .201 F2
Carter Ho Gosport PO13 . .155 B5
 18 Portsmouth PO1 . . . . .182 A5
Carter's Clay Rd SO51 . . . .26 B5
Carter's La 3 BH15 . . . . . .202 C2
Carters Ave BH15 . . . . . . .201 D4
Carthage CI SO53 . . . . .55 F8
Cartref CI BH31 . . . . .114 F6
Cartwright CI BH10 . . . . . .189 C4
Cartwright Dr PO15 . . . . . .129 F2
Carvers Ind Est BH24 . . . .141 A7
Carvers La BH24 . . . . .141 A7
Cascade Ave BH9 . . . . . . .190 E2
Cascades Sh Ctr PO1 . . . .216 B3
Cases Bakery CI PO17 . . . .108 A4
Cashmoor CI 4 BH12 . . . .203 F7
Caslake CI BH25 . . . . .194 F1
Caspar John CI PO14 . . . .179 B6
Caspian CI PO15 . . . . .129 B7
Casselles Ct 8 BH25 . . . . .195 A2
Casterbridge Ct 5 BH4 . .204 C3
Casterbridge Rd BH23 . . .165 C3
Castle Ave
 Christchurch BH23 . . . . . .208 E8
 Havant PO9 . . . . .136 B1
 Winchester SO23 . . . . . . .215 D6
Castle CI
 Milford on S SO41 . . . . . .211 E3
 Portsmouth PO5 . . . . . . .216 B1
 BH21 . . . . .186 B7
Castle Ct
 2 Bitterne Pk SO18 . . . . . .79 E1
 2 Christchurch BH23 . . . .209 A7
 Southampton,Millbrook
 SO15 . . . . .102 A6
Castle Farm La PO17 . . . . .108 B2
Castle Gate CI BH9 . . . . . .190 C2
Castle Gr GU32 . . . . .40 E3
Castle Gr PO16 . . . . .156 D7
Castle Hill Poole BH14 . . .203 B4
 Winchester SO23 . . . . . . .215 D6
Castle Hill La
 Burley BH24 . . . . .142 E3
 Edmondsham BH21 . . . . . .91 A7
Castle Hts 1 SO18 . . . . . . .79 F1
Castle La Calshot SO45 . . .178 F7
 Chandler's Ford SO53 . . . .55 B4
 North Baddesley SO52 . . . .54 D4
 1 Southampton SO18 . . . . .79 F1
Castle La W BH9 . . . . .190 C2
Castle Lane E BH7 . . . . . . .206 C8
Castle Malwood Lodge
 SO43 . . . . .98 B5
Castle Marina PO13 . . . . .179 F1
Castle Mdw SP5 . . . . .46 F7
Castle Mews SO14 . . . . . .102 F3
Castle Pier BH7 . . . . .206 D7
Castle Prim Sch PO16 . . . .156 D7
Castle Rd
 Bournemouth BH9 . . . . . .190 A1
 Netley SO31 . . . . .127 A6
 Portsmouth PO5 . . . . . . .216 B1
 Rowlands Castle PO9 . . . .113 B1
 Southampton SO19 . . . . . .79 E2
 Southwick PO17 . . . . . . .132 F6
Castle Sq 3 SO14 . . . . . . .102 F3

Castle St
 Christchurch BH23 . . . . . .207 B6
 Poole BH15 . . . . .202 C1
 Portchester PO16 . . . . . . .156 D7
 Southampton SO14 . . . . .103 A7
Castle Trad Est PO16 . . . .156 E8
Castle View PO12 . . . . . . .101 D3
Castle View Rd PO16 . . . .156 E6
Castle Way SO14 . . . . . . .102 F3
Castle Woods SP5 . . . . . . .47 D6
Castledene Cres BH14 . . . .203 A2
Castlemain Ave BH6 . . . . .206 C5
Castleman Ct BH22 . . . . . .138 D3
Castleman Way BH24 . . . .141 A6
Castlemans La PO11 . . . . .160 A1
Castlemews BH24 . . . . . . .140 C5
Castlepoint BH8 . . . . .190 E2
Castleshaw CI SO16 . . . . .101 F7
Castleton Ave BH10 . . . . .189 D6
Castleton Ct PO5 . . . . .216 A1
Castleway PO9 . . . . .136 B1
Castlewood BH24 . . . . . . .140 D5
Catalina CI BH23 . . . . .208 A6
Catalina Dr BH15 . . . . . . .202 E1
Catamaran CI SO31 . . . . . .128 F1
Cateran CI SO16 . . . . .101 F8
Cathay Gdns SO45 . . . . . .125 C3
Cathedral View 4 SO23 . .215 F4
Catherine CI SO30 . . . . . . .80 E2
Catherine Cres SP5 . . . . . .46 D7
Catherine Gdns SO30 . . . . .80 E2
Catherine Wheel Gdns
 BH23 . . . . .191 E3
Catherington CE Inf Sch
 P08 . . . . .88 B1
Catherington La
 Horndean PO8 . . . . .112 B7
 Horndean,Catherington P08 .88 B1
Catherington Way PO9 . . .135 F3
Catisfield Ho 3 PO1 . . . . .216 C4
Catisfield La PO15 . . . . . . .130 B1
Catisfield Rd
 Fareham PO15 . . . . .130 C1
 Portsmouth PO4 . . . . . . .183 B4
Catmint CI SO53 . . . . .54 F7
Caton CI BH12 . . . . .204 B8
Cattistock Rd BH8 . . . . . . .190 E2
Catways SO21 . . . . .30 B7
Causeway SO51 . . . . .52 D6
Causeway Cres SO40 . . . .101 A8
Causeway Farm 6 SO18 . .103 E8
Causeway Farm PO8 . . . . .12 C1
Causeway The
 Petersfield GU31 . . . . .40 E1
 Portchester PO16 . . . . . . .131 E1
Causton Gdns SO50 . . . . . .56 A3
Cavalier CI SO45 . . . . .125 D3
Cavalier Ct PO6 . . . . .158 D8
Cavan Cres BH17 . . . . . . .187 B1
Cavanna CI PO13 . . . . . . .155 B3
Cavell Dr PO6 . . . . .133 E1
Cavendish CI
 Romsey SO51 . . . . .28 B2
 Waterlooville PO7 . . . . . .134 F8
Cavendish Corner Mobile
 Home Pk 8 BH24 . . . . .141 B8
Cavendish Ct 1 BH4 . . . .204 C3
Cavendish Gr
 Southampton SO17 . . . . .102 F8
 Winchester SO23 . . . . .2 B3
Cavendish Hall BH1 . . . . .205 A5
Cavendish Mews 3
 SO15 . . . . .102 F8
Cavendish PI BH1 . . . . . . .205 A5
Cavendish Rd
 Bournemouth BH1 . . . . . .205 A5
 Portsmouth PO5 . . . . . . .216 C1
Caversham CI
 Hamworthy BH15 . . . . . .201 E3
 Southampton SO19 . . . . .104 A4
Cawdor Rd BH3 . . . . .204 D7
Cawte Rd SO15 . . . . .102 D6
Cawte's PI PO16 . . . . .156 D7
Caxton Ave SO19 . . . . . . .104 B6
Caxton CI BH23 . . . . .206 A8
Cecil Ave Ashurst SO40 . . .100 C2
 Bournemouth BH8 . . . . . .205 B8
 Southampton SO19 . . . . . .78 B1
Cecil CI BH21 . . . . .186 E6
Cecil Ct BH8 . . . . .205 B8
Cecil Gr PO5 . . . . .216 A1
Cecil Hill PO5 . . . . .216 A1
Cecil Rd
 Bournemouth BH5 . . . . . .205 E4
 Poole BH12 . . . . .203 D7
 Southampton SO19 . . . . .103 F3
Cecil Villas SO17 . . . . .79 C1
Cedar Ave
 Bournemouth BH10 . . . . .189 D6
 Christchurch BH23 . . . . . .208 E8
 Southampton SO15 . . . . .102 D8
 St Leonards BH24 . . . . . .139 E3
Cedar CI Burisedon SO31 .127 F3
 Gosport PO12 . . . . .156 A1
 Hedge End SO30 . . . . . .105 C7
 Kings Worthy SO23 . . . . . .2 B8
 Upton BH16 . . . . .202 A3
 Waterlooville PO7 . . . . . .134 E6
Cedar Cres
 North Baddesley SO52 . . . .53 F5
 Waterlooville PO8 . . . . . .112 C5

Cedar Ct
Bishop's Waltham SO32 83 D8
Bournemouth BH4 204 B2
[10] Fareham PO16 131 C1
Portsmouth PO5 216 C1
Cedar Dr Hordle SO41 211 D8
Wimborne Minst BH21 164 A5
Cedar Gdns Havant PO9 136 A2
Old Milton BH25 194 F1
Southampton SO14 103 A8
Cedar Gr PO3 183 B7
Cedar Grange [18] BH13 204 A4
Cedar Lawn SO51 28 C1
Cedar Manor BH4 204 C3
Cedar Pl BH23 169 B1
Cedar Rd Eastleigh SO50 55 E1
Hythe SO45 150 A7
Southampton SO14 103 A7
Cedar Sch The SO16 77 E4
Cedar Trad Pk BH21 164 F6
Cedar Way
Fareham PO14 154 E8
Ferndown BH22 165 C8
Cedar Wlk SO22 215 C5
Cedar Wood Cl
Fair Oak SO50 57 E2
Totton SO40 100 C8
Cedarmount SO43 121 F4
Cedars The
Bournemouth BH4 204 C4
Fareham PO16 130 F3
Cedars View SP5 4 E7
Cedarwood SO23 2 C7
Cedarwood Lodge [6]
PO16 131 B2
Ceder Ho SO14 103 B3
Cedric Cl SO45 177 F8
Celandine Ave
Locks Heath SO31 128 F2
Waterlooville PO8 112 B3
Celandine Cl
Chandler's Ford SO53 54 F5
Christchurch BH23 208 B8
Celia Cl PO7 135 B8
Cellars Farm Rd BH6 207 A3
Cement Terr [2] SO14 102 F3
Cemetery Ave BH15 202 F6
Cemetery Junc BH2 204 F5
Cemetery La
Denmead PO7 110 F5
Westbourne PO10 137 D3
Cemetery Rd
Southampton SO15 102 F8
Wimborne Minst BH21 163 B5
Centaur St PO2 182 D8
Centaury Gdns SO50 81 C7
Centenary Cl SO41 172 C2
Centenary Gdns PO9 135 F2
Centenary Ho BH23 207 B7
Centenary Way BH1 205 E5
Central Ave
Corfe Mullen BH21 186 D7
Poole BH12 203 E6
Central Bridge SO14 103 B3
Central Dr
Bournemouth BH2 204 E5
West Moors BH24 166 B8
Central Point PO3 183 B6
Central Prec The SO53 55 C5
Central Rd Cosham PO6 158 C7
Portchester PO16 156 B7
Southampton SO14 103 A2
Central Sq PO1 182 A4
Central St PO1 216 C4
Central Station Bridge
SO15 102 E5
Central Way N SO45 151 E2
Centre La SO41 196 E1
Centre Pl BH24 140 F7
Centre Way SO31 129 A3
Centurion Ct [24] PO1 182 A4
Centurion Gate PO4 183 D3
Centurion Ho SO18 103 C7
Centurion Ind Pk SO18 103 C7
Cerdic Mews SO31 128 A4
Cerne Abbas BH13 204 A1
Cerne Cl
Bournemouth BH9 190 B4
North Baddesley SO52 53 F4
West End SO18 80 B1
Cessac Ho PO12 181 C2
Chadderton Gdns PO1 182 B3
Chaddesley Glen BH13 214 E6
Chaddesley Grange
BH13 214 F6
Chaddesley Pines BH13 214 E6
Chaddesley Wood Rd
BH13 214 E5
Chadswell Mdw PO9 135 D1
Chadwell Ave SO19 104 B4
Chadwick Rd SO50 55 F2
Chadwick Way SO31 127 F2
Chafen Rd SO18 103 D7
Chaffey Cl BH24 141 C8
Chaffinch Cl
Broadstone BH17 186 F2
New Milton BH25 194 F2
Totton SO40 100 C8
Chaffinch Gn PO8 111 E4
Chaffinch Way
Lee-on-t-S PO13 179 F4
Portchester PO16 155 F8
Chalbury Cl BH17 188 A2
Chalbury Ct [2] BH14 203 B4
Chalcroft Distribution Pk
SO30 81 B5
Chaldecott Gdns BH10 189 C4
Chaldon Rd BH17 187 F2
Chale Cl PO13 155 C2
Chalewood Rd SO45 177 E7
Chalfont Ave BH23 191 D3
Chalfont Ct [7] SO16 78 A1
Chalice Cl BH14 203 A4
Chalice Ct SO30 105 B6
Chalk Hill Soberton SO32 85 C5
West End SO18 80 C1
Chalk Hill Rd PO8 112 C8
Chalk La PO17 131 B7
Chalk Pit Cotts PO17 131 B7
Chalk Ridge
Horndean PO8 88 D3
Winchester SO23 11 D7
Chalk's Cl SP5 47 D7
Chalkpit Rd PO6 133 B1
Chalkridge Rd PO6 134 A1
Chalky La SO32 83 D8
Challenge Ent Ctr The
PO3 158 B3
Challenger Dr PO12 181 C8
Challenger Way SO45 125 D2
Challis Ct [10] SO14 103 A3
Chalmers Way SO31 127 E3
Chaloner Cres SO45 126 A1
Chalton Cres PO9 135 D4
Chalton Ho PO1 216 B4
Chalton La PO8 88 D6
Chalvington Ct SO53 55 C5
Chalvington Rd SO53 55 D4
Chalwyn Ind Est BH15,
BH12 203 A7
Chalybeate Cl SO16 78 B2
Chalybeate Hospl SO16 78 B2
Chamberlain Gr PO14 155 A8
Chamberlain Hall SO16 79 A4
Chamberlain Rd SO17 79 A3
Chamberlayne Ct SO52 54 B4
Chamberlayne Ho SO31 127 B6
Chamberlayne Park Sch
SO19 104 A1
Chamberlayne Rd
Bursledon SO31 127 F8
Eastleigh SO50 56 A2
Netley SO31 127 B6
Chambers Ave SO51 53 B7
Chambers Cl SO16 77 C5
Champion Cl SO41 211 F4
Chancel Rd SO31 129 B3
Chancellors La SO32 81 F4
Chanctonbury Ho PO5 216 B1
Chander Cl BH22 165 E4
Chandler's Ford Ind Est
SO53 55 B5
Chandler's Ford Inf Sch
SO53 55 D6
Chandler's Ford Sta
SO53 55 C6
Chandlers Cl
Bournemouth BH7 206 B8
South Hayling PO11 185 C2
Chandlers Ct [29] SO14 103 A3
Chandlers Pl SO31 127 B6
Chandlers Way SO31 129 B6
Chandos Ave BH12 204 A8
Chandos Ho [3] SO14 103 A3
Chandos St [12] SO14 103 A3
Channel Ct
Barton on S BH25 209 E7
Bournemouth BH6 206 D3
Channel Mouth Rd
SO45 151 F1
Channel Way SO14 103 C3
Channels Farm Rd SO16 79 D5
Channon Ct [11] SO15 102 E7
Channon Ret Pk SO50 55 E3
Chant Cl BH23 207 D7
Chantrell Wlk PO15 130 D3
Chantry Cl BH23 193 F1
Chantry Mead SO22 215 C7
Chantry Rd
Gosport PO12 181 A8
Horndean PO8 112 B7
Southampton SO14 103 B3
Chantry The
Bournemouth BH1 205 A4
Locks Heath PO14 129 C3
Chapel Cl Braishfield SO51 28 C6
Corfe Mullen BH21 186 C6
West End SO30 80 D2
Chapel Cres SO19 104 A4
Chapel Ct [1] PO1 182 C7
Chapel Dro
Hedge End SO30 105 B6
Horton Heath SO50 81 C7
Chapel Gate BH23 190 C8
Chapel La Bishopstone SP5 22 B7
Blackfield SO45 177 E8
Bransgore BH23 193 A8
Burley BH24 143 B3
Corfe Mullen BH21 186 C5
Curdridge SO32 106 E8
East Boldre SO42 175 D6
East Parley BH23 190 C8
Fawley SO45 151 A2
Lockerley SO51 26 A5
Lyndhurst SO43 121 F4
Michelmersh SO51 27 D8
Nomansland SP5 73 C7
Otterbourne SO21 31 B1
Poole BH15 202 C2
Redlynch SP5 47 E6
Sway SO41 172 D1
Totton SO40 100 E5
Chapel La *continued*
[5] Waterlooville PO7 134 E7
Wimborne Minst BH21 163 B5
Winchester SO21 12 B8
Chapel Rd Droxford SO32 61 C3
Poole BH14 203 A4
Sarisbury SO31 128 E6
Soberton SO32 85 B2
Southampton SO14 103 B4
Swanmore SO32 84 B5
West End SO30 80 E2
Chapel Rise BH24 140 D2
Chapel Sq PO12 180 F7
Chapel St East Meon GU32 38 D1
Gosport PO12 181 B9
Petersfield GU32 40 F3
[3] Portsmouth PO5 216 A1
Portsmouth,Buckland PO2 182 D8
Southampton SO14 103 B4
Chapelside PO14 154 A8
Chaplains Ave PO8 111 D3
Chaplains Cl PO8 111 D3
Charborough Rd BH18 187 B3
Charden Ct SO18 104 B7
Charden Rd
Bishopstoke SO50 57 A2
Gosport PO13 180 D8
Charfield Cl
Fareham PO14 154 D8
Winchester SO22 215 C3
Charing Cl BH24 141 A6
Charity View PO17 130 E7
Chark La PO13 179 F5
Charlcot Lawn PO9 135 D6
Charlecote Dr SO53 55 A8
Charlecote Ho SO15 102 D5
Charlecote Mews [14]
SO22 215 D6
Charlemont Dr [2] PO16 131 D1
Charles Cl
Waterlooville PO7 134 D6
Winchester SO23 215 F8
Charles Cres BH25 195 B5
Charles Dickens Birthplace
Mus* PO1 182 C7
Charles Dickens Inf Sch
PO1 182 D7
Charles Dickens Jun Sch
PO1 182 D7
Charles Dickens St PO1 216 B3
Charles Gdns BH10 189 D2
Charles Ho PO12 181 E6
Charles Keightley Ct
BH21 163 D4
Charles Knott Gdns
SO15 102 F7
Charles Ley Ct SO45 151 B3
Charles Miller Ct [9]
SO15 102 F8
Charles Norton-Thomas Ct [4]
PO1 182 B5
Charles Rd
Christchurch BH23 207 F8
Poole BH15 202 D3
Charles St
Petersfield GU32 40 E3
Portsmouth PO1 216 C4
Southampton SO14 103 A3
Charles Watts Way
SO30 105 B8
Charles Wyatt Ho [3]
SO14 103 A7
Charles's La BH24 141 E3
Charlesbury Ave PO12 180 F4
Charleston Cl PO11 184 E4
Charleston Rd SO45 150 D8
Charlesworth Dr PO7 111 D2
Charlesworth Gdns
PO7 111 D1
Charlie Soar Ct [1] SO50 56 A2
Charliejoy Gdns [1]
SO14 103 C6
Charlott Ct PO5 216 B1
Charlotte Cl
Christchurch BH23 208 A6
[3] New Milton BH25 195 A2
Poole BH12 204 C7
Charlotte Ct
Chandler's Ford SO53 55 E7
Southampton SO19 103 F2
Charlotte Dr PO12 181 C8
Charlotte Mews PO12 181 A3
Charlotte Pl SO14 103 A6
Charlotte St PO1 216 B4
Charlton Cl
Bournemouth BH9 190 C4
Hordle SO41 195 F3
Charlton Dr GU31 41 A5
Charlton Rd SO15 102 D7
Charltons The BH2 204 F5
Charminster [6] PO5 182 E2
Charminster Ave BH9 190 B1
Charminster Cl
Bournemouth BH8 190 B2
Waterlooville PO7 134 E8
Charminster Pl BH8 190 C2
Charminster Rd BH8 205 B7
Charmouth Gr BH14 203 A4
Charmouth Terr [6] SO16 78 A1
Charmus Rd SO40 76 B2
Charmwen Cres SO30 80 C2
Charnock Cl SO41 195 F3
Charnwood PO13 155 D2
Charnwood Ave BH9 190 B3
Charnwood Cl
Chandler's Ford SO53 30 C2
Totton SO40 76 D1
West Moors BH22 138 E2
Charnwood Cres SO53 30 C2
Charnwood Dr SP6 69 E3
Charnwood Gdns SO53 30 C2
Charnwood Way SO45 177 E7
Chartcombe BH13 214 E8
Charter Ho [2] PO5 216 A2
Charter Rd BH11 188 D6
Chartergrove Ho [12]
GU31 40 F3
Charterhouse Way SO30 81 C1
Chartwell [5] BH13 204 B3
Chartwell Cl
Eastleigh SO50 56 B6
Titchfield PO14 129 C1
Chartwell Dr PO9 136 C3
Chase Cl GU33 21 A4
Chase Farm Cl SO32 83 E3
Chase Gr SO32 83 E3
Chase Rd GU33 21 A4
Chase The Gosport PO12 180 F4
St Leonards BH24 140 D5
Titchfield PO14 129 D2
Verwood BH31 115 C5
Chaseside BH7 206 A8
Chasewater Ave PO3 183 A7
Chatburn Ave PO8 111 F3
Chatfield Ave PO2 182 A8
Chatfield Ho [10] PO1 216 C4
Chatfield Rd PO13 155 C4
Chatham Cl PO12 181 C8
Chatham Dr PO1 182 B3
Chatham Rd SO22 215 A3
Chatsworth GU33 21 B1
Chatsworth Ave
Cosham PO6 158 A6
Portsmouth PO6 157 F6
Chatsworth Cl PO15 130 C1
Chatsworth Ct PO5 216 C1
Chatsworth Rd
Bournemouth BH8 205 C6
Eastleigh SO50 56 B6
Poole BH14 203 B5
Southampton SO19 104 A6
Chatsworth Way BH25 194 E1
Chaucer Ave PO6 132 E1
Chaucer Bsns Pk SO23 2 C1
Chaucer Cl
Fareham PO16 130 F2
Waterlooville PO7 111 E2
Wimborne Minst BH21 163 C6
Chaucer Dr SO41 211 D5
Chaucer Rd Poole BH13 214 F8
Southampton SO19 104 D6
Chaucombe Pl BH25 194 F1
Chaundler Rd SO23 215 E8
Chaveney Cl SO45 125 F1
Chavy Water SO51 52 E6
Chawton Cl
Southampton SO18 104 D8
Winchester SO22 1 D4
Cheam Rd BH18 186 F4
Cheam Way SO40 76 D1
Cheater's La SP6 92 C8
Cheddar Cl SO19 103 E3
Cheddington Rd BH9 190 A4
Chedington Cl BH17 187 E2
Chedworth Cres PO6 133 A1
Cheeryble Ho [16] PO1 182 D7
Cheesecombe Farm La
GU33 19 F6
Chellowdene SO53 55 C5
Chelmsford Rd
Portsmouth PO2 157 F2
Upton BH16 201 A7
Chelsea Rd PO5 216 C1
Cheltenham Cres PO13 179 F4
Cheltenham Ct [10] SO17 79 A1
Cheltenham Gdns SO30 81 C3
Cheltenham Rd
Cosham PO6 157 C8
Poole BH12 203 C5
Chelveston Cres SO16 78 A4
Chelwood Gate SO16 78 F5
Chene Rd BH21 163 D4
Cheping Gdns SO30 106 A6
Chepstow Cl
Chandler's Ford SO53 55 B6
Totton SO40 100 C8
Chepstow Ct PO7 112 B1
Cheqhers Ho [4] PO16 131 B1
Chequers Cl SO41 197 B3
Chequers Quay [8] PO10 161 A8
Cherbourg Prim Sch
SO50 56 A1
Cherbourg Rd SO50 56 A1
Cherford Rd BH11 189 B2
Cherita Ct BH15 202 F6
Cheriton [7] BH4 204 C2
Cheriton Ave
Bournemouth BH7 206 C8
Southampton SO18 104 D7
Cheriton Cl Havant PO9 135 D4
Horndean PO8 112 B7
Winchester SO22 215 B7
Cheriton Ct [5] SO15 102 C6
Cheriton La
Bramdean SO24 15 C8
Cheriton SO24 14 F8
Cheriton Prim Sch SO24 14 C6
Cheriton Rd
Eastleigh SO50 55 F1
Gosport PO12 180 F4
Portsmouth PO4 183 C4
Winchester SO22 215 C6
Cheriton Way BH21 163 C6
Cherque La PO13 180 A8
Cherque Way PO13 180 A7
Cherrett Cl BH11 188 F4
Cherries Dr BH9 189 E2
Cherry Blossom Ct [19]
PO1 182 D7
Cherry Cl
Lee-on-t-S PO13 179 F2
Poole BH14 203 B4
Cherry Ct Poole BH14 203 B5
[16] Southampton SO17 103 A8
Cherry Dro SO50 81 D6
Cherry Gdns SO32 83 D7
Cherry Gr BH22 165 C6
Cherry Hill Gdns BH16 201 B6
Cherry Hill Gr BH16 201 B6
Cherry Tree Ave
Fareham PO14 154 D8
Waterlooville PO8 112 B2
Cherry Tree Cl
Hordle SO41 211 D8
St Leonards BH24 139 D3
Cherry Tree Ct [4] BH25 195 B1
Cherry Tree Dr BH25 194 E5
Cherry Wlk SO15 102 C8
Cherrygarth Rd PO15 130 C1
Cherryton Gdns SO45 150 B3
Cherrywood SO30 105 B6
Cherrywood Gdns
South Hayling PO11 185 A4
Totton SO40 100 C7
Chervil Cl
Chandler's Ford SO53 54 F6
Horndean PO8 88 C1
Cherville Ct SO51 52 E7
Cherville Mews SO51 52 E8
Cherville St SO51 52 E8
Cherwell Cres SO16 101 E8
Cherwell Gdns SO53 55 D5
Cherwell Ho SO16 101 E8
Cheshire Cl PO15 129 F5
Cheshire Dr BH8 191 A2
Cheshire Way PO10 137 D2
Chesil Gdns BH12 203 B8
Chesil St SO23 215 F5
Chesil Terr SO23 215 F5
Chesil Wood SO23 11 C7
Chesilbourne Gr BH8 190 D3
Chesildene Ave BH8 190 D3
Chesildene Dr BH8 190 D3
Chessel Ave
Bournemouth BH5 205 F4
Southampton SO19 103 E6
Chessel Cres SO19 103 F7
Chester Cres PO13 180 B4
Chester Ct SO16 78 C2
Chester Cts [8] PO12 181 C5
Chester Pl [7] PO5 182 D2
Chester Rd Poole BH13 204 A2
Southampton SO18 80 A1
Winchester SO23 215 F6
Chesterfield Cl BH13 214 F8
Chesterfield Ct BH1 205 C3
Chesterfield Rd PO3 183 A8
Chesterton Gdns PO8 111 E3
Chesterton Pl PO15 129 C8
Chestnut Ave
Barton on S BH25 210 A8
Bournemouth BH6 206 C4
Christchurch BH23 206 D8
[2] Colden Common SO21 31 F1
Eastleigh SO50 55 F1
Eastleigh SO53 55 D1
Ellingham BH24 116 B6
Havant PO9 135 B3
Littleton SO22 1 C4
Portsmouth PO4 182 F4
Waterlooville PO8 112 C5
Chestnut Cl
Chandler's Ford SO53 55 C2
Denmead PO7 110 F4
Romsey SO51 53 D6
West End SO30 80 D3
Chestnut Ct
Durrants PO9 136 B8
Southampton SO17 79 B2
Chestnut Dr
Ashurst SO40 100 C3
Petersfield GU31 40 F1
Chestnut Gr BH21 164 E6
Chestnut Lodge [4] SO16 78 E3
Chestnut Rd
Brockenhurst SO42 146 A1
Southampton SO16 78 A2
Chestnut Rise
Droxford SO32 61 B2
Eastleigh SO53 55 D1
Chestnut Way
Burton BH23 192 C3
Titchfield PO14 129 C1
Chestnut Wlk
Botley SO30 105 F8
Gosport PO12 156 A1
Chestnuts The SO31 129 A2
Chetnole Cl BH17 188 A1
Chettle Rd SO19 104 E5
Chetwode Way BH17 187 B2
Chetwynd Dr SO16 78 F4
Chetwynd Rd
Portsmouth PO4 182 E3
Southampton SO16 78 F5
Chevening Ct [4] PO4 183 B5
Cheviot Court Flats
BH23 207 F8
Cheviot Cres SO16 101 E8
Cheviot Dr SO45 125 D3
Cheviot Gn SO31 152 D10
Cheviot Rd SO16 101 E8
Cheviot Way BH31 114 F5
Cheviot Wlk PO14 154 F7
Cheviots The BH14 203 C3

Chevron Bsns Pk SO45 ... 150 B6
Chewter Cl PO4 ... 182 E1
Chewton Common Rd
BH23 ... 209 B8
Chewton Farm Rd BH23 ... 194 C1
Chewton Lodge BH23 ... 209 B8
Chewton Mews BH23 ... 194 A2
Chewton Way BH23 ... 194 B1
Cheyne Gdns BH4 ... 204 C2
Cheyne Way PO13 ... 179 F2
Chichester Ave PO11 ... 185 A3
Chichester Cl
Gosport PO13 ... 155 B2
Hedge End SO30 ... 81 C1
Sarisbury SO31 ... 128 E3
West Wellow SO51 ... 51 B2
Chichester Ho PO9 ... 136 A3
Chichester Rd
North Hayling PO11 ... 160 C1
Portsmouth PO2 ... 182 E8
Ringwood BH24 ... 117 C1
Southampton SO18 ... 104 A7
Chichester Way BH23 ... 208 A5
Chichester Wlk BH21 ... 163 E1
Chickenhall La SO50 ... 56 C2
Chickerell Cl BH9 ... 190 B3
Chidden Cl GU32 ... 38 D1
Chidden Holt SO53 ... 55 A5
Chideock Cl BH12 ... 203 E6
Chidham Cl PO9 ... 135 E2
Chidham Dr PO9 ... 135 E2
Chidham Rd PO6 ... 134 A1
Chidham Sq PO9 ... 135 E2
Chidham Wlk 2 PO9 ... 135 E2
Chigwell Rd BH8 ... 190 B1
Chilbolton Ave SO22 ... 215 B6
Chilbolton Ct
11 Havant PO9 ... 136 B6
Winchester SO22 ... 215 A5
Chilcomb Cl PO13 ... 179 F3
Chilcomb La
Chilcomb SO21 ... 11 E5
Winchester SO23 ... 11 C5
Chilcomb Rd SO18 ... 104 C8
Chilcombe Cl PO9 ... 135 F3
Chilcombe Hts SO23 ... 215 F5
Chilcombe Rd BH6 ... 206 B5
Chilcote Rd PO3 ... 183 A7
Childe Sq PO2 ... 157 C2
Chilfrome Cl BH17 ... 187 C1
Chilgrove Rd PO6 ... 158 C8
Chilham Cl SO50 ... 56 A7
Chillenden Ct SO40 ... 100 C6
Chillerton SO31 ... 127 C7
Chilling La SO31 ... 152 F7
Chillington Gdns 5
SO53 ... 30 B1
Chilly Hill SP6 ... 94 F7
Chilmark Ct GU33 ... 20 F4
Chilsdown Way PO7 ... 134 E4
Chiltern Cl
Old Milton BH25 ... 194 F1
Poole BH4 ... 204 B5
Totton SO40 ... 100 D5
Chiltern Ct
5 Christchurch BH23 ... 207 F8
Gosport PO12 ... 181 B6
2 Portsmouth PO5 ... 182 D1
Chiltern Dr
Barton on S BH25 ... 209 E8
Verwood BH31 ... 114 F6
Chiltern Gn SO16 ... 101 E8
Chiltern Wlk PO14 ... 154 F7
Chilworth Cl SO16 ... 54 D1
Chilworth Dro SO16 ... 54 D1
Chilworth Gdns PO8 ... 88 D4
Chilworth Gr PO12 ... 181 A6
Chilworth Old Village
SO16 ... 54 C2
Chilworth Rd SO16 ... 54 E1
Chimes The BH4 ... 204 B3
Chine Ave SO19 ... 103 E6
Chine Cl SO31 ... 129 A4
Chine Cres BH2 ... 204 D2
Chine Crescent Rd BH2 ... 204 D2
Chine The PO13 ... 155 E1
Chine Wlk BH22 ... 165 E1
Chinham Rd SO40 ... 99 C6
Chipstead Ho 9 PO6 ... 157 F8
Chipstead Rd 8 PO6 ... 157 F8
Chirk Pl SO51 ... 53 A7
Chisels La BH23 ... 193 B6
Chisholm Cl SO16 ... 77 F5
Chislehurst 16 BH4 ... 204 C3
Chiswell Rd BH17 ... 187 D1
Chitty Rd PO4 ... 183 A2
Chivers Cl PO5 ... 216 B1
Chloe Gdns BH12 ... 203 D7
Chorley Cl BH15 ... 202 C6
Chris Cres BH16 ... 201 C7
Christ the King RC Prim Sch
BH11 ... 189 A5
Christ's Hospl 13 SO23 ... 215 D5
Christchurch Bay Rd
BH25 ... 209 F7
Christchurch By-Pass
BH23 ... 207 D8
Christchurch Castle*
BH23 ... 207 B6
Christchurch Gdns
Cosham PO7 ... 134 B2
1 Winchester SO23 ... 215 D3
Christchurch Hospl
BH23 ... 206 F8
Christchurch Jun Sch
BH23 ... 207 A7
Christchurch Prim Sch
BH23 ... 207 A7
Christchurch Priory*
BH23 ... 207 C6
Christchurch Rd
Barton on S BH25 ... 209 D8
Bournemouth,Boscombe
BH1,BH7 ... 205 D4
Bournemouth,Iford BH7 ... 206 B6
Ferndown BH22 ... 165 C1
Hordle SO41 ... 211 C8
Hurn BH23 ... 191 C5
Ringwood BH24 ... 140 F7
Ringwood,Moortown BH24 ... 141 A4
Winchester SO23 ... 215 D4
Winchester SO23 ... 215 D5
Christchurch Sta BH23 ... 207 A7
Christie Ave PO15 ... 129 C8
Christine Ct 8 SO18 ... 103 E8
Christopher Cres BH15 ... 202 C6
Christopher Way PO10 ... 136 F2
Christyne Ct PO7 ... 134 D4
Church Cl
Bishopstoke SO50 ... 56 D4
Clanfield PO8 ... 88 B6
Locks Heath SO31 ... 129 B3
Minstead SO43 ... 98 C2
North Baddesley SO52 ... 54 A4
Church End SO15 ... 102 C8
Church Farm SP6 ... 93 F8
Church Farm Cl SO45 ... 125 B6
Church Hatch SP5 ... 47 A8
Church Hill
Milford on S SO41 ... 211 E4
Redlynch SP5 ... 47 F5
Verwood BH31 ... 114 E6
West End SO30 ... 80 C1
Church La Awbridge SO51 ... 26 E3
Botley SO30 ... 106 A5
Braishfield SO51 ... 28 D7
Bramdean SO24 ... 15 C4
Brockenhurst SO42 ... 173 B8
Burley BH24 ... 143 B3
Bursledon SO31 ... 128 B8
Christchurch BH23 ... 207 B6
Colden Common SO21 ... 56 F8
Compton PO18 ... 90 F2
Curdridge SO32 ... 106 D8
Damerham SP6 ... 68 D4
Durley SO32 ... 81 F6
East Boldre SO42 ... 175 D5
Easton Down SO21 ... 2 F5
Fawley SO45 ... 151 A3
Ferndown BH22 ... 189 F7
Hambledon PO7 ... 86 D3
Havant PO9 ... 160 B8
Hedge End SO30 ... 105 B5
Highfield SO17 ... 79 B2
Kings Worthy SO23 ... 2 C6
Littleton SO22 ... 1 A6
Lymington SO41 ... 197 E3
Lyndhurst SO43 ... 121 F5
Meonstoke SO32 ... 61 C7
Mottisfont SO51 ... 5 F2
North Hayling PO11 ... 160 C3
Nursling SO16 ... 76 F6
Old Milton BH25 ... 194 F1
Pilley SO41 ... 173 F2
Plaitford SO51 ... 50 B5
Romsey SO51 ... 52 E7
Sherfield English SO51 ... 25 D3
12 Southampton SO14 ... 102 F3
Swanmore SO32 ... 84 C6
Sway SO41 ... 172 B1
Twyford SO21 ... 32 A7
West Meon GU32 ... 37 B5
Church Leat SP5 ... 47 A8
Church Mead 9 SO41 ... 197 E2
Church Path
1 Emsworth PO10 ... 160 F8
Fareham PO16 ... 131 C1
Gosport PO12 ... 181 D5
Horndean PO8 ... 112 D6
Titchfield PO14 ... 154 A8
Church Path N PO1 ... 216 B4
Church Pl Fareham PO16 ... 131 C2
Romsey SO51 ... 52 E7
Church Rd
Bishopstoke SO50 ... 56 D5
Bournemouth BH6 ... 206 F3
Ferndown BH22 ... 165 C5
Gosport PO12 ... 181 A3
Locks Heath SO31 ... 129 B3
Michelmersh SO51 ... 6 D2
Poole BH14 ... 203 A4
Portchester PO16 ... 156 E6
Portsmouth PO1 ... 216 C4
Privett GU34 ... 17 C3
Romsey SO51 ... 52 E7
Shedfield SO32 ... 107 E7
Soberton PO17 ... 109 C6
South Hayling PO11 ... 185 A5
Southampton SO19 ... 103 D2
Southbourne PO10 ... 161 E8
Steep GU32 ... 40 E7
Swanmore SO32 ... 84 B5
Thorney Island PO10 ... 161 D1
Three Legged Cross BH21 ... 114 E1
Warsash SO31 ... 152 D10
Westbourne PO10 ... 137 B3
Church St
Christchurch BH23 ... 207 B6
East Meon GU32 ... 38 E1
Fordingbridge SP6 ... 93 F8
Liss GU33 ... 20 E6
Poole BH15 ... 202 B1
Portsmouth PO1 ... 216 C4
Romsey SO51 ... 52 E7
Southampton SO15 ... 78 C1
Titchfield PO14 ... 154 A8
Church St *continued*
Upham SO32 ... 58 F6
6 Wimborne Minst BH21 ... 163 B5
Church View
Portsmouth PO4 ... 183 A5
Shedfield SO32 ... 107 F7
Southampton SO19 ... 103 D2
Westbourne PO10 ... 137 B3
Church View Cl SO19 ... 104 A3
Church Wlk SP5 ... 48 A5
Churcher Cl PO12 ... 180 D3
Churcher Rd PO10 ... 137 B4
Churcher Wlk 2 PO12 ... 180 D3
Churcher's Coll GU31 ... 41 A4
Churchers Coll Jun Sch
GU32 ... 40 E3
Churchfield BH31 ... 114 E6
Churchfield Cres BH15 ... 202 E4
Churchfield Ct 2 BH15 ... 202 E3
Churchfield La BH24 ... 93 E2
Churchfield Rd
Petersfield GU31 ... 41 B4
Poole BH15 ... 202 E3
Churchfields
Fawley SO45 ... 151 B3
Twyford SO21 ... 32 A6
Churchfields Rd SO21 ... 32 A6
Churchill Ave SO32 ... 59 A1
Churchill Cl Alderholt SP6 ... 92 E5
Titchfield PO14 ... 129 C1
Churchill Cres BH12 ... 203 C6
Churchill Ct
Farlington PO6 ... 158 E8
New Milton BH25 ... 194 F2
Waterlooville PO8 ... 112 A6
Churchill Dr PO10 ... 136 F4
Churchill Dro BH21 ... 91 C7
Churchill Gdns BH12 ... 203 C5
Churchill Ho SO18 ... 104 C8
Churchill Mews PO12 ... 181 A7
Churchill Rd
Bournemouth BH1 ... 205 E5
Poole BH12 ... 203 D6
Wimborne Minst BH21 ... 163 E3
Churchill Sq 3 PO4 ... 183 B2
Churchill Yard Ind Est
PO7 ... 111 E1
Churchmoor Rd BH21 ... 164 A5
Churchward Gdns SO30 ... 81 C2
Cinderford Cl 21 PO6 ... 133 B1
Cinnamon Ct 3 SO15 ... 102 E6
Cinnamon La 7 BH15 ... 202 B1
Circle The
3 Bournemouth BH9 ... 190 A4
Poole BH13 ... 214 F7
Portsmouth PO5 ... 182 D2
Wickham PO17 ... 108 A4
Circular Rd PO1 ... 182 C7
Circus The PO6 ... 133 A2
Cirrus Gdns SO31 ... 127 F2
City Bldgs PO1 ... 216 B4
City Bsns Ctr SO23 ... 215 E6
City Commerce Ctr 6
SO14 ... 103 B3
City Ct 27 SO14 ... 103 A3
City Ind Pk SO15 ... 102 E4
City of Portsmouth Boys Sch
PO2 ... 157 E4
City of Portsmouth Girls' Sch
PO1 ... 182 E6
City of Toronto Homes
SO16 ... 101 F8
City Rd SO23 ... 215 E6
Civic Centre Rd
Havant PO9 ... 135 F2
Southampton SO14 ... 102 F5
Civic Way PO16 ... 131 C1
Clacton Rd PO6 ... 157 D8
Claire Ct 6 BH23 ... 209 A7
Claire Gdns PO8 ... 88 C2
Clamp Gn SO21 ... 56 F8
Clandon Dr SO50 ... 55 F5
Clanfield Cl SO53 ... 55 D6
Clanfield Dr SO53 ... 55 D6
Clanfield Ho 7 PO1 ... 216 C4
Clanfield Jun Sch PO8 ... 88 B7
Clanfield Rd SO18 ... 104 C7
Clanfield Way SO53 ... 55 D6
Clanwilliam Rd PO13 ... 179 F3
Clare Cl PO14 ... 129 C2
Clare Gdns
Blackfield SO45 ... 177 F7
Petersfield GU31 ... 41 C3
Clare Ho PO12 ... 180 F7
Clare Lodge Cl BH23 ... 169 A1
Claremont Ave BH9 ... 190 B2
Claremont Cl SO50 ... 56 A6
Claremont Cres SO15 ... 102 A7
Claremont Gdns PO7 ... 134 E4
Claremont Rd
Bournemouth BH9 ... 190 B2
Portsmouth PO1 ... 216 D3
Southampton SO15 ... 102 A7
Clarence Espl PO5 ... 182 C1
Clarence Ho 5 SO14 ... 103 C6
Clarence Par PO5 ... 182 C2
Clarence Park Rd BH7 ... 206 A6
Clarence Pl BH23 ... 206 F8
Clarence Rd
Gosport PO12 ... 181 D6
Lyndhurst SO43 ... 121 F5
3 Poole BH14 ... 203 A3
Portsmouth PO5 ... 182 D1
Clarence St PO1 ... 216 B4
Clarendon Cl
Broadstone BH18 ... 187 A4
Denmead PO7 ... 110 F5
10 Romsey SO51 ... 28 B1
Clarendon Cres PO14 ... 129 C1
Clarendon Ct
3 Bournemouth BH2 ... 204 D2
6 Portsmouth PO5 ... 182 D1
Clarendon Pk SO41 ... 197 D2
Clarendon Pl
1 Portsmouth PO1 ... 216 B3
Portsmouth PO1 ... 216 C4
Clarendon Rd
Bournemouth BH4 ... 204 D3
Broadstone BH18 ... 186 F4
Christchurch BH23 ... 207 A7
Havant PO9 ... 135 E1
Portsmouth,Southsea PO5 ... 182 D2
Southampton SO16 ... 102 A8
Clarendon St PO1 ... 216 C4
Clark's Cl BH24 ... 141 A7
Clarkes Rd PO1 ... 182 F6
Claude Ashby Cl SO18 ... 79 E4
Claudeen Cl SO18 ... 79 E5
Claudeen Ct SO19 ... 104 E6
Claudia Ct PO12 ... 180 F6
Claudius Cl SO53 ... 55 F7
Claudius Gdns SO53 ... 55 F7
Clausen Way SO41 ... 197 C1
Clausentum Cl SO53 ... 55 E7
Clausentum Ho SO18 ... 103 C7
Clausentum Rd
Southampton SO14 ... 103 B7
Winchester SO23 ... 215 D3
Claxton St PO1 ... 216 C3
Clay Hill SO43 ... 122 A3
Clay St SP5 ... 24 A3
Claybank Rd PO3 ... 158 A1
Claybank Spur PO3 ... 158 A1
Claydon Ave PO4 ... 183 A4
Clayford Ave BH22 ... 165 B7
Clayford Cl BH17 ... 187 D2
Clayhall Rd PO12 ... 181 B3
Clayhill Cl SO32 ... 83 D4
Claylake Dr BH31 ... 115 A5
Claylands Ct SO32 ... 83 B8
Claylands Rd SO32 ... 83 B8
Claylands Road Ind Est
SO32 ... 83 B8
Claypit Rd SO51 ... 29 C6
Claypits La SO45 ... 125 D4
Claypitt La GU32 ... 18 D6
Clearwater Apartments 5
PO4 ... 182 E1
Cleasby Cl SO16 ... 101 E7
Cleasby Grange 2 BH5 ... 205 F3
Clease Way SO21 ... 31 C7
Clee Ave PO14 ... 154 D8
Cleek Dr SO16 ... 78 F5
Cleethorpes Rd SO19 ... 104 B4
Cleeve Cl PO6 ... 133 B1
Cleeve Ho BH25 ... 209 F7
Cleeves Cl BH12 ... 188 D2
Cleeves The SO40 ... 100 C6
Clegg Rd PO4 ... 183 A3
Clem's Way SO51 ... 5 A1
Clematis Cl BH23 ... 208 C8
Clement Attlee Way
PO6 ... 157 B8
Clement Mews BH4 ... 204 B3
Cleric Ct PO14 ... 129 C3
Cleveland Cl BH25 ... 209 D7
Cleveland Ct
4 Bournemouth BH2 ... 204 D2
3 Southampton SO18 ... 80 A1
Cleveland Dr
Fareham PO14 ... 154 D8
Hythe SO45 ... 125 D2
Cleveland Gdns BH1 ... 205 C5
Cleveland Rd
Bournemouth BH1 ... 205 D5
Gosport PO12 ... 181 B4
Portsmouth PO5 ... 216 D2
Southampton SO18 ... 79 F1
Clevelands Cl SO53 ... 30 B1
Cleverley Ho 26 PO1 ... 182 A5
Clewers Hill SO32 ... 83 D4
Clewers La SO32 ... 83 E4
Cliff Cres BH25 ... 209 F7
Cliff Dr
Christchurch BH23 ... 208 C6
Poole BH13 ... 214 E6
Cliff Rd Milford on S SO41 ... 211 B4
Southampton SO15 ... 102 D5
Stubbington PO14 ... 153 F1
Cliff The SO19 ... 103 D3
Cliff Way SO21 ... 31 D7
Cliff Wlk 17 BH4 ... 204 C2
Cliffdale Gdns PO6 ... 134 A1
Cliffdale Prim Sch PO2 ... 157 F2
Cliffe Ave SO31 ... 127 E3
Cliffe Rd BH25 ... 209 E7
Clifford Dibben Mews 1
SO14 ... 103 A8
Clifford Pl SO50 ... 57 C2
Clifford Rd BH9 ... 190 A1
Clifford St SO14 ... 103 B5
Clifton Cres PO7 ... 111 B4
Clifton Ct
1 Bournemouth BH7 ... 205 F4
Hamworthy BH15 ... 201 D4
3 New Milton BH25 ... 195 A1
2 Southampton SO15 ... 102 A8
Clifton Gdns
Ferndown BH22 ... 165 C4
1 Southampton SO15 ... 102 A8
West End SO18 ... 80 C1
Clifton Hill SO22 ... 215 D6
Clifton Lodge SO15 ... 102 A8
Clifton Lodge No 1 18
SO22 ... 215 D6
Clifton Lodge No 2 19
SO22 ... 215 D6
Clifton Rd
Bournemouth BH6 ... 206 D3
Lee-on-t-S PO13 ... 180 A4
Poole BH14 ... 203 E2
10 Portsmouth PO5 ... 182 C2
Southampton SO15 ... 102 A8
Winchester SO22 ... 215 D6
Clifton St Gosport PO12 ... 180 F6
Portsmouth PO1 ... 216 D4
Clifton Terr
11 Portsmouth PO5 ... 182 C2
Winchester SO22 ... 215 D6
Clingan Rd BH6 ... 206 D7
Clinton Cl BH23 ... 194 B2
Clinton Rd
Lymington SO41 ... 197 E5
Waterlooville PO7 ... 111 C2
Clipper Cl SO31 ... 128 E1
Clitheroe Cotts SO42 ... 148 F1
Clive Ct 23 BH4 ... 204 C3
Clive Gr PO16 ... 156 C7
Clive Rd
Bournemouth BH9 ... 189 F1
Christchurch BH23 ... 193 E2
Portsmouth PO1 ... 182 E6
Cliveden Cl BH22 ... 165 C7
Clock Ho 4 PO7 ... 134 E7
Clock House The SO40 ... 76 A2
Clock St 7 PO1 ... 182 A5
Clocktower Dr 1 PO4 ... 183 B2
Cloisters The
3 Christchurch BH23 ... 207 B6
Fareham PO15 ... 130 C2
Lymington SO41 ... 197 E3
Ringwood BH24 ... 141 C6
3 Romsey SO51 ... 52 E8
Southampton SO16 ... 79 A3
Close Bellfield The
PO14 ... 153 F7
Close The
Barton on S BH25 ... 210 B8
Broadstone BH18 ... 186 E3
Colden Common SO50 ... 31 D1
Cosham PO6 ... 158 A7
Fordingbridge SP6 ... 94 C7
Hamble-le-R SO31 ... 128 A4
Hedge End SO30 ... 105 B6
Holbury SO45 ... 150 D4
Langrish GU32 ... 39 C3
Portchester PO16 ... 156 C8
Redlynch SP5 ... 47 D7
Ringwood BH24 ... 140 F7
Southampton SO18 ... 104 D7
St Leonards,Avon Castle
BH24 ... 140 D4
St Leonards,St Ives BH24 ... 140 A4
Sway SO41 ... 172 A2
Whitsbury SP6 ... 45 B3
Closewood Rd PO7 ... 111 A2
Clough La BH24 ... 142 F3
Clough's Rd BH24 ... 141 B7
Clovelly Rd Breach PO10 ... 137 D1
Emsworth PO10 ... 160 E8
North Hayling PO11 ... 160 C4
Portsmouth PO4 ... 183 A4
Southampton SO14 ... 103 B6
Clover Cl
Christchurch BH23 ... 208 B8
Gosport PO13 ... 155 B3
Locks Heath SO31 ... 128 E2
Clover Ct
New Milton BH25 ... 195 D4
Waterlooville PO7 ... 135 A6
Clover Dr BH17 ... 186 F1
Clover Nooke SO15 ... 101 C8
Clover Way
Hedge End SO30 ... 105 A6
Romsey SO51 ... 53 C8
Clovers The BH12 ... 204 A8
Clowes Ave BH6 ... 207 B3
Clubhouse La SO32 ... 83 D3
Clump Hill BH21 ... 114 B1
Cluster Ind Est PO4 ... 183 A5
Clyde Ct PO12 ... 180 F6
Clyde Ho 7 SO14 ... 103 C5
Clyde Rd Gosport PO12 ... 180 F6
Poole BH17 ... 187 B2
Clydebank Rd PO2 ... 182 D8
Clydes Dale Ct 5 SO17 ... 79 B1
Clydesdale Rd PO15 ... 129 B7
Clydesdale Way SO40 ... 100 B8
Coach Hill PO14 ... 153 F8
Coach Hill Cl SO53 ... 55 B7
Coach Hill La BH24 ... 142 E5
Coach Ho The SO22 ... 1 B2
Coach House Mews
BH22 ... 165 F7
Coach House Pl BH1 ... 205 A5
Coach Rd SO31 ... 127 E3
Coach Rd The SP5 ... 4 C7
Coach-House Mews
PO4 ... 183 C4
Coachmakers Mews 6
SO51 ... 52 E7
Coachmans Copse SO18 ... 80 A2
Coachmans Halt PO7 ... 86 C2
Coal Park La SO31 ... 128 D8
Coalville Rd SO19 ... 104 B4
Coastguard Cl PO12 ... 180 F2
Coastguard Cotts
Barton on S BH25 ... 209 E8
Exbury SO45 ... 178 A2
Langstone PO9 ... 159 F6

Coastguard Cotts *continued*
Lymington SO41 198 A2
Coastguard Way BH23 207 F5
Coat Gdns SO45 126 A3
Coates Rd SO19 104 D4
Coates Way PO7 134 E5
Cobalt Ct 3 PO13 180 C6
Cobb's Rd BH21 163 E6
Cobbett Cl SO22 215 A3
Cobbett Ct 3 SO18 103 E7
Cobbett Rd SO18 103 E8
Cobbett Way SO30 105 F7
Cobblers Cnr SO41 173 B3
Cobblewood PO10 136 F3
Cobbs La BH15 202 E6
Cobden Ave
Portsmouth PO3 183 A8
Southampton SO18 103 E8
Cobden Cres SO18 103 F8
Cobden Ct SO18 103 E8
Cobden Dell 4 SO18 103 E8
Cobden Gdns SO18 79 E1
Cobden Hts SO18 79 E1
Cobden Marine Ct
SO17 103 D8
Cobden Rise SO18 79 E1
Cobden St PO12 181 B6
Cobham Gr PO15 129 F5
Cobham Rd
Bournemouth BH9 190 A3
Ferndown BH21 165 A8
Cobham Way BH21 163 E1
Coblands Ave SO40 100 D7
Coburg Ho 6 SO14 103 C6
Coburg St
Portsmouth PO1 216 C3
Southampton SO14 103 C6
Cochcrane Cl PO13 180 D6
Cochrane Ho 13 PO1 182 A5
Cockerell Cl
Locks Heath PO15 129 C5
Merley BH21 163 F1
Cockleshell Cl SO31 128 E1
Cockleshell Gdns PO4 183 C3
Cockleshell Sq PO12 181 D6
Cocklydown La SO40 100 E5
Cockshott La GU32 19 C2
Codogan Ct 3 BH1 205 B3
Cogdean Cl BH21 186 E8
Cogdean Way BH21 186 E8
Cogdean Wlk BH21 186 E8
Cogdeane Rd BH17 187 D2
Coghlan Cl PO16 131 B2
Coker Cl SO22 215 C6
Colborne Ave BH21 163 F6
Colborne Cl
Lymington SO41 197 E5
Poole BH15 202 D1
Colbourne Cl BH23 193 A8
Colbourne Ct 7 SO23 215 E8
Colburn Cl SO16 77 D2
Colbury Gr PO9 135 C4
Colchester Ave SO50 56 E4
Colchester Rd PO6 133 E1
Cold Harbour Cl PO17 107 F4
Coldeast Cl SO31 128 E5
Coldeast Hospl SO31 128 F5
Coldeast Way SO31 128 F5
Colden Common Prim Sch
SO21 56 F8
Coldharbour Farm Rd
PO10 136 F1
Coldharbour La SO16,
SO51 77 B8
Coldhill La PO8 111 F7
Cole Hill SO32 85 C5
Colebrook Ave
Portsmouth PO3 183 B7
Southampton SO15 78 C1
Colebrook Pl SO23 215 F5
Colebrook St SO23 215 E5
Colehill Cres BH9 190 B3
Colehill Fst Sch BH21 164 A7
Colehill Gdns SO32 83 A8
Colehill La Colehill BH21 163 F8
Wimborne Minst BH21 164 A8
Coleman Rd BH11 189 A3
Coleman St SO14 103 B4
Colemere Gdns BH23 208 F8
Colemore Rd BH7 206 C7
Colemore Sq PO9 135 F4
Colenso Rd PO16 131 A2
Coleridge Cl SO31 128 D1
Coleridge Ct SO19 104 D5
Coleridge Gdns PO8 111 F4
Coleridge Gn BH23 207 F8
Coleridge Rd PO6 132 F1
Coles Ave BH15 201 E2
Coles Cl SO21 32 A7
Coles Gdns BH15 201 E2
Coles Mede SO21 31 B3
Coles's La SP5 48 E5
Colesbourne Rd PO6 133 B1
Coleson Rd SO18 103 E8
Coleville Ave SO45 151 B3
Colin Cl BH21 186 D5
Colinton Ave PO16 132 D1
Coll of Air Traffic Control
BH23 190 F7
Collard Way 4 GU33 20 F4
College Cl
Hamble-le-R SO31 127 F2
Rowlands Castle PO9 113 C1
College Keep SO14 103 B3
College La 28 PO1 182 A5
College Park Inf Sch
PO2 157 E1
College Pl 9 SO15 103 A6
College Rd
Bournemouth BH5 206 A4
Portsmouth PO1 182 A5
Ringwood BH24 141 A7
Southampton SO19 103 E2
Waterlooville PO7 134 F3
College St
Petersfield GU32 40 F3
Portsmouth PO1 182 A5
Southampton SO14 103 A3
Winchester SO23 215 E5
College Wlk SO23 215 E4
Collett Cl SO30 81 B2
Colley Cl SO23 2 A3
Collier Cl SO17 103 C8
Collingbourne Ave BH6 206 D7
Collingbourne Dr SO53 55 A6
Collington Cres PO6 133 B1
Collingwood Ho PO15 130 D2
Collingwood Rd
Portsmouth PO5 182 D2
West Moors BH21 138 E6
Collingwood Ret Pk
PO14 155 B6
Collingwood Way GU31 41 A5
Collingworth Cl SO31 129 B6
Collingworth Rise SO31 129 B6
Collins Cl SO53 54 F6
Collins La Compton GU31 66 F7
Ringwood BH24 141 A7
Collins Rd PO4 183 A2
Collins' La SO21 30 C7
Collis Rd PO3 183 A8
Collwood Cl BH15 202 C7
Collyers Rd SO42 172 F7
Colman Ct BH1 205 C3
Colne Ave SO16 77 D2
Colne Ct SO16 77 E2
Colonnade Rd 3 BH5 206 A5
Colonnade Road W 2
BH5 206 A5
Colonnade The SO19 103 D3
Colpoy St PO5 216 A2
Colson Cl SO23 215 F6
Colson Rd SO23 215 F6
Colt Cl Rownhams SO16 77 F5
Wimborne Minst BH21 164 B6
Colton Copse SO53 54 F6
Colts Rd SO16 77 E7
Coltsfoot Cl SO30 105 B7
Coltsfoot Dr
Locks Heath SO31 128 E2
3 Waterlooville PO7 134 F5
Coltsfoot Wlk SO51 28 C1
Coltsmead PO6 156 F8
Columbia Rd BH10 189 C2
Columbia Trees La
BH10 189 C1
Columbian Way BH10 189 C2
Columbine Cl BH23 193 B1
Colvedene Cl SO21 31 F1
Colville Cl 4 BH5 206 A5
Colville Dr SO32 83 D8
Colville Rd
5 Bournemouth BH5 206 A5
Cosham PO6 158 A8
Colvin Gdns SO53 55 B8
Colwell Cl SO16 101 D8
Colwell Rd PO6 157 F7
Combe Down SO21 31 E7
Combe Rd GU33 21 B1
Comber Rd 1 BH9 190 A3
Comet Way BH23 208 A6
Comfrey Cl Horndean PO8 88 C1
Romsey SO51 28 C1
Comines Way SO30 104 F7
Comley Ct 11 SO51 52 E7
Comley Hill PO9 136 D5
Comley Rd BH9 189 F2
Commercial Pl PO1 216 B4
Commercial Rd
Bournemouth BH2 204 E3
Poole BH14 203 A4
Portsmouth PO1 216 B4
Southampton SO14 102 F5
Southampton SO15 102 E5
Totton SO40 101 A7
Commercial St SO18 104 B7
Commodore Ct 1 SO14 103 B3
Commodore Pl PO12 181 D7
Common Barn La
Lee-on-t-S PO13 179 F4
Lee-on-t-S PO13 180 A5
Common Cl SO53 55 C8
Common Gdns SO53 55 C8
Common Hill Rd SO51 28 D6
Common La
Southwick PO17 132 E7
Titchfield PO14 153 E8
Common Rd
Chandler's Ford SO53 55 C8
Emsworth PO10 137 F5
Whiteparish SP5 24 B2
Common St PO1 216 C4
Common The SP6 68 D3
Commonside PO10 137 B5
Compass Cl
Gosport PO13 180 D6
Southampton SO19 104 A4
Compass Ct 21 SO17 79 A1
Compass Point
Fareham PO16 155 A8
Hamble-le-R SO31 127 E2
Compass Rd PO6 157 B8
Compton & Up Marden CE
Prim Sch PO18 90 F2
Compton Acres Gdns*
BH13 214 E7
Compton All Saints CE Prim
Sch SO21 31 D8
Compton Ave BH14 203 D1
Compton Beeches
BH24 140 A5
Compton Cl
Eastleigh SO50 55 F6
Havant PO9 135 F3
9 Lee-on-t-S PO13 179 F3
Verwood BH31 114 F6
Winchester SO22 10 B3
Compton Cotts
Compton SO20 6 D7
Minstead SO43 98 C3
Compton Cres BH22 139 B1
Compton Ct
4 Bournemouth BH6 206 F4
4 Havant PO9 135 E2
Poole BH14 203 D3
Compton Dr BH14 203 C2
Compton Gdns BH14 203 C2
Compton Ho 6 SO16 102 B8
Compton Lo 26 BH4 204 C3
Compton Rd
New Milton BH25 195 A2
Portsmouth PO2 157 F3
Totton SO40 101 A8
Winchester SO23 215 D5
Compton St SO21 31 D8
Compton Way SO22 10 B3
Compton Wlk 1 SO14 103 A5
Compton's Dr SO51 50 A6
Conan Rd PO2 157 E4
Concorde Cl PO15 129 D5
Concorde Way PO15 129 D5
Condor Ave PO16 155 F8
Condor Cl
Southampton SO19 103 D3
Three Legged Cross BH21 139 B5
Coney Gn 5 SO23 215 E8
Coneygar La BH22 165 B3
Conference Dr SO31 129 B3
Conference Pl 5 SO41 197 F2
Conford Ct PO9 135 D6
Congleton Cl SO43 98 C3
Conifer Ave BH14 203 B2
Conifer Cl
Christchurch BH23 191 D3
Ferndown BH22 165 F1
Hythe SO45 125 F3
St Leonards BH24 139 D4
Waterlooville PO8 112 A2
Winchester SO22 215 D7
Conifer Cres SO41 197 B3
Conifer Gr PO13 155 C4
Conifer Mews PO16 132 D1
Conifer Rd SO16 78 A4
Conifers 4 BH13 204 B3
Conigar Rd PO10 136 F3
Coniston Ave
Bournemouth BH11 188 F6
4 Portsmouth PO3 183 A8
Coniston Cl BH31 114 E5
Coniston Gdns SO30 105 B5
Coniston Ho 8 PO6 133 B1
Coniston Rd
Eastleigh SO50 55 F2
Ringwood BH24 141 B6
Southampton SO16 101 C8
Coniston Wlk PO14 154 E7
Connaught Cl BH25 194 E1
Connaught Cres BH12 203 E6
Connaught Hall SO18 79 D4
Connaught La PO6 156 F8
Connaught Pl 3 PO9 136 A1
Connaught Rd
Bournemouth BH5 206 B5
Havant PO9 136 A1
Portsmouth PO2 157 D2
Connell Rd BH15 202 C5
Connemara Cres PO15 129 B7
Connigar Cl PO13 180 C7
Conqueror Way PO14 179 D6
Conrad Gdns PO15 129 C8
Conservatory The 6
SO23 215 F5
Consort Cl Eastleigh SO50 56 B5
Poole BH12 203 C5
Consort Ct 5 PO16 131 C1
Consort Ho
Ferndown BH22 165 D6
3 Portsmouth PO1 182 D7
Consort Mews 7 PO17 130 E7
Consort Rd SO50 56 B5
Constable Cl
Ferndown BH22 165 C4
Gosport PO12 181 C2
Southampton SO19 104 C2
Constable's Gate 10
SO23 215 D5
Constantine Ave SO53 55 F6
Constantine Cl SO53 55 F6
Constitution Hill Gdns
BH14 203 A5
Constitution Hill Rd
BH14 203 A5
Consulate Ho 3 SO14 103 B3
Convent Ct PO10 160 E8
Convent La PO10 160 F8
Convent Meadow Mobile
Home Site BH23 207 C5
Conway Cl
Chandler's Ford SO53 55 B3
New Milton BH25 195 B3
Conway Ct 10 BH25 195 B3
Conways Dr BH14 203 A4
Cook Cl BH24 141 C8
Cook Row BH21 163 B4
Cook St SO14 103 A4
Cooke Gdns BH12 203 F6
Cooke Rd BH12 203 F6
Cooks La Awbridge SO51 27 A4
Breach PO10 137 E1
Lockerley SO51 25 E8
Totton SO40 76 C2
Cooley Ho PO13 155 B5
Coolhurst BH14 214 C7
Coombe Ave BH10 189 E3
Coombe Farm Ave
PO16 155 A8
Coombe Gdns BH10 189 E2
Coombe La Awbridge SO51 26 F3
Sway SO41 196 D8
West Meon GU32 37 E4
Coombe Rd
East Meon GU32 63 D8
Gosport PO12 181 B8
Coombe Road Terr GU32 63 D8
Coombedale SO31 129 B2
Coombs Cl PO8 88 C1
Cooper Dean Dr BH8 190 F1
Cooper Dean Rdbt The
BH7,BH8 191 A1
Cooper Gr PO16 156 D6
Cooper Rd Ashurst SO40 100 C3
Portsmouth PO3 183 B8
Cooper's Cl
West End SO18 80 C1
West Wellow SO51 51 B2
Cooper's La SO19 103 D3
Coopers Ct 20 SO14 103 A3
Coopers La BH31 114 F8
Coopers Rise PO8 112 D7
Copeland Dr BH14 203 B2
Copeland Rd SO16 77 D1
Copenhagen Twrs SO19 126 F8
Copinger Cl SO40 100 C6
Copnor Bridge Bsns Ctr
PO3 183 A7
Copnor Inf & Jun Sch
PO3 158 A1
Copnor Rd PO2 157 F3
Copper Beech Cl BH13 204 A4
Copper Beech Dr PO6 158 E8
Copper Beech Gdns
BH10 189 D2
Copper Beeches
Blackfield SO45 150 F2
2 Bournemouth BH2 204 F4
Copper St 5 PO5 216 A1
Coppercourt Leaze 5
BH21 163 C4
Copperfield Ho 17 PO1 182 D7
Copperfield Rd SO16 79 A5
Copperfields SO40 100 B7
Coppers Cl SP6 93 A6
Coppice Ave BH22 165 B7
Coppice Cl
New Milton BH25 195 D4
St Leonards BH24 139 F4
Winchester SO22 215 A7
Coppice Hill SO32 83 D7
Coppice Rd SO40 76 C2
Coppice The
Brockenhurst SO42 145 D1
Christchurch BH23 208 B6
Gosport PO13 155 D2
Netley SO31 127 C5
Waterlooville PO8 112 A6
Coppice View
Bournemouth BH10 189 E3
Whiteley PO15 129 D7
Coppice Way PO15 130 D3
Coppins Gr PO16 156 C6
Copse Ave BH25 195 B2
Copse Cl Liss GU33 21 A4
North Baddesley SO52 53 F4
Otterbourne SO21 31 C4
Petersfield GU31 41 C4
Poole BH14 202 F3
Totton SO40 100 F6
Waterlooville PO7 134 D2
Copse Cvn Pk The SO40 99 D5
Copse La Chilworth SO16 54 F1
Gosport PO13 155 D1
Hamble-le-R SO31 127 F2
North Hayling PO11 185 A8
Copse Rd Burley BH24 142 F2
New Milton BH25 195 B2
Southampton SO18 80 A2
Verwood BH31 114 F6
Copse The
Chandler's Ford SO53 55 E5
Fareham PO15 130 D4
Romsey SO51 28 C1
West Moors BH24 166 C8
Copse View SO19 104 E5
Copse Way BH23 208 E8
Copsewood Ave BH8 190 E1
Copsewood Rd
Ashurst SO40 100 C3
Hythe SO45 125 F3
Southampton SO18 79 E2
Copsey Cl PO6 158 D8
Copsey Gr PO6 158 D8
Copthorne Cotts SO45 151 C3
Copthorne La SO45 151 B3
Copythorn Rd PO2 157 F1
Copythorne CE Inf Sch
SO40 75 B2
Copythorne Cl BH8 190 D2
Copythorne Cres SO40 75 C3
Coracle Cl SO31 128 F1
Coral Cl PO16 156 C6
Coral Ct 6 Gosport PO13 180 C6
2 Poole BH13 204 A4
Coralin Gr PO7 112 B1
Coram Cl 3 SO23 215 E8
Corbar Rd BH23 206 E8
Corbett Rd PO7 134 D5
Corbiere Ave BH12 188 D1
Corbiere Cl SO16 77 E3
Corbin Ave BH22 166 A6
Corbin Ct SO41 197 B2
Corbin Rd SO41 197 B2
Corbould Rd SO45 149 F8
Corby Cres PO3 158 B4
Cordelia Cl SO45 125 D3
Corfe Cl PO14 179 A7
Corfe Halt Cl BH21 162 E1
Corfe Hills Sch BH18 186 F6
Corfe Lodge Rd BH18 186 D3
Corfe Mews BH15 202 D4
Corfe View Rd
Corfe Mullen BH21 186 C5
Poole BH14 203 C3
Corfe Way BH18 186 E3
Corfu BH13 214 E6
Corhampton Cres PO9 135 D4
Corhampton Ho 11 PO1 216 C4
Corhampton La
Droxford SO32 60 D6
Meonstoke SO32 61 A5
Corhampton Rd BH6 206 C6
Coriander Dr SO40 100 C7
Coriander Way PO15 129 D8
Corinna Gdns SO45 125 D3
Corinthian Rd SO53 55 E7
Cork La SO40 101 F2
Cormorant Cl PO16 155 F8
Cormorant Dr SO45 126 C2
Cormorant Wlk PO13 155 B2
Corn Mkt SO51 52 E7
Cornaway La PO16 156 B8
Cornbrook Gr PO7 112 C1
Cornel Rd SO19 103 F5
Cornelia Cres BH12 204 A6
Cornelius Dr PO7 112 B1
Corner Mead PO7 110 F4
Corner The SO22 215 C7
Cornerways Ct 3 BH25 195 B2
Cornes Cl SO22 215 B5
Cornfield PO16 131 B4
Cornfield Cl SO53 54 F6
Cornfield Rd PO13 179 F3
Cornflower Cl SO31 128 E3
Cornflower Dr BH23 208 C8
Cornford Way BH23 208 D8
Cornforth Rd SO40 76 C1
Cornish Gdns BH10 189 D1
Cornmarket Cl 7 BH21 163 B5
Cornpits La SP6 68 C3
Cornwall Cl 4 SO18 80 A2
Cornwall Cres SO18 79 F2
Cornwall Rd
Chandler's Ford SO53 55 C3
Portsmouth PO1 182 E5
Southampton SO18 79 F2
Cornwallis Cres PO1 216 C4
Cornwallis Ho PO1 216 C4
Cornwallis Rd SO41 211 B4
Cornwell Cl
Gosport PO13 180 D7
Portsmouth PO2 157 B2
Coronado Rd PO12 181 B8
Coronation Ave
Bournemouth BH9 189 F2
Upton BH16 201 B7
Coronation Cl BH31 114 F7
Coronation Eventide Homes
4 PO2 157 E4
Coronation Homes
SO18 104 D8
Coronation Par SO31 127 E3
Coronation Rd
South Hayling PO11 185 E1
Swanmore SO32 84 B5
Verwood BH31 114 F7
Waterlooville PO7 134 E8
Coronation Terr SP6 69 A2
Corporation Rd BH1 205 C5
Corpus Christi RC Prim Sch
Bournemouth BH5 206 A5
Portsmouth PO2 157 D2
Corsair Dr SO45 125 D3
Corscombe Cl BH17 187 E2
Cort Way PO15 130 C4
Cortina Way SO30 105 C5
Cortmerron 20 BH4 204 C2
Cortry Cl BH12 204 A
Corvette Ave SO31 128 F
Corylus Ct SO40 76 B
Cosford Cl SO50 57 A
Cosham Park Ave PO6 157 F
Cosham Sta PO6 157 F
Cossack Gn 1 SO14 103 A
Cossack La 23 SO23 215 E
Cossack Lane Ho 26
SO23 215 E
Cosworth Dr SO45 125 D
Cotes Ave BH14 203 A
Cotes Ct BH14 203 A
Cotlands Rd BH8 205 B
Cotsalls SO50 57 D
Cotswold Cl Havant PO9 135 E
Hythe SO45 125 D
Verwood BH31 114 F
Cotswold Ct
6 Christchurch BH23 207 F
5 Southampton SO17 79 A

Cotswold Ho [3] PO6 ....157 C8
Cotswold Rd SO16 ....101 F8
Cotswold Wlk [1] PO14 ..154 F7
Cott La BH24 ....143 B2
Cott St SO32 ....84 D4
Cott Street La SO32 ....91 E1
Cottage Cl PO7 ....110 F3
Cottage Gdns BH12 .....203 C5
Cottage Gr Gosport PO12 .181 B6
Portsmouth PO5 ....216 B2
Cottage Grove Prim Sch
PO5 ....216 B1
Cottage La GU32,GU33 ....19 F3
Cottage Mews SP6 ....69 E2
Cottage View PO1 ....216 C3
Cottagers La SO41 ....196 A4
Cotteridge Ho [1] PO5 ...216 C2
Cottes Way PO14 ....179 B6
Cottesway E PO14 ....179 B6
Cotton Cl
Bishopstoke SO50 ....56 E3
Corfe Mullen BH18 ....186 F5
Cotton Dr PO10 ....136 E3
Cotwell Ave PO8 ....112 B4
Coulmere Rd PO12 ....181 A7
Coulsdon Rd SO30 ....105 C6
Coultas Rd SO53 ....30 E2
Council Hos
Horton Heath BH21 ....114 A1
Lockerley SO51 ....26 B5
Sopley BH23 ....167 F2
Countess Cl BH21 ....187 E8
Countess Gdns BH7 ......205 F8
Country View
Stubbington PO14 ....154 B4
West Wellow SO51 ....50 E3
County Gates La [10] BH4 .204 B4
County Gdns PO14 ....154 C8
Course Park Cres PO14 .129 D2
Court Barn Cl PO13 ......179 F4
Court Barn La PO13 ......179 F4
Court Cl
[3] Christchurch BH23 ....207 E7
Cosham PO6 ....158 B7
Lymington SO41 ....197 D2
Southampton SO18 ....104 A6
Totton SO40 ....76 D2
Court Hill SP6 ....68 E5
Court House Cl SO45 .....126 A4
Court La PO6 ....158 B7
Court Lane Inf Sch PO6 .158 A7
Court Lane Jun Sch
PO6 ....158 A7
Court Mead PO6 ....158 B7
Court Rd
Bournemouth BH9 ....190 B1
Kings Worthy SO23 ....2 C5
Lee-on-t-S PO13 ....179 E4
Southampton SO15 ....102 F7
Court Royal Mews SO15 .102 F8
Court The SO41 ....197 D2
Courtenay Dr BH21 ....163 C6
Courtenay Pl SO41 ....197 E3
Courtenay Rd
Poole BH14 ....203 B4
Winchester SO23 ....2 A3
Courthill Fst Sch BH14 ..203 D4
Courthill Rd BH14 ....203 C4
Courtier Cl SO45 ....125 C3
Courtland Gdns SO16 .....79 B5
Courtlands [3] SO41 ....197 E4
Courtlands Terr PO8 ....112 A4
Courtleigh Manor [6]
BH5 ....205 D4
Courtmount Gr PO6 .....158 A8
Courtnay Cl PO15 ....129 D3
Courtney Pl BH21 ....186 C5
Courtyard Cl SO42 ....145 F1
Courtyard Mews SO42 ...145 F1
Courtyard The
Christchurch BH23 ....207 D6
Finchdean PO8 ....113 B7
[11] Petersfield GU31 ....40 F3
Poole BH12 ....188 C1
[4] Romsey SO51 ....52 E7
Wimborne Minst BH21 ...164 A1
Cousins Gr PO4 ....182 F2
Cove Rd BH10 ....189 C2
Covena Rd BH6 ....206 E6
Coventry Cl BH21 ....186 C4
Coventry Cres BH17 ......187 A1
Coventry Ct
Gosport PO13 ....180 D6
[8] Winchester SO23 ....215 E8
Coventry Rd SO15 ....102 F6
Coverack Way PO6 ....157 B7
Covert Gr PO7 ....135 A5
Covert The SO51 ....53 B6
Covindale Ho [2] PO4 .....183 A3
Covington Rd PO10 ....137 B5
Cow La Cosham PO6 .....157 D7
Portchester PO16 ....156 D7
Cowan Rd PO7 ....134 D5
Coward Rd PO12 ....180 F2
Cowdown La PO18 ....90 D4
Cowdray Cl
Bishopstoke SO50 ....56 F2
Southampton SO16 ....78 B4
Cowdray Ho
Portsmouth PO1 ....216 C3
[25] Winchester SO23 ....215 D6
Cowdray Pk PO14 ....179 A7
Cowdrey Gdns BH8 ....190 F2
Cowdrys Field [2] BH21 ....163 B6
Cowell Dr BH7 ....206 B8
Cowes La SO31 ....152 D8
Cowgrove Rd BH21 ....162 F5
Cowleas Cl SO51 ....26 E5
Cowleas Cotts SO51 ....26 E5
Cowley Cl SO16 ....77 E2
Cowley Rd
Lymington SO41 ....197 C4
Poole BH17 ....202 D8
Cowleys Rd BH23 ....192 C2
Cowper Ave BH25 ....193 A1
Cowper Rd
Bournemouth BH9 ....189 F2
Portsmouth PO1 ....182 E7
Southampton SO19 ....104 D6
Cowpitts La BH24 ....117 D2
Cowplain Com Sch PO8 .111 F2
Cowslip Cl Gosport PO13 .155 C2
Locks Heath SO31 ....128 E2
Cowslip Rd BH18 ....186 F2
Cowslip Way SO51 ....28 C1
Cox Ave BH9 ....190 B4
Cox Cl BH9 ....190 B4
Cox Dale PO14 ....129 C1
Cox Row SO53 ....55 D3
Cox's Dr SO19 ....104 B2
Cox's La SO19 ....103 D3
Coxes Mdw GU32 ....40 E5
Coxford Cl SO16 ....78 A2
Coxford Dro SO16 ....78 A3
Coxford Rd SO16 ....78 C4
Coxs Hill SO21 ....32 A8
Coxstone La [2] BH24 .....141 A6
Coy Pond Rd BH12 ....204 B5
Cozens Cl SO19 ....103 E1
Crab Orchard Way
BH21 ....114 F2
Crabapple Cl SO40 ....100 C7
Crabbe Ct PO5 ....216 B2
Crabbs Way SO40 ....100 B7
Crabbswood La SO41 .....195 E8
Crabden La PO8 ....88 E1
Crableck La SO31 ....128 D5
Crabthorn Farm La
PO14 ....179 B8
Crabton Close Rd BH5 ..205 F4
Crabtree SO16 ....77 F1
Crabtree Cl BH23 ....192 C2
Crabwood Cl SO16 ....77 F2
Crabwood Ct PO9 ....135 D7
Crabwood Dr SO30 ....80 E1
Crabwood Rd SO16 ....77 E2
Cracknore Hard
Marchwood SO40 ....102 A1
Marchwood SO40 ....102 C2
Cracknore Hard La
SO40 ....102 A1
Cracknore Rd SO15 ....102 D5
Craddock Ho
[11] Portsmouth PO1 ....182 A5
[2] Winchester SO23 ....11 C8
Crafts La GU31 ....41 A5
Craig Ho [3] PO5 ....182 D2
Craigmoor Ave BH8 ....190 F1
Craigmoor Cl BH8 ....190 F1
Craigmoor Way BH8 ......190 E2
Craigside Rd BH24 ....139 D4
Craigwell Rd PO7 ....134 E4
Craigwood Dr BH22 ......165 E4
Crampmoor La SO51 ....28 E1
Cranberry Cl SO40 ....101 F1
Cranborne Cres BH12 ...203 E8
Cranborne Ct
[17] Bournemouth,Westbourne
BH4 ....204 C3
Bournemouth,Winton BH9 .205 B8
Cranborne Gdns [8] SO53 ..30 B1
Cranborne Pl BH25 ....194 E3
Cranborne Rd
Alderholt SP6 ....92 A5
Bournemouth BH2 ....204 E2
Cosham PO6 ....134 A1
Wimborne Minst BH21 ...163 C7
Cranborne Wlk PO14 ....154 E7
Cranbourne Cl SO15 ....78 D1
Cranbourne Ct BH17 .....188 A2
Cranbourne Dr SO21 ......31 B3
Cranbourne Pk SO30 ....105 C4
Cranbourne Rd PO12 ....181 C4
Cranbrook Mews BH12 ..203 B6
Cranbrook Rd BH12 ......203 B6
Cranbury Ave SO14 ....103 B6
Cranbury Cl Downton SP5 ..46 F6
Otterbourne SO21 ....31 B3
Cranbury Ct SO19 ....103 F3
Cranbury Gdns SO31 .....104 F1
Cranbury Pl SO14 ....103 A6
Cranbury Rd
Eastleigh SO50 ....56 A1
Eastleigh SO50 ....56 A2
Southampton SO19 ....103 F3
Cranbury Terr [5] SO14 ..103 A6
Cranbury The [4] SO14 ...103 A6
Cranbury Twrs [6] SO14 ..103 A6
Crane Cl Gosport PO13 ..155 B2
Verwood BH31 ....114 E6
Crane Dr BH31 ....114 E6
Crane Way BH21 ....139 B6
Cranemoor Ave BH23 ....193 E2
Cranemoor Cl BH23 ......193 E2
Cranemoor Gdns BH23 ..193 F2
Cranes Mews BH15 ....202 D3
Craneswater Ave PO4 ...182 E2
Craneswater Gate [10]
PO4 ....182 E1
Craneswater Jun Sch
PO4 ....182 F2
Craneswater Mews [5]
PO4 ....182 E2
Craneswater Pk PO4 .....182 E2
Cranfield Ave BH21 ....163 D5
Cranford Gdns SO53 ....55 B8
Cranford Ho [6] SO17 ......79 A2
Cranford Rd GU32 ....40 E2
Cranford Way SO17 ....79 A2
Cranleigh Ave PO1 ....182 E6
Cranleigh Ct BH6 ....206 E5
Cranleigh Gdns BH6 .....206 E5
Cranleigh Ho
Hedge End SO30 ....81 C3
Southampton SO17 ....103 A8
Cranleigh Paddock
SO43 ....121 F6
Cranleigh Rd
Bournemouth BH6 ....206 D5
Hedge End SO30 ....105 C6
Portchester PO16 ....156 A7
Portsmouth PO1 ....182 E6
Cranmer Dr SO16 ....77 C5
Cranmer Rd BH9 ....204 F8
Cranmore SO31 ....127 C7
Cransley Ct
Bournemouth BH4 ....204 C2
[4] Bournemouth BH4 .....204 C2
Crantock Gr BH8 ....190 F2
Cranwell Cl
Bournemouth BH11 ....188 E4
Bransgore BH23 ....169 B1
Cranwell Ct SO16 ....77 F5
Cranworth Rd SO22 ......215 D7
Crasswell St PO1 ....216 C4
Craven Ct PO15 ....130 D3
Craven Rd SO53 ....55 D6
Craven St [9] SO14 ....103 A5
Crawford Cl SO16 ....77 D5
Crawford Dr PO16 ....130 F3
Crawley Ave PO9 ....136 A6
Crawley Hill SO51 ....50 F2
Crawshaw Rd BH14 ....203 B2
Crawte Ave SO45 ....150 D2
Crawters La [6] GU31 ......40 F3
Cray Ho PO12 ....181 D5
Creasey Rd BH11 ....189 A5
Credenhill Rd PO6 ....133 C1
Creech Rd BH12 ....203 C5
Creech View PO7 ....110 E4
Creech Wood Forest Wlk*
PO7 ....110 D3
Creedy Dr BH23 ....207 B5
Creedy Gdns SO18 ....80 A3
Creek End PO10 ....160 F7
Creek Rd Gosport PO12 ..181 D5
South Hayling PO11 ....185 D1
Creekmoor La BH17 ......202 A8
Creighton Rd SO15 ....101 F6
Cremorne Pl [7] GU32 ......40 F4
Cremyll Cl PO14 ....179 C7
Crescent Cl SO22 ....10 B4
Crescent Ct
Barton on S BH25 ....209 F7
[14] Bournemouth BH2 .....204 D2
Crescent Dr BH25 ....209 F7
Crescent Ho SO50 ....56 B3
Crescent Prim Sch The
SO50 ....56 A3
Crescent Rd
Bournemouth BH2 ....204 E3
Fareham PO16 ....131 A1
Gosport PO12 ....181 A2
Locks Heath SO31 ....128 F2
North Baddesley SO52 .....53 F5
Poole BH14 ....203 E4
Verwood BH31 ....115 A6
Wimborne Minst BH21 ...163 C4
Crescent The
Barton on S BH25 ....209 D8
[3] Bournemouth BH1 .....205 E4
Eastleigh SO50 ....56 B4
Exbury SO45 ....177 B5
Marchwood SO40 ....101 E1
Netley SO31 ....127 C6
Romsey SO51 ....53 B8
Southampton SO19 ....104 A2
Southbourne PO10 ....161 D8
Twyford SO21 ....32 A6
Upham SO32 ....58 C2
Waterlooville PO7 ....134 C4
West Moors BH24 ....166 B8
Woodlands SO40 ....99 E3
Crescent Wlk BH22 ....165 E2
Cressey Rd SO51 ....52 F7
Cressy Rd PO2 ....182 D7
Crest Cl PO16 ....131 D1
Crest Rd BH12 ....203 C6
Crest The PO7 ....134 C2
Crest Way SO19 ....104 C4
Cresta Ct [6] PO4 ....182 F2
Cresta Gdns BH22 ....165 E2
Crestland Cl PO8 ....112 B3
Crestwood Coll for Bsns &
Enterprise SO50 ....55 F5
Crete Cotts SO45 ....125 E1
Crete La SO45 ....125 F1
Crete Rd SO45 ....125 F1
Cribb Cl BH17 ....202 E7
Crichel Mount Rd BH14 .214 C7
Crichel Rd BH9 ....205 A8
Crichton Ho SO31 ....127 B6
Cricket Chambers BH1 ..205 A4
Cricket Cl BH23 ....207 F5
Cricket Dr PO8 ....112 A5
Cricklemede SO32 ....83 D7
Cricklewood Cl SO32 ......83 D7
Crigdon Cl SO16 ....101 E8
Crimea Rd BH9 ....204 F7
Cringle Ave BH6 ....207 A4
Crinoline Gdns PO4 ......183 B2
Cripple Gate La SO42 ...175 D5
Crispin Cl
Christchurch BH23 ....208 F8
Crispin Cl continued
Horton Heath SO50 ....81 C6
Locks Heath SO31 ....129 B4
Crispstead La SO23 ....215 D3
Crisspyn Cl PO8 ....112 B6
Criterion Arc [16] BH1 .....204 F3
Crittall Cl SO41 ....172 C2
Croad Ct [1] PO16 ....131 C1
Crockford Cl BH25 ....195 B5
Crockford Rd PO10 ....137 B4
Croft Cl BH21 ....186 D7
Croft Hts SP5 ....24 B3
Croft La PO11 ....159 F1
Croft Rd
Bournemouth BH9 ....189 F2
Bransgore BH23 ....193 B6
Christchurch BH23 ....207 F7
Poole BH12 ....203 B6
Portsmouth PO2 ....157 D1
Ringwood BH24 ....117 C1
Croft The Bishopstone SP5 .22 B8
Chandler's Ford SO53 .....55 C3
Stubbington PO14 ....154 C4
Totton SO40 ....76 C2
[7] Eastleigh SO50 ....56 A2
Croftlands Ave PO14 .....179 C8
Crofton Anne Dale Inf Sch
PO14 ....179 C7
Crofton Anne Dale Jun Sch
PO14 ....179 C7
Crofton Ave PO13 ....179 C5
Crofton Cl
Christchurch BH23 ....191 E1
Southampton SO17 ....79 A1
Waterlooville PO7 ....134 D5
Crofton Ct PO14 ....179 C7
Crofton Hammond Inf Sch
PO14 ....179 C7
Crofton Hammond Jun Sch
PO14 ....179 C7
Crofton La PO14 ....179 B6
Crofton Rd
Portsmouth,Milton PO4 ..183 B5
Portsmouth,North End
PO2 ....157 E2
Crofton Sch PO14 ....179 E7
Crofton Way
Swanmore SO32 ....84 A5
Warsash SO31 ....128 C1
Cromalt Cl SO45 ....125 D2
Cromarty Ave PO4 ....183 B4
Cromarty Cl PO14 ....154 B4
Cromarty Rd SO16 ....77 E5
Crombie Cl PO8 ....111 F4
Cromer Gdns BH12 ....203 F5
Cromer Rd
Bournemouth BH8 ....205 D7
Poole BH12 ....203 F5
Portsmouth PO6 ....133 E1
Southampton SO16 ....77 D1
Cromhall Cl PO14 ....154 C8
Crompton Way PO15 .....129 C5
Cromwell Pl [2] BH5 ....206 B5
Cromwell Rd
Bournemouth BH5 ....206 B5
Poole BH12 ....203 D5
Portsmouth PO4 ....183 B2
Southampton SO15 ....102 F7
[4] Wimborne Minst BH21 .163 D4
Winchester SO22 ....215 C4
Crondall Ave PO9 ....135 E6
Crooked Hays Cl SO40 ...101 F1
Crooked Walk La PO17 ..132 F4
Crookham Cl PO9 ....135 C4
Crookham Rd SO19 ....126 F8
Crookhorn Coll of
Technology PO7 ....134 F4
Crookhorn La
Soberton SO32 ....85 C8
Waterlooville PO7 ....134 E3
Crosby Rd BH4 ....204 C1
Crosfield Cl SO51 ....51 B2
Cross House Ctr SO14 ...103 C3
Cross Keys Pas [6] SO23 .215 E5
Cross La
Bishop's Waltham SO32 ...59 A2
Waterlooville PO8 ....112 A5
Cross Lanes BH24 ....117 C7
Cross Rd Lee-on-t-S PO13 .180 A4
Southampton SO19 ....103 E7
Cross St
[1] Bishop's Waltham
SO32 ....83 C7
Portsmouth PO5 ....216 C2
Portsmouth,Portsea PO1 .182 A6
Winchester SO23 ....215 D6
Cross The Bishopstone SP5 .22 B7
Burley BH24 ....143 A3
East Meon GU32 ....38 D1
Cross Trees SP6 ....45 F1
Cross Way
Christchurch BH23 ....191 D1
Compton SO21 ....31 D5
Havant PO9 ....135 E2
Cross Ways BH23 ....169 D5
Crossbill Cl PO8 ....112 A7
Crossfell Wlk PO14 ....154 E7
Crosshouse Rd SO14 .....103 C3
Crossland Cl PO12 ....181 C4
Crossland Dr PO9 ....136 A3
Crossley Ct [2] SO15 ......102 C6
Crossley Pl [5] SO15 ......102 E6
Crossmead Ave BH25 ....195 A2
Crossway The PO16 ......156 C8
Crossways SO41 ....196 D1
Crossways Cl SP5 ....46 E7
Crossways The
Denmead PO7 ....111 B7
Crossways The continued
Gosport PO12 ....181 B7
Upton BH16 ....201 C7
Crosswell Cl SO19 ....104 C5
Crouch La PO8 ....112 A7
Croucher's Croft SO22 ..215 A7
Crow Arch La BH24 ......141 B6
Crow Arch Lane Ind Est
BH24 ....141 B5
Crow Cotts BH24 ....141 D4
Crow Hill Top BH24 ......142 A4
Crow La BH24 ....141 C5
Crowder Terr SO22 ....215 D5
Crowders Gn SO21 ....56 F8
Crowe Hill Ct [2] BH15 ...202 E4
Crowlin Ho [1] PO17 ......130 E8
Crown Cl Poole BH12 ....203 C5
Waterlooville PO7 ....134 E3
Crown Ct
Portsmouth PO1 ....216 C4
[4] Wimborne Minst BH21 .163 B5
Crown Mead BH21 ....163 C4
Crown Mews [1] PO12 ...181 D5
Crown St
Portsmouth PO1 ....216 C4
Southampton SO15 ....102 B8
Crows Nest La SO32 ....81 F1
Crowsbury Cl PO10 ......136 E3
Crowsport SO31 ....128 A3
Crowther Cl SO19 ....104 C4
Croxton Rd PO1 ....182 B3
Croydon Cl SO16 ....78 A4
Crummock Rd SO53 ....55 A8
Crundles GU31 ....41 B3
Crusader Ct
[3] Bournemouth BH4 .....204 B4
[4] Gosport PO12 ....181 C8
Crusader Rd
Bournemouth BH11 ......188 D4
Hedge End SO30 ....105 D6
Crusaders Way SO53 .....54 F6
Cruse Cl SO41 ....172 B2
Cruxton Farm Ctyd
BH21 ....163 D2
Crystal Way PO7 ....135 B8
Cucklington Gdns BH9 ..190 B4
Cuckmere La SO16 ....101 D8
Cuckoo Bushes La SO53 ..55 C8
Cuckoo Hill Rly* SP6 ......94 C1
Cuckoo Hill Way BH23 ..169 C1
Cuckoo La
[17] Southampton SO14 ....102 F3
Stubbington PO14 ....179 B8
Cuckoo Rd BH12 ....203 A8
Cudnell Ave BH11 ....189 A6
Cudworth Mead SO30 .....81 D1
Cuffnells Cl BH24 ....117 B8
Cul-De-Sac BH25 ....209 C8
Culford Ave SO40 ....100 F6
Culford Cl BH8 ....190 F2
Culford Ct [1] BH8 ....205 A5
Culford Way SO40 ....100 F6
Cull Cl BH12 ....204 C8
Cull La BH25 ....195 B5
Culliford Cres BH17 ......187 E2
Culloden Cl PO15 ....130 E2
Culloden Rd PO14 ....154 F6
Cullwood La BH25 ....195 B5
Cully Terr PO13 ....155 C4
Culver SO31 ....127 C7
Culver Cl SO16 ....77 D2
Culver Dr PO11 ....185 C1
Culver Mews SO23 ....215 E5
Culver Rd
New Milton BH25 ....194 F2
[2] Portsmouth PO4 ....183 A2
Winchester SO23 ....215 D4
Culverhayes Cl [5] BH21 .163 B6
Culverhayes Pl BH21 .....163 B6
Culverhayes Rd BH21 ...163 B6
Culverin Sq PO3 ....158 A4
Culverlands Bsns Pk
SO32 ....107 E6
Culverlands Cl SO32 .....107 E7
Culverley Cl SO42 ....145 F1
Culverwell Gdns [6]
SO23 ....215 D5
Culvery Gdns SO18 ....80 B2
Cumber Rd SO31 ....128 E3
Cumberland Ave
Chandler's Ford SO53 .....55 E6
Emsworth PO10 ....136 F4
Cumberland Bsns Ctr
PO1 ....216 C3
Cumberland Cl SO53 ......55 E6
Cumberland Ho PO1 .....182 A6
Cumberland House Natural
History Mus* PO4 ....182 F1
Cumberland Inf Sch
PO4 ....183 A3
Cumberland Pl SO15 ....102 F5
Cumberland Rd PO5 .....216 D3
Cumberland St
Portsmouth PO1 ....182 A6
Southampton SO14 ....103 B4
Cumberland Way SO45 ..125 D3
Cumbrian Way SO16 ....101 F8
Cummins Gn SO31 ....105 A1
Cumnor Rd BH1 ....205 A3
Cunard Ave SO15 ....102 C8
Cunard Rd SO14 ....103 A2
Cundell Way SO23 ....2 B8
Cunningham Ave SO32 ...83 A8
Cunningham Cl
Bournemouth BH11 ......189 A3

Cunningham Cl *continued*
Christchurch BH23 ....208 A6
Portsmouth PO2 ....157 D4
Ringwood BH24 ....141 C8
Cunningham Cres
Bournemouth BH11 ....189 B3
Southampton SO19 ....104 B4
Cunningham Ct
New Milton BH25 ....194 F3
16 Portsmouth PO5 ....182 D2
Cunningham Dr
Gosport PO13 ....155 D4
Locks Heath SO31 ....129 B4
Cunningham Gdns SO31 .127 F8
Cunningham Ho SO32 ...83 B8
Cunningham Pl BH11 ...189 A3
Cunningham Rd
Horndean PO8 ....112 C7
Waterlooville PO7 ....134 D5
Cupernham Cl SO51 ....28 A1
Cupernham Inf Sch SO51 .28 B1
Cupernham Jun Sch
SO51 ....28 B1
Cupernham La SO51 ....28 A2
Curdridge Cl 2 PO9 ....136 A5
Curdridge La SO32 ....83 C3
Curdridge Prim Sch
SO32 ....106 D8
Curlew Cl
Emsworth PO10 ....160 E7
Ferndown BH22 ....165 B7
Hythe SO45 ....126 B2
Southampton SO16 ....78 B5
Curlew Dr Hythe SO45 ...126 B2
Portchester PO16 ....155 F8
Curlew Gdns PO8 ....111 F4
Curlew Path 3 PO4 ....183 B5
Curlew Rd
Bournemouth BH8 ....190 D2
Christchurch BH23 ....208 A6
Curlew Sq SO50 ....55 E2
Curlew Wlk
Gosport PO13 ....155 A3
Hythe SO45 ....126 B2
Curlews The BH31 ....115 A5
Curlieu Rd BH15 ....202 E6
Curtis Mead PO2 ....157 F4
Curtis Rd BH12 ....203 C5
Curtiss Gdns PO12 ....180 F4
Curve The Gosport PO13 ..155 B2
Horndean PO8 ....111 F6
Curzon Ct
46 Bournemouth BH4 ....204 C3
Southampton SO16 ....78 D4
Curzon Howe Rd PO1 ...182 A5
Curzon Pl SO41 ....197 D2
Curzon Rd
Bournemouth BH1 ....205 D6
Poole BH14 ....203 A3
Waterlooville PO7 ....134 E7
Curzon Way BH23 ....208 D8
Custards Rd SO43 ....121 F6
Custards The SO43 ....122 A6
Cut Throat La
Droxford SO32 ....61 B2
Swanmore SO32 ....84 C6
Cutbush La
Southampton SO18 ....104 B8
West End SO18 ....80 A3
Cuthbert Rd PO1 ....182 F6
Cuthburga Rd BH21 ....163 C4
Cuthbury Cl BH21 ....163 A4
Cuthbury Gdns BH21 ....163 A5
Cutler Cl
New Milton BH25 ....195 C3
Poole BH12 ....204 C7
Cutlers La PO14 ....179 C8
Cutlers Pl BH21 ....164 A5
Cutter Ave SO31 ....128 E1
Cutts Arch SO32 ....85 B7
Cygnet Ct PO16 ....155 F8
Cygnet Ho PO12 ....181 B8
Cygnet Rd PO6 ....158 F7
Cygnus Gdns SO45 ....125 C3
Cynthia Cl BH12 ....203 B7
Cynthia Ho BH12 ....203 B7
Cynthia Rd BH12 ....203 B7
Cypress Ave SO19 ....103 F5
Cypress Cres PO8 ....112 A5
Cypress Gdns
Botley SO30 ....106 A7
Totton SO40 ....100 C7
Cypress Gr SO41 ....211 D8
Cyprus Rd
Portsmouth PO2 ....182 E8
Titchfield PO14 ....129 C1
Cyril Rd BH8 ....205 C6

D

D Ave SO45 ....150 E5
D-Day Mus* PO5 ....182 C1
Dacombe Cl BH16 ....201 C7
Dacombe Dr BH16 ....201 C7
Dacres Wlk 3 SO41 ....211 D5
Daffodil Rd SO16 ....79 C4
Daggons Rd SP6 ....92 D6
Dagmar Mews 24 PO5 ...182 C2
Dahlia Ct BH15 ....202 E6
Dahlia Rd SO16 ....79 A4
Daintree Cl SO19 ....104 D3
Dairy Cl
Christchurch BH23 ....207 D7
Corfe Mullen BH21 ....186 B4
Dairy Cl *continued*
Redlynch SP5 ....47 D6
Dairy La SO16 ....77 B5
Dairymoor PO17 ....108 A4
Daisy Cl BH15 ....202 D6
Daisy La Gosport PO12 ...181 B5
Locks Heath SO31 ....129 C3
Daisy Mead PO7 ....135 A7
Daisy Rd SO16 ....79 B4
Dakota Cl BH23 ....208 B7
Dale Cl Littleton SO22 ....1 A5
Poole BH15 ....202 F6
Dale Dr PO13 ....155 B5
Dale Gn SO53 ....55 B8
Dale Park Ho 4 PO1 ....216 B3
Dale Rd Hythe SO45 ....125 F3
Poole BH15 ....202 F6
Southampton SO16 ....78 C2
Stubbington PO14 ....179 D8
Dale The PO7 ....134 D2
Dale Valley Cl SO16 ....78 C2
Dale Valley Gdns SO16 ...78 C2
Dale Valley Rd
Poole BH15 ....202 F7
Southampton SO16 ....78 C3
Dales Cl BH21 ....164 C6
Dales Dr BH21 ....164 B5
Dales La BH23 ....190 E7
Dales Way SO40 ....100 B8
Dalewood Ave BH11 .....188 E5
Dalewood Rd PO15 .....130 D1
Dalkeith Arc BH1 ....204 F3
Dalkeith Rd
Corfe Mullen BH21 ....186 D4
Poole BH13 ....204 A1
Dalley Way 6 GU33 ....20 F4
Dalling Rd BH12 ....204 A5
Dallington Cl PO14 .....179 C6
Dalmally Gdns SO18 .....103 F8
Dalmeny Rd BH6 ....207 A3
Dalzell 19 SO23 ....215 E8
Damask Gdns PO7 ....112 B1
Dame Elizabeth Kelly Ct 3
PO2 ....157 E4
Damen Cl SO30 ....105 A5
Damerham Rd BH8 .....190 D3
Damerham Trout Lakes*
SP6 ....68 D2
Dampier Cl PO13 ....180 C7
Damson Cres SO50 ....57 B1
Damson Hill SO32 ....60 B1
Danbury Ct PO10 ....137 A2
Dances Way PO11 ....184 E4
Dandelion Cl PO13 ....155 B2
Dando Rd PO7 ....111 A4
Dandy's Ford La SO51 ....25 F1
Dane Cl SO45 ....150 F1
Dane Ct BH14 ....203 A4
Dane Dr BH22 ....165 E3
Dane Rd SO41 ....211 A6
Danebury Cl PO9 ....135 E6
Danebury Gdns SO53 .....55 A4
Danebury Way SO16 ....77 D3
Danecourt Cl BH14 ....202 F4
Danecourt Rd BH14 ....202 F4
Danecrest Rd SO41 ....195 F3
Danehurst SO41 ....211 A6
Danehurst New Rd
SO41 ....195 C8
Danehurst Pl SO31 ....129 A2
Danemark Ct 5 SO23 ...215 E6
Danes Cl BH25 ....210 A7
Danes Rd Awbridge SO51 ..26 D3
Portchester PO16 ....132 B1
4 Winchester SO23 ....215 E7
Danesbrook La PO7 ....135 A7
Danesbury Ave BH6 ....206 F4
Danesbury Mdws BH25 ..195 C5
Danestead Ho 8 BH25 ..195 A3
Danestream Cl SO41 .....211 D4
Danestream Ct SO41 .....211 E4
Daneswood Rd BH25 .....195 C3
Daniel Gdns 2 BH15 ....202 C1
Daniell's Cl SO41 ....197 E3
Daniell's Wlk SO41 .....197 E3
Daniels Wlk SO40 ....76 B1
Dansie Cl BH14 ....203 B4
Dapple Pl SO40 ....102 A1
Darby's Cl BH15 ....202 D6
Darby's Cnr BH17 ....187 C2
Darby's La BH15 ....202 D6
Darby's La N BH17 ....202 D8
Dark La Blackfield SO45 ...150 F1
Cheriton SO24 ....14 D5
Hinton BH23 ....194 A4
Darley Rd BH22 ....165 C3
Darlington Gdns SO15 ....78 D1
Darlington Rd PO4 ....182 E3
Darnan Ho 6 SO14 ....103 A7
Darracott Rd BH5 ....206 B5
Darren Cl PO14 ....154 D4
Darren Ct 9 PO16 ....131 B2
Darrian Ct BH16 ....201 B7
Dart Ho SO18 ....103 F8
Dart Rd SO18 ....80 B3
Dartington Rd SO50 ....56 D5
Dartmouth Bldgs 5
PO14 ....155 A6
Dartmouth Cl 6 PO12 ..181 C8
Dartmouth Ct 5 PO12 ..181 C8
Dartmouth Mews PO5 ....216 A1
Dartmouth Rd PO3 ....158 A2
Darwin Ave BH23 ....191 E1
Darwin Cl PO13 ....179 F4
Darwin Ct 4 BH13 ....204 A4
Darwin Ho PO1 ....216 C4
Darwin Rd Eastleigh SO50 ..56 B4
Southampton SO15 ....102 E7
Darwin Way PO13 ....180 D6
Daubney Gdns PO9 ....135 C6
Daulston Rd PO1 ....182 F7
Davenport Cl
Gosport PO13 ....180 C6
Upton BH16 ....201 C7
Daventry La PO3 ....158 C4
David Cowan Ho 23
SO23 ....215 D6
David Ct SO51 ....53 A6
David Hart Bsns Ctr SP5 ..46 E8
David Newberry Dr
PO13 ....180 A6
David Way BH15 ....201 D2
David's La BH24 ....140 D5
Davidia Ct PO7 ....135 A6
Davidson Cl SO45 ....126 B4
Davidson Ct 42 PO1 .....182 A5
Davis Cl PO13 ....180 C8
Davis Ct BH12 ....203 E5
Davis Field BH25 ....194 F2
Davis Rd BH12 ....203 E5
Davis Way PO14 ....155 A6
Daw La PO11 ....184 F8
Dawkins Bsns Ctr BH15 .201 D3
Dawkins Rd BH15 ....201 D3
Dawkins Way BH25 ....195 A2
Dawlish Ave SO15 ....102 D8
Dawn Cl BH10 ....189 C2
Dawn Gdns SO22 ....215 A4
Dawnay Cl SO16 ....79 D5
Daws Ave BH11 ....189 B2
Dawson Rd SO19 ....104 C2
Day La PO8 ....111 E7
Day's Ct BH21 ....163 D4
Daylesford Cl BH14 .....203 A2
Dayrell Cl SO40 ....76 B1
Dayshes Cl PO13 ....155 B3
Dayslondon Rd PO7 .....134 D5
Daytona BH14 ....214 C7
De Courtenai Cl BH11 ...188 E5
De Grouchy La SO17 ....79 A1
De Haviland Cl BH21 ....163 F2
De Havilland Ho BH23 ..208 A6
De Havilland Way BH23 .208 A6
De La Warr Rd SO41 .....211 C4
De Lisle Cl PO2 ....157 F4
De Lisle Rd BH3 ....204 F7
De Lunn Bldgs 8 SO23 ..215 E6
De Mauley Ct BH13 ....214 E8
De Mauley Rd BH13 ....214 E8
De Montfort Rd BH21 ...163 D1
De Mowbray Way SO41 .197 D2
De Port Hts SO32 ....61 C6
De Redvers Rd BH14 .....203 C2
Deacon Cl SO19 ....104 A5
Deacon Cres SO19 ....104 A6
Deacon Gdns BH11 ....189 A5
Deacon Rd
Bournemouth BH11 ....189 A5
Locks Heath SO31 ....129 B2
Southampton SO19 ....104 A5
Deacon Trad Est SO50 ....56 C2
Deadman Hill SP6 ....71 D5
Deakin Ct SO53 ....55 C5
Deal Cl PO14 ....154 C4
Deal Rd PO6 ....133 E1
Dean Cl Hamworthy BH15 .201 E3
Winchester SO22 ....215 A8
Dean Court (Bournemouth
FC) BH7 ....205 F6
Dean Ct Hedge End SO30 .105 C7
Southampton SO18 ....104 A8
3 Southampton,Bitterne Manor
SO18 ....103 E8
Dean Farm PO17 ....131 A5
Dean La
Bishop's Waltham SO32 .....59 E3
Finchdean PO8,PO9 ....113 D5
Whiteparish SP5 ....24 B4
Winchester SO22 ....1 B2
Dean Park Cres BH1 .....204 F3
Dean Park Rd BH1 ....204 F4
Dean Pl SO53 ....55 C6
Dean Rd Cosham PO6 .....157 F8
Fair Oak SO50 ....57 C1
Southampton SO18 ....104 A7
West Dean SP5 ....3 B2
West Tytherley SP5 ....3 E5
Dean St PO1 ....182 A5
Dean Sta SP5 ....3 D3
Dean Swift Cres BH14 ..214 C8
Dean Villas PO17 ....130 E7
Dean's Rd 6 BH5 ....206 B5
Deane Ct 22 PO9 ....136 B5
Deane Down Dro SO22 .....1 B4
Deane Gdns 5 PO13 .....179 F3
Deane's Park Rd PO16 ..131 D1
Deanery The SO53 ....55 B8
Deanfield Cl SO31 ....127 F3
Deanfields Ct SO18 .....104 B8
Deans Court La BH21 ...163 C4
Deans Ct SO41 ....211 D5
Deans Dell GU32 ....18 E1
Deans Gate PO14 ....179 C6
Deans Gr BH21 ....163 D7
Deans The BH1 ....204 F4
Deanscroft Rd BH10 .....189 E4
Deansfield Cl SO51 ....53 B8
Deansleigh Rd BH7 ....191 B1
Deanswood Dr PO7 ....111 E1
Dear Hay La BH15 ....202 C2
Dearing Cl SO43 ....121 F4
Debney Lodge PO7 ....134 F7
Decies Rd BH14 ....203 B5
Dee Cl SO53 ....55 A5
Dee Way BH15 ....202 B1
Deep Dell PO8 ....112 B5
Deepdene SO18 ....103 E8
Deepdene La BH11 ....188 E5
Deeping Cl SO19 ....103 F1
Deeping Gate PO7 ....135 A7
Deer Leap PO15 ....130 D5
Deer Park Cl BH25 ....194 F4
Deer Park Farm Ind Est
SO50 ....57 E1
Deer Wlk SO30 ....105 D8
Deerhurst Cl SO40 ....100 D6
Deerhurst Cres PO6 ....133 A1
Deerhurst Ho 3 PO6 ....133 A1
Deerleap Cl SO45 ....126 A3
Deerleap La SO40 ....100 D2
Deerleap Way
Hythe SO45 ....126 A3
New Milton BH25 ....195 B5
Defender Rd SO19 ....103 D3
Defender Wlk SO19 .....103 D3
Defoe Cl PO15 ....129 C8
Delamere Gdns BH10 ....189 E3
Delamere Rd PO4 ....182 F3
Delaval Ho 2 PO1 ....182 B5
Delft Cl SO31 ....128 F3
Delft Gdns PO8 ....111 D2
Delft Mews BH23 ....207 D6
Delhi Cl BH14 ....203 D3
Delhi Rd BH9 ....189 F2
Delilah Rd BH15 ....201 D2
Delius Ave SO19 ....104 D3
Delius Wlk PO7 ....134 E5
Delkeith Ct BH22 ....165 D4
Dell Cl Broadstone BH18 ..186 E4
Cosham PO7 ....134 B2
Fair Oak SO50 ....57 C1
Dell Cotts SO24 ....15 F1
Dell Piece E PO8 ....112 D5
Dell Piece W PO8 ....112 C5
Dell Quay Cl PO13 ....155 B2
Dell Rd Southampton SO18 ..79 F2
Winchester SO23 ....11 C6
Dell The
Barton on S BH23 ....209 C8
Havant PO9 ....135 B2
Portchester PO16 ....131 D1
Southampton SO15 ....102 E6
Dellcrest Path PO6 .....134 B2
Dellfield GU32 ....18 E2
Dellfield Cl 11 PO6 .....133 A1
Delme Ct 4 PO16 ....131 A1
Delme Dr PO16 ....131 D2
Delme Sq 7 PO16 ....131 B1
Delph Rd BH21 ....187 D8
Delph Woods Woodland
Trail* BH18,BH21 ....187 C7
Delphi Way PO7 ....134 F2
Delta Bsns Pk PO16 .....155 B7
Delta Cl BH23 ....208 A7
Dempsey Cl SO19 ....104 B4
Denbigh Cl Eastleigh SO50 .55 F5
Totton SO40 ....100 D5
Denbigh Dr PO16 ....130 F2
Denbigh Gdns SO16 ....78 F4
Denby Rd BH15 ....202 E4
Dene Cl Chilworth SO16 ....78 F7
Ringwood BH24 ....117 C1
Sarisbury SO31 ....128 E4
Dene Hollow PO6 ....158 D8
Dene Rd SO40 ....100 C2
Dene The BH13 ....204 A2
Dene Way SO40 ....100 C3
Dene Wlk BH22 ....165 E1
Denecote Lodge BH13 ..214 H8
Deneside Copse SO41 ..197 B1
Deneve Ave BH17 ....187 C1
Denewood Copse BH22 .138 D3
Denewood Rd
Bournemouth BH4 ....204 B3
West Moors BH22 ....138 D4
Denewulf Cl 2 SO32 .....83 C8
Denham Cl Poole BH17 ....187 E3
Stubbington PO14 ....179 B7
Winchester SO23 ....215 D8
Denham Dr BH23 ....193 F1
Denham Fields SO50 .....57 B3
Denham Gdns SO31 ....127 B5
Denham's Cnr SO32 ....81 D5
Denhill Cl PO11 ....184 E5
Denholm Cl BH24 ....117 D1
Denison Rd BH17 ....187 C1
Denmark La BH15 ....202 D3
Denmark Rd
Bournemouth BH9 ....189 F1
Poole BH15 ....202 D3
Denmark Terr BH1 ....205 E6
Denmead BH25 ....195 D4
Denmead Ho PO1 ....216 C4
Denmead Inf Sch PO7 ....111 A4
Denmead Jun Sch PO7 .111 A4
Denmead Pk PO7 ....111 A4
Denmead Rd
Bournemouth BH6 ....206 D7
Southampton SO18 ....104 C8
Dennet Ho SO23 ....2 D1
Denning Mews PO5 ....216 B3
Dennis Rd BH21 ....186 D5
Dennis Way GU33 ....21 A3
Dennison Ct 18 SO15 ....102 B8
Dennistoun Ave BH23 ....207 F7
Denny Cl SO45 ....151 B3
Densome Cnr SP6 ....71 A6
Denville Ave PO16 ....156 D6
Denville Cl PO6 ....158 F8
Denvilles Cl PO9 ....136 B2
Denzil Ave Netley SO31 ..127 C6
Southampton SO14 ....103 B6
Depden Gdns SO45 ....125 D1
Depedene Cl SO45 ....150 B4
Derby Ct 12 PO13 ....180 C6
Derby Ho SO50 ....56 A1
Derby Rd
Bournemouth BH1 ....205 C4
Eastleigh SO50 ....55 F2
Portsmouth PO2 ....157 D1
Southampton SO14 ....103 B6
Dereham Way BH12 ....203 F6
Deridene Ct SO40 ....100 C6
Derlyn Rd PO16 ....131 A1
Derritt La BH23 ....192 D8
Derrybrian Gdns BH25 ..195 A2
Dersingham Cl PO6 .....133 E1
Derwent Cl
Bournemouth BH9 ....190 A2
Ferndown BH22 ....166 A6
Horndean PO8 ....88 C2
Stubbington PO14 ....154 D4
West End SO18 ....80 B1
Derwent Dr SO40 ....100 B8
Derwent Rd
Lee-on-t-S PO13 ....179 F3
New Milton BH25 ....195 B5
Southampton SO16 ....77 E1
Derwentwater Rd BH21 .163 C2
Desborough Cl 6 PO6 ..133 A1
Desborough Rd SO50 ....56 A2
Devenish Rd SO22 ....1 D3
Deverel Cl BH23 ....207 A8
Deverell Pl PO7 ....134 C3
Devine Gdns SO50 ....56 E2
Devon Cl SO53 ....55 C3
Devon Dr SO53 ....55 C3
Devon Mews 6 SO15 ...102 E5
Devon Rd
Christchurch BH23 ....206 E8
Poole BH15 ....202 E5
Portsmouth PO3 ....158 A3
Devonshire Ave PO4 ....183 A3
Devonshire Gdns
Bursledon SO31 ....105 A2
Hythe SO45 ....150 A8
Devonshire Inf Sch PO4 .182 F4
Devonshire Mans 10
SO15 ....102 F6
Devonshire Rd SO15 ....102 F6
Devonshire Sq PO4 ....182 F4
Devonshire Way PO14 ...154 C8
Dew La SO50 ....55 F3
Dewar Cl PO15 ....129 C5
Deweys La BH24 ....140 F7
Dewlands Pk BH31 ....114 D6
Dewlands Rd BH31 ....114 D6
Dewlands Way BH31 .....114 E6
Dewlish Cl BH17 ....188 A2
Dewsbury Ct 3 SO18 .....80 A2
Dhekelia Ct PO1 ....216 C4
Dial Cl BH23 ....169 D2
Diamond Cl SP6 ....93 E8
Diamond Ct
Fordingbridge SP6 ....93 E8
2 Waterlooville PO7 .....134 E8
Diamond St 2 PO5 ....216 A1
Diana Cl Emsworth PO10 ..136 E4
Ferndown BH22 ....165 D6
Gosport PO12 ....180 E4
Diana Ct 7 BH23 ....209 A7
Diana Way BH21 ....186 E7
Dibben Wlk SO51 ....28 C1
Dibble Dr SO52 ....53 F3
Dibden Cl
Bournemouth BH8 ....190 D3
Havant PO9 ....135 C4
Dibden Lodge Cl SO45 ..125 F5
Dibles Pk SO31 ....128 E1
Dibles Rd
Locks Heath SO31 ....128 D1
Locks Heath SO31 ....128 E1
Dickens Cl PO2 ....182 D7
Dickens Dell SO40 ....100 B7
Dickens Dr PO15 ....106 C1
Dickens Ho PO4 ....183 B4
Dickens Rd BH6 ....206 D7
Dickins La GU31 ....41 A5
Dickinson Rd PO4 ....182 F5
Dickson Pk PO17 ....108 A4
Didcot Rd Poole BH17 ...202 D7
Southampton SO15 ....78 C1
Dieppe Cres PO2 ....157 E4
Dieppe Gdns PO12 ....180 F4
Dight Rd PO12 ....181 C3
Diligence Cl SO31 ....105 A1
Dillington Ho 4 PO7 ....134 E8
Dilly La BH25 ....210 A7
Dimond Cl SO18 ....79 E1
Dimond Hill SO18 ....79 E1
Dimond Rd SO18 ....79 E2
Dingle Rd BH5 ....206 B4
Dingle Way SO31 ....129 A4
Dingley Rd BH15 ....202 D6
Dinham Ct BH25 ....195 D4
Dinham Rd BH25 ....195 D4
Diprose Rd BH21 ....186 E7
Disa Ho SO15 ....102 E6
Discovery Cl PO14 ....154 C5
Discovery Court Bsns Ctr
BH12 ....188 E2
Disraeli Rd BH23 ....207 D6
Ditcham Cres PO9 ....135 E4
Ditcham Park Sch GU31 ..89 F8
Ditchbury SO41 ....197 D6
Ditton Cl PO14 ....154 C4
Ditton Cotts SO42 ....148 F
Dock La SO42 ....149 A
Dock Mill Cotts 18 PO5 ..182 D
Dock Rd PO12 ....181 C
Dockenfield Cl PO9 ....135 C
Doctor's Hill SO51 ....26 A

Eastbourne Ave
Gosport PO12 180 F8
Southampton SO15 102 D8
Eastbourne Rd PO3 183 A8
Eastbrook Cl
Gosport PO12 180 F8
Locks Heath SO31 129 A5
Eastbrook Row BH21 163 C4
Eastbury Ct BH23 207 F4
Eastchurch Cl SO16 77 F4
Eastcliff Cl PO13 179 E4
Eastcot Cl SO45 150 C3
Eastcott Cl BH7 206 A8
Eastcroft Rd PO12 180 F5
Easter Rd BH9 190 A2
Eastern Ave PO4 183 B6
Eastern Ind Ctr PO6 158 C6
Eastern Par
Fareham PO16 155 B7
Portsmouth PO4 182 F2
Eastern Rd Fawley SO45 151 E2
Havant PO9 136 A2
Lymington SO41 197 D4
Portsmouth,Anchorage Park PO6 158 C4
Portsmouth,Baffins PO3 183 C7
Portsmouth,Whale Island PO2 157 B1
West End SO30 80 D1
Eastern Terr 3 PO4 183 A2
Eastern Villas Rd PO4 182 D1
Eastern Way
Fareham PO16 131 C1
Milford on S SO41 211 F4
Eastfield Ave PO14 154 F7
Eastfield Ct BH24 141 C7
Eastfield La
Ringwood,Hightown BH24 141 C7
Ringwood,Poulner BH24 141 C8
Eastfield Rd
Portsmouth,Eastney PO4 183 A3
Portsmouth,Ports Down PO6 133 C2
Southampton SO17 103 C8
Eastfields PO5 216 C1
Eastgate St
Southampton SO14 103 A3
Winchester SO23 215 F5
Eastlake Ave BH12 203 C6
Eastlake Cl GU31 41 C3
Eastlake Hts PO4 183 D3
Eastlands BH25 195 B1
Eastleigh Coll SO50 56 A1
Eastleigh Coll of F Ed SO50 56 A2
Eastleigh Lakeside Rly* SO50 79 F8
Eastleigh Rd
Fair Oak SO50 57 C1
Havant PO9 136 D4
Eastleigh Sta SO50 56 B3
Eastleigh Town Mus* SO50 56 A2
Eastman Cl SP5 47 A6
Eastmeare Ct SO40 100 C6
Eastney Farm Rd PO4 183 C3
Eastney Rd PO4 183 B3
Eastney St 6 PO4 183 A2
Eastoke Ave PO11 185 E2
Eastoke Corner Sta* PO11 185 B2
Easton La
Easton Down SO21 2 E3
Winchester SO23 2 C1
Easton Lane Bsns Ctr SO23 215 F6
Eastover Ct PO9 135 D6
Eastville Rd SO50 57 C1
Eastways SO32 83 C7
Eastwood SO51 25 C1
Eastwood Ave BH22 165 E6
Eastwood Cl PO11 185 B5
Eastwood Rd 5 PO2 157 E4
Eastworth Rd BH31 114 E7
Eaton Rd BH13 204 A2
Ebblake Cl BH31 115 C3
Ebblake Ent Pk BH31 115 C5
Ebblake Ind Est BH31 115 C4
Ebden Rd SO23 215 F6
Ebenezer La BH24 140 F7
Ebor Gr PO3 183 C7
Ebor Cl BH22 165 E2
Ebor Rd BH12 203 D6
Ebury Ct 7 BH4 204 C3
Eccles Rd BH15 202 A2
Ecton La PO3 158 C3
Eddystone Rd SO40 76 D2
Edelvale Rd SO18 80 B1
Eden Ct
9 Bournemouth BH1 205 B3
11 Bournemouth,Westbourne BH4 204 C2
Eden Gr BH21 163 D3
Eden Grange 5 SO14 103 A7
Eden Rd SO18 80 B2
Eden Rise PO16 155 B8
Eden St PO1 216 B4
Eden Terr 1 PO2 157 D2
Eden Wlk SO53 55 A5
Edenbridge Rd PO4 183 C5
Edenbridge Way SO31 128 F6
Edenhurst 12 BH4 204 C3
Edgar Cres PO16 156 D6
Edgar Rd SO23 215 D4
Edgar Villas SO23 215 D4
Edgarton Rd BH17 187 D3
Edgbaston Ho PO5 216 B2
Edgecombe Cres PO13 180 C8
Edgefield Gr PO7 112 C1
Edgehill Rd
Bournemouth BH9 189 F1
Southampton SO18 79 F1
Edgell Rd PO10 137 B4
Edgemoor Rd BH22 139 B1
Edgerly Gdns PO6 157 F6
Edgeware Rd PO4 183 B5
Edgewood Ct GU33 21 B2
Edifred Rd BH9 190 A4
Edinburgh Ct 2 SO15 102 A6
Edinburgh Ho 4 SO22 215 D6
Edinburgh Rd PO1 216 A3
Edington Cl SO32 83 B8
Edington Rd SO23 215 E7
Edith Haisman Cl SO15 102 D5
Edmondsham Ho 16 BH2 204 E3
Edmondsham House Gdns* BH21 91 A4
Edmondsham Rd BH31 114 E8
Edmund Rd PO4 182 F3
Edmunds Cl
Hedge End SO30 105 D5
8 Old Milton BH25 195 A1
Edneys La PO7 111 B6
Edward Ave SO50 56 D4
Edward Cl SO45 150 E1
Edward Gdns PO9 135 C1
Edward Gr PO16 132 E1
Edward May Ct BH11 189 A4
Edward Rd
Bournemouth BH11 189 B3
Christchurch BH23 207 F8
Hythe SO45 126 A4
Poole BH14 203 C5
Southampton SO15 102 C7
Winchester SO23 215 D3
Edward's Cl 18 PO6 133 B1
Edwards Cl
Lymington SO41 197 B3
Waterlooville PO8 111 F2
Edwards Ct BH23 209 A8
Edwin Jones Gn SO15 102 E8
Edwina Cl
North Baddesley SO52 54 B4
Ringwood BH24 117 C1
Southampton SO19 104 A6
Edwina Dr BH17 187 B2
Edwina Ho SO18 79 E4
Effingham Gdns SO19 104 C4
Efford Ct SO41 197 B2
Efford Farm Cotts SO41 197 A1
Efford Way SO41 197 B2
Egan Cl PO2 157 F3
Egbert Rd SO23 215 E7
Egdon Cl BH22 165 B3
Egdon Ct BH16 201 B7
Egdon Dr BH21 187 E8
Egerton Ct BH8 205 D6
Egerton Gdns BH8 205 D6
Egerton Rd BH8 205 D6
Eglantine Cl PO8 112 B4
Eglantine Wlk PO8 112 C4
Egmont Cl BH24 140 D2
Egmont Dr BH24 140 D2
Egmont Gdns BH24 140 D2
Egmont Rd BH16 201 B4
Eight Acres SO51 53 B7
Eileen Beard Ho 1 PO9 136 A5
Elaine Gdns PO8 112 A5
Elan Cl SO18 80 B1
Elcombes Cl SO43 121 F5
Elder Cl
Locks Heath SO31 128 F2
Marchwood SO40 102 A1
Winchester SO22 215 A2
Elder Gn SO21 57 A8
Elder Rd PO9 136 B3
Elderberry Cl
Clanfield PO8 88 D4
Fair Oak SO50 57 B1
Elderberry La BH23 207 F6
Elderberry Way PO8 112 C4
Elderfield Cl PO10 137 A3
Elderfield Rd PO9 135 D7
Eldon Ave BH25 209 E8
Eldon Cl BH25 209 E8
Eldon Ct 5 Poole BH14 203 A4
Portsmouth PO5 216 B2
Eldon Ho 9 SO14 103 A3
Eldon Pl BH4 204 B3
Eldon Rd
Bournemouth BH9 189 E1
Compton SO20 7 A5
Eldon St PO5 216 B2
Eldridge Gdns SO51 52 F8
Eleanor Ct BH25 194 F1
Eleanor Dr BH11 188 D5
Eleanor Gdns BH23 206 E8
Electron Way SO53 55 C5
Elettra Ave PO7 134 C8
Eleven Cross SP6 68 B5
Elfin Ct 11 SO17 103 A8
Elfin Dr BH22 165 C7
Elgar Cl Gosport PO12 181 A3
Portchester PO6 156 E8
Southampton SO19 104 C3
Elgar Ct SO41 197 F4
Elgar Rd
Bournemouth BH10 189 D4
Southampton SO19 104 C3
Elgar Wlk PO7 134 F5
Elgin Cl Fareham PO15 130 F2
Hythe SO45 126 A3
Elgin Rd
Bournemouth BH4 204 D6
Cosham PO6 157 F6
Poole BH14 203 C2
Southampton SO15 102 D5
Elijah Cl BH15 201 E2
Eling Cl SO22 1 D3
Eling Ct PO9 135 D6
Eling Hill SO40 101 B5
Eling Inf Sch SO40 101 A6
Eling La SO40 101 A6
Eling Tide Mill* SO40 101 A6
Eling View SO15 101 C7
Eling Wharf SO40 101 B6
Elingfield Ct SO40 101 A7
Eliot Ho
8 New Milton BH25 195 A2
Southampton SO17 79 C2
Elise Cl BH7 206 B8
Eliza Pl 6 PO12 181 C6
Elizabeth Ave BH23 206 F8
Elizabeth Cl Downton SP5 46 D7
West End SO30 80 D1
Wickham PO17 107 F4
Elizabeth Cres SO41 196 B2
Elizabeth Ct
Aldermoor SO16 78 A3
1 Bournemouth BH1 205 B3
3 Cosham PO6 157 F8
Eastleigh SO50 56 A4
Fareham PO14 154 F7
4 Gosport PO12 181 A7
8 New Milton BH25 195 B2
Portswood SO17 79 C1
West End SO30 80 D1
Ferndown BH22 165 D6
Elizabeth Gdns
Christchurch BH23 208 D7
Hythe SO45 126 A1
Portsmouth PO4 182 F2
Elizabeth Ho SO40 76 B2
Elizabeth Rd Poole BH15 202 D3
Stubbington PO14 179 D7
Upton BH16 201 C7
Waterlooville PO7 134 E5
Wickham PO17 108 A4
Wimborne Minst BH21 163 C5
Elizabeth Way
Bishop's Waltham SO32 83 B7
Eastleigh SO50 56 B5
Elkhams Cl SO41 196 D1
Elkstone Rd PO6 133 B1
Ellachie Gdns PO12 181 B2
Ellachie Mews PO12 181 B2
Ellachie Rd PO12 181 B2
Elland Cl SO50 57 C1
Elldene Ct SO40 100 E5
Ellen Gdns SO53 55 A5
Ellen Wren Ho SO18 79 E4
Ellerslie Cl PO14 179 A6
Ellery Gr SO41 197 E5
Ellesfield Dr BH22 165 D2
Ellesmere Orch PO10 137 B5
Ellingham Cross BH24 116 F5
Ellingham Dr BH24 116 D5
Ellingham Dro BH24 117 B5
Ellingham Rd BH25 209 D8
Elliot Cl SO40 100 D7
Elliot Rise SO30 81 C2
Elliott Rd BH11 188 F3
Ellis Rd SO19 104 E5
Ellisfield Rd PO9 135 E4
Ellwood Ave SO19 104 E5
Ellwood Cl SO19 104 E6
Elm Ave
Christchurch BH23 191 E1
Lymington SO41 197 C1
New Milton BH25 195 A2
Elm Cl
South Hayling PO11 185 A3
Southampton SO16 78 F4
Elm Close Est PO11 184 F3
Elm Cotts BH24 141 A7
Elm Cres Hythe SO45 150 A7
Upham SO32 58 E5
Elm Ct
Chandler's Ford SO53 30 C1
5 New Milton BH25 195 A2
Southampton,Sholing SO19 103 F3
24 Westwood Park SO17 79 A1
Winchester SO22 215 C6
Elm Dr GU31 40 E1
Elm Gdns
Bournemouth BH4 204 C5
West End SO30 80 D3
Elm Gr Eastleigh SO50 55 F2
Gosport PO12 181 B6
Portsmouth PO5 216 B1
South Hayling PO11 185 A3
Elm La PO9 135 F1
Elm Lodge PO5 216 C1
Elm Park Rd PO9 135 F2
Elm Rd
Bishop's Waltham SO32 83 E8
Havant PO9 160 A8
Winchester SO22 215 C6
Elm St Portsmouth PO5 216 A1
Southampton SO14 103 B4
Elm Terr Liss GU33 20 E5
Southampton SO14 103 B3
Elm Tree Cl SO40 100 B2
Elm Tree Wlk BH22 189 E8
Elmdale GU31 41 A4
Elmdale Cl SO31 152 D10
Elmdale Gr SO51 51 B1
Elmers Way BH23 169 B1
Elmes Dr SO15 101 F7
Elmes Rd BH9 189 F2
Elmeswelle Rd PO8 112 A6
Elmfield Cl SP5 47 D5
Elmfield La SO45 178 E7
Elmfield North Block SO15 102 D5
Elmfield West Block SO15 102 D5
Elmgate Dr BH7 206 A7
Elmhurst Rd
Bournemouth BH11 189 A5
Fareham PO16 155 B8
Gosport PO12 181 C5
West Moors BH22 138 F2
Elmhurst Way BH22 138 F1
Elmleigh Rd PO9 135 F2
Elmore Ave PO13 180 A5
Elmore Cl PO13 179 F2
Elmore Dr BH24 139 E6
Elmore Rd PO13 179 F2
Elmrise Prim Sch BH11 189 A4
Elms Ave BH14 203 A1
Elms Cl Fordingbridge SP6 69 B2
Poole BH14 203 A1
Elms Rd PO16 155 B7
Elms Way BH6 206 E4
Elmsdown Ct BH24 140 F7
Elmsleigh Ct SO17 79 A4
Elmsleigh Gdns SO16 79 A4
Elmslie Gdns SO31 104 F1
Elmstead Rd BH13 214 F8
Elmtree Gdns SO51 53 C6
Elmtree Rd PO6 158 E8
Elmwood Ave
Fordingbridge SP6 69 D2
Waterlooville PO7 134 E6
Elmwood Ct SO16 78 B2
Elmwood Lodge 2 PO16 131 B2
Elmwood Rd PO2 157 E4
Elmwood Way BH23 209 A7
Elphinstone Rd
Portsmouth PO5 182 C2
Walkford BH23 194 B1
Elsfred Rd PO14 179 A6
Elson Inf Sch PO12 181 A9
Elson Jun Sch PO12 181 A9
Elson La PO12 181 A9
Elson Rd PO12 181 A9
Elstead Gdns PO7 134 C4
Elstree Rd SO19 103 E5
Eltham Cl BH7 206 B8
Elvin Cl SO41 195 F3
Elwell Gn PO11 184 F3
Elwyn Rd BH1,BH8 205 C5
Ely Ct 8 PO13 180 D5
Elysium Ct BH22 165 E3
Emanuel St PO2 182 D7
Embankment Way BH24 141 B6
Embassy Ct PO4 216 D2
Emberley Cl BH22 166 A6
Embley Cl SO40 76 D2
Embley La SO51 51 E7
Embley Park Ind Est SO51 51 E7
Embley Park Jun Sch SO51 52 E7
Embley Park Sch SO51 51 E6
Embsay Rd SO31 128 D8
Emer Cl SO52 54 A5
Emerald Cl
Southampton SO19 104 B6
St Leonards BH24 139 E6
Waterlooville PO7 135 A7
Emerald Cres SO45 126 B4
Emerson Cl 12 BH15 202 C2
Emerson Rd BH15 202 D2
Emily Cl BH23 192 A1
Emily Ct BH14 203 E5
Emmadale Ct 7 SO14 103 A6
Emmanuel CE Mid Sch BH31 114 E5
Emmanuel Cl PO14 129 C2
Emmett Rd SO16 77 F5
Emmons Cl SO31 128 A1
Emperor Ho SO18 103 C7
Empire Ct 6 PO9 135 F1
Empress Pk SO14 103 B7
Empress Rd
Lyndhurst SO43 121 F5
Southampton,Bevois Valley SO14 103 B7
Empshott Rd PO4 182 F4
Empson Wlk PO13 179 F4
Emsbrook Dr PO10 136 F2
Emsworth Common Rd PO10 136 F6
Emsworth House Cl PO10 136 E1
Emsworth Mus* PO10 160 F8
Emsworth Prim Sch PO10 136 E1
Emsworth Rd
Havant PO9 136 B1
Lymington SO41 197 E4
Portsmouth PO2 157 E1
Southampton SO15 102 B8
Thorney Island PO10 161 B2
Emsworth Sta PO10 136 F1
Encombe Cl BH12 203 F8
Endeavour Bsns Pk PO9 159 E7
Endeavour Cl
Gosport PO12 181 D5
Southampton SO15 102 B7
Endeavour Ct 5 SO14 103 B3
Endeavour Pk BH24 141 B6
Endeavour Way SO45 126 A5
Enderleigh Ho PO9 135 E1
Enderwood Cl SO40 100 B8
Endfield Cl BH23 191 F1
Endfield Rd
Bournemouth BH9 190 A2
Christchurch BH23 191 E1
Endle St SO14 103 C3
Endofield Cl PO14 154 F6
Enfield Ave BH15 202 E6
Enfield Cres BH15 202 E6
Enfield Gr SO19 103 E3
Enfield Rd BH15 202 E6
Englands Way BH11 188 D4
Englefield Ct SO31 127 A6
Englefield Rd SO18 103 D7
English Ct
15 Bournemouth BH2 204 D4
7 Romsey SO51 52 F7
English Rd SO15 102 B7
Enmill La SO22 9 E5
Ennel Copse SO52 54 A4
Ennerdale Cl PO8 88 C2
Ennerdale Gdns SO18 80 B1
Ennerdale Rd
Southampton SO16 77 E2
Stubbington PO14 154 D4
Ensbury Ave BH10 189 D1
Ensbury Cl BH10 189 D1
Ensbury Ct BH10 189 E2
Ensbury Park Rd BH9 189 E2
Ensign Dr PO13 180 D6
Ensign Pk SO31 127 E2
Ensign Way SO31 127 E2
Enterprise Cl SO31 128 E1
Enterprise Ind Est PO8 112 C8
Enterprise Pk PO16 131 E2
Enterprise Rd
Chilworth SO16 54 C1
Horndean PO8 112 C8
Enterprise Way BH23 190 C8
Eperston Rd PO8 112 A6
Epiphany CE Prim Sch The BH9 190 B4
Epping Cl SO18 80 B1
Epsom Cl SO50 81 D7
Epsom Ct PO15 129 C8
Epworth Rd PO2 157 F1
Erasmus Park Student Village SO23 2 C1
Eric Rd PO14 179 D7
Erica Cl Locks Heath SO31 128 F3
Waterlooville PO8 112 B3
Erica Dr BH21 186 D6
Erica Way PO8 112 B3
Ericksen Rd BH11 189 C3
Erinbank Mans BH1 205 C3
Ernest Cl PO10 136 F1
Ernest Rd Havant PO9 135 C3
Portsmouth PO1 182 E7
Erpingham Rd BH12 204 A5
Errington Ho 3 SO50 56 A2
Erskine Ct SO16 77 F5
Erskine Rd SO22 215 C5
Escombe Rd SO50 56 D3
Escur Cl PO2 157 F4
Esdaile La BH24 142 F3
Esher Gr PO7 111 C2
Eskdale Cl PO8 88 C2
Eskdale Ho 5 PO6 133 B1
Esmond Cl PO10 160 F8
Esmonde Cl PO13 179 F3
Esmonde Way BH17 202 F8
Esplanade Poole BH13 214 F7
Portsmouth PO4 183 B2
Esplanade Gdns PO4 183 C2
Esplanade The PO12 181 E5
Essex Ave BH23 191 F1
Essex Gn SO53 55 C2
Essex Rd PO4 183 A4
Esslemont Rd PO4 182 F3
Estancia Cl PO13 179 F4
Estella Rd PO2 182 D8
Estridge Cl SO31 105 A1
Ethel Rd PO1 182 E6
Ethelbert Rd BH21 163 D4
Ethelburt Ave SO16 79 C5
Ethelred Gdns SO40 100 C6
Eton Gdns BH4 204 C4
Eton Mans 2 BH6 206 E3
Eton Rd PO5 216 D2
Ettrick Rd BH13 204 A1
Eucalyptus Ave BH24 140 A2
European Way SO14 103 B2
Euryalus Rd PO14 154 F6
Euston Gr BH24 141 A6
Euston Rd PO4 183 B5
Eva Allaway Ct 33 PO1 182 A5
Evans Cl
Bournemouth BH11 188 F
Portsmouth PO2 157 B
St Leonards BH24 139 E
Evans Rd PO4 183 A
Evans St SO14 103 A
Evelegh Rd PO6 158 D
Evelyn Cl SO32 83 E
Evelyn Cres SO15 102 D
Evelyn Mews 1 BH9 189 F
Evelyn Rd BH9 190 A
Evening Glade BH22 165 E
Evenlode Rd SO16 77 E
Eventide Homes BH8 190 E
Everdene Cl BH22 165 C
Everdon La PO3 158 C
Everest Rd BH23 207 E
Everglades Ave PO8 111 F
Everglades Cl BH22 165 D
Evergreen Cl
Marchwood SO40 101 F
Three Legged Cross BH21 138

Evergreen Cl *continued*
Waterlooville PO7 ....134 D7
Evergreens
St Leonards BH24 ....139 E5
Totton SO40 ....101 A6
Evering Ave BH12 ....188 D1
Evering Gdns BH12 ......188 C1
Everlea Cl SO41 ....196 D1
Everon Gdns BH25 ....195 B1
Evershot Rd BH8 ....190 E2
Eversleigh 10 BH2 ......204 D2
Eversley Cres PO9 ....135 E4
Eversley Pl SO22 ....215 B3
Everton Rd SO41 ....196 B2
Evesham Cl
Bournemouth BH7 ....206 B8
Southampton SO16 ....79 B5
Evesham Ct BH13 ....204 A1
Ewart Ct SO45 ....126 A5
Ewart Rd PO1 ....182 E7
Ewell Way SO40 ....76 D1
Ewer Comm PO12 ....181 B3
Ewhurst Cl PO9 ....135 D4
Exbourne Manor BH1 ...205 C3
Exbury Central Sta
SO45 ....177 A6
Exbury Cl SO50 ....56 F2
Exbury Dr BH11 ....188 F5
Exbury Gdns* SO45 .....177 A5
Exbury Rd Beaulieu SO42 .149 D2
Blackfield SO45 ....150 E1
Havant PO9 ....136 A5
Excellent Rd PO14 ....154 F5
Excelsior Rd BH14 ....203 C3
Exchange Ho PO2 ....157 D1
Exchange Rd PO1 ....216 A3
Exchange The 3 PO4 ....182 E2
Exeter Cl Eastleigh SO50 ...55 F5
Emsworth PO10 ....136 F2
Locks Heath SO31 ....128 F3
Southampton SO18 ....80 A1
Exeter Cres BH2 ....204 F3
Exeter Ct
5 Christchurch BH23 ....209 B7
Gosport PO13 ....180 C6
Exeter La BH2 ....204 F2
Exeter Park Mans BH2 ..204 F2
Exeter Park Rd BH2 .....204 F2
Exeter Rd
Bournemouth BH2 ....204 F3
Portsmouth PO4 ....182 F2
Southampton SO18 ....104 A8
Exford Ave SO18 ....104 C8
Exford Dr SO18 ....104 C7
Exleigh Cl SO18 ....104 B6
Exmoor Cl
Swanwick PO15 ....129 B7
Totton SO40 ....100 B7
Exmoor Rd SO14 ....103 B6
Exmouth Gdns SO50 .....81 C7
Exmouth Rd
Gosport PO12 ....181 A9
Portsmouth PO5 ....182 D2
Exmouth St SO14 ....103 A5
Explosion Mus of Naval Firepower* PO12 ......181 D8
Exton Gdns PO16 ....132 C2
Exton Rd
Bournemouth BH6 ....206 D7
Havant PO9 ....136 B5
Eyebright Cl SO50 ....81 C6
Eyeworth Wlk SO45 .....125 C4
Eynham Ave SO19 ....104 C6
Eynham Cl SO19 ....104 B6
Eynon Mews BH24 ....140 F6
Eyre Cl SO40 ....100 D6

F

F Ave SO45 ....150 F6
Faber Cl PO9 ....136 A4
Faber Mews SO51 ....53 B8
Fabers Yd 12 SO22 ......215 D6
Fabian Cl PO7 ....135 A8
Factory Rd Eastleigh SO50 .56 A2
Upton BH16 ....201 C6
Fair Field SO51 ....28 A1
Fair Gn SO19 ....104 B5
Fair Isle Cl PO14 ....179 B8
Fair La SO21 ....11 F8
Fair Lea BH2 ....204 E2
Fair Oak Ct Fair Oak SO50 .57 D2
5 Gosport PO12 ....180 D3
Fair Oak Dr PO9 ....135 F3
Fair Oak Inf Sch SO50 ....57 D1
Fair Oak Jun Sch SO50 ....57 C1
Fair Oak Rd PO4 ....183 C4
Fair View 2 SO50 ....56 A3
Fairacre Rise PO14 ......154 B8
Fairacre Wlk PO14 ......154 B8
Fairbairn Wlk SO53 ....54 F6
Fairbourne Cl PO8 ....111 E2
Fairclose Dr SO22 ....1 B5
Faircourt 8 BH25 ....195 B3
Faircross Cl SO45 ....150 C3
Fairdown Cl SO23 ....11 C7
Fairfax Cl SO22 ....10 B5
Fairfax Ct SO19 ....104 E6
Fairfax Mews SO19 ......104 E6
Fairfield
Christchurch BH23 ....207 B7
Denmead PO7 ....110 F5
Fairfield Ave PO14 ....154 F7
Fairfield Cl
Christchurch BH23 ....207 B7
Emsworth PO10 ....136 F2
Hythe SO45 ....125 F4
Fairfield Cl *continued*
Lymington SO41 ....197 E3
Wimborne Minst BH21 ....163 F5
Fairfield Inf Sch PO9 ....136 A1
Fairfield Rd
Barton on S BH25 ....209 E7
Compton SO21 ....31 D5
Havant PO9 ....135 F1
Wimborne Minst BH21 ...163 D4
Winchester SO22 ....215 D7
Fairfield Sq PO6 ....157 E8
Fairfield Terr 7 PO9 .....135 F1
Fairgate Ctr The SP6 .....70 A4
Fairhaven Ct 9 BH5 .....205 E4
Fairholme Ct 1 SO50 .....56 A3
Fairhome Cl PO12 ....181 B8
Fairies Dr BH22 ....165 F3
Fairisle Inf Sch SO16 .....77 E4
Fairisle Jun Sch SO16 ....77 E4
Fairisle Rd SO16 ....77 E4
Fairlands Montessori Sch
SO32 ....107 E7
Fairlawn BH22 ....165 D5
Fairlawn Cl SO16 ....77 F6
Fairlawn Ho 9 SO22 ....215 D5
Fairlea Grange 3 SO16 ...78 F4
Fairlea Rd
Emsworth PO10 ....136 F3
Lymington SO41 ....197 E5
Fairlead Dr PO13 ....180 D6
Fairlie BH24 ....117 C1
Fairlie Cl SO30 ....81 C3
Fairlie Pk BH24 ....117 B1
Fairlight Holiday Chalets
PO11 ....185 C2
Fairlight La SO41 ....195 D8
Fairmead Ct
Locks Heath SO31 ....128 E1
South Hayling PO11 ......184 E3
Fairmead Way SO40 .....100 E5
Fairmead Wlk PO8 ......112 B3
Fairmile Par BH23 ....191 F1
Fairmile Rd BH23 ....191 F1
Fairoak Rd
Bishopstoke SO50 ....56 E2
Bishopstoke SO50 ....56 F2
Fair Oak SO50 ....57 B2
Fairthorn Ct 3 BH2 .....204 F4
Fairthorne Gdns PO12 ...181 A5
Fairview Cl Hythe SO45 ..126 A3
Romsey SO51 ....28 B1
Fairview Cres BH18 ......187 A5
Fairview Ct PO12 ....180 E4
Fairview Dr
Broadstone BH18 ....187 A5
Hythe SO45 ....126 A3
Romsey SO51 ....28 B1
Fairview Par 1 SO45 ....126 A2
Fairview Pk BH14 ....203 C3
Fairview Rd BH18 ....187 A5
Fairwater Cl PO13 ....155 B1
Fairway Bsns Ctr PO3 ...158 C2
Fairway Dr BH23 ....206 F6
Fairway Gdns SO16 ....77 E5
Fairway Rd Hythe SO45 ..125 F4
Poole BH14 ....214 C8
Fairway The
Barton on S BH25 ....210 B7
Gosport PO13 ....155 C1
Locks Heath SO31 ....128 F1
Portchester PO16 ....156 C8
Rowlands Castle PO9 .....113 C2
Fairways BH22 ....165 F6
Fairwinds BH13 ....214 B3
Fairwood Rd BH31 ....115 C5
Fairy Cross Way PO8 ....112 B2
Falaise Cl SO16 ....78 C4
Falcon Cl
2 Gosport PO12 ....181 C8
Portchester PO16 ....155 F8
Falcon Ct PO7 ....110 F3
Falcon Dr BH23 ....208 A5
Falcon Fields SO45 ......151 B3
Falcon Gn PO6 ....158 F7
Falcon Rd PO8 ....112 A7
Falcon Sq SO50 ....55 E1
Falcon View SO22 ....215 A2
Falcon Way SO32 ....81 F1
Falconer Ct SO45 ....150 C6
Falconer Dr BH15 ....201 E4
Falconwood Cl SP6 ....69 D1
Falkland Ct SO53 ....55 C3
Falkland Rd
Chandler's Ford SO53 .....55 C3
1 Portsmouth PO2 ......157 E4
Southampton SO15 ....102 A8
Falkland Sq 2 BH15 ....202 C2
Falklands Cl PO13 ....179 F4
Fallow Cres SO30 ....105 D8
Fallow Field SO22 ....215 B2
Fallows The BH25 ......195 B5
Falmouth Rd PO6 ....132 F1
Falstaff Way SO40 ....100 E5
Fancy Rd BH12 ....203 B8
Fanshawe St SO14 ....103 A6
Far Ends 4 BH14 ....203 B4
Far Meadow Way PO10 ..160 D8
Farcroft Rd BH12 ....203 B5
Faregrove Ct 8 PO16 ...131 A1
Fareham Coll PO14 ......130 E1
Fareham Ent Ctr 3
PO14 ....155 A6
Fareham Hts PO16 ....131 D3
Fareham Ind Pk PO16 ....131 C3
Fareham Park Rd PO15 ..130 C3
Fareham Rd
Gosport PO13 ....155 D4
Southwick PO17 ....132 E6
Fareham Rd *continued*
Wickham PO17 ....108 A3
Fareham Sta PO15 ....130 F1
Faringdon Ct 17 SO23 ...215 E8
Faringdon Rd SO18 ......104 D7
Farleigh Cl PO9 ....135 D5
Farley Cl Fair Oak SO50 ....57 D1
Winchester SO22 ....10 B4
Farley Ct SO16 ....78 D2
Farley La SO51 ....7 E2
Farley Mount Ctry Pk*
SO21 ....9 B8
Farley Mount Rd SO21 .....9 A3
Farlington Ave PO6 ......134 D1
Farlington Marshes (Nature Reserve)* PO6 ....158 F5
Farlington Rd PO2 ....182 E8
Farm Cl
Hamble-le-R SO31 ....128 A2
Ringwood BH24 ....141 A8
Farm Ct BH21 ....164 A4
Farm Edge Rd PO14 .....179 C6
Farm House Cl PO14 ....154 C5
Farm La
Christchurch BH23 ....208 A5
Southbourne PO18 ....161 F7
Farm La N BH25 ....210 A8
Farm La S BH25 ....210 A8
Farm Lane Cl PO7 ....134 D6
Farm Rd Titchfield PO14 ..129 E2
West Moors BH22 ....138 D2
Farm View PO10 ....136 F3
Farm View Ave PO8 ....88 B5
Farmdene Cl BH23 ....208 D8
Farmers Wlk
Hordle SO41 ....211 D8
1 Wimborne Minst BH21 .163 B6
Farmery Cl SO18 ....79 D4
Farmhouse Way PO8 ....112 A5
Farmlea Rd PO6 ....157 A8
Farmside Gdns PO3 .....157 F4
Farnham Rd Liss GU33 ....20 E4
Poole BH12 ....204 A7
Steep GU32 ....41 B7
Farnleys Mead SO41 .....197 E2
Faroes Cl PO14 ....179 B8
Farrier Way PO16 ....155 B6
Farriers Cl BH21 ....164 B6
Farriers Ct 4 PO5 ....182 D2
Farriers Way PO7 ....112 C1
Farriers Wlk PO12 ....181 D6
Farringdon Rd PO9 ......136 A4
Farringford Rd SO19 ....104 D5
Farrington 24 BH4 ......204 C2
Farthing Cl PO12 ....181 A6
Farthing La PO1 ....182 A3
Farthingale Terr 11
PO1 ....182 A3
Farthings Ct The 13
BH1 ....205 A3
Farthings Gate PO7 .....134 E3
Farthings The PO14 .....153 C8
Farwell Cl BH23 ....192 C3
Farwell Rd BH12 ....188 C2
Fastnet Cl SO16 ....77 E5
Fastnet Ho 9 PO5 ....182 D1
Fastnet Way PO14 ....154 B4
Fathersfield SO42 ....145 F2
Fathoms Reach PO11 ....184 F4
Faulston Cotts SP5 ....22 D8
Faversham 9 BH2 ....204 D2
Fawcett Rd
New Milton BH25 ....194 F2
Portsmouth PO4 ....216 D2
Fawley Bsns Ctr SO45 ...151 A3
Fawley By Pass SO45 ....151 B3
Fawley Ct 24 PO9 ....136 B5
Fawley Gn BH8 ....190 D3
Fawley Inf Sch SO45 .....151 A3
Fawley La Owslebury SO21 .33 A8
Privett GU34 ....17 B4
Fawley Rd Fawley SO45 ...150 E3
Hythe SO45 ....126 A2
Hythe,Buttsash SO45 .....150 B8
Portsmouth PO2 ....157 E5
Southampton SO15 ....102 A6
Fawn Cres SO30 ....105 D8
Fawn Gdns BH25 ....194 F4
Fay Cl PO14 ....179 C7
Fayre Rd PO16 ....155 A8
Fayrewood Ct BH31 ......114 F7
Fearon Rd PO2 ....157 E1
Felix Rd PO12 ....181 B8
Fell Cl SO31 ....129 A4
Fell Dr PO13 ....179 F3
Felmer Dr SO23 ....2 C7
Feltham Cl SO51 ....53 C8
Felton Cres BH23 ....208 F8
Felton Ct BH14 ....202 F5
Felton Rd BH14 ....202 F5
Feltons Pl PO3 ....157 F5
Fen Ave PO16 ....155 B7
Fenleigh Cl BH25 ....195 B1
Fennel Gdns SO41 ....197 E5
Fennell Cl PO7 ....111 D1
Fenton Rd BH6 ....206 C5
Fenwick Ct BH8 ....205 B5
Fenwick Hospl SO43 .....121 E6
Fern Bank
5 Bournemouth BH2 .....204 F3
Three Legged Cross BH21 .138 E7
Fern Barrow BH12 ....204 B7
Fern Cl Alderholt SP6 .....93 A5
Burton BH23 ....192 C2
Petersfield GU31 ....41 C3
Fern Cotts 2 PO16 ......131 C2
Fern Ct SO18 ....103 E7
Fern Dr PO9 ....136 A2
Fern Hill La SO51 ....28 E8
Fern Rd Hythe SO45 ......125 F3
Southampton SO19 ....103 F2
Fern Way PO15 ....129 D3
Fernacre Bsns Pk SO51 ...27 E1
Ferncroft Cl PO14 ....179 C6
Ferncroft Gdns BH10 ....189 D5
Ferncroft Rd BH10 ......189 D5
Ferndale
Hedge End SO30 ....105 D5
Waterlooville PO7 ....135 A8
Ferndale Mews PO13 ....155 B4
Ferndale Rd
Marchwood SO40 ....101 F1
New Milton BH25 ....195 B4
Ferndene Way SO18 .....103 F8
Ferndown Ct SP6 ....69 D1
Ferndown Fst Sch BH22 .165 C5
Ferndown Ind Est BH21 .164 F7
Ferndown Mid Sch
BH22 ....165 C5
Ferndown Upper Sch
BH22 ....165 B6
Ferneham Rd PO15 ....130 C2
Fernglade BH25 ....195 A3
Fernheath Cl BH11 ......189 A3
Fernheath Rd BH11 ......189 A3
Fernhill SO53 ....55 E6
Fernhill Cl BH17 ....188 A2
Fernhill Flats 6 BH2 ....204 F3
Fernhill Gate BH25 ......195 A5
Fernhill La BH25 ....195 A4
Fernhill Rd BH25 ....195 A3
Fernhills Rd SO45 ....126 B1
Fernhurst Cl PO11 ....184 D3
Fernhurst Jun Sch PO4 ..182 F4
Fernhurst Rd PO4 ....182 F4
Fernie Cl PO14 ....179 B7
Fernlea BH23 ....207 D6
Fernlea Ave BH22 ....165 D4
Fernlea Cl
Ferndown BH22 ....165 D4
St Leonards BH24 ....139 E4
Fernlea Gdns
Ferndown BH22 ....165 D4
Southampton SO16 ....78 E3
Fernlea Way SO45 ....125 D3
Fernside Ave BH14 ......202 F4
Fernside Bsns Pk BH22 .165 A7
Fernside Cl
Holbury SO45 ....150 C3
Southampton SO16 ....101 F8
Fernside Ct BH15 ....202 E4
Fernside Rd
Bournemouth BH9 ....204 E8
Poole BH15 ....202 E4
West Moors BH22 ....138 E2
Fernside Way SO50 ....57 E2
Fernside Wlk SO50 ....57 E2
Fernway Cl BH21 ....164 B4
Fernwood Cl BH24 ....140 B5
Fernwood Cres SO18 .....103 F8
Fernwood Ho PO8 ....112 A2
Fernyhurst Ave SO16 .....77 F6
Ferris Ave BH8 ....190 D2
Ferris Cl BH8 ....190 D2
Ferris Pl BH8 ....190 D2
Ferrol Rd PO12 ....181 C7
Ferry Rd
Bournemouth BH6 ....206 F3
Hythe SO45 ....125 F3
Poole BH19 ....214 A1
Poole,Lower Hamworthy
BH15 ....202 B1
Portsmouth PO4 ....183 D3
Portsmouth PO4 ....183 E4
South Hayling PO11 ......184 B4
Ferry Way BH13 ....214 B3
Ferrybridge Gn 4 SO30 .105 C6
Ferrymans Quay SO31 ...127 B5
Ferrypoint SO41 ....198 A4
Festing Bldgs 1 PO4 ....182 F2
Festing Gr PO4 ....183 A2
Festing Mews 2 PO4 ....182 F2
Festing Rd PO4 ....182 F2
Feversham Ave BH8 .....190 E1
Fey Rd PO12 ....181 C6
Fibbards Rd SO42 ....145 F1
Field Cl Compton SO21 ....31 C6
Gosport PO13 ....155 B5
Locks Heath SO31 ....129 A2
Romsey SO51 ....53 A7
Southampton SO16 ....79 C5
Field End SO23 ....2 C7
Field Pl Barton on S BH25 .209 D8
Verwood BH31 ....114 E7
Field View SO53 ....54 F6
Field Way
Christchurch BH23 ....193 D1
Compton SO21 ....31 C6
Corfe Mullen BH21 ....186 E8
Denmead PO7 ....110 F4
Godshill SP6 ....70 D2
Field Wlk SO41 ....197 D5
Fielden Cl SO52 ....53 F4
Fielder Dr 1 PO14 ......155 A6
Fielders Ct
Waterlooville PO7 ....134 C4
West End SO30 ....80 E1
Fielders' Way SO51 ....51 B2
Fieldfare Cl PO8 ....88 C4
Fieldfare Ct SO40 ....100 C8
Fieldhouse Dr PO13 .....179 F4
Fieldmore Rd PO12 ......181 B8
Fields Cl SO45 ....150 E1
Fields The BH31 ....114 F7
Fieldway BH24 ....141 B8
Fifth Ave Cosham PO6 ....157 E8
Fifth Ave *continued*
Havant PO9 ....136 B2
Fifth St PO1 ....182 F6
Filmer Cl PO13 ....180 D8
Filmorehill La GU34 ......17 B3
Filton Cl SO40 ....76 C1
Filton Rd SO41 ....197 D4
Finch Ho 11 PO4 ....183 B2
Finch Rd PO4 ....183 D3
Finch's La SO21 ....31 F6
Finchdean Rd
Havant PO9 ....135 D4
Rowlands Castle PO9 .....113 D3
Finches The SO17 ....79 B2
Finchfield Ave BH11 .....188 F6
Finchmead La GU32 ......40 B4
Finchwood Farm Ind Units
PO11 ....160 B1
Findon Rd PO12 ....181 B9
Fineshade 7 BH13 ......214 F7
Finisterre Cl PO14 ....154 B4
Finlay Cl SO19 ....104 C4
Finley Cl SO40 ....76 B1
Finzi Cl SO19 ....104 C3
Fiona Cl SO23 ....11 C8
Fir Ave BH25 ....195 B2
Fir Cl Lyndhurst SO43 ....121 F4
West Moors BH22 ....138 E3
Fir Copse Rd PO7 ....134 D4
Fir Croft Dr SO53 ....55 D5
Fir Rd SO40 ....100 B2
Fir Tree Cl
Horton Heath SO50 ....81 C7
St Leonards BH24 ....139 D2
Fir Tree Cotts GU33 ......21 E4
Fir Tree Ct SO18 ....104 B8
Fir Tree Gdns PO8 ......112 C5
Fir Tree Hill SP6 ....93 A6
Fir Tree La
Christchurch BH23 ....193 D1
Horton Heath SO50 ....81 B7
Fir Tree Rd Bartley SO40 ...99 A7
South Hayling PO11 ......185 A3
Fir Vale Rd BH1 ....204 F3
Firbank Rd BH9 ....205 B8
Firecrest Cl SO16 ....78 B6
Firefly Cl PO13 ....180 A5
Firgrove Cl SO52 ....53 F4
Firgrove Cres PO3 ......157 F5
Firgrove Ct SO15 ....102 C7
Firgrove La PO17 ....108 F2
Firgrove Rd
North Baddesley SO52 .....54 A5
Southampton SO15 ....102 C7
Firlands Rise PO9 ....135 A1
Firmain Rd BH12 ....188 D1
Firmount Cl SO41 ....196 E1
Firmstone Rd SO23 ....11 C8
Firs Ave PO8 ....111 F2
Firs Cres SO23 ....2 B8
Firs Dr SO30 ....105 A5
Firs Glen Rd
Bournemouth BH9 ....204 E8
Verwood BH31 ....115 A4
West Moors BH22 ....138 E2
Firs La BH14 ....214 B8
Firs Pk GU31 ....41 C3
Firs The
Bournemouth BH1 ....205 A4
Chandler's Ford SO53 .....55 C3
Gosport PO13 ....155 D1
Southampton SO16 ....78 F4
Winchester SO22 ....215 C7
Firshill BH23 ....208 E8
Firside Rd BH21 ....186 C4
First Ave Cosham PO6 ....157 F8
Farlington PO6 ....158 E8
Havant PO9 ....136 B2
Horndean PO8 ....88 C3
Southampton SO15 ....101 D7
Southbourne PO10 ....161 D8
First Marine Ave BH25 ...209 F7
First St SO45 ....150 E8
Firsway BH16 ....201 C7
Firtree Cres SO41 ....195 F3
Firtree Gdns PO8 ....112 C5
Firtree Way SO19 ....104 B5
Firwood Cl SO53 ....55 D8
Fisgard Rd PO12 ....181 B8
Fisher Cl PO14 ....179 B8
Fisher Rd PO13 ....155 C3
Fisher's Rd SO40 ....101 A6
Fisherman's Ave BH5 ....206 B4
Fisherman's Bank BH23 .207 E5
Fisherman's Wlk BH5 ....206 B4
Fishermans Rd BH15 .....202 C1
Fishermans The PO10 ....161 A8
Fishermans Wlk PO11 ....185 E2
Fishers Gr PO6 ....158 E7
Fishers Hill PO15 ....130 B2
Fishery La PO11 ....185 C2
Fishlake Mdws SO51 ......27 F1
Fitzgerald Cl PO15 ....129 C8
Fitzharris Ave BH9 ......205 A7
Fitzherbert Rd PO6 ......158 D7
Fitzherbert Spur PO6 ....158 E7
Fitzherbert St PO1 ....216 B4
Fitzhugh Ho 8 SO15 .....102 E6
Fitzhugh Pl SO15 ....102 F7
Fitzhugh St 3 SO15 .....102 F5
Fitzmaurice Rd BH23 ....206 E8
Fitzpain Cl BH22 ....165 D2
Fitzpain Rd BH22 ....165 D2
Fitzpatrick Ct PO6 ....133 D1
Fitzroy Cl SO16 ....78 F7

Fitzroy Dr PO13 180 A7
Fitzroy Wlk PO1 216 C4
Fitzwilliam Ave PO14 179 A7
Fitzwilliam Cl BH11 188 F5
Fitzworth Ave BH16 201 C4
Fitzwygram Cres PO9 135 F3
Five Bridges Rd SO23 215 C1
Five Elms Dr SO51 53 C6
Five Heads Rd PO8 112 C8
Five Post La PO12 181 B7
Fivefields Cl SO23 11 C6
Fivefields Rd SO23 11 C7
Flag Wlk PO8 111 F5
Flaghead BH13 214 E6
Flaghead Chine Rd
BH13 214 E6
Flaghead Rd BH13 214 E7
Flagstaff Gn PO12 181 D7
Flambard Ave BH23 192 A1
Flambard Rd BH14 203 C2
Flamborough Cl SO16 77 D3
Flamingo Ct PO16 155 F8
Flamstone St SP5 22 B8
Flanders Ho 1 PO14 154 E8
Flanders Ind Pk SO30 105 B8
Flanders Rd SO30 105 B8
Flathouse Rd PO1 182 C7
Flaxfields End SP6 69 E1
Flazen Cl BH11 188 D3
Fleet Cl PO13 155 D1
Fleet End Bottom
SO31 152 F10
Fleet End Rd
Locks Heath SO31 128 F1
Warsash SO31 152 F10
Fleet Farm Cvn & Camping
Ctr PO11 185 A8
Fleet Terr SO21 31 B1
Fleet Way PO1 182 B6
Fleet's Cnr BH17 202 B7
Fleetend Cl PO9 135 E6
Fleets Est BH15 202 B6
Fleets La BH15 202 C6
Fleetsbridge Bsns Ctr
BH17 202 B7
Fleetspoint Bsns Ctr
BH15 202 B5
Fleetwood Ct BH15 202 C7
Fleming Ave SO52 54 B4
Fleming Cl PO15 129 D4
Fleming Ct
North Baddesley SO52 54 B4
Southampton SO19 103 D2
Fleming Pl
Colden Common SO21 31 F1
1 Romsey SO51 52 F7
Fleming Rd
Southampton SO16 79 D4
Winchester SO22 1 C3
Fletcher Cl
Bournemouth BH10 189 D3
Hythe SO45 125 D3
Fletcher Rd BH10 189 D3
Fletchwood La
Totton SO40 100 B4
Woodlands SO40 99 F2
Fleur de Lys Mobile Home Pk
SO41 173 F1
Fleuret Cl SO45 126 A1
Flexford Cl SO53 30 A1
Flexford Gdns PO9 136 A3
Flexford La SO41 196 C6
Flexford Rd SO52,SO53 54 E7
Flinders Ct 4 PO4 183 B2
Flint Cl SO19 104 E4
Flint St PO5 216 A1
Floating Bridge Rd
SO14 103 C3
Floral Farm BH21 164 A2
Florence Cl SO51 51 B2
Florence Ct 2 SO18 103 E8
Florence Rd
Bournemouth BH5 205 F4
Poole BH14 203 D4
Portsmouth PO5 182 D1
Southampton SO19 103 D2
Florentine Way PO7 135 A8
Florins The
Locks Heath PO14 129 A1
Waterlooville PO7 134 E3
Floriston Gdns BH25 195 D3
Floud La GU32 37 B5
Flower Bldgs PO13 179 E2
Flower Ct BH21 163 D3
Flowerdown Cl SO40 100 C8
Flowerdown Ho SO22 1 C4
Flowerdown Mobile Home Pk
SO22 1 C5
Flowers Cl SO31 127 E3
Flowers La SO51 50 D6
Flume Rd SO45 151 C4
Flushards SO41 197 F3
Flying Bull Cl 3 PO2 182 D8
Flying Bull La PO2 182 D8
Flying Bull Prim Sch
PO2 182 D8
Foldsgate Cl SO43 121 F6
Foley Ho PO1 216 B4
Folkestone Rd PO3 183 A8
Folland Cl SO52 54 A4
Folly Farm La BH24 140 C6
Folly Field SO32 83 D7
Folly La GU32 40 F3
Folly Mkt 7 GU31 40 F3
Font Cl PO14 129 C3
Fontley Rd PO15 130 A5
Fontmell Rd BH18 187 C3
Fontwell Cl SO40 76 C1
Fontwell Gdns SO50 81 D7
Fontwell Mews 5 PO7 112 B1
Fontwell Rd 5 PO5 182 D2
Foord Rd SO30 105 B5
Football Gn SO43 98 D3
Footner Cl SO51 28 C2
Footners La BH23 192 C2
Forbes Almshouses
GU32 38 E1
Forbes Cl SO16 77 F6
Forbes Rd SO23 2 B8
Forbury Rd 2 PO5 216 C2
Ford Ave SO53 55 D4
Ford Cl BH22 165 F7
Ford La BH22 166 A7
Ford Rd PO12 180 F6
Fordingbridge Bsns Pk
SP6 69 D1
Fordingbridge Hospl SP6 69 F1
Fordingbridge Inf Sch
SP6 69 F3
Fordingbridge Jun Sch
SP6 69 F3
Fordingbridge Rd
Alderholt SP6 93 B7
Portsmouth PO4 183 B3
Fordington Ave SO22 215 C6
Fordington Rd SO22 215 C7
Fore Bridge GU31 40 F2
Foreland Cl BH23 191 D4
Foreland Ct PO11 185 C2
Foreland Rd BH16 201 C4
Forelle Ctr The BH31 115 C4
Foremans Cotts PO12 181 E3
Foreshore N SO45 151 B6
Foreshore S SO45 151 B6
Forest Ave PO8 111 F3
Forest Cl
Chandler's Ford SO53 55 C8
Christchurch BH23 193 D1
North Baddesley SO52 53 E5
Verwood BH31 115 D4
Waltham Chase SO32 83 E3
Waterlooville PO8 111 F3
Forest Cnr GU33 21 A7
Forest Ct
Fordingbridge SP6 69 F1
Lymington SO41 197 B2
New Milton BH25 195 B2
Forest Edge
Fawley SO45 151 B3
New Milton BH25 195 C4
Forest Edge Cl
St Leonards BH24 139 D5
Sway SO41 172 A3
Forest Edge Dr BH24 139 D6
Forest Edge Rd BH24 141 E5
Forest Edge Sch SO40 100 E7
Forest End PO7 134 D7
Forest Front SO45 150 A8
Forest Gate SO45 177 F7
Forest Gate Gdns SO41 197 D1
Forest Gdns
Lyndhurst SO43 121 F5
Waltham Chase SO32 83 E3
Forest Glade Cl SO42 145 D1
Forest Hall SO42 146 A1
Forest Hill Way SO45 125 F2
Forest Hills Ct BH24 141 D6
Forest Hills Dr SO18 79 F3
Forest Ho 14 BH1 205 A3
Forest La Fareham PO17 131 B8
Hardley SO45 150 B6
Ringwood BH24 141 F6
Verwood BH31 114 E7
Forest Links Rd BH22 138 B1
Forest Mdw SO45 150 A8
Forest Mead PO7 110 F3
Forest Oak Dr BH25 195 A5
Forest Park Rd SO42 145 E2
Forest Pines BH25 195 A4
Forest Rd
Bransgore BH23 169 F4
Burley Street BH24 142 F5
Chandler's Ford SO53 55 D8
Denmead PO7 110 D4
Liss GU33 21 A6
Nomansland SP5 73 C7
Poole BH13 204 A2
Waltham Chase SO32 83 F3
West Moors BH22 138 F3
Woodgreen SP6 47 E3
Forest Rise
Christchurch BH23 193 D2
Liss GU33 21 A6
Forest Side Gdns BH24 117 C1
Forest View
Beckley BH25 194 D5
Brockenhurst SO42 145 D1
4 Southampton SO14 102 F4
Forest View Cl BH9 190 A2
Forest View Dr BH21 165 A5
Forest View Rd BH9 190 A3
Forest Way
Christchurch BH23 193 D1
Everton SO41 196 D1
Ferndown BH21 165 A5
Gosport PO13 155 E1
Totton SO40 76 A2
Forest Wlks (Blackwater)*
SO42 144 E6
Forester Rd SO32 85 B1
Foresters Gate SO45 177 D7
Foresters Pk SO23 2 A4
Foresters Rd SO45 150 F2
Forestlake Ave BH24 141 D6
Forestside Ave PO9 136 A5
Forestside The BH31 115 D5
Forge Cl SO31 105 A1
Forge La SO45 151 B3
Forge Rd SO45 177 F7
Forneth Gdns PO15 154 B8
Forres Sandle Manor
SP6 69 D2
Forster Rd SO14 103 B7
Forsyth Gdns BH10 189 C1
Forsythia Cl Havant PO9 136 C4
Hedge End SO30 105 B8
Hythe SO45 150 A7
Forsythia Pl SO19 103 F5
Fort Brockhurst* PO12 155 F1
Fort Cumberland* PO4 183 E3
Fort Cumberland Cl
BH15 201 D2
Fort Cumberland Rd
PO4 183 D3
Fort Fareham Ind Est
PO14 155 A6
Fort Fareham Rd PO14 154 F6
Fort Nelson* PO17 132 B3
Fort Rd Gosport PO12 181 B2
Southampton SO19 103 E3
Fort Wallington Ind Est
PO16 131 D2
Fort Widley Married Quarters
PO6 133 F1
Fortescue Rd
Bournemouth BH3 205 A6
Poole BH12 203 D6
Forth Cl
Chandler's Ford SO53 55 B5
Stubbington PO14 179 B8
Forth Ho 11 SO14 103 C6
Forties Cl PO14 154 B4
Forton Cl BH10 189 E4
Forton Lodge 3 PO12 181 C6
Forton Rd Gosport PO12 181 B6
Portsmouth PO1 182 E6
Fortune Ct SO53 55 C6
Fortune Ho PO12 181 A6
Fortunes Way PO9 134 F1
Forty Acre La GU31 66 D3
Forum The 6 PO9 135 E2
Forward Dr SO41 197 C2
Foster Cl PO14 154 C4
Foster Rd Gosport PO12 181 B4
Portsmouth PO1 216 C4
Founders Way PO13 155 D2
Foundry Cres SO31 127 F8
Foundry Ct 23 PO1 182 A5
Foundry La SO15 102 B7
Foundry Lane Prim Sch
SO15 102 B7
Foundry Rd SP5 47 D7
Fountain Ct
4 Colden Common SO21 31 F1
Hedge End SO30 105 B6
Poole BH13 204 B2
Fountain Rdbt BH23 207 B6
Fountain Sq PO11 184 E4
Fountain St PO1 216 B3
Fountain Way BH23 207 B6
Fountains Pk SO31 127 A7
Four Acre SO30 106 A6
Four Cnrs SP6 68 A4
Four Marks Gn 3 PO9 136 B6
Four Wells Rd BH21 164 A7
Fourposts Hill 3 SO15 102 E5
Fourshells Cl SO45 150 F2
Fourth Ave Cosham PO6 157 E8
Havant PO9 136 B2
Fourth St PO1 182 F6
Fowey Cl SO53 55 B6
Fowey The SO45 150 E2
Fowlers Rd SO30 105 B8
Fowlers Wlk SO16 54 D2
Fox Cl SO50 56 F2
Fox Field SO41 196 D1
Fox La
Wimborne Minst BH21 164 C5
Winchester SO22 215 A3
Fox Pond La SO41 197 D1
Fox's Wlk SO45 177 F7
Foxbury Cl SO45 126 A2
Foxbury Gr PO16 156 B7
Foxbury La
Gosport PO13 155 D4
Westbourne PO10 137 D4
Foxbury Rd BH24 166 F8
Foxcombe Cl SO32 84 A5
Foxcote Gdns BH25 194 F3
Foxcote Ho 6 PO6 132 F2
Foxcott Cl SO19 126 F8
Foxcott Gr PO9 135 F5
Foxcroft Dr
Holbury SO45 150 B3
Wimborne Minst BH21 164 B5
Foxdale Ct 17 BH2 204 E3
Foxes Cl Verwood BH31 114 F5
Waterlooville PO7 134 E6
Foxes La SO51 50 F5
Foxglade SO45 177 F7
Foxglove Cl BH23 208 C8
Foxglove Pl BH25 195 D4
Foxgloves Fareham PO16 131 C3
Upton BH16 201 B7
Foxgloves The SO30 105 D5
Foxhayes La SO45 177 F7
Foxhills Ashurst SO40 100 C4
Verwood BH31 115 B6
Foxhills Cl SO40 100 C4
Foxhills Inf Sch SO40 100 D4
Foxhills Jun Sch SO40 100 D4
Foxholes 1 BH6 206 F4
Foxholes Rd
Bournemouth BH6 206 F4
Poole BH15 202 F6
Foxlands SO45 177 F7
Foxlea 3 SO15 102 E7
Foxlea Gdns PO12 181 B8
Foxlease Terr SO43 121 F4
Foxley Dr PO3 158 B4
Foxtail Dr SO45 125 F1
Foxwood Ave BH23 207 F5
Foxy Paddock SO45 177 F7
Foy Gdns SO31 128 C1
Foyes Ct SO15 102 D6
Foyle Rd SO53 55 B6
Frampton Cl
1 Colden Common SO21 31 F1
New Milton BH25 195 C5
Frampton Pl BH24 141 A7
Frampton Rd BH9 205 A8
Frampton Way
Kings Worthy SO23 2 C7
Totton SO40 100 F6
Frances Ct 7 BH23 209 B7
Frances Rd
Bournemouth BH1 205 C4
Waterlooville PO7 134 D3
Frances Sheldon Ct
SO22 215 C5
Francesca Ct 5 BH23 207 E7
Francesca Grange 4
BH23 207 E7
Francesca Lo 1 BH23 207 E6
Francis Ave
Bournemouth BH11 188 D3
Portsmouth PO4 182 F3
Francis Avenue Ind Est
BH11 188 D3
Francis Cl PO13 180 A5
Francis Gdns SO23 2 B3
Francis Pl PO14 179 D7
Francis Rd Horndean PO8 88 C3
Poole BH12 203 E5
Franconia Dr SO16 77 B3
Frank Judd Ct 36 PO1 182 A5
Frank Miles Ho 1 PO5 216 B2
Frank Wareham Cottage
Homes The BH9 190 A4
Frankland Cres BH14 203 E3
Frankland Terr 4 PO10 161 A8
Franklin Rd
Bournemouth BH9 190 A3
Gosport PO13 180 C7
New Milton BH25 195 C4
Twyford SO21 32 A7
Franklyn Ave SO19 104 A4
Franklyn Cl BH16 201 B7
Franks Way BH12 203 B7
Frankston Rd BH6 206 C4
Frankton Way PO12 181 D6
Frarydene PO10 161 D8
Fraser Cl SO16 77 F6
Fraser Ct BH25 194 F3
Fraser Gdns PO10 137 E2
Fraser Rd Gosport PO13 155 C4
Havant PO9 135 D2
Kings Worthy SO23 2 C8
Poole BH12 203 F8
Portsmouth PO5 216 C2
Portsmouth,Whale Island
PO2 157 B2
Frater La PO12 156 A1
Fratton Ct PO1 216 D3
Fratton Park (Portsmouth
FC) PO4 183 A5
Fratton Rd PO1 216 D4
Fratton Sta PO1 182 E5
Fratton Way
Fair Oak SO50 57 C1
Portsmouth PO4 182 F5
Frattton Ind Est PO4 183 A5
Frayslea 4 SO45 126 A2
Freda Rd BH23 206 F6
Freda Routh Gdns SO50 57 D2
Frederica Rd BH9 204 E8
Frederick St
Portsmouth PO1 216 B4
Southampton SO14 103 B6
Free St SO32 83 D8
Freedom Ct SO45 126 A3
Freefolk Gn 1 PO9 136 B5
Freegrounds Ave SO30 105 C6
Freegrounds Cl 1
SO30 105 C6
Freegrounds Inf Sch
SO30 105 D6
Freegrounds Jun Sch
SO30 105 D6
Freegrounds Rd SO30 105 C6
Freemans Cl BH21 164 B6
Freemans La BH21 164 B5
Freemantle Bsns Ctr
SO15 102 C5
Freemantle CE Inf Sch
SO15 102 C6
Freemantle Cl SO19 103 F5
Freemantle Common Rd
SO19 103 F6
Freemantle Rd PO12 181 B8
Freestone Rd 10 PO5 182 D2
Fremington Ct 6 BH25 195 B3
French Rd BH17 187 B1
French St
8 Portsmouth PO1 182 A3
Southampton SO14 102 F3
French's Farm Rd BH16 201 A7
Frenches La SO51 51 C8
Frenchies View PO7 110 E4
Frenchmans Rd GU32 40 E4
Frenchmoor La
East Dean SP5 3 F2
West Tytherley SP5 3 F4
Frendstaple Rd PO7 135 A6
Frensham Cl
Bournemouth BH10 189 E3
Hedge End SO30 105 C6
Frensham Ct
Hedge End SO30 105 C6
Portsmouth PO4 182 F4
Frensham Rd PO4 182 F4
Freshfield Gdns PO7 134 E8
Freshfield Rd SO15 102 B7
Freshfield Sq SO15 102 B7
Freshwater Ct
Chandler's Ford SO53 30 E1
Lee-on-t-S PO13 179 E3
Freshwater Dr BH15 201 D3
Freshwater Rd
Christchurch BH23 208 C6
Cosham PO6 157 E7
Frewen Liby PO1 182 B4
Friars Croft SO40 76 C2
Friars Gate BH23 208 C6
Friars Pond Rd PO15 130 C1
Friars Rd
Christchurch BH23 208 B6
Eastleigh SO50 55 F1
Friars Way SO18 79 D4
Friars Wlk BH25 210 A8
Friarscroft SO31 127 B7
Friarsgate SO23 215 E6
Friary Cl 6 PO5 182 C2
Friary Gdns 7 SO23 215 D5
Friary The 5 PO5 182 C2
Friday's Ct BH24 140 F7
Friendly Societies' Homes
PO4 183 B3
Friends Provident St Mary's
Stadium (Southampton FC)
The SO14 103 B5
Friendship Ho PO5 216 B1
Frinton Ct 2 BH14 203 A4
Frith La PO17 108 B7
Frith Lane End PO17 108 B8
Fritham Cl SO40 100 C7
Fritham Gdns BH8 190 D3
Fritham Rd SO18 104 D8
Frobisher Ave BH12 188 F1
Frobisher Cl
Christchurch BH23 207 F6
Gosport PO13 180 C6
Ringwood BH24 117 C1
Frobisher Ct SO40 102 A3
Frobisher Gdns
6 Emsworth PO10 160 F8
Southampton SO19 104 C4
Frobisher Gr PO16 156 C7
Frobisher Ho 6 PO1 182 A5
Frobisher Ind Ctr SO51 27 E1
Froddington Rd PO5 216 C2
Frog La Fordingbridge SP6 93 E7
Titchfield PO14 154 A8
Froghall SO45 126 A1
Frogham Cross SP6 94 E6
Frogham Gn PO9 135 D6
Frogham Hill SP6 94 D6
Frogmore PO14 154 C8
Frogmore La
Nursling SO16 77 D3
Waterlooville PO8 112 A6
Frome Cl SO40 102 A1
Frome Rd SO18 80 A3
Fromond Cl SO41 197 E5
Fromond Rd SO22 1 D3
Front Lawn Inf Sch PO9 135 F5
Front Lawn Jun Sch
PO9 135 F5
Frost La SO45 126 B1
Frost Rd BH11 188 F3
Frosthole Cl PO15 130 E3
Frosthole Cres PO15 130 E3
Froud Way BH21 186 C4
Froude Ave PO12 181 C3
Froude Rd PO12 181 D3
Froxfield CE Inf Sch
GU32 18 E2
Froxfield Cl SO22 1 D4
Froxfield Gdns PO16 132 C1
Froxfield Ho PO1 216 C4
Froxfield Rd PO9 136 B5
Froyle Ct 19 PO9 136 B5
Fry Cl Blackfield SO45 150 F2
Hamble-le-R SO31 128 A4
Fry's La SO32 61 D4
Fryer Cl BH11 189 B5
Fryern Arc SO53 55 E7
Fryern Cl SO53 55 E6
Fryern Court Rd SP6 69 E5
Fryern Ct SO53 55 E7
Fryern Inf Sch SO53 55 E6
Fryern Jun Sch SO53 55 E6
Fryers Cl SO23 2 C8
Fryers Copse BH21 164 C6
Fryers Rd BH21 138 D8
Frys La SO41 196 D2
Fuchsia Gdns SO15 78 D2
Fulcrum Ctr The BH12 188 C2
Fulflood Ct 2 SO22 215 C5
Fulflood Rd PO9 135 E5
Fullegar Cotts SO32 84 B6
Fullerton Cl
7 Havant PO9 136 B
Southampton SO19 126 F
Fullerton Rd SO41 197 C
Fulmar Cl SO16 78 B
Fulmar Dr SO45 126 B

Fulmar Rd BH23 208 A5
Fulmar Wlk PO13 155 A3
Fulmer Wlk PO8 111 E4
Fulwood Ave BH11 188 E5
Funtington Rd PO2 182 F8
Funtley Ct PO16 130 E4
Funtley Hill PO16 130 E4
Funtley La PO17 130 E5
Funtley Rd PO17 130 E5
Furdies PO7 110 E4
Furley Cl 8 SO23 215 F6
Furlong Mews BH24 140 F7
Furlong The BH24 140 F7
Furlonge Ho PO10 136 E1
Furneaux Gdns PO16 131 B3
Furnell Rd BH15 202 D1
Furness Rd 13 PO5 182 D1
Furniss Way PO11 184 D4
Furnston Gr PO10 137 E1
Fury Way PO14 179 B8
Furze Cl SO19 104 A5
Furze Croft BH25 195 A2
Furze Hall PO16 131 B4
Furze Hill Dr BH14 203 C1
Furze La PO4 183 D4
Furze Rd SO19 104 A5
Furze Way PO8 112 B4
Furzebrook Cl BH17 187 E3
Furzedale Gdns SO45 126 B1
Furzedale Pk SO45 126 B2
Furzedown Cotts SO20 7 B7
Furzedown Cres 4 PO9 136 A5
Furzedown Ho SO20 7 B6
Furzedown Mews 2 SO45 126 B1
Furzedown Rd
Compton SO20 7 B8
Southampton SO17 79 A2
Furzehall Ave PO16 131 B3
Furzehill BH21 163 C8
Furzelands Rd BH21 138 E8
Furzeley Rd PO7 110 F2
Furzey Ave SO45 126 B2
Furzey Cl SO45 150 F1
Furzey Gdns* SO43 98 A3
Furzey La SO42 148 B1
Furzey Rd BH16 201 B6
Furzley Ct PO9 135 C6
Furzley La SO43 74 D6
Furzley Rd SO40 74 E3
Furzy Whistlers Cl BH23 169 B1
Fushia Cl PO9 136 C4
Futcher Sch The PO6 158 C8
Fyeford Cl SO16 77 F6
Fyfield Cl PO15 129 C8
Fyfield Way SO22 1 B5
Fyning St PO1 216 C4

G

G Ave SO45 150 F6
Gable Mews PO11 185 A4
Gablehurst BH16 201 C7
Gables Ct SO16 78 F5
Gadbridge Ct 14 BH4 204 C2
Gage Cl SO40 102 A2
Gain's Rd PO4 182 E2
Gainsborough Ave BH25 195 B5
Gainsborough Cl SO19 104 C2
Gainsborough Ct
4 Bournemouth BH5 206 B5
Lymington SO41 197 D2
North Baddesley SO52 54 B4
Gainsborough Ho
Barton on S BH25 210 A6
2 Portsmouth PO4 182 E2
Gainsborough Mews PO14 153 F8
Gainsborough Rd
Bournemouth BH7 205 F7
St Leonards BH24 139 F5
Gainsford Rd SO19 103 E5
Galaxie Rd PO8 112 B4
Gale Moor Ave PO12 180 D4
Galleon Cl SO31 128 F1
Gallia Ct SO17 78 F1
Gallop Way BH12 204 C7
Gallops The PO14 129 D2
Galloway Rd BH15 201 D4
Gallows Dr BH22 165 E1
Galsworthy Rd SO40 100 D7
Galt Rd PO6 158 D8
Galton Ave BH23 206 F6
Gamble Cl SO19 103 F4
Gamble Rd PO2 182 D8
Gambledon La SO51 25 F5
Gamblins La SO32 107 F8
Ganger Farm La SO51 28 C2
Ganger Rd SO51 28 C2
Gannet Cl Hythe SO45 126 B2
Southampton SO16 78 B5
Gannets The PO14 179 B8
Gar St SO23 215 D5
Garage Cotts GU32 40 E4
Garbett Rd SO23 11 C8
Garden City SO45 125 A6
Garden Cl
Lyndhurst SO43 121 E5
New Milton BH25 195 A1
South Hayling PO11 184 F3
Garden Court Cotts BH22 138 D3
Garden Ct
Bournemouth BH1 205 D6
Portchester PO16 156 D8
Garden Ho 6 BH1 205 B3
Garden La
Portsmouth PO5 216 B1
25 Winchester SO23 215 E6
Garden Mews
10 Petersfield GU32 40 F3
Warsash SO31 128 C1
Garden Rd BH24 142 F3
Garden Terr 14 PO5 182 D2
Garden Wlk BH22 165 E7
Garden-La BH24 139 E3
Gardeners Cotts BH24 141 A4
Gardeners La SO51 52 A4
Gardenia Dr PO15 129 E3
Gardens Cres BH14 214 B8
Gardens Ct 5 BH15 202 E3
Gardens Rd BH14 214 B8
Gardens The
Fareham PO16 131 C3
Hambledon PO7 86 C3
Havant PO9 136 B1
Gardiner Cl SO40 102 A2
Gardiners Cnr SO51 28 D6
Gardner Ct BH23 206 E8
Gardner Rd
Christchurch BH23 206 E8
Ringwood BH24 141 B6
Titchfield PO14 153 F7
Gardner Way SO53 55 B8
Garendon Ct SP6 69 E2
Garfield Ave BH1 205 D5
Garfield Cl SO32 83 C8
Garfield Rd
Bishop's Waltham SO32 83 C8
Netley SO31 127 A6
Portsmouth PO2 182 D8
Southampton SO19 103 E7
Garland Ave PO10 136 F3
Garland Ct 5 PO12 181 B6
Garland Rd BH15 202 D4
Garland Way SO40 100 B8
Garnett Cl PO14 154 C4
Garnier Pk PO17 108 A4
Garnier Rd SO23 215 E3
Garnier St PO1 216 D3
Garnock Rd SO19 103 D2
Garratt Cl SO30 81 D2
Garrett Cl SO19 104 A1
Garrick Gdns SO19 104 B2
Garrick Ho 4 PO2 157 F4
Garrison Hill SO32 61 B2
Garrow Dr SO41 197 E5
Garsdale Cl BH11 189 A6
Garsons Rd PO10 161 D8
Garston Cl GU32 63 D8
Garstons Cl PO14 153 F8
Garstons Rd PO14 153 F8
Garth Cl BH24 139 D4
Garth Rd BH9 190 A1
Garth The SO45 125 F2
Garton Rd SO19 103 D3
Gashouse Hill SO31 127 C5
Gaston Gdns SO51 52 F8
Gatcombe SO31 127 C7
Gatcombe Ave PO3 158 A2
Gatcombe Dr PO2 157 F3
Gatcombe Gdns
Fareham PO14 154 B8
West End SO18 80 A2
Gatcombe Park Prim Sch PO2 157 F4
Gate House Rd PO16 156 A7
Gatehouse The
11 Southampton SO18 103 E8
West End SO30 80 C2
Gatekeeper Cl 7 SO23 11 C8
Gateway The BH13 203 F4
Gatwick Cl SO16 78 A4
Gaulter Cl PO9 136 A3
Gavan St SO19 104 D5
Gawn Pl PO12 181 D3
Gaydon Rise BH11 188 E4
Gaylyn Way PO14 154 B8
Gaza Ave SO42 175 C6
Gaza Ho PO15 130 D3
Gazelle Cl PO13 180 D5
Gazing La SO51 50 E3
Gazings The SO51 50 E3
Geddes Way GU31 41 C4
Gemini Cl SO16 77 F4
General Johnson Ct 4 SO22 215 A4
Geneva Ave BH6 206 D5
Genoa Cl SO41 197 C1
Genoa Ho PO6 157 A7
Gento Cl SO30 105 E6
Geoffrey Ave PO7 134 B2
Geoffrey Cres PO16 155 B6
George Byng Way PO2 182 C8
George Ct PO5 182 D2
George Ct The 10 PO1 182 A3
George Curl Way SO18 79 F6
George Eyston Dr SO22 215 B4
George Mews The BH24 140 F7
George Rd SO41 211 C5
George Rdbt The BH15 202 C3
George St Eastleigh SO50 56 B3
Gosport PO12 181 C6
Portsmouth PO1,PO2 182 F7
George Wright Cl SO50 55 F2
Georges Mews BH21 186 D7
Georgia Cl Havant PO9 135 E3
Lee-on-t-S PO13 179 F4
Georgian Cl BH24 141 A8
Georgian Way BH10 189 F4
Georgina Cl Poole BH12 204 C8
Totton SO40 76 B1
Georgina Talbot Ho BH12 204 B8
Gerald Rd BH3 205 A6
Gerard Cres SO19 104 D6
Gerard Ho 6 PO2 157 E4
Germaine Cl BH23 208 F8
Gervis Cres BH14 203 A1
Gervis Pl BH1 204 F3
Gervis Rd BH1 205 B3
Gibbs Cl SO45 150 A8
Gibbs Rd SO14 102 F5
Giblet Ore PO14 179 A6
Gibraltar Cl PO15 130 D2
Gibraltar Rd
Fareham PO14 154 F6
Portsmouth PO4 183 D3
Gibson Cl
Lee-on-t-S PO13 179 F4
Whiteley PO15 129 E5
Gibson Rd BH17 202 E7
Giddylake BH21 163 D6
Gifford Cl PO15 130 E3
Gilbert Cl Alderholt SP6 93 B6
Gosport PO13 180 D8
Lymington SO41 197 D2
Gilbert Mead PO11 184 E4
Gilbert Rd BH8 205 D6
Gilbert Way PO7 134 E5
Gilbury Cl SO18 79 E4
Gilchrist Gdns SO31 152 C9
Giles Cl Fareham PO16 131 B3
Gosport PO12 181 A7
Hedge End SO30 81 D1
Giles La SP5 50 A4
Gilkicker Rd PO12 181 C2
Gillam Rd BH10 189 D5
Gillcrest PO14 129 C4
Gillett Rd BH12 204 C7
Gillies The 6 PO16 131 A1
Gillingham Cl
Bournemouth BH9 190 C4
Kings Worthy SO23 2 C7
Gillingham Rd SO41 211 D4
Gillion Ct 2 BH23 207 E6
Gillman Rd PO6 134 E1
Gilpin Cl Pilley SO41 173 F1
Southampton SO19 104 E5
Gilpin Hill SO41 172 B2
Gilpins Folly SO41 172 A3
Gins La SO42 176 E1
Girton Cl PO14 129 C1
Gisors Rd PO4 183 B4
Gitsham Gdns PO7 134 C3
Gladdis Rd BH11 188 F3
Glade The
Blackfield SO45 177 E7
Chandler's Ford SO53 30 F1
Christchurch BH23 191 E1
Fareham PO15 130 D4
South Hayling PO11 185 C1
St Leonards BH24 139 E5
Waterlooville PO7 135 A8
Gladelands Cl BH18 186 E4
Gladelands Pk BH22 165 F7
Gladelands Way BH18 186 E4
Glades The SO31 129 A4
Gladstone Cl BH23 207 D6
Gladstone Gdns PO16 156 C7
Gladstone Pl 4 PO2 182 D8
Gladstone Rd
Bournemouth BH7 205 F5
Gosport PO12 181 A8
Poole BH12 203 C5
Southampton SO19 104 B5
Gladstone Rd E BH7 205 F5
Gladstone Rd W BH1 205 E5
Gladstone St SO23 215 D6
Gladys Ave
Portsmouth PO2 157 D2
Waterlooville PO8 112 A4
Glamis Ave BH10 189 E5
Glamis Cl PO7 135 A8
Glamis Ct PO14 179 C8
Glamorgan Rd PO8 88 B3
Glasgow Rd PO4 183 B3
Glasslaw Rd SO18 104 A8
Glasspool PO7 110 E5
Gleadowe Ave BH23 207 A6
Glebe Cl PO11 184 E5
Glebe Cnr PO17 108 B3
Glebe Ct Botley SO30 106 A8
Fair Oak SO50 57 D2
Southampton SO17 79 A2
Glebe Dr PO13 155 C1
Glebe La SP5 49 D4
Glebe Mdw SP5 4 A2
Glebe Park Ave PO9 135 A1
Glebe Rd Buriton GU31 65 D5
Southampton SO14 103 B3
Glebe The PO14 179 C6
Glebefield Gdns 1 PO6 157 E8
Glebefields 6 SO41 211 D5
Glen Cl BH25 209 D8
Glen Dale PO9 113 C1
Glen Eyre Cl SO16 79 A4
Glen Eyre Dr SO16 79 A5
Glen Eyre Hall SO16 79 A5
Glen Eyre Rd SO16 78 F5
Glen Eyre Way SO16 79 A4
Glen Fern Rd BH1 205 A3
Glen Ho PO12 180 F3
Glen Park Mobile Home Pk SO21 57 B8
Glen Rd
Bournemouth BH5 205 F4
Poole BH14 203 B4
Sarisbury SO31 128 F6
Southampton SO19 103 D2
Glen Spey BH25 195 D2
Glen The Gosport PO13 155 E1
Poole BH12 203 D6
Poole,Canford Cliffs BH13 214 E8
Glenair Ave BH14 203 A3
Glenair Cres BH14 203 A3
Glenair Rd BH14 203 A3
Glenavon BH25 195 C2
Glenavon Rd BH23 193 F1
Glenbrook Wlk PO14 154 C8
Glencarron Way 3 SO16 78 E3
Glencoe Rd
Bournemouth BH7 205 F7
Poole BH12 203 D5
Portsmouth PO1 182 F7
Glencoyne Gdns SO16 77 F2
Glenda Cl SO31 152 D10
Glendale
Locks Heath SO31 129 B2
Swanmore SO32 84 B4
Glendale Ave BH22 165 E6
Glendale Cl
Christchurch BH23 191 D3
Wimborne Minst BH21 163 C5
Glendale Ct BH23 191 D3
Glendale Rd BH6 207 A4
Glendeep Cl SO23 2 B6
Glendon Ave BH10 189 C6
Glendowan Rd SO53 55 A7
Glendrive BH25 209 C8
Gleneagles
Christchurch BH23 206 F6
Poole BH13 204 B2
Gleneagles Ave BH14 203 D2
Gleneagles Cl BH22 165 F6
Gleneagles Dr PO7 112 B2
Glenelg PO15 130 F2
Glenesha Gdns PO15 130 D2
Glenferness Ave BH4 204 D5
Glenfield Ave SO18 103 F7
Glenfield Cres SO18 103 F7
Glenfield Inf Sch SO18 103 F7
Glenfield Way SO18 103 F7
Glengariff Rd BH14 203 C2
Glengarry BH25 195 C2
Glengarry Way BH23 208 C6
Glenhurst Sch PO9 136 A1
Glenives Cl BH24 140 A4
Glenlea Cl SO30 80 D1
Glenlea Dr SO30 80 D1
Glenleigh Ave 6 PO6 157 F7
Glenleigh Ct 5 PO6 157 F7
Glenleigh Pk PO9 136 B2
Glenmeadows Dr BH10 189 B5
Glenmoor Cl BH10 189 D1
Glenmoor Rd
Bournemouth BH9 204 E8
Ferndown BH22 165 D3
Glenmoor Sch BH10 189 D1
Glenmore Ct SO17 103 A8
Glenmore Gdns PO8 111 F2
Glenmount Dr BH14 203 B4
Glenn Rd SO30 80 D2
Glenny Cl PO13 180 A6
Glenroyd Gdns BH6 206 E4
Glenside
Barton on S BH23,BH25 209 B7
Hythe SO45 125 F3
Glenside Ave SO19 104 D4
Glenthorne Cl PO14 179 D6
Glenthorne Mdw GU32 38 E1
Glenthorne Rd PO3 158 A1
Glenville Cl BH23 194 B2
Glenville Gdns BH10 189 C2
Glenville Rd
Bournemouth BH10 189 C2
Walkford BH23 194 B2
Glenwood Ave SO16 79 A5
Glenwood Cl BH22 138 E2
Glenwood Ct SO50 57 E2
Glenwood Gdns PO8 111 F3
Glenwood La BH22 138 E2
Glenwood Rd
Breach PO10 137 E1
Verwood BH31 114 F5
West Moors BH22 138 E2
Glenwood Sch PO10 136 F1
Glenwood Way BH22 138 E2
Glidden Cl PO1 216 C3
Glidden La PO7 86 E3
Glissons BH22 165 A2
Globe La BH15 202 C2
Gloster Ct PO15 129 C5
Gloucester Cl GU32 40 D3
Gloucester Ct 3 GU32 40 F4
Gloucester Ho 1 PO12 181 C5
Gloucester Mews PO5 216 B2
Gloucester Pl PO5 216 B1
Gloucester Rd
Bournemouth BH7 205 F5
Poole BH12 203 E5
Portsmouth PO1 182 A6
Waterlooville PO7 134 F6
Gloucester Sq 28 SO14 103 A3
Gloucester Terr PO5 216 B1
Gloucester View PO5 216 B2
Glyn Dr PO14 179 C7
Glyn Jones Cl SO45 150 F2
Glyn Way PO14 179 C7
Glynville Cl BH21 164 A7
Glynville Ct BH21 164 A7
Glynville Rd BH21 164 A7
Goathorn Cl BH16 201 D4
Goathouse La PO17 109 B4
Goddard Cl SO51 50 E3
Godfrey Olson Ho SO50 56 B3
Godfrey Pink Way SO32 83 D7
Godiva Lawn PO4 183 C3
Godmanston Cl BH17 188 A1
Godshill Cl BH8 190 D3
Godson Ho 27 SO23 215 E6
Godwin Cl
Emsworth PO10 136 E3
Winchester SO22 1 C3
Godwin Cres PO8 88 C3
Godwins Field SO21 31 C8
Godwit Cl PO12 181 B9
Godwit Rd PO4 183 C6
Gofton Ave PO6 158 B7
Gogg's La SP5 47 F6
Gold Mead Cl 5 SO41 197 E2
Gold Oak SP6 91 F7
Gold St PO5 216 A1
Goldcrest Cl
Fareham PO16 155 E8
Horndean PO8 112 A7
Goldcrest Gdns SO16 78 A5
Goldcrest La SO40 100 C7
Golden Cres SO41 196 D1
Golden Ct
Waterlooville PO7 134 E7
West End SO30 80 F3
Golden Gates BH13 214 B3
Golden Gr SO14 103 B5
Golden Hind Pk SO45 125 F2
Golden Sands BH13 214 B3
Goldenleas Ct BH11 188 D3
Goldenleas Dr BH11 188 D3
Goldfinch Cl BH25 194 F2
Goldfinch La PO13 179 F4
Goldfinch Rd BH17 201 E8
Goldring Cl PO11 185 A3
Goldsmith Ave PO4 182 F4
Goldsmith Cl SO40 100 D7
Goldsmith Inf Sch PO4 182 E4
Goldsmith Rd SO50 55 F1
Goldsmiths Ct 17 SO14 103 A3
Goldwire Dr SO53 54 F5
Golf Course Rd SO16 78 E6
Golf Links Rd
Broadstone BH18 187 B5
Ferndown BH22 165 E4
Goliath Rd BH15 201 D2
Gomer Ct PO12 180 E3
Gomer Inf Sch PO12 180 E3
Gomer Jun Sch PO12 180 E3
Gomer La PO12 180 E3
Good Rd BH12 203 C7
Goodacre Dr SO53 54 F5
Goodall Ct 18 PO16 131 B1
Goodens The SO24 14 C5
Goodison Cl SO50 57 B1
Goodlands Vale SO30 105 A7
Goodsell Cl PO14 179 B7
Goodwin Cl SO16 77 D2
Goodwood Cl
Gosport PO12 181 B9
Titchfield PO14 129 D2
Waterlooville PO8 112 B1
Goodwood Ct PO10 161 E8
Goodwood Gdns SO40 100 C8
Goodwood Rd
Eastleigh SO50 55 E4
Gosport PO12 181 B9
Portsmouth PO5 216 D1
Gooseberry La BH24 140 F7
Gordleton Ind Pk SO41 196 F5
Gordon Ave
Southampton SO14 103 A8
Winchester SO23 11 C6
Winchester SO23 11 C7
Gordon Bldgs SO15 102 C8
Gordon Ct 7 BH4 204 C4
Gordon Mount BH23 209 B8
Gordon Rd
Bournemouth BH1 205 D4
Chandler's Ford SO53 30 D1
Christchurch BH23 209 A8
Curdridge SO32 83 A1
Emsworth PO10 161 B8
Fareham PO16 131 A1
Gosport PO12 181 A5
Lymington SO41 197 C3
Poole BH12 204 A5
Portsmouth PO1 182 B3
Waterlooville PO7 134 D6
Wimborne Minst BH21 163 E4
Winchester SO23 215 E6
Gordon Rd S BH12 204 A5
Gordon Terr SO19 104 A2
Gordon Watson Ho SO23 215 D3
Gordon Way BH23 192 D1
Gore Grange BH25 194 F2
Gore Rd BH25 194 E2
Gore Rd Ind Est BH25 194 F2
Gorey Rd BH12 188 D1
Goring Ave PO8 88 D4
Goring Field SO22 215 A7
Gorleston Rd BH12 203 F5
Gorley Cross SP6 94 B4
Gorley Ct PO9 135 C6
Gorley Lynch SP6 94 D4
Gorley Rd BH24 117 C1
Gorran Ave PO13 155 C1
Gorse Cl
Locks Heath SO31 128 F2
New Milton BH25 195 D4
St Leonards BH24 139 D4
Gorse Down SO21 33 B4
Gorse Hill Cl BH15 202 F5
Gorse Hill Cres BH15 202 E5
Gorse Hill Rd BH15 202 F5

Gorse Knoll Dr BH31 ....114 E7
Gorse La BH16 ....201 D7
Gorse Rd
Corfe Mullen BH21 ....186 C5
Petersfield GU31 ....41 C3
Gorsecliff Ct 7 BH5 ....205 D4
Gorsecliff Rd BH10 .....189 D1
Gorsefield Rd BH25 .....195 B4
Gorseland Ct BH22 ......165 E3
Gorselands Rd SO18 .....80 B1
Gorselands Way PO13 ...180 D8
Gorseway PO11 ....184 D3
Gorseway The PO11 .....184 D3
Gort Cres SO19 ....104 B4
Gort Rd
Bournemouth BH11 ....189 B3
Poole BH17 ....187 A1
Gosling Cl BH17 ....202 F7
Gosport Ho 29 PO9 ......136 B5
Gosport La SO43 ....122 A4
Gosport Mus* PO12 ....181 D5
Gosport Rd
Fareham PO16 ....155 B7
Lee-on-t-S PO13 ....179 F2
Stubbington PO14 ....179 E7
Gosport Sh Prec 6
PO12 ....181 D5
Gosport St SO41 ....197 F4
Gough Cres BH17 ....187 B2
Gover Rd SO16 ....101 C8
Goyda Ho PO12 ....180 F6
Grace Ct 15 PO5 ....182 C2
Grace Darling Ho BH15 .202 D1
Grace Dieu Gdns SO31 ..104 F1
Grace La SP6 ....70 E8
Gracefields PO15 ....154 B8
Graddidge Way SO40 ...100 D6
Graemar Cotts SO51 .....25 C3
Graemar La SO51 ....25 C2
Grafton Cl
Bournemouth BH3 ....205 A7
Christchurch BH23 ....207 D6
Gosport PO12 ....181 C8
Grafton Gdns
Lymington SO41 ....197 C1
Southampton SO16 ....78 C5
Grafton Rd
Bournemouth BH3 ....205 A6
Winchester SO23 ....215 D4
Grafton St PO2 ....182 D7
Graham Ct SO19 ....104 B6
Graham Ho 4 SO14 .....103 C6
Graham Norris Bsns Ctr The
SO45 ....150 E1
Graham Rd
Gosport PO12 ....181 A8
Portsmouth PO4 ....182 E3
Southampton SO14 ....103 B6
Graham St SO14 ....103 C6
Grainger Gdns SO19 ....104 C3
Grammar School La
BH21 ....163 B4
Granada Cl PO8 ....112 A4
Granada Rd
Hedge End SO30 ....105 B6
Portsmouth PO4 ....182 E1
Granary Mews BH24 ....140 F7
Granary The BH24 ......140 F7
Granby Gr SO17 ....79 B3
Granby Rd BH9 ....190 A4
Grand Ave BH6 ....206 C4
Grand Division Row 1
PO4 ....183 B3
Grand Par 13 Poole BH15 .202 B1
Portsmouth PO1 ....182 A3
South Hayling PO11 ......185 A2
Grange Cl Gosport PO12 ..180 F6
Havant PO9 ....136 B2
Hordle SO41 ....211 E8
Southampton SO18 ....79 E4
Winchester SO23 ....215 C2
Grange Cotts SO30 .....105 E7
Grange Cres PO12 ......180 F6
Grange Ct
5 Bournemouth BH1 .....205 B3
Netley SO31 ....127 B7
Grange Dr SO30 ....105 D8
Grange Gdns BH12 ......203 E8
Grange Inf Sch PO13 ....180 C7
Grange Jun Sch PO13 ...180 C7
Grange La PO13 ....180 C7
Grange Mews SO51 ......28 C1
Grange Park Mobile Homes
SO30 ....81 C1
Grange Rd
Bournemouth BH6 ....206 D3
Broadstone BH18 ....187 A4
Christchurch BH23 ....208 B7
Gosport PO13 ....180 D6
Hedge End SO30 ....105 C8
Netley SO31 ....127 B7
Petersfield GU32 ....40 E2
Portsmouth PO2 ....157 D1
2 Southampton SO16 .....78 B1
St Leonards BH24 ....139 E1
Winchester SO23 ....215 C1
Grange Road Bsns Ctr
BH23 ....208 A7
Grange Sch The BH23 ...207 E7
Grange The Hordle SO41 .211 E8
1 Southampton SO16 .....78 B1
Grangewood Ct SO50 .....57 B2
Grangewood Gdns SO50 ..57 B2
Grangewood Hall BH21 .163 D5
Grant Rd PO6 ....158 D8
Grant's Ave BH1 ....205 D6
Grantham Ave SO31 .....127 E3
Grantham Ct 9 SO50 ....56 A2
Grantham Rd
Bournemouth BH1 ....205 E5
Eastleigh SO50 ....55 F2
Southampton SO19 ....103 F6
Grantley Rd 3 BH5 .....205 F4
Grants Cl BH1 ....205 E6
Granville Cl PO9 ....160 A8
Granville Ct SO15 ....102 E7
Granville Pl
9 Bournemouth BH1 .....204 F3
Winchester SO23 ....215 F4
Granville Rd
Bournemouth BH5 ....206 A5
Poole BH12 ....203 B5
Granville St SO14 ....103 B4
Grasdean Cl 1 SO18 .....80 A1
Grasmere SO50 ....55 F2
Grasmere Cl
Christchurch BH23 ....191 D3
West End SO18 ....80 B1
Grasmere Ct SO16 ....77 E2
Grasmere Gdns BH25 ...195 B5
Grasmere Ho 7 PO6 ....133 B1
Grasmere Rd
Bournemouth BH5 ....206 A4
Poole BH13 ....214 B3
Grasmere Way PO14 ....154 D4
Grassmere Way PO7 ....112 C1
Grassymead PO14 ....129 C4
Grateley Cl SO19 ....126 F8
Grateley Cres PO9 ......135 C4
Gravel Cl SP5 ....46 E8
Gravel Hill
Broadstone BH17,BH18,
BH21 ....187 D5
Swanmore SO32 ....84 B3
Gravel La BH24 ....140 F8
Gray Cl Locks Heath SO31 .128 F2
Poole BH17 ....202 F8
Gray's Yd 5 BH15 ......202 C1
Graycot Cl BH10 ....189 C5
Grayland Cl PO11 ....184 E4
Grayling Mead SO51 .....27 F1
Grays Ave SO45 ....126 B3
Grays Cl
Colden Common SO21 ......56 F8
Gosport PO12 ....180 E3
Romsey SO51 ....53 A7
Grays Ct PO1 ....182 A4
Grayshott Cl SO22 ....1 D4
Grayshott Rd
Gosport PO12 ....180 F4
Portsmouth PO4 ....182 F4
Grayson Cl PO13 ....180 A6
Great Copse Dr PO9 .....135 E6
Great Elms Cl SO45 .....150 B3
Great Farm Rd SO50 .....55 F3
Great Field Rd SO22 ....1 D3
Great Gays PO14 ....153 F1
Great Hanger GU31 ......41 B3
Great Mead
Denmead PO7 ....111 A3
Lyndhurst SO43 ....121 F4
Great Minster St 2
SO23 ....215 E5
Great Posbrook Cotts
PO14 ....153 E6
Great Southsea St PO5 ..216 B1
Great Well Dr SO51 ......53 A8
Greatbridge Rd SO51 .....27 E1
Greater Horseshoe Way 3
PO17 ....130 E8
Greatfield Way PO9 .....113 B3
Greatwood Cl SO45 .....126 A2
Greaves Cl BH10 ....189 C3
Grebe Cl
Broadstone BH17 ....201 E8
Christchurch BH23 ....208 A6
Milford on S SO41 ....211 E4
Portchester PO16 ....155 F8
Waterlooville PO8 ....111 E4
Westbourne PO10 ....137 B4
Green Acres BH23 ......207 F7
Green Acres Cl BH24 ....140 D5
Green Bottom BH21 .....164 A7
Green Cl Hythe SO45 ....126 A4
Kings Worthy SO23 ....2 A5
Poole BH15 ....202 D1
Whiteparish SP5 ....24 B4
Woodlands SO40 ....99 F4
Green Cres PO13 ....155 C1
Green Dr SP6 ....93 B6
Green Farm Gdns PO3 ..157 F4
Green Gdns BH15 ....202 D1
Green Hollow Cl PO16 ..130 F4
Green Jacket Cl SO22 ...215 C3
Green La Ampfield SO51 ...53 E8
Barton on S BH25 ....210 B8
Bishop's Waltham SO32 ....83 D7
Blackfield SO45 ....177 F8
Bournemouth BH10 ......189 D3
Burridge SO31 ....106 A1
Bursledon SO31 ....104 F1
Chilworth SO16 ....54 F1
Clanfield PO8 ....88 D5
Denmead PO7 ....110 E4
Downton SP5 ....46 F8
Ferndown BH22 ....165 A1
Fordingbridge SP6 ....69 F2
Gosport,Alverstoke PO12 ..181 A5
Gosport,Elson PO12 ......181 C9
Hamble-le-R SO31 ....128 A2
Hambledon PO7 ....86 B4
High Cross GU32 ....18 F5
Locks Heath SO31 ....128 F1
Green La *continued*
Lower Swanwick SO31 ....128 D8
Ossemsley BH25 ....194 E8
Portsmouth PO3 ....158 A3
Ringwood BH24 ....141 A7
Ringwood,Upper Kingston
BH24 ....141 C4
Soberton PO7 ....86 C7
South Hayling PO11 ......184 E3
Southampton SO16 ....77 E2
Swanmore SO32 ....84 D7
Totton SO40 ....76 B4
Whitsbury SP6 ....69 C7
Green Loaning BH23 ....207 F5
Green Park Cl SO23 .....215 F8
Green Park Rd SO16 ....101 E7
Green Pastures Cvn Site
SO51 ....75 E4
Green Pk BH1 ....205 D3
Green Pond Cnr 2 PO9 .136 B1
Green Pond La SO51 .....29 C3
Green Rd
Bournemouth BH9 ....205 A8
Gosport PO12 ....181 A3
Poole BH15 ....202 D1
Portsmouth PO5 ....216 B2
Stubbington PO14 ....154 C4
Green The Burton BH23 ..192 D2
East Meon GU32 ....38 D1
Liss GU33 ....20 E5
Romsey SO51 ....28 C1
Rowlands Castle PO9 .....113 C2
Sarisbury SO31 ....128 E6
Whiteparish SP5 ....24 B4
Green Wlk PO15 ....130 E3
Green's Cl SO50 ....57 A1
Greenacre BH25 ....210 A8
Greenacre Cl BH16 .....201 C6
Greenacre Gdns PO7 ...134 D4
Greenacres
32 Bournemouth BH4 .....204 C3
Downton SP5 ....46 D8
Greenacres Cl BH10 .....189 E6
Greenacres Dr SO21 .....31 C3
Greenaway La
Locks Heath SO31 ....128 E2
Warsash SO31 ....128 D2
Greenbank Cres SO16 ....78 F5
Greenbanks Cl SO41 ....211 D5
Greenbanks Gdns PO16 .131 D2
Greenclose La BH21 ....163 D4
Greendale Cl
Chandler's Ford SO53 ......55 E6
Fareham PO15 ....130 D4
Greendale The PO15 ....130 D4
Greenfield Cres PO8 ....112 C4
Greenfield Gdns BH25 ...210 B8
Greenfield Rd BH15 .....202 E7
Greenfield Rise PO8 ....112 B3
Greenfields Liss GU33 .....21 A4
1 Poole BH12 ....203 F7
Greenfields Ave SO40 ....76 F1
Greenfields Cl SO40 ......76 F1
Greenfinch Cl
Broadstone BH17 ....186 F1
Eastleigh SO50 ....55 D1
Greenfinch Wlk BH24 ...141 C6
Greenhayes BH18 ....187 C2
Greenhays Rise BH21 ...163 C5
Greenhill Ave SO22 .....215 C6
Greenhill Cl
Wimborne Minst BH21 ....163 D6
Winchester SO22 ....215 C6
Greenhill La
Rownhams SO16 ....77 E8
Wimborne Minst BH21 ....163 D6
Greenhill Rd
Wimborne Minst BH21 ....163 D6
Winchester SO22 ....215 B6
Greenhill Terr SO22 .....215 C6
Greenidge Ct 8 SO15 ...102 F8
Greenlea Cl PO7 ....134 B2
Greenlea Cres SO16 ......79 D5
Greenlea Rd PO12 ......180 F7
Greenmead Ave SO41 ....196 D1
Greens Cl SO32 ....83 B8
Greens Meade SP5 ....47 D6
Greenside Ct BH25 ......210 B6
Greensleeves Ave BH18 .187 B6
Greensome Dr BH22 .....165 F6
Greenway GU32 ....38 F1
Greenway Cl SO41 ....197 C3
Greenway Cres BH16 ....201 A7
Greenway La GU31 ....65 C6
Greenway Rd PO12 .....181 B7
Greenway The PO10 .....136 F4
Greenways
Chandler's Ford SO53 ......55 E6
Christchurch BH23 ....208 F8
Milford on S SO41 ....211 C5
Southampton SO16 ....79 D5
Swanmore SO32 ....84 B5
Greenways Ave BH8 .....190 C3
Greenways Ct BH22 .....165 E3
Greenways Rd SO42 .....146 A1
Greenwich The
Blackfield SO45 ....150 E2
24 Southampton SO14 ....103 A3
Greenwood Ave
Cosham PO6 ....157 D8
Ferndown BH22 ....165 E6
Poole BH14 ....214 C8
Rownhams SO16 ....77 D6
Greenwood Cl
Eastleigh SO50 ....55 F1
Fareham PO16 ....131 A4
Romsey SO51 ....53 A8
Greenwood Copse
BH24 ....140 A4
Greenwood La SO32 .....82 A8
Greenwood Rd BH9 .....204 E8
Greenwood Way BH24 ..140 A4
Greenwoods 6 BH25 ....195 B1
Greetham St PO5 ....216 B3
Gregg Sch The SO18 .....80 A3
Gregory Gdns SO40 ......76 C1
Gregory La SO32 ....82 C5
Gregson Ave PO13 ......155 C4
Gregson Cl PO13 ....155 C3
Grenadier Cl SO31 ......129 B2
Grendon Cl SO16 ....79 B5
Grenehurst Way GU31 ....40 F4
Grenfell Rd BH9 ....189 F3
Grenfield Ct PO10 ......136 F3
Grenville Cl BH24 ....117 D1
Grenville Ct
Bitterne Pk SO18 ....79 F3
11 Bournemouth BH4 .....204 D4
15 Poole BH15 ....202 C2
Grenville Gdns SO45 ....126 A1
Grenville Ho 32 PO1 ....182 A5
Grenville Rd
Portsmouth PO4 ....216 D1
Wimborne Minst BH21 ....163 D4
Gresham Rd BH9 ....190 B1
Gresley Gdns SO30 ....81 C2
Greville Gn PO10 ....136 E3
Greville Rd SO15 ....102 D7
Grevillea Ave PO15 .....129 E3
Greycot Cl BH21 ....138 E8
Greyfriars 2 SO23 ......215 F6
Greyfriars Ct PO5 ......216 B1
Greyfriars Rd PO15 .....130 C2
Greyhound Cl SO30 ......81 B3
Greyladyes SO31 ....128 B7
Greys Farm Cl SO24 .....14 D4
Greyshott Ave PO14 .....154 C8
Greystoke Ave BH11 .....188 F5
Greywell Ave SO16 ....78 C4
Greywell Ct SO16 ....78 C4
Greywell Sq PO9 ....135 F5
Griffen Cl SO50 ....56 E2
Griffin Ct
Southampton SO17 ....103 C8
Wimborne Minst BH21 ....163 D3
Griffin Ind Pk SO40 ......76 E2
Griffin Wlk PO13 ....180 C6
Griffiths Gdns BH10 .....189 B5
Griffon Cl SO31 ....105 A2
Grigg La SO42 ....146 A1
Grindle Cl PO16 ....132 C1
Gritanwood Rd PO4 .....183 B3
Grosvenor Cl
Southampton SO17 ....79 C2
St Leonards BH24 ....139 D5
Grosvenor Ct
8 Bournemouth BH1 .....205 B3
2 Bournemouth,Springbourne
BH1 ....205 D4
Christchurch BH23 ....209 B8
Farlington PO6 ....158 F8
Romsey SO51 ....53 C7
1 Southampton SO17 .....79 C1
Stubbington PO14 ....179 D7
Grosvenor Dr SO23 .....215 F8
Grosvenor Gdns
Bournemouth BH1 ....205 E4
Southampton SO17 ....79 C2
West End SO30 ....104 D8
Grosvenor Ho
4 Portsmouth PO5 ....216 B2
12 Southampton SO15 ....102 F6
6 Bournemouth BH4 .....204 C3
Grosvenor Lo 8 BH4 ....204 C3
Grosvenor Lodge 5
SO17 ....79 C2
Grosvenor Mews
5 Gosport PO12 ....181 C6
7 Highfield SO17 ....79 C2
Lymington SO41 ....197 D5
2 Southampton SO17 .....79 C1
Grosvenor Pines 13
BH4 ....204 C3
Grosvenor Rd
Bournemouth BH4 ....204 C3
Chandler's Ford SO53 ......30 E1
Southampton SO17 ....79 C2
Grosvenor Sq SO15 .....102 F6
Grosvenor St PO5 ......216 B2
Grove Ave Gosport PO12 .181 C6
Portchester PO16 ....156 C6
Grove Bldgs 7 PO12 ....181 C5
Grove Ct 5 PO9 ....135 F1
Grove Gdns
Barton on S BH25 ....210 A7
Southampton SO19 ....104 B2
Grove Ho
Portsmouth PO5 ....216 B1
Portsmouth PO5 ....216 C1
Grove La SP5 ....47 F7
Grove Mans 10 BH1 .....205 B3
Grove Mews SO19 ....104 B2
Grove Pastures SO41 ....197 E3
Grove Pl Lymington SO41 .197 E3
Southampton SO19 ....104 B2
Grove Rd
Barton on S BH25 ....210 A7
Bournemouth BH1 ....205 B3
Compton SO21 ....31 D5
Cosham PO6 ....158 C7
Fareham PO16 ....131 A1
Gosport PO12 ....181 B8
Havant PO9 ....135 F1
Lee-on-t-S PO13 ....179 E3
Lymington SO41 ....197 F3
Grove Rd *continued*
Poole BH12 ....203 B6
Southampton SO15 ....102 C7
Wimborne Minst BH21 ....163 D4
Grove Rd N PO5 ....216 B1
Grove Rd S PO5 ....216 B1
Grove Road E BH23 .....207 A8
Grove Road W BH23 ....206 F8
Grove St SO14 ....103 B4
Grove The
Bournemouth BH9 ....189 F3
Bursledon SO31 ....105 A1
Christchurch BH23 ....191 E1
Ferndown BH22 ....165 C4
Netley SO31 ....127 D7
Southampton SO19 ....104 B1
Stubbington PO14 ....179 B7
Verwood BH31 ....115 A5
Westbourne PO10 ....137 B3
Grovebury SO31 ....129 A2
Grovelands Rd SO22 ....1 B1
Groveley Bsns Ctr BH23 .207 E6
Groveley Rd
Bournemouth BH4 ....204 B2
Christchurch BH23 ....207 E6
Groveley Way SO51 ......28 E1
Grovely Ave BH5 ....205 F3
Groves Down SO51 ....50 E4
Grower Gdns BH11 ......189 A4
Gruneisen Rd PO2 ......157 C2
Guardhouse Rd PO1 ....182 B7
Guardian Ct 23 SO17 .....79 A1
Guardroom Rd PO2 .....157 B1
Gudge Heath La PO15 ...130 E2
Guelders The PO7 ....134 E3
Guernsey Cl SO16 ....77 E3
Guernsey Rd BH12 ......188 D1
Guessens La PO14 ....153 F8
Guest Ave BH12 ....204 A6
Guest Cl BH12 ....204 A6
Guest Rd
Bishopstoke SO50 ....56 D3
Upton BH16 ....201 B7
Guild Ho 18 SO14 ....103 A3
Guildford Cl PO10 ......137 E1
Guildford Ct
2 Bournemouth BH4 .....204 C4
15 Gosport PO13 ....180 D5
Guildford Dr SO53 ....55 B3
Guildford Rd PO1 ....182 E6
Guildford St 1 SO14 ....103 C5
Guildhall Ct BH15 ....202 B2
Guildhall Mus* BH15 ....202 B2
Guildhall Sq PO1 ....216 B3
Guildhall Wlk PO1 ......216 A3
Guildhill Rd BH6 ....206 E4
Guillemot Cl SO45 ......126 B2
Guillemot Gdns PO13 ...155 B3
Gull Cl PO13 ....155 B2
Gulliver Cl BH14 ....214 C8
Gulliver Ct 1 BH21 .....163 C5
Gulls The SO40 ....101 F2
Gullycroft Mead SO30 ...105 B7
Gunners Bldgs PO3 .....157 F4
Gunners Mews SO32 .....83 E8
Gunners Pk SO32 ....83 E7
Gunners Row PO4 ......183 B2
Gunners Way PO12 .....155 F1
Gunstore Rd PO3 ....158 A4
Gunville Cres BH9 ......190 B3
Gunwharf Quays PO1 ...181 F6
Gunwharf Quays (Sh Ctr)
PO1 ....182 A4
Gunwharf Rd PO1 ......182 A4
Gurjun Cl BH16 ....201 A8
Gurkha Mus The*
SO23 ....215 D5
Gurnard Rd PO6 ....157 E7
Gurnays Mead SO51 ......50 E3
Gurney Rd
Corfe Mullen BH21 ....186 E6
Portsmouth PO4 ....183 B4
Southampton SO15 ....102 C8
Gussage Rd BH12 ....203 F8
Gutner La PO11 ....160 C1
Guttridge Dro SO51 ......29 B7
Guy's Cl BH24 ....141 B6
Gwatkin Cl PO9 ....135 C3
Gwen-Rhian Ct 4 SO15 .102 F7
Gwenlyn Rd BH16 ....201 C6
Gwessin Terr 6 PO12 ...181 C5
Gwynne Rd BH12 ....203 E5
Gypsy La Ringwood BH24 .141 B8
Waterlooville PO8 ....111 F5

H

H Ave SO45 ....150 F6
Ha'penny Dell PO7 ......134 E3
Haarlem Mews BH23 ....207 D7
Haccupps La SO51 ....6 D1
Hack Dr SO21 ....56 F8
Hackett Way 2 PO14 ...155 A6
Hacketts La SO32 ....60 F2
Hackleys La SO51 ....51 B5
Hackworth Gdns SO30 ...81 C3
Hadden Rd BH8 ....205 D8
Haddon Cl PO14 ....130 E1
Haddon Dr SO50 ....56 A5
Haddons Dr BH21 ......138 D7
Hadleigh Gdns SO50 .....56 A5
Hadleigh Rd 3 PO6 .....157 D8
Hadley Field SO45 ....150 B5
Hadley Way BH18 ....186 E3
Hadow Rd BH10 ....189 C3
Hadrian Cl BH22 ....165 D2

Hadrian Way
Chilworth SO16 78 E7
Corfe Mullen BH21 186 E8
Hadriana Cl SO53 55 E7
Haflinger Dr PO15 129 B8
Haglane Copse SO41 197 C2
Hahnemann Rd BH2 204 E2
Haig Ave BH13 203 E1
Haig Ct 6 PO2 157 E3
Haig Rd SO50 57 A1
Haileybury Gdns SO30 81 C1
Hainault Dr BH31 115 A6
Haking Rd BH23 207 D7
Halcyon Ct BH15 202 C6
Halden Cl 2 SO51 28 B1
Hale Ave BH25 195 B2
Hale Ct PO1 182 E7
Hale Gdns BH25 195 B2
Hale La SP6 47 B3
Hale Prim Sch SP6 47 C3
Hale Rd SP6 70 E8
Hale St N PO1 216 C4
Hale St S PO1 216 C4
Hales Dr SO30 105 A5
Halesowen Ho 4 PO5 216 A2
Halewood Way BH23 206 F8
Half Moon St 1 PO1 182 A5
Halfpenny La PO1 182 A3
Halfway Rd SO45 151 E1
Halifax Ct SO30 80 C2
Halifax Rise PO7 134 F7
Halifax Way BH23 208 B7
Hall Cl SO32 83 D8
Hall Ct SO32 107 A7
Hall Lands La SO50 57 D2
Hall of Aviation (Mus)*
SO14 103 B3
Hall Rd BH11 188 F3
Hall Way The SO22 1 B5
Hallet Cl SO18 80 A2
Hallett Rd PO9 136 B2
Halletts Cl PO14 179 C8
Halliards The PO16 155 B7
Halliday Cl PO12 181 B6
Halliday Cres PO4 183 C3
Halliday Ho 12 PO4 183 B2
Hallowell Ho PO1 216 B4
Halls Farm Cl SO22 1 E3
Halsey Cl PO12 180 F3
Halstead Rd
Cosham PO6 157 D8
Southampton SO18 79 F2
Halstock Cres BH17 187 D2
Halter Path BH15 201 E3
Halter Rise BH21 164 C6
Halterworth Cl SO51 53 B7
Halterworth Com Prim Sch
SO51 53 C7
Halterworth La SO51 53 C7
Halton Cl BH23 193 B8
Haltons Cl SO40 76 D1
Halyard Cl PO13 180 D7
Halyards SO31 128 A4
Ham La Gosport PO12 156 A1
Hampreston BH21 164 E3
Horndean PO8 112 A8
Southbourne PO10 161 D7
Wimborne Minst BH21 164 C5
Hambert Way SO40 100 E5
Hamble Cl SO31 128 C1
Hamble Com Sports Coll
SO31 127 E5
Hamble Court Bsns Pk
SO31 127 E3
Hamble Ct
Chandler's Ford SO53 55 D5
Stubbington PO14 179 B8
3 Waterlooville PO8 111 F4
Hamble Ho PO16 155 A7
Hamble House Gdns
SO31 128 A2
Hamble La
Bursledon SO31 104 F2
Bursledon SO31 127 F8
Hamble-le-R SO31 127 F2
Waterlooville PO7 134 E5
Hamble Manor SO31 128 A2
Hamble Pk SO31 128 F1
Hamble Prim Sch SO31 127 E4
Hamble Rd Gosport PO12 180 F4
Poole BH15 203 A6
Hamble Springs SO32 83 D7
Hamble Sta SO31 127 E5
Hamblecliff Ho SO31 127 D3
Hambledon Cl SO22 1 D4
Hambledon Gdns BH6 206 C6
Hambledon Inf Sch PO7 86 D3
Hambledon La PO7,SO32 85 E3
Hambledon Par PO7 111 C2
Hambledon Rd
Bournemouth BH7 206 B7
Bournemouth,West Southbourne
BH6 206 C6
Clanfield PO8 88 B6
Denmead PO7 111 B3
Hambledon PO7 110 D8
Waterlooville PO7 134 E7
Hambleside Ct SO31 127 F2
Hamblewood SO30 106 A6
Hamblewood Ct SO30 106 A6
Hamblin Way BH8 190 E2
Hambrook Rd 1 PO12 181 A7
Hambrook St PO5 216 A1
Hamdown Cres SO51 51 B2
Hameldon Cl SO16 101 E7
Hamfield Dr PO11 184 E4
Hamilton Bsns Pk BH25 194 E2
Hamilton Cl
Bournemouth BH1 205 D5
Christchurch BH23 207 F4
Hamworthy BH15 201 E2
Langstone PO9 159 F8
Hamilton Cres BH15 201 E2
Hamilton Ct
1 Bournemouth BH8 205 B5
Milford on S SO41 211 C4
16 Portsmouth PO5 182 C2
16 Southampton SO17 79 A1
1 Wimborne Minst BH21 163 B5
Hamilton Gr PO13 155 B2
Hamilton Ho PO1 216 D4
Hamilton Mews
Bransgore BH23 193 B8
4 Hythe SO45 126 B1
Lymington SO41 197 F4
Hamilton Pk SP5 47 A8
Hamilton Pl SO41 197 D3
Hamilton Rd
Bishopstoke SO50 56 D3
Bournemouth BH1 205 D4
Corfe Mullen BH21 186 E5
Hamworthy BH15 201 E2
Hythe SO45 150 B8
Portchester PO6 156 E8
Portsmouth PO5 182 D2
Hamilton Way BH25 194 E2
Hamlet Ct SO45 151 B3
Hamlet Way PO12 156 A1
Hammond Cl PO15 130 D2
Hammond Ho 9 PO12 181 E5
Hammond Ind Pk PO14 179 D6
Hammond Rd PO15 130 E2
Hammond's Gn SO40 100 D8
Hammonds Cl SO40 100 E8
Hammonds La SO40 100 E8
Hammonds Way SO40 100 E8
Hampage Gn PO9 135 D7
Hampden La BH6 206 B5
Hampreston CE Fst Sch
BH21 164 E3
Hampshire Cl BH23 191 F2
Hampshire Corporate Pk
SO53 55 B2
Hampshire Ct
3 Bournemouth BH2 204 F3
Chandler's Ford SO53 55 C3
Hampshire Hatches La
BH24 141 A4
Hampshire Ho 2 BH2 204 F3
Hampshire St PO1 182 E7
Hampshire Terr PO1 216 A2
Hampton Cl
Blackfield SO45 177 E8
Waterlooville PO7 135 A7
Hampton Ct 5 BH2 204 D4
Hampton Dr BH24 117 B1
Hampton Farm La SO32 84 A6
Hampton Gdns SO45 177 E8
Hampton Gr PO15 130 B1
Hampton Hill SO32 84 B6
Hampton La
Blackfield SO45 150 E1
Winchester SO22 215 A7
Hampton Twrs SO19 126 E8
Hamptworth Rd SP5 48 D4
Hamtun Cres SO40 76 E1
Hamtun Gdns SO40 76 E1
Hamtun Rd SO19 104 C3
Hamtun St 6 SO14 102 F3
Hamwic Ho 3 SO14 103 A6
Hamworthy Fst Sch
BH15 201 F1
Hamworthy LODGE
BH15 201 F2
Hamworthy Mid Sch
BH15 201 F1
Hamworthy Sta BH16 201 D4
Hanbidge Cres PO13 155 D4
Hanbidge Wlk PO13 155 D4
Hanbury Sq GU31 41 A5
Handel Rd SO15 102 F5
Handel Terr SO15 102 E6
Handford Pl 2 SO15 102 F6
Handley Ct BH24 140 F7
Handley Lodge 2 BH12 203 F7
Handley Rd PO12 180 F6
Handsworth Ho PO5 216 C2
Handy Villas 22 SO23 215 E6
Hanger Way GU31 41 B3
Hangers The SO32 59 E2
Hanham Ct BH12 204 B8
Hanham Rd
Corfe Mullen BH21 186 D5
Wimborne Minst BH21 163 C5
Hankinson Rd BH9 205 A8
Hanley Rd SO15 102 D8
Hanlon Cl BH11 189 B4
Hann Rd SO16 77 E6
Hannah Gdns PO7 134 F8
Hannah Way SO41 196 F5
Hannay Rise SO19 104 D5
Hannington Pl BH7 206 A5
Hannington Rd
Bournemouth BH7 206 A5
Havant PO9 135 D7
Hanns Way SO50 56 A2
Hanover Bldgs SO14 103 A4
Hanover Cotts SO32 36 E3
Hanover Ct Hythe SO45 126 A4
7 Portsmouth PO1 182 A4
Hanover Gdns PO16 131 B3
Hanover Gn BH17 202 F7
Hanover Ho
Gosport PO13 155 B5
Poole BH15 202 D3
Hanover Ho *continued*
7 Southampton SO14 103 A4
Totton SO40 101 A8
Hanover Lodge SO23 215 D4
Hanover St PO1 182 A5
Hanoverian Way PO15 129 C7
Hanway Rd PO1,PO2 100 E7
Harbeck Rd BH8 190 C3
Harborough Rd SO15 102 F6
Harbour Cl
Marchwood SO40 102 C2
Poole BH13 214 D6
Harbour Cres BH23 207 E5
Harbour Ct
Barton on S BH25 209 E7
Christchurch BH23 207 E6
8 Emsworth PO10 160 F8
Poole BH13 214 E6
Harbour Hill Cres BH15 202 E5
Harbour Hill Rd BH15 202 E5
Harbour Hospl The
BH15 202 D3
Harbour Lights BH15 202 E4
Harbour Par SO15 102 F4
Harbour Prospect BH14 214 C8
Harbour Rd
Bournemouth BH6 207 A3
Gosport PO1 181 E6
South Hayling PO11 184 C4
Harbour Side Cvn & Camping
Site PO3 158 D1
Harbour Twr 10 PO12 181 E5
Harbour View PO16 156 C6
Harbour View Cl BH14 203 A5
Harbour View Ct BH23 207 B5
Harbour View Rd BH14 203 A5
Harbour Watch BH14 214 C7
Harbour Way
Emsworth PO10 161 A8
Portsmouth PO2 157 C2
Harbourgate Bsns Pk
PO6 157 B8
Harbourne Gdns SO18 80 B2
Harbourside PO9 159 F6
Harbridge Ct
Havant PO9 135 D7
Verwood BH24 115 F6
Harbridge Dro BH24 93 C3
Harcombe Cl BH17 187 E3
Harcourt Cl PO8 112 A4
Harcourt Mews 6 BH5 206 A5
Harcourt Rd
Bournemouth BH5 206 A5
Fareham PO14 154 B7
Gosport PO12 181 A6
Portsmouth PO1 182 E7
Southampton SO18 103 E8
Hard The PO1 182 A5
Harding La SO50 57 B3
Harding Rd PO12 180 F6
Hardley Ind Est SO45 150 B6
Hardley La SO45 150 B8
Hardley Rdbt SO45 150 B6
Hardley Sch & Sixth Form
SO45 150 C5
Hardman Ct PO3 158 B4
Hardwick Rd SO53 55 D6
Hardwicke Cl SO16 77 F2
Hardwicke Way SO31 127 E3
Hardy Ave GU31 41 A5
Hardy Cl
Locks Heath SO31 129 B4
New Milton BH25 194 F3
Southampton SO15 102 B6
West Moors BH22 138 F1
Hardy Cres BH21 163 D4
Hardy Dr SO45 126 B1
Hardy Rd Eastleigh SO50 56 A1
Farlington PO6 158 E7
Poole BH14 203 D4
West Moors BH22 138 F1
Hare La Alderholt BH21 91 F5
New Milton BH25,SO41 195 E3
Twyford SO21 32 A4
Harebell Cl PO16 131 C3
Harefield Ct SO51 53 B8
Harefield Inf Sch SO18 104 B8
Harefield Jun Sch SO18 104 B8
Harefield Rd SO17 79 C3
Hares Gn BH7 206 A8
Harestock Cl SO22 1 D5
Harestock Cnr SO22 1 C3
Harestock Prim Sch SO22 1 D3
Harestock Rd
Havant PO9 135 D3
Winchester SO22 1 C4
Harewood Ave BH7 206 A6
Harewood Cl SO50 56 A5
Harewood Cres BH7 205 F8
Harewood Gdns BH7 205 F7
Harewood Gn SO41 212 A4
Harewood Pl BH7 206 B6
Harford Cl SO41 197 C1
Harford Rd BH12 203 C8
Harkness Dr PO7 135 B8
Harkwood Dr BH15 201 E4
Harland Cres SO15 78 D1
Harland Rd BH6 207 A3
Harlaxton Cl SO50 55 F5
Harlech Dr SO53 55 A4
Harlequin Gr PO15 130 F1
Harleston Rd PO6 133 D1
Harleston Villas 5
BH21 163 D4
Harley Ct SO31 128 D1
Harley Wlk PO1 216 C4
Harlyn Rd SO16 77 F1
Harman Rd PO13 155 C3
Harness Cl BH21 164 B6
Harold Cl SO40 100 C6
Harold Rd
Portsmouth PO4 182 E3
South Hayling PO11 185 B2
Southampton SO15 102 C7
Stubbington PO14 179 D8
Westbourne PO10 137 B4
Harold Terr PO10 136 F1
Harper Way 15 PO16 131 B1
Harpway La BH23 192 C6
Harraby Gn BH18 187 A3
Harrage The SO51 52 F7
Harrier Cl Horndean PO8 112 A7
Lee-on-t-S PO13 179 F3
Southampton SO16 78 B6
Harrier Dr BH21 163 D2
Harrier Gn SO45 150 B6
Harrier Mews SO31 127 E3
Harrier Way
Hardley SO45 150 B6
Petersfield GU31 41 C2
Harriers Cl BH23 208 D8
Harriet Cl PO14 179 B7
Harrington Ct BH23 208 F7
Harris Ave SO30 105 C8
Harris La PO8 89 E5
Harris Rd PO13 155 C3
Harris Way
New Milton BH25 195 B6
North Baddesley SO52 54 A4
Harrison Ave BH1 205 D6
Harrison Cl BH23 192 C3
Harrison Ho 3 PO2 157 D2
Harrison Prim Sch
PO16 131 B2
Harrison Rd
Fareham PO16 131 B2
Southampton SO17 79 C3
Harrison Way BH22 138 E3
Harrison's Cut SO14 103 A4
Harrow Cl BH23 193 B7
Harrow Down SO22 215 B2
Harrow La GU32 40 F6
Harrow Rd
Bransgore BH23 193 B6
Portsmouth PO5 216 D2
Harrowgate La PO7,PO8 87 B1
Harry Barrow Cl 1
BH24 141 A6
Harry Law Hall PO1 216 B3
Hart Cl BH25 194 F4
Hart Ct SO19 103 F3
Hart Hill SO45 126 C2
Hart Plain Ave
Waterlooville PO8 111 D3
Waterlooville PO8 111 F2
Hart Plain Jun & Inf Schs
PO7,PO8 111 E2
Hartford Ho PO1 216 A1
Harthill Dro SP5 47 E6
Harting Cl PO8 88 D4
Harting Down GU31 41 B4
Harting Gdns PO16 132 C1
Harting Rd BH6 206 D7
Hartington Rd
Gosport PO12 180 F6
Southampton SO14 103 B6
Hartland Ct PO10 137 D1
Hartland's Rd PO16 131 B1
Hartley Ave SO17 79 B3
Hartley Cl
Bishopstoke SO50 57 A1
Hythe SO45 126 A1
Hartley Ct 5 SO17 103 A8
Hartley Gr SO16 79 A4
Hartley Rd
Bishopstoke SO50 57 A1
Portsmouth PO2 157 E3
Hartley Wlk 1 SO45 126 A1
Hartnell Ct BH21 186 D5
Harts Farm Way PO9 159 C8
Harts Way SO41 196 D1
Hartsbourne Dr BH7 206 B8
Hartsgrove Ave SO45 150 E1
Hartsgrove Cl SO45 150 E1
Hartwell Rd PO3 158 B4
Hartwood Gdns PO8 111 E2
Harvard Cl PO13 180 A5
Harvest Cl SO22 215 B2
Harvest La SP5 22 C8
Harvest Rd
Chandler's Ford SO53 54 F6
Denmead PO7 110 E4
Harvester Dr PO15 130 B1
Harvester Way SO41 197 D6
Harvestgate Wlk PO9 135 D6
Harvesting La GU32 64 C5
Harvey Brown Ho PO11 185 A5
Harvey Cres SO31 128 F2
Harvey Ct SO45 150 E2
Harvey Gdns SO45 126 B3
Harvey Ho 13 PO4 183 B2
Harvey Rd
Bishopstoke SO50 56 E2
Bournemouth BH5 206 A5
Oakley BH21 187 E8
Harwell Rd BH17 202 D7
Harwich Rd PO6 133 D1
Harwood Cl
Gosport PO13 155 C4
Totton SO40 100 D8
Harwood Ct BH25 194 F3
Harwood Pl SO23 2 C8
Harwood Rd PO13 155 C4
Haselbury Rd SO40 100 F7
Haselfoot Gdns SO30 104 E7
Haselworth Dr PO12 181 B2
Haselworth Prim Sch
PO12 181 B4
Haskells Cl SO43 121 E4
Haskells Rd BH12 203 B7
Haslar Cres PO7 111 D2
Haslar Marina PO12 181 F4
Haslar Rd
Gosport,Clayhall PO12 181 D3
Gosport,Newtown PO12 181 E5
Haslar Terr PO12 181 D3
Haslegrave Ho 2 PO2 182 D8
Haslemere Ave BH23 209 A8
Haslemere Gdns PO11 185 F2
Haslemere Pl BH23 209 A8
Haslemere Rd
Breach PO10 137 D2
Portsmouth PO4 182 F3
Hasler Rd BH17 187 D2
Haslop Rd BH21 164 A7
Hassocks The 7 PO7 135 A7
Hastings Ave PO12 180 F8
Hastings Ho 3 PO2 157 C2
Hastings Rd
Bournemouth BH8 190 F2
Poole BH17 187 B2
Hatch Ct PO9 135 C7
Hatch La GU33 21 C4
Hatch Mead SO30 80 C2
Hatch Pond Rd BH17 202 C8
Hatchers La SO21 33 A5
Hatchet Cl SP6 47 D3
Hatchet La SO42 175 D8
Hatchley La SO32 58 B5
Hatfield Ct BH25 194 E3
Hatfield Gdns BH7 206 B8
Hatfield Rd 1 PO4 183 A3
Hathaway Cl SO50 56 B4
Hathaway Gdns PO7 112 B1
Hathaway Rd BH6 206 D4
Hatherden Ave BH14 202 F5
Hatherell Cl SO30 80 D1
Hatherley Cres PO16 156 B8
Hatherley Dr PO16 156 B8
Hatherley Mans 4
SO15 102 C7
Hatherley Rd
Portsmouth PO6 133 A1
Winchester SO22 215 D7
Hatley Rd SO18 104 B8
Hatt La SO51 5 E2
Havant Bsns Ctr PO9 159 D8
Havant Coll PO9 135 E2
Havant Education PRU
PO8 111 F2
Havant Farm Cl PO9 135 F3
Havant Mus & Arts Ctr*
PO9 136 A1
Havant Rd Cosham PO6 157 F8
Emsworth PO10 160 D8
Farlington PO6 158 D8
Horndean PO8 112 D6
North Hayling PO11 160 A5
North Hayling,Fleet PO11 185 A7
Portsmouth PO2 157 E1
Stoke PO11 159 F2
Havant Ret Pk PO9 135 B1
Havant St PO1 182 A5
Havant Sta PO9 135 F2
Havant War Meml Hospl
PO9 135 E2
Havant-by-pass PO9 160 A8
Havelock Ct SO31 128 C1
Havelock Mans PO5 216 D2
Havelock Rd Poole BH12 204 A5
Portsmouth PO5 216 C2
Southampton SO14 102 F5
Warsash SO31 128 C1
Havelock Way BH23 193 D2
Haven Cotts BH23 208 A4
Haven Cres PO14 153 F1
Haven Ct
4 Milford on S SO41 211 C4
Poole BH13 214 B3
Haven Gdns BH25 195 B2
Haven Rd
Corfe Mullen BH21 186 C6
Poole BH13 214 E7
South Hayling PO11 185 E1
Haven The Eastleigh SO50 56 B5
Gosport PO12 181 B3
Locks Heath SO31 129 B4
Portsmouth PO4 183 B5
Southampton SO19 103 E4
Havendale SO30 105 D5
Havenhurst BH13 214 E6
Havenstone Way SO18 79 E4
Haverstock Rd BH9 190 B2
Haviland Mews BH7 205 F5
Haviland Rd
Bournemouth BH7 205 F5
Ferndown BH21 165 A7
Haviland Rd E BH7 205 F5
Haviland Rd W BH1 205 F5
Havisham Rd PO2 182 C7
Havre Twrs SO19 126 E8
Hawden Rd BH11 189 A1
Haweswater Cl SO16 77 F1
Hawfinch Cl SO16 78 B6
Hawk Cl
Stubbington PO14 179 B7
Wimborne Minst BH21 164 A7
Hawkchurch Gdns BH17 187 E2
Hawke St PO1 182 A5
Hawker Cl BH21 163 F1
Hawkers Cl SO40 76 E1

Hawkeswood Rd SO18 ... 103 C7
Hawkewood Ave PO7 ... 111 D2
Hawkhill SO45 ... 125 C3
Hawkhurst Cl SO19 ... 104 A1
Hawkins Cl BH24 ... 117 C1
Hawkins Ct SO40 ... 101 F3
Hawkins Rd
Gosport PO13 ... 155 D2
Poole BH12 ... 188 F1
Hawkley Cl PO9 ... 135 E6
Hawkley Gn SO19 ... 126 F8
Hawkley Rd GU33 ... 20 C5
Hawks Mead GU33 ... 20 E5
Hawkwell PO16 ... 155 F8
Hawkwood Rd BH1,BH5 ... 205 F4
Haworth Cl BH23 ... 192 A1
Hawstead Gn PO9 ... 135 D6
Hawthorn Cl
Colden Common SO21 ... 57 A8
Fair Oak SO50 ... 57 C2
Hedge End SO30 ... 105 D6
New Milton BH25 ... 195 C4
Portchester PO16 ... 132 B1
Hawthorn Cres PO6 ... 158 B6
Hawthorn Ct GU31 ... 41 C3
Hawthorn Dr
Broadstone BH17 ... 186 F1
Sway SO41 ... 172 B2
Hawthorn La SO31 ... 128 E5
Hawthorn Rd
Bournemouth BH9 ... 204 F8
Burton BH23 ... 192 E4
Denmead PO7 ... 110 E4
Horndean PO8 ... 88 C2
Hythe SO45 ... 125 F3
Southampton SO17 ... 79 A2
Hawthorn Wlk 6 PO13 ... 179 F3
Hawthorne Gr PO11 ... 185 B4
Hawthorne Rd SO40 ... 100 D8
Hawthorns The
Bishop's Waltham SO32 ... 83 A8
Christchurch BH23 ... 207 F6
Eastleigh SO50 ... 55 E1
Marchwood SO40 ... 102 A1
Hawthorns The Urban Wildlife Ctr* SO15 ... 102 F8
Hayburn Rd SO16 ... 77 D2
Haydens Ct SO41 ... 197 F4
Haydn Cl SO23 ... 2 B8
Haydock Cl SO40 ... 100 C8
Haydock Mews PO7 ... 112 B1
Haydon Rd BH13 ... 204 B1
Hayes Ave BH7 ... 205 E6
Hayes Cl Fareham PO15 ... 130 D3
Wimborne Minst BH21 ... 164 A4
Hayes La BH21 ... 164 B5
Hayes Mead SO45 ... 150 B6
Hayeswood Fst Sch BH21 ... 164 B6
Hayeswood Rd BH21 ... 164 A6
Hayle Rd SO18 ... 80 B2
Hayley Cl SO45 ... 149 F8
Hayling Ave PO3 ... 183 B7
Hayling Billy Bsns Ctr PO11 ... 184 D4
Hayling Cl
Fareham PO14 ... 154 D8
Gosport PO12 ... 181 C9
Hayling Sch The PO11 ... 185 A5
Haymoor Mid Sch BH17 ... 187 E1
Haymoor Rd BH15 ... 203 A7
Haynes Ave BH15 ... 202 D4
Haynes Way SO45 ... 125 E1
Hays Cotts GU32 ... 40 D7
Haysoms Cl BH25 ... 195 B1
Hayter Gdns SO51 ... 53 A8
Hayters Way SP6 ... 93 A6
Hayton Ct 2 SO40 ... 100 F7
Hayward Bsns Ctr PO9 ... 136 B3
Hayward Cl SO40 ... 100 D7
Hayward Cres BH31 ... 114 E5
Hayward Ct SO45 ... 150 C4
Hayward Way BH31 ... 114 E5
Haywards Ct 11 PO1 ... 182 A4
Haywards Farm Cl BH31 ... 114 E5
Haywards La BH21 ... 186 C7
Hazel Cl Alderholt SP6 ... 93 A5
Chandler's Ford SO53 ... 30 C1
Christchurch BH23 ... 193 C1
Colden Common SO21 ... 57 A8
Hazel Ct
Bournemouth BH9 ... 190 C4
1 New Milton BH25 ... 195 B1
Portsmouth PO4 ... 182 F4
Winchester SO22 ... 215 A8
Hazel Dr BH22 ... 165 D8
Hazel Farm Rd SO40 ... 100 C7
Hazel Gr
Locks Heath SO31 ... 129 B2
Winchester SO22 ... 215 B3
Woodlands SO40 ... 99 F3
Hazel Rd Clanfield PO8 ... 88 C5
Lymington SO41 ... 197 A4
Southampton SO19 ... 103 D3
Hazel Wlk GU31 ... 40 F1
Hazel Wood Inf Sch SO40 ... 100 C7
Hazelbank Cl GU31 ... 41 B4
Hazeldale Villas SO45 ... 126 A5
Hazeldean Ct PO9 ... 113 B1
Hazeldean Dr PO9 ... 113 B1
Hazeldown Rd SO16 ... 77 E5
Hazeleigh Ave SO19 ... 103 E2
Hazeley Farm Cotts SO21 ... 32 E7
Hazeley Gn PO9 ... 136 B5
Hazeley Rd SO21 ... 32 D6
Hazelgrove PO8 ... 88 C5
Hazelholt Dr PO9 ... 135 D3
Hazell Ave BH10 ... 189 B2
Hazelton Cl BH7 ... 206 A8
Hazelwood PO14 ... 154 B5
Hazelwood Ave
Havant PO9 ... 135 B3
New Milton BH25 ... 194 F4
Hazelwood Dr BH31 ... 115 B4
Hazelwood Rd SO18 ... 80 A1
Hazlebury Rd BH17 ... 202 A7
Hazlemere Dr BH24 ... 139 E3
Hazleton Way PO8 ... 112 B4
Head Down GU31 ... 41 B3
Head's La BH10 ... 189 E5
Headbourne Worthy Ho SO23 ... 2 B5
Headinglea 9 BH13 ... 204 B3
Headland Dr SO31 ... 129 A4
Headlands Bsns Pk BH24 ... 117 A2
Headlands The SP5 ... 46 E7
Headless Cross BH10 ... 189 D5
Headley Cl PO13 ... 179 F3
Headon View GU32 ... 37 C5
Heads Farm Cl BH10 ... 189 E5
Headswell Ave BH10 ... 189 E4
Headswell Cres BH10 ... 189 E4
Headswell Gdns BH10 ... 189 E4
Heanor Cl BH10 ... 189 C2
Hearne Gdns SO32 ... 84 A1
Hearts of Oak Mews SO41 ... 197 D4
Heath Ave BH15 ... 202 D6
Heath Cl Fair Oak SO50 ... 57 D1
Horndean PO8 ... 112 B7
Wimborne Minst BH21 ... 164 B7
Heath Ct GU31 ... 40 F2
Heath Farm Cl BH22 ... 165 C3
Heath Farm Rd BH22 ... 165 C3
Heath Farm Way BH22 ... 165 C3
Heath Gdns SO31 ... 127 D7
Heath House Cl SO30 ... 105 B4
Heath House Gdns SO30 ... 105 B4
Heath House La SO30 ... 105 C4
Heath La SO42 ... 175 C7
Heath Lawns PO15 ... 130 D1
Heath Lodge GU31 ... 40 F2
Heath Rd Hordle SO41 ... 195 F3
Locks Heath SO31 ... 129 A3
North Baddesley SO52 ... 54 A3
Petersfield GU31 ... 41 A3
Soberton SO32 ... 85 A1
Southampton SO19 ... 104 A5
St Leonards BH24 ... 139 D4
Walkford BH23 ... 194 B1
Heath Rd E GU31 ... 41 B2
Heath Rd N SO31 ... 128 F3
Heath Rd S SO31 ... 128 F3
Heath Rd W GU31 ... 41 A2
Heath The PO7 ... 111 A4
Heathcote Ct 2 BH7 ... 205 F4
Heathcote Pl SO21 ... 30 B7
Heathcote Rd
Bournemouth BH5,BH7 ... 205 F4
Chandler's Ford SO53 ... 55 D6
Portsmouth PO2 ... 157 F1
Heathen St SO32 ... 82 B4
Heather Chase SO50 ... 57 A2
Heather Cl
Bournemouth BH8 ... 190 D4
Corfe Mullen BH21 ... 186 E6
Gosport PO13 ... 155 B2
Hordle SO41 ... 196 A3
St Leonards BH24 ... 139 E3
Totton SO40 ... 100 E7
Walkford BH23 ... 194 A2
Waterlooville PO7 ... 134 F6
Heather Ct SO18 ... 104 D7
Heather Dr BH22 ... 165 D7
Heather Gdns PO15 ... 130 D3
Heather Lo 1 BH25 ... 195 A3
Heather Rd
Blackfield SO45 ... 150 F2
Bournemouth BH10 ... 189 D3
Petersfield GU31 ... 41 C3
Heather View Rd BH12 ... 203 F7
Heather Way BH22 ... 165 D7
Heatherbank Rd BH4 ... 204 C3
Heatherbrae Gdns SO52 ... 53 F4
Heatherbrae La BH16 ... 201 B6
Heatherdeane Rd SO17 ... 79 A2
Heatherdell BH16 ... 201 B6
Heatherdene Rd SO53 ... 30 E1
Heatherdown Rd BH22 ... 139 A1
Heatherdown Way BH22 ... 139 A1
Heatherfield GU31 ... 65 D5
Heatherlands Fst Sch BH12 ... 203 E5
Heatherlands Rd SO16 ... 78 F8
Heatherlands Rise BH12 ... 203 D5
Heatherlea Rd BH6 ... 206 D4
Heatherley Ct PO5 ... 216 C1
Heatherstone Ave
Dibden Purlieu SO45 ... 125 F1
Hythe SO45 ... 126 A1
Heatherton Mews PO10 ... 136 F2
Heatherview Cl SO52 ... 53 F5
Heathfield SO45 ... 125 F2
Heathfield Ave
Fareham PO15 ... 130 D1
Poole BH12 ... 204 A8
Heathfield Cl
Chandler's Ford SO53 ... 30 C2
Southampton SO19 ... 104 B3
Heathfield Cvn Pk BH23 ... 169 F2
Heathfield Ho BH23 ... 169 F1
Heathfield Jun Sch SO19 ... 104 C3
Heathfield Rd
Chandler's Ford SO53 ... 30 C2
Petersfield GU31 ... 41 C3
Portsmouth PO2 ... 157 D1
Southampton SO19 ... 104 B3
West Moors BH22 ... 139 A1
Heathfield Specl Sch PO14 ... 154 C8
Heathfield Way BH22 ... 138 F1
Heathlands SO32 ... 107 E7
Heathlands Ave BH22 ... 165 D2
Heathlands Cl
Burton BH23 ... 192 C3
Chandler's Ford SO53 ... 55 C8
Verwood BH31 ... 115 A6
Heathlands Ct SO45 ... 149 E8
Heathlands Prim Sch BH11 ... 189 A3
Heathlands Rd SO53 ... 55 C8
Heathwood Ave BH25 ... 209 E8
Heathwood Rd BH9 ... 204 E8
Heathy Cl BH25 ... 209 F8
Heaton Rd
Bournemouth BH10 ... 189 B2
Gosport PO12 ... 181 A8
Heavytree Rd BH14 ... 203 B4
Hebrides Cl PO14 ... 179 B8
Heckfield Cl 10 PO9 ... 136 B5
Heckford La BH15 ... 202 D3
Heckford Rd
Corfe Mullen BH21 ... 186 C5
Poole BH15 ... 202 D4
Hector Cl PO7 ... 134 E2
Hector Rd PO14 ... 155 A6
Hedera Rd SO31 ... 128 F3
Hedge End Bsns Ctr SO30 ... 81 B1
Hedge End Ret Pk SO30 ... 105 A7
Hedge End Sta SO30 ... 81 D3
Hedge End Trad Pk SO30 ... 81 A1
Hedge End Wlk 7 PO9 ... 136 B6
Hedgerley BH25 ... 210 B8
Hedgerow Cl SO16 ... 77 E7
Hedgerow Dr SO18 ... 80 B1
Hedgerow Gdns PO10 ... 136 F3
Hedley Cl SO45 ... 150 F1
Hedley Gdns SO30 ... 81 B2
Heidelberg Rd PO4 ... 182 F4
Heights App BH16 ... 201 C7
Heights Rd BH16 ... 201 C8
Heights The
Fareham PO16 ... 131 D2
Hedge End SO30 ... 105 A4
Heinz Burt Cl SO50 ... 55 F3
Helena Rd PO4 ... 182 F2
Helford Gdns SO18 ... 80 B2
Helic Ho 2 BH21 ... 163 C5
Hellyer Rd PO4 ... 183 A3
Helm Cl PO13 ... 180 D6
Helsby Cl PO14 ... 154 E8
Helsted Cl PO12 ... 180 E4
Helston Dr PO10 ... 136 F3
Helston Rd PO6 ... 132 F1
Helvellyn Rd SO16 ... 101 F8
Helyar Rd BH8 ... 190 F2
Hemdean Gdns SO30 ... 80 D1
Hemlock Rd PO8 ... 111 E4
Hemlock Way SO53 ... 54 F5
Hemming Cl SO40 ... 100 E6
Hemmingway Gdns PO15 ... 129 C8
Hempland La GU34 ... 17 C4
Hempsted Rd PO6 ... 133 B1
Hemsley Wlk PO8 ... 112 A4
Henbest Cl BH21 ... 164 C5
Henbury Cl
Corfe Mullen BH21 ... 186 D6
Poole BH17 ... 188 A2
Henbury Rise BH21 ... 186 D6
Henbury View Fst Sch BH21 ... 186 C6
Henbury View Rd BH21 ... 186 D6
Henchard Cl BH22 ... 165 C2
Henderson Pk PO4 ... 183 C3
Henderson Rd PO4 ... 183 C3
Hendford Gdns BH10 ... 189 D2
Hendford Rd BH10 ... 189 D2
Hendy Cl PO5 ... 216 B1
Henery St 10 PO12 ... 181 C5
Hengist Cvn Pk BH6 ... 207 B4
Hengist Rd BH1 ... 205 D4
Hengistbury Head Nature Reserve* BH6 ... 207 E2
Hengistbury Head Nature Trail* BH6 ... 207 C3
Hengistbury Rd
Barton on S BH25 ... 209 E8
Bournemouth BH6 ... 207 A3
Henley Ct SO41 ... 211 E3
Henley Gdns
Bournemouth BH7 ... 206 A7
Fareham PO15 ... 130 D4
Henley Rd PO4 ... 182 F3
Henning's Park Rd BH15 ... 202 E5
Henry Beaufort Sch SO22 ... 1 E3
Henry Cl SO45 ... 150 B6
Henry Cort Com Coll The PO15 ... 130 B3
Henry Cort Dr PO15 ... 130 C3
Henry Player Ave PO12 ... 181 D7
Henry Rd
Bishopstoke SO50 ... 56 D4
Southampton SO15 ... 102 C7
Henry St SO15 ... 102 F6
Henstead Ct 9 SO15 ... 102 F6
Henstead Rd SO15 ... 102 F6
Hensting La SO50 ... 32 E2
Henty Rd SO16 ... 102 B8
Henville Cl PO13 ... 180 D8
Henville Rd 6 BH8 ... 205 C5
Henwood Down GU31 ... 41 A3
Hepworth Cl SO19 ... 104 C2
Herald Ind Est SO30 ... 81 B1
Herald Rd SO30 ... 81 B1
Herbert Ave BH12 ... 203 D7
Herbert Ct BH12 ... 203 D7
Herbert Hospl BH4 ... 204 B2
Herbert Rd Gosport PO12 ... 180 F5
New Milton BH25 ... 195 B3
Poole BH4 ... 204 B2
Portsmouth PO4 ... 182 E2
Redlynch SP5 ... 47 D6
Herbert St PO1 ... 182 C7
Herbert Walker Ave
Southampton SO15 ... 102 C4
Southampton SO15 ... 102 E3
Herberton Rd BH6 ... 206 C5
Hercules Rd BH15 ... 201 D3
Hercules St PO2 ... 182 D8
Hereford Ct
10 Gosport PO13 ... 180 C6
Portsmouth PO5 ... 216 C1
Hereford Rd PO5 ... 216 C1
Hereward Cl SO51 ... 53 B7
Heritage Bsns Pk PO12 ... 155 F1
Heritage Ct BH13 ... 214 F7
Heritage Gdns PO16 ... 156 A7
Heritage Way PO12 ... 155 F1
Heritage Way,Priddy's Hard PO12 ... 181 C9
Herm Rd BH12 ... 188 D1
Hermes Ct 10 PO12 ... 181 C9
Hermes Rd PO13 ... 179 D4
Hermitage Cl
Bishop's Waltham SO32 ... 83 A8
Havant PO9 ... 135 E4
Three Legged Cross BH21 ... 138 E8
Hermitage Gdns PO7 ... 134 F8
Hermitage Rd BH14 ... 203 A5
Hermitage The BH14 ... 203 A5
Hern La SP6 ... 94 B6
Herne Jun Sch GU31 ... 41 A4
Herne Rd Cosham PO6 ... 157 E8
Petersfield GU31 ... 41 A3
Heron Cl Portsmouth PO4 ... 183 B5
Sway SO41 ... 172 B2
Heron Court Rd BH3, BH9 ... 205 A7
Heron Dr BH21 ... 164 A8
Heron Ho 1 PO5 ... 182 E2
Heron La SO51 ... 27 D6
Heron Quay PO10 ... 161 A7
Heron Sq SO50 ... 55 E2
Heron Way PO13 ... 155 B3
Herons Cl PO14 ... 154 C4
Herons Ct PO11 ... 185 B5
Heronswood SO40 ... 76 D2
Herrick Cl SO19 ... 104 D4
Herriot Ho PO8 ... 112 A2
Herriott Cl PO8 ... 112 A5
Herstone Cl BH17 ... 187 F1
Hertford Cl SP6 ... 69 F3
Hertford Ct 6 BH23 ... 209 B7
Hertford Pl PO1 ... 182 D7
Hertsfield PO14 ... 129 C4
Hesketh Cl BH24 ... 140 A5
Hesketh Ho 4 SO15 ... 102 C6
Hestan Cl BH23 ... 191 D4
Hester Rd PO4 ... 183 B4
Hestia Cl SO51 ... 53 C8
Heston Way BH22 ... 138 D3
Heston Wlk PO12 ... 180 E3
Hewett Cl PO14 ... 153 F7
Hewett Ho PO14 ... 153 F7
Hewett Rd
Portsmouth PO2 ... 157 E2
Titchfield PO14 ... 153 F7
Hewetts Rise SO31 ... 152 C10
Hewitt Cl PO12 ... 181 A8
Hewitt Rd BH15 ... 201 E4
Hewitt's Rd SO15 ... 102 D5
Heyes Dr SO19 ... 104 C3
Heysham Rd
Broadstone BH18 ... 187 A3
Southampton SO15 ... 102 B7
Heyshott Gdns PO8 ... 88 D4
Heyshott Rd PO4 ... 182 F4
Heytesbury Rd BH6 ... 206 D5
Heyward Rd PO4 ... 182 E4
Heywood Gdns PO9 ... 135 D6
Heywood Gn SO19 ... 104 E5
Hibbard Ct BH10 ... 189 D1
Hibberd Way BH10 ... 189 D1
Hibberds Field BH21 ... 91 A7
Hibbs Cl BH16 ... 201 C7
Hickes Cl BH11 ... 188 F4
Hickory Cl BH16 ... 201 A8
Hickory Dr SO22 ... 1 C4
Hickory Gdns SO30 ... 80 D3
High Barn Cotts SO32 ... 36 F3
High Brow BH22 ... 165 D5
High Cross GU32 ... 18 E2
High Cross La GU32 ... 18 D1
High Ct PO4 ... 183 A3
High Dr PO13 ... 155 C1
High Firs Gdns SO51 ... 53 C7
High Firs Rd Romsey SO51 ... 53 C7
Southampton SO19 ... 104 C5
High Howe Cl BH11 ... 188 E4
High Howe Gdns BH11 ... 188 E4
High Howe La BH11 ... 188 E4
High Lawn Way PO9 ... 135 F5
High Marryats BH25 ... 210 A7
High Mdw SO19 ... 104 C6
High Mead
Fareham PO15 ... 130 E4
Ferndown BH22 ... 165 A2
High Mead La BH22 ... 165 A1
High Oaks Cl SO31 ... 129 A3
High Oaks Gdns BH11 ... 188 E4
High Park Rd BH18 ... 186 E4
High Pines BH23 ... 208 D7
High Point SO18 ... 103 E8
High Rd Bishopstone SP5 ... 22 B8
Southampton SO16 ... 79 D4
High Ridge Cres BH25 ... 195 C2
High St Beaulieu SO42 ... 148 F1
Bishop's Waltham SO32 ... 83 C7
Botley SO30 ... 106 A7
Buriton GU31 ... 65 D5
Bursledon SO31 ... 128 B7
Christchurch BH23 ... 207 B6
Cosham PO6 ... 157 F7
Damerham SP6 ... 68 C5
Downton SP6 ... 47 A8
Droxford SO32 ... 61 B1
East Meon GU32 ... 38 E1
Eastleigh SO50 ... 56 A2
Emsworth PO10 ... 160 F8
Fareham PO16 ... 131 C1
Fordingbridge SP6 ... 69 F1
Gosport PO12 ... 181 D5
Hamble-le-R SO31 ... 128 A2
Hambledon PO7 ... 86 D3
Hythe SO45 ... 126 A5
Lee-on-t-S PO13 ... 179 E2
Lymington SO41 ... 197 E4
Lyndhurst SO43 ... 121 F5
Meonstoke SO32 ... 61 C4
Milford on S SO41 ... 211 D4
Petersfield GU32 ... 40 F3
Poole BH15 ... 202 C2
Portsmouth PO1 ... 182 A3
Ringwood BH24 ... 140 F7
Shedfield SO32 ... 107 F7
Soberton SO32 ... 85 B4
16 Southampton SO14 ... 103 A3
Southwick PO17 ... 132 F6
St Leonards BH24 ... 139 F6
Titchfield PO14 ... 153 F8
Totton SO40 ... 101 A7
Twyford SO21 ... 32 A5
Twyford,Northfields SO21 ... 32 A7
West End SO30 ... 80 D1
West Meon GU32 ... 37 C5
Wimborne Minst BH21 ... 163 B4
Winchester SO23 ... 215 D6
Winchester SO23 ... 215 E5
Winchester SO23 ... 215 F5
Woodgreen SP6 ... 70 E7
High St N BH15 ... 202 D3
High Trees Fair Oak SO50 ... 57 E2
Poole BH13 ... 214 G8
Waterlooville PO7 ... 134 F8
High Trees Dr SO22 ... 215 C8
High Trees Wlk BH22 ... 165 D7
High View PO16 ... 132 C1
High View Way SO18 ... 103 F8
High Walls PO16 ... 131 C1
High Way BH18 ... 186 F3
High Wlk PO15 ... 130 E3
Highbank Ave PO7 ... 134 C3
Highbank Gdns SP6 ... 69 F1
Highbridge Rd
Colden Common,Highbridge SO50 ... 56 D7
Colden Common,Twyford SO21 ... 31 F2
Poole BH14 ... 203 C3
Highbury Bldgs PO6 ... 157 F6
Highbury Cl Fair Oak SO50 ... 57 C1
New Milton BH25 ... 195 B2
Highbury Coll PO6 ... 158 A6
Highbury Gr
Cosham PO6 ... 158 A6
Portsmouth PO6 ... 157 F6
Highbury Prim Sch PO6 ... 158 A6
Highbury St 6 PO1 ... 182 A4
Highbury Way PO6 ... 157 F6
Highclere Ave PO9 ... 135 E4
Highclere Rd SO16 ... 78 D3
Highclere Way SO53 ... 55 B3
Highcliff Ave SO14 ... 103 A8
Highcliffe Castle* BH23 ... 208 E7
Highcliffe Cnr BH23 ... 209 B8
Highcliffe Dr SO50 ... 56 A7
Highcliffe Rd
Christchurch BH23 ... 208 C7
Gosport PO12 ... 180 F4
Winchester SO23 ... 215 F4
Highcliffe Sch BH23 ... 193 D1
Highcliffe St Marks's Prim Sch BH23 ... 193 F1
Highcroft Ind Est PO8 ... 112 C8
Highcroft La PO8 ... 112 C7
Highcrown Mews SO17 ... 79 A2
Highcrown St SO17 ... 79 A2
Higher Blandford Rd BH18,BH21 ... 186 F6
Higher Merley La BH21 ... 186 E8
Highfield
Lymington SO41 ... 197 D3
Twyford SO21 ... 32 A5
Highfield Ave
Fareham PO14 ... 154 F8

Highfield Ave *continued*
Lymington SO41 197 C3
Ringwood BH24 141 A8
Southampton SO17 78 F3
Twyford SO21 32 A5
Waterlooville PO7 111 F1
Highfield Campus (Univ of Southampton) SO17 79 A3
Highfield CE Prim Sch (Inf) SO17 79 B2
Highfield CE Prim Sch (Jun) SO17 79 A2
Highfield Cl
Chandler's Ford SO53 55 E6
Corfe Mullen BH21 186 E5
Southampton SO17 79 A2
Sway SO41 172 B2
Waterlooville PO7 111 F1
Highfield Cres SO17 79 B2
Highfield Ct SO32 83 B8
Highfield Dr BH24 141 A8
Highfield Gdns Liss GU33 21 B4
Sway SO41 172 B2
Highfield Hall SO17 79 A2
Highfield Ho 3 BH14 203 B4
Highfield La Redlynch SP5 47 D5
Southampton SO17 79 B2
Highfield Lodge 3 SO17 79 A2
Highfield Par PO7 112 A1
Highfield Rd
Bournemouth BH9 189 E2
Chandler's Ford SO53 55 E6
Corfe Mullen BH21 186 E5
Gosport PO12 180 F6
Lymington SO41 197 C3
Petersfield GU32 40 F4
Portsmouth PO1 216 C3
Ringwood BH24 141 A8
Southampton SO17 79 A2
West Moors BH22 138 E4
Highfield Terr 1 SO22 215 D5
Highfields SO31 128 F1
Highgate Rd PO3 158 A1
Highgrove Cl SO40 100 D5
Highgrove Ind Pk PO3 158 B3
Highgrove Rd PO3 183 B8
Highland Ave BH23 194 B1
Highland Cl PO10 160 E8
Highland Rd
Emsworth PO10 136 E1
Poole BH14 203 B5
Portsmouth PO4 183 A3
Wimborne Minst BH21 163 D6
Highland St 4 PO4 183 A2
Highland Terr PO4 182 F3
Highland View Cl BH21 163 D5
Highlands Cl Hythe SO45 126 A2
North Baddesley SO52 53 E5
Highlands Cres BH10 189 C4
Highlands Ho SO19 103 D3
Highlands Rd
Barton on S BH25 210 A8
Fareham PO15,PO16 130 D3
Farlington PO6 158 D8
Highlands Way
Hythe SO45 125 F2
Whiteparish SP5 24 B4
Highmoor Cl
Corfe Mullen BH21 186 D5
Poole BH14 203 B3
Highmoor Rd
Bournemouth BH11 189 A1
Corfe Mullen BH21 186 D5
Poole BH14 203 B3
Highmount Cl SO23 11 C7
Highnam Gdns SO31 128 F4
Hightown Gdns BH24 141 C6
Hightown Hill BH24 141 F7
Hightown Ind Est BH24 141 B6
Hightown Prim Sch SO19 104 E4
Hightown Rd
Ringwood,Hightown BH24 141 C6
Ringwood,Moortown BH24 141 A6
Hightown Twrs SO19 104 E4
Hightrees Ave BH8 190 F1
Highview Cl BH23 191 E3
Highview Gdns BH12 203 C7
Highways Rd SO21 31 C5
Highwood Cl SP6 92 D6
Highwood La
North Baddesley SO51 53 D7
Ringwood BH24 117 E3
Highwood Lawn PO9 135 D7
Highwood Rd
Brockenhurst SO42 172 F8
Gosport PO13 180 C7
Poole BH14 203 E4
Higworth Cvn Site PO11 184 F5
Higworth La PO11 184 F5
Hilary Ave PO6 158 A7
Hilary Ct PO13 180 D6
Hilary Rd BH17 187 C1
Hilda Ct 1 SO15 102 F7
Hilda Gdns PO7 111 A4
Hilda Pl 3 SO14 103 C5
Hilda Rd BH12 203 E7
Hilden Ct PO11 184 F3
Hilden Way SO22 1 B5
Hiley Rd BH15 202 C6
Hill Brow Cl PO9 113 B1
Hill Brow Rd GU33 21 B2
Hill Cl Bransgore BH23 193 A8
Fair Oak SO50 57 C5
Hill Close Est SP6 70 E8
Hill Croft PO15 129 E3
Hill Dr PO15 130 D3
Hill Farm Rd SO15 102 E6
Hill Grove La SO32 84 C5
Hill Head Rd PO14 179 A6
Hill House Sch SO41 173 D1
Hill Houses La SO24 14 B6
Hill La Bransgore BH23 193 A8
Burton BH23 192 F2
Colden Common SO21 31 F1
Southampton SO15 78 E2
Hill Park Rd
Fareham PO15 130 D4
Gosport PO12 180 F6
Hill Pl SO31 128 B8
Hill Rd PO16 132 D1
Hill Rise Meonstoke SO32 61 C5
Twyford SO21 32 A5
Hill St Poole BH15 202 C2
Totton SO40 76 C5
Hill Terr Fair Oak SO50 57 C5
Wimborne Minst BH21 164 A2
Hill View GU32 38 D1
Hill View Cvn Pk SO50 57 B5
Hill View Prim Sch BH10 189 E3
Hill View Rd
Braishfield SO51 28 C6
Ferndown BH22 165 C7
Michelmersh SO51 27 C8
Portchester PO16 132 D1
Hill Way BH24 139 F5
Hill Wlk PO15 130 D3
Hillary Cl Fareham PO16 130 F2
Lyndhurst SO43 122 A3
Hillary Rd BH23 207 E8
Hillborough Cres 2 PO5 216 C1
Hillborough Ct 1 PO5 216 C1
Hillbourne Com Fst & Mid Schs BH17 187 B2
Hillbourne Rd BH17 187 A2
Hillbrow Cl PO15 130 D3
Hillbrow Rd BH6 206 B6
Hillbury Pk SP6 93 B5
Hillbury Rd SP6 93 B5
Hillcrest Ave
Chandler's Ford SO53 55 E6
Ferndown BH22 165 C8
Hillcrest Cl
Bournemouth BH9 190 A3
North Baddesley SO52 53 F5
Hillcrest Dr SO53 55 D6
Hillcrest Gdns SO32 83 E4
Hillcrest Hospl BH10 189 D1
Hillcrest Rd
Bournemouth BH9 190 A3
Corfe Mullen BH21 186 C5
Poole BH12 203 A5
Hillcroft SP5 47 D6
Hillcroft Cl SO41 197 E4
Hilldene Way SO30 80 E1
Hillditch SO41 197 D6
Hilldown Rd SO17 79 B2
Hilldowns Ave PO2 157 C2
Hiller Wlk 2 PO13 179 F3
Hillgrove Rd SO18 79 F3
Hillier Way SO23 215 E8
Hillman Rd BH14 203 D5
Hillmead Gdns PO9 135 B2
Hillmeadow BH31 115 A4
Hillsea Mkt PO2 157 E5
Hillside Curdridge SO32 106 F8
Littleton SO22 1 C5
Hillside Ave Romsey SO51 53 A7
Southampton SO18 79 E1
Waterlooville PO7 134 B2
Hillside Cl
Chandler's Ford SO53 55 D6
Horndean PO8 88 C3
West Dean SP5 3 D2
Winchester SO22 215 A8
Hillside Cotts GU33 21 B2
Hillside Cres PO6 132 F1
Hillside Dr BH23 191 D3
Hillside Fst Sch BH31 114 F7
Hillside Gdns BH21 186 C4
Hillside Ind Est PO8 112 C8
Hillside Mews BH21 186 C4
Hillside Rd
Corfe Mullen BH21 186 C5
Lymington SO41 197 C3
Poole BH12 188 F1
Verwood BH31 114 F7
Winchester SO22 215 A7
Woodlands Common BH21 114 A6
Hillside Wlk BH21 114 A6
Hillsley Rd PO6 132 F2
Hillson Dr PO15 130 C3
Hillson Ho PO15 130 D3
Hillsons Rd SO30 106 B7
Hilltop SO22 1 C5
Hilltop Cl BH22 165 B7
Hilltop Cres PO6 134 C2
Hilltop Dr SO19 104 D4
Hilltop Gdns PO8 88 D3
Hilltop Rd
Corfe Mullen BH21 186 E5
Ferndown BH22 165 B7
Portsmouth PO6 133 A2
Hillview PO8 112 C5
Hillview Rd
Bournemouth BH10 189 D3
Hythe SO45 125 F3
Hillway The
Chandler's Ford SO53 55 D7
Portchester PO16 156 C8
Hilly Cl SO21 33 B4
Hillyfields SO16 77 C3
Hilsea Cres PO2 157 E5
Hilsea Mkt PO2 157 E5
Hilsea Sta PO3 158 A4
Hiltingbury Cl SO53 30 D1
Hiltingbury Ct 4 SO53 30 B1
Hiltingbury Inf Sch SO53 30 C1
Hiltingbury Jun Sch SO53 30 C1
Hiltingbury Rd
Chandler's Ford SO53 30 D1
3 Havant PO9 136 A5
Hiltom Rd BH24 141 B7
Hilton Cl BH15 203 A6
Hilton Rd Gosport PO12 181 C4
Hedge End SO30 105 C7
New Milton BH25 195 B4
Hinchliffe Cl BH15 201 F2
Hinchliffe Rd BH15 201 F2
Hinkler Ct SO19 104 D4
Hinkler Rd SO19 104 E5
Hinton Admiral Mews BH23 193 E2
Hinton Admiral Sta BH23 193 E2
Hinton Ampner Ho* SO24 14 E3
Hinton Cl PO9 135 C4
Hinton Cres SO19 104 E4
Hinton Fields SO23 2 C6
Hinton Hill SO24 14 F4
Hinton Ho 3 PO7 134 E8
Hinton House Dr SO23 2 C6
Hinton Manor La PO8 87 F2
Hinton Rd BH1 204 F3
Hinton Wood BH1 205 A2
Hinton Wood Ave BH23 193 E1
Hintonwood La BH23 193 E2
Hipley Rd PO9 136 A3
Hirst Rd SO45 126 B3
Hispano Ave PO15 129 C7
Hither Gn PO10 137 E2
Hitherwood Cl 9 PO7 112 B1
Hive Gdns BH13 214 D6
Hives Way SO41 197 D6
HMS Victory* PO1 181 F7
HMS Warrior* PO1 181 F6
Hoad's Hill PO17 108 B2
Hoadlands GU31 41 B4
Hobart Dr SO45 126 B3
Hobart Rd BH25 194 F2
Hobb La SO30 105 D6
Hobbs Ct 2 PO12 181 E5
Hobbs Pk BH24 139 F4
Hobbs Rd BH12 203 C8
Hobby Cl
Portsmouth PO3 158 A4
Waterlooville PO8 111 E4
Hobson Way SO45 150 D3
Hoburne Ct BH23 193 C1
Hoburne Cvn Pk BH23 208 C8
Hoburne Gdns BH23 193 C1
Hoburne La BH23 208 C8
Hockham Ct PO9 135 C7
Hockley Cl 4 PO6 157 D8
Hockley Cotts
Cheriton SO24 13 E3
Twyford SO21 32 A8
Hockley Link SO21 10 E1
Hocombe Dr SO53 30 B2
Hocombe Park Cl SO53 30 B2
Hocombe Rd SO53 30 D2
Hocombe Wood Rd SO53 30 B2
Hodder Cl SO53 55 B5
Hodges Cl Havant PO9 136 A3
Poole BH17 202 E7
Hoe La SO51,SO52 53 D3
Hoe Rd SO32 83 E7
Hoe St PO7 109 F7
Hoe The PO13 155 E1
Hoeford Cl PO16 155 B6
Hogarth Cl
7 Romsey SO51 28 B1
Southampton SO19 104 C2
Hogarth Way BH8 191 A2
Hoggarth Cl GU31 41 A4
Hogs Lodge La PO8 88 E8
Hogue Ave BH10 189 D5
Hogwood La SO30 80 E6
Holbeach Cl PO6 133 E1
Holbein Lodge SO41 198 B3
Holbrook Pl 3 SO51 52 E7
Holbrook Prim Sch PO13 155 C3
Holbrook Rd
Fareham PO16 155 B8
Portsmouth PO1 216 C3
Holburne Naish BH25 209 D8
Holbury Cl BH8 190 E3
Holbury Ct 6 PO9 136 B5
Holbury Dro SO45 150 C4
Holbury La SO51 4 D3
Holbury Prim Sch SO45 150 C3
Holcombe Rd BH16 201 B6
Holcot La PO3 158 C4
Holcroft Rd SO19 104 E5
Holdaway Cl SO23 2 C7
Holden La SO24 34 F7
Holdenbury Ct PO3 158 C5
Holdenhurst Ave BH7 206 C7
Holdenhurst Cl PO8 88 C1
Holdenhurst Rd
Bournemouth BH8 205 C5
Bournemouth,Holdenhurst BH8 191 B3
Holdings The BH24 141 B5
Hole La Curdridge SO32 83 A1
Soberton PO7 110 A8
Holes Bay North Rdbt BH17 202 A6
Holes Bay Pk BH15 202 B4
Holes Bay Rd BH15 202 B4
Holes Bay Rdbt BH15 202 B5
Holes Cl SO41 195 F4
Holkham Cl SO16 77 E3
Hollam Cl PO14 154 B8
Hollam Cres PO14 154 B8
Hollam Dr PO14 154 B8
Hollam Rd PO4 183 B4
Holland Cl SO53 55 C3
Holland Pk SO31 128 F3
Holland Pl Gosport PO13 155 D2
Southampton SO16 78 B1
Holland Rd
Portsmouth PO4 216 D2
Southampton SO19 103 D2
Totton SO40 100 C7
Holland Way BH18 186 F5
Hollands Cl SO22 1 B5
Hollands Wood Cvn & Camping Site SO42 146 A4
Hollands Wood Dr BH25 195 B5
Hollenden 9 BH13 204 A4
Hollies Cl SO41 172 B1
Hollies The Horndean PO8 88 C2
West Wellow SO51 50 E2
Hollingbourne Cl SO18 103 D8
Hollman Dr SO51 52 D7
Hollow La PO11 184 F3
Holloway Ave BH11 188 F5
Holly Bank Cl PO8 112 C5
Holly Cl Hythe SO45 150 A7
Sarisbury SO31 128 E3
St Leonards BH24 139 D4
Upton BH16 201 A7
West Moors BH22 138 D2
Holly Ct Lymington SO41 197 B2
Poole BH15 202 D4
West Moors BH22 138 D2
Holly Dell SO16 78 E5
Holly Dr PO7 135 A6
Holly Gdns Burton BH23 192 D1
Milford on S SO41 211 C5
West End SO30 80 D3
Holly Gr Fareham PO16 130 E4
Verwood BH31 114 E5
Holly Green Rise BH11 188 E4
Holly Hatch Rd SO40 100 E6
Holly Hedge La BH17 202 C8
Holly Hill SO16 78 E5
Holly Hill Cl SO16 78 E5
Holly Hill La SO31 128 C4
Holly Hill Mans SO31 128 E4
Holly Hill Woodland Pk* SO31 128 C4
Holly Ho SO19 103 E2
Holly La Boldre SO41 174 B1
New Milton BH25 195 C4
Walkford BH23 194 C2
Holly Lo 13 BH13 204 A4
Holly Lodge
Chandler's Ford SO53 55 C3
Southampton SO17 79 B1
Holly Mdws SO22 215 A8
Holly Oak Ct SO16 78 A4
Holly Oak Rd SO16 78 A3
Holly Rd Ashurst SO40 100 B2
Blackfield SO45 177 E8
Holly St PO12 181 C5
Hollybank PO13 179 F2
Hollybank Cl SO45 126 A3
Hollybank Cres SO45 125 F4
Hollybank La PO10 136 F4
Hollybank Rd SO45 125 F4
Hollybrook Appartments PO16 156 B8
Hollybrook Ave SO16 78 C3
Hollybrook Cl SO16 78 B2
Hollybrook Gdns SO31 129 A5
Hollybrook Inf Sch SO16 78 D3
Hollybrook Jun Sch SO16 78 D3
Hollybrook Rd SO16 78 C2
Hollydene Villas SO45 126 A4
Hollywell Dr PO6 157 B7
Hollywood Cl SO52 53 F4
Hollywood Ct SO41 197 D5
Hollywood La SO41 197 D5
Holm Cl BH24 117 C1
Holm Ct PO11 184 F2
Holm Hill La BH23,BH25 194 B7
Holm Oak Cl Littleton SO22 1 B5
Verwood BH31 114 E8
Holman Cl PO8 112 A2
Holmbush Ct PO5 216 B1
Holmdale Rd PO12 180 F7
Holme Rd BH23 209 B8
Holmefield Ave PO14 154 F7
Holmes Cl SO31 127 B6
Holmesland Dr SO30 105 F7
Holmesland La SO30 105 F8
Holmesland Wlk SO30 105 F7
Holmfield Ave BH7 206 C7
Holmgrove PO14 129 C3
Holmhurst Ave BH23 193 F1
Holmsley Cl
Lymington SO41 197 B2
Southampton SO18 104 C7
Holmsley Ct SO40 100 B8
Holmsley Pas BH24 170 C7
Holmsley Rd BH25 170 E2
Holmwood Ct SO16 79 A4
Holmwood Garth BH24 141 D6
Holne Ct PO4 183 C3
Holnest Rd BH17 187 D1
Holst Way PO7 134 E5
Holt Cl Lee-on-t-S PO13 180 A6
Wickham PO17 107 F4
Holt Ct SO19 126 E8
Holt Down GU31 41 B3
Holt Gdns PO9 113 B3
Holt Ho BH8 205 D5
Holt Pl BH22 165 F7
Holt Rd Poole BH12 203 F6
Southampton SO15 102 F6
Three Legged Cross BH21 138 D8
Holt View SO50 56 F2
Holworth Cl BH11 188 E3
Holy Family RC Prim Sch SO16 77 D2
Holy Rood Est SO14 103 A3
Holy Rood Pl 1 SO14 103 A3
Holyborne Rd SO51 53 B7
Holybourne Rd PO9 135 F3
Holyrood Ave SO17 79 B2
Holyrood Cl Poole BH17 202 A8
2 Waterlooville PO7 135 A7
Holyrood Ho 5 SO14 103 A3
Holywell Cl BH17 187 D3
Home Farm BH25 210 E8
Home Farm Bsns Ctr SO51 4 E5
Home Farm Cl SO45 126 B3
Home Farm Office Village PO16 155 D8
Home Farm Rd BH31 114 E7
Home Farm Way BH31 114 E6
Home Field Dr SO16 77 C5
Home Mead PO7 110 F4
Home Rd BH11 189 B6
Home Rule Rd SO31 129 B4
Home Way GU31 41 C3
Homeborough Ho SO45 126 A5
Homebridge Ho 2 SP6 69 F2
Homecliffe Ho BH23 209 B8
Homecorfe Ho BH18 187 B5
Homedale Ho BH2 204 F5
Homedene Ho BH15 202 D3
Homefayre Ho 3 PO16 131 B1
Homefield SO51 28 A1
Homefield Cotts
Hawkley GU33 19 E7
Liss GU33 20 E5
Homefield Ho 7 BH25 195 A2
Homefield Ind Prep Sch BH6 206 F5
Homefield Rd
Cosham PO6 158 C7
Westbourne PO10 137 B4
Homefield Way PO8 88 B6
Homeforde Ho SO42 146 A1
Homefort Ho 2 PO12 181 B5
Homegrange Ho SO41 211 D4
Homegrove Ho PO5 216 C1
Homeheights 8 PO5 182 C2
Homelake Ho BH14 203 B3
Homelands Est BH23 206 F6
Homelands Ho BH22 165 D5
Homeleigh Ho 5 BH8 205 A5
Homelife Ho BH8 205 B4
Homemead Ho SO51 52 E6
Homemill Ho 5 BH25 195 A3
Homeoaks Ho BH2 204 F5
Homepoint Ho SO18 104 A7
Homer Cl Gosport PO13 180 B8
Waterlooville PO8 111 E2
Homer Farm La SO45 177 E6
Homer Mobile Home Pk SO45 177 E6
Homerise Ho 1 SO23 215 E6
Homerose Ho PO5 216 B2
Homeryde Ho PO13 179 E2
Homesea Ho PO5 216 B2
Homeside Rd BH9 190 A2
Homespinney Ho SO18 79 D1
Homestour Ho 1 BH23 207 A6
Hometide Ho PO13 179 E2
Homeview Ho BH15 202 D3
Homewater Ho 8 PO7 134 E8
Homeway Cotts SO40 101 B5
Homewell PO9 135 F1
Homewood Cl BH25 195 C3
Homewood Ho SO41 197 C2
Homington Rd SP5 23 F8
Honey La Burley BH24 142 E2
Fareham PO15 130 D5
Honeybourne Cres BH6 207 A4
Honeycritch La GU32 19 C3
Honeysuckle Cl
Gosport PO13 155 B3
Locks Heath SO31 129 A5
Winchester SO22 215 C2
Honeysuckle Ct
Locks Heath SO31 129 A5
3 Southampton SO18 104 B7
Waterlooville PO7 135 A5
Winchester SO22 1 C3
Honeysuckle Gdns SO41 196 C1
Honeysuckle La BH17 186 F1
Honeysuckle Rd SO16 79 B4
Honeysuckle Way
Chandler's Ford SO53 55 A6
Christchurch BH23 208 B8
Honeywood Cl
Portsmouth PO3 157 F4
Totton SO40 76 D1
Honeywood Ho BH14 214 C7
Honister Cl SO16 101 E8
Hood Cl
Bournemouth BH10 189 B1
Locks Heath SO31 129 B4
Hood Cres BH10 189 B1
Hood Rd SO18 104 A8

Hook Cl SO51 30 A2
Hook Cotts SO31 152 F9
Hook Cres SO51 30 A2
Hook La PO14,SO31 153 B8
Hook Park Rd SO31 152 E8
Hook Rd SO51 29 F2
Hook Water Cl SO53 30 B2
Hook Water Rd SO53 30 B2
Hook with Warsash CE Prim Sch SO31 152 D10
Hook's Farm Way PO9 135 D3
Hook's La PO9 135 D3
Hooke Cl BH17 188 A2
Hookpit Farm La SO23 2 B8
Hookwood La SO51 29 F2
Hop Cl BH16 201 A7
Hop Gdns The SP5 24 A3
Hope Lodge Sch SO18 103 E7
Hope Rd SO30 80 E2
Hope St PO1 216 B4
Hopfield Cl PO7 134 E7
Hopfield Ho PO7 134 E6
Hopfield Mews PO7 134 E6
Hopkins Cl
Bournemouth BH8 191 A2
Portchester PO6 156 E8
Hopkins Ct PO4 183 B2
Hopwood Ct PO16 130 F3
Horace Rd 7 BH5 205 E4
Horder Cl SO16 78 F3
Hordle CE Prim Sch SO41 196 A3
Hordle La SO41 196 A2
Hordle Rd PO9 135 C4
Hordle Walhampton Sch SO41 198 A6
Horlock Rd SO42 146 A2
Hornbeam Cl 2 SO30 105 D6
Hornbeam Gdns SO30 80 D3
Hornbeam Rd
Chandler's Ford SO53 54 F6
Havant PO9 136 B3
Hornbeam Sq BH15 202 D2
Hornbeam Way BH21 163 E5
Hornby Cl SO31 152 D10
Hornby Halt* PO11 185 A2
Hornchurch Rd SO16 77 F4
Horndean CE Jun Sch PO8 112 C7
Horndean Ho 6 PO1 216 C4
Horndean Inf Sch PO8 112 C7
Horndean Prec PO8 112 D7
Horndean Rd PO9 136 E3
Horndean Tech Coll PO8 112 B7
Hornet Cl Fareham PO15 130 D2
Gosport PO12 181 C4
Hornet Rd Fareham PO14 154 F5
Thorney Island PO10 161 A3
Horning Rd BH12 203 F5
Horns Dro SO16 77 E6
Horns Hill Nursling SO16 77 D6
Soberton SO32 85 B2
Horns Hill Cl SO16 77 D6
Horsa Cl BH6 206 E4
Horsa Ct BH6 206 E4
Horsa Rd BH6 206 E4
Horse Sands Cl PO4 183 D3
Horsea La PO2 157 E4
Horsea Rd PO2 157 E5
Horsebridge Rd PO9 136 A4
Horsebridge Way SO16 77 E6
Horsecroft SO51 52 F8
Horsefair Mews SO51 52 E7
Horsefair The SO51 52 E7
Horsepost La PO7,PO8 87 B2
Horseshoe Bridge SO14 103 C8
Horseshoe Cl
Titchfield PO14 129 D2
Wimborne Minst BH21 164 B6
Horseshoe Common Rdbt BH1 204 F3
Horseshoe Ct
5 Bournemouth BH1 204 F4
Downton SP5 46 F7
Horseshoe Dr
Romsey SO51 28 B2
Totton SO40 76 A2
Horseshoe Lodge SO31 128 F1
Horseshoe Paddocks Bsns Ctr PO15 130 B6
Horseshoe The BH13 214 C4
Horsham Ave BH10 189 C6
Horton Cl BH9 190 C3
Horton Ho BH22 165 F7
Horton Rd Gosport PO13 155 C4
Horton Heath BH21 114 B1
Ringwood BH24 140 C6
St Leonards BH24 139 E6
Horton Way
Bishopstoke SO50 56 F1
Verwood BH31 114 D5
Hosker Rd BH5 206 B5
Hoskins Ho PO1 182 B6
Hospital La PO16 156 E6
Hospital Rd PO17,SO32 108 B8
Hotspur Cl SO45 125 F5
Houchin St SO32 83 C7
Houghton Cl 1 PO9 136 B6
Houlton Rd BH15 202 E4
Hound Cl SO31 127 D5
Hound Farm SO31 127 E6
Hound Manor SO31 127 E6
Hound Rd SO31 127 D6
Hound Road Gdns SO31 127 D6
Hound Way SO31 127 D6
Hounds Way BH21 164 B5
Houndwell Pl SO14 103 A4
Hounsdown Ave SO40 100 F5
Hounsdown Bsns Pk SO40 101 A3
Hounsdown Cl SO40 100 F5
Hounsdown Sch SO40 100 F4
Hounslow Cl BH15 201 F1
House Farm Rd PO12 180 E4
Hove Ct PO13 179 E3
Hoverfly Cl PO13 180 A5
Hoveton Gr SO53 55 B8
Howard Cl Burley BH24 143 A3
Chandler's Ford SO53 55 D4
Christchurch BH23 207 F6
Fair Oak SO50 57 C2
Lee-on-t-S PO13 180 A7
Southampton SO18 79 E4
Howard Lo 20 PO5 182 C2
Howard Oliver Ho SO45 126 B3
Howard Rd
Bournemouth BH8 205 C8
Portsmouth PO2 157 E4
Southampton SO15 102 D6
Verwood BH31 114 F6
Howard's Gr SO15 102 C8
Howards Mead SO41 197 B2
Howe Cl
Christchurch BH23 207 F5
New Milton BH25 194 F3
Howe La BH31 114 F5
Howe Rd PO13 180 C5
Howell Cl SO14 103 C5
Howell Ho BH21 163 F7
Howerts Cl SO31 152 D10
Howeth Cl BH10 189 D3
Howeth Rd BH10 189 D3
Howlett Cl SO41 197 C4
Howton Cl BH10 189 C5
Howton Rd BH10 189 C5
Hoxley Rd BH10 189 D4
Hoyal Rd BH15 201 D3
Hoylake Cl PO13 155 C1
Hoylake Rd PO6 134 C1
Hoyle Cl SO32 58 D3
Hoylecroft Cl PO15 130 E3
Hubert Rd SO23 215 C2
Hudson Cl Gosport PO13 180 C6
Poole BH12 188 C2
Ringwood BH24 141 C8
Hudson Ct SO40 100 D6
Hudson Davies Cl SO41 173 F1
Hudson Rd PO5 216 C2
Hughes Bsns Ctr BH23 208 A7
Hughes Cl SO45 150 E1
Hulbert Jun Sch PO7 134 F6
Hulbert Rd Havant PO9 135 B4
Waterlooville PO7 134 F7
Hull Cres BH11 188 D4
Hull Rd BH11 188 E4
Hull Way BH11 188 E4
Hulles Way SO52 53 F4
Hulse Lodge 5 SO15 102 F8
Hulse Rd SO15 102 F8
Hulton Cl SO19 103 D1
Humber Cl PO14 179 B8
Humber Gdns SO31 105 A1
Humber Rd BH22 166 A6
Hummicks The SO42 176 C8
Hundred Acres PO17 108 F4
Hundred Acres Rd PO17 108 E4
Hundred La SO41 198 A7
Hundred The
5 Fordingbridge SP6 69 F1
Romsey SO51 52 E7
Waterlooville PO7 111 D1
Hunger Hill BH15 202 C2
Hungerfield Cl BH23 169 A1
Hungerford SO31 128 A7
Hungerford Hill SP6 94 D5
Hungerford Rd BH8 190 D3
Hunt Ave SO31 127 C6
Hunt Rd
Christchurch BH23 207 F8
Poole BH15 202 E4
Hunter Cl
Christchurch BH23 208 A7
Gosport PO13 180 D7
Hardley SO45 150 B6
Wimborne Minst BH21 164 C6
Hunter Ct 4 SO16 78 B1
Hunter Rd
Portsmouth PO4 182 F3
Thorney Island PO10 161 A3
Hunter's Ride SO21 29 E4
Hunters Chase SO32 84 C3
Hunters Cl BH31 115 C5
Hunters Cres
Romsey SO51 28 C1
Totton SO40 100 B6
Hunters Ct SO31 105 B3
Hunters Hill SO40 100 D3
Hunters Lodge PO15 130 B1
Hunters Ride PO7 134 E6
Hunters Way SO50 57 A2
Huntfield Rd BH9 190 B2
Huntingdon Cl
Titchfield PO14 129 C1
Totton SO40 76 E1
Huntingdon Dr BH21 163 E1
Huntingdon Gdns
Christchurch BH23 192 A2
Horton Heath SO50 81 D7
Huntley Cl 19 PO6 133 B1
Huntly Rd BH3 204 D7
Huntly Way SO18 103 F7
Hunton Cl SO16 78 D3
Hunts Pond Rd SO31 129 C3
Huntsbottom La GU33 21 B3
Huntsman Cl PO8 111 F5
Huntvale Rd BH9 190 B3
Hurdle Way SO21 31 C7
Hurdles Mead SO41 211 D3
Hurdles The
Christchurch BH23 206 E8
Titchfield PO14 129 D2
Hurlingham Gdns SO16 79 A5
Hurn Cl BH24 140 D6
Hurn Court La BH23 190 F6
Hurn Ct
Bournemouth BH8 191 A4
12 Havant PO9 136 B6
Hurn La BH24 140 D6
Hurn Rd
Christchurch BH23 191 D3
St Leonards BH24 140 C3
Hurn Way BH23 191 D1
Hurricane Dr SO16 77 E6
Hursley Cl BH7 206 C8
Hursley Ct 2 SO53 30 B1
Hursley Dr SO45 177 E7
Hursley Park Rd SO21 30 A6
Hursley Rd
Chandler's Ford SO53 55 C7
Havant PO9 135 D5
Hurst Castle* SO41 212 D1
Hurst Cl
Barton on S BH25 209 D8
Chandler's Ford SO53 55 A4
Stubbington PO14 179 A6
Totton SO40 100 F8
Walkford BH23 194 C2
Hurst Ct
4 Christchurch BH23 209 A7
5 Milford on S SO41 211 C4
Hurst Gn PO13 155 B2
Hurst Green Cl
Southampton SO19 104 A1
Waterlooville PO8 112 B2
Hurst Hill BH14 214 C8
Hurst La
Colden Common SO21,SO50 58 A7
High Cross GU34 18 B3
Hurst Rd
Milford on S SO41 211 E3
Ringwood BH24 117 A1
Hurstbourne Ave BH23 193 E1
Hurstbourne Cl PO9 135 D5
Hurstbourne Pl SO19 126 F8
Hurstdene Rd BH8 190 C2
Hurstly La SO41 173 B4
Hurstville Dr PO7 134 F6
Hurstwood Ave PO10 137 E1
Hussar Cl BH23 206 F7
Hussar Ct PO7 111 C1
Hussey Cl 2 SO23 215 E8
Hutfield Ct 1 PO12 181 B6
Hutwood Rd SO16 79 A8
Huxley Cl SO31 129 B2
Huxley Ct SO45 125 C2
Hyacinth Cl BH17 186 F1
Hyde Abbey Rd SO23 215 E6
Hyde CE Prim Sch SP6 94 D5
Hyde Church La SO23 215 E7
Hyde Church Path 6 SO23 215 E7
Hyde Cl Southampton SO15 78 C1
Sway SO41 172 B2
Totton SO40 100 B7
Winchester SO23 215 E7
Hyde Gate 10 SO23 215 E7
Hyde House Gdns 5 SO23 215 E7
Hyde La SP6 94 C6
Hyde Lodge SO23 215 D7
Hyde Park Ho PO5 216 B2
Hyde Park Rd PO5 216 B3
Hyde Rd BH10 189 C5
Hyde St Portsmouth PO5 216 B2
Winchester SO23 215 E7
Hyde The BH25 194 E4
Hyden Cross GU32 63 E2
Hyden Farm La
East Meon GU32 63 D1
Hambledon PO8 87 D7
Hyden Wood GU32 63 E2
Hylton Rd GU32 40 F3
Hymans Way SO40 100 E7
Hynes Ct 1 SO17 103 B8
Hynesbury Rd BH23 208 C6
Hyssop Cl PO15 129 D7
Hythe By Pass SO45 149 E8
Hythe Hospl SO45 126 A2
Hythe Prim Sch SO45 126 A4
Hythe Rd Cosham PO6 157 E8
Marchwood SO40 124 F8
Poole BH15 203 A7

I

I O Ctr The PO15 129 E2
Ibbertson Cl BH8 190 F2
Ibbertson Rd BH8 190 F2
Ibbertson Way BH8 190 F2
Ibbett Rd BH10 189 C3
Ibbotson Way SO40 100 D5
Ibsen Cl PO15 129 C8
Ibsley Cl BH8 205 C6
Ibsley Dro BH24 94 B1
Ibsley Gr PO9 135 D3
Icarus Pl PO7 134 F2
Iddesleigh Rd BH3 205 A6
Ideal Park Homes Cvn Pk SO50 56 E6
Idsworth Cl PO8 112 E6
Idsworth Ho PO1 216 B4
Idsworth Rd
Portsmouth PO3 183 A8
Waterlooville PO8 112 B2
Iford Bridge Home Pk BH6 206 D7
Iford Ct 15 PO9 136 B6
Iford Gdns BH7 206 C7
Iford La BH6 206 E6
Ilex Cl SO23 2 B8
Ilex Cres SO31 129 A3
Ilex Wlk PO11 185 C2
Ilford Cl BH6 206 F5
Illustrious Rd PO14 179 B6
Imber Dr BH23 208 F8
Imber Rd SO23 11 C8
Imber Way SO19 104 C4
Imbrecourt BH13 214 E7
Imperial Appartments 8 SO14 103 B3
Imperial Ave SO15 102 B7
Imperial Ct 4 BH13 214 F7
Imperial Pk SO14 103 B7
Imperial Rd SO14 103 B7
Imperial Way SO15 102 C5
Implacable Rd PO13 179 E4
Ingarth 7 BH6 206 E3
Ingersley Rise SO30 80 D1
Ingle Glen SO45 126 A1
Ingle Gn SO40 76 B1
Ingledene Cl
Gosport PO12 181 B5
Havant PO9 135 D2
Inglegreen Cl BH25 194 F1
Inglesham Way BH15 201 E4
Ingleside SO31 127 C7
Ingleside Cl PO14 154 B8
Ingleton Rd SO16 77 D1
Inglewood Ave BH8 190 F1
Inglewood Dr BH25 195 B2
Inglewood Gdns SO50 57 C3
Inglis Rd PO5 216 D1
Ingoldfield La PO17, SO32 109 C7
Ingram Ct SO17 103 C8
Ingram Wlk 1 BH21 163 D4
Ingworth Rd BH12 204 A5
Inhams La PO7 110 D5
Inhurst Ave PO7 135 A8
Inhurst Rd PO2 157 E2
Inkerman Rd SO19 103 D3
Inkpen Wlk PO9 135 D7
Inlands Rd PO18 161 F8
Inmans La GU32 41 B5
Insley Cres BH18 186 E5
Intech* SO21 12 B7
International Pk SO18 79 F6
International Way SO19 126 F8
Inveravon BH23 207 F4
Inverclyde Ho BH14 203 B4
Inverclyde Rd BH14 203 C4
Invergordon Ave PO6 158 B7
Inverkip Cl PO13 179 E4
Inverleigh Rd BH6 206 C6
Inverness Ave PO15 130 E3
Inverness Rd
Gosport PO12 181 A7
Poole BH13 214 E7
Portsmouth PO1 182 E7
Invincible Rd PO14 179 B6
Inwood Rd GU33 21 A4
Ionic Cl SO53 55 F7
Iping Ave PO9 135 E4
Ipley Way SO45 126 A2
Ipswich Rd BH12 204 B4
Ireland Way PO7 134 E5
Irene Ct SO16 78 B2
Irequois Ct SO14 103 B7
Iris Rd Bournemouth BH9 189 F1
Southampton SO16 79 B4
Iron Mill Cl PO15 130 D3
Ironbridge Cres SO31 129 A6
Ironbridge La PO4 183 C4
Ironmill La PO15 130 B5
Ironside Ct 7 SO14 102 F3
Irvine Cl PO16 131 A3
Irvine Way BH23 207 E8
Irving La BH6 206 D5
Irving Rd
Bournemouth BH6 206 D5
Southampton SO16 77 F1
Irwell Cl SO53 55 A5
Irwin Hts PO12 181 A9
Isaacs Cl BH12 204 B7
Isambard Brunel Jun Sch PO2 182 E8
Isambard Brunel Rd PO1 216 B3
Isis Cl SO16 101 E8
Island Cl PO11 160 A3
Island Point SO41 197 F4
Island View SO41 172 B3
Island View Ave BH23 208 B5
Island View Cl SO41 211 E3
Island View Gdns SO41 211 E4
Island View Rd BH25 209 C7
Island View Terr PO2 157 C1
Island View Wlk PO16 132 C1
Islay Gdns PO6 133 F1
Itchen Ave SO50 56 F2
Itchen Cl Petersfield GU31 40 E2
West Wellow SO51 50 D3
Itchen Coll SO19 104 A5
Itchen Ct
4 Waterlooville PO8 111 F4
Itchen Ct continued
3 Winchester SO23 215 F6
Itchen Rd PO9 136 B6
Itchen Valley Ctry Pk* SO30 80 C5
Itchen Valley Ctry Pk Visitor Ctr* SO30 80 C5
Itchen View SO18 79 E4
Itchenor Rd PO11 185 F2
Itchenside Cl SO18 79 F4
Itchin Cl SO40 100 D6
Ithica Cl PO11 185 A4
Ivamy Pl BH11 188 F2
Ivanhoe Rd SO15 78 D1
Ivor Cl SO45 150 C4
Ivor Rd
Corfe Mullen BH21 186 D4
Poole BH15 202 A1
Ivy Cl St Leonards BH24 139 D4
Totton SO40 76 E2
Winchester SO22 215 C3
Ivy Cotts SO21 31 A1
Ivy Ct Southampton SO16 78 D3
Waterlooville PO7 134 D4
7 Whiteley PO15 129 D8
Ivy Dene SO19 104 D4
Ivy Ho 2 PO12 181 C5
Ivy La Portsmouth PO1 182 A6
Ringwood BH24 117 B4
West End SO30 80 C2
Ivy Orch PO8 88 B6
Ivy Rd Oakley BH21 187 D8
Southampton SO17 103 C8
Ivydene Gdns PO8 112 A4
Ivyhouse La GU32 18 E3
Iwerne Cl BH9 190 B4

J

J Ave SO45 151 A6
Jacaranda Cl PO15 129 E3
Jacey Ho 6 BH1 205 A3
Jack Cl SO53 54 E6
Jack Cockerill Way 8 PO5 182 D1
Jackdaw Cl PO8 111 E4
Jackdaw Rise SO50 55 D1
Jackie Wigg Gdns SO40 101 A7
Jacklin Ct BH18 187 B5
Jackman's Hill SO21 33 A6
Jackmans Cl SO19 103 D3
Jackson Cl PO6 158 C6
Jackson Gdns BH12 203 C6
Jackson Rd BH12 203 C6
Jacmar Ct 4 BH25 195 B2
Jacob's Gutter La SO40 101 A4
Jacob's St PO1 216 B4
Jacobean Cl BH23 194 B1
Jacobs Cl Clanfield PO8 88 C5
Romsey SO51 53 A7
Jacobs Ct PO9 135 E1
Jacobs Rd BH15 201 E2
Jacobs Wlk SO40 100 E5
Jacomb Pl PO13 155 D2
Jacqueline Ave PO7 134 D4
Jacqueline Rd BH12 203 C7
Jade Ct 1 Gosport PO13 180 C6
7 Waterlooville PO7 134 E8
Jago Rd PO1 181 F7
Jamaica Pl PO12 181 C5
Jamaica Rd PO12 181 D6
James Butcher Ct 11 PO5 182 D1
James Callaghan Dr PO6 133 B2
James Cl Gosport PO13 155 C4
South Hayling PO11 184 E4
James Copse Rd PO8 111 F5
James Ct SO51 53 A6
James Grieve Ave SO31 129 B2
James Howell Ct PO7 110 F4
James Rd Gosport PO13 155 C4
Havant PO9 135 E2
Poole BH12 204 A5
James St SO14 103 B4
Jameson Rd
Bournemouth BH9 189 F1
Southampton SO19 103 F3
Janaway Gdns SO17 103 D8
Janes Cl SO45 177 E8
Janred Ct BH25 209 E7
Janson Rd SO15 102 D8
Japonica Way PO9 136 C4
Jarndyce Wlk PO2 182 D7
Jarvis Fields SO31 128 B8
Jasmine Ct
2 Gosport PO13 180 C6
Lymington SO41 197 C4
1 Southampton SO15 102 F8
Whiteley PO15 106 D1
Jasmine Gr PO7 135 A6
Jasmine Rd SO30 105 B8
Jasmine Way PO8 88 C5
Jasmine Wlk 5 PO14 154 E8
Jasmond Rd PO6 157 F6
Jason Pl PO7 134 E2
Jason Way PO12 180 F8
Jaundrells Cl BH25 195 C3
Java Dr PO15 129 C7
Javelin Rd PO10 161 A3
Jay Cl Horndean PO8 112 A7
Stubbington PO14 154 B5
Jay's Ct BH23 209 B8
Jealous La SO41 173 A2
Jefferson Ave BH1 205 D6
Jeffries Cl SO16 77 E5
Jellicoe Ave PO12 180 F3

Jellicoe Cl BH14 202 F5
Jellicoe Dr BH23 207 F6
Jellicoe Ho 8 PO1 216 C4
Jenkins Gr PO3 183 B7
Jenkyns Cl SO30 106 A7
Jenner Cl BH31 114 E7
Jenner Way SO51 53 C8
Jennings Rd Poole BH14 203 C2
Totton SO40 101 A8
Jensen Ct SO15 102 F7
Jephcote Rd BH11 188 F4
Jermyns La SO51 28 E4
Jerome Ct SO19 104 D6
Jerram Cl PO12 180 F3
Jerrett's La SO16 77 D3
Jersey Cl Poole BH12 188 D1
Southampton SO16 77 E3
Stubbington PO14 179 D6
Jersey Rd Poole BH12 188 D1
Portsmouth PO2 182 E8
Jervis Court La SO32 84 A7
Jervis Dr PO12 181 B7
Jervis Rd PO2 157 C2
Jesmond Ave BH23 208 F8
Jesmond Gr SO31 129 A1
Jessamine Rd SO16 78 B2
Jessica Ave BH31 114 D7
Jessica Cl 1 PO7 112 B1
Jessica Cres SO40 76 B1
Jessie Rd Gosport PO12 181 A5
Havant PO9 135 C3
Portsmouth PO4 182 E4
Jessie Terr 23 SO14 103 A3
Jessop Cl SO45 125 F5
Jessop Wlk SO45 125 F5
Jessopp Cl BH10 189 F4
Jessopp Ho 6 BH21 163 C5
Jessopp Rd BH21 164 B6
Jetty Rd SO45 151 C5
Jewell Rd BH8 191 A2
Jewry St SO23 215 E6
Jex Blake Cl SO16 78 B4
Jimmy Brown Ave BH21 138 F5
Jinny La SO51 27 E5
Jo Benson Ct 3 PO4 182 F2
Joanna Cl SP5 46 D7
Jockey La SO50 56 E5
Jodrell Cl PO8 112 C7
Joe Bigwood Cl SO16 77 D5
John Bunyan Cl PO15 129 C8
John Darling Mall SO50 56 A4
John Keble CE Prim Sch
SO21 30 B6
John King Shipyard 10
PO10 161 A8
John St SO14 103 A3
John's Rd SO19 103 D3
Johns Rd PO16 155 B7
Johnson Rd BH21 165 A8
Johnson St 4 SO14 103 A4
Johnson View PO15 129 E6
Johnston Rd BH15 202 D7
Johnstone Rd BH23 207 E6
Jolliffe Ave BH15 202 D4
Jolliffe Ct 13 GU32 40 F3
Jolliffe Rd BH15 202 D4
Jonas Nichols Sq SO14 103 B4
Jonathan Cl SO41 197 E5
Jonathan Rd PO15 130 E1
Jones La SO45 126 A5
Jopps Cnr BH23 192 C4
Jordan Ho SO15 102 C5
Jordans La
Portmore SO41 198 B8
Sway SO41 172 C2
Joseph Nye Ct 41 PO1 182 A5
Joseph St 9 PO12 181 C5
Joshua Cl BH15 201 E2
Josian Wlk SO14 103 B5
Jowitt Dr BH25 194 F2
Joyce Dickson Cl BH24 141 B6
Joys La SO41 198 E8
Joys Rd BH21 138 E8
Jubilee Ave PO6 156 E8
Jubilee Bsns Ctr PO7 134 E8
Jubilee Cl
Corfe Mullen BH21 186 E7
Eastleigh SO50 55 F1
Fordingbridge SP6 69 C1
Ringwood BH24 141 C8
Jubilee Cotts GU32 37 C4
Jubilee Cres BH12 203 D5
Jubilee Ct Alderholt SP6 92 E5
Fareham PO14 155 A7
Sway SO41 172 B1
Jubilee Gdns
Bournemouth BH10 189 D2
Southampton SO18 104 B7
Jubilee Ho PO10 136 E1
Jubilee Mews PO10 161 C8
Jubilee Rd
Corfe Mullen BH21 186 E7
Fordingbridge SP6 69 C1
Gosport PO12 181 B6
Poole BH12 203 D5
Portchester PO16 156 D7
Portsmouth PO4 182 F3
Romsey SO51 52 E8
Waterlooville PO7 111 E1
Jubilee Terr
Portsmouth PO5 216 A1
Westbourne PO10 137 B3
Jukes Wlk SO30 80 F2
Julia Cl BH23 208 F8
Julian Cl SO16 78 F6
Julian Ct SO18 79 E2
Julian Rd SO19 104 B3
Julian's Rd BH21 163 A4
Julie Ave PO15 130 E1
Juliet Ct PO7 135 A8
Julius Cl SO53 55 E6
Julyan Ave BH12 204 A8
Jumar Cl SO31 152 D9
Jumpers Ave BH23 206 E8
Jumpers Rd BH23 206 F8
Junction Rd
Bournemouth BH9 204 F8
Hamworthy BH16 201 D4
Totton SO40 101 A7
Juniper Cl
Ferndown BH22 165 C8
Lymington SO41 197 B2
North Baddesley SO52 53 F5
Three Legged Cross BH21 138 E8
Winchester SO22 215 B3
Juniper Ct 5 SO18 103 E7
Juniper Flats BH23 206 E8
Juniper Rd Horndean PO8 88 C1
Southampton SO18 103 F7
Juniper Sq PO9 159 F8
Jupiter Cl SO16 77 E3
Jupiter Ct PO1 182 A4
Jupiter Way BH21 186 E8
Jura Cl PO6 134 A1
Jurd Way SO31 104 F1
Jurds Lake Way SO19 103 E1
Justin Cl Fareham PO14 154 E8
Gosport PO12 181 D7
Justin Gdns BH10 189 E4
Justine Ct 2 SO18 104 B7
Justinian Cl SO53 55 F7
Jute Cl PO16 132 B1
Jutland Cl PO15 129 B7
Juventu Cl PO9 136 A3

K

K&B Est BH17 202 B8
Kamptee Copse BH25 195 B6
Kanes Hill SO19 104 F5
Kanes Hill Cvn Site
SO19 104 F4
Kanes Hill Prim Sch
SO19 104 E6
Kangaw Pl BH15 201 D2
Karen Ave PO6 158 C6
Kassassin St PO4 183 A2
Kassel Cl PO7 135 B8
Katherine Chance Cl
BH23 192 C3
Kathleen Rd SO19 104 B4
Kathryn Cl SO40 76 B1
Katrina Gdns PO11 185 A5
Katrine Cres SO53 55 A8
Katterns Cl BH23 191 E2
Kay Cl BH23 207 E6
Kayak Cl SO31 128 E1
Kayleigh Cl SO40 100 D6
Kealy Rd PO12 181 A7
Kearsney Ave PO2 157 E2
Keast Wlk PO13 155 D4
Keats Ave
Milford on S SO41 211 D5
Portchester PO6 132 E1
Keats Cl Swanwick PO15 106 B1
Waterlooville PO8 111 F4
Winchester SO22 215 A2
Keats Ho Havant PO9 135 F4
1 New Milton BH25 195 A1
Keats Rd SO19 104 C6
Keble Cl
Chandler's Ford SO53 55 C4
Hursley SO21 30 B8
Keble Rd SO53 55 C4
Keble St SO22 215 A4
Keeble Cl BH10 189 D6
Keeble Cres BH10 189 D6
Keeble Rd BH10 189 D6
Keel Cl Gosport PO13 180 D7
Portsmouth PO3 158 C3
Keelan Ct PO5 182 D2
Keenans Cotts GU33 20 E5
Keep The PO16 156 D7
Keepers Cl SO53 55 B6
Keepers La Dunbridge SO51 5 C2
Wimborne Minst BH21 164 F4
Kefford Cl PO8 112 B6
Keighley Ave BH18 186 F1
Keith Cl PO12 181 B7
Keith Ho 24 PO1 182 A5
Keith Rd BH3 204 D7
Kelburn Cl SO53 55 B7
Kellaway Rd BH17 202 F8
Kellett Rd SO15 102 E8
Kelly Cl BH17 202 F8
Kelly Ct
10 Fareham PO16 131 B2
Southampton SO16 78 C5
1 Southampton,Bitterne
SO18 103 E8
Kelly Ho SO18 79 E4
Kelly Rd PO7 134 E5
Kelmscott Gdns SO53 30 B1
Kelsall Gdns BH25 195 A3
Kelsey Ave PO10 137 E1
Kelsey Cl Liss GU33 21 A5
Locks Heath PO14 129 B1
Kelsey Head PO6 157 A7
Kelston Cl SO15 102 A7
Kelvin Cl SO45 126 A3
Kelvin Gr Netley SO31 127 C6
Portchester PO16 156 D8
Kelvin Rd SO50 55 F2
Kemp Rd BH9 204 F8
Kemp Welch Ct BH12 204 B8
Kempfelt Ho 20 PO1 182 A5
Kemps Quay Ind Pk
SO18 103 D7
Kempton Ct PO15 129 C8
Kempton Pk 3 PO7 112 B1
Kemshott Ct PO9 135 D6
Ken Berry Ct PO9 130 D6
Ken Rd BH6 206 E4
Kench The PO11 183 F4
Kendal Ave
Portsmouth PO3 158 A1
Southampton SO16 101 D8
Kendal Cl
Chandler's Ford SO53 55 E7
Waterlooville PO8 112 A4
Kendal Ct SO16 77 D1
Kenilworth Cl
Lee-on-t-S PO13 179 F4
New Milton BH25 195 B3
Kenilworth Ct
2 Christchurch BH23 207 A7
1 Poole BH13 214 F8
9 Winchester SO23 215 E8
Kenilworth Dr SO50 56 A6
Kenilworth Gdns SO30 80 E1
Kenilworth Ho 15 SO14 103 C6
Kenilworth Rd
Portsmouth PO5 182 D1
Southampton SO15 102 F6
Kenmore Cl SO40 100 E5
Kennard Ct BH25 194 F3
Kennard Rd BH25 194 F3
Kennart Rd BH17 202 B7
Kennedy Ave PO15 130 E3
Kennedy Cl PO7 134 E4
Kennedy Cres PO12 180 F2
Kennedy Rd SO16 77 F3
Kennel La SO22 1 C4
Kennet Cl Gosport PO12 181 B2
West End SO18 80 B3
Kennet Rd GU31 40 E2
Kenneth Ct 9 BH23 209 B7
Kennett Cl SO51 53 C7
Kennett Rd SO51 53 C7
Kennington La SO40 99 B7
Kennington Rd BH17 202 D8
Kensington Cl SO50 56 D5
Kensington Ct
14 Gosport PO12 181 C9
14 Poole BH13 204 B3
3 Southampton SO17 79 C2
Kensington Dr 1 BH2 204 D4
Kensington Fields SO45 125 D2
Kensington Gdns PO14 129 C2
Kensington Pk SO41 211 C4
Kensington Rd
Gosport PO12 181 C4
Portsmouth PO2 157 F1
Kenson Gdns SO19 104 A4
Kent Gdns SO40 100 D5
Kent Gr PO16 156 C6
Kent Ho
28 Bournemouth BH4 204 C3
4 Southampton SO14 103 C5
Kent La BH24 93 D1
Kent Rd
Chandler's Ford SO53 55 C3
Gosport PO13 155 B4
Poole BH12 203 E6
Portsmouth PO5 216 B1
Southampton SO17 79 C1
Kent St Portsmouth PO1 182 A5
Southampton SO14 103 C6
Kentidge Rd PO7 134 D5
Kentish Rd SO15 102 C7
Kenwood Bsns Pk PO9 136 A2
Kenwood Rd PO16 156 D6
Kenwyn Cl SO18 80 B2
Kenya Rd PO16 156 B7
Kenyon Cl BH15 202 E7
Kenyon Rd Poole BH15 202 E7
Portsmouth PO2 157 F2
Keppel Cl BH24 141 B7
Kerley Rd BH2 204 E2
Kern Cl SO16 77 F3
Kernells Ct 2 BH4 204 B4
Kerrfield SO22 215 B5
Kerrfield Mews SO22 215 B5
Kerrigan Ct SO17 103 A7
Kerry Cl
Chandler's Ford SO53 55 C6
Lymington SO41 197 C3
Kerry Gdns SP6 69 B2
Kersley Gdns SO19 104 A4
Kesteven Way SO18 80 B1
Kestrel Cl
Bishop's Waltham SO32 83 A8
Botley SO32 81 F1
Clanfield PO8 88 C4
Ferndown BH22 165 B7
Marchwood SO40 101 E1
Southampton SO16 78 B5
Stubbington PO14 154 B4
Upton BH16 201 B8
Winchester SO22 215 B2
Kestrel Ct BH24 141 A8
Kestrel Dr BH23 208 A6
Kestrel Pl PO6 158 F7
Kestrel Rd Eastleigh SO50 55 E2
Portsmouth PO3 158 A4
Kestrel Way SP6 93 B5
Kestrels The SO31 127 F8
Keswick Ave PO3 183 A8
Keswick Ct BH25 195 B5
Keswick Rd
Bournemouth BH5 205 F4
New Milton BH25 195 B5
Southampton SO19 103 D2
Keswick Way BH31 114 E5
Kettering Terr PO2 182 C8
Keverstone Ct BH1 205 D3
Kevlyn Cres SO31 104 F1
Kew La SO31 128 A7
Kewlake La SO40 74 D1
Keydell Ave PO8 112 A5
Keydell Cl PO8 112 A5
Keyes Cl
Christchurch BH23 207 F6
Gosport PO13 155 C3
Poole BH12 188 F1
Keyes Ct 4 PO5 216 C1
Keyes Rd PO13 155 C3
Keyhaven Cl PO13 155 A2
Keyhaven Dr PO9 135 C5
Keyhaven Rd SO41 212 A4
Keynsham Rd SO19 104 B6
Keysworth Ave BH25 209 F8
Keysworth Rd BH16 201 C4
Khandala Gdns PO7 134 F4
Khartoum Rd SO17 79 A2
Khyber Rd BH12 203 D5
Kidmore La PO7 110 F6
Kidson Ct PO2 182 D8
Kielder Cl SO53 55 A7
Kielder Gr PO13 155 D2
Kilbride Path 5 PO2 182 D8
Kilderkin Dr PO8 112 D7
Kilford Ct SO30 106 A6
Kilham La SO22 10 B6
Killarney Cl SO19 104 E3
Killock 6 BH13 214 F7
Kilmarnock Rd BH9 189 F1
Kilmeston Cl PO9 135 F6
Kilmeston Rd
Cheriton SO24 14 D4
Kilmeston SO24 14 D2
Kilmington Way BH23 208 F8
Kilmiston Cl PO1 182 E7
Kilmiston Dr PO16 132 C1
Kiln Acre PO16 131 B3
Kiln Cl Corfe Mullen BH21 186 C4
Hythe SO45 125 E3
Kiln Field GU33 20 E5
Kiln Gn SO21 57 A8
Kiln Hill SO32 109 B8
Kiln La Braishfield SO51 28 C6
Buriton GU31 65 D5
Otterbourne SO21 31 C2
Redlynch SP5 47 E7
Southwick PO7 109 D4
Kiln Rd Fareham PO16 131 A3
Portsmouth PO3 158 A1
Kiln Way BH31 115 C3
Kilnside PO7 110 F3
Kilnyard Cl SO40 76 D1
Kilpatrick Cl 6 PO2 182 D8
Kilwich Way PO16 156 B6
Kimber Rd BH11 188 F3
Kimberley Cl
Christchurch BH23 206 F8
Fair Oak SO50 57 D2
Hedge End SO30 105 B5
Kimberley Ct SO19 103 E2
Kimberley Rd
Bournemouth BH6 206 C5
Poole BH14 203 B3
Portsmouth PO4 183 A2
Kimbers GU32 40 E4
Kimbolton Rd PO3 183 A6
Kimbridge Cnr SO51 27 B8
Kimbridge Cres PO9 136 A6
Kimbridge La SO51 26 F7
Kimmeridge Ave BH12 203 C8
Kimpton Cl PO13 179 F3
Kimpton Ct 9 PO9 136 B6
Kineton Rd SO15 78 E1
King Albert Ct PO1 216 C4
King Albert St PO1 216 C4
King Alfred Pl SO23 215 E7
King Alfred Terr 13
SO23 215 E7
King Arthur's Ct PO6 158 D8
King Charles St 9 PO1 182 A4
King Cl BH24 139 F4
King Cup Ave SO31 128 F3
King Edward Ave
Bournemouth BH9 190 A2
Southampton SO16 102 A8
King Edward Cres PO2 157 D2
King Edward Ct BH9 189 F2
King Edward Cvn Pk The
SO52 30 A1
King Edward Pk (Cvn Pk)
SO52 55 A8
King Edward VI Sch
SO15 102 E8
King George Ave
Bournemouth BH9 189 F2
Petersfield GU32 40 F4
King George Mews 4
GU32 40 F4
King George Mobile Home Pk
BH25 194 F1
King George Rd PO16 156 D7
King George's Ave SO15 101 F7
King Harold Ct SO23 215 D4
King Henry 1 St PO1 216 A3
King James Terr 2
PO1 182 A3
King John Ave
Bournemouth BH11 188 D5
Portchester PO16 156 B7
King John Cl BH11 188 D6
King La GU32 39 F8
King Richard 1 Rd PO1 216 A3
King Richard Cl PO6 157 D8
King Richard Dr BH11 188 D5
King Richard Sec Sch
PO6 156 F8
King St Emsworth PO10 161 A8
Gosport PO12 181 D6
Portsmouth PO5 216 B2
Southampton SO14 103 A3
Westbourne PO10 137 B3
Wimborne Minst BH21 163 B4
King William St PO1 182 A6
King's Ave BH23 206 F6
King's Cl SO53 55 D7
King's Copse Rd SO45 177 D8
King's Cres BH14 203 E2
King's Croft La PO9 135 C2
King's Ho 6 SO14 103 A3
King's La GU32 18 D4
King's Park Dr BH7,BH1 205 E6
King's Park Prim Sch
BH1 205 E5
King's Park Rd BH7 205 E6
King's Prim Sch The
SO30 80 E3
King's Rd
Bournemouth BH3 205 A7
Emsworth PO10 160 E8
Fareham PO16 131 B1
Lee-on-t-S PO13 179 E4
Portsmouth PO5 216 B1
Waterlooville PO8 111 F3
King's Royal Hussars Mus
The* SO23 215 D5
King's Saltern Rd SO41 198 A2
King's Terr
4 Emsworth PO10 160 F8
Portsmouth PO1,PO5 216 A1
King's Wlk 8 SO23 215 E5
Kingcome Ho PO1 216 B4
Kingcup Cl BH18 186 E2
Kingdom Cl PO15 129 D5
Kingfisher Cl
Bournemouth BH6 206 E6
Hamble-le-R SO31 128 A4
Rowlands Castle PO9 113 B1
South Hayling PO11 185 C2
Waterlooville PO8 111 E4
West Moors BH22 138 F2
Kingfisher Copse SO31 129 B3
Kingfisher Ct
Bournemouth BH8 205 D6
Havant PO9 136 B2
Portsmouth PO3 158 A4
1 Southampton SO17 79 A2
Kingfisher Cvn Pk PO13 180 C3
Kingfisher Dr PO10 137 B4
Kingfisher Park Homes 3
BH10 189 F4
Kingfisher Pk BH21 138 E6
Kingfisher Rd SO50 55 E2
Kingfisher Way
Christchurch BH23 208 A5
Marchwood SO40 101 E1
Ringwood BH24 117 B1
Romsey SO51 52 F8
Kingfishers
4 Christchurch BH23 207 A5
Portchester PO16 155 F8
Kingfishers The BH31 115 A5
Kingland Cres 4 BH15 202 C2
Kingland Rd BH15 202 D2
Kings Arms La BH24 140 F7
Kings Arms Row BH24 140 F7
Kings Ave
Hamble-le-R SO31 127 E3
Poole BH14 203 D2
Winchester SO22 215 C3
Kings Bench Alley 19
PO1 182 A5
Kings Cl Lymington SO41 197 D4
Lyndhurst SO43 121 F5
Poole BH15 202 D5
Rowlands Castle PO9 113 A1
Twyford SO21 32 A7
West Moors BH22 138 E1
Kings Copse Ave SO30 105 D5
Kings Copse Prim Sch
SO30 105 C5
Kings Copse Rd SO30 105 D5
Kings Cote Villas 3
PO5 182 E1
Kings Court Sch PO8 88 A1
Kings Cres SO41 197 D4
Kings Ct SP6 69 F1
Kings Field SO31 105 A1
Kings Field Gdns SO31 105 A1
Kings Grange 11 BH4 204 D2
Kings Head Yd 1 SO23 215 E5
Kings High Sch BH10 189 C3
Kings Huts SO41 197 A3
Kings La Chilcomb SO21 11 F6
Sway SO41 196 E8
Kings Mede PO8 112 B5
Kings Mews PO5 182 D2
Kings Park Com Hospl
BH7 205 F5
Kings Park Rd SO15 103 A6
Kings Rd
Chandler's Ford SO53 55 D6
Gosport PO12 181 B6
Lymington SO41 197 D4
New Milton BH25 195 C3
Petersfield GU32 40 D4
South Hayling PO11 185 A5
Winchester SO22 215 A4
Kings Ride SO45 177 E7

Kings Row 3 SO22 215 D6
Kings Sch The SO50 57 B1
Kings Somborne Rd SO51 7 D2
Kings Way PO9 113 A1
Kings Worthy Prim Sch
SO23 2 C6
Kings' Sch SO22 10 B7
Kingsbere Ave BH10 189 B2
Kingsbere Gdns BH23 209 A8
Kingsbere Rd BH15 202 E5
Kingsbridge Rd BH14 203 C3
Kingsbury Ct PO8 88 B6
Kingsbury Rd SO14 103 B7
Kingsbury's La BH24 140 F7
Kingsclere Ave
Havant PO9 135 D5
Southampton SO19 126 F8
Kingsclere Cl SO19 103 F1
Kingscote Ho 7 PO6 132 F2
Kingscote Rd
Portchester PO6 132 F2
Waterlooville PO8 111 D3
Kingscroft Ct PO9 135 D1
Kingsdale Ct 9 SO22 215 D6
Kingsdown Pl PO1 216 D3
Kingsdown Rd PO7 111 C2
Kingsdown Way SO18 80 A2
Kingsey Ave PO10 160 E8
Kingsfernsden La GU31,
GU32 41 A5
Kingsfield
Lymington SO41 198 A2
Ringwood BH24 141 A7
Kingsfold Ave SO18 79 F3
Kingsford Cl SP5 47 D5
Kingsgate 10 BH13 204 B3
Kingsgate Rd SO23 215 D4
Kingsgate St SO23 215 E4
Kingsland Cl PO6 133 C1
Kingsland Ct Poole BH13 214 F7
3 Southampton SO14 103 A4
Kingsland Ho 4 SO14 103 A5
Kingsland Mkt SO14 103 A4
Kingsland Sq 5 SO14 103 A4
Kingsleigh Prim Sch
BH10 189 C3
Kingsley Ave BH6 207 A4
Kingsley Cl BH6 207 A4
Kingsley Gdns SO40 100 B7
Kingsley Gn PO9 135 E6
Kingsley Pl SO22 215 C3
Kingsley Rd
Gosport PO12 180 F7
Portsmouth PO4 183 C4
Southampton SO15 102 B7
Kingsmead PO17 108 D8
Kingsmead Ave PO14 179 D6
Kingsmead Cotts PO17 108 C7
Kingsmead Ct
7 Southampton SO15 78 B1
6 Wimborne Minst BH21 163 B5
Kingsmill Cl PO12 180 F4
Kingsmill Rd BH17 202 E7
Kingston SO31 127 C7
Kingston Cres PO2 182 D8
Kingston Cross PO2 182 D8
Kingston Ct SO16 77 F2
Kingston Gdns PO15 130 D4
Kingston Lacy Ho*
BH21 162 B7
Kingston Pk
Lymington SO41 197 D2
West Wellow SO51 74 E8
Kingston Rd
Gosport PO12 180 F5
Poole BH15 202 D4
Portsmouth PO1,PO2 182 E8
Southampton SO15 102 D6
Kingsway
Chandler's Ford SO53 55 D6
Chandler's Ford SO53 55 E8
Ferndown BH22 165 B8
North Hayling PO11 160 A3
Southampton SO14 103 A5
Kingsway Cl BH23 191 F1
Kingsway Ct SO53 55 F8
Kingsway Gdns SO53 55 E8
Kingsway The PO16 156 C8
Kingswell Cl BH10 189 D2
Kingswell Gdns BH10 189 B2
Kingswell Gr BH10 189 B2
Kingswell Path PO1 216 B4
Kingswell Rd BH10 189 C2
Kingswell St PO1 216 B3
Kingswood
Marchwood SO40 102 A1
15 Bournemouth BH4 204 C2
Kingswood Cl PO15 129 D8
Kingswood Ct 3 PO15 129 D8
Kingswood Pl PO17 130 E7
Kingsworthy Rd PO9 135 F3
Kinloss Ct SO16 78 A5
Kinnell Cl PO10 160 F8
Kinross Cres PO6 158 B7
Kinross Rd
Bournemouth BH3 204 E6
Totton SO40 100 F7
Kinsbourne Ave BH10 189 D2
Kinsbourne Cl SO19 104 E6
Kinsbourne Rise SO19 104 F5
Kinsbourne Way SO19 104 E6
Kinsford Ct SO42 145 F1
Kinson Ave BH15 203 A7
Kinson Gr BH10 189 C6
Kinson Park Rd BH10 189 D6
Kinson Pottery Ind Est
BH14 203 A6
Kinson Prim Sch BH11 189 B5
Kinson Rd BH10 189 C3
Kinterbury Ct 10 SO17 103 A8
Kintyre Rd PO6 133 F1
Kinver Cl SO51 28 B1
Kiosks The 9 BH15 202 C1
Kipling Bldgs 3 PO2 157 E3
Kipling Cl PO15 106 B1
Kipling Ct SO19 103 F1
Kipling Rd Eastleigh SO50 55 F3
Poole BH14 203 B5
Portsmouth PO2 157 E3
Kirby Cl BH15 202 F6
Kirby Ct 4 PO2 157 E2
Kirby Rd PO2 157 F2
Kirby Way BH6 206 D4
Kirk Gdns SO40 100 F5
Kirkham Ave BH23 192 C3
Kirkstall Rd PO4 182 E1
Kirkway BH18 187 B4
Kirpal Rd PO3 183 B6
Kirtley Cl PO6 158 C6
Kirton Rd PO6 158 C7
Kitchener Cres BH17 187 B2
Kitchener Rd SO17 79 C2
Kitchers Cl SO41 172 B2
Kite Cl PO8 111 E4
Kites Croft Bsns Pk
SO31 129 E2
Kites Croft Cl PO14 129 C1
Kitnocks Hill SO32 106 F8
Kitscroft Rd BH10 189 C5
Kitt's La GU32,SO24 16 C2
Kittiwake Cl
Bournemouth BH6 206 D6
Gosport PO13 155 B2
Kitwalls La SO41 211 D5
Kitwood Gn 26 PO9 136 B5
Kivernell Pl 1 SO41 211 C4
Kivernell Rd SO41 211 D4
Kiwi Cl BH15 202 E3
Kleves Ct SO19 104 B6
Knapp Cl BH23 207 A8
Knapp La SO51 29 D4
Knapp Mill Ave BH23 207 A8
Knapps Hard GU32 37 B5
Knatchbull Cl SO51 52 F7
Knellers La SO40 100 D4
Knight Cl SO23 215 E8
Knight Gdns PO6 158 E7
Knightcrest Pk SO41 196 E1
Knighton Cnr PO8 112 C7
Knighton Cvn Pk SO41 196 E1
Knighton Heath Cl
BH11 188 E4
Knighton Heath Ind Est
BH11 188 E2
Knighton Heath Rd
BH11 188 E4
Knighton La BH21 188 D7
Knighton Pk BH25 209 E8
Knighton Rd SO19 103 F4
Knights Bank Rd PO14 153 F1
Knights Cl SO31 128 E1
Knights Rd BH11 188 D5
Knightsbridge Ct BH2 204 E2
Knightsfield GU32 40 E3
Knightstone Ct 3 PO2 157 F4
Knightstone Gr BH22 138 D2
Knightstone Grange 2
SO45 126 A2
Knightwood Ave
Havant PO9 136 A5
Lyndhurst SO43 121 F5
Knightwood Cl
Ashurst SO40 100 B2
Christchurch BH23 208 D8
Lyndhurst SO43 121 F5
Knightwood Glade SO53 54 F7
Knightwood Oak*
SO43 120 F1
Knightwood Prim Sch
SO53 54 F7
Knightwood Rd
Chandler's Ford SO53 55 A6
Hythe SO45 126 B3
Knightwood View SO53 55 C5
Knobcrook Rd 3 BH21 163 B6
Knole Ct 5 BH1 205 D4
Knole Gdns BH1 205 D4
Knole Rd BH1 205 D4
Knoll Gdns*
Ferndown BH21 164 F4
St Leonards BH24 139 F4
Knoll La BH21 186 B7
Knoll Manor BH2 204 F5
Knotgrass Rd SO31 128 E2
Knowland Dr SO41 211 D5
Knowle Ave PO17 130 E8
Knowle Hill SO50 56 B7
Knowle La SO50 57 E1
Knowle Rd
Brockenhurst SO42 145 E2
Fareham PO17 131 A7
Knowle Village PO17 130 F7
Knowle Village Bsns Pk
PO17 130 D8
Knowles Cl
Christchurch BH23 207 E7
Nursling SO16 77 D5
Knowles Mdw GU33 21 B1
Knowlton Gdns BH9 190 B3
Knowlton Rd BH17 187 F2
Knowsley Cres PO6 158 A7
Knowsley Rd PO6 157 F7
Knox Rd Havant PO9 135 D1
Knox Rd *continued*
Portsmouth PO2 157 C1
Knyght Cl SO51 53 A6
Knyveton Ho BH1 205 B4
Knyveton Rd BH1 205 C4
Kootenay Ave SO18 104 E7
Kooyong Cl SO51 51 B2
Kornwestheim Way SO50 55 E3
Kynegils Rd SO22 215 B8
Kynon Cl 2 PO12 181 C9
Kyoto Wlk PO9 136 A3
Kyrchil La BH21 163 F6
Kyrchil Way BH21 163 F7
Kytes La SO32 82 C6

L

Labrador Dr BH15 202 D1
Laburnum Ave PO6 158 C7
Laburnum Cl
Ferndown BH22 165 B6
North Baddesley SO52 54 A5
Verwood BH31 115 C5
Laburnum Cres SO45 150 B8
Laburnum Ct SO19 103 D3
Laburnum Dr
Everton SO41 211 D8
Kings Worthy SO23 2 B8
Laburnum Gr
Eastleigh SO50 56 A3
Portsmouth PO2 157 E1
South Hayling PO11 185 B4
Laburnum Ho
8 Bournemouth BH10 189 F4
Hedge End SO30 105 D6
Laburnum Rd
Fareham PO16 155 B6
Hedge End SO30 105 D6
Southampton SO16 79 C4
Waterlooville PO7 134 D6
Lacey Cres BH15 203 A6
Lackford Ave SO40 100 E6
Lacon Cl SO18 103 E8
Lacy Cl BH21 163 C6
Lacy Dr BH21 163 C6
Ladram Rd PO12 180 E4
Lady Betty's Dr PO15 129 E5
Ladybridge Rd PO7 134 C4
Ladycross Rd SO45 126 A2
Ladysmith Cl BH23 207 E7
Ladysmith Terr SO32 83 C7
Ladywood SO50 55 F6
Ladywood Ho PO5 216 B2
Lagado Cl BH14 214 C8
Lagland Ct 14 BH15 202 C2
Lagland St BH15 202 C2
Lagoon Cl BH14 214 B8
Lagoon Rd BH14 214 B8
Laidlaw Cl BH12 204 B8
Laidlaw Gdns SO53 30 B1
Lainston Cl SO22 215 A8
Lake Ave BH15 201 D1
Lake Cres BH15 201 E3
Lake Dr Hamworthy BH15 201 D1
Poole BH15 201 D2
Winchester SO22 10 B3
Lake Farm Cl
Ferndown BH22 189 B8
Hedge End SO30 105 C8
Lake Grove Rd BH25 195 A4
Lake Ho SO15 102 C6
Lake Rd
Bournemouth BH11 189 C6
Chandler's Ford SO53 55 E8
Curdridge SO32 106 F8
Hamworthy BH15 201 E2
Portsmouth PO1 216 C4
Southampton SO19 103 D2
Verwood BH31 115 B5
Lake View Manor BH25 195 A3
Lakeland Gdns SO40 101 E1
Lakelands Dr SO15 102 C6
Laker Ho SO15 102 F7
Lakes The SO32 84 A4
Lakeside Fareham PO17 130 E5
Lee-on-t-S PO13 179 F1
Ower SO51 75 D6
Ringwood BH24 141 C6
Lakeside Ave
Portsmouth PO3 183 B7
Rownhams SO16 77 E5
Lakeside Ct PO4 182 F2
Lakeside Ctry Pk* SO50 79 F8
Lakeside Gdns PO9 136 A2
Lakeside Pines BH25 195 A4
Lakeside Rd BH13 204 A1
Lakeside Sch SO53 55 F8
Lakesmere Rd PO8 112 C6
Lakeview Dr BH24 141 D6
Lakewood Cl SO53 55 D8
Lakewood Rd
Ashurst SO40 100 C3
Chandler's Ford SO53 30 E1
Chandler's Ford SO53 55 D8
Christchurch BH23 193 F1
Lamberhurst Cl SO19 127 A8
Lambert Cl PO7 134 E5
Lambourn Cl PO14 154 D8
Lambourn Sq SO53 55 B6
Lambourne Cl SO45 125 F1
Lambourne Dr SO31 129 B3
Lambourne Ho SO30 105 A6
Lambourne Rd SO18 80 B2
Lambs Cl BH17 187 C1
Lambs Lease GU33 21 A3
Lambsgreen La BH21 162 F2
Lammas Rd SO45 126 B2
Lampeter Ave PO6 158 B8
Lampton Gdns 5 BH9 189 F1
Lamward Mans 1 SO14 103 A7
Lanark Cl BH15 201 E2
Lancaster Cl
Bursledon SO31 105 A1
Christchurch BH23 208 C7
Corfe Mullen BH18 186 F5
Lee-on-t-S PO13 180 B4
Portchester PO16 132 B1
Lancaster Ct SO30 80 C2
Lancaster Dr
Corfe Mullen BH18 186 F5
Verwood BH31 114 E6
Lancaster Rd
Ferndown BH21 165 A8
Southampton SO16 77 F3
Lancaster Way PO7 134 F6
Lance's Hill SO18 103 F7
Lancer Cl BH23 206 F7
Lancer Ho PO7 111 C1
Lander Cl BH15 202 D1
Landford CE Prim Sch
SP5 49 D4
Landford Common Farm
SP5 49 E2
Landford Gdns BH8 190 D2
Landford Way BH8 190 D2
Landguard Rd
Portsmouth PO4 183 A3
Southampton SO15 102 D6
Landon Ct PO12 181 A3
Landon Rd PO13 155 D1
Landport St
Portsmouth PO1 216 C4
Portsmouth,Southsea PO5 216 A2
Landport Terr PO1 216 A2
Landport View PO1 216 B4
Lands End Rd SO31 128 C7
Landsdowne St PO5 216 A2
Landseer Rd
1 Bournemouth BH4 204 C3
Southampton SO19 104 C3
Lane End SO24 17 C8
Lane End Cotts SP5 49 D3
Lane End Dr PO10 160 F8
Lane Lowther Gdns The 4
BH8 205 C5
Lane The Fawley SO45 151 B3
Gosport PO12 181 A2
Portsmouth PO4 182 F2
Lanehays Rd SO45 125 F3
Lanes End PO14 179 C7
Lanes The BH25 195 A5
Lanesbridge Cl SO40 99 F5
Langbar Cl SO19 103 E6
Langbrook Cl PO9 159 F8
Langdale Ave PO6 158 B7
Langdale Cl SO16 101 F8
Langdon Ct BH14 203 D4
Langdon Rd BH14 203 D4
Langdown Firs SO45 126 A3
Langdown Lawn SO45 126 A3
Langdown Lawn Cl
SO45 126 A2
Langdown Rd SO45 126 B3
Langford Ct 12 PO16 131 B1
Langford La SP5 47 E8
Langford Rd PO1 182 F7
Langham Cl SO52 53 F4
Langham Ct BH23 191 F1
Langhorn Rd SO16 79 C4
Langley Chase BH24 140 A5
Langley Gdn SP6 70 A3
Langley Lodge Gdns
SO45 177 F7
Langley Rd
Christchurch BH23 193 E1
Poole BH14 203 F4
Portsmouth PO2 182 E8
Southampton SO15 102 A6
Langrish Cl PO9 136 A6
Langrish Prim Sch GU32 40 A3
Langrish Rd SO16 78 B4
Langside Ave BH12 204 A8
Langside Sch BH12 204 A8
Langstone Ave PO9 159 F7
Langstone Harbour Nature
Reserve* PO9 159 A3
Langstone High St PO9 159 F6
Langstone Ho
Fareham PO16 155 A7
Havant PO9 136 A3
Langstone Inf Sch PO3 183 A7
Langstone Jun Sch PO3 183 A7
Langstone Marina Hts
PO4 183 D3
Langstone Rd
Langstone PO9 159 F7
Portsmouth PO3 183 A6
Langstone Wlk
Fareham PO14 154 C8
Gosport PO13 155 B2
Langton Cl
Barton on S BH25 210 B8
Lee-on-t-S PO13 180 A6
Winchester SO22 215 C7
Langton Farm Gdns
PO1 182 E7
Langton Rd
Bishop's Waltham SO32 83 C8
Bournemouth BH7 205 F5
Lanham La SO22 1 B1
Lankhills Rd SO23 215 E7
Lansdell Ct 4 BH15 202 E3
Lansdown Ave PO16 156 D6
Lansdown Terr PO10 137 B5
Lansdowne Ave
Waterlooville PO7 134 B2
Winchester SO23 215 D3
Lansdowne Cl 2 SO51 52 E8
Lansdowne Cres BH1 205 B3
Lansdowne Ct
1 Romsey SO51 52 E8
3 Winchester SO23 215 D3
Lansdowne Gdns
Bournemouth BH1 205 A4
Romsey SO51 52 E8
Lansdowne Hill 4 SO14 102 F3
Lansdowne Ho 3 PO12 181 A7
Lansdowne Rd
Bournemouth BH1 205 A5
Southampton SO15 102 A7
Lansdowne Rdbt The
BH1 205 A3
Lantana Cl PO7 134 F6
Lantern Ct SO23 215 C4
Lanyard Dr PO13 180 D6
Lapthorn Cl PO13 155 B4
Lapwing Cl Gosport PO12 181 B8
Horndean PO8 112 A7
Lapwing Dr SO40 100 C8
Lapwing Gr PO16 155 F8
Lapwing Rd
Portsmouth PO4 183 C5
Wimborne Minst BH21 164 A7
Lara Cl BH8 190 D3
Larch Ave SO45 150 C5
Larch Cl
Broadstone BH17 186 E1
Hordle SO41 195 F3
Kings Worthy SO23 2 B8
Lee-on-t-S PO13 180 A5
St Leonards BH24 140 A4
West End SO30 80 D2
Larch Ct PO1 216 C4
Larch Rd SO16 78 A3
Larch Row SP6 70 D2
Larch Way
Bursledon SO31 127 F8
Ferndown BH22 165 C7
Larchdale Cl SO31 152 D10
Larches Gdns PO15 130 C1
Larchfield Way PO8 112 C5
Larchwood Ave PO9 135 B4
Larchwood Rd SO40 100 C6
Larcombe Rd GU32 40 D2
Larg Dr SO22 1 C4
Lark Hill Rise SO22 215 B2
Lark Rd BH23 208 A6
Lark Way PO10 137 C4
Larkhill Rd PO3 157 F4
Larks Cl BH22 165 B7
Larks Rise BH22 165 B7
Larksfield Ave BH9 190 C3
Larkshill Cl BH25 195 B4
Larkspur Chase SO19 104 E5
Larkspur Cl
Locks Heath SO31 128 F2
Swanmore SO32 84 A5
Larkspur Dr
Chandler's Ford SO53 54 F6
Marchwood SO40 124 F8
Larkspur Gdns
7 Hedge End SO30 105 C6
Holbury SO45 150 B4
Larkwhistle Wlk PO9 135 C7
Lascelles Ct 1 BH7 206 B6
Lascelles Rd BH7 206 B6
Laser Cl SO31 128 E1
Lasham Gn 28 PO9 136 B5
Lasham Ho 5 SO16 102 B8
Lasham Wlk PO14 154 D7
Lashly Mdw PO7 86 C3
Latch Farm Ave BH23 207 A8
Latchmore Dr SO45 125 C4
Latchmore Forest Gr
PO8 112 A3
Latchmore Gdns PO8 111 F3
Latelie Cl SO31 127 C5
Latham Cl SO50 57 B2
Latham Ct SO15 102 B7
Latham Rd Fair Oak SO50 57 B2
Romsey SO51 53 A8
Latimer Ct
Portsmouth PO3 158 B4
4 Southampton SO17 79 A1
Latimer Gate 22 SO14 103 A3
Latimer Ho 5 SO15 102 F5
Latimer Rd BH9 204 F8
Latimer St Romsey SO51 52 E7
Southampton SO14 103 A3
Latimers Cl BH23 193 F1
Lauder Cl PO10 137 D2
Launcelyn Cl SO52 53 F3
Launceston Cl 3 PO12 181 C8
Launceston Dr SO50 55 F5
Laundry La SO41 211 E4
Laundry Rd SO16 78 B2
Laurel Cl
Christchurch BH23 193 D1
Corfe Mullen BH21 186 D6
8 Gosport PO12 181 C8
Hordle SO41 195 E4
Hythe SO45 125 F3
Locks Heath SO31 129 B4
Southampton SO19 103 D3
St Leonards BH24 139 E3
Laurel Dr BH18 187 C4
Laurel Gdns
Broadstone BH18 187 C4
Locks Heath SO31 129 B4
Laurel La BH24 139 E3
Laurel Rd
Locks Heath SO31 129 B4

Laurel Rd *continued*
Waterlooville PO8 112 C4
Laurels The
Broadstone BH18 187 B4
Brockenhurst SO42 172 F8
Ferndown BH22 165 C7
Lauren Mews PO11 184 E2
Lauren Way SO40 76 B1
Laurence Ct SO50 57 C2
Laurence Gn PO10 136 F4
Laurence Mews SO51 52 F8
Lauriston Dr 7 SO53 30 B1
Laurus Cl PO7 135 A5
Laurus Wlk 4 PO13 179 F3
Lavant Cl PO8 112 B1
Lavant Ct GU32 40 E4
Lavant Dr PO9 136 A3
Lavant St GU32 40 E3
Lavender Cl
Southampton SO19 103 F5
Verwood BH31 115 C5
Lavender Rd
Bournemouth BH8 190 D4
Hordle SO41 195 E3
Waterlooville PO7 135 A6
Lavender Villas BH23 209 A8
Lavender Way BH18 186 D3
Lavender Wlk BH8 190 D4
Laverock Lea PO16 132 C1
Laverstock 3 BH5 205 F3
Laverstoke Cl SO16 77 E6
Lavey's La PO15 130 B6
Lavington Gdns SO52 53 F3
Lavinia Rd Gosport PO12 181 B6
Poole BH12 203 C7
Lawford Rd BH9 190 A4
Lawford Way SO40 100 E7
Lawn Cl Gosport PO13 180 D8
Milford on S SO41 211 E4
Lawn Ct
13 Bournemouth BH2 204 D4
Southampton SO17 103 A7
Lawn Dr SO31 129 A2
Lawn Ho 24 SO23 215 E6
Lawn Rd Eastleigh SO50 56 B5
Littleton SO22 1 C5
Lymington SO41 197 B3
Milford on S SO41 211 E4
Southampton SO17 103 B8
Lawn St SO23 215 E6
Lawn View BH25 194 D5
Lawns Cl BH21 164 C6
Lawns Rd BH21 164 B6
Lawns The BH23 209 B8
Lawnside Rd SO15 102 A8
Lawnswood SO50 57 D1
Lawnswood Cl
Dibden Purlieu SO45 125 E1
Waterlooville PO8 111 F2
Lawrence Ave PO8 111 E2
Lawrence Ct
Bournemouth BH8 205 C6
Southampton SO19 103 F3
Lawrence Dr BH13 203 E1
Lawrence Gr SO19 103 F2
Lawrence Ho SO45 126 B4
Lawrence La SP6 94 B4
Lawrence Mans PO5 216 D1
Lawrence Rd
Fareham PO15 130 F2
Portsmouth PO5 216 D1
Ringwood BH24 117 D2
Lawrence Sq 3 PO12 181 D5
Lawrence Way 4 SO23 215 E8
Lawrence Wlk PO13 180 D6
Lawson Cl SO31 128 D8
Lawson Ct 3 SO16 78 B1
Lawson Rd Poole BH12 203 B6
Portsmouth PO5 216 D2
Laxton Cl
Locks Heath SO31 129 B3
Southampton SO19 104 A2
Layard Dr BH21 163 D1
Laymoor La BH21 164 D5
Layton Ct BH12 203 D5
Layton Rd Gosport PO13 155 C3
Poole BH12 203 D5
Lazy Acre PO10 161 D8
Le Patourel Cl BH23 207 D7
Le Tissier Ct 6 SO15 102 E6
Lea Rd SO45 177 E7
Lea The BH31 115 A5
Lea Way BH11 188 E6
Lea-Oak Gdns PO15 130 D3
Leabrook SO31 129 A5
Leacock Cl SO32 84 B5
Leafy La PO15 129 E6
Lealand Gr PO6 158 D8
Lealand Rd PO6 158 D7
Leamington Cres PO13 179 F3
Leamington Ho 9 PO5 216 B2
Leamington Rd BH9 205 A7
Leander Cl SO50 56 A5
Leander Dr 7 PO12 181 C8
Leaphill Rd BH7 206 B6
Lear Rd PO12 181 B6
Learoyd Rd BH17 202 E7
Leaside Way SO16 79 C5
Leatherhead Gdns SO30 81 D2
Leaway The PO16 156 D8
Lebanon Rd SO15 101 D7
Lebern Ho SO30 105 D7
Lechlade Gdns
Bournemouth BH7 206 B8
Fareham PO15 130 E4
Leckford Cl
Portchester PO16 132 B2
Southampton SO18 104 D8
Leckford Rd PO9 136 B6
Ledbury Rd
Christchurch BH23 207 F5
Portsmouth PO6 133 C1
Lederle La PO13 155 C5
Ledgard Cl BH14 203 B4
Ledwell Ct PO12 181 D7
Lee Church La SO51 76 F8
Lee Ct BH22 165 D4
Lee Dro SO51 53 B1
Lee Ground PO15 129 F5
Lee La SO16,SO51 53 A2
Lee Lands SO41 197 D1
Lee Rd PO12 181 A7
Lee-on-the-Solent Inf Sch
PO13 179 F2
Lee-on-the-Solent Jun Sch
PO13 179 F2
Leedam Rd BH10 189 D4
Leep La PO12 181 B3
Lees Cl BH23 191 D4
Lees La PO12 181 B6
Lees Lane N 9 PO12 181 B6
Leesland CE Inf Sch
PO12 181 A5
Leesland CE Jun Sch
PO12 181 B5
Leesland Rd PO12 181 A6
Leeson Dr BH22 165 B8
Leeson Rd BH7 205 E7
Legg La BH21 163 D4
Legion Cl
Hamworthy BH15 201 E2
Southampton SO16 79 C4
Legion La SO23 2 C7
Legion Rd
Hamworthy BH15 201 E2
South Hayling PO11 185 A4
Leicester Ct 11 PO13 180 D5
Leicester Rd Poole BH13 203 F3
Southampton SO15 78 D2
Leicester Way SO23 2 C1
Leigh Cl BH21 163 E4
Leigh Comm BH21 163 E5
Leigh Cotts PO9 136 A4
Leigh Ct SO50 55 E3
Leigh Gdns BH21 163 D4
Leigh House Hospl SO21 11 E7
Leigh La BH21 163 F5
Leigh Mans 2 SO17 79 A1
Leigh Pk SO41 197 C3
Leigh Rd Eastleigh SO50 55 E3
Fareham PO16 131 A2
Havant PO9 135 F2
New Milton BH25 195 A3
Southampton SO17 79 A1
Wimborne Minst BH21 163 E4
Leigham Vale Rd BH6 206 D4
Leighton Ave 19 SO15 102 B8
Leighton Lo 3 BH2 204 D4
Leighton Rd SO19 103 F3
Leisure The PO13 155 D4
Leith Ave PO16 132 E1
Lemon Rd SO15 102 B7
Len Williams Terr PO2 182 E7
Lendorber Ave PO6 158 A8
Lennox Cl
Chandler's Ford SO53 55 E7
Gosport PO12 181 C2
Southampton SO16 77 F5
Lennox Ct 9 PO5 182 D2
Lennox Mans PO5 182 D1
Lennox Rd N PO5 182 D2
Lennox Rd S PO5 182 D2
Lensyd Gdns PO8 111 F6
Lent Hill Ct SO22 215 B4
Lentham Cl BH17 187 D1
Lentune Way SO41 197 D2
Leofric Ct PO4 183 C3
Leominster Ho PO6 133 B1
Leominster Rd PO6 133 B1
Leonard Rd PO12 181 C6
Leonards Ct SO16 101 C8
Leopold Dr SO32 83 B7
Leopold St PO4 182 E2
Lepe Ctry Pk* SO45 178 B2
Lepe Rd SO45 178 A3
Leroux Cl SO15 102 F5
Lerryn Rd PO13 155 D2
Leslie Loader Ct SO50 56 A4
Leslie Loader Ho SO19 103 E5
Leslie Rd
Bournemouth BH9 204 F7
Poole BH14 203 A3
Lesser Horseshoe Cl 2
PO17 130 E8
Lester Ave PO9 135 C2
Lester Rd PO12 180 F5
Lester Sq BH24 143 C3
Leven Ave BH4 204 D5
Leven Cl
Bournemouth BH4 204 D4
Chandler's Ford SO53 55 A7
Leventhorpe Ct PO12 181 C5
Leveret Cl PO12 181 C9
Leveson Cl PO12 180 F3
Levet's La 4 BH15 202 B1
Leviathan Cl PO14 179 D7
Lewens Cl BH21 163 C4
Lewens La BH21 163 C4
Lewes Cl SO50 56 A6
Lewesdon Dr BH18 186 F4
Lewin Cl SO21 56 F8
Lewins Wlk SO31 104 F1
Lewis Cl SO45 125 C2
Lewis Ho 5 SO14 103 A5
Lewis Rd PO10 137 A3
Lewis Silkin Way SO16 78 A4
Lewry Cl SO30 105 C7
Lexby Rd SO40 101 A6
Lexden Gdns PO11 184 E4
Leybourne Ave
Bournemouth BH10 189 D4
Southampton SO18 104 A8
Leybourne Cl BH10 189 C5
Leydene Ave BH8 190 F1
Leydene Cl BH8 190 F1
Leydene Pk GU32 63 E3
Leyland Cl PO12 181 B4
Leyland Rd BH12 188 E2
Leyside BH23 207 F6
Leyton Conyers 11 BH13 214 F7
Leyton Rd SO14 103 C6
Liam Cl PO9 136 A4
Liberty Cl BH21 139 B6
Liberty Ct BH23 206 F7
Liberty Rd PO17 109 A8
Liberty Row SO31 128 A2
Liberty The PO7 110 E3
Library Gdns PO9 135 E3
Library Mews BH12 203 D5
Library Rd
Bournemouth BH9 189 F1
Ferndown BH22 165 D5
Poole BH12 203 E5
Totton SO40 101 A7
Lichen Way SO40 101 F2
Lichfield Ct 4 PO13 180 D5
Lichfield Dr PO12 181 C8
Lichfield Rd
Locks Heath PO14 129 C3
Portsmouth PO3 183 A6
Liddel Way SO53 55 B5
Liddiard Gdns PO4 183 B2
Liddiards Way PO7 134 E3
Lidiard Gdns PO4 183 B2
Liederbach Dr BH31 115 C4
Lightfoot Lawn PO4 183 C3
Lighthouse The 18 PO1 182 A4
Lightning Cl SO45 150 F2
Lights Cl BH23 207 B7
Lilac Cl Havant PO9 136 C3
Ringwood BH24 141 B8
Lilac Rd SO16 79 B4
Lilley Cl SO40 101 F2
Lillies The SO50 81 D7
Lilliput CE Fst Sch
BH14 214 C8
Lilliput Ct BH14 203 B3
Lilliput Rd BH14 214 D8
Lily Ave PO7 134 B2
Limberline Rd PO3 158 A4
Limberline Spur PO3 158 A5
Lime Ave SO19 104 A5
Lime Cl
Colden Common SO21 57 A8
Hythe SO45 125 E2
Poole BH15 202 F6
Southampton SO19 104 A5
Lime Gdns SO30 80 D3
Lime Gr Hordle SO41 211 D8
Portsmouth PO6 133 B1
South Hayling PO11 184 C3
Lime Kiln La SO45 150 B5
Lime Kiln Lane Estate Mobile Home Pk SO45 150 B5
Lime St SO14 103 A3
Lime Tree Cl SP6 92 F6
Lime Tree Ho 1 SO41 197 E4
Lime Wlk Botley SO30 105 F7
Hythe SO45 125 E2
Limekiln La
Bishop's Waltham SO32 59 F4
East Meon GU32 64 D6
Limes Cl GU33 20 F4
Limes The Gosport PO13 155 D1
Langstone PO9 159 F8
Marchwood SO40 102 A1
Waterlooville PO7 134 D3
Limetree Wlk 3 SO23 11 D8
Limited Rd BH9 190 A1
Lin Brook Dr BH24 117 C2
Linacre Rd SO19 104 D5
Linbrook Ct BH24 117 A1
Lincoln Ave
Bournemouth BH1 205 D5
Christchurch BH23 191 F2
Lincoln Cl
Locks Heath PO14 129 C3
Romsey SO51 28 B1
Lincoln Ct
9 Gosport PO13 180 D5
Southampton SO15 78 E2
West End SO30 80 C2
Lincoln Pl SO53 55 D4
Lincoln Rd Poole BH12 203 D7
Portsmouth PO1 182 E5
Lincoln Rise PO8 112 B4
Lincolns Rise SO50 31 B1
Lind Cl PO7 134 F3
Lind Rd PO12 181 C2
Linda Gr PO8 111 F3
Linda Rd SO45 151 B3
Lindal Ct SO30 105 C7
Lindbergh Cl PO13 180 D5
Lindbergh Rd BH21 165 A8
Lindbergh Rise PO15 129 E6
Linden Cl
Ferndown BH22 165 D1
Waltham Chase SO32 83 E3
Linden Ct
Locks Heath SO31 129 C4
Ringwood BH24 140 F8
6 Romsey SO51 52 F7
West End SO18 80 B3
Linden Dr GU33 20 F4
Linden Gdns
Hedge End SO30 105 D5
Ringwood BH24 140 F8
Linden Gr
Chandler's Ford SO53 55 C8
Gosport PO12 181 B4
South Hayling PO11 185 A3
Linden Lea PO16 132 C1
Linden Rd
Bournemouth BH9 190 A3
Ferndown BH22 165 D1
Poole BH12 203 C6
Romsey SO51 52 F7
Southampton SO16 78 A4
Linden Way Havant PO9 135 F3
Lymington SO41 197 C4
Waterlooville PO8 112 C5
Linden Wlk SO52 53 F5
Lindens Cl PO10 136 F2
Lindens The BH23 192 D3
Lindford Rd BH24 117 D1
Lindisfarne Cl PO6 158 A7
Lindley Ave PO4 183 A2
Lindon Ct PO4 182 F4
Lindsay Ct 19 BH13 204 A4
Lindsay Ho 8 PO5 182 D2
Lindsay Manor 11 BH13 204 A4
Lindsay Pk 15 BH13 204 A4
Lindsay Rd Poole BH13 203 F4
Southampton SO19 104 E6
Lindum Ct 3 BH13 204 A4
Lindway SO31 129 A5
Liners Ind Est SO15 102 C6
Lineside BH23 207 C8
Linford Cl BH25 195 B4
Linford Cres SO16 78 D3
Linford Ct Fair Oak SO50 57 C2
Havant PO9 135 D7
Linford Ho BH24 117 F3
Linford Rd BH24 117 D1
Ling Dale SO16 78 F7
Ling Rd BH12 188 B1
Lingdale Pl 3 SO17 103 A8
Lingdale Rd BH6 206 D6
Lingfield Ct PO1 182 B3
Lingfield Gdns SO18 79 F2
Lingfield Grange 11
BH13 204 B3
Lingwood Ave BH23 207 F6
Lingwood Cl SO16 78 F7
Lingwood Wlk SO16 78 F7
Linhorns La BH25 195 A5
Link Ho PO3 158 B3
Link Rd Portsmouth PO6 133 B2
Ringwood BH24 141 C8
Southampton SO16 77 F3
Link Rise BH21 186 E6
Link The PO7 112 A1
Linkenholt Way PO9 135 C4
Linklater Path PO1 182 D7
Links Cl PO9 113 B1
Links Dr BH23 191 D1
Links La
Rowlands Castle PO9 113 B2
South Hayling PO11 184 C3
Links Rd Poole BH14 203 D2
Winchester SO22 215 B7
Links The PO13 155 C1
Links View Ave BH14 203 E2
Links View Way SO16 78 F6
Linkside Ave BH7 205 F8
Linkway PO14 179 C6
Linmead Dr BH11 189 A6
Linnet Cl Petersfield GU31 41 C2
Ringwood BH24 141 C6
Waterlooville PO8 111 E4
Linnet Ct Gosport PO12 180 F6
New Milton BH25 194 F3
Linnet Rd BH17 201 F8
Linnet Sq SO50 55 D1
Linnets The
Portchester PO16 155 F8
Totton SO40 100 C8
Linnies La SO41 196 B7
Linthorpe Rd BH15 202 E4
Linton Lawns BH22 165 E3
Linwood Cl SO45 126 A2
Linwood Rd BH9 205 B7
Linwood Sch BH9 205 A7
Lion Brewery The 1
PO2 182 D8
Lion Ho PO17 108 A4
Lion Rd PO1 181 F8
Lion St PO1 182 B5
Lion Terr PO1 182 B5
Lionheart Cl BH11 188 D5
Lionheart Way SO31 105 A1
Lions Hall 4 SO22 215 D5
Lions La BH24 139 D5
Lions Wood BH24 139 E4
Liphook Ho 30 PO9 136 B5
Lipizzaner Fields PO15 129 B8
Lippen La SO32 36 F4
Lisbon Rd SO15 102 D6
Lisle Cl Lymington SO41 197 D3
Winchester SO22 10 A3
Lisle Court Rd SO41 198 C3
Lisle Ct SO22 215 C4
Lisle Way PO10 136 E3
Liss Inf & Jun Schs GU33 21 A3
Liss Rd PO4 182 F4
Liss Sta GU33 20 F4
Lissenden 1 BH13 204 B3
Litchfield Cres SO18 79 F1
Litchfield Rd
Southampton SO18 79 F1
Winchester SO22 1 D4
Litchford Rd BH25 195 C3
Lith Ave PO8 112 C8
Lith La PO8 88 C1
Little Abshot Rd PO14 153 B8
Little Anglesey PO12 181 B3
Little Anglesey Rd
PO12 181 A2
Little Arthur St PO2 182 E7
Little Ashton La SO32 59 E3
Little Barn Pl GU33 21 B4
Little Barrs Dr BH25 195 B4
Little Bull La SO32 83 D2
Little Burn SO41 172 B2
Little Cnr PO7 111 A3
Little Coburg St PO1 216 C3
Little Croft Rd BH12 203 B6
Little Ct Poole BH14 214 C7
Poole,Canford Cliffs BH13 214 F8
Little Dene Copse SO41 197 B2
Little Dewlands BH31 114 D6
Little Dro SP6 70 E7
Little Forest Mans 12
BH1 205 A3
Little Forest Rd BH4 204 E5
Little Fosters BH13 214 E6
Little Fox Dr 2 SO31 129 B5
Little Gays PO14 153 F2
Little George St PO1 182 E7
Little Gn PO12 181 A3
Little Green Orch PO12 181 A3
Little Hambrook St 6
PO5 216 A1
Little Holbury Park Homes Mobile Home Pk SO45 150 B5
Little Hyden La PO8 88 B7
Little Kimble Wlk 3
SO30 105 C6
Little La PO12 181 A3
Little Lance's Hill SO19 103 F6
Little Lonnen
Colehill BH21 163 F8
Wimborne Minst BH21 164 A8
Little Mead PO7 111 A3
Little Minster St SO23 215 E5
Little Oak Rd SO16 78 F4
Little Park Cl SO30 105 B6
Little Park Farm Rd
PO15 129 C5
Little Park Mans PO17 107 E4
Little Quob La SO30 80 E2
Little Reynolds SO40 100 D5
Little Shore La SO32 83 D7
Little Southsea St PO5 216 A1
Little Stodham Ho GU33 20 D2
Little Toller SO16 78 F7
Little Woodfalls Dr SP5 47 D4
Little Woodham La
PO13 180 C5
Littlecroft Ave BH9 190 B3
Littledown Ave BH7 205 F7
Littledown Dr BH7 205 F7
Littlefield Cres SO53 54 E6
Littlegreen Ave PO9 136 B4
Littlegreen Sch PO18 90 E4
Littlemead Cl BH17 202 A7
Littlemeads SO51 52 D7
Littlemill La SP6 68 C6
Littlemoor Ave BH11 188 D4
Littlepark Ave PO9 135 B3
Littleton Gr PO9 135 F4
Littleton La SO21,SO22 1 A5
Littleton Rd SO22 1 B4
Littlewood SO51 50 F3
Littlewood Gdns
Sarisbury SO31 128 E3
West End SO30 80 D1
Liverpool Ct 2 PO13 180 D5
Liverpool Rd
Fareham PO14 154 F6
Portsmouth PO1 182 E5
Liverpool St SO14 103 A7
Livesay Gdns PO1 182 F6
Livingstone Ct PO13 180 D6
Livingstone Rd
Bournemouth BH5 206 B5
Christchurch BH23 207 D7
Poole BH12 203 C6
Portsmouth PO5 216 C1
Southampton SO14 103 A8
Wimborne Minst BH21 163 E4
Llewellin Ct BH16 201 C7
Llewelyn Cl BH16 201 C7
Lloyd Ave SO40 101 E1
Loader Cl SO23 2 C7
Loaders Cl BH9 205 A8
Loane Rd SO19 103 F3
Lobelia Ct PO7 135 A6
Lobelia Rd SO16 79 C5
Locarno Rd PO3 158 A2
Loch Rd BH14 203 E5
Lock App PO6 157 A7
Lock View PO6 157 A7
Lock's Cotts SO45 125 D5
Locke Rd SO30 105 C8
Lockerley CE Prim Sch
SO51 5 A1
Lockerley Cl SO41 197 E2
Lockerley Cres SO16 77 F1
Lockerley Rd
Awbridge SO51 26 D5
Dunbridge SO51 26 C8
Havant PO9 136 A3
Lockhams Rd SO32 106 F8
Locks Heath Ctr SO31 129 A3
Locks Heath Jun & Inf Schs
SO31 129 A1

Locks Rd SO31 129 A3
Locksheath Cl PO9 135 D6
Locksheath Park Rd SO31 129 B2
Locksley Ct SO15 102 F7
Locksley Dr BH22 165 C3
Locksley Rd SO50 55 E1
Locksway Rd PO4 183 C4
Lockswood Keep SO31 129 A4
Lockswood Rd SO31 128 F3
Lockyer Ct GU32 41 B5
Lockyer's Mid Sch BH21 186 D8
Lockyers Dr BH22 165 F6
Lockyers Rd BH21 186 E8
Lode Hill SP5 47 B8
Loders Cl BH17 187 D3
Lodge Ave PO6 158 A8
Lodge Cl BH14 203 E4
Lodge Ct BH14 203 E4
Lodge Dr SO45 126 A1
Lodge Dro SP5 47 D4
Lodge Gdns PO12 181 A4
Lodge Hill PO17 109 B6
Lodge Rd
Christchurch BH23 206 E8
Havant PO9 135 B1
Locks Heath SO31 129 B3
Lymington SO41 197 B3
Southampton SO14 103 A7
Lodge The
Bournemouth BH2 204 E4
Southampton SO15 102 F7
Waterlooville PO7 135 A6
Lodge Vale SO51 51 B1
Lodgebury Cl PO10 161 E8
Lodsworth Cl PO8 88 D4
Lodsworth Ho PO1 216 C4
Loewy Cres BH12 188 D2
Lofting Cl SO50 56 E2
Logan Cl SO16 77 F5
Lomax Cl SO30 81 C1
Lombard Ave BH6 206 D5
Lombard Ct 8 PO1 182 A4
Lombard St PO1 182 A3
Lombardy Cl
Gosport PO13 155 E2
Verwood BH31 115 B5
Lombardy Rise PO7 134 F5
Lomer La BH24 93 C3
Lomond Cl PO2 182 D8
Londesborough Rd PO4 182 E3
London Ave PO2 157 D2
London La BH23 167 F2
London Rd
Blendworth PO8 112 D8
Clanfield PO8 88 D4
Clanfield PO8 88 E5
Cosham PO6 157 F8
Hill Brow GU33 21 B1
Horndean PO8 88 D2
Kings Worthy SO23 2 B5
Petersfield GU31 41 D6
Portsmouth PO2 157 E3
Southampton SO15 103 A6
Waterlooville PO7,PO8 111 F1
Waterlooville,Purbrook PO7 134 C4
London Tavern Cvn Pk The BH24 141 C8
Lone Barn La SO32 60 E7
Lone Pine Dr BH22 165 E3
Lone Pine Pk BH22 165 F3
Lone Pine Way BH22 165 F2
Lone Valley PO7 134 C3
Long Acre Ct PO1 182 E7
Long Beech Dr SO40 100 D6
Long Cl SO23 215 C3
Long Cl W SP5 46 E8
Long Copse SO45 150 E3
Long Copse Ct PO10 136 F4
Long Copse La PO10 137 A4
Long Curtain Rd PO5 182 A2
Long Down GU31 41 B4
Long Dr Gosport PO13 155 C1
West End SO30 80 E2
Long La Bursledon SO31 105 A1
Colehill BH21 163 E8
Holbury SO45 150 C5
Marchwood SO40 101 D1
Ringwood BH24 141 B4
Long Lane Cl SO45 150 D3
Long Meadow Ind Est BH21 138 E7
Long Priors GU32 37 B5
Long Rd
Bournemouth BH10 189 C5
Petersfield GU32 41 A5
Soberton SO32 85 D6
Long Steeple La SP6 45 D2
Long Water Dr PO12 181 C2
Long Wlk SO21 2 E3
Longacre Cl GU33 21 A4
Longacre Dr BH22 165 C4
Longacres PO14 129 C4
Longbarrow Cl BH8 191 A1
Longbridge Cl SO40 76 D2
Longbridge Ct SO40 76 D2
Longbridge Ho 8 PO5 216 B2
Longbridge Ind Pk SO14 103 C3
Longclose Rd SO30 105 D7
Longcroft PO9 135 E1
Longdean Cl 1 PO6 133 A1
Longdon Dr PO13 179 F4
Longdown Activity Farm* SO40 100 D2
Longespee Rd BH21 187 E8
Longfield Ave PO14 154 E7
Longfield Cl PO4 183 C5
Longfield Dr
Bournemouth BH11 189 A6
Ferndown BH22 189 E8
Longfield Rd
Emsworth PO10 136 E3
Fair Oak SO50 57 D1
Hordle SO41 196 B2
Winchester SO23 11 D8
Longfleet CE Comb Sch BH15 202 D4
Longfleet Rd BH15 202 E4
Longford Pl SO41 197 D1
Longham Bsns Ctr BH22 165 B2
Longhouse Gn 6 SO23 11 C8
Longlands Rd PO10 161 D8
Longleat Gdns
New Milton BH25 194 E3
Southampton SO16 78 B4
Longman Ct 28 PO5 182 C2
Longmead GU33 20 F4
Longmead Ave SO50 56 D4
Longmead Ct PO9 159 F7
Longmead Gdns PO9 159 F7
Longmead Rd
Burley Street BH24 142 F4
1 Southampton SO18 80 A2
Longmeadow Gdns SO45 126 A4
Longmeadow La BH17 201 E8
Longmore Ave SO19 103 D2
Longmore Cres SO19 103 D2
Longmynd Dr PO14 154 D8
Longridge Rd SO30 105 C6
Longs La PO14 179 C8
Longs Wlk PO1 182 D7
Longshore Way PO4 183 D4
Longspee Sch BH17 202 D7
Longstaff Gdns PO16 130 F3
Longstock Cl SO19 127 A8
Longstock Cres SO40 100 D7
Longstock Rd PO9 136 B6
Longwood Ave PO8 111 F3
Longwood Dean La SO21 34 B5
Longwood Rd SO21 33 C5
Longworthy 3 SO45 125 E1
Lonnen Rd BH21 164 A8
Lonnen Wood Cl BH21 164 A8
Lonsdale Ave
Cosham PO6 158 A7
Portchester PO16 156 D6
Lonsdale Rd BH3 204 F6
Loosehanger SP5,SP6 47 F3
Loperwood SO40 76 A2
Loperwood La SO40 76 A3
Loraine Ave BH23 209 C8
Lord Cl BH17 202 F7
Lord Montgomery Way 1 PO1 216 A2
Lord Mountbatten Cl SO18 79 E4
Lord Wilson Sch SO31 128 F4
Lord's Hill Ctr E SO16 77 F4
Lord's Hill Ctr W SO16 77 F4
Lord's Hill District Ctr SO16 77 F4
Lord's Hill Way SO16 78 B5
Lordington Cl PO6 158 B8
Lords Ct PO1 216 C4
Lords St PO1 216 C4
Lordshill Rdbt SO16 77 E4
Lordswood SO50 56 E7
Lordswood Cl SO16 78 D4
Lordswood Ct SO16 78 C4
Lordswood Gdns SO16 78 D4
Lordswood Rd SO16 78 C4
Loreille Gdns SO16 77 E7
Loring Ho 7 PO2 157 E4
Lorne Park Rd BH1 205 A3
Lorne Pl SO18 104 A7
Lorne Rd PO5 216 D1
Lortemore Pl 5 SO51 52 E7
Loughwood Cl SO50 56 A6
Louis Flagg Ho 2 PO5 216 B2
Lovage Gdns SO40 100 C7
Lovage Rd PO15 129 D7
Lovage Way PO8 88 C1
Lovatt Gr PO15 130 D3
Love La
Milford on S SO41 211 D5
Petersfield GU31 41 A4
Petersfield GU31 41 B4
Romsey SO51 52 E7
Twyford SO21 32 B5
Upham SO24,SO32 35 B4
West Meon GU32 37 C4
Woodgreen SP6 70 E8
Lovedean La
Horndean PO8 111 F6
Waterlooville PO8 112 A4
Lovedon La SO23 2 C7
Lovelock Terr 13 PO13 180 C6
Loveridge Way SO50 56 A3
Lovett Rd PO3 158 A3
Lovett Wlk SO22 1 C3
Lowcay Rd PO5 182 E2
Lowden Cl SO22 215 B2
Lower Alfred St SO14 103 B6
Lower Ashley Rd BH25 195 D2
Lower Banister St 7 SO15 102 F6
Lower Bartons SP6 69 F1
Lower Baybridge La SO21 33 C2
Lower Bellfield PO14 153 F7
Lower Bere Wood PO7 134 F7
Lower Blandford Rd BH18 187 B3
Lower Brook St SO23 215 E6
Lower Brookfield Rd PO1 182 E6
Lower Brownhill Rd SO16 77 D3
Lower Buckland Rd SO41 197 D5
Lower Canal Wlk SO14 103 A3
Lower Chase Rd SO32 83 F4
Lower Church Path PO1 216 B3
Lower Church Rd PO14 129 C3
Lower Common La BH21 139 A7
Lower Common Rd SO51 50 E3
Lower Crabbick La PO7 110 B5
Lower Densome Wood SP6 70 E8
Lower Derby Rd PO2 157 C1
Lower Drayton La PO6 158 C7
Lower Duncan Rd SO31 129 B5
Lower Farlington Rd PO6 158 E8
Lower Farm Dr PO6 157 E7
Lower Farm La SO51 29 B3
Lower Forbury Rd PO5 216 C2
Lower Golf Links Rd BH18 187 B5
Lower Gr SP6 45 B2
Lower Grove Rd PO9 160 A8
Lower Heyshott GU31 41 A3
Lower La SO32 83 C8
Lower Lamborough La SO24 14 D5
Lower Mead GU31 41 B4
Lower Mead End Rd SO41 171 F1
Lower Moors Rd SO21 31 F1
Lower Mortimer Rd SO19 103 D3
Lower Mullin's La SO45 125 E4
Lower New Rd SO30 80 D2
Lower Northam Rd SO30 105 C7
Lower Pennington La SO41 212 D7
Lower Preshaw La SO32 59 F8
Lower Quay PO16 155 B8
Lower Quay Cl PO16 155 B8
Lower Quay Rd PO16 155 B8
Lower Rd PO9 135 C1
Lower Sandy Down La SO41 173 C3
Lower Spinney SO31 152 C9
Lower St SO51 28 B7
Lower St Helens Rd SO30 105 C5
Lower Stanmore La SO23 215 C3
Lower Swanwick Rd SO31 128 D8
Lower Tye Cvn & Camping Ctr PO11 160 C1
Lower Vicarage Rd SO19 103 D3
Lower Wardown GU31 41 B4
Lower William St SO14 103 D6
Lower William St Ind Est SO14 103 D6
Lower Wingfield St PO1 216 C4
Lower Woodside SO41 212 E8
Lower York St SO14 103 D6
Lowesmore Ct BH14 203 C4
Lowestoft Rd PO6 133 D1
Loweswater Ho 10 PO6 133 B1
Lowford Hill Cl SO31 105 A1
Lowland Rd PO7 110 E4
Lowry Gdns SO19 104 C2
Lowther Gdns 3 BH8 205 C5
Lowther Rd BH8 205 B6
Loxwood Rd PO8 111 F6
Loyd-Lindsay Sq SO22 215 B8
Luard Ct 4 PO9 136 B1
Lucas Cl SO16 77 F5
Lucas Rd Poole BH15 202 B1
Poole,Upper Parkstone BH12 203 C6
Luccombe Pl SO15 78 D2
Luccombe Rd SO15 78 D2
Lucerne Ave
Bournemouth BH6 206 D5
Waterlooville PO7 111 D2
Lucerne Gdns SO30 105 B7
Lucerne Rd SO41 211 D4
Lucia Foster Welch Coll Student Village 7 SO14 103 B3
Luckham Cl BH9 190 B2
Luckham Gdns BH9 190 C2
Luckham Pl BH9 190 B2
Luckham Rd BH9 190 B2
Luckham Rd E BH9 190 B2
Lucknow St PO1 216 D3
Lucky La SO41 174 A1
Ludcombe PO7 110 F5
Ludlow Inf Sch SO19 103 E4
Ludlow Jun Sch SO19 103 E4
Ludlow Rd
Portsmouth PO6 133 C1
Southampton SO19 103 E4
Ludwell's La SO32 83 F4
Lugano Cl PO7 111 D1
Lukes Cl SO31 128 A2
Lukin Dr SO16 77 C6
Lulworth Ave BH15 201 E1
Lulworth Bsns Ctr SO40 76 E2
Lulworth Cl
Chandler's Ford SO53 55 B3
Hamworthy BH15 201 E1
South Hayling PO11 185 A5
Southampton SO16 77 E2
Lulworth Cres BH15 201 E1
Lulworth Ct BH15 201 E2
Lulworth Gn SO16 77 E2
Lulworth Rd PO13 179 E2
Lumby Dr BH24 141 B8
Lumby Drive Mobile Home Pk 2 BH24 141 B8
Lumley Gdns PO10 161 A8
Lumley Path 7 PO10 161 A8
Lumley Rd PO10 137 A1
Lumley Terr PO10 137 A1
Lumsden Ave SO15 102 D7
Lumsden Mans 3 SO15 102 C7
Lumsden Rd PO4 183 D3
Lundy Cl SO16 77 E5
Lundy Wlk PO14 179 B8
Lunedale Rd SO45 149 E8
Lupin Gdns SO22 1 B2
Lupin Rd SO16 79 C5
Luscombe Rd BH14 203 C2
Luther Rd BH9 204 F8
Lutman St PO10 136 E4
Luton Rd SO19 104 B4
Luxor Pk PO9 159 E7
Luxton Cl SO30 105 F8
Luzborough La SO51 53 D6
Lyburn Cl SO16 78 C4
Lyburn Ct SO16 78 C4
Lyburn Ho SP5 73 B7
Lyburn Rd
Nomansland SP5 73 B8
Redlynch SP5 48 F1
Lych Gate Ct BH24 141 C6
Lychgate Dr PO8 112 B7
Lychgate Gn PO14 154 C5
Lydden Ct PO13 155 D2
Lydford Gdns BH11 189 A2
Lydford Rd BH11 189 A2
Lydgate
Milford on S SO41 211 A5
Totton SO40 100 D7
Lydgate Cl SO19 104 D4
Lydgate Gn SO19 104 D4
Lydgate Rd SO19 104 D4
Lydiard Cl SO50 56 A5
Lydlinch Cl BH22 165 D1
Lydlynch Inf Sch SO40 100 E7
Lydlynch Rd SO40 100 F7
Lydney Cl PO6 157 C8
Lydney Rd SO31 128 F3
Lydwell Cl BH11 188 F5
Lyell Rd BH12 203 C6
Lymbourn Rd PO9 136 A1
Lyme Cl SO50 55 F5
Lyme Cres BH23 208 F8
Lymefields SO41 211 E6
Lymer La SO16 77 C6
Lymer Villas SO16 77 C6
Lymington CE Inf Sch SO41 197 D4
Lymington Hospl SO41 197 D4
Lymington Jun Sch SO41 197 D4
Lymington Pier Sta SO41 198 A3
Lymington Rd
Brockenhurst SO42 146 A1
Christchurch BH23 208 F7
East End SO41 199 B7
Milford on S SO41 211 E6
New Milton BH25 195 C1
Lymington Rehabilitation Unit SO41 197 E4
Lymington Town Sta SO41 197 F4
Lymington Vineyard* SO41 197 B2
Lymore La SO41 211 F6
Lymore Valley SO41 211 E6
Lynch Cl SO22 215 C8
Lynch La GU32 37 C4
Lyndale Cl SO41 211 E5
Lyndale Rd SO31 129 C4
Lynden Cl PO14 154 B8
Lynden Gate SO19 104 A3
Lyndhurst Cl
South Hayling PO11 185 A3
Winchester SO22 1 D4
Lyndhurst Ho PO9 135 E6
Lyndhurst Jun Sch PO2 157 F1
Lyndhurst Rd
Ashurst SO40 100 B2
Bransgore BH23 193 D6
Brockenhurst SO42 146 A2
Burley BH24 143 C5
Cadnam SO40 98 E7
Christchurch BH23 193 D2
Gosport PO12 181 A5
Landford SP5 49 D3
Portsmouth PO2 157 F1
Lyndock Cl SO19 103 E2
Lyndock Pl SO19 103 E2
Lyndon Ct BH23 191 F1
Lyndum Cl GU32 40 F4
Lyne Pl PO8 112 B6
Lynes La BH24 140 F7
Lynford Ave SO22 215 C8
Lynford Way SO22 215 C8
Lynn Cl SO18 80 B3
Lynn Rd Poole BH17 187 F1
Portsmouth PO2 182 F8
Lynn Way SO23 2 C7
Lynric Cl BH25 210 A7
Lynton Cres BH23 191 D3
Lynton Ct SO40 100 E6
Lynton Gdns PO16 130 F3
Lynton Gr PO3 183 A8
Lynton Rd
Hedge End SO30 105 C7
Petersfield GU32 40 E4
Lynwood Ave PO8 111 D3
Lynwood Cl BH22 165 D7
Lynwood Ct
Lymington SO41 197 D3
Winchester SO22 215 D8
Lynwood Dr BH21 187 E8
Lynx Cl SO50 56 F2
Lyon Ave BH25 195 B3
Lyon Rd BH12 188 E2
Lyon St SO14 103 A6
Lyons Pl SO30 105 B5
Lysander Cl BH23 208 C7
Lysander Ct 21 PO1 182 A4
Lysander Way PO7 135 A8
Lyse Ct GU33 20 F4
Lysses Ct PO16 131 C1
Lyster Rd SP6 70 A2
Lystra Rd BH9 190 A3
Lytchett Dr BH18 186 F2
Lytchett Way BH16 201 B6
Lyteltane Rd SO41 197 D2
Lytham Rd
Broadstone BH18 187 A3
Southampton SO18 80 A1
Lythe La GU32 40 A5
Lytton Rd
Bournemouth BH1,BH8 205 C5
Hythe SO45 126 B2

M

Mabey Ave BH10 189 D2
Mabey Cl PO12 181 C3
Mablethorpe Rd PO6 133 E1
Macandrew Rd BH13 214 F7
Macarthur Cres SO18 104 A8
Macaulay Ave PO6 132 F1
Macaulay Rd BH18 187 A4
Macklin Ho 21 SO22 215 D6
Maclaren Rd BH9 189 F3
Maclean Rd BH11 188 F3
Macnaghten Rd SO18 103 D8
Madden Cl PO12 180 F3
Maddison St 5 SO14 102 F4
Maddoxford La SO32 82 A1
Maddoxford Way SO32 81 F2
Madeira Rd
Bournemouth BH1 205 A4
Poole BH14 203 D5
Portsmouth PO2 157 F3
Madeline Cl BH12 203 B7
Madeline Cres BH12 203 B7
Madeline Rd GU31 40 F4
Madison Ave BH1 205 D6
Madison Cl PO13 180 E8
Madison Ct 8 PO16 131 C1
Madrisa Ct SO41 197 E4
Mafeking Rd PO4 182 F3
Maffey Ct SO30 106 A7
Mag's Barrow BH22 165 E2
Magazine La SO40 102 A3
Magdala Rd Cosham PO6 157 F7
South Hayling PO11 184 E3
Magdalen Ct 4 PO2 157 E3
Magdalen Hill SO23 215 F5
Magdalen La BH23 207 A6
Magdalen Mews 8 SO23 215 F5
Magdalen Rd PO2 157 E3
Magdalene Way PO14 129 C2
Magennis Cl PO13 180 D7
Magenta Ct 4 PO13 180 C6
Magister Dr PO13 180 A5
Magna Cl BH11 188 F6
Magna Gdns BH11 188 F6
Magna Rd BH21 188 C7
Magnolia Cl
Bournemouth BH6 207 A5
Fareham PO14 154 E8
Hythe SO45 125 C4
Verwood BH31 115 C4
Magnolia Gr SO50 57 E2
Magnolia Ho 6 BH10 189 F4
Magnolia Rd SO19 103 F5
Magnolia Terr PO7 134 E6
Magnolia Way PO8 112 C4
Magpie Cl
Bournemouth BH8 190 C3
Fareham PO16 155 E8
Magpie Cotts PO8 113 C4
Magpie Dr SO40 100 C7
Magpie Gdns SO19 104 C4
Magpie Gr BH25 194 F2
Magpie La Eastleigh SO50 55 E1
Lee-on-t-S PO13 179 F4
Magpie Rd PO8 113 C5
Magpie Wlk PO8 111 D4
Maiden La SO41 197 F1
Maidford Gr PO3 158 C4
Maidment Cl BH11 188 E4
Maidstone Cres PO6 133 E1
Main Rd PO17 133 A6
Main Rd
Colden Common SO21 32 A1
East End SO41 199 B8

Main Rd *continued*
Gosport PO13 155 D5
Hardley SO45 150 C6
Hermitage PO10,PO18 161 D8
Hythe SO45 125 C5
Littleton SO22 1 B5
Marchwood SO40 101 F1
Marchwood SO40,SO45 125 A6
Otterbourne SO21 31 C3
Owslebury SO21 33 B3
Portmore SO41 198 B7
Portsmouth PO1 181 F7
Totton SO40 100 E4
Twyford SO21 31 F2
Mainline Bsns Ctr GU33 20 F4
Mainsail Dr PO16 155 B8
Mainstone SO51 52 D6
Mainstream Ct SO50 56 D3
Maisemore Gdns PO10 160 D8
Maitland Ct SO41 197 D3
Maitland St PO1 182 D7
Maitlands The 2 BH2 204 D2
Maizemore Wlk 7 PO13 179 F3
Majestic Rd SO16 77 B4
Major Ct PO12 181 B8
Majoram Way PO15 129 D7
Majorca Mans 4 BH2 204 E3
Malan Cl BH17 202 E8
Malcolm Cl
Chandler's Ford SO53 30 E1
Locks Heath SO31 129 B3
Malcolm Rd SO53 30 E1
Malcomb Cl BH6 207 A3
Malcroft Mews SO40 102 A1
Maldon Cl SO50 56 D3
Maldon Rd
2 Cosham PO6 157 D8
Southampton SO19 103 E4
Malibres Rd SO53 55 F8
Malin Cl
Southampton SO16 77 E4
Stubbington PO14 179 B8
Malins Rd PO2 182 D8
Malins Road Apts 18 PO2 182 D7
Mall The Burley BH24 143 A3
Chandler's Ford SO53 55 E7
Portsmouth PO2 157 D1
Mallard Bldgs 6 BH25 195 A3
Mallard Cl
Bishop's Waltham SO32 83 A8
Bournemouth BH8 190 C1
Christchurch BH23 208 A6
Hordle SO41 196 A3
Romsey SO51 52 F8
Mallard Gdns
Gosport PO13 155 B2
Hedge End SO30 81 C2
Mallard Rd
Bournemouth BH8 190 D1
Portsmouth PO4 183 B5
Rowlands Castle PO9 113 B1
Wimborne Minst BH21 164 A7
Mallard Way PO10 137 C4
Mallards Rd SO31 127 F8
Mallards The
Fareham PO16 131 A3
Langstone PO9 159 F7
Mallett Cl SO30 81 E2
Mallory Cl BH23 207 F8
Mallory Cres PO16 131 A3
Mallow Cl
Broadstone BH18 186 E3
Christchurch BH23 208 C8
2 Cosham PO6 157 F8
Locks Heath SO31 128 F2
Waterlooville PO7 134 F6
Mallow Rd SO30 105 A6
Mallows The BH25 195 D4
Malmesbury Cl SO50 57 C2
Malmesbury Ct BH8 205 C6
Malmesbury Gdns SO22 215 B8
Malmesbury Park Pl 7 BH8 205 C5
Malmesbury Park Prim Sch BH8 205 B5
Malmesbury Park Rd BH8 205 B6
Malmesbury Pl SO15 102 D7
Malmesbury Rd
Romsey SO51 52 E8
Southampton SO15 102 D7
St Leonards BH24 139 E3
Malmsbury Cl 6 BH23 207 A5
Maloney Mews PO11 185 E1
Maloren Way BH22 139 A1
Malory Cl SO19 104 D6
Malt La SO32 83 C7
Malta Rd PO2 182 E8
Malthouse 7 BH15 202 C2
Malthouse Cl
Easton Down SO21 2 F4
Romsey SO51 52 E8
Malthouse Cotts SO51 77 A8
Malthouse Gdns SO40 101 F1
Malthouse La PO16 131 B1
Malthouse Rd PO2 182 D8
Maltings The
Bournemouth BH11 188 F6
Fareham PO16 131 D2
Petersfield GU31 40 F3
3 Poole BH15 202 E3
Malus Cl PO14 154 F7
Malvern Ave PO14 154 E8
Malvern Bsns Ctr SO15 78 D2
Malvern Cl
Bishop's Waltham SO32 83 D7

Malvern Cl *continued*
Bournemouth BH9 190 A3
Malvern Ct
4 Bournemouth BH9 190 A2
2 Christchurch BH23 207 F8
Malvern Dr SO45 125 D3
Malvern Gdns SO30 81 D2
Malvern Mews PO10 136 F1
Malvern Rd
Bournemouth BH9 190 A2
Gosport PO12 180 F5
Hill Brow GU33 21 B2
Portsmouth PO5 182 D1
Southampton SO16 78 C2
Malvern Terr SO16 78 D2
Malwood Ave SO16 78 D3
Malwood Cl PO9 136 A6
Malwood Gdns SO40 100 C8
Malwood Rd SO45 126 A4
Malwood Rd W SO45 125 F4
Manaton Way SO30 81 B1
Manchester Ct 10 PO13 180 D5
Manchester Rd
Netley SO31 127 A5
Portsmouth PO1 182 E5
Sway SO41 172 B3
Manchester Terr PO10 137 B4
Mancroft Ave PO14 179 C7
Mandalay Cl BH31 114 E5
Mandale Cl BH11 189 A4
Mandale Rd BH11 188 F3
Mandarin Way PO13 180 C6
Mandela Way SO15 102 E5
Manderley SO41 211 E3
Manington Hall 5 BH4 204 C2
Manley Rd SO31 104 F1
Manners La PO4 182 E4
Manners Rd PO4 182 E4
Manning Ave BH23 193 C1
Manningford Cl SO23 2 A3
Mannings Heath Rd BH12 188 B1
Mannings Heath Rdbt BH17 188 B2
Mannings Heath Ret Pk BH12 203 A8
Mannington Pl 12 BH2 204 E3
Mannington Way BH22 138 D2
Manns Cl SO18 80 C2
Mannyngham Way SO51 27 D7
Manor Ave BH12 188 C1
Manor Cl Bursledon SO31 104 F1
Ferndown BH22 165 E5
Fordingbridge SP6 69 F1
8 Havant PO9 135 F1
Milford on S SO41 211 D6
Totton SO40 100 E6
Wickham PO17 108 A3
7 Winchester SO23 215 F6
Manor Cres
Bursledon SO31 104 F1
Cosham PO6 158 B7
Manor Ct Havant PO9 135 D1
Ringwood BH24 140 F8
Titchfield PO15 129 D4
Verwood BH31 114 F6
Manor Farm SO24 14 D1
Manor Farm Cl
Bishopstoke SO50 56 E2
Old Milton BH25 194 F1
Manor Farm Cotts
Exton SO32 61 C7
Rockbourne SP6 44 E2
South Hayling PO11 185 A6
Whitsbury SP6 45 A5
Manor Farm Ctry Pk* SO31 105 D3
Manor Farm Gn SO21 31 F5
Manor Farm Gr SO50 56 E2
Manor Farm La SO51 6 E1
Manor Farm Mus* SO30 105 F4
Manor Farm Rd
Bournemouth BH10 189 C7
Fordingbridge SP6 69 C1
Southampton SO18 79 D2
Manor Farmyard BH8 191 B3
Manor Flats SO21 31 F5
Manor Gdns
Breach PO10 137 D1
Ringwood BH24 140 F8
Verwood BH31 114 F6
Manor Ho BH18 187 A4
Manor House Ave SO15 101 E6
Manor Inf Sch
Holbury SO45 150 B4
Portsmouth PO1 182 F7
Manor La BH31 114 F5
Manor Lodge Rd PO9 113 A1
Manor Mews PO6 158 C8
Manor Park Ave 5 PO3 183 A8
Manor Park Ho 1 SO18 103 E7
Manor Pk BH15 202 B5
Manor Quay SO18 103 D7
Manor Rd
Bishopstoke SO50 56 E2
Bournemouth BH1 205 C3
Breach PO10 137 D1
Chilworth SO16 54 D1
Christchurch BH23 207 A6
Durley SO32 82 D7
East Tytherley SP5 4 E7
Holbury SO45 150 C4
Hythe SO45 125 A4
Milford on S SO41 211 D6
New Milton BH25 195 B3
Portsmouth PO1 182 E7
Ringwood BH24 141 B7

Manor Rd *continued*
South Hayling PO11 184 F5
Twyford SO21 31 F5
Verwood BH31 114 F6
Manor Rd N SO19 103 E4
Manor Rd S SO19 103 E3
Manor Terr
Bursledon SO31 104 E1
Durley SO32 82 E7
Manor Villas PO17 108 A3
Manor Way Breach PO10 137 D1
Lee-on-t-S PO13 179 E3
South Hayling PO11 185 A2
Verwood BH31 114 F7
Manor Wharf SO18 103 C7
Manor Wks SO40 101 B7
Manorside Comb Sch BH12 188 D1
Mansard Ct BH13 214 B3
Mansbridge Cotts SO18 79 F4
Mansbridge Prim Sch SO18 79 E4
Mansbridge Rd
Eastleigh SO50 56 A1
Southampton SO18 79 F4
Mansel Cl BH12 204 C7
Mansel Ct SO16 77 E2
Mansel Inf Sch SO16 77 D2
Mansel Jun Sch SO16 77 D2
Mansel Rd E SO16 77 E1
Mansel Rd W SO16 77 D2
Mansell Cl SO45 125 E1
Mansergh Wlk SO40 100 B8
Mansfield Ave BH14 203 C4
Mansfield Cl
Ferndown BH22 165 D2
Poole BH14 203 C4
Mansfield La SO32 107 B4
Mansfield Rd
Bournemouth BH9 189 E1
Gosport PO13 180 C8
Poole BH14 203 C4
Ringwood BH24 140 F7
Mansion Ct 6 PO4 182 E1
Mansion Rd
Portsmouth PO4 182 E1
Southampton SO15 102 D6
Manston Ct SO16 77 F4
Mansvid Ave PO6 158 B7
Mantle Cl PO13 180 D7
Mantle Sq PO2 157 B2
Manton Cl BH15 201 E3
Manton Rd BH15 201 E3
Maple Bsns Pk BH21 164 F7
Maple Cl
Barton on S BH25 210 B7
Bursledon SO31 127 F8
Christchurch BH23 208 F7
Emsworth PO10 136 F2
Fareham PO15 130 C1
Lee-on-t-S PO13 179 F2
Romsey SO51 53 C6
Maple Cres PO8 88 D6
Maple Ct Lymington SO41 197 B2
Southampton,Sholing SO19 104 B4
Southampton,Woolston SO19 103 E2
Maple Dr Denmead PO7 111 A4
Ferndown BH22 165 C8
Kings Worthy SO23 2 B8
Maple Gdns SO40 100 C6
Maple Ho Havant PO9 136 A2
Southampton SO16 78 F7
Maple Lo BH16 201 C7
Maple Rd
Bournemouth BH9 204 F8
Hythe SO45 150 B8
Poole BH15 202 D3
Portsmouth PO5 182 D2
Southampton SO18 103 E7
Maple Sq SO50 55 E1
Maple Wlk GU31 40 F1
Maple Wood PO9 135 B1
Mapleleaf Gdns 5 SO50 56 A2
Maples The SO53 55 C8
Mapleton Rd SO30 105 D6
Mapletree Ave PO8 112 C4
Maplewood Cl SO40 100 C6
Maplin Rd SO16 77 D2
Mapperton Cl BH17 187 F2
Marabout Cl BH23 207 D7
Maralyn Ave PO7 134 E6
Marathon Pl SO50 57 B2
Marazan Rd PO3 158 B2
Marbrean Cl SP6 69 C2
Marchesi Ct PO14 154 C4
Marchwood By Pass
Marchwood SO40 124 E8
Totton SO40 101 B3
Marchwood CE Inf Sch SO40 124 E8
Marchwood Ct 8 PO12 180 D3
Marchwood Ind Pk SO40 102 A3
Marchwood Jun Sch SO40 101 F1
Marchwood Priory Hospl SO40 125 A7
Marchwood Rd
Bournemouth BH10 189 C3
Havant PO9 135 E6
Southampton SO15 102 B6
Totton SO15 101 C4
Marchwood Terr SO40 101 F2
Marcus Cl SO50 57 B2
Mardale Rd SO16 101 D8
Mardale Wlk SO16 101 D8

Marden Paddock SO42 145 F1
Marden Way GU31 41 A3
Mardon Cl SO18 79 E5
Mare La SO21 32 F6
Margam Ave SO19 103 F5
Margards La BH31 114 E5
Margaret Cl PO7 111 D1
Margaret Rule Hall 5 PO1 216 B3
Margarita Rd PO15 130 E2
Margate Rd PO5 216 C2
Margery's Ct 31 PO1 182 A5
Marian Cl BH21 186 C4
Marian Rd BH21 186 C4
Marianne Cl SO15 101 F6
Marianne Rd Poole BH12 204 C8
Wimborne Minst BH21 164 A7
Marie Ave SP5 46 D7
Marie Cl BH12 203 D7
Marie Ct 6 PO7 134 E8
Marie Rd SO19 104 C3
Marigold Cl PO15 130 E2
Marina Bldgs 3 PO12 181 B5
Marina Cl PO10 161 A7
Marina Ct
2 Bournemouth BH5 205 E3
Christchurch BH23 209 A7
Marina Dr
Hamble-le-R SO31 128 A2
Poole BH14 203 B1
Marina Gr
Portchester PO16 156 C6
Portsmouth PO3 183 B7
Marina Keep PO6 157 A6
Marina The BH5 205 E3
Marina Twrs 5 BH5 205 E3
Marina View
1 Christchurch BH23 207 A5
Netley SO31 126 F7
Marine Cotts 7 PO12 181 B6
Marine Ct
Barton on S BH25 209 D7
Portsmouth PO4 183 A2
Marine Dr BH25 209 E7
Marine Dr E BH25 210 A6
Marine Drive W BH25 209 E7
Marine Par SO14 103 B4
Marine Par E PO13 179 F2
Marine Par W PO13 179 D4
Marine Point BH25 209 F7
Marine Prospect BH25 209 F7
Marine Rd BH6 206 D3
Marine Wlk PO11 185 D3
Mariner's Cl SO31 128 A4
Mariners Ct
Christchurch BH23 208 A6
Lymington SO41 197 F2
South Hayling PO11 185 D1
Mariners Mews SO45 126 A4
Mariners Reach BH25 210 A6
Mariners The SO31 127 B6
Mariners Way
Gosport PO12 181 D4
Warsash SO31 128 C1
Mariners Wlk PO4 183 B5
Marion Rd PO4 182 E2
Maritime Ave SO40 102 A3
Maritime Chambers SO14 103 B2
Maritime Way SO14 103 A2
Maritime Wlk SO14 103 B2
Marjoram Cres PO8 112 B3
Mark Anthony Ct PO11 184 F3
Mark Cl Portsmouth PO3 157 F4
Southampton SO15 102 A7
Mark Ct PO7 134 E8
Mark Way SO51 4 D3
Mark's La BH25 195 A6
Mark's Rd PO14 179 E7
Markall Cl SO24 14 D5
Marken Cl SO31 128 E3
Market Bldgs SO16 79 D4
Market Cl BH15 202 C2
Market La SO23 215 E5
Market Par PO9 135 F1
Market Pl
Fordingbridge SP6 69 F1
Ringwood BH24 140 F7
Romsey SO51 52 E7
19 Southampton SO14 103 A3
Market St Eastleigh SO50 56 B1
Eastleigh SO50 56 B2
Poole BH15 202 B2
Winchester SO23 215 E5
Market Way BH21 163 D4
Marketway PO1 216 B4
Markham Ave BH10 189 D7
Markham Cl BH10 189 D6
Markham Rd BH9 205 A8
Marks Rd BH9 189 F3
Marks Terr SO32 83 B8
Marks Tey Rd PO14 154 C5
Markway Cl PO10 136 D1
Marl La SP6 69 D2
Marlands Lawn PO9 135 C6
Marlands Sh Ctr SO14 102 F4
Marlborough Cl PO7 134 D5
Marlborough Ct
30 Bournemouth BH4 204 C3
Chandler's Ford SO53 55 A4
15 Gosport PO12 181 C9
Hythe SO45 125 E2
3 Wimborne Minst BH21 163 C5
Marlborough Gdns SO30 81 C3
Marlborough Gr PO16 156 C7
Marlborough Ho
3 Highfield SO17 79 A1
Southampton SO15 102 F8

Marlborough Mans 2 BH7 206 B6
Marlborough Pines 25 BH4 204 C3
Marlborough Pk PO9 136 C3
Marlborough Pl
Lymington SO41 197 D5
Wimborne Minst BH21 163 D5
Marlborough Rd
Bournemouth BH4 204 C3
Chandler's Ford SO53 30 F1
Gosport PO12 180 F6
Poole BH14 203 C4
Southampton SO15,SO16 102 B8
Marlborough Row PO1 182 A6
Marldell Cl PO9 136 A5
Marler Ho 9 BH4 204 B4
Marles Cl PO13 180 D8
Marley Ave BH25 194 F3
Marley Cl BH25 194 F3
Marley Mount SO41 171 E1
Marlhill Cl SO18 79 F2
Marlin Cl PO13 180 D6
Marline Rd BH12 203 D6
Marlott Rd BH15 202 C5
Marlow Cl PO15 130 E4
Marlow Dr BH23 191 E3
Marlow Rd SO32 83 A8
Marlowe Ct
Southampton SO19 103 F1
Waterlooville PO7 111 D1
Marlpit Dr BH23 194 A2
Marlpit La BH25 195 A8
Marls Rd SO30 105 E7
Marmion Ave PO5 182 D2
Marmion Gn BH23 207 F7
Marmion Rd PO5 182 D2
Marne Ho 8 PO14 154 E8
Marne Rd SO18 104 A7
Marnhull Rd BH15 202 D4
Marnhull Rise SO22 215 A5
Marpet Cl BH11 188 F6
Marples Way PO9 135 D1
Marquis Way BH11 188 D5
Marram Cl SO41 197 E5
Marrelswood Gdns PO7 134 C4
Marryat Ct
Christchurch BH23 209 B7
New Milton BH25 194 F3
Marryat Rd BH25 194 F3
Marsden Rd PO6 157 B8
Marsh Cl PO6 158 C6
Marsh Gdns SO30 81 C2
Marsh Ho 8 SO14 103 A3
Marsh La Breamore SP6 70 A8
Christchurch BH23 191 F2
Fawley SO45 151 B4
Lymington SO41 197 E5
Southampton SO14 103 B3
Upton BH16 201 A7
Marsh Par SO45 126 A4
Marsh The SO45 126 A4
Marshal Rd BH17 187 B1
Marshall Ct 10 SO15 102 F8
Marshall Dr SO30 80 F1
Marshall Pl 1 SO16 78 E3
Marshall Rd PO11 185 C2
Marshall Sq SO15 102 F8
Marshfield BH21 163 F7
Marshfield Cl SO40 101 D1
Marshfield Ho PO6 158 C7
Marshlands Cl BH23 207 D6
Marshlands Rd PO6 158 D7
Marshlands Spur PO6 158 E7
Marshwood Ave
Poole BH17 187 F3
Waterlooville PO7 135 A7
Marston Cl BH25 195 B5
Marston Gate 6 SO23 215 E6
Marston Gr BH23 193 E1
Marston La PO3 158 B4
Marston Rd
New Milton BH25 195 B5
Poole BH15 202 B2
Southampton SO19 104 E5
Martello Cl PO12 180 D3
Martello Ho 5 BH13 214 F8
Martello Pk BH13 214 F7
Martello Rd BH13 203 F1
Martello Rd S BH13 214 F8
Martello Twrs BH13 214 F7
Martells Ct 1 PO1 182 A4
Martells The BH25 210 B7
Martin Ave
Denmead PO7 111 A4
Stubbington PO14 179 D7
Martin Cl
Broadstone BH17 201 F8
Lee-on-t-S PO13 179 F4
Swanmore SO32 84 B4
Martin Down National Nature Reserve* SP5,SP6 42 C3
Martin Rd Havant PO9 136 A4
Portsmouth PO3 183 A8
Stubbington PO14 179 D7
Martin St SO32 83 B7
Martin's Rd SO42 146 A2
Martindale Ave BH21 164 B5
Martindale Terr 1 SO16 101 E7
Martingale Cl BH16 201 D7
Martins Cl BH22 165 E7
Martins Dr BH22 165 E7
Martins Fields SO21 10 C1
Martins Hill Cl BH23 192 C1

Martins Hill La BH23 192 C1
Martins Rise SP5 24 A3
Martins The SO50 57 D1
Martins Way BH22 165 E7
Martlet Cl PO13 180 A5
Martley Gdns SO30 81 D2
Marvic Ct PO9 135 E6
Marvin Cl SO30 105 D7
Marvin Way
Hedge End SO30 105 D7
Southampton SO18 104 C6
Marwell Cl BH7 206 A7
Marwell Zoological Pk*
SO21 57 E8
Mary Coombs Ct PO11 185 A3
Mary La BH22 138 D2
Mary Mitchell Cl BH24 140 F7
Mary Rose* PO1 181 F7
Mary Rose Cl PO15 130 E3
Mary Rose St The PO1 216 B3
Marybridge Cl SO40 100 E6
Marycourt Sch PO12 181 A2
Maryfield SO14 103 B4
Maryland Cl SO18 79 F3
Maryland Ct 3 SO41 211 B4
Maryland Gdns SO41 211 B4
Maryland Rd BH16 201 C4
Masefield Ave PO6 132 F1
Masefield Cl SO50 55 F3
Masefield Cres PO8 111 F4
Masefield Gn SO19 104 D6
Mason Moor Prim Sch
SO16 101 F8
Masseys La SO42 175 C7
Masten Cres PO13 180 C8
Masters Ct BH4 204 D3
Masterson Cl BH23 207 D7
Matapan Rd PO2 157 E4
Matchams Cl BH24 167 B7
Matchams La BH23 167 B4
Matheson Rd SO16 78 A5
Matilda Pl 4 SO23 215 E6
Matley Gdns SO40 100 B7
Matlock Rd BH22 165 C3
Matrix Pk PO15 129 E3
Matthews Cl PO9 135 C3
Matthews La SO42 175 C6
Matthews Pl PO7 134 E6
Maturin Cl SO41 197 D3
Maundeville Cres BH23 206 E8
Maundeville Rd BH23 206 E8
Maunsell Way SO30 81 D2
Maureen Cl BH12 203 B8
Maurepas Way PO7 134 D7
Mauretania Ho 13 SO14 103 C6
Mauretania Rd SO16 77 B4
Maurice Rd
Bournemouth BH8 205 D8
Portsmouth PO4 183 C4
Maury's La SO51 50 D4
Mavis Cres PO9 135 F2
Mavis Rd BH9 190 B1
Maxstoke Cl PO5 216 C3
Maxwell Rd
Bournemouth BH9 205 A7
Broadstone BH18 186 E3
Poole BH13 214 F7
Portsmouth PO4 183 A3
Southampton SO19 104 A3
May Ave SO41 197 D5
May Bush La SO32 85 B1
May Cl SO45 150 D3
May Copse SO45 150 D3
May Cres SO45 150 D3
May Gdns
Bournemouth BH11 188 E4
Walkford BH23 194 B2
May La SO41 174 A1
May Rd SO15 102 C7
May Tree Cl SO22 215 A2
Maybray King Way
SO18,SO19 104 A7
Maybush Ct 2 SO16 78 A1
Maybush Rd SO16 77 F2
Maycroft Ct 4 SO15 102 F8
Mayday Ct SO40 101 A7
Maydman Sq PO3 183 A6
Mayfair BH4 204 C2
Mayfair Ct Botley SO30 106 A7
Poole BH13 204 B2
Mayfair Gdns
Bournemouth BH11 189 A4
Southampton SO15 102 F7
Mayfield PO13 179 E2
Mayfield Ave Poole BH14 203 E3
Totton SO40 100 F8
Mayfield Cl
Ferndown BH22 165 C6
Stubbington PO14 179 D8
Mayfield Dr BH22 165 C6
Mayfield Rd
Bournemouth BH9 190 A2
Fordingbridge SP6 69 C2
Gosport PO12 181 C4
Portsmouth PO2 157 F2
Southampton SO17 79 C3
Mayfield Sch PO2 157 F2
Mayfield Way BH22 165 C6
Mayflower Cl
Chandler's Ford SO53 55 B5
Lymington SO41 198 A2
Stubbington PO14 179 C6
Mayflower Ct
10 Southampton SO16 102 B8
Mayflower Ct continued
7 Southampton,Banister's Park
SO15 102 F7
Mayflower Dr PO4 183 C5
Mayflower Rd SO15 102 B8
Mayflowers The SO16 79 A4
Mayfly Cl SP6 69 F2
Mayford Rd BH12 204 B6
Mayhall Rd PO3 158 A1
Mayhill La SO32 84 E8
Maylands Ave PO4 183 A5
Maylands Rd PO9 135 B2
Mayles Cl PO17 108 A3
Mayles Cnr PO17 130 D8
Mayles La
Knowle Village PO17 130 E8
Wickham PO17 107 F1
Mayles Rd PO4 183 B5
Maylings Farm Rd PO16 130 F3
Maylyn Rd BH16 186 A2
Maynard Cl PO13 155 C4
Maynard Pl PO8 112 B7
Maynard Rd SO40 100 F7
Mayo Cl PO1 182 D7
Maypole Villas SO50 56 B8
Mayridge PO14 129 C3
Mays Firs SP6 47 F2
Mays La PO14 154 C4
Mays Yd PO8 112 C8
Maytree Cl Fair Oak SO50 57 D2
Locks Heath SO31 129 A3
Maytree Gdns PO8 111 E3
Maytree Inf Sch SO14 103 B6
Maytree Rd
Chandler's Ford SO53 30 D2
5 Fareham PO16 131 A1
Southampton SO18 104 A6
Waterlooville PO8 111 E3
Mayvale Cl SO40 101 F1
Mayville High Sch PO5 182 D2
McGovern Mews SO31 152 D10
McIntyre Rd BH23 191 A8
McKinley Rd BH4 204 C2
McWilliam Cl BH12 204 C8
McWilliam Rd 2 BH9 190 A2
Meacher Cl SO40 100 E8
Mead Cl
Broadstone BH18 187 A1
Romsey SO51 53 B7
Mead Cres SO18 79 D3
Mead Ct
Chandler's Ford SO53 55 C6
Southampton SO16 78 A3
Mead End Rd
Denmead PO7 111 A3
Sway SO41 171 F2
Mead Rd
Chandler's Ford SO53 55 C6
Lymington SO41 197 B2
Winchester SO23 215 C2
Mead The Gosport PO13 155 B3
Hythe SO45 125 F3
Liss GU33 20 F4
Petersfield GU32 40 D2
Mead Way PO16 131 B3
Meadbrook Gdns SO53 55 C6
Meadcrest Wood SO42 145 D1
Meadcroft Cl SO31 152 D10
Meadend Cl PO9 136 B5
Meadow Ave
Fordingbridge SP6 69 E2
Locks Heath SO31 129 A4
Meadow Cl
Bransgore BH23 193 A8
Burley BH24 142 F2
Ferndown BH22 165 D1
Fordingbridge SP6 69 E2
North Baddesley SO52 54 A3
Ringwood BH24 141 B8
Sopley BH23 192 B7
Stoke PO11 159 F3
Totton SO40 100 F5
Waltham Chase SO32 83 E4
West End SO30 80 E2
Meadow Court Cl BH9 190 A3
Meadow Ct
2 Bournemouth BH9 190 A3
2 Emsworth PO10 160 F8
Fordingbridge SP6 69 E2
Verwood BH31 115 A4
Whiteparish SP5 24 C4
3 Wimborne Minst BH21 163 D4
Meadow Edge PO7 134 B2
Meadow Farm La BH21 186 D8
Meadow Gdns SO32 83 E4
Meadow Gr
Chandler's Ford SO53 55 C4
Verwood BH31 115 B5
Meadow La Burton BH23 192 C2
Eastleigh SO50 56 A2
Hamble-le-R SO31 128 A2
Meadow Rd
Lymington SO41 197 C2
New Milton BH25 195 B4
Ringwood BH24 141 B8
Meadow Rise
Corfe Mullen BH18 186 F5
Waterlooville PO8 112 B3
Meadow St PO5 216 A2
Meadow Terr 1 PO16 131 A1
Meadow The
Denmead PO7 110 F4
Romsey SO51 27 F1
Meadow View Rd BH11 188 E4
Meadow Way
Barton on S BH25 210 A7
Fawley SO45 151 B3
Ringwood BH24 141 B8
Meadow Way continued
Verwood BH31 115 B5
Winchester SO22 215 A2
Meadow Wlk
Gosport PO13 155 B5
1 Liss GU33 20 F4
Portsmouth PO1 216 B4
Meadowbank BH16 201 C8
Meadowbank Rd PO15 130 D1
Meadowcroft Cl SO21 31 C3
Meadowhead Rd SO16 78 F3
Meadowland
Christchurch BH23 207 F6
Kings Worthy SO23 2 B7
Meadowlands
Havant PO9 136 A1
Lymington SO41 197 C4
Ringwood BH24 141 A4
Rowlands Castle PO9 113 C3
Meadowlands Jun & Inf Schs
PO8 111 E5
Meadowmead Ave
SO15 102 A7
Meadows Cl BH16 201 C7
Meadows Dr BH16 201 C7
Meadows The
Fareham PO16 131 C3
Lyndhurst SO43 122 A4
Waterlooville PO7 134 C8
Meadowside Cl SO18 79 E4
Meadowsweet PO7 112 C1
Meadowsweet Rd BH17 201 E8
Meadowsweet Way
Horton Heath SO50 81 C6
Portsmouth PO6 133 D1
Meads The
Chandler's Ford SO53 55 A5
Romsey SO51 52 D7
Meadway PO7 112 A1
Meadway The BH23 193 D2
Mears Rd SO50 57 D1
Meath Cl PO11 185 C1
Medina Cl SO53 55 E5
Medina Ct PO13 179 D4
Medina Ho PO16 155 A7
Medina Prim Sch PO6 157 E7
Medina Rd Cosham PO6 157 E8
Southampton SO15 78 B1
Medina Way BH23 208 C6
Medlar Cl Burton BH23 192 D1
1 Hedge End SO30 105 D6
Medley Pl SO15 102 A7
Medlicott Way SO32 84 B4
Medstead Rd PO9 135 F3
Medwall Gn SO19 104 D5
Medway Dr SO53 55 A8
Medway Rd BH22 166 A6
Meerut Rd SO42 145 F2
Meeting House La BH24 140 F7
Megan Ct 7 PO6 157 F7
Megan Rd SO30 80 D2
Megana Way SO51 28 C5
Meggeson Ave SO18 80 A2
Megson Dr PO13 180 A6
Melbourne Gdns 6
SO30 105 C6
Melbourne Ho PO1 216 B3
Melbourne Pl PO5 216 B2
Melbourne Rd
Bournemouth BH8 205 C6
Christchurch BH23 191 E1
5 Hedge End SO30 105 C6
Melbourne St SO14 103 B4
Melbury Ave BH12 203 E7
Melbury Cl
Ferndown BH22 165 D4
Lymington SO41 197 D3
Melbury Ct 12 SO17 79 A1
Melchet Cl SO51 25 B1
Melchet Rd SO18 104 C8
Melford Ct BH1 205 A3
Melick Cl SO40 101 F2
Mellor Cl 1 PO6 157 D8
Mellstock Rd BH15 202 D5
Melrose Cl PO4 183 B4
Melrose Ct
New Milton BH25 195 C3
Totton SO40 76 C1
Melrose Gdns PO12 180 F7
Melrose Rd SO15 78 D2
Melton Ct BH13 203 F4
Melverley Gdns BH21 163 D5
Melville Cl SO16 78 C5
Melville Rd
Bournemouth BH9 204 E8
Gosport PO12 181 B8
Portsmouth PO4 183 D3
Melvin Jones Ho PO14 154 C4
Mendip Cl
New Milton BH25 195 B2
Verwood BH31 114 F5
Mendip Ct 4 BH23 207 F8
Mendip Gdns SO45 125 D2
Mendip Rd
Southampton SO16 101 F8
Verwood BH31 114 F6
Mendips Rd PO14 154 E8
Mendips Wlk PO14 154 D8
Mengham Ave PO11 185 A3
Mengham Ct PO11 185 B3
Mengham Inf Sch PO11 185 A4
Mengham Jun Sch
PO11 185 A4
Mengham La PO11 185 A3
Mengham Rd PO11 185 A3
Menin Ho PO15 130 C2
Menslands La
Hambledon PO7 86 B1
Menslands La continued
Soberton PO7 109 F8
Mentone Rd 2 BH14 203 A3
Menzies Cl SO16 77 F5
Meon Cl Clanfield PO8 88 D4
Gosport PO13 155 B2
Petersfield GU32 40 E4
Romsey SO51 53 C7
Meon Cres SO53 55 D5
Meon Ct SO18 104 D8
Meon Gdns SO32 84 B5
Meon Ho Fareham PO16 155 A7
Winchester SO23 215 F4
Meon Jun & Inf Schs
PO4 183 B4
Meon Rd
Bournemouth BH7 206 B7
Portsmouth PO4 183 B5
Romsey SO51 53 C7
Meon Shore Chalets
PO14 153 D2
Meoncross Sch PO14 154 D4
Meonside Ct PO17 108 A3
Meonstoke CE Inf Sch
SO32 61 C4
Meonwara Cres GU32 37 D5
Mercer Way SO51 53 A8
Merchants Pl 19 SO23 215 E6
Merchants Row 6 PO1 182 A3
Merchants Wlk 16 SO14 102 F3
Merchistoun Rd PO8 112 C7
Mercury Cl SO16 77 F4
Mercury Gdns SO31 128 A4
Mercury Pl PO7 134 E2
Merdon Ave SO53 55 D8
Merdon Cl SO53 55 D8
Merdon Ct SO53 55 D7
Merdon Jun Sch SO53 55 D7
Mere Croft PO15 129 D3
Meredith Cl BH23 207 D7
Meredith Gdns SO40 100 D6
Meredith Inf Sch PO2 182 E8
Meredith Lodge 5 PO7 135 A7
Meredith Rd PO2 157 E3
Meredith Twrs SO19 104 E4
Meredun Cl SO21 30 B7
Merepond La GU34 17 F3
Merganser Cl PO12 181 B8
Meriden Cl BH13 214 F7
Meriden Ct 11 SO23 215 E8
Meriden Rd PO5 216 A2
Meridian Ctr 12 PO9 135 F1
Meridians The BH23 206 F6
Merino Way BH22 138 F1
Merlewood Cl BH2 204 F4
Merlewood Ct 9 BH25 195 B3
Merley Court Touring Pk
BH21 163 C1
Merley Dr BH23 209 A8
Merley Fst Sch BH21 163 D1
Merley Gdns BH21 163 E1
Merley Ho BH21 163 B1
Merley House Holiday Pk
BH21 163 B1
Merley House La BH21 163 C1
Merley La BH21 163 E1
Merley Park Rd
Ashington BH21 187 B8
Corfe Mullen BH21 186 F8
Merley BH21 163 C1
Merley Ways BH21 163 D2
Merlin Cl
Bishop's Waltham SO32 83 B8
Ringwood BH24 141 C6
Waterlooville PO8 111 E4
Merlin Cotts SO45 151 B3
Merlin Dr PO3 158 A4
Merlin Gdns
Hedge End SO30 105 B7
Portchester PO16 132 B1
Merlin Lodge SO19 103 D3
Merlin Mews 4 SO32 83 C7
Merlin Way
Chandler's Ford SO53 54 F7
Christchurch BH23 208 A5
Mermaid Ct 3 BH5 205 E3
Mermaid Rd PO14 154 F5
Mermaid Way SO14 103 B2
Merrick Way SO53 55 A8
Merridale Rd SO19 103 E5
Merriefield Ave BH18 187 B5
Merriefield Cl BH18 187 B6
Merriefield Dr BH18 187 B6
Merrieleas Cl SO53 55 C7
Merrieleas Dr SO53 55 C7
Merriemeade Cl 2
SO45 125 E1
Merriemeade Par 1
SO45 125 E1
Merrifield BH21 163 E8
Merritown La BH23 190 D7
Merritt Ct SO53 55 C3
Merrivale Ave BH6 206 E5
Merrivale Cl SO45 125 E3
Merrivale Ct PO10 137 D1
Merrivale Rd PO2 157 F3
Merrow Ave BH12 204 B7
Merrow Chase 1 BH13 214 F7
Merrow Cl PO16 156 A8
Merry Gdns SO52 54 A5
Merryfield PO14 129 C4
Merryfield Ave PO9 135 D5
Merryfield Cl
Bransgore BH23 193 A8
Verwood BH31 114 F6
Merryfield Ct BH10 189 C4
Merryfield La BH10 189 C4
Merryfield Rd GU31 41 B4
Merryoak Gn SO19 103 F5
Merryoak Rd SO19 103 F5
Merrytree Cl SO51 50 E3
Merryweather Est BH24 141 C8
Mersea Gdns SO19 104 A4
Mersham Gdns SO18 104 A7
Merstone Rd PO13 155 C2
Merthyr Ave PO6 158 B8
Merton Ave PO16 156 D6
Merton Cl SP6 69 F3
Merton Cres PO16 156 D6
Merton Ct
2 Christchurch BH23 209 B7
3 Poole BH15 202 E4
3 Portsmouth PO5 216 C1
Merton Gr BH24 140 F8
Merton Rd
Portsmouth PO5 216 C1
Southampton SO17 79 B3
Merville Gdns BH9 204 F8
Meryl Rd PO4 183 C4
Mesh Pond SP5 46 D7
Mesh Rd SO51 6 B2
Metcalfe Ave PO14 179 D8
Meteor Rd PO10 161 A3
Methuen Cl 2 BH8 205 C5
Methuen Rd
Bournemouth BH8 205 B5
Poole BH17 187 B2
Portsmouth PO4 183 A3
Methuen St SO14 103 A7
Metuchen Way SO30 105 C4
Mews Ct SO21 31 B3
Mews La SO22 215 D5
Mews The
Blackfield SO45 177 F7
Bournemouth BH2 204 D3
Chandler's Ford SO53 55 C3
7 Gosport PO12 181 E5
Havant PO9 135 E4
Petersfield GU31 41 A4
Rownhams SO16 77 F6
Southampton SO19 104 D4
Verwood BH31 115 A4
Mewsey Ct PO9 135 D7
Mey Cl PO7 135 A7
Meynell Cl SO50 55 F3
Meyrick Cl BH23 193 A7
Meyrick Ho 1 PO2 157 C1
Meyrick Park Cres BH3 204 F6
Meyrick Park Mans 7
BH2 204 F4
Meyrick Rd
Bournemouth BH1 205 B3
Havant PO9 135 D1
Portsmouth PO2 157 C1
Micawber Ho 23 PO1 182 D7
Michael Crook Cl PO9 135 C3
Michael's Way SO45 125 F4
Michaels Way SO50 57 D2
Michelgrove Rd BH5 205 E3
Michelmersh Cl SO16 77 E5
Michelmersh Gn BH8 190 D2
Michigan Way SO40 100 B8
Mickleham Cl BH12 204 B8
Midanbury Cres SO18 79 F1
Midanbury Ct 9 SO18 103 E8
Midanbury La SO18 79 F1
Midanbury Wlk SO18 103 F8
Midas Cl PO7 134 F4
Middle Brook BH11 189 A6
Middle Brook St SO23 215 E6
Middle Common Rd
SO41 197 A3
Middle Ct PO1 182 E7
Middle La BH24 141 A7
Middle Mdw GU33 21 A4
Middle Mead PO14 154 B8
Middle Park Way PO9 135 D6
Middle Rd
Bournemouth BH10 189 C5
Locks Heath SO31 129 B5
Lymington SO41 197 D3
North Baddesley SO52 54 A4
Poole BH15 202 E6
Southampton SO19 104 A4
Sway SO41 172 B2
Tiptoe SO41 195 E8
Winchester SO22 215 C6
Middle St
Portsmouth PO5 216 B2
Southampton SO14 103 A7
Middlebere Cres BH16 201 C4
Middlebridge St SO51 52 E6
Middlebrook 3 SO32 83 C8
Middlecroft La PO12 180 F6
Middlehill Dr BH21 164 B6
Middlehill Rd BH21 164 A6
Middlesex Rd PO4 183 B3
Middleton Cl
Fareham PO14 154 E7
Southampton SO18 80 A1
Middleton Mews
Locks Heath SO31 129 B5
Old Milton BH25 194 F1
Middleton Rd
Bournemouth BH9 189 E2
Ringwood BH24 141 A8
Middleton Rise PO8 88 D4
Middleton Wlk 1 PO14 154 E7
Midfield Cl PO14 154 F7
Midgham Farm Cotts
SP6 93 D6
Midhurst Ho PO1 216 C4
Midland Rd BH9 189 F1
Midlands Est SO30 80 C1
Midlington Barns SO32 85 A7
Midlington Hill SO32 85 A7

Midlington Ho SO32 ...85 A7
Midlington Rd SO32 ...85 B8
Midway SO45 ...125 F3
Midway Path BH13 ...214 C3
Midway Rd PO2 ...157 E5
Midways PO14 ...179 C6
Midwood Ave BH8 ...190 F1
Milbeck Cl PO8 ...112 A3
Milborne Cres BH12 ...203 E8
Milbourne Rd BH22 ...165 C6
Milburn Cl 3 BH4 ...204 C4
Milburn Rd BH4 ...204 B4
Milburns The SO51 ...27 D7
Milbury Cres SO18 ...104 A6
Milbury Ho PO6 ...133 A2
Mildenhall 5 BH2 ...204 D2
Mildmay Ct 2 SO23 ...215 F5
Mildmay St SO22 ...215 B3
Mile End Rd PO2 ...182 C7
Milebush Rd PO4 ...183 C5
Miles Ct PO11 ...185 D1
Miles's La SP5 ...24 C5
Milestone Point 1 PO9 ...135 F1
Milestone Rd BH15 ...202 D5
Milford Cl Havant PO9 ...135 D3
West Moors BH22 ...138 F2
Milford Cres SO41 ...211 E4
Milford Ct
1 Gosport PO12 ...180 D3
Milford on S SO41 ...211 E4
4 Portsmouth PO4 ...183 B4
Milford Dr BH11 ...188 F5
Milford Gdns SO53 ...55 E6
Milford Ho
Milford on S SO41 ...211 E5
Southampton SO19 ...104 B6
Winchester SO23 ...215 D3
Milford on Sea CE Prim Sch
SO41 ...211 E6
Milford Rd
Barton on S BH25 ...210 C7
Lymington SO41 ...197 C1
Portsmouth PO1 ...216 C3
Milford Trad Est SO41 ...211 E4
Military Rd
Fareham PO16 ...131 D2
Gosport,Alverstoke PO12 ...181 A2
Gosport,Alverstoke PO12 ...181 B1
Gosport,Brockhurst PO12 ...180 E6
Gosport,Clayhall PO12 ...181 C2
Portsmouth,Hilsea PO3 ...157 F5
Portsmouth,Landport PO1 ...182 B7
Milkwood Ct SO40 ...100 C7
Milky Down Back La
BH24 ...141 E7
Mill Cl Denmead PO7 ...111 B4
Nursling SO16 ...77 D5
Stoke PO11 ...159 F2
Mill Cross PO7 ...111 A4
Mill Ct Fordingbridge SP6 ...69 E1
4 Southampton SO17 ...79 C2
Mill End Damerham SP6 ...68 D4
Emsworth PO10 ...161 B8
Mill Gate Ho 30 PO1 ...182 A5
Mill Hill SO30 ...106 B6
Mill Hill Cl BH14 ...203 B3
Mill Ho SO18 ...80 A4
Mill House Bsns Ctr
SO19 ...103 D4
Mill House Ctr SO40 ...101 A7
Mill House Lodge SO50 ...56 C3
Mill La Bishopstone SP5 ...22 C8
Brockbridge SO32 ...61 C2
Brockenhurst SO42 ...146 B1
Burley BH24 ...143 C4
Christchurch BH23 ...209 B8
Droxford SO32 ...61 B1
Durley SO32 ...82 D3
Emsworth PO10 ...137 B2
Gosport PO12 ...181 B7
Havant,Bedhampton PO9 ...135 C1
Hawkley GU33 ...19 F8
Hurn BH23 ...191 B6
Kings Worthy SO21 ...2 D6
Langstone PO9 ...159 F6
Lymington SO41 ...197 F4
Minstead SO43 ...98 E2
Nursling SO16 ...76 F4
Petersfield GU32 ...41 B6
Poole BH14 ...203 B3
Portsmouth,Landport PO1 ...182 C7
Portsmouth,Wymering
PO6,PO7 ...133 F3
Romsey SO51 ...52 D7
Sherfield English SO51 ...25 E1
South Baddesley SO41 ...198 F4
Steep Marsh GU32 ...19 F1
Sway SO41 ...196 E7
Titchfield PO15 ...130 A2
Wickham PO17 ...108 A5
Wimborne Minst BH21 ...163 C5
Mill Mdw SO41 ...211 D5
Mill Pond Rd PO12 ...181 B7
Mill Pond The SO45 ...150 B6
Mill Quay PO10 ...161 A7
Mill Race View SP5 ...46 F8
Mill Rd
Christchurch BH23 ...207 A8
Denmead PO7 ...111 A4
Fareham PO16 ...155 A8
Gosport PO12 ...181 A7
Liss GU33 ...21 A5
Southampton SO15 ...102 A5
Totton SO40 ...101 A7
Waterlooville PO7 ...134 E6
Westbourne PO10 ...137 B4
Mill Rd N BH8 ...190 E3
Mill Rd S BH8 ...190 D2
Mill Rise SO51 ...5 D1
Mill Rythe Inf Sch PO11 ...185 B6
Mill Rythe Jun Sch
PO11 ...185 B6
Mill Rythe La PO11 ...185 A7
Mill St Corfe Mullen BH21 ...162 A1
Eastleigh SO50 ...56 B4
Mill Way SO40 ...100 E5
Mill Yd The SO16 ...77 C5
Millais Rd SO19 ...103 E3
Milland Rd SO23 ...215 F4
Millbank Ho
14 Southampton SO14 ...103 C6
5 Wimborne Minst BH21 ...163 C5
Millbank St SO14 ...103 C5
Millbridge Gdns SO19 ...104 B4
Millbrook Cl
Chandler's Ford SO53 ...55 B5
Liss GU33 ...21 A4
Millbrook Com Sch SO16 ...77 E3
Millbrook Dr PO9 ...136 A6
Millbrook Flyover SO15 ...101 E7
Millbrook Point Rd
SO15 ...102 A6
Millbrook Rd W SO15 ...101 F6
Millbrook Road E SO15 ...102 D5
Millbrook Road W SO15 ...102 A6
Millbrook Sta SO15 ...102 B6
Millbrook Trad Est
SO15 ...101 D7
Millcourt SO50 ...57 D2
Millennium Ct PO7 ...134 E5
Millennium Sq 11 PO16 ...131 B1
Miller Cl BH25 ...195 C4
Miller Dr PO16 ...130 F3
Miller Rd BH23 ...207 D7
Miller's Pond Gdns
SO19 ...103 F3
Millers La SO22 ...9 F3
Millers Quay Ho PO16 ...155 B8
Millers Way SO45 ...125 F2
Millfield
New Milton BH25 ...194 E3
Poole BH17 ...202 A7
Millhams Cl BH10 ...189 B6
Millhams Dr BH10 ...189 B6
Millhams Rd BH10 ...189 B6
Millhams St BH23 ...207 B6
Millhams Street N 2
BH23 ...207 B6
Milliken Cl SO45 ...150 F2
Mills Rd PO2 ...157 D1
Mills The BH12 ...203 E7
Millstream Cl
Poole BH17 ...202 A7
Wimborne Minst BH21 ...163 C4
Millstream Rise SO51 ...52 D7
Millstream Trad Est
BH24 ...141 A5
Millverton Ct 1 SO18 ...104 B7
Millvina Cl SO40 ...99 F4
Millway SO32 ...82 B5
Millyford Cl BH25 ...209 D8
Milman Ct 12 SO23 ...215 E6
Milne Cl SO45 ...125 C2
Milne Rd BH17 ...187 B1
Milner Ct SO15 ...102 C8
Milner Pl SO22 ...215 C4
Milner Rd BH4 ...204 C1
Milnthorpe La SO22 ...215 C5
Milton Bsns Ctr BH25 ...194 E2
Milton Cl BH14 ...203 D3
Milton Ct
Ferndown BH22 ...165 D5
3 Portsmouth PO4 ...183 A5
Milton Gr
Locks Heath SO31 ...129 B2
New Milton BH25 ...195 B2
Milton La PO4 ...183 A5
Milton Mead BH25 ...194 F2
Milton Par PO8 ...111 E2
Milton Park Ave 1 PO4 ...183 B4
Milton Park Jun & Inf Schs
PO4 ...183 B4
Milton Rd
Bournemouth BH8 ...205 A6
Eastleigh SO50 ...56 B5
Poole BH14 ...203 D3
Portsmouth PO4 ...183 A5
Southampton SO15 ...102 F6
Waterlooville PO7,PO8 ...111 E3
Wimborne Minst BH21 ...163 C6
Milton Villas BH8 ...205 A5
Miltoncross Sch PO3 ...183 A6
Milverton Cl
Christchurch BH23 ...193 E1
Totton SO40 ...101 A6
Milverton Ho PO5 ...216 B2
Milverton Rd
Totton SO40 ...101 A6
Winchester SO22 ...215 C6
Milvil Ct PO13 ...179 E3
Milvil Rd PO13 ...179 E3
Mimosa Ave BH21 ...187 E8
Mimosa Cl PO15 ...129 E3
Mimosa Dr SO50 ...57 E2
Mincingfield La SO32 ...82 D5
Mincingfield Terr SO32 ...82 D5
Minden Ho
Fareham PO14 ...154 F8
Romsey SO51 ...53 B7
Minden Way SO22 ...215 A3
Minerva Cl PO7 ...134 E2
Minerva Cres 20 PO1 ...182 A4
Minerva Ct 2 PO4 ...182 E1
Minerva Dr 9 PO12 ...181 C8
Minley Ct 10 PO9 ...136 B5
Minnitt Rd PO12 ...181 E5
Minstead Ave SO18 ...104 D8
Minstead Cl SO22 ...1 D4
Minstead Ct 4 SO17 ...103 A8
Minstead Rd
Bournemouth BH10 ...189 C3
Portsmouth PO4 ...183 B3
Minster Cl PO15 ...130 C2
Minster Ct 9 SO15 ...102 C6
Minster La 3 SO23 ...215 E5
Minster Pk BH21 ...138 E5
Minster The BH21 ...163 B4
Minster View BH21 ...163 C5
Minster Way BH16 ...201 B7
Mint Rd GU33 ...21 B6
Mint The GU31,GU32 ...40 F2
Minter's Lepe PO7 ...134 E3
Mintern Cl SO50 ...56 D5
Minterne Grange BH14 ...214 C7
Minterne Rd
3 Bournemouth BH9 ...190 A2
Christchurch BH23 ...207 E5
Poole BH14 ...214 C7
Minters Ct 28 SO23 ...215 D6
Minton Mews BH2 ...204 F5
Mintys Hill SP6 ...68 F8
Mintys Yd 4 BH24 ...141 A6
Mirabella Cl SO19 ...103 D2
Mirror Cl SO31 ...128 F1
Mislingford Rd SO32 ...84 D3
Missenden Acres SO30 ...105 C8
Missenden Pl SO50 ...56 A1
Mission La
Broadstone BH18 ...187 A2
Waterlooville PO8 ...112 A3
Mission Rd BH18 ...187 A2
Misslebrook La SO16,
SO52 ...54 D3
Mistletoe Gdns SO31 ...128 E6
Mistral 11 SO14 ...103 B3
Mitchell Cl
Barton on S BH25 ...210 A7
Locks Heath PO15 ...129 D5
Mitchell Dr SO50 ...57 C3
Mitchell Point SO31 ...127 F2
Mitchell Rd
Eastleigh SO50 ...56 B2
Ferndown BH21 ...165 A7
Havant PO9 ...135 B3
Poole BH17 ...202 F8
Mitchell Way
Eastleigh SO18,SO50 ...80 A8
Portsmouth PO3 ...158 B3
Mitchells Cl Redlynch SP5 ...47 D6
Romsey SO51 ...52 F7
Mitre Copse SO50 ...56 F2
Mitre Ct
5 Christchurch BH23 ...207 A7
5 Fareham PO14 ...154 E7
Mizen Ho PO6 ...157 A7
Mizen Way PO13 ...180 D6
Mizpah Villas SO32 ...83 E3
Moat Cl SO45 ...150 B3
Moat Ct
Bournemouth BH4 ...204 C5
Gosport PO12 ...180 D4
Moat Dr PO12 ...180 D3
Moat Hill SO18 ...79 F3
Moat La BH25 ...209 F8
Moat Wlk PO12 ...180 D3
Mockbeggar La BH24 ...117 A7
Moffat Rd BH23 ...207 D7
Moggs Mead GU31 ...41 A3
Mole Hill PO7 ...134 F5
Molefields SO41 ...211 E5
Molesworth Rd PO12 ...181 C4
Mollison Rise PO15 ...129 D6
Molyneux Rd BH25 ...195 D3
Momford Rd SO22 ...10 B3
Mon Cres SO18 ...104 C7
Monaco Ct BH9 ...205 B8
Monarch Cl
Locks Heath SO31 ...129 A2
3 Waterlooville PO7 ...135 A7
Monarch Ct 23 BH4 ...204 C3
Monarch Way
West End SO30 ...80 F2
Winchester SO22 ...215 A4
Monastery Rd SO18 ...103 E7
Monckton Rd
Gosport PO12 ...181 B2
Portsmouth PO3 ...158 A2
Moneyfield Ave PO3 ...158 B1
Moneyfield La 3 PO3 ...183 A8
Moneyfly Rd BH31 ...115 B5
Monk's Hill PO10 ...137 B5
Monks Brook Cl SO50 ...55 E1
Monks Brook Ind Pk
SO53 ...55 B5
Monks Cl BH22 ...166 A8
Monks Ct 4 SO41 ...197 F2
Monks Hill PO13 ...179 C5
Monks Orch GU32 ...40 F5
Monks Pl SO40 ...100 D6
Monks Rd Netley SO31 ...127 B6
Winchester SO23 ...215 E7
Monks Way
Bournemouth BH11 ...188 D5
Eastleigh SO50 ...55 F1
Southampton SO18 ...79 E4
Stubbington PO14 ...179 B5
Monks Wlk SO45 ...149 F8
Monks Wood GU32 ...40 F5
Monks Wood Cl SO16 ...79 B6
Monkshood Cl BH23 ...193 B1
Monkswell Gn BH23 ...207 D6
Monkton Cl BH22 ...165 D6
Monkton Cres BH12 ...203 E8
Monkton La SO40 ...100 C6
Monkwood Cl PO9 ...135 D5
Monkworthy Dr BH24 ...139 F5
Monmouth Cl
Chandler's Ford SO53 ...55 B6
Verwood BH31 ...115 B4
Monmouth Ct
Lymington SO41 ...197 E3
Ringwood BH24 ...140 F7
Monmouth Dr BH31 ...115 B4
Monmouth Gdns SO40 ...100 D5
Monmouth Rd PO2 ...157 D1
Monmouth Sq SO22 ...10 B5
Monnow Gdns SO18 ...80 B1
Monroe Cl PO12 ...180 E3
Mons The 17 SO23 ...215 D6
Monsal Ave BH22 ...165 C3
Montacute Sch BH17 ...187 C2
Montacute Way BH21 ...187 E8
Montagu Cl PO12 ...181 C9
Montagu Pk BH23 ...209 A7
Montagu Rd BH23 ...209 B8
Montague Ave SO19 ...104 D3
Montague Cl SO19 ...104 D3
Montague Ct SO45 ...149 E8
Montague Gdns GU31 ...41 B3
Montague Rd
Bishopstoke SO50 ...56 D3
Bournemouth BH5 ...206 B4
Portsmouth PO2 ...157 E1
Montague Wallis Ct 40
PO1 ...182 A5
Montana Ct PO7 ...135 A6
Montefiore Ho SO18 ...79 D4
Monteray Dr SO41 ...195 F4
Monterey Dr Havant PO9 ...136 A4
Locks Heath SO31 ...129 A2
Montfort Cl SO51 ...53 C7
Montfort Coll SO51 ...53 C7
Montfort Hts SO51 ...53 C7
Montfort Rd SO51 ...53 C6
Montgomerie Rd PO5 ...216 C2
Montgomery Ave
Bournemouth BH11 ...189 B3
Totton SO40 ...100 D8
Montgomery Cl SO22 ...215 A3
Montgomery Rd
Gosport PO13 ...155 C3
Havant PO9 ...136 A1
Southampton SO18 ...104 A8
Montgomery Way SO53 ...55 B3
Montgomery Wlk PO7 ...134 D5
Montpelier Cl SO31 ...129 C3
Montrose Ave PO16 ...132 E1
Montrose Cl
Hedge End SO30 ...105 E6
Verwood BH31 ...114 F6
Montrose Dr BH10 ...189 B2
Montserrat Rd PO13 ...179 E3
Monument Ct SO14 ...103 A2
Monument La
Portchester PO17 ...132 B4
Walhampton SO41 ...198 A5
Woodmancote PO18 ...137 F7
Monxton Gn 13 PO9 ...136 B6
Moody Rd PO14 ...179 C6
Moody's Hill SP5 ...3 C2
Moon Cl SO40 ...101 E1
Moonhills La SO42 ...149 B2
Moonrakers Way BH23 ...193 E1
Moonscross Ave SO40 ...100 F4
Moor La SP5 ...48 C8
Moor Pk PO7 ...112 B1
Moor Rd BH18 ...187 B5
Moor Side BH24 ...166 B8
Moor View Rd BH15 ...202 E6
Moorcroft Ave BH23 ...192 C2
Moordown Cl BH9 ...190 A4
Moordown St John's CE Prim
Sch BH9 ...189 F1
Moore Ave BH11 ...189 A4
Moore Cl BH25 ...194 F1
Moore Cres SO31 ...127 C7
Moore Gdns PO12 ...180 F4
Moorfield Gr BH9 ...189 F2
Moorfields Rd BH13 ...214 F8
Moorgreen Hospl SO30 ...80 E1
Moorgreen Rd
Havant PO9 ...136 A5
West End SO30 ...80 F2
Moorhaven BH22 ...165 D6
Moorhead Ct SO14 ...103 C2
Moorhill Gdns SO18 ...104 E7
Moorhill Rd Burley BH24 ...143 A2
West End SO18,SO30 ...104 D8
Moorhills 2 BH21 ...163 D4
Moorings Cl BH15 ...201 F1
Moorings The
2 Christchurch BH23 ...207 A5
Fareham PO16 ...155 B7
Moorings Way PO4 ...183 C6
Moorings Way Inf Sch
PO4 ...183 C6
Moorland Ave BH25 ...209 F8
Moorland Cl Hythe SO45 ...125 D3
Locks Heath SO31 ...129 A4
Moorland Cres BH16 ...201 B7
Moorland Ct BH22 ...138 D2
Moorland Gate BH24 ...141 A5
Moorland Par BH16 ...201 B7
Moorland Rd
Bournemouth BH1 ...205 D4
Portsmouth PO1 ...182 E6
Moorland Way BH16 ...201 B7
Moorlands Cl SO42 ...145 D1
Moorlands Coll BH23 ...192 B6
Moorlands Cres SO18 ...104 B8
Moorlands Inf Sch SO18 ...80 B1
Moorlands Rd
Swanmore SO32 ...84 A7
Verwood BH31 ...114 F7
West Moors BH22 ...138 E3
Moorlands Rise BH22 ...138 F3
Moorlea 2 BH8 ...205 B5
Moors Cl
Colden Common SO21 ...31 F1
Hurn BH23 ...191 B7
Moors Valley Ctry Park
Visitor Ctr* BH24 ...139 D8
Moors Valley Ctry Pk*
BH24 ...115 E1
Moors Valley Rly*
BH24 ...115 C1
Moorside Cl BH11 ...189 B3
Moorside Gdns BH11 ...189 B3
Moorside Rd
Bournemouth BH11 ...189 B3
Corfe Mullen BH21 ...186 D5
West Moors BH22 ...138 E2
Winchester SO23 ...2 C2
Moortown Ave PO6 ...134 D1
Moortown Dr
Bournemouth BH21 ...188 B8
Wimborne Minst BH21 ...164 B1
Moortown Farm BH21 ...188 B8
Moortown Ho BH24 ...141 A5
Moortown La BH24 ...141 C4
Moorvale Rd BH9 ...190 A2
Moot Cl SP5 ...47 A7
Moot Garden The* SP5 ...47 A7
Moot Gdns SP5 ...46 F6
Moot La SP5 ...46 F5
Mopley SO45 ...177 F7
Mopley Cl SO45 ...177 F7
Morant Ct 4 BH25 ...195 B3
Morant Rd BH24 ...117 B1
Moraunt Cl 1 PO12 ...181 C9
Moraunt Dr PO16 ...156 B6
Moray Ct 11 BH21 ...163 B5
Mordaunt Rd SO14 ...103 A7
Morden Ave BH22 ...165 C4
Morden Rd BH9 ...189 E1
Morecombe Ct 4 PO5 ...216 C2
Moreland Rd PO12 ...181 B6
Morelands Ct PO7 ...134 F4
Morelands Prim Sch
PO7 ...134 E2
Morelands Rd PO7 ...134 E4
Moresby Ct 5 PO16 ...131 B1
Morestead Rd
Winchester SO21 ...11 E3
Winchester SO23 ...215 F2
Moreton Rd BH9 ...190 B4
Morgan Le Fay Dr SO53 ...54 F7
Morgan Rd
Hedge End SO30 ...105 C5
Portsmouth PO4 ...183 C4
Morgan's La SP5 ...42 A1
Morgan's Vale & Woodfalls
CE Prim Sch SP5 ...47 D7
Morgans Dr PO14 ...154 C5
Morgans Rise Rd SP5 ...47 D7
Morgans Vale Rd SP5 ...47 D6
Moriconium Quay BH15 ...201 D1
Morington Ct 8 BH8 ...205 A5
Morland Rd SO15 ...78 C1
Morley Cl
Bournemouth BH5 ...206 A5
Burton BH23 ...192 C3
Southampton SO19 ...103 F6
Morley Cres PO8 ...112 A3
Morley Dr SO32 ...83 C8
Morley Gdns SO53 ...55 C8
Morley Rd
Bournemouth BH5 ...206 A5
Portsmouth PO4 ...183 A2
Morley Way BH22 ...165 F3
Morleys La SO51 ...29 C3
Morningside Ave PO16 ...132 E1
Mornington Dr SO22 ...215 A8
Mornish Rd BH13 ...203 F2
Morpeth Ave SO40 ...100 F8
Morris Cl Gosport PO13 ...155 B5
Hythe SO45 ...125 D4
Morris Rd Poole BH17 ...202 D8
Southampton SO15 ...102 E5
Morrison Ave BH12 ...203 F6
Morse Ct SO31 ...127 A6
Morshead Cres PO16 ...130 F3
Mortimer Cl
Christchurch BH23 ...208 A6
Kings Worthy SO23 ...2 C6
Netley SO31 ...127 B6
Totton SO40 ...76 D1
Mortimer Lawn PO9 ...135 D7
Mortimer Rd
Botley SO30 ...106 A6
Bournemouth BH8 ...190 B1
Portsmouth PO6 ...133 C1
Southampton SO19 ...103 E4
Mortimer Way SO52 ...53 F3
Mortimer's Ind Units
SO51 ...75 E5
Mortimers Dr SO50 ...57 D2
Mortimers La SO50 ...57 E2
Mortimore Rd PO12 ...180 F6
Mosaic Cl SO19 ...104 F4
Mosdell Rd PO10 ...161 E8
Mosedale Wlk 2 SO16 ...101 E7
Moselle Ct SO15 ...102 C5
Moss Cl GU33 ...21 A4
Moss Dr SO40 ...101 F2
Moss Rd SO23 ...215 F6

Mossleigh Ave SO16 ......77 F5
Mossley Ave Poole BH12 .189 A1
Poole BH12 ....204 A8
Motcombe Rd BH13 .....204 A2
Mottisfont Abbey (NT)*
SO51 ....5 F3
Mottisfont Abbey Gdns*
SO51 ....5 F3
Mottisfont Cl [1] SO15 ...102 A6
Mottisfont Lodge [5]
SO51 ....52 F7
Mottisfont Rd SO50 ......56 A4
Moulin Ave PO5 ....182 E2
Mound Cl PO12 ....181 A4
Mount Ave BH25 ....195 A1
Mount Cl
New Milton BH25 ....195 A1
Winchester SO22 ....1 E3
Mount Dr
Chandler's Ford SO53 ......55 E4
Fareham PO15 ....154 B8
Mount Grace Dr BH14 ..214 D7
Mount Heatherbank [7]
BH1 ....204 F3
Mount Hospl The SO50 ...56 D5
Mount House Cl SO45 ...126 A5
Mount La SO51 ....25 F7
Mount Pleasant
Christchurch BH23 ....208 A5
Denmead PO7 ....110 F2
Kings Worthy SO23 ....2 C6
Ringwood BH24 ....141 A7
Romsey SO51 ....52 E6
Mount Pleasant Dr
Bournemouth BH8 ....190 F1
Bransgore BH23 ....169 C1
Mount Pleasant Ind Pk
SO14 ....103 B7
Mount Pleasant Jun Sch
SO14 ....103 B7
Mount Pleasant La
SO41 ....197 A7
Mount Pleasant Rd
Gosport PO12 ....181 B4
Poole BH15 ....202 D3
Southampton SO14 ....103 B6
Mount Rd
Bournemouth BH11 ....189 B4
Poole BH14 ....203 B5
Mount Temple SO51 ......53 A7
Mount The
[5] Bassett SO16 ....78 F4
Gosport PO13 ....155 E1
[9] Old Shirley SO16 ....78 A1
Ringwood BH24 ....141 D8
Mount View SO50 ....56 B4
Mount View Rd SO22 .....10 B4
Mountain Ash Cl SO18 ..104 C7
Mountbatten Ave SO51 ...52 F7
Mountbatten Bsns Ctr
SO15 ....102 E5
Mountbatten Bsns Pk
PO6 ....158 C6
Mountbatten Cl
Christchurch BH23 ....208 A5
Gosport PO13 ....155 C4
Mountbatten Ct
New Milton BH25 ....194 F3
Winchester SO22 ....1 E3
Mountbatten Dr
Ferndown BH22 ....165 C5
Waterlooville PO7 ....134 D6
Mountbatten Gdns BH8 .190 F2
Mountbatten Pl SO23 ......2 C8
Mountbatten Rd
Eastleigh SO50 ....56 A5
Poole BH13 ....204 B1
Totton SO40 ....100 D8
Mountbatten Sch & Language
Coll The SO51 ....53 C6
Mountbatten Sq [6] PO4 .183 B2
Mountbatten Way
Portsmouth PO1 ....182 B7
Southampton SO15 ....102 C5
Mountfield SO45 ....125 E4
Mountjoy Cl BH21 ....163 F2
Mountjoy Ct [4] PO1 .....182 A3
Mountview Ave PO16 ....132 E1
Mountwood Rd PO10 ....137 D1
Mousehole La
Hythe SO45 ....126 A3
Southampton SO18 ....103 F8
Mousehole Rd PO6 ......132 F1
Mowbray Rd SO19 ....104 B4
Moxhams SP6 ....69 F1
Moyles Court Sch BH24 .117 C5
Muccleshell Cl PO9 .....136 A4
Muddyford Rd SP5 ....47 D8
Mude Gdns BH23 ....208 A5
Mudeford Com Inf Sch
BH23 ....207 E6
Mudeford Green Cl
BH23 ....207 F5
Mudeford Jun Sch
BH23 ....207 F6
Mudeford La BH23 ......207 F6
Muir Ho SO45 ....125 E1
Muira Est SO14 ....103 C5
Mulberry Ave
Cosham PO6 ....158 A7
Stubbington PO14 ....179 C6
Mulberry Cl PO12 ....181 B5
Mulberry Ct [4] BH23 .....207 A7
Mulberry Gdns SP6 ....93 E8
Mulberry Gr SO41 ....211 D8
Mulberry La
Cosham PO6 ....158 A7
Sarisbury SO31 ....128 E5
Mulberry Mews SP6 ......93 E8
Mulberry Rd SO40 ....101 F1
Mulberry Wlk SO15 .....102 C8
Mullen Cl SO19 ....103 E4
Mullins Cl BH12 ....204 C8
Mullion Cl PO6 ....157 B7
Mumby Rd PO12 ....181 D6
Mundays Row PO8 ....88 C1
Munro Cres SO15 ....101 F7
Munster Rd Poole BH14 ..203 D3
Portsmouth PO2 ....157 D2
Murefield Rd PO1 ....216 C3
Muriel Rd PO7 ....134 E8
Murley Rd BH9 ....205 A8
Murray Cl Fareham PO15 .130 E2
Southampton SO19 ....104 E6
Murray Cotts SO32 ......107 D7
Murray Rd PO8 ....112 B6
Murray's La PO1 ....181 F7
Murrills Est PO16 ....156 E8
Mus of Electricity*
BH23 ....207 B7
Muscliff Prim Sch BH9 ..190 C4
Muscliffe Ct [8] PO9 .....136 B5
Muscliffe La BH9 ....190 B5
Muscliffe Rd BH9 ....189 F1
Museum of Archaeology*
SO14 ....103 A2
Museum Rd PO1 ....182 B4
Mussett Cl SO40 ....100 E7
Mustang Ave PO15 ......129 C7
My Lords La PO11 ....185 B3
Myers Cl SO32 ....84 B5
Myrtle Ave
Portchester PO16 ....156 D7
Totton SO40 ....100 D6
Myrtle Cl Gosport PO13 ...155 B3
Hordle SO41 ....195 F4
Myrtle Gr PO3 ....183 B7
Myrtle Rd
Bournemouth BH8 ....205 C6
Southampton SO16 ....78 B4
Myvern Cl SO45 ....150 D3

N

Nada Rd BH23 ....193 D1
Nailsworth Rd PO6 ......133 B1
Nairn Ct BH3 ....204 E7
Nairn Rd
Bournemouth BH3 ....204 E6
Poole BH13 ....214 E7
Naish Ct PO9 ....135 C7
Naish Dr PO12 ....156 A1
Naish Rd BH25 ....209 E7
Namu Rd BH9 ....189 E1
Nancy Rd PO1 ....216 D3
Nansen Ave BH15 ....202 D5
Napier Cl PO13 ....180 D5
Napier Cres PO15 ....130 C1
Napier Rd
Hamworthy BH15 ....201 C3
Horndean PO8 ....112 C6
Portsmouth PO5 ....182 D2
Southampton SO19 ....104 E5
Narrow La
Ringwood,North Poulner
BH24 ....117 D1
Ringwood,Poulner BH24 ...141 D8
[9] Romsey SO51 ....52 E7
Narvik Rd PO2 ....157 D4
Naseby Cl [5] PO6 ....133 A1
Naseby Rd BH9 ....190 A2
Nash Cl SO45 ....125 D1
Nash Rd SO45 ....125 D2
Nashe Cl PO15 ....130 D3
Nashe Ho PO15 ....130 C3
Nashe Way PO15 ....130 C3
Nasmith Cl PO12 ....180 D4
Nat Gonella Sq [4] PO12 .181 D5
Natanbury SP5 ....47 A7
Nathen Gdns BH15 ......201 D3
National Air Traffic Services
Hq PO15 ....129 F8
National Motor Mus The*
SO42 ....148 E2
Nations Hill SO23 ....2 B6
Navarac Ct BH14 ....203 C3
Navigator's Way SO30 ...105 C8
Navy Rd PO1 ....182 A6
Nea Cl BH23 ....208 D8
Nea Dr BH24 ....116 B5
Nea Rd BH23 ....208 E8
Neacroft Cl BH25 ....209 D8
Neath Way SO53 ....55 A5
Needles Ct [1] SO41 ......211 C4
Needles Ho PO16 ....155 A7
Needles Point SO41 ......211 D3
Neelands Gr PO6 ....156 E8
Neighbourhood Ctr
BH17 ....187 E2
Neilson Cl SO53 ....55 C7
Nelson Ave
Portchester PO16 ....156 B8
Portsmouth PO2 ....157 D2
Nelson Cl Holbury SO45 ..150 C3
New Milton BH25 ....194 F3
Romsey SO51 ....52 F8
Nelson Cres PO8 ....112 C7
Nelson Ct Fareham PO14 .154 F6
[1] Hythe SO45 ....126 B1
[18] Poole BH15 ....202 C2
[8] Portsmouth PO1 ....182 D7
Nelson Ctr The PO3 .....158 B2
Nelson Dr BH23 ....207 F6
Nelson Ho [8] PO12 ......181 E5
Nelson Ind Pk SO30 ....81 B1
Nelson La PO17 ....132 C2
Nelson Pl SO41 ....197 F3
Nelson Rd
Bishopstoke SO50 ....56 D4
Gosport PO12 ....181 B5
Poole BH4,BH12 ....204 B4
Portsmouth PO5 ....216 C1
Portsmouth,Landport PO1 .182 D7
Southampton SO15 ....102 C6
Winchester SO23 ....11 C6
Nelsons Gdns SO30 ....81 C3
Nepean Cl PO12 ....181 B2
Neptune Ct
[14] Portsmouth PO1 ....182 A4
Southampton SO16 ....77 F4
Neptune Ho
[1] Cosham PO6 ....157 F8
Southampton SO14 ....103 B2
Neptune Rd
Fareham,Hill Park PO15 ...130 C2
Fareham,West End PO14 ..154 F5
Neptune Way SO14 ......103 B2
Nerissa Cl PO7 ....135 B8
Nerquis Cl SO51 ....53 B8
Nesbitt Cl PO13 ....155 B3
Nessus St PO2 ....182 D8
Nest Bsns Pk PO9 ....136 B4
Nethercliffe Sch SO22 ...215 C7
Netherfield Cl PO9 ......136 A1
Netherhall Gdns BH4 ....204 C3
Netherhill SO32 ....82 C3
Netherhill La SO32 ....82 B2
Netherton Rd PO12 ......180 F7
Netherwood Pl BH21 ....163 A5
Netley Abbey* SO31 ......127 A7
Netley Abbey Inf Sch
SO31 ....127 B7
Netley Abbey Jun Sch
SO31 ....127 B7
Netley Cl
Chandler's Ford SO53 ......55 B3
Poole BH15 ....203 A7
Netley Cliff SO31 ....127 B5
Netley Court Sch SO31 ..127 B5
Netley Ct [8] PO12 ....181 C9
Netley Firs Rd
Hedge End SO19 ....104 F4
Hedge End SO30 ....105 A6
Netley Hill Est SO19 .....104 F4
Netley Lodge Cl SO31 ...127 C5
Netley Mans [10] PO5 .....182 D1
Netley Marsh CE Inf Sch
SO40 ....100 A7
Netley Marsh Workshops
SO40 ....100 A7
Netley Rd
[13] Portsmouth PO5 ....182 C2
Titchfield PO14 ....129 C1
Netley Sta SO31 ....127 C6
Netley Terr [14] PO5 ......182 C2
Nettlecombe Ave PO4 ...182 E1
Nettlestone SO31 ....127 C7
Nettlestone Rd [1] PO4 ...183 A2
Nettleton Cl BH17 ....202 E7
Netton Cl SP5 ....22 B8
Netton St SP5 ....22 C8
Neva Rd SO18 ....103 F8
Neville Ave PO16 ....156 D6
Neville Dr SO51 ....27 F1
Neville Gdns PO10 ......136 E3
Neville Lovett Com Sch The
PO14 ....154 F8
Neville Rd PO3 ....183 A7
Neville Shute Rd PO3 ...158 A3
New Borough Rd BH21 ..163 D3
New Brighton Rd PO10 ..136 F2
New Cliff Ho SO19 ....103 E1
New Cliffe Gdns SO30 ...105 B6
New Coll (Univ of
Southampton) SO15 ...102 F7
New Cotts Ashurst SO40 ..123 F7
Exbury SO45 ....177 B5
Fareham PO16 ....155 A8
Hampreston BH21 ....164 E2
Nursling SO16 ....77 C2
South Baddesley SO41 ....199 A5
New Ct BH24 ....140 E7
New Cut PO11 ....159 F3
New Down La PO6,PO7 ..134 A2
New Fields Bsns Pk
BH17 ....202 D8
New Forest Dr SO42 .....145 D1
New Forest Ent Ctr
SO40 ....100 E5
New Forest Mus & Visitor
Ctr* SO43 ....122 A5
New Forest Otter, Owl &
Wildlife Pk* SO40 ....123 E8
New Forest Reptile Ctr*
SO43 ....121 A3
New Harbour Rd BH15 ...202 B1
New Harbour Rd S
BH15 ....213 B8
New Harbour Road W
BH15 ....202 A1
New Inn Cotts SO42 .....175 C5
New Inn La Bartley SO40 ..99 B6
East Boldre SO42 ....175 C5
New Inn Rd SO40 ....99 B7
New La Bashley BH25 ....194 F6
Havant PO9 ....136 A3
Milford on S SO41 ....211 F3
New Marsh Ho SO45 .....126 A4
New Merrifield BH21 ....163 F7
New Milton Inf Sch
BH25 ....195 A1
New Milton Jun Sch
BH25 ....195 A1
New Milton Sta BH25 ...195 A3
New Orch BH15 ....202 B2
New Par
Bournemouth BH10 ....189 E3
Portchester PO16 ....156 D8
New Park Rd BH6 ....206 C4
New Quay Rd BH15 .....202 B1
New Rd Ashurst SO40 ....100 C2
Bishop's Waltham SO32 ....59 D2
Blackfield SO45 ....150 E1
Bournemouth BH10 ....189 E7
Clanfield PO8 ....88 C5
Colden Common SO21 ......31 F1
Fair Oak SO50 ....57 B2
Fareham PO16 ....131 A1
Ferndown BH22 ....165 E3
Havant PO9 ....135 E2
Holbury SO45 ....150 C7
Horndean PO8 ....111 E6
Hythe SO45 ....126 A4
Hythe,Buttsash SO45 .....150 B7
Ibsley BH24 ....117 B8
Landford SP5 ....49 F2
Littleton SO22 ....1 B6
Meonstoke SO32 ....61 D3
Michelmersh SO51 ....27 D8
Milford on S SO41 ....212 A4
Netley SO31 ....127 B6
Poole BH12 ....203 D6
Portsmouth PO2 ....182 F7
Ringwood BH24 ....141 A4
Rockbourne SP6 ....44 E1
Romsey SO51 ....53 A8
Southampton SO14 ....103 A5
Southbourne PO10 ....161 E8
Swanmore SO32 ....84 A5
Swanwick SO31 ....128 F8
Warsash SO31 ....152 E10
Westbourne PO10 ....137 B3
Woodlands Common BH21 .114 A6
New Rd E PO2 ....182 F8
New St Lymington SO41 ...197 E4
[5] Poole BH15 ....202 B1
Ringwood BH24 ....141 A6
New Street Mews SO41 .197 E4
New Town PO16 ....156 D8
New Valley Rd SO41 .....211 C5
Newbarn La PO18 ....137 F8
Newbarn Rd Buriton GU31 .65 C2
Havant PO9 ....135 C3
Newbolt Cl PO8 ....111 E3
Newbolt Rd PO6 ....132 F1
Newbridge SO31 ....127 C6
Newbridge Jun Sch
PO2 ....182 F7
Newbridge Rd
Cadnam SO40 ....75 A1
Newbridge SO40 ....74 F3
Newbridge Way SO41 ...197 C1
Newbroke Rd PO13 ......180 E8
Newburgh St SO23 ......215 D6
Newbury Cl SO50 ....57 B2
Newbury Dr BH10 ....189 D1
Newbury Pl SO31 ....128 F2
Newbury Rd SO15 ....78 C1
Newcombe Rd
Bournemouth BH6 ....206 E5
Southampton SO15 ....102 E6
West Moors BH22 ....138 D3
Newcome Rd PO1 ....182 E6
Newcomen Ct [8] PO2 ...157 C2
Newcomen Rd PO2 ......157 C2
Newcroft Gdns BH23 ....207 A8
Newenham Rd SO41 .....197 E2
Newfield Rd GU33 ....21 A6
Newfoundland Dr BH15 .202 D2
Newfoundland Drive Rdbt
BH15 ....202 D1
Newgate La PO14 ....155 A4
Newgate Lane Ind Est
PO14 ....155 B6
Newitt Pl SO16 ....78 F6
Newland Ave PO12 ......181 A5
Newlands PO15 ....130 C1
Newlands Ave SO15 .....102 D7
Newlands Cl
Blackfield SO45 ....150 E1
Chandler's Ford SO53 ......54 E5
Newlands Copse SO45 ...150 F1
Newlands La
Denmead PO7 ....111 A1
Waterlooville PO7 ....134 A6
Newlands Manor SO41 ..211 D7
Newlands Prim Sch SO16 .77 E1
Newlands Rd
Blackfield SO45 ....150 E2
Bournemouth BH7 ....206 A6
Christchurch BH23 ....207 F7
New Milton BH25 ....195 B1
Waterlooville PO7 ....134 D5
Newlands The [2] SO17 ....79 C2
Newlands Way BH18 ....186 D3
Newlease Rd PO7 ....134 F5
Newlyn Way Poole BH12 ..203 E7
Portsmouth PO6 ....157 A7
Newlyn Wlk SO51 ....28 A1
Newman St [2] SO16 .....102 B8
Newman's La BH22 .....138 C4
Newmans Cl
West Moors BH21 ....138 E5
Wimborne Minst BH21 ....163 D3
Newmans Copse Rd
SO40 ....101 A4
Newmans Hill PO17 ......84 D1
Newmarket Cl SO50 ......81 D7
Newmer Ct PO9 ....135 C6
Newmorton Rd BH9 .....190 A4
Newney Cl PO2 ....157 F4
Newnham Ct PO9 ....136 B5
Newport Cl SO53 ....55 A4
Newport La SO51 ....28 C6
Newport Rd PO12 ....180 F5
Newstead Rd BH6 ....206 D4
Newton Bglws SP5 ....24 A3
Newton Cl
Stubbington PO14 ....154 C4
Whiteparish SP5 ....24 A3
Newton La Romsey SO51 ..52 E6
Whiteparish SP5 ....24 A3
Newton Morrell BH14 ....203 D3
Newton Pl PO13 ....179 E4
Newton Rd
Barton on S BH25 ....210 B8
Poole BH13 ....214 F8
Southampton SO18 ....79 E1
Twyford SO21 ....32 A7
Newtown Bsns Ctr
BH12 ....203 A7
Newtown CE Prim Sch
PO12 ....181 C6
Newtown Ct SO31 ....128 C1
Newtown La
Corfe Mullen BH21 ....186 D8
Ibsley BH24,SP26 ....94 C1
South Hayling PO11 ......184 E4
Verwood BH31 ....115 A5
Newtown Rd
Eastleigh SO50 ....56 A3
Sherfield English SO51 .....26 B3
Southampton SO19 ....104 B1
Verwood BH31 ....115 A5
Verwood BH31 ....115 A6
Warsash SO31 ....152 C10
Newtown Soberton Inf Sch
PO17 ....109 C6
Nichol Rd SO53 ....30 D1
Nichola Ct BH12 ....203 B7
Nicholas Cl BH23 ....194 B2
Nicholas Cres PO15 .....130 F2
Nicholas Ct
Lee-on-t-S PO13 ....179 E2
South Hayling PO11 ......184 E3
Nicholas Gdns BH10 .....189 C2
Nicholas Rd SO45 ....177 F7
Nicholl Pl PO13 ....155 C2
Nichols Rd SO14 ....103 B5
Nicholson Cl BH17 ......202 E8
Nicholson Gdns [1] PO1 ..216 C3
Nicholson Way PO9 .....135 E3
Nicholson Wlk SO16 ......77 D6
Nickel Cl SO23 ....215 F6
Nickel St [4] PO5 ....216 A1
Nickleby Gdns SO40 .....100 B7
Nickleby Ho [10] PO1 .....182 D7
Nickleby Rd PO8 ....88 B6
Nickson Cl SO53 ....55 B8
Nightingale Ave SO50 ....55 D1
Nightingale Cl
Bursledon SO31 ....127 F8
Gosport PO12 ....180 F6
Romsey SO51 ....53 B7
Rowlands Castle PO9 .....113 A1
Verwood BH31 ....115 A5
West Wellow SO51 ....50 D3
[5] Winchester SO22 ......215 A4
Nightingale Cres SO32 ..107 F8
Nightingale Ct
Cosham PO6 ....158 B8
Southampton SO16 ....78 A4
Westbourne PO10 ....137 B4
Nightingale Dr SO40 ....100 C8
Nightingale Gr SO15 ....102 C7
Nightingale Ho SO51 .....53 A8
Nightingale Mews
Locks Heath SO31 ....129 B3
Netley SO31 ....127 C5
Nightingale Pk [1] PO9 ..136 B1
Nightingale Prim Sch
SO50 ....55 D1
Nightingale Rd
Petersfield GU32 ....40 E2
Portsmouth PO5 ....182 B2
Southampton SO15 ....102 C7
Nightingale Wlk SO31 ...127 C4
Nightingdale Ct [3]
SO15 ....102 C6
Nightjar Cl
Broadstone BH17 ....201 F8
Waterlooville PO8 ....112 A6
Nile Rd SO17 ....79 A2
Nile St PO10 ....160 F8
Nimrod Dr PO13 ....180 D6
Nimrod Way BH21 ....164 F6
Nine Acres GU32 ....20 B1
Nine Elms La PO17 ......131 E4
Ninian Cl SO50 ....57 C1
Ninian Park Rd PO3 .....158 A2
Nirvana Mans [12] PO5 ...182 D1
Niton Cl PO13 ....155 C2
Noads Cl SO45 ....125 F2
Noads Way SO45 ....125 E2
Noadswood Sec Sch
SO45 ....125 E2
Nob's Crook SO50 ....57 A2
Nobbs La PO1 ....182 A4
Nobes Ave PO13 ....155 C2
Nobes Cl PO13 ....155 D2
Noble Cl BH11 ....188 F
Noble Rd SO30 ....105 D
Noctule Ct PO17 ....130 D
Noel Cl SO42 ....146 A
Noel Rd BH10 ....189 B

Noel The BH25 195 C3
Nomad Cl SO18 80 B1
Nomansland & Hamptworth CE Prim Sch SP5 73 C8
Nook The Eastleigh SO50 56 B5
Gosport PO13 155 E1
Noon Gdns BH31 115 B6
Noon Hill Dr BH31 115 B6
Noon Hill Rd BH31 115 B6
Norbury Cl SO53 55 B7
Norbury Gdns SO31 127 E2
Norcliffe Cl BH11 189 B3
Norcliffe Rd SO17 103 A8
Norcroft Ct SO15 78 C2
Nordik Gdns SO30 105 C5
Nore Cres PO10 136 D1
Nore Farm Ave PO10 136 D1
Noreuil Rd GU32 40 D3
Norfolk Ave BH23 191 F2
Norfolk Cres PO11 184 E2
Norfolk Ct SO53 55 C3
Norfolk Ho 2 PO9 136 A1
Norfolk Mews PO11 184 E2
Norfolk Rd Gosport PO12 180 F7
Southampton SO15 102 D7
Norfolk St PO5 216 B2
Norgett Way PO16 156 B7
Norham Ave SO16 78 C2
Norham Cl SO16 78 C2
Norland Rd PO4 216 D1
Norlands Dr SO21 31 C4
Norley Cl PO9 135 E5
Norleywood BH23 208 F8
Norleywood Rd SO41 198 E8
Norman Ave BH12 204 A6
Norman Cl PO16 156 D6
Norman Ct 4 PO4 182 E2
Norman Gdns
Hedge End SO30 105 A5
Poole BH12 204 A6
Norman Ho 16 SO14 103 C6
Norman Rd
Blackfield SO45 177 F8
Gosport PO12 181 A6
Portsmouth PO4 182 E3
South Hayling PO11 185 B2
Southampton SO15 102 D5
Winchester SO23 215 D4
Norman Way PO9 135 C2
Normandy Cl
Rownhams SO16 77 E6
Sway SO41 172 A2
Normandy Ct
Warsash SO31 128 C1
Wickham PO17 108 B4
Normandy Dr BH23 207 D7
Normandy Gdns 1
PO12 180 F4
Normandy Ho SO51 53 B7
Normandy La SO41 198 A1
Normandy Rd PO2 157 E4
Normandy Way
Fordingbridge SP6 69 E1
Hamworthy BH15 201 D2
Marchwood SO40 102 A1
Normanhurst Ave BH8 190 E1
Normans SO23 215 D4
Normanton Cl BH23 191 F1
Norris Cl Romsey SO51 28 C2
St Leonards BH24 139 E4
Norris Gdns Havant PO9 160 A8
New Milton BH25 195 A1
Norris Hill SO18 79 E1
Norrish Ct PO2 182 E7
Norrish Rd BH12 203 C5
Norset Rd PO15 130 D2
North Ave
Bournemouth BH10 189 D6
Portsmouth PO2 157 E5
North Baddesley Inf Sch
SO52 54 B4
North Baddesley Jun Sch
SO52 54 B4
North Battery Rd PO2 157 B2
North Bay PO10 161 A3
North Cl Gosport PO12 180 F4
Havant PO9 160 A8
Lymington SO41 197 E4
Romsey SO51 28 C1
North Common La
Landford SP5 49 B6
Sway SO41 196 F7
North Cres PO11 185 B3
North Cross St PO12 181 D5
North Ct PO1 182 E7
North Dr Littleton SO22 1 B5
Ossemsley BH25 194 E8
Southwick PO17 132 F6
West Moors BH24 166 B8
North East Cl SO19 104 C5
North East Rd SO19 104 B4
North End Ave PO2 157 D2
North End Cl SO53 55 C4
North End Farm Cotts
SO24 14 C7
North End Gr PO2 157 D2
North End La
Cheriton SO24 14 D7
Ibsley BH24,SP6 93 D4
North Fields Cotts SO21 32 A7
North Greenlands SO41 197 C2
North Head SO41 211 A5
North Hill Fareham PO16 131 B3
Portsmouth PO6 133 B2
North Hill Cl SO22 215 D8
North Hill Ct SO22 215 D7
North La Beaulieu SO42 148 E5
Buriton GU31 65 E5
North La *continued*
Clanfield PO8 88 C7
East Meon PO8 64 C2
Nomansland SP5 73 C7
North Lodge Rd BH14 203 E4
North Millers Dale SO53 55 B8
North Park Bsns Ctr
PO17 130 D8
North Poulner Rd BH24 117 B2
North Rd
Bournemouth BH7 205 E5
Brockenhurst SO42 146 A1
Dibden Purlieu SO45 125 E1
Horndean PO8 88 C2
Kings Worthy SO23 2 B8
Petersfield GU32 40 F4
Poole BH14 203 A4
Portsmouth PO6 133 A2
Southampton SO17 103 C8
North Road E PO17 133 A6
North Road W PO17 133 A6
North Shore Rd PO11 184 D4
North Sq 2 PO17 130 E7
North St Emsworth PO10 136 F1
Gosport PO12 181 D6
Havant PO9 135 F1
Havant,Bedhampton PO9 135 D2
Lymington SO41 197 C2
Poole BH15 202 C2
Portsmouth PO1 216 C4
Portsmouth,Portsea PO1 182 A5
Westbourne PO10 137 B4
North Street Arc 11
PO9 135 F1
North Stroud La GU32 39 E3
North Trestle Rd SO45 151 C6
North View SO22 215 C6
North Wallington PO16 131 C3
North Walls SO23 215 E6
North Way PO9 135 E1
North Weirs SO42 145 D1
Northam Bsns Ctr 21
SO14 103 C6
Northam Mews PO1 216 C3
Northam Rd SO14 103 B5
Northam St PO1 216 C3
Northampton La SO45 177 E8
Northarbour Rd PO6 157 D7
Northarbour Spur PO6 157 D8
Northbourne Ave BH10 189 D5
Northbourne Cl 5
SO45 126 A1
Northbourne Gdns
BH10 189 E5
Northbourne Pl 3
BH10 189 D5
Northbourne Rdbt BH10 189 E5
Northbrook Ave SO23 11 C7
Northbrook Bower SO32 83 D8
Northbrook Cl
Portsmouth PO1 182 D7
Winchester SO23 11 C7
Northbrook Ho SO32 83 D8
Northbrook Ind Est SO16 78 C2
Northbrook Rd
Broadstone BH18 187 A2
Southampton SO14 103 B5
Northbrook Springs
Vineyard* SO32 59 C1
Northbrooke Ct SO23 11 C7
Northcote Gdns PO10 161 E8
Northcote Rd
Bournemouth BH1 205 C4
Portsmouth PO4 182 E3
Southampton SO17 79 C2
Northcott Cl PO12 180 F3
Northcroft Rd PO12 180 F6
Northdene Rd SO53 55 C5
Northend La SO32 61 B2
Northern Access Rd
SO45 151 D2
Northern Anchorage
SO19 103 D3
Northern Bldgs 10 PO6 157 F8
Northern Galleries 4
PO14 155 A6
Northern Inf Sch PO16 132 C1
Northern Jun Com Sch
PO16 132 C1
Northern Par PO2 157 E3
Northern Parade Inf Sch
PO2 157 E3
Northern Parade Jun Sch
PO2 157 E3
Northern Rd
Cosham PO6 157 F7
Cosham PO6 157 F8
Fawley SO45 151 E2
Northern Way PO1 181 F8
Northerwood Ave SO43 121 E5
Northerwood Cl SO52 53 F4
Northerwood Ho SO43 121 E6
Northesk Ho PO1 216 C4
Northey Rd BH6 206 E6
Northfield Ave PO14 154 F7
Northfield Cl
Bishop's Waltham SO32 59 A1
Horndean PO8 88 C2
Northfield Pk PO16 132 B1
Northfield Rd
Milford on S SO41 211 F4
Ringwood BH24 117 B1
Southampton SO18 79 F2
Northfields Farm La
PO17 108 B5
Northgate Ave PO2 182 F8
Northgate Chambers 10
SO23 215 E6
Northgate Lodge 2
SO23 215 E6
Northlands Cl SO40 100 D8
Northlands Dr SO23 215 E8
Northlands Gdns SO15 102 E7
Northlands Rd
Eastleigh SO50 56 A3
Romsey SO51 53 C6
Southampton SO15 102 E8
Totton SO40 100 E8
Northleigh Cnr SO18 79 E5
Northleigh La BH21 163 E6
Northmead Dr BH17 201 F8
Northmere Dr BH12 203 F7
Northmere Rd BH12 203 F7
Northmore Cl SO31 129 B5
Northmore Rd SO31 129 B5
Northney La PO11 160 C4
Northney Rd PO11 160 B4
Northolt Gdns SO16 78 A5
Northover BH3 204 F6
Northover La SO41 195 E7
Northover Rd
Lymington SO41 197 A4
Portsmouth PO3 183 B8
Northshore BH13 214 C4
Northumberland Ct
BH24 140 F7
Northumberland Rd
Portsmouth PO5 216 D3
Southampton SO14 103 B6
Northway Gosport PO13 155 C4
Titchfield PO15 129 E3
Northways PO14 179 D7
Northwood Cl SO16 79 A6
Northwood La PO11 160 A1
Northwood Rd PO2 157 E4
Northwood Sq 8 PO16 131 B2
Nortoft Rd BH8 205 B6
Norton Cl
Christchurch BH23 207 D7
Southampton SO19 103 E3
Southwick PO17 132 F6
Waterlooville PO7 134 D7
Norton Dr PO16 131 A3
Norton Gdns BH9 189 E1
Norton Rd
Bournemouth BH9 204 E8
Southwick PO17 132 F6
Norton Way BH15 202 A1
Norton Welch Cl SO52 54 B4
Norway Cl 3 BH9 189 F1
Norway Rd PO3 158 A4
Norwich Ave BH2 204 D3
Norwich Ave W BH2 204 D3
Norwich Cl SO31 128 E4
Norwich Ct 5 BH2 204 E3
Norwich Mans BH2 204 D3
Norwich Pl PO13 179 E4
Norwich Rd
Bournemouth BH2 204 E3
Portsmouth PO6 133 D1
Southampton SO18 79 F2
Norwood Pl BH5 206 B5
Norwood Prim Sch SO50 56 A3
Nottingham Pl PO13 179 E4
Nouale La BH24 141 D7
Novello Gdns PO7 134 E6
Noyce Dr SO50 57 D1
Noyce Gdns BH8 191 B2
Nuffield Ind Est BH17 202 D8
Nuffield Rd BH17 202 D7
Nugent Rd BH6 207 A4
Nunns Pk SP5 24 B4
Nuns Rd SO23 215 E7
Nuns Wlk SO23 215 F8
Nurse's Path SO21 32 A5
Nursery Cl
Emsworth PO10 136 F3
Gosport PO13 155 B3
Nursery Cotts SP6 46 E1
Nursery Field GU33 20 E3
Nursery Gdns
Chandler's Ford SO53 55 C3
Romsey SO51 53 A7
Southampton SO19 104 B6
Waterlooville PO8 112 A5
Winchester SO22 215 B6
Nursery Gr SO30 105 C5
Nursery Ho SO53 55 C6
Nursery La PO14 179 C6
Nursery Rd
Bournemouth BH9 190 A3
Havant PO9 135 C2
Ringwood BH24 141 A6
Southampton SO18 79 D1
Nursling CE Prim Sch
SO16 77 C5
Nursling Cres PO9 136 A5
Nursling Gn BH8 190 D2
Nursling Ind Est SO16 77 B4
Nursling St SO16 77 C5
Nutash PO14 129 C4
Nutbeem Rd SO50 56 A2
Nutbourne Ho PO6 158 D7
Nutbourne Pk PO18 161 F7
Nutbourne Rd
Farlington PO6 158 D7
South Hayling PO11 185 E1
Nutburn Rd SO52 54 B5
Nutfield Ct SO16 77 E3
Nutfield Pl PO1 216 C4
Nutfield Rd SO16 77 D6
Nuthatch Cl
Broadstone BH17 201 F8
Ferndown BH22 165 B8
Rowlands Castle PO9 113 B1
Nutley Cl BH11 188 F4
Nutley Rd PO9 135 D5
Nutley Way BH11 188 F4
Nutsey Ave SO40 76 D2
Nutsey Cl SO40 76 E3
Nutsey La SO40 76 E2
Nutshalling Ave SO16 77 E5
Nutshalling Cl SO40 76 C2
Nutwick Rd PO9 136 B3
Nutwood Way SO40 76 E2
Nyewood Ave PO16 132 D1
Nyria Way PO12 181 D5

O

O' Jays Ind Pk PO3 158 A2
O'connell Rd SO50 55 F2
Oak Ave BH23 206 D8
Oak Cl Corfe Mullen BH21 186 C5
Dibden Purlieu SO45 125 E1
Ferndown BH22 165 E1
Lyndhurst SO43 121 F4
Southampton SO15 101 C8
Upham SO32 58 F5
Waterlooville PO8 111 E2
Oak Coppice Cl SO50 57 A2
Oak Coppice Rd PO15 129 D8
Oak Ct Fareham PO15 130 C2
Lymington SO41 197 C2
Oak Dr Fair Oak SO50 57 C1
Petersfield GU31 40 E1
Poole BH15 202 D2
Oak Gdns
Bournemouth BH11 189 B1
Hordle SO41 211 D8
Oak Green Way SO18 104 A8
Oak La BH24 141 B8
Oak Leaf Cl SO40 124 E8
Oak Lodge 4 PO2 157 C2
Oak Lodge Specl Sch
SO45 125 C3
Oak Meadow CE Prim Sch
PO15 130 C3
Oak Mews BH12 203 C5
Oak Park Dr PO9 136 A3
Oak Park Ind Est PO6 157 D8
Oak Rd Alderholt SP6 92 F5
Bishop's Waltham SO32 83 E8
Bournemouth BH8 205 C6
Bursledon SO31 127 F8
Clanfield PO8 88 C5
Dibden Purlieu SO45 125 E1
Fareham PO15 130 D2
New Milton BH25 195 C3
Southampton SO19 103 E2
Upton BH16 201 C6
Oak St PO12 181 C5
Oak Tree Cl SO21 56 F8
Oak Tree Dr
Emsworth PO10 136 F4
Liss GU33 21 A4
Oak Tree Gdns SO30 105 B6
Oak Tree Way SO50 56 A5
Oak Vale SO18 80 B3
Oak Wlk SO50 57 C1
Oakapple Gdns PO6 158 E8
Oakbank Rd
Bishopstoke SO50 56 D3
Southampton SO19 103 D3
Oakcroft La PO14 154 C5
Oakdale Rd BH15 202 E6
Oakdale South Road Mid Sch
BH15 202 C5
Oakdean Rd PO4 183 C4
Oakdene Gosport PO13 155 D1
Southampton SO17 79 B2
Totton SO40 100 C7
Oakdene Cl BH21 163 D5
Oakdene Gdns SO50 57 C2
Oakdown Rd PO14 179 D8
Oaken Botton Cvn Site
BH25 171 E5
Oakenbrow Hythe SO45 125 D2
Sway SO41 172 A2
Oakes The PO14 154 B4
Oakfield Ct 13 PO9 136 B5
Oakfield Prim Sch SO40 76 E1
Oakfield Rd Bartley SO40 99 B7
Poole BH15 202 C6
Totton SO40 100 F7
Oakfields SO50 56 A7
Oakford Ct BH8 190 D3
Oakgrove Gdns SO50 56 E2
Oakgrove Rd SO50 56 E2
Oakham Grange BH22 165 E5
Oakhill SO31 105 B1
Oakhill Cl
Bursledon SO31 105 B1
Chandler's Ford SO53 55 E5
Oakhill Ct SO53 55 E5
Oakhill Terr SO31 105 B1
Oakhurst BH23 207 F7
Oakhurst Cl Netley SO31 127 C6
West Moors BH22 138 F2
Oakhurst Com Fst Sch
BH22 138 F2
Oakhurst Dr PO7 135 A8
Oakhurst Gdns PO7 134 B2
Oakhurst La BH22 138 F2
Oakhurst Rd
Southampton SO17 79 A3
West Moors BH22 138 F2
Oakhurst Way SO31 127 C6
Oakland Dr SO40 101 F1
Oakland Wlk BH22 165 F1
Oaklands
14 Chandler's Ford SO53 30 B1
Lymington SO41 197 F2
Oaklands *continued*
Waterlooville PO7 135 A6
Oaklands Ave SO40 100 F8
Oaklands Cl
Fordingbridge SP6 69 E2
Verwood BH31 114 E6
6 Winchester SO22 215 A4
Oaklands Com Sch SO16 77 F5
Oaklands Gdns PO14 129 C1
Oaklands Gr PO8 111 E3
Oaklands Ho 9 PO6 132 F2
Oaklands RC Sch PO7 134 F5
Oaklands Rd Havant PO9 136 A1
Petersfield GU32 40 E4
Oaklands The SO53 55 C3
Oaklands Way
Hythe SO45 125 D2
Southampton SO16 78 F4
Titchfield PO14 129 C1
Oaklea Cl PO7 134 B2
Oakleafe Pl SO53 55 C6
Oakleigh Cres SO40 100 E6
Oakleigh Dr SP5 73 D8
Oakleigh Gdns SO51 53 A7
Oakleigh Way BH23 208 F7
Oakley Cl SO45 150 C4
Oakley Ct 11 SO16 102 B8
Oakley Gdns BH16 201 A7
Oakley Hill BH21 163 D2
Oakley Ho
Portsmouth PO5 216 B1
12 Southampton SO15 102 B8
3 Southampton,Banister's Pk
SO15 102 F7
Oakley La Merley BH21 163 E2
Mottisfont SO51 5 F4
Wimborne Minst BH21 164 A2
Oakley Rd Havant PO9 135 D5
Mottisfont SO51 5 E3
Southampton,Shirley SO16 102 A8
Southampton,Wimpson
SO16 101 F8
Wimborne Minst BH21 163 D2
Oakley Sh Ctr BH21 163 E1
Oakley Straight BH21 163 E1
Oakmead Coll of Tech
BH11 188 F4
Oakmead Gdns BH11 188 F4
Oakmead Rd BH17 201 F7
Oakmeadow Cl PO10 137 A3
Oakmont Dr PO8 111 F2
Oakmount Ave
Chandler's Ford SO53 55 D4
Southampton SO17 79 A1
Totton SO40 100 F8
Oakmount Mans SO17 78 F1
Oakmount Rd SO53 55 E5
Oakridge Rd SO15 101 D8
Oaks Coppice PO8 112 A6
Oaks Dr BH24 139 D3
Oaks Mead BH31 115 A6
Oaks The Bursledon SO31 127 F8
Southampton SO19 103 F5
Verwood BH31 114 E7
Waterlooville PO8 112 A2
Oakshott Dr PO9 136 A5
Oakthorn Cl PO13 180 C6
Oaktree Ct
Milford on S SO41 211 C4
Southampton SO16 78 E3
Oaktree Par BH23 169 B1
Oaktree Pk SO30 80 C4
Oaktree Rd SO18 79 E2
Oakum Ho PO3 183 A6
Oakville Mans 11 SO15 102 F6
Oakwood BH3 204 E7
Oakwood Ave
Havant PO9 135 B3
New Milton BH25 195 C4
Otterbourne SO21 31 C3
Oakwood Cl
Bournemouth BH9 190 B2
Chandler's Ford SO53 30 D1
Otterbourne SO21 31 C4
Romsey SO51 28 C1
Warsash SO31 152 D10
Oakwood Ct
Chandler's Ford SO53 30 D1
New Milton BH25 195 B3
West End SO30 80 E2
Oakwood Ctr The PO9 136 B3
Oakwood Dr SO16 78 C5
Oakwood Ho SO21 31 C4
Oakwood Inf Sch SO16 78 B5
Oakwood Jun Sch SO16 78 B5
Oakwood Lodge SO21 31 C4
Oakwood Rd
Bournemouth BH9 190 B2
Chandler's Ford SO53 55 D8
Christchurch BH23 193 E1
Portsmouth PO2 157 E4
South Hayling PO11 184 F3
Oakwood Way SO31 128 A3
Oasis Mews BH16 201 A7
Oasis The 12 BH13 204 A4
Oates Rd BH9 189 E1
Oatfield Gdns SO40 76 C1
Oatlands SO51 52 F8
Oatlands Cl SO32 81 F1
Oatlands Rd SO32 81 F1
Oban Rd BH3 204 E7
Obelisk Ct SO19 103 D2
Obelisk Rd SO19 103 E2
Ober Rd SO42 145 E2
Oberfield Rd SO42 145 D1

Oberland Ct SO41 197 D4
Oberon Cl PO7 135 A8
Occupation La PO14 153 E7
Ocean Cl PO15 130 D2
Ocean Ct PO11 184 E3
Ocean Hts 4 BH5 205 F3
Ocean Pk PO3 158 B1
Ocean Rd Fareham PO14 154 F5
Southampton SO14 103 A1
Ocean Way SO14 103 B2
Oceana Ho SO15 102 E5
Oceanarium* BH2 204 F2
Ockendon Cl PO5 216 B2
Ocknell Camping Site SO43 97 B6
Ocknell Gr SO45 125 C3
Octavia Gdns SO53 55 F7
Octavia Hill SO22 215 B4
Octavia Rd SO18 79 E4
Octavius Ct 2 PO7 112 B1
Odell Cl PO16 130 F3
Odeon Bldgs 7 PO6 157 F8
Odiham Cl
Chandler's Ford SO53 55 B3
Southampton SO16 77 F4
Officers Quarters The PO12 181 D6
Oglander Rd SO23 215 E8
Ogle Rd SO14 102 F4
OK Mobile Home Pk BH23 208 B8
Okeford Rd BH18 187 C2
Okement Cl SO18 80 B2
Olave Cl PO13 179 E3
Old Agwi Rd SO45 151 C5
Old Auction Ho 13 PO12 181 E5
Old Barn Cl
Christchurch BH23 191 D2
Ringwood BH24 141 C7
Old Barn Cres PO7 86 C2
Old Barn Farm Rd BH21 139 B6
Old Barn Gdns PO8 111 F6
Old Barn Rd BH23 191 D2
Old Bound Rd BH16 201 C6
Old Brewery The 10 BH15 202 C2
Old Brickyard Rd SP6 69 B2
Old Bridge Cl SO31 128 B8
Old Bridge House Rd SO31 128 B8
Old Bridge Rd
Bournemouth BH6 206 D7
Portsmouth PO4 182 E2
Old Canal 3 PO4 183 B4
Old Christchurch La 12 BH1 204 F3
Old Christchurch Rd
Bournemouth BH1 204 F3
Everton SO41 196 D1
Old Coach Mews BH14 203 A4
Old Coastguard Cotts SO41 212 A3
Old Coastguard Rd BH13 214 B4
Old Comm SO31 129 A4
Old Commercial Rd PO1 182 C7
Old Common Gdns SO31 129 A4
Old Copse Rd PO9 136 A3
Old Cottage Cl SO51 50 E3
Old Cracknore Cl SO40 101 F2
Old Cricket Mews SO15 102 F8
Old Farm Cl BH24 117 C2
Old Farm Copse SO51 50 F3
Old Farm Dr SO18 79 F3
Old Farm La
Stubbington PO14 179 C6
Westbourne PO10 137 D3
Old Farm Rd BH15 202 E6
Old Farm Way PO6 158 E7
Old Farm Wlk SO41 197 D3
Old Farmhouse Mews SO41 197 E5
Old Forge Cl SP6 92 F6
Old Forge Ct SO41 197 D2
Old Forge Rd BH21 164 F6
Old Forge The SO32 107 D7
Old Garden Cl SO31 129 C2
Old Gdns SO22 215 D8
Old Generator Ho The BH12 204 A5
Old Gosport Rd PO16 155 B8
Old Granary The SP5 46 F8
Old Ham La BH21 164 D4
Old Highway Mews BH21 163 D4
Old Hillside Rd SO22 215 A8
Old Infirmary Ho 13 PO1 182 A4
Old Ivy La SO30 80 B2
Old Kennels Cl SO22 10 A3
Old Kennels La SO22 10 B3
Old Kiln Rd BH16 201 D6
Old Laundry The SO21 32 A5
Old Lifeboat Ho* BH15 202 C1
Old Litten La GU32 19 D3
Old London Rd PO2 157 F4
Old Lyndhurst Rd SO40 98 F8
Old Magazine Cl SO40 101 F2
Old Maltings The SO41 197 D3
Old Manor Cl BH21 163 D4
Old Manor Farm PO9 135 B1
Old Manor Way PO6 158 B7
Old Market Rd
Corfe Mullen BH21 186 A8
Cosham PO6 157 F8
Old Mill Ho BH24 140 F6
Old Mill La
Denmead PO7,PO8 111 B8
Hambledon PO8 87 D3
Petersfield GU31 41 C5
Old Mill Way SO16 78 A1
Old Milton Gn BH25 194 F1
Old Milton Rd BH25 195 A2
Old Mulberry Cl BH10 189 A1
Old Orch BH15 202 C1
Old Orchards SO41 197 E2
Old Park Rd SO24 15 F8
Old Parsonage Ct SO21 31 C3
Old Pines Cl BH22 165 E4
Old Priory Cl SO31 128 A2
Old Priory Rd BH6 206 F4
Old Rd Gosport PO12 181 C4
Romsey SO51 53 A7
Southampton SO14 103 B2
Wimborne Minst BH21 163 B5
Old Rd The PO6 157 F6
Old Rectory Cl
Corfe Mullen BH21 186 D8
Westbourne PO10 137 B3
Old Rectory Ct SO40 101 B5
Old Rectory Gdns SO21 2 D6
Old Rectory La SO21 32 A6
Old Rectory Rd PO6 158 F8
Old Redbridge Rd SO15 101 C8
Old Reservoir Rd PO6 158 D7
Old River PO7 110 F3
Old Romsey Rd SO40 98 E8
Old Rope Wlk The BH15 201 F1
Old Ropewalk BH15 202 A1
Old Salisbury La SO51 27 B2
Old Salisbury Rd SO51 75 F7
Old Sandpit La BH16 186 A2
Old Sawmill Cl BH31 114 E7
Old School Cl
Ferndown BH22 165 C5
Hardley SO45 150 B6
Netley SO31 127 D7
Poole BH14 203 A4
Old School Dr PO11 185 B2
Old School Gdns SO30 80 E2
Old School Rd GU33 20 F4
Old Shamblehurst La SO30 81 C2
Old Spring La SO32 84 B5
Old St Stubbington PO14 154 B4
Stubbington,Hill Head PO14 179 A7
Old St John's Mews BH9 189 F3
Old Stacks Gdns BH24 141 C6
Old Star Pl 2 PO1 182 A5
Old Station App SO23 215 F5
Old Swanwick La SO31 128 D8
Old Tannery The SP5 47 A8
Old Timbers PO11 184 F3
Old Town Mews 8 BH15 202 C2
Old Turnpike PO16 131 B3
Old Van Diemans Rd PO7 134 C5
Old Vicarage Cl BH10 189 E6
Old Vicarage La SO41 196 C8
Old Vineries The SP6 69 D1
Old Wareham Rd
Corfe Mullen BH16,BH21 186 A3
Poole BH12 203 A7
Old Well Cl The SO19 104 C3
Old Winchester Hill La
Warnford SO32 37 B2
West Meon GU32 37 D2
Old Winchester Hill Nature Reserve* SO32 62 C6
Old Winchester Hill Nature Trail* GU32 62 D6
Old Wymering La PO6 157 E8
Oldbarn Cl SO40 76 C2
Oldbury Ct SO16 77 D2
Oldbury Ho 6 PO5 216 B2
Oldbury Way PO14 154 C8
Oldenburg PO15 129 B8
Oldgate Gdns 1 PO2 157 F4
Oldhouse La SO51 50 E7
Oleander Cl SO31 129 A5
Oleander Dr SO40 100 B8
Olinda St PO1 182 E6
Olive Cres PO16 156 D6
Olive Rd SO16 78 A3
Oliver Rd
Lymington SO41 197 C3
Portsmouth PO4 183 A3
Southampton SO18 79 D3
Oliver's Battery Cres SO22 10 B4
Oliver's Battery Gdns SO22 10 B3
Oliver's Battery Prim Sch SO22 215 A1
Oliver's Battery Rd N SO22 10 B5
Oliver's Battery Rd S SO22 10 B4
Olivers Cl SO40 100 B7
Olivers Ct PO2 182 E8
Olivers Rd BH21 164 A6
Olivers Way BH21 164 A6
Olivia Cl PO7 112 A1
Olympic Way SO50 57 B2
Omdurman Ct 2 SO17 79 A2
Omdurman Rd SO17 79 A2
Omega Ho PO5 216 C3
Omega St PO5 216 C3
Onibury Cl SO18 80 A1
Onibury Rd SO18 80 A1
Onslow Gdns BH21 163 D6
Onslow Ho BH21 163 D6
Onslow Rd
4 Portsmouth PO5 182 D1
Southampton SO14 103 A6
Ophir Gdns 1 BH8 205 C5
Ophir Rd
Bournemouth BH8 205 B5
Portsmouth PO2 157 E3
Oracle Dr PO7 134 E3
Orange Gr PO13 155 D1
Orange Row PO10 160 F8
Oratory Gdns BH13 214 F8
Orchard Ave
Bishopstoke SO50 56 F1
Poole BH14 202 F2
Orchard Bglws PO17 109 A2
Orchard Cl
Christchurch BH23 207 A6
Colden Common SO21 31 F1
Corfe Mullen BH21 186 D7
Edmondsham BH21 91 A4
Fawley SO45 151 B3
Ferndown BH22 165 E5
Fordingbridge SP6 69 F2
Gosport PO12 156 A1
Horndean PO8 112 C6
North Baddesley SO52 53 F5
Ringwood BH24 141 A8
South Hayling PO11 184 F2
Totton SO40 100 F5
Orchard Ct Cadnam SO40 98 F8
Hedge End SO30 105 E7
Verwood BH31 115 A5
Orchard Cvn Pk The SO40 99 D5
Orchard Gdns 1 SP6 69 F1
Orchard Gr
New Milton BH25 195 A1
Portchester PO16 156 B7
Waterlooville PO8 111 F3
Orchard Ho
4 Southampton SO14 103 A3
Winchester SO22 215 C5
Orchard Inf Sch SO45 125 E2
Orchard Jun Sch SO45 125 E3
Orchard La
Corfe Mullen BH21 186 D7
Emsworth PO10 161 A8
Romsey SO51 52 E7
Southampton SO14 103 A3
Orchard Lea Inf Sch PO15 130 E4
Orchard Lea Jun Sch PO15 130 E4
Orchard Leigh 2 BH25 195 B2
Orchard Mead 2 BH24 141 A8
Orchard Mews 2 BH23 207 A6
Orchard Mount 3 BH24 141 A8
Orchard Pl SO14 103 A3
Orchard Rd Fair Oak SO50 57 C2
Gosport PO12 181 D7
Havant PO9 159 F8
Locks Heath SO31 128 F2
Portsmouth PO4 182 E4
Redlynch SP5 47 D6
South Hayling PO11 185 A2
Orchard St BH2 204 E3
Orchard The
Bournemouth BH11 188 D6
Bransgore BH23 193 C8
Chilworth SO16 54 E1
Cosham PO6 157 F7
Denmead PO7 110 F4
Milford on S SO41 211 D4
Southampton SO16 79 B5
Orchard Way SO45 125 F2
Orchard Wlk
15 Bournemouth BH2 204 E3
Winchester SO22 215 B8
Orchardlea SO32 84 C3
Orchards Way
Southampton SO17 79 A2
West End SO30 80 D1
Orcheston Rd BH8 205 C6
Orchid Way BH23 207 C7
Ordnance Ct PO3 158 A5
Ordnance Rd
Gosport PO12 181 D5
Southampton SO15 103 A6
Ordnance Row PO1 182 A5
Ordnance Way SO40 102 A3
Oregon Cl SO19 104 A4
Orestes Gate BH23 208 A5
Orford Cl BH23 191 D4
Orford Ct 4 PO6 157 F7
Oriana Way SO16 77 B4
Oriel Dr PO14 129 B1
Oriel Rd PO2 157 D2
Orient Dr SO22 1 C3
Orion Ave PO12 181 C8
Orion Cl
Southampton SO16 77 F4
Stubbington PO14 179 D7
Orion Ind Ctr SO18 79 E5
Orkney Cl SO16 77 E4
Orkney Rd PO6 133 F1
Ormesby Dr SO53 55 B8
Ormond Cl SO50 57 B2
Ormonde Rd BH13 204 A2
Ormsby Rd PO5 216 B1
Orpen Rd SO19 104 C4
Orpine Cl PO15 129 F3
Orsmond Cl PO7 134 F6
Orwell Cl Gosport PO12 181 C8
Orwell Cl *continued*
Southampton SO16 77 E1
Orwell Cres PO14 129 C2
Orwell Rd GU31 40 E2
Osborn Cres PO13 155 B4
Osborn Ct PO3 158 B4
Osborn Mall 3 PO16 131 C1
Osborn Rd PO16 131 B1
Osborn Rd S PO16 131 B1
Osborn Sq 2 PO16 131 C1
Osborne Cl Netley SO31 127 C5
1 Waterlooville PO7 135 A7
Osborne Ct
7 Milford on S SO41 211 C4
Southampton SO17 79 C1
Osborne Dr SO53 55 E5
Osborne Gdns
Fair Oak SO50 57 E1
Southampton SO17 79 C1
Osborne Ho
Southampton SO14 103 B3
West Wellow SO51 50 E3
Osborne Rd
Bournemouth BH9 204 E8
Gosport PO12 181 D6
Lee-on-t-S PO13 179 E3
New Milton BH25 195 B3
Petersfield GU32 40 F4
Poole BH14 203 B3
Portsmouth PO5 182 C2
Totton SO40 101 A7
Warsash SO31 152 D10
Wimborne Minst BH21 163 D4
Osborne Rd N SO17 79 C1
Osborne Rd S SO17 103 C8
Osborne Sch SO23 215 D7
Osborne View Rd PO14 179 A6
Osbourne Ho 4 BH25 195 A3
Osier Cl PO2 157 C3
Osier Rd GU31 40 D1
Oslands La SO31 128 D7
Oslo Twrs SO19 126 E8
Osprey Cl
Christchurch BH23 208 A5
Farlington PO6 158 E7
Marchwood SO40 101 E1
Southampton SO16 78 B5
Osprey Ct PO16 155 F8
Osprey Dr PO11 185 B3
Osprey Gdns PO13 179 F3
Osprey Quay PO10 161 B7
Ossemsley Manor Ho BH23 194 D6
Ossemsley South Dr BH25 194 F8
Osterley Cl SO30 105 E6
Osterley Ct BH23 207 A8
Osterley Rd SO19 103 E5
Ostlers The SO41 196 A3
Oswald Cl BH9 189 E2
Oswald Rd BH9 189 F2
Othello Dr PO7 135 A8
Otter Cl Bishopstoke SO50 57 A2
3 Gosport PO13 180 D5
Upton BH16 201 B6
Verwood BH31 115 A5
Otter Rd BH15 202 F6
Otterbourne 14 BH2 204 D4
Otterbourne CE Prim Sch SO21 31 B2
Otterbourne Cres PO9 135 D5
Otterbourne Hill SO21 31 B2
Otterbourne Ho SO21 31 B2
Otterbourne House Gdns SO21 31 B2
Otterbourne Rd SO21 31 D6
Otters Wlk BH25 195 C5
Our Lady & St Joseph RC Prim Sch SO41 197 A4
Ouse Cl SO53 55 A8
Outer Circ SO16 78 A4
Outlands La SO30 106 D7
Outram Rd PO5 216 C1
Outwick Cross SP6 69 F8
Oval Gdns PO12 180 F4
Oval Rd SO51 5 A1
Oval The GU33 20 F4
Oven Camping Site The PO11 184 F5
Over Links Dr BH14 203 D2
Overbrook SO45 125 F2
Overbrook Way SO52 53 E5
Overbury Manor BH12 204 B5
Overbury Rd BH14 203 C3
Overcliff Rise SO16 78 E4
Overcliffe Mans BH1 205 C3
Overcombe Cl BH17 187 E2
Overdell Ct 8 SO15 102 E7
Overstand Cres SO41 211 D3
Overton Cres PO9 135 D5
Overton Rd PO10 137 E1
Oviat Cl SO40 100 B7
Ovington Ave BH7 206 C7
Ovington Ct SO18 104 D8
Ovington Gdns BH7 206 C7
Ovington Rd SO50 56 A1
Owen Cl PO13 180 C7
Owen Rd SO50 55 F2
Owen St PO4 183 A2
Owen's Rd SO22 215 D7
Ower La SO45 178 E8
Owls Rd
Bournemouth BH5 205 E3
Verwood BH31 115 A5
Owlshotts BH13 214 F7
Owslebury Bottom SO21 33 A5
Owslebury Gr PO9 135 F5
Owslebury Prim Sch SO21 33 A4
Oxburgh Cl SO50 55 F5
Oxendown SO32 61 C4
Oxenwood Gn PO9 135 D6
Oxey Cl BH25 195 A1
Oxford Ave
Bournemouth BH6 206 B5
Southampton SO14 103 B6
Oxford Cl PO16 131 A2
Oxford La
Bournemouth BH11 189 B6
Swanmore SO32 84 F7
Oxford Rd
Bournemouth BH8 205 B4
Gosport PO12 180 F5
Portsmouth PO5 216 D1
Southampton SO14 103 A7
Oxford St SO14 103 A3
Oxford Terr SO41 172 C2
Oxlease Cl SO51 28 A1
Oxleys Cl PO14 154 B8
Oxted Ct 5 PO4 183 B5
Oyster Ct PO13 179 D4
Oyster Est The PO6 158 C6
Oyster Mews
5 Emsworth PO10 160 F8
7 Portsmouth PO1 182 A3
Oyster Quay PO6 157 B7
Oyster St PO1 182 A3
Ozier Rd SO18 80 A2

P

Pacific Cl SO14 103 C2
Packridge La SO51,SO52 53 F1
Padbury Cl PO2 157 F4
Paddington Cl BH11 188 D4
Paddington Gr BH11 188 D3
Paddington Rd PO2 157 F1
Paddock Cl
Ferndown BH21 165 A5
Poole BH12 203 B7
St Leonards BH24 139 F4
Paddock End PO7 110 F3
Paddock Gdns SO41 197 D5
Paddock Gr BH31 115 A5
Paddock The
Brockenhurst SO42 145 F1
Eastleigh SO50 56 B6
Fordingbridge SP6 94 E6
Gosport PO12 181 A4
Kings Worthy SO23 2 C5
Stubbington PO14 154 C4
Totton SO40 76 C2
West Moors BH24 166 C8
Paddock Way GU32 40 D2
Paddock Wlk PO6 157 A8
Paddocks The
Bournemouth BH10 189 D4
Fawley SO45 151 B3
Padfield Cl BH6 206 E6
Padget Rd BH24 117 C1
Padnell Ave PO8 112 A2
Padnell Inf Sch PO8 112 A3
Padnell Jun Sch PO8 112 B3
Padnell Pl PO8 112 B2
Padnell Rd PO8 112 B3
Padstow Pl SP6 93 E8
Padwell Rd SO14 103 A7
Padwick Ave PO6 158 A8
Padwick Ct PO11 184 E3
Paffard Cl PO13 180 C7
Page Cl SO45 150 D2
Pages La SO42 175 C6
Paget Cl BH21 164 A7
Paget Rd
Bournemouth BH11 189 A4
Gosport PO12 181 A3
Paget St SO14 103 B4
Pagham Cl PO10 161 A8
Pagham Gdns PO11 185 F2
Paignton Ave PO3 183 A8
Paignton Rd SO16 77 F1
Paimpol Pl SO51 52 E6
Pain's Rd PO5 216 C2
Painswick Cl
Cosham PO6 157 C8
Sarisbury SO31 128 F6
Painter Cl PO3 158 B3
Painters Field SO23 215 C2
Paisley Rd BH6 206 C5
Palace Ho* SO42 148 F2
Palace La SO42 148 F1
Palace Mews SO32 83 C7
Palfrey Rd BH10 189 D5
Paling Bsns Pk SO30 105 B4
Palk Rd PO9 135 D1
Pallant Gdns PO16 131 D2
Pallant The PO9 135 F1
Pallet Cl SO21 56 F8
Pallot Cl SO31 104 F1
Palm Ct 1 PO5 182 C2
Palm Hall Cl SO23 215 F5
Palm Rd SO16 78 A3
Palma Ct BH23 209 A7
Palmer Pl BH25 195 A4
Palmer Rd BH15 202 C5
Palmer's Rd PO10 136 F1
Palmers Cl SO50 57 D1
Palmerston Ave
Christchurch BH23 207 D6
Fareham PO16 131 B1
Palmerston Bsns Pk PO14 155 B7
Palmerston Cl BH16 201 D7

Palmerston Ct
28 Portsmouth PO5 ....182 C2
4 Winchester SO23 ....215 D3
Palmerston Dr PO14 .....155 A7
Palmerston Mans 3
PO5 ....182 C2
Palmerston Rd
Bournemouth BH1 ....205 A6
Poole BH14 ....203 D4
Portsmouth POE ....100 DE
South Hayling SO31 .....185 A4
Southampton SO14 ......103 A4
Upton BH16 ....201 C7
Palmerston Road Prec 4
PO5 ....182 C2
Palmerston St SO51 ......52 F7
Palmerston Way PO12 ...180 F2
Palmyra Rd PO14 ....181 A8
Palomino Dr PO15 ....130 E2
Pamela Ave PO6 ....132 F1
Pamphill CE Fst Sch
BH21 ....162 E5
Pamplyn Cl SO41 ....197 C4
Pan St PO1 ....216 B4
Pangbourne Ave PO6 ....181 A8
Pangbourne Cl SO19 ....104 A4
Pannall Rd PO12 ....181 A8
Panorama Ct PO13 ......179 E3
Panorama Rd BH13 ......214 B3
Pans Cnr BH22 ....165 F3
Pansy Rd SO16 ....79 A4
Pantheon Rd SO53 ....55 F7
Pantiles The SP6 ....69 D1
Panton Cl PO41 ....136 E3
Panwell Rd SO18 ....104 A7
Parade Ct PO2 ....157 E5
Parade The
4 Bournemouth BH6 .....206 E3
Cadnam SO40 ....98 F8
New Milton BH25 ....195 D3
Old Milton BH25 ....194 F1
Poole BH17 ....187 B1
Portsmouth PO1 ....182 A6
Paradise La Bartley SO40 ..99 D6
Bishop's Waltham SO32 ...83 F6
Fareham PO16 ....131 E2
Westbourne PO10 ....137 B4
Paradise St
14 Poole BH15 ....202 B1
Portsmouth PO1 ....216 B4
Parchment St SO23 .....215 E6
Parchment The PO9 .....135 F1
Pardoc Cl SO30 ....105 C5
Pardys Hill PO31 ....186 D8
Parham Cl BH25 ....194 E3
Parham Dr SO50 ....55 F4
Parham Rd
Bournemouth BH10 ......189 C2
Gosport PO12 ....181 C7
Parish Ct SO41 ....197 E4
Parish Rd BH15 ....202 E3
Park App PO17 ....130 E7
Park Ave
Bournemouth BH10 ......189 C6
Lymington SO41 ....197 D4
Waterlooville PO7 ......134 C3
Winchester SO23 ....215 E6
Park Cl
Brockenhurst SO42 .....146 A2
Burton BH23 ....192 C3
Gosport PO12 ....180 F6
Hythe SO45 ....126 B4
Lyndhurst SO43 ....122 A3
Marchwood SO40 ....101 D1
Milford on S SO41 ......211 E4
New Milton BH25 ....195 C5
Winchester SO23 ....215 E8
Park Com Sch PO9 ......135 C5
Park Cotts PO17 ....108 A3
Park Court Flats 7
SO15 ....102 C6
Park Ct
14 Milford on S SO41 ....211 C4
1 Petersfield GU32 ......40 F3
12 Poole BH13 ....204 B3
Portsmouth PO5 ....216 B1
Romsey SO51 ....53 D5
1 Winchester SO23 .....215 E8
Park Dr BH31 ....114 E7
Park Farm Ave PO15 ....130 D3
Park Farm Cl PO15 .....130 D3
Park Farm Rd PO7 ......134 D4
Park Gate BH25 ....195 A2
Park Gate Bsns Ctr
SO31 ....129 B6
Park Gate Mews 7 BH21 ..204 E3
Park Gate Prim Sch
SO31 ....129 B4
Park Gdns BH25 ....207 E7
Park Glen SO31 ....129 C4
Park Gr PO6 ....157 F7
Park Heritage Ctr The*
SO31 ....127 C4
Park Ho SO41 ....150 C3
Park Ho
9 Portsmouth PO5 ......182 C2
Winchester SO23 ....215 E6
Park Homer Dr BH21 ...164 A6
Park Homer Rd BH21 ...163 F6
Park La Alderholt SP6 ...92 F6
Bournemouth BH10 .....189 F4
Cosham PO6 ....158 A7
Droxford SO32 ....61 B1
Fareham PO16 ....131 A2
Havant,Bedhampton PO9 .135 C3

Park La *continued*
Holbury SO45 ....150 B4
Kings Worthy SO21 ......2 D6
Marchwood SO40 ....101 C1
Milford on S SO41 ......211 D4
Otterbourne SO21 ....56 B8
Rowland's Castle PO10 ..137 C8
1 Southampton SO15 ...102 F5
Stubbington PO14 ......179 C8
Swanmore SO32 ....60 A3
Swanmore SO32 ....84 B8
Twyford SO21 ....32 A5
Waterlooville PO8 ......112 A2
West Dean SP5 ....3 B8
Wimborne Minst BH21 ..163 C4
Park Lake Rd BH15 .....202 E2
Park Mans 2 PO6 ....158 A7
Park Par PO9 ....135 F4
Park Pl PH14 ....202 F4
Park Rd
Bishop's Waltham SO32 ..83 A8
Bournemouth BH8 ......205 A5
Breach PO10 ....137 D1
Chandler's Ford SO53 ...55 C7
Denmead PO7 ....110 F5
Eastleigh SP6 ....69 F2
Gosport PO12 ....181 B4
Lymington SO41 ....197 D4
Milford on S SO41 ......211 E4
Netley SO31 ....195 C5
Old Milton BH25 ....194 F1
2 Petersfield GU32 .....40 F3
Poole BH15,BH14 ....202 B5
Portsmouth PO1 ....182 B5
South Hayling PO11 ....184 C4
Southampton SO15 .....102 D6
Waterlooville PO8 ......112 A2
Winchester SO22,SO23 ..215 D8
Park Rd N PO9 ....135 F2
Park Rd S PO9 ....135 F1
Park Royal 2 PO2 ......157 E3
Park St Gosport PO12 ..181 B6
Portsmouth PO5 ....216 A2
Southampton SO15,SO16 ..102 B8
Park Terrs 11 PO12 ....181 C5
Park The
Barton on S BH25 .....209 C7
Droxford SO32 ....61 A1
Wimborne Minst BH21 ..164 A1
Park View Botley SO30 ..106 A7
Compton SO21 ....31 E6
Durrants PO9 ....136 B8
Hedge End SO30 ....105 B7
Lockerley SO51 ....4 E3
New Milton BH25 ......195 A2
Otterbourne SO21 ......31 A1
7 Poole BH15 ....202 E3
Portsmouth PO2 ....157 D8
Winchester SO23 ......215 A8
Park View Ct BH8 .....205 C7
Park View Mews BH25 ..195 A2
Park Villas SO32 ....61 B1
Park Vista GU32 ....38 D1
Park Way Fair Oak SO50 ..57 F2
Havant PO9 ....135 E2
New Milton BH22 ....138 E2
Park Wlk Fareham PO15 ..130 D3
Southampton SO14 .....103 A5
Parker Cl PO12 ....156 A1
Parker Gdns PO7 ....134 C2
Parker Rd BH9 ....204 F7
Parkers Cl BH24 ....117 C1
Parkfield Ho 11 PO6 ...132 F2
Parkhouse Farm Way
PO9 ....135 C5
Parkland Cl BH31 ......115 D4
Parkland Dr BH25 ......209 F8
Parkland Pl
New Milton BH25 ......195 A2
18 Southampton SO17 ..103 A8
Parklands
Locks Heath SO31 ......129 A4
Southampton SO18 .....79 E1
Totton SO40 ....101 A8
11 Bournemouth BH4 ...204 C3
Parklands Ave PO8 .....112 A5
Parklands Bsns Pk PO7 ..110 F3
Parklands Cl
Chandler's Ford SO53 ...55 C8
Gosport PO12 ....181 B7
Parkside
Christchurch BH23 .....193 D1
Havant PO9 ....135 C2
4 Highfield SO17 ....79 A2
Ringwood BH24 ....141 A6
Totton SO40 ....100 F5
Parkside Ave SO16 .....101 D8
Parkside Gdns
Bournemouth BH10 .....189 E2
Winchester SO22 ......215 A8
Parkside Rd BH14 ......203 C4
Parkside The SO16 .....102 A8
Parkstone Ave
Poole BH14 ....203 D4
Parkstone Gram Sch
BH17 ....187 B1
Parkstone Hts
Poole BH14 ....202 F5
Poole BH14 ....203 A5
Parkstone Rd BH15 .....202 E3
Parkstone Sta BH14 ....203 A4
Parkstone Rd BH2 .....204 E4
Parkville Rd SO18 ......79 D4
Parkwater Rd SP5 ......24 D2
Parkway PO15 ....129 F7
Parkway Dr BH8 ....205 E8
Parkway Gdns SO53 ....55 C7

Parkway S Rdbt PO15 ...129 D7
Parkway The
Gosport PO13 ....155 B2
Southampton SO16 ......79 B5
Parkwood Cl SO30 ......105 C7
Parkwood Ctr PO7 .....134 E8
Parkwood La 7 BH5 ....206 B5
Parkwood Rd
Bournemouth BH5 ......206 A4
Wimborne Minst BH21 ..163 C4
Parley Cl BH22 ....165 F1
Parley Cross BH22 .....189 E8
Parley Fst Sch BH22 ...165 D3
Parley Green La BH23 ..190 B7
Parley La BH23 ....190 D7
Parley Rd BH9 ....190 A2
Parliament Pl SO22 ....215 A2
Parmiter Dr BH21 ......163 E4
Parmiter Ho 5 SO23 ...215 F6
Parmiter Rd BH21 ......163 E4
Parmiter Way BH21 ....163 E4
Parnell Rd SO50 ....55 F2
Parr Ho 1 BH14 ....203 A4
Parr Rd PO6 ....157 D8
Parr St BH14 ....203 A4
Parr Cl PO6 ....156 E8
Parry Rd SO19 ....104 D4
Parsonage Barn La
BH24 ....141 B7
Parsonage Cl
Fordingbridge SP6 ......69 F2
Petersfield GU32 ....41 B5
Parsonage Ct 9 BH8 ...205 A5
Parsonage La SO32 .....82 B5
Parsonage Park Dr SP6 ..69 E2
Parsonage Rd
Bournemouth BH1 ......205 A3
Southampton SO14 .....103 C6
Parsons Cl PO3 ....157 F5
Partridge Cl
Christchurch BH23 .....208 A5
Fareham PO16 ....155 E8
Partridge Down SO22 ...10 B3
Partridge Dr BH14 .....203 C1
Partridge Gdns PO8 ...111 D4
Partridge Gn BH25 ....195 B6
Partridge Hill SP5 ......50 A3
Partridge Rd
Brockenhurst SO42 ....172 F8
Dibden Purlieu SO45 ...125 F1
Partridge Wlk BH14 ...203 B1
Partry Cl SO31 ....55 A8
Pascoe Cl BH14 ....203 A4
Passage La SO31 ......128 B1
Passfield Ave SO50 ....55 E2
Passfield Cl SO50 ......55 E2
Passfield Wlk 2 PO9 ..136 B5
Passingham Wlk PO8 ..112 A4
Paston Ho 8 PO17 .....130 E7
Pastures The
Cheriton SO24 ....14 C6
Denmead PO7 ....110 E3
6 Eastleigh SO50 ......56 A2
Locks Heath PO14 .....129 C4
Pat Bear Cl SO15 ......101 C8
Patchins Rd BH16 .....201 B4
Patchins The BH14 ....214 C8
Patchway Dr PO14 .....154 D8
Paternoster Ho 4 SO23 ..215 F5
Paternoster Row 5
SO23 ....215 E5
Patricia Cl SO30 ....80 D2
Patricia Dr SO30 ....105 D7
Patrick Howard-Dobson Ct
8 PO6 ....11 F4
Patrick's Cl GU33 ......21 A4
Patrick's Copse Rd GU33 ..21 A4
Patterdale Ho 6 PO6 ...133 B1
Paulet Cl SO18 ....80 A1
Paulet Lacave Ave SO16 ..77 F6
Paulet Pl SO22 ....215 C3
Pauletts La SO40 ......76 B3
Pauls La SO41 ....196 E8
Paulsgrove Ent Ctr PO6 ..158 D7
Paulsgrove Ind Ctr PO6 ..157 B8
Paulsgrove Prim Sch
PO6 ....157 C8
Paulsgrove Rd PO2 ....182 F8
Paultons Cl SO45 ......125 C8
Paultons Pk* SO51 .....75 C6
Pauncefoot Hill SO51 ...52 C5
Pauncefote Rd BH5 ....206 A5
Pauntley Rd BH23 .....207 E5
Pavan Gdns BH10 .....189 C2
Pavilion Cl SO50 ....81 D8
Pavilion Ct SO53 ......55 C8
Pavilion Rd SO30 ......105 C5
Pavilion The 2 BH4 ....204 C2
Paxton Cl SO30 ....105 D5
Paxton Rd PO14 ....155 A8
Payne Cl BH22 ....138 E5
Payne's La SO50 ....57 C3
Payne's Rd SO15 ......102 B6
Paynes Hay Rd SO51 ...28 C8
Peace Cl BH23 ....193 A8
Peach Rd SO16 ....78 A4
Peacock Cl PO16 ......155 E8
Peacock La PO1 ....182 A3
Peacock Pl 4 SO23 ....11 C3
Peak Cl SO16 ....101 F8
Peak Dr PO14 ....154 D8
Peak La Fareham PO14 ..154 D7
Upham SO32 ....59 B4
Peak Rd PO8 ....88 A5
Peak The PO9 ....113 C2
Peake New Rd SO32 ...61 F8

Peaked Post SP5 ....42 A1
Peakfield PO7 ....110 E4
Pealsham Gdns SP6 ....69 E2
Pear Cl BH12 ....204 B4
Pear Tree Cl Alderholt SP6 ..92 F6
Botley SO32 ....81 F2
Bransgore BH23 ....193 B8
Pear Tree Dr SP5 ......73 D8
Pearce Ave SO19 ......104 A4
Pearce Ct PO12 ....181 C6
Pearce Gdns BH14 ....203 A1
Pearce Rd BH10 ......201 B6
Pearce-Smith Cl BH25 ..209 E7
Pearl Gdns BH10 .....189 C4
Pearl Rd BH10 ....189 C4
Pearmain Dr 8 SO41 ..197 E2
Pearman Ct SO41 .....197 C2
Pears Gr PO10 ....161 D4
Pearson Ave BH14 ....203 B5
Pearson Gdns BH10 ...189 D6
Peartree Ave SO19 ...103 E5
Peartree Cl
Southampton SO19 ....103 D8
Stubbington PO14 .....179 D8
West Wellow SO51 .....50 C3
Peartree Ct
6 Lymington SO41 .....197 E2
Southampton SO19 ....103 E4
Peartree Ho Hythe SO45 ..125 E2
Southampton SO19 ....103 D4
Pebble Cl PO11 ....185 B2
Pebble Ct
Marchwood SO40 ......101 F2
South Hayling PO11 ...185 D1
Pebmarsh Rd 5 PO6 ..157 D8
Peckham Ave BH25 ...195 A2
Peckham Cl PO14 .....129 C2
Pedham Cl PO4 ....183 A3
Pedlars Wlk BH24 ....140 F7
Pedula Way SO50 ......56 E5
Peeks Mews BH6 .....206 F5
Peel Cl Poole BH12 ...203 C5
Romsey SO51 ....28 C1
Verwood BH31 ....114 E7
Peel Common Inf Sch
PO13 ....155 B2
Peel Common Jun Sch
PO13 ....155 B2
Peel Pl PO5 ....216 B2
Peel Rd PO12 ....181 B5
Peel St SO14 ....103 C5
Peelers Gate 10 PO6 ..157 F7
Peewit Hill SO31 ......105 A3
Peewit Hill Cl SO31 ...105 B3
Pegasus Ave SO41 ....196 B2
Pegasus Cl
Gosport PO13 ....180 D5
Hamble-le-R SO31 ....127 F2
Southampton SO16 ....77 F4
Pegasus Ct
Bournemouth BH1 .....205 A5
8 New Milton BH25 ...195 A3
Pegasus Lodge BH22 ..165 D5
Peggotty Ho 2 PO1 ...182 D7
Pegham Bsns Ctr PO15 ..130 B6
Pegham Coppice PO15 ..130 B6
Pegham Ind Pk PO15 ..130 B6
Pelham 21 BH14 ....204 A4
Pelham Cl BH23 ....207 D6
Pelham Rd Gosport PO12 ..181 B6
Portsmouth PO5 ....216 B1
Pelham Terr 3 PO10 ...161 A8
Pelican Cl PO15 ....130 D2
Pelican Ct SO21 ....30 B7
Pelican Mead BH24 ...141 C6
Pelican Rd PO14 ......154 F5
Pembers Cl SO50 .....57 D2
Pemberton Rd SO43 ...122 A5
Pembrey Cl SO16 .....78 A5
Pembridge Rd SO45 ..150 F3
Pembroke Cl
Eastleigh SO50 ....55 F5
Portsmouth PO1 ......182 A3
Romsey SO51 ....52 F7
Totton SO40 ....101 A8
Pembroke Cres PO14 ..179 A7
Pembroke Ct
4 Christchurch BH23 ..209 B7
Gosport PO13 ....155 C1
Southampton SO17 ....79 B1
Pembroke Rd
Bournemouth BH4 .....204 B2
Poole BH12 ....203 D7
Portsmouth PO1 ......182 A3
Southampton SO19 ....104 B4
Pembury Rd Havant PO9 ..160 A8
Stubbington PO14 .....179 B8
Pemerton Rd SO22 .....1 D3
Pen Craig 2 BH13 .....204 B3
Penarth Ave PO6 .....158 B8
Penarth Cl SO19 ......104 C5
Pendennis Rd PO6 ....132 F1
Pendle Cl SO16 ....101 F8
Pendle Gn SO51 ....4 F1
Pendleton Gdns SO45 ..150 E3
Penelope Cl 12 BH23 ..209 B7
Penelope Gdns SO31 ..104 F2
Penfords Paddock SO32 ..83 D7
Pengelly Ave BH10 ...189 E5
Penhale Gdns PO14 ...179 B8
Penhale Inf Sch PO1 ..182 E5
Penhale Rd PO1 ......182 E5
Penhale Way SO40 ...100 E5
Penhurst Rd PO9 .....135 B2
Peninsula Rd SO22 ...215 A4
Peninsula Sq SO23 ...215 D6
Penistone Cl SO19 ...104 B1
Penjar Ave PO7 ....134 C4

Penk Ridge PO9 ....158 F8
Penn Cl BH25 ....194 E1
Penn Ct BH22 ....138 D3
Penn Hill Ave BH14 ...203 D3
Penn Way PO12 ....180 E3
Pennant Hills PO7 ....110 DE
Pennant Pk PO15 .....131 C3
Pennant Way SO53 ...207 F7
Pennard Way SO53 ...55 E4
Penner Rd PO9 ....159 E7
Pennerly Ct PO9 .....135 D7
Pennine Cl 8 BH23 ...207 F8
Pennine Gdns SO45 ..125 D2
Pennine Ho SO16 .....101 F7
Pennine Rd BH12 .....204 A6
Pennine Way
Chandler's Ford SO53 ..55 D4
Lee-on-t-S PO13 ......180 A4
Verwood BH31 ....114 F5
Pennine Wlk PO14 ....154 E7
Pennings Dro SP5 .....23 E8
Pennington CE Jun Sch
.......................197 C3
Pennington Cl
Colden Common SO21 ..56 F8
Lymington SO41 ......197 C5
West Moors BH22 .....23 D1
Pennington Cres BH22 ..138 C2
Pennington Cross SO41 ..197 B2
Pennington Ho 6 BH4 ..204 C2
Pennington Inf Sch
SO41 ....197 C3
Pennington Oval SO41 ..197 B2
Pennington Rd BH22 ..138 C2
Pennington Way PO15 ..130 D3
Penns Pl GU31 ....40 E4
Penns Rd GU32 ....40 E4
Penny Ct
1 Gosport PO12 ....181 C6
8 Petersfield GU31 ....40 F3
Penny Hedge BH5 ....210 B8
Penny La PO10 ....161 B8
Penny Pl PO7 ....134 E3
Penny St PO1 ....182 A3
Penny Way BH23 .....208 C6
Penny's Cl SP6 ....69 F3
Penny's Cnr SO41 ....195 F4
Penny's Cres SP6 .....69 F3
Penny's Ct BH22 .....165 D5
Penny's Wlk BH24 ....140 E8
Pennycress SO31 .....128 E2
Pennys La SP6 ....69 F3
Pennywell Gdns BH25 ..195 D4
Penrhyn Ave PO6 .....158 B8
Penrhyn Cl SO50 ....55 F5
Penrith Cl BH31 ......114 E5
Penrith Ct SO16 ......101 E7
Penrose Cl 2 PO2 ....157 D2
Penrose Rd BH22 .....165 D6
Penshurst Way SO50 ..56 A4
Pentagon The SO45 ..115 A2
Pentere Cl PO10 .....112 A6
Pentire Ave SO15 .....78 D2
Pentire Way SO15 ....78 D2
Pentland Cl SO45 ....125 D2
Pentland Rise PO16 ..132 D1
Penton Cr PO9 ....136 B6
Penton Pl 8 SO23 ....215 F4
Penton Rd SO21 ......32 A7
Pentons Hill SP6 ......94 D6
Pentridge Way SO40 ..100 B8
Penwood Gn 15 PO9 ..136 B5
Peper Harow SO22 ...112 B6
Peppard Cl SO18 .....104 A7
Pepper Cl PO11 ......185 A5
Peppercorn Cl BH23 ..81 B3
Peppercorn Way SO30 ..81 B3
Pepys Ave SO19 ......104 D5
Pepys Cl Gosport PO12 ..181 B2
Portsmouth PO4 .....182 F2
Percival Rd PO2 ......182 F2
Percivale Rd SO53 ....54 F4
Percy Chandler St PO1 ..216 C4
Percy Cl SO45 ....125 F5
Percy Rd
Bournemouth BH5 ....205 F4
Gosport PO12 ....181 C5
Portsmouth PO4 ......182 F3
Southampton SO16 ...102 A8
Peregrine Cl SO40 ....100 C6
Peregrine Rd BH23 ...208 A5
Peregrines The PO16 ..155 F8
Pergin Cres BH17 ....187 F2
Pergin Way BH17 ....187 F2
Perkins Ho 8 PO1 ....182 E5
Pern Dr SO30 ....106 A7
Peronne Cl PO3 ......157 F5
Peronne Rd PO3 .....157 F5
Perran Rd SO16 ......77 D1
Perry Gdns SO51 .....202 C1
Perryfield Gdns BH7 ..206 B8
Perrywood Cl SO45 ...150 C3
Perrywood Gdns SO40 ..100 B8
Perseus Pl PO7 ....134 A1
Perseus Terr 15 PO1 ..182 A4
Pershore Cl SO31 ....129 B3
Persian Dr PO15 .....129 D2
Persley Rd BH10 .....189 F5
Perth Cl BH23 ....193 E1
Perth Ho PO1 ....216 C3
Perth Rd Gosport PO13 ..180 A4
Portsmouth PO4 .....183 A4
Pervin Rd PO6 ....157 F8
Pest Hos GU32 ....16 C1

Peststead La SO32 ... 85 C4
Peter Ashley Activity Ctr PO6 ... 134 D1
Peter Ashley Rd PO6 ... 134 D1
Peter Grant Way BH22 ... 165 C5
Peter Symonds Coll SO22 ... 215 D7
Peterborough Ct 12 PO13 ... 180 D5
Peterborough Rd
Portsmouth PO6 ... 133 E1
Southampton SO14 ... 103 A7
Peters Cl Sarisbury SO31 ... 128 E3
Upton BH16 ... 201 C6
Peters Rd
Ferndown BH22 ... 165 F3
Locks Heath SO31 ... 128 F3
Peterscroft Ave SO40 ... 100 B2
Petersfield Bsns Pk GU32 ... 40 D3
Petersfield Ho PO1 ... 216 C4
Petersfield Hospl GU32 ... 40 E3
Petersfield Inf Sch GU32 ... 40 F3
Petersfield La PO8 ... 88 C6
Petersfield Mus* GU32 ... 40 F3
Petersfield Pl BH7 ... 206 B7
Petersfield Rd
Bournemouth BH7 ... 206 B7
Bramdean SO24 ... 15 B5
Buriton GU31 ... 65 D6
Cheriton SO24 ... 14 D4
Chilcomb SO21 ... 11 D7
Clanfield PO8 ... 88 D7
Havant PO9 ... 136 A6
Winchester SO23 ... 11 C7
Petersfield Sch The GU32 ... 40 E2
Petersfield Sta GU32 ... 40 E4
Petersgate Inf Sch PO8 ... 88 C4
Petersham Cl PO7 ... 111 D1
Petersham Ho 5 PO5 ... 182 D1
Petersham Rd BH17 ... 202 A8
Petit Rd BH9 ... 190 A3
Petrel Wlk PO13 ... 155 B2
Petrie Rd PO13 ... 179 F3
Petticoat La SP5 ... 47 E7
Pettinger Gdns SO17 ... 103 D8
Petty Cl SO51 ... 53 A6
Pettycot Cres PO13 ... 155 B3
Petworth Gdns
Eastleigh SO50 ... 56 A5
Southampton SO16 ... 78 B5
Petworth Rd PO3 ... 183 B6
Petwyn Cl BH22 ... 166 A6
Pevensey Cl SO16 ... 77 D1
Peverell Rd BH16 ... 201 B4
Peverells Rd SO53 ... 55 E7
Peverells Wood Ave SO53 ... 55 E7
Peverells Wood Cl SO53 ... 55 F6
Peveril Cl BH24 ... 139 F6
Peveril Rd SO19 ... 103 E4
Pewsey Pl SO15 ... 78 D2
Phelipps Rd BH21 ... 186 E6
Pheonix Way PO13 ... 155 C1
Philip Green Meml Sch BH21 ... 67 B2
Philip Rd PO7 ... 134 F5
Phillimore Rd SO16 ... 79 D4
Phillips Cl SO16 ... 77 E6
Philpott Dr SO40 ... 101 F1
Phoenix Bldgs PO3 ... 158 A2
Phoenix Cl SO31 ... 105 A2
Phoenix Ctr The SO40 ... 76 D2
Phoenix Pk SO50 ... 56 C2
Phoenix Sq PO2 ... 157 E4
Phyldon Cl BH12 ... 203 B5
Phyldon Rd BH12 ... 203 B6
Pickard Rd BH22 ... 165 F7
Pickering Cl BH18 ... 187 A2
Picket Cl SP6 ... 69 F2
Pickford Rd BH9 ... 189 E1
Pickwick Cl SO40 ... 100 B7
Pickwick Ho 12 PO1 ... 182 D7
Picton Ho
10 Portsmouth PO5 ... 216 B2
Waterlooville PO7 ... 111 C1
Pier Head Rd PO2 ... 157 B1
Pier Rd PO1 ... 182 B3
Pier St PO13 ... 179 E3
Pig Shoot La BH23 ... 190 F5
Pigeon House La PO7 ... 133 D4
Pikes Hill SO43 ... 121 F6
Pikes Hill Ave SO43 ... 121 E6
Pilbrow Ct 8 PO12 ... 180 F4
Pilchards Ave SO50 ... 57 B3
Pilford Heath Rd BH21 ... 164 B7
Pilgrim Park Homes BH24 ... 141 C8
Pilgrim Pl
Lymington SO41 ... 197 E3
Southampton SO18 ... 79 E4
Pilgrim's Cl BH25 ... 195 C3
Pilgrims Cl SO53 ... 55 A4
Pilgrims Gate
Bishop's Waltham SO32 ... 83 B8
Winchester SO22 ... 215 C7
Pilgrims Sch The SO23 ... 215 E5
Pilgrims Way
Poole BH17 ... 202 A7
Stubbington PO14 ... 179 B6
Pill Hill SP5 ... 24 A4
Pilley Bailey SO41 ... 174 A2
Pilley Gn SO41 ... 174 A1
Pilley Hill SO41 ... 173 E1
Pilley St SO41 ... 174 A1
Pilning Cl PO14 ... 154 C8
Pilot Hight Rd BH11 ... 189 A4
Pilsdon Dr BH17 ... 187 E3
Pimpern Cl BH17 ... 187 F2
Pimpernel Cl SO31 ... 128 E2
Pine Ave
Bournemouth BH6 ... 206 C4
Poole BH12 ... 203 F6
Pine Cl Ashurst SO40 ... 100 C3
Barton on S BH25 ... 209 E8
Ferndown BH22 ... 165 C7
Hythe SO45 ... 125 F2
Landford SP5 ... 49 D2
North Baddesley SO52 ... 53 F5
Winchester SO22 ... 10 B3
Pine Cotts GU33 ... 21 A7
Pine Cres
Chandler's Ford SO53 ... 30 C1
Christchurch BH23 ... 208 E8
Pine Ct PO10 ... 136 F4
Pine Dr Clanfield PO8 ... 88 C5
Poole BH13 ... 203 F3
Southampton SO18 ... 104 D7
St Leonards BH24 ... 139 F4
Pine Dr E SO18 ... 104 E7
Pine End BH22 ... 165 F3
Pine Glen Ave BH22 ... 165 C8
Pine Gr PO9 ... 136 A1
Pine Grange 4 BH1 ... 205 A3
Pine Ho New Milton BH25 ... 195 A3
Southampton SO16 ... 78 F7
Pine Lodge 10 BH13 ... 214 F7
Pine Manor Rd BH24 ... 139 D5
Pine Mans 3 BH1 ... 205 D4
Pine Park Mans 16 BH13 ... 204 A4
Pine Rd Alderholt SP6 ... 92 F5
Bishop's Waltham SO32 ... 83 D8
Bournemouth BH9 ... 205 A8
Chandler's Ford SO53 ... 55 C8
East End BH21 ... 162 F1
Romsey SO51 ... 53 C6
Pine Top Cvn Site BH25 ... 171 F5
Pine Tree Cl BH21 ... 163 D5
Pine Tree Gdns PO8 ... 112 A2
Pine Tree Glen BH4 ... 204 C3
Pine Trees Cl PO14 ... 154 D8
Pine Vale Cres BH10 ... 189 F3
Pine View Cl
Redlynch SP5 ... 47 D4
Upton BH16 ... 201 C6
Verwood BH31 ... 114 D7
Pine View Rd BH31 ... 114 D7
Pine Way SO16 ... 78 F7
Pine Wlk Chilworth SO16 ... 78 F7
Liss GU33 ... 21 A6
Locks Heath SO31 ... 129 A5
Verwood BH31 ... 115 B5
West Moors BH22 ... 138 E3
Pinebeach Ct BH13 ... 214 G8
Pinecliff Rd BH13 ... 214 G8
Pinecliffe Ave BH6 ... 206 C4
Pinecliffe Rd BH25 ... 209 C7
Pinefield Rd SO18 ... 79 F2
Pinegrove Rd SO19 ... 103 F4
Pineholt Cl BH24 ... 140 A5
Pinehurst
10 Milford on S SO41 ... 211 C4
6 Southampton SO17 ... 79 A1
Pinehurst Ave BH23 ... 207 F5
Pinehurst Cl PO7 ... 112 C2
Pinehurst Pk BH22 ... 165 F8
Pinehurst Rd
Southampton SO16 ... 78 F7
West Moors BH22 ... 138 F1
Pinelands Ct SO16 ... 78 C4
Pinelands Rd SO16 ... 78 F8
Pines The Godshill SP6 ... 70 E2
Poole BH13 ... 204 A2
Portchester PO16 ... 132 A1
Southampton SO16 ... 78 B3
Pineside BH9 ... 205 A8
Pinesprings Dr BH18 ... 186 E2
Pinetops Cl SO41 ... 197 B3
Pinetree Wlk BH17 ... 201 F8
Pineview Cl SO31 ... 105 A1
Pinewood Gosport PO13 ... 155 E1
Southampton SO16 ... 78 F6
Pinewood Ave
Bournemouth BH10 ... 189 D5
Havant PO9 ... 135 B3
Pinewood Cl
Bournemouth BH10 ... 189 D5
Romsey SO51 ... 28 C1
Stubbington PO14 ... 154 D4
Upton BH16 ... 201 A7
Walkford BH23 ... 194 A2
Pinewood Cres SO45 ... 126 B2
Pinewood Ct BH22 ... 138 D2
Pinewood Dr SO45 ... 126 B1
Pinewood Gdns BH22 ... 165 D7
Pinewood Lodge 5 PO16 ... 131 B2
Pinewood Pk SO19 ... 104 F5
Pinewood Rd
Christchurch BH23 ... 193 F1
Ferndown BH22 ... 165 C7
Hordle SO41 ... 195 F3
Poole BH13 ... 204 B1
St Leonards BH24 ... 139 F4
Upton BH16 ... 201 B7
Pink Rd PO2 ... 182 E8
Pinkney La SO43 ... 121 E3
Pinks Hill PO16 ... 131 D2
Pinnacle The 7 BH1 ... 205 A3
Pinsley Dr PO17 ... 133 B5
Pinto Cl PO15 ... 129 C7
Pipers Ash BH24 ... 141 C8
Pipers Cl SO40 ... 100 D6
Pipers Dr BH23 ... 208 A7
Pipers Mead PO8 ... 88 A5
Pipers Wood Ind Est PO7 ... 134 C8
Piping Cl SO21 ... 56 F8
Piping Gn SO21 ... 56 F8
Piping Rd SO21 ... 56 F8
Pipistrelle Wlk 4 PO17 ... 130 E8
Pipit Cl Gosport PO12 ... 181 B8
Waterlooville PO8 ... 112 A6
Pippin Cl
Christchurch BH23 ... 191 E2
8 Lymington SO41 ... 197 E2
Pirelli St SO15 ... 102 F4
Pirelli Way SO50 ... 56 A2
Pirrie Cl SO15 ... 78 D1
Pitcairn Mews 8 PO4 ... 183 B2
Pitchponds Rd SO31 ... 152 C10
Pitcot La SO21 ... 33 B3
Pitcroft La GU31 ... 65 F5
Pitcroft Rd PO2 ... 157 D1
Pitmore Cl SO50 ... 56 B8
Pitmore La
Sway,Bowling Green SO41 ... 196 F7
Sway,Durns Town SO41 ... 172 D1
Pitmore Rd SO50 ... 56 B8
Pitreavie Rd PO6 ... 157 F6
Pitt Hill La PO7 ... 86 F1
Pitt Rd SO15 ... 102 C6
Pitt Rdbt SO22 ... 10 B5
Pitter Cl SO22 ... 1 B5
Pitthouse La BH23 ... 191 D8
Pittmore Rd BH23 ... 192 C2
Pitts Deep La SO41 ... 199 C4
Pitts La SP5 ... 22 C8
Pitts Pl BH25 ... 195 D2
Pitwines Cl BH15 ... 202 D2
Pitymoor La PO17 ... 133 B4
Place Cres PO7 ... 134 F5
Place House Cl PO15 ... 130 C1
Place La SO21 ... 31 E8
Plaitford Gr PO9 ... 135 C5
Plaitford Wlk SO16 ... 77 F1
Plant Cl SO51 ... 51 B2
Plant Park Rd BH24 ... 140 C2
Plantagenet Cres BH11 ... 188 D5
Plantation SO41 ... 211 E8
Plantation Ct
Lymington SO41 ... 197 D4
Poole BH17 ... 187 C1
Plantation Dr
Marchwood SO40 ... 101 E1
Walkford BH23 ... 194 A2
Plantation Rd
Hill Brow GU33 ... 21 B2
Poole BH17 ... 187 C1
West Wellow SO51 ... 74 D8
Plantation The SO32 ... 82 E2
Plassey Cres BH10 ... 189 C5
Platform Rd SO14 ... 103 A2
Platoff Rd SO41 ... 212 E8
Player Ct SP6 ... 69 F3
Players Cres SO40 ... 100 E5
Playfair Rd PO5 ... 216 C2
Playfields Dr BH12 ... 203 E6
Plaza Mews 3 SO51 ... 52 F7
Plaza Par 4 SO51 ... 52 F7
Pleasance Way BH25 ... 194 F3
Pleasant La PO10 ... 161 C1
Pleasant Rd PO4 ... 183 B4
Plecy Cl BH22 ... 165 D2
Plemont Cl BH12 ... 188 E1
Pless Rd SO41 ... 211 B5
Plough La SO32 ... 85 C2
Plough Way SO22 ... 215 B2
Plover Cl
Southampton SO16 ... 78 B5
Stubbington PO14 ... 179 B7
Plover Dr SO41 ... 211 F4
Plover Rd SO40 ... 100 C7
Plover Reach PO4 ... 183 B5
Plovers Down SO22 ... 10 B3
Plovers Rd PO8 ... 112 A6
PLPH Rd SO45 ... 151 B5
Plumer Rd BH17 ... 187 A1
Plumley Wlk PO9 ... 135 D7
Plumpton Gdns PO3 ... 158 B3
Plumpton Gr 4 PO7 ... 112 B1
Pluto Rd SO50 ... 55 F3
Plymouth Dr PO14 ... 179 B8
Plymouth St PO5 ... 216 B2
Pococks La GU33 ... 19 F7
Poets Way SO22 ... 215 B6
Poinsettia Cl PO15 ... 129 E3
Point The BH5 ... 205 E3
Pointout Cl SO16 ... 78 E3
Pointout Rd SO16 ... 78 E3
Pokesdown Com Prim Sch BH5 ... 206 B5
Pokesdown Sta BH7 ... 206 A5
Poles La Hursley SO21 ... 30 D6
Lymington SO41 ... 197 E1
Otterbourne SO21 ... 31 B5
Polesden Cl SO53 ... 55 B8
Police Station La SO32 ... 61 B1
Police Training Ctr SO31 ... 127 D5
Pollards Moor Rd SO40 ... 75 B1
Polygon Ct SO15 ... 102 E5
Polygon Sch The SO15 ... 102 E6
Polygon The SO15 ... 102 F5
Pomona Cl BH22 ... 165 D6
Pompey Ctr PO4 ... 182 F5
Pompey Ctr Trad Pk The PO4 ... 182 F5
Pompey's Cnr BH21 ... 165 A4
Pompey's La BH22 ... 165 B2
Pond Cl Marchwood SO40 ... 101 F2
New Milton BH25 ... 195 A3
Pond Cotts GU32 ... 39 C1
Pond La PO8 ... 88 B6
Pond Piece PO7 ... 110 F3
Pond Rd SO31 ... 128 F6
Pondhead Cl SO45 ... 150 C3
Pondside Flats SO42 ... 148 F1
Pondside La SO32 ... 83 C8
Ponsonby Ho PO5 ... 216 B2
Ponsonby Rd BH14 ... 203 D4
Pony Dr BH16 ... 201 D7
Pook La Fareham PO17 ... 131 C4
Havant PO9 ... 160 A8
Pooksgreen SO40 ... 101 D1
Pool Lane Rdbt BH11 ... 188 E4
Poole Aquarium & Serpentarium* BH15 ... 202 C1
Poole Commerce Ctr BH12 ... 203 F5
Poole Gram Sch BH17 ... 187 D2
Poole High Sch BH15 ... 202 C4
Poole Hill BH2 ... 204 D3
Poole Hospl BH15 ... 202 D3
Poole La BH11 ... 189 B5
Poole Rd
Bournemouth BH4 ... 204 C3
Poole BH13 ... 204 A4
Southampton SO19 ... 103 E4
Upton BH16 ... 201 D7
Wimborne Minst BH21 ... 163 C4
Poole Sta BH15 ... 202 C3
Popes La Totton SO40 ... 100 F7
Upham SO32 ... 58 C4
Popes Rd BH15 ... 202 D6
Popham Ct PO9 ... 135 C6
Poplar Cl
Bransgore BH23 ... 193 C8
Christchurch BH23 ... 209 B8
3 Poole BH15 ... 202 B1
Wimborne Minst BH21 ... 163 D5
Poplar Cres BH24 ... 141 B7
Poplar Dr Fareham PO14 ... 154 E8
Marchwood SO40 ... 101 D1
Poplar Gr PO11 ... 185 A4
Poplar La BH23 ... 193 C8
Poplar Rd
New Milton BH25 ... 195 D4
Southampton SO19 ... 103 F6
Poplar Way
Hedge End SO30 ... 105 D6
North Baddesley SO52 ... 53 F5
Ringwood BH24 ... 141 B7
Poplar Wlk GU31 ... 40 E1
Poplars The SO32 ... 83 E3
Poppy Cl
Christchurch BH23 ... 208 C8
Locks Heath SO31 ... 128 F2
Poppy Rd SO16 ... 79 C5
Poppyfields SO53 ... 55 A6
Porchester Rd SO19 ... 103 E3
Porlock Rd SO16 ... 77 D2
Port La Hursley SO21 ... 30 C8
Winchester SO22 ... 10 A2
Port Royal St PO5 ... 216 C3
Port Way PO6 ... 157 B7
Portadene 1 BH4 ... 204 D2
Portal Rd
Bishopstoke SO50 ... 56 D3
Gosport PO13 ... 155 C3
Southampton SO19 ... 104 B4
Totton SO40 ... 100 D7
Winchester SO23 ... 215 F4
Portarlington Cl BH4 ... 204 D2
Portarlington Ct 44 BH4 ... 204 C3
Portarlington Rd BH4 ... 204 C2
Portchester Bsns Ctr PO16 ... 156 D8
Portchester Castle* PO16 ... 156 F6
Portchester Com Sch PO16 ... 156 D7
Portchester Ct 3 BH8 ... 205 B5
Portchester Ho 5 PO17 ... 130 E8
Portchester Hts PO16 ... 132 D1
Portchester La PO17 ... 132 D4
Portchester Pl BH8 ... 205 B5
Portchester Rd
Bournemouth BH8 ... 205 A5
Portchester PO16 ... 156 A8
Portsmouth PO2 ... 182 E8
Portchester Rise SO50 ... 56 A7
Portchester Sch BH7 ... 206 A7
Portchester Sta PO16 ... 156 D8
Portcreek Cotts PO6 ... 158 B5
Portelet Cl BH12 ... 188 D2
Portelet Ho SO16 ... 77 D3
Portelet Pl SO30 ... 105 C5
Porteous Cres SO53 ... 55 F6
Porter Rd BH17 ... 202 B7
Porter's La SO14 ... 102 F3
Porters La BH21 ... 164 C6
Portersbridge Mews 1 SO51 ... 52 E7
Portersbridge St SO51 ... 52 E7
Portesham Gdns BH9 ... 190 B4
Portesham Way BH17 ... 187 E3
Portfield Cl BH23 ... 207 A7
Portfield Rd
Christchurch BH23 ... 207 A7
Portsmouth PO3 ... 158 B3
Portfield Sch
Christchurch BH23 ... 207 A6
East Parley BH23 ... 189 B8
Portiere Ho BH11 ... 189 A4
Portland Bldgs 5 PO12 ... 181 C5
Portland Dr PO12 ... 180 D3
Portland Ho 7 PO12 ... 181 D5
Portland Pl BH2 ... 204 F4
Portland Rd
Bournemouth BH9 ... 205 A8
Portsmouth PO5 ... 182 C2
Waterlooville PO7 ... 134 E7
Portland Sq 5 GU33 ... 20 F4
Portland St
Portsmouth PO1 ... 182 B5
Southampton SO14 ... 102 F4
Portland Terr
2 Portsmouth PO5 ... 182 C2
Southampton SO14 ... 102 F4
Portland's Cl GU32 ... 41 B5
Portman Cres BH5 ... 206 B4
Portman Rd BH7 ... 205 F5
Portman Terr BH5 ... 206 B4
Portmore Cl BH18 ... 187 C6
Portobello Gr PO16 ... 132 D1
Portsdown Ave PO6 ... 158 C8
Portsdown Hill Rd
Cosham PO6 ... 134 C1
Havant PO9 ... 135 A1
Portchester PO17 ... 132 D2
Portsmouth PO6 ... 133 E1
Portsdown Prim Sch PO6 ... 157 F8
Portsdown Rd PO16 ... 156 E8
Portside Cl SO40 ... 102 A3
Portsmouth & Southsea Sta PO1 ... 216 B3
Portsmouth Cath (CE) PO1 ... 182 A3
Portsmouth City Mus & Art Gallery* PO1 ... 182 B3
Portsmouth Coll PO3 ... 183 C7
Portsmouth Ent Ctr PO3 ... 158 B2
Portsmouth Gram Sch The PO1 ... 182 B3
Portsmouth Harbour Sta PO1 ... 181 F6
Portsmouth High Sch for Girls PO5 ... 216 A1
Portsmouth High Sch for Girls (Juns) PO5 ... 182 C2
Portsmouth Hospl (Bupa) PO9 ... 136 D5
Portsmouth RC Cath* PO1 ... 216 A4
Portsmouth Rd
Bursledon SO31 ... 105 A1
Colden Common SO50 ... 57 C6
Cosham PO6 ... 157 F6
Horndean PO8 ... 112 C6
Lee-on-t-S PO13 ... 180 A4
Southampton SO19 ... 104 C2
Portsview Ave PO16 ... 156 E8
Portsview Gdns PO16 ... 132 D1
Portswood Ave SO17 ... 103 B8
Portswood Ctr SO17 ... 79 B1
Portswood Dr 2 BH10 ... 190 A4
Portswood Pk SO17 ... 103 B8
Portswood Prim Sch SO17 ... 79 C2
Portswood Rd
Havant PO9 ... 135 D6
Portsmouth PO2 ... 157 E5
Southampton SO17 ... 79 C2
Portuguese Fireplace* SO43 ... 120 F4
Portview Rd SO18 ... 79 F1
Portway Cl SO18 ... 104 B7
Posbrooke La PO14 ... 153 E6
Posbrooke Rd PO4 ... 183 B4
Post Office Bldgs BH9 ... 204 F8
Post Office La BH24 ... 140 A5
Post Office Rd
18 Bournemouth BH1 ... 204 F3
Waterlooville PO7 ... 134 C5
Postern Cl PO16 ... 156 D8
Postern Ct 9 SO14 ... 102 F3
Potash Terr PO9 ... 135 E1
Potteries The PO16 ... 131 B3
Potterne Way BH21 ... 115 A4
Potterne Wood Cl BH31 ... 115 C4
Potters Ave PO16 ... 131 A4
Potters Field GU33 ... 21 A4
Potters Heron Cl SO51 ... 29 E3
Potters Heron La SO51 ... 29 E3
Potters Way BH14 ... 203 C2
Pottery Junc BH14 ... 203 E5
Pottery Rd BH14 ... 203 B2
Poulner Cl SO19 ... 104 A1
Poulner Ct PO9 ... 135 C6
Poulner Hill BH24 ... 141 E8
Poulner Inf & Jun Schs BH24 ... 117 C2
Poulner Pk BH24 ... 117 C1
Pound Cl Gosport PO13 ... 180 D8
Poole BH15 ... 202 F5
Ringwood BH24 ... 141 A8
Pound Cotts SO32 ... 61 D5
Pound Ct SO18 ... 104 A7
Pound Gate Dr PO14 ... 129 C1
Pound Hill SO51 ... 50 C5
Pound La Ampfield SO51 ... 29 B2
Ashurst SO40 ... 100 E3
Burley BH24 ... 142 F2
Cadnam SO40 ... 75 C1
1 Christchurch BH23 ... 207 B6
Damerham SP6 ... 68 B5
Meonstoke SO32 ... 61 D5
Plaitford SO51 ... 50 C5
Poole BH15 ... 202 E5
Sherfield English SO51 ... 25 F4
Pound Lea PO11 ... 185 A5

Pound Rd
Bursledon SO31 104 E1
Kings Worthy SO23 2 C8
Lymington SO41 197 B2
Portsmouth PO6 133 B2
Pound St SO18 104 A7
Pound Tree Rd SO14 103 A4
Poundbury Ct SO31 129 A6
Pounds Terr PO1 182 A6
Powell Cres SO40 100 F5
Powell Rd BH14 203 B3
Powell Sq [8] PO1 182 A5
Power Rd PO1 182 E6
Powerscourt Rd
Barton on S BH25 209 E7
Portsmouth PO2 182 E8
Powis Cl BH25 195 B3
Powlett Rd SO41 197 E3
Poyner Cl PO16 131 B2
Poynings Pl PO1 182 A3
Precinct The
Holbury SO45 150 C4
Waterlooville PO7 134 E7
Precosa Rd SO30 105 E6
Prelate Way PO14 129 D2
Premier Ctr The SO51 53 D5
Premier Par SO18 79 F3
Premier Way SO51 53 D5
Preshaw Cl SO16 78 B4
Preshaw Est SO32 35 B3
Presidents Ct [12] PO12 181 C9
Presseys Cnr SP6 93 A7
Preston Cl BH16 201 C7
Preston La BH23 192 D3
Preston Rd Poole BH15 202 C6
Portsmouth PO2 182 F8
Preston Way BH23 208 D8
Prestwood Cl BH25 194 F1
Prestwood Rd SO30 105 C6
Pretoria Rd
Hedge End SO30 105 B5
Portsmouth PO4 182 F3
Prettyjohn Ho [14] PO4 183 B2
Pricketts Hill PO17,SO32 108 A6
Prideaux-Brune Ave
PO13 155 C4
Priest Croft SO45 150 E2
Priest Croft Dr SO45 150 E2
Priest La BH23 192 B7
Priest's House Mus & Gdns*
BH21 163 B4
Priestfields PO14 129 C2
Priestlands SO51 52 E8
Priestlands Cl SO40 100 A6
Priestlands La SO41 197 C3
Priestlands Pl SO41 197 D3
Priestlands Rd SO41 197 C3
Priestlands Sch SO41 197 D2
Priestley Cl SO40 100 D7
Priestley Rd BH10 189 B1
Priestwood Cl SO18 104 D7
Primate Rd PO14 129 D2
Primrose Cl
Chandler's Ford SO53 54 F4
Gosport PO13 155 C5
Hedge End SO30 105 C5
Primrose Ct PO7 135 A6
Primrose Gdns BH17 186 F1
Primrose La Rake GU33 21 D4
Redlynch SP5 47 C6
Primrose Rd SO16 79 A4
Primrose Terr SO32 59 D2
Primrose Way
Christchurch BH23 208 C8
Corfe Mullen BH21 186 E7
Locks Heath SO31 128 F2
Romsey SO51 28 C1
Prince Albert Rd PO4 183 A3
Prince Alfred St PO12 181 B4
Prince George St
Havant PO9 135 F1
Portsmouth PO1 182 A5
Prince Of Wales Ave
SO15 102 A8
Prince Of Wales Cl [4]
PO7 135 A7
Prince Of Wales Rd
Bournemouth BH4 204 C4
[3] Gosport PO12 181 C5
Prince Rd Fareham PO14 154 F6
Rownhams SO16 77 E6
Prince Regent Ct PO5 216 B2
Prince William Ct SO50 56 F2
Prince's Bldgs [21] SO23 215 E6
Prince's Ct
Ferndown BH22 165 D5
[4] Portsmouth PO1 182 D7
Prince's Mead Sch SO21 2 E6
Prince's Pl
New Milton BH25 195 C3
[1] Portsmouth PO1 182 D7
Prince's Rd SO51 52 E8
Prince's St
Portsmouth PO1 182 D7
Southampton SO14 103 C6
Princes Cl
Bishop's Waltham SO32 83 B8
Redlynch SP5 47 E7
Princes Cotts GU32 63 D8
Princes Cres SO43 122 B5
Princes Ct
Lyndhurst SO43 122 B5
[1] Poole BH13 204 A4
[2] Southampton SO14 103 C6
Princes Dr PO7 112 A1
Princes Hill SP5 47 E7
Princes Ho
Portsmouth PO5 216 A1

Princes Ho *continued*
[3] Southampton SO14 103 C6
Princes Pl SO22 215 C3
Princes Rd
Ferndown BH22 165 D5
Petersfield GU32 40 D4
Southampton SO15 102 D6
Princess Anne Hospl
SO16 78 B3
Princess Ave BH23 207 B6
Princess Cl SO30 80 E2
Princess Ct [11] SO23 215 E6
Princess Gdns PO8 112 C7
Princess Rd
Ashurst SO40 100 B2
Bournemouth BH4 204 B4
Poole BH13 204 A4
Pringles Cl BH22 165 E5
Pringles Dr BH22 165 E5
Prinstead Cl [6] SO23 215 F4
Prinsted Cres PO6 158 D7
Prinsted La PO10 161 D7
Prinsted Wlk PO14 154 D8
Printers Row [13] SO23 215 D6
Priors Barton SO23 215 D3
Priors Cl Breach PO10 137 E1
Christchurch BH23 208 C7
Priors Dean Rd SO22 1 D4
Priors Hill La SO31 127 E8
Priors Leaze La PO18 137 F1
Priors Rd BH17 202 A8
Priors Way SO22 10 B3
Priors Wlk [3] BH21 163 B5
Priorsdean Ave PO3 183 A6
Priorsdean Cres PO9 135 D3
Priory Ave SO17 79 D1
Priory CE Prim Sch The
BH23 207 B6
Priory Cl
Bishop's Waltham SO32 83 B8
Southampton SO17 79 D1
Priory Cres PO4 183 A4
Priory Ct
Bishop's Waltham SO32 83 B8
Portchester PO6 156 E8
Portsmouth PO5 216 D2
Priory Gdns
Portchester PO16 156 C7
Waterlooville PO7 111 E1
West Moors BH22 166 A8
[13] Winchester SO23 215 E6
Priory Ho
Christchurch BH23 207 C5
[6] Southampton SO14 103 A5
Priory Ind Pk BH23 208 B7
Priory Quay BH23 207 C5
Priory Rd
Bournemouth BH2 204 E2
Eastleigh SO50 55 F1
Fareham PO15 130 D2
Gosport PO12 181 B9
Gosport PO12 181 C9
Netley SO31 127 B6
[5] Portsmouth PO4 183 A2
Southampton,Portswood
SO17 79 D1
Southampton,St Denys
SO17 103 C8
Southwick PO17 133 A6
West Moors BH22 166 A8
Priory Sch SO32 83 B8
Priory Sch (Sports Coll)
PO4 216 D2
Priory The SO32 83 B7
Priory View Ct [4] BH23 207 B6
Priory View Pl [3] BH9 190 A3
Priory View Rd
Bournemouth BH9 190 A3
Burton BH23 192 C2
Private Rd SO41 197 E5
Privet Rd BH9 204 F8
Privett Ho PO1 182 A6
Privett Pl PO12 180 E4
Privett Rd Fareham PO15 130 C2
Gosport PO12,PO13 180 D3
High Cross GU32 18 E2
Waterlooville PO7 134 D3
Prochurch Rd PO8 112 B4
Proctor Cl SO19 104 D5
Proctor Dr SO52 53 F3
Proctor La PO1 182 F5
Promenade BH23 208 B5
Promenade Ct PO13 179 E3
Promenade The
Emsworth PO10 160 F7
Hythe SO45 126 A5
[5] Portsmouth PO2 157 D1
Prospect La
Durrants PO9 136 B7
Havant PO9 136 B5
Prospect Pl
Chandler's Ford SO53 55 C6
Hythe SO45 126 A5
Prospect Rd PO1 182 C7
Prosperous St [1] BH15 202 C1
Protea Gdns PO14 130 A1
Provene Cl SO32 83 E4
Provene Gdns SO32 83 E4
Providence Ct [2] PO1 182 C7
Providence Hill SO31 105 A2
Providence Pk SO16 78 F5
Provost St SP6 69 F1
Pruetts La GU31 20 F1
Prunus Cl
Ferndown BH22 165 B7
Southampton SO16 78 C5
Prunus Dr BH22 165 B7
Pudbrook Ho SO30 106 A6

Pudbrooke Gdns SO30 105 B8
Pudding La SO23 2 B5
Puddleslosh La SP6 69 D3
Puddletown Cres BH17 187 F2
Puffin Cl SO16 78 B5
Puffin Cres PO14 154 B4
Puffin Gdns PO13 155 B3
Puffin Wlk PO8 111 D4
Pug's Hole SP5 4 B7
Pulens Cres GU31 41 C4
Pulens La GU31 41 B4
Pullman Bsns Pk BH24 141 B6
Pullman Ct BH22 138 D2
Pullman Way BH24 141 B6
Pump La Gosport PO13 155 C1
Waterlooville PO8 112 A5
Pundle Green Est SO40 99 B6
Punsholt La SO24 16 F5
Purbeck Ave BH15 201 E1
Purbeck Cl BH16 201 B7
Purbeck Ct
Bournemouth BH5 206 B3
[3] Christchurch BH23 207 F8
Purbeck Dr
Fareham PO14 154 D8
Verwood BH31 114 F5
Purbeck Gdns BH14 202 F5
Purbeck Hts BH14 203 B5
Purbeck Rd
Barton on S BH25 209 D7
Bournemouth BH2 204 E2
Purbeck Wlk PO14 154 D7
Purbrook Chase Prec
PO7 134 E3
Purbrook Cl SO16 78 C4
Purbrook Gdns PO7 134 C5
Purbrook Heath Rd
PO7 134 B5
Purbrook Ho PO7 134 C5
Purbrook Inf Sch PO7 134 D5
Purbrook Jun Sch PO7 134 D5
Purbrook Park Sch PO7 134 D3
Purbrook Rd PO1 182 E5
Purbrook Way
Havant PO9 135 C4
Waterlooville PO7 134 F4
Purcell Cl PO7 134 E5
Purcell Rd SO19 104 D4
Purchase Rd BH12 204 C7
Purdy Ho BH11 189 A4
Purewell BH23 207 D6
Purewell Cl BH23 207 E6
Purewell Cross BH23 207 E6
Purewell Cross Rd
BH23 207 D7
Purewell Ct [2] BH23 207 E7
Purewell Rdbt BH23 207 E6
Purkess Cl SO53 55 D7
Purkiss Cl SO40 99 C5
Purley Way SO51 50 B3
Purlieu La SP6 70 F3
Purrocks The GU32 40 F5
Purslane Gdns PO15 129 E3
Purvis Gdns SO19 104 B2
Pussex La BH23 191 A7
Putmans La GU31 66 F7
Pycroft Cl
North Hayling PO11 160 C3
Southampton SO19 104 A5
Pye Cl BH21 186 E7
Pye Cnr BH21 163 B4
Pye La Alderholt BH21 91 E6
Wimborne Minst BH21 163 B4
Pye St PO1 216 B4
Pyland's La SO31 105 B3
Pyle Cl PO8 112 A4
Pylehill SO50 57 C3
Pylewell Park Gdns*
SO41 198 E4
Pylewell Rd SO45 126 A4
Pyramid Ctr PO3 158 B3
Pyramids L Ctr The
PO5 182 D1
Pyrford Cl Gosport PO12 180 E3
Waterlooville PO7 111 E2
Pyrford Gdns [3] SO41 197 E2
Pyrford Mews SO41 197 E2
Pytchley Cl PO14 179 A7

Q

Quadra Point PO3 158 B3
Quadrangle The
Eastleigh SO50 56 A4
Romsey SO51 53 D6
Quadrant SP6 93 E8
Quadrant Ctr The BH1 204 F3
Quail Way PO8 112 A6
Quaker Ct BH24 140 F6
Quantock Ct [7] BH23 207 F8
Quantock Rd SO16 101 E8
Quantocks The SO45 125 D2
Quarely Rd PO9 135 C6
Quarr Ho SO41 172 A3
Quarry Chase [4] BH4 204 C3
Quarry Cl BH21 164 B7
Quarry Dr BH21 164 B7
Quarry Rd
Wimborne Minst BH21 164 B7
Winchester SO23 11 C7
Quarterdeck Ave PO2 157 B1
Quarterdeck The PO1 181 E6
Quarterjack Mews [1]
BH21 163 C4
Quartremaine Rd PO3 158 B3
Quavey Rd SP5 47 E6
Quay 2000 SO14 103 C8

Quay Haven SO31 128 D8
Quay Hill SO41 197 F4
Quay Ho SO31 128 B1
Quay La PO12 156 B1
Quay Point
[8] Poole BH15 202 C1
Portsmouth PO6 157 C8
Quay Rd
Christchurch BH23 207 B6
Lymington SO41 197 F4
Quay St Fareham PO16 131 C1
Fareham PO16 155 B8
Lymington SO41 197 F4
Quay The
Hamble-le-R SO31 128 A2
Poole BH15 202 C1
Quayle Dr BH11 188 F6
Quayside SO30 106 A6
Quayside Commerce Ctr
PO16 155 B8
Quayside Rd
Fawley SO45 151 F1
Southampton SO18 103 D7
Quayside Wlk SO40 101 F3
Quebec Gdns SO31 104 F1
Queen Alexandra Hospl
PO6 157 F8
Queen Anne Dr
Oakley BH21 187 E8
Wimborne Minst BH21 164 A1
Queen Anne's Dr PO9 135 C2
Queen Elizabeth Ave
SO41 197 D4
Queen Elizabeth Country
Park Visitor Ctr* PO8 64 F4
Queen Elizabeth Ct
Southampton SO17 79 C3
Wimborne Minst BH21 163 B4
Queen Elizabeth Ctry Pk*
GU31 65 B3
Queen Elizabeth's Sch
BH21 162 F6
Queen Katherine Rd
SO41 197 F3
Queen Mary Ave BH9 189 F2
Queen Mary Rd PO16 156 D7
Queen Rd PO14 154 F6
Queen St Emsworth PO10 161 A8
Lymington SO41 197 D3
Portsmouth PO1 182 A5
Twyford SO21 31 F5
Woodgreen SP6 47 B2
Queen's Ave BH23 207 B5
Queen's Cl SO51 53 A7
Queen's Cres PO5 216 B1
Queen's Ct SO15 102 E5
Queen's Gr PO5 216 B1
Queen's Inclosure Prim Sch
PO7 112 A1
Queen's Par
Lyndhurst SO43 121 F5
[1] Waterlooville PO7 134 E7
Queen's Park Ave BH8 205 D8
Queen's Park Gdns BH8 205 D7
Queen's Park Inf Sch
BH8 190 C1
Queen's Park Jun Sch
BH8 190 B1
Queen's Park Rd BH8 205 D7
Queen's Park South Dr
BH8 205 D7
Queen's Park West Dr
BH8 205 D7
Queen's Pl PO5 216 B1
Queen's Rd
Bournemouth BH3 204 D4
Chandler's Ford SO53 30 D1
Christchurch BH23 207 E6
Corfe Mullen BH21 186 D5
Fareham PO16 131 B1
Gosport PO12 181 C5
Poole BH14 203 D4
Portsmouth PO1 181 F7
Portsmouth,Buckland PO2 182 E8
Southampton SO15 78 C2
Warsash SO31 152 C10
Waterlooville PO7 111 F1
Winchester SO22 215 B5
Queen's Terr PO5 216 B1
Queen's Terr SO14 103 A3
Queen's Way PO5 216 B1
Queens Cl Hythe SO45 126 B3
Lee-on-t-S PO13 179 E3
West Moors BH22 138 D1
Queens Cres
Horndean PO8 112 C7
Stubbington PO14 179 D8
Queens Ct
[16] Bournemouth BH4 204 D4
Bournemouth,Charminster
BH8 205 B8
New Milton BH25 195 D3
[12] Winchester SO23 215 D5
Queens Gate PO1 182 B2
Queens Gdns
Bournemouth BH2 204 D4
Fordingbridge SP6 69 F2
Queens Gr
New Milton BH25 195 C4
Waterlooville PO7 134 D5
Queens Ho [2] SO14 103 A3
Queens Keep
[22] Portsmouth PO5 182 C2
[4] Southampton SO15 102 F5
Queens Mead SO22 215 A4
Queens Rd
Ferndown BH22 165 D7
Lee-on-t-S PO13 179 F1

Queens Rd *continued*
Lyndhurst SO43 122 B5
Petersfield GU32 40 D4
Queens Ride SO52 53 E4
Queens View SO31 127 B6
Queens Way BH24 141 B7
Queensbury Mans [9]
BH1 205 A3
Queensland Rd BH5 206 A5
Queensmead
Burton BH23 192 A1
[4] Wimborne Minst BH21 163 C5
Queenstown Rd SO15 102 D6
Queensway
New Milton BH25 194 E3
North Hayling PO11 160 A3
Southampton SO14 103 A3
Queensway The PO16 156 B8
Queenswood Ave BH8 190 E1
Queenswood Dr BH22 165 D7
Querida Cl SO31 128 D8
Quilter Cl SO19 104 D4
Quince La BH21 163 E6
Quintin Cl BH23 208 F8
Quinton Cl PO5 216 C2
Quintrell Ave PO16 156 A8
Quob Farm Cl SO30 80 E3
Quob La SO30 80 E3
Quomp The BH24 141 A7
Quoyne Ct SO51 52 E7

R

R L Stevenson Ave BH4 204 B3
Racecourse La PO6 157 B8
Racecourse View SO43 121 F6
Rachel Cl Fair Oak SO50 57 B2
Poole BH12 203 C7
Rachel Madocks Sch
PO8 111 D4
Racton Ave PO6 158 B7
Racton Rd PO10 136 F3
Radcliffe Ct SO14 103 B5
Radcliffe Rd SO14 103 B6
Radclyffe Rd PO16 131 C2
Radipole Rd BH17 188 A2
Radleigh Gdns SO40 100 B8
Radley Cl SO30 81 C1
Radnor St PO5 216 B2
Radstock Rd SO19 103 E3
Radway Cres SO15 102 D8
Radway Rd SO15 78 E1
Raebarn Cl SO24 14 D5
Raeburn Dr SO30 105 C7
Raglan Cl SO53 55 A4
Raglan Ct Eastleigh SO50 56 A6
Gosport PO12 181 A5
Locks Heath SO31 129 A5
Raglan Gdns BH11 189 A2
Raglan St PO5 216 C3
Raglan Terr PO10 137 A1
Ragmore La GU32 18 E5
Rails La PO11 185 C2
Railway Cotts
Southampton SO15 101 C8
West Dean SP5 3 D3
West Meon GU32 37 C4
West Tisted GU34 17 C6
Railway Flats PO1 182 E5
Railway Terr SO42 172 F8
Railway Triangle Ind Est
PO6 158 B6
Railway View PO1 216 C3
Railway View Rd SO17 103 C8
Rainbow Pl SO15 102 C6
Rake Bsns Pk GU33 21 E4
Rake CE Fst Sch GU33 21 F5
Rake Rd GU33 21 B4
Raleigh Cl
Christchurch BH23 207 F5
New Milton BH25 194 F3
Ringwood BH24 141 C8
Raleigh Ho [37] PO1 182 A5
Raleigh Rd BH12 188 E1
Raleigh Wlk PO13 180 D6
Raley Rd SO31 129 A2
Ralph Jessop Ct BH12 203 D7
Ralph La SO51 28 A1
Ralph Rd BH21 186 E7
Ramalley La SO53 55 B8
Rambler Dr PO13 180 C6
Ramblers Way PO7 112 C1
Ramillies Ho
[3] Fareham PO14 154 E7
[16] Gosport PO12 181 C5
Ramley Rd SO41 197 B3
Rampart Gdns PO3 157 F5
Rampart Rd SO18 103 D7
Rampart Row PO12 181 E4
Rampart The SO41 197 D5
Rams Wlk GU32 40 F3
Ramsay Pl PO13 155 C2
Ramsay Rd SO23 2 C8
Ramsdale Ave PO9 135 C5
Ramsdean Rd GU32 39 E2
Ramsey Ct BH25 194 F3
Ramsey Rd PO11 185 A3
Ramshill GU31 41 A4
Rances Way SO22 215 C3
Randall Cl SO40 76 C2
Randall Rd SO53 30 D2
Randall's La BH24 142 E5
Randolph Rd
[2] Bournemouth BH1 205 E4

Randolph Rd *continued*
Poole BH14 203 C5
Portsmouth PO2 157 E2
Randolph St SO15 102 C7
Ranelagh Ct 9 SO17 103 A8
Ranelagh Gdns SO15 102 E7
Ranelagh Rd
Christchurch BH23 208 F7
Havant PO9 135 D1
Portsmouth PO2 157 C1
Winchester SO23 215 D4
Ranfurly Gdns SO45 125 E1
Range Gdns SO19 104 B3
Range Gn PO2 157 C3
Ranger Ct SO14 103 B2
Ranmore Ct SO45 125 C4
Rannoch Cl PO15 130 E3
Ransome Cl PO14 153 F7
Ranvilles Jun & Inf Schs
PO14 154 C8
Ranvilles La PO14 154 B7
Rapley Ct PO11 184 E3
Rapson Cl PO6 133 C1
Raptor & Reptile Ctr*
BH24 141 C5
Rareridge La SO32 83 E8
Rashley Mews SO41 197 E3
Ratcliffe Rd
Dibden Purlieu SO45 125 F1
Hedge End SO30 105 C7
Rathdora Mews SO31 127 F8
Ratlake La SO21 29 F4
Rattigan Gdns PO15 129 C8
Ravana Ct 4 BH8 205 A5
Raven Cl PO13 180 C6
Raven Croft PO5 216 B1
Raven Rd SO14 103 B6
Raven Sq SO50 55 D2
Raven Way BH23 208 A5
Ravens Cl PO14 179 D7
Ravens Way SO41 211 D4
Ravenscourt Rd
Bournemouth BH6 206 C5
Lymington SO41 197 D2
Ravenscroft Cl SO31 104 F1
Ravenscroft Way SO32 81 F1
Ravensdale Cl BH12 203 C6
Ravenshall 7 BH2 204 D2
Ravenswood PO14 129 C3
Ravenswood Gdns 12
PO5 182 D2
Ravenswood House Hospl
PO17 130 E8
Ravine Ct BH13 214 F7
Ravine Gdns 5 BH13 214 F7
Ravine Rd
Bournemouth BH5 206 B4
Poole BH13 214 F8
Rawlinson Terr PO1 182 A6
Raymond Cl
Holbury SO45 150 D3
Verwood BH31 115 B6
West End SO30 80 F3
Raymond Rd
Portchester PO6 132 E1
Southampton SO15 102 D7
Rayners Dr BH12 203 D6
Rayners Gdns SO16 79 D4
Raynes Rd PO13 180 A4
Rayscliff 21 BH4 204 C2
Reading Room La SO32 106 D8
Readon Cl GU31 41 A4
Readon Ho GU31 41 A4
Rebbeck Rd BH7 206 A6
Recess The SO50 56 B5
Record Rd PO10 136 E1
Recreation Cotts SO51 50 E3
Recreation Rd BH12 203 E6
Rectory Ave
Corfe Mullen BH21 162 D1
Farlington PO6 158 F8
Rectory Cl Gosport PO12 181 A3
Stubbington PO14 179 C8
Rectory Ct SO30 105 F7
Rectory Hill SP5 3 D3
Rectory La Breamore SP6 46 B1
Meonstoke SO32 61 C5
Rectory Rd
Langstone PO9 159 F8
Poole BH15 202 C6
Red Barn Ave PO16 132 C1
Red Barn Com Prim Sch
PO16 156 C8
Red Barn La PO16 130 E4
Red Deer Ct 4 SO22 215 C6
Red Hill Cres SO16 78 E4
Red Hill Way SO16 78 E4
Red Horn Cl BH16 201 C4
Red House Mews SO41 197 E3
Red House Mus & Gdns*
BH23 207 B6
Red La Corfe Mullen BH21 186 A8
Upham SO32 58 B6
West Tytherley SP5 4 A7
Red Leaves SO32 83 E2
Red Lodge SO53 55 B3
Red Lodge Sch SO16 78 E4
Red Oaks Cl BH22 165 B7
Red Oaks Dr SO31 129 B5
Redan Cl BH23 208 F7
Redan The PO12 181 C2
Redbreast Rd BH9 190 A3
Redbreast Rd N BH9 190 A3
Redbridge Com Sch
SO16 101 D8
Redbridge Cswy SO15,
SO16,SO40 101 B8
Redbridge Flyover
SO16 101 C8
Redbridge Gr PO9 135 D3
Redbridge Hill SO16 77 F1
Redbridge La
Nursling SO16 77 D4
Southampton SO16 77 C2
Redbridge Prim Sch
SO15 101 D8
Redbridge Rd SO15 101 D8
Redbridge Sta SO15 101 C8
Redbridge Twrs SO16 101 C8
Redbrook Cotts SP6 94 A7
Redcar Ave PO3 158 A1
Redcliffe Cl BH23 192 C3
Redcote Cl SO18 104 B7
Redcotts La BH21 163 B5
Redcotts Rd BH21 163 B5
Redcourt 2 SO16 78 F4
Redcroft La SO31 105 A1
Redfords The SO40 76 E1
Redhill SO16 78 E4
Redhill Ave BH9 189 F3
Redhill Cl
Bournemouth BH10 189 E3
Southampton SO16 78 E4
Redhill Cres BH9 189 F3
Redhill Ct 1 BH10 190 A4
Redhill Dr BH10 189 E3
Redhill Ho PO1 216 C4
Redhill Park Homes 1
BH10 189 F4
Redhill Rd PO9 113 B1
Redhill Rdbt BH10 189 F4
Redhoave Rd BH17 187 E2
Redhouse Park Gdns
PO12 180 F7
Redlands
Christchurch BH23 208 A7
Poole BH12 203 F5
Redlands Dr SO19 103 F6
Redlands Gr PO4 183 C4
Redlands La
Emsworth PO10 136 F4
Fareham PO14,PO16 155 A8
Redlands Prim Sch
PO16 155 B7
Redlynch CE Prim Sch
SP5 48 A5
Redlynch Cl PO9 136 B4
Redmans View BH31 114 E6
Redmoor Cl SO19 103 F6
Rednal Ho PO5 216 C3
Redoubt Ct PO14 154 F6
Redrise Cl SO45 150 B3
Redsails BH13 214 B3
Redshank Cl BH17 186 F1
Redshank Rd PO8 112 A7
Redvers Cl SO41 197 D2
Redvers Rd BH23 207 E7
Redward Rd SO16 77 F5
Redwing Ct PO4 183 C5
Redwing Gdns SO40 100 C8
Redwing Rd PO8 88 C4
Redwood Cl Hythe SO45 125 C3
Lymington SO41 197 D5
Ringwood BH24 141 B7
West End SO30 80 C2
Redwood Ct Bassett SO16 79 A6
5 Waterlooville PO7 134 E8
Redwood Dr
Ferndown BH22 165 C8
Portchester PO16 156 B8
Redwood Gdns SO40 100 C7
Redwood Gr PO9 136 A4
Redwood Lodge 4
PO16 131 B2
Redwood Park Sch PO6 158 A6
Redwood Rd BH16 201 A8
Redwood Way SO16 79 A6
Reed Dr SO40 101 F2
Reed's Pl PO12 181 B7
Reeder Cl SP6 69 E1
Reedling Dr PO4 183 C5
Reedmace Cl PO7 135 A6
Reeds La GU33 21 D6
Reeds Mdw GU32 39 D4
Reeds Rd PO12 181 B8
Reeves Cl SO51 50 E3
Reeves Way SO31 104 F1
Regal Cl PO6 157 F8
Regency Cres BH23 206 F8
Regency Ct 12 PO1 182 A4
Regency Gdns PO7 134 D6
Regency Pl
Fareham PO15 130 E1
Ringwood BH24 141 A8
Regent Cl SO21 31 C4
Regent Ct
2 Portsmouth PO1 182 D7
17 Southampton SO17 79 A1
18 Winchester SO23 215 E8
Regent Dr BH7 205 F8
Regent Ho SO30 81 C3
Regent Mews GU32 40 D4
Regent Pl PO5 216 A1
Regent Rd SO53 55 D6
Regent St
Portsmouth PO1 182 C7
Southampton SO14 102 F4
Regent Way BH23 207 B6
Regent's Gr 1 SO16 102 B8
Regent's Park Gdns
SO15 102 B7
Regent's Park Rd SO15 102 A7
Regents Ct
11 Knowle Village PO17 130 E7
Langstone PO9 159 F8
8 Southampton SO16 102 B8
Regents Gate SO31 128 E5
Regents Park Com Coll
SO16 102 A8
Regents Pl PO12 181 D7
Reginald Rd PO4 183 A3
Reid St BH23 207 A8
Reigate Ho PO1 216 C4
Relay Rd PO7 134 D8
Reldas The 9 PO1 182 A3
Reliant Cl SO53 55 B4
Rempstone Rd BH21 187 D8
Renault Dr BH18 187 A1
Renda Rd SO45 150 C4
Renny Rd PO1 182 F5
Renouf Cl SO41 197 C3
Renown Cl SO53 55 B5
Renown Gdns PO8 111 F5
Renown Ho 15 PO12 181 C5
Repton Cl PO12 180 E4
Repton Gdns SO30 81 D2
Reservoir La
Hedge End SO30 105 A6
Petersfield GU32 40 F6
Resolution Ho 14 PO12 181 C5
Rest-A-Wyle Ave PO11 185 A5
Restharrow BH1 205 A4
Restynge Ho BH31 114 F7
Retreat Rd BH21 163 D4
Retreat The
Eastleigh SO50 56 B4
Portsmouth PO5 216 B1
Totton SO40 101 A5
Revenge Cl PO4 183 C6
Revenge Ho 13 PO12 181 C5
Rewlands Dr SO22 1 C4
Rex Est SO53 55 D5
Reynard Ct BH15 202 F3
Reynolds Ct SO51 53 A6
Reynolds Dale SO40 100 D5
Reynolds Rd
Fair Oak SO50 57 D1
Gosport PO12 181 C3
Southampton SO15 102 C8
Rhinefield Cl
Bishopstoke SO50 56 F2
Brockenhurst SO42 145 E1
Havant PO9 135 C4
Rhinefield Forest Walks*
SO42 145 A2
Rhinefield Ornamental Dr*
SO42 144 F6
Rhinefield Rd
Brockenhurst SO42 145 C2
New Milton BH25 170 E2
Rhiners Cl SO41 172 B2
Rhyme Hall Mews SO45 151 B3
Rhys Ct PO4 183 A4
Ribble Cl
Broadstone BH18 187 A2
Chandler's Ford SO53 55 D5
Ribble Ct SO16 77 E1
Ribbonwood Hts BH14 203 B4
Ricardo Cres BH23 208 A6
Ricardo Way SO41 197 D7
Rice Gdns BH16 201 D4
Rice Terr BH16 201 D4
Richard Cl BH16 201 B8
Richard Gr PO12 156 A1
Richard Moss Ho 9
SO23 215 E6
Richard Taunton Pl SO17 79 A2
Richards Cl
Blackfield SO45 150 F2
Locks Heath SO31 129 B3
Richards Ct 6 SO15 78 B1
Riches Mews 9 PO16 131 A1
Richlans Rd SO30 105 C6
Richmond Cl
Chandler's Ford SO53 30 C1
South Hayling PO11 184 E4
Totton SO40 76 B1
Richmond Ct
12 Milford on S SO41 211 C4
7 New Milton BH25 195 A3
Richmond Dr PO11 184 E4
Richmond Gdns
Bournemouth BH1 204 F3
Southampton SO17 79 B1
Waterlooville PO7 134 C5
Richmond Hall 6 SO17 79 C2
Richmond Hill BH2 204 F3
Richmond Hill Dr BH2 204 F3
Richmond Ho
1 Southampton SO15 102 C6
5 Winchester SO22 215 D6
Richmond La SO51 28 A1
Richmond Park Ave
BH8 205 C7
Richmond Park Cl BH8 205 D6
Richmond Park Cres
BH8 205 C7
Richmond Park Rd BH8 205 C7
Richmond Pk SO21 31 D4
Richmond Pl
Portsmouth,Portsea PO1 182 B5
Portsmouth,Southsea PO5 182 C2
Richmond Rd
Gosport PO12 181 A5
Lee-on-t-S PO13 179 D3
Poole BH14 203 C4
Portsmouth PO5 182 D2
Southampton SO15 102 C6
Wimborne Minst BH21 163 D4
Richmond Rise
Bournemouth BH8 205 D6
Portchester PO16 132 C1
Richmond St SO14 103 B3
Richmond Terr 12 PO5 182 C2
Richmond Wood Rd
BH8 205 C7
Richville Rd SO16 102 A8
Ridding Cl SO15 78 C1
Riders Inf Sch PO9 135 E5
Riders Jun Sch PO9 135 E5
Riders La PO9 135 E4
Ridge Cl PO8 88 C4
Ridge Common La GU32 40 C6
Ridge La Curbridge SO30 106 D3
Romsey SO51 76 C8
Ridge The SP5 47 D5
Ridge Top La
Froxfield Green GU32 39 E6
Froxfield Green GU32 40 B8
Ridgefield Gdns BH23 208 D8
Ridgemede Jun Sch
SO32 83 D8
Ridgemount Ave SO16 78 F5
Ridgemount Gdns BH15 201 E3
Ridgemount La SO16 78 F5
Ridgeway
Broadstone BH18 187 B4
Corfe Mullen BH21 186 D8
Ferndown BH22 189 E8
Winchester SO22 215 A3
Ridgeway Cl
Chandler's Ford SO53 55 E5
Fair Oak SO50 57 C3
Portchester PO6 132 F1
Ridgeway House Sch
SO19 103 F5
Ridgeway La SO41 197 D1
Ridgeway The PO16 131 E1
Ridgeway Wlk SO53 55 E5
Ridgewood Cl SO45 125 C4
Ridgway PO9 135 D1
Ridings The Fair Oak SO50 57 A2
Liss GU33 21 B4
Portsmouth PO2 157 F3
Waltham Chase SO32 83 E4
Ridley Cl SO45 150 C4
Ridley Rd BH9 204 F8
Ridout Cl BH10 189 B1
Rigby Rd SO17 103 B8
Riggs Gdns BH11 188 F2
Rigler Rd BH15 202 A2
Rimbury Way BH23 207 A8
Rimington Gdns 1 SO51 28 B1
Rimington Rd PO8 111 E3
Ring The SO16 78 E7
Ringbury SO41 197 D6
Ringlet Way 5 SO23 11 C8
Ringwood CE Inf Sch
BH24 141 A7
Ringwood Dr SO52 53 E4
Ringwood Ho PO9 135 F5
Ringwood Jun Sch
BH24 141 A6
Ringwood Rd
Alderholt SP6 93 A4
Bournemouth BH11 188 E4
Bransgore BH23 193 D5
Burley Street BH24 142 E5
Ferndown BH22 165 C4
Fordingbridge SP6 94 A4
Fordingbridge SP6 94 C4
Poole BH12 203 B7
Portsmouth PO4 183 B3
Ringwood BH24 140 C6
Sopley BH23 192 A7
St Leonards BH24 139 D2
Three Legged Cross BH21 139 B7
Totton SO40 100 C7
Verwood BH31 115 F5
Walkford BH23 194 B1
West Moors BH22 166 A8
Ringwood Rd Nature Reserve
BH11 188 E5
Ringwood Road Ret Pk
BH11 188 E3
Ringwood Sch BH24 141 A7
Ringwood Terr SO42 146 A2
Ringwood Trad Est
BH24 141 A6
Ringwood Waldorf Sch
BH24 140 D6
Ripley Ct BH22 165 F7
Ripley Gr PO3 183 A8
Ripon Ct SO50 81 D7
Ripon Gdns 6 PO7 112 B1
Ripon Rd BH9 190 A1
Ripplewood SO40 102 A1
Ripstone Gdns SO17 79 B3
Rise The
Brockenhurst SO42 145 F1
Waterlooville PO7 134 D2
Ritchie Cl PO11 185 A3
Ritchie Ct SO19 104 B4
Ritchie Pl BH22 138 D4
Ritchie Rd BH11 189 B4
Rival Moor Rd GU31 41 C2
River Cl BH21 163 C6
River Ct SO41 197 F4
River Gdns SO41 211 E4
River Gn SO31 128 A2
River La PO15 130 C6
River Mews SO50 56 D3
River Pk BH6 206 F6
River Rd SP6 70 D2
River St PO10 137 B4
River View Ho SO19 103 D3
River View Rd SO18 79 D2
River Way
Christchurch BH23 191 D2
Havant PO9 136 A3
River Wlk SO18 79 E3
River's St PO5 216 C2
Riverbourne Ct SO18 103 D8
Riverdale Ave PO7 135 A7
Riverdale Cl SP6 69 F2
Riverdale Cotts PO16 131 D3
Riverdale La BH23 207 A6
Riverdene Pl SO18 103 D8
Riverhead Cl PO4 183 B5
Riverland Ct 4 BH23 207 A6
Riverlea Rd BH23 207 A6
Rivermead Cl SO51 52 D7
Rivermead Ct PO10 137 A3
Rivermead Gdns BH23 191 E2
Riverpark Ct SO18 79 D1
Rivers Reach SO41 197 F3
Riversdale 8 BH21 163 C4
Riversdale Cl SO19 126 E8
Riversdale Gdns PO9 135 F2
Riversdale Rd BH6 207 A4
Riverside
Bishopstoke SO50 56 D3
4 Bournemouth BH10 189 F4
Ringwood BH24 140 F6
Riverside Ave
Bournemouth BH7 191 C1
Fareham PO16 131 D3
Riverside Bsns Pk SO41 197 F4
Riverside Cl Bartley SO40 99 C6
Liss GU33 20 F4
Riverside Cotts SO21 31 F6
Riverside Ct
7 Bournemouth BH4 204 D4
Southampton,Bitterne
SO18 103 D8
Southampton,Bitterne Manor
SO18 103 C7
West Moors BH22 138 D3
Riverside Gdns SO51 52 E6
Riverside Ho 4 SO23 215 F6
Riverside La BH6 206 F5
Riverside Mews PO17 108 A3
Riverside Pk BH23 207 A5
Riverside Pk Cvn & Campsite
SO31 128 A5
Riverside Pk Ind Est
BH21 163 D3
Riverside Pl SP6 69 F1
Riverside Rd
Bournemouth BH6 206 F5
West Moors BH22 138 D2
Riverside Sch PO7 134 F4
Riverside Terr 5 PO10 161 A8
Riverslea Mews BH23 207 D6
Riversmeet Ct BH23 207 D6
Riverview SO40 100 F5
Riverview Terr SO31 128 D8
Riviera 11 BH1 205 B3
Riviera Ct
Bournemouth BH2 204 D3
8 Poole BH13 214 F7
RN Submarine Mus & HMS
Alliance* PO12 181 E4
RNLI Mus* BH15 202 C2
Road View PO2 182 C8
Roads Hill PO8 88 A1
Robann Cvn Pk SO31 129 D3
Robere Ho SO19 103 D3
Robert Cecil Ave SO18 79 E4
Robert Mack Ct 39 PO1 182 A5
Robert Whitworth Dr
SO51 27 F1
Roberts Cl Everton SO41 196 E1
Wickham PO17 108 A4
Roberts La BH17 201 F7
Roberts Rd
Bournemouth BH7 206 A6
Gosport PO12 180 F6
Hythe SO45 125 F4
Poole BH17 187 B1
Southampton SO15 102 E5
Totton SO40 100 F6
Robertshaw Ho SO43 121 F6
Robin Cres BH25 194 D5
Robin Ct SO15 102 F8
Robin Gdns
Christchurch BH23 207 A8
Totton SO40 100 C8
Waterlooville PO8 111 D4
Robin Gr BH25 194 F2
Robin Sq SO50 55 C2
Robina Cl PO7 135 A7
Robinia Gn SO16 78 C5
Robins Cl PO14 179 C8
Robins Ct 7 BH21 163 C4
Robins Mdw PO14 129 C1
Robins Way BH23 208 B5
Robinson Ct
Lee-on-t-S PO13 179 E2
Portchester PO16 132 C1
Robinson Rd PO14 179 B6
Robinson Way PO3 158 C3
Robinswood Dr BH22 165 D2
Robsall Cl BH12 203 E4
Robville Ct 3 BH7 206 B6
Rochester Ct 1 PO13 180 D5
Rochester Rd
Bournemouth BH11 189 B4
Portsmouth PO4 182 F3
Rochester St SO14 103 C5
Rochford Rd PO6 157 D8
Rockall Cl SO16 77 E5
Rockbourne Cl PO9 135 C4
Rockbourne Gdns BH25 209 D
Rockbourne La SP6 68 D

Rockbourne Rd SO22 ......1 D4
Rockbourne Roman Villa* SP6 ......68 F7
Rockery Cl SO45 ......125 C4
Rockford Cl BH6 ......206 F3
Rockford Ho SO50 ......57 B1
Rockingham Way PO16 ..156 B8
Rockleigh Dr SO40 ......100 D5
Rockleigh Rd SO16 ......78 D3
Rockley Mews BH15 ....201 E2
Rockley Pk Cvn Est BH15,BH16 ......201 B3
Rockley Rd BH15 ......201 E1
Rockpit Cotts GU33 ......21 B4
Rockram Cl SO40 ......99 B7
Rockram Gdns SO45 ......125 C4
Rockrose Way PO6 ......133 A2
Rockstone Ct 2 SO14 ...103 A6
Rockstone La SO14 ......103 A6
Rockstone Pl SO15 ......102 F6
Rockville Dr PO7 ......134 E7
Rodbard Ho SO31 ......104 F1
Rodbourne Cl SO41 ......211 D8
Rodfield La SO21,SO24 ....13 C5
Rodlease La SO41 ......173 E2
Rodney Cl Gosport PO13 .180 D6
Poole BH12 ......204 A8
Rodney Ct
Christchurch BH23 ......208 A6
7 Poole BH15 ......202 C1
Southampton SO19 ......104 C4
Rodney Dr BH23 ......207 F6
Rodney Ho 10 PO12 ......181 D5
Rodney Rd PO4 ......183 A5
Rodney Way PO8 ......112 B6
Rodway BH21 ......163 C4
Rodwell Cl BH10 ......189 C6
Roebuck Ave PO15 ......130 D5
Roebuck Cl Cosham PO6 .157 F7
New Milton BH25 ......195 B3
Roebuck Dr PO12 ......181 C8
Roeshot Cres BH23 ......193 E1
Roeshot Hill BH23 ......193 C2
Roewood Cl SO45 ......150 C3
Roewood Rd SO45 ......150 C3
Rogate Gdns PO16 ......132 C1
Rogate Ho 1 PO1 ......216 C4
Roger Penny Way
Brook SO43 ......73 C2
Fordingbridge,Bramshaw, SP5 ......72 D6
Fordingbridge,Godshill SP6 ..71 B5
Rogers Cl
Bishopstoke SO50 ......56 E4
Gosport PO12 ......181 B7
Rogers Ho PO13 ......179 F2
Rogers Mead PO11 ......160 A3
Rogers Rd SO50 ......56 E4
Roi-mar Home Pk BH8 .190 D4
Roker Way SO50 ......57 B1
Roland Cl PO8 ......112 B6
Rollesbrook Gdns SO15 .102 E6
Rollestone Rd SO45 ......150 C2
Rolls Dr BH6 ......207 B3
Roman Cl SO53 ......55 E7
Roman Ct PO10 ......137 D1
Roman Dr SO16 ......78 E7
Roman Gdns SO45 ......125 D1
Roman Gn PO7 ......110 E4
Roman Gr PO16 ......156 D6
Roman Ho SO18 ......103 C7
Roman Hts BH21 ......186 E8
Roman Mdw SP5 ......46 F7
Roman Quay SP6 ......69 F1
Roman Rd Chilworth SO16 .78 E8
Corfe Mullen BH18 ......186 E5
Dibden Purlieu SO45 ......149 E8
Dibden Purlieu,Applemore SO45 ......125 C2
Hardley SO45 ......150 B6
Havant PO10 ......136 C1
Twyford SO21 ......32 A5
Roman Row SO32 ......83 D8
Roman Way
Dibden Purlieu SO45 ......125 D1
Havant PO9 ......135 C2
Pamphill BH21 ......162 C5
Romans' Rd SO23 ......215 D4
Romford Rd SO31 ......152 D10
Romill Cl SO18 ......80 B3
Romney Cl BH10 ......189 E3
Romney Ct 51 BH4 ......204 C3
Romney Rd BH10 ......189 E4
Romsey Abbey* SO51 ......52 E7
Romsey Abbey CE Prim Sch SO51 ......52 E7
Romsey Ave
Portchester PO16 ......156 A8
Portsmouth PO3 ......183 B6
Romsey Cl SO50 ......56 A3
Romsey Ct SO15 ......102 D6
Romsey Hospl SO51 ......53 A7
Romsey Ind Est SO51 ......52 F8
Romsey Inf Sch SO51 ......52 F7
Romsey Jun Sch SO51 ......53 A8
Romsey Lodge 8 SO16 ...78 A1
Romsey Rd Awbridge SO51 .26 E4
Cadnam SO40,SO51 ......75 C3
Compton SO20 ......6 D8
Eastleigh SO50 ......56 A3
Horndean PO8 ......88 C2
Lyndhurst SO43 ......121 F5
Ower SO51 ......75 F6
Southampton SO16 ......78 A1
West Wellow SO51 ......51 A3
Whiteparish SP5 ......24 F3
Winchester SO22 ......215 A4
Romsey Sch The SO51 ....52 E8
Romsey Sta SO51 ......52 F8
Romyns Ct PO14 ......130 F1
Ronald Bowker Ct 1 SO22 ......215 C6
Ronald Pugh Ct SO18 ....79 E4
Rook Hill Rd BH23 ......208 B6
Rookcliff 13 SO41 ......211 C4
Rookcliff Way SO41 ......211 C4
Rooke Ho 17 PO1 ......182 A5
Rookery Ave PO15,SO31 ..129 B7
Rookery Grange SO31 ....129 B7
Rookery La SP6 ......45 F1
Rookery The
Lumley PO10 ......137 A1
West Dean SP5 ......3 D3
Rookes Cl PO8 ......112 B6
Rookes La SO41 ......197 E2
Rookes Mews GU31 ......41 A4
Rookesbury Park Sch PO17 ......108 D4
Rookesbury Pk Cvn Club Site PO17 ......108 D5
Rookley SO31 ......127 C7
Rooks Down Rd SO22 ...215 B3
Rooksbridge SO45 ......125 C4
Rooksbury Croft PO9 ...136 A5
Rooksway Gr PO16 ......155 F8
Rookwood 3 SO41 ......211 C4
Rookwood Cl SO50 ......56 B6
Rookwood Gdns SP6 ......69 D1
Rookwood View PO7 ......110 F5
Roosevelt Cres BH11 ......189 B6
Rope Hill SO41 ......173 D1
Rope Wlk SO31 ......128 A2
Rope Wlk The PO16 ......155 B8
Ropers La BH16 ......201 D7
Ropewalk Ho 7 SO23 ...215 E6
Ropley Cl SO19 ......127 A8
Ropley Rd
Bournemouth BH7 ......206 C7
25 Havant PO9 ......136 B5
Rosamund Ave BH21 ......163 E1
Roscrea Cl BH6 ......207 B4
Roscrea Dr BH6 ......207 B4
Rose Bowl The* SO30 ......80 F1
Rose Cl Hedge End SO30 ..105 C8
Hythe SO45 ......126 A2
Rose Cott PO8 ......112 D7
Rose Cres BH15 ......202 F6
Rose Ct BH15 ......202 E3
Rose Farm Cl BH22 ......165 B3
Rose Gdn The BH23 ......191 D1
Rose Gdns BH9 ......190 A3
Rose Hill PO8 ......112 A5
Rose Rd
Southampton SO14 ......103 A8
Totton SO40 ......101 A6
Rosebank Cl SO16 ......77 E5
Rosebank Lodge SO16 ......77 E5
Rosebay Cl SO50 ......81 C6
Rosebay Ct 2 PO7 ......134 F5
Rosebery Ave
Cosham PO6 ......158 A7
Hythe SO45 ......126 A2
Rosebery Cl BH31 ......115 C5
Rosebery Cres SO50 ......56 B6
Rosebery Rd BH5 ......206 A5
Rosebrook Ct 4 SO18 ...103 E7
Rosebud Ave 1 BH9 ......190 A2
Rosecrae Cl BH25 ......194 F4
Rosedale Ave SO51 ......53 A7
Rosedale Cl
3 Christchurch BH23 ......207 E6
Titchfield PO14 ......153 F8
Rosehill Cl BH23 ......169 B1
Rosehill Dr BH23 ......169 B1
Rosehip Cl SO50 ......57 A1
Roselands
Waterlooville PO8 ......112 A5
West End SO30 ......104 D8
Roselands Cl SO50 ......57 B3
Roselands Gdns SO17 ......79 A2
Roseleigh Dr SO40 ......100 E6
Rosemary Ct 8 BH23 ......209 B7
Rosemary Gdns
Hedge End SO30 ......105 C5
Poole BH12 ......203 B7
Whiteley PO15 ......129 D8
Rosemary La 29 PO1 ......182 A5
Rosemary Rd BH12 ......203 C7
Rosemary Way PO8 ......112 B5
Rosemary Wlk 3 PO13 ...179 F3
Rosemoor Gr SO53 ......30 B1
Rosemount Rd BH4 ......204 B2
Rosendale Rd SO53 ......55 D4
Rosery The PO12 ......181 B2
Rosetta Rd PO4 ......183 B4
Rosewall Rd SO16 ......77 F3
Rosewarne Ct 9 SO23 ...215 E7
Rosewood PO13 ......155 E1
Rosewood Gdns
Clanfield PO8 ......88 C5
Marchwood SO40 ......102 A1
New Milton BH25 ......194 F4
Rosida Gdns SO15 ......102 E6
Rosina Cl PO7 ......135 B8
Roslin Gdns BH3 ......204 D7
Roslin Rd BH3 ......204 E7
Roslin Rd S BH3 ......204 E7
Roslyn Ho PO5 ......216 B1
Rosoman Ct SO19 ......103 F4
Rosoman Ho SO19 ......103 F4
Rosoman Rd SO19 ......103 F4
Ross Gdns
Bournemouth BH11 ......188 C5
Southampton SO16 ......78 A2
Ross Glades BH3 ......204 E6
Ross Mews SO31 ......127 A6
Ross Rd BH24 ......117 C1
Ross Way PO13 ......179 F4
Rossan Ave SO31 ......152 D9
Rossington Ave SO18 ......103 F8
Rossington Way SO18 ......103 F7
Rossiters La SO40 ......99 E5
Rossiters Quay BH23 ......207 C6
Rossley Cl BH23 ......193 E2
Rosslyn Cl SO52 ......54 A4
Rossmore Com Coll BH12 ......203 D8
Rossmore Par BH12 ......203 B8
Rossmore Rd BH12 ......203 D7
Rostrevor La 9 PO4 ......182 E1
Rostrevor Mans 8 PO4 .182 E1
Rostron Cl SO18 ......80 A3
Rosyth Rd SO18 ......103 F7
Rotary Cl BH21 ......163 F7
Rotary Ct SO31 ......127 B6
Rotary Ho SO15 ......102 D8
Rothbury Cl
Southampton SO19 ......104 A4
Totton SO40 ......76 D1
Rothbury Pk BH25 ......195 B2
Rother Cl Petersfield GU31 .41 C4
West End SO18 ......80 B1
Rother Dale SO19 ......104 E3
Rother Ho GU33 ......20 F3
Rotherbank Farm La GU33 ......21 A6
Rothercombe La GU32 ...40 A4
Rotherfield Rd
Bournemouth BH5 ......206 B3
Walkford BH23 ......194 A1
Rotherley GU32 ......40 E4
Rotherwick Cl PO9 ......136 B5
Rothesay Dr BH23 ......208 E7
Rothesay Rd
Bournemouth BH4 ......204 C5
Gosport PO12 ......181 A8
Rothsbury Dr SO53 ......55 B6
Rothschild Cl SO19 ......103 E1
Rothville Pl SO53 ......30 B2
Rothwell Cl 9 PO6 ......133 A1
Rotterdam Dr BH23 ......207 D7
Rotterdam Twrs SO19 ....126 F8
Roughdown La SO45 ......150 C1
Roumelia La BH1,BH5 ...205 E4
Round Hill SP6 ......69 F1
Roundabouts The GU33 ...21 A5
Roundcopse SO45 ......125 C3
Roundhaye Gdns BH11 ....188 F6
Roundhaye Rd BH11 ......188 F6
Roundhill Cl SO18 ......80 A1
Roundhill Cross SP6 ......45 E1
Roundhouse Ct
Lymington SO41 ......197 D3
South Hayling PO11 ......185 B2
Roundhouse Dr SO40 ......100 C6
Roundhouse Mdw PO10 .161 A7
Roundhuts Rise 3 SO23 ...11 C8
Roundway PO7 ......134 F8
Roundways BH11 ......188 F3
Routs Way SO16 ......77 F7
Row The SP5 ......47 D7
Row Wood La PO13 ......155 B1
Rowallan Ave PO13 ......180 C8
Rowan Ave PO8 ......112 B2
Rowan Cl Bursledon SO31 .127 F8
Christchurch BH23 ......208 D8
Lee-on-t-S PO13 ......179 F2
Romsey SO51 ......53 C6
Southampton SO16 ......78 A3
St Leonards BH24 ......139 D4
Swanmore SO32 ......84 B4
Sway SO41 ......172 B1
Totton SO40 ......100 D6
Rowan Ct
Portsmouth PO4 ......182 F4
Southampton SO19 ......103 F3
Rowan Dr
Broadstone BH17 ......186 E1
Christchurch BH23 ......208 D8
Verwood BH31 ......115 B4
Rowan Gdns SO30 ......105 D6
Rowan Rd PO9 ......136 C3
Rowan Tree Cl GU33 ......21 A4
Rowan Way PO14 ......154 C7
Rowans Pk SO41 ......197 D3
Rowans The SO40 ......101 E1
Rowbarrow Cl BH17 ......187 E2
Rowborough Rd SO18 ......103 F8
Rowbury Rd PO9 ......135 D6
Rowden Cl SO51 ......50 E2
Rowe Asheway SO31 ......128 F3
Rowe Gdns 6 BH12 ......203 F7
Rowena Ct PO5 ......216 C2
Rowena Rd BH6 ......206 F5
Rowes La SO41 ......199 B7
Rowhay La SO32 ......58 C5
Rowhill Dr SO45 ......125 C3
Rowin Cl PO11 ......185 D2
Rowland Ave BH15 ......202 E6
Rowland Rd
Fareham PO15 ......130 F2
Portchester PO6 ......132 E1
Rowlands Ave PO7 ......111 E1
Rowlands Castle Rd
Blendworth PO8 ......112 E6
Blendworth PO8 ......112 F7
Rowlands Castle St John's CE Prim Sch PO9 ......136 B8
Rowlands Castle Sta PO9 ......113 C2
Rowlands Cl SO53 ......55 A4
Rowlands Hill BH21 ......163 D6
Rowlands Wlk 2 SO18 ......80 A2
Rowley Cl SO30 ......105 F8
Rowley Dr SO30 ......105 F8
Rowlings Rd SO22 ......1 D3
Rowner Cl PO13 ......155 C1
Rowner Inf Schs PO13 ..155 D1
Rowner Jun Sch PO13 ..155 D1
Rowner La PO13 ......155 C1
Rowner Rd PO13 ......180 D8
Rownhams Cl SO16 ......77 E6
Rownhams Ct SO16 ......77 F8
Rownhams La
North Baddesley SO52 ......53 F5
Rownhams SO16 ......77 F7
Rownhams,Toot Hill SO16, SO52 ......53 F1
Rownhams Pk SO16 ......77 E8
Rownhams Rd
Bournemouth BH8 ......190 D3
Havant PO9 ......135 D5
North Baddesley SO52 ......54 A4
Southampton SO16 ......77 F3
Rownhams Rd N SO16 ......77 F5
Rownhams St John's CE Prim Sch SO16 ......77 E6
Rownhams Way SO16 ......77 E6
Rowse Cl SO51 ......27 F1
Roxan Ct 5 SO15 ......102 F7
Roxborough 47 BH4 ......204 C3
Roxburgh Ho SO31 ......129 A3
Roy's La SO32 ......109 D8
Royal Arc 5 BH1 ......205 E4
Royal Armouries Mus of Artillery* PO17 ......132 B3
Royal Bournemouth Gen Hospl The BH7 ......191 B1
Royal Crescent Rd 10 SO14 ......103 B3
Royal Ct
Chandler's Ford SO53 ......55 C6
Southampton SO17 ......79 C2
Royal Gate PO4 ......183 B2
Royal Gdns
Rowlands Castle PO9 ......113 A1
Southampton SO15 ......101 F7
Royal Greenjackets Mus* SO23 ......215 D5
Royal Hampshire Cty Hospl SO22 ......215 C5
Royal Hampshire Regiment Mus* SO23 ......215 D5
Royal Hospl Haslar PO12 ......181 D3
Royal London Pk SO30 ..105 B8
Royal Marines Mus* PO4 ......183 B2
Royal Mews 15 PO5 ......182 D2
Royal Naval Cotts PO17 .132 F6
Royal Naval Mus* PO1 ..181 F7
Royal Oak Rd BH10 ......189 C5
Royal South Hants Hospl SO14 ......103 A6
Royal Sovereign Ave PO14 ......155 A5
Royal The PO11 ......184 E2
Royal Victoria Ctry Pk* SO31 ......127 C4
Royal Victoria Mews BH4 ......204 D3
Royal Way PO7 ......135 A7
Royal Winchester Mews SO22 ......215 A5
Royden La SO41 ......173 D3
Roydon Cl SO22 ......215 C3
Royster Cl BH17 ......187 C1
Royston Ave SO50 ......56 A5
Royston Cl SO17 ......79 B2
Royston Ct SO40 ......76 E1
Royston Dr BH21 ......163 D5
Royston Pl BH25 ......210 B8
Rozel Ct SO16 ......77 E3
Rozel Manor BH13 ......204 B2
Rozelle Cl SO22 ......1 A5
Rozelle Rd BH14 ......203 C4
Ruben Dr BH15 ......201 D2
Rubens Cl BH25 ......195 B3
Ruby Cl SO40 ......76 B1
Ruby Ct 1 PO7 ......134 E8
Ruby Rd SO19 ......104 A6
Rudd La SO51 ......27 E7
Rudgwick Cl PO16 ......156 B8
Rudmore Ct 3 PO2 ......157 C1
Rudmore Rd PO2 ......182 C8
Rudmore Sq PO2 ......182 C8
Rudolph Ct PO7 ......134 C5
Ruffield Cl SO22 ......215 A8
Rufford Cl SO50 ......56 A6
Rufford Gdns BH6 ......206 E5
Rufus Cl
Chandler's Ford SO53 ......55 E8
Rownhams SO16 ......77 D6
Rufus Ct SO43 ......122 A5
Rufus Gdns SO40 ......100 C7
Rufus Stone* SO43 ......98 A6
Rugby Rd Poole BH17 ....187 A1
Portsmouth PO5 ......216 D2
Rumbridge Ct SO40 ......101 A6
Rumbridge Gdns SO40 ...101 A7
Rumbridge St SO40 ......101 A6
Runnymede
Fareham PO15 ......130 D4
West End SO30 ......80 D1
Runnymede Ave BH11 ....188 E6
Runton Rd BH12 ......203 F5
Runway The BH23 ......208 B7
Rushall La BH21 ......186 A5
Rushcombe Fst Sch BH21 ......186 D5
Rushcombe Way BH21 ....186 E6
Rushes Ct GU32 ......40 E4
Rushes Farm GU32 ......40 E4
Rushes Rd GU32 ......40 E4
Rushes The SO40 ......101 F2
Rushfield Rd GU33 ......20 F3
Rushford Warren BH23 ..207 F5
Rushin Ho PO10 ......136 D8
Rushington Ave SO40 ....100 F6
Rushington Bsns Pk SO40 ......100 E5
Rushington La SO40 ....100 E6
Rushmere Gate PO7 ......86 C2
Rushmere La PO7 ......110 E8
Rushmere Rd BH6 ......206 D7
Rushmere Wlk PO9 ......135 D6
Rushpole Ct SO45 ......125 C3
Rushton Cres BH3 ......204 F6
Ruskin Ave BH9 ......190 B3
Ruskin Rd Eastleigh SO50 ..56 B5
Portsmouth PO4 ......183 A4
Ruskin Way PO8 ......111 F4
Rusland Cl SO53 ......55 B7
Russel Rd BH10 ......189 C6
Russell Bldgs PO16 ......156 C7
Russell Churcher Ct PO12 ......180 F7
Russell Cl PO13 ......179 F3
Russell Cotes Art Gall & Mus* BH1 ......205 A2
Russell Cotes Rd BH1 ...205 A2
Russell Ct 2 BH25 ......195 A3
Russell Dr
Christchurch BH23 ......207 D6
Dunbridge SO51 ......5 D1
Russell Gdns
Hamworthy BH16 ......201 C4
St Leonards BH24 ......140 B5
Russell Pl Fareham PO16 .131 A1
Southampton SO17 ......79 B1
Russell Rd Havant PO9 ..135 F2
Lee-on-t-S PO13 ......179 F3
Winchester SO23 ......215 E8
Russell St Gosport PO12 ..181 A7
11 Southampton SO14 ....103 A3
Russell Way GU31 ......41 A2
Russet Cl
Ferndown BH22 ......165 D6
3 Lymington SO41 ......197 F2
Russet Gdns PO10 ......161 B8
Russet Ho SO30 ......105 A6
Russett Cl SO32 ......84 B4
Rustan Cl Fair Oak SO50 ...57 D2
Hedge End SO30 ......105 B6
Rustington Ho 3 PO1 ....216 B3
Rustlings Mews PO8 ....112 B7
Rutland Ct SO18 ......104 A7
Rutland Gdns SO31 ......105 A1
Rutland Manor 10 BH13 .204 A4
Rutland Rd
Bournemouth BH9 ......205 B8
Christchurch BH23 ......191 F1
Rutland Way SO18 ......80 A1
Ruxley Cl SO45 ......150 C4
Ryall Rd BH17 ......187 D1
Ryan Cl BH22 ......165 C7
Ryan Gdns
Bournemouth BH11 ......189 B6
Ferndown BH22 ......165 C7
Rydal Cl
Christchurch BH23 ......191 D4
9 Portsmouth PO6 ......133 B1
Rydal Ho
2 Bournemouth BH4 ......204 C2
11 Portsmouth PO6 ......133 B1
Rydal Mews BH21 ......163 D5
Rydal Rd PO12 ......181 A9
Ryde Pl PO13 ......180 A4
Ryde Terr SO14 ......103 B3
Rye Cl SO53 ......54 F6
Rye Dale SO40 ......100 C3
Rye Paddock La SO45 ...151 B4
Ryecroft Havant PO9 ....136 B1
Titchfield PO14 ......129 C2
Ryecroft Ave BH11 ......188 E5
Ryedown La SO51 ......51 E4
Ryefield Cl GU31 ......41 C3
Rylandes Ct SO16 ......77 F3

S

Sabre Rd PO10 ......161 A3
Sackville St PO5 ......216 B2
Saddle Cl BH21 ......164 C6
Saddlers Cl
Eastleigh SO50 ......56 A6
2 Fordingbridge SP6 ......69 F1
Sadlers La SO45 ......126 A1
Sadlers Wlk 9 PO10 ......161 A8
Saffron Ct
Bournemouth BH11 ......188 D3
Locks Heath SO31 ......128 E2
Saffron Dr BH23 ......208 B8
Saffron Way
Bournemouth BH11 ......188 D3
Whiteley PO15 ......129 D8
Sage Cl PO7 ......135 A6
Sages La GU34 ......17 D5
Sailor's La SO32 ......35 E1
Sailors La SO32 ......60 C8
Sainsbury Lodge PO1 ...216 D3
Saints Cl BH21 ......138 E8
St Adlem's CE Comb Sch BH12 ......204 A6
St Agatha's Rd SO31 ....128 A4
St Agathas Way PO1 ....216 B4

St Alban's Ave BH8 ....205 C7
St Alban's CE Prim Sch
PO9 ....136 A3
St Alban's Cres BH8 ....205 B8
St Alban's Rd
Bournemouth BH8 ....205 B7
Havant PO9 ....136 A4
Southampton SO14 ....103 B5
St Albans Ct 14 PO13 ....180 D5
St Albans Rd PO4 ....182 F3
St Aldhelm's BH14 ....203 F4
St Aldhelm's Cl BH13 ....203 F3
St Aldhelm's Pl BH13 ....203 F4
St Aldhelm's Rd BH13 ....203 F4
St Andrew Cl PO8 ....88 C2
St Andrew's Bldgs SO31 .128 A2
St Andrew's Rd
Farlington PO6 ....158 F8
Gosport PO12 ....181 B5
Portsmouth PO5 ....216 C2
South Hayling PO11 ....185 B2
St Andrews 3 BH23 ....207 A6
St Andrews Cl
Michelmersh SO51 ....27 D6
North Baddesley SO52 ....53 E5
St Andrews Gn SO32 ....61 C5
St Andrews Ho 3 SO17 .103 B8
St Andrews Pk SO50 ....81 D6
St Andrews Rd
Broadstone BH18 ....187 A5
Southampton SO14 ....103 A5
St Ann's Cres PO12 ....181 A7
St Ann's Ct 1 BH1 ....205 E5
St Ann's Hospl BH13 ....214 E6
St Ann's Rd
Horndean PO8 ....112 C7
Portsmouth PO4 ....182 F3
St Anne's Ave BH6 ....206 E5
St Anne's Gdns SO19 ....103 E2
St Anne's Gr PO14 ....154 F7
St Anne's RC Sch SO15 ..102 F6
St Anne's Rd
Southampton SO19 ....103 E2
Upton BH16 ....201 B7
St Anne's Sch PO13 ....179 E3
St Annes Cl SO22 ....215 A2
St Annes Gdns SO41 ....197 D3
St Annes Ho SO51 ....52 E6
St Annes La SO32 ....107 E7
St Annes Mews 18 SO14 .103 A8
St Anns Ct SO17 ....79 B2
St Anthony's RC Prim Sch
PO14 ....129 D1
St Anthony's Rd BH2 ....204 F5
St Antony's 6 BH4 ....204 D2
St Aubin's Ave SO19 ....104 B5
St Aubin's Pk PO11 ....184 D3
St Aubyns Ct BH15 ....202 B2
St Aubyns La BH24 ....117 E1
St Augustin's Rd BH2 ....204 F5
St Augustine Gdns SO17 .79 D1
St Augustine Rd PO4 ....182 F3
St Austell Cl SO50 ....56 E3
St Barbara Way PO2 ....157 F4
St Barbe Cl SO51 ....53 A6
St Barbe Mus* SO41 ....197 E4
St Bartholomew's Gdns
PO5 ....216 C1
St Bede CE Prim Sch
SO23 ....215 E6
St Bede's Ct 8 SO23 ....215 E7
St Bernard Ho 15 SO14 ..103 A3
St Birinus Rd SP5 ....47 D6
St Blaize Rd SO51 ....53 C8
St Boniface Ct SO52 ....54 B3
St Bonnet Dr SO32 ....83 C8
St Brelade Pl SO16 ....77 D3
St Brelades Ave BH12 ....188 D1
St Catherine St PO5 ....182 D1
St Catherine's Par BH23 .191 F1
St Catherine's RC Prim Sch
BH21 ....164 B6
St Catherine's Rd
Bournemouth BH6 ....206 F3
Eastleigh SO50 ....56 B5
South Hayling PO11 ....184 C4
Southampton SO18 ....79 E1
Winchester SO23 ....215 F4
St Catherine's Way
BH23 ....191 D3
St Catherines BH21 ....163 C4
St Catherines Ct PO11 ....184 C3
St Catherines Rd SO50 ....56 A5
St Catherines View
SO30 ....105 A6
St Catherines Way
PO16 ....131 E1
St Chad's Ave PO2 ....157 E2
St Christopher Ave
PO16 ....131 C3
St Christopher Ct 1
PO5 ....182 E1
St Christopher's Rd
PO9 ....135 C4
St Christophers Cl SO52 ..54 A4
St Christophers Gdns
PO13 ....155 C2
St Christophers Hospl
PO16 ....131 B3
St Christophers Mobile Home
Pk PO8 ....88 D3
St Christophers Sch
SO18 ....103 E8
St Clair Rd BH13 ....214 F7
St Clares Ave PO9 ....135 D7
St Cleeve Way BH22 ....165 C3
St Clement St 2 SO23 ..215 D5
St Clement's & St John's CE
Inf Sch BH1 ....205 D5
St Clement's Gdns BH1 .205 D5
St Clement's Rd BH1 ....205 D5
St Clements Cl SO51 ....52 E8
St Clements Rd BH15 ....203 A7
St Colman's Ave PO6 ....158 A8
St Contest Way SO40 ....124 F8
St Cross Ct 4 SO23 ....215 D3
St Cross Hospl* SO23 ....215 D2
St Cross Mede SO23 ....215 C2
St Cross Rd SO23 ....215 D3
St Cuthberts Cl SO31 ....129 B4
St Cuthberts La SO31 ....129 B4
St Cyres Meml Cotts
SO41 ....197 F5
St David's Cl SO40 ....76 C1
St David's Ct
3 Bournemouth BH1 ....205 E5
Gosport PO13 ....180 C6
North Baddesley SO52 ....54 A3
St David's Rd
Clanfield PO8 ....88 C5
Portsmouth PO5 ....216 C2
Upton BH16 ....201 B7
St Davids Rd SO31 ....128 F3
St Denys 2 BH25 ....195 B1
St Denys Prim Sch SO17 .79 C1
St Denys Rd SO17 ....79 C1
St Denys Wlk PO9 ....135 D6
St Denys' Sta SO17 ....103 C8
St Edmondsbury Ct 6
PO13 ....180 D5
St Edmund Cl PO14 ....129 B1
St Edmund's Rd SO16 ...102 B8
St Edmunds RC Sch
PO1 ....216 C3
St Edward's RC/CE Sch
BH15 ....202 F7
St Edward's Rd
Gosport PO12 ....181 B5
Portsmouth PO5 ....216 B1
St Edward's Sch SO51 ....25 A1
St Edward's Terr 6
PO12 ....181 A7
St Edwards Rd SO31 ....127 B7
St Elizabeth's Ave SO18 .104 B7
St Evox Cl SO16 ....77 F5
St Faith's CE Prim Sch
SO22 ....215 D3
St Faith's Cl PO12 ....181 A6
St Faith's Rd
Portsmouth PO1 ....216 B4
Winchester SO23 ....215 D3
St Francis Ave SO18 ....104 B8
St Francis CE Prim Sch
SO53 ....55 A5
St Francis Cl SO45 ....177 E7
St Francis Ct
Locks Heath PO14 ....129 C3
2 Portsmouth PO2 ....157 E4
St Francis Pl PO9 ....135 E3
St Francis Rd
Blackfield SO45 ....177 E7
Gosport PO12 ....181 C2
St Francis Specl Sch
PO14 ....154 C8
St Gabriel's Rd SO18 ....104 B7
St George Cl SO31 ....104 F1
St George RC Sch (Boys)
SO17 ....79 C6
St George's Almshos 6
BH15 ....202 B1
St George's Ave
Bournemouth BH8 ....205 C8
Havant PO9 ....136 B1
Poole BH12 ....203 B8
St George's Beneficial CE
Prim Sch PO1 ....182 A5
St George's Bsns Ctr 44
PO1 ....182 A5
St George's Cl
Bournemouth BH8 ....205 C8
Christchurch BH23 ....208 D8
St George's Cotts SP6 ....47 D3
St George's Cres SP6 ....69 F3
St George's Ct
2 Bournemouth BH1 ....205 E5
North Baddesley SO52 ....54 A3
St George's Ct BH12 ....203 B8
St George's Ct 7 PO5 ....216 A1
St George's Dr BH22 ....165 C4
St George's Ho 16 SO23 .215 E6
St George's Rd
Cosham PO6 ....157 F8
Portsmouth,Eastney PO4 ..183 A2
Portsmouth,Old Portsmouth
PO1 ....182 A4
South Hayling PO11 ....184 D3
St George's Sq 2 SO32 ..83 C7
St George's St SO23 ....215 E6
St George's Way PO1 ....182 A5
St George's Wlk 3 PO7 ..134 E7
St Georges Cotts
Martin SP6 ....43 C3
Woodgreen SP6 ....70 D8
St Georges Ct
Fareham PO16 ....155 B8
Ferndown BH22 ....165 E5
St Georges Dr
Bournemouth BH11 ....188 D3
Bransgore BH23 ....193 B8
St Georges Ho 4 SO17 ....103 B8
St Georges Ind Est PO4 .183 A5
St Georges Mans 5
BH5 ....205 F4
St Georges Rd
Fordingbridge SP6 ....69 F2
Locks Heath SO31 ....128 F3
St Georges Sq PO1 ....182 A5
St Georges St SO14 ....103 A4
St Georges Wlk PO12 ....181 D6
St Giles Cl SO23 ....215 F5
St Giles Hill SO23 ....215 F5
St Giles Way PO8 ....88 C2
St Helen's Mans 7
PO4 ....182 E1
St Helen's Par PO4 ....182 E1
St Helen's Rd
Gosport PO12 ....180 E3
South Hayling PO11 ....184 D3
St Helena Gdns SO18 ....79 F3
St Helena Way PO16 ....156 C8
St Helens Cl PO4 ....182 F2
St Helens Mews SO50 ....57 D2
St Helier Pl SO16 ....77 E3
St Helier Rd
Gosport PO12 ....181 C9
Poole BH12 ....188 D1
St Hellen's Rd PO6 ....158 D8
St Hermans Cvn Est
PO11 ....185 C2
St Hermans Mans PO11 .185 C2
St Hermans Rd PO11 ....185 C2
St Hilda Ave PO8 ....88 C2
St Hubert Rd PO8 ....88 C2
St Ives End La BH24 ....140 A4
St Ives Fst Sch BH24 ....140 B5
St Ives Gdns BH2 ....204 F5
St Ives Pk BH24 ....140 A5
St Ives Wood BH24 ....140 C5
St James CE Fst Sch SP6 .93 A6
St James CE Prim Sch
PO10 ....136 F2
St James Cl Clanfield PO8 .88 C4
2 Poole BH15 ....202 B1
Southampton SO15 ....78 C1
St James Cvn Pk SO52 ....30 A1
St James Ho 14 SO14 ....103 A3
St James Hospl PO4 ....183 C5
St James Park Rd SO16 ..78 C2
St James Pk (Cvn Pk)
SO52 ....55 A8
St James Rd
Ferndown BH22 ....165 A6
Sway SO41 ....172 C2
Upper Shirley SO15 ....78 C1
West End SO30 ....80 D2
St James Way PO16 ....156 C8
St James' CE Prim Sch
Bournemouth BH7 ....206 B6
West End SO30 ....80 F2
St James' La SO22,SO23 .215 D5
St James' Rd PO10 ....136 F1
St James' Terr SO22,
SO23 ....215 D5
St James' Villas SO23 ....215 D5
St James's 1 BH5 ....205 E3
St James's Rd
Portsmouth PO5 ....216 B2
Southampton SO15 ....102 D8
St James's Sq BH5 ....206 A5
St James's St PO1 ....182 B5
St John the Baptist CE Prim
Sch
Titchfield PO14 ....129 C2
Waltham Chase SO32 ....83 E2
St John's Ave PO7 ....134 E3
St John's CE Prim Sch
PO12 ....181 B8
St John's Cl
Gosport PO12 ....181 B6
Wimborne Minst BH21 ....163 D4
St John's Coll PO5 ....216 C1
St John's Ct
4 Bournemouth BH1 ....205 E5
North Baddesley SO52 ....54 B3
2 Portsmouth PO2 ....157 C1
St John's Ctr SO30 ....105 B6
St John's Gdns 2 BH9 ..189 F1
St John's Hill BH21 ....163 D5
St John's Hospital
(Almshouses)(N) 1
SO23 ....215 F5
St John's Hospital
(Almshouses)(S) 3
SO23 ....215 F5
St John's Rd
Bournemouth BH5 ....205 E4
Breach PO10 ....137 D1
Christchurch BH23 ....207 A6
Cosham PO6 ....158 A8
Eastleigh SO50 ....56 B4
Havant PO9 ....135 C4
Hedge End SO19,SO30 ....105 B5
Locks Heath SO31 ....129 B2
Poole BH15 ....202 D4
Winchester SO23 ....215 F6
St John's St Hythe SO45 .126 A4
Winchester SO23 ....215 F5
St Johns CE Fst Sch
BH21 ....163 D4
St Johns Cl
Rownhams SO16 ....77 E7
South Hayling PO11 ....184 F2
St Johns Ct SO40 ....101 F1
St Johns Dr SO40 ....101 E1
St Johns Gdns SO51 ....52 F8
St Johns Glebe SO16 ....77 F6
St Johns Inf Sch SO14 ...102 F3
St Johns La SO32 ....107 E7
St Johns Mews
Locks Heath SO31 ....129 C3
Portsmouth PO5 ....216 C1
St Johns RC Prim Sch
PO1 ....216 C3
St Johns Rd BH25 ....195 A7
St Johns Sq 6 PO12 ....181 B6
St Joseph Cl SO31 ....129 B3
St Joseph's RC Comb Sch
BH12 ....203 E7
St Joseph's RC Prim Sch
BH23 ....208 A8
St Josephs Mews PO5 ..216 C1
St Jude's CE Prim Sch
PO1 ....182 B3
St Jude's RC Prim Sch
PO14 ....130 E1
St Judes Cl PO5 ....216 B1
St Julien's Hospl
(Almshouses) SO14 ....103 A2
St Just Cl BH22 ....165 C3
St Katharine's CE Prim Sch
BH6 ....207 B4
St Kitts Ho 4 PO6 ....132 F2
St Lawrence Cl SO30 ....81 D2
St Lawrence Rd
Eastleigh SO50 ....56 A4
2 Southampton SO14 ....103 B3
St Ledger's Pl BH8 ....205 D6
St Ledger's Rd BH8 ....205 D6
St Leonard's Ave PO11 ..185 A3
St Leonard's Rd
Bournemouth BH8 ....205 B6
Winchester SO23 ....11 C6
St Leonards Cl PO15 ....129 E3
St Leonards Farm Pk
BH22 ....166 A8
St Leonards Hospl
BH24 ....139 C1
St Leonards Rd SO41 ....199 B8
St Leonards Way BH24 ..139 D4
St Lucia Ho 2 PO6 ....132 F2
St Luke's CE Prim Sch
Bournemouth BH9 ....204 F8
Sway SO41 ....172 B1
St Luke's CE Sec Sch
PO5 ....216 B3
St Luke's Rd
Bournemouth BH3 ....204 F7
Gosport PO12 ....181 A7
St Lukes Cl SO30 ....81 C1
St Maradox La BH9 ....189 F2
St Margaret's Almshouses
BH21 ....163 A5
St Margaret's Ave BH23 .207 B5
St Margaret's Cl SO18 ...104 B7
St Margaret's Cotts SO32 .59 D2
St Margaret's Hill BH21 .163 A6
St Margaret's Rd
Bishopstoke SO50 ....56 D4
Bournemouth BH10 ....189 C2
Poole BH15 ....202 D4
St Margarets BH2 ....204 F5
St Margarets Cl BH21 ...163 A5
St Margarets Hill BH21 .163 A5
St Margarets La PO14 ...129 E1
St Margarets Rd PO11 ....185 A3
St Mark's CE Jun Sch
SO15 ....102 D7
St Mark's CE Prim Sch
BH10 ....189 C1
St Mark's Cl PO12 ....181 B2
St Mark's Pl PO12 ....181 B3
St Mark's Rd
Bournemouth BH11 ....189 B3
Gosport PO12 ....181 A3
Portsmouth PO2 ....157 D1
St Marks Cl SO53 ....30 F1
St Marks Ct 2 PO12 ....181 A6
St Marks Rd
Lymington SO41 ....197 B3
Southampton SO14 ....103 B5
St Martin's Cl
Southampton SO16 ....77 E3
Winchester SO23 ....215 F6
St Martin's Ho 1 PO5 ..182 D1
St Martins Cl SO50 ....56 D4
St Martins Rd BH16 ....201 A7
St Martins Trad Pk
SO23 ....215 F6
St Mary Gr SO41 ....196 B2
St Mary Magdalen
Almshouses 4 SO23 ...215 F5
St Mary St
Southampton SO14 ....103 B4
Winchester SO22 ....215 B3
St Mary's SO51 ....52 E6
St Mary's Ave PO12 ....181 A3
St Mary's CE Prim Sch
SO14 ....103 B4
St Mary's Church Cl
SO18 ....79 D4
St Mary's Cl
Droxford SO32 ....61 B1
Kings Worthy SO21 ....2 C5
Redlynch SP5 ....47 F4
St Mary's Coll SO18 ....103 F8
St Mary's Ct BH6 ....206 E3
St Mary's Ho PO1 ....182 F6
St Mary's Hospl East Wing
PO3 ....183 A6
St Mary's Hospl West Wing
PO1 ....182 F6
St Mary's Maternity Hospl
BH15 ....202 D3
St Mary's Mews BH22 ....165 D4
St Mary's Pl SO14 ....103 A4
St Mary's RC Comb Sch
BH15 ....202 E5
St Mary's RC Prim Sch
PO12 ....181 A6
St Mary's Rd
Bishopstoke SO50 ....56 D4
Bournemouth BH1 ....205 D6
Ferndown BH22 ....165 D5
Liss GU33 ....20 F4
Netley SO31 ....127 C6
Poole BH15 ....202 E4
Portsmouth PO1 ....182 F6
South Hayling PO11 ....184 F3
Southampton SO14 ....103 A6
Stubbington PO14 ....154 C4
St Mary's Terr SO21 ....32 A6
St Marys Cl BH23 ....193 C8
St Mathews Rd SO22 ....215 B8
St Matthew's Rd PO6 ....157 F8
St Matthews Cl 2 SO14 .103 A5
St Matthews Ct PO12 ....181 D6
St Merrin's Cl BH10 ....189 C4
St Michael & All Angels CE
Inf Sch SO43 ....121 F5
St Michael's BH2 ....204 D3
St Michael's CE Mid Sch
BH21 ....163 E7
St Michael's CE Prim Sch
BH2 ....204 D3
St Michael's Ct 17 PO6 ..133 B1
St Michael's Gdns 8
SO23 ....215 D5
St Michael's Gr PO14 ....154 F7
St Michael's Ho PO14 ....154 F8
St Michael's Mews 9
BH2 ....204 E3
St Michael's Pas SO23 ....215 E4
St Michael's Pl 11 BH2 ..204 E3
St Michael's Rd
Bournemouth BH2 ....204 E2
Havant PO9 ....135 C3
Portsmouth PO1 ....216 A2
Winchester SO23 ....215 D4
St Michael's Rdbt BH4 ..204 D3
St Michael's Sq 11 SO14 .102 F3
St Michael's St 13 SO14 .102 F3
St Michaels Cl
Blackfield SO45 ....150 F1
Hamworthy BH15 ....201 E3
Verwood BH31 ....114 F5
St Michaels Ct 1 BH6 ..206 C4
St Michaels Rd
Locks Heath SO31 ....129 A2
Totton SO40 ....100 F8
Verwood BH31 ....114 F4
St Michaels Way PO8 ....88 C2
St Monica Inf Sch SO19 .104 A3
St Monica Jun Sch
SO19 ....104 A3
St Monica Rd SO19 ....104 A3
St Nicholas Ave PO13 ....180 C7
St Nicholas Flats 3
PO2 ....157 D1
St Nicholas Rise SO23 ....2 B6
St Nicholas Row PO17 ...108 A3
St Nicholas St PO1 ....182 A3
St Nicholas' Rd PO9 ....135 C3
St Osmund's Rd BH14 ....203 D3
St Patrick's Ct SO52 ....54 A3
St Patrick's La GU33 ....21 D5
St Patrick's RC Prim Sch
SO19 ....103 E3
St Paul's Hill SO22 ....215 D6
St Paul's La BH8 ....205 B4
St Paul's Pl BH8 ....205 B4
St Paul's Rd
Bournemouth BH8 ....205 B4
Portsmouth PO5 ....216 A2
Sarisbury SO31 ....128 E6
St Paul's Sq PO5 ....216 A2
St Pauls Ct 15 SO22 ....215 D6
St Pauls Pl 26 SO23 ....215 D6
St Pauls RC Prim Sch
PO6 ....157 B8
St Peter St SO23 ....215 E6
St Peter's Ave PO11 ....160 C2
St Peter's Ct
14 Petersfield GU32 ....40 F3
3 Poole BH14 ....203 A4
St Peter's Gate 13 BH1 ..204 F3
St Peter's Gr PO5 ....216 C1
St Peter's RC Comp Sch
BH6 ....206 F4
St Peter's RC Prim Sch
SO22 ....10 B5
St Peter's RC Sch BH7 ..206 B8
St Peter's Rd
Bournemouth BH1 ....205 A3
Petersfield GU32 ....40 F3
Poole BH14 ....203 A4
St Peter's Rdbt BH1 ....205 A3
St Peter's Sq 7 PO10 ....160 F8
St Peter's St SO32 ....83 C8
St Peter's Wlk 15 BH1 ....204 F3
St Peters Cl SO32 ....106 D8
St Peters Ct
3 Bournemouth BH1 ....205 A3
1 Emsworth PO10 ....161 A8
St Peters RC Prim Sch
PO7 ....134 F5
St Peters Rd PO11 ....160 C3
St Philip's Way SO18 ....104 B7
St Pirans Ave PO3 ....183 A7
St Quentin Ho 2 PO14 ..154 E7
St Richards Gdns PO7 ....134 C5
St Ronan's Ave PO4 ....182 E2
St Ronan's Rd PO4 ....182 E2
St Saviours Cl BH7 ....206 C7
St Sebastian Cres PO16 .131 B1
St Simon Cl SO31 ....129 B3
St Simons Rd PO5 ....182 D1
St Stephen's Ct BH2 ....204 E

St Stephen's Rd
Bournemouth BH2 ....204 E3
Winchester SO22 ....215 B8
St Stephen's Way 4 BH2 ....204 F3
St Stephens La BH31 ....115 A7
St Stephens Rd PO2 ....182 E8
St Swithun Cl SO32 ....83 B8
St Swithun St SO23 ....215 F5
St Swithun Wells RC Prim Sch SO53 ....55 E5
St Swithun's Cl SO51 ....28 D1
St Swithun's RC Prim Sch PO5 ....182 D2
St Swithun's Rd BH1 ....205 B4
St Swithun's Rd S BH1 ..205 B4
St Swithun's Rdbt BH1 ..205 B3
St Swithun's Sch SO21 ...11 D8
St Swithuns Ct 8 SO14 .103 A6
St Swithuns Rd PO2 ....157 F2
St Theresas Cl PO9 ....135 C3
St Thomas Ave PO11 ....184 D3
St Thomas Cl
Bournemouth BH10 ....189 D2
Fareham PO16 ....131 C3
St Thomas Ct SO50 ....57 D2
St Thomas Garnet's RC Sch BH5 ....206 A5
St Thomas Mews 3 SO23 ....215 D5
St Thomas More's RC Prim Sch PO9 ....135 D3
St Thomas Pk SO41 ....197 D3
St Thomas St SO23 ....215 D5
St Thomas's Ct 5 PO1 ..182 A4
St Thomas's Rd PO12 ..181 B9
St Thomas's St
Lymington SO41 ....197 E3
Portsmouth PO1 ....182 A3
St Tristan Cl SO31 ....129 B2
St Ursula Gr PO5 ....216 C1
St Valerie Rd
Bournemouth BH2 ....204 F5
Gosport PO12 ....181 B4
St Vigor Way SO21 ....56 F8
St Vincent Coll PO12 ....181 B6
St Vincent Cres PO8 ....112 B6
St Vincent Rd
Gosport PO12 ....181 B7
Portsmouth PO5 ....182 D2
St Vincent St PO5 ....216 A2
St Walburga's RC Prim Sch BH9 ....190 B1
St Winifred's Rd
Bournemouth BH2 ....204 F5
Southampton SO16 ....78 C2
St Winifred's Sch SO17 ..79 A1
Salcombe Ave PO3 ....158 A1
Salcombe Cl SO53 ....55 B4
Salcombe Cres SO40 ....100 E6
Salcombe Rd
Southampton SO15 ....102 C7
Totton SO40 ....100 E6
Salcot Rd SO23 ....215 E8
Salem St SO15 ....78 C1
Salerno Dr PO12 ....180 F4
Salerno Ho
Fareham PO14 ....154 F7
Romsey SO51 ....53 B7
Salerno Pl BH15 ....201 D2
Salerno Rd
Portsmouth PO2 ....157 D4
Southampton SO16 ....78 C5
Salet Way PO7 ....112 B1
Salisbury Cl SO50 ....56 B4
Salisbury Ct 1 SO50 ....56 B4
Salisbury Rd
Awbridge SO51 ....52 B6
Bournemouth BH1 ....205 E4
Breamore SP6 ....46 C2
Burton BH23 ....192 D2
Cosham PO6 ....158 A7
Ellingham BH24 ....116 F5
Fordingbridge SP6 ....70 A5
Ibsley BH24 ....94 A1
Ower SO51 ....75 D8
Ower,Stonyford SO51 ....75 F4
Poole BH14 ....203 C5
Portsmouth PO4 ....182 F2
Ringwood BH24 ....140 F8
Sopley,Winkton BH23 ....192 B5
Southampton SO17 ....79 A3
Totton SO40 ....76 C3
West Wellow SO51 ....51 B1
Salisbury Road Arc 4 SO40 ....100 F7
Salisbury St
Fordingbridge SP6 ....69 F1
6 Southampton SO15 ....102 F6
Salisbury Terr PO13 ....179 F2
Salmon Dr SO50 ....56 F2
Salt La SO24,SO32 ....34 E3
Salt Meat La PO12 ....181 D7
Salter Rd BH13 ....214 C3
Salterne Ho 2 SO41 ....197 E2
Salterns Ave PO4 ....183 B6
Salterns Cl PO11 ....185 C3
Salterns Ct BH14 ....214 B8
Salterns Est PO16 ....155 B7
Salterns La
Bursledon SO31 ....128 A7
Fareham PO16 ....155 B7
South Hayling PO11 ....185 C3
Salterns Point BH14 ....214 B8
Salterns Quay BH14 ....214 B8
Salterns Rd Poole BH14 ..203 A3
Stubbington PO13,PO14 ....179 B5
Salterns Sch SO40 ....101 A7
Salterns Way BH14 ....214 B8
Salters Acres SO22 ....1 C3
Salters La SO22 ....1 B2
Saltgrass La SO41 ....212 A3
Saltings Rd BH16 ....201 B6
Saltings The
Farlington PO6 ....158 E7
Langstone PO9 ....159 F6
Saltmarsh La PO11 ....184 F5
Saltmarsh Rd SO14 ....103 B3
Saltmead SO17 ....79 C1
Salvia Cl PO7 ....135 A6
Salwey Rd SO30 ....105 D5
Samantha Cl BH10 ....189 E3
Samber Cl SO41 ....197 C4
Sammy Miller Motorcycle Mus* BH25 ....194 E5
Sampan Cl SO31 ....128 E1
Samphire Cl SO41 ....197 E5
Samples Way BH17 ....202 F8
Sampson Rd
Fareham PO14 ....154 F6
Portsmouth PO1 ....181 F7
Samson Cl PO13 ....180 D7
Samson Rd BH15 ....201 D2
Samuel Rd PO1 ....182 F6
San Diego Rd PO12 ....181 B7
San Remo Twrs 4 BH5 ..205 E3
Sancreed Rd BH12 ....203 E7
Sancroft Ho BH21 ....164 A1
Sand Cl SO51 ....50 E3
Sandbanks Bsns Ctr BH13 ....214 B3
Sandbanks Rd BH14, BH15 ....203 A2
Sandbourne Rd
Bournemouth BH4 ....204 C1
Poole BH15 ....202 D4
Sandcroft Cl PO12 ....180 E3
Sandecotes Rd BH14 ....203 C3
Sandell Ct SO16 ....79 B5
Sanderling Rd PO4 ....183 D5
Sanderlings BH24 ....141 C6
Sanderlings The PO11 ....185 A2
Sandford Ave PO12 ....180 D4
Sandford Cl BH9 ....190 C3
Sandford Way BH18 ....186 F2
Sandhill La PO13 ....180 A6
Sandhills Cl BH17 ....187 D2
Sandhurst Ct PO5 ....216 C1
Sandhurst Dr BH21 ....139 A7
Sandhurst Rd SO15 ....102 E6
Sandilands Way 7 SO45 ....126 A1
Sandisplatt PO14 ....154 C8
Sandle Copse SP6 ....69 B2
Sandleford Rd PO9 ....135 D7
Sandleheath Ind Est SP6 .69 B2
Sandleheath Rd SP6 ....92 F8
Sandlewood Cl
Clanfield PO8 ....88 C5
Totton SO40 ....100 C8
Sandmartin Cl BH25 ....209 F7
Sandown Cl PO12 ....180 D3
Sandown Rd
Christchurch BH23 ....207 E6
Cosham PO6 ....157 E7
Southampton SO15 ....78 B1
Sandpiper Cl
Broadstone BH17 ....186 F1
Horndean PO8 ....112 A7
Marchwood SO40 ....101 E1
Sandpiper Rd SO16 ....78 B6
Sandpipers PO6 ....158 E7
Sandpit La SO41 ....199 D5
Sandport Gr PO16 ....156 B7
Sandringham Cl
Bournemouth BH9 ....190 B4
Chandler's Ford SO53 ....54 F4
Sandringham Ct
Bournemouth BH8 ....205 C6
13 Gosport PO12 ....181 C9
5 Southampton,Millbrook SO15 ....102 A6
14 Westwood Park SO17 ....79 A1
Sandringham Gdns BH9 .190 B4
Sandringham La PO1 ..216 D3
Sandringham Rd
Fareham PO14 ....154 C8
Petersfield GU32 ....40 F4
Poole BH14 ....203 C3
Portsmouth PO1 ....216 D3
Southampton SO18 ....79 E1
Sandsbury La GU32 ....40 C5
Sandy Balls Holiday Ctr SP6 ....70 D2
Sandy Beach Est PO11 ..185 F1
Sandy Brow PO7 ....134 D3
Sandy Cl Petersfield GU31 .41 C3
Wimborne Minst BH21 ....164 A8
Sandy Down SO41 ....173 C4
Sandy La
Abbotswood SO51 ....28 B3
Bournemouth BH6 ....206 B5
Christchurch BH23 ....191 E2
Fair Oak SO50 ....57 B2
Lyndhurst SO43 ....121 F4
North Baddesley SO52 ....54 B5
Pamphill BH21 ....162 B5
Rake GU33 ....21 E4
Redlynch SP5 ....47 E7
St Leonards BH24 ....140 A5
Steep Marsh GU32 ....41 B8
Three Legged Cross BH21 .114 E2
Titchfield PO14 ....153 F8
Upton BH16 ....201 B6
Verwood BH31 ....115 A6
Waltham Chase SO32 ....83 C2
Sandy La *continued*
Wimborne Minst BH21 ....164 A8
Sandy Mead Rd BH8 ....190 F1
Sandy Plot BH23 ....207 C8
Sandy Point Rd PO11 ....185 E1
Sandy Way BH10 ....189 E4
Sandyfield Cres PO8 ....111 E3
Sandyhurst Cl BH17 ....187 C1
Sanross Cl PO14 ....179 A6
Santoy BH13 ....214 D5
Saplings The SO45 ....150 B5
Sapphire Cl 1 PO12 ....181 C8
Sapphire Ridge PO7 ....135 A7
Saracen Cl SO41 ....197 C1
Saracens Rd SO53 ....55 F7
Sarah Cl BH7 ....206 B8
Sarah Robinson Ho 22 PO1 ....182 A5
Sarah Sands Cl BH23 ...207 D8
Sarisbury CE Jun Sch SO31 ....128 E5
Sarisbury Gate 4 SO31 .129 B5
Sarisbury Inf Sch SO31 ..128 E4
Sark Rd BH12 ....203 D8
Sarnia Ct SO16 ....77 E3
Sarum Ave BH22 ....138 E4
Sarum Cl SO22 ....215 A5
Sarum Ct Poole BH14 ....203 C4
Winchester SO22 ....215 B5
Sarum Rd
Chandler's Ford SO53 ....55 E6
Winchester SO22 ....10 B7
Sarum Road Hospl SO22 ....215 A5
Sarum St 12 BH15 ....202 B1
Sarum View SO22 ....10 B7
Sarum Wlk SO41 ....197 D6
Satchell La SO31 ....128 A4
Saturn Cl SO16 ....77 F4
Saulfland Dr BH23 ....208 D8
Saulfland Ho BH23 ....208 D8
Saulfland Pl BH23 ....208 D8
Saunders Cl PO13 ....180 A7
Saunders Ho PO6 ....132 E1
Saunders La SO51 ....26 E6
Saunders Mews 5 PO4 .183 B2
Savernake Cl
Gosport PO13 ....155 D2
9 Romsey SO51 ....28 B1
Saville Cl
Bishopstoke SO50 ....56 D5
Gosport PO12 ....180 F3
Saville Ct BH21 ....163 D3
Saville Gdns PO16 ....131 A3
Savoy Bldgs 6 PO16 ....131 B1
Savoy Ho SO40 ....101 A7
Sawmills The SO32 ....82 B5
Sawyer Cl SO22 ....1 B1
Saxe Ct 12 PO17 ....130 E7
Saxholm Cl SO16 ....78 F6
Saxholm Dale SO16 ....78 F6
Saxholm Way SO16 ....78 F6
Saxley Ct PO9 ....135 C6
Saxon Cl Horndean PO8 ...88 C3
Locks Heath SO31 ....128 E1
Portchester PO16 ....132 B1
Saxon Ct 17 SO23 ....215 E6
Saxon Gdns SO30 ....105 A5
Saxon Ho 17 SO14 ....103 C6
Saxon Hts BH6 ....206 E5
Saxon King Gdns BH6 ...207 B4
Saxon Mdw SP5 ....46 F7
Saxon Pl SO41 ....197 D6
Saxon Rd Blackfield SO45 .150 F1
Southampton SO15 ....102 D5
Winchester SO23 ....215 E7
Saxon Shore Inf Sch PO6 ....156 E8
Saxon Sq Sh Ctr BH23 ...207 B6
Saxon Way Alderholt SP6 ..93 A5
Romsey SO51 ....53 C7
Saxon Wlk SO53 ....55 E5
Saxonbury Rd BH6 ....206 E5
Saxonford Rd BH23 ....208 C7
Saxonhurst SP5 ....47 A7
Saxonhurst Cl BH10 ....189 E5
Saxonhurst Gdns BH10 ..189 E4
Saxonhurst Rd BH10 ....189 E4
Sayers Rd SO50 ....56 E3
Scafell Ave PO14 ....154 D8
Scallows La SO51 ....50 E6
Scantabout Ave SO53 ....55 F7
Scantabout Prim Sch SO53 ....55 F7
Scarf Rd BH17 ....202 F7
Scarff Ct PO11 ....185 B2
Scholars' Wlk PO6 ....158 C7
School Cl
Chandler's Ford SO53 ....55 B5
Verwood BH31 ....115 A7
School Hill SO32 ....85 C6
School La
Bournemouth BH11 ....189 B6
Bransgore BH23 ....169 E4
Chandler's Ford SO53 ....55 B5
Compton PO18 ....90 F2
Denmead PO7 ....110 D5
Emsworth PO10 ....160 F8
Hamble-le-R SO31 ....128 A2
Kings Worthy SO23 ....2 B4
3 Liss GU33 ....20 F4
Lymington SO41 ....197 E4
Lymington,Warborne SO41 .197 F8
Milford on S SO41 ....211 E6
Petersfield GU32 ....41 B6
Poole BH15 ....202 C5
Ringwood BH24 ....141 A7
Southbourne PO18 ....161 F7
School La *continued*
St Leonards BH24 ....140 A4
Three Legged Cross BH21 .138 F7
Westbourne PO10 ....137 B5
Wimborne Minst BH21 ....163 B5
School Pl SO19 ....103 E4
School Rd
Bransgore BH23 ....169 E4
Bursledon SO31 ....128 A8
Fawley SO45 ....151 B3
Gosport PO12 ....155 F1
Havant PO9 ....135 E1
Hythe SO45 ....126 A4
Nomansland SP5 ....73 C8
Redlynch SP5 ....48 A5
Romsey SO51 ....28 C1
Totton SO40 ....101 A6
Twyford SO21 ....31 F5
West Wellow SO51 ....50 F2
Wickham PO17 ....108 A3
Schooner Way
Locks Heath SO31 ....128 E1
Portsmouth PO4 ....183 C6
Schooners Cl PO13 ....179 F4
Scimitars The PO14 ....179 B8
Scivier's La SO32 ....58 C2
Scotland Cl SO50 ....57 E2
Scotney Ct 18 PO9 ....136 B6
Scott Cl Poole BH12 ....188 F1
Stubbington PO14 ....154 C4
Scott Ho 2 PO2 ....157 C2
Scott Rd Eastleigh SO50 ....55 F2
Poole BH12 ....188 F1
Poole BH12 ....203 F8
Portsmouth,Hilsea PO3 ....157 F5
Portsmouth,Hilsea PO3 ....158 A5
Portsmouth,Portsea Island PO1 ....181 F7
Southampton SO19 ....103 F1
Scott's Gn BH23 ....207 F8
Scott-Paine Dr SO45 ....126 B4
Scotter Rd
Bishopstoke SO50 ....56 D3
Bournemouth BH7 ....206 B6
Scotter Sq SO50 ....56 D3
Scotts Cl
Colden Common SO21 ....57 A8
Downton SP5 ....46 E8
Scotts Hill La BH23 ....207 D7
Scratchface La
Havant PO9 ....135 B2
Waterlooville PO7 ....134 F4
Scullards La 1 SO14 ....102 F4
Scylla Ind Est SO23 ....11 C8
Sea Breeze Gdns PO4 ....183 C3
Sea Crest Rd PO13 ....179 F2
Sea Front PO11 ....184 E3
Sea Front Est PO11 ....185 B2
Sea Grove Ave PO11 ....185 A2
Sea Kings PO14 ....179 B7
Sea La PO14 ....179 C5
Sea Mill Gdns 35 PO1 ...182 A5
Sea Pines 9 SO41 ....211 C4
Sea Point 8 BH13 ....214 F7
Sea Rd Barton on S BH25 ..209 E8
Bournemouth BH5 ....205 E4
Bournemouth,Southbourne BH6 ....206 F3
Milford on S SO41 ....211 E4
Southampton SO19 ....103 D4
Sea View Cotts PO10 ....160 F8
Sea View Est SO31 ....127 B5
Sea View Rd
Cosham PO6 ....134 D1
Poole BH15 ....203 A6
Upton BH16 ....201 A7
Sea Vixen Ind Est BH23 ..208 A8
Seabank Cl BH16 ....201 A7
Seabird Way PO16 ....155 B7
Seabourne Pl 5 BH5 ....206 B5
Seabourne Rd BH5 ....206 B5
Seabreeze Way SO41 ....211 B6
Seacliff Ct BH6 ....206 D3
Seacombe Gn SO16 ....77 D1
Seacombe Rd BH13 ....214 B3
Seacroft Ave BH25 ....209 E8
Seafarers Wlk PO11 ....185 F1
Seafield Cl BH25 ....209 F7
Seafield Dr BH6 ....206 E5
Seafield Park Rd PO14 ..179 B6
Seafield Rd
Barton on S BH25 ....209 E8
Bournemouth BH6 ....206 D4
Christchurch BH23 ....208 C7
Portchester PO16 ....156 B7
Portsmouth PO3 ....158 A1
Southampton SO16 ....77 E3
Seafield Terr PO12 ....181 C4
Seafields PO10 ....160 E8
Seaford Cl SO31 ....104 F1
Seagarth Cl SO16 ....78 D3
Seagarth La SO16 ....78 D3
Seager's Ct PO1 ....181 F4
Seagrim Rd BH8 ....190 C3
Seagrove Rd PO2 ....157 D1
Seagull Cl PO4 ....183 C6
Seagull Ct PO10 ....136 F1
Seagull La PO10 ....136 F1
Seagull Rd BH8 ....190 C1
Seagulls The PO13 ....180 A4
Seahorse Wlk PO12 ....181 D6
Sealark Rd PO12 ....181 B8
Seaman's La SO43 ....98 C4
Seamead PO14 ....179 C5
Seamoor La BH4 ....204 B3
Seamoor Rd BH4 ....204 B3
Searles Hill SO21 ....32 A6
Seathrift Cl PO13 ....179 E3
Seathwaite Ho 15 PO6 ..133 B1
Seaton Ave PO3 ....183 A8
Seaton Cl
Christchurch BH23 ....209 B8
Lymington SO41 ....197 E5
Stubbington PO14 ....179 C7
West End SO18 ....80 C1
Seaton Rd BH23 ....209 B8
Seatown Cl BH17 ....188 A1
Seaview Ave PO16 ....132 E1
Seaview Ct
9 Gosport PO12 ....180 D3
Lee-on-t-S PO13 ....179 F2
Seaview Rd
Barton on S BH25 ....209 D7
South Hayling PO11 ....185 D3
Walkford BH23 ....194 C1
Seaward Ave
Barton on S BH25 ....209 F7
Bournemouth BH6 ....206 B4
Seaward Gdns SO19 ....103 E4
Seaward Rd SO19 ....103 E4
Seaward Twr 11 PO12 ...181 E5
Seaway BH25 ....210 B8
Seaway Ave BH23 ....208 C7
Seaway Cres PO4 ....183 D4
Seaway Gr PO16 ....156 C6
Seaweed Cl SO19 ....126 E8
Seawinds SO41 ....211 A5
Sebastian Gr PO7 ....135 A8
Second Ave Cosham PO6 .157 E8
Farlington PO6 ....158 E8
Havant PO9 ....136 B2
Southampton SO15 ....101 D7
Southbourne PO10 ....161 D8
Second Marine Ave BH25 ....210 A6
Second St SO45 ....150 E8
Sedberg Ho SO16 ....77 D1
Sedbergh Rd SO16 ....77 D1
Seddon Cl BH25 ....210 B8
Seddul-Bahr SO30 ....80 E5
Sedgefield Cl
Portchester PO6 ....156 F8
Totton SO40 ....100 C8
Sedgeley Gr PO12 ....181 A8
Sedgemead SO31 ....127 B5
Sedgemead Ct SO31 ....127 B5
Sedgewick Cl PO13 ....180 C8
Sedgewick Rd SO19 ....104 C5
Sedgley Cl PO5 ....216 C2
Sedgley Rd BH9 ....204 E8
Sedgwick Cl SO50 ....56 D3
Sedgwick Rd SO50 ....56 D3
Seed Warehouse The 3 BH15 ....202 C1
Segars La SO21 ....31 F5
Segensworth E Ind Est PO15 ....129 D5
Segensworth N Ind Est PO15 ....129 E5
Segensworth Rd PO15 ..129 E3
Segensworth W Ind Est PO15 ....129 C5
Selangor Ave PO10 ....136 D1
Selborne Ave
Havant PO9 ....135 D5
Southampton SO18 ....104 C8
Selborne Cl GU32 ....40 F5
Selborne Ct 3 SO51 ....28 B1
Selborne Gdns PO12 ....181 A5
Selborne Pl SO22 ....215 B3
Selborne Wlk SO18 ....104 C8
Selbourne Dr SO50 ....56 A4
Selbourne Rd
Havant PO9 ....135 E1
Totton SO40 ....100 D8
Selbourne Terr PO1 ....216 D3
Selby Cl BH18 ....187 A3
Seldon Cl SO22 ....10 B4
Seldown BH15 ....202 D3
Seldown Bridge BH15 ...202 D2
Seldown La BH15 ....202 D3
Seldown Rd BH15 ....202 D3
Self Rd BH15 ....202 A2
Selfridge Ave BH6 ....207 B3
Selfridge Cl BH6 ....207 B3
Selhurst Ho PO1 ....216 C4
Selhurst Way SO50 ....57 C1
Seliot Cl BH15 ....202 D5
Selkirk Cl BH21 ....163 E1
Sellwood Rd SO31 ....127 C6
Sellwood Way BH25 ....209 D8
Selma Ct 1 PO5 ....182 D2
Selman Cl SO45 ....126 B4
Selsdon Ave SO51 ....53 B8
Selsey Ave Gosport PO12 .181 A9
Portsmouth PO4 ....183 A2
Selsey Cl
South Hayling PO11 ....185 F2
Southampton SO16 ....77 E2
Selsmore Ave PO11 ....185 C3
Selsmore Rd PO11 ....185 B3
Selwood Pk BH10 ....189 C7
Selworth La SO32 ....85 B3
Selworthy Cl BH14 ....203 A2
Selwyn Ct 8 PO6 ....157 F7
Selwyn Gdns SO50 ....56 A5
Sengana Cl SO30 ....105 D6
Senlac Rd SO51 ....53 B7
Sennen Pl PO6 ....157 A7
Sentinal Ct BH15 ....202 E3
Sentinel Cl PO7 ....112 B1
Seps 4 Rd SO45 ....151 C4
September Cl SO30 ....80 D1

Serle Cl SO40 ....100 B7
Serle Gdns SO40 ....100 D6
Sermon Rd SO22 ....215 A7
Serotine Cl PO17 ....130 E7
Serpentine Rd
Fareham PO16 ....131 B2
Poole BH15 ....202 C3
7 Portsmouth PO5 ....182 C2
Waterlooville PO7 ....134 C3
Service Rd PO6 ....157 D8
Set Oaks Cvn Site BH25 .171 E5
Set Thorns Rd SO41 ....172 C2
Setley Gdns BH8 ....190 E3
Setters Cl SO21 ....56 F8
Settle Cl 4 SO16 ....102 B8
Settlers Cl PO1 ....216 C4
Sevenoaks Dr BH7 ....206 A8
Sevenoaks Rd PO6 ....157 E8
Severn Cl
Portchester PO16 ....156 A8
Portsmouth PO6 ....133 B1
Severn Rd
Ferndown BH22 ....166 A5
Southampton SO16 ....101 E8
Severn Way SO30 ....80 D1
Seward Rd SO45 ....126 B3
Seward Rise SO51 ....53 C8
Seymour Cl
Chandler's Ford SO53 ....55 E5
Portsmouth PO2 ....182 D7
Southampton SO16 ....78 C3
Totton SO40 ....76 C1
Seymour Gdns BH24 ....117 B1
Seymour Ho SO16 ....78 D3
Seymour La SO52 ....53 F4
Seymour Rd
Lee-on-t-S PO13 ....180 A4
Ringwood BH24 ....117 B1
Southampton SO16 ....78 D3
Shackleton Ho 2 PO2 ..157 E2
Shackleton Rd PO13 ....180 D8
Shackleton Sq BH23 ....169 B1
Shadwell Ct 9 PO2 ....157 C2
Shadwell Rd PO2 ....157 D2
Shaftesbury Ave
Chandler's Ford SO53 ....55 C4
Southampton SO17 ....79 B2
Waterlooville PO7 ....134 E5
Shaftesbury Cl BH22 ....138 F2
Shaftesbury Ct BH3 ....204 F6
Shaftesbury Rd
Bournemouth BH8 ....205 C6
Gosport PO12 ....181 C4
Poole BH15 ....202 D3
Portsmouth,Southsea PO5 .182 C2
West Moors BH22 ....138 F2
Shaftesbury St SP6 ....69 F1
Shaftsbury Rd
Gosport PO12 ....181 C4
Gosport PO12 ....181 C5
Shaggs Mdw SO43 ....122 A5
Shakespeare Ave SO17 ..103 B8
Shakespeare Bsns Ctr
SO50 ....56 B4
Shakespeare Dr SO40 ....76 D2
Shakespeare Gdns PO8 .111 E3
Shakespeare Inf Sch
SO50 ....56 A5
Shakespeare Jun Sch
SO50 ....56 A5
Shakespeare Mews
PO14 ....154 A8
Shakespeare Rd
Bournemouth BH6 ....206 D7
Eastleigh SO50 ....56 A4
Portsmouth PO1 ....182 E7
Wimborne Minst BH21 ....163 C6
Shakespeare Terr 12
PO1 ....182 A3
Shalbourne Rd PO12 ....181 A8
Shalcombe SO31 ....127 C7
Shaldon Cl SO16 ....78 C4
Shaldon Rd 8 PO9 ....136 B6
Shales Rd SO18 ....104 B7
Shallow La SO41 ....197 E8
Shallows The SP6 ....70 C7
Shamblehurst La N SO32 .81 D3
Shamblehurst La S SO30 .81 C1
Shamblehurst Prim Sch
SO30 ....105 C8
Shamrock Cl PO12 ....181 D5
Shamrock Ct 2 BH21 ....163 C4
Shamrock Quay SO14 ....103 D5
Shamrock Rd SO19 ....103 D3
Shamrock Villas 3 SO17 .79 C1
Shamrock Way SO45 ....126 A5
Shanklin Cres SO15 ....78 D1
Shanklin Rd
Portsmouth PO4 ....182 E4
Southampton SO15 ....78 D2
Shannon Cl PO15 ....130 D2
Shannon Ct 7 PO12 ....181 C9
Shannon Ho 9 SO14 ....103 C5
Shannon Rd
Gosport PO14 ....155 A5
Stubbington PO14 ....179 B8
Shannon Way SO53 ....55 B6
Shapland Ave BH11 ....188 E5
Shappen Hill La BH24 ....142 F1
Shapton Cl SO45 ....150 B4
Shapwick Rd BH15 ....202 A1
Shard Cl BH31 ....115 A6
Sharland Pl 6 PO14 ....154 E7
Sharlands Cl BH18 ....187 B3
Sharlands Rd PO14 ....155 A6
Sharon Ct 4 PO12 ....181 C6
Sharon Rd SO30 ....80 C2
Sharp Rd BH12 ....204 A7
Sharp's Copse Prim Sch
PO9 ....136 B5
Sharp's Rd PO9 ....136 B5
Sharpley Cl SP6 ....69 E3
Sharpness Cl PO14 ....154 C8
Sharps Cl PO3 ....158 B3
Sharps Rd PO9 ....136 B5
Sharvells Rd SO41 ....211 C5
Shavard La SO32 ....61 D6
Shaves La BH25 ....195 A5
Shaw Cl Totton SO40 ....100 D7
West End SO18 ....80 A2
Shaw Rd BH24 ....117 C2
Shawcross Ind Pk PO3 ..158 A5
Shawford Cl
Southampton SO16 ....78 E4
Totton SO40 ....100 B7
Shawford Gdns BH8 ....190 D2
Shawford Gr PO9 ....135 C5
Shawford Rd
Bournemouth BH8 ....190 D3
Twyford SO21 ....31 F6
Shawford Sta SO21 ....31 E6
Shayer Rd SO15 ....78 C1
Shear Hill GU31 ....41 B5
Sheardley La SO32 ....62 A1
Shearer Rd PO1 ....182 E7
Shears Brook Cl BH23 ..169 B1
Shears Rd SO50 ....56 E3
Shearwater Ave PO16 ..155 E8
Shearwater Cl PO13 ....155 B2
Shearwater Ct PO11 ....185 D1
Shearwater Dr PO6 ....158 F7
Sheep Pond La SO32 ....61 B3
Sheep St GU32 ....40 F3
Sheepwash La PO7 ....133 F8
Sheet Prim Sch GU32 ....41 B6
Sheffield Cl SO50 ....56 D5
Sheffield Ct 11 PO13 ....180 C6
Sheffield Rd PO1 ....216 D3
Sheiling Sch The BH24 ..140 C6
Shelbourne Cl BH8 ....205 D6
Shelbourne Rd BH8 ....205 B6
Sheldrake Gdns
Hordle SO41 ....196 B3
Southampton SO16 ....78 B5
Sheldrake Rd BH23 ....208 A5
Shelford Rd PO4 ....183 B5
Shell Bay Sailing Ctr*
BH19 ....214 A1
Shell Ct SO40 ....101 F2
Shellcroft SO31 ....152 D10
Shelley Ave PO6 ....132 E1
Shelley Cl
Bournemouth BH1 ....205 E5
Christchurch BH23 ....208 C7
St Leonards BH24 ....139 E5
Winchester SO22 ....215 B6
Shelley Ct
10 Bournemouth BH4 ....204 C3
Ferndown BH22 ....165 D5
Southampton SO15 ....102 E5
Shelley Gdns
Bournemouth BH1 ....205 E5
Waterlooville PO8 ....111 E3
Shelley Hamlets BH23 ..208 D7
Shelley Hill BH23 ....208 D7
Shelley Ho 9 BH25 ....195 A2
Shelley La SO51 ....75 E8
Shelley Rd
Bournemouth BH1 ....205 E5
Eastleigh SO50 ....55 F1
Poole BH12 ....203 D5
Southampton SO19 ....104 E6
Totton SO40 ....76 D2
Shelley Rd E BH7 ....205 F5
Shelley Way SO41 ....211 D5
Shelton Rd BH6 ....206 C6
Shenley Cl PO15 ....130 C2
Shenstone Ct 2 BH25 ..195 A1
Shepards Cl PO14 ....154 C8
Shepheard's Way PO12 .181 C3
Shepherd Cl BH23 ....193 F1
Shepherds Cl
Bartley SO40 ....99 B6
Winchester SO22 ....10 B4
Shepherds Down Specl Sch
SO21 ....31 C6
Shepherds Hey Rd SO40 .76 B1
Shepherds Hill BH24 ....116 C6
Shepherds La
Compton SO21 ....31 C6
Ellingham BH24 ....116 B6
Shepherds Purse Cl
SO31 ....128 F2
Shepherds Rd
Bartley SO40 ....99 C6
Winchester SO23 ....11 C8
Shepherds Way
Bournemouth BH7 ....206 A7
Everton SO41 ....196 D1
Nursling SO16 ....77 C5
Sheppard Cl PO8 ....112 A6
Sheppards Field 4
BH21 ....163 B6
Shepperd Terr 14 PO13 ..180 C6
Sherborn Cres BH17 ....188 A2
Sherborne Ct SO50 ....56 A6
Sherborne Dr BH22 ....165 D4
Sherborne House Sch
SO53 ....55 D8
Sherborne Rd SO17 ....79 B3
Sherborne Way SO30 ....105 C6
Sherbrooke Cl
Kings Worthy SO23 ....2 C8
Sherbrooke Cl *continued*
Lee-on-t-S PO13 ....180 A6
Sherecroft Gdns SO30 ..106 B7
Sherfield Ave PO9 ....136 A5
Sherfield Cl BH8 ....190 D2
Sherfield English La
SO51 ....50 C6
Sherfield English Rd SP5 .50 B4
Sherfield Ho 10 SO15 ....102 E7
Sheridan Cl
Southampton SO19 ....104 D5
Winchester SO22 ....215 A3
Sheridan Gdns
Swanwick PO15 ....129 C8
Totton SO40 ....100 D7
Sheringham Rd
Poole BH12 ....203 F5
Portsmouth PO6 ....133 D1
Sherley Gn SO31 ....105 A1
Sherrin Cl BH15 ....202 D5
Sherringham Cl SO45 ....151 B3
Sherwin Wlk PO12 ....181 A4
Sherwood Ave
Ferndown BH22 ....165 C3
Hedge End SO30 ....105 C4
Poole BH14 ....203 A3
Sherwood Cl
Christchurch BH23 ....206 F7
Liss GU33 ....21 A7
Southampton SO16 ....78 E3
Sherwood Dr BH31 ....115 B6
Sherwood Gdns SO31 ....128 E4
Sherwood Rd
Chandler's Ford SO53 ....30 E1
Gosport PO12 ....181 A5
Sherwood Way SO45 ....177 E7
Shetland Cl
Portsmouth PO6 ....133 F1
Totton SO40 ....100 B8
Shetland Rise PO15 ....129 B7
Shetland View BH31 ....115 A6
Shillinglee PO7 ....134 E4
Shillingstone Dr BH9 ....190 B3
Shillingstone Gdns 3
BH12 ....203 F7
Shillito Rd BH12 ....203 E5
Shinewill Gdns 4 SO16 .101 E8
Shingle Bank Dr SO41 ..211 D4
Shinwell Ct 8 SO15 ....78 B1
Ship Leopard St 12 PO1 .182 A5
Shipbuilding Rd PO1 ....181 F8
Shipcote La SO32 ....59 D2
Shipley Rd SO21 ....32 A7
Shipstal Cl BH16 ....201 C4
Shipton Gn PO9 ....135 D6
Shipwrights Wlk SO41 ..212 B3
Shire Cl Swanwick PO15 ..129 B7
Waterlooville PO7 ....112 C1
Shires Cl BH24 ....141 A4
Shires Copse BH6 ....206 F3
Shires Mead BH31 ....115 A6
Shires The SO30 ....105 A6
Shires Wlk SO40 ....100 B7
Shirley Ave
Portsmouth PO4 ....183 C4
Southampton SO15 ....102 C8
Shirley Cl
Bransgore BH23 ....169 B1
West Moors BH22 ....138 E2
Shirley High St SO15,
SO16 ....102 B8
Shirley Holms SO41 ....173 B1
Shirley Inf Sch SO15 ....78 C1
Shirley Park Rd SO16 ....102 B8
Shirley Pk SO16 ....78 C2
Shirley Rd
Bournemouth BH9 ....190 A1
Poole BH12 ....203 B6
Portsmouth PO5 ....182 E2
Southampton SO15 ....102 C7
Upton BH16 ....201 C7
Shirley Twrs SO15 ....102 C8
Shirley Warren Prim Sch
SO16 ....78 A2
Shirrel Ct 7 PO12 ....180 D3
Shoblands Way 6 SO45 .126 A1
Shoe La Meonstoke SO32 ..61 C6
Upham SO32 ....58 F6
Sholing Ct PO9 ....135 D6
Sholing Inf Sch SO19 ....104 A5
Sholing Jun Sch SO19 ....104 A5
Sholing Rd SO19 ....103 E4
Sholing Sta SO19 ....103 F2
Sholing Tech Coll The
SO19 ....104 A4
Shoot Hill PO7,PO17 ....109 D3
Shoot La PO13 ....180 A8
Shooters Hill Cl SO19 ....104 B3
Shop La SO19,SO31 ....104 E2
Shore Ave
Portsmouth PO4 ....183 B6
Upton BH16 ....201 C6
Shore Cl
Milford on S SO41 ....211 D4
Upton BH16 ....201 C6
Shore Cres SO32 ....83 D7
Shore Gdns BH16 ....201 B6
Shore Ho SO31 ....128 C1
Shore La
Bishop's Waltham SO32 ....83 D7
Upton BH16 ....201 C6
Shore Rd Hythe SO45 ....126 B3
Poole BH13 ....214 D6
Warsash SO31 ....128 C1
Shoreacres BH13 ....214 C3
Shorefield Country Pk
SO41 ....211 A6
Shorefield Cres SO41 ....211 C5
Shorefield Rd
Marchwood SO40 ....101 F2
Milford on S SO41 ....211 A6
Shorefield Way SO41 ....211 C5
Shorehaven PO6 ....156 F8
Shorewood Cl SO31 ....128 F1
Short Cl BH12 ....204 A8
Short Hill Nomansland SP5 .73 B8
Romsey SO51 ....28 C1
Short Rd PO14 ....179 A7
Short Row PO1 ....182 A6
Short's Farm SO51 ....50 D7
Shorts Cl BH23 ....192 C1
Shorts Rd SO50 ....57 C2
Shorwell SO31 ....127 C7
Shotterfield Terr GU33 ....20 F4
Shotters Hill Cl SO30 ....80 D1
Shotts La SO41 ....198 C4
Shottsford Rd BH15 ....202 C5
Shraveshill Cl SO40 ....76 D1
Shrubb's Ave SO41 ....197 E4
Shrubbery Cl PO16 ....156 C7
Shrubbery The PO12 ....180 F7
Shrubbs Hill Gdns SO43 .121 F4
Shrubbs Hill Rd SO43 ..121 F4
Shrubland Cl SO18 ....104 B8
Sibland Cl PO14 ....154 D8
Siblings The SO19 ....104 E6
Sicily Ho 7 PO14 ....154 E7
Siddal Cl SO19 ....104 C4
Sidings The Downton SP5 ..47 A8
Netley SO31 ....127 D5
Sidlesham Cl PO11 ....185 F2
Sidmouth Ave 1 PO3 ....183 A8
Sidney Gdns 2 BH9 ....190 B4
Sidney Smith Ct BH17 ..187 E2
Sidney St SO41 ....196 A2
Silchester Cl BH2 ....204 F5
Silchester Pl 11 SO23 ..215 E7
Silchester Rd PO3 ....183 B7
Silhouette Ct PO11 ....185 D1
Silkin Gdns SO40 ....100 D6
Silkstead Ave PO9 ....135 F6
Silkstead La SO21 ....30 F7
Sillen La SP6 ....43 A3
Silver Birch Ave PO14 ..154 E8
Silver Birch Cl Liss GU33 ..21 A4
Poole BH13 ....204 A4
Southampton SO19 ....104 C4
Silver Birch Way 1
PO15 ....129 D8
Silver Birches SO31 ....127 F8
Silver Bsns Pk BH23 ....207 F7
Silver Hill SO23 ....215 E5
Silver St
5 Christchurch BH23 ....207 B6
Hordle SO41 ....196 C5
Lyndhurst SO43 ....121 D5
1 Portsmouth PO5 ....216 A1
Silver Way BH23 ....208 E7
Silverdale BH25 ....210 B7
Silverdale Cl BH18 ....186 E4
Silverdale Cres SP6 ....93 A6
Silverdale Ct 5 SO15 ....102 E7
Silverdale Dr PO7 ....111 C3
Silverdale Rd SO15 ....102 E7
Silverlock Pl PO10 ....137 B5
Silvers End 2 SO45 ....126 A1
Silvers Wood SO40 ....76 C1
Silversands Ct PO11 ....184 F3
Silversands Gdns PO11 ..185 B2
Silverthorne Way PO7 ..134 D8
Silvertrees
Emsworth PO10 ....136 F2
Sarisbury SO31 ....128 E6
Silverweed Ct SO53 ....54 F7
Silverweed Ct SO31 ....128 E2
Silverwood Cl
Merley BH21 ....163 D2
Winchester SO22 ....215 B3
Silvester Rd PO8 ....111 F2
Silwood Cl SO22 ....215 C7
Simmonds Cl BH15 ....202 D5
Simmons Cl SO30 ....105 C8
Simmons Gn PO11 ....185 C3
Simnel St 8 SO14 ....102 F3
Simon Ct SO18 ....104 E7
Simon Way SO18 ....104 E6
Simonds Ct 6 SO23 ....215 E8
Simpkins Ct 13 SO53 ....30 B1
Simpson Cl PO16 ....156 C8
Simpson Rd PO2 ....157 C1
Sinah La PO11 ....184 C4
Sinclair Ct 4 BH14 ....203 A4
Sinclair Prim Sch SO16 ..78 A5
Sinclair Rd SO16 ....78 A5
Singleton Dr BH10 ....189 C2
Singleton Gdns PO8 ....88 D4
Singleton Way SO40 ....100 B8
Sir Christopher Ct SO45 .126 B4
Sir Galahad Rd SO53 ....54 F6
Sir George's Rd SO15 ....102 D6
Sir Harold Hillier Gardens &
Arboretum* SO51 ....28 D4
Sir John's Mews SO32 ....35 B3
Sir Lancelot Cl SO53 ....54 F6
Sirdar Ho SO17 ....79 C3
Sirdar Rd SO17 ....79 C3
Sirius Ct PO5 ....216 B2
Sirius Ho 11 PO5 ....182 D2
Siskin Cl
Bishop's Waltham SO32 ....83 A8
Ferndown BH22 ....165 B7
Southampton SO16 ....78 A5
Siskin Gr PO7 ....135 A6
Siskin Inf Sch PO13 ....180 D6
Siskin Jun Sch PO13 ....180 D6
Siskin Rd PO4 ....183 C5
Sissinghurst Cl SO19 ....104 A1
Sissinghurst Rd PO16 ..156 A7
Siward Ho GU32 ....40 E3
Six Dials SO14 ....103 A5
Six Oaks Rd SO52 ....54 A4
Sixpenny Cl
Locks Heath PO14 ....129 A1
Poole BH12 ....203 F7
Sixth Ave PO6 ....157 E8
Sizer Way SO45 ....125 B3
Skew Rd PO17 ....132 D2
Skinner St BH15 ....202 C1
Skintle Gn SO21 ....56 F8
Skipper Cl SO40 ....102 A3
Skipper Way PO13 ....180 A5
Skipton Cl BH18 ....187 A2
Skipton Rd SO53 ....55 D4
Sky End La SO41 ....196 A2
Skye Cl PO6 ....133 F1
Skylark Ct PO4 ....183 C5
Skylark Mdws
Fareham PO15 ....130 A6
Whiteley PO15 ....129 F5
Skys Wood Rd SO53 ....54 F6
Slab La Redlynch SP5 ....47 C6
West Wellow SO51 ....50 E3
Slade Cl SO41 ....196 A3
Slade The GU32 ....18 F2
Slade's La BH10 ....204 C8
Slader Bsns Pk BH17 ....187 E1
Slades Farm Rd BH10 ....189 D2
Slades Hill SO45 ....150 F2
Slater App PO2 ....157 A1
Slater Cl SO40 ....100 B8
Sleepbrook Cl BH31 ....114 E6
Sleeper's Hill SO22 ....215 B4
Sleeper's Hill Ho SO22 ..215 B4
Sleepers Delle Gdns
SO22 ....215 C4
Sleepers Hill Gdns
SO22 ....215 B4
Sleight La BH21 ....186 C8
Slepe Cres BH12 ....203 F8
Slindon Cl PO8 ....88 D5
Slindon Gdns 4 PO9 ....135 F1
Slindon St PO1 ....216 B3
Slingsby Cl PO1 ....216 A1
Slinn Rd BH23 ....207 E7
Slip Way BH15 ....202 B2
Slipper Cvn Pk PO10 ....161 A8
Slipper Rd PO10 ....161 A8
Slipway The PO6 ....157 A7
Sloane Ave SO45 ....150 D4
Sloane Pk SO32 ....107 D7
Sloane Stanley Ct PO12 .181 B7
Slocum Ho 18 PO12 ....181 C5
Sloe Tree Cl SO31 ....129 C2
Slough La BH16 ....201 A6
Small Cl GU31 ....41 A5
Smallcutts Ave PO10 ....137 D1
Smeaton Cl PO15 ....129 E4
Smeaton St 7 PO2 ....157 C2
Smeeton Rd PO13 ....179 F3
Smith Cl SO45 ....150 F2
Smith Gr SO30 ....105 C5
Smith La PO10 ....161 D1
Smith St PO12 ....181 A6
Smith's Field SO51 ....28 A1
Smithe Cl SO50 ....56 A3
Smithfield Pl BH9 ....189 F1
Smiths La SO32 ....107 F8
Smithson Cl BH12 ....204 C8
Smithy La BH25 ....194 F6
Smithy The PO7 ....110 E4
Smugglers La BH21 ....163 E7
Smugglers La N BH23 ....193 E1
Smugglers La S BH23 ....208 E8
Smugglers Reach BH23 .208 A5
Smugglers Wood Rd
BH23 ....193 D1
Smythe Rd SO19 ....104 D3
Snailing La GU33 ....20 C8
Snails La BH24 ....117 B3
Snakemoor La SO32 ....81 E5
Snapdragon Cl SO31 ....128 F2
Snape Cl PO13 ....180 C8
Snell's Cnr PO8 ....88 D3
Snellgrove Cl SO40 ....76 C2
Snellgrove Pl SO40 ....76 C2
Snooks La SO41 ....198 B6
Snowberry Cres PO9 ....136 C3
Snowdon Dr PO14 ....154 E8
Snowdon Rd BH4 ....204 C4
Snowdrop Cl SO31 ....128 F2
Snowdrop Gdns BH23 ....193 B1
Soake Rd PO7 ....111 B3
Soalwood La GU32 ....18 F1
Soberton Ho
Portsmouth PO1 ....216 C4
29 Southampton SO17 ....79 A1
Soberton Rd
Bournemouth BH8 ....205 D6
Havant PO9 ....135 E4
Soberton Twrs SO32 ....85 B6
Solar Ct BH13 ....204 A2
Soldridge Cl 5 PO9 ....136 B6
Solent Ave
Lymington SO41 ....198 A3
Southampton SO19 ....104 E6
Solent Breezes Cvn Site
SO31 ....152 F6
Solent Bsns Ctr SO15 ....102 B6
Solent Bsns Pk PO15 ....129 E2
Solent Cl
Chandler's Ford SO53 ....55 E6
Lymington SO41 ....197 F3
Solent Ct
6 Milford on S SO41 ....211 C4

Solent Ct *continued*
25 Portsmouth PO5 . . . . . . 182 C2
Southampton SO19 . . . . . . 103 E1
Stubbington PO14 . . . . . . 179 C7
Solent Ctr PO15 . . . . . . 129 E7
Solent Dr
Barton on S BH25 . . . . . . 210 A7
Hythe SO45 . . . . . . 125 F4
South Hayling PO11 . . . . . . 184 F2
Warsash SO31 . . . . . . 152 D8
Solent Gate
Gosport PO14 . . . . . . 155 B5
12 Portsmouth PO5 . . . . . . 182 E1
Solent Ho Fareham PO16 . 155 A7
Havant PO9 . . . . . . 136 A3
Solent Homes SO19 . . . . 104 E6
Solent Hts
Lee-on-t-S PO13 . . . . . . 179 E2
Portsmouth PO4 . . . . . . 183 D3
Solent Ind Ctr SO15 . . . . 102 C6
Solent Ind Est SO30 . . . . 81 B1
Solent Inf Sch PO6 . . . . 158 D8
Solent Jun Sch PO6 . . . . 158 D8
Solent Lo 5 BH25 . . . . 195 A1
Solent Mdws SO31 . . . . 128 A2
Solent Mead SO41 . . . . 197 E3
Solent Pines 2 SO41 . . . 211 B4
Solent Rd
Barton on S BH25 . . . . . . 209 D7
Bournemouth BH6 . . . . . . 207 A3
Cosham PO6 . . . . . . 158 C8
Havant PO9 . . . . . . 135 E1
Hythe SO45 . . . . . . 149 E8
Southampton SO15 . . . . . . 102 E4
Stubbington PO14 . . . . . . 179 A6
Walkford BH23 . . . . . . 194 B2
Solent View
Bournemouth BH6 . . . . . . 207 A3
Calshot SO45 . . . . . . 178 F8
Lee-on-t-S PO13 . . . . . . 179 D4
Portchester PO16 . . . . . . 132 B1
Walhampton SO41 . . . . . . 198 B3
Solent Village PO15 . . . . 129 E6
Solent Way
Beaulieu SO42 . . . . . . 148 F8
Gosport PO12 . . . . . . 180 F3
Milford on S SO41 . . . . . . 211 F4
Solihull Ho PO5 . . . . . . 216 A2
Solly Cl BH12 . . . . . . 203 E7
Solomon Way BH15 . . . . 201 D2
Solomons La SO32 . . . . . . 83 F2
Solona Cl SO53 . . . . . . 55 F7
Solway Ho 10 SO14 . . . . 103 C6
Somborne Ct 27 SO17 . . . 79 A1
Somborne Dr PO9 . . . . . 135 F5
Somborne Ho SO19 . . . . 103 F1
Somerby Rd BH15 . . . . . 202 D6
Somerford Ave BH23 . . . 208 B8
Somerford Bsns Pk
BH23 . . . . . . 208 A7
Somerford Cl SO19 . . . . 104 A6
Somerford Ct BH23 . . . . 208 E7
Somerford Prim Com Sch
BH23 . . . . . . 207 E7
Somerford Rd BH23 . . . . 207 F7
Somerford Rdbt BH23 . . 208 A8
Somerford Way BH23 . . . 207 E6
Somerley Rd BH9 . . . . . . 205 A8
Somerley View 1 BH24 . 141 A8
Somers Cl SO22 . . . . . . 215 B3
Somers Park Prim Sch
PO5 . . . . . . 216 C3
Somers Rd
Portsmouth PO5 . . . . . . 216 C2
Portsmouth PO5 . . . . . . 216 C3
Somers Rd N PO1 . . . . . . 216 D3
Somerset Ave SO18 . . . . 104 C7
Somerset Cres SO53 . . . . 55 D3
Somerset Ct 6 SO15 . . . 102 C6
Somerset Ho PO7 . . . . . . 111 C1
Somerset Rd
Bournemouth BH7 . . . . . . 206 A5
Christchurch BH23 . . . . . . 206 E8
Portsmouth PO5 . . . . . . 182 D1
Southampton SO17 . . . . . . 79 C2
Somerset Terr SO15 . . . . 102 C6
Somerstown Flats PO9 . 136 A1
Somerton Ave SO18 . . . . 104 B7
Somerton Cl BH25 . . . . . 195 D3
Somervell Cl PO12 . . . . . 181 A3
Somervell Dr PO16 . . . . . 131 A3
Somerville Ct BH25 . . . . 194 F3
Somerville Pl 1 PO2 . . . 157 C2
Somerville Rd
Bournemouth BH2 . . . . . . 204 D3
Kings Worthy SO23 . . . . . . 2 C8
Ringwood BH24 . . . . . . 141 C8
Sommers Ct SO19 . . . . . 103 C3
Sonata Ho PO6 . . . . . . 157 A7
Sonnet Way PO7 . . . . . . 135 B8
Sonning Way BH8 . . . . . . 190 B2
Sopers La
Christchurch BH23 . . . . . . 207 A6
Poole BH17 . . . . . . 187 B1
Sopley Cl BH25 . . . . . . 209 D8
Sopley Common Nature Reserve* BH23 . . . . . . 191 C8
Sopley Ct 16 PO9 . . . . . 136 B6
Sopley Farm Bldgs
BH23 . . . . . . 192 B6
Sopley Prim Sch BH23 . . 168 C1
Sopwith Cl BH23 . . . . . . 208 B6
Sopwith Cres BH21 . . . . 163 E2
Sopwith Rd SO50 . . . . . . 55 F3
Sopwith Way SO31 . . . . . 128 F8
Sorrel Cl Romsey SO51 . . . 28 C1
Waterlooville PO7 . . . . . . 135 A6
Sorrel Dr PO15 . . . . . . 129 D7
Sorrel Gdns BH18 . . . . . 186 F2
Sorrell Cl SO31 . . . . . . 128 F2
Sorrell Ct BH23 . . . . . . 208 B8
Sorrell Way BH23 . . . . . 208 B8
South Ave Fawley SO45 . . 150 E3
Holbury SO45 . . . . . . 150 C5
New Milton BH25 . . . . . . 195 B2
Portsmouth PO2 . . . . . . 157 E4
South Baddesley Rd
SO41 . . . . . . 198 B4
South Baddesley CE Prim Sch
SO41 . . . . . . 198 E6
South Bay PO10 . . . . . . 161 A3
South Cl Gosport PO12 . . 180 F2
Havant PO9 . . . . . . 160 A8
Romsey SO51 . . . . . . 28 C1
South Cliff Rd BH2 . . . . 204 F2
South Cross St PO12 . . . 181 D5
South Ct
Hamble-le-R SO31 . . . . . . 127 E2
Milford on S SO41 . . . . . . 211 E4
South Downs Coll PO7 . . 135 A3
South Dr Awbridge SO51 . . 27 B3
Littleton SO22 . . . . . . 1 B4
West Moors BH24 . . . . . . 166 B7
South East Cres SO19 . . 104 A4
South East Rd SO19 . . . . 104 A4
South End Cl SO21 . . . . . 30 B7
South Front
9 Romsey SO51 . . . . . . 52 F7
Southampton SO14 . . . . . . 103 A4
South Gr SO41 . . . . . . 197 F3
South Hampshire Ind Pk
SO40 . . . . . . 76 D2
South Haven Cl BH16 . . . 201 B3
South Hill Alderholt SP6 . . 93 A6
Droxford SO32 . . . . . . 85 A8
Southampton SO16 . . . . . . 79 A4
South Kinson Dr BH11 . . 189 B4
South La Breach PO10 . . . 137 E2
Buriton GU31 . . . . . . 65 D4
Clanfield PO8 . . . . . . 88 B6
Downton SP5 . . . . . . 46 E7
Horndean PO8 . . . . . . 89 B3
Nomansland SP5 . . . . . . 73 C7
Woodmancote PO10 . . . . . . 137 D3
South Lodge
Fareham PO15 . . . . . . 130 B1
Poole BH13 . . . . . . 214 G7
South Mill Rd SO15 . . . . 102 A7
South Millers Dale SO53 . 55 B7
South Normandy 4
PO1 . . . . . . 182 A4
South Par
Portsmouth PO5 . . . . . . 182 D1
5 Totton SO40 . . . . . . 100 F7
South Parade Pier*
PO4 . . . . . . 182 E1
South Park Rd BH12 . . . 204 A8
South Pl PO13 . . . . . . 180 A4
South Rd
Bournemouth BH1 . . . . . . 205 E5
Corfe Mullen BH21 . . . . . . 186 E6
Cosham PO6 . . . . . . 158 C7
Horndean PO8 . . . . . . 88 C1
Poole BH15 . . . . . . 202 C2
Portsmouth,Paulsgrove
PO6 . . . . . . 133 A2
Portsmouth,Portsea Island
PO1 . . . . . . 182 E7
South Hayling PO11 . . . . . . 184 F3
Southampton SO17 . . . . . . 103 C8
Southwick PO17 . . . . . . 133 A6
South Road Comb Sch
BH15 . . . . . . 202 C2
South Spur PO6 . . . . . . 133 B2
South Sq 9 PO17 . . . . . . 130 E7
South St Eastleigh SO50 . . 80 A8
Emsworth PO10 . . . . . . 160 F8
Gosport PO12 . . . . . . 181 D5
Havant PO9 . . . . . . 135 F1
Hythe SO45 . . . . . . 126 A4
Lymington SO41 . . . . . . 197 C2
Portsmouth PO5 . . . . . . 216 A1
Titchfield PO14 . . . . . . 153 F8
South Stoneham Ho
SO18 . . . . . . 79 D3
South Sway La SO41 . . . . 196 D7
South Terr PO1 . . . . . . 182 A5
South Trestle Rd SO45 . . 151 D5
South View
Bournemouth BH2 . . . . . . 204 F5
Waterlooville PO8 . . . . . . 112 A3
Winchester SO22 . . . . . . 215 C6
South View Park Homes
SO22 . . . . . . 215 A1
South View Pl 10 BH2 . . 204 E3
South View Rd
Christchurch BH23 . . . . . . 207 A6
Southampton SO15 . . . . . . 102 D8
Winchester SO22 . . . . . . 10 B4
South Weirs SO42 . . . . . 172 D8
South Western Cres
BH14 . . . . . . 203 B2
South Wood Gdns SO31 . 128 F3
Southampton Airport (Parkway) Sta SO18 . . . . 79 F6
Southampton Central Sta
SO15 . . . . . . 102 E5
Southampton City Coll
SO14 . . . . . . 103 B4
Southampton Gen Hospl
SO16 . . . . . . 78 B2
Southampton Hill PO14 . 129 F1
Southampton Ho 6
PO9 . . . . . . 136 A5
Southampton International Airport SO18 . . . . . . 79 F6
Southampton Maritime Mus* SO14 . . . . . . 102 F3
Southampton Oceanography Ctr SO14 . . . . . . 103 B2
Southampton Rd
Bartley SO40 . . . . . . 99 B7
Brockenhurst SO42,SO41 . . 173 A4
Cadnam SO40 . . . . . . 98 E8
Eastleigh SO50 . . . . . . 56 D1
Fareham PO16 . . . . . . 131 B2
Fordingbridge SP6 . . . . . . 70 B1
Hythe SO45 . . . . . . 125 F4
Locks Heath PO15 . . . . . . 129 C5
Locks Heath SO31 . . . . . . 129 C4
Lymington SO41 . . . . . . 197 D5
Lyndhurst SO43 . . . . . . 122 B6
Portsmouth PO6 . . . . . . 157 D8
Ringwood BH24 . . . . . . 141 B8
Romsey SO51 . . . . . . 53 A6
Titchfield PO14 . . . . . . 129 D3
Southampton Solent Univ
SO14 . . . . . . 103 A5
Southampton Solent Univ Marine Operations Ctr
SO40 . . . . . . 102 A2
Southampton St 3
SO15 . . . . . . 102 F6
Southbourne Ave
Cosham PO6 . . . . . . 158 B7
Emsworth PO10 . . . . . . 161 B8
Holbury SO45 . . . . . . 150 C4
Southbourne Coast Rd
BH6 . . . . . . 206 F3
Southbourne Cross Roads 5
BH6 . . . . . . 206 E3
Southbourne Gr BH6 . . . . 206 C4
Southbourne Jun & Inf Schs
PO10 . . . . . . 161 E8
Southbourne Lane Central 6
BH6 . . . . . . 206 C4
Southbourne Lane E 5
BH6 . . . . . . 206 C4
Southbourne Lane W
BH6 . . . . . . 206 B4
Southbourne Overcliff Dr
BH6 . . . . . . 206 D3
Southbourne Rd
Bournemouth BH6 . . . . . . 206 C4
Lymington SO41 . . . . . . 197 C3
Southbourne Sands
BH6 . . . . . . 206 D3
Southbourne Sta PO10 . . 161 E8
Southbrook Cl
Langstone PO9 . . . . . . 159 F8
Poole BH17 . . . . . . 188 A2
Southbrook Mews 5
SO32 . . . . . . 83 C8
Southbrook Rd
Langstone PO9 . . . . . . 159 F8
5 Southampton SO15 . . . . 102 E5
Southcliff PO13 . . . . . . 179 E4
Southcliff Rd SO14 . . . . 103 A7
Southcliffe Ho 1 SO14 . 103 A6
Southcliffe Rd
Barton on S BH25 . . . . . . 209 D7
Christchurch BH23 . . . . . . 208 C6
Southcote Rd BH1 . . . . . 205 C4
Southcroft Rd PO12 . . . . 180 F5
Southdale Ct SO53 . . . . . 55 C6
Southdene Rd SO53 . . . . . 55 C5
Southdown Ct 1 BH23 . . 207 F8
Southdown Rd
Compton SO21 . . . . . . 31 D5
Cosham PO6 . . . . . . 158 A8
Horndean PO8 . . . . . . 88 B2
Horndean PO8 . . . . . . 88 C3
Southdown View PO7 . . . 111 C2
Southdown Way BH22 . . 138 F1
Southend La SO32 . . . . . 109 D8
Southern Ave BH22 . . . . 139 A1
Southern Gdns SO40 . . . . 100 E7
Southern La
Barton on S BH25 . . . . . . 209 F8
Old Milton BH25 . . . . . . 194 F1
Southern Oaks BH25 . . . . 194 F1
Southern Rd
Bournemouth BH6 . . . . . . 206 C4
Fawley SO45 . . . . . . 151 F1
Lymington SO41 . . . . . . 197 D3
Southampton SO15 . . . . . . 102 E4
West End SO30 . . . . . . 80 E1
Southernhay PO7 . . . . . . 110 F4
Southernhay Rd BH31 . . . 115 B6
Southey Rd BH23 . . . . . . 207 F7
Southfield BH24 . . . . . . 141 A6
Southfield La BH24 . . . . 143 D2
Southfield Mews 6
BH24 . . . . . . 141 A6
Southfield Wlk PO9 . . . . 135 C7
Southfields Cl SO32 . . . . 83 C8
Southgate St SO23 . . . . . 215 D5
Southgate Villas SO23 . . . 215 D5
Southill Ave BH12 . . . . . 203 C6
Southill Gdns BH9 . . . . . 190 A1
Southill Rd
Bournemouth BH9 . . . . . . 190 A1
Poole BH12 . . . . . . 203 D7
Southlands Cosham PO6 . 158 A8
Lymington SO41 . . . . . . 197 C2
Southlands Ave
Bournemouth BH6 . . . . . . 206 F4
Corfe Mullen BH21 . . . . . . 186 D6
Southlands Cl BH21 . . . . 186 D6
Southlands Ct BH18 . . . . 187 A3
Southlands Sch & The Wing Ctr SO41 . . . . . . 197 F7
Southlawns Wlk BH25 . . . 194 F1
Southlea Ave BH6 . . . . . 206 F4
Southleigh Gr PO11 . . . . 184 F4
Southleigh Rd
Emsworth PO10 . . . . . . 136 F3
Havant PO9 . . . . . . 136 C3
Southmead Rd PO15 . . . . 130 E1
Southmoor La PO9 . . . . . 159 D7
Southsea Castle* PO5 . . . 182 C1
Southsea Cvn Pk PO4 . . . 183 D2
Southsea Inf Sch PO5 . . . 182 F2
Southsea Terr PO5 . . . . . 216 A1
Southview Droxford SO32 . . 61 B1
4 Portsmouth PO4 . . . . . . 182 F2
Southville Rd BH5 . . . . . 206 B5
Southwater PO13 . . . . . . 179 E3
Southway Gosport PO13 . . 155 C3
Titchfield PO15 . . . . . . 129 E3
Southways PO14 . . . . . . 179 D7
Southwick Ave PO16 . . . . 132 E1
Southwick Cl SO22 . . . . . . 1 D4
Southwick Ct PO14 . . . . . 155 A6
Southwick Hill Rd PO6 . . 133 E1
Southwick Ho 5 PO1 . . . 216 C4
Southwick Pl BH6 . . . . . . 206 C7
Southwick Rd
Bournemouth BH6 . . . . . . 206 C6
Denmead PO7 . . . . . . 110 E4
Portsmouth PO6 . . . . . . 133 C2
Wickham PO17 . . . . . . 108 C3
Southwood Ave
Bournemouth BH6 . . . . . . 206 C4
Walkford BH23 . . . . . . 194 B1
Southwood Cl
Ferndown BH22 . . . . . . 165 C6
Walkford BH23 . . . . . . 194 A1
Southwood Rd
Portsmouth PO2 . . . . . . 157 E4
South Hayling PO11 . . . . . . 185 D1
Sovereign Ave PO12 . . . . 181 C8
Sovereign Bsns Ctr
BH15 . . . . . . 202 B6
Sovereign Cl
Bournemouth BH7 . . . . . . 205 F8
Portsmouth PO4 . . . . . . 183 C5
Totton SO40 . . . . . . 100 C8
Sovereign Cres PO14 . . . 129 A1
Sovereign Ct
4 Eastleigh SO50 . . . . . . 56 A2
13 Southampton SO17 . . . . 79 A1
Sovereign Ctr 6 BH1 . . . 205 E4
Sovereign Dr
Hedge End SO30 . . . . . . 105 E6
Portsmouth PO4 . . . . . . 183 C5
Sovereign La PO7 . . . . . . 134 E3
Sovereign Pl BH24 . . . . . 140 F7
Sovereign Way SO50 . . . . 55 F6
Sowden Cl SO30 . . . . . . 105 B7
Sowley La SO41 . . . . . . 199 D5
Spain Bldgs GU32 . . . . . . 40 E3
Spain The GU32 . . . . . . 40 E3
Spalding Rd SO19 . . . . . 104 E5
Spaniard's La SO51 . . . . . 53 A3
Sparkford Cl
Bournemouth BH7 . . . . . . 206 B8
Winchester SO22 . . . . . . 215 C4
Sparkford Rd SO22 . . . . . 215 C5
Sparrow Cl PO8 . . . . . . 111 F4
Sparrow Ct PO13 . . . . . . 179 F4
Sparrow Sq SO50 . . . . . . 55 D2
Sparrowgrove SO21 . . . . . 31 D4
Sparrowhawk Cl PO3 . . . 158 A4
Sparsholt Cl PO9 . . . . . . 135 B5
Sparsholt Rd
Southampton SO19 . . . . . . 126 F8
Winchester SO21,SO22 . . . . . 9 C3
Spartan Cl
Stubbington PO14 . . . . . . 154 C5
Thorney Island PO10 . . . . . . 161 A3
Spartina Dr SO41 . . . . . . 197 E5
Spear Rd SO14 . . . . . . 103 A8
Spearywell Wood Woodland Wlk* SO51 . . . . . . 5 C4
Specks La PO4 . . . . . . 183 A5
Speedfield Pk PO14 . . . . 155 A5
Speedwell Cl
Chandler's Ford SO53 . . . . . 55 B5
Locks Heath SO31 . . . . . . 128 F2
Speedwell Dr BH23 . . . . 208 B8
Speggs Wlk 2 SO30 . . . . 105 C6
Speltham Hill PO7 . . . . . . 86 D2
Spencer Cl PO11 . . . . . . 185 A3
Spencer Ct
1 New Milton BH25 . . . . . . 195 B2
2 Portsmouth PO5 . . . . . . 182 D2
Stubbington PO14 . . . . . . 179 E7
Spencer Dr PO13 . . . . . . 179 F2
Spencer Gdns PO8 . . . . . 111 E3
Spencer Rd
Bournemouth BH1 . . . . . . 205 C4
Eastleigh SO50 . . . . . . 55 E2
Emsworth PO10 . . . . . . 136 E4
New Milton BH25 . . . . . . 195 B2
Poole BH13 . . . . . . 214 F8
Portsmouth PO4 . . . . . . 182 F2
Southampton SO19 . . . . . . 104 D6
Spenlow Cl PO2 . . . . . . 182 D8
Spenser Cl SO31 . . . . . . 152 D10
Spetisbury Cl BH9 . . . . . 190 B3
Spice Quay 1 PO1 . . . . . 182 A3
Spicer Ho PO1 . . . . . . 182 B6
Spicer La BH11 . . . . . . 188 E5
Spicer St PO1 . . . . . . 216 B4
Spicer's Hill SO40 . . . . . 100 F5
Spicer's Way SO40 . . . . . 100 E6
Spicers Ct 2 SO22 . . . . . 215 D6
Spicewood PO15 . . . . . . 130 E2
Spinacre BH25 . . . . . . 210 B8
Spindle Cl
Broadstone BH18 . . . . . . 186 F2
Spindle Cl *continued*
Havant PO9 . . . . . . 136 C3
Spindle Warren PO9 . . . . 136 C3
Spindlewood Cl
10 Old Milton BH25 . . . . . . 195 A1
Southampton SO16 . . . . . . 79 A6
Spindlewood Way SO40 . . 124 F8
Spinnaker Cl
Gosport PO13 . . . . . . 180 D7
South Hayling PO11 . . . . . . 184 E4
Spinnaker Ct
Netley SO31 . . . . . . 127 B6
21 Portsmouth PO1 . . . . . . 182 A5
Spinnaker Dr PO2 . . . . . 157 D4
Spinnaker Grange PO11 . 160 C4
Spinnaker Ho PO6 . . . . . 157 A7
Spinnaker Pl 6 PO10 . . . 161 A8
Spinnaker Quay PO1 . . . 181 F4
Spinnaker Twr* PO1 . . . 181 F5
Spinnaker View PO9 . . . . 135 A1
Spinnakers The PO13 . . . 179 E2
Spinners Cl BH22 . . . . . . 138 E1
Spinners Gdn* SO41 . . . . 173 E1
Spinney Cl
St Leonards BH24 . . . . . . 139 D4
Waterlooville PO8 . . . . . . 111 E3
Spinney Dale SO45 . . . . . 126 B2
Spinney Gdns SO45 . . . . 126 B2
Spinney The
Bramdean SO24 . . . . . . 15 C5
Compton SO21 . . . . . . 31 C7
Denmead PO7 . . . . . . 110 F3
8 Eastleigh SO50 . . . . . . 56 A2
Fair Oak SO50 . . . . . . 57 A2
Gosport PO13 . . . . . . 155 D1
Portchester PO16 . . . . . . 131 F1
Southampton SO16 . . . . . . 79 A6
St Leonards BH24 . . . . . . 139 F6
Totton SO40 . . . . . . 76 C1
Waterlooville PO8 . . . . . . 112 A6
Spinney Way BH25 . . . . . 195 B6
Spinney Wlk SO18 . . . . . . 79 F3
Spinneys La BH22 . . . . . 165 D5
Spinningfield Ho 1
GU32 . . . . . . 40 F4
Spitfire Ct SO19 . . . . . . 103 D3
Spitfire End 2 SO23 . . . . . 11 D8
Spitfire Quay SO19 . . . . 103 C4
Spitfire Way SO31 . . . . . 127 F3
Spithead Ave PO12 . . . . . 181 C2
Spithead Ho PO16 . . . . . 155 A7
Spithead Hts PO4 . . . . . 183 D3
Spittlefields BH24 . . . . . 141 B7
Sportsman Pl SO30 . . . . . 80 E1
Spouts La SO51 . . . . . . 50 D6
Spring Cl Fair Oak SO50 . . 57 C2
Southampton SO19 . . . . . . 103 F4
Verwood BH31 . . . . . . 114 F5
Spring Cres SO17 . . . . . . 103 B8
Spring Ct Poole BH12 . . . 203 D5
1 Southampton SO15 . . . . 102 E5
Spring Firs SO19 . . . . . . 103 E3
Spring Garden La PO12 . 181 C6
Spring Gdns
2 Emsworth PO10 . . . . . . 161 A8
North Baddesley SO52 . . . . . 54 A4
Poole BH12 . . . . . . 203 D5
Portsmouth PO1 . . . . . . 216 A3
Spring Gr SO31 . . . . . . 105 A1
Spring Hills SO19 . . . . . . 104 D4
Spring House Cl SO21 . . . 32 A1
Spring La
Bishopstoke SO50 . . . . . . 56 D3
Colden Common SO21 . . . . . 31 F1
New Milton BH25 . . . . . . 195 D2
Swanmore SO32 . . . . . . 84 B5
Spring Pl 2 SO51 . . . . . . 52 E7
Spring Rd
Bournemouth BH1 . . . . . . 205 D5
Hythe SO45 . . . . . . 126 A4
Lymington SO41 . . . . . . 198 A2
Sarisbury SO31 . . . . . . 128 F6
Southampton SO19 . . . . . . 104 A5
Southampton,Itchen SO19 . 103 F4
Southampton,Merry Oak
SO19 . . . . . . 103 F6
Spring St PO1 . . . . . . 216 B3
Spring The PO7 . . . . . . 110 F3
Spring Vale
Swanmore SO32 . . . . . . 84 A4
Waterlooville PO8 . . . . . . 112 B4
Spring Wlk PO1 . . . . . . 216 B4
Springbank Rd BH7 . . . . 205 F8
Springbourne Ct BH1 . . . 205 D5
Springbourne Mews
BH1 . . . . . . 205 C5
Springcroft PO13 . . . . . . 155 B5
Springdale Ave BH18 . . . 186 F5
Springdale Ct 3 SO40 . . . 100 F7
Springdale Fst Sch
BH18 . . . . . . 186 E4
Springdale Gr BH21 . . . . 186 E4
Springdale Rd BH18,
BH21 . . . . . . 186 E4
Springfield 2 GU33 . . . . . 20 F4
Springfield Ave
Bournemouth BH6 . . . . . . 207 A4
Christchurch BH23 . . . . . . 191 D2
Holbury SO45 . . . . . . 150 D3
Springfield Cl
Havant PO9 . . . . . . 135 B2
Lymington SO41 . . . . . . 198 A3
Verwood BH31 . . . . . . 114 F5
Wickham PO17 . . . . . . 108 A4

Springfield Cres
Poole BH14 .... 203 B4
Redlynch SP5 .... 47 D5
Springfield Ct SO19 .... 103 F2
Springfield Dr SO40 .... 100 E6
Springfield Gdns BH25 .. 195 D2
Springfield Gr SO45 .... 150 D4
Springfield Rd
Poole BH14 .... 203 A4
Verwood BH31 .... 114 F5
Springfield Sch PO6 .... 158 C7
Springfield Way PO14 ... 179 C6
Springfields Cl 3 SO21 ... 31 F1
Springford Cl SO16 .... 78 B4
Springford Cres SO16 .... 78 B3
Springford Gdns SO16 .... 78 B4
Springford Rd SO16 .... 78 B4
Springhill RC Prim Sch SO15 .... 102 E6
Springhill Rd SO53 .... 55 D6
Springles La PO15 .... 130 A5
Springvale Ave
Bournemouth BH7 .... 205 F8
Kings Worthy SO23 .... 2 B6
Springvale Rd SO23 .... 2 B7
Springwater Cl BH11 ... 189 A3
Springwater Ct BH23 ... 207 D6
Springwater Dr BH23 ... 207 D6
Springwater Rd BH11 ... 189 A3
Springwell 3 PO9 .... 135 F1
Springwood Ave PO7 .... 134 F6
Spruce Ave PO7 .... 135 A6
Spruce Cl
Broadstone BH17 .... 186 E1
Warsash SO31 .... 152 D10
Spruce Dr
Southampton SO19 .... 104 E5
Totton SO40 .... 100 B8
Spruce Wlk 8 PO13 .... 179 F3
Spur Cl BH21 .... 164 C6
Spur Hill Ave BH14 .... 203 D3
Spur Rd Cosham PO6 .... 157 F8
Poole BH14 .... 203 D3
Waterlooville PO7 .... 134 E7
Spur The Gosport PO12 ... 180 F2
Wickham PO17 .... 108 A4
Spurgeon Rd BH7 .... 206 B6
Spurlings Ind Est PO17 ... 131 D3
Spurlings Rd PO17 .... 131 D4
Square Cl BH21 .... 164 F3
Square The
Bournemouth BH2 .... 204 F3
Compton PO18 .... 90 F2
Fawley SO45 .... 151 B3
Gosport PO12 .... 181 C9
Hamble-le-R SO31 .... 128 A2
Lymington SO41 .... 197 C3
Petersfield GU32 .... 40 F3
Sherfield English SO51 .... 26 B4
Southbourne PO10 .... 161 D7
Titchfield PO14 .... 153 F8
West Moors BH24 .... 166 B8
Westbourne PO10 .... 137 B3
Wickham PO17 .... 108 A3
Wimborne Minst BH21 ... 163 B5
Winchester SO23 .... 215 E5
Squarey Cl SP5 .... 46 F6
Squires Wlk SO19 .... 103 E1
Squirrel Cl
Bishopstoke SO50 .... 56 F2
1 Locks Heath SO31 .... 129 B5
Squirrel Dr SO19 .... 104 A3
Squirrel Wlk BH31 .... 114 F5
Squirrel's Cl BH23 .... 191 D2
Squirrels Wlk SO45 .... 125 F2
Stable Cl PO14 .... 129 D2
Stable Cotts SO43 .... 74 A3
Stable La 8 GU31 .... 40 F3
Stables The
Christchurch BH23 .... 206 F7
Locks Heath SO31 .... 129 A2
Stacey Cl BH12 .... 203 C7
Stacey Ct Havant PO9 .... 135 D7
Portsmouth PO5 .... 182 C1
Stacey Gdns BH8 .... 190 F2
Stadium Way BH15 .... 202 C3
Staff Rd SO51 .... 6 B1
Stafford Rd
Bournemouth BH1 .... 205 A4
Petersfield GU32 .... 40 F5
Portsmouth PO5 .... 216 C1
Southampton SO15 .... 102 D6
Staffwise Bsns Ctr PO6 .. 157 F7
Stag Bsns Pk BH24 .... 141 A5
Stag Cl Bishopstoke SO50 ... 56 F2
New Milton BH25 .... 194 E4
Stag Dr SO30 .... 105 D8
Stag Gates SO45 .... 150 E1
Stag Way PO15 .... 130 D5
Stagbrake Cl SO45 .... 150 B3
Stags La SO21 .... 33 A5
Stagshorn Rd PO8 .... 112 C7
Stagswood BH31 .... 114 D6
Stainer Cl SO19 .... 104 D3
Staith Cl SO19 .... 104 C5
Stake's La SO32 .... 59 E8
Stakes Hill Inf Sch PO7 .. 134 F6
Stakes Hill Rd PO7 .... 134 F6
Stakes La SO32 .... 58 F4
Stakes Rd PO7 .... 134 D4
Stalbridge Dr BH22 .... 165 D4
Stalbridge Rd BH17 .... 202 A7
Stalham Rd BH12 .... 203 F6
Stallard Cl PO10 .... 136 E1
Stallards La BH24 .... 140 F7
Stalybridge Cl SO31 .... 129 A6
Stamford Ave PO11 .... 184 E3
Stamford Lodge PO11 ... 184 E3
Stamford Rd BH6 .... 206 D5
Stamford St PO1 .... 216 D4
Stamford Way SO50 .... 57 C1
Stampsey Ct 5 PO2 .... 157 C2
Stamshaw Ct 2 PO2 .... 157 D1
Stamshaw Inf Sch PO2 .. 157 D2
Stamshaw Rd PO2 .... 157 D1
Stanbridge Earls Sch SO51 .... 27 B3
Stanbridge La SO51 .... 27 B3
Stanbridge Rd PO9 .... 136 B3
Standard Way PO16 .... 131 D3
Standen Rd SO16 .... 77 C5
Standford St SO14 .... 103 B4
Standing Hill SP5 .... 3 F8
Stanfield Cl BH12 .... 203 D7
Stanfield Rd
Bournemouth BH9 .... 204 E8
Ferndown BH22 .... 165 C6
Poole BH12 .... 203 D7
Stanford Cl PO6 .... 157 D8
Stanford Ct
23 Havant PO9 .... 136 B5
Southampton SO19 .... 104 D3
Stanford Gdns SO41 .... 197 D2
Stanford Hill SO41 .... 197 D3
Stanford Rd SO41 .... 197 D3
Stanford Rise SO41 .... 172 B2
Stanhope Gate 1 PO5 .... 182 C2
Stanhope Rd PO1 .... 216 B3
Stanier Way SO30 .... 81 C2
Staniforth Ct BH23 .... 207 D6
Stanley Ave PO3 .... 183 B8
Stanley Cl
Bishopstone SP5 .... 22 B8
Fareham PO15 .... 130 E2
Gosport PO12 .... 156 A1
Verwood BH31 .... 115 A5
Stanley Ct
Bournemouth BH1 .... 205 C5
Poole BH15 .... 202 C6
Stanley Green Cres BH15 .... 202 C5
Stanley Green Fst Sch BH15 .... 202 C6
Stanley Green Ind Est BH15 .... 202 B5
Stanley Green Rd
Poole BH15 .... 202 C5
Poole BH15 .... 202 C6
Stanley La PO5 .... 182 C2
Stanley Pearce Ho BH17 .... 187 C1
Stanley Pk (Cvn & Chalet Site) BH25 .... 195 C6
Stanley Rd
Bournemouth BH1 .... 205 C5
Christchurch BH23 .... 209 A8
Emsworth PO10 .... 161 A8
Holbury SO45 .... 150 D4
Lymington SO41 .... 198 A2
Poole BH15 .... 202 C1
Portsmouth PO2 .... 157 C1
Southampton SO17 .... 79 C1
Totton SO40 .... 76 D1
Stanley St PO5 .... 182 C2
Stanmore La SO22 .... 215 B3
Stanmore Prim Sch SO22 .... 215 C3
Stannington Cl BH25 .... 195 B2
Stannington Cres SO40 .. 100 F8
Stannington Way SO40 .. 100 F8
Stanpit BH23 .... 207 E5
Stanstead Rd SO50 .... 55 F4
Stansted Cl PO9 .... 113 C1
Stansted Cres PO9 .... 136 B6
Stansted Ct PO9 .... 113 C2
Stansted Rd PO5 .... 216 D2
Stanswood Rd
Blackfield SO45 .... 178 C6
Havant PO9 .... 135 D6
Stanton Bldgs SO15 .... 102 A7
Stanton Lacy 12 BH13 .... 214 F7
Stanton Rd
Bournemouth BH10 .... 189 C2
Petersfield GU32 .... 40 E4
Southampton SO15 .... 102 A7
Stanton Rd Ind Est SO15 .... 102 A7
Stapehill Cres BH21 .... 164 C5
Stapehill Mus & Gdns* BH21 .... 164 E5
Stapehill Rd BH21 .... 164 F4
Staple Ash La GU32 .... 39 C7
Staple Cl PO7 .... 111 D1
Staple Close La BH15 .... 202 C6
Staple Cross
Burton BH23 .... 207 E8
Southwick PO17 .... 132 C8
Staple Gdns 31 SO23 .... 215 D6
Staplecross La BH23 .... 207 D8
Stapleford Ave BH22 .... 165 F6
Stapleford Cl SO51 .... 28 B2
Stapleford La SO32 .... 81 F5
Staplehurst Cl SO19 .... 104 B1
Staplers Reach PO13 .... 155 B2
Stapleton Rd 6 PO3 .... 183 A8
Staplewood La
Ashurst SO40 .... 124 C7
Marchwood SO40 .... 101 C1
Star Cotts PO17 .... 108 A3
Star La BH24 .... 140 F7
Stares Cl PO13 .... 180 C7
Starina Gdns PO7 .... 135 B8
Starlight Farm Cl BH31 .. 115 A7
Starling Sq SO50 .... 55 D2
Station App
Broadstone BH18 .... 187 A4
Brockenhurst SO42 .... 146 A1
25 Portsmouth PO1 .... 182 A5
Station Cl PO17 .... 108 A4
Station Cotts SO42 .... 123 D1
Station Hill Botley SO30 .. 106 C7
Bursledon SO31 .... 128 B8
Eastleigh SO50 .... 56 B3
Winchester SO23 .... 215 D6
Station La SO53 .... 55 C5
Station Rd Alderholt SP6 ... 92 F6
Bishop's Waltham SO32 .... 83 C7
Burley BH24 .... 170 D7
Bursledon SO31 .... 128 B8
Christchurch BH23 .... 207 A7
Christchurch,Highcliffe BH23 .... 193 E2
Cosham PO6 .... 158 C7
Fordingbridge SP6 .... 69 D1
Gosport PO12 .... 180 F7
Liss GU33 .... 20 F4
Locks Heath SO31 .... 129 A5
Netley SO31 .... 127 B5
New Milton BH25 .... 195 A2
Nursling SO16 .... 77 A5
Petersfield GU32 .... 40 E4
Poole,Lower Hamworthy BH15 .... 202 A1
Poole,Lower Parkstone BH14 .... 203 B4
Portchester PO16 .... 156 D8
Portsmouth PO3 .... 183 A8
Romsey SO51 .... 52 E7
Soberton SO32 .... 85 C7
South Hayling PO11 .... 184 E4
Southampton,Redbridge SO15 .... 101 C8
Southampton,Sholing SO19 .... 103 F3
Sway SO41 .... 172 B1
Verwood BH31 .... 114 D7
West Meon GU32 .... 37 C4
West Moors BH22 .... 138 D2
Wickham PO17 .... 108 A4
Wimborne Minst BH21 .... 163 D3
32 Winchester SO23 .... 215 D6
Station Rd N SO40 .... 101 A7
Station Rd S SO40 .... 101 A7
Station St
Lymington SO41 .... 197 F4
Portsmouth PO1 .... 216 B3
Station Terr Twyford SO21 . 31 E6
Wimborne Minst BH21 ... 163 D4
Station Yd SP6 .... 92 E6
Staunton BH2 .... 204 F2
Staunton Ave PO11 .... 184 D3
Staunton Ctry Pk* PO9 . 136 A7
Staunton Ctry Pk Vistors Ctr* PO9 .... 136 A6
Staunton Park Com Sch PO9 .... 136 B7
Staunton Rd PO9 .... 135 E2
Staunton St PO1 .... 216 B4
Stead Cl PO11 .... 185 B3
Stedman Rd BH5 .... 206 B5
Steel St PO5 .... 216 A1
Steele Cl SO53 .... 55 D4
Steels Dro SP6 .... 70 E7
Steels La SP6 .... 68 C4
Steep CE Prim Sch GU32 . 40 F7
Steep Cl
Portchester PO16 .... 132 C1
Southampton SO18 .... 104 C8
Steepdene BH14 .... 203 B3
Steeple Cl BH17 .... 187 D3
Steeple Way PO14 .... 129 D3
Steepleton Rd BH18 .... 187 C3
Steerforth Cl PO2 .... 182 D8
Stein Rd PO10 .... 137 D2
Steinbeck Cl PO15 .... 129 C8
Stella Ct
13 Christchurch BH23 .... 209 B7
Southampton SO16 .... 78 C4
Stem La BH25 .... 194 E4
Stenbury Way SO31 .... 127 C7
Stenhurst Rd BH15 .... 202 E6
Step Terr SO22 .... 215 C6
Stephen Cl PO8 .... 112 B2
Stephen Langton Dr BH11 .... 188 D5
Stephen Lodge PO5 .... 216 B1
Stephen Martin Gdns SP6 .... 69 E2
Stephen Rd PO15 .... 130 F1
Stephens Ct SO51 .... 52 E6
Stephens Wlk BH24 .... 140 F7
Stephenson Cl PO12 .... 181 A3
Stephenson Rd SO40 .... 76 D2
Stephenson Way SO30 .... 81 C3
Steplake La SO51 .... 25 C1
Steplake Rd SO51 .... 50 D7
Stepnell Reach BH16 .... 201 D5
Sterte Ave BH15 .... 202 B4
Sterte Avenue W BH15 .... 202 B4
Sterte Cl BH15 .... 202 C4
Sterte Ct BH15 .... 202 C4
Sterte Espl BH15 .... 202 C3
Sterte Ind Est BH15 .... 202 B4
Sterte Rd BH15 .... 202 C4
Steuart Rd SO18 .... 103 D7
Stevenson Cres BH14 .... 203 E3
Stevenson Rd BH6 .... 207 A3
Stevensons Cl 3 BH21 .... 163 C4
Steventon Rd SO18 .... 104 C7
Stewart Cl 5 BH8 .... 205 C5
Stewart Ho SO53 .... 30 C1
Stewart Pl PO1 .... 182 E7
Stewart Rd BH8 .... 205 B6
Stewarts Gn PO7 .... 86 C3
Stewarts Way BH22 .... 165 E7
Stibbs Way BH23 .... 169 C1
Stillmore Rd BH11 .... 188 D3
Stillwater Pk BH24 .... 117 C2
Stinchar Dr SO53 .... 55 A5
Stinsford Cl BH9 .... 190 B4
Stinsford Rd BH17 .... 187 D1
Stirling Ave PO7 .... 134 F7
Stirling Bsns Pk BH21 ... 164 F7
Stirling Cl
New Milton BH25 .... 195 B3
Totton SO40 .... 77 A1
Stirling Cres
Hedge End SO30 .... 81 C1
Totton SO40 .... 101 A8
Stirling Ct
3 Bournemouth BH4 .... 204 C2
Fareham PO15 .... 130 E3
11 New Milton BH25 .... 195 B3
Stirling Rd BH3 .... 204 E7
Stirling St PO2 .... 182 D8
Stirling Way BH23 .... 208 B6
Stirling Wlk SO51 .... 52 E7
Stirrup Cl Upton BH16 ... 201 D7
Wimborne Minst BH21 .... 164 C6
Stoborough Dr BH18 .... 187 A2
Stock La SP5 .... 49 D6
Stock's Cross SO43 .... 73 F4
Stock's La SO32 .... 61 E5
Stockbridge Cl
Havant PO9 .... 136 B5
Poole BH17 .... 188 B2
Stockbridge Rd
Michelmersh SO51 .... 27 C7
Winchester SO22 .... 215 B7
Stocker Pl PO13 .... 155 D1
Stockers Ave SO22 .... 215 B7
Stockheath La PO9 .... 135 E3
Stockheath Rd PO9 .... 135 F4
Stockheath Way PO9 .... 135 F4
Stockholm Dr SO30 .... 105 C5
Stockley Cl SO45 .... 150 C3
Stocks La GU34 .... 17 B2
Stockton Cl SO30 .... 105 C7
Stoddart Ave SO19 .... 103 F6
Stodham La
Hill Brow GU33 .... 21 A2
Liss GU33 .... 20 F1
Stoke Common Rd SO50 .. 56 E5
Stoke Gdns PO12 .... 181 C5
Stoke Hts SO50 .... 57 B3
Stoke Park Dr SO50 .... 56 D4
Stoke Park Inf Sch SO50 .. 56 F2
Stoke Park Jun Sch SO50 .... 56 E2
Stoke Park Rd SO50 .... 56 D4
Stoke Rd Gosport PO12 ... 181 C5
Southampton SO16 .... 78 A1
Winchester SO23 .... 2 A3
Stoke Wood Cl SO50 .... 57 B2
Stoke Wood Rd BH3 .... 204 F6
Stokes Ave BH15 .... 202 D4
Stokes Bay Mobile Home Pk PO12 .... 180 D2
Stokes Bay Rd PO12 .... 180 E2
Stokes Ct 2 SO15 .... 102 E6
Stokesay Cl SO45 .... 150 A8
Stokeway 4 PO12 .... 181 C5
Stone Crop Cl SO31 .... 128 F2
Stone Gdns BH8 .... 191 A2
Stone La Gosport PO12 .... 181 B4
5 Gosport PO12 .... 181 B5
Wimborne Minst BH21 .... 163 A6
Stone Lane Ind Est BH21 .... 163 B6
Stone Sq PO9 .... 135 F4
Stone St PO5 .... 216 A1
Stone Terr SO21 .... 31 A1
Stonechat Cl
Ferndown BH22 .... 165 B8
Petersfield GU31 .... 41 C2
Stonechat Ct BH23 .... 207 F7
Stonechat Dr SO40 .... 100 B8
Stonechat Rd PO8 .... 112 A7
Stonecrop Cl BH18 .... 186 E2
Stoneham Cemetery Rd SO18 .... 79 F4
Stoneham Cl
Petersfield GU32 .... 40 D4
Southampton SO16 .... 79 D5
Stoneham Ct SO16 .... 79 B5
Stoneham Gdns SO31 .... 104 F1
Stoneham La SO16 .... 79 D6
Stoneham Pk GU32 .... 40 D4
Stoneham Way SO16, SO18 .... 79 E5
Stonehills SO45 .... 151 C3
Stoneleigh 3 BH13 .... 214 F8
Stoneleigh Ave SO41 .... 195 F4
Stoneleigh Cl PO16 .... 156 B8
Stoner Hill Rd GU32 .... 19 B1
Stoners Cl PO13 .... 155 B3
Stoney Croft Rise SO53 .... 55 C2
Stoney Ct SO22 .... 215 C8
Stoney La SO22 .... 215 C8
Stony La Burton BH23 .... 192 C2
Christchurch BH23 .... 207 C7
Damerham SP6 .... 68 B4
Portsmouth PO1 .... 182 A6
Stony Lane S BH23 .... 207 D6
Stonymoor Cl SO45 .... 150 C3
Stopples La SO41 .... 195 F3
Storrington Rd PO8 .... 88 D5
Story La BH18 .... 187 B4
Stour Cl Ferndown BH21 ... 164 D4
Stour Cl *continued*
Petersfield GU31 .... 40 E2
West End SO18 .... 80 A3
West Wellow SO51 .... 50 D3
Stour Ct 6 BH13 .... 204 A4
Stour Pk BH10 .... 189 E6
Stour Rd
Bournemouth BH8 .... 205 D6
Christchurch BH23 .... 207 A6
Stour Rdbt BH23 .... 206 F5
Stour View Gdns BH21 ... 162 E1
Stour Way BH23 .... 191 D1
Stour Wlk
Bournemouth BH8 .... 190 D4
Wimborne Minst BH21 .... 163 D3
Stourbank Rd BH23 .... 207 A6
Stourcliffe Ave BH6 .... 206 C4
Stourcroft Dr BH23 .... 191 E1
Stourfield Inf & Jun Schs BH6 .... 206 D6
Stourfield Rd BH5 .... 206 B4
Stourpaine Rd BH17 .... 187 D2
Stourton Ct 21 BH4 .... 204 C3
Stourvale Ave BH23 .... 206 D8
Stourvale Gdns SO53 .... 55 D5
Stourvale Pl 3 BH5 .... 206 B5
Stourvale Rd BH6 .... 206 C6
Stourwood Ave BH6 .... 206 D4
Stourwood Mans 4 BH6 .... 206 C4
Stourwood Rd BH6 .... 206 D4
Stouts La BH23 .... 169 B1
Stow Cres PO15 .... 130 D2
Stowe Cl SO30 .... 81 D1
Stowe Rd PO4 .... 183 B4
Stradbrook PO13 .... 155 B1
Stragwyne Cl SO52 .... 53 F5
Straight Mile The SO51 ... 28 E2
Strand SO14 .... 103 A4
Strand St BH15 .... 202 C1
Strand The PO11 .... 185 C1
Stranding St SO50 .... 55 F2
Stratfield Dr 9 SO53 .... 30 B1
Stratfield Gdns PO9 .... 135 D7
Stratfield Pk PO7 .... 134 C8
Stratfield Pl BH25 .... 194 E3
Stratford Ct 10 SO23 .... 215 E8
Stratford Ho PO5 .... 216 B2
Stratford Pl
Eastleigh SO50 .... 56 B4
Lymington SO41 .... 197 D5
Stratford Rd PO7 .... 135 A8
Strathmore Dr BH31 .... 115 B6
Strathmore Rd
Bournemouth BH9 .... 190 A4
Gosport PO12 .... 181 C5
Stratton Cl PO6 .... 157 C8
Stratton Rd
Bournemouth BH9 .... 190 C3
Southampton SO15 .... 78 C1
Winchester SO23 .... 11 C7
Strawberry Fields
East Boldre SO42 .... 175 D6
Hedge End SO30 .... 105 A6
Strawberry Hill SO31 .... 128 F3
Strawberry Mead SO50 ... 57 B1
Streamleaze PO14 .... 129 C2
Street End SO52 .... 54 B5
Street The SP5 .... 24 A4
Streets La BH24 .... 141 C4
Strete Mount 1 BH23 .... 207 E7
Stretton Ct BH14 .... 203 B4
Stride Ave PO3 .... 183 B6
Strides La BH24 .... 140 F7
Strides Way SO40 .... 100 B7
Strode Gdns BH24 .... 140 B5
Strode Rd PO2 .... 157 C2
Strongs Cl SO51 .... 53 B8
Stroud Cl
Portsmouth PO6 .... 133 A1
Wimborne Minst BH21 .... 164 A6
Stroud End GU32 .... 40 B4
Stroud Gdns BH23 .... 207 E6
Stroud Green La PO14 .... 154 D5
Stroud La BH23 .... 207 F6
Stroud Park Ave BH23 ... 207 E6
Stroud Sch SO51 .... 53 E8
Strouden Ave BH8 .... 205 C8
Strouden Court Prec PO9 .... 135 D7
Strouden Ct PO9 .... 135 D7
Strouden Rd BH9 .... 190 A1
Stroudley Ave PO6 .... 158 C6
Stroudley Way SO30 .... 81 D2
Stroudwood Rd
Fair Oak SO32 .... 58 A4
Havant PO9 .... 136 A3
Struan Cl BH24 .... 139 F6
Struan Ct BH24 .... 140 A6
Struan Dr BH24 .... 140 A6
Struan Gdns BH24 .... 139 F6
Stuart Bridgewater Ho SO18 .... 104 A7
Stuart Cl
Stubbington PO14 .... 179 C7
Upton BH16 .... 201 B7
Stuart Cres SO22 .... 215 C3
Stuart Ct 4 PO6 .... 157 F8
Stuart Rd BH23 .... 209 B8
Stubbermere PO10 .... 136 E7
Stubbington Ave PO2 .... 157 E1
Stubbington Gn PO14 .... 179 C8
Stubbington La PO14 .... 179 D6
Stubbington Way SO50 ... 57 D1
Stubbs Dro SO30 .... 105 D7
Stubbs Rd SO19 .... 104 C2
Stuckton Rd SP6 .... 94 B8
Student Village BH12 ... 204 D8

Studland Cl SO16 ....77 D1
Studland Ct 20 BH4 ....204 C3
Studland Dr SO41 ....211 C5
Studland Rd
Bournemouth BH4 ....204 C1
Lee-on-t-S PO13 ....179 E3
Southampton SO16 ....77 D1
Studley Ave SO45 ....150 C3
Studley Cl BH23 ....209 C8
Studley Ct BH25 ....209 D8
Sturgess Ct 14 PO16 ....131 B1
Sturminster Ho 4 SO16 ....78 A1
Sturminster Rd 1 BH9 ....190 B4
Styles The SP5 ....22 C8
Sudbury Rd PO6 ....157 D8
Suetts La SO32 ....83 F7
Suffolk Ave
Christchurch BH23 ....191 F2
Southampton SO15 ....102 D7
Suffolk Cl
Chandler's Ford SO53 ....55 C2
Wimborne Minst BH21 ....164 C6
Suffolk Dr
Chandler's Ford SO53 ....55 C2
Swanwick PO15 ....129 B7
Suffolk Gn SO53 ....55 C2
Suffolk Rd
Bournemouth BH2 ....204 E3
Portsmouth PO4 ....183 B3
Suffolk Rd S BH2 ....204 D3
Sullivan Cl PO6 ....156 E8
Sullivan Rd SO19 ....104 D3
Sullivan Way PO7 ....134 E5
Sultan Rd
Emsworth PO10 ....136 F1
Portsmouth PO1,PO2 ....182 D7
Sumar Cl PO14 ....154 D5
Summer Field Cl BH21 ....164 A4
Summer Flds BH31 ....114 F4
Summer La SO42 ....176 F8
Summercroft Way BH22 ....138 E3
Summerfield Cl BH23 ....192 C2
Summerfield Ct PO3 ....158 B4
Summerfield Gdns SO16 ....79 D5
Summerfields
Bournemouth BH7 ....205 F7
Locks Heath SO31 ....129 B1
Summerhill Rd PO8 ....112 A3
Summerlands BH22 ....165 D6
Summerlands Rd SO50 ....57 C2
Summerlands Wlk 17
PO9 ....136 B5
Summerleigh Wlk PO14 ....154 D5
Summers Ave BH11 ....189 B6
Summers La BH23 ....192 D1
Summers St SO14 ....103 C6
Summersfield GU33 ....20 F3
Summertrees Ct BH25 ....195 D4
Summit Way SO18 ....79 F1
Sumner Rd GU31 ....65 D5
Sun Ct PO5 ....216 C2
Sun St PO1 ....182 A5
Sun Valley Bsns Pk SO23 ....2 C1
Sunbeam Way PO12 ....181 B4
Sunbury Cl BH11 ....189 A6
Sunbury Ct
24 Bournemouth BH4 ....204 C3
Fareham PO15 ....130 E4
Suncourt Villas PO12 ....180 F8
Sunderland Dr BH23 ....208 B7
Sunderton La PO8 ....88 C5
Sundew Cl
Christchurch BH23 ....193 C1
New Milton BH25 ....195 D4
Sundew Rd BH18 ....186 E2
Sundowner SO14 ....103 B2
Sundridge Cl PO6 ....157 F8
Sunlight Cotts SO21 ....29 E8
Sunningdale
41 Bournemouth BH4 ....204 C3
Christchurch BH23 ....206 F6
Colden Common SO21 ....31 F1
Hythe SO45 ....125 F3
6 Poole BH15 ....202 E3
Sunningdale Cl
Bishopstoke SO50 ....56 F2
Gosport PO13 ....155 C1
Sunningdale Cres BH10 ....189 C4
Sunningdale Gdns
Broadstone BH18 ....187 A5
Southampton SO18 ....104 B7
Sunningdale Rd
Portchester PO16 ....156 D7
Portsmouth PO3 ....183 A7
Sunny Hill Ct BH12 ....203 D5
Sunny Hill Rd BH12 ....203 D5
Sunny Way SO40 ....100 F7
Sunny Wlk PO1 ....182 A6
Sunnybank Dr BH21 ....164 B6
Sunnybank Rd BH21 ....164 B6
Sunnybank Way BH21 ....164 B6
Sunnydown Rd SO22 ....10 A3
Sunnyfield Rd BH25 ....210 A8
Sunnyfield Rise SO31 ....105 A1
Sunnyfields PO6 ....158 C7
Sunnyheath PO9 ....135 E4
Sunnyhill Rd BH6 ....206 C5
Sunnylands Ave BH6 ....206 F4
Sunnymead Dr PO7 ....111 D2
Sunnymoor Rd BH11 ....189 A1
Sunnyside Pk BH24 ....140 C5
Sunnyside Rd BH12 ....203 D6
Sunnyside Wlk PO9 ....135 D7
Sunridge Cl BH12 ....204 A6
Sunrise Ct BH22 ....165 D5
Sunset Ave SO40 ....100 E8
Sunset Lo BH13 ....204 A2
Sunset Rd SO40 ....100 E8
Sunshine Ave PO11 ....185 B2
Suntrap Gdns PO11 ....185 B2
Sunvale Cl SO19 ....104 B3
Sunwood Rd PO9 ....135 D5
Surbiton Rd SO50 ....56 B5
Surrey Cl
Christchurch BH23 ....191 F2
Totton SO40 ....100 D5
Surrey Ct
Chandler's Ford SO53 ....55 D3
Southampton SO15 ....102 C6
Surrey Gdns BH4 ....204 C4
Surrey Lo 8 BH4 ....204 D4
Surrey Point 7 SO16 ....78 E3
Surrey Rd
Bournemouth BH4,BH12 ....204 B4
Chandler's Ford SO53 ....55 D4
Southampton SO19 ....103 D2
Surrey Rd S BH4 ....204 C4
Surrey St PO1 ....216 B3
Sussex Cl BH9 ....190 B4
Sussex Ct
6 Gosport PO12 ....181 C9
Portsmouth PO5 ....216 B1
Sussex Gdns GU31 ....40 F2
Sussex Pl
Portsmouth PO5 ....216 B1
Portsmouth,Landport PO1 ....216 B4
Sussex Rd
Chandler's Ford SO53 ....55 D3
Petersfield GU31 ....41 B1
Portsmouth PO5 ....216 B1
Southampton SO14 ....103 A4
Sussex St SO23 ....215 D6
Sussex Terr PO5 ....216 B1
Sutherland Ave BH18 ....186 E5
Sutherland Cl 6 SO51 ....28 B1
Sutherland Rd
Portsmouth PO4 ....182 E4
Southampton SO16 ....77 F5
Sutherlands Ct SO53 ....55 C6
Sutherlands Way SO53 ....55 B6
Sutton Cl Poole BH17 ....188 B2
Portsmouth PO3 ....158 B4
Waterlooville PO8 ....111 D3
Sutton Ct PO14 ....130 F1
Sutton Gdns SO23 ....215 E6
Sutton Hill Camping Site
BH21 ....114 B8
Sutton Pl SO42 ....146 A1
Sutton Rd
Bournemouth BH9 ....190 B1
Totton SO40 ....76 E1
Waterlooville PO8 ....111 D3
Swale Dr SO53 ....55 A7
Swallow Cl
Broadstone BH17 ....201 F8
Havant PO9 ....136 B2
Totton SO40 ....100 C6
Swallow Ct Clanfield PO8 ....88 B6
Lee-on-t-S PO13 ....179 F4
Swallow Dr SO41 ....211 E4
Swallow Sq SO50 ....55 D2
Swallow Way BH21 ....164 A7
Swallow Wood PO16 ....131 B3
Swan Cl Emsworth PO10 ....161 A8
Lower Swanwick SO31 ....128 D7
Swan Ct Bursledon SO31 ....128 C8
Gosport PO13 ....155 B4
Swan Ctr The SO50 ....56 B2
Swan Gn 3 BH23 ....207 A5
Swan La SO23 ....215 E6
Swan Mead BH24 ....141 C6
Swan Quay
Portchester PO16 ....155 D8
Southampton SO18 ....103 D8
Swan St GU32 ....40 E3
Swanage Cl SO19 ....103 E3
Swanage Rd PO13 ....179 E3
Swancote PO16 ....155 F8
Swanley Cl SO50 ....56 A5
Swanmore Ave SO19 ....104 C3
Swanmore Bsns Pk SO32 ....83 F5
Swanmore CE Prim Sch
SO32 ....84 B5
Swanmore Cl
Bournemouth BH7 ....206 B7
Winchester SO22 ....1 D4
Swanmore Coll of Tech
SO32 ....84 A4
Swanmore Park Ho SO32 ....84 C8
Swanmore Rd
Bournemouth BH7 ....206 B7
Droxford SO32 ....84 E7
Havant PO9 ....135 D7
Swanmore SO32 ....84 A6
Swans Wlk PO11 ....185 B3
Swansbury Dr BH8 ....191 B2
Swanton Cl PO14 ....179 D8
Swanton Gdns SO53 ....55 B7
Swanwick Bsns Ctr
SO31 ....128 D7
Swanwick La
Lower Swanwick SO31 ....128 E8
Swanwick SO31 ....129 A8
Swanwick Nature Reserve*
SO31 ....128 F8
Swanwick Shore Rd
SO31 ....128 D7
Swanwick Sta SO31 ....129 B6
Swarraton Rd PO9 ....136 A3
Sway Ct 20 Havant PO9 ....136 B5
Sway SO41 ....196 C8
Sway Gdns BH8 ....190 D2
Sway Park Ind Est SO41 ....172 B1
Sway Rd
Brockenhurst SO42 ....172 F7
Lymington SO41 ....197 B6
Sway Rd *continued*
New Milton BH25,SO41 ....195 C6
Sway Sta SO41 ....172 B1
Swaythling Prim Sch
SO17 ....79 B3
Swaythling Rd
Havant PO9 ....135 D6
West End SO30 ....80 B2
Swaythling Sta SO18 ....79 D4
Swedish Hos SO41 ....198 E8
Sweep The BH24 ....140 F7
Sweetbriar Gdns PO7 ....134 F5
Sweethills Cres PO15 ....129 C8
Sweyns Lease SO42 ....175 C6
Swift Cl Broadstone BH17 ....201 F8
Eastleigh SO50 ....55 D2
Horndean PO8 ....112 A7
Lee-on-t-S PO13 ....179 F4
Winchester SO22 ....215 B3
Swift Gdns SO19 ....103 D1
Swift Hollow SO19 ....103 D1
Swift Rd
Southampton SO19 ....103 D1
Thorney Island PO10 ....161 A3
Swinburn Gdns PO8 ....111 F4
Swincombe Rise SO18 ....80 B1
Swiss Rd PO7 ....134 E7
Switch House Rd SO45 ....151 E2
Swivelton La PO17 ....132 A3
Sword Cl Clanfield PO8 ....88 B5
Gosport PO12 ....180 E2
Sword Sands Rd PO2 ....183 C7
Swordfish Dr BH23 ....208 B7
Sycamore Ave SO53 ....30 C1
Sycamore Cl
Broadstone BH17 ....186 F1
Bursledon SO31 ....127 F8
Christchurch BH23 ....206 D8
Clanfield PO8 ....88 D5
Gosport PO13 ....155 E1
Milford on S SO41 ....211 C5
North Baddesley SO52 ....53 F5
Romsey SO51 ....53 C6
Titchfield PO14 ....129 C1
Waterlooville PO8 ....111 E3
Sycamore Ct
4 Fordingbridge SP6 ....69 F1
Ringwood BH24 ....117 C2
Sycamore Dr
Holbury SO45 ....150 B5
Kings Worthy SO23 ....2 B8
South Hayling PO11 ....184 F4
Sycamore Pl BH21 ....164 D5
Sycamore Rd
Bishop's Waltham SO32 ....83 E7
Hordle SO41 ....195 F4
Hythe SO45 ....125 F3
Southampton SO16 ....78 A2
Sycamore Wlk
Botley SO30 ....105 F7
Petersfield GU31 ....40 E1
Sycamores The SO45 ....126 A4
Sydenham Ct PO1 ....216 D3
Sydenham Terr
Portsmouth PO1 ....216 D3
Westbourne PO10 ....137 B5
Sydling Cl BH17 ....188 B2
Sydmanton Cl SO51 ....53 A6
Sydmonton Ct 2 PO9 ....136 B6
Sydney Ave SO31 ....127 E3
Sydney Ho PO1 ....216 B4
Sydney Rd
Bishopstoke SO50 ....56 D4
Broadstone BH18 ....187 A3
Christchurch BH23 ....191 E1
Gosport PO12 ....181 B5
Southampton SO15 ....78 B1
Syers Cl GU33 ....20 F4
Syers Rd GU33 ....20 F4
Sylmor Gdns BH9 ....190 A2
Sylvan Ave SO19 ....104 C6
Sylvan Cl Hordle SO41 ....196 B2
St Leonards BH24 ....139 D4
Sylvan Dr SO52 ....53 F3
Sylvan Fst Sch BH12 ....203 B6
Sylvan La SO31 ....128 A2
Sylvan Rd BH12 ....203 B6
Sylvan View PO7 ....134 F6
Sylvans The SO45 ....125 D3
Sylvia Cres SO40 ....76 E1
Symes Rd
Hamworthy BH15 ....201 E4
Romsey SO51 ....53 B7
Symonds Cl SO53 ....55 D4
Symonds St SO23 ....215 E5
Synor Ho 12 SO15 ....103 A6
Sywell Cres PO3 ....158 C4

T

Tadburn Cl
Chandler's Ford SO53 ....55 D5
Romsey SO51 ....53 B7
Tadburn Gn SO51 ....52 E6
Tadburn Rd SO51 ....53 A6
Tadden Cotts BH21 ....162 D7
Tadden Wlk BH18 ....186 F2
Tadfield Cres SO51 ....53 A7
Tadfield Rd SO51 ....53 A7
Tadhurst Ho 4 PO1 ....216 C3
Tait Cl BH17 ....202 E7
Tait Pl PO13 ....155 D1
Talbot Ave BH3 ....204 E7
Talbot Cl Havant PO9 ....135 D3
Southampton SO16 ....78 F4
Talbot Comb Sch BH12 ....204 B8
Talbot Ct
Bournemouth BH9 ....189 F1
21 Southampton SO14 ....103 A3
Talbot Dr
Christchurch BH23 ....193 F2
Poole BH12 ....204 B8
Talbot Heath Sch BH4 ....204 C5
Talbot Hill Rd BH9 ....204 D8
Talbot House Prep Sch
BH9 ....204 E7
Talbot Manor BH3 ....204 D8
Talbot Mdws BH12 ....204 B8
Talbot Mews BH10 ....189 B1
Talbot Rd
Bournemouth BH9 ....204 E7
Dibden Purlieu SO45 ....125 E1
Havant PO9 ....135 D3
Portsmouth PO4 ....182 E4
Titchfield PO15 ....129 E2
Talbot Rdbt BH3 ....204 D7
Talbot Rise BH10 ....189 C2
Talisman Bsns Ctr SO31 ....129 B6
Talland Rd PO14 ....129 B1
Tamar Cl Ferndown BH22 ....166 A5
Portchester PO16 ....132 A1
Tamar Down PO7 ....135 A7
Tamar Gdns SO18 ....80 B2
Tamar Gr SO45 ....125 E3
Tamarisk Cl
Portsmouth PO4 ....183 C3
Stubbington PO14 ....179 C6
Waterlooville PO7 ....135 A5
Tamarisk Gdns SO18 ....103 E8
Tamarisk Rd SO30 ....105 B8
Tamella Rd SO30 ....105 E6
Tammys Turn PO14 ....154 B8
Tamorisk Dr SO40 ....100 C6
Tamworth Ct 3 PO12 ....181 B4
Tamworth Rd
Bournemouth BH7 ....205 F5
Portsmouth PO3 ....183 A6
Tan Howse Cl BH7 ....206 B8
Tanfield La PO17 ....108 A3
Tanfield Pk PO17 ....108 A3
Tangier La SO32 ....83 A8
Tangier Rd PO3 ....183 B7
Tanglewood
Fareham PO16 ....131 A3
Marchwood SO40 ....102 A1
Tanglewood Cl PO7 ....134 C4
Tanglewood Ct 1 BH25 ....195 B3
Tanglewood Lo BH17 ....201 F8
Tangley Wlk PO9 ....136 B5
Tangmere Cl BH23 ....208 B6
Tangmere Dr SO16 ....78 A4
Tangmere Pl BH17 ....202 E7
Tangmere Rise SO53 ....55 D4
Tangyes Cl PO14 ....179 D8
Tanhouse Cl SO30 ....105 D5
Tanhouse La SO30 ....105 D5
Tankerdale La GU33 ....41 C8
Tankerton Cl 2 PO6 ....157 E8
Tankerville Rd SO19 ....103 D3
Tanner St 7 SO23 ....215 E5
Tanner's Brook Inf Sch
SO15 ....101 F7
Tanner's Brook Jun Sch
SO15 ....101 F7
Tanner's Brook Way
SO15 ....101 F6
Tanner's La PO7 ....111 A5
Tanner's Ridge PO7 ....134 E3
Tanneries Ind Est The
PO9 ....135 E1
Tanneries The PO14 ....154 A8
Tanners La
Fareham PO14 ....154 F5
Sandleheath SP6 ....68 F3
South Baddesley SO41 ....199 A4
West Wellow SO51 ....51 D7
Tanners Rd SO52 ....54 A3
Tanners The PO14 ....129 C1
Tansy Cl PO7 ....135 A6
Tansy Mdw SO53 ....54 F4
Tanyard Cotts GU32 ....41 B6
Tanyards The SO53 ....30 B1
Taplin Dr SO30 ....105 C8
Taplings Cl SO22 ....1 D3
Taplings Rd SO22 ....1 D3
Tapper Ct BH21 ....163 E4
Taranto Rd SO16 ....78 C4
Tarbery Cres PO8 ....112 C7
Tardif Ho SO16 ....78 B2
Target Rd PO2 ....157 C2
Tarius Cl PO13 ....155 D3
Tarleton Rd PO6 ....133 B1
Tarn Dr BH17 ....201 F8
Tarn Rise PO8 ....88 C2
Tarrant Cl BH17 ....187 E2
Tarrant Gdns PO9 ....135 D3
Tarrant Rd BH9 ....190 B3
Tarrants The 12 BH2 ....204 D4
Tasman Cl
Christchurch BH23 ....206 F8
Southampton SO14 ....103 B2
Tasman Ct SO14 ....103 B2
Taswell Rd PO5 ....182 D2
Tatchbury La SO40 ....99 F8
Tatchbury Mount Hopsl
SO40 ....76 A2
Tate Ct SO15 ....101 C7
Tate Mews SO15 ....101 C8
Tate Rd SO15 ....101 C8
Tates Rd SO45 ....126 B3
Tatnam Cres BH15 ....202 C3
Tatnam Rd BH15 ....202 C4
Tattenham Rd SO42 ....172 F8
Tattershall Cres PO16 ....156 B7
Tatwin Cl SO19 ....104 D5
Tatwin Cres SO19 ....104 D5
Taunton Dr SO18 ....104 B7
Taunton Row SO53 ....55 D3
Taunton's Coll SO15 ....78 E1
Tavell's La SO40 ....101 E1
Tavells Cl SO40 ....101 E1
Taverner Cl BH15 ....202 D2
Taverners Cl SO19 ....104 D3
Tavistock Cl 4 SO51 ....28 B1
Tavistock Gdns 3 PO9 ....136 B1
Tavy Cl SO53 ....55 B6
Taw Dr SO53 ....55 B6
Tawny Owl Cl PO14 ....154 B4
Taylor Cl SO19 ....103 D1
Taylor Dr BH8 ....190 D4
Taylor Rd PO12 ....181 C3
Taylor Way BH31 ....115 A6
Taylor's Bldgs 6 BH15 ....202 C1
Taylors Cnr SO23 ....2 B5
Teachers Terr 7 GU33 ....20 F4
Teachers Way SO45 ....150 B4
Teak Cl BH13 ....214 H8
Teal Cl Horndean PO8 ....112 A7
Portchester PO16 ....155 F8
South Hayling PO11 ....185 B3
Totton SO40 ....100 C7
Teal Wlk PO13 ....155 B3
Teapot Row 2 PO4 ....183 B2
Teasel Way BH22 ....138 E1
Teazle Cl GU31 ....41 C2
Tebourba Cotts SO41 ....172 B1
Tebourba Dr PO12 ....181 A4
Tebourba Ho 6 PO14 ....154 E8
Tebourba Way
Curdridge SO30 ....106 D7
Southampton SO16 ....101 F7
Technology Rd BH17 ....202 A8
Ted Bates Ct 7 SO15 ....102 E6
Ted Bates Rd 9 SO14 ....103 B3
Ted Kelly Ct 43 PO1 ....182 A5
Tedder Cl BH11 ....189 B3
Tedder Gdns BH11 ....189 B3
Tedder Rd
Bournemouth BH11 ....189 B3
Gosport PO13 ....155 D3
Southampton SO18 ....104 A8
Tedder Way SO40 ....100 D7
Teddington Rd PO4 ....183 A3
Tee Ct 10 SO51 ....52 E7
Tees Cl SO53 ....55 A7
Tees Farm Rd SO21 ....56 F8
Tees Gn SO21 ....56 F8
Teg Down GU31 ....41 B4
Teg Down Meads SO22 ....215 A7
Teglease Gn PO9 ....135 D7
Teignmouth Rd
Gosport PO12 ....180 F7
Portsmouth PO3 ....183 A8
Telegraph Rd SO30 ....80 E1
Telegraph Way SO21 ....12 B7
Telephone Rd PO4 ....182 E4
Telford Gdns SO30 ....81 E2
Telford Pl SO41 ....211 E4
Telford Rd
Ferndown BH21 ....165 A8
Portsmouth PO2 ....157 E3
Telford Way SO31 ....129 C5
Teme Cres SO16 ....101 E8
Teme Rd SO16 ....101 E8
Temeraire 11 SO15 ....102 F8
Tempest Ave PO7 ....135 A8
Templar Ct 2 SO14 ....103 A7
Templars Mede SO53 ....55 B3
Templars Way SO53 ....55 B3
Temple Gdns SO19 ....103 F2
Temple La GU32 ....63 E8
Temple Mews BH1 ....205 D6
Temple Rd Liss GU33 ....21 A6
Southampton SO19 ....103 F2
Temple St PO1 ....216 B4
Temple Trees 45 BH4 ....204 C3
Templecombe Rd SO50 ....56 F1
Templemere PO14 ....154 B7
Templer Cl BH11 ....188 F1
Templeton Cl PO2 ....157 E3
Tenby Cl SO18 ....104 A8
Tenby Dr SO53 ....55 A4
Tench Way SO51 ....52 F8
Tennyson Cl
Bishop's Waltham SO32 ....83 E8
Holbury SO45 ....150 B5
Tennyson Cres PO7 ....111 D1
Tennyson Ct
2 Portswood SO17 ....79 B1
22 Southampton SO17 ....79 A1
Tennyson Gdns PO16 ....131 A2
Tennyson Rd
Bournemouth BH9 ....189 F2
Eastleigh SO50 ....55 F2
1 Poole BH14 ....203 A3
Portsmouth PO2 ....182 F8
Southampton SO17 ....79 B1
Totton SO40 ....76 D2
Wimborne Minst BH21 ....163 C6
Tenon Ct BH23 ....207 B7
Tensing Cl PO16 ....131 A3
Tensing Rd BH23 ....207 E8
Tenterton Ave SO19 ....104 B1
Terence Ave BH17 ....187 C1
Terence Gdns PO4 ....182 E2
Terence Rd BH21 ....186 C5
Terminus Terr SO14 ....103 B3
Tern Cl SO45 ....126 B2
Tern Ct BH6 ....206 D6

Tern Wlk Gosport PO13 ... 155 B3
6 Portsmouth PO4 ... 183 B5
Terrace Rd BH2 ... 204 E3
Terrace The
Damerham SP6 ... 68 D5
Rockbourne SP6 ... 68 F8
Terrier Cl SO30 ... 81 C3
Terrington Ave BH23 ... 193 E1
Terriote Cl SO53 ... 55 C7
Test Cl GU31 ... 40 E2
Test Ho SO23 ... 215 F4
Test La SO16 ... 77 B2
Test Rd SO14 ... 126 B8
Test Valley Bsns Ctr
SO16 ... 77 C2
Test Valley Bsns Pk
SO52 ... 54 A5
Testbourne Ave SO40 ... 100 D7
Testbourne Cl SO40 ... 100 D7
Testbourne Rd SO40 ... 100 D6
Testcombe Rd PO12 ... 181 B4
Testlands Ave SO16 ... 77 D6
Testwood Ave SO40 ... 76 E1
Testwood Cres SO40 ... 76 D2
Testwood La SO40 ... 76 F1
Testwood Pl SO40 ... 101 A8
Testwood Rd
Havant PO9 ... 135 D5
Southampton SO15 ... 102 B6
Testwood Sch SO40 ... 76 F1
Tethering Dro SP6 ... 47 D3
Tetney Cl SO16 ... 77 E3
Tetsome Cotts PO17 ... 130 E7
Teviot Ho 9 SO14 ... 103 C6
Teviot Rd SO53 ... 55 A5
Tewkesbury Ave
Fareham PO15 ... 130 C3
Gosport PO12 ... 181 B8
Tewkesbury Cl PO6 ... 157 D8
Texas Dr SO22 ... 10 B3
Thackeray Mall 10 PO16 ... 131 B1
Thackeray Rd SO17 ... 103 B8
Thackeray Sq 1 PO16 ... 131 C1
Thacking Gn SO21 ... 56 F8
Thames Cl
Ferndown BH22 ... 166 A6
West End SO18 ... 80 B3
Thames Ct 1 PO8 ... 111 F4
Thames Dr PO15 ... 130 D4
Thames Mews 11 BH15 ... 202 B1
Thames St BH15 ... 202 B1
Thamesmead Cl PO12 ... 180 F7
Thatched Cottage Cvn Pk
SO43 ... 122 B6
Thatchers La
Norleywood SO41 ... 198 F8
Sopley BH23 ... 168 F3
Theatre Mews 17 PO5 ... 182 D2
Theobold Rd BH23 ... 191 A8
Theseus Rd PO13 ... 179 D4
Thessaly Ct 4 BH5 ... 205 F4
Thetchers Cl BH25 ... 195 B5
Thetford Gdns SO53 ... 55 A7
Thetford Rd
Gosport PO12 ... 180 F7
Poole BH12 ... 203 F5
Thicket The
Gosport PO13 ... 155 E1
Portchester PO16 ... 131 F1
Portsmouth PO5 ... 216 C1
Romsey SO51 ... 53 C6
Waterlooville PO7 ... 134 D3
Third Ave Cosham PO6 ... 157 E8
Havant PO9 ... 136 A2
Southampton SO15 ... 101 F6
Thirlmere SO50 ... 55 F2
Thirlmere Cl PO14 ... 154 D4
Thirlmere Ho 12 PO6 ... 133 B1
Thirlmere Rd SO16 ... 77 E2
Thirlstane Firs SO53 ... 55 B4
Thistle Cl BH23 ... 208 C8
Thistle Rd
Chandler's Ford SO53 ... 54 F5
Hedge End SO30 ... 105 B6
Thistlebarrow Rd BH7 ... 205 E6
Thistledown PO8 ... 112 B5
Thistledowne Gdns
PO10 ... 161 B8
Thomas Cl SO40 ... 100 D6
Thomas Grant Ave
PO12 ... 181 D7
Thomas Lewis Way SO17 ... 79 C2
Thomas Lockyer Cl
BH31 ... 115 A5
Thomas Rd
North Baddesley SO52 ... 54 A4
Petersfield GU31 ... 41 A5
Thompson's La
Colden Common SO50,SO21 ... 57 E7
Colden Common,Hensting
SO50 ... 57 C7
Thompsons La PO7 ... 110 C6
Thoresby Ct BH25 ... 194 E3
Thorn Cl Eastleigh SO50 ... 56 A5
Petersfield GU31 ... 41 C2
Thorn Rd BH17 ... 187 D3
Thornbrake Rd PO12 ... 181 C4
Thornbury 18 BH4 ... 204 C3
Thornbury Ave
Blackfield SO45 ... 177 F8
Southampton SO15 ... 102 E7
Thornbury Cl PO14 ... 154 C8
Thornbury Ho 10 PO6 ... 132 F2
Thornbury Hts SO53 ... 30 F1
Thornbury Rd BH6 ... 207 A4
Thornbury Wood SO53 ... 30 F1
Thornby Ct PO3 ... 158 B4
Thorncliffe Cl PO2 ... 157 F4
Thorncombe Cl
Bournemouth BH9 ... 190 B4
Poole BH17 ... 187 E2
Thorncroft Rd PO1 ... 182 E5
Thornden Sch SO53 ... 55 F8
Thorndike Cl SO16 ... 78 A2
Thorndike Rd SO16 ... 77 F2
Thorne Cl BH31 ... 114 E6
Thorne Way BH21 ... 139 B6
Thorner's Homes,Centre Ct
15 SO15 ... 102 B8
Thorner's Homes,North Ct 14
SO15 ... 102 B8
Thorner's Homes,South Ct 16
SO15 ... 102 B8
Thorner's Homes,West Ct 13
SO15 ... 102 B8
Thorners Ct 8 SO15 ... 102 F6
Thorness Cl SO16 ... 77 C1
Thorney Cl PO14 ... 154 D8
Thorney Island Com Prim Sch
PO10 ... 161 A3
Thorney Old Pk PO10 ... 161 D1
Thorney Rd PO10 ... 161 B6
Thorney View PO11 ... 160 C2
Thornfield Cl PO8 ... 88 C2
Thornfield Dr BH23 ... 193 F1
Thorngate SP5 ... 4 B8
Thorngate Ct 5 PO12 ... 181 A7
Thorngate Way 5
PO12 ... 181 D5
Thornham La PO10 ... 161 C6
Thornham Rd BH25 ... 195 D3
Thornhill Ave SO19 ... 104 D6
Thornhill Cl SO45 ... 150 F2
Thornhill Park Rd SO18 ... 104 D7
Thornhill Prim Sch
SO19 ... 104 C5
Thornhill Rd
Blackfield SO45 ... 150 F2
Southampton SO16 ... 78 D4
Thorni Ave PO15 ... 130 C3
Thornleigh Rd SO19 ... 103 E2
Thornley Rd BH10 ... 189 D4
Thorns La SO41 ... 199 F6
Thornton Ave SO31 ... 128 C1
Thornton Cl
Corfe Mullen BH21 ... 186 C5
Cosham PO7 ... 134 B2
Thornton Rd PO12 ... 181 B9
Thornworthy 4 SO45 ... 125 E1
Thornycroft Ave SO19 ... 103 D2
Thorogood Ct 4 BH15 ... 202 E4
Thorold Ct SO18 ... 79 E1
Thorold Rd
Chandler's Ford SO53 ... 30 E1
Southampton SO18 ... 79 E1
Three Acre Dr BH25 ... 209 F8
Three Acres PO7 ... 111 A3
Three Cross Rd BH21 ... 138 E6
Three Horse Shoes La
SO24 ... 16 E2
Three Legged Cross Fst Sch
BH21 ... 114 E1
Three Lions Cl 9 BH21 ... 163 B5
Three Oaks SO19 ... 104 E5
Three Tun Cl 33 PO1 ... 182 A5
Threefield La SO14 ... 103 A3
Thresher Cl PO7 ... 112 C1
Throop Cl BH8 ... 191 A2
Throop Rd
Bournemouth,Holdenhurst
BH8 ... 191 A2
Bournemouth,Throop BH8 ... 190 E4
Throopside Ave BH9 ... 190 D4
Thrush Rd BH12 ... 188 C1
Thrush Wlk PO8 ... 111 E4
Thruxton Ct SO19 ... 103 E5
Thruxton Rd PO9 ... 135 C5
Thurbern Rd PO2 ... 157 E2
Thurmell Cl SO30 ... 105 C4
Thurmell Wlk SO30 ... 105 C4
Thurmond Cres SO22 ... 215 A4
Thurmond Rd SO22 ... 215 A4
Thursby Rd BH23 ... 193 F1
Thurston Cl SO53 ... 55 D7
Thwaite Rd BH12 ... 204 B5
Thyme Ave PO15 ... 129 D8
Thyme Ct 2 PO15 ... 129 D8
Tichborne Gr PO9 ... 135 D5
Tichborne Rd
Eastleigh SO50 ... 80 A8
Southampton SO18 ... 104 D8
Tichborne Way PO13 ... 155 D1
Tichbourne Ho SO30 ... 105 C7
Tickleford Dr SO19 ... 104 A1
Tickner Cl SO30 ... 105 E5
Ticonderoga Gdns
SO19 ... 103 E1
Tidcombe Gn PO9 ... 135 C7
Tidemill Cl BH23 ... 207 A8
Tides Reach SO18 ... 103 D8
Tides Way SO40 ... 101 F2
Tideway Gdns PO4 ... 183 C4
Tidworth Rd PO9 ... 135 F4
Tiffany Cl SO41 ... 195 F4
Tiffield Cl PO3 ... 158 C4
Tiger Rd PO1 ... 181 F8
Tilbrook Rd SO15 ... 102 A8
Tilburg Rd BH23 ... 207 D7
Tilden Rd SO21 ... 31 D5
Tile Barn Camp Site
SO42 ... 173 A8
Tilebarn La SO42 ... 173 A6
Tilford Rd PO8 ... 111 F6
Tiller Gdns BH11 ... 189 A5
Tillingbourn PO14 ... 129 C3
Tillington Gdns PO8 ... 88 D4
Tilmore Gdns GU32 ... 40 F5
Tilmore Rd GU32 ... 40 E5
Timberlane PO7 ... 134 D4
Timberley Ho 2 PO1 ... 216 C3
Timberley La SP5 ... 48 A6
Timberly Cl SO45 ... 150 C4
Timbermill Ct SP6 ... 93 F8
Timbers The PO15 ... 130 C1
Timor Cl PO15 ... 129 C8
Timothy Cl BH10 ... 189 D5
Timpson Rd PO1 ... 216 D4
Timsbury Cres PO9 ... 135 E2
Timsbury Ct SO19 ... 103 F4
Timsbury Dr SO16 ... 77 F1
Timson Cl SO40 ... 100 C6
Tincleton Gdns BH9 ... 190 B4
Tindale Rd SO16 ... 77 E2
Tinker Alley SO30 ... 80 A7
Tinkers Cross SP6 ... 69 E4
Tinneys Cl SP5 ... 47 D4
Tintagel Cl SO16 ... 78 C6
Tintagel Way PO6 ... 157 B7
Tintern Cl PO6 ... 133 A1
Tintern Gr 2 SO15 ... 102 E5
Tintern Rd PO12 ... 181 A5
Tipner Gn PO2 ... 157 C3
Tipner La PO2 ... 157 B3
Tipner Rd PO2 ... 157 C2
Tiptoe Gn 17 PO9 ... 136 B6
Tiptoe Prim Sch SO41 ... 195 D8
Tiptoe Rd BH25 ... 171 B1
Tipton Ho PO5 ... 216 B2
Tiptree Cl SO50 ... 56 A5
Tisted Ct 9 PO9 ... 136 B5
Titchfield Abbey*
PO15 ... 130 A2
Titchfield Haven Visitor Ctr*
PO14 ... 153 F1
Titchfield Hill PO14 ... 154 A8
Titchfield La PO17 ... 107 D3
Titchfield Park Rd
PO15 ... 129 D3
Titchfield Prim Sch
PO14 ... 129 F1
Titchfield Rd PO14 ... 154 B6
Tithe Barn SO41 ... 197 E5
Tithe Mead SO51 ... 27 F1
Tithe The PO7 ... 110 F3
Tithelands La SO24 ... 15 F4
Tithewood Cl SO53 ... 30 B2
Titus Gdns PO7 ... 135 A8
Tiverton Ct
34 Bournemouth BH4 ... 204 C3
1 Fareham PO16 ... 131 C2
Tivoli Cl SO53 ... 55 F7
Tivoli Ct PO2 ... 182 F8
Toby St PO1 ... 216 B4
Todber Cl BH11 ... 188 D3
Tokar St PO4 ... 183 A2
Tokio Rd PO3 ... 158 A1
Tolefrey Gdns SO53 ... 54 F6
Tollard Cl BH12 ... 203 E8
Tollbar Way SO30 ... 81 B2
Tollerford Rd BH17 ... 187 D2
Tollgate SO53 ... 55 C2
Tollgate Ests SO51 ... 27 B3
Tollgate Rd SO31 ... 128 D8
Tollgate The
Fareham PO16 ... 131 B2
3 Winchester SO23 ... 215 E7
Tolpuddle Gdns BH9 ... 190 B4
Tolstoi Rd BH14 ... 203 A6
Tomkyns Cl SO53 ... 54 F6
Tommy Green Wlk SO50 ... 55 F3
Toms La BH24 ... 118 B8
Tonbridge St PO5 ... 182 C2
Tonge Rd BH11 ... 189 B6
Tonnant Cl PO14 ... 179 D7
Toogoods Way SO16 ... 77 D5
Toomer Cl SO45 ... 150 F2
Toothill Rd SO51 ... 53 D1
Top La BH24 ... 141 A7
Topaz Gr PO7 ... 135 B8
Topiary Gdns SO31 ... 129 B4
Topiary The BH14 ... 202 F5
Tor Cl Portchester PO16 ... 131 E1
Waterlooville PO7 ... 134 F3
Tor Way GU31 ... 41 A3
Torbay Rd BH14 ... 203 C3
Torberry Dr GU31 ... 41 B2
Torch Cl SO50 ... 57 B2
Torcross Cl SO19 ... 103 E2
Torfrida Ct PO4 ... 183 C3
Tormead SO45 ... 125 F3
Tornay Gr SO52 ... 53 F4
Toronto Pl PO12 ... 181 B6
Toronto Rd PO2 ... 182 E7
Torquay Ave
Gosport PO12 ... 181 A9
Southampton SO15 ... 102 D8
Torque Cl SO19 ... 104 E4
Torre Cl SO50 ... 56 A6
Torridge Gdns SO18 ... 80 B3
Torrington Cl SO19 ... 104 A4
Torrington Rd PO2 ... 157 F3
Tortworth Cl PO14 ... 154 D8
Torvain Pk BH14 ... 203 A5
Torwood Gdns SO50 ... 56 F2
Tosson Cl 3 SO16 ... 101 E8
Totland Cl SO16 ... 101 E8
Totland Ct 8 SO41 ... 211 C4
Totland Rd Cosham PO6 ... 157 E7
Gosport PO13 ... 155 C2
Totmel Rd BH17 ... 188 A2
Totnes Cl SO50 ... 55 F5
Tottehale Cl SO52 ... 53 F3
Tottenham Rd PO1 ... 216 D4
Totton & Eling Heritage Ctr*
SO40 ... 101 A6
Totton By Pass SO40 ... 101 A7
Totton Coll SO40 ... 100 D8
Totton Sta SO40 ... 101 A7
Totton Western By-Pass
SO40 ... 100 C5
Totton Wlk PO9 ... 135 D6
Tournerbury La PO11 ... 185 B4
Tourney Rd BH11 ... 188 E6
Tovey Pl SO23 ... 2 C7
Towans The BH13 ... 214 C3
Tower Cl PO12 ... 180 D3
Tower Ct
Bournemouth BH2 ... 204 E2
Warsash SO31 ... 128 C1
10 Winchester SO22 ... 215 D6
Tower Gdns 4 SO16 ... 78 F4
Tower Ho SO19 ... 103 E1
Tower Ind Est The SO50 ... 56 C2
Tower La Eastleigh SO50 ... 56 C2
Wimborne Minst BH21 ... 163 D6
Tower Park Rdbt BH15 ... 202 F7
Tower Pl SO30 ... 80 D1
Tower Rd
Bournemouth BH1 ... 205 E5
Poole BH13 ... 204 B2
Portsmouth PO4 ... 182 F3
Winchester SO23 ... 215 D6
Tower Rd W BH13 ... 204 A1
Tower St Emsworth PO10 ... 161 A8
Portsmouth PO1 ... 181 F4
Winchester SO23 ... 215 D6
Tower The 3 PO12 ... 181 B6
Towers Farm BH21 ... 186 D7
Towers Gdn PO9 ... 159 F6
Towers The SO31 ... 127 B5
Towers Way BH21 ... 186 D7
Town Hall Rd PO9 ... 135 F1
Town La GU32 ... 41 B5
Town Quay
Portsmouth PO1 ... 181 F4
Southampton SO15 ... 102 F2
Towngate Bridge BH15 ... 202 C3
Towngate Sh Ctr 1
BH15 ... 202 C2
Townhill Inf Sch SO18 ... 80 A2
Townhill Jun Sch SO18 ... 80 A2
Townhill Way SO18 ... 80 B2
Townsend Cl BH11 ... 189 B6
Townsend La Martin SP6 ... 43 A4
Pentridge SP6 ... 42 E4
Townsend Prim Sch
BH8 ... 191 A2
Townsville Rd BH9 ... 190 B2
Towpath Mead PO4 ... 183 C4
Toynbee Cl SO50 ... 56 A3
Toynbee Rd SO50 ... 56 A3
Toynbee Sch The SO53 ... 55 E5
Tozer Cl BH11 ... 188 F2
Tracey Ct 8 BH23 ... 209 A7
Trafalgar Cl
Chandler's Ford SO53 ... 55 B5
Hermitage PO10 ... 161 D8
Trafalgar Ct
Christchurch BH23 ... 207 F5
Fareham PO14 ... 154 F7
6 Portsmouth PO5 ... 182 D2
Trafalgar Ho SO45 ... 126 B3
Trafalgar Pl
Lymington SO41 ... 197 F4
Portsmouth PO1 ... 216 D4
Trafalgar Rd
Bournemouth BH9 ... 204 F7
Southampton SO14 ... 103 A2
Southampton,Freemantle
SO15 ... 102 C6
Trafalgar Sq PO12 ... 181 B6
Trafalgar St SO23 ... 215 D6
Trafalgar Way 3 SO45 ... 126 B1
Trafford Rd SO50 ... 57 B1
Trampers La PO17 ... 109 A4
Tranby Rd SO19 ... 103 E4
Tranmere Cl SO41 ... 197 F2
Tranmere Rd PO4 ... 183 B4
Treadwheel Rd PO8 ... 113 B6
Treagore Rd SO40 ... 76 C1
Trearnan Cl SO16 ... 101 F8
Treasury Ct 27 SO23 ... 215 D6
Treble Cl SO22 ... 10 B4
Tredegar Rd PO4 ... 183 A3
Tree Hamlets BH16 ... 201 C5
Tree Side Way PO7 ... 111 E1
Treebys Cl BH23 ... 192 D1
Treeside BH23 ... 193 C2
Treeside Ave SO40 ... 101 A7
Treeside Rd SO15 ... 102 C8
Treetops 9 BH13 ... 214 F7
Trefoil Cl 8 PO7 ... 135 A7
Trefoil Way BH23 ... 208 C8
Tregantle Mews PO12 ... 181 A5
Tregaron Ave PO6 ... 158 B7
Tregonwell Ct 18 BH2 ... 204 E3
Tregonwell Rd BH2 ... 204 E2
Treloar Rd PO11 ... 185 F1
Treloen Ct 3 BH8 ... 205 A5
Treloyhan Cl SO53 ... 55 D4
Tremona Ct SO16 ... 78 B2
Tremona Rd SO16 ... 78 B2
Trenley Cl SO45 ... 150 C3
Trent Cl SO18 ... 79 F1
Trent Ho 8 SO14 ... 103 C5
Trent Rd SO18 ... 79 F1
Trent Way
Ferndown BH22 ... 166 A6
Lee-on-t-S PO13 ... 179 F3
Trent Way *continued*
West End SO30 ... 80 D2
Trent Wlk PO16 ... 156 A8
Trentham Ave BH7 ... 206 B8
Trentham Cl BH7 ... 206 B8
Tresillian Cl BH23 ... 194 B2
Tresillian Gdns SO18 ... 80 B2
Tresillian Way BH23 ... 194 B2
Trevis Rd PO4 ... 183 C4
Trevone 5 BH25 ... 195 B3
Trevone Cl SO40 ... 100 E5
Trevor Rd PO4 ... 182 E3
Trevose Cl
Chandler's Ford SO53 ... 55 D4
Gosport PO13 ... 155 C1
Trevose Cres SO53 ... 55 D5
Trevose Way PO14 ... 129 B1
Triangle Gdns SO16 ... 77 D3
Triangle La PO14 ... 153 E4
Triangle The
Bournemouth BH2 ... 204 E3
Upton BH16 ... 201 B7
Whiteparish SP5 ... 24 B4
Tribe Rd PO12 ... 181 A6
Tricketts La BH22 ... 165 F6
Trigon Rd BH15 ... 202 D7
Trimaran Cl SO31 ... 128 E1
Trimaran Rd SO31 ... 128 E1
Trimm's Dro SP6 ... 70 E8
Trimmer's Ct PO1 ... 181 F5
Trinadad Ho 1 PO6 ... 132 F2
Trinidad Cres BH12 ... 203 C8
Trinidad Ho BH12 ... 203 C8
Trinity 2 BH1 ... 205 A3
Trinity CE Fst Sch BH31 ... 114 F8
Trinity Cl PO12 ... 181 E5
Trinity Ct
Chandler's Ford SO53 ... 55 D6
8 Southampton SO15 ... 102 C6
Totton SO40 ... 76 E2
Trinity Gdns
Fareham PO16 ... 131 A1
20 Winchester SO23 ... 215 E6
Trinity Gn PO12 ... 181 E5
Trinity Ind Est
Southampton SO15 ... 101 F7
Wimborne Minst BH21 ... 163 E3
Trinity Rd
Bournemouth BH1 ... 205 A4
Southampton SO14 ... 103 A5
Trinity St PO16 ... 131 B1
Tripps Mobile Home Pk
SO30 ... 105 D7
Tristan Cl SO45 ... 178 E7
Tristram Cl SO53 ... 54 F4
Triton Ctr The SO51 ... 53 D5
Triumph Cl PO15 ... 130 D2
Triumph Rd PO14 ... 154 F5
Troak Cl BH23 ... 207 E8
Trojan Way PO7 ... 134 F3
Troon Cres PO6 ... 134 C1
Troon Rd BH18 ... 187 A5
Trooper Bottom GU32 ... 19 B3
Trosnant Inf Sch PO9 ... 135 E3
Trosnant Jun Sch PO9 ... 135 E3
Trosnant Rd PO9 ... 135 E2
Trotters La BH21 ... 164 B6
Trotts La SO40 ... 101 C3
Troublefield Nature
Reserve* BH23 ... 191 A8
Troubridge Ct 7 PO1 ... 182 D7
Trowbridge Cl SO16 ... 77 E5
Trowbridge Ct 18 SO23 ... 215 E6
Truman Rd BH11 ... 189 B6
Truro Ct PO13 ... 180 C6
Truro Rd PO6 ... 132 F1
Truro Rise SO50 ... 56 E3
Truscott Ave BH9 ... 205 A7
Trussell Cl SO22 ... 1 D3
Trussell Cres SO22 ... 1 D3
Trystworthy 3 BH2 ... 204 E3
Tuckers La BH15 ... 201 F1
Tucks Cl BH23 ... 193 A8
Tuckton Cl BH6 ... 206 D4
Tuckton Rd
Bournemouth,Southbourne
BH6 ... 206 F5
Bournemouth,West Southbourne
BH6 ... 206 E4
Tuckton Rdbt BH6 ... 206 F5
Tudor Ave PO10 ... 136 F4
Tudor Cl Alderholt SP6 ... 93 A5
Gosport PO13 ... 180 D8
Portchester PO16 ... 132 B1
South Hayling PO11 ... 184 F2
Totton SO40 ... 100 C8
Tudor Cres PO6 ... 157 F6
Tudor Ct
Bournemouth BH1 ... 205 A5
5 Cosham PO6 ... 157 F8
2 Fareham PO14 ... 154 F7
Poole BH15 ... 202 E6
3 Portsmouth PO5 ... 182 D1
Tudor Gdns SO30 ... 105 A5
Tudor House Mus & Gdn*
SO14 ... 102 F3
Tudor Rd BH18 ... 187 B4
Tudor Way SO23 ... 2 B8
Tudor Wood Cl SO16 ... 78 F4
Tuffin Cl SO16 ... 77 C5
Tukes Ave PO13 ... 155 B4
Tulip Gdns Havant PO9 ... 135 C1
Sarisbury SO31 ... 128 F3
Tulip Rd SO16 ... 79 C4
Tumulus Cl SO19 ... 104 F4
Tunstall Rd
Portsmouth PO6 ... 133 D1
Southampton SO19 ... 104 E4

Tunworth Ct PO9 136 B5
Tupman Ho 21 PO1 182 D7
Tuppenny La PO10 161 C8
Turbary Cl BH12 203 D8
Turbary Ct
Bournemouth BH12 189 A1
Ferndown BH22 165 F6
Upton BH16 201 C8
Turbary Hts BH11 188 F1
Turbary Park Ave BH11 189 A2
Turbary Rd
Ferndown BH22 165 F6
Poole BH12 203 D8
Turbary Ret Pk BH11 188 E3
Turf Croft Ct BH23 194 B2
Turk's La BH14 203 A1
Turlin Moor Com Fst Sch BH16 201 C4
Turlin Moor Com Mid Sch BH16 201 C4
Turlin Rd BH16 201 C4
Turnberry Cl BH23 206 F6
Turner Ave PO13 180 E8
Turner Rd PO1 182 D7
Turners Farm Cres SO41 196 A2
Turners Oak Ct SO15 78 C1
Turnpike Down SO23 11 C8
Turnpike Way SO30 105 B7
Turnstone Gdns SO16 78 B5
Turnworth Cl BH18 187 C3
Turtle Cl PO14 154 B4
Turvy King Ct PO7 110 F4
Tuscan Wlk SO53 55 E6
Tuscany Way PO7 135 B8
Tussocks The SO40 101 F2
Tutland Rd SO52 53 F4
Tutor Cl SO31 127 F3
Tutt's La SO51 50 E4
Tweed Cl SO53 55 A7
Tweed La SO41 197 D8
Tweedale Rd BH9 190 C3
Twemlow Ave BH14 202 F3
Twiggs End Cl SO31 128 F4
Twiggs La
Marchwood SO40 124 E7
Marchwood SO40 124 E8
Twiggs Lane End SO40 124 C5
Twin Oak Pk BH23 192 D6
Twin Oaks SO19 103 F3
Twin Oaks Cl BH18 187 A3
Twittens Way PO9 135 F1
Twyford Ave
Portsmouth PO2 157 D1
Southampton SO15 78 C1
Twyford Cl BH8 190 D2
Twyford Ct 16 SO23 215 E8
Twyford Dr PO13 179 F3
Twyford Ho
Southampton SO15 102 F7
Trickett's Cross BH22 165 F6
Twyford Rd SO50 56 B5
Twyford Sch SO21 32 A6
Twyford St Mary's CE Prim Sch SO21 31 F5
Twyford Way BH17 188 A2
Twynham Ave BH23 207 A7
Twynham Cl SP5 46 F6
Twynham Rd BH6 206 F4
Twynham Sch BH23 207 A6
Twynhams Hill SO32 108 A8
Tyler Ct PO9 135 E5
Tylers Cl SO41 197 D5
Tyleshades The SO51 53 A6
Tyne Cl SO53 55 A5
Tyne Way SO30 80 E2
Tynedale Cl
Bournemouth BH9 190 B4
Gosport PO12 180 F8
Tyneham Ave BH12 203 C8
Tynham Ct BH23 207 C6
Tyrells La BH24 142 E4
Tyrrel Lawn PO9 135 D7
Tyrrel Rd SO53 55 C7
Tyrrell Gdns BH8 191 A2
Tyrrells Ct BH23 169 B1
Tyseley Rd PO5 216 B2
Tytherley Gn
Bournemouth BH8 190 D2
5 Havant PO9 136 B5
Tytherley Rd SO18 104 C8

U

Ubsdell Cl BH25 195 A3
Uddens Dr BH21 164 D7
Uddens Trad Est BH21 164 E6
Ullswater SO50 56 A1
Ullswater Ave SO18 80 B1
Ullswater Ho 4 PO6 133 B1
Ullswater Rd
Southampton SO16 77 E1
Wimborne Minst BH21 163 C2
Undercliff Dr BH1 205 C2
Undercliff Gdns SO16 78 E4
Undercliff Rd BH5 205 E3
Underdown Ave PO7 134 D2
Undershore SO41 197 E6
Undershore Rd SO41 198 A4
Underwood Cl
Poole BH17 187 B1
Southampton SO16 78 E4
Underwood Rd
Bishopstoke SO50 56 E3
Southampton SO16 78 E4
Unicorn Rd
Lee-on-t-S PO13 179 D4
Unicorn Rd *continued*
Portsmouth PO1 216 B4
Unicorn Training Ctr The PO1 216 A4
Union La SO32 61 A1
Union Pl PO1 216 C4
Union Rd Havant PO9 135 E1
Southampton SO14 103 C6
Union St Fareham PO16 131 C1
16 Portsmouth PO1 182 A5
Winchester SO23 215 F6
Univ Coll Winchester SO22 215 C5
Univ of Portsmouth PO1 216 A3
Univ of Portsmouth (Eldon Bldg) PO1 216 B2
Univ of Portsmouth (Langstone Campus) PO4 183 D5
Universal Marina SO31 128 C6
University Cres SO17 79 B3
University Parkway SO16 54 D1
University Rd SO17 79 B3
University Rdbt BH10 204 C8
Unwin Cl SO19 103 D1
Upham CE Prim Sch SO32 58 E5
Upham St SO32 58 D5
Uphill Rd SO22 1 C5
Upland La GU33 20 B7
Uplands Ave BH25 210 A8
Uplands Cl BH22 166 A8
Uplands Cres PO16 131 B2
Uplands Gdns BH8 190 C2
Uplands Prim Sch PO16 131 A3
Uplands Rd
Bournemouth BH8 190 C2
Cosham PO6 158 C8
Denmead PO7 110 C6
Rowlands Castle PO9 113 C2
West Moors BH22 139 A1
Winchester SO22 1 E3
Uplands Sch BH14 203 C3
Uplands Way SO17 79 A2
Uplyme Cl BH17 188 A2
Upmill Cl SO18 80 B3
Uppark (NT)* GU31 90 F8
Upper Arundel St PO1 216 B3
Upper Banister St 1 SO15 102 F6
Upper Barn Copse SO50 57 B3
Upper Bere Wood PO7 134 E7
Upper Brook Dr SO31 128 F2
Upper Brook St SO23 215 E6
Upper Brownhill Rd SO16 77 F3
Upper Bugle St SO14 102 F3
Upper Church Rd SO32 107 E7
Upper Common Rd SO41 196 F4
Upper Cornaway La PO16 132 B1
Upper Crabbick La PO7 110 C6
Upper Crescent Rd SO52 53 F5
Upper Deacon Rd SO19 104 C6
Upper Gn GU33 19 E7
Upper Golf Links Rd BH18 187 B5
Upper Gordon Rd BH23 194 A1
Upper Heyshott GU31 41 A3
Upper High St SO23 215 D6
Upper Hinton Rd BH1 204 F3
Upper House Ct PO17 108 A3
Upper House Farm SO24 16 D2
Upper Market St SO50 56 B3
Upper Mead Cl SO50 57 D2
Upper Moors Rd
Brambridge SO50 31 F1
Colden Common SO21,SO50 56 F8
Upper Mount GU33 20 E3
Upper Mullins La SO45 125 E3
Upper New Rd SO30 80 D1
Upper Northam Cl SO30 105 A6
Upper Northam Dr SO30 104 F6
Upper Northam Rd SO30 105 B6
Upper Norwich Rd 6 BH2 204 E3
Upper Old St PO14 154 B4
Upper Piece PO7 111 A3
Upper Rd BH12 203 C6
Upper Shaftesbury Ave SO17 79 B2
Upper Shirley Ave SO15 78 C1
Upper Spinney SO31 152 C10
Upper St Helens Rd SO30 105 B5
Upper St Michael's Gr PO14 154 F8
Upper Terrace Rd BH2 204 E3
Upper Toothill Rd SO16, SO51 53 E1
Upper Wardown GU31 41 B4
Upper Weston La SO19 104 A2
Upper Wharf PO16 155 C8
Uppleby Rd BH12 203 C6
Upton Cl Havant PO9 135 D7
Upton BH16 201 B7
Upton Cres SO16 77 D7
Upton Cross Mobile Home Pk BH16 201 C7
Upton Ct BH16 201 C7
Upton Ctry Pk* BH17 201 F6
Upton Grey Cl SO22 1 D3
Upton Heath Est BH16 201 D7
Upton Ho 3 SO16 78 A1
Upton Ind Est BH16 201 D6
Upton Inf Sch BH16 201 A7
Upton Jun Sch BH16 201 A7
Upton La SO16 77 C6
Upton Rd BH17 201 F7
Upton Way BH18 186 F3
Upwey Ave BH15 201 E3
Usborne Cl PO13 179 F4
Utrecht Ct BH23 207 D7
Uxbridge Cl SO31 128 F6

V

Vadne Gdns PO12 181 B7
Vaggs La SO41 195 E6
Vale Cl BH14 203 E4
Vale Dr SO18 79 F1
Vale Gr PO12 181 A8
Vale Lodge BH1 205 D5
Vale Mans 4 BH1 205 D4
Vale Rd
Bournemouth BH1 205 D4
Poole BH14 203 E4
Redlynch SP5 47 D6
Winchester SO23 11 C6
Vale The Horndean PO8 88 C1
Hythe SO45 125 F3
Locks Heath SO31 129 B2
Portsmouth PO5 182 C2
Vale View Pk SO41 195 F7
Valencia Cl BH23 191 D4
Valentine Ave SO19 104 C3
Valentine Cl PO15 130 C2
Valentine Ct
Southampton SO19 104 C3
Waterlooville PO7 135 A8
Valentines Inf Sch SO19 104 C2
Valerian Ave PO15 129 F3
Valerian Cl SO50 81 C6
Valerian Rd SO30 105 C6
Valetta Pk PO10 160 E8
Valetta Rd PO10 161 D1
Valette Rd BH9 190 A3
Valiant Gdns PO2 157 D4
Valiant Rd PO10 161 D1
Valiant Way BH23 208 B7
Valley Cl Blackfield SO45 150 F1
Christchurch BH23 191 E3
Colden Common SO21 56 F8
Redlynch SP5 47 D6
Waterlooville PO7 134 C3
Valley Ct The SO22 215 B4
Valley La BH23 169 E4
Valley Park Dr PO8 88 D4
Valley Rd
Bournemouth BH8 190 F3
Chandler's Ford SO53 55 C7
Littleton SO22 1 B5
Totton SO40 100 F5
Valley Rise SO31 128 E4
Valley The SO22 215 B4
Valley View Poole BH12 204 B7
Southampton,Sholing SO19 104 A4
Southampton,Sholing Common SO19 104 A5
Valleydene SO45 125 F2
Vallis Cl BH15 202 D1
Valsheba Dr PO14 179 B6
Vanburgh Way 6 SO53 30 B1
Vancouver Wharf SO19 103 C4
Vanguard Ct PO4 183 D3
Vanguard Rd
Bournemouth BH8 190 E1
5 Gosport PO12 181 C9
6 Poole BH15 202 C2
Southampton SO18 104 A8
Vanstone Rd PO13 180 D7
Vantage Way BH12 188 B2
Vardy Cl SO19 104 D3
Varna Rd SO15 102 C6
Varos Cl PO12 181 A7
Varsity Rd PO10 161 D1
Vaudrey Cl SO15 78 C1
Vaughan Cl SO19 104 E5
Vaughan Rd SO45 125 C4
Vauxhall Way GU32 40 E3
Veal's La SO40 125 A7
Vear's La SO21 57 A8
Vecta Cl BH23 208 C6
Vectis Ct 1 SO16 78 F4
Vectis Rd
Barton on S BH25 209 D7
Gosport PO12 180 E3
Vectis Way PO6 157 F7
Velder Ave PO4 183 B5
Vellan Ct SO16 77 C1
Velmore Rd SO53 55 B4
Velsheda Ct SO45 126 A5
Velvet Lawn Rd BH25 194 F4
Venator Pl BH21 163 C6
Venerable Rd PO14 155 A5
Vengeance Rd PO13 179 E4
Venice Cl PO7 135 A8
Venning Ave BH11 188 E5
Ventnor Ct SO16 79 C5
Ventnor Rd
Gosport PO13 155 B3
Portsmouth PO4 182 E4
Ventnor Way PO16 131 E1
Ventry Cl BH13 203 F4
Ventura Ctr The BH16 201 D6
Ventura Pl BH16 201 D6
Venture Ct PO3 158 A5
Venture Ind Pk PO3 158 A5
Venture Rd SO16 54 D1
Verbena Cres PO8 112 B4
Verbena Way SO30 105 C6
Verdon Ave SO31 127 F3
Verger Cl PO14 129 C3
Verity Cres BH17 188 A1
Vermont Cl SO16 78 F4
Vermont Sch SO16 78 E4
Vernalls Cl BH10 189 D6
Vernalls Ct BH25 195 C5
Vernalls Gdns BH10 189 D5
Verne Rd BH31 115 A5
Verney Cl BH11 189 B3
Verney Rd BH11 189 A3
Vernham Rd SO22 215 C8
Verno La BH23 193 C1
Vernon Ave PO4 183 A5
Vernon Cl
Bishop's Waltham SO32 59 D2
Gosport PO12 181 A6
Vernon Ct 3 PO2 157 E2
Vernon Hill SO32 59 D2
Vernon Mews 2 PO4 183 A5
Vernon Rd Gosport PO12 181 A6
Portsmouth PO3 158 A2
Vernon Wlk 5 SO15 102 F6
Verona Ave BH6 206 D5
Verona Rd SO53 55 F6
Verulam Pl 8 BH1 204 F3
Verulam Rd Poole BH14 202 F4
Southampton SO14 103 B7
Verwood CE Fst Sch BH31 114 E5
Verwood Cres BH6 207 B4
Verwood Ind Est BH31 115 A6
Verwood Rd
Ellingham BH24 116 A1
Havant PO9 136 B6
Ringwood BH24 140 C8
Three Legged Cross BH21 114 F1
Woodlands Common BH21 114 A7
Veryan PO14 130 E1
Vesca Ho SO31 129 B6
Vespasian Ct SO18 103 D7
Vespasian Rd SO18 103 D7
Vespasian Way SO53 55 E7
Vesta Way SO53 55 E7
Vetch Cl BH23 208 C8
Vian Cl PO13 155 C4
Vian Ct BH25 194 F3
Vian Pl SO23 2 C8
Vian Rd PO7 134 E5
Vicarage Cotts BH8 190 F3
Vicarage Dr SO30 105 B5
Vicarage Farm Bsns Pk SO50 57 C5
Vicarage Gdns SO41 196 A2
Vicarage La Cadnam SO40 75 B1
Curdridge SO32 106 C8
Hambledon PO7 86 D3
Hordle SO41 196 A2
Stubbington PO14 179 C8
Swanmore SO32 84 C6
Vicarage Pk SP5 47 D6
Vicarage Rd
Bournemouth BH9 189 F1
Marchwood SO40 101 F1
Poole BH15 202 C6
Redlynch SP5 48 A5
Verwood BH31 114 F6
Vicarage Terr PO12 180 F8
Vicarage Way BH23 192 D2
Vice La SO43 74 A4
Viceroy Rd SO19 104 A3
Vickers Cl BH8 191 B2
Vickery Way BH23 207 D8
Victena Rd SO50 57 C2
Victor Ct SO18 104 D6
Victor Rd
Portsmouth PO1 182 F7
Thorney Island PO10 161 D1
Victor St SO15 78 B1
Victoria Ave
Bournemouth BH9 189 E1
Portsmouth PO1 182 B3
South Hayling PO11 184 F3
Waterlooville PO7 134 B3
Victoria Bldgs SO32 83 B8
Victoria Cl
Corfe Mullen BH21 186 D5
Locks Heath SO31 129 A1
Victoria Cottage Hospl PO10 160 F8
Victoria Cres BH12 203 D6
Victoria Ct Durley SO32 82 C7
Netley SO31 127 A6
6 Portsmouth PO1 182 D7
South Hayling PO11 184 E3
Victoria Gdns
Ferndown BH22 165 D6
Fordingbridge SP6 69 D1
Ringwood BH24 141 A6
Victoria Glade SO31 127 C5
Victoria Gr PO5 216 C1
Victoria Ho
1 Fareham PO16 131 B1
33 Winchester SO23 215 D6
Victoria Hospl BH21 163 A5
Victoria Mews 6 PO17 130 E7
Victoria Park Pl 4 BH9 189 F1
Victoria Park Rd BH9 189 E1
Victoria Pl
Bournemouth BH1,BH8 205 C5
6 Gosport PO12 181 B5
4 Lymington SO41 197 E2
Romsey SO51 52 E7
Wimborne Minst BH21 163 B5
Victoria Rd
Bishop's Waltham SO32 83 B8
Bournemouth BH1 205 C5
Christchurch BH23 207 E5
Eastleigh SO50 56 B5
Emsworth PO10 136 E1
Ferndown BH22 165 D6
Fordingbridge SP6 69 D1
Milford on S SO41 211 C4
Netley SO31 127 A6
Poole BH12 203 C6
Portsmouth PO1 182 A6
Southampton SO19 103 D2
Stoke PO11 159 F2
Waterlooville PO7 134 E7
Wimborne Minst BH21 163 B5
Winchester SO23 215 D7
Victoria Rd N PO5 216 C2
Victoria Rd S PO5 182 D2
Victoria Sch BH13 203 F4
Victoria Sq PO13 179 E3
Victoria St Gosport PO12 181 C6
Portsmouth PO1 182 D7
Southampton SO14 103 C5
Victoria Terr
3 Cosham PO6 157 F7
Lumley PO10 137 A1
Southbourne PO10 161 C8
Westbourne PO10 137 B3
Victoria Wlk SO30 80 E2
Victory Ave PO8 112 A6
Victory Cl
Chandler's Ford SO53 55 B4
Three Legged Cross BH21 139 B6
Victory Cotts SO31 128 D7
Victory Cres SO15 102 B6
Victory Ct PO13 155 D1
Victory Gn PO2 157 C2
Victory Ho PO6 157 A7
Victory Rd
27 Portsmouth PO1 182 A5
Southampton SO15 102 B6
Stubbington PO14 179 D7
Victory Ret Pk PO2 182 C7
Victory Sq SO15 102 B6
Victory Trad Est PO3 158 B2
Victory Way SO16 77 E7
Viewside Cl BH21 186 C5
Viking Cl Blackfield SO45 177 F8
Bournemouth BH6 207 A4
Southampton SO16 77 E4
Stubbington PO14 179 B8
Viking Way
Bournemouth BH6 207 A4
Christchurch BH23 208 A5
Horndean PO8 88 C3
Vikings The SO51 53 B7
Villa Gdns PO7 134 F8
Village Cl PO14 179 C7
Village Ctr SO40 101 F1
Village Gate PO14 153 F8
Village Mews SO40 101 F1
Village Rd PO12 181 A3
Village St GU32 41 B6
Village The SP5 4 A8
Villas The BH25 194 E5
Ville De Paris Rd PO14 155 A5
Villeneuve St Georges Way SO50 55 E3
Villette Cl BH23 192 A1
Villiers Ct
18 Portsmouth PO5 182 C2
Winchester SO23 215 D5
Villiers Rd Hythe SO45 149 F8
Portsmouth PO5 182 C2
Southampton SO15 102 C8
Vimoutiers Ct SP6 69 E1
Vimy Ho 3 PO14 154 E8
Vince Cl BH11 189 B5
Vincent Ave SO16 78 C2
Vincent Cl 2 BH25 195 A2
Vincent Gr PO16 156 C7
Vincent Rd
1 New Milton BH25 195 A2
Southampton SO15 102 C8
Vincent St SO15 102 C8
Vincent's Gr SO15 102 B8
Vincent's Wlk SO14 103 A4
Vine Bank SO18 104 B8
Vine Cl Bournemouth BH7 206 A7
Warsash SO31 128 D3
Vine Coppice PO7 134 E4
Vine Ct 9 PO6 157 F7
Vine Farm Cl BH12 204 C8
Vine Farm Rd BH12 204 B8
Vine Hill BH21 162 E5
Vine Ho SO31 129 A5
Vine Rd SO16 78 B3
Vine Sch The SO32 106 D8
Vinegar Hill SO41 211 D5
Vineries Cl BH21 163 F6
Vineries The BH21 163 F6
Vinery Gdns SO16 78 C1
Vinery Rd SO16 78 C2
Vinery The BH25 195 B2
Vineside PO13 155 E1
Viney Ave SO51 53 B8
Viney Rd SO41 197 F1
Vineyard Cl SO19 103 D3
Vineyards The SO52 54 A4
Vinnells La GU32 37 D6
Vinneys Cl BH23 192 C2
Vinson Rd GU33 21 A4
Violet Ave PO14 179 B7
Violet Cl SO53 55 A6

Violet Farm Cl BH21 186 D8
Violet La BH25 195 A4
Violet Rd SO16 79 A4
Virginia Cl BH12 203 C7
Virginia Park Rd PO12 180 F6
Viscount Cl BH11 188 D5
Viscount Ct BH11 188 D5
Viscount Dr BH23 208 B7
Viscount Wlk BH11 188 D5
Vista Marina BH13 214 D6
Vita Rd PO2 157 E3
Vitre Gdns SO41 197 E2
Vivash Rd PO1 216 D3
Vixen Cl PO14 179 B7
Vixen Wlk BH25 195 B5
Vokes Cl SO19 104 B5
Vokes Cotts SO23 2 A5
Vulcan Cl SO15 101 F7
Vulcan Rd
  Southampton SO15 101 F7
  Thorney Island PO10 161 D1
Vulcan The 19 PO1 182 A4
Vulcan Way BH23 208 B7
Vyse La 15 SO14 102 F3

W

Wade Court Rd PO9 160 A8
Wade La PO9 160 A8
Wadham Rd PO2 157 D2
Wadhurst Gdns SO19 127 A8
Wadhurst Rd SO30 105 C6
Wadmore Cl SO45 126 B4
Wagtail Dr BH25 194 F2
Wagtail Rd PO8 112 A6
Wagtail Way PO16 155 F8
Wainscot Rd PO4 183 A2
Wainsford Cl SO41 197 B2
Wainsford Ct SO41 197 C2
Wainsford Rd SO41 196 E2
Wainwright Cl PO6 158 C6
Wainwright Gdns SO30 81 C3
Wait End Rd PO7 134 E6
Waite End Prim Sch PO7 134 E6
Wake Lawn PO4 183 C3
Wakefield Ave
  Bournemouth BH10 189 E5
  Fareham PO16 130 F3
Wakefield Ct 2 SO18 80 A1
Wakefield Pl PO12 181 A3
Wakefield Rd SO18 80 A1
Wakeford Ct 8 SO51 52 F7
Wakeford Pl SO31 129 A1
Wakefords Way PO9 136 B6
Wakely Gdns BH11 189 A5
Wakely Rd BH11 189 B5
Walberant Bldgs 2 PO3 157 F4
Walberton Ave PO6 158 A8
Walberton Ct 1 PO6 158 A8
Walburton Way PO8 88 D4
Walcheren Pl BH15 201 C3
Walcote Pl 30 SO23 215 D6
Walcott Ave BH23 191 F1
Waldegrave Cl SO19 103 D1
Walden Gdns PO8 112 B7
Walden Rd PO2 157 C2
Walditch Gdns BH17 187 E2
Waldon Gdns SO18 80 B2
Waldren Cl BH15 202 E2
Wales St SO23 215 F6
Walford Bldgs PO3 183 A7
Walford Cl BH21 163 C6
Walford Gdns BH21 163 B6
Walford Mill Craft Ctr* BH21 163 B6
Walford Rd PO6 133 C1
Walhampton Hill SO41 197 F5
Walker Gdns SO30 81 C1
Walker Pl Gosport PO13 155 D1
  Hamble-le-R SO31 127 F2
Walker Rd PO2 157 C2
Walker's La S SO45 177 F8
Walkers Cl SO50 57 D2
Walkers La N SO45 150 F1
Walkford La BH25 194 D3
Walkford Rd BH23 194 C2
Walkford Way BH23 194 B1
Walking Field La BH15 202 D2
Walkwood Ave BH7 206 B8
Wallace Ct BH18 187 A3
Wallace La SO42 175 C6
Wallace Rd
  Broadstone BH18 187 A3
  Portsmouth PO2 182 F8
  Southampton SO19 103 F1
Wallington Ct PO14 154 F6
Wallington Dr SO53 55 B8
Wallington Hill 3 PO16 131 C2
Wallington Rd PO2 157 F1
Wallington Shore Rd
  Fareham PO16 131 C2
  1 Portchester PO16 131 D1
Wallington Way PO16 131 C2
Wallis Gdns PO7 111 E1
Wallis Rd
  Bournemouth BH10 189 B1
  Waterlooville PO7 111 E1
Walliscott Rd BH11 189 A1
Wallisdean Ave
  Fareham PO14 154 F8
  Portsmouth PO3 183 B7
Wallisdean Jun & Inf Schs PO14 154 F8
Wallisdown Rd BH10 204 C8
Wallisdown Rdbt BH12 189 A1
Wallrock Wlk PO10 136 F4
Walmer Cl SO50 56 A7
Walmer Rd PO1 182 E5
Walnut Ave SO18 79 E5
Walnut Cl
  Chandler's Ford SO53 30 C2
  New Milton BH25 194 F3
  Southampton SO16 77 F1
Walnut Dr PO14 179 B7
Walnut Gr
  Southampton SO16 77 F1
  Winchester SO22 215 B7
Walnut Tree Cl PO11 184 F3
Walnut Tree Dr PO10 137 E3
Walpole La SO31 128 E8
Walpole Rd
  Bournemouth BH1 205 E5
  Gosport PO12 181 D5
  Winchester SO22 215 A3
Walpole Terr 2 PO12 181 B4
Walsall Rd PO3 183 A6
Walsford Rd BH4 204 C5
Walsingham Cl PO6 133 D1
Walsingham Dene BH7 205 F8
Walsingham Gdns SO18 79 F3
Waltham Bsns Pk SO32 84 A4
Waltham Cl Droxford SO32 61 A2
  Portchester PO16 132 C2
Waltham Cres SO16 78 B4
Waltham Rd BH7 206 B6
Waltham St PO5 216 A2
Walton Cl Gosport PO12 181 A5
  Waterlooville PO7 134 E5
Walton Ct Fareham PO15 130 D4
  10 Portsmouth PO1 182 A4
Walton Pl SO22 215 B3
Walton Rd
  Bournemouth BH10 189 C2
  Cosham PO6 158 C5
  Gosport PO12 181 A5
  Poole BH15 203 A6
  Southampton SO19 104 D3
Waltons Ave SO45 150 D4
Wandesford Pl PO12 156 A1
Wangfield La SO32 82 C1
Wansbeck Cl SO53 55 B5
Wanstead Cl BH24 117 B1
War Meml Hospl
  Gosport PO12 181 A5
  Milford on S SO41 211 E4
Warbler Cl
  Horndean PO8 112 A7
  Southampton SO16 78 B6
  Upton BH16 201 B8
Warblington Ave PO9 136 B1
Warblington Cl SO53 55 B3
Warblington Ct 2 PO1 182 A4
Warblington Rd PO10 160 E8
Warblington Sch PO9 136 B1
Warblington St PO1 182 A4
Warblington Sta PO9 136 B1
Warborne La SO41 197 F8
Warbrook Ct 3 PO9 136 B5
Warburton Cl SO19 104 E4
Warburton Rd
  Poole BH17 202 E8
  Southampton SO19 104 E4
Ward Cres PO10 137 A3
Ward Ct PO11 184 E2
Ward Ho PO1 182 A6
Ward Rd PO4 183 A2
Warden Cl SO30 80 D1
Wardens Cl PO11 184 F5
Warders Ct 2 PO12 181 B6
Wardle Rd SO50 56 D7
Wardroom Rd PO2 157 B1
Wareham Ct
  Bournemouth BH7 206 B6
  Hamworthy BH15 201 E2
Wareham Rd BH21 186 D5
Warfield Ave PO7 134 E7
Warfield Cres PO7 134 F7
Warland Way BH21 186 E7
Warlock Cl SO19 104 D3
Warmwell Cl
  Bournemouth BH9 190 B4
  Poole BH17 187 F2
Warnborough Ct 6 PO9 136 B6
Warner Ct 12 SO23 215 E8
Warner Mews SO30 106 A7
Warnes La BH24 142 F2
Warnford Cl PO12 181 A5
Warnford Cres PO9 135 D5
Warnford Ct SO15 102 F7
Warnford Rd
  Bournemouth BH7 206 B7
  Meonstoke SO32 61 D7
Warren Ave
  Chandler's Ford SO53 55 E5
  Christchurch BH23 207 F5
  Portsmouth PO4 183 B5
  Southampton SO16 78 B2
Warren Cl
  Chandler's Ford SO53 55 E5
  South Hayling PO11 184 C4
  Southampton SO16 78 A2
  St Leonards BH24 140 D5
Warren Cres SO16 78 A2
Warren Dr BH24 140 D5
Warren Edge Cl BH6 206 F3
Warren Edge Ct BH6 206 F3
Warren Edge Rd BH6 206 F3
Warren Gdns SO51 28 B1
Warren La
  Bucklers Hard SO42 200 E7
  Owslebury SO21 33 E8
  St Leonards BH24 140 D5
  Warren Corner GU32 19 B5
Warren Park Prim Sch PO9 135 D7
Warren Pk SO41 211 A6
Warren Pl SO40 76 C2
Warren Rd
  Bournemouth BH4 204 B2
  Liss GU33 21 B7
  Poole BH14 203 D4
  Winchester SO23 11 C8
Warren The SO45 150 B5
Warren Wlk BH22 165 B7
Warrior Bsns Ctr The PO6 158 E7
Warrior Cl SO53 55 B4
Warrior Pk SO53 55 B4
Warrys Cl SO45 150 A8
Warsash Cl PO9 135 E6
Warsash Ct SO31 128 C1
Warsash Gr PO13 155 B2
Warsash Maritime Ctr (Southampton Solent Univ) SO31 152 C9
Warsash Rd
  Locks Heath PO14 153 C8
  Warsash SO31 128 E1
Warspite Cl PO2 157 D4
Warton Cl SO42 175 C6
Warwick Ave BH25 195 B3
Warwick Cl
  Chandler's Ford SO53 55 A4
  Lee-on-t-S PO13 180 A4
  14 Winchester SO23 215 E8
Warwick Cres PO5 216 B2
Warwick Ct
  3 Emsworth PO10 160 F8
  15 Winchester SO23 215 E8
Warwick Ho 19 SO14 103 C6
Warwick Pl
  1 Bournemouth BH7 206 A5
  West Wellow SO51 50 E3
Warwick Rd
  Bournemouth BH7 206 A5
  Poole BH14 203 C3
  Southampton SO15 78 D2
  Totton SO40 100 F8
Warwick Way PO17 108 A4
Wasdale Cl PO8 88 C2
Washbrook Rd PO6 133 D1
Washington Ave BH1 205 D6
Washington Ct 4 PO4 183 A5
Washington Rd
  Emsworth PO10 136 F1
  Portsmouth PO2 182 D8
Wastwater Ho 14 PO6 133 B1
Watcombe Rd BH6 206 D5
Water Cl SO23 215 E5
Water La
  Bournemouth BH6 206 D7
  Hythe SO45 125 E2
  2 Southampton SO15 102 F5
  Totton SO40 100 E8
  Winchester SO23 215 F5
Water Lane Farm BH10 189 E6
Water's Edge SO30 105 B6
Waterbeech Dr SO30 105 C8
Waterberry Dr PO7 111 C1
Waterditch Rd BH23 193 A4
Waterford Cl
  Lymington SO41 197 F3
  Poole BH14 203 A2
Waterford Gdns BH23 209 A7
Waterford La SO41 197 F2
Waterford Lodge BH23 208 B6
Waterford Pl BH23 209 B7
Waterford Rd
  Christchurch BH23 209 B7
  New Milton BH25 195 C3
Waterfront Mus* BH15 202 B1
Watergardens BH8 205 A5
Watergate 12 PO12 181 E5
Waterhouse La SO15 102 B7
Waterhouse Way SO15 102 B7
Waterlock Gdns PO4 183 D4
Waterloo Cl PO8 111 D3
Waterloo Ho BH17 187 B1
Waterloo Ind Est SO30 81 B1
Waterloo Rd
  Bournemouth BH9 204 F7
  Corfe Mullen BH21 186 B5
  Gosport PO12 181 C2
  Havant PO9 135 F2
  Lymington SO41 197 F4
  Poole BH17 202 C8
  Southampton SO15 102 D6
Waterloo Sch The PO7 134 E7
Waterloo St PO5 216 B2
Waterloo Terr SO15 102 F6
Waterloo Way BH24 141 A6
Waterman Terr PO5 216 D1
Watermans La SO45 125 E1
Watermead 5 BH23 207 A5
Watermead Rd PO6 158 E7
Watermill Ct 2 PO9 135 F1
Watermill Rd BH23 207 A8
Waters Edge
  Lee-on-t-S PO13 179 F1
  Poole BH13 214 D6
Waters Edge Gdns PO10 160 F8
Waters Gn SO42 146 A2
Waters Green Ct SO42 146 A2
Waters The PO17 130 E5
Watersedge PO17 108 A4
Watersedge Rd PO6 157 A8
Watershed Ct 2 PO6 133 A1
Watership Dr BH24 141 D6
Waterside
  Christchurch BH23 207 F4
  Downton SP5 47 A7
  Hythe SO45 126 A5
Waterside Cl BH24 117 B1
Waterside Gdns PO16 131 D1
Waterside Heritage Ctr* SO45 126 B4
Waterside La PO16 156 E6
Waterside Prim Sch SO45 126 B2
Waterside Rd SO51 28 A1
Waterside Sch PO2 157 B3
Waterside Sch (Unit) PO4 183 C4
Waterside Sq SO45 125 F5
Watersmead SO23 215 D3
Watersmeet
  Fareham PO16 155 B7
  5 Winchester SO23 215 F5
Watersmeet Ct BH23 207 B5
Waterston Cl BH17 187 D1
Waterworks Rd
  Farlington PO6 158 D7
  Otterbourne SO21 31 D4
  Petersfield GU32 41 A6
Watery La
  Christchurch BH23 208 A8
  Upton BH16 201 A7
Watkin Rd
  6 Bournemouth BH5 205 F4
  Hedge End SO30 81 D2
Watley Cl SO16 77 D5
Watley La SO21 32 B6
Watson Wlk SO40 100 C7
Watton Cl BH8 191 A2
Watton La SO32 61 E2
Watton Rd SO45 150 C3
Watts Cl SO16 77 F3
Watts Rd
  Hedge End SO30 105 C7
  Portsmouth PO1 182 D7
Wavecrest Cl SO40 102 A3
Wavell Ave BH17 187 A1
Wavell Rd
  Bournemouth BH11 189 B4
  Gosport PO13 155 D3
  Southampton SO18 104 A8
Wavell Way SO22 215 A3
Wavendon Ave BH25 209 E8
Waveney Cl PO13 179 F3
Waveney Gn SO16 77 E1
Waverley 14 BH4 204 C3
Waverley Ave SO31 127 C5
Waverley Cl
  Fordingbridge SP6 69 F3
  Romsey SO51 28 B1
Waverley Cres BH15 202 D6
Waverley Ct SO31 127 C5
Waverley Gr PO4 182 E2
Waverley Ho 9 BH25 195 B2
Waverley Path PO12 180 E3
Waverley Rd
  Cosham PO6 158 C7
  Fordingbridge SP6 69 F3
  New Milton BH25 195 B2
  Portsmouth PO4 182 E2
  Southampton SO15 102 D5
Wayfarer Cl
  Locks Heath SO31 128 F1
  Portsmouth PO4 183 C5
Wayfarers PO13 180 D7
Wayground Rd BH21 162 E1
Waylands Pl SO30 105 B4
Wayman Rd BH21 186 E6
Wayne Rd BH12 203 B6
Waynflete Cl 1 SO32 83 C8
Waynflete Pl SO22 215 A4
Wayside SO31 128 D8
Wayside Cl SO41 211 D5
Wayside Rd
  Bournemouth BH6 206 E4
  St Leonards BH24 166 F8
Wayte St PO6 157 F7
Waytown Cl BH17 187 D1
Weald Cl SO31 129 A4
Weardale Rd SO53 55 D4
Weavers Cl BH22 138 E1
Weavers Gn PO9 136 C3
Weavers Pl SO53 55 B8
Weavills Rd SO50 57 A1
Webb Cl PO11 185 A2
Webb La PO11 185 A2
Webb Rd PO16 156 D6
Webb's Way BH11 188 F1
Webbers Way PO12 181 C3
Webbs Cl BH24 139 D6
Webbs Gn SO32 85 C3
Webbs Way BH24 139 E6
Webburn Gdns SO18 80 A3
Webster Rd
  Bournemouth BH9 190 A3
  Winchester SO22 215 A7
Wedgewood Cl
  Holbury SO45 150 C4
  Stubbington PO14 179 A6
Wedgewood Way PO8 111 E2
Wedgwood Dr BH14 203 A2
Wedgwood Gdns BH23 169 C1
Wedmore Cl SO22 10 A3
Weeke Cl SP5 46 D7
Weeke Manor Cl SO22 215 B8
Weeke Prim Sch SO22 215 B8
Weevil La PO12 181 D7
Weirs The 3 SO23 215 F4
Welbeck Ave SO17 79 B2
Welbeck Ct SO17 79 B2
Welburn Ct SO18 80 A1
Welch Rd Gosport PO12 181 A8
  Portsmouth PO4 182 E2
Welch Way SO16 77 F5
Welchwood Cl PO8 111 F6
Weldon Ave BH11 188 E5
Well Cl BH25 194 F2
Well Copse Cl PO8 88 C1
Well Hill PO7 110 D7
Well House Cl SP6 45 B3
Well House La SO22 1 E5
Well La Godshill SP6 70 E2
  Hamble-le-R SO31 128 A2
  Poole BH15 202 C4
  Swanmore SO32 84 B7
Well Mdw PO9 135 E6
Welland Gdns SO18 80 B2
Welland Gn SO16 101 E8
Welland Rd BH21 163 D4
Wellands Rd SO43 122 A5
Wellbrooke Gdns SO53 55 B7
Weller Ho 15 PO1 182 D7
Wellers Cl SO40 100 B7
Welles Rd SO53 55 D6
Wellesley Ave BH23 208 C7
Wellesley Cl PO7 134 E7
Wellington Ave
  Christchurch BH23 208 C7
  Southampton SO18 104 B7
Wellington Cl
  Dibden Purlieu SO45 125 D1
  Horndean PO8 112 D6
Wellington Ct
  7 Bournemouth,Dean Park BH8 205 A5
  Bournemouth,Westbourne BH2 204 D3
  11 Gosport PO12 181 C9
  10 Havant PO9 135 F1
  New Milton BH25 195 A3
  Southampton SO15 102 D6
  West End SO30 80 C2
Wellington Dr PO13 180 A5
Wellington Gr PO16 156 C7
Wellington Pk SO30 81 A1
Wellington Pl SO40 98 F8
Wellington Rd
  Bournemouth BH8 205 A5
  Poole BH14 203 C3
  Southampton SO18 79 E2
Wellington St PO5 216 B2
Wellington Way 2 PO7 134 E7
Wellingtonia Gdns SO41 195 F4
Wellman Ct 2 SO16 78 E3
Wellow Cl Havant PO9 135 D3
  Southampton SO18 104 C7
Wellow Ct 10 SO18 103 E8
Wellow Dro SO51 50 E7
Wellow Gdns PO14 129 C1
Wellow Sch SO51 50 F3
Wellow Wood Rd SO51 50 D8
Wellowbrook Cl SO53 55 A6
Wells Cl Portsmouth PO3 183 B6
  Swanwick PO15 129 C8
Wells Pl SO50 56 B2
Wells Rd SO50 56 B2
Wellsmoor PO14 129 C2
Wellswood Gdns PO9 113 C3
Wellsworth La PO9 113 C3
Wellworthy Rd SO41 197 D6
Wembley Gr PO6 158 B6
Wembley Way SO50 57 C1
Wendover Cl BH25 194 F1
Wendover Rd PO9 135 E2
Wendy Cres BH22 165 F3
Wenlock Ct 9 BH23 207 F8
Wensley Gdns PO10 136 F3
Wentwood Gdns BH25 195 D2
Wentworth BH14 214 C7
Wentworth Ave BH5 206 B4
Wentworth Cl BH5 206 B3
Wentworth Coll BH5 206 A4
Wentworth Dr
  Broadstone BH18 187 B5
  Christchurch BH23 206 F6
  Horndean PO8 112 B7
Wentworth Gdns
  Holbury SO45 150 D3
  Southampton SO19 104 B1
Wentworth Gr SO45 150 D3
Wentworth Grange
  Ferndown BH22 165 D7
  Winchester SO22 215 C4
Wescott Way BH11 188 E4
Wesermarsch Rd PO8 112 A4
Wesley Cl
  8 Bournemouth BH8 205 C5
  Southampton SO19 104 D4
Wesley Ct PO1 216 D3
Wesley Gr PO3 158 A3
Wesley Grange 48 BH4 204 C3
Wesley Ho
  Trickett's Cross BH22 165 F6
  15 Winchester SO23 215 E6
Wesley Rd
  Kings Worthy SO23 2 C7
  Poole BH12 203 C5
  Wimborne Minst BH21 163 E5
Wessex Ave BH25 195 A2
Wessex Cl
  Blackfield SO45 177 F8
  Christchurch BH23 208 C7
  Lee-on-t-S PO13 180 A6

Wessex Ct
Southampton,Sholing SO19 ... 104 A4
8 Southampton,Westwood Pk SO17 ... 103 A8
22 Winchester SO23 ... 215 D6
Wessex Dr SO22 ... 215 C6
Wessex Est BH24 ... 141 C8
Wessex Gate
Bournemouth BH8 ... 205 C6
2 Southampton SO15 ... 102 E7
Wessex Gate Ind Est PO8 ... 112 C6
Wessex Gate Ret Pk BH15 ... 202 B6
Wessex Gdns
Portchester PO16 ... 156 B7
Romsey SO51 ... 53 B7
Wessex La SO18 ... 79 D4
Wessex Nuffield Hospl SO53 ... 31 A1
Wessex Rd Horndean PO8 ... 88 D3
Poole BH14 ... 203 A3
Ringwood BH24 ... 141 B8
Wessex Trade Ctr BH12 ... 203 A7
Wessex Way
Bournemouth,Springbourne BH8 ... 205 C5
Bournemouth,Westbourne BH2,BH4 ... 204 D3
Colden Common SO21 ... 57 A8
West Ave BH21 ... 138 E8
West Bargate 2 SO14 ... 102 F4
West Battery Rd PO2 ... 157 B1
West Bay Rd SO15 ... 102 C5
West Borough BH21 ... 163 B5
West Cl Lymington SO41 ... 197 B2
Verwood BH31 ... 114 D6
West Cliff 9 BH2 ... 204 F4
West Cliff Cotts BH2 ... 204 E2
West Cliff Ct 40 BH4 ... 204 C3
West Cliff Gdns BH2 ... 204 E2
West Cliff Mews BH2 ... 204 E2
West Cliff Rd BH4 ... 204 C2
West Close Ho BH6 ... 207 A4
West Comm SO45 ... 177 E6
West Ct
Portsmouth,Buckland PO1 ... 182 E7
Portsmouth,Eastney PO4 ... 183 A3
Southampton SO19 ... 103 F1
West Downs Cl PO16 ... 131 A4
West Downs Student Village SO22 ... 215 B5
West Dr Bishopstoke SO50 ... 56 D4
West Moors BH24 ... 166 B8
West End Cl SO22 ... 215 C6
West End Cotts 2 PO16 ... 131 A1
West End Local History Mus & Heritage Ctr* SO30 ... 80 D1
West End Rd
Bursledon SO31 ... 104 F3
Southampton SO18 ... 104 A8
West End Terr SO22 ... 215 C6
West Haye Rd PO11 ... 185 D1
West Hayes
Lymington SO41 ... 197 F3
Winchester SO22 ... 215 B5
West Hill Ct SO15 ... 102 E5
West Hill Dr Hythe SO45 ... 125 F5
Winchester SO22 ... 215 C6
West Hill Park Sch PO14 ... 153 E8
West Hill Pk SO22 ... 215 B6
West Hill Pl 8 BH2 ... 204 E3
West Hill Rd BH2 ... 204 E2
West Hoe La SO32 ... 83 F7
West Horton Cl SO50 ... 56 F2
West Horton La SO50 ... 56 F1
West Howe Cl BH11 ... 189 A4
West Howe Ind Est BH11 ... 188 E3
West La Everton SO41 ... 196 E1
North Baddesley SO52 ... 53 E5
North Hayling PO11 ... 184 F6
West Links SO53 ... 55 C2
West Lodge PO13 ... 179 D4
West Mans 3 BH4 ... 204 C3
West Marlands Rd SO14 ... 102 F5
West Meon CE Prim Sch GU32 ... 37 B5
West Mews 4 PO17 ... 130 E7
West Mills Rd SP6 ... 69 E1
West Moors Mid Sch BH22 ... 138 F1
West Moors Rd
Ferndown BH22 ... 165 D7
Three Legged Cross BH21 ... 138 E7
West Moors BH22 ... 138 D5
West Moors St Mary's CE Fst Sch BH22 ... 138 D3
West Overcliff Dr BH4 ... 204 D1
West Park Dr SP6 ... 68 D5
West Park La SP6 ... 68 C5
West Park Lo 30 SO17 ... 79 A1
West Park Rd SO15 ... 102 F5
West Point PO13 ... 179 E3
West Quay SO14 ... 102 F4
West Quay Rd
Poole BH15 ... 202 B2
Southampton SO15 ... 102 E4
West Rd
Bournemouth BH5 ... 206 B4
Bransgore BH23 ... 193 A8
Dibden Purlieu SO45 ... 125 D1
Emsworth PO10 ... 160 E8
Fawley SO45 ... 150 C8
Hedge End SO30 ... 104 F6
West Rd *continued*
Milford on S SO41 ... 211 A5
Southampton,Woolston SO19 ... 103 E2
Southwick PO17 ... 133 A6
West Row BH21 ... 163 B4
West Row Mews BH21 ... 163 B4
West St Emsworth PO10 ... 160 F8
Fareham PO16 ... 131 B1
Fordingbridge SP6 ... 69 E1
Hambledon PO7 ... 86 C2
Havant PO9 ... 135 F1
Havant,Bedhampton PO9 ... 135 E1
Hythe SO45 ... 125 F5
Poole BH15 ... 202 B2
Portchester PO16 ... 156 C8
Portchester PO16 ... 156 D8
Portsmouth PO1 ... 181 F4
Ringwood BH24 ... 140 E7
Soberton SO32 ... 85 C5
Southampton SO14 ... 102 F3
Southwick PO17 ... 132 E6
Titchfield PO14 ... 153 F8
Wimborne Minst BH21 ... 163 B5
West Station Terr BH4 ... 204 D3
West Street Ct 8 BH21 ... 163 B5
West Tytherley CE Prim Sch SP5 ... 4 A8
West Undercliff Prom BH2 ... 204 D1
West View Cotts PO10 ... 137 E2
West View Rd
Christchurch BH23 ... 207 E6
Poole BH15 ... 202 C4
West Walk (North) Forest Wlk* PO17 ... 108 E7
West Walk (South) Forest Wlk* PO17 ... 108 F5
West Way
Bournemouth BH9 ... 190 B2
Broadstone BH18 ... 186 F3
Lymington SO41 ... 197 C2
West Way Cl BH9 ... 190 B1
Westbeams Rd SO41 ... 172 B1
Westborn Rd PO16 ... 131 B1
Westbourne Ave
Emsworth PO10 ... 137 A2
Holbury SO45 ... 150 C4
Westbourne Cl
Bournemouth BH4 ... 204 C3
Emsworth PO10 ... 137 A2
Westbourne Cres SO17 ... 79 A1
Westbourne Ct 5 PO9 ... 135 E2
Westbourne Gate 15 BH4 ... 204 C3
Westbourne Mans 1 SO17 ... 79 A1
Westbourne Park Rd BH4 ... 204 B2
Westbourne Prim Sch PO10 ... 137 B4
Westbourne Rd
Portsmouth PO2 ... 182 F8
Westbourne PO10 ... 137 A3
Westbroke Gdns SO51 ... 27 F1
Westbrook Cl
Bournemouth BH10 ... 189 D2
Locks Heath SO31 ... 129 A6
Westbrook Ctr The 7 PO7 ... 112 B1
Westbrook Gr PO7 ... 134 D4
Westbrook Rd PO16 ... 156 D6
Westbrook Way SO18 ... 79 D4
Westbrooke Cl PO8 ... 112 A6
Westbrooke Cotts GU32 ... 38 E1
Westbury Cl
Barton on S BH25 ... 210 B8
Bransgore BH23 ... 193 A7
Christchurch BH23 ... 193 D1
20 Portsmouth PO6 ... 133 B1
Westbury Ct
Hedge End SO30 ... 105 C6
1 Poole BH14 ... 203 B4
Westbury Mall 8 PO16 ... 131 B1
Westbury Manor Mus* PO16 ... 131 B1
Westbury Rd
Fareham PO16 ... 131 B1
Ringwood BH24 ... 141 B7
Southampton SO15 ... 101 F7
Westbury Sq 9 PO16 ... 131 B1
Westby Rd BH5 ... 205 F4
Westcliff Cl PO13 ... 179 E4
Westcliff Ho 8 BH4 ... 204 C2
Westcliff Mews SO19 ... 103 D3
Westcliff Palms 18 BH4 ... 204 C2
Westcliff Wlk SO45 ... 125 F5
Westcot Rd SO45 ... 150 B3
Westcroft Par 7 BH25 ... 195 B2
Westcroft Pk BH18 ... 187 C4
Westcroft Rd PO12 ... 180 F5
Westdown Rd BH11 ... 189 A5
Westerham 7 BH13 ... 204 B3
Westerham Cl PO6 ... 157 E8
Westerham Rd BH4 ... 204 B3
Westering SO51 ... 53 C8
Westerleigh 12 BH4 ... 204 C2
Westerley Cl SO31 ... 128 E1
Western Ave
Barton on S BH25 ... 209 D8
Bournemouth BH10 ... 189 D4
Emsworth PO10 ... 160 D8
Poole BH13 ... 203 F2
Southampton SO15 ... 102 A6
Western CE Prim Sch SO22 ... 215 B6
Western Cl BH10 ... 189 D5
Western Com Hospl SO16 ... 77 F1
Western Ct 3 PO16 ... 131 A1
Western District Cut SO15 ... 102 D7
Western Downland CE Prim Sch
Damerham SP6 ... 68 D4
Rockbourne SP6 ... 44 F1
Western Espl
Southampton SO14,SO15 ... 102 F3
Southampton SO15 ... 102 E5
Western Par
Emsworth PO10 ... 160 E7
Portsmouth PO5 ... 182 B2
Western Rd
Chandler's Ford SO53 ... 30 E1
Fareham PO16 ... 131 B1
Fawley SO45 ... 151 E1
Havant PO9 ... 135 E2
Liss GU33 ... 20 F4
Lymington SO41 ... 197 D4
Poole BH13 ... 204 A2
Poole,Canford Cliffs BH13 ... 214 F8
Portsmouth PO6 ... 157 D7
West End SO30 ... 80 D1
Winchester SO22 ... 215 C6
Western Terr PO2 ... 157 C2
Western Way
Fareham PO16 ... 131 A1
Gosport PO12 ... 180 E2
Portsmouth PO1 ... 181 F8
Westerngate 13 BH13 ... 204 B3
Westfield 10 BH21 ... 163 B5
Westfield Ave
Fareham PO14 ... 154 F8
South Hayling PO11 ... 184 F3
Westfield Cl
Hamble-le-R SO31 ... 127 E2
Horton Heath SO50 ... 81 D7
Wimborne Minst BH21 ... 163 B5
Westfield Cnr SO18 ... 79 E5
Westfield Comm SO31 ... 127 E2
Westfield Cres SO53 ... 55 C4
Westfield Dr SO32 ... 84 D2
Westfield Dro SO24 ... 34 F8
Westfield Ho SO18 ... 79 E4
Westfield Ind Est
Gosport PO12 ... 181 A5
Horndean PO8 ... 112 D7
Westfield Jun Sch PO6 ... 156 E8
Westfield Oaks PO11 ... 184 F3
Westfield Rd
Bournemouth BH6 ... 206 E4
Chandler's Ford SO53 ... 55 C3
Gosport PO12 ... 181 A5
Littleton SO22 ... 1 B5
Lymington SO41 ... 198 A2
Portsmouth PO4 ... 183 A3
Southampton SO15 ... 102 A7
Totton SO40 ... 100 F8
Westgate PO14 ... 179 C6
Westgate Mews SO30 ... 80 E1
Westgate Mus* SO23 ... 215 D6
Westgate Pk BH4 ... 204 B3
Westgate Sch The SO22 ... 215 C7
Westgate St 14 SO14 ... 102 F3
Westgrove SP6 ... 69 E1
Westgrove Gdns PO10 ... 160 F8
Westham Cl BH17 ... 187 E3
Westheath Rd BH18 ... 187 B4
Westland Dr PO7 ... 134 F4
Westland Gdns PO12 ... 181 A4
Westlands Ct BH23 ... 193 A8
Westlands Dr BH13 ... 214 F8
Westlands Gr PO16 ... 156 C7
Westley Cl SO22 ... 215 B7
Westley Gr PO14 ... 154 F8
Westlink SO51 ... 28 A3
Westman Rd SO22 ... 1 D3
Westmarch Ct 1 SO17 ... 79 C2
Westmead Cl PO11 ... 184 E3
Westminster Ct BH25 ... 209 F7
Westminster Gate SO22 ... 10 B5
Westminster Gdns PO14 ... 129 C3
Westminster Pl PO1 ... 182 D7
Westminster Rd
Milford on S SO41 ... 211 A4
Poole BH13 ... 204 B1
Westminster Rd E BH13 ... 204 B1
Westmoreland Ct SO41 ... 195 F3
Westmorland Way SO53 ... 55 E5
Weston Ave PO4 ... 183 B4
Weston Cl SO19 ... 103 F1
Weston Cres SO18 ... 104 C7
Weston Ct SO19 ... 126 F8
Weston Dr BH1 ... 205 B3
Weston Grove Rd SO19 ... 103 D2
Weston Ho GU32 ... 40 E3
Weston La Nursling SO16 ... 77 A4
Southampton SO19 ... 103 F1
Weston GU32 ... 65 C8
Weston Par SO19 ... 126 E8
Weston Park Boys Sch SO19 ... 104 B1
Weston Park Inf Sch SO19 ... 104 A1
Weston Park Jun Sch SO19 ... 104 A1
Weston Rd Colehill BH21 ... 163 F7
Eastleigh SO50 ... 56 A3
Petersfield GU31 ... 41 A3
Weston Shore Inf Sch SO19 ... 126 F8
Westover La BH24 ... 140 D5
Westover Prim Sch PO3 ... 183 B8
Westover Rd
Bournemouth BH1 ... 204 F3
Milford on S SO41 ... 211 D4
Portsmouth PO3 ... 183 B8
Southampton SO16 ... 101 C8
Westover Retail Pk BH9 ... 190 A4
Westquay Ho 6 PO16 ... 131 C1
Westray Hall BH4 ... 204 C1
Westridge Ct 4 SO17 ... 79 B1
Westridge Rd
Portswood SO17 ... 79 B1
Southampton SO17 ... 103 B8
Westrow Gdns SO15 ... 102 F7
Westrow Rd SO15 ... 102 E7
Westside View PO7 ... 111 C1
Westview Rd SO22 ... 1 A2
Westward Rd SO30 ... 105 C8
Westway PO15 ... 129 E3
Westways Havant PO9 ... 158 F8
Stubbington PO14 ... 179 D7
Westways Cl SO16 ... 77 D5
Westwood Ave BH22 ... 165 D6
Westwood Cl PO10 ... 137 A2
Westwood Ct
12 Southampton SO17 ... 103 A8
Totton SO40 ... 76 E2
West End SO30 ... 80 D1
Westwood Gdns SO53 ... 55 E7
Westwood Mans 23 SO17 ... 79 A1
Westwood Rd
Lyndhurst SO43 ... 121 F6
Netley SO31 ... 127 B7
Portsmouth PO2 ... 157 E4
Southampton SO17 ... 103 A8
Westwood Park SO17 ... 79 A1
Westwood View SO24 ... 14 E1
Westwoods & Glendene Pk BH25 ... 194 D6
Wetherby Cl BH18 ... 187 A2
Wetherby Ct SO40 ... 100 D8
Wetherby Gdns SO40 ... 100 C8
Wetherdown GU31 ... 41 A3
Weybridge Cl SO31 ... 128 F6
Weyhill Cl Havant PO9 ... 135 D5
Portchester PO16 ... 132 C1
Weyman's Ave BH10 ... 189 C6
Weymans Dr BH10 ... 189 C6
Weymouth Ave PO12 ... 180 F8
Weymouth Rd
Poole BH14 ... 203 C5
1 Portsmouth PO2 ... 157 D1
Whaddon Chase PO14 ... 179 B7
Whaddon Ct PO9 ... 135 C6
Whaddon La
Colden Common SO21 ... 58 A8
Owslebury SO21 ... 33 A3
Whale Island Way PO2 ... 157 C1
Whalesmead Cl SO50 ... 56 F1
Whalesmead Rd SO50 ... 56 F1
Whaley Rd PO2 ... 157 B1
Wharf Cl BH12 ... 203 E6
Wharf Hill SO23 ... 215 F4
Wharf Mill 1 SO23 ... 215 F4
Wharf Rd
Portsmouth PO2 ... 182 C8
Southampton SO19 ... 103 D3
Wharfdale Rd
Bournemouth BH4 ... 204 D4
Poole BH12 ... 203 E6
Wharncliffe Ct BH23 ... 208 F7
Wharncliffe Gdns BH23 ... 209 A7
Wharncliffe Ho SO19 ... 103 D3
Wharncliffe Rd
Bournemouth BH5 ... 205 D4
Christchurch BH23 ... 209 A7
Southampton SO19 ... 103 D3
Whartons Cl SO40 ... 100 C3
Whartons La SO40 ... 100 C3
Whatleigh Cl BH15 ... 202 C1
Wheat Cl SO53 ... 54 F6
Wheatcroft Dr SO18 ... 80 D1
Wheatcroft Rd PO13 ... 179 F3
Wheatear Dr GU31 ... 41 C2
Wheatears Dr SO51 ... 50 E3
Wheatland Cl SO22 ... 215 B3
Wheatlands PO14 ... 129 C4
Wheatlands Ave PO11 ... 185 E1
Wheatlands Cres PO11 ... 185 E1
Wheatley Gn PO9 ... 135 C6
Wheaton Grange 4 BH4 ... 204 D4
Wheaton Rd BH7 ... 206 A5
Wheatplot Park Homes 2 BH10 ... 189 F4
Wheatsheaf Ct SO30 ... 105 B6
Wheatsheaf Dr PO8 ... 111 D3
Wheatstone Rd PO4 ... 182 F3
Wheeler Cl PO12 ... 181 B7
Wheelers La BH11 ... 188 D6
Wheelers Mdw SO31 ... 104 F1
Wheelers Wlk SO45 ... 177 F8
Wheelhouse Cvn Pk SO52 ... 30 A1
Wheelwright Mews SP5 ... 46 E7
Whernside Cl SO16 ... 101 F8
Wherwell Ct 14 PO9 ... 136 B5
Whichers Cl PO9 ... 136 B8
Whichers Gate Rd PO9 ... 136 B8
Whimbrel Cl PO4 ... 183 C5
Whimbrel Ct BH23 ... 208 A6
Whinchat Cl
Fareham PO15 ... 130 C4
Southampton SO16 ... 78 B6
Whincroft Cl BH22 ... 165 E7
Whincroft Dr BH22 ... 165 E6
Whinfield Rd SO45 ... 149 E8
Whinwhistle Rd SO51 ... 51 B2
Whippingham Cl PO6 ... 157 D7
Whistler Cl SO19 ... 104 C3
Whistler Rd SO19 ... 104 C3
Whitaker Cres SO41 ... 197 C3
Whitby Ave BH18 ... 187 A2
Whitby Cl BH23 ... 191 D4
Whitby Cres BH18 ... 187 A2
Whitby Ct 4 SO41 ... 211 D1
Whitby Rd SO41 ... 211 B4
Whitchurch Ave BH18 ... 187 C3
Whitchurch Ct SO19 ... 103 F3
Whitcombe Cl SO40 ... 100 E7
Whitcombe Gdns PO1 ... 182 F6
White Barn Cres SO41 ... 196 A3
White Beam Rise PO8 ... 88 C5
White Cl BH15 ... 203 A7
White Cloud Pk PO4 ... 182 F3
White Cloud Pl PO4 ... 182 F3
White Cotts SP5 ... 47 D7
White Dirt La PO8 ... 88 C3
White Farm Cl BH10 ... 204 D8
White Gates SO32 ... 82 B5
White Harmony Acres Ind Est SO30 ... 80 E5
White Hart La
Cadnam SO40 ... 98 F8
Portchester PO16 ... 156 C7
White Hart Rd
Fair Oak SO50 ... 57 C1
4 Gosport PO12 ... 181 B5
Portsmouth PO1 ... 182 A3
White Heather Ct SO45 ... 126 A6
White Ho The SO41 ... 211 D3
White Horse Dr BH15 ... 202 C5
White Horse La PO7 ... 111 A6
White Horses BH25 ... 209 E7
White House Gdns GU32 ... 40 E5
White Knights BH25 ... 209 F7
White La SO21 ... 32 A8
White Ladies SO51 ... 28 B7
White Ladies Cl PO9 ... 136 A1
White Lion Ctyd BH24 ... 140 F7
White Lion Wlk PO12 ... 181 D6
White Lodge Gdns PO16 ... 130 E4
White Oak Wlk 12 PO9 ... 136 B5
White Oaks Ct 9 SO16 ... 102 B8
White Rd SO50 ... 56 D4
White Row SP5 ... 46 C8
White Swan Rd PO1 ... 216 A3
White Way The
Meonstoke SO32 ... 61 A7
Warnford SO32 ... 36 A1
White Wings Ho PO7 ... 110 F3
White's Rd SO19 ... 104 A6
Whiteacres Cl 4 PO12 ... 181 B6
Whitebeam Cl
Colden Common SO21 ... 57 A8
2 Fareham PO14 ... 154 E8
Waterlooville PO8 ... 112 C5
Whitebeam Rd SO30 ... 105 D6
Whitebeam Way
North Baddesley SO52 ... 54 A5
Verwood BH31 ... 115 B5
Whitechimney Row PO10 ... 137 B3
Whitecliff Cres BH14 ... 203 A2
Whitecliff Rd BH14 ... 202 F2
Whitecliffe Ave PO3 ... 183 A7
Whitecliffe Ct PO12 ... 180 D4
Whitecroft SO45 ... 126 A2
Whitecross Cl BH17 ... 187 E3
Whitecross Gdns 1 PO2 ... 157 F3
Whitedell La PO17 ... 131 D5
Whitefield Farm SO45 ... 177 F6
Whitefield Rd
Holbury SO45 ... 150 C3
New Milton BH25 ... 195 A2
Poole BH14 ... 203 A2
Whitehall BH23 ... 207 B6
Whitehart Fields BH24 ... 141 C8
Whitehaugh Ct SO50 ... 56 D4
Whitehaven
Horndean PO8 ... 112 D6
Portchester PO16 ... 156 B7
Whitehaven Cvn Pk SO45 ... 177 E8
Whitehaven Home Pk SO45 ... 177 E8
Whitehayes Cl BH23 ... 192 D2
Whitehayes Rd BH23 ... 192 C1
Whitehill Cl SO18 ... 104 C7
Whitehorn Dr SP5 ... 73 D8
Whitehouse Gdns SO15 ... 102 A6
Whitehouse Rd BH21 ... 163 D2
Whitelands
Bransgore BH23 ... 169 D4
Droxford SO32 ... 85 B8
Whitelaw Rd SO15 ... 102 B7
Whiteleaf La PO7 ... 86 C8
Whitelegg Way BH10 ... 189 F5
Whiteley Farm Rdbt PO15 ... 106 E1
Whiteley La
Swanwick PO15 ... 106 C1
Whiteley PO15 ... 129 F5
Whiteley Prim Sch PO15 ... 129 C7
Whiteley Sh Ctr PO15 ... 129 E8
Whiteley Way PO15 ... 129 E7
Whitemoor La SO40,SO51 ... 75 E3
Whitemoor Rd SO42 ... 145 D2
Whitenap Cl SO51 ... 53 B6
Whitenap La SO51 ... 53 C6

Whiteparish All Saints CE Prim Sch SP5 ....24 B3
Whites Ct 4 PO2 ....157 D1
Whites Hill SO21 ....33 A3
Whites La SO45 ....151 B3
Whiteshoot SP5,SP6 ....47 F4
Whiteshoot Hill SP5 ....47 E4
Whiteshute La SO23 ....215 C3
Whitestone Cl SO16 ....101 F8
Whitethorn Rd PO11 ....185 B3
Whitewater Rise SO45 ....125 F1
Whiteways BH21 ....163 E6
Whitfield Pk BH24 ....140 B5
Whithedwood Ave SO15 ....102 D8
Whithers La SO42 ....175 C7
Whitingham Ct 1 BH5 ....206 B5
Whitley Cl PO10 ....137 B5
Whitley Row PO4 ....183 C5
Whitley Way BH25 ....195 B5
Whitmore La BH21 ....114 A7
Whitsbury Cl BH8 ....190 D2
Whitsbury Cross SP6 ....69 C8
Whitsbury Rd
Fordingbridge SP6 ....69 E3
Havant PO9 ....136 A5
Whitstable Rd PO6 ....157 E8
Whittington Cl SO45 ....125 F3
Whittle Ave PO15 ....129 C5
Whittle Rd BH21 ....164 F7
Whittles Way BH15 ....202 B2
Whitwell SO31 ....127 C7
Whitwell Rd PO4 ....182 E1
Whitworth Cl PO12 ....181 B5
Whitworth Cres SO18 ....103 D8
Whitworth Ct SO18 ....103 D7
Whitworth Rd
Gosport PO12 ....181 A6
Portsmouth PO2 ....182 F8
Southampton SO18 ....103 D8
Whyke Ct 3 PO9 ....135 E2
Whyte Cl SO45 ....150 B3
Whyteways SO50 ....55 F4
Wick 1 Ind Est BH25 ....194 E2
Wick 2 Ind Est BH25 ....194 E2
Wick Cl BH25 ....194 E2
Wick Dr BH25 ....194 E2
Wick Farm BH6 ....207 B5
Wick La
Bournemouth BH6 ....207 A5
Christchurch BH23 ....207 B6
Downton SP5 ....46 B8
Wick Point Mews BH23 ....207 B5
Wicket Rd BH10 ....189 C5
Wicket The SO45 ....125 F2
Wickfield Ave BH23 ....207 B6
Wickfield Cl BH23 ....207 B6
Wickford Ho BH23 ....207 A6
Wickham CE Prim Sch PO17 ....108 A4
Wickham Croft PO17 ....108 A3
Wickham Ct
Ferndown BH22 ....165 E6
3 Gosport PO12 ....180 D3
Wickham Dr BH21 ....186 D4
Wickham Ho
3 Portswood SO17 ....79 B1
10 Southampton SO17 ....79 A1
Wickham Rd
Bournemouth BH7 ....206 A5
Droxford SO32 ....85 A5
Fareham PO16,PO17 ....131 B5
Wickham St PO1 ....182 A5
Wickham Vineyard* SO32 ....107 B7
Wicklea Rd BH6 ....207 B4
Wicklow Dr SO53 ....55 A5
Wickmeads Rd BH6 ....207 A5
Wickor Cl PO10 ....137 A2
Wickor Way PO10 ....137 A2
Wicor Mill La PO16 ....156 B7
Wicor Path PO16 ....156 D6
Wicor Prim Sch PO16 ....156 B8
Widbury Rd SO41 ....197 C2
Widden Cl SO41 ....172 B2
Widdicombe Ave BH14 ....203 E2
Wide La SO18 ....79 E5
Wide Lane Cl SO42 ....145 F1
Widecombe Dr SO45 ....125 E3
Widgeon Cl
Gosport PO12 ....181 B8
Southampton SO16 ....78 B6
Widgeon Ct PO16 ....155 F8
Widget Cl BH11 ....189 B2
Widlers La SO32 ....58 F6
Widley Court Dr PO6 ....158 A7
Widley Ct
3 Cosham PO6 ....158 A7
Fareham PO14 ....155 A6
Widley Gdns PO7 ....134 D3
Widley Rd Cosham PO6 ....158 A8
Portsmouth PO2 ....157 C2
Widley Wlk PO6,PO7 ....133 F3
Widworthy Dr BH18 ....186 F5
Wield Cl PO9 ....135 C4
Wigan Cres PO9 ....135 B2
Wight View
Lee-on-t-S PO13 ....179 D4
South Hayling PO11 ....185 C1
Wight Wlk BH22 ....165 E2
Wightway Mews SO31 ....128 C1
Wigmore Ho PO1 ....216 C4
Wilberforce Cl 2 SO22 ....215 A4
Wilberforce Rd
Gosport PO12 ....181 C2
Wilberforce Rd *continued*
Portsmouth PO5 ....216 B1
Wilby La PO3 ....158 C4
Wilcon Ct SO50 ....81 D7
Wild Arum Way SO53 ....54 F5
Wild Cherry Way SO53 ....55 A6
Wild Grounds Nature Reserve* PO13 ....180 C6
Wild Ridings PO14 ....154 C8
Wild Rose Cres SO31 ....128 E2
Wildburn Cl SO40 ....76 C2
Wilde Cl SO40 ....100 D7
Wildern Cl SO31 ....128 F3
Wildern Ct SO30 ....105 B8
Wildern La SO30 ....105 C7
Wildern Sch SO30 ....105 C7
Wilderness Hts SO18 ....80 C1
Wilderton Rd BH13 ....203 F3
Wilderton Rd W BH13 ....204 A4
Wildfell Cl BH23 ....192 A1
Wildground Inf Sch SO45 ....125 F1
Wildground Jun Sch SO45 ....125 F1
Wildground La 4 SO45 ....126 A1
Wildmoor Wlk 4 PO9 ....136 B5
Wildown Gdns BH6 ....207 A3
Wildown Rd BH6 ....207 A3
Wilfred Rd BH5 ....205 F4
Wilkins Cl PO8 ....88 B6
Wilkins Way BH15 ....202 B2
Wilkinson Dr BH8 ....191 B2
Wilkinson Ho 15 PO4 ....183 B2
Wilks Cl SO16 ....77 C5
Willersley Cl PO6 ....133 C1
Willett Rd BH21 ....163 A2
William Booth Ho 1 PO1 ....182 B5
William Cl
Stubbington PO14 ....179 D6
Walkford BH23 ....194 A2
William Ct
11 Christchurch BH23 ....209 B7
5 Portsmouth PO4 ....183 B4
William George Ct PO13 ....179 E2
William Gilpin CE Prim Sch SO41 ....173 F1
William Macleod Way SO16 ....78 A1
William Panter Ct 2 SO50 ....56 A2
William Price Gdns PO16 ....131 B2
William Rd
Bournemouth BH7 ....205 F7
Lymington SO41 ....197 E5
William St SO14 ....103 C5
William's Ind Pk BH25 ....194 E2
Williams Cl
Gosport PO13 ....180 D7
Holbury SO45 ....150 D3
Williams Rd PO3 ....158 B3
Willis Ave SO52 ....54 B4
Willis Rd Gosport PO12 ....181 C5
Portsmouth PO1 ....216 B3
Southampton SO16 ....79 D5
Willis Way BH15 ....202 B6
Willis Waye SO23 ....2 C6
Willment Marine & Bsns Pk SO19 ....103 D5
Willow Ave SP6 ....69 F2
Willow Cl
Bournemouth BH4 ....204 B5
Havant PO9 ....136 A1
Hedge End SO30 ....105 D6
St Leonards BH24 ....139 D4
Upton BH16 ....201 D5
West End SO30 ....80 E3
Willow Ct
Bournemouth BH7 ....206 C6
Fareham PO14 ....130 D1
Southampton SO16 ....78 A3
Willow Dr
Christchurch BH6 ....207 A5
Marchwood SO40 ....124 F8
Ringwood BH24 ....141 A5
Wimborne Minst BH21 ....164 C6
Willow Gdns
North Baddesley SO52 ....53 F5
Westbourne PO10 ....137 B4
Willow Gn SO21 ....57 A8
Willow Gr SO50 ....57 D2
Willow Herb Cl SO31 ....128 E2
Willow La BH23 ....169 D3
Willow Lo 1 BH1 ....205 D4
Willow Mead
Bournemouth BH8 ....190 D4
Hedge End SO30 ....105 B8
Willow Pk BH14 ....203 A3
Willow Pl
Christchurch BH23 ....207 C6
Gosport PO12 ....181 B6
Willow Rd
Bishop's Waltham SO32 ....83 E7
Liss GU33 ....21 A4
Willow Tree Ave PO8 ....112 B2
Willow Tree Gdns PO14 ....154 E8
Willow Tree Ho SO41 ....197 C2
Willow Tree Rise BH11 ....189 B3
Willow Tree Wlk SO19 ....104 B3
Willow View BH16 ....201 C4
Willow Way
Christchurch BH23 ....207 A5
Ferndown BH22 ....165 D7
Willow Wlk BH25 ....210 B7
Willow Wood Rd PO11 ....185 A3
Willowdale Cl GU32 ....40 A4
Willowdene Cl
Havant PO9 ....135 B4
New Milton BH25 ....195 C3
Willows The
Barton on S BH25 ....210 B8
Chandler's Ford SO53 ....55 C3
Denmead PO7 ....110 F4
Wills Cl BH21 ....186 D4
Wills Rd BH12 ....203 F4
Wills Way SO51 ....53 A6
Willwood Cl BH17 ....187 E3
Wilmcote Gdns 5 PO5 ....216 C3
Wilmcote Ho PO5 ....216 C3
Wilmer Rd SO50 ....56 A2
Wilmington Cl SO18 ....79 F3
Wilmot Cl SO50 ....56 E5
Wilmott Cl PO12 ....180 F5
Wilmott La PO12 ....180 F5
Wilmur Cres BH15 ....202 E6
Wilson Ct 6 SP6 ....69 F1
Wilson Gr PO5 ....216 C1
Wilson Rd
Bournemouth BH1 ....205 E6
Poole BH14 ....203 C4
Portsmouth PO2 ....157 C2
Wilson St SO14 ....103 C5
Wilton Ave SO15 ....102 F6
Wilton Cl
Christchurch BH23 ....191 D1
5 Gosport PO12 ....180 F4
Wilton Cres SO15 ....78 D1
Wilton Ct SO15 ....102 D8
Wilton Dr PO8 ....112 A5
Wilton Gdns
New Milton BH25 ....194 F3
Southampton SO15 ....78 D1
Wilton Pl
19 Bournemouth BH4 ....204 C2
Portsmouth PO5 ....182 D2
Wilton Rd
Bournemouth BH7 ....205 F5
Southampton SO15 ....78 D1
Wilton Terr PO5 ....182 D2
Wiltshire Gdns BH23 ....192 F8
Wiltshire Rd
Bransgore BH23 ....192 F8
Chandler's Ford SO53 ....55 D3
Wiltshire St PO5 ....216 A2
Wilverley Ave
Bournemouth BH8 ....190 F2
Havant PO9 ....136 A4
Wilverley Cl SO41 ....197 B2
Wilverley Inclosure Forest Walks* BH25 ....171 C7
Wilverley Pl SO45 ....150 E1
Wilverley Rd
Brockenhurst SO42 ....145 F1
Christchurch BH23 ....208 A7
New Milton BH25 ....170 F3
Wimbledon Park Rd PO5 ....182 D2
Wimborne Fst Sch BH21 ....163 B5
Wimborne Ho
Southampton SO16 ....77 F1
Trickett's Cross BH22 ....165 F7
Wimborne Inf & Jun Schs PO4 ....183 A4
Wimborne Minster Model Town & Gdns* BH21 ....163 B4
Wimborne Rd
Bournemouth,Dean Park BH9 ....204 F5
Bournemouth,Kinson BH11 ....189 C6
Bournemouth,Moordown BH9 ....204 F8
East End BH21 ....162 F1
Poole,Longfleet BH15 ....202 D4
Poole,Oakdale BH15 ....202 D6
Portsmouth PO4 ....183 A4
Wimborne Minst BH21 ....163 E6
Wimborne Rd E
Ferndown BH22 ....165 B6
Trickett's Cross BH22 ....165 E7
Wimborne Rd W
Ferndown BH21 ....164 E6
Wimborne Minst BH21 ....164 B4
Wimpole Ct PO1 ....216 C4
Wimpole St PO1 ....216 C4
Wimpson Gdns SO16 ....77 F1
Wimpson La SO16 ....101 E8
Wincanton Way PO7 ....112 B1
Winchcombe Rd PO6 ....133 B1
Winchelsea Specl Sch BH12 ....188 D1
Winchester By Pass SO23 ....2 C3
Winchester Cath* SO23 ....215 E5
Winchester Christian Sch SO22 ....215 B3
Winchester City Mill* SO23 ....215 F5
Winchester Cl SO31 ....127 B6
Winchester Coll SO23 ....215 E4
Winchester Ct
13 Gosport PO13 ....180 D5
5 Romsey SO51 ....28 B1
Southampton SO15 ....78 C1
Winchester Cty Mus* SO23 ....215 E5
Winchester Hill SO51 ....53 B8
Winchester Ho
8 Havant PO9 ....136 A5
Romsey SO51 ....53 A7
Winchester Mews 19 SO17 ....103 A8
Winchester Pl 5 BH15 ....202 C2
Winchester Rd
Bishop's Waltham SO32 ....83 B8
Chandler's Ford SO53 ....55 E7
Durley SO32 ....81 E4
Fair Oak SO50 ....57 C4
Langrish GU32 ....39 E4
New Milton BH25 ....195 C4
Petersfield GU32 ....40 D4
Petersfield,Stroud GU32 ....40 B4
Portsmouth PO2 ....182 E8
Romsey SO51 ....52 F7
Romsey,Woodley SO51 ....28 C1
Shedfield SO32,PO17 ....107 E6
Southampton SO16 ....78 C2
Upham SO21,SO32 ....58 C3
Waltham Chase SO32 ....83 E2
Wickham PO17 ....108 A3
Winchester Sch of Art SO23 ....215 F6
Winchester St
Botley SO30 ....106 A7
4 Southampton SO15 ....102 F6
Winchester Sta SO22 ....215 D6
Winchester Trad Pk SO23 ....2 C1
Winchester Way SO40 ....100 C7
Winchfield Cl SO19 ....104 A1
Winchfield Cres PO9 ....135 C4
Winchfield Ho 4 PO12 ....181 E5
Wincombe Cl BH22 ....165 D3
Wincombe Dr BH22 ....165 D4
Windbury Rd SO16 ....77 E2
Windermere Ave
Southampton SO16 ....77 E2
Stubbington PO14 ....154 D4
Windermere Gdns SO40 ....100 E8
Windermere Ho PO6 ....157 B8
Windermere Rd
Bournemouth BH3 ....205 A7
Portsmouth PO2 ....157 F3
West End SO18 ....80 B1
Windfield Dr SO51 ....53 B8
Windgreen Est BH21 ....186 E7
Windham Mews BH1 ....205 D5
Windham Rd BH1 ....205 D5
Windmill Cl Clanfield PO8 ....88 C6
5 Milford on S SO41 ....211 D5
St Leonards BH24 ....140 D4
Windmill Copse SO45 ....125 F1
Windmill Field PO7 ....111 A4
Windmill Gr PO16 ....156 C6
Windmill La
Bursledon SO31 ....105 A2
St Leonards BH24 ....140 D4
Windover Cl SO19 ....104 C6
Windrush Gdns PO7 ....134 D7
Windrush Rd SO16 ....101 E8
Windrush Way SO45 ....126 A3
Windsor Cl Hordle SO41 ....195 E4
St Leonards BH24 ....139 F4
Windsor Ct
Bishopstoke SO50 ....56 D4
3 Christchurch BH23 ....209 A7
6 Cosham PO6 ....157 F8
Poole BH14 ....203 B3
19 Portsmouth PO5 ....182 C2
14 Southampton,Bevois Mount SO17 ....103 A8
2 Southampton,Bitterne SO18 ....103 E7
3 Southampton,Millbrook SO15 ....102 A6
6 Southampton,Westwood Pk SO17 ....103 A8
Windsor Gate SO50 ....56 A6
Windsor Ho
3 Portsmouth PO1 ....216 C3
1 Winchester SO23 ....215 F6
Windsor Mans 1 BH6 ....206 E3
Windsor Rd
Bournemouth BH5 ....205 E4
Christchurch BH23 ....206 E7
Cosham PO6 ....157 F7
Gosport PO12 ....181 A5
Petersfield GU32 ....40 F4
Poole BH14 ....203 B3
Portchester PO16 ....156 D6
Waterlooville PO7 ....111 D2
Windsor Way SP6 ....93 A6
Windward Ct 12 PO12 ....181 C5
Wine Cross PO17 ....109 A1
Winecross Cotts PO17 ....109 A2
Winfield Way PO10 ....136 F4
Winfrid Ho SO40 ....100 D7
Winfrith Cres BH12 ....203 E8
Winfrith Way SO16 ....77 D5
Wingate Dr SO19 ....104 B5
Wingate Rd
Gosport PO12 ....155 F1
Totton SO40 ....100 D8
Wingfield Ave
Christchurch BH23 ....193 D1
Poole BH15 ....202 D6
Wingfield Ct BH1 ....205 C3
Wingfield St PO1 ....182 D7
Winghams La SO51 ....29 B3
Wingrove Rd SO40 ....100 C3
Winifred Cl SO50 ....57 C3
Winifred Rd Poole BH15 ....202 E5
Waterlooville PO7 ....134 E8
Winkfield Row PO8 ....112 B5
Winkle St SO14 ....103 A2
Winkton Cl Burton BH23 ....192 C3
Havant PO9 ....135 E3
Winkton Gn BH23 ....192 C5
Winkton Ho BH23 ....192 C4
Winn Ct SO17 ....102 E7
Winn Mans 18 SO17 ....79 A1
Winn Rd SO17 ....79 A1
Winnall Cl SO23 ....2 C1
Winnall Manor Rd SO23 ....11 C8
Winnall Prim Sch SO23 ....11 C8
Winnall Trad Est
Winchester SO23 ....11 C8
Winchester SO23 ....2 C1
Winnall Valley Rd SO23 ....11 C8
Winnards Cl BH22 ....165 E2
Winnards Pk SO31 ....128 D4
Winnham Dr PO16 ....132 A1
Winnington PO15 ....130 D4
Winnington Cl PO15 ....130 D4
Winscombe Ave PO8 ....112 A2
Winsford Ave SO50 ....57 A1
Winsford Cl
Bishopstoke SO50 ....57 A1
Christchurch BH23 ....193 D1
Winsford Gdns SO50 ....57 A1
Winslade Rd Havant PO9 ....135 D5
Winchester SO22 ....1 C4
Winsley Ave BH6 ....206 C4
Winslow Ct PO6 ....158 D8
Winsor Cl PO11 ....185 D1
Winsor La SO40 ....99 E7
Winsor Rd Bartley SO40 ....99 B8
Cadnam SO40 ....75 D1
Totton SO40 ....101 A6
Winspit Cl BH15 ....201 E3
Winstanley Rd
Nursling SO16 ....77 C5
Portsmouth PO2 ....157 C1
Winston Ave BH12 ....204 A6
Winston Churchill Ave PO5 ....216 B2
Winston Cl Eastleigh SO50 ....56 A4
South Hayling PO11 ....184 E3
Southampton SO16 ....77 F2
Winston Ct
1 Christchurch BH23 ....207 A7
4 Old Milton BH25 ....195 A1
Winston Gdns BH12 ....204 A6
Winston Par 6 BH25 ....195 A1
Winston Pk BH12 ....204 A6
Winston Rd BH9 ....190 A3
Winston Way BH24 ....141 B8
Winstone Bldgs SO16 ....78 E3
Winstone Cres SO52 ....54 A3
Winter Rd PO4 ....183 A3
Winterbarrow Cotts SO32 ....36 E3
Winterbourne Cl BH15 ....202 D4
Winterbourne Rd
Poole BH15 ....202 D5
Portchester PO6 ....132 F1
Romsey SO51 ....28 B1
Winterhayes Cl BH17 ....187 E3
Winterhill Rd PO6 ....157 D8
Winters Cl SO45 ....150 D3
Winters Hill SO32 ....82 E8
Winters Rd SO32 ....84 A1
Winterslow Dr PO9 ....135 E6
Winton Boys' Sch BH10 ....189 D1
Winton Cl
Lymington SO41 ....197 F3
Winchester SO22 ....215 D8
Winton Ct
3 Petersfield GU32 ....40 F3
West End SO30 ....80 D1
Winton Prim Sch BH9 ....189 E2
Winton Rd
Petersfield GU32 ....40 F4
Portsmouth PO2 ....157 F2
Winton St 8 SO14 ....103 A5
Winton Way
Bournemouth BH10 ....189 D1
New Milton BH25 ....195 B5
Wisbech Way SO41 ....195 F3
Wisborough Rd PO5 ....182 E2
Wises Ct 1 PO12 ....181 E5
Wish Pl PO5 ....216 D1
Wishart Gdns BH9 ....190 B5
Wistaria Ho 7 BH10 ....189 F4
Wisteria Dr BH31 ....115 C4
Wisteria Gdns PO9 ....136 B4
Witchampton Cl PO9 ....136 A5
Witchampton Rd BH18 ....186 F2
Witham Cl SO53 ....55 A6
Witherbed La
Titchfield PO15 ....129 D4
Titchfield PO15 ....129 E5
Withermoor Rd BH9 ....204 E8
Withewood Mans 2 SO15 ....102 C7
Withies Rd PO13 ....180 D8
Withingham Rd BH13 ....203 F3
Withington Cl 3 PO6 ....133 B1
Withy Cl SO51 ....52 F8
Witley BH14 ....214 C7
Witley Rd PO8 ....111 F6
Witney Rd BH17 ....187 D1
Witt Rd SO50 ....57 C2
Wittensford La SO43 ....98 C8
Wittering Rd
South Hayling PO11 ....185 F2
Southampton SO16 ....78 A4
Witts Hill SO18 ....79 F1
Wivenhoe Ho BH22 ....165 F6
Woburn Cl SO50 ....56 A6
Woburn Ct PO13 ....179 F1
Woburn Rd SO16 ....78 B5
Wode Cl PO8 ....88 C3
Wodehouse Rd SO19 ....103 E4
Woking Rd BH14 ....203 C4
Wolfe Cl
Christchurch BH23 ....207 D7
Winchester SO22 ....215 A3
Wollaston Rd BH6 ....206 F3
Wollaton Cres BH22 ....165 C3
Wollaton Rd BH22 ....165 C3

Wollstonecraft Rd **1**
BH5 . . . . .205 F3
Wolseley Rd Poole BH12 .203 D6
Southampton SO15 . . . . . .102 C7
Wolsey Way SO41 . . . . . . .211 D5
Wolterton Rd BH12 . . . . . .204 A5
Wolverley Ct
19 Bournemouth BH4 . . . .204 C3
Southampton SO16 . . . . . .78 D3
Wolverton Rd
Bournemouth BH7 . . . . . .205 F5
Havant PO9 . . . . .135 E5
Southampton SO14 . . . . . .103 B5
Wolvesey Castle (Old
Bishop's Palace)*
SO23 . . . . .215 E5
Wolvesey Pl SO3 . . . . . . .55 A4
Wolvesey Terr **2** SO23 . . .215 F4
Wonderholm Par BH11 .189 B2
Wonston Ct PO9 . . . . . . .136 C6
Wonston Rd SO16 . . . . . . .78 B4
Wood Cl SO19 . . . . .104 C3
Wood End Rd BH24 . . . . .141 E5
Wood End Way SO53 . . . . .55 A6
Wood Glade Cl SO40 . . . .101 F1
Wood Ho **6** BH13 . . . . . .204 B3
Wood La
Bournemouth BH11 . . . . . .188 E6
Bramdean SO24 . . . . .15 E6
Milford on S SO41 . . . . . .211 C4
Southwick PO17 . . . . .133 A6
Wood Lawn Cl BH25 . . . .209 F8
Wood Lodge SO40 . . . . . .76 B1
Wood Rd SO40 . . . . .100 B2
Wood Row BH9 . . . . .190 E4
Wood View BH21 . . . . . . .164 A8
Wood's Cnr BH24 . . . . . . .45 C5
Woodacre Gdns BH22 . . .165 E4
Woodberry La
Emsworth PO10 . . . . .137 A6
Rowland's Castle PO9 . . . .158 E8
Rowlands Castle PO9 . . . .113 D1
Woodbind Wlk SO31 . . . .128 F2
Woodbourne Cl
Fareham PO15 . . . . .130 D1
Liss GU33 . . . . .21 A4
Woodbury
Bournemouth BH1 . . . . . .205 A2
Brockenhurst SO42 . . . . . .145 D1
Woodbury Ave
Bournemouth BH8 . . . . . .190 F2
Langstone PO9 . . . . .159 F8
Petersfield GU32 . . . . .40 E5
Woodbury Cl BH23 . . . . .191 E3
Woodbury Gr PO8 . . . . . .111 F5
Woodcock La SO41 . . . . .196 B4
Woodcocks Cres BH7 . . .206 A8
Woodcot Cres PO9 . . . . .136 B5
Woodcot Prim Sch
PO13 . . . . .155 B4
Woodcote Cotts SO24 . . .15 D4
Woodcote Dr BH16 . . . . .201 B6
Woodcote La PO14 . . . . .155 A3
Woodcote Rd SO17 . . . . . .79 C3
Woodcroft Gdns PO8 . . . .111 F5
Woodcroft La PO8 . . . . . .111 F5
Wooden House La SO41 .174 B2
Woodend Rd BH9 . . . . . .204 E8
Wooderson SO500 . . . . . . .57 B3
Woodfalls Cross SP5 . . . . .47 D4
Woodfern SP6 . . . . .70 D2
Woodfield Ave PO6 . . . . .134 F1
Woodfield Cotts GU32 . . .19 B3
Woodfield Dr SO22 . . . . . .10 B6
Woodfield Gdns BH23 . .193 D1
Woodfield Ho **7** PO2 . . .157 E3
Woodfield Park Rd
PO10 . . . . .161 B8
Woodfield Rd BH11 . . . . .189 A5
Woodford Cl BH24 . . . . . .141 C7
Woodford Ho PO15 . . . . .130 D2
Woodford Rd BH1 . . . . . .205 C4
Woodgaston La PO10 . . .160 C1
Woodgreen Ave PO9 . . . .135 D3
Woodgreen Dr BH11 . . . .188 D4
Woodgreen Rd SO22 . . . . .1 D4
Woodgreen Wlk SO40 . . .76 B1
Woodhall Way PO15 . . . .130 E3
Woodhay SO43 . . . . .121 E5
Woodhay Wlk **17** PO9 . .136 B6
Woodhayes Ave BH23 . . .193 E2
Woodhill Sch
Botley SO30 . . . . .105 F7
Chandler's Ford SO53 . . . . .55 D7
Woodhouse Ct SO30 . . . .105 C8
Woodhouse La
Finchdean PO8 . . . . .113 A6
Hedge End SO30 . . . . . . .105 E8
Rowlands Castle PO8,PO9 .113 C4
Woodhouse Rd PO8 . . . . .112 F7
Woodington Ed Ctr SO41 . .51 C6
Woodington Rd SO51 . . . . .51 C6
Woodlake BH17 . . . . .187 E1
Woodland Ave BH5 . . . . .206 A4
Woodland Cl
Southampton SO18 . . . . . .104 D7
Verwood BH31 . . . . .114 D7
West Wellow SO51 . . . . . .52 C7
Woodland Ct BH7 . . . . . .205 F5
Woodland Dro SO21 . . . . .36 B2
Woodland Mans BH14 . . .203 B5
Woodland Mews SO30 . . .80 D1
Woodland Pl **1** SO15 . .102 E7
Woodland St PO1 . . . . . . .216 D4
Woodland View
Burslandon SO31 . . . . . . .127 F8
Horndean PO8 . . . . .111 F6

Woodland Way
Christchurch BH23 . . . . . .208 D8
Milford on S SO41 . . . . . .211 C4
Woodland Wlk
Bournemouth BH5 . . . . . .206 A4
Ferndown BH22 . . . . .165 F7
Woodlands
Fareham PO16 . . . . .131 D2
20 Poole BH13 . . . . .204 A4
Woodlands Ave
Emsworth PO10 . . . . .136 F3
Hamworthy BH15 . . . . . . .201 F3
Woodlands Cl
Bransgore BH23 . . . . .193 A8
Chandler's Ford SO53 . . . . .30 D2
Dibden Purlieu SO45 . . . .125 F1
Gosport PO13 . . . . .180 C6
Sarisbury SO31 . . . . .128 F6
Woodlands Com Sch
SO18 . . . . .104 D8
Woodlands Cotts SO24 . . .16 D2
Woodlands Cres BH15 . .201 F3
Woodlands Ct
Dibden Purlieu SO45 . . . .125 F1
Poole BH12 . . . . .204 B8
1 Winchester,Hyde SO23 .215 E7
Winchester,Weeke SO22 . .215 A8
Woodlands Cvn Pk
SO41 . . . . .196 A3
Woodlands Dr SO31 . . . . .127 D6
Woodlands Dro SO40 . . .100 A3
Woodlands Ed Ctr PO8 . .111 E4
Woodlands Gdns **8**
SO51 . . . . .28 B1
Woodlands Gr PO7 . . . . .134 D5
Woodlands La
Hill Brow GU33 . . . . .21 B3
South Hayling PO11 . . . . .184 E5
Woodlands Rd
Barton on S BH25 . . . . . .209 E7
Brockenhurst SO42 . . . . .172 F7
Woodlands SO40 . . . . .99 E3
Woodlands The
Chandler's Ford SO53 . . . . .30 A1
Kings Worthy SO23 . . . . . . .2 C2
Woodlands Way
Burslandon SO31 . . . . . . .127 F8
Havant PO9 . . . . .135 F4
New Milton BH25 . . . . . . .195 B5
North Baddesley SO52 . . . .53 F4
Southampton SO15 . . . . . .102 F8
St Leonards BH24 . . . . . . .139 F4
Woodlane Cl SO24 . . . . . .15 D5
Woodlark Gdns GU31 . . . .41 C3
Woodlea Cl SO22 . . . . . .215 C8
Woodlea Gdns SO30 . . . . .80 E1
Woodlea Ho SO53 . . . . . . .55 C3
Woodlea Way SO51 . . . . . .29 F2
Woodleaze Cl BH18 . . . . .187 B6
Woodleigh Cl PO9 . . . . . .136 C3
Woodley Cl SO51 . . . . .28 C2
Woodley Close Flats
SO51 . . . . .28 C2
Woodley Gdns SO41 . . . .197 D5
Woodley La SO51 . . . . . . .28 B2
Woodley Rd
Gosport PO12 . . . . .181 C5
Southampton SO19 . . . . . .103 D3
Woodley Way SO51 . . . . . .28 A2
Woodling Cres SP6 . . . . . .70 D2
Woodlinken Cl BH31 . . . .115 B4
Woodlinken Dr BH31 . . . .115 B5
Woodlinken Way BH31 . . .115 B5
Woodmancote La PO10 . .137 E4
Woodmancote Rd PO4 . .183 A4
Woodmill La SO18 . . . . . . .79 E2
Woodmoor Cl SO40 . . . . .102 A1
Woodpath PO5 . . . . .216 B1
Woodpath Ho PO5 . . . . . .216 B1
Woodpecker Cl
Havant PO9 . . . . .136 B1
Verwood BH31 . . . . .114 F5
Woodpecker Copse
SO31 . . . . .129 B3
Woodpecker Dr
Broadstone BH17 . . . . . . .201 F8
Marchwood SO40 . . . . . . .101 E1
Woodpecker Way
Eastleigh SO50 . . . . .55 C7
Portsmouth PO3 . . . . .158 A4
Woodpeckers SO23 . . . . .215 E8
Woodpeckers Dr SO22 . .215 A8
Woodrising BH13 . . . . . . .214 B3
Woodrisings The **6**
BH2 . . . . .204 D4
Woodroffe Wlk PO10 . . . .136 F4
Woodrow PO7 . . . . .110 E4
Woodruff Cl BH23 . . . . . .208 C8
Woodrush Cres SO31 . . . .128 E2
Woods Edge BH18 . . . . . .187 A2
Woods Ho **5** SO32 . . . . . .96 D1
Woods View Rd BH9 . . . .204 D8
Woodsedge PO7 . . . . .135 A6
Woodside
Brockenhurst SO42 . . . . . .173 A8
Chilworth SO16 . . . . .78 A3
Gosport PO13 . . . . .155 B5
Portsmouth PO5 . . . . .216 B1
Woodside Ave
Eastleigh SO50 . . . . .55 F4
Lymington SO41 . . . . .197 E1
Woodside Cl
Ferndown BH22 . . . . .165 E6
10 Lymington SO41 . . . .197 E2
Marchwood SO40 . . . . . . .101 E1
Woodside Cres SO16 . . . . .54 E2
Woodside Ct **5** SO17 . . .103 B8
Woodside Gdns SO40 . . .100 C3

Woodside La SO41 . . . . . .197 E1
Woodside Rd
Bournemouth BH5 . . . . . .206 B4
Eastleigh SO50 . . . . .55 E4
Ferndown BH22 . . . . .165 E6
North Baddesley SO52 . . . .53 F4
Poole BH14 . . . . .203 C3
Southampton SO17 . . . . . .102 D0
West Moors BH22 . . . . . . .138 D4
Woodside Way SO30 . . . .105 A5
Woodstock Ave PO8 . . . .112 A5
Woodstock Cl
Fareham PO14 . . . . .130 E1
Hedge End SO30 . . . . . . .105 D5
Poole BH14 . . . . .203 B2
Woodstock Dr SO17 . . . . .79 A1
Woodstock La BH24 . . . .141 A6
Woodstock Rd
Burton BH23 . . . . .192 D2
Gosport PO12 . . . . .181 C4
Havant PO9 . . . . .135 D2
Poole BH14 . . . . .203 A2
Woodthorpe Gdns SO41 .128 F6
Woodvale PO15 . . . . .130 D2
Woodvale Gdns BH25 . . .195 C4
Woodville Cl SO16 . . . . . . .79 A6
Woodview Pk SO30 . . . . .106 C7
Woodville Dr PO1 . . . . . . .182 B3
Woodville Rd
Fawley SO45 . . . . .151 B3
Havant PO9 . . . . .135 B2
Woodward Cl PO12 . . . . .180 F4
Wooferton Rd PO6 . . . . .133 A1
Woolley Ho **2** SO14 . . . .203 B8
Woolfield La GU32,GU34 .18 B3
Woolford Cl **1** SO22 . . . .215 A4
Woolley Ho **2** SO14 . . . .103 A5
Woolmer Cl **11** PO9 . . . .136 B5
Woolmer La BH24 . . . . . .117 A2
Woolmer St PO10 . . . . . .136 E4
Woolner Ave
Cosham PO6 . . . . .158 A8
Petersfield GU32 . . . . .40 F4
Woolsbridge Ind Est
BH21 . . . . .139 A6
Woolsbridge Rd BH24 . .139 E5
Woolslope Cl BH22 . . . . .138 E1
Woolslope Gdns BH22 . .138 F1
Woolslope Rd BH22 . . . .138 E1
Woolston Cl **4** PO12 . . .180 D3
Woolston Inf Sch SO19 . .103 E2
Woolston Rd
Havant PO9 . . . . .135 C6
Netley SO31 . . . . .127 C7
Woolston Sch (Language
Coll) SO19 . . . . .103 F2
Woolston Sta SO19 . . . . .103 D3
Woolven Cl BH14 . . . . . . .203 A5
Woolverston SO22 . . . . . .115 C7
Woolwich Cl SO31 . . . . . .104 F2
Wootton SO31 . . . . .127 C7
Wootton Farm Rd BH25 .170 E2
Wootton Gdns BH1 . . . . .205 A3
Wootton Mount BH1 . . . .205 A3
Wootton Rd
Lee-on-t-S PO13 . . . . .180 A4
Tiptoe BH25 . . . . .195 D7
Wootton Rough BH25 . . .195 B8
Wootton St PO6 . . . . .157 F7
Worbarrow Gdns BH12 . .203 C8
Worcester Cl **5** PO5 . . .216 C2
Worcester Ct **9** PO13 . .180 C6
Worcester Pl
1 Lymington SO41 . . . .197 F2
Southampton SO19 . . . . . .104 B2
Wordsworth Ave
Bournemouth BH8 . . . . . .190 E1
Portchester PO6 . . . . .132 E1
Wordsworth Cl
Bishop's Waltham SO32 . . . .83 E8
Winchester SO22 . . . . . . .215 B6
Wordsworth Inf Sch
SO15 . . . . .78 B1
Wordsworth Rd PO15 . . .106 C1
Wordsworth SO15 . . . . . . .78 C1
Worgret Rd BH15 . . . . . .202 D7
Workman's La GU32 . . . . . .38 D1
Workmans's La SO31 . . . .152 E8
Workshop Rd PO6 . . . . . .133 A2
Worldham Rd PO9 . . . . . .136 B6
Worrell Dr BH12 . . . . .203 C8
Worsley Rd PO5 . . . . .216 B1
Worsley St PO4 . . . . .183 A2
Worth Apts PO5 . . . . .182 D1
Worthing Ave PO12 . . . . .180 F8
Worthing Rd PO5 . . . . . . .182 D2
Worthington Cres BH23 . .203 A3
Worthy La SO23 . . . . .215 B6
Worthy Ho SO16 . . . . .78 B1
Worthy La SO23 . . . . .215 E7
Worthy Rd
New Milton BH25 . . . . . . .195 A3
Winchester SO23 . . . . . . .215 E8
Wortley Rd BH23 . . . . . . .209 A7
Wr Twr Rd BH18 . . . . . . .187 C4
Wraxall Cl BH17 . . . . .187 D1
Wraysbury Park Dr
PO10 . . . . .136 F4
Wren Cl
Christchurch BH23 . . . . . .208 B5
New Milton BH25 . . . . . . .194 F2
Ringwood BH24 . . . . .141 C6
Winchester SO22 . . . . . . .215 B3
Wren Cres BH12 . . . . .203 D8
Wren Ctr The PO10 . . . . .137 A3
Wren Gdns SP6 . . . . .93 B5
Wren Rd SO50 . . . . .55 E1
Wrenway PO16 . . . . .155 F8

Wrexham Gr PO8 . . . . .88 B2
Wright Cl PO15 . . . . .129 F6
Wright Way SO45 . . . . . . .151 E1
Wright's Hill SO19 . . . . . .104 A2
Wrights Wlk SO31 . . . . . .104 F1
Wriothesley Ct PO14 . . . .153 F8
Wroxham Rd BH12 . . . . .203 F5
Wryneck Cl SO16 . . . . .78 B6
Wyatts Cl BH12 . . . . .186 D6
Wyatts La BH21 . . . . .186 C6
Wyborn Cl BH6 . . . . .206 A3
Wych La PO13 . . . . .155 B3
Wychwood **58** BH4 . . . . .204 C3
Wychwood Cl BH2 . . . . .204 F4
Wychwood Dr
Blackfield SO45 . . . . .177 E7
Bournemouth BH2 . . . . . .204 F4
Wychwood Gr SO53 . . . . . .55 E8
Wychwood Grange **1**
BH2 . . . . .204 F4
Wycliffe Rd
Bournemouth BH9 . . . . . .204 F8
Southampton SO18 . . . . . . .80 A1
Wycote Rd PO13 . . . . . . .155 B4
Wyeford Cl **4** PO9 . . . . .136 B6
Wyelands Ave BH21 . . . .164 D5
Wyke Mark SO22 . . . . . .164 A7
Wykeham Ave PO2 . . . . .157 E1
Wykeham Cl Netley SO31 .127 B6
Southampton SO18 . . . . . . .78 E4
Wykeham Field PO17 . . .108 A3
Wykeham House Sch
SO16 . . . . .131 C1
Wykeham Ind Est The
SO23 . . . . .2 C2
Wykeham La SO21 . . . . . .12 A7
Wykeham Pl
Lymington SO41 . . . . .197 E3
Winchester SO22 . . . . . . .215 B4
Wykeham Rd
Netley SO31 . . . . .127 B6
Portsmouth PO2 . . . . .157 E1
Wykeham Terr **7** SO23 .215 F4
Wylde Green La GU33 . . . .21 B5
Wylds La GU32 . . . . .65 C8
Wyllie Rd PO2 . . . . .157 E4
Wylye Cl SO18 . . . . .80 B3
Wymering La PO6 . . . . . .133 E1
Wymering Manor (Youth
Hostel)* PO6 . . . . .157 D8
Wymering Manor Cl **8**
PO6 . . . . .157 D8
Wymering Rd PO2 . . . . . .182 E8
Wyn Sutcliffe Ct **7** PO4 .183 A3
Wyncombe Rd BH5 . . . . .206 B5
Wyndcliffe Rd PO4 . . . . .182 E3
Wyndham Cl
Walkford BH23 . . . . .194 B2
Waterlooville PO8 . . . . . . .112 B4
Wyndham Ct SO15 . . . . .102 E5
Wyndham Pl **4** SO15 . .102 E5
Wyndham Rd
Poole BH14 . . . . .203 B3
Wynford Rd BH23 . . . . . .194 B2
Poole BH14 . . . . .203 C4
Wynford Rd
Bournemouth BH9 . . . . . .190 B4
Poole BH14 . . . . .203 C4
Wynne Cl BH18 . . . . .186 F4
Wynter Cl SO18 . . . . .205 F7
Wynter Rd SO18 . . . . . . .104 B8
Wynton Way PO15 . . . . .130 C3
Wynyards Gap SO52 . . . . .53 F4
Wyre Cl SO15 . . . . .55 B6
Wyvern Cl
Chandler's Ford SO53 . . . . .55 D6
Poole BH12 . . . . .203 D7
Wyvern Tech Coll SO50 . .57 C1

Y

Yachtsman Cl SO31 . . . . .128 C8
Yaldhurst Ct **20** PO9 . . .136 B6
Yaldhurst La SO41 . . . . . .197 B3
Yapton St PO1 . . . . .216 B3
Yarborough Rd PO5 . . . . .216 B1
Yardlea Cl PO9 . . . . .113 C4
Yardley Cl PO17 . . . . .158 C4
Yardley Rd SO30 . . . . . . .105 C5
Yarmouth Cl BH12 . . . . .204 A5
Yarmouth Gdns **5** SO15 . .78 B1
Yarmouth Rd BH12 . . . . .203 F6
Yarrell Mead SO41 . . . . . .197 B3
Yarrells Cl BH16 . . . . .201 C6
Yarrells Dr BH16 . . . . .201 C6
Yarrells La BH16 . . . . .201 C6
Yarrells Sch BH16 . . . . . .201 B7
Yarrow Cl BH23 . . . . .208 B8
Yarrow Rd BH12 . . . . . . .203 A8
Yarrow Way SO31 . . . . . .128 E2
Yateley Cl PO9 . . . . .135 C5
Yaverland SO31 . . . . .127 C6
Yeatman Old Mill **10**
BH15 . . . . .202 B1
Yeatminster Rd BH17 . . .187 F2
Yeatton Ho SO41 . . . . . . .196 A1
Yelverton Ave SO45 . . . . .150 A8
Yelverton Rd **10** BH1 . . .204 F3
Yeo Ct PO4 . . . . .183 C4
Yeoman Pk SO16 . . . . .77 C1
Yeoman Pl Poole BH8 . . .190 F2
Yeomans Lodge **6**
BH25 . . . . .195 B2
Yeomans Rd BH8 . . . . . .190 E3

Yeomans Way
Bournemouth BH8 . . . . . .190 E2
Totton SO40 . . . . .100 F8
Yeovil Chase SO18 . . . . .104 B8
Yeovilton Cl SO41 . . . . . .196 E1
Yerville Gdns SO11 . . . . .105 F7
Yew La BH25 . . . . .195 C4
Yew Rd SO18 . . . . .104 A8
Yew Tree Ave PO8 . . . . . .112 B2
Yew Tree Cl
Fair Oak SO50 . . . . .57 C3
Hedge End SO30 . . . . . . .105 B6
Wimborne Minst BH21 . . .163 D5
Yew Tree Ct
Fordingbridge SP6 . . . . . . .93 E8
5 New Milton BH25 . . . .195 B1
Swanwick PO15 . . . . .129 B7
Yew Tree Dr PO15 . . . . . .129 C7
Yew Tree Gdns
Denmead PO7 . . . . .110 E4
3 Ringwood BH24 . . . . .141 A6
Yew Tree Pl GU33 . . . . . . .21 A4
Yew Tree Rd PO11 . . . . . .185 A8
Yewberry Way SO53 . . . . .54 E6
Yews The PO8 . . . . .110 E6
Yewside PO13 . . . . .155 D2
Yewtree Cl SO45 . . . . . . .150 A8
Yewtree La SO16 . . . . .77 C3
Yoells Cres PO8 . . . . .111 F6
Yoells La PO8 . . . . .111 F6
Yokesford Hill SO51 . . . . .27 E4
Yokesford Hill Est SO51 . . .27 F5
Yonge Cl SO50 . . . . .56 B3
York Ave BH25 . . . . .195 B3
York Bldgs SO14 . . . . . . .103 A4
York Cl Broadstone BH18 .187 A2
Chandler's Ford SO53 . . . . .54 F4
Christchurch BH23 . . . . . .206 F7
Horton Heath SO50 . . . . . .81 D7
Petersfield GU32 . . . . .40 D3
Southampton SO19 . . . . . .103 C6
Totton SO40 . . . . .101 A8
York Cres PO13 . . . . .180 A4
York Dro Nomansland SP5 . .73 D8
Southampton SO18 . . . . . .104 B7
York Gdns PO16 . . . . .156 E6
York Ho Fareham PO14 . .130 E1
Gosport PO12 . . . . .181 D5
20 Southampton SO14 .103 C6
Southampton SO14 . . . . . .215 E8
York Pl Bournemouth BH7 .206 A5
7 New Milton BH25 . . . .195 B3
Portsmouth PO1 . . . . .182 B6
York Rd
Bournemouth BH1 . . . . . .205 B4
Broadstone BH18 . . . . . . .187 A2
Eastleigh SO50 . . . . .56 A5
Netley SO31 . . . . .127 A6
Southampton SO15 . . . . . .102 F2
York Terr PO2 . . . . .157 F5
Yorkdale SO31 . . . . .128 C3
Yorke St PO5 . . . . .216 A2
Yorke Way SO31 . . . . . . .127 E3
Yorkwood GU33 . . . . .20 F4
Youngbridge Ct PO12 . . .155 A7
Youngs Rd BH11 . . . . . . .189 A5
Yves Mews PO5 . . . . .182 D2

Z

Zamek Cl BH11 . . . . .189 A5
Zetland Ct BH4 . . . . .204 B1
Zetland Rd
Farlington PO6 . . . . .158 D7
Gosport PO12 . . . . .181 B6
Zeus La PO7 . . . . .134 F3
Zinnia Cl BH10 . . . . .189 E2

Addresses

Name and Address	Telephone	Page	Grid reference

Any feature in this atlas can be given a unique reference to help you find the same feature on other Ordnance Survey maps of the area, or to help someone else locate you if they do not have a Street Atlas.

The grid squares in this atlas match the Ordnance Survey National Grid and are at 500 metre intervals. The small figures at the bottom and sides of every other grid line are the National Grid kilometre values (**00** to **99** km) and are repeated across the country every 100 km (see left).

To give a unique National Grid reference you need to locate where in the country you are. The country is divided into 100 km squares with each square given a unique two-letter reference. Use the administrative map to determine in which 100 km square a particular page of this atlas falls.

The bold letters and numbers between each grid line (**A** to **F**, **1** to **8**) are for use within a specific Street Atlas only, and when used with the page number, are a convenient way of referencing these grid squares.

Example   *The railway bridge over DARLEY GREEN RD in grid square B1*

Step 1: Identify the two-letter reference, in this example the page is in **SP**

Step 2: Identify the 1 km square in which the railway bridge falls. Use the figures in the southwest corner of this square: Eastings **17**, Northings **74**. This gives a unique reference: **SP 17 74**, accurate to 1 km.

Step 3: To give a more precise reference accurate to 100 m you need to estimate how many tenths along and how many tenths up this 1 km square the feature is (to help with this the 1 km square is divided into four 500 m squares). This makes the bridge about **8** tenths along and about **1** tenth up from the southwest corner.

This gives a unique reference: **SP 178 741**, accurate to 100 m.

Eastings (read from left to right along the bottom) come before Northings (read from bottom to top). If you have trouble remembering say to yourself "Along the hall, THEN up the stairs"!

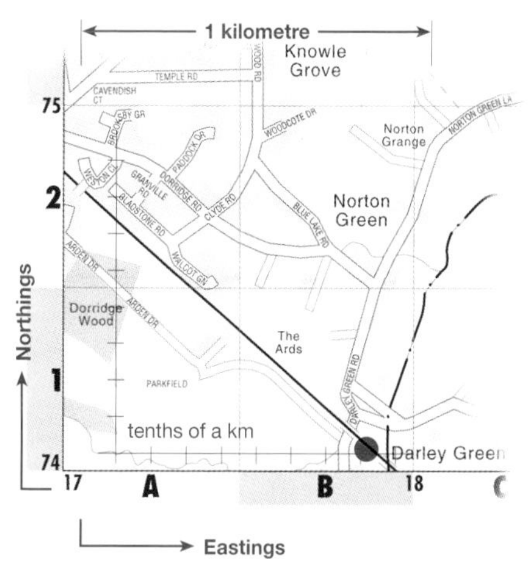

PHILIP'S MAPS

the Gold Standard for drivers

◆ **Philip's street atlases cover every county in England, Wales, Northern Ireland and much of Scotland**

◆ Every named street is shown, including alleys, lanes and walkways

◆ Thousands of additional features marked: stations, public buildings, car parks, places of interest

◆ Route-planning maps to get you close to your destination

◆ Postcodes on the maps and in the index

◆ Widely used by the emergency services, transport companies and local authorities

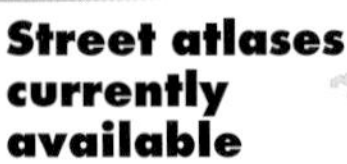

For national mapping, choose
Philip's Navigator Britain
the most detailed road atlas available of England, Wales and Scotland. Hailed by Auto Express as 'the ultimate road atlas', the atlas shows every road and lane in Britain.

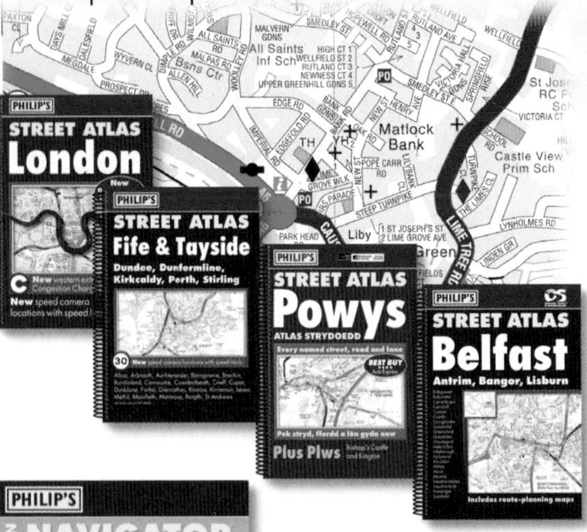

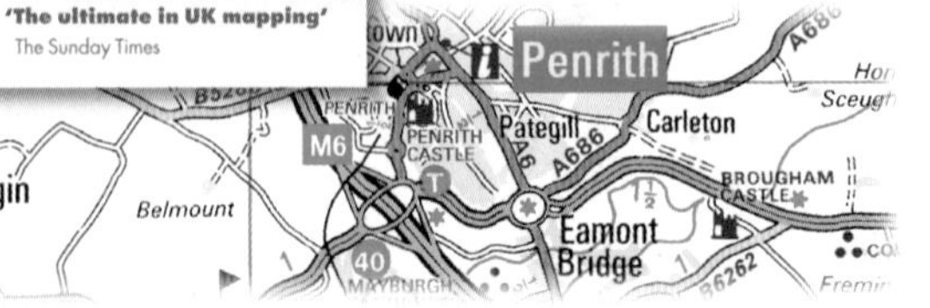

Street atlases currently available

England
Bedfordshire and Luton
Berkshire
Birmingham and West Midlands
Bristol and Bath
Buckinghamshire and Milton Keynes
Cambridgeshire and Peterborough
Cheshire
Cornwall
Cumbria
Derbyshire
Devon
Dorset
County Durham and Teesside
Essex
North Essex
South Essex
Gloucestershire and Bristol
Hampshire
North Hampshire
South Hampshire
Herefordshire Monmouthshire
Hertfordshire
Isle of Wight
Kent
East Kent
West Kent
Lancashire
Leicestershire and Rutland
Lincolnshire
Liverpool and Merseyside
London
Greater Manchester
Norfolk
Northamptonshire
Northumberland
Nottinghamshire
Oxfordshire
Shropshire
Somerset
Staffordshire
Suffolk

Surrey
East Sussex
West Sussex
Tyne and Wear
Warwickshire and Coventry
Wiltshire and Swindon
Worcestershire
East Yorkshire Northern Lincolnshire
North Yorkshire
South Yorkshire
West Yorkshire

Wales
Anglesey, Conwy and Gwynedd
Cardiff, Swansea and The Valleys
Carmarthenshire, Pembrokeshire and Swansea
Ceredigion and South Gwynedd
Denbighshire, Flintshire, Wrexham
Herefordshire Monmouthshire
Powys

Scotland
Aberdeenshire
Ayrshire
Dumfries and Galloway
Edinburgh and East Central Scotland
Fife and Tayside
Glasgow and West Central Scotland
Inverness and Moray
Lanarkshire
Scottish Borders

Northern Ireland
County Antrim and County Londonderry
County Armagh and County Down
Belfast
County Tyrone and County Fermanagh

How to order
Philip's maps and atlases are available from bookshops, motorway services and petrol stations. You can order di from the publisher by phoning **0207 531 8473** or online at **www.philips-maps.co.uk**
For bulk orders only, e-mail philips@philips-maps.co.uk